H. D. Thoreau   Henry D. Thoreau

Countee Cullen   D. H. Lawrence

Charles Dickens   Jonathan Swift   Daniel Defoe

G. Bernard Shaw   Phillis Wheatley   Stephen Crane

Langston   Bret Harte   Henry W. Longfellow
Langston Hughes

Oscar Wilde   Thornton Wilder   Edgar A Poe

Ernest Hemingway   J. Austen

Sinclair Lewis   Herman Melville   R. Emerson

Ed   Ivan Turgenev   A Bradstreet

T. S. Eliot   Jack London   Thomas Hardy

IN THE TRADITION OF
CHARLES SCRIBNER'S SONS,
THE PUBLISHER OF
SUCH LITERARY GIANTS AS
F. SCOTT FITZGERALD,
ERNEST HEMINGWAY,
EDITH WHARTON, AND
THOMAS WOLFE,

WE PROUDLY PRESENT THE

SCRIBNER LITERATURE SERIES

Signature Edition

INTRODUCING LITERATURE

APPRECIATING LITERATURE

UNDERSTANDING LITERATURE

ENGLISH LITERATURE WITH WORLD MASTERPIECES

AMERICAN LITERATURE

ENJOYING LITERATURE

SCRIBNER Laidlaw
Ordinary Students—Extraordinary Results

Respected and current research into teaching and learning will help you reach your goal of developing students' understanding and love of literature.

The *Scribner Literature Series,* Signature Edition, provides you with the following advantages.

■ Classic and contemporary literature, crossing periods, cultures, and genres

■ Strategies for *actively* involving students with literature

■ Features that help you improve students' abilities in reading, thinking, writing, and speaking

■ Practical time-saving teacher's materials for motivating students, conducting lessons, and evaluating results

■ Captivating illustrations including fine art, classic photography, and original artwork by the best of today's illustrators

from *Introducing Literature*

from *English Literature with World Masterpieces*

CLASSIC AND CONTEMPORARY LITERATURE, CROSSING PERIODS, CULTURES, AND GENRES

- Literature that helps students develop a sense of themselves by exploring the lives and experiences of others

- Literature that covers a vast variety of times and places: long ago, far away, here and now, the future

- Literature that creates the sense of wonder that has inspired generations of avid readers

- Literature that captures the beauty of language

- Literature that entices students with outstanding illustrations

Great literature that is enjoyable literature

from *Understanding Literature*

UNRIVALED STRATEGIES FOR *ACTIVELY* INVOLVING STUDENTS WITH LITERATURE

■ **Purpose-Setting Questions** to propel the student into the literary selection

■ **Writing-Before-Reading** or **Discussing-Before-Reading Activities** to prepare the student for the topic or theme of the literary selection

■ **Prereading Vocabulary Activities** to remove obstacles to comprehension and enjoyment

■ **Unit Introductions** and **Biographical Headnotes** to capture the student's interest and to provide a frame of reference for the literary selection

■ **Reading Guides** to give a sense of confidence to students as they tackle demanding selections

■ **Three-Part Questioning Strategy** (imitated but never equaled) to focus the student's attention on different cognitive levels—Recalling, Interpreting, Extending

from *Appreciating Literature*

from *American Literature*

- **Challenge** and **Viewpoint Activities** to encourage different modes of response and to engage all students in dialogue with literary experts

- **Postreading Vocabulary Activities** to allow the student to demonstrate mastery

- **Consistent Two-Pronged Composition Assignments** to provide options for analytical and creative responses to literature

- **Comparing Activities** to suggest new ways of looking at literature

- **Annotated Models for Active Reading** to demonstrate how an alert reader approaches a literary selection—the ideas that such a reader considers, the questions that such a reader asks, while reading

- **Guides for Reading Each Genre** to help the student transfer learning and enjoyment to selections outside the anthology

- **Active Reading Features** to help the student extract the most meaning and enjoyment from the selections in each unit

- **Thematic Reviews** to generate yet additional ways of thinking about the literature that the student has read

- **Literary Maps, Timelines,** and **Overhead Transparencies** to capture the interest of the student who learns best in a visual mode

from *Understanding Literature*

FEATURES THAT HELP YOU IMPROVE STUDENTS' ABILITIES IN READING, THINKING, WRITING, AND SPEAKING

In each anthology a unique section to help you integrate all aspects of the language-arts curriculum while teaching literature:

STUDENT'S RESOURCES: LESSONS IN ACTIVE LEARNING

■ **Speaking and Listening Handbook**—four two-page step-by-step lessons that teach the student how to present a public speech, listen effectively, participate in a group discussion, perform literature through oral interpretation, and interact in collaborative-learning activities

■ **Thinking Skills Handbook**—six two-page lessons that show students how to apply higher-order thinking processes that underlie the understanding and enjoyment of all literature: problem solving, inductive inquiry, logical reasoning, evaluation, representation, and synthesis

■ **Reading and Study Skills Handbook** (grades 7–10)—four two-page lessons that reinforce the methodologies most important to students who want to manage their learning—for example, finding the main idea, making inferences, using graphic organizers

■ **Writing About Literature Handbook**—ten to twelve lessons that demonstrate how to apply the prewriting-writing-revising process to a wide variety of literature-based assignments

■ **Research Paper Casebook** (grades 11–12)—a comprehensive guide for writing a literary research paper based on primary and secondary sources; reprinted secondary sources to use in writing a full-fledged research paper on one of the selections or authors in the anthology

PRACTICAL TIME-SAVING TEACHER'S MATERIALS FOR MOTIVATING STUDENTS, CONDUCTING LESSONS, AND EVALUATING RESULTS

TEACHER'S ANNOTATED EDITION

Reproduced student pages surrounded by sidebar annotations and bottom-of-the-page annotations that provide on-the-spot teaching help:

- **At a Glance** to remind you of the major developments on each page of a selection

- **Literary Options** and **Thematic Options** to help you clarify your purposes for teaching each selection

- **Annotations Keyed to the Selection** to point out significant passages and to encourage student involvement

- **Guided Reading Questions** to provide you with additional options of literal and inferential questions to ask on a page-by-page basis

- **Answers** to all end-of-selection questions and **Guidelines for Evaluating** all end-of-selection composition assignments

- **Additional Annotations** to give you an overview of all other unit and back-of-book features

from *Enjoying Literature*

from *English Literature with World Masterpieces*

A WEALTH OF ADDITIONAL MATERIALS FOR USE BEFORE, DURING, AND AFTER EACH LESSON

TEACHER'S CLASSROOM RESOURCES

On a selection-by-selection basis (grades 7–10) or on an author-by-author basis (grades 11–12) you can choose from

- **Teaching Notes** (additional background and a quick summary of all the materials provided within the *Scribner Literature Series* for each selection or author)
- **Prereading Vocabulary Blackline Masters**
- **Selection Test Blackline Masters**

In addition, within the *Teacher's Classroom Resources* you will find

- **Literary Skills and Active Learning Guides** (blackline masters offering additional reinforcement and enrichment activities)
- **Unit Tests** (short answer and essay)
- **Answer Key**
- **Overhead Transparencies**

THE SCRIBNER LITERATURE SERIES, SIGNATURE EDITION
THE MARK OF EXCELLENCE

The *Scribner Literature Series* was published in an earlier edition under the title *Macmillan Literature Series* by Macmillan Publishing Company.
Scribner Laidlaw is a division of Macmillan, Inc.

SCRIBNER LITERATURE SERIES

ENJOYING LITERATURE

Signature Edition

TEXAS TEACHER'S ANNOTATED EDITION

SCRIBNER Laidlaw
NEW YORK

Scribner Laidlaw
866 Third Avenue
New York, New York 10022
Collier Macmillan Canada, Inc.

Printed in the United States of America
ISBN 0-02-195590-5

CONTENTS

SIGNATURE EDITION

The *Scribner Literature Series* was first published in 1984–1985 under the title *Macmillan Literature Series.* That original edition won adoption after adoption all across the country as teachers, supervisors, and community leaders recognized its innovations and commitment to making high-quality literature accessible to *all* students. While following in the tradition of time-tested literature anthologies, the *Macmillan Literature Series* broke new ground both in the literary options it offered and in the structure, quality, and variety of its study aids—all designed to create independent readers who would continue reading and learning long after they finished the textbook.

The Signature Edition offers everything the original books offered and more. This edition places even greater emphasis on the student as an active learner, an active participant in the experience of literature. Through literature-based lessons in thinking, reading, study skills, writing, research, speaking, and listening, these books encourage students to interact with the selections.

Of course, each student interacts with literature differently; after all, each student is an individual. This brings us to the edition title—Signature Edition. The word *signature* underscores, first and foremost, the whole notion of individual differences. No two signatures are alike, as no two active learners are alike. A signature, ultimately, is a sign of authenticity and a personal mark of commitment. The Signature Edition stands for the authentic experience of literature and a commitment to help *every* student participate in that experience.

The following pages discuss the purpose and elements of the *Teacher's Annotated Edition.* We think of this teacher's edition as a kind of signature too—a sign of the kind of book a publisher can produce when working closely with teachers in the development of educational materials.

INTRODUCTION TO THE
TEACHER'S ANNOTATED EDITION

Classroom teachers and curriculum supervisors suggested to us the idea of a teacher's edition for a literature anthology. They suggested a teacher's edition that reprints student pages and provides teaching aids in the form of annotations for each page. These on-the-page annotations help teachers focus and enrich the discussion of literature; they help teachers to conveniently direct students' attention to critical passages, encouraging close, attentive, active reading of literature.

Classroom teachers and supervisors reviewed our prototypes for this *Teacher's Annotated Edition* during its development. Indeed, teachers and supervisors—novices and veterans—were the driving force behind this book. Why weren't teachers satisfied with the traditional paperback teacher's *manual* or *guide* that publishers have long provided for literature series, and why did teachers help us shape the *Scribner Literature Teacher's Annotated Editions* to create the particular kind of book you are now examining?

THE NEED FOR A *TEACHER'S ANNOTATED EDITION* FOR A LITERATURE ANTHOLOGY

A brief review of elementary-secondary publishing of the last decade indicates that teacher's annotated editions have begun to accompany student books for an increasing range of grades and for a broadening array of disciplines. However, full-blown teacher's annotated editions for 7–12 literature anthologies have been unheard of. Instead, student literature anthologies have traditionally been accompanied only by a teacher's manual, which includes strategies for teaching, answers to questions, and bibliographies.

As important as such a teacher's manual is, it is not enough, according to the classroom teachers and supervisors who shared their opinions with us. A teacher's manual, no matter how detailed or novel, cannot help teachers who are working through a literary selection or a skills page with their classes. At such times teachers need on-the-spot help—and very specific help. Broad generalizations in a teacher's manual about an aspect of an author's technique—be it imagery or diction or implication of theme—are all well and good, but *what busy teachers need are clear, specific notes about particular techniques right at the point where the techniques occur. What busy teachers need, in other words, are on-the-page annotations to highlight the particular and varied techniques that an author uses in a given work of literature.* Such annotations form the heart of the *Scribner Literature Teacher's Annotated Editions.* They allow teachers to direct a class discussion to certain aspects of a selection—easily, authoritatively. Teachers, of course, have total control over which annotations to work into any given class lesson, and the physical format of the annotated pages generally includes space for teachers to write in annotations of their own.

SUPPORT FOR THE *SCRIBNER LITERATURE TEACHER'S ANNOTATED EDITIONS*

Teachers who participated in shaping this *Teacher's Annotated Edition* clearly voiced their needs and preferences, which are reflected in the particular kinds of annotations you will find on the hundreds of textbook pages that follow. Here, we wish to share with you the criteria used in creating the annotations. According to our teacher-reviewers, page-by-page annotations must

1. be written by experienced teachers familiar with the literature and its successful presentation to students

2. save time for teachers rather than demand more time

3. be brief enough for a teacher to scan quickly

4. be simply and visibly tied to discrete passages within a selection

5. treat topics covered within the student book itself (literary terms, historical development) rather than random esoterica

6. include ideas that can be shared with students of various abilities

FEATURES OF THE
TEACHER'S ANNOTATED EDITION

As a result of the development process, which involved teachers and supervisors, the *Scribner Literature Teacher's Editions* include six varieties of on-page annotations:

SIDEBAR ANNOTATIONS FOR SELECTIONS

These are the most numerous of the annotations. There are five kinds of sidebar annotations.

1. **At a Glance.** Under this head, teachers will find one or more sentences summarizing the major developments *on that page* of the selection. Through this annotation teachers can find out "what happens where" within a selection without having to reread the entire selection. "At a Glance" functions like guide words in dictionaries, allowing the user to see the parameters of a page.

> **AT A GLANCE**
> - Franklin works as an apprentice on his brother's newspaper—Boston, 1720–1721.
> - Franklin publishes articles in the paper anonymously but then reveals his secret.
> - His brother is jailed for publishing a politically offensive article, and Franklin is questioned by the authorities.

annotation for Ben Franklin's *Autobiography,* Grade 11, p. T58

2. **Literary Options.** Here teachers will find a list of the most obvious literary elements or techniques associated with the piece of literature. If teachers wish to focus their teaching of a selection on one or more dominant elements or techniques, this list will be particularly helpful.

> **LITERARY OPTIONS**
> - autobiography
> - tone

Grade 11, p. T58

3. **Thematic Options.** Teachers can use this annotation to select one or more themes to focus on in the teaching of the selection.

> **THEMATIC OPTIONS**
> - striving for self-improvement
> - political and personal liberty

Grade 11, p. T58

4. **Annotations Keyed to the Text.** By virtue of simple numerical coding and shading (for prose selections) or citation of lines (for poetry selections), each annotation refers clearly to a certain passage and elucidates that

passage. Each annotation provides the teacher with an insight about the passage and, often, about its relation to the selection as a whole.

1 BACKGROUND

During this time many English people went to India to seek their fortunes.

2 CHARACTERIZATION

Roylott is shown to be a violent and dangerous man.

3 CHARACTERIZATION

Roylott keeps exotic animals from India. He is unafraid of these dangerous animals.

4 READING SKILLS: CAUSE AND EFFECT

Julia's white hair reveals the desolation and fear she felt at Stoke Moran before she died.

5 PLOT: SUSPENSE

Helen's sister died two weeks before she was to marry. Helen is to marry shortly. This information creates a sense of danger.

annotations for Arthur Conan Doyle's *Speckled Band,* Grade 7, p. T27

RESPONSE JOURNAL

Ask students to jot down a few rhymes they remember from *their* childhood. What associations do they have with the rhymes?

annotation for Lorraine Hansberry's "On Summer," Grade 8, p. T325

These annotations are similar to the marginal notes that effective teachers have long squeezed into their personal copies of literature anthologies. Now, at last, with the *Scribner Literature Teacher's Editions* there is room for substantial marginal annotations—to make in-class discussions richer and easier to manage.

Each *Teacher's Edition* contains thousands of annotations for teachers, who may use them all or select only some, according to their own best judgments. Teachers may find these annotations sufficient for a sound discussion of the selection, or teachers may replace or supplement these annotations with observations or insights of their own.

These keyed-to-text annotations fall into the following categories:

- literary elements
- background
- vocabulary
- paraphrasing the passage
- reading skills
- response journal

Special Note About Response Journals: Sidebar annotations headed "Response Journal" provide suggestions for student writing based on a particular passage in the selection. These annotations are designed to help teachers capitalize on what research has shown about the importance of literature-based writing assignments.

5. **Reflecting on the Selection.** The final sidebar annotation for each selection or group of selections suggests an overview question for teachers to ask students; the annotation also includes a possible response. The point of this question is to give students an opportunity to respond holistically, to react in general, to the selection before beginning a detailed postselection analysis with the suggested Study Questions or a teacher's own questions.

NOTE: In the *Teacher's Edition* for *English Literature with World Masterpieces,* an additional annotation appears from time to time, to suggest pairings of selections in English literature and selections in world literature.

"GUIDED READING" ANNOTATIONS

These bottom-of-the-page annotations include one or more pairs of literal and inferential questions about the portion of the literary selection on that page. Teachers may use these questions, which address different thinking skills, to check students' comprehension on a page-by-page basis before working through the end-of-selection Study Questions. A suggested answer is provided for each Guided Reading question.

GUIDED READING

LITERAL QUESTIONS

1a. According to Thomas, what were postmen fond of? (walking, dogs, Christmas, and snow)

2a. What does Thomas say about the "Useful" tam-o'-shanters and balaclavas? (The tam-o'-shanters were blinding and the balaclavas would only fit shrunken heads.)

INFERENTIAL QUESTIONS

1b. What do you make of his answer and the fact that the child does not question it? (He's joking, but his literal-minded companion neither questions the statement nor sees the humor in it.)

2b. What can you infer about the child Thomas from the adult's description of these gifts? (He regarded the gifts as neither "Useful" nor desirable.)

for Dylan Thomas' "Child's Christmas in Wales," Grade 10, p. T284

ANSWERS

All end-of-selection questions are answered on the page. Teachers no longer have to juggle a separate answer guide as they evaluate student responses to questions in the anthology. The annotation "Guidelines for Evaluation" provides advice for teacher critiques of written responses to Composition assignments. (In its first edition the *Scribner Literature Series* pioneered providing evaluation criteria for each and every Composition assignment.)

ANNOTATIONS FOR UNIT INTRODUCTIONS

These annotations provide teachers with an overview of key concepts to be treated in the unit. In the *Teacher's Editions* for *American Literature* and *English Literature with World Masterpieces,* these annotations include a list of key characteristics of each historical period.

ANNOTATIONS FOR ENDS OF UNITS

These annotations offer suggestions for using the Active Reading feature, the Review feature, and other-end-of-unit features that appear in the student textbook. If questions or activities are part of the textbook feature, these annotations include suggested answers.

ANNOTATIONS FOR "STUDENT'S RESOURCES"

Each volume of the *Scribner Literature Series* contains four handbooks to help students become actively and independently involved in the study of literature. These handbooks, grouped under the label "Student's Resources: Lessons in Active Learning," encourage students to integrate the study of literature with a variety of skills: thinking skills, speaking skills, listening skills, reading skills, study skills, writing skills, research skills. The annotations at the head of each handbook explain the philosophy, structure, or application of its lessons. Additionally, you will find annotations for other back-of-the-book features, including the Glossary and various indexes.

HOW TO USE THIS *TEACHER'S ANNOTATED EDITION*

To meet the needs of their classes and to accommodate their own preferences, teachers have always customized the student anthologies from which they have worked. Similarly, teachers may customize the *Scribner Literature Teacher's Annotated Editions* to reflect their own teaching styles and to meet local or state curriculum and methodology guidelines.

The six main categories of annotations—and the subclasses of selection-specific sidebar annotations—are there for teachers to choose among depending on their interests at the moment and the demands of their particular instructional load. A teacher's choice of which annotations to incorporate into a lesson may vary from year to year depending on how familiar and comfortable that teacher is at that particular time with a given selection, genre, or historical period.

One simple way to begin to feel "at home" with this *Teacher's Annotated Edition* and to see its advantages for yourself is to consider using it in three distinct ways: BEFORE, DURING, and AFTER teaching a selection.

USING THE *TEACHER'S ANNOTATED EDITION* BEFORE TEACHING A SELECTION

As you prepare to teach a selection, consider in particular the following annotations:

- **Annotations for Unit Introduction.** To remind yourself of the context into which this work fits
- **At a Glance.** To refresh yourself on the key points in the selection
- **Literary Options.** To decide which literary elements you want to emphasize
- **Thematic Options.** To decide which theme or themes you want to highlight

USING THE *TEACHER'S ANNOTATED EDITION* DURING THE TEACHING OF A SELECTION

As you undertake a class reading or discussion of the selection, you will find the following annotations offer a wealth of material:

- **Annotations Keyed to the Text.** To point out the author's use of literary elements and vocabulary; to provide additional background for students; to help students understand and appreciate difficult passages; to provide suggestions for journal entries
- **"Guided Reading" Annotations.** To monitor students' grasp of the selection, page by page, on literal and inferential levels
- **Reflecting on the Selection.** To allow you to have notable closure and to generate class response

USING THE *TEACHER'S ANNOTATED EDITION* AFTER TEACHING A SELECTION

As you and your class engage in detailed analysis of the literary selection, you can use at least the following two kinds of annotations:

- **Answers.** To help you assess your students' responses to the postselection study aids
- **Annotations for "Student's Resources."** To help you link these skills lessons to the selection just read

CREATING A FILE SYSTEM

The booklets in the *Teacher's Classroom Resources* have been designed so that you may pull out the individual pages and place them in a binder or file. Then when it comes time to reproduce those pages for class distribution, you need only take them to the photocopier.

Alternatively, you may wish to keep the booklets intact. In such a case, you may either photocopy multiple copies for class distribution directly from the booklet, or you may wish to make one master copy. Then you will be able to keep the original booklets intact in a safe place and make class copies as necessary from the master copy, which you will punch and place appropriately in a binder or file.

ADDITIONAL TEACHING MATERIALS:
TEACHER'S CLASSROOM RESOURCES

The *Scribner Literature Teacher's Annotated Editions* were produced to help teachers conduct effective lessons on literature. These *Teacher's Editions* free teachers (who often teach literature to several different grades and to more than one ability level) from the need to do extensive research on their own or to work from more than one book at the same time. The *Teacher's Editions* are, in effect, an attempt to streamline lesson preparation by putting the imaginative, lesson-enhancing ideas that teachers need *as* they teach right alongside *what* they teach and, thus, save time.

Nevertheless, there are additional materials that teachers need—above and beyond the annotations in the *Teacher's Edition.* Teachers, for example, need materials ranging from scope-and-sequence charts of all the skills presented in the series to blackline masters for additional student practice. For each grade level the *Scribner Literature Series* offers such materials—and more—in a separate component, the *Teacher's Classroom Resources.*

Here is an annotated list of the elements that make up the *Teacher's Classroom Resources* for each grade:

- ***Teacher's Professional Resources.*** This element contains articles about issues in the teaching of literature in Grades 7–12; complete scope-and-sequence charts for skills treated throughout the series (including the skills highlighted in each anthology's "Student's Resources"); correlations to simplify overall curriculum planning.

- ***Unit Booklets.*** Each of these booklets corresponds to one or two units of the anthology and contains a variety of important teaching materials.

  For teaching the unit as a whole, you will find the following:

  - A scope-and-sequence chart for the unit
  - Introductory material for the unit, a list of objectives, a bibliography, and suggested audiovisual aids
  - In Grades 7–10 a blackline-master guide for studying the genre covered in the unit
  - Blackline masters to provide practice in the topics covered in the anthology's Active Reading segment
  - Unit multiple-choice and essay tests in blackline-master form.

  Then you will find material arranged on a **selection-by-selection basis** (Grades 7–10) or on an **author-by-author basis** (Grades 11–12).

  - Additional teaching notes, including a synopsis of the selection and a statement of its theme; a suggested motivational activity, which often can involve **writing before reading;** a list of Glossary words for the selection; additional projects; references to all correlated blackline masters

- Prereading Vocabulary blackline master to introduce and give practice in difficult words from the selection
- Reading Guide blackline master to help less-able students note key points of the selection as they read
- Check Test blackline master to get a quick sense of your students' grasp of the selection on a literal level
- Writing Process Guide blackline master to help students use prewriting, writing, and revising techniques in completing the analytical Composition assignments
- Selection Test blackline master (multiple choice)

- *Literary Skills and Active Learning Guides.* The first part of this booklet contains blackline masters that provide further practice in identifying and applying their understanding of literary elements, terms, and techniques. Rather than being limited to specific selections, these blackline masters can be used with many different selections in the book—and with more than one genre.

  The second part of this booklet contains blackline masters correlated to the material highlighted in the "Student's Resources: Lessons in Active Learning" at the back of the student anthology. These blackline masters include checklists, forms, and charts to help students with the speaking, listening, thinking, writing, reading, study, and research activities suggested in the "Student's Resources"—and, in fact, throughout the textbook.

- *Answer Key.* For quick and easy reference, a single booklet contains answers and guidelines for evaluation for all of the blackline masters and tests in the *Teacher's Classroom Resources.*

- *Overhead Transparencies.* The *Scribner Literature Series* offers an alternative medium for instruction in the active reading of literature. Research suggests that students often benefit from a graphic—rather than strictly verbal—approach to content. Therefore, we offer two types of graphic overhead transparencies, which take full advantage of this medium.

  The first kind of overhead transparency is a group of graphic organizers, which help students grasp the overall content and organization of an anthology unit. The second kind of overhead transparency is a group of fine-art reproductions, selected to teach or reinforce important *literary* concepts.

SPECIAL MATERIAL
FOR TEXAS TEACHERS

For teachers in Texas the *Scribner Literature Series* offers the **Texas** *Teacher's Annotated Edition* and the **Texas** *Teacher's Classroom Resources.* All the features outlined in the preceding pages appear in the special Texas versions of the *Teacher's Annotated Edition* and the *Teacher's Classroom Resources,* but in addition Texas teachers will find the following features:

- **Texas Essential Elements box in the Texas** *Teacher's Annotated Edition.* On the first page of each selection or group of selections in Grades 7–10 and alongside the biography for each author in Grades 11–12, you will find a box itemizing the Essential Elements that are covered in the immediately following anthology pages.

- *Texas Teacher's Resources* **in the** *Texas Teacher's Classroom Resources.* This booklet contains three important items.

    1. You will find a full correlation between the Essential Elements itemized in the box just described and their coverage in the anthology.

       The box itself serves as a shorthand summary of which elements are covered. The fuller correlation chart is especially useful in filling out lesson plans or other required documentation.

    2. You will find a chart showing how the *Scribner Literature Series* can be used to meet the requirements of the Texas Teacher Appraisal system.

    3. You will find TEAMS blackline masters. These pages will provide practice in content and test-taking skills as your students prepare for the Texas Educational Assessment of Minimum Skills.

SCRIBNER LITERATURE SERIES

Signature Edition

INTRODUCING LITERATURE

ENJOYING LITERATURE

UNDERSTANDING LITERATURE

APPRECIATING LITERATURE

AMERICAN LITERATURE

ENGLISH LITERATURE

WITH WORLD MASTERPIECES

COVER: The central image is an original woodcut of William Shakespeare. The woodcut is framed by handmade marbleized paper. The combination of these two art forms suggests the sources of the finest literature—imaginative power and delicate craft.

GENERAL ADVISERS

READING AND INSTRUCTIONAL METHODS
Jack Cassidy
Professor of Education
Millersville University
Millersville, Pennsylvania

THINKING SKILLS
Eric Cooper
Director, Comprehension and Cognition Project
The College Board
New York, New York

TEACHER'S PROFESSIONAL RESOURCES
Robert DiYanni
Associate Professor of English
Pace University
Pleasantville, New York

SPEAKING AND LISTENING SKILLS
R. Brian Loxley
Communications Consultant
New York, New York

CONSULTANTS

Jean Canning, English Coordinator K–9, Summit School System, Summit, New Jersey

Pat Endsley, Assistant Principal, Berkeley Unified School District, Berkeley, California

Marta McMahon Heise, English Teacher, Churchill Junior High School, East Brunswick, New Jersey

Beverly McColley, English Teacher, Brandon Junior High School, Virginia Beach, Virginia

Jean Morgan, English Teacher, Indian Hill Schools, Cincinnati, Ohio

L. Carol O'Neal, Coordinator of English and Language Arts, Clayton County Public Schools, Jonesboro, Georgia

Judi Purvis, Secondary Language Arts Appraiser, Carrollton–Farmers Branch Independent School District, Texas

Donna Rosenberg, English Teacher, Author, Consultant, Winnetka, Illinois

WRITERS
Instructional Text

Cosmo F. Ferrara, Writer and Consultant, Former Department Chair

Gale Cornelia Flynn, Poet and Writer, Former English Teacher

Richard Foerster, Educational Writer

Meish Goldish, Educational Writer, Former English Teacher

Philip McFarland, English Teacher

Eileen Hillary Oshinsky, Educational Writer

Derrick Tseng, Educational Writer

WRITERS
Thinking Skills Handbook

Beau F. Jones-Davis, North Central Regional Educational Laboratory, Elmhurst, Illinois

Susan Sardy, Yeshiva University, New York, New York

John Sherk, University of Missouri, Kansas City, Missouri

Teacher's Classroom Resources

Stanlee Brimberg, Bank Street School for Children, New York, New York

Ellen Davis, Friendswood Independent School District, Texas

Judith H. McGee, Coordinator of Secondary Education, Athens Independent School District, Texas

David Nicholson, Riverdale Country School, Bronx, New York

The publisher is grateful for assistance and comments from the following people:

Gerald Dwight, Cherry Hill High School West, Cherry Hill, New Jersey

José Flores, Center for Mexican American Studies, University of Texas, Austin

Francisco Jiménez, Santa Clara University, Santa Clara, California

Nancy Murvine, Tatnall Middle School, Wilmington, Delaware

James S. Russell, Aptos, California

ii

SCRIBNER LITERATURE SERIES

ENJOYING LITERATURE

Signature Edition

SCRIBNER Laidlaw
NEW YORK

ACKNOWLEDGMENTS

Grateful acknowledgment is given authors, publishers, and agents for permission to reprint the following copyrighted material. Every effort has been made to determine copyright owners. In the case of any omissions, the Publisher will be pleased to make suitable acknowledgments in future editions.

George Allen & Unwin

THOR HEYERDAHL: Excerpt from *Kon-Tiki Expedition*. Reprinted by permission of George Allen & Unwin (Publishers) Ltd.

Associated Book Publishers Ltd.

E. V. RIEU: "Night Thought of a Tortoise Suffering from Insomnia on a Lawn" from *The Flattered Flying Fish and Other Poems*. Published by Methuen & Co. Reprinted by permission of Associated Book Publishers Ltd.

Atheneum Publishers, Inc.

WILLIAM GIBSON: Adaptation of Act III, Scenes 2 and 3 from *The Miracle Worker*. Copyright © 1956, 1957 by William Gibson; copyright © 1959 by Tamarack Production Ltd. and George S. Klein and Lee Garel as Trustees and three separate Deeds of Trust. Reprinted by permission of Atheneum Publishers, Inc.

Patricia Ayres

EVE MERRIAM: "Simile: Willow and Ginkgo" from *It Doesn't Always Have to Rhyme*. Published by Atheneum. Copyright © 1964 by Eve Merriam. Reprinted by permission of Eve Merriam.

Julian Bach Literary Agency, Inc.

ALICE WALKER: "For My Sister Molly" from *Revolutionary Petunias and Other Poems*. Copyright © 1972 by Alice Walker. Reprinted by permission of Julian Bach Literary Agency, Inc.

Baker's Plays

EDMOND ROSTAND: *The Romancers*, adapted and abridged by Aurand Harris. Copyright © 1979 by Aurand Harris. Reprinted by permission of Baker's Plays, Boston, MA 02111.

Scribner Laidlaw
866 Third Avenue
New York, New York 10022
Collier Macmillan Canada, Inc.

Printed in the United States of America

Pupil's Edition ISBN 0-02-195430-5

Texas Teacher's Annotated Edition ISBN 0-02-195590-5
987654321

The Bodley Head

CYRUS MACMILLAN: "The Indian Cinderella" retitled ("Strong Wind, the Invisible") from *Canadian Wonder Tales*. Reprinted by permission of The Bodley Head.

Brandt & Brandt Literary Agents, Inc.

SHIRLEY JACKSON: "Charles" from *The Lottery*. Copyright 1948, 1949, by Shirley Jackson. Copyright renewed © 1976, 1977 by Laurence Hyman, Barry Hyman, Mrs. Sarah Webster, and Mrs. Joanne Schnurer. Reprinted by permission of Brandt & Brandt Literary Agents, Inc.

Jonathan Cape Ltd.

ROBERT FROST: "A Minor Bird," "A Time to Talk," "The Road Not Taken," and "Stopping by Woods on a Snowy Evening" from *The Poetry of Robert Frost*, edited by Edward Connery Lathem. Reprinted by permission of Jonathan Cape Ltd. and the Estate of Robert Frost.
ERNEST HEMINGWAY: "A Day's Wait" from *The First Forty-Nine Stories*. Reprinted by permission of Jonathan Cape Ltd. and the Executors of the Ernest Hemingway Estate.

The Caxton Printers

TOSHIO MORI: "The Six Rows of Pompons" from *Yokohama, California*. Reprinted by permission of The Caxton Printers, Caldwell, Idaho.

B.J. Chute

B.J. CHUTE: "Come of Age" from *One Touch of Nature*. Copyright, E. P. Dutton, 1965. Reprinted by permission of B.J. Chute.

Don Congdon Associates, Inc.

EDWARD ABBEY: "Havasu" from *Desert Solitaire*. Copyright © 1968 by Edward Abbey.
RUSSELL BAKER: Excerpts from *Growing Up*. Copyright © 1982 by Russell Baker.
The preceding selections were reprinted by permission of Don Congdon Associates, Inc.

Harold Courlander

HAROLD COURLANDER: "Paul Bunyan's Cornstalk" from *Ride with the Sun*. Copyright © 1955 by McGraw-Hill Book Company. Copyright renewed 1983 by Harold Courlander. Reprinted by permission of Harold Courlander.

Coward-McCann

WALTER BLAIR: "The Amazing Crockett Family" from *Tall Tale America*. Copyright 1944, copyright renewed © 1972 by Walter Blair. Reprinted by permission of Coward-McCann.

v

A LETTER TO THE STUDENT

Enjoying Literature is a collection of stories, poems, plays, and other works of literature, all carefully chosen with you in mind. Some of the events you will read about will be familiar to you, and some of the characters will seem like people you know. Other events and characters will be new to you. With every selection you read, however, you will find yourself *thinking about literature*.

Whether a selection contains familiar or unfamiliar details, you are bound to enjoy it more if you think about it. You may read about a character and think about why that character makes a certain decision. You may read about an unfamiliar setting and think about what it has in common with your own time and place. In fact, thinking is a part of reading, and both thinking and reading make enjoying possible.

This anthology has been designed to help you think about literature in an organized way. Before a selection you will find a short introductory paragraph that ends with a question or a statement. This question or statement will help you to decide what to look for as you read the selection. After each selection you will find Study Questions that ask you to *recall* the details of the selection, *interpret* the meaning of those details, and *extend* the meaning of those details into your own experience.

Near the back of this book you will find a special section called "Student's Resources: Lessons in Active Learning." The handbooks that make up this section are practical guides for responding to literature by speaking, thinking, reading and studying, and writing. Each handbook lesson is designed to help you grow as an active, independent reader and thinker, to help you take charge of your own learning.

A writer once said, "Literature is news that *stays* news." Great literature, in other words, is always fresh. By thinking about what you read, you'll find that the literature in this book will remain meaningful and valuable long after you have closed this book and gone on to another.

CONTENTS

ENJOYING LITERATURE

The first unit presents four types of literature.
Each selection in this unit focuses on the general theme "communication."

THE SHORT STORY

The selections in Enjoying Literature *were carefully chosen. The annotations in this column indicate the literary skill or element that each selection illustrates.*

Contents vii

viii   *Contents*

POETRY

Contents ix

NONFICTION

DRAMA

GREEK MYTHS AND AMERICAN FOLK TALES

Contents   xi

THE NOVEL

xii   *Contents*

STUDENT'S RESOURCES

LESSONS IN ACTIVE LEARNING 588

Related blackline masters in *Teacher's Classroom Resources.*

Instruction and literature-based activities for oral/aural skills. Students may use lessons with *any* selection.

Definition, example, explanation for each skill plus procedures for application to literature. Students may use lessons with *any* selection.

Focused instruction on skills most essential to extracting meaning and demonstrating mastery. Students may use handbook as *constant* reference.

Composition assignments throughout the text refer to these lessons, which reinforce prewriting, writing, and revising skills.

Enjoying Literature

Preview Enjoying Literature

Why do we read literature? The title of this book gives the answer. We read literature to enjoy it. Stories, poems, nonfiction, and drama enable us to enjoy sharing the thoughts and experiences of interesting characters. We meet these characters just as we meet people in our own lives. We may travel with literary characters to places that we might otherwise never visit. Through literature we may enjoy new adventures, challenges, and victories.

Enjoying literature, however, means much more than getting pleasure from our reading. Enjoyment also includes understanding. Literature is a kind of mirror that enables us to see ourselves better and to understand what we see. When we read about a character who faces up to a challenge, we may better understand how to face our own challenges. In other words, literature helps us to think about ourselves and understand our own lives. That understanding is one of our greatest sources of enjoyment.

People write literature because they want to say something about life. To express themselves, writers select the form of literature best suited to their ideas. One writer may create a drama. Another may write a poem. Each form of literature gives an author a different way of presenting his or her view of the world.

This unit presents four different types of literature, or literary forms: story, poem, nonfiction, and drama. You will study one example of each form in order to recognize its distinct qualities. Later in this book you will find additional examples of each.

Even though the types of literature may look different on the pages of a book, they can deal with the same idea, or topic. In this unit all the selections show individuals trying to communicate with one another. As you read each selection, think about the problems that are created when characters fail to make their thoughts and emotions clear. Ask yourself what these characters help you to understand about communicating.

Enjoying Literature 1

Begin this unit by asking students to name some of the reasons why people read. Answers will probably include such ideas as to become informed and to be entertained. Invite students to name some of the types of entertaining reading materials they have enjoyed. Then have the Preview real aloud in class. Reiterate that there are many different types of literature but that only four of these types will be introduced in other units of this book. Emphasize that though they will undoubtedly get much pleasure from reading the selections in this unit, they will also come away from it with a better understanding of themselves and other people.

AT A GLANCE

- Nine-year-old Schatz, after a doctor's examination, is sent to bed with flu and a temperature of 102°.
- His father reads to him, but Schatz seems detached.

LITERARY OPTIONS

- short story
- theme
- dialogue

THEMATIC OPTIONS

- communication
- courage
- selflessness

1 DIALOGUE

Hemingway uses characteristically sparse dialogue to set the short story's plot in motion: The boy is sick.

2 POINT OF VIEW

Because the story is told from the father's point of view, the reader shares his adult perception of potential danger.

3 SETTING

Schatz's confinement to his room during his illness contributes to his sense of fear *and isolation.*

TEXAS ESSENTIAL ELEMENTS GRADE 8

1A writing process
1C support for main idea
1E appropriate language
1I sentence structure
2A varied sentences
2E grammar, punctuation, spelling
3A plot and character development
3C setting and mood
3D literary genres
4F point of view
To locate treatment of an Element, see *Texas Teacher's Resources.*

Ernest Hemingway (1899–1961) is one of America's greatest writers. In 1953 he won the Pulitzer Prize for *The Old Man and the Sea,* his novel of a battle between an old man and an enormous fish. In 1954 he won the Nobel Prize for Literature. Hemingway's characters are famous for their courage. Hemingway based the following story on the actual experience of one of his sons.

■ What thoughts might the boy have during his illness?

Ernest Hemingway

A Day's Wait

He came into the room to shut the windows while we were still in bed, and I saw he looked ill. He was shivering, his face was white, and he walked slowly as though it ached to move.

"What's the matter, Schatz?"[1]

"I've got a headache."

"You better go back to bed."

"No, I'm all right."

"You go to bed. I'll see you when I'm dressed."

But when I came downstairs he was dressed, sitting by the fire, looking a very sick and miserable boy of nine years. When I put my hand on his forehead I knew he had a fever.

"You go up to bed," I said, "you're sick."

"I'm all right," he said.

When the doctor came he took the boy's temperature.

"What is it?" I asked him.

"One hundred and two."

Downstairs, the doctor left three different medicines in different colored capsules with instructions for giving them. One was to bring down the fever, another a purgative, the third to overcome an acid condition. The germs of influenza can only exist in an acid condition, he explained. He seemed to know all about influenza and said there was nothing to worry about if the fever did not go above one hundred and four degrees. This was a light epidemic of flu and there was no danger if you avoided pneumonia.

Back in the room I wrote the boy's temperature down and made a note of the time to give the various capsules.

"Do you want me to read to you?"

"All right. If you want to," said the boy. His face was very white and there were dark areas under his eyes. He lay still in the bed and seemed very detached from what was going on.

I read aloud from Howard Pyle's *Book of Pirates;* but I could see he was not following what I was reading.

---

1. **Schatz:** [shäts]: German nickname meaning "dear."

GUIDED READING

LITERAL QUESTION

1a. How does Schatz respond when his father offers to read to him? (He says, "All right" but seems very detached.)

INFERENTIAL QUESTION

1b. Why do you think Schatz is so detached? (He is sick and feverish; he may be worried.)

"How do you feel, Schatz?" I asked him.

"Just the same, so far," he said.

1 I sat at the foot of the bed and read to myself while I waited for it to be time to give another capsule. It would have been natural for him to go to sleep, but when I looked up he was looking at the foot of the bed, looking very strangely.

"Why don't you try to go to sleep? I'll wake you up for the medicine."

"I'd rather stay awake."

2 After a while he said to me, "You don't have to stay in here with me, Papa, if it bothers you."

"It doesn't bother me."

"No, I mean you don't have to stay if it's going to bother you."

I thought perhaps he was a little light-headed and after giving him the prescribed capsules at eleven o'clock I went out for a while.

It was a bright, cold day, the ground covered with a sleet that had frozen so that it seemed as if all the bare trees, the bushes, the cut brush and all the grass and the bare ground had been varnished with ice. I took the young Irish setter for a little walk up the **3** road and along a frozen creek, but it was difficult to stand or walk on the glassy surface, and the red dog slipped and slithered and I fell twice, hard, once dropping my gun and having it slide away over the ice.

We flushed a covey of quail[2] under a high clay bank with overhanging brush and I killed two as they went out of sight over the top of the bank. Some of the covey lit in trees, but most of them scattered into brush piles and it was necessary to jump on the ice-coated mounds of brush several times before they would flush. Coming out while you were

poised unsteadily on the icy, springy brush they made difficult shooting, and I killed two, missed five, and started back pleased to have found a covey close to the house and happy there were so many left to find on another day.

4 At the house they said the boy had refused to let anyone come into the room.

"You can't come in," he said. "You mustn't get what I have."

I went up to him and found him in exactly the position I had left him, white-faced, but with the tops of his cheeks flushed by the fever, staring still, as he had stared, at the foot of the bed.

I took his temperature.

"What is it?"

"Something like a hundred," I said. It was one hundred and two and four tenths.

"It was a hundred and two," he said.

"Who said so?"

---

2. **flushed a covey of quail:** drove a small flock of quail from under cover. Quail are small game birds.

A Day's Wait 3

GUIDED READING

LITERAL QUESTIONS

1a. What does Schatz tell his father about staying in his room? ("You don't have to stay if it bothers you.")

2a. What is Schatz doing when his father looks up? (looking strangely at the foot of the bed)

INFERENTIAL QUESTIONS

1b. Why do you think he says this? (He doesn't want to cause any inconvenience; he doesn't want his father to get sick; he may be trying to hint that he's worried.)

2b. Why doesn't the father try to find out what's bothering his son? (He attributes Schatz's behavior to his fever and medication; he believes there is nothing seriously wrong with the boy.)

- Schatz asks what time he will die, finally revealing his confusion about Fahrenheit and Centigrade.
- His father explains the difference and realizes how much his son has suffered during the day.
- Schatz begins his physical and emotional recovery.

1 PLOT: CLIMAX

Hemingway uses dialogue to bring about this emotion-packed climax, in which the father finally asks what's wrong and the boy finally admits his fear.

2 CHARACTERIZATION

Details about Schatz's emotional recovery show how much he has held in and how the truth relieves him.

REFLECTING ON THE STORY

Do you think the lack of communication between father and son in this story is believable? Why or why not? (Students may believe that the misunderstanding is typical, arising out of differences in character or generation; others may believe that most parents would have gotten at the truth sooner.)

STUDY QUESTIONS

1. 102°F; influenza
2. reads aloud; stares and seems detached
3. that he is going to die; doesn't know there are two temperature scales and two types of thermometers
4. He refuses to let anyone in the room, lies in same position all day, asks when he'll die, relaxes slowly after father explains thermometers.
5. consideration for father; *courageous*—boy believes all know he's dying but none will speak to him about it; *foolish*—could have been helped early if he'd admitted fears
6. Possible answers: Fear of being rejected or of hurting another; prevents one from seeing another's point of view or feelings

---

"The doctor."

"Your temperature is all right," I said. "It's nothing to worry about."

"I don't worry," he said, "but I can't keep from thinking."

"Don't think," I said. "Just take it easy."

"I'm taking it easy," he said and looked straight ahead. He was evidently holding tight on to himself about something.

"Take this with water."

"Do you think it will do any good?"

"Of course it will."

I sat down and opened the *Pirate* book and commenced to read, but I could see he was not following, so I stopped.

1 "About what time do you think I'm going to die?" he asked.

"What?"

"About how long will it be before I die?"

"You aren't going to die. What's the matter with you?"

"Oh, yes, I am. I heard him say a hundred and two."

"People don't die with a fever of one hundred and two. That's a silly way to talk."

"I know they do. At school in France the boys told me you can't live with forty-four degrees. I've got a hundred and two."

He had been waiting to die all day, ever since nine o'clock in the morning.

"You poor Schatz," I said. "Poor old Schatz. It's like miles and kilometers. You aren't going to die. That's a different thermometer. On that thermometer thirty-seven is normal. On this kind it's ninety-eight."

"Are you sure?"

"Absolutely," I said. "It's like miles and kilometers. You know, like how many kilometers we make when we do seventy miles in the car?"

"Oh," he said.

2 But his gaze at the foot of the bed relaxed slowly. The hold over himself relaxed too, finally, and the next day it was very slack and he cried very easily at little things that were of no importance.

STUDY QUESTIONS

Recalling

1. What is the boy's temperature? What illness does he have?
2. How does the father try to entertain his son? How does the boy respond to the attempts?
3. What does the boy fear is going to happen to him? What misunderstanding is the basis of his fear?

Interpreting

4. How can you tell that the boy has been under a great deal of pressure all day?
5. Why do you think the boy hides his fears all day? Do you consider his behavior courageous or foolish? Explain.

4   *Enjoying Literature: The Short Story*

Extending

6. Why do you think people often are reluctant to reveal their true thoughts to others? Why might this lack of communication lead to misunderstandings?

READING AND LITERARY FOCUS

The Short Story

A **short story** is a fictional account of events written in prose paragraphs. Usually each event in a story leads to the next event. Often the beginning of a story introduces a problem that becomes more complicated as the story develops. By the end of the story, the difficulty is somehow settled.

Think of a story you may be familiar with—*A Christmas Carol,* for example. At the beginning of the story, Scrooge is a mean and heartless character. He refuses to donate money on Christmas Eve to some men who are collecting for charity. They also ask for and remind Scrooge of his former partner, Marley, who is now dead. The problem gets more complicated when Marley's ghost comes to Scrooge in a dream and shows Scrooge his past, present, and future. At the end of the story, Scrooge changes his cruel ways.

The events of a story usually occur in a specific time and place. For example, *A Christmas Carol* takes place in the nineteenth century in London, England, on a Christmas Eve and Christmas Day.

Authors write to entertain readers. However, authors also write stories to express their personal views about life. The author of *A Christmas Carol* wanted to express the idea that the benefits of kindness and generosity outweigh those of greed.

You will find more stories beginning on page 31.

Thinking About the Short Story

1. Who are the main characters in "A Day's Wait"?
2. What problems do the characters in "A Day's Wait" face? How are the problems solved?

VOCABULARY

Synonyms

A **synonym** is a word that has the same or nearly the same meaning as another word. *Try* and *attempt* are synonyms. The italicized words below are from "A Day's Wait." Choose the word that is *nearest* the meaning of each italicized word. Write the number of each item and the letter of your choice on a separate sheet.

1. *commenced* to study
   - (a) read
   - (b) began
   - (c) stopped
   - (d) meant
2. *epidemic* of measles
   - (a) event
   - (b) result
   - (c) widespread appearance
   - (d) itchiness
3. *slithered* through the grass
   - (a) slid
   - (b) cut
   - (c) grew
   - (d) tripped
4. a *slack* rope
   - (a) thick
   - (b) tight
   - (c) loose
   - (d) old
5. the *prescribed* medicine
   - (a) tasty
   - (b) helpful
   - (c) bottled
   - (d) recommended

COMPOSITION

Answering an Essay Question

Write an essay that answers the following question: Why do the father and son fail to communicate with each other? First make a general statement. Then quote a specific conversation in which they misunderstand each other. Next explain what each character thinks the other person means by his remarks. Finally, explain what each speaker actually means or is thinking at the time. *For help with this assignment, see Lesson 1 in the Writing About Literature Handbook at the back of this book.*

Writing a Story

Write a short story in which the main character's conflict develops from a misunderstanding about something. For example, the character may not understand an important instruction. Make sure that the events in the story are logical and that the characters and setting are described clearly. *For help with this assignment, see Lesson 4 in the Writing About Literature Handbook at the back of this book.*

CHALLENGE

Bibliography

Imagine you had a friend who was ill and had to stay in bed. Make a bibliography, or list, of five books you would recommend to your friend. Include a brief reason for each recommendation.

A Day's Wait 5

1. Schatz and his father
2. ■ Both have a problem communicating; Schatz can't tell his father of his fear that he is dying; Papa doesn't know that the boy misunderstands the temperature scales.
   - ■ Schatz tells Papa he knows no one can live with a temperature of 44° and his is 102°; Papa explains the difference between the two temperature scales, using miles and kilometers to make his point.

VOCABULARY

1. (b) began
2. (c) widespread appearance
3. (a) slid
4. (c) loose
5. (d) recommended

CHALLENGE

Bibliography should include
- ■ at least titles and authors of five books
- ■ reasons for recommending each

ANSWERING AN ESSAY QUESTION

Objective

To analyze a central element of the story

Guidelines for Evaluation
- ■ suggested length: 1–2 paragraphs
- ■ should answer "Why do father and son fail to communicate?"
- ■ should make general statement and give a specific example of this failure

WRITING A STORY

Objective

To write a short story about a misunderstanding

Guidelines for Evaluation
- ■ suggested length: 100–300 words
- ■ story's focus: a problem related to a misunderstanding by the main character
- ■ should relate logical events, characters, setting
- ■ should resolve the problem at end of story

Robert Frost (1875–1963) is one of the most famous and most honored of twentieth-century American poets. He wrote many poems about the land and people of New England, where he spent much of his life as a farmer and a teacher. One of Frost's finest qualities is the way his poems seem to speak in a warm and friendly way to each reader.

■ What would be an appropriate occasion to stop work and talk?

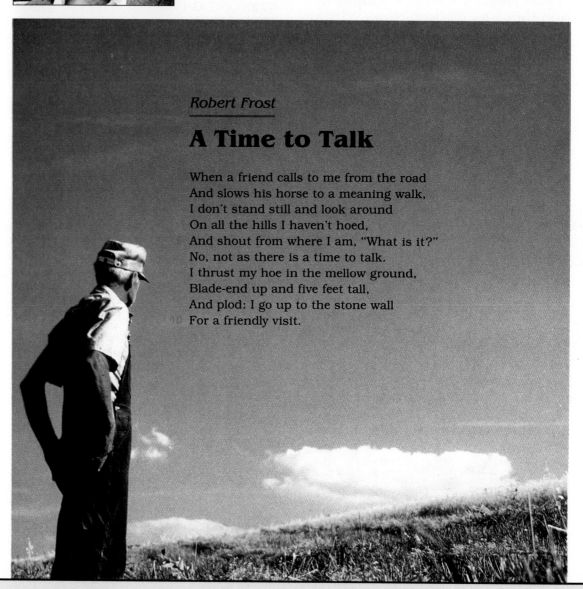

Robert Frost

A Time to Talk

When a friend calls to me from the road
And slows his horse to a meaning walk,
I don't stand still and look around
On all the hills I haven't hoed,
And shout from where I am, "What is it?"
No, not as there is a time to talk.
I thrust my hoe in the mellow ground,
Blade-end up and five feet tall,
And plod: I go up to the stone wall
For a friendly visit.

STUDY QUESTIONS

Recalling

1. According to lines 1–4, what kind of work is the poet doing when his friend calls to him?
2. Name three things the poet does *not* do when a friend calls.
3. Name two things he *does* when a friend calls.

Interpreting

4. To what is the poet saying "No" in line 6? What does he mean by "a time to talk"?
5. Does the poet seem to enjoy both his work and his friends? How can you tell?

Extending

6. Why do you think it is important to make time both for work and for friends?

READING AND LITERARY FOCUS

Poetry

Poetry is imaginative writing in which language, images, sound, and rhythm combine to create a special emotional effect. The poet carefully selects the exact words to suggest a particular picture or to stir certain emotions. In "A Time to Talk," for example, the words *mellow ground* create a vivid picture of soft, rich earth. They also convey a sense of the poet's gentle and comfortable feeling for the land.

The speaker of a poem is the person or thing that "speaks" or "tells" the poem. Usually the speaker is the poet. Sometimes, however, the speaker is another person, an animal, or even an object. The speaker of "A Time to Talk" is the poet, Frost.

Poems are generally written in lines. Often the lines are grouped in units called **stanzas.** "A Time to Talk," however, is not divided into stanzas.

The sound of a poem helps reflect the feeling of the speaker. In Frost's poem, for example, the sound is the natural rhythm of a plain and simple conversation. In fact, nearly every word in the poem has just one syllable. By using this simple style, Frost helps to convey the picture of a plain, gentle farmer doing his chores. Many poems also contain rhyme. For example, in lines 1 and 4 of Frost's poem, the words *road* and *hoed* rhyme.

Poets, like story writers, wish to express their ideas about life. For example, in "A Time to Talk" Frost expresses his belief in the importance of friendship and communicating with others.

You will find more poems beginning on page 219.

Thinking About Poetry

1. Besides lines 1 and 4, which other lines of the poem rhyme?
2. Which of the following emotions does the poem best convey: relaxation, hurriedness, or sadness? What specific words or phrases in the poem help to create that emotion?

COMPARING THEMES

■ The father in "A Day's Wait" and the speaker in "A Time to Talk" both want to communicate with another person. Which person more easily succeeds in communicating? Why?

A Time to Talk 7

- Russell enters his final year of high school with little hope of finding a job.
- His only interest is writing.
- He thinks of writing as a vocation of the rich.

LITERARY OPTIONS

- nonfiction
- style
- audience

THEMATIC OPTIONS

- communication
- discoveries
- adolescence

1 PURPOSE

Baker begins his autobiographical account with a scene most people have experienced themselves. Choosing a scene or emotion with which his audience can identify is crucial to his purpose: to entertain.

2 BACKGROUND

In the 1930s many high school graduates could not afford a college education; they had to go to work to help support their families.

3 INTERNAL CONFLICT

Russell is torn between his desire to be a writer and his conviction that it is "not real work."

TEXAS ESSENTIAL ELEMENTS GRADE 8

3A character development
3C setting and mood
3D literary genres
3E types of nonfiction
4A appropriate meaning of multimeaning words
4B implied main idea
4C fact vs. nonfact
4E cause/effect
4F author's purpose
To locate treatment of an Element, see *Texas Teacher's Resources.*

Russell Baker (born 1925) has been a columnist for the *New York Times* since 1962. He won the Pulitzer Prize in 1979 for his distinguished journalism and in 1982 for his book *Growing Up.* The book is Baker's humorous and loving recollection of growing up with his family during the Great Depression of the 1930s, a time of poverty and hardship. This selection from the book tells of the young man's attempt to decide on a career.

■ Does Baker's experience seem realistic and believable?

Russell Baker

from Growing Up

1   "Something will come along."

That became my mother's battle cry as I plowed into the final year of high school. Friends began asking her what Russell planned to do when he graduated, and her answer was, "Something will come along." She didn't know what, and nothing was in sight on the horizon, but she'd survived so long now on faith that something always came along for people who did their best. "Russ hasn't made up his mind yet, but something will come along," she told people.

2   I saw no possibilities and looked forward to the end of school days with increasing glumness. It was assumed I would get a job. Boys of our economic class didn't ordinarily go to college. My education, however, hadn't fitted me for labor. While I was reading the Romantic poets[1] and learning Latin syntax,[2] practical boys had been taking shop, mechanical drawing, accounting, and typing. I couldn't drive a nail without mashing my thumb. When I mentioned my inadequacies to my mother she said, "Something will come along, Buddy."

3   The only thing that truly interested me was writing, and I knew that sixteen-year-olds did not come out of high school and become writers. I thought of writing as something to be done only by the rich. It was so obviously not real work, not a job at which you could earn a living. Still, I had begun to think of myself as a writer. It was the only thing for which I seemed to have the smallest talent, and, silly though it sounded when I told people I'd like to be a writer, it gave me a way of thinking about myself which satisfied my need to have an identity.

The notion of becoming a writer had flickered off and on in my head since the Belleville[3] days, but it wasn't until my third year in high

---

1. **Romantic poets:** group of British poets writing in the late 1700s and early 1800s.
2. **syntax:** sentence structure.

3. **Belleville:** town in northeastern New Jersey where Baker had lived earlier.

8   *Enjoying Literature: Nonfiction*

GUIDED READING

LITERAL QUESTION

1a. What two reasons does Russell give for wanting to be a writer? (only thing in which he had any talent; gave him an "identity")

INFERENTIAL QUESTION

1b. In what way might writing have given him an "identity"? (It provided him with a way to refer to himself, to think of himself, and to see the world.)

school that the possibility took hold. Until then I'd been bored by everything associated with English courses. I found English grammar dull and baffling. I hated the assignments to turn out "compositions," and went at them like heavy labor, turning out leaden, lackluster paragraphs that were agonies for teachers to read and for me to write. The classics thrust on me to read seemed as deadening as chloroform.[4]

When our class was assigned to Mr. Fleagle for third-year English I anticipated another grim year in that dreariest of subjects. Mr. Fleagle was notorious among City students for dullness and inability to inspire.

He constantly sprinkled his sentences with "don't you see." It wasn't a question but an exclamation of mild surprise at our ignorance. "Your pronoun needs an antecedent,[5] don't you see," he would say, very primly. "The purpose of the Porter's scene,[6] boys, is to provide comic relief from the horror, don't you see."

Late in the year we tackled the informal essay. "The essay, don't you see, is the . . ." My mind went numb. Of all forms of writing, none seemed so boring as the essay. Naturally we would have to write informal essays. Mr. Fleagle distributed a homework sheet offering us a choice of topics. None was quite so simpleminded as "What I Did on My Summer Vacation," but most seemed to be almost as dull. I took the list home and dawdled until the night before the essay was due. Sprawled on the sofa, I finally faced up to the grim task, took the list out of my notebook, and scanned it. The topic on which my eye stopped was "The Art of Eating Spaghetti."

4. **chloroform** [klôr′ə fôrm]: type of anesthetic, or substance used to cause sleep.
5. **antecedent:** [an′tə sēd′ənt]: noun to which the pronoun refers.
6. **Porter's scene:** comic scene in *Macbeth*, a tragic play by William Shakespeare.

This title produced an extraordinary sequence of mental images. Surging up out of the depths of memory came a vivid recollection of a night in Belleville when all of us were seated around the supper table—Uncle Allen, my mother, Uncle Charlie, Doris, Uncle Hal—and Aunt Pat served spaghetti for supper. Spaghetti was an exotic treat in those days. Neither Doris nor I had ever eaten spaghetti, and none of the adults had enough experience to be good at it. All the good humor of Uncle Allen's house reawoke in my mind as I recalled the laughing arguments we had that night about the socially respectable method for moving spaghetti from plate to mouth.

Suddenly I wanted to write about that, about the warmth and good feeling of it, but I wanted to put it down simply for my own joy, not for Mr. Fleagle. It was a moment I wanted to recapture and hold for myself. I wanted to relive the pleasure of an evening at New Street. To write it as I wanted, however, would violate all the rules of formal composition I'd learned in school, and Mr. Fleagle would

Russell Baker in 1943.

Growing Up 9

AT A GLANCE
- Dull Mr. Fleagle becomes Russell's English teacher.
- Russell is bored with English class until he discovers a composition topic that excites him.
- He recalls a scene from his past and wishes to write about it for his own gratification.

1 STYLE: HUMOR

Baker's humor grows from his use of the simile "as deadening as chloroform"—an exaggerated way to describe the classics he had to read.

2 CHARACTERIZATION

Mr. Fleagle's dullness is deftly and humorously evoked by quoting his speech patterns.

3 AUDIENCE

Baker's choice of details ("What I Did on My Summer Vacation," "dawdled until the night before") encourages his audience to identify personally with his conflict.

4 THEME

The composition topic about eating spaghetti causes Russell to discover "an extraordinary sequence of mental images." The writer in him comes alive at this moment.

5 THEME

Russell makes another discovery: Writing for one's own gratification is a first crucial step toward good writing.

GUIDED READING

LITERAL QUESTIONS

1a. How does Russell feel about writing the informal essays Mr. Fleagle assigns? (They are boring for him to write and for teachers to read.)

2a. What happens when Russell writes the title for his essay on eating spaghetti? (The title produces "an extraordinary sequence of mental images.")

INFERENTIAL QUESTIONS

1b. Why do you think he finds most of the compositions so boring? (The topics don't excite him or seem to touch on his life.)

2b. What type of writing seems to appeal most to Russell? (informal, humorous writing based on his own experiences; writing he can do for his own pleasure)

AT A GLANCE

- Russell writes the essay for himself; there is no time to write a *proper* essay.
- Mr. Fleagle reads the essay to the class; Russell discovers the thrill of making an audience laugh.
- Russell's dreams of becoming a writer are solidified.

1 STYLE: HUMOR

Baker pokes fun at himself by reporting that the same phrase that had annoyed him so often— "Don't you see"—now "put the final seal on my happiness."

REFLECTING ON THE SELECTION

Do you think Russell's life would be different today if the composition list had not contained the topic "The Art of Eating Spaghetti"? (Most students will probably say that Russell may have found other inspiration for writing.)

STUDY QUESTIONS

1. writing
2. recalled laughing arguments his family had about proper way to eat spaghetti; wanted to capture warmth and good feelings
3. that he would give it a failing grade; read essay aloud, calls it "of the very essence of the essay"
4. pure ecstasy that his words had the power to make people laugh
5. Answers will vary. Most will agree the moment was decisive—it made a writing career seem a real possibility—but other events would be necessary to make the career a reality.
6. ■ He calls "something will come along" his mother's battle cry.
   ■ end of 5th paragraph: "The classics thrust on me to read seemed as deadening as chloroform."
   ■ of Mr. Fleagle's phrase "don't you see" says, "It wasn't a question, but an exclamation of mild surprise at our ignorance."

7. Most will agree that the essay was successful because it conveyed feelings as well as ideas.
8. fame or money; knowledge that they are communicating ideas to others; immortality; sense of creating

---

surely give it a failing grade. Never mind. I would write something else for Mr. Fleagle after I had written this thing for myself.

When I finished it the night was half gone and there was no time left to compose a proper, respectable essay for Mr. Fleagle. There was no choice next morning but to turn in my private reminiscence of Belleville. Two days passed before Mr. Fleagle returned the graded papers, and he returned everyone's but mine. I was bracing myself for a command to report to Mr. Fleagle immediately after school for discipline when I saw him lift my paper from his desk and rap for the class's attention.

"Now, boys," he said, "I want to read you an essay. This is titled 'The Art of Eating Spaghetti.' "

And he started to read. My words! He was reading *my words* out loud to the entire class. What's more, the entire class was listening. Listening attentively. Then somebody laughed, then the entire class was laughing, and not in contempt and ridicule, but with openhearted enjoyment. Even Mr. Fleagle stopped two or three times to repress a small prim smile.

I did my best to avoid showing pleasure, but what I was feeling was pure ecstasy at this startling demonstration that my words had the power to make people laugh. In the eleventh grade, at the eleventh hour as it were, I had discovered a calling. It was the happiest moment of my entire school career. When Mr. Fleagle finished he put the final seal on my happiness by saying, "Now that, boys, is an essay, don't you see. It's—don't you see it's of the very essence of the essay, don't you see. Congratulations, Mr. Baker."

For the first time, light shone on a possibility. It wasn't a very heartening possibility, to be sure. Writing couldn't lead to a job after high school, and it was hardly honest work, but Mr. Fleagle had opened a door for me. After that I ranked Mr. Fleagle among the finest teachers in the school.

STUDY QUESTIONS

Recalling

1. What was Russell's main interest in school?
2. Why did Russell want to write about eating spaghetti?
3. What did Russell think Mr. Fleagle's reaction to his essay would be? What was Mr. Fleagle's actual reaction?
4. What reaction does Russell have when Mr. Fleagle reads his essay to the class?

Interpreting

5. Do you think the incident described in the selection could really be important enough to decide Russell Baker's career? Why or why not?

6. Cite passages in this selection that indicate Baker's sense of humor.
7. What does Baker suggest about the ability of writing to communicate ideas and emotions?

Extending

8. What rewards might people derive from a career as a writer?

READING AND LITERARY FOCUS

Nonfiction

Nonfiction is factual prose writing. Its subject matter is real experiences. A story or poem may be about imaginary incidents, but nonfiction deals only with actual events. "A Day's Wait" is a fictional

10 *Enjoying Literature: Nonfiction*

story concerned with temperature scales. An encyclopedia article about centigrade and Fahrenheit temperature scales is an example of nonfiction.

Nonfiction may be placed into two main categories: (1) essays and (2) biographies and autobiographies. An **essay** is a composition that expresses the writer's knowledge or thoughts on one particular subject. Essays may be written on any subject, including sports, politics, or science.

A **biography** is the story of someone's life, written by another person. Often authors write biographies about celebrities such as past presidents, sports heroes, or famous scientists. An **autobiography** is the story of a person's life written by that person. Many politicians, for example, write their autobiographies after retiring.

Nonfiction writers, like story authors and poets, create their work partly to express their personal views on life. They may convey these ideas directly or merely suggest them through details in their writing. For example, a person who feels strongly about the importance of a college education could state this belief directly in an essay. Another author with the same belief could express the idea indirectly by writing the biography of an individual who completed college and benefited by it later in life.

You will find more nonfiction selections beginning on page 297.

Thinking About Nonfiction

1. Would you categorize *Growing Up* as an essay, a biography, or an autobiography? Why?
2. What personal ideas about writing did Baker express through his account of one particular high school assignment?

VOCABULARY

Context Clues

Sometimes you can figure out the meaning of a word by its **context,** or the words and sentences that surround it. Look at the following sentence from *Growing Up:*

When our class was assigned to Mr. Fleagle for third-year English I anticipated another grim year in that dreariest of subjects.

Suppose you did not know the meaning of *grim.* The writer talks about English as the "dreariest" of subjects. From this clue you may conclude that *grim* means "dreary" and "uninviting."

The following sentences come from the selection. Choose the best meaning for each italicized word by studying its *context.* That is, examine the ideas found in the sentence in which the word appears or in surrounding sentences. Write your answers on a separate sheet.

1. I hated the assignments to turn out "compositions," and went at them like heavy labor, turning out leaden, *lackluster* paragraphs that were agonies for teachers to read and for me to write.
   (a) exciting   (c) puzzling
   (b) dull   (d) long
2. He constantly sprinkled his sentences with "don't you see." It wasn't a question but an *exclamation* of mild surprise at our ignorance.
   (a) solution   (c) denial
   (b) outcry   (d) pattern
3. *Surging* up out of the depths of memory came a vivid recollection of a night in Belleville. . . .
   (a) knowing   (c) ending
   (b) swelling   (d) drowning
4. I did my best to avoid showing pleasure, but what I was feeling was pure *ecstasy* at this startling demonstration that my words had the power to make people laugh.
   (a) sorrow   (c) indifference
   (b) anger   (d) joy

COMPARING THEMES

1. Compare Mr. Fleagle's communication skills with those of the father in "A Day's Wait."
2. In what ways is Mr. Fleagle's success in communicating with Russell similar to the speaker's success in "A Time to Talk"?

Growing Up 11

TEXAS ESSENTIAL ELEMENTS
GRADE 8

1A writing process
1B purpose and audience
1C support for main idea
1D evaluation of content and
organization
1E appropriate language
3A plot development and
character development
3C setting and mood
3D literary genres
4B implied main idea
4E cause/effect
4K library references
To locate treatment of an
Element, see *Texas
Teacher's Resources*.

William Gibson (born 1914) is best known for his drama *The Miracle Worker* (1959). This play was a great Broadway success and was later made into a movie. It presents an emotional account of the early life of Helen Keller. Before she was two years old, Helen lost her sight, hearing, and ability to speak. In spite of these handicaps, Helen became a world-famous author and representative for improving conditions for the blind.

The following scenes come from Act III of *The Miracle Worker*. Annie has been staying with the Kellers for about a month, trying to break through seven-year-old Helen's blindness and deafness. Her task has been made more difficult by Helen's parents, who have always given in to their willful daughter. Annie persuaded the Kellers to allow her and Helen to spend two weeks apart from the family in a small garden house on their property. During these two weeks Annie taught Helen to obey her and to spell a number of words in the finger alphabet for the deaf.

At the opening of the following scene, the two weeks in the garden house are ending.

■ What is life like for Helen, who cannot see, hear, or speak?

William Gibson

from **The Miracle Worker**

CHARACTERS

ANNIE SULLIVAN: young teacher trained to work with the blind and deaf; twenty years old

HELEN KELLER: child who has been blind and deaf since infancy; now seven years old

KATE KELLER: Helen's mother; in her late twenties

CAPTAIN KELLER: Helen's father; middle-aged

JAMES KELLER: Captain Keller's grown son by a previous marriage; in his early twenties

AUNT EV: Captain Keller's sister; middle-aged

Scene: *The action takes place on the Keller homestead in Tuscumbia, Alabama. The time is the 1880s.*

12 *Enjoying Literature: Drama*

The garden house.
Late afternoon.

1 [HELEN *is quietly working with wool and a crochet hook,*[1] *doing simple stitches.* ANNIE *is writing a letter, occasionally looking up spellings in a dictionary.*]

ANNIE. "—my. mind. is. undisciplined. full. of. skips. and. jumps. and—" [*She halts, re-reads. frowns.*] Hm.

[ANNIE *puts her nose again in the dictionary, flips back to an earlier page, and fingers down the words.* KATE *presently comes down toward the bay window with a trayful of food.*]

Disinterested. disjoin—where's discipline?

[*She goes a page or two back, searching with her finger, muttering.*]

What a dictionary! Have to know how to spell it before you can look up how to spell it, dis-ciple, *discipline!* Diskipline. . . .

[*But her eyes are bothering her, she closes them in exhaustion.* KATE *watches her through the window.*]

KATE. What are you doing to your eyes?

[ANNIE *glances around; she puts her smoked glasses*[2] *on, and gets up to come over, assuming a cheerful energy.*]

ANNIE. It's worse on my vanity! I'm learning to spell. . . .

KATE. You're not to overwork your eyes, Miss Annie.

ANNIE. Well. Whatever I spell to Helen I'd better spell right.

---

1. **crochet** [krō shā′] **hook:** small hook used to loop and weave together strands of thread or yarn.
2. **smoked glasses:** Annie has very bad eyesight and uses dark glasses to ease her eyestrain.

KATE. [*Almost wistful.*] How—serene she is.

ANNIE. She learned this stitch yesterday. Now I can't get her to stop! . . .

2 KATE. You've taught her so much, these two weeks. I would never have—

ANNIE. Not enough. [*She is suddenly gloomy, shakes her head.*] Obedience isn't enough. Well, she learned two nouns this morning, key and water, brings her up to eighteen nouns and three verbs.

KATE. [*Hesitant.*] But—not—

ANNIE. No. Not that they mean things. It's still a finger-game, no meaning. [*She turns to* KATE *abruptly.*] Mrs. Keller—[*But she defers it; she comes back, to sit in the bay and lift her hand.*] Shall we play our finger-game?[3]

KATE. How will she learn it?

ANNIE. It will come.

[*She spells a word;* KATE *does not respond.*]

KATE. How?

3 ANNIE. [*A pause.*] How does a bird learn to fly? [*She spells again.*] We're born to use words, like wings, it has to come.

KATE. How?

ANNIE. [*Another pause, wearily.*] All right. I don't know how. [*She pushes up her glasses, to rub her eyes.*] I've done everything I could think of. Whatever she's learned here—keeping herself clean, knitting, stringing beads, meals, setting-up exercises each morning, we climb trees, hunt eggs, yesterday a chick was born in her hands—all of it I spell, everything we do, we never stop spelling. I go to bed with—writer's cramp from talking so much!

---

3. **finger-game:** Annie has been teaching Kate the finger alphabet used by the deaf, so that Kate will be able to communicate with Helen.

The Miracle Worker 13

GUIDED READING

LITERAL QUESTIONS

1a. How does Annie feel when she says, "Obedience isn't enough"? (gloomy)

2a. To what does Annie compare a person learning to communicate? (a bird learning to fly)

INFERENTIAL QUESTIONS

1b. Why do you think she feels gloomy? (Her hopes for Helen are so much higher than Kate's; she wants to teach Helen to communicate.)

2b. In what way is a person's learning to communicate like a bird's learning to fly? (Words come as naturally to humans as flying does to birds; like flight, communication is a power that allows us to explore the world in new ways.)

1 CHARACTERIZATION

Annie again affirms her faith in Helen's inborn power to communicate.

2 EXTERNAL CONFLICT

Kate and Annie are in conflict again. Kate wants her daughter back, but she is intimidated by Annie's strength.

KATE. I worry about you, Miss Annie. You must rest.

ANNIE. Now? She spells back in her *sleep,* her fingers make letters when she doesn't know! In her bones those five fingers know, that hand aches to—speak out, and something in her mind is asleep, how do I—nudge that awake? That's the one question.

KATE. With no answer.

ANNIE. [*Long pause.*] Except keep at it. Like this.

[*She again begins spelling—"I, need"—and* KATE'*s brows gather, following the words.*]

KATE. More—time? [*She glances at* ANNIE, *who looks her in the eyes, silent.*] Here?

14   *Enjoying Literature: Drama*

GUIDED READING

LITERAL QUESTION

1a. What is the one question that Annie says she's trying to answer? (How can she nudge Helen's mind awake?)

INFERENTIAL QUESTION

1b. What do you think Kate means when she says the question has "no answer"? (either that Annie has been unable to find an answer or that there really is no answer, that Helen will never learn to communicate)

ANNIE. Spell it.

[KATE *spells a word—"no"—shaking her head;* ANNIE *spells two words—"why, not"—back, with an impatient question in her eyes; and* KATE *moves her head in pain to answer it.*]

KATE. Because I can't—

ANNIE. Spell it! If she ever learns, you'll have a lot to tell each other, start now.

[KATE *painstakingly spells in air. In the midst of this the rear door opens, and* KELLER *enters with the setter* BELLE *in tow.*]

1 **KELLER.** Miss Sullivan? On my way to the office, I brought Helen a playmate—

ANNIE. Outside please, Captain Keller. . . .

[*She escorts* KELLER *by the arm over the threshold; he obeys, leaving* BELLE.]

KELLER. Miss Sullivan, you are a tyrant.

ANNIE. Likewise, I'm sure. You can stand there, and close the door if she comes.

KATE. I don't think you know how eager we are to have her back in our arms—

ANNIE. I do know, it's my main worry.

KELLER. It's like expecting a new child in the house. Well, she *is*, so—composed, so—[*Gently.*] Attractive. You've done wonders for her, Miss Sullivan.

2 **ANNIE.** [*Not a question.*] Have I.

KELLER. If there's anything you want from us in repayment tell us, it will be a privilege to—

ANNIE. I just told Mrs. Keller. I want more time.

KATE. Miss Annie—

ANNIE. Another week. . . .

KELLER. And what would another week ac-complish? We are more than satisfied, you've done more than we ever thought possible, taught her constructive—

ANNIE. I can't promise anything. All I can—

3 **KELLER.** —things to do, to behave like—even look like—a human child, so manageable, contented, cleaner, more—

ANNIE. Cleaner.

KELLER. Well. We say cleanliness is next to godliness, Miss—

ANNIE. Cleanliness is next to nothing, she has to learn that everything has its name! That **4** words can be her *eyes*, to everything in the world outside her, and inside too, what is she without words? With them she can think, have ideas, be reached, there's not a thought or fact in the world that can't be hers. You publish a newspaper, Captain Keller, do I have to tell you what words are? And she has them already—

KELLER. Miss Sullivan.

ANNIE. —eighteen nouns and three verbs, **5** they're in her fingers now, I need only time to push *one* of them into her mind! One, and everything under the sun will follow. Don't you see what she's learned here is only clearing the way for that? I can't risk her unlearning it, give me more time alone with her, another week to—

KELLER. Look.

[*He points, and* ANNIE *turns.* HELEN *is playing with the dog's claws; she makes letters with her fingers, shows them to the dog, waits with her palm, then manipulates the dog's claws.*]

KELLER. What is she spelling? [*A silence.*]

KATE. Water?

[ANNIE *nods.*]

The Miracle Worker 15

AT A GLANCE

- *Scene 1 (continued):* Helen's parents are determined to have her back.
- Annie pleads for one more week with Helen.

1 EXTERNAL CONFLICT

Annie and Captain Keller are well-matched antagonists, each of whom recognizes the other's strength. For the moment Annie wins.

2 STAGE DIRECTIONS

The directions indicate that Annie's "Have I" is in disagreement with Keller's "You've done wonders. . . ."

3 STYLE: REPETITION

When Annie repeats "Cleaner," she is commenting ironically on how little Keller expects for Helen in contrast to how much Annie expects of the child.

4 THEME

Annie explains her passionate belief that words can be Helen's "eyes," allowing the blind girl to "see" the world—and herself—through the power of communication.

5 FORESHADOWING

Annie's words foreshadow the climactic moment of the play.

GUIDED READING

LITERAL QUESTIONS

1a. When Kate says that Annie doesn't know how eager the family is to have Helen back, what does Annie say? (She does know; it's her main worry.)

2a. What does Annie say about cleanliness? (It is "next to nothing.")

INFERENTIAL QUESTIONS

1b. What does Annie mean by her reply? (that she's afraid the family's low expectations of Helen are keeping her from learning)

2b. What does Annie mean? (It is such a small accomplishment, compared to what Annie wants for Helen: the ability to communicate.)

■ *Scene 1 (continued):* Helen must be returned to her parents by six o'clock.

■ Annie spends her final day in the garden house stil! striving for a breakthrough with Helen.

1 CHARACTERIZATION

Annie finally surrenders to the combined strength of Captain Keller and Kate, but she still insists on keeping Helen until six o'clock sharp.

2 PLOT: SUSPENSE

Suspense builds as Annie spells *water* into Helen's hand, then thrusts her hand into the tumbler.

3 IRONY

One would expect the Kellers to want more for their daughter than they want for their dog, Annie implies, but they don't seem to.

4 THEME

Annie eloquently expresses her passionate commitment to Helen and to the wonders of communication.

5 RESPONSE JOURNAL

So far in the play, Annie has compared words to wings, eyes, and light. Ask students to write in their journals about which image best describes the power of words.

KELLER. Teaching a dog to spell. [*A pause.*] The dog doesn't know what she means, any more than she knows what you mean. Miss Sullivan, I think you ask too much, of her and yourself. God may not have meant Helen to have the—eyes you speak of.

ANNIE. [*Toneless.*] I mean her to. . . .

1 KELLER. An agreement *is* an agreement.

ANNIE. Mrs. Keller?

KATE. [*Simply.*] I want her back.

[*A wait;* ANNIE *then lets her hands drop in surrender, and nods.*] . . .

ANNIE. Not until six o'clock. I have her till six o'clock.

KELLER. Six o'clock. Come, Katie.

[*They leave.* . . . ANNIE *stands watching* HELEN *work the dog's claws. Then she settles beside them on her knees, and stops* HELEN's *hand.*]

ANNIE. [*Gently.*] No.

[*She shakes her head, with* HELEN's *hand to her face, then spells.*]

Dog, D, o, g.

[*She touches* HELEN's *hand to* BELLE. HELEN *dutifully pats the dog's head, and resumes spelling to its paw.*]

Not water.

2 [ANNIE *rolls to her feet, brings a tumbler of water back from the tray, and kneels with it, to seize* HELEN's *hand and spell.*]

Here. Water. *Water.*

[*She thrusts* HELEN's *hand into the tumbler.* HELEN *lifts her hand out dripping, and taking the tumbler from* ANNIE, *endeavors to thrust* BELLE's *paw into it.* ANNIE *sits watching wearily.*]

16   *Enjoying Literature: Drama*

I don't know how to tell you. Not a soul in the world knows how to tell you. Helen, Helen.

[*She bends in compassion to touch her lips to* HELEN's *temple, and instantly* HELEN *pauses, her hands off the dog, her head slightly averted.*[4] . . . ANNIE *sits back.*]

3 Yes, what's it to me? They're satisfied. Give them back their child and dog, both housebroken, everyone's satisfied. But me, and you.

[HELEN's *hand comes out into the light, groping.*]

Reach. *Reach!*

[ANNIE *extending her own hand grips* HELEN's; *the two hands are clasped, tense in the light, the rest of the room changing in shadow.*]

4 I wanted to teach you—oh, everything the earth is full of, Helen—everything on it that's ours for a wink and it's gone, and what we are on it; the—light we bring to it and leave 5 behind in—words. Why, you can see five thousand years back in a light of words, everything we feel, think, know—and share, in words, so not a soul is in darkness, or done with, even in the grave. And I know, I *know*, one word and I can—put the world into your hand—and whatever it is to me, I won't take less. How, how, how do I tell you that *this* [*She spells.*] means a *word*, and the word means this *thing*, wool?

[*She thrusts the wool into* HELEN's *hand;* HELEN *sits puzzled.*]

Or this—s, t, o, o, l—means this *thing*, stool?

[*She clasps* HELEN's *palm to the stool.* HELEN *waits, uncomprehending.* ANNIE *snatches up her napkin, spells:*]

---

4. **averted:** turned away.

GUIDED READING

LITERAL QUESTIONS

1a. Who does Annie say is not satisfied with Helen's progress? (Annie and Helen herself)

2a. To what does Annie compare words on a page? (light)

INFERENTIAL QUESTIONS

1b. Why do you think Annie says Helen is dissatisfied? (She senses that somewhere inside, a part of Helen is struggling to reach out.)

2b. What does Annie mean when she says that because of this light "not a soul is in darkness . . . even in the grave"? (Our words create a light of understanding between us; people remember them even after we die.)

Napkin!

[*She forces it on* HELEN'*s hand, waits, discards it, lifts a fold of the child's dress, spells:*]

Dress!

[*She lets it drop, spells:*]

F, a, c, e, face!

1 [*She draws* HELEN'*s hand to her cheek, and pressing it there, staring into the child's unresponsive eyes, hears the distant belfry[5] toll, slowly: one, two, three, four, five, six.*] . . .

The dining room of the main house. Shortly afterward.

The KELLERS *are celebrating* HELEN'*s homecoming with a special dinner. The group includes* ANNIE *and* HELEN, CAPTAIN KELLER, KATE, AUNT EV (CAPTAIN KELLER'*s sister*), *and* JAMES (KELLER'*s grown son by an earlier marriage*). *The dinner seems to be going smoothly, and* HELEN *has been behaving herself.*

KATE. Pickles, Aunt Ev?

AUNT EV. Oh, I should say so, you know my opinion of your pickles—

KATE. This is the end of them, I'm afraid. I didn't put up nearly enough last summer, this year I intend to—

2 [*She interrupts herself, seeing* HELEN *deliberately lift off her napkin and drop it to the floor. She bends to retrieve it, but* ANNIE *stops her arm*. . . . ANNIE *puts the napkin on* HELEN. HELEN *yanks it off, and throws it down*. ANNIE *rises, lifts* HELEN'*s plate, and bears it away.* HELEN, *feeling it gone, slides*

---

5. **belfry:** tower in which bells are hung.

3 down and commences to kick up under the table; the dishes jump.* ANNIE *takes* HELEN'*s wrists firmly and swings her off the chair.* HELEN, *struggling, gets one hand free, and catches at her mother's skirt; when* KATE *takes her by the shoulders,* HELEN *hangs quiet.*]

KATE. Miss Annie.

ANNIE. No.

4 **KATE.** [*A pause.*] It's a very special day.

ANNIE. [*Grimly.*] It will be, when I give in to that. . . .

AUNT EV. But what's the child done?

ANNIE. She's learned not to throw things on the floor and kick. It took us the better part of two weeks and—

AUNT EV. But only a napkin, it's not as if it were breakable!

ANNIE. And everything she's learned *is?* . . .

KATE. What do you wish to do?

ANNIE. Let me take her from the table. . . .

KATE. [*Distressed.*] Will once hurt so much, Miss Annie? I've—made all Helen's favorite foods, tonight.

KELLER. [*Gently.*] It's a homecoming party, Miss Annie.

5 [ANNIE *after a moment releases* HELEN. *But she cannot accept it.*]

ANNIE. She's testing you. You realize? . . .

JAMES. [*To* ANNIE.] She's testing *you.*

KELLER. [*Testily.*] Jimmie. . . .

ANNIE. Of course she's testing me. Let me keep her to what she's learned and she'll go on learning from me. Take her out of my hands and it all comes apart.

The Miracle Worker **17**

GUIDED READING

LITERAL QUESTIONS

1a. How does Helen behave at dinner? (She throws her napkin on the floor, kicks under the table, and struggles physically with Annie.)

2a. What does Annie think will happen to Helen's learning now? (It will be lost unless the Kellers return Annie's authority.)

INFERENTIAL QUESTIONS

1b. Why do you think Helen misbehaves as soon as she returns to the main house? (She knows she can do what she likes there; she wants to see what Annie will do about it.)

2b. Do you think Annie is right? Why or why not? (Yes. Everyone needs some level of discipline in order to learn things that don't come easily.)

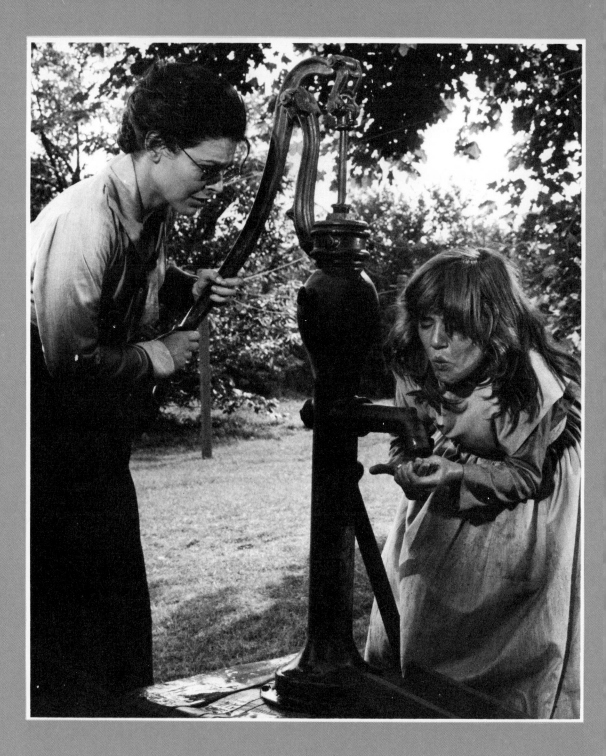

[KATE *closes her eyes, digesting it;* ANNIE *sits again, with a brief comment for her.*]

1 ANNIE. Be bountiful,[6] it's at her expense. [*She turns to* JAMES, *flatly.*] Please pass me more of—her favorite foods.

[*Then* KATE *lifts* HELEN'*s hand, and turning her toward* ANNIE, *surrenders her.*] . . .

KATE. [*Low.*] Take her, Miss Annie.

ANNIE. Thank you.

2 [*But the moment* ANNIE *rising reaches for her hand,* HELEN *begins to fight and kick, clutching to the tablecloth, and uttering laments.*] . . .

JAMES. [*Wearily.*] I think we've started all over. . . .

[ANNIE *moves in to grasp* HELEN'*s wrist, and* HELEN *flinging out a hand encounters the pitcher; she swings with it at* ANNIE: ANNIE *falling back blocks it with an elbow, but the water flies over her dress.* ANNIE *gets her breath, then snatches the pitcher away in one hand, hoists* HELEN *up bodily under the other arm and starts to carry her out, kicking.* KELLER *stands.*]

ANNIE. [*Savagely polite.*] Don't get up!

KELLER. Where are you going?

3 ANNIE. Don't smooth anything else out for me, don't interfere in any way! I treat her like a seeing child because I *ask* her to see. I *expect* her to see, don't undo what I do!

KELLER. Where are you taking her?

ANNIE. To make her fill this pitcher again! . . .

[ANNIE *pulls* HELEN *downstairs by one hand, the pitcher in her other hand, down the porch steps, and across the yard to the*

---

6. **bountiful:** generous.

pump. She puts HELEN'*s hand on the pump handle, grimly.*]

ANNIE. All right. Pump.

[HELEN *touches her cheek,[7] waits uncertainly.*]

ANNIE. No, she's not here. Pump!

[*She forces* HELEN'*s hand to work the handle, then lets go. And* HELEN *obeys. She pumps till the water comes, then* ANNIE *puts the pitcher in her other hand and guides it under the spout, and the water tumbling half into and half around the pitcher douses* HELEN'*s hand.* ANNIE *takes over the handle to keep water coming, and does automatically what she has done so many times before, spells into* HELEN'*s free palm:*]

ANNIE. Water. W, a, t, e, r. *Water.* It has a—name—

[*And now the miracle happens.* HELEN *drops the pitcher on the slab under the* **4** *spout, it shatters. She stands transfixed.[8]* ANNIE *freezes on the pump handle: There is a change in the sundown light, and with it a change in* HELEN'*s face, some light coming into it we have never seen there, some struggle in the depths behind it; and her lips tremble, trying to remember something the muscles around them once knew, till at last it finds its way out, painfully, a baby sound buried under the debris[9] of years of dumbness.*]

5 HELEN. Wah. Wah. [*And again, with great effort.*] Wah. Wah.

[HELEN *plunges her hand into the dwindling water, spells into her own palm.*

---

7. **Helen . . . cheek:** Touching her cheek is Helen's sign for her mother.
8. **transfixed:** motionless, as if spellbound.
9. **debris** [də brē′]: rubbish.

The Miracle Worker 19

AT A GLANCE

- *Scene 2 (continued):* Annie carries Helen to the water pump to make her refill the pitcher she has spilled.
- The water falls on Helen's hand, and she links the sensation with her baby word for "water."

1 THEME

Annie's cutting words "Be bountiful, it's at her expense" tell the Kellers that their indulgence is preventing Helen from developing into a human being.

2 INTERNAL CONFLICT

Helen's behavior shows the terrible confusion and frustration of someone completely shut out from any kind of communication.

3 THEME

Annie's commitment to Helen shines through her words: "I *ask* her to see. I *expect* her to see . . ."

4 THEME

As Helen is on the verge of her breakthrough into communication, her face is lighted up by "some light coming into it we have never seen there." The description builds on Annie's earlier comparison of words to light.

5 PLOT: CLIMAX

Helen says the word she learned as a baby before her illness, and the play reaches its emotional high point.

GUIDED READING

LITERAL QUESTIONS

1a. What happens to Helen at the pump when the water spills over her hand? (She remembers her baby word for "water," and she connects the water with its name.)

2a. What changes in light are called for in the stage directions? (changes in the sundown light and on Helen's face)

INFERENTIAL QUESTIONS

1b. Why is this event called a "miracle"? (because the breakthrough that seemed impossible has happened—Helen finally connects a word and the thing it represents.)

2b. What do you think the changes in light are meant to signify? (that Helen is "seeing the light"; that her mind has opened to communication)

■ *Scene 2 (continued):* Annie spells other words into Helen's hand, and Helen understands them.

■ Helen's parents come, and Helen understands the words *Mother* and *Papa.* She then acknowledges Annie as *Teacher.*

1 THEME

Helen's discovery that she can communicate overwhelms her.

2 METAPHOR

Helen's bell ringing provides a beautiful metaphor for her discovery that she can communicate with the world.

3 THEME

By "seizing Helen's hand" Keller communicates with his daughter for the first time.

4 THEME

Helen and Annie share a poignant moment of discovery and communication as Annie spells "Teacher" and Helen acknowledges her.

Then she gropes frantically, ANNIE *reaches for her hand, and* HELEN *spells into* ANNIE's *hand.*]

ANNIE. [*Whispering.*] Yes.

[HELEN *spells into it again.*]

ANNIE. Yes!

[HELEN *grabs at the handle, pumps for more water, plunges her hand into its spurt and grabs* ANNIE's *to spell it again.*]

ANNIE. *Yes!* Oh, my dear—

[*She falls to her knees to clasp* HELEN's *hand, but* HELEN *pulls it free, stands almost bewildered, then drops to the ground, pats it swiftly, holds up her palm.* ANNIE *spells into it:*]

ANNIE. Ground.

[HELEN *spells it back.*]

ANNIE. Yes!

[HELEN *whirls to the pump, pats it, holds up her palm, and* ANNIE *spells into it.*]

ANNIE. Pump.

[HELEN *spells it back.*]

ANNIE. Yes! Yes!

1 [Now HELEN *is in such an excitement she is possessed, wild, trembling, cannot be still, turns, runs, falls onto the porch step, claps it, reaches out her palm, and* ANNIE *is at it instantly to spell:*]

ANNIE. Step.

[HELEN *has not time to spell back now, she whirls groping, to touch anything, encounters the trellis, shakes it, thrusts out her palm, and* ANNIE *while spelling to her cries wildly at the house.*]

ANNIE. Trellis. Mrs. Keller! *Mrs. Keller!*

20   *Enjoying Literature: Drama*

---

2 [*Inside* KATE *starts to her feet.* HELEN *scrambles back onto the porch, groping, and finds the bell string, tugs it, the bell rings, the distant chimes begin tolling the hour, all the bells in town seem to break into speech while* HELEN *reaches out and* ANNIE *spells feverishly into her hand.* KATE *hurries out, with* KELLER *after her. . . .* HELEN, *ringing the bell, with her other hand encounters her mother's skirt; when she throws a hand out,* ANNIE *spells into it:*]

ANNIE. Mother.

3 [KELLER *now seizes* HELEN's *hand, she touches him, gestures a hand, and* ANNIE *again spells:*]

ANNIE. Papa—She *knows!*

[KATE *and* KELLER *go to their knees, stammering, clutching* HELEN *to them, and* ANNIE *steps unsteadily back to watch the threesome,* HELEN *spelling wildly into* KATE's *hand, then into* KELLER's, KATE *spelling back into* HELEN's; *they cannot keep their hands off her, and rock her in their clasp.*

Then HELEN *gropes, feels nothing, turns all around, pulls free, and comes with both hands groping, to find* ANNIE. *She encounters* ANNIE's *thighs,* ANNIE *kneels to her,* HELEN's *hand pats* ANNIE's *cheek impatiently, points a finger, and waits; and* ANNIE *spells into it:*]

ANNIE. Teacher.

[HELEN *spells it back, slowly;* ANNIE *nods.*]

Teacher.

[*She holds* HELEN's *hand to her cheek. Presently* HELEN *withdraws it, then turns again and stumbles back to her parents.* ANNIE, *with her own load of emotion, has retreated, her back turned, toward the*

GUIDED READING

LITERAL QUESTIONS

1a. How do Helen's parents react when Helen learns to spell their names? (They stammer, clutch Helen, and rock her.)

2a. What name does Annie spell out when Helen points at finger at her? (Teacher)

INFERENTIAL QUESTIONS

1b. Do you think they had been expecting a moment like this to happen? (No; they never really believed in Annie's dream for Helen.)

2b. Why do you think she spells out "Teacher" instead of "Annie"? ("Teacher" is the name that means the most to Annie at that moment; it gives her a role in Helen's life along with "Mother" and "Papa.")

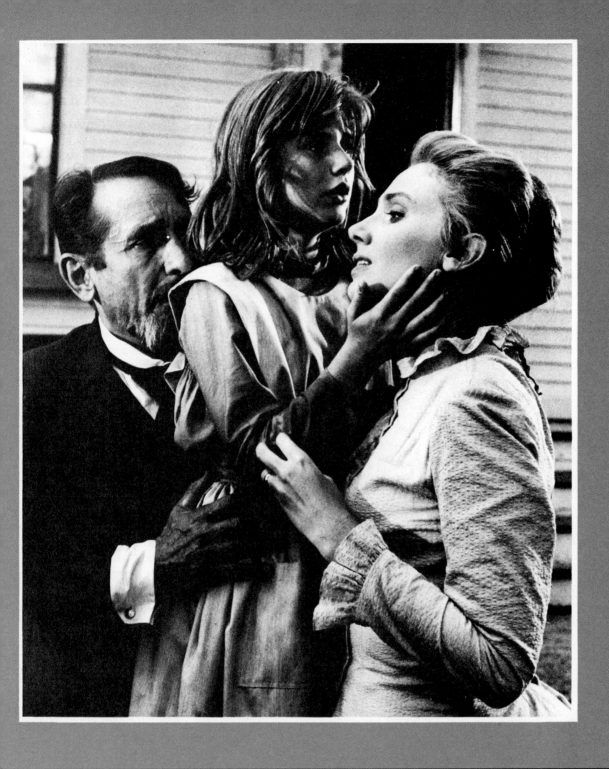

- Helen spells "Teacher" into Kate's hand and goes seeking Annie.
- Helen kisses Annie. Annie gathers Helen into her arms and spells "I love Helen."

1 PLOT: RESOLUTION

Annie and Helen, who have seemed bitter enemies at times, acknowledge their love for one another.

2 REFLECTING ON THE SELECTION

There are two kinds of love in this play, Annie's and the Kellers'. Which love was better for Helen and why? (Annie's, because while it was harsh at times, it brought Helen independence and opened the world to her)

STUDY QUESTIONS

1. to obey, keep herself clean, knit, finger-spell, behave at meals, do setting-up exercises; that the letters she spells create words that are names for things
2. another week alone with Helen; no
3. wants to take her from the table; feels Helen won't learn if others indulge her poor behavior
4. recalls baby sound for water—*wah wah;* connects letters for water with water itself; realizes that everything has a name
5. spells "teacher" looking for Annie; feels wonder, gratitude, and loss
6. *finds:* can reach Helen with words; *loses:* knows Annie will be best to continue teaching Helen
7. Answers will vary. Possibilities: patience, consistency, love for Helen, understanding, knowledge, and persistence.
8. They make possible thinking, speaking, and writing.
9. Possible answer: Language is basic to communication but is possible without words; examples, body language and infants making needs clear without words.

---

pump, to sit. KATE *moves to* HELEN, *touches her hand questioningly, and* HELEN *spells a word to her.* KATE *comprehends it, their first act of verbal communication, and she can hardly utter the word aloud, in wonder, gratitude, and deprivation;*[10] *it is a moment in which she simultaneously finds and loses a child.*]

KATE. Teacher?

---

10. **deprivation** [dep′rə vā′shən]: loss.

[HELEN *feels her way across the yard, rather shyly, and when her moving hands touch* ANNIE'S *skirt she stops. For a moment neither of them moves. Then* HELEN *slides into* ANNIE'S *arms, and lifting away her smoked glasses, kisses her on the cheek.* ANNIE *gathers her in.* . . .

ANNIE *has found* HELEN'S *hand, almost without knowing it, and she spells slowly into it, her voice unsteady, whispering.*]

ANNIE. I, love, Helen.

STUDY QUESTIONS

Recalling

1. Name six things that Annie has taught Helen in the garden house. What does she still want Helen to learn?
2. What request does Annie make of the Kellers in the garden house? What is their response?
3. In what way does Annie respond to Helen's poor behavior at the homecoming dinner? Why does Annie respond this way?
4. What happens to Helen at the water pump?
5. What is Helen's first act of verbal communication with her mother, Kate? According to the author, how does this moment affect Kate?

Interpreting

6. At the end of the selection, the author speaks of a moment in which Kate "simultaneously finds and loses a child." What does he mean?
7. What special qualities of Annie's ultimately help her to communicate with Helen?
8. According to this selection, what is the importance of words and language in communication?

Extending

9. To what extent do you think it is possible to communicate without a language? Explain.

22 *Enjoying Literature: Drama*

READING AND LITERARY FOCUS

Drama

A **drama** is a play or story performed on stage in front of an audience. The script, or written version of the drama, has two parts. One part is the dialogue, or lines that the characters speak. The other part is the stage directions, or instructions for performing the play.

Look at the following excerpt from *The Miracle Worker:*

KATE. [*Simply.*] I want her back.
[*A wait;* ANNIE *then lets her hands drop in surrender, and nods.*]

The stage directions are shown in brackets. The first direction tells the actress playing Kate how to speak. The second direction tells the actress playing Annie when and how to move. The dialogue that Kate speaks is "I want her back."

A drama is often divided into acts, which may be further divided into scenes. A new act or scene usually begins whenever the time or place of the action changes.

One reason that **playwrights**—the authors of plays—create their work is to express their personal views about life. The actions that occur on stage reflect how playwrights view life in general.

For example, a play about a beloved doctor who serves in the same neighborhood for forty years may convey the playwright's ideas about the importance and rewards of dedication to a career.

You will find more drama selections beginning on page 349.

Thinking About a Drama

1. Give three examples of stage directions that tell the actors how to move as they perform *The Miracle Worker*. Then give three more examples of directions that tell the performers how to speak their lines.
2. Based on the play's action, what main idea do you feel the playwright is trying to convey?

COMPOSITION

Writing a Drama Review

▨ Write a drama review of *The Miracle Worker*. Begin by giving general information about the drama and its author. Then describe the setting of the play. Next describe the main characters, and summarize the plot. End your review by stating your opinion of the drama, backed by details from the play. *For help with this assignment, see Lesson 9 in the Writing About Literature Handbook at the back of this book.*

Writing a Scene

▨ Imagine the conversation that might take place between Captain Keller and Annie after Helen demonstrates her ability to learn the meaning of language. Write a dramatic scene that reveals what the two characters might say to one another. Make sure the characters and plot remain believable, based on previous events. *For help with this assignment, see Lesson 10 in the Writing About Literature Handbook at the back of this book.*

CHALLENGE

Research Report

▨ Go to the library, and research the accomplishments of Helen Keller. Prepare a brief report that outlines the highlights of her career. As an alternative you may do a report on another accomplished individual who has overcome a serious handicap. Subjects might include Wilma Randolph and Stevie Wonder.

COMPARING THEMES

1. Tell how the father in "A Day's Wait," Mr. Fleagle, and Annie Sullivan use teaching as a means of communicating successfully. Then tell who you think had the hardest job of communicating and why.
2. Tell how a commitment to friendship is important to both the speaker in "A Time to Talk" and Annie Sullivan. Then compare how this commitment helps each of them to communicate with others.

The Miracle Worker 23

The activities in this lesson will help students recognize similarities and differences in literary genres and to identify the audience, purpose, and suitable reading speed for different types of literature. Suggested answers for these activities are provided here. In addition, you will find among the materials for this unit in your *Teacher's Resource Book* the following related blackline masters: Recognizing Differences and Similarities; Understanding Purpose and Audience; Adjusting Rate of Reading; Skimming and Scanning.

Activity 1

1. "A Day's Wait": the paragraph starting "It was a cold day" (p. 3); "A Time to Talk": poem, lines 7–9 (p. 6); *Growing Up:* the paragraph starting "This title produced" (p. 9); *The Miracle Worker:* in stage directions at the bottom of column 1, p. 19.

2. "A Day's Wait": last sentence (p. 4); "A Time to Talk": poem, lines 9–10 (p. 6). *Growing Up:* "I . . . looked forward to the end of school days with increasing glumness" (p. 8); *The Miracle Worker:* Annie spells two words—"Why, not"—back, with an impatient question in her eyes (p. 15).

3. Frost: " . . . as there is a time to talk . . . I go up. . . ." (p. 6); Baker: "The only thing that truly interested me was writing . . . ." (p. 8)

Active Reading

Enjoying Literature

Recognizing Differences and Similarities

The opening unit presents four types of literature—a story, a poem, a nonfiction selection, and a drama. These types of literature take different shapes on the page. For example, in "A Day's Wait" and "Growing Up" the sentences group into paragraphs. In "A Time to Talk" the lines occur in stanzas. *The Miracle Worker* contains a mixture of dialogue and stage directions.

Despite their differences, the four selections do have similarities. For instance, all the selections involve characters in a specific time and place, or *setting.* In the story and nonfiction selection you learn about the setting through prose description. In the drama you find the setting established in stage directions. In the poem setting is revealed in the pictures, or images, that the words suggest. Similarly, all four literature selections have *plots, characters,* and *themes.*

There are further similarities and differences in the ways you discover the authors' personal ideas. In the poem and nonfiction piece you can discover the authors' personal beliefs easily. That is, Frost and Baker state their beliefs directly. In the story and drama, however, Hemingway and Gibson do not indicate their ideas about life in a direct statement. Instead, you must "read between the lines" and figure out their beliefs based on the content and style of their work. Nevertheless, all four authors share a common goal. They all wish to emphasize the need for individuals to communicate effectively with one another.

Activity 1 Look back at the four selections in this unit to answer each item below.

1. Find a description of setting in each of the four selections. Also tell whether each description appears in a paragraph, in a poem, or in stage directions.

2. In each of the four selections, identify a passage that indicates the feelings of a character.

3. In the selections by Frost and Baker, the authors state their personal beliefs directly. Identify a passage from each of these selections that expresses a personal belief of the author.

24   *Enjoying Literature*

Understanding Purpose and Audience

As a reader you probably encounter many types of writing. At one time you may be in the mood for a good mystery story, while at another time you may need to read an encyclopedia article to do a school report. At home at night you may glance through newspaper advertisements. Each type of writing differs because the authors wrote each one for a specific purpose and audience.

The *purpose* is the reason an author writes something. The author of a mystery story wishes to *entertain* you. On the other hand, the writer of an encyclopedia article wants to *inform* readers about a subject. Different still, the people who write newspaper advertisements want to *persuade* readers to buy merchandise. Part of your job as a good reader is to identify the author's purpose. Is the purpose to entertain? If so, has the author succeeded in entertaining you? Is the purpose to inform? If so, what information have you learned? Is the purpose to persuade? If so, what arguments has the author used, and do you agree with them? Asking all these questions will enable you to benefit fully from your reading.

Writers are also concerned with their readers, or *audience*. Before writing, they consider who will read their work. Knowing their audience helps authors decide on a style, or how they will word their ideas. For example, authors of nursery stories are likely to use very simple vocabulary and short sentences. By contrast, contributors to a law journal may use many complex legal terms that they assume their readers understand. In evaluating your reading you should always consider the intended audience for the work. If you find an article difficult, think about whether the author wrote it for an audience different from yourself. Also, before you recommend reading something to friends, consider whether they are a proper audience for that type of writing.

Activity 2   Identify the purpose of each type of writing below as *to entertain, to inform,* or *to persuade.*

1. an almanac
2. a book of riddles
3. a magazine advertisement
4. a campaign speech
5. a front-page news story
6. a bedtime story

Activity 3   Identify a likely audience for each work below.

1. a high school textbook
2. a newspaper editorial
3. a thank-you letter
4. a cookbook
5. a movie script
6. a business letter

Activity 4
1. fast
2. slow
3. average
4. slow
5. average
6. slow
7. slow
8. fast
9. slow
10. fast

Adjusting Rate of Reading

You do not always walk at the same speed. For example, you may stroll slowly through a beautiful park but walk briskly to get some exercise. Similarly, your reading rate changes depending on the type of material you are reading and on your purpose for reading.

First let's consider how your reading rate might vary with different types of reading material. A poem is much shorter than a story. However, each word in a poem is packed with meaning, and you must read the poem slowly to appreciate it fully. Most stories, on the other hand, can be read fairly quickly in comparison.

Second let's consider how your reading rate might change depending on the specific reason you are reading the material. For example, if you are reading *The Miracle Worker* for your own enjoyment, you may read it quickly one time through. However, if you are an actor memorizing a role in the play, you will probably want to read the lines slowly and repeatedly.

Activity 4   For each situation below, identify whether your reading rate would be *slow, average,* or *fast.* Be prepared to explain why you chose the rate you did.

1. You read a book of humorous essays for your own pleasure.

2. You read a chapter of a history textbook to prepare for a test.

3. You read a magazine review of a play you wish to see.

4. You read an autobiography in order to do a book review.

5. You read a bedtime story to a young child.

6. You read a play in order to design the scenery.

7. You read a newspaper article to do a class report on current events.

8. You read a friendly letter from a neighbor who is away at summer camp.

9. You read the instructions for operating a cassette recorder.

10. You read a copy of the school newspaper for relaxation.

Skimming and Scanning

You probably read the literature in this book at an average reading rate. There are occasions, however, when you may wish to do a much faster kind of reading, called skimming. *Skimming* is looking over material very rapidly to get a general impression of its content. In the library you may skim a book to decide if its material is suitable for a report. In the classroom you may skim a chapter that you plan to read more thoroughly later on. At home you may skim newspaper headlines.

To skim an entire book, first glance at its title, the table of contents, and the index (if it has one). These features will give you a general idea of the material in the book. When skimming a single chapter or selection, look first at its title and any subheads that appear. Also note any words in bold print or italics, and glance at any pictures and captions that accompany the text. Previewing the selection in this way will give you an overall idea of the content.

Another way of reading rapidly is scanning. This kind of reading is even faster than skimming. *Scanning* is looking over a page for one particular item of information. You might be searching for a specific word, fact, or number. Suppose, for example, you could not recall the nickname of the boy in "A Day's Wait." You would run your eyes across each page of the story until they fell on the name Schatz.

Activity 5 Answer each item below by scanning or skimming the necessary material in this book.

1. What kind of literature is *not* included in the book: American folk tales, European fables, or Greek myths?

2. Scan the Table of Contents to discover the title of a selection by Arthur C. Clarke.

3. Based on its title and pictures, what do you think the selection by Langston Hughes (page 306) is about?

4. Scan the Table of Contents to identify the author of the poem "The Heron."

5. What is the first line of dialogue spoken in *The Miracle Worker*?

1. European fables
2. "Crime on Mars"
3. the life of Harriet Tubman
4. Theodore Roethke
5. "—my mind, is, undisciplined, full, of, skips, and, jumps, and—"

At the end of every unit in this book, you will find a Literary Skills Review covering the major literary terms taught in the unit. The Literary Skills Review for the unit "Enjoying Literature" focuses on the most significant differences among the four genres introduced in the unit: short story, poetry, nonfiction, and drama. You may want to use this Review as a summary of the material covered in the unit. You may also encourage students to use the Guide for Reading Literature as a checklist for reading any story, poem, nonfiction work, or play.

Literary Skills Review

Enjoying Literature

Guide for Reading Literature

Use this guide to help you understand and appreciate the characteristics of the four types of literature presented so far in this book—stories, poems, nonfiction, and drama. The other units of the book will deal with each type in more detail and will also present three other types of literature—myths, folk tales, and the novel.

The Short Story

1. Who are the **characters**? What **problems** do they face?
2. What **events** take place to make the characters' problems more complicated? What happens at the end of the story?
3. **When and where** does the story take place?
4. What **idea about life** does the story express?

Poetry

1. What **vivid pictures** does the poem present?
2. Does the poem have a regular **rhythm**? Which lines **rhyme**?
3. Which lines in the poem form separate **stanzas**?
4. Whats **idea about life** does the poem express?

Nonfiction

1. What is the subject of the **essay**? What main **fact or detail** does the essay include?
2. Who is the subject of the **biography** or **autobiography**? What main **event** in the person's life is mentioned?
3. What **idea about life** does the writer express?

Drama

1. Who are the characters who speak the **dialogue**?
2. **When and where** does the play take place? What additional information do the **stage directions** provide?
3. What major event takes place in each **act** and **scene** of the play?
4. What **idea about life** does the play express?

Themes Review

Enjoying Literature

Writers throughout history have returned again and again to certain general themes—such universally important matters as love, ideals, family life, and communication. For example, many stories, poems, plays, and other works have focused on people's need to communicate with one another. However, each writer who treats the general theme "communication" says something very specific and personal about it.

When we read two works dealing with a common theme, we should notice that each writer presents a different specific view of that theme. For example, both "A Day's Wait" (page 2) and *The Miracle Worker* (page 12) are concerned with the general theme "communication." "A Day's Wait" expresses the following specific view of that general theme: "Misunderstandings may arise when we do not communicate openly." *The Miracle Worker* presents a different specific theme: "Language is essential in human communication." A general theme can be a word or phrase, such as "communication." A specific theme can be stated as a complete sentence.

1. What specific views of the general theme "communication" are expressed by "A Time to Talk" and *Growing Up*?

2. What does each of the following selections say about the value people place on communication?
   "A Day's Wait"   *Growing Up*
   "A Time to Talk"   *The Miracle Worker*

3. What does each of the following selections say about both the power and the limitations of language to communicate what we think and feel?
   "A Day's Wait"   *Growing Up*
   "A Time to Talk"   *The Miracle Worker*

Enjoying Literature 29

At the end of every unit in this book, you will find a Themes Review comparing the selections in the unit in light of certain themes. The questions in the Themes Review for the unit "Enjoying Literature" recall the theme of "Communication" as it is portrayed in the selections in this unit. Suggested answers to these questions are presented here.

1. "A Time to Talk": Always find time to communicate with friends.
   Growing Up: Good writing is that which best communicates thoughts and feelings.

2. "A Day's Wait": The boy learns to value communication as a means to alleviate fear.
   "A Time to Talk": The farmer values communication as a way of keeping in touch with friends.
   Growing Up: Russell values communication because it allows him to reminisce and to express himself.
   The Miracle Worker: Annie knows that communication will liberate Helen.

3. "A Day's Wait": Language can communicate our fears, but only if we know how to express ourselves.
   "A Time to Talk": Words can express feelings of friendship, but only if the speaker takes the time to mean them.
   Growing Up: Words can communicate powerfully only if we have something we really want to say.
   The Miracle Worker: To make communication possible, all parties must speak the same language.

For more information about the other themes portrayed in these selections, see the Theme Index beginning on page 666.

30   *The Short Story*

Preview
The Short Story

A **short story** is a brief work of prose fiction. Usually we can read a short story in one sitting. Small as it is, a short story can contain almost anything. For example, a story can show us events that remind us of our own lives and introduce us to people and places that we recognize. On the other hand, a story can take us to fantastic lands where people and events are like nothing we have ever known before. In either case, a story always communicates ideas about life and human nature.

Most short stories have five major elements: plot, character, setting, point of view, and theme. These are the events, people, places, and ideas that an author uses to create a fictional world. Each element has its own role in a story. In most good stories the five elements work together so closely that we often cannot talk about one without also mentioning the others. This combination of elements forms a story's total effect, or the overall impression that a story creates in our minds.

The stories on the following pages are divided into six groups. Each of the first five groups represents one of the elements: plot, character, setting, point of view, and theme. A final group shows how the elements combine to create a story's total effect. Knowing the five elements is an important step to understanding the short story. This understanding adds to the pleasure that we can find in any short story.

Begin this unit by asking students to discuss their favorite reading material. Fiction will most probably be near the top of the list for many students. Ask students why they think fiction is so popular. After they have suggested reasons, have the Preview read aloud in class. Reiterate that fiction is the work of the imagination. Emphasize its ability to provide escape and entertainment, to carry us to places and times both distant and near, while also ultimately showing us something about human nature and about life all over the world. Explain to students that they will be reading examples of one of the most popular literary types—the short story.

- Food has dwindled to a three-day supply of bread, and the narrator's father is sick.
- His mother must find a way for the family to survive until spring.
- She instructs the children to leave her alone to think.

LITERARY OPTIONS

- plot
- characterization
- setting

THEMATIC OPTIONS

- family life
- survival
- nature

1 PLOT: CONFLICT

The mother introduces the main conflict of the plot: facing a hard winter and economic hardship.

2 PLOT: FORESHADOWING

The description of how the mother puts a new bottom in the chair foreshadows an important element of the plot.

3 CHARACTERIZATION

Especially in contrast to his sister Sophie, the narrator seems sensitive to his mother's moods and to the family crisis.

**TEXAS ESSENTIAL ELEMENTS
GRADE 8**

1A writing process
1B purpose and audience
1C support for main idea
1D evaluation of content and organization
1E appropriate language
2A varied sentences
3A plot and character development
3D literary genres
4B implied main idea
4F point of view
To locate treatment of an Element, see *Texas Teacher's Resources.*

PLOT

Jesse Stuart (1907–1984) began writing in his spare time between chores on the family's farm in Kentucky. Sometimes he scratched poems on tobacco leaves and potato sacks. At the age of seventeen, he became a schoolteacher. Most of Stuart's stories are about the hard-working farmers of the Kentucky hills. In "Spring Victory" one farm family struggles for survival.

■ What difficulties do they face? What personal qualities help them to succeed?

Jesse Stuart

Spring Victory

1 "I don't know what to do," Mom said. "We've just enough bread for three more days. We don't have much of anything else to eat with our bread. This is a terrible winter and your father down sick."

Mom sat on a hickory-split-bottomed chair. She put the bottom in the chair last spring. I went to the woods after the sap got up and peeled the green hickory bark from the small hickory sapling. **2** Mom took a case knife and scraped the green from the slats of bark and wove them across the bottom of a chair that Pa wanted to throw away.

"If your father was only well," Mom said and looked at the blazing forestick.[1] "I'll have to think of something. You children run along and play. Leave me alone to think."

Sophie and I crossed the floorless dog-trot[2] between the two big log-pens of our house. We

called this dog-trot the "entry." We kept our stovewood and firewood stacked in the entry. This was a place where the rain, snow and sleet couldn't touch the wood. It was easy to walk out of the kitchen and carry an arm load of the stovewood for the kitchen stove when Mom was getting a meal. It was easy for me to carry firewood from the big stack in the entry to the fireplace where Mom was looking into the fire and dreaming now.

3 "There's not any place for us to run and play," Sophie said. "The only place we have to run and play is in the entry. And the cold wind blows through here."

"You are right," I said. "But Mom wants us to get away from her for a little while. Mom is worried."

Sophie stood by the firewood pile. She put her small white hand upon a big oak backlog that had part of the dead bark slipped from it. Sophie's long blond hair was lifted from her shoulders by a puff of wind. The cold wind

---

1. **forestick:** log placed at the front of a fireplace.
2. **dog-trot:** outdoor passageway with a roof.

32   *The Short Story*

GUIDED READING

LITERAL QUESTION

1a. Why does Mom ask the children to run along and play? (She has to think of a way to provide food for the family for the winter.)

INFERENTIAL QUESTION

1b. Do you think Mom is used to making decisions for the family all alone? How can you tell? (No; she says, *If your father was only well.*)

brought tears to her eyes. Beyond the entry we saw the pine tops upon the mountainside sagging with snow. We couldn't see any briar thickets on the high hill slopes. They were snowed under. The garden fence posts barely stuck out of the snow. Four paths led away from our house—one to the barn, one to the smokehouse, one to the well and one to the hollow back of our house where Mom and I hauled wood with our horse. The big logs that Fred pulled with a long chain around them made a path through the deep snow from the dark hollow under the pines to our woodyard.

"This snow has been on the ground since last November," Sophie said. "That was 1917. Now it is January, 1918. You are ten years old and I am thirteen years old."

We stood in the entry by the woodpile and talked until we got cold, then Sophie opened the door and we walked into the room. We hurried to the big bright fire to warm our cold hands. Mom was staring into the fireplace with her eagle-gray eyes. She looked steadily toward the fire. She was holding James on her lap. Mary was sitting in a small rocking chair beside her. Pa turned over in bed and asked for water.

Mom got up from the rocking chair with James in her arms. She walked toward Pa's bed. Mom poured a glass of water from a pitcher that was on a stand at the head of Pa's bed.

"Do you feel any better, Mick?" Mom said.

"Nope, I don't, Sal," he said. "I feel weak as water. I'll tell you that flu is bad stuff. I got up too soon and took a back-set."

Pa took the glass of water and drank. Mom stood and watched him with James in her arms.

"Is the firewood holding out?" Pa asked as he handed Mom the empty glass.

"Yes, it is," Mom said. "We have plenty of wood."

"How about food for the family and for the livestock?"

"We're getting along all right," Mom said. "Don't worry, Mick. We'll take care of everything. You get well just as soon as you can. You won't get well if you keep on worrying."

"I can't keep from worrying," Pa said. "Here I'm down sick and can't get out of bed. Crops failed us last year and we don't have bread for the children. And I've never seen such snow on the ground. This is a dark winter to me."

"It's a dark winter for all of us," Mom said. "But remember the snow will leave the hills one of these days and the sun will shine on blue violets under the last year's leaves."

Mom put the water glass back on the standtable beside the water pitcher. She walked back to her rocking chair. The firelight glowed over the room and tiny shadows flickered on the newspaper-papered walls.

"Son, we are not whipped yet," Mom said to me. "Your Pa is asleep now. I'll tell you what we are going to do."

I walked over beside Mom's chair. Sophie stood beside her too.

"Sophie can do the cooking," Mom said. "Can't you bake bread and cook potatoes, Sophie?"

"Yes, Mom."

"And you can use an ax well for a boy ten years old," Mom said.

"It's easy for me to chop with my pole-ax."

"Then you take your ax and go to the hills," Mom said, pointing from the front window to the steep snow-covered bluff east of our house. "You can find all kinds of tough-butted white oaks on the bluff over there. Cut them down, trim them and scoot them over the hill. We're going to make baskets out of them."

I kept my pole-ax in the entry by the firewood pile, where it would not be snowed under. As I walked out of the front room I pulled my toboggan cap low over my ears. I wrapped

Spring Victory 33

- Pa worries about how the family is getting along without him; Mom reassures him.
- Mom sends the boy to cut wood.
- She will make baskets to sell.

1 SETTING

The story is set on a remote farm during the bitter winter of 1918. The details about the *four paths* reiterate the farm's remoteness and the family's need for self-sufficiency.

2 STYLE

The reader is presented with details of setting and character in a simple, straightforward style. This style is in keeping with the family's simple, straightforward life.

3 VOCABULARY: DIALECT

The phrase *took a back-set* means to have a setback or relapse. It is one of many examples of Kentucky hill dialect in the story.

4 CHARACTERIZATION

The father shows his concern for his family and the deep responsibility he feels to take care of them all: He takes the *dark winter* personally.

5 CHARACTERIZATION

In contrast to her husband, Mom responds to the crisis with optimism, resolve, and practicality.

GUIDED READING

LITERAL QUESTIONS

1a. What is Mom's plan? To whom does she confide it? (She is going to make baskets. She confides it to the boy and Sophie.)

2a. How many children are in the family? Is the boy the oldest? (There are four children. The boy's sister Sophie is the oldest, at thirteen; the boy is ten.)

INFERENTIAL QUESTIONS

1b. Why do you think Mom discusses her plan with the children but not with Pa? (She needs the children's help; she doesn't want to worry Pa; she may be afraid Pa would talk her out of the idea.)

2b. Why do you think Mom seems to depend most on the boy? (He seems more mature and sensitive than Sophie; he has been trained to use an ax.)

1 EXTERNAL CONFLICT

The image of the boy climbing uphill in waist-deep snow powerfully evokes the difficulty of the family's physical struggle to survive the winter.

2 THEME

Although the boy struggles with nature, he also appreciates the beauty of this frozen moment, as the sound of his hammer echoes from hill to hill.

3 CHARACTERIZATION

The boy's selflessness and efficiency are apparent as he returns from his hard labor and asks what more there is to do.

my overalls close around my legs so the snow wouldn't get around my feet. I picked up my pole-ax and walked down the path toward the barn. The cold whistling January wind stung my face. Fred nickered to me as I passed the barn. The creek was frozen over and the snow had covered the ice save for a hole that I had chopped so the cow and horse could get water.

1 I passed the water-hole and the empty hog pen. I started up the steep bluff toward the white-oak trees. The snow came to my waist. I held to bushes and pulled up the hills—breaking a tiny path through the waist-deep snow. Finally, I reached the white-oak grove and stood beneath a shaggy-topped white-oak sapling. The dead last year's leaves were still clinging to its boughs. These clusters of dead leaves were weighted with snow. When the

2 sharp bit of my pole-ax hit the frozen white-oak wood, a loud ring struck the distant frozen hill across the valley. The sounds came back to my ears. Snow rained on me from the top of the white-oak sapling. I felled the white oak down the bluff toward the barn. I trimmed its branches and cut its top away. I slid the sapling over the bluff toward the barn. I cut twelve white-oak saplings, and trimmed and topped them and slid them over the bluff toward the barn.

It was easier for me to get down the bluff than it had been to climb it. The white-oak saplings had made a path through the deep snow. I followed this broken path toward the barn. I carried the white-oak saplings from

3 the barn to the entry. I carried one at a time on my shoulder; the green, white-oak timber was heavy. After I'd carried them to the entry I went into the house to see what Mom wanted me to do next.

"After you warm yourself," Mom said, "I want you to take a handsaw and saw these white-oak saplings into six-foot lengths. After you saw them into lengths, I want you to split the lengths into four quarters and bring them to me."

By the time that Mom had given me in-

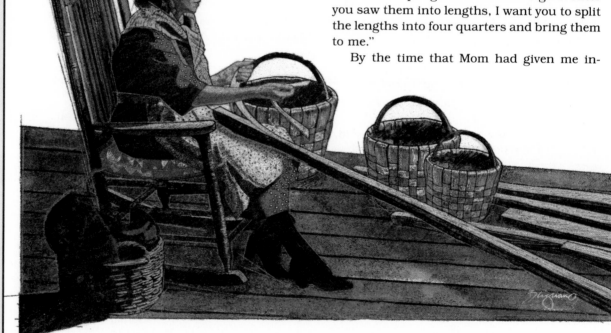

GUIDED READING

LITERAL QUESTION

1a. Where does the boy have to go to get the wood for the baskets? (to the oak-tree grove up the steep bluff)

INFERENTIAL QUESTION

1b. Why do you think the author spends so much time on the details of this errand? (The errand shows an example of the family's struggle to survive.)

structions, I was warm enough to go to work again. I sawed the poles into six-foot lengths and split them with my pole-ax. I carried them into our front room and stacked them in a pile of small green fence rails. Mom looked the pile over and picked up one of the cuts and started to work. She used a butcher knife, a drawing knife and a case knife. She split the lengths again and again and ripped long splits from each length. She split one length into coarser splits to make ribs for the baskets. Another length she split into basket handles.

"I'm going to make feed baskets," Mom said. "People will always need feed baskets. I'm going to make them in three different sizes. I'm going to make peck baskets. Men will want peck baskets to carry eggs to town on Saturdays. They'll want them to carry salt, sugar and coffee from the store where they have a long way to walk. I'm going to make a half-bushel basket for it will be about the right size to carry corn to the mules, nubbins to the cows and ears of corn to the fattening hogs. And I'm going to make bushel feed baskets."

1 Sophie got supper that night and I fed Fred and fed and milked Gypsy. I found two more hens under our chicken-roost on the snow. They were frozen stiff as boards. I felt of their craws and I could feel only a few grains of corn. I didn't tell Mom about the chickens. I buried them in the snow. Every day a chicken, guinea or a turkey froze to death. Some days as many as six fowls would freeze to death. I found sparrows frozen to death around the barn. When I put hay down for Gypsy and gave her corn nubbins in a feed box I milked cold milk from her into the bucket. There was an icy stillness in the January night air and millions of bright stars shivered in a cold blue sky.

By the time that Sophie had steaming-hot corn bread baked, and I had done the feeding,

the milking and carried in firewood and stove-wood for the night, Mom had made two baskets. Sophie had crossed the entry from the kitchen to tell Mom that supper was ready, and I was putting my kindling wood in the corner to start the morning fire when Mom held up a basket to us.

"Look, children," she said. "I'm not quite as good as I used to be when I helped Pap make baskets. I need practice."

"Mom, that's a pretty basket," I said.

"Supper is ready," Sophie said.

2 We crossed the entry for supper. The starlight from the winter skies couldn't shine in at our entry. Mom carried a pine torch to light our way to the kitchen. Sophie led James across the entry and Mary held to Mom's skirt. The hot steaming corn bread was sweet to our taste. We had milk and bread and hot boiled potatoes.

"Tomorrow," Mom said, "I want you to saddle Fred and ride to Greenwood with four baskets. I'll have two more made by morning. Sell the peck basket for thirty-five cents. Sell the half-bushel basket for sixty cents. Sell the two bushel baskets for a dollar apiece. That will be two dollars and ninety-five cents if you sell all the baskets."

"I'll do it, Mom, just as soon as I get the feeding done," I said.

I went to bed that night and dreamed of riding Fred to town. I dreamed that my baskets sold. I dreamed that men wanted more baskets and I came home with my pockets filled with money and a load of corn meal, flour, lard and candy on Fred's back—all that he could carry.

I awoke and built a fire in the front room to warm it for Mom. She slept in a bed with Sophie and Mary just across from Pa's bed—in the other corner of the room. I slept upstairs with James. After I'd built the fire in the front room, I crossed the entry with a pine

- Mom begins to make baskets.
- Sophie cooks, and the boy does the farm chores.
- He buries hens and turkeys that freeze to death.
- Mom tells him to sell the baskets in town tomorrow.
- He dreams of the money the sale of baskets will bring.

1 PLOT: RISING ACTION

As the chickens freeze to death, the reader realizes the extremeness of the cold. Whether the family can survive the winter becomes a more serious question.

2 SETTING

It is 1918, but little seems to have changed since pioneer days, as Mom lights the entry with a pine torch, and the family eats a supper of milk, corn bread, and potatoes.

GUIDED READING

LITERAL QUESTIONS

1a. What does the boy find under the chicken roost? (two hens frozen to death)

2a. What does the family have for dinner that night? (milk, corn bread, and potatoes)

INFERENTIAL QUESTIONS

1b. Why doesn't the boy tell Mom about the chickens? (He wants to protect her from the grim news because she already has so much to worry about.)

2b. Do you think the boy is used to having much better dinners than this? (Probably not too often; he doesn't express any shock or distaste at how little there is to eat.)

- Mom instructs the boy on traveling and on selling the baskets.
- The boy sets out for town.
- The boy sells the baskets and takes an order for two more.

1 RESPONSE JOURNAL

Let students imagine they are the boy and describe, in detail, their feelings about setting out on such an important mission for the first time in the dead of winter.

2 IMAGERY

Stuart indicates the boy's vulnerability with specific images of nature: "dark hollow," "rough sides," "black-oak," "shadowy ghosts."

3 POINT OF VIEW

The first-person point of view allows the reader to know the boy's feelings of satisfaction in assuming his father's role in the family.

torch. It was yet before daylight on the short winter day. I put a fire in the stove and took my milk bucket and feed basket and started toward the barn. I fed Fred corn in his box and threw down hay from the loft. I forked hay to Gypsy's manger and gave her corn nubbins to eat while I milked her.

When I finished my work, Mom had cooked our breakfast. She made griddle cakes for us and we ate sorghum molasses with hot griddle cakes. After breakfast while Mom was feeding Pa, I put the saddle on Fred and bridled him. I rode to our front door. Mom came out with four baskets. She carried two in each hand.

"Watch old Fred," Mom said. "Do be careful. If the snow balls on his feet, get off his back and find you a sharp-edged rock or a sharp stick and knock the snowballs from his feet. If he falls with you and hurts you—what are we going to do then?"

Mom looked serious when she spoke to me. I wasn't afraid of Fred falling with me. I was glad to get on my way. I wasn't afraid. I wanted to ride Fred to town. It was the first time in my life that I had ever been allowed to ride to town to sell anything.

"You get a sack of meal if you sell a basket," Mom said. "It will cost you fifty cents. If you sell all your baskets, get a sack of flour too. That's a dollar. That will make a dollar and a half. You'll have a dollar and forty-five cents left. Get a quarter's worth of salt, a quarter's worth of sugar and a small bucket of lard. If you have a penny left, bring it home to me; I've got a use for every penny."

I tied the basket handles together and put two baskets on each side of me behind the saddle. I pulled my toboggan cap low over my ears and rode Fred up the hollow toward Greenup. My feet were warm in my wool socks and brogan shoes. The cold wind hit my face as I rode away in the winter morning mists. Mom stood in the door and watched me out

of sight. I rode up the dark hollow where frost filled the air and where the rough sides of the black-oak trees that stood on the rocky bluffs were white with frost and looked like shadowy ghosts. The frozen snow crunched beneath Fred's big feet.

As I rode over the hill toward the town, a man was feeding his cattle.

"Would you like to buy a basket, Mister?" I asked.

"How do you sell them, Sonnie?" he asked.

"Thirty-five cents for the peck basket," I said. "Sixty cents for the half-bushel basket and a dollar apiece for the bushel baskets."

"I'll take both of the bushel baskets," he said as he pulled his billfold from his pocket and reached me two one-dollar bills. I untied the baskets from the saddle and gave them to him. Two dollars in my pocket and two baskets to sell. The next log shack I passed, I climbed down from my saddle and knocked at the door. A man came to the door.

"Do you want to buy a basket, Mister?" I asked.

"Sonnie, it's cold weather to sell baskets, isn't it?" he said. "You're out awfully early too. What time did you start this morning?"

"Daylight."

As we talked, the man stepped out into the yard and looked at my baskets. He asked me the price and I told him.

"I'll take both your baskets," he said. "These are well-made baskets and I need feed baskets. I'll take a couple of bushel baskets if you'll make them for me."

"I'll bring 'em to you in two days from now," I said, "if I live and Mom lives."

"Does your mother make these baskets?"

"Yes."

"She certainly put them together well," he said. "I've made baskets and I know a basket."

I said good-by to the tall beardy-faced man. I felt good to take Pa's place and go to town. I

GUIDED READING

LITERAL QUESTIONS

1a. What does Mom tell the boy to buy if he sells all the baskets? (meal, flour, sugar, salt, and lard)

2a. What does the boy add after he tells a customer he'll be back in two days? ("if I live and Mom lives")

INFERENTIAL QUESTIONS

1b. Why is Mom so specific about the cost of the meal and the flour? (The boy isn't accustomed to buying food or handling money at all; every penny matters.)

2b. Why do you think he says this? Is he serious? (He seems to take his family's situation very seriously and to believe that there is danger of their not being able to survive.)

felt like I was helping run the place. I got off Fred's back twice and knocked the balls of snow from his feet with a stick. I rode to town and got my meal and flour. I put a sack of flour in one end of a coffee sack and a sack of meal in the other and balanced it across Fred's broad back—tied the coffee sack to a ring in my saddle. I carried the sugar, salt and lard in another sack in front of my saddle. Slowly, I went over the hill home.

When I rode back home, Mom came out the front door to meet me. I showed her my meal, flour, sugar, salt and lard. Mom's face brightened with a smile. She stood beside the horse and held the bridle reins when I climbed from the saddle a little stiff with cold.

"And here's twenty-five cents left," I said as I pulled my mitten from my right hand and pulled a quarter from my pocket.

1 "We'll make it," Mom said. "The winter is dark now but after a while spring will come. Violets are budding under the dead leaves beneath the snow right now!"

When I went to the woods to haul wood for the fireplace and the kitchen stove, Mom put on Pa's clothes and went with me. Pa's boots **2** fit tightly on Mom's legs. Mom's long slender body fit well in Pa's corduroy pants. His coat was not too broad for Mom's shoulders.

I tied Fred to a tree by his bridle rein. Then Mom and I took the double-bitted ax and the crosscut saw down to a tall dead oak. I cut a notch part of the way into the dead tree the way I wanted it to fall. Mom took the ax and finished chopping the notch. We got down on our knees together and pulled the long crosscut saw through the hard dead oak tree. After we sawed awhile, we heard a crack and the tree bent earthward and hit the snow-covered hill below with a slash. The snow dashed in a white powdery cloud high into the air. I took the ax and trimmed the knots from the tree while Mom led Fred up to the tree, hooked the

snaking chain around the log and fastened the trace chains to the singletree.

"He's ready," Mom said.

I climbed on Fred's back and reined him with the bridle reins down the path. Clouds of snow blew from under Fred's feet as he moved the big dead log toward the woodyard. Mom followed with the ax in her ungloved hand and the crosscut saw across her shoulder. When Fred got to the woodyard, he stopped. I got off his back—unhitched the traces and took him to the barn. I came back **3** to the woodyard. All afternoon Mom got down on her knees in the snow on one side of the log and I got down on the other side of the big dead log. We dragged the crosscut saw across the bone-dry seasoned oak log. We cut stovewood lengths and firewood lengths until we finished the log. Then we split the wood lengths with our axes. I used my pole-ax on the stovewood lengths for the cookstove. Mom used the double-bitted ax and split the longer firewood lengths. After we split the lengths into finer wood, I carried it and stacked it in the entry where it was safe from rain, sleet and snow.

4 "When your Pa gets well again," Mom said, "I won't have so much work to do. He always took care of the wood getting."

Mom would sit up on the long winter evenings when the wind blew around the house and weave baskets. Sophie would often help her with the white-oak splits after she had washed the supper dishes. Sophie would take the case knife and smooth the splinters from the splits. I would take the drawing knife and rip off long splits from the white-oak sapling **5** lengths. It was fun for us to do this around the winter fire while we laughed and talked and parched corn in a skillet. Mary parched the corn while Sophie and I helped Mom. Pa lay in bed—his face pale on the white pillow in the dim flicker of the pine torch above our

Spring Victory 37

- The boy returns with supplies.
- Mom is optimistic and looks forward to spring.
- Mom and the boy cut trees, haul wood, and saw logs for the fire; she weaves more baskets.
- Pa is no better.

1 PLOT: FORESHADOWING

Mom's basket making is a success: In her optimism she looks ahead to spring and imagines new life budding under the snow.

2 POINT OF VIEW

Through the boy's eyes Mom fits Pa's clothes as she does his job, hauling wood for the fireplace.

3 THEME

The family's daily struggle for survival is made vivid in the detailed description of an arduous and necessary job.

4 CHARACTERIZATION

Mom's strength and optimism are evident as she looks ahead to a time when her workload will be easier.

5 THEME

Despite their difficult situation, the family enjoys evenings of fun and intimacy around the fire.

GUIDED READING

LITERAL QUESTIONS

1a. What does Mom wear when she goes to haul wood? (Pa's clothes)

2a. Who helps Mom haul and saw the wood? (the boy)

INFERENTIAL QUESTIONS

1b. Why doesn't Mom wear her own clothes to haul wood? (Since Pa always hauled the wood, she would not have suitable clothes to wear.)

2b. Why doesn't Sophie help? (She may be watching the smaller children or cooking; she may not be strong enough.)

AT A GLANCE

- Pa talks about spring and plowing.
- Mom makes twelve baskets in one day, and the boy worries that she will get sick.
- He continues to cut down trees, and he becomes a good salesperson.
- He is sent to buy animal feed.

1 MOOD

As Pa talks about spring and making changes in planting, the mood of the story becomes more hopeful.

2 THEME

The concern family members show one another shines through this story. Here, Mom wishes her basket making could give Pa an easier life.

3 CHARACTERIZATION

Mom epitomizes the level-headed, practical pioneer woman as she gives the boy a lesson in bargaining with Broughton.

---

1 mantel and the leaping blazes from the fore-stick. Sometimes Pa talked to us about spring and when he would be plowing again. He told us he'd never plant the swamps in the hollow again and have the craw-dads to cut down the young corn soon as it sprouted from the furrow. One day when Mom worked steadily all day and Sophie and I helped her in the evening, she made twelve baskets.

2 "It's one of the biggest day's work I've ever done in my life," Mom said. "If I could make twelve baskets one day with another, your Pa wouldn't have to worry about spring and plowing."

"Mom wanted me to be careful about the horse falling," I thought. "She told me to keep the snow knocked from his feet so it wouldn't ball and throw him when I rode him to Greenwood—Mom doesn't know what she would do without me—well, she'd better watch about making twelve baskets one day with another. What would we do if Mom would get sick?"

As I walked toward the barn over the frozen snow, I had these thoughts about my mother.

Every weekday, I took baskets to Greenwood. I sold them almost any place I stopped

When I sold all my baskets one day, I learned to take orders for the next day. There was a ready sale for the baskets my mother made. And I learned to be a good salesman for a boy of ten. After I'd go to Greenup in the morning and sell baskets and bring back the things Mom told me to get, I'd climb the bluff above the hog pen and cut the bushy-topped white-oak saplings and slide them over the bluff to the barn. Then I'd carry them to the entry and saw them into lengths with a handsaw, split them into quarters and carry them into the house for Mom.

When our feed ran out, Mom sent me to Broughton's to see about feed.

"I think John Broughton's got corn and I know he's got fodder to sell," Mom said. "You get the saddle on Fred and ride out there and 3 see. Don't pay over twenty cents a shock for fodder. Offer him fifteen cents at first and if he won't take that, then offer him twenty cents. We have to have feed for Fred and Gypsy. Offer him ninety cents a barrel for corn and don't give him over a dollar a barrel."

When I rode away to Broughton's to see about feed, I left Mom at home making baskets. I rode down the hollow and turned up

38 *The Short Story*

GUIDED READING

LITERAL QUESTION

1a. Why is the boy worried after Mom makes twelve baskets in one day? (He's afraid she will get sick.)

INFERENTIAL QUESTION

1b. Besides his love for Mom, what else does he show by his worrying about Mom's health? (that he knows the rest of the family could not easily survive without her)

the left fork of Ragweed Hollow. The snow was nearly to Fred's neck in places. I found my way to Broughton's barn where Mr. Broughton was feeding his cows.

"I'll take fifteen cents a shock for thirty shocks of fodder," Mr. Broughton said. "That's all I have to sell. That ought to winter your horse and cow until grass gets here this spring. I won't take ninety cents a barrel for my corn. I'll take a dollar a barrel for it and put it in your corncrib. I can let you have ten barrels of corn."

"All right, Mr. Broughton," I said. "I'll pay you for the corn and fodder right now if you'll promise me you'll deliver the fodder while you're bringing the corn."

Mr. Broughton's eyes looked big when I told him I'd pay him now. I know he wondered where I got the money. He knew Pa was sick, for he had been around home a couple of times to see him and talked to him far into the night. I paid Mr. Broughton a ten-dollar bill, four one-dollar bills, and I gave him a half dollar, and then I rode toward home. The next day we had feed in our barn to last until the hills got green again.

1 "How's the feed holding out?" Pa asked.

"Mick, we've got plenty of feed."

"That feed's lasting the longest of any feed yet."

"We've got enough to last until the pastures get green."

Pa would curve his thin lips in a smile. He would lie on the bed and ask questions about the horse, the cow and the chickens.

Often when I walked along the creek I found rabbits dead—frozen hard as an icicle. I found dead quails. I found dead possums. **2** Maybe they had starved to death for something to eat. I found still life wherever I went. The weather had been so cold and all life had shrunk to the bone, perished for food or had frozen to death.

The snow didn't show any signs of melting.

All we did at home was get wood, feed the horse and cow, cook, eat, sleep and make baskets. I took four, six, eight and often ten baskets away each day to Greenup. People called me the "Basket Boy." I brought back meal, flour, lard and groceries. Every day I brought back a piece of dry goods for Mom. She'd write down on paper what she wanted and I'd bring it back. Each day I brought back some money to Mom. I never spent all that I got for the baskets. Mom planned the spending so I'd bring the money home.

"A body needs a little money about the house," Mom said. "We never know what time we might need it. I've got to keep a little ahead to buy medicine for your Pa. He's liable to get worse any time. It's hard to tell. He's had a long lingering spell this winter and his face is awful white. His jawbones look like they'll come through the skin any minute, his face is so thin."

As the winter days dragged on toward spring and the great sheets of snow remained **3** on the steep hill slopes, Mom did not go to the woodyard and help me cut wood like she had. I cut the wood with my pole-ax. Mom sat in her chair before the fire and wove baskets. She seldom got up for anything. Pa talked more to Mom now than he had ever talked. She propped him up in bed with his pillow behind his back and he watched her weave baskets. He talked to her about when the snow would leave and the ground would show—dark with melted snow-water running down over the hills leaping like fish in the sunlight.

"Go to Greenwood and get the Doctor," Mom said one day. "Get on Fred and hurry to town!"

"Is Pa worse?" I asked.

"Don't ask questions but hurry," Mom said.

I rode Fred over the snow fast as I could go. I got Doctor Morris out of bed. He rode his

Spring Victory 39

AT A GLANCE

- The boy buys feed and surprises the farmer with cash.
- Mom says the family may need extra money.
- Mom no longer helps with the arduous jobs; she and Pa talk.
- Mom sends the boy for the doctor.

1 THEME

In this brief dialogue we see the deep love between Mom and Pa. Pa knows that Mom is taking care of things; Mom knows that he knows. Yet pride and traditional values are maintained.

2 THEME

The narrator, in describing the "still life," allows us to contrast the animals' death with the family's survival.

3 PLOT: FORESHADOWING

The change in Mom foreshadows the climax of the story. She seldom leaves her chair, and she and Pa have talks.

GUIDED READING

LITERAL QUESTION

1a. When Pa asks about the feed, what does Mom say? (There's plenty.)

INFERENTIAL QUESTION

1b. Why doesn't she tell him she's bought more with the money she's earned? Do you think he knows anyway? (She may not want to hurt his pride; his comment about the length of time the grain has lasted indicates that he may.)

- A baby is born to the family.
- As the snow melts Pa begins to recover.
- The family begins working the land again.

1 PLOT: CLIMAX

The climax of the story is reached with the birth of a baby, a symbol of hope and survival for the family.

2 PLOT: RESOLUTION

The story began inside the cold house; it ends outside, with Mom holding the baby and finding violets, the boy clearing the way for the plow, and Pa at the plow. The family not only has survived but also is flourishing.

REFLECTING ON THE STORY

What does the boy learn in the story? (He learns firsthand how to shoulder responsibility, to overcome fear, etc.)

STUDY QUESTIONS

1. Little food left in house; father is ill; winter is terribly cold.
2. Mom will make baskets to sell; Sophie will cook, help make baskets; boy will cut wood, sell baskets, buy necessities.
3. Mother has a baby boy.
4. healthier; debts are paid, and spring has arrived
5. willingness and ability to work hard; capacity to sustain hope
6. They survive a difficult time; come out of it with a new child and even some extra money.
7. Father's health improves; Mother has a baby; violets bloom; pasture grass is growing.
8. Answers will vary. Possibilities: *winter*—restful quiet, solitude; *spring*—renewal, hope; *summer*—joy; *fall*—sadness

horse and we raced back over the snow in the winter moonlight and starlight. When we got to the house, I saw a light from the front window. Sophie met me at the front door and told me that we'd have to sit by a fire in the kitchen stove. Doctor Morris went into the house.

1 It was some time before daylight when I heard a baby cry.

"I hear a baby crying, Sophie," I said.

"Yes, didn't you know?"

"But I never would have thought that."

"Come in the front room, you children," Doctor Morris said as he looked in at the kitchen door. "You will be very happy when you see the big fine brother I have brought you."

Sophie and I ran into the room to see our brother. We had a lamp in our front room now. I could understand why Mom had me to buy it. I could understand about the cloth she had me to get. I thought of these things as I looked at Mom lying on the bed with the quilts turned down enough for us to see our brother. We stood beside the bed watching the quilts shake when he kicked. And he cried like he was mad at everybody. There was a smile on Mom's lips.

It was March and the sun had shone brightly for three days. The snow melted and the snow-water ran in tiny streams down the small drains on the steep bluffs.

When Pop saw the dark hills again he sat up in bed. There was more color in his face now. Each day he looked at the hills and talked to Mom. Soon as Mom got up from the bed, Pa was up walking about. Color was coming back rapidly to his face. Flesh was coming back to his skeleton body. Sophie did the cooking and I did the feeding. I got the wood. Mom had paid all of our bills and she had a little money left after she paid Doctor Morris.

"All our debts are paid, Mick," Mom said. "The hard winter is over. Violets are in bloom and pasture grass is coming back to the pastures."

2 Mom stood in the late March wind with our tiny brother wrapped in a blanket in her arms. She kicked the dead leaves away with the toe of her shoe from a clump of blooming violets. I walked ahead of Pa and cut stalks and sprouts with a grubbing hoe. Pa rested between the handles of the plow and looked at Mom standing at the edge of the field with the early buds of spring about her.

STUDY QUESTIONS

Recalling

1. List three problems that Mom mentions at the beginning of the story.
2. What is Mom's plan to raise money for the family? Tell how Sophie and the boy help.
3. What happens after the boy brings the doctor to the farm?
4. What is the father's condition at the end of the story? What good news does Mom give him?

Interpreting

5. What qualities or virtues help the family to succeed?
6. What do you think is the "victory" that the family wins?
7. What signs of hope and new life appear at the end of the story?

Extending

8. What moods and feelings do people sometimes associate with the different seasons?

40   *The Short Story*

READING AND LITERARY FOCUS

Plot

The **plot** is the sequence of events, or what happens in a story. Each event in a plot causes or leads to the next. For example, in Charles Dickens' "Christmas Carol" Scrooge's stinginess causes the visits of four ghosts. Each ghost leads to the next one. As we read a story, we wonder how it will end, and we become involved in the chain of events. Our interest in the story rises according to the following pattern:

The **climax** is the point of our highest interest and involvement in the story. At that part of the plot, we know how the story will end. After the climax events continue to a **resolution,** the end of the story, when we learn the final outcome. For example, in "A Christmas Carol" the climax happens in the morning when Scrooge decides to be a kinder person. The resolution shows examples of his new generosity.

Thinking About Plot

1. List three major events in the plot of "Spring Victory" in the order that they happen.
2. What is the climax of "Spring Victory"? What is the resolution of the story?

VOCABULARY

Synonyms

A **synonym** is a word that has the same or nearly the same meaning as another word. *Help* and *aid* are synonyms. The italicized words in the following numbered items are from "Spring Victory." Choose the word that is nearest the meaning of each italicized word, *as the word is used in the story.* Write the number of each item and the letter of your choice on a separate sheet.

1. *hauled* wood with our horse
   - (a) found
   - (b) dragged
   - (c) searched for
   - (d) invented
2. steep snow-covered *bluff*
   - (a) cliff
   - (b) ocean
   - (c) jungle
   - (d) building
3. long *lingering* illness
   - (a) beginning
   - (b) eager
   - (c) cheerful
   - (d) continuing
4. The weather is *liable* to get worse.
   - (a) likely
   - (b) unable
   - (c) different
   - (d) free
5. newly planted *sapling*
   - (a) sweet odor
   - (b) sharp tool
   - (c) wide field
   - (d) young tree

COMPOSITION

Writing About Plot

■ Does the outcome of the plot of "Spring Victory" follow logically from the events of the story? Explain your opinion in an essay. First state your opinion clearly. Then give at least two reasons for your opinion of the outcome. Support each reason with examples from the story. *For help with this assignment, see Lesson 2 in the Writing About Literature Handbook at the back of this book.*

Writing a Newspaper Story

■ Write a newspaper story about one family's struggle to survive dangerous weather conditions (for example, a flood, a blizzard, a tornado). Like a newspaper writer, include the who, what, where, when, and why of the story. Begin by telling the size of the family, the type of weather they survive, the time, and the place. Second, describe the dangerous weather conditions. Finally, tell what the family does to survive.

Spring Victory 41

READING AND LITERARY FOCUS

1. Mother thinks of a way to make money for food; the boy sells baskets; by spring, father is well.
2. The climax is the birth of the baby. The resolution occurs with the arrival of spring.

VOCABULARY

1. (b) dragged
2. (a) cliff
3. (d) continuing
4. (a) likely
5. (d) young tree

COMPOSITION: GUIDELINES FOR EVALUATION

WRITING ABOUT PLOT

Objective

To analyze the plot's development

Guidelines for Evaluation

■ suggested length: 1–3 paragraphs
■ composition should discuss whether plot's outcome is logical; should include at least two reasons
■ should support each reason with examples

WRITING A NEWSPAPER STORY

Objective

To write a news story

Guidelines for Evaluation

■ suggested length: 3–4 paragraphs
■ story should identify event being reported
■ should answer the questions *who? what? where? when?* and *why?* with specific details

- The story takes place in a village of foolish people.
- Shmelka and Shmelkicha's four daughters mix their feet up and cannot get out of bed.
- Shmelka consults the wise Elder of Chelm.

LITERARY OPTIONS

- cause-effect relationships
- plot
- humor

THEMATIC OPTIONS

- foolishness and wisdom
- communities
- family life

1 SETTING/BACKGROUND

Although the towns are fictional, and the story resembles a folk tale, many details reflect Jewish peasants' way of life in Eastern Europe at the turn of the century.

2 STYLE: HUMOR

Much of the story's humor derives from the matter-of-fact tone in which ridiculous events are described. The words *so of course they couldn't get up* prepare the reader to leave ordinary reasoning behind.

TEXAS ESSENTIAL ELEMENTS
GRADE 8

1A writing process
1B purpose and audience
3A plot development and character development
3D literary genres
4B implied main idea
4E cause/effect
4G prediction of outcomes
To locate treatment of an Element, see *Texas Teacher's Resources.*

© 1982 Jill Krementz

Isaac Bashevis Singer (born 1904) came to the United States from Poland in 1935. He is one of a few modern authors who write in Yiddish, the language spoken by many Jews in eastern Europe. Singer has also translated some of his own stories into English. In 1978 he was awarded the Nobel Prize for Literature. The following story takes place in the fictional town of Chelm, which is inhabited entirely of fools.

■ What truths about humans does the silly behavior reveal?

Isaac Bashevis Singer

The Mixed-Up Feet and the Silly Bridegroom

1 Near the village of Chelm[1] there was a hamlet[2] called East Chelm, where there lived a tenant farmer called Shmelka[3] and his wife, Shmelkicha.[4] They had four daughters, all of whom slept in the same broad bed. Their names were Yenta, Pesha, Trina, Yachna.[5]

As a rule the girls got up early in the morning to milk the cows and help their mother with the household chores. But one winter morning they stayed in bed later than usual. When their mother came to see what was keeping them, she found all four struggling and screaming in the bed. Shmelkicha demanded to know what all the commotion was about and why they were pulling each other's hair. The girls replied that in their sleep they

2 had gotten their feet mixed up, and now they didn't know whose feet belonged to whom, and so of course they couldn't get up.

As soon as she learned about her daughters' mixed-up feet, Shmelkicha, who was from Chelm proper, became exceedingly frightened. She remembered that a similar event had taken place in Chelm many years before and, oh, how much trouble there had been. She ran at once to a neighbor and begged her to milk the cows, and she herself set off for Chelm to ask the town's Elder[6] what to do. Before she left, she said to the girls, "You stay in bed and don't budge until I return. Because once you get up with the wrong feet, it will be very difficult to set things right."

When Shmelkicha arrived in Chelm and told the Elder about what had happened to her daughters, he clutched his white beard

---

1. **Chelm** [кнelm]
2. **hamlet:** small country town.
3. **Shmelka** [shmel′kä]
4. **Shmelkicha** [shmel kē′кнä]
5. **Yenta, Pesha, Trina, Yachna** [yen′tä, pesh′ä, trē′nä, yäкн′nä]

6. **Elder:** respected older member of a community often consulted for wisdom and advice.

GUIDED READING

LITERAL QUESTION

1a. How does the mother respond to her daughters' problem? (She goes off to consult the Elder for advice.)

INFERENTIAL QUESTION

1b. What does the mother's response tell you about her? (She is foolish; she doesn't trust her own common sense.)

with one hand, placed the other on his forehead, and was immediately lost in thought. As he pondered he hummed a Chelm melody.

After a while he said, "There is no perfect solution for a case of mixed-up feet. But there is something that sometimes helps."

He told Shmelkicha to take a long stick, walk into the girls' room, and unexpectedly whack the blanket where their feet were. "It is possible," explained the wise Elder, "that in surprise and pain each girl will grab at her own feet and jump out of bed." A similar remedy had once been used in such a case, and it had worked.

Many townspeople were present when the Elder made his pronouncement, and as always they admired his great wisdom. The Elder stated further that in order to prevent **1** such an accident in the future, it would be advisable to gradually marry off the girls. Once each girl was married and had her own house and her own husband, there would be no danger that they would get their feet mixed up again.

Shmelkicha returned to East Chelm, picked up a stick, walked into her daughters' room, and whacked the quilt with all her might. The girls were completely taken aback, but before a moment had passed, they were out of bed, screaming in pain and fright, each jumping on her own feet. Shmelka, their father, and a number of neighbors who had followed Shmelkicha into the house and witnessed what had happened, again came to the conclusion that the wisdom of the Elder of Chelm knew no bounds.

Shmelka and Shmelkicha immediately decided to carry out the rest of the Elder's advice **2** and started looking for a husband for their eldest daughter. They soon found a young man of Chelm called Lemel.[7] His father was a coachman, and Lemel himself already owned a horse and wagon. It was clear that Yenta's future husband would be a good provider.

When they brought the couple together to sign the marriage agreement, Yenta began to **3** cry bitterly. Asked why she was crying, she replied, "Lemel is a stranger, and I don't want to marry a stranger."

"Didn't I marry a stranger?" her mother asked.

"You married Father," Yenta answered, "and I have to marry a total stranger." And her face became wet with tears.

The match would have come to nothing, but luckily they had invited the Elder of

_____

7. **Lemel** [le′məl]

The Mixed-Up Feet and the Silly Bridegroom 43

GUIDED READING

LITERAL QUESTIONS

1a. What two pieces of advice does the Elder give? (to whack the daughters' blanket and to marry off the daughters)

2a. How does Yenta answer when her mother says, "Didn't I marry a stranger?" ("You married Father, and I have to marry a total stranger.")

INFERENTIAL QUESTIONS

1b. Are the two pieces of advice foolish or wise? (Each is a foolish overreaction, but each has an underlying wisdom: Scaring the girls will get them out of bed, and separating them may prevent future problems.)

2b. What is wrong with Yenta's reasoning? (Her mother did marry a stranger, who later became Yenta's father.)

1 ALLUSION

In the Bible King Solomon was known for his ability to help people solve seemingly impossible problems. The reference provides humorous contrast to the so-called problems in this story.

2 READING SKILLS: CONTRAST

Since Shmelka "was not a native of Chelm," his rational thinking is at odds with Lemel's lack of common sense.

3 READING SKILLS: CAUSE AND EFFECT

Lemel breaks the jar of chicken fat because he tries to apply Shmelka's advice about the penknife to an inappropriate situation.

4 CHARACTERIZATION

"Didn't you tell me to?" sums up Lemel's character. He is easygoing and doesn't think for himself, blindly following any advice he gets.

Chelm to be present. And, after some pondering, he again found the way out. He said to Yenta, "Sign the marriage contract. The moment you sign it, Lemel becomes your betrothed.[8] And when you marry, you will not be marrying a stranger, you will be marrying your betrothed."

When Yenta heard these words, she was overjoyed. Lemel kissed the Elder three times on his huge forehead, and the rest of the company praised the wisdom of the Elder of Chelm, which was even greater than that of wise King Solomon.

But now a new problem arose. Neither Lemel nor Yenta had learned to sign their names.

Again the Elder came to the rescue: "Let Yenta make three small circles on the paper, and Lemel three dashes. These will serve as their signatures and seal the contract."

Yenta and Lemel did as the Elder ordered, and everybody was gay and happy. Shmelkicha treated all the witnesses to cheese blintzes and borscht,[9] and the first plate naturally went to the Elder of Chelm, whose appetite was particularly good that day.

Before Lemel returned to Chelm proper, from where he had driven in his own horse and wagon, Shmelka gave him as a gift a small penknife with a mother-of-pearl handle. It happened to be the first day of Hanukkah,[10] and the penknife was both an engagement gift and a Hanukkah present.

Since Lemel often came to East Chelm to buy from the peasants the milk, butter, hay, oats, and flax which he sold to the townspeople of Chelm, he soon came to visit Yenta again. Shmelka asked Lemel whether his

---

8. **betrothed:** one who is engaged to be married; fiancé.
9. **cheese blintzes** [blints'əz] **and borscht** [bôrsht]: pancakes filled with cheese and beet soup.
10. **Hanukkah** [hä'nə kə]: joyous winter Jewish holiday that lasts for eight days.

44 *The Short Story*

---

friends in Chelm had liked his penknife, and Lemel replied that they had never seen it.

"Why not?" Shmelka asked.

"Because I lost it."

"How did you lose it?"

"I put the penknife into the wagon and it got lost in the hay."

Shmelka was not a native of Chelm but came from another nearby town, and he said to Lemel, "You don't put a penknife into a wagon full of straw and hay and with cracks and holes in the bottom to boot. A penknife you place in your pocket, and then it does not get lost."

"Future Father-in-law, you are right," Lemel answered. "Next time I will know what to do."

Since the first gift had been lost, Shmelka gave Lemel a jar of freshly fried chicken fat to replace it. Lemel thanked him and returned to Chelm.

Several days later, when business again brought Lemel to East Chelm, Yenta's parents noticed that his coat pocket was torn, and the entire left side of his coat was covered with grease stains.

"What happened to your coat?" Shmelkicha asked.

Lemel replied, "I put the jar of chicken fat in my pocket, but the road is full of holes and ditches and I could not help bumping against the side of the wagon. The jar broke, and it tore my pocket and the fat ran out all over my clothes."

"Why did you put the jar of chicken fat into your pocket?" Shmelka asked.

"Didn't you tell me to?"

"A penknife you put into your pocket. A jar of chicken fat you wrap in paper and place in the hay so that it will not break."

Lemel replied, "Next time I will know what to do."

Since Lemel had had little use out of the

GUIDED READING

LITERAL QUESTIONS

1a. What advice does the Elder give to persuade Yenta to marry a stranger? (to sign the marriage contract so that he would no longer be a stranger)

2a. Why does Lemel put a jar of chicken fat in his pocket? (He remembers Shmelka's advice about protecting a penknife.)

INFERENTIAL QUESTIONS

1b. Is the advice foolish or wise? (Logically, it is foolish; psychologically, it is wise because it succeeds in resolving Yenta's fears.)

2b. Do you think Lemel will know what to do the next time a new situation arises? (No; he will probably apply old advice to an inappropriate situation again.)

AT A GLANCE

- Yenta give Lemel a silver gulden, which he loses.
- He applies her advice about the gulden to her next gift, eggs, and breaks them.

1 PLOT: SUSPENSE

The reader always knows in advance exactly what Lemel will do wrong the next time. There is a feeling of suspense, though, about how long the foolish family will allow their gifts to be wasted and how they will correct the situation.

2 STYLE: REPETITION

Lemel's repetition of this line after each mishap ironically underscores his lack of common sense and contributes to the humor of the story.

first two gifts, Yenta herself gave him a silver gulden,[11] which her father had given her as a Hanukkah gift.

When Lemel came to the hamlet again, he was asked how he had spent the money.

"I lost it," he replied.

"How did you lose it?"

"I wrapped it in paper and placed it in the hay. But when I arrived in Chelm and unloaded my merchandise, the gulden was gone."

1 "A gulden is not a jar of chicken fat," Shmelka informed him. "A gulden you put into your purse."

---

11. **silver gulden:** Polish money of the time.

"Next time I will know what to do."

Before Lemel returned to Chelm, Yenta gave her fiancé some newly laid eggs, still warm from the chickens.

On his next visit he was asked how he had enjoyed the eggs, and he replied that they had all been broken.

"How did they break?"

"I put them into my purse, but when I tried to close it, the eggs broke."

"Nobody puts eggs into a purse," Shmelka said. "Eggs you put into a basket bedded with straw and covered with a rag so that they will not break."

2 "Next time I will know what to do."

Since Lemel had not been able to enjoy the

The Mixed-Up Feet and the Silly Bridegroom 45

GUIDED READING

LITERAL QUESTION

1a. Why does Lemel put the silver gulden in the hay? (He is following the advice given for the jar of chicken fat.)

INFERENTIAL QUESTION

1b. How could the family have prevented the loss of Lemel's gifts? (by giving him specific instructions for carrying each gift)

- Lemel inadvertently kills Yenta's gifts.
- The Elder suggests a quick marriage to avert further catastrophes.
- The couple have a child, and Lemel is amazed when the Elder guesses its sex in two questions.

1 THEME

The story deals humorously with a common stress of family life: exasperation with an in-law.

2 PLOT: CLIMAX

All of the preceding action has been building to the emotional high point of the wedding.

3 READING SKILLS: CAUSE AND EFFECT

This episode resolves the story but leaves us with the conviction that Lemel's naiveté could precipitate many more similarly humorous incidents.

REFLECTING ON THE STORY

What points do you think the story makes about giving and taking advice? (Some people are too eager to seek and believe in the advice of others; nothing can replace common sense and thinking for yourself.)

STUDY QUESTIONS

1. because of their mixed-up feet; to whack girls' feet with a stick; so they might grab their own feet in pain and jump out of bed
2. doesn't want to marry a stranger; says once she signs marriage contract, Lemel will be her betrothed, not a stranger
3. possible answers: *lost:* penknife, gulden; *broken:* jar of chicken fat, eggs; *killed:* duck, goldfish
4. blames problem on Lemel's traveling to see Yenta; recommends that they marry
5. tells Lemel his baby is a girl after only one wrong guess

---

gifts he had received, Yenta decided to present him with a live duck.

When he returned, he was asked how the duck was faring, and he said she had died on the way to Chelm.

"How did she die?"

"I placed her in a basket with straw and covered it well with rags, just as you had told me to. When I arrived home, the duck was dead."

"A duck has to breathe," Shmelkicha said. "If you cover her with rags, she will suffocate. A duck you put in a cage, with some corn to eat, and then she will arrive safely."

"Next time I will know what to do."

Since Lemel had gained neither use nor pleasure from any of his gifts, Yenta decided to give him her goldfish, a pet she had had for several years.

And again on his return, when asked about the goldfish, he replied that it was dead.

"Why is it dead?"

"I placed it in a cage and gave it some corn, but when I arrived it was dead."

1 Since Lemel was still without a gift, Yenta decided to give him her canary, which she loved dearly. But Shmelka told her that it seemed pointless to give Lemel any more gifts, because whatever you gave him either died or got lost. Instead Shmelka and Shmelkicha decided to get the advice of the Elder of Chelm.

The Elder listened to the whole story, and as usual clutched his long white beard with one hand and placed the other on his high forehead.

After much pondering and humming, he proclaimed, "The road between East Chelm and Chelm is fraught[12] with all kinds of dangers, and that is why such misfortunes occur. The best thing to do is to have a quick marriage. Then Lemel and Yenta will be together, and Lemel will not have to drag his gifts from one place to another, and no misfortunes will befall them."

2 This advice pleased everyone, and the marriage was soon celebrated. All the peasants of the hamlet of East Chelm and half of the townspeople of Chelm danced and rejoiced at the wedding. Before the year was out, Yenta give birth to a baby girl and Lemel went to tell the Elder of Chelm the good tidings that a child had been born to them.

3 "Is the child a boy?" the Elder asked.

"No."

"Is it a girl?"

"How did you guess?" Lemel asked in amazement.

And the Elder of Chelm replied, "For the wise men of Chelm there are no secrets."

---

12. **fraught** [frôt]: filled, or loaded.

STUDY QUESTIONS

Recalling

1. Why do the four daughters stay in bed late? What is the Elder's advice for solving the problem?
2. Why does Yenta not want to marry Lemel? In what way does the Elder convince her?
3. Name four gifts that Lemel receives from Yenta's family. Tell what happens to each gift.
4. What is the Elder's solution to the problem with the gifts?
5. Tell how the Elder amazes Lemel at the end of the story.

46   *The Short Story*

Interpreting

6. In what way does Yenta's family cause the problem with the gifts? In what way is Lemel responsible?
7. What traits of human nature are suggested by the Elder and his advice?
8. What serious ideas are suggested by the silly events of the story?

READING AND LITERARY FOCUS

Chronology; Cause and Effect

Just as in everyday life, events in the plot of a story are related. Each event leads to or causes the next. Most stories are told in **chronological order,** the time order in which events naturally happen. For example, a runner trains *before* an important race and rests *after* it.

Events are also arranged by cause and effect. In a **cause-and-effect** relationship each event makes others happen. For example, a person may get a job *because* of his or her past record. An *effect* of the new job may be the ability to buy a new car or home. The plot of a story should be logical. We should understand why and in what order events happen.

Thinking About Chronology; Cause and Effect

1. List in chronological order the events in "The Mixed-Up Feet and the Silly Bridegroom."
2. Tell how the mixed-up feet help to cause Yenta's marriage.
3. Reread the part of the story about Lemel's gifts. In what way are the events in this section related by cause and effect?

VOCABULARY

Sentence Completions

Each of the following sentences contains a blank with four possible words for completing the sentence. The words are from "The Mixed-Up Feet and the Silly Bridegroom." Choose the word that best completes each sentence. Write the number of each item and the letter of your choice on a separate sheet.

1. Anne was ___ grateful for the neighbors' kindness. She thanked them again and again.
   (a) gradually   (c) bitterly
   (b) exceedingly   (d) unexpectedly
2. The judge ___ a long time before reaching a decision.
   (a) proclaimed   (c) witnessed
   (b) clutched   (d) pondered
3. The syrup that the doctor gave him was an effective ___ for Alan's cough.
   (a) contract   (c) remedy
   (b) tenant   (d) tidings
4. Mr. Reed has more customers because of the higher quality of the ___ he sells.
   (a) merchandise   (c) provider
   (b) misfortunes   (d) chores
5. The ___ caused when the team entered the rally was exciting and noisy.
   (a) commotion   (c) peasants
   (b) pronouncement   (d) wisdom

CHALLENGE

Children's Book

■ In "The Mixed-Up Feet and the Silly Bridegroom" the people of Chelm are all fools. Illustrate a story for children about another fictional town where all the people share one trait (for example, extreme laziness, unusual clothing, or skill at acrobatics). Briefly describe the town and the people's main trait. Then draw a series of pictures or create collages that show the town, its people, and their main trait. You may want to donate your book to a kindergarten class.

The Mixed-Up Feet and the Silly Bridegroom   47

6. Family never gives advice until too late. Lemel follows advice unthinkingly.
7. Answers will vary. Possible answers are that people in quandaries are relieved to simply follow advice, sensible or not; highly respected people may not truly be wise.
8. Possible answers: some like to be told what to do; some can't think for themselves; following orders without thinking causes trouble.

1. Girls mix up feet, can't get up; Mother goes to Elder for advice; he says whack girls' feet and begin marrying them off; girls get up; parents find Lemel for eldest; daughter won't marry a stranger; Elder brought into solve problem; he says once contract is signed, they are no longer strangers; Mother gives Lemel penknife; he loses it; Lemel gets other gifts and loses or ruins them; Elder brought in; says Yenta and Lemel should marry because misfortunes are caused by road Lemel travels to see Yenta; marriage occurs; Yenta has baby; Lemel visits Elder; Elder guesses baby's sex after hearing that it is not a boy.
2. Elder's solution for solving that problem includes marrying off girls.
3. Lemel loses knife through own stupidity, then seeks advice about how to keep each gift safely. Because he's so stupid, with each new gift he follows advice for the last gift, losing or destroying each gift in turn.

1. (b) exceedingly
2. (d) pondered
3. (c) remedy
4. (a) merchandise
5. (a) commotion

Students should
■ choose a particular trait, such as laziness, acrobatic skill
■ imagine a town whose inhabitants share this trait
■ briefly describe it in words
■ depict it in a drawing or collage

AT A GLANCE

- The setting is a hot and dry October.
- The narrator remembers walking with his older brother Paul and is playing with a match.

LITERARY OPTIONS

- plot
- setting
- conflict

THEMATIC OPTIONS

- family life
- confronting obstacles
- nature

1 POINT OF VIEW

The first-person narrator immediately prepares the reader for what will follow: a boyhood memory involving a forest fire and an injustice to his older brother.

2 CHARACTERIZATION

The narrator's description of his mother as more a "referee than parent" suggests that the children and Grandfather were often in conflict. The adult siblings still can't decide whether Grandfather was "quite mad" or "full of wisdom."

3 SETTING

The description of the weather as "hot and still and dry" hints at the crisis to come.

4 PLOT: FORESHADOWING

The narrator's discussion of the kitchen matches foreshadows what is about to happen.

John D. MacDonald (1916–1986) is famous for his popular detective novels. The hero of many of these novels is detective Travis McGee. MacDonald also writes more serious stories. His work has been the basis of many movies and television shows. His stories often have exciting action.

■ In "Fire!" what problems does a forest fire create for one twelve-year-old boy?

John D. MacDonald

Fire!

Not long ago, coming back home on a night flight, I saw the sullen ember of a distant forest fire in the hills and felt a small twist of anguish. I knew it was the memory of the injustice of my grandfather toward my big brother Paul in a long-ago October.

There were seven of us children in all. Now, when we all get together with wives and husbands and children, we end up telling Grandfather stories, marveling at that strange, wild old man who raised us, with our mother acting more as referee than parent. Sometimes we judge him quite mad. At other times we think he was full of wisdom. Perhaps it was both. He never explained. Paul and I can laugh about the fire now.

It was a strange October that year. Hot and still and dry, day after day, the sun rising and setting in a weird mist. The creek ran nearly dry. We all lugged water to the growing things and worried about the well. I remember that the three littlest ones, Tom, Nan, and Bunny volunteered to give up washing—as an effort to save water. It was denied. The woodlands which began a half dozen miles north of the farm had dozens of fires. When the winds were right, you could smell the stink of burning forest, a strange dirty stench, somehow frightening.

Paul was fifteen that year, and I was twelve. I did the thoughtless, stupid thing on the way back from the creek. I'd gone down there with Paul on a hot Sunday afternoon to see if any fish were trapped in the pools. We were walking back. I had some kitchen matches in my pocket. When out in the wide world I liked to carry one in the corner of my mouth. I felt it gave me a certain devil-may-care[1] air.

In those years all small boys knew that if you hold a match in a certain way and throw it downward at a stone or a sidewalk, it will pop and burn. I was not skilled, but I had

---

1. **devil-may-care:** without caution, carefree.

48   *The Short Story*

GUIDED READING

LITERAL QUESTION

1a. What do "all small boys know," according to the narrator? (how to ignite a match by throwing it on the sidewalk)

INFERENTIAL QUESTION

1b. Given the dryness of the weather, what do you predict will happen to the narrator and the match he holds in the corner of his mouth? (He will start a forest fire.)

tried so many times it required no thought. As we passed a gray rock half buried in the dry weeds along the fence line, I hurled my match at it. It struck properly for once. The head popped and bounced into the weeds, and in an instant the sun-paled flames were high and spreading. For once Paul did not take time out to tell me how stupid I was. He yanked his shirt off and began stomping and flailing, and yelled at me to run for help and water.

I was a hundred yards from the dooryard, and I think I made as good time and as much noise as a fire engine. In a very short and confusing time, all seven kids and my mother and my grandfather were out there with wet sacks and blankets. It was a very near thing. I think that if there had been eight of us instead of nine, it might have gotten away. As it was, it burned off a very large area.

Tom was nine, and as responsible as any of us, and Grandfather left him out there with a bucket of water and orders to patrol the edges, looking for any spark which could have survived the battle.

When we got back to the porch, Grandfather sat down to catch his wind. He had been wonderful out in the pasture, like a great windmill hammering at the flames, yelling at them as he beat them out.

"Who was there?" he demanded.

That was one area where he had always been predictable. When any punishable offense occurred, Grandfather solved the problem of blame by walloping everyone who had been in the immediate area. Thus we were forever united, policing each other, with no tattletales.

Paul and I admitted our presence at the scene, knowing that we would sit down very carefully for the next day or so. The other kids drifted away, and we were left there facing the old man. I remember the black streaks of burned grasses on his big hands.

"All right," he said. "Which one of you did it?"

The simple question surprised us. Without warning, he had changed the rules. Paul straightened himself slightly and said, "I did it!" He was fifteen. He used a tone of voice we younger ones did not yet dare to use. Grandfather sighed and he looked at me, blue eyes under those angry white brows. I believe I tried to speak. But the thing I had done was so shamefully stupid, I wasted too much time trying to think of a way to confess which would make it believable.

Before I could find the beginning words, Grandfather got up and went into the house, Mother trotting along behind him, asking nervous questions.

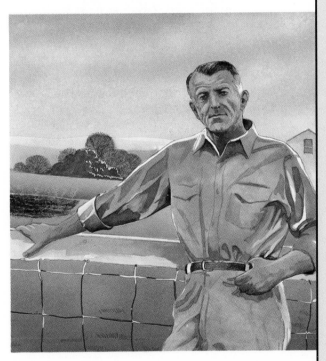

Fire! 49

AT A GLANCE
- The boy's match ignites a fire.
- His brother Paul takes charge.
- The family puts out the fire.
- Grandfather asks who started it, and Paul takes the blame.

1 CHARACTERIZATION

Paul's maturity and sense of responsibility are apparent as he leaps into action, fighting the fire and instructing the narrator to get help.

2 STYLE: SIMILE

Remembering how he perceived Grandfather's strength and relentlessness during the fire, the narrator compares the old man's actions to those of a powerful, tireless machine: a windmill.

3 INTERNAL CONFLICT

The boy struggles inwardly to find the courage to admit his blame, but, stunned by Grandfather's unexpected changing of the rules, Paul's sudden confession, and Grandfather's anger, he lets the moment pass.

GUIDED READING

LITERAL QUESTIONS

1a. How did the fire begin? (The boy was playing a game with a match, and it ignited.)

2a. How did Grandfather change the rules? (He asked, "Which one of you did it?")

INFERENTIAL QUESTIONS

1b. What did the boy's action with the match show about him? (He was immature and thoughtless.)

2b. Why do you think Paul confessed to starting the fire? (He wanted to protect his younger brother from Grandfather's anger.)

- Grandfather takes Paul along to help fight a forest fire, hoping to teach him a lesson.
- The boy remains at home; the well runs dry; and the boy is expected to take charge.

1 EXTERNAL CONFLICT

The crew of "rough, weary men" and their tools, as well as Mother's pleading for her son, suggest the deadliness of the fire.

2 PLOT: CLIMAX

The story reaches its emotional high point as the narrator recalls the ordeal of guilt he experienced while his brother was experiencing his own ordeal with the forest fire.

3 THEME

The narrator links several of the story's themes as he explains how circumstances allow him to transform his guilt into a new sense of family responsibility.

I tried to explain myself to Paul, but he turned away. There was a great silence that night at the supper table. I was an outcast. I wanted the normal punishment. The change of ground rules made me feel lost and sick.

Grandfather got up from the table and looked at Paul and said, "I made some arrangements. You are excused from school. You'll get a better look at a fire, boy."

Early Monday morning one of the county trucks stopped and picked up Grandfather **1** and Paul. There was a crew of rough, weary men aboard the truck and a crude bunch of tools in a steel drum—axes, shovels, mattocks. I remember Mother pleading with Grandfather, saying, "But he's just a boy!"

I did not hear his answer. I know now they needed every strong pair of arms they could round up. It was a fearful time in the powder-dry forests.

50 *The Short Story*

I went off to school with the others. I did **2** not hear much that day in school. I had the horrible vision of Paul encircled by a roar of flames, running and screaming. It was a horrible injustice. It was all my fault. I plotted to sneak off that night and join them in the hills. Somehow I would rescue Paul, and everyone would forgive me.

When the five of us got home from school, we learned that the well had gone dry. And that too seemed to be my fault. We had used a lot of water fighting that stupid grass fire. Mother got me aside and said, "What do you think we should do?"

The question astonished me. It made me **3** realize that with Grandfather and Paul gone, I was the eldest male on the farm. I forgot the feeling of being an outcast. The creek water was sweet. The creek was nearly three hundred yards from the well. Mother had turned

GUIDED READING

LITERAL QUESTION

1a. How does the boy feel at the supper table after Paul has taken the blame? (lost, sick, like an outcast)

INFERENTIAL QUESTION

1b. Why does he feel like an outcast if no one else but Paul knows what he did? (The boy's guilt makes him feel cut off from the rest of the family.)

off the pump when it had sucked dry.

I organized the four eldest of us, Christine, Sheila, Tom, and me, into a water brigade.[2] We scoured out big containers and loaded them on the pickup, and I drove it as close to the creek as I could get it. Then we filled them, bucket by bucket, drove back, and dumped the water into the well. It was very hard work. After several loads, I primed[3] the old pump and started it again. After Tom and Sheila were too exhausted to continue, Christine and I managed two more trips by ourselves.

1 As I lay in my bed that moonlight night, a smell of burning forest came in the window. I was in a soft bed, while Paul and Grandfather were in the hills. There was more penance[4] to

---

2. **brigade** [bri gād′]: people organized for a job.
3. **primed:** poured water into a dry pump to start it.
4. **penance:** voluntary self-punishment.

do. I could not manage the truck system by myself, but I could carry water. I dressed and went quietly out into the night. I could not guess how many trips I made that night. Toward the end I could not manage full buckets.

I remember sitting on the edge of the well, **2** the dawn rose-gray at the horizon line, opening and closing my aching hands, summoning up the will to make yet another trip to the creek. I remember seeing my mother come across the side yard in her robe. She led me back to the house. I can remember fighting tears, and losing just as we reached the steps.

The heavy rains began at dawn on Thursday, and before we left for school, Paul and our grandfather were home, dirty, exhausted, walking in a strange dazed, dragging way, as though they were walking up hill. When we came home from school, they were still sleeping. Grandfather got up for supper, but Paul did not, and Mother had me take him up hot soup and milk and apple pie. He told me of digging endless trenches, chopping through thousands of tough forest roots. He showed me his hands. We were friends again, somehow, but in a different way.

3 When I went back downstairs to my place at the table, I found Mother telling Grandfather how well I had managed the water problem. When there was a pause I blurted, "I set that fire Sunday."

"Don't interrupt your mother," he said.

I sat with my head bowed. I could not eat. When she had finished, Grandfather said, "Mary, if I didn't think the boy could manage, I wouldn't have taken Paul with me."

4 He gave me a rough pat on the shoulder as he left the table. I wore it like medals. And suddenly I was hungry. Grandfather never explained, and we never knew what he would do next. He was as wild and random as the winds that blew.

Fire! 51

AT A GLANCE
- The narrator organizes the children to fill the well; they work hard before the rains begin.
- The narrator confesses to Grandfather, who pats his shoulder.

1 CHARACTERIZATION

The boy's new sense of responsibility will not allow him to rest when he remembers what the other men in the family are enduring.

2 RESPONSE JOURNAL

In their journals have students comment on how much they think the boy has grown up as a result of this experience.

3 PLOT: FALLING ACTION

The boy finally makes his confession, making possible the resolution that follows.

4 PLOT: RESOLUTION

Grandfather's pat on the shoulder suggests that he has known the identity of the real culprit. "I wore it like medals" colorfully conveys the boy's sense of pride at Grandfather's approval.

REFLECTING ON THE STORY

Why do you think the narrator remembers this episode in his life so vividly? (It stirred up powerful emotions; it changed his relationships in his family; it evoked all his mixed feelings about Grandfather.)

GUIDED READING

LITERAL QUESTIONS

1a. How does the boy feel after Paul tells him about the forest fire and shows his hands? (that they are friends again but in a different way)

2a. When does the boy finally confess to causing the fire? (after hearing his mother boast about how responsible and helpful he was while Grandfather and Paul were away)

INFERENTIAL QUESTIONS

1b. What does the boy mean by saying they were friends in a different way? (Because of what they've been through, Paul will not be as protective in the future, and the boy will not want him to be.)

2b. Why do you think he confesses then? (He has learned what it feels like to take responsibility; he wants to live up to his mother's high opinion of him.)

1. at times, wise; at others, quite mad
2. thinks fondly of his youth; is male, adult now, married, probably a father; twelve years old
3. He hurls match at rock to see if it will ignite on impact; feels it would take too long to find words to make story believable; since Grandfather changed rules, he's unprepared to confess.
4. arranges that he help fight a fire
5. organizes older children into water brigade to prime dry pump; later continues filling well alone
6. Mother tells Grandfather about water brigade; boy confesses he set fire; Grandfather tells him not to interrupt; rewards him with rough pat.
7. *mad:* strange method of punishing everyone at scene of wrongdoing, his unpredictability; *wise:* assigns each boy to job he's best suited for
8. Answers will vary. Possible answers: Paul takes younger brother's punishment, showing protective love; narrator remained guilty, and his actions toward Paul may be shaped by guilt.
9. Paul and narrator both learn from physical work. Paul confronts danger with the firefighters like a true adult; narrator forms a water brigade and realizes that he can be responsible and capable.

READING AND LITERARY FOCUS

1. He knows he's guilty, but lets brother accept punishment he deserves.
2. people battling drought and fire

CHALLENGE

Students should
- use resources at library to find out about forest fires
- take notes and prepare an outline
- present information to class orally

STUDY QUESTIONS

Recalling

1. According to the second paragraph, what do the grown children think of Grandfather?
2. From the first four paragraphs find two facts about the storyteller. What age was he at the time of the fire?
3. In what way does the person who tells the story start a fire? Why does he fail to confess?
4. What punishment does Paul receive from Grandfather?
5. What work does the storyteller do while Paul and Grandfather are away?
6. What happens after Paul and Grandfather return home?

Interpreting

7. What actions do you think make Grandfather seem "mad"? What actions show his wisdom?
8. Why do you think that Paul and the storyteller become friends "in a different way" at the end of the story?

Extending

9. Tell how physical labor can sometimes be the best teacher. Use examples from the story to support your opinion.

READING AND LITERARY FOCUS

Conflict

A good plot usually contains a conflict. A **conflict** is a struggle between two opposing forces. When we read a story, we become interested because we want to know how this struggle will be settled. At the climax we learn what the solution will be. We see the final outcome at the resolution.

The conflict in a story can be external or internal. An **external conflict** is a struggle against an outside force, such as nature or another person. For example, imagine a story about a farmer trying to save a crop from poor weather. This story has a conflict of a person against nature. Imagine a

story about a rookie baseball player in debate with the coach about a spot in the lineup. This story has a conflict of one person against another.

An **internal conflict** is a struggle that takes place within a person's mind. For example, a person tries to decide between going to a party and sitting with a sick friend.

Thinking About Conflict

1. What internal conflict does the storyteller of "Fire!" have?
2. Give an example from the story of a conflict against nature.

COMPOSITION

Writing About Plot

■ Write an essay about the plot of "Fire!" First choose three or four major events of the story. Show how each event causes the next one. Then tell what part of the story is the climax. Finally, tell what part of the story is the resolution.

Writing a Journal Entry

■ Imagine that you are Paul. You have just returned home from fighting the forest fire. Write a journal entry about the events of "Fire!" You may want to answer the following questions: Why did you take the blame for the fire? What did you do to help put out the forest fire? What is your opinion of Grandfather and your brother?

CHALLENGE

Research and Oral Report

■ Do research in the library on forest fires in the United States. Then present an oral report. You may want to answer the following questions in your report: How much damage is done by forest fires every year? What are some effects of forest fires? What methods are used to put out fires? How can people prevent them?

COMPOSITION: GUIDELINES FOR EVALUATION

WRITING ABOUT PLOT

Objective
To write an essay about the plot of "Fire!"

Guidelines for Evaluation
- suggested length: three to four paragraphs
- should explain cause-effect relationship of three or four important events
- should clearly explain climax and resolution
- should use an informal style

WRITING A JOURNAL ENTRY

Objective
To write from the point of view of a character

Guidelines for Evaluation
- suggested length: 150–200 words
- be written from Paul's point of view and explain motivations for his actions
- should give opinion of other characters
- should use informal style and first person

Shirley Jackson (1919–1965) is famous for haunting tales of horror and for warm, humorous stories of family life. The mother of four children, she found time for writing in between her many household chores. Her stories contain people who behave in unusual ways.

■ As you read "Charles," decide what is odd about the actions of each member of this family.

AT A GLANCE
- Laurie begins kindergarten and changes from a baby to a "swaggering" boy.
- He comes home on the first day being generally rude and talking about Charles, the bad boy of the class.

LITERARY OPTIONS
- plot
- characterization
- point of view

THEMATIC OPTIONS
- growing up
- family life
- communication

Shirley Jackson

Charles

1   The day my son Laurie started kindergarten he renounced[1] corduroy overalls with bibs and began wearing blue jeans with a belt; I watched him go off the first morning with the older girl next door, seeing clearly that an era of my life was ended, my sweet-voiced, nursery-school tot replaced by a long-trousered, swaggering[2] character who forgot to stop at the corner and wave goodbye to me.

2   He came home the same way, the front door slamming open, his cap on the floor, and the voice suddenly become raucous[3] shouting, "Isn't anybody *here*?"

   At lunch he spoke insolently to his father, spilled his baby sister's milk, and remarked that his teacher said we were not to take the name of the Lord in vain.

   "How *was* school today?" I asked, elaborately casual.

---

1. **renounced** [ri nounst′]: gave up.
2. **swaggering** [swag′ər ing]: arrogant; walking in a proud way.
3. **raucous** [rô′kəs]: rough-sounding.

   "All right," he said.

   "Did you learn anything?" his father asked.

   Laurie regarded his father coldly. "I didn't learn nothing," he said.

   "Anything," I said. "Didn't learn anything."

   "The teacher spanked a boy, though," Laurie said, addressing his bread and butter. "For being fresh," he added, with his mouth full.

   "What did he do?" I asked. "Who was it?"

3   Laurie thought. "It was Charles," he said. "He was fresh. The teacher spanked him and made him stand in a corner. He was awfully fresh."

   "What did he do?" I asked again, but Laurie slid off his chair, took a cookie, and left, while his father was still saying, "See here, young man."

   The next day Laurie remarked at lunch, as soon as he sat down, "Well, Charles was bad again today." He grinned enormously and said, "Today Charles hit the teacher."

   "Good heavens," I said, mindful of the

Charles   53

1 **POINT OF VIEW**

Through the mother's eyes the reader sees Laurie change from a baby to a boy in "blue jeans with a belt." The mother's first-person narration creates a sense of poignancy, humor, and suspense throughout the story.

2 **CHARACTERIZATION**

Laurie's behavior after the first day of kindergarten suggests that his character, as well as his clothing, is undergoing some change, spelling trouble for his parents.

3 **PLOT: FORESHADOWING**

Laurie's hesitation here is a clue, which his mother notices but does not stop to analyze or question Laurie about.

TEXAS ESSENTIAL ELEMENTS
GRADE 8

3A plot and character development
3D literary genres
4B implied main idea
4D sequential order
4E cause/effect
4F point of view
4K library references
To locate treatment of an Element, see *Texas Teacher's Resources.*

GUIDED READING

LITERAL QUESTION

1a. How does Laurie's appearance change on his first day at kindergarten? (He changes his bib overalls for blue jeans and a belt.)

INFERENTIAL QUESTION

1b. Do you think Laurie's changed appearance might signify a change in how he feels? (Yes. He might feel more grown up, more independent, and free to act differently.)

- The mother gives a chronology of Charles's misdeeds for the rest of the week.
- She begins to worry about the effect of kindergarten on Laurie.

1 THEME

Laurie's new sense of himself is creating tensions in the family, tensions that *he* seems to enjoy enormously but that his mother hastens to smooth over.

2 CHARACTERIZATION

Laurie's emphatic "but everybody did" suggests that he approves of Charles's disruptive behavior, even enjoys it.

Lord's name, "I suppose he got spanked again?"

"He sure did," Laurie said. "Look up," he said to his father.

1 "What?" his father said, looking up.

"Look down," Laurie said. "Look at my thumb. Gee, you're dumb." He began to laugh insanely.

"Why did Charles hit the teacher?" I asked quickly.

"Because she tried to make him color with red crayons," Laurie said. "Charles wanted to color with green crayons so he hit the teacher

54   *The Short Story*

2 and she spanked him and said nobody play with Charles but everybody did."

The third day—it was Wednesday of the first week—Charles bounced a seesaw onto the head of a little girl and made her bleed, and the teacher made him stay inside all during recess. Thursday Charles had to stand in a corner during storytime because he kept pounding his feet on the floor. Friday Charles was deprived of blackboard privileges because he threw chalk.

On Saturday I remarked to my husband, "Do you think kindergarten is too unsettling

GUIDED READING

LITERAL QUESTION

1a. What does Laurie's mother do when Laurie starts laughing at his father? (She quickly changes the subject back to Charles.)

INFERENTIAL QUESTION

1b. Why do you think she changes the subject? (She probably senses that the father is about to lose his temper with Laurie, so she tries to distract their attention back to the more terrible Charles.)

for Laurie? All this toughness, and bad grammar, and this Charles boy sounds like such a bad influence."

"It'll be all right," my husband said reassuringly. "Bound to be people like Charles in the world. Might as well meet them now as later."

On Monday Laurie came home late, full of news, "Charles," he shouted as he came up the hill; I was waiting anxiously on the front steps. "Charles," Laurie yelled all the way up the hill, "Charles was bad again."

"Come right in," I said, as soon as he came close enough. "Lunch is waiting."

"You know what Charles did?" he demanded, following me through the door. "Charles yelled so in school they sent a boy in from first grade to tell the teacher she had to make Charles keep quiet, and so Charles had to stay after school. And so all the children stayed to watch him."

"What did he do?" I asked.

"He just sat there," Laurie said, climbing into his chair at the table. "Hi, Pop, y'old dust mop."

"Charles had to stay after school today," I told my husband. "Everyone stayed with him."

"What does this Charles look like?" my husband asked Laurie. "What's his other name?"

"He's bigger than me," Laurie said. "And he doesn't have any rubbers and he doesn't ever wear a jacket."

Monday night was the first Parent-Teachers meeting, and only the fact that the baby had a cold kept me from going; I wanted passionately to meet Charles's mother. On Tuesday Laurie remarked suddenly, "Our teacher had a friend come to see her in school today."

"Charles's mother?" my husband and I asked simultaneously.

"Naaah," Laurie said scornfully. "It was a man who came and made us do exercises, we had to touch our toes. Look." He climbed down from his chair and squatted down and touched his toes. "Like this," he said. He got solemnly back into his chair and said, picking up his fork, "Charles didn't even *do* exercises."

"That's fine," I said heartily. "Didn't Charles want to do exercises?"

"Naaah," Laurie said. "Charles was so fresh to the teacher's friend he wasn't *let* do exercises."

"Fresh again?" I said.

"He kicked the teacher's friend," Laurie said. "The teacher's friend told Charles to touch his toes like I just did and Charles kicked him."

Charles 55

AT A GLANCE

■ Laurie brings home more accounts of Charles's escapades.
■ Laurie's mother cannot attend the Parent-Teachers meeting.

RESPONSE JOURNAL

Have students comment on the father's opinion, "Bound to be people . . . now as later."

1 CHARACTERIZATION

Laurie offers both an excuse for being late and one possible motive for Charles's behavior: The misbehaving boy wins a great deal of attention.

2 THEME

Laurie dodges his father's attempt to discover Charles's last name, signaling poor communication.

3 CHARACTERIZATION

Laurie is proud of the exercise he learned, at the same time that he admires Charles for refusing to join in.

GUIDED READING

LITERAL QUESTIONS

1a. How does Laurie act toward his father after telling about Charles's latest misdeed? (He insults his father.)

2a. Why does Laurie's mother want to go to the first Parent-Teachers meeting? (to meet Charles's mother)

INFERENTIAL QUESTIONS

1b. Do you see any relationship between the behavior of Laurie and Charles? (Charles is rude in school; Laurie is rude at home.)

2a. Why do you think she wants to meet Charles's mother? (She wants to see what kind of mother has brought up a child who misbehaves so badly.)

1 POINT OF VIEW/HUMOR

Because the story is told from the mother's point of view, the reader shares the parents' intense curiosity and humorous preoccupation with the sudden change in Charles's behavior.

2 STYLE: DIALOGUE

The narrator steps back into the story as a character. The dialogue she uses builds reader interest and effectively heightens tension.

3 CHARACTERIZATION

Laurie, who seemed disappointed while Charles was behaving himself, is overjoyed to share once again in the attention Charles gets for misbehaving.

4 PLOT: SUSPENSE

As Laurie's mother sets out for the P.T.A. meeting, the story approaches its peak of humor and suspense: Will she meet Charles's mother there?

"What are they going to do about Charles, do you suppose?" Laurie's father asked him.

Laurie shrugged elaborately. "Throw him out of school, I guess," he said.

Wednesday and Thursday were routine; Charles yelled during story hour and hit a boy in the stomach and made him cry. On Friday Charles stayed after school again and so did all the other children.

1 With the third week of kindergarten Charles was an institution in our family; the baby was being a Charles when she cried all afternoon; Laurie did a Charles when he filled his wagon full of mud and pulled it through the kitchen; even my husband, when he caught his elbow in the telephone cord and pulled telephone, ashtray, and a bowl of flowers off the table, said, after the first minute, "Looks like Charles."

During the third and fourth weeks it looked like a reformation in Charles; Laurie reported grimly at lunch on Thursday of the third week, "Charles was so good today the teacher gave him an apple."

"What?" I said, and my husband added warily,[4] "You mean Charles?"

"Charles," Laurie said. "He gave the crayons around and he picked up the books afterward and the teacher said he was her helper."

"What happened?" I asked incredulously.[5]

"He was her helper, that's all," Laurie said, and shrugged.

2 "Can this be true, about Charles?" I asked my husband that night. "Can something like this happen?"

"Wait and see," my husband said cynically.[6] "When you've got a Charles to deal with, this may mean he's only plotting."

He seemed to be wrong. For over a week

---

4. **warily** [wâr′ə lē]: cautiously.
5. **incredulously** [in krej′ə ləs lē]: with doubts.
6. **cynically** [sin′i klē]: without trust.

Charles was the teacher's helper; each day he handed things out and he picked things up; no one had to stay after school.

"The P.T.A. meeting's next week again," I told my husband one evening. "I'm going to find Charles's mother there."

"Ask her what happened to Charles," my husband said. "I'd like to know."

"I'd like to know myself," I said.

On Friday of that week things were back to normal. "You know what Charles did today?" Laurie demanded at the lunch table, in a voice slightly awed. "He told a little girl to say a word and she said it and the teacher washed her mouth out with soap and Charles laughed.

3 "What word?" his father asked unwisely, and Laurie said, "I'll have to whisper it to you, it's so bad." He got down off his chair and went around to his father. His father bent his head down and Laurie whispered joyfully. His father's eyes widened.

"Did Charles tell the little girl to say *that*?" he asked respectfully.

"She said it *twice*," Laurie said. "Charles told her to say it *twice*."

"What happened to Charles?" my husband asked.

"Nothing," Laurie said. "He was passing out the crayons."

Monday morning Charles abandoned the little girl and said the evil word himself three or four times, getting his mouth washed out with soap each time. He also threw chalk.

4 My husband came to the door with me that evening as I set out for the P.T.A. meeting. "Invite her over for a cup of tea after the meeting," he said. "I want to get a look at her."

"If only she's there," I said prayerfully.

"She'll be there," my husband said. "I don't see how they could hold a P.T.A. meeting without Charles's mother."

At the meeting I sat restlessly, scanning

GUIDED READING

LITERAL QUESTION

1a. What has Charles become to the family? (an institution)

INFERENTIAL QUESTION

1b. How do you think Laurie feels about this development? (He probably feels important because the stories he tells have captured the family's attention and imagination.)

each comfortable matronly face, trying to determine which one hid the secret of Charles. None of them looked to me haggard[7] enough. No one stood up in the meeting and apologized for the way her son had been acting. No one mentioned Charles.

After the meeting I identified and sought out Laurie's kindergarten teacher. She had a plate with a cup of tea and a piece of chocolate cake; I had a plate with a cup of tea and a piece of marshmallow cake. We maneuvered up to one another cautiously, and smiled.

"I've been so anxious to meet you," I said. "I'm Laurie's mother."

"We're all so interested in Laurie," she said.

---

7. **haggard:** worn-out.

"Well, he certainly likes kindergarten," I said. "He talks about it all the time."

__1__ "We had a little trouble adjusting, the first week or so," she said primly, "but now he's a fine little helper. With occasional lapses,[8] of course."

"Laurie usually adjusts very quickly," I said. "I suppose this time it's Charles's influence."

"Charles?"

"Yes," I said, laughing, "you must have your hands full in that kindergarten, with Charles."

__2__ "Charles?" she said. "We don't have any Charles in the kindergarten."

---

8. **lapses:** mistakes.

STUDY QUESTIONS

Recalling

1. Name three ways that Laurie changes when he starts kindergarten.
2. Give four examples of Charles's poor behavior in school.
3. Give two examples of Laurie's misbehaving at home.
4. What doubt does Laurie's mother have about sending Laurie to kindergarten? What is her husband's opinion?
5. At the P.T.A. meeting what does the teacher say about Laurie? What does she say about Charles?

Interpreting

6. Who is Charles? Why do you think Laurie tells stories about him?
7. Why do you think Laurie's parents are misled by his stories and never suspect the truth?

Extending

8. What do you think happens after the end of the story?

READING AND LITERARY FOCUS

Suspense; Foreshadowing; Predicting Outcomes

When we read a good story, we become involved in the plot. We wait to see what will happen next. We want to know how the conflict will be settled. This growing interest as the plot of a story nears its climax is called **suspense.** One way in which authors create suspense is foreshadowing. **Foreshadowing** is the use of clues by an author to prepare readers for events that will happen later in a story. Foreshadowing makes us curious about what will happen. It builds our interest. In fact, we can often use the author's clues to predict the outcome of a story. Predicting the outcome of a story can add to our reading pleasure.

Charles 57

1. She expects Charles's mother to look wild. Her expectations become the reader's, so the reader is now as anxious to "find" mother as she is.

2. Laurie's misbehavior at home is a clue to Charles's identity. When his mother asks who the disobedient student is, "Laurie thought." It is his first and only hesitation in his storytelling. It is at that moment he decides to call the miscreant "Charles." At end of story, the teacher's euphemistic statements ("We're all so interested in Laurie" and "We had a little trouble adjusting . . . With occasional lapses, of course") all reveal the trouble she had with Laurie.

VOCABULARY

1. INSTITUTION: an act or process of starting

2. REFORMATION: ref/or/ma/tion

3. RENOUNCE: origins in Middle English, Middle French, and Latin

4. HAGGARD: M.F., *hagard,* of a hawk

5. CORDUROY: a durable cotton cloth with vertical ribs or wales

Thinking About Suspense; Foreshadowing

1. What does Laurie's mother expect Charles's mother to look like? Tell how this adds suspense to the scene at the P.T.A. meeting.

2. During the story what clues does the author give about who Charles really is?

VOCABULARY

Using the Dictionary

A **dictionary** is a book that lists words in alphabetical order and gives meanings and other information about those words. A dictionary presents information about a word as shown in the sample entry that follows:

> **kin·der·gar·ten** (kin′dər gärt′ən, -gärd′ən) *n.* class or division of school for children from four to six years old, preceding the first grade of elementary school. [German *Kindergarten* literally, children's garden, from *Kind* child + *Garten* garden.]
>
> —*Scribner Dictionary*

Each word listed is called an **entry word.** Entry words are divided into syllables by dots or spaces. For example, *kindergarten,* the entry word in the sample, has four syllables. The division tells us where to break the word when we write it on two lines.

Pronunciation is the way a word is spoken. The dictionary gives a word's pronunciation in parentheses after the entry word. The letters used in the pronunciation are called a **phonetic alphabet.**

Every dictionary has a **pronunciation key** to explain the sounds of these phonetic letters.

A word's **part of speech** tells how it is used in a sentence. The abbreviation for a word's part of speech is usually given after the pronunciation. For example, *kindergarten* is a noun and is marked *n.*

The **definition,** or meaning, of a word is usually given after the part of speech. Many words have more than one definition, and these different definitions are numbered. The most common meaning is usually given first.

Some dictionaries also give a word's etymology. The **etymology** is the origin and history of a word. It is usually given in brackets either before or after the definition. For example, *kindergarten* comes from two German words: *Kind* meaning "child" and *Garten* meaning "garden."

To make finding a word easier, each dictionary page has two guide words at the top. The **guide words** are the first and last entry words on the page. All other entry words on the page fall alphabetically between the two guide words.

The italicized words in the following questions are from "Charles." Use a dictionary to answer the questions.

1. What is the first meaning of *institution*?
2. Where would you divide *reformation* if you could not write the word on one line?
3. From what languages do we get the word *renounce*?
4. What is the meaning in French for *haggard*?
5. What is the first meaning of *corduroy*?

58   *The Short Story*

Pearl S. Buck (1892–1973) is the only American woman to have won the Nobel Prize for Literature. She was born in West Virginia, but she grew up in China because her parents were Presbyterian ministers there. Many of her works take place in China, including *The Good Earth*. In such works Buck hoped to create better understanding among different peoples. "Christmas Day in the Morning" is not about China. However, it is about human understanding.

■ What understanding does the man reach by the story's end?

AT A GLANCE

- Robert wakes very early and mourns the lost traditions of family Christmases.
- He remembers when he was fifteen and on his father's farm.

LITERARY OPTIONS

- plot
- characterization
- flashback

THEMATIC OPTIONS

- love
- traditions
- family life

1 PLOT: INTERNAL CONFLICT

Robert's romantic attachment to the traditional Christmases of his past causes him to mourn the lost magic.

2 FLASHBACK

The words "He slipped back in time" and "He was fifteen years old" signal the beginning of Robert's flashback.

TEXAS ESSENTIAL ELEMENTS GRADE 8

1A writing process
1B purpose and audience
1C support for main idea
1E appropriate language
1H grammatical conventions
3A plot and character development
3D literary genres
4B implied main idea
4D sequential order
4F point of view
To locate treatment of an Element, see *Texas Teacher's Resources*.

Pearl S. Buck

Christmas Day in the Morning

He woke suddenly and completely. It was four o'clock, the hour at which his father had always called him to get up and help with the milking. Strange how the habits of his youth clung to him still! Fifty years ago, and his father had been dead for thirty years, and yet he woke at four o'clock in the morning. He had trained himself to turn over and go to sleep, but this morning, because it was Christmas, he did not try to sleep.

1 Yet what was the magic of Christmas now? His childhood and youth were long past, and his own children had grown up and gone. Some of them lived only a few miles away, but they had their own families, and they would come in as usual toward the end of the day. They had explained with infinite gentleness that they wanted their children to build Christmas memories about their houses, not his. He was left alone with his wife.

Yesterday she had said, "It isn't worthwhile, perhaps—"

And he had said, "Oh, yes, Alice, even if there are only the two of us, let's have a Christmas of our own."

Then she had said, "Let's not trim the tree until tomorrow, Robert. Just so it's ready when the children come. I'm tired."

He had agreed, and the tree was still out in the back entry.

Why did he feel so awake tonight? For it was still night, a clear and starry night. No moon, of course, but the stars were extraordinary! Now that he thought of it, the stars seemed always large and clear before the dawn of Christmas Day. There was one star now that was certainly larger and brighter than any of the others. He could even imagine it moving, as it had seemed to him to move one night long ago.

2 He slipped back in time, as he did so easily nowadays. He was fifteen years old and still on his father's farm. He loved his father. He had not known it until one time a few days before Christmas, when he had overheard what his father was saying to his mother.

Christmas Day in the Morning 59

GUIDED READING

LITERAL QUESTION

1a. What does Robert miss in Christmas now? (the magic)

INFERENTIAL QUESTION

1b. How do you think he would like to celebrate Christmas now? (in the same way he did in the past, with his family around him)

Christmas Day . . . **T-59**

- Robert recalls how he discovered that his father loved him.
- He remembers rising early on a Christmas Day and doing the milking by himself as a gift to his father.

1 THEME

His father's expressed love for him awakens love in Robert.

2 POINT OF VIEW

The story is told in the third person, but the narrator knows Robert's thoughts, feelings, and past intimately. This paragraph contrasts the financial poverty of Robert's past with the affluence but emotional emptiness of the present.

3 SETTING

The father's answer to the child, "It's a barn like ours," shows the family's simple yet strong connection with the Christmas tradition.

4 FLASHBACK

The past becomes especially immediate as the reader is made intensely aware of the slow passage of time during the Christmas Eve of long ago.

"Mary, I hate to call Rob in the mornings. He's growing so fast and he needs his sleep. If you could see how he sleeps when I go in to wake him up! I wish I could manage alone."

"Well, you can't, Adam." His mother's voice was brisk. "Besides, he isn't a child anymore. It's time he took his turn."

1 "Yes," his father said slowly. "But I sure do hate to wake him."

When he heard these words, something in him woke. His father loved him! He had never thought of it before, taking for granted the tie of their blood. Neither his father nor his mother talked about their children; they had no time for such things. There was always so much to do on a farm.

Now he knew his father loved him, there would be no more loitering in the mornings and having to be called again. He got up after that, stumbling blind with sleep, and pulled on his clothes, his eyes tight shut, but he got up.

And then on the night before Christmas, that year when he was fifteen, he lay for a few **2** minutes thinking about the next day. They were poor, and most of the excitement was in the turkey they had raised themselves and in the mince pies his mother made. His sisters sewed presents, and his mother and father always bought something he needed, not only a warm jacket, maybe, but something more, such as a book. And he saved and bought them each something too.

He wished, that Christmas he was fifteen, he had a better present for his father. As usual he had gone to the ten-cent store and bought a tie. It had seemed nice enough until he lay thinking the night before Christmas, and then he wished that he had heard his father and mother talking in time for him to save for something better.

He lay on his side, his head supported by his elbow, and looked out his attic window. The stars were bright, much brighter than he ever remembered seeing them, and one star in particular was so bright that he wondered if it were really the Star of Bethlehem.

3 "Dad," he had once asked, when he was a little boy, "what is a stable?"

"It's just a barn," his father had replied, "like ours."

Then Jesus had been born in a barn, and to a barn the shepherds and the Wise Men had come, bringing their Christmas gifts!

The thought had struck him like a silver dagger. Why should he not give his father a special gift too, out there in the barn? He could get up early, earlier than four o'clock, and he could creep into the barn and get all the milking done. He'd do it alone, milk and clean up, and then when his father went in to start the milking he'd see it all done. And he could know who had done it.

He laughed to himself as he gazed at the stars. It was what he would do, and he mustn't sleep too sound.

4 He must have waked twenty times, scratching a match each time to look at his old watch—midnight, and half past one, and then two o'clock.

At a quarter to three he got up and put on his clothes. He crept downstairs, careful of the creaky boards, and let himself out. The big star hung lower over the barn roof, a reddish gold. The cows looked at him, sleepy and surprised. It was early for them too.

"So, boss," he whispered. They accepted him placidly, and he fetched some hay for each cow, and then got the milking pail and the big milk cans.

He had never milked all alone before, but it seemed almost easy. He kept thinking about his father's surprise. His father would come in and call him, saying that he would get things started while Rob was getting dressed. He'd go to the barn, open the door, and then he'd go to get the two big empty milk cans. But they wouldn't be waiting or empty; they'd

GUIDED READING

LITERAL QUESTIONS

1a. What does Robert's father say that affects Robert so deeply? ("But I sure do hate to wake him.")

2a. Does the job of milking seem difficult to him? (It seems "almost easy.")

INFERENTIAL QUESTIONS

1b. Is it believable that Robert could be so moved by such a simple statement? (Students who can imagine how little emotion was openly expressed in the family will find Robert's reaction believable.)

2b. Why do you think Robert finds the work almost easy? (He is full of joy imagining how surprised his father will be to find the job done.)

AT A GLANCE

- Robert finishes milking the cows and then returns to bed.
- His father wakes him as usual and then goes out to the barn.
- His father returns, laughing and sobbing.

1 THEME

A gift given in love, the passage suggests, is "not a chore."

2 RESPONSE JOURNAL

Have students comment on this description of how intense anticipation makes time seem to slow down.

3 CHARACTERIZATION

In just a few words the father's emotional state is made vivid. A man not accustomed to expressing emotion is overcome with deep love and gratitude for his son and attempts to express those feelings.

---

be standing in the milkhouse, filled.

"What the—" he could hear his father exclaiming.

He smiled and milked steadily, two strong streams rushing into the pail, frothing and fragrant. The cows were still surprised but acquiescent. For once they were behaving well, as though they knew it was Christmas.

1 The task went more easily than he had ever known it to before. Milking for once was not a chore. It was something else, a gift to his father, who loved him. He finished, the two milk cans were full, and he covered them and closed the milkhouse door carefully, making sure of the latch. He put the stool in its place by the door and hung up the clean milk pail. Then he went out of the barn and barred the door behind him.

Back in his room he had only a minute to pull off his clothes in the darkness and jump into bed, for he heard his father up. He put the covers over his head to silence his quick breathing. The door opened.

"Rob!" his father called. "We have to get up, son, even if it is Christmas."

"Aw right," he said sleepily.

"I'll go on out," his father said. "I'll get things started." The door closed and he lay **2** still, laughing to himself. In just a few minutes his father would know. His dancing heart was ready to jump from his body.

The minutes were endless—ten, fifteen, he did not know how many—before he heard his father's footsteps again. The door opened and he lay still.

"Rob!"

"Yes, Dad—"

3 "Son—" His father was laughing, a queer, sobbing sort of a laugh. "Thought you'd fool me, did you?" His father was standing beside his bed, feeling for him, pulling away the cover.

Christmas Day in the Morning 61

GUIDED READING

LITERAL QUESTION

1a. What is the father doing as he returns to Robert's room? (laughing and sobbing at the same time)

INFERENTIAL QUESTION

1b. Why do you think he is so moved by the gift? (The gift is so unexpected, and, since he is a farmer, he appreciates the love in his son's hard work; he knows how hard it is for his son to get up early.)

- Robert's father hugs him and thanks him, and they go downstairs to see the Christmas tree. The flashback ends.
- In the present Robert decorates the Christmas tree for his wife.

1 CHARACTERIZATION

The boy Robert's suppressed emotions come tumbling forth in this powerful outburst. He had probably never spoken to his father like this before.

2 FLASHBACK

Robert's flashback ends, and he is back in the present, but with a difference. His boyhood act of love, a simple but deeply meaningful gesture, warms this later Christmas morning.

3 THEME

Robert's realization is the story's main idea: "Love alone could waken love." His memory of loving and being loved has reawakened his ability to express his love and redeems this Christmas day for him.

REFLECTING ON THE STORY

Do you think the present Christmas will be different for Robert from other recent Christmases? (yes, because his gift of love has reawakened his ability to appreciate the joys of the present)

He found his father and clutched him in a great hug. He felt his father's arms go around him. It was dark and they could not see each other's faces.

"Son, I thank you. Nobody ever did a nicer thing—"

1 "Oh, Dad, I want you to know—I do want to be good!" The words broke from him of their own will. He did not know what to say. His heart was bursting with love.

"Well, I reckon I can go back to bed and sleep," his father said after a moment. "No, hark, the little ones are waked up. Come to think of it, son, I've never seen you children when you first saw the Christmas tree. I was always in the barn. Come on!"

He got up and pulled on his clothes again, and they went down to the Christmas tree, and soon the sun was creeping up to where the star had been. Oh, what a Christmas, and how his heart had nearly burst again with shyness and pride as his father told his mother and made the younger children listen about how he, Rob, had got up all by himself.

"The best Christmas gift I ever had, and I'll remember it, son, every year on Christmas morning, so long as I live."

2 They had both remembered it, and now that his father was dead he remembered it alone, that blessed Christmas dawn when, alone with the cows in the barn, he had made his first gift of true love.

Outside the window now the great star slowly sank. He got up out of bed and put on his slippers and bathrobe and went softly upstairs to the attic and found the box of Christmas-tree decorations. He took them downstairs into the living room. Then he brought in the tree. It was a little one—they had not had a big tree since the children went away—but he set it in the holder and put it in the middle of the long table under the win-

dow. Then carefully he began to trim it.

It was done very soon, the time passing as quickly as it had that morning long ago in the barn. He went to his library and fetched the little box that contained his special gift to his wife, a star of diamonds, not large but dainty in design. He had written the card for it the day before. He tied the gift on the tree and then stood back. It was pretty, very pretty, and she would be surprised.

But he was not satisfied. He wanted to tell her, to tell her how much he loved her. It had been a long time since he had really told her, although he loved her in a very special way, much more than he ever had when they were young.

He had been fortunate that she had loved him, and how fortunate that he had been able to love! Ah, that was the true joy of life, the ability to love! For he was quite sure that some people were genuinely unable to love anyone. But love was alive in him; it still was.

3 It occurred to him suddenly that it was alive because long ago it had been born in him when he knew his father loved him. That was it: love alone could waken love.

And he could give the gift again and again. This morning, this blessed Christmas morning, he would give it to his beloved wife. He could write it down in a letter for her to read and keep forever. He went to his desk and began his love letter to his wife: "My dearest love. . . ."

When it was finished he sealed it and tied it on the tree where she would see it the first thing when she came into the room. She would read it, surprised and then moved, and realize how very much he loved her.

He put out the light and went tiptoeing up the stairs. The star in the sky was gone, and the first rays of the sun were gleaming the sky. Such a happy, happy Christmas!

GUIDED READING

LITERAL QUESTIONS

1a. Could Robert and his father see each other's faces as they hugged? (No, it was dark.)

2a. What does Robert do once his memory of the past is over and he is still lying awake? (He goes downstairs to decorate the Christmas tree.)

INFERENTIAL QUESTIONS

1b. Why do you think the author points out this fact? (Neither the boy nor his father is used to expressing emotion; they might have been embarrassed if they had seen each other's faces.)

2b. In what way is this action like his childhood gift to his father? (Again he rises early on Christmas morning to create a surprise for someone he loves.)

STUDY QUESTIONS

Recalling

1. According to the second paragraph, why does Christmas have less magic now for Robert?
2. Tell how fifteen-year-old Robert realizes that his father loves him.
3. What Christmas gift does fifteen-year-old Robert give his father?
4. What two gifts does Robert give to his wife?
5. Why does Robert think that love is alive inside him?

Interpreting

6. Why is Robert's gift to his father special? Why do you think the work he does for the gift is easy?
7. Tell how the story shows that "love alone could waken love."
8. Tell why Robert's feelings about Christmas change during the story.

Extending

9. Why do you think that holidays often help us to appreciate more the people we love?

READING AND LITERARY FOCUS

Flashback

The events of a plot are usually arranged in chronological order. Sometimes authors interrupt that order to show us an event from the past. A **flashback** is a scene that breaks the normal time order of a plot to show events that happened in the past. For example, when an adult in a story remembers a childhood experience, the story is using a flashback.

Thinking About Flashback

1. What part of "Christmas Day in the Morning" is a flashback?
2. Find the beginning of the flashback in the story. What words warn us that we are seeing an event from the past?

COMPOSITION

Answering an Essay Question

■ According to "Christmas Day in the Morning," should the past be forgotten or remembered? Write an essay that answers this question. First state your opinion clearly. Then tell how the story shows its attitude about the past. Be sure to use examples from the story to support your opinions. *For help with this assignment, see Lesson 1 in the Writing About Literature Handbook at the back of this book.*

Writing a Flashback

■ Write a brief story in which a person remembers an important event from the past. First write one or two sentences about the present. Then use a flashback to show the event from the past. Finally, end your story with one or two sentences in the present again. You may want to use one of the following events: (a) The winner of a dance contest remembers his first dance lesson. (b) A person remembers the first time she saw her dog.

COMPARING STORIES

1. "Spring Victory," "The Mixed-Up Feet and the Silly Bridegroom," and "Fire!" create suspense. Compare the suspense in two or more of these stories. Tell what events in each story cause the suspense. Then tell what outcome ends the suspense. Which story is most suspenseful?
2. Compare the conflicts in two or more of the following stories: "Spring Victory," "Charles," and "Christmas Day in the Morning." Choose one conflict from each story. Show what forces are involved in the conflict. Tell how the conflict is solved.
3. Compare the climaxes of two or more of the following stories: "Charles," "Christmas Day in the Morning," and "Fire!" Tell what event is the climax of each story. Which climax do you think is most exciting? Why?

Christmas Day in the Morning 63

STUDY QUESTIONS

1. Children and grandchildren want to spend morning in own homes.
2. He overhears father say he doesn't like to wake Robert.
3. He gets up early to milk cows.
4. love letter, pin
5. Memory of father rekindles his ability to love.
6. Father understands how hard it is for son to get up early; it was done willingly and with love
7. Robert feels father's love; learns to give love; later feels specialness of love for wife.
8. He stops feeling sorry for himself; can still give love.
9. Possible answers: It's time for gift giving, opportunity to give something special to loved ones.

READING AND LITERARY FOCUS

1. story of Robert's gift to father
2. "He slipped back in time."

COMPARING STORIES

1. "Spring Victory": cause—problems solved slowly; end—father's recovery; "Mixed-Up Feet": cause—Lemel's mishaps; end—marriage; "Fire!": cause—boy's misgivings, failure to act; end—grandfather's praise; *most suspenseful:* Opinions will vary.
2. "Spring Victory": family vs. hunger, sickness; resolved through persistence, optimism; "Charles": Laurie vs. authority; not resolved; "Christmas . . .": narrator vs. his own longing for Christmas to be special; resolved when he writes letter to wife
3. "Charles": discovery that there is no Charles; "Christmas . . .": Robert's decision to get up early and trim tree for wife; "Fire!": boy's confession; *most exciting:* Opinions will vary.

COMPOSITION: GUIDELINES FOR EVALUATION

ANSWERING AN ESSAY QUESTION

Objective

To write an essay that answers a question

Guidelines for Evaluation

■ suggested length: one to two paragraphs
■ should answer "Should the past be forgotten or remembered?" using examples from story
■ should tell how story shows writer's attitude about the past

WRITING A FLASHBACK

Objective

To write a story containing a flashback

Guidelines for Evaluation

■ suggested length: two to three short paragraphs
■ should establish character in present
■ should use flashback to show important event in past concerning character; end in present
■ should use an informal narrative style

AT A GLANCE

- A woman is walking alone on a city street, and a young boy tries to snatch her purse.
- He falls. The woman kicks him, then holds him and questions him.

LITERARY OPTIONS

- character
- conflict

THEMATIC OPTIONS

- compassion
- communication
- discoveries

1 READING SKILLS: MAKING INFERENCES

From the author's choice of words—"large," "hammer and nails," "slung"—the reader can infer that the woman is capable of taking care of herself.

2 EXTERNAL CONFLICT

The boy's need to escape conflicts with the woman's desire to discover the motive for the robbery. Since she is more powerful, she wins this round.

TEXAS ESSENTIAL ELEMENTS GRADE 8

1A writing process
1B purpose and audience
1C support for main idea
1E appropriate language
1H grammatical conventions
3A plot and character development
3D literary genres
4E cause/effect
4F point of view
To locate treatment of an Element, see *Texas Teacher's Resources.*

CHARACTER

Langston Hughes (1902–1967) began writing poetry while he was in high school. Later he worked in a restaurant in Washington, D.C. One day he waited on the poet Vachel Lindsay and left some of his poems near Lindsay's plate. Lindsay was impressed and helped Hughes to publish his first book of poetry. In addition to poetry, Hughes wrote stories, plays, songs, movie scripts, and essays. "Thank You, M'am" begins on a city street.

■ What unexpected things happen after the story moves inside?

Langston Hughes

Thank You, M'am

1   She was a large woman with a large purse that had everything in it but hammer and nails. It had a long strap and she carried it slung across her shoulder. It was about eleven o'clock at night, and she was walking alone, when a boy ran up behind her and tried to snatch her purse. The strap broke with the single tug the boy gave it from behind. But the boy's weight, and the weight of the purse combined, caused him to lose his balance so, instead of taking off full blast as he had hoped, the boy fell on his back on the sidewalk, and his legs flew up. The large woman simply turned around and kicked him right square in his blue-jeaned sitter. Then she reached down, picked the boy up by his shirt front, and shook him until his teeth rattled.

After that the woman said, "Pick up my pocketbook, boy, and give it here."

She still held him. But she bent down enough to permit him to stoop and pick up 2 her purse. Then she said, "Now ain't you ashamed of yourself?"

Firmly gripped by his shirt front, the boy said, "Yes'm."

The woman said, "What did you want to do it for?"

The boy said, "I didn't aim to."

She said, "You a lie!"

By that time two or three people passed, stopped, turned to look, and some stood watching.

"If I turn you loose, will you run?" asked the woman.

"Yes'm," said the boy.

"Then I won't turn you loose," said the woman. She did not release him.

"I'm very sorry, lady, I'm sorry," whispered the boy.

"Um-hum! And your face is dirty. I got a

64   *The Short Story*

GUIDED READING

LITERAL QUESTION

1a. What does the woman do after she kicks the boy? (asks him about himself)

INFERENTIAL QUESTION

1b. Why do you think the woman asks these questions? (She may want to learn about the boy—if he is hungry or in trouble. She is upset with him but may also be concerned.)

great mind to wash your face for you. Ain't you got nobody home to tell you to wash your face?"

"No'm," said the boy.

"Then it will get washed this evening," said the large woman starting up the street, dragging the frightened boy behind her.

1 He looked as if he were fourteen or fifteen, frail and willow-wild, in tennis shoes and blue jeans.

The woman said, "You ought to be my son. I would teach you right from wrong. Least I can do right now is to wash your face. Are you hungry?"

"No'm," said the being-dragged boy. "I just want you to turn me loose."

"Was I bothering *you* when I turned that corner?" asked the woman.

"No'm."

"But you put yourself in contact with *me*," said the woman. "If you think that that contact is not going to last awhile, you got another thought coming. When I get through with you, sir, you are going to remember Mrs. Luella Bates Washington Jones."

Sweat popped out on the boy's face and he **2** began to struggle. Mrs. Jones stopped, jerked him around in front of her, put a half nelson[1] about his neck, and continued to drag him up the street. When she got to her door, she dragged the boy inside, down a hall, and into a large kitchenette-furnished room at the rear of the house. She switched on the light and left the door open. The boy could hear other roomers laughing and talking in the large house. Some of their doors were opened, too, so he knew he and the woman were not alone. The woman still had him by the neck in the middle of her room.

She said, "What is your name?"

"Roger," answered the boy.

---

1. **half nelson:** wrestling hold made with one arm.

"Then, Roger, you go to that sink and wash your face," said the woman, whereupon she **3** turned him loose—at last. Roger looked at the door—looked at the woman—looked at the door—*and went to the sink.*

"Let the water run until it gets warm," she said. "Here's a clean towel."

4 "You gonna take me to jail?" asked the boy, bending over the sink.

"Not with that face, I would not take you nowhere," said the woman. "Here I am trying to get home to cook me a bite to eat and you snatch my pocketbook! Maybe you ain't been to your supper either, late as it be. Have you?"

AT A GLANCE

- The woman brings the reluctant boy home and makes him wash.
- She asks him if he has had his supper.

1 POINT OF VIEW AND CHARACTER

The story is told in the third person, but the narrator's impressions of the boy are also the woman's impressions. She sees how vulnerable he really is.

2 STYLE: HUMOR

The vivid image of the purse snatcher being dragged home by his intended victim is so unexpected that it is funny.

3 INTERNAL AND EXTERNAL CONFLICT

The boy sizes up his opponent and hesitates for a moment, looking for a chance to escape. Finally, he gives up and does as he's told.

4 DIALOGUE/CHARACTERIZATION

The way the woman and the boy communicate points up their differences. The boy directly expresses his fear of going to jail. The woman expresses her compassion in a gruff, almost bullying way.

GUIDED READING

LITERAL QUESTION

1a. What does Mrs. Jones tell the boy that makes him sweat? ("When I get through with you, sir, you are going to remember Mrs. Luella Bates Washington Jones.")

INFERENTIAL QUESTION

1b. What do you think Mrs. Jones means by that statement? (She is going to make sure that he never tries to steal again.)

- The boy tells the woman he wanted the money to buy blue suede shoes.
- The woman tells him she has done things she is ashamed of too.
- They eat dinner, and she gives him ten dollars to buy the shoes.
- The boy thanks her and leaves.

1 CHARACTERIZATION

The surprising Mrs. Jones offers her biggest surprise. Instead of lecturing the boy, she admits to having "done things" she's not proud of herself. This moment of sharing is a turning point.

2 CHARACTERIZATION

By admitting her own past desperation and misdeeds, the woman has forged a bond of understanding between herself and the boy. He now yearns for her trust and respect.

3 PLOT: CLIMAX

With the gift of money, the story reaches its emotional high point. Mrs. Jones is able to express both her compassion for the boy and her expectations for him.

4 PLOT: RESOLUTION

The resolution of the plot, the parting, shows the boy unable to communicate his feelings for what Mrs. Jones has done for him.

REFLECTING ON THE STORY

Mrs. Jones clearly does something important for the boy, but does he do something for her as well? (He gives her a chance to show her compassion and feel she's made a difference in someone's life.)

"There's nobody home at my house," said the boy.

"Then we'll eat," said the woman. "I believe you're hungry—or been hungry—to try to snatch my pocketbook."

"I wanted a pair of blue suede shoes," said the boy.

"Well, you didn't have to snatch *my* pocketbook to get some suede shoes," said Mrs. Luella Bates Washington Jones. "You could of asked me."

"M'am?"

The water dripping from his face, the boy looked at her. There was a long pause. A very long pause. After he had dried his face and not knowing what else to do dried it again, the boy turned around, wondering what next. The door was open. He could make a dash for it down the hall. He could run, run, run, run, *run!*

The woman was sitting on the daybed. After a while she said, "I were young once and I wanted things I could not get."

There was another long pause. The boy's mouth opened. Then he frowned, but not knowing he frowned.

The woman said, "Um-hum! You thought I was going to say *but*, didn't you? You thought I was going to say, *but I didn't snatch people's pocketbooks.* Well, I wasn't going to say that." Pause. Silence. "I have done things, too, which I would not tell you, son—neither tell God, if he didn't already know. So you set down while I fix us something to eat. You might run that comb through your hair so you will look presentable."

In another corner of the room behind a screen was a gas plate and an icebox. Mrs. Jones got up and went behind the screen. The woman did not watch the boy to see if he was going to run now, nor did she watch her purse which she left behind her on the daybed. But the boy took care to sit on the far side of the

66   *The Short Story*

room where he thought she could easily see him out of the corner of her eye, if she wanted to. He did not trust the woman *not* to trust him. And he did not want to be mistrusted now.

"Do you need somebody to go to the store," asked the boy, "maybe to get some milk or something?"

"Don't believe I do," said the woman, "unless you just want sweet milk yourself. I was going to make cocoa out of this canned milk I got here."

"That will be fine," said the boy.

She heated some lima beans and ham she had in the icebox, made the cocoa, and set the table. The woman did not ask the boy anything about where he lived, or his folks, or anything else that would embarrass him. Instead, as they ate, she told him about her job in a hotel beauty shop that stayed open late, what the work was like, and how all kinds of women came in and out, blondes, redheads, and brunettes. Then she cut him a half of her ten-cent cake.

"Eat some more, son," she said.

When they were finished eating she got up and said, "Now, here, take this ten dollars and buy yourself some blue suede shoes. And next time, do not make the mistake of latching on to *my* pocketbook *nor nobody else's*—because shoes come by devilish like that will burn your feet. I got to get my rest now. But I wish you would behave yourself, son, from here on in."

She led him down the hall to the front door and opened it. "Good night! Behave yourself, boy!" she said, looking out into the street.

The boy wanted to say something else other than, "Thank you, m'am," to Mrs. Luella Bates Washington Jones, but he couldn't do so as he turned at the barren stoop and looked back at the large woman in the door. He barely managed to say, "Thank you," before she shut the door. And he never saw her again.

GUIDED READING

LITERAL QUESTIONS

1a. What does Mrs. Jones say about her youth? (that she too wanted things she couldn't have, that she did things she was ashamed of)

2a. What does Mrs. Jones do after they finish eating? (She gives the boy money to buy the shoes he wants.)

INFERENTIAL QUESTIONS

1b. What do you think the boy feels toward Mrs. Jones on hearing this information? (He is probably surprised by it and begins to respect her for understanding him.)

2b. Why do you think Mrs. Jones gives the boy the money? (She wants to help him, to keep him from stealing, to tell him that what he does matters to somebody.)

STUDY QUESTIONS

Recalling

1. What happens to Mrs. Jones as she is walking home from work? In what way does she continue to walk home?
2. Name two points in the story where Roger can run away but does not.
3. What reason does Roger give for wanting money? What is Mrs. Jones's reaction?
4. Name two things that Mrs. Jones gives Roger.
5. Tell what happens in the last paragraph of the story.

Interpreting

6. Why do you think Roger does not run away when he can?
7. Why do you think Mrs. Jones treats Roger the way she does?
8. At the end of the story, for what is Roger really thanking Mrs. Jones?

READING AND LITERARY FOCUS

Character

A **character** is a person in a story. When we read a story, we become aware of the personality of each important character. A character's personality is made up of different qualities, or **character traits.** For example, in "Christmas Day in the Morning" Robert may be called a warm, giving person. He possesses the following character traits: generosity, honesty, affection, and helpfulness.

In stories some characters show only one major trait. Others are more like real people: They show a number of different traits. Some characters change during a story. For example, Robert changes his attitude toward Christmas. Other characters remain the same all through a story.

Thinking About Character

■ Name three character traits for Mrs. Jones. Name two traits for Roger.

COMPOSITION

Writing About Character

■ Write about the ways that Roger changes during the story. First give your opinion of his personality at the beginning of the story. Then tell what new traits he learns during the story. Finally, tell whether or not you think the change is believable and why. Be sure to use examples from the story to support your opinions.

Writing a Character Description

■ Write a character description of a person who shows only one personality trait. Begin with a general statement about the character (for example, "Anne has a sense of humor," or "Paul is very considerate"). Then tell a brief story that shows the character's trait.

CHALLENGE

Research

■ Do research in a library about Langston Hughes's life and his work. Use your findings to write a report about his life. Include information about the following: his youth, his early success as a writer, and his later fame.

Thank You, M'am   67

STUDY QUESTIONS

1. A boy tries to snatch her purse. She drags him home with her.
2. when Mrs. Jones lets him go to wash his face, and when she is talking to him after he has dried his face
3. wants suede shoes; says that he just had to ask her
4. dinner, ten dollars, interest in him, compassion
5. Roger can barely speak to thank Mrs. Jones, and she closes door.
6. Answers will vary. He is probably curious to see what will happen next; also, he feels her concern.
7. She understands what it is like to want things you can't have; she too has done things she's not proud of, wants to help him see there are better ways than crime to get what he wants.
8. her humanity and understanding

READING AND LITERARY FOCUS

Some possible answers: *Mrs. Jones:* tough, courageous, compassionate, generous, humble, honest; *Roger:* frail, sloppy, needy, lonely, sometimes desperate

CHALLENGE

Students should
■ use resources at library to find information about Langston Hughes
■ write a report about his life and career as a writer

COMPOSITION: GUIDELINES FOR EVALUATION

WRITING ABOUT CHARACTER

Objective

To describe the changes in a character

Guidelines for Evaluation

■ suggested length: three paragraphs
■ should give writer's opinion of character's personality at beginning of story
■ should explain what new traits are learned, whether change is believable, and why
■ should use specific examples from story

WRITING A CHARACTER DESCRIPTION

Objective

To describe a person, developing a single trait

Guidelines for Evaluation

■ suggested length: one paragraph
■ should make a general statement about person, highlighting a specific trait
■ should illustrate trait with a brief story
■ should use vivid descriptive words

- The narrator recalls his first day of high school in a new town.
- He sees a girl standing apart from the others.
- He meets her on his new paper route, and they talk.

LITERARY OPTIONS

- characterization
- setting
- conflict

THEMATIC OPTIONS

- friendship
- adolescence
- isolation and poverty

1 CHARACTERIZATION

The narrator's self-described behavior indicates that he is an outsider, shy about revealing himself. These traits motivate his behavior in the story.

2 POINT OF VIEW

The first-person narrator, an adult reflecting on his boyhood, expresses intimately the adolescent's longing for friendship, increasing the poignancy of the story.

3 SETTING

The description of the plains as a "big swoop of nothing" helps create a feeling of isolation in the story.

TEXAS ESSENTIAL ELEMENTS GRADE 8

1I word choice
3A plot and character development
3C setting and mood
3D literary genres
4E cause/effect
4F point of view
4H generalizations
To locate treatment of an Element, see *Texas Teacher's Resources.*

William Stafford (born 1914) grew up in Kansas. Many of Stafford's poems and stories are about the American Midwest. The following story takes place during the Great Depression of the 1930s. At that time many businesses closed, and people lost their jobs. In addition, low prices, droughts, and dust storms ruined many midwestern farms.

■ How are the two young people in this story affected by hard times?

William Stafford

The Osage Orange Tree[1]

1   On that first day of high school in the prairie town where the tree was, I stood in the sun by the flagpole and watched, but pretended not to watch, the others. They stood in groups and talked and knew each other, all except one—a girl though—in a faded blue dress, carrying a sack lunch and standing near the corner looking everywhere but at the crowd.

I might talk to her, I thought. But of course it was out of the question.

That first day was easier when the classes started. Some of the teachers were kind; some were frightening. Some of the students didn't care, but I listened and waited; and at the end of the day I was relieved, less conspicuous from then on.

2   But that day was not really over. As I hurried to carry my new paper route, I was thinking about how in a strange town, if you are quiet, no one notices, and some may like you,

later. I was thinking about this when I reached the north edge of town where the 3 scattering houses dwindle. Beyond them to the north lay just openness, the plains, a big swoop of nothing. There, at the last house, just as I cut across a lot and threw to the last customer, I saw the girl in the blue dress coming along the street, heading on out of town, carrying books. And she saw me.

"Hello."

"Hello."

And because we stopped we were friends. I didn't know how I could stop, but I didn't hurry on. There was nothing to do but to act as if I were walking on out too. I had three papers left in the bag, and I frantically began to fold them—box them, as we called it—for throwing. We had begun to walk and talk. The girl was timid; I became more bold. Not much, but a little.

"Have you gone to school here before?" I asked.

"Yes, I went here last year."

A long pause. A meadowlark sitting on a

---

1. **Osage** [ō′sāj] **Orange Tree:** spiny tree native to the U.S. with orange-colored wood.

68   *The Short Story*

GUIDED READING

LITERAL QUESTION

1a. Where and when does the boy speak to the girl for the first time? (on the north edge of town, after school)

INFERENTIAL QUESTION

1b. Why do you think he speaks to her the second time? (No one is watching them, so he feels bolder than at school; he needs a friend.)

fencepost hunched his wings and flew. I kicked through the dust of the road.

1 I began to look ahead. Where could we possibly be walking to? I couldn't be walking just because I wanted to be with her.

Fortunately, there was one more house, a gray house by a sagging barn, set two hundred yards from the road.

"I thought I'd see if I could get a customer here," I said, waving toward the house.

"That's where I live."

"Oh."

We were at the dusty car tracks that turned off the road to the house. The girl stopped. There was a tree at that corner, a straight but little tree with slim branches and shiny dark leaves.

"I could take a paper tonight to see if my father wants to buy it."

A great relief, this. What could I have said to her parents? I held out a paper, dropped it, picked it up, brushing off the dust. "No, here's a new one"—a great action, putting the dusty paper in the bag over my shoulder and pulling out a fresh one. When she took the paper we stood there a minute. The wind was coming in over the grass. She looked out with a tranquil expression.

2 She walked away past the tree, and I hurried quickly back toward town. Could anyone in the houses have been watching? I looked back once. The girl was standing on the small bridge halfway into her house. I hurried on.

The next day at school I didn't ask her whether her father wanted to take the paper. When the others were there I wouldn't say anything. I stood with the boys. In American history the students could choose their seats, **3** and I saw that she was too quiet and plainly dressed for many to notice her. But I crowded in with the boys, pushing one aside, scrambling for a seat by the window.

That night I came to the edge of town. Two papers were left, and I walked on out. The meadowlark was there. By some reeds in a ditch by the road a dragonfly—snake feeders, we called them—glinted. The sun was going down, and the plains were stretched out and lifted, some way, to the horizon. Could I go on up to the house? I didn't think so, but I walked on. Then, by the tree where her road turned off, she was standing. She was holding her books. More confused than ever, I stopped.

"My father will take the paper," she said.

She told me always to leave the paper at the foot of the tree. She insisted on that, saying their house was too far; and it is true that I was far off my route, a long way, a half-mile out of my territory. But I didn't think of that.

And so we were acquainted. What I remember best in that town is those evening walks to the tree. Every night—or almost every night—the girl was there. Evangeline was her name. We didn't say much. On Friday night of the first week she gave me a dime, the cost of the paper. It was a poor newspaper, by the **4** way, cheap, sensational, unreliable. I never went up to her house. We never talked together at school. But all the time we knew each other; we just happened to meet. Every evening.

There was a low place in the meadow by that corner. The fall rains made a pond there, and in the evenings sometimes ducks would be coming in—a long line with set wings down the wind, and then a turn, and a skimming **5** glide to the water. The wind would be blowing and the grass bent down. The evenings got colder and colder. The wind was cold. As winter came on the time at the tree was dimmer, but not dark. In the winter there was snow. The pond was frozen over; all the plains were white. I had to walk down the ruts of the road and leave the paper in the crotch of the tree,

The Osage Orange Tree 69

AT A GLANCE

- The girl says her father will subscribe to the paper; she insists that it be left at the tree rather than at the house.
- Evangeline meets the boy at the tree each night.

1 INTERNAL CONFLICT

The boy's adolescent shyness will not allow him to admit, even to himself, that he wants to be with the girl.

2 THEME

The themes of adolescent self-consciousness and the need for friendship intertwine here. "Could anyone . . . have been watching?" conveys adolescent fear of being observed—even in an innocent friendship.

3 CHARACTERIZATION

The boy's observations characterize the girl as poorer than the others and even more isolated than he. His observations also characterize himself: He wants to be her friend—but privately, not in public.

4 RESPONSE JOURNAL

Have students write about the unusual friendship described in this passage.

5 SETTING

The description of the onset of winter reinforces the mood of bleakness and isolation.

GUIDED READING

LITERAL QUESTIONS

1a. What explanation does the boy give the girl for his continuing to walk away from town? (He says he's looking for a new customer.)

2a. What does the girl tell the boy to do with the newspapers? (leave them at the foot of the tree)

INFERENTIAL QUESTIONS

1b. Why does he say this? (He does not want the girl to know that he is walking along just for her company.)

2b. What reasons might the girl have for keeping the boy away from her house? (She might be ashamed of her poverty; she might want to see him alone.)

1 READING SKILLS: INFERENCE

The fact that the boy strikes out after approaching Evangeline's brother shows, without explicitly telling, that the incident has upset him.

2 SETTING

The abject poverty of the Depression is summed up in the narrator's words: "poor in a way you can't understand." The depth of Evangeline's poverty is an important element in the story's outcome.

3 STYLE: WORD CHOICE

The adjectives "dark," "straight," "heavy," "thick," and "black" contribute to the somber, regretful mood of the story.

sometimes, when it was cold. The wind made a sound through the black branches. But usually, even on cold evenings, Evangeline was there.

At school we played ball at noon—the boys did. And I got acquainted. I learned that Evangeline's brother was janitor at the school. A big dark boy he was—a man, middle-aged I thought at the time. He didn't ever let on that he knew me. I would see him sweeping the halls, bent down, slow. I would see him and Evangeline take their sack lunches over to the **1** south side of the building. Once I slipped away from the ball game and went over there, but he looked at me so steadily, without moving, that I pretended to be looking for a book, and quickly went back, and got in the game and struck out.

You don't know about those winters, and

especially that winter. Those were the dust years.[2] Wheat was away down in price. Every **2** one was poor—poor in a way that you can't understand. I made two dollars a week, or something like that, on my paper route. I could tell about working for ten cents an hour—and then not getting paid; about families that ate wheat, boiled, for their main food, and burned wheat for fuel. You don't know how it would be. All through that hard winter I carried a paper to the tree by the pond, in the evening, and gave it to Evangeline.

In the cold weather Evangeline wore a **3** heavier dress, a dark, straight, heavy dress, under a thick black coat. Outdoors she wore

---

2. **dust years:** the Great Depression in the 1930s; the Midwest and Southwest suffered droughts.

70   *The Short Story*

GUIDED READING

LITERAL QUESTION

1a. What new character is introduced here? What do you learn about him? (We meet Evangeline's brother, a janitor: He is bent over and moves slowly; he is not friendly.)

INFERENTIAL QUESTION

1b. What does this information suggest about Evangeline's family? (They are worn down by poverty; isolation is a family trait.)

a knitted cap that fastened under her chin. She was dressed this way when we met and she took the paper. The reeds were broken now. The meadowlark was gone.

And then came the spring. I have forgotten to tell just how Evangeline looked. She was of medium height, and slim. Her face was pale, **[1]** her forehead high, her eyes blue. Her tranquil face I remember well. I remember her watching the wind come in over the grass. Her dress was long, her feet small. I can remember her by the tree, with her books, or walking on up the road toward her house and stopping on the bridge halfway up there, but she didn't wave, and I couldn't tell whether she was watching me or not. I always looked back as I went over the rise toward town.

And I can remember her in the room at school. She came into American history one spring day, the first really warm day. She had changed from the dark heavy dress to the dull blue one of the last fall; and she had on a new belt, a gray belt, with blue stitching along the edges. As she passed in front of Jane Wright, a girl who sat on the front row, I heard Jane say to the girl beside her, "Why look at Evangeline—that old dress of hers has a new belt!"

"Stop a minute, Evangeline," Jane said; "let me see your new dress."

[2] Evangeline stopped and looked uncertainly at Jane and blushed. "It's just made over," she said, "it's just. . . ."

"It's cute, Dear," Jane said; and as Evangeline went on Jane nudged her friend in the ribs and the friend smothered a giggle.

Well, that was a good year. Commencement[3] time came, and—along with the newspaper job—I had the task of preparing for finals and all. One thing, I wasn't a student who took part in the class play or anything like that. I was just one of the boys—twenty-fourth in line to get my diploma.

---
3. **Commencement:** graduation.

And graduation was bringing an end to my paper-carrying. My father covered a big territory in our part of the state, selling farm equipment; and we were going to move at once to a town seventy miles south. Only because of my finishing the school year had we stayed till graduation.

I had taught another boy my route, always leaving him at the end and walking on out, by myself, to the tree. I didn't really have to go around with him that last day, the day of graduation, but I was going anyway.

At the graduation exercises, held that May afternoon, I wore my brown Sunday suit. My mother was in the audience. It was a heavy day. The girls had on new dresses. But I didn't see her.

3 I suppose that I did deserve old man Sutton's "Shhh!" as we lined up to march across the stage, but I for the first time in the year forgot my caution, and asked Jane where Evangeline was. She shrugged, and I could see for myself that she was not there.

We marched across the stage; our diplomas were ours; our parents filed out; to the strains of a march on the school organ we trailed to the hall. I unbuttoned my brown suit coat, stuffed the diploma in my pocket, and sidled out of the group and upstairs.

Evangeline's brother was emptying wastebaskets at the far end of the hall. I sauntered toward him and stopped. I didn't know what I wanted to say. Unexpectedly, he solved my problem. Stopping in his work, holding a partly empty wastebasket over the canvas sack he wore over his shoulder, he stared at me, as if almost to say something.

4 "I noticed that your sister wasn't here," I said. The noise below was dwindling. The hall was quiet, an echoey place; my voice sounded terribly loud. He emptied the rest of the wastebasket and shifted easily. He was a man, in big overalls. He stared at me.

"Evangeline couldn't come," he said. He

The Osage Orange Tree   71

AT A GLANCE

- The boy observes his classmates' cruelty to Evangeline.
- The boy's family plans to move.
- Evangeline is not at graduation.
- The narrator seeks out her brother for an explanation.

1 CHARACTERIZATION

Even to the grown-up narrator looking back on his youth, Evangeline is something of a mystery. He may "remember well" her "tranquil face" but will never fully understand what conflicts and suffering lay behind it.

2 EXTERNAL CONFLICT

Evangeline is so innocent and straightforward that she seems unable to fight back against the cruel teasing of her classmates—or even to recognize it as cruel.

3 INTERNAL CONFLICT

The narrator finally overcomes his internal conflict and asks someone at school about Evangeline. His behavior suggests he is worried and wants to see her one last time.

4 CHARACTERIZATION

The fact that the boy's voice sounds "terribly loud" even to himself suggests how nervous he is about approaching Evangeline's brother.

GUIDED READING

LITERAL QUESTIONS

1a. How does Evangeline react when the girls tease her? (She blushes and says, "It's just made over . . .")

2a. What one thing does the narrator do alone when he is training the new boy on the paper route? (goes to meet Evangeline)

INFERENTIAL QUESTIONS

1b. What does Evangeline's reaction show about her? (She is too trusting and innocent of other people's intentions; she is honest.)

2b. Why do you think the narrator does this? (He does not want to give up his friendship with the girl until he has to. Also, he wants to keep the friendship secret.)

- Evangeline's brother says she has stolen the money intended for her graduation dress.
- The narrator tries unsuccessfully to find Evangeline at home.
- He finds all the newspapers hidden under the bridge.

1 SETTING

The gray, "lopsided" house, the barren yard, and the dishwater tossed out back all suggest that Evangeline's family are careless about their surroundings and discouraged by their poverty.

2 THEME

The tree bears inedible fruit, and its thorny branches were used for fencing before barbed wire came into use. With its green leaves and thorns, the tree represents the tentative, stunted friendship of the boy and girl.

3 READING SKILLS: INFERENCE

From the description of the papers as "boxed" (folded) and "worn and weathered by rain, by snow," it is clear that Evangeline threw them one by one under the bridge.

REFLECTING ON THE STORY

If the narrator could relive the time of the story, what do you think he would change? (Perhaps he would be more open in his feelings for Evangeline.)

---

stopped, looked at me again, and said, "She stole."

"Stole?" I said. "'Stole what?'"

He shrugged and went toward the next wastebasket, but I followed him.

"She stole the money from her bank—the money she was to use for her graduation dress," he said. He walked stolidly[4] on, and I stopped. He deliberately turned away as he picked up the next wastebasket. But he said something else, half to himself. "You knew her. You talked to her . . . I know." He walked away.

I hurried downstairs and outside. The new carrier would have the papers almost delivered by now; so I ran up the street toward the north. I took a paper from him at the end of the street and told him to go back. I didn't pay any more attention to him.

No one was at the tree, and I turned, for the first time, up the road to the house. I walked over the bridge and on up the narrow, **1** rutty tracks. The house was gray and lopsided. The ground of the yard was packed; nothing grew there. By the back door, the door to which the road led, there was a grayish-white place on the ground where the dishwater had been thrown. A gaunt shepherd dog trotted out growling.

And the door opened suddenly, as if someone had been watching me come up the track. A woman came out—a woman stern-faced, with a shawl over her head and a dark lumpy dress on—came out on the back porch and shouted, "Go 'way, go 'way! We don't want no papers!" She waved violently with one hand, holding the other on her shawl, at her throat. She coughed so hard that she leaned over and put her hand against one of the uprights of the porch. Her face was red. She glanced to-

---

4. **stolidly** [stol′id lē]: unemotionally.

72   *The Short Story*

---

ward the barn and leaned toward me. "Go 'way!"

Behind me a meadowlark sang. Over all the plains swooped the sky. The land was drawn up somehow toward the horizon.

I stood there, half-defiant, half-ashamed. The dog continued to growl and to pace around me, stiff-legged, his tail down. The windows of the house were all blank, with blinds drawn. I couldn't say anything.

I stood a long time and then, lowering the newspaper I had held out, I stood longer, waiting, without thinking of what to do. The meadowlark bubbled over again, but I turned and walked away, looking back once or twice. The old woman continued to stand, leaning forward, her head out. She glanced at the barn, but didn't call out any more.

My heels dug into the grayish place where the dishwater had been thrown; the dog skulked along behind.

At the bridge, halfway to the road, I stopped and looked back. The dog was lying down again; the porch was empty; and the door was closed. Turning the other way, I **2** looked toward town. Near me stood our ragged little tree—an Osage orange tree it was. It was feebly coming into leaf, green all over the branches, among the sharp thorns. I hadn't wondered before how it grew there, all alone, in the plains country, neglected. Over our pond some ducks came slicing in.

Standing there on the bridge, still holding the folded-boxed-newspaper, that worthless paper, I could see everything. I looked out along the road to town. From the bridge you would see the road going away, to where it went over the rise.

Glancing around, I flipped that last newspaper under the bridge and then bent far over **3** and looked where it had gone. There they were—a pile of boxed newspapers, thrown in a heap, some new, some worn and weathered, by rain, by snow.

GUIDED READING

LITERAL QUESTIONS

1a. According to Evangeline's brother, why isn't Evangeline at graduation? (She "stole" money intended for a graduation dress from her bank.)

2a. Where does the boy discover all the papers he had left at the tree? How do they look? (He discovers them under the bridge. They are boxed and weathered.)

INFERENTIAL QUESTIONS

1b. Why do you think Evangeline took the money? (to buy the papers and make friends with the boy)

2b. What does the condition of the papers tell you about how they got there? (Evangeline probably threw each one from the bridge each night.)

STUDY QUESTIONS

Recalling

1. According to paragraph one, what is the boy doing when he first sees Evangeline? What is Evangeline doing?
2. Where does Evangeline live? Why does the boy walk there every day?
3. According to her brother, why does Evangeline miss graduation?
4. What happens when the boy goes to Evangeline's house after graduation? Describe the newspapers that he finds under the bridge.

Interpreting

5. Why do you think the boy wants to be Evangeline's friend?
6. What do you think Evangeline does with her graduation-dress money? Why?
7. Who do you think threw the newspapers under the bridge? Why?

Extending

8. When young people transfer to a new school, why is making friends sometimes difficult?

READING AND LITERARY FOCUS

Making Inferences from Details of Character

Details make a story realistic, colorful, and interesting. They can also provide important information about characters. To enjoy a story completely, we should notice details and make inferences from them. An **inference** is a conclusion that we draw from the information we have. For example, a new boy transfers into a school. He joins the basketball team and the honor society. We can infer that he is a well-rounded student.

Details about appearance or behavior give us clues to a character's personality. For example, in "Thank You, M'am" (page 64) Mrs. Jones works late in a beauty shop. From this detail we can infer that she needs the money that she gives to Roger. The detail helps us to see her generosity.

Thinking About Making Inferences

■ What inferences about Evangeline can you make from each of the following details?
  a. She wears a faded blue dress.
  b. She lives far outside the town.
  c. She waits at the tree every day for the boy.

VOCABULARY

Analogies

Analogies are comparisons that are stated as double relationships. For example, A is to B as C is to D. On tests analogies are written as two pairs of words, A : B :: C : D. You may be given the first pair and asked to find or complete a second pair that has the same kind of relationship as the first. For example, in the analogy HOT : COLD :: BRIGHT : DARK, the first word in each pair is the opposite of the second word.

Analogies can state the following kinds of relationships, among others:

- synonyms (KIND : CARING)
- cause and effect (PRACTICE : SKILL)
- different grammatical forms of the same word (COMPLETE : COMPLETION)

The following numbered items are analogies that need to be completed. The third word in each item is from "The Osage Orange Tree." Decide how the first two words in each item are related. Then, from the four choices that follow each numbered item, choose the word that best completes the second pair. Write the number of each item and the letter of your choice on a separate sheet.

1. TROPHY : RACE :: DIPLOMA :
   (a) school   (c) sports
   (b) memory   (d) prize

2. GREEDY : SELFISH :: GAUNT :
   (a) thin   (c) colorful
   (b) generous   (d) selfish

3. EXCITING : STADIUM :: TRANQUIL :
   (a) gymnasium   (c) calm
   (b) church   (d) quiet

The Osage Orange Tree   73

1. watching the other students, pretending not to; standing alone, watching the others
2. on the edge of town; to deliver newspaper
3. She stole from her own bank the money to be used for her graduation dress.
4. ■ A woman says they don't want any newspaper.
   ■ Newspapers are heaped in a box under bridge, some worn, others new
5. Answers will vary. Possibilities: She is an outsider like him, is friendly to him, and desperately needs a friend.
6. She pays for the newspapers so he will visit her every day.
7. Evangeline; so that no one would know that she was spending her graduation money
8. Answers will vary. Some possible answers: The other students know each other and have made friends before transfer students arrive, and groups of people sometimes feel more privileged when they exclude newcomers.

READING AND LITERARY FOCUS

a. She is poor.
b. She is poor; her family may prefer to live away from others; the location of her home has helped to isolate Evangeline.
c. She likes him; she has nothing more important to do.

VOCABULARY

1. (a) diploma: school
2. (a) gaunt: thin
3. (b) tranquil: church

- Monk and Glennie, two seventh-graders, are playing catch on the firehouse lawn when Scho sees them.
- Scho joins them, but he doesn't have a glove.
- The boys throw him easy grounders, then a bumpy one that Scho misses and has to chase after.

LITERARY OPTIONS

- characterization
- internal/external conflict
- plot

THEMATIC OPTIONS

- peer acceptance and rejection
- friendship
- isolation

1 THEME

Vivid, precise verbs—"lob," "snag," "burn," "spank"—suggest how skilled Monk and Glennie are at the game and how well-matched they are as friends.

2 POINT OF VIEW

The third-person narrator compares the look of the game of catch to a dance, then indicates that Glennie sees Scho dawdling. The narrator's shifting perspective reveals what each character sees.

3 CHARACTERIZATION

Scho has upset the game for the two friends, so Monk sends Scho a "fast, bumpy grounder" to discourage him from playing.

TEXAS ESSENTIAL ELEMENTS GRADE 8

1A writing process
1D evaluation of content and organization
2A varied sentences
3A plot and character development
3D literary genres
4B implied main idea
4E cause/effect
4F point of view
To locate treatment of an Element, see *Texas Teacher's Resources*.

Richard Wilbur was born in New York City in 1921. Wilbur is best know as a poet. However, he has also written stories, a children's book, and translations of classic French plays. The following story begins with a simple game of catch.

■ In what way are the events that happen next both funny and sad?

Richard Wilbur

A Game of Catch

Monk and Glennie were playing catch on the side lawn of the firehouse when Scho caught sight of them. They were good at it, for seventh-graders, as anyone could see right away. Monk, wearing a catcher's mitt, would lean easily sidewise and back, with one leg lifted and his throwing hand almost down to the grass, and then lob the white ball straight up into the sunlight. Glennie would shield his eyes with his left hand and, just as the ball fell past him, snag it with a little dart of his glove. Then he would burn the ball straight toward Monk, and it would spank into the round mitt and sit, like a still-life apple on a plate, until Monk flipped it over into his right hand and, with a negligent flick of his hanging arm, gave Glennie a fast grounder.

They were going on and on like that, in a kind of slow, mannered,[1] luxurious dance in the sun, their faces perfectly blank and entranced, when Glennie noticed Scho dawdling along the other side of the street and called hello to him. Scho crossed over and stood at the front edge of the lawn, near an apple tree, watching.

"Got your glove?" asked Glennie after a time. Scho obviously hadn't.

"You could give me some easy grounders," said Scho. "But don't burn 'em."

"All right," Glennie said. He moved off a little, so the three of them formed a triangle, and they passed the ball around for about five minutes, Monk tossing easy grounders to Scho, Scho throwing to Glennie, and Glennie burning them in to Monk. After a while, Monk began to throw them back to Glennie once or twice before he let Scho have his grounder, and finally Monk gave Scho a fast, bumpy grounder that hopped over his shoulder and went into the brake[2] on the other side of the street.

"Not so hard," called Scho as he ran across to get it.

"You should've had it," Monk shouted.

It took Scho a little while to find the ball among the ferns and dead leaves, and when

---

1. **mannered:** with noticeable style.

2. **brake:** clump of brush or shrubs.

GUIDED READING

LITERAL QUESTION

1a. When Scho complains about the bumpy grounder, What does Monk say? ("You should've had it.")

INFERENTIAL QUESTION

1b. How do you think Monk feels when he says this? (resentful of Scho for disturbing the game and for complaining; perhaps glad that Scho has to run after the ball) he saw it, he grabbed it up and threw it toward Glennie. It struck the tree trunk of the apple tree, bounced back at an angle, and rolled steadily and stupidly onto the cement apron in front of the firehouse, where one of the trucks was parked. Scho ran hard and stopped it just before it rolled under the truck, and this time he carried it back to his former position on the lawn and threw it carefully to Glennie.

1 "I got an idea," said Glennie. "Why don't Monk and I catch for five minutes more, and then you can borrow one of our gloves?"

"That's all right with me," said Monk. He socked his fist into his mitt, and Glennie burned one in.

"All right," Scho said, and went over and sat under the tree. There in the shade he watched them resume their skillful play. They threw lazily fast or lazily slow—high, low, or wide—and always handsomely, their expressions serene, changeless, and forgetful. When Monk missed a low backhand catch, he walked indolently[3] after the ball and, hardly even looking, flung it sidearm for an imaginary put-out. After a good while of this, Scho said, "Isn't it five minutes yet?"

"One minute to go," said Monk, with a fraction of a grin.

Scho stood up and watched the ball slap back and forth for several minutes more, and then he turned and pulled himself up into the crotch of the tree.

2 "Where you going?" Monk asked.

"Just up the tree," Scho said.

"I guess he doesn't want to catch," said Monk.

Scho went up and up through the fat light-gray branches until they grew slender and bright and gave under him. He found a place where several supple branches were knit to

_____
3. **indolently** [ind'əl ənt lē]: lazily.

make a dangerous chair, and sat there with his head coming out of the leaves into the sunlight. He could see the two other boys down below, the ball going back and forth between them as if they were bowling on the grass, and Glennie's crew-cut head looking like a sea urchin.

3 "I found a wonderful seat up here," Scho said loudly. "If I don't fall out." Monk and Glennie didn't look up or comment, and so he began jouncing gently in his chair of branches and singing "Yo-ho, heave ho" in an exaggerated way.

"Do you know what, Monk?" he announced in a few moments. "I can make you

A Game of Catch 75

GUIDED READING

LITERAL QUESTION

1a. What does Scho do when Glennie and Monk don't let him back in the game? (climbs a tree)

INFERENTIAL QUESTION

1b. Why do you think he does this? (He feels rejected and frustrated; he doesn't know what else to do; he is trying to get some attention.)

- Scho plays a game: Every time Monk and Glennie do or say something, Scho tells them he made them do or say it.
- The boys get angry and stop playing catch.
- Monk climbs the tree, shakes it, and Scho falls.

1 CHARACTERIZATION

Scho devises a sad strategy to gain some satisfaction from the situation. By taunting the boys and claiming to control them, he distracts them from their game and eventually brings it to an end.

2 INTERNAL CONFLICT

Scho has a moment of hesitation: Glennie offers acceptance, but Scho doesn't trust him. Scho continues to taunt the boys, perhaps wondering if he missed an opportunity to be friends with Glennie and Monk.

3 PLOT: SUSPENSE

With Monk feeling "furious and foolish" and Scho feeling "exuberant" but "panicky," the situation is quickly getting out of control—perhaps dangerous.

4 PLOT: CLIMAX

Scho's fall from the tree marks the emotional high point of the story. The description of Scho's stillness and the boys' fear encourages the reader's concern for his welfare.

---

two guys do anything I want. Catch that ball, Monk! Now you catch it, Glennie!"

"I was going to catch it anyway," Monk suddenly said. "You're not making anybody do anything when they're already going to do it anyway."

1 "I made you say what you said," Scho replied joyfully.

"No, you didn't," said Monk, still throwing and catching but now less serenely absorbed in the game.

"That's what I wanted you to say," Scho said.

The ball bounded off the rim of Monk's mitt and plowed into a gladiolus bed beside the firehouse, and Monk ran to get it while Scho jounced in his treetop and sang, "I wanted you to miss that. Anything you do is what I wanted you to do."

"Let's quit for a minute," Glennie suggested.

"We might as well, until the peanut gallery[4] shuts up," Monk said.

They went over and sat crosslegged in the shade of the tree. Scho looked down between his legs and saw them on the dim, spotty ground, saying nothing to one another. Glennie soon began abstractedly[5] spinning his glove between his palms; Monk pulled his nose and stared out across the lawn.

"I want you to mess around with your nose, Monk," said Scho, giggling. Monk withdrew his hand from his face.

"Do that with your glove, Glennie," Scho persisted. "Monk, I want you to pull up hunks of grass and chew on it."

Glennie looked up and saw a self-delighted, intense face staring down at him through the leaves. "Stop being a dope and come down and we'll catch for a few minutes," he said.

---

4. **peanut gallery:** slang for the highest section in the balcony of a theater.
5. **abstractedly** [ab strak'tid lē]: while thinking about something else.

76　*The Short Story*

---

2 Scho hesitated, and then said, in a tentatively[6] mocking voice, "That's what I wanted you to say."

"All right, then, nuts to you," said Glennie.

"Why don't you keep quiet and stop bothering people?" Monk asked.

"I made you say that," Scho replied, softly.

"Shut up," Monk said.

"I made you say that, and I want you to be standing there looking sore. And I want you to climb up the tree. I'm making you do it!"

3 Monk was scrambling up through the branches, awkward in his haste, and getting snagged on twigs. His face was furious and foolish, and he kept telling Scho to shut up, shut up, shut up, while the other's exuberant[7] and panicky voice poured down upon his head.

"*Now* you shut up or you'll be sorry," Monk said, breathing hard as he reached up and threatened to shake the cradle of slight branches in which Scho was sitting.

4 "I *want*—"Scho screamed as he fell. Two lower branches broke his rustling, crackling fall, but he landed on his back with a deep thud and lay still, with a strangled look on his face and his eyes clenched. Glennie knelt down and asked breathlessly, "Are you O.K., Scho? Are you O.K.?," while Monk swung down through the leaves crying that honestly he hadn't even touched him, the crazy guy just let go. Scho doubled up and turned over on his right side, and now both the other boys knelt beside him, pawing at his shoulder and begging to know how he was.

Then Scho rolled away from them and sat partly up, still struggling to get his wind but forcing a species of smile onto his face.

"I'm sorry, Scho," Monk said. "I didn't mean to make you fall."

Scho's voice came out weak and gravelly,

---

6. **tentatively** [ten'tə tiv lē]: doubtfully.
7. **exuberant** [ig zoo'bər ənt]: enthusiastic.

GUIDED READING

LITERAL QUESTIONS

1a. What do Glennie and Monk do when they decide to quit playing for a minute? (They sit under a tree and do not speak.)

2a. What does Scho do when Glennie tells him to come down from the tree and play catch? (He hesitates, then says, "That's what I wanted you to say.")

INFERENTIAL QUESTIONS

1b. Why don't they speak? (They are afraid Scho will claim to be controlling them again; they are trying to think of a way out of the situation.)

2b. Why doesn't Scho accept the offer to play catch? (He doesn't trust the boys; now he would rather continue to get revenge on them than to risk playing with them.)

in gasps. "I meant—you to do it. You—had to. You can't do—anything—unless I want—you to."

Glennie and Monk looked helplessly at him as he sat there, breathing a bit more easily and smiling fixedly, with tears in his eyes. Then they picked up their gloves and the ball, walked over to the street, and went slowly away down the sidewalk, Monk punching his fist into the mitt, Glennie juggling the ball between glove and hand.

From under the apple tree, Scho, still bent over a little for lack of breath, croaked after them in triumph and misery, "I want you to do whatever you're going to do for the whole rest of your life!"

STUDY QUESTIONS

Recalling

1. Find two ways that Scho tries to join the game of catch. What happens each time?
2. What does Scho yell down from the tree? What effect does he have on the game of catch?
3. What happens when Monk climbs the tree?
4. Tell what happens after Scho and Monk are out of the tree.
5. What is Scho's condition in the last paragraph? What does he say as the other boys leave?

Interpreting

6. Do Monk and Glennie want Scho to play catch with them? Why or why not?
7. Why does Scho feel both "triumph and misery"?

Extending

8. In many disagreements between people, no one really wins. Use the story as an example to explain this idea.

READING AND LITERARY FOCUS

Character Motivation

Like people in everyday life, the characters in a story should have clear motivations for their actions. **Motivation** is a feeling or goal that causes a character to act. For example, in "The Osage Orange Tree" (page 68) Evangeline orders the newspaper from the boy. Her motivation is her loneliness. She wants to see the boy every day.

A character's motivation should be clear, at least by the end of the story. A character may do something that surprises us. However, the action must fit the character's personality and have a clear motivation. For example, Evangeline spends the money saved for her graduation dress. This is a surprising action. However, the act shows us how deep her loneliness is.

Thinking About Character Motivation

■ Why do you think Scho teases the other boys from the tree? Why does he pretend to have power over them?

COMPOSITION

Writing About Character

■ Do you think that Monk is a true-to-life character? Write an essay about his personality. First state your opinion clearly. Then give reasons. You may want to include (a) the different traits he shows, (b) the ways in which he changes, and (c) the motivations for his actions. Be sure to use examples from the story to support your opinions. *For help with this assignment, see Lesson 3 in the Writing About Literature Handbook at the back of this book.*

Writing a Description of a Character

■ Describe an imaginary character. Tell what your character looks like. Include descriptions of his or her clothing, voice, and way of moving. Be sure to use realistic details.

A Game of Catch 77

COMPOSITION: GUIDELINES FOR EVALUATION

WRITING ABOUT CHARACTER

Objective
To evaluate portrayal of a character

Guidelines for Evaluation
■ suggested length: one or two paragraphs
■ should clearly state opinion about the character Monk; give reasons for opinion
■ use examples from story that focus on the character's traits, motivations, and actions

WRITING A DESCRIPTION OF A CHARACTER

Objective
To write a description of an imaginary character

Guidelines for Evaluation
■ suggested length: one or two paragraphs
■ should describe character's physical appearance, clothing, voice, way of moving
■ should use details to make character realistic
■ should use an informal style

- Monk apologizes, but Scho continues to taunt the boys.
- Monk and Glennie leave, and in "triumph and misery" Scho shouts after them.

1 THEME

Scho's "triumph" in getting the last word is desperate and poignant: Ultimately he is more alone than ever.

REFLECTING ON THE STORY

Who do you think is to blame for what happens? (Monk and Glennie are cruel, but Scho contributes to his own humiliation.)

STUDY QUESTIONS

1. ■ The first time, Scho dawdles along far side of street, watching; the second time, he asks if the five minutes they wanted to play by themselves are up.
   ■ The first time, the boys throw the ball so it's hard for him to catch; the second time, they just ignore him.
2. He tells boys he can make them do anything he wants, takes pleasure out of game. Boys stop playing.
3. Scho falls from his perch.
4. Scho sits up, struggles to smile, asserts again that he is controlling the boys.
5. He is both triumphant and miserable; he wants boys to do whatever they are going to do for rest of their lives.
6. He is not as good a player, is younger, has no glove; they are enjoying the game as it stands.
7. *Triumph:* He survived fall, has boys' attention, still claims to be controlling them. *Miserable:* He is still alone.
8. Glennie and Monk lose because they do not enjoy the game after Scho appears; Scho loses because the others never accept him.

READING AND LITERARY FOCUS

- Scho feels left out.
- He feels powerless. He pretends to be controlling the boys who won't let him play.

Jessamyn West (1907–1984) grew up in California, where she attended a one-room schoolhouse. Her most famous book is *The Friendly Persuasion*. Another work, *Cress Delahanty*, is a collection of stories about a young girl. The stories follow Cress from the age of twelve to sixteen. Like West, Cress is the daughter of a California rancher. In fact, the stories are inspired by West's own life.

■ What makes Cress especially true-to-life?

Jessamyn West

Then He Goes Free

While her mother and father awaited the arrival of Mr. and Mrs. Kibbler, who had called asking to speak to them "about Cress and Edwin, Jr.," Mr. Delahanty reminded his wife how wrong she had been about Cress.

"Not two months ago," he said, "in this very room you told me you were worried because Cress wasn't as interested in the boys as a girl her age should be. In this very room. And now look what's happened."

Mrs. Delahanty, worried now by Mrs. Kibbler's message, spoke more sharply than she had intended. "Don't keep repeating, 'in this very room,'" she said, "as if it would have been different if I'd said it in the back porch or out of doors. Besides, what has happened?"

Mr. Delahanty took off his hat, which he'd had on when Mrs. Kibbler phoned, and sailed it out of the living room toward the hall table, which he missed. "Don't ask me what's happened," he said. "I'm not the girl's mother."

Mrs. Delahanty took off her own hat and jabbed the hatpins back into it. "What do you mean, you're not the girl's mother? Of course you're not. No one ever said you were."

Mr. Delahanty picked up his fallen hat, put it on the chair beside the hall table and came back into the living room. "A girl confides in her mother," he told his wife.

"A girl confides in her mother!" Mrs. Delahanty was very scornful. "Who tells you these things, John Delahanty? Not *your* mother. She didn't have any daughter. Not me. Cress doesn't confide in anyone. How do you know these things, anyway, about mothers and daughters?"

John Delahanty seated himself upon the sofa, legs extended, head back, as straight and unrelaxed as a plank.

"Don't catch me up that way, Gertrude," he said. "You know I don't know them." Without giving his wife any opportunity to crow over this victory he went on quickly: "What I'd like

78　*The Short Story*

to know is, why did the Kibblers have to pick a Saturday night for this call? Didn't they know we'd be going into town?"

Like most ranchers, John Delahanty stopped work early on Saturdays so that, after a quick cleanup and supper, he and his wife could drive into town. There they did nothing very important: bought groceries, saw a show, browsed around in the hardware stores, visited friends. But after a week of seeing only themselves—the Delahanty ranch was off the main highway—it was pleasant simply to saunter along the sidewalks looking at the cars, the merchandise, the people in their town clothes. This Saturday trip to town was a jaunt they both looked forward to during the week, and tonight's trip, because of February's warmer air and suddenly, it seemed, longer twilight, would have been particularly pleasant.

"Five minutes more," said Mr. Delahanty, "and we'd have been on our way."

"Why didn't you tell Mrs. Kibbler we were just leaving?"

"I did. And she said for anything less important she wouldn't think of keeping us."

Mrs. Delahanty came over to the sofa and stood looking anxiously down at her husband. **2** "John, exactly what did Mrs. Kibbler say?"

"The gist of it," said Mr. Delahanty, "was that . . ."

"I don't care about the gist of it. That's just what you think she said. I want to know what she really said."

Mr. Delahanty let his head fall forward, though he still kept his legs stiffly extended. "What she really said was, 'Is this Mr. John Delahanty?' And I said, 'Yes.' Then she said, 'This is Mrs. Edwin Kibbler, I guess you remember me.' "

"Remember her?" Mrs. Delahanty exclaimed. "I didn't know you even knew her."

"I don't," said Mr. Delahanty, "but I remem-**3** ber her all right. She came before the school board about a month ago to tell us we ought to take those two ollas[1] off the school grounds. She said it was old-fashioned to cool water that way, that the ollas looked messy and were unhygienic."[2]

"Did you take them off?" Mrs. Delahanty asked, without thinking. As a private person John Delahanty was reasonable and untalkative. As clerk of the school board he inclined toward dogmatism[3] and long-windedness. Now he began a defense of the ollas and the school board's action in retaining them.

"Look, John," said Mrs. Delahanty, "I'm not interested in the school board or its water coolers. What I want to know is, what did Mrs. Kibbler say about Cress?"

"Well, she said she wanted to have a little talk with us about Cress—and Edwin, Jr."

"I know that." Impatience made Mrs. Delahanty's voice sharp. "But what about them?"

Mr. Delahanty drew his feet up toward the sofa, then bent down and retied a shoelace. "About what Cress did to him—Edwin, Jr."

"*Did* to him!" said Mrs. Delahanty aghast.

"That's what his mother said."

Mrs. Delahanty sat down on the hassock **4** at her husband's feet. "Did to him," she repeated again. "Why, what could Cress do to him? He's two or three years older than Cress, fifteen or sixteen anyway. What could she do to him?"

Mr. Delahanty straightened up. "She could hit him, I guess," he ventured.

"Hit him? What would she want to hit him for?"

"I don't know," said Mr. Delahanty. "I don't

---

1. **ollas** [ol′əz]: wide-mouthed jars or pots used for holding water.
2. **unhygienic** [un′hī′jē en′ik]: unhealthful, not clean.
3. **dogmatism** [dôg′mə tiz′əm]: positive, often arrogant declarations of opinions or beliefs.

Then He Goes Free 79

- On Saturday evenings the Delahantys usually go into town, but the Kibblers' visit will detain them.
- Mr. Delahanty says Mrs. Kibbler once asked the school board to remove water jars from the school grounds.
- According to Mrs. Kibbler, Cress "did" something to Edwin.

1 SETTING

The isolation of the ranch and the simple pleasures of the town are emphasized in this description of a typical week in the Delahantys' life.

2 CHARACTERIZATION

The humorous bickering between the Delahantys seems to be something each is accustomed to. Knowing each other intimately, they probably often engage in this sort of give-and-take.

3 PLOT: FORESHADOWING

Mrs. Kibbler's strong feelings about the ollas foreshadow a key element in the plot and indicate that she is a person who will make a fuss.

4 PLOT: SUSPENSE

Suspense builds as Cress's parents wonder what a thirteen-year-old girl could have done to a fifteen-year-old boy to upset his parents so much.

GUIDED READING

LITERAL QUESTIONS

1a. Which of the Delahantys spoke to Mrs. Kibbler on the phone? (Mr. Delahanty)

2a. Why does Mr. Delahanty remember Mrs. Kibbler? (She asked that the school board remove water jars from the school grounds.)

INFERENTIAL QUESTIONS

1b. How does this fact add to the humor and suspense of the situation? (Mrs. Delahanty is impatient to know what she said; her taciturn husband reveals the information only gradually.)

2b. What does Mr. Delahanty's memory of Mrs. Kibbler suggest about her? (She is likely to make a fuss about seemingly insignificant matters.)

AT A GLANCE

- Mr. Delahanty explains that Edwin has teeth missing; the family is expected to pay the dentist's bill.
- Mrs. Delahanty wants to question Cress, but Cress left the house during the phone call.
- The Kibblers arrive.

1 CHARACTERIZATION

The Delahantys' speculations about Cress allow contrasting views of her. Her mother claims she is "tenderhearted" while her father implies she is capable of hitting a boy. Both impressions of her ultimately contain truth.

2 HUMOR

Although Mrs. Delahanty claims it "isn't any joking matter," the author's tone is humorous as Mr. and Mrs. Delahanty speculate on how Cress could have knocked out Edwin's teeth.

3 THEME

Mr. Delahanty's perceptive remark underscores the fact that Cress's sympathetic interest in Edwin has brought on the present situation.

4 CHARACTERIZATION

Mrs. Kibbler—characterized by her "determined" nose and "cage-shaped" hair—seems both ridiculous and overbearing. By contrast her husband seems meek and vulnerable.

know that she did hit him. Maybe she kicked him. Anyway, his mother seems to think the boy's been damaged in some way."

"Damaged," repeated Mrs. Delahanty angrily. "Damaged! Why, Cress is too tenderhearted to hurt a fly. She shoos them outside instead of killing them. And you sit there talking of hitting and kicking."

"Well," said Mr. Delahanty mildly, "Edwin's got teeth out. I don't know how else she could get them out, do you?"

"I'm going to call Cress," said Mrs. Delahanty, "and ask her about this. I don't believe it for a minute."

"I don't think calling her will do any good. She left while I was talking to Mrs. Kibbler."

"What do you mean, left?"

"Went for a walk, she said."

"Well, teeth out," repeated Mrs. Delahanty unbelievingly. "Teeth out! I didn't know you could get teeth out except with pliers or a chisel."

"Maybe Edwin's teeth are weak."

"Don't joke about this, John Delahanty. It isn't any joking matter. And I don't believe it. I don't believe Cress did it or that that boy's teeth are out. Anyway I'd have to see them to believe it."

"You're going to," Mr. Delahanty said. "Mrs. Kibbler's bringing Edwin especially so you can."

Mrs. Delahanty sat for some time without saying anything at all. Then she got up and walked back and forth in front of her husband, turning her hat, which she still held, round and round on one finger. "Well, what does Mrs. Kibbler expect us to do now?" she asked. "If they really are out, that is?"

"For one thing," replied Mr. Delahanty, "she expects us to pay for some new ones. And for another . . ." Mr. Delahanty paused to listen. Faintly, in the distance a car could be heard. "Here she is now," he said.

Mrs. Delahanty stopped her pacing. "Do

you think I should make some cocoa for them, John? And maybe some marguerites?"[4]

"No, I don't," said Mr. Delahanty. "I don't think Mrs. Kibbler considers this a social visit."

As the car turned into the long driveway which led between the orange grove on one side and the lemon grove on the other to the Delahanty house, Mrs. Delahanty said, "I still don't see why you think this proves I'm wrong."

Mr. Delahanty had forgotten about his wife's wrongness. "How do you mean wrong?" he asked.

"About Cress's not being interested in the boys."

"Oh," he said. "Well, you've got to be pretty interested in a person—one way or another—before you hit him."

"That's a perfectly silly notion," began Mrs. Delahanty, but before she could finish, the Kibblers had arrived.

Mr. Delahanty went to the door while Mrs. Delahanty stood in the back of the room by the fireplace unwilling to take one step toward meeting her visitors.

Mrs. Kibbler was a small woman with a large, determined nose, prominent blue eyes and almost no chin. Her naturally curly hair—she didn't wear a hat—sprang away from her head in a great cage-shaped pompadour[5] which dwarfed her face.

Behind Mrs. Kibbler was Mr. Kibbler, short, dusty, soft-looking, bald, except for a fringe of hair about his ears so thick that the top of his head, by contrast, seemed more naked than mere lack of hair could make it.

Behind Mr. Kibbler was Edwin, Jr. He was as thin as his mother, as mild and soft-look-

---

4. **marguerites** [mär′gə rētz′]: frosted cookies.
5. **pompadour** [pom′pə dôr′]: hairstyle in which hair is combed back from the forehead and puffed high in front.

80   *The Short Story*

GUIDED READING

LITERAL QUESTIONS

1a. When Mr. and Mrs. Delahanty are discussing Edwin's teeth, what does Mrs. Delahanty tell her husband not to do? (joke about the situation)

2a. How are the Kibblers' appearances described? (she—*small; large, determined nose; hair sprang away;* etc.; he—*dusty; soft-looking; naked;* etc.)

INFERENTIAL QUESTIONS

1b. Why do you think Mr. Delahanty jokes about the situation? (He may be trying to offset his wife's anger and relieve tension; he may find the idea of his daughter "damaging" a boy amusing.)

2b. Which of the Kibblers do you think is the dominant one? (Mrs. Kibbler) ing as his father; and to these qualities he added an unhappiness all of his own. He gave one quick look at the room and the Delahantys through his thick-lensed spectacles, after which he kept his eyes on the floor.

Mr. Delahanty closed the door behind the callers, then introduced his wife to Mrs. Kibbler. Mrs. Kibbler in turn introduced her family to the Delahantys. While the Kibblers were seating themselves—Mrs. Kibbler and Edwin, Jr., on the sofa, Mr. Kibbler on a straight-backed chair in the room's darkest corner—Mrs. Delahanty, out of nervousness, bent and lit the fire, which was laid in the fireplace, though the evening was not cold enough for it. Then she and Mr. Delahanty seated themselves in the chairs on each side of the fireplace.

Mrs. Kibbler looked at the fire with some surprise. "Do you find it cold this evening, Mrs. Delahanty?" she asked.

"No," said Mrs. Delahanty, "I don't. I don't know why I lit the fire."

To this Mrs. Kibbler made no reply. Instead, without preliminaries, she turned to her son. "Edwin," she said, "show the Delahantys what their daughter did to your teeth."

Mrs. Delahanty wanted to close her eyes, look into the fire, or find, as Edwin, Jr., had done, a spot of her own on the floor to examine. There was an almost imperceptible ripple along the length of the boy's face as if he had tried to open his mouth but found he lacked the strength. He momentarily lifted his eyes from the floor to dart a glance into the dark corner where his father sat. But Mr. Kibbler continued to sit in expressionless silence.

"Edwin," said Mrs. Kibbler, "speak to your son."

"Do what your mother says, Son," said Mr. Kibbler.

Very slowly, as if it hurt him, Edwin opened his mouth.

His teeth were white, and in his thin face they seemed very large, as well. The two middle teeth, above, had been broken across in a slanting line. The lower incisor appeared to be missing entirely.

"Wider, Edwin," Mrs. Kibbler urged. "I want the Delahantys to see exactly what their daughter is responsible for."

But before Edwin could make any further effort, Mrs. Delahanty cried, "No, that's enough."

"I didn't want you to take our word for anything," Mrs. Kibbler said reasonably. "I wanted you to see."

"Oh, we see, all right," said Mrs. Delahanty earnestly.

Mr. Delahanty leaned forward and spoke to Mrs. Kibbler. "While we see the teeth, Mrs. Kibbler, it just isn't a thing we think Crescent would do. Or in fact how she could do it. We think Edwin must be mistaken."

"You mean lying?" asked Mrs. Kibbler flatly.

"Mistaken," repeated Mr. Delahanty.

"Tell them, Edwin," said Mrs. Kibbler.

Then He Goes Free 81

AT A GLANCE

- Mrs. Delahanty nervously lights a fire.
- Mrs. Kibbler forces Edwin to show his teeth.
- Mr. Delahanty defends Cress.

1 CHARACTERIZATION

Edwin reveals his shyness and embarrassment by keeping his eyes on the floor.

2 STYLE: DIALOGUE

The author uses dialogue to reveal how Mrs. Kibbler manipulates her family to get what she wants.

3 THEME

Mr. Delahanty becomes serious and shows his pride in and concern for Cress as he defends her to Mrs. Kibbler.

GUIDED READING

LITERAL QUESTIONS

1a. Where does Mr. Kibbler sit? (in the room's darkest corner)

2a. What does Mrs. Delahanty say when Mrs. Kibbler wants Edwin to open his mouth wider? ("No, that's enough.")

INFERENTIAL QUESTIONS

1b. What does this choice of seats show about how he feels? (He does not want to be a part of the affair.)

2b. Why does Mrs. Delahanty say that? (She sees the point Mrs. Kibbler is making; perhaps she does not want Edwin to suffer any more embarrassment.)

AT A GLANCE

- Edwin says Cress knocked him down for fun.
- Mrs. Kibbler says Edwin's "damage" was caused by the olla that fell on him.
- She expects the Delahantys to pay the dentist's bill and Cress to apologize.
- Cress appears, apologizes to Edwin, and offers to help pay the costs.

1 HUMOR

By mentioning the role of the ollas in the incident, Mrs. Kibbler implicates Mr. Delahanty in Cress's offense. Her ironic triumph in her son's moment of pain has a touch of humor.

2 STYLE: SIMILE

By comparing Edwin to "a frightened colt," the narrator emphasizes the boy's extreme vulnerability.

3 CHARACTERIZATION

Cress's quick and sincere apology and offer to pay for the dental work help establish her as a caring person and suggest that the whole story has not yet been told.

4 THEME

The Delahantys' behavior (in the aftermath of the damaging evidence against Cress) shows them to be a loving, trusting family. Cress's parents do not threaten to punish her; she offers to punish herself.

"She knocked me down," said Edwin, very low.

Mrs. Delahanty, although she was already uncomfortably warm, held her hands nearer the fire, even rubbed them together a time or two.

"I simply can't believe that," she said.

"You mean hit you with her fist and knocked you down?" asked Mr. Delahanty.

"No," said Edwin even lower than before. "Ran into me."

"But not on purpose," said Mrs. Delahanty.

Edwin nodded. "Yes," he said. "On purpose."

"But why?" asked Mr. Delahanty. "Why? Cress wouldn't do such a thing, I know—without some cause. Why?"

"Tell them why, Edwin," said his mother.

Edwin's head went even nearer the floor—as if the spot he was watching had diminished or retreated.

"For fun," he said.

It was impossible not to believe the boy as he sat there hunched, head bent, one eyelid visibly twitching. "But Cress would never do such a thing," said Mrs. Delahanty.

1 Mrs. Kibbler disregarded this. "It would not have been so bad, Mr. Delahanty, except that Edwin was standing by one of those ollas. When your daughter shoved Edwin over she shoved the olla over, too. That's probably what broke his teeth. Heavy as cement and falling down on top of him and breaking up in a thousand pieces. To say nothing of his being doused with water on a cold day. And Providence alone can explain why his glasses weren't broken."

"What had you done, Edwin?" asked Mrs. Delahanty again.

"Nothing," whispered Edwin.

"All we want," said Mrs. Kibbler, "is what's perfectly fair. Pay the dentist's bill. And have that girl of yours apologize to Edwin."

Mrs. Delahanty got up suddenly and

82   *The Short Story*

2 walked over to Edwin. She put one hand on his thin shoulder and felt him twitch under her touch like a frightened colt.

"Go on, Edwin," she said. "Tell me the truth. Tell me why."

Edwin slowly lifted his head. "Go on, Edwin," Mrs. Delahanty encouraged him.

"He told you once," said Mrs. Kibbler. "Fun. That girl of yours is a big, boisterous thing from all I hear. She owes my boy an apology."

Edwin's face continued to lift until he was looking directly at Mrs. Delahanty.

He started to speak—but had said only three words, "Nobody ever wants," when Cress walked in from the hall. She had evidently been there for some time, for she went directly to Edwin.

3 "I apologize for hurting you, Edwin," she said.

Then she turned to Mrs. Kibbler. "I've got twelve seventy-five saved for a bicycle. That can go to help pay for his teeth."

After the Kibblers left, the three Delahantys sat for some time without saying a word. The fire had about died down and outside an owl, hunting finished, flew back toward the hills, softly hooting.

4 "I guess if we hurried we could just about catch the second show," Mr. Delahanty said.

"I won't be going to shows for a while," said Cress.

The room was very quiet. Mrs. Delahanty traced the outline of one of the bricks in the fireplace.

"I can save twenty-five cents a week that way. Toward his teeth," she explained.

Mrs. Delahanty took the poker and stirred the coals so that for a second there was an upward drift of sparks; but the fire was too far gone to blaze. Because it had not yet been completely dark when the Kibblers came, only one lamp had been turned on. Now that night had arrived the room was only partially

---

GUIDED READING

LITERAL QUESTIONS

1a. When does Cress step into the room to apologize? (when Edwin is saying to Cress's mother, "Nobody ever wants . . .")

2a. What happens after the Kibblers leave? (The Delahantys sit silently; Mr. Delahanty asks if they still want to go to the movies.)

INFERENTIAL QUESTIONS

1b. Why do you think she chooses this moment? (Perhaps she senses that Edwin is about to say something she doesn't want him to have to say.)

2b. Do you think Cress's parents still have faith in her? How can you tell? (Yes; they are silently waiting for her to explain, rather than confronting her angrily or punishing her.)

lighted; but no one seemed to care. Mr. Delahanty, in Mr. Kibbler's dark corner, was almost invisible. Mrs. Delahanty stood by the fireplace. Cress sat where Edwin had sat, looking downward, perhaps at the same spot at which he had looked.

"One day at school," she said, "Edwin went out in the fields at noon and gathered wildflower bouquets for everyone. A lupine, a poppy, two barley heads, four yellow violets. He tied them together with blades of grass. They were sweet little bouquets. He went without his lunch to get them fixed, and when we came back from eating there was a bouquet on every desk in the study hall. It looked like a flower field when we came in and Edwin did it to surprise us."

After a while Mr. Delahanty asked, "Did the kids like that?"

"Yes, they liked it. They tore their bouquets apart," said Cress, "and used the barley beards to tickle each other. Miss Ingols made Edwin gather up every single flower and throw it in the wastepaper basket."

After a while Cress said, "Edwin has a collection of bird feathers. The biggest is from a buzzard, the littlest from a hummingbird. They're all different colors. The brightest is from a woodpecker."

"Does he kill birds," Mr. Delahanty asked, "just to get a feather?"

"Oh, no!" said Cress. "He just keeps his eyes open to where a bird might drop a feather. It would spoil his collection to get a feather he didn't find that way."

Mr. Delahanty sighed and stirred in his wooden chair so that it creaked a little.

"Edwin would like to be a missionary to China," said Cress. Some particle in the fireplace, as yet unburned, blazed up in a sudden spurt of blue flame. "Not a preaching missionary," she explained.

AT A GLANCE

- After the Kibblers leave, Cress explains that Edwin picked bouquets for the class.
- She tells about Edwin's feather collection and that he wants to be a missionary to China.

1 POINT OF VIEW

The third-person narrator sets the scene so that the reader feels like an observer in the room. By having Cress take Edwin's seat, the narrator indicates Cress's ability to appreciate Edwin's situation.

2 CHARACTERIZATION

Edwin's sacrifice of his lunch to pick the bouquets suggests his sweetness and eagerness to please.

3 THEME

Edwin has obviously confided many things about himself to Cress, and she feels a fondness for him.

GUIDED READING

LITERAL QUESTION

1a. What things does Cress tell her parents about Edwin? (He once picked flowers for the class; he collects feathers; he wants to be a missionary to China.)

INFERENTIAL QUESTION

1b. What does Cress reveal about herself by saying these things? (She has often talked to Edwin; she is fond of him and realizes how vulnerable he is.)

- Cress tells her parents more about Edwin's dreams and "fancies."
- She explains that no one chooses Edwin for a teammate in a playground game.
- Cress describes how she chose him for her team and, in "rescuing" him, ran too hard and knocked him down.

1 READING SKILLS: INFERENCES

Cress's remark that Edwin has had to "take too much medicine" suggests that Edwin was a sickly child. This possibility would account for his lack of competence in sports and games.

2 SETTING

The description of the "surf-like" sound outside creates a peaceful feeling appropriate to this moment of real communication within the family.

3 CHARACTERIZATION

Cress's description of Edwin's predicament reveals how sorry she feels for him and suggests one reason she has tried to be his friend.

4 PLOT: CLIMAX

The story reaches its emotional high point as Cress finally explains how her good intentions were responsible for causing Edwin additional pain.

"A medical missionary?" asked Mr. Delahanty.

1 "Oh, no! Edwin says he's had to take too much medicine to ever be willing to make other people take it."

There was another long silence in the room. Mrs. Delahanty sat down in the chair her husband had vacated and once more held a hand toward the fire. There was just enough life left in the coals to make the tips of her fingers rosy. She didn't turn toward Cress at all or ask a single question. Back in the dusk Cress's voice went on.

"He would like to teach them how to play baseball."

Mr. Delahanty's voice was matter-of-fact. "Edwin doesn't look to me like he would be much of a baseball player."

"Oh he isn't," Cress agreed. "He isn't even any of a baseball player. But he could be a baseball authority. Know everything and teach by diagram. That's what he'd have to do. And learn from them how they paint. He says some of their pictures look like they had been painted with one kind of bird feather and some with another. He knows they don't really paint with bird feathers," she explained. "That's just a fancy[6] of his."

2 The night wind moving in off the Pacific began to stir the eucalyptus trees in the wind-break. Whether the wind blew off sea or desert didn't matter; the long eucalyptus leaves always lifted and fell with the same watery, surf-like sound.

"I'm sorry Edwin happened to be standing by that olla," said Mr. Delahanty. "That's what did the damage, I suppose."

"Oh, he had to stand there," said Cress. "He didn't have any choice. That's the mush pot."

"Mush pot," repeated Mr. Delahanty.

---

6. **fancy:** imaginative idea.

84   *The Short Story*

"It's a circle round the box the olla stands on," said Crescent. "Edwin spends about his whole time there. While we're waiting for the bus anyway."

"Crescent," asked Mr. Delahanty, "what is this mush pot?"

"It's prison," said Cress, surprise in her voice. "It's where the prisoners are kept. Only at school we always call it the mush pot."

"Is this a game?" asked Mr. Delahanty.

"It's dare base," said Crescent. "Didn't you ever play it? You choose up sides. You draw two lines and one side stands in the middle and tries to catch the other side as they run 3 by. Nobody ever chooses Edwin. The last captain to choose just gets him. Because he can't help himself. They call him the handicap. He gets caught first thing and spends the whole game in the mush pot because nobody will waste any time trying to rescue him. He'd just get caught again, they say, and the whole game would be nothing but rescue Edwin."

"How do you rescue anyone, Cress?" asked her father.

"Run from home base to the mush pot without being caught. Then take the prisoner's hand. Then he goes free."

"Were you trying to rescue Edwin, Cress?"

Cress didn't answer her father at once. Fi- 4 nally she said, "It was my duty. I chose him for our side. I chose him first of all and didn't wait just to get him. So it was my duty to rescue him. Only I ran too hard and couldn't stop. And the olla fell down on top of him and knocked his teeth out. And humiliated him. But he was free," she said. "I got there without being caught."

Mrs. Delahanty spoke with a great surge of warmth and anger. "Humiliated him! When you were only trying to help him. Trying to rescue him. And you were black-and-blue for days yourself! What gratitude."

Cress said, "But he didn't want to be res-

GUIDED READING

LITERAL QUESTIONS

1a. What was Cress trying to do when she knocked Edwin down? What did she succeed in doing? (rescue him; humiliate him)

2a. When is the first time Mrs. Delahanty speaks on this page? (In the last paragraph she speaks out in defense of Cress.)

INFERENTIAL QUESTIONS

1b. How do you think Cress feels about what happened? (sorry that her attempt to help made Edwin feel worse)

2b. Why do you think Mrs. Delahanty keeps quiet so long? (She probably wants to understand all that Cress is feeling about Edwin.)

cued, Mother. Not by me anyway. He said he liked being in the mush pot. He said . . . he got there on purpose . . . to observe. He gave me back the feathers I'd found for him. One was a road-runner feather. The only one he had."

"Well, you can start a feather collection of your own," said Mrs. Delahanty with energy. "I often see feathers when I'm walking through the orchard. After this I'll save them for you."

"I'm not interested in feathers," said Cress. Then she added, "I can get two bits an hour anytime suckering trees[7] for Mr. Hudson or cleaning blackboards at school. That would be two fifty a week at least. Plus the twelve seventy-five. How much do you suppose his teeth will be?"

"Cress," said her father, "you surely aren't going to let the Kibblers go on thinking you knocked their son down on purpose, are you? Do you want Edwin to think that?"

---

7. **suckering trees:** removing buds from trees.

"Edwin doesn't really think that," Cress said. "He knows I was rescuing him. But now I've apologized—and if we pay for the new teeth and everything, maybe after a while he'll believe it."

She stood up and walked to the hall doorway. "I'm awfully tired," she said. "I guess I'll go to bed."

"But Cress," asked Mrs. Delahanty, "why do you want him to believe it? When it isn't true?"

Cress was already through the door, but she turned back to explain. "You don't knock people down you are sorry for," she said.

After Cress had gone upstairs Mrs. Delahanty said, "Well, John, you were right, of course."

"Right?" asked Mr. Delahanty, again forgetful.

"About Cress's being interested in the boys."

"Yes," said Mr. Delahanty. "Yes, I'm afraid I was."

STUDY QUESTIONS

Recalling

1. According to Edwin and his mother, what did Cress do to Edwin?
2. List two ways in which Cress tries to make up for Edwin's injury.
3. What explanation does Cress give her parents?
4. Why does Cress want Edwin to believe that she knocked him down on purpose?

Interpreting

5. Why do you think Cress feels sorry for Edwin?
6. What does Cress mean when she says, "You don't knock people down you are sorry for"?

Extending

7. What we think about ourselves is more important than what others think of us. Use the story as an example to explain this opinion.

READING AND LITERARY FOCUS

Characterization

The term *characterization* has two meanings in literature. First, **characterization** is the personality of a character; second, it is the way in which an author shows that personality. An author may make direct statements about a character. For example, in "Then He Goes Free" West tells us directly that Edwin has "an unhappiness all of his own."

Then He Goes Free 85

1. Possible answers: Mr. Delahanty sits "legs extended, head back, as straight and unrelaxed as a plank"; Mrs. Delahanty "spoke more sharply than she intended" and was "unwilling to take one step toward meeting her visitors"; both look forward to the trips to town.

2. Possible answers:
   ■ apologizes and offers to help pay for Edwin's teeth; shows she is direct, self-assured, and wants to help him
   ■ refuses to go to the show and tells her parents how she will raise money for Edwin's teeth; shows she takes responsibility

VOCABULARY

1. (a) stroll
2. (c) short trip
3. (a) main point
4. (a) drenched
5. (b) become smaller

COMPARING STORIES

1. ■ "The Osage Orange Tree": Evangeline buys a newspaper so the paper boy will visit daily.
   ■ "A Game of Catch": Scho hurts himself and irritates Monk and Glennie getting their attention
   ■ "Then He Goes Free": Edwin pretends to like being a tag prisoner and not want rescuing.
   ■ Answers will vary. Scho and Edwin keep their pride for less.

2. ■ "Thank You M'am": Mrs. Jones is courageous, tough, generous, and caring. Her honesty and solution to the boy's desire for suede shoes are disarming.
   ■ "The Osage Orange Tree": Evangeline's shyness and willingness to sacrifice for companionship; and the boy's lack of confidence, awkwardness, awareness of nature and Evangeline's appearance are appealing.

An author may also reveal a character's personality indirectly by reporting (1) the character's appearance, (2) the character's words and actions, and (3) the comments that others make about the character. For example, Edwin's appearance shows that he is quiet and sickly: He is "thin as his mother, as mild and soft-looking as his father." Edwin's words show that he does not want anyone to feel sorry for him: He says that Cress pushed him over "on purpose" and "for fun." His actions show his shyness: He stares quietly at the floor. Finally, what Cress says about Edwin shows that he is not athletic but is smart: "He isn't even any of a baseball player. But he could be a baseball authority."

Thinking About Characterization

1. Find an example of what the author says directly about Mr. Delahanty. About Mrs. Delahanty.
2. Find something Cress says and something she does. Tell what we learn about her from each example.
3. Name two things we learn about Cress from what her parents say about her.

VOCABULARY

Context Clues

Sometimes we can learn the meaning of a word by studying its **context,** or the words around it. For example, the following passage is from "Then He Goes Free":

Why, Cress is too *tenderhearted* to hurt a fly. She shoos them outside instead of killing them.

Cress is *tenderhearted.* As a result, she does not hurt flies but shoos them outside instead. *Tenderhearted* must mean "sympathetic."

The following sentences are from "Then He Goes Free." Choose the best meaning for each italicized word by studying its *context.* That is, study the ideas found in the sentence in which the

■ "A Game of Catch": Scho's desire for acceptance, denial of helplessness, and assertion he controls those who exclude him is typical. He is plucky.

word appears. Write the number of each item and the letter of your choice on a separate sheet.

1. It was pleasant simply to *saunter* along the sidewalks looking at the cars, the merchandise, the people in their town clothes.
   (a) stroll   (c) argue
   (b) crawl   (d) litter

2. This Saturday trip to town was a *jaunt* they both looked forward to during the week.
   (a) problem   (c) short trip
   (b) dumpy house   (d) long journey

3. "I don't care about the *gist* of it. That's just what you think she said. I want to know what she really said."
   (a) main point   (c) end
   (b) beginning   (d) happy event

4. "To say nothing of his being *doused* with water on a cold day."
   (a) drenched   (c) boiled
   (b) stuffed   (d) dried

5. Edwin's head went even nearer the floor—as if the spot he was watching had *diminished* or retreated.
   (a) exploded   (c) grown larger
   (b) become smaller (d) doubled

COMPARING STORIES

1. Compare two or more of the following stories: "The Osage Orange Tree," "A Game of Catch," and "Then He Goes Free." For each story name a young person who does not have many friends. Tell how each character behaves as a result of this problem. Which character seems to have a more sensible way of reacting to the problem?

2. Compare two or more of the following stories: "Thank You, M'am," "The Osage Orange Tree," and "A Game of Catch." Choose one character from each story. Which character seems more likable? Why? Give at least one action by each character to support your opinion.

SETTING

Arthur C. Clarke (born 1917) is a writer of science fiction, stories that take place in the future and are based on scientific discoveries. Clarke was born in England. He studied physics, the science of matter and energy. One of his stories is the basis for the film *2001: A Space Odyssey.* "Crime on Mars" is a science-fiction detective story.

■ What details in the story tell you what Mars is like?

Arthur C. Clarke

Crime on Mars

1 "We don't have much crime on Mars," said Detective-Inspector Rawlings, a little sadly. "In fact, that's the chief reason I'm going back to the Yard.[1] If I stayed here much longer, I'd get completely out of practice."

We were sitting in the main observation lounge of the Phobos Spaceport, looking out across the jagged sun-drenched crags of the tiny moon. The ferry rocket that had brought us up from Mars had left ten minutes ago and was now beginning the long fall back to the ocher-tinted globe hanging there against the stars. In half an hour we would be boarding the liner for Earth—a world on which most of the passengers had never set foot, but which they still called "home."

"At the same time," continued the Inspec- **2** tor, "now and then there's a case that makes life interesting. You're an art dealer, Mr. Maccar; I'm sure you heard about that spot of

bother at Meridian City a couple of months ago."

3 "I don't think so," replied the plump, olive-skinned little man I'd taken for just another returning tourist. Presumably the Inspector had already checked through the passenger list; I wondered how much he knew about me, and tried to reassure myself that my conscience was—well, reasonably clear. After all, everybody took *something* out through Martian Customs—

"It's been rather well hushed up," said the Inspector, "but you can't keep these things quiet for long. Anyway, a jewel thief from Earth tried to steal Meridian Museum's greatest treasure—the Siren Goddess."

"But that's absurd!" I objected. "It's priceless, of course—but it's only a lump of sandstone. You couldn't sell it to anyone—you might just as well steal the Mona Lisa."[2]

---

1. **Yard:** Scotland Yard, headquarters of the London police.

2. **Mona Lisa** [mō′nə lē′zə]: priceless portrait by Italian painter Leonardo da Vinci (1452–1519).

Crime on Mars 87

GUIDED READING

LITERAL QUESTION

1a. Who does Detective-Inspector Rawlings first address when he starts to tell about the attempted theft? (Mr. Maccar)

INFERENTIAL QUESTION

1b. Why do you think the Inspector addresses Maccar first? (Since the attempted theft was from a museum, he assumes the art dealer will be interested.)

- The Inspector states that someone paid Danny Weaver to commit the crime.
- Weaver planned the theft for Sunday, when Martian cities are dead.
- The city, Meridian, stands in two hemispheres.

1 PLOT: SUSPENSE

Two details increase the suspense in the story: that Weaver was paid to steal the goddess, and that he would have succeeded but for "fantastically bad luck."

2 PLOT: FORESHADOWING

The prevalence of replicas of the goddess foreshadows an important element of the thief's plan.

3 PLOT: RISING ACTION

The thief's plan revolves around the fact that the colonists in the Martian community stay at home on Sundays.

4 SETTING

In an offhand way the Inspector mentions another aspect of the setting. The city is on the line between two hemispheres. This fact will prove critical to the outcome of the crime.

The Inspector grinned, rather mirthlessly. "*That's* happened too," he said. "Maybe the motive was the same. There are collectors who would give a fortune for such an object, even if they could only look at it themselves. Don't you agree, Mr. Maccar?"

"That's perfectly true," said the art dealer. "In my business you meet all sorts of crazy people."

1 "Well, this chappie—name's Danny Weaver— had been well paid by one of them. And if it hadn't been for a piece of fantastically bad luck, he might have brought it off."

The Spaceport P.A. system apologized for a further slight delay owing to final fuel checks, and asked a number of passengers to report to Information. While we were waiting for the announcement to finish, I recalled what little I knew about the Siren Goddess.

2 Although I'd never seen the original, like most other departing tourists I had a replica in my baggage. It bore the certificate of the Mars Bureau of Antiquities, guaranteeing that "this full-scale reproduction is an exact copy of the so-called Siren Goddess, discovered in the Mare Sirenium by the Third Expedition, A.D 2012 (A.M. 23)."

It's quite a tiny thing to have caused so much controversy. Only eight or nine inches high—you wouldn't look at it twice if you saw it in a museum on Earth. The head of a young woman, with slightly oriental features, elongated earlobes, hair curled in tight ringlets close to the scalp, lips half parted in an expression of pleasure or surprise—and that's all.

But it's an enigma[3] so baffling that it has inspired a hundred religious sects,[4] and driven quite a few archeologists[5] out of their minds. For a perfectly human head has no right whatsoever to be found on Mars, whose only intelligent inhabitants were crustaceans[6]—"educated lobsters," as the newspapers are fond of calling them. The aboriginal[7] Martians never came near to achieving space flight, and in any event, their civilization died before men existed on Earth.

No wonder the Goddess is the Solar System's Number One mystery. I don't suppose we'll find the answer in my lifetime—if we ever do.

3 "Danny's plan was beautifully simple," continued the Inspector. "You know how absolutely dead a Martian city gets on Sunday, when everything closes down and the colonists stay home to watch the TV from Earth. Danny was counting on this when he checked into the hotel in Meridian West, late Friday afternoon. He'd have Saturday for reconnoitering[8] the museum, and undisturbed Sunday for the job itself, and on Monday morning he'd be just another tourist leaving town. . . .

4 "Early Saturday he strolled through the little park and crossed over into Meridian East, where the museum stands. In case you don't know, the city gets its name because it's exactly on longitude one-eighty degrees; there's a big stone slab in the park with the Prime Meridian engraved on it, so that visitors can get themselves photographed standing in two hemispheres at once. Amazing what simple things amuse some people.

"Danny spent the day going over the museum, exactly like any other tourist determined to get his money's worth. But at closing

---

3. **enigma** [i nig′mə]: mystery.
4. **sects:** groups of people who have the same beliefs.
5. **archeologists** [är′kē ol′ə jists]: scientists who study the remains of earlier civilizations.

6. **crustaceans** [krus tā′shənz]: water creatures with shells, such as crabs, lobsters, and shrimp.
7. **aboriginal** [ab′ə rij′ən əl]: earliest inhabitants of a place.
8. **reconnoitering** [rē′kə noi′tər ing]: exploring, inspecting.

GUIDED READING

LITERAL QUESTION

1a. What is the narrator carrying in his baggage? (a replica of the Siren Goddess)

INFERENTIAL QUESTION

1b. How might such a replica be used in a plot to steal the original Goddess? (A replica could be substituted for the statue; also, the thief could claim that the real statue he is carrying is only a replica.)

time he didn't leave; he'd holed up in one of the galleries not open to the public, where the museum had been arranging a Late Canal Period reconstruction but had run out of money before the job could be finished. He stayed there until about midnight, just in case there were any enthusiastic researchers still in the building. Then he emerged and got to work."

"Just a moment," I interrupted. "What about the night watchman?"

"My dear chap! They don't have such luxuries on Mars. There weren't even any burglar alarms, for who would bother to steal lumps of stone? True, the Goddess was sealed up neatly in a strong glass-and-metal cabinet, just in case some souvenir hunter took a fancy to her. But even if she were stolen there was nowhere the thief could hide, and of course all outgoing traffic would be searched as soon as the statue was missed."

That was true enough. I'd been thinking 1 in terms of Earth, forgetting that every city on Mars is a closed little world of its own beneath the force-field that protects it from the freezing near-vacuum. Beyond those electronic shields is the utterly hostile emptiness of the Martian Outback, where a man will die in seconds without protection. That makes law enforcement very easy; no wonder there's so little crime on Mars. . . .

"Danny had a beautiful set of tools, as specialized as a watchmaker's. The main item was a microsaw no bigger than a soldering iron; it had a wafer-thin blade, driven at a million cycles a second by an ultrasonic power pack. It would go through glass or metal like butter—and leave a cut only about as thick as a hair. Which was very important for Danny, as he could not leave any traces of his handiwork.

"I suppose you've guessed how he intended to operate. He was going to cut through the base of the cabinet and substitute one of those souvenir replicas for the genuine Goddess. It might be a couple of years before some inquisitive expert discovered the awful truth, and long before then the original would have been taken to Earth, perfectly disguised as a copy of itself. Pretty neat, eh?

"It must have been a weird business, working in that darkened gallery with all those million-year-old carvings and unexplainable artifacts around him. A museum on Earth is bad enough at night, but at least it's—well, *human*. And Gallery Three, which houses the Goddess, is particularly unsettling. It's full of 2 bas-reliefs[9] showing quite incredible animals fighting each other; they look rather like giant beetles, and most paleontologists[10] flatly deny that they could ever have existed. But imaginary or not, they belonged to this world, and they didn't disturb Danny as much as the Goddess, staring at him across the ages and defying him to explain her presence here. She gave him the creeps. How do I know? He told me.

3 "Danny set to work on that cabinet as carefully as any diamond cutter preparing to cleave a gem. It took most of the night to slice out the trapdoor, and it was nearly dawn when he relaxed and put down the saw. There was still a lot of work to do, but the hardest part was over. Putting the replica into the case, checking its appearance against the photos he'd thoughtfully brought with him, and covering up his traces might take a good part of Sunday, but that didn't worry him in the least. He had another twenty-four hours, and would positively welcome Monday's first visitors so that he could mingle with them and make his inconspicuous exit.

---

9. **bas-reliefs** [bä′ri lēfs′]: carvings made on a flat surface, such as a wall.
10. **paleontologists** [pā′lē on tol′ə jists]: scientists who study ancient forms of life.

Crime on Mars 89

- The Inspector explains that Danny hid in the museum one Saturday night.
- He took his time to cut through the display case, expecting that he would have all of Sunday to finish the job.

1 SETTING

The hostile environment of Mars discourages crime, so there are no watchmen or burglar alarms in Martian communities, a fact that makes the thief's job easier.

2 MOOD

The Inspector's description of the bizarre exhibits in the gallery creates an eerie, unsettling mood.

3 PLOT: SUSPENSE

The Inspector clearly admires the thief's skill, planning, and persistence. Suspense increases as we wonder what could possibly have gone wrong: What was the bad luck that ruined the scheme?

GUIDED READING

LITERAL QUESTIONS

1a. What details of the thief's tools and procedure does the Inspector relate? (The tools were beautiful, specialized, and modern; the thief's work was painstaking.)

2a. Who asks the Inspector a question about the night watchman? (the narrator)

INFERENTIAL QUESTIONS

1b. Why do you think the Inspector describes the theft in such detail? (He may want to build suspense, to make his listeners appreciate how well the crime was carried out.)

2b. Why do you think the narrator asks questions, and why does the art dealer remain silent? (The narrator is obviously curious about the crime. Answers about the art dealer will vary: Some students may be suspicious of him.)

"It was a perfectly horrible shock to his nervous system, therefore, when the main doors were noisily unbarred at eight thirty and the museum staff—all six of them—started to open up for the day. Danny bolted for the emergency exit, leaving everything behind—tools, Goddesses, the lot.

"He had another big surprise when he found himself in the street: it should have been completely deserted at this time of day, with everyone at home reading the Sunday papers. But here were the citizens of Meridian East, as large as life, heading for plant or office on what was obviously a normal working day.

"By the time poor Danny got back to his hotel we were waiting for him. We couldn't claim much credit for deducing that only a visitor from Earth—and a very recent one at that—could have overlooked Meridian City's chief claim to fame. And I presume you know what *that* is."

"Frankly, I don't," I answered. "You can't see much of Mars in six weeks, and I never went east of the Syrtis Major."

"Well, it's absurdly simple, but we shouldn't be too hard on Danny—even the locals occasionally fall into the same trap. It's something that doesn't bother us on Earth, where we've been able to dump the problem in the Pacific Ocean. But Mars, of course, is all dry land; and that means that *somebody* is forced to live with the International Date Line.[11] . . .

"Danny, you see, had planned the job from Meridian West. It was Sunday over there all right—and it was still Sunday there when we picked him up at the hotel. But over in Merid-

---

11. **International Date Line:** imaginary north-south line that marks the beginning of time zones, each of which is an hour later than the next. When it is Saturday on one side of the International Date Line, it is Sunday on the other side.

ian East, half a mile away, it was only Saturday. That little trip across the park had made all the difference! I told you it was rotten luck."

There was a long moment of silent sympathy, then I asked, "What did he get?"

"Three years," said Inspector Rawlings.

"That doesn't seem very much."

"Mars years—that makes it almost six of ours. And a whopping fine which, by an odd coincidence, came to exactly the refund value of his return ticket to Earth. He isn't in jail, of course—Mars can't afford that kind of nonproductive luxury. Danny has to work for a living, under discreet surveillance. I told you that the Meridian Museum couldn't afford a night watchman. Well, it has one now. Guess who?"

"All passengers prepare to board in ten minutes! Please collect your hand baggage!" ordered the loudspeakers.

As we started to move toward the airlock, I couldn't help asking one more question.

"What about the people who put Danny up to it? There must have been a lot of money behind him. Did you get them?"

"Not yet; they'd covered their tracks pretty thoroughly, and I believe Danny was telling the truth when he said he couldn't give us a lead. Still, it's not my case. As I told you, I'm going back to my old job at the Yard. But a policeman always keeps his eyes open—like an art dealer, eh, Mr. Maccar? Why, you look a bit green about the gills. Have one of my space-sickness tablets."

"No, thank you," answered Mr. Maccar, "I'm quite all right."

His tone was distinctly unfriendly; the social temperature seemed to have dropped below zero in the last few minutes. I looked at Mr. Maccar, and I looked at the Inspector. And suddenly I realized that we were going to have a very interesting trip.

Crime on Mars 91

---

1. Rawlings—a detective-inspector; Mr. Maccar—an art dealer; in a spaceport on Mars
2. a small sandstone head of a young woman with slightly Oriental features; because a replica of a human head is on Mars
3. Friday, check into hotel; Saturday, reconnoiter museum; Sunday, steal statue; Monday, leave town
4. Time is one day ahead of what he thought it was. He is interrupted by museum staff when they come to work that Monday.
5. unknown even to Danny; looks sick
6. He thinks Mr. Maccar is suspect.
7. *fact:* airport details, human interactions, techniques of thieves and detectives; *fantasy:* cultural life of knowledgeable crustaceans, Martian environment
8. Answers will vary. Possible answers: *Fantastic:* It might give readers nothing to relate to. *Realistic:* It might work if writer were knowledgeable and manipulated plot imaginatively.

READING AND LITERARY FOCUS

1. Phobos Spaceport; city of Meridian, primarily at the museum
2. Each city is isolated from the next under force-field protecting it from a freezing near-vacuum, where unprotected humans die in seconds; isolation limits crime
3. a strange and mysterious one

CHALLENGE

Students should
- create a collage which could be used as an ad for vacations to Mars
- create an alluring image of Mars

STUDY QUESTIONS

Recalling

1. What are the names and occupations of the two men to whom the storyteller is speaking? Where are they talking?
2. Describe the Siren Goddess. Why is it a mystery?
3. What is Danny Weaver's plan for each day of his weekend on Mars?
4. What is the error in Danny's plan? Tell how he is caught.
5. At the end of the story, what does the inspector say about the people who hired Danny? What is Mr. Maccar's reaction?

Interpreting

6. At the end of the story, why does the storyteller think they will have an interesting trip?
7. What parts of this story seem based on scientific fact? What parts are fantasy?

Extending

8. Do you think science fiction should be completely fantastic or more realistic? Why?

READING AND LITERARY FOCUS

Setting

Setting is the place and time in which a story happens. Setting can include place, climate, historical period, and time of year and day. For example, "Then He Goes Free" (page 78) is set in California in modern times. It takes place in a ranch house on a warm evening in February.

Setting often creates an **atmosphere,** or mood, that runs through an entire story. Atmosphere can make a story seem cheerful, sad, gloomy, or mysterious. For example, in "Then He Goes Free" the uncomfortable warmth and the growing darkness create a mood of sadness. This mood is fitting to Cress's unhappiness at hurting a friend.

When we read a story we should try to picture the setting. This mental picture puts us into the proper mood for the story. For example, in "Then He Goes Free" we feel Cress's sadness. As a result, we feel that we are part of the story.

Thinking About Setting

1. Name two different places in which the events of "Crime on Mars" take place.
2. Tell how the climate on Mars affects the amount of crime there.
3. Reread the description of Gallery Three. The paragraph begins, "It must have been a weird business. . . ." What is the atmosphere?

COMPOSITION

Writing About Setting

■ Write an essay about the importance of setting in "Crime on Mars." First describe Mars as it is in the story. Then tell why the story could take place only on another planet like Mars.

Describing a Setting

■ In "Crime on Mars" each city on the planet is surrounded by "the utterly hostile emptiness of the Martian Outback." Write a description of what you imagine that dangerous wilderness to be like. First tell what the area looks like. Second describe conditions of climate. Then tell why the area is very dangerous.

CHALLENGE

Collage

■ A **collage** is a picture made from assembling scraps of materials (magazine pictures, paint, cloth, colored paper, and so on). Imagine an advertisement for vacations on Mars. Create a collage that shows what vacations on Mars might look like. You may want to take one or more of the following scenes from "Crime on Mars": a spaceport, the park at the meridian, the art museum, the outback.

COMPOSITION: GUIDELINES FOR EVALUATION

WRITING ABOUT SETTING

Objective
To analyze importance of setting in story

Guidelines for Evaluation
- suggested length: two paragraphs
- should describe Mars as in story
- should tell why story could take place only on another planet like Mars

DESCRIBING A SETTING

Objective
To write a description of the Martian Outback

Guidelines for Evaluation
- suggested length: two or three paragraphs
- should imaginatively describe the Martian outback and its climactic conditions
- should explain why area is very dangerous
- should use vivid details

Juan A. A. Sedillo (1902–1982) was born in New Mexico. He worked as a lawyer and held public office. He wrote about Mexico and the southwestern United States. The following story is based on an actual legal case.

■ As you read the story, decide what gives the land its great value for the people of Río en Medio.

Juan A. A. Sedillo

Gentleman of Río en Medio[1]

It took months of negotiation to come to an understanding with the old man. He was in no hurry. What he had the most of was time. He lived up in Río en Medio, where his people had been for hundreds of years. He tilled the same land they had tilled. His house was small and wretched, but quaint. The little creek ran through his land. His orchard was gnarled and beautiful.

The day of the sale he came into the office. His coat was old, green and faded. I thought of Senator Catron,[2] who has been such a power with these people up there in the mountains. Perhaps it was one of his old Prince Alberts.[3] He also wore gloves. They were old and torn and his fingertips showed through them. He carried a cane, but it was only the skeleton of a worn-out umbrella. Behind him walked one of his innumerable kin—a dark young man with eyes like a gazelle.

The old man bowed to all of us in the room. Then he removed his hat and gloves, slowly and carefully, Chaplin[4] once did that in a picture, in a bank—he was the janitor. Then he handed his things to the boy, who stood obediently behind the old man's chair.

There was a great deal of conversation about rain and about his family. He was very proud of his large family. Finally we got down to business. Yes, he would sell, as he had agreed, for twelve hundred dollars, in cash. We would buy, and the money was ready. "Don[5] Anselmo," I said to him in Spanish, "we

---

1. **Río en Medio** [rē´ō en mä´dē ō]
2. **Senator Catron** [ka´trən]: Thomas Benton Catron, Senator from New Mexico, 1912–1917.
3. **Prince Alberts:** long, double-breasted coats.

4. **Chaplin:** Charlie Chaplin (1889–1977), silent film comedian.
5. **Don:** Spanish title of respect, much like *Sir* in English.

Gentleman of Río en Medio   93

AT A GLANCE

■ Don Anselmo's people have lived in Río en Medio in rural New Mexico for centuries.
■ He comes to the office to conclude a sale of his property.

LITERARY OPTIONS

■ setting
■ characterization
■ point of view

THEMATIC OPTIONS

■ family life
■ communities
■ traditions

1 SETTING

We can infer that the old man loves his land because it has been part of his family for "hundreds of years." We can also infer that the beauty of the land is what makes it attractive to potential buyers.

2 CHARACTERIZATION

Don Anselmo's faded but formal clothes indicate that he is poor but dignified and that he has his own sense of what is correct dress and behavior for important occasions.

3 POINT OF VIEW

The reference to silent film comedian Charlie Chaplin suggests that the first-person narrator finds the old man's formality touching and perhaps slightly comic.

TEXAS ESSENTIAL ELEMENTS GRADE 8

3A plot and character development
3C setting and mood
3D literary genres
4B implied main idea
4F point of view
4I use of parts of a book
To locate treatment of an Element, see *Texas Teacher's Resources*.

GUIDED READING

LITERAL QUESTION

1a. What does Don Anselmo talk about when he first comes to the office? (the weather and his family)

INFERENTIAL QUESTION

1b. How is Don Anselmo's approach to the meeting different from the narrator's? (The narrator is businesslike; Don Anselmo wants to talk about other matters. Perhaps Don Anselmo is uncomfortable about the sale.)

AT A GLANCE

- The narrator tells Don Anselmo that he owns more land than he thought. The Americans are willing to pay double what they offered.
- Don Anselmo feels insulted.

1 THEME

Don Anselmo's unexpected reaction ("Friend, I do not like you to speak to me in that manner") reveals that Don Anselmo and the narrator come from different communities with very different attitudes and traditions.

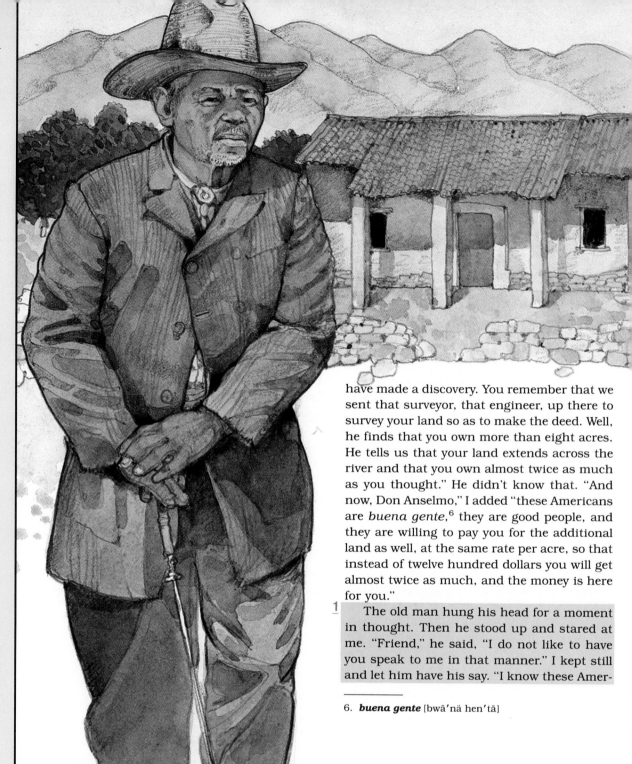

have made a discovery. You remember that we sent that surveyor, that engineer, up there to survey your land so as to make the deed. Well, he finds that you own more than eight acres. He tells us that your land extends across the river and that you own almost twice as much as you thought." He didn't know that. "And now, Don Anselmo," I added "these Americans are *buena gente*,[6] they are good people, and they are willing to pay you for the additional land as well, at the same rate per acre, so that instead of twelve hundred dollars you will get almost twice as much, and the money is here for you."

The old man hung his head for a moment in thought. Then he stood up and stared at me. "Friend," he said, "I do not like to have you speak to me in that manner." I kept still and let him have his say. "I know these Amer-

6. *buena gente* [bwā′nä hen′tä]

GUIDED READING

LITERAL QUESTION

1a. What does the narrator tell Don Anselmo about his land? (that he owns twice as much as he'd thought and that the Americans are willing to buy all of it)

INFERENTIAL QUESTION

1b. Why is Don Anselmo's reaction to this news surprising? (He seems insulted, and most people would probably be pleased that they are getting more money.)

1 icans are good people, and that is why I have agreed to sell to them. But I do not care to be insulted. I have agreed to sell my house and land for twelve hundred dollars and that is the price."

I argued with him but it was useless. Finally he signed the deed and took the money but refused to take more than the amount agreed upon. Then he shook hands all around, put on his ragged gloves, took his stick and walked out with the boy behind him.

A month later my friends had moved into Río en Medio. They had replastered the old adobe house, pruned the trees, patched the fence and moved in for the summer. One day they came back to the office to complain. The children of the village were overrunning their property. They came every day and played under the trees, built little play fences around them, and took blossoms. When they were spoken to, they only laughed and talked back good-naturedly in Spanish.

2 I sent a messenger up to the mountains for Don Anselmo. It took a week to arrange another meeting. When he arrived he repeated his previous preliminary performance. He wore the same faded cutaway,[7] carried the same stick and was accompanied by the boy again. He shook hands all around, sat down with the boy behind his chair, and talked about the weather. Finally I broached the subject. "Don Anselmo, about the ranch you sold to these people. They are good people and want to be your friends and neighbors always. When you sold to them you signed a document, a deed, and in that deed you agreed to several things. One thing was that they were to have the complete possession of the property. Now, Don Anselmo, it seems that every

---

7. **cutaway:** man's formal coat.

day the children of the village overrun the orchard and spend most of their time there. We would like to know if you, as the most respected man in the village, could not stop them from doing so in order that these people may enjoy their new home more in peace."

Don Anselmo stood up. "We have all learned to love these Americans," he said, "because they are good people and good neighbors. I sold them my property because I knew they were good people, but I did not sell them the trees in the orchard."

This was bad. "Don Anselmo," I pleaded, "when one signs a deed and sells real property one sells also everything that grows on the land, and those trees, every one of them, are on the land and inside the boundaries of what you sold."

"Yes, I admit that," he said. "You know," he added, "I am the oldest man in the village. Almost everyone there is my relative and all the children of Río en Medio are my *sobrinos* and *nietos*,[8] my descendants. Every time a child has been born in Río en Medio since I took possession of that house from my mother I have planted a tree for that child. The trees in that orchard are not mine, *señor*, they belong to the children of the village. Every person in Río en Medio born since the railroad came to Santa Fe owns a tree in that orchard. I did not sell the trees because I could not. They are not mine."

3 There was nothing we could do. Legally we owned the trees but the old man had been so generous, refusing what amounted to a fortune for him. It took most of the following winter to buy the trees, individually, from the descendants of Don Anselmo in the valley of Río en Medio.

---

8. *sobrinos* [sō brē′nōs] **and** *nietos* [nyä′tōs]: Spanish for "nieces and nephews" and "grandchildren."

Gentleman of Río en Medio 95

- Don Anselmo will not take more than the first-agreed price.
- The buyers complain that children play in the orchard.
- Don Anselmo explains that those trees belong to the children.
- The buyers must buy the trees individually from the children.

1 **CHARACTERIZATION**

Sedillo reveals Don Anselmo to be a proud man with his own set of standards.

2 **SETTING**

From the narrator's explanation of the difficulties in setting up a meeting with Don Anselmo, we can infer how isolated and primitive the setting is.

3 **THEME**

Sedillo touches on the themes of family life, communities, and traditions by revealing the community of Río en Medio to be one big family, bound together by the orchard.

REFLECTING ON THE STORY

How do Don Anselmo and the new buyers differ in the way they regard their property? (To the Americans the land is probably just real estate; to Don Anselmo it represents centuries of family tradition.)

GUIDED READING

LITERAL QUESTIONS

1a. What does Don Anselmo do every time a child is born in the village? (plants a tree for the child)

2a. According to Don Anselmo, whom do the trees belong to? (his individual descendants)

INFERENTIAL QUESTIONS

1b. Why do you think Don Anselmo does this? (He wants every child to have a sense of community and a share in the land.)

2b. Why do you think Don Anselmo didn't tell the narrator about the trees before the sale? (Answers will vary. Possible answers: He assumed the narrator understood about the trees; he realized the new owners would find out soon enough and could pay then.)

1. He wears old, faded green coat and old gloves, carries skeleton of umbrella as cane; bows and carefully removes hat and gloves, speaks cordially.
2. He discovers Don Anselmo owns almost twice as much land as he thought; insulted, he insists on adhering to original deal.
3. Village children play on their property. Children are his relatives; he planted a tree when each was born. He can't sell the trees because they belong to the children.
4. Americans buy trees individually from Don Anselmo's descendants.
5. He is poor but dignified and courteous.
6. Answers will vary. Most will agree that Don Anselmo has made an agreement and wants to keep his word; also, people are more important to him than money.
7. It doesn't matter to him how much land he owns or what its monetary value is. Land's real value is the fact that it can sometimes hold families together.

READING AND LITERARY FOCUS

The land is beautiful with its old gnarled orchard, its running creek, and the quaint old house.

VOCABULARY

1. *Negotiation:* discussion in order to come to an agreement
2. No, many *wretched* things are merely poor and are not also *quaint,* or charming.
3. *Preliminary:* word or action serving as introduction to main event

STUDY QUESTIONS

Recalling

1. List at least three details of Don Anselmo's appearance or manners.
2. In the beginning of the story, why does the storyteller offer Don Anselmo more money? What is Don Anselmo's reaction?
3. Why do the Americans complain to the storyteller about their new land? What is Don Anselmo's explanation for the problem?
4. In what way is the problem with the ownership of the trees solved?

Interpreting

5. What do we learn about Don Anselmo from his appearance and manners?
6. Why do you think Don Anselmo reacts as he does to the offer of more money?
7. What do you think is Don Anslemo's attitude toward land?

READING AND LITERARY FOCUS

Making Inferences from Details of Setting

Because of their limited length, many stories contain only a few details of setting. However, we can use the hints contained in these details to imagine a whole world. To do so, we must make inferences. An **inference** is a conclusion that we draw from the information we have. For example, we see a house with a beautiful, well-kept garden. Inside the fence we find toys and a playful dog. We can infer that the house is warm and comfortable and that a happy, loving family lives there.

Details of setting help us to picture the place and time in which a story happens. This mental picture allows us to enter the world of a story. Therefore, we should notice details of setting in order to enjoy a story more. For example, the spaceport in "Crime on Mars" has a public address system over which announcements are made. From this detail we can infer that a Martian space-

port might look and sound much like an airport or a train station of today.

Thinking About Making Inferences

■ Study the details of setting in the first paragraph of "Gentleman of Río en Medio." What can you infer from these details about why the Americans want to buy Don Anselmo's land?

VOCABULARY

Using a Glossary

A **glossary** is an alphabetical list of words. It is usually found at the end of a textbook and gives information about words that appear in the book. Like a dictionary, a glossary gives the definitions, or meanings, of the words. Many glossaries also provide help with pronunciation and note the part of speech. **Pronunciation,** the way a word is spoken, usually follows the word. The letters used in the pronunciation are called a **phonetic alphabet.** Many glossaries have **pronunciation keys** to explain the sounds of these letters. The **part of speech** tells how a word is used in a sentence. The abbreviation for a word's part of speech is often given after the pronunciation.

Unlike a dictionary, a glossary includes only words that are found within the textbook. The words are often special words that are related to the subject of the book. For example, the glossary in a biology textbook lists scientific terms. The Glossary at the back of this book lists words from the literature selections. Many words have more than one meaning. The words in this Glossary are defined as they are used in the literature.

The italicized words in the following questions are from "Gentleman of Río en Medio." Use the Glossary at the back of this book to answer the questions.

1. What is the meaning of *negotiation*?
2. Are all *wretched* houses *quaint*?
3. What is the meaning of *preliminary*?

Mark Twain (1835–1910) is one of America's greatest writers. He was born Samuel Clemens near Hannibal, Missouri. His famous works include *The Prince and the Pauper, A Connecticut Yankee in King Arthur's Court, The Adventures of Tom Sawyer,* and *The Adventures of Huckleberry Finn.*

■ What do you think makes "Jim Baker's Blue-jay Yarn" hard to believe? Why do you think so many people consider the yarn funny?

Mark Twain

Jim Baker's Blue-jay Yarn

1   Animals talk to each other, of course. There can be no question about that; but I suppose there are very few people who can understand them. I never knew but one man who could. I knew he could, however, because he told me so himself. He was a middle-aged, 2 simple-hearted miner who had lived in a lonely corner of California, among the woods and mountains, a good many years, and had studied the ways of his only neighbors, the beasts and the birds, until he believed he could accurately translate any remark which they made. This was Jim Baker. According to Jim Baker, some animals have only a limited education, and use only very simple words, and scarcely ever a comparison or a flowery figure; whereas, certain other animals have a large vocabulary, a fine command of language and a ready and fluent delivery; consequently these latter talk a great deal; they like it; they are conscious of their talent, and they enjoy "showing off." Baker said, that after long and careful observation, he had come to the conclusion that the blue-jays were the best talkers he had found among birds and beasts. Said he:—

3   "There's more *to* a blue-jay than any other creature. He has got more moods, and more different kinds of feelings than other creatures; and mind you, whatever a blue-jay feels, he can put into language. And no mere commonplace language, either, but rattling, out-and-out book-talk—and bristling with metaphor, too—just bristling! And as for command of language—why *you* never see a blue-jay get stuck for a word. No man ever did. They just boil out of him! And another thing: I've noticed a good deal, and there's no bird, or cow, or anything that uses as good grammar as a blue-jay. You may say a cat uses good grammar. Well, a cat does—but you let a cat get excited, once; you let a cat get to pulling fur with another cat on a shed, nights, and you'll hear grammar that will give you the lockjaw.

Jim Baker's Blue-jay Yarn   97

GUIDED READING

LITERAL QUESTION

1a. What does Jim Baker say about the relative speaking abilities of the "birds and beasts"? (Some animals use simple words and little or no figurative language. Others have large vocabularies and speak fluently. Blue-jays have superior grammar.)

INFERENTIAL QUESTION

1b. From these comments, what can we infer about the world of the story? (The world of the story is whimsical, humorous, and fantastic.)

- Jim discusses blue-jay grammar.
- He begins his account of a blue-jay finding a knot-hole in a roof.
- The blue-jay is puzzled by the disappearance of an acorn into the hole.

**1 READING SKILLS:
SENTENCE STRUCTURE**

Baker uses a long, ten-line sentence to set the stage for the beginning of the yarn. Its extraordinary length builds excitement for the appearance of the blue-jay himself.

2 PERSONIFICATION

As the jay begins to talk, the author sets up a parallel between two realms of experience—the blue-jay's experience and the human's experience.

3 PLOT: CONFLICT

Baffled by the lack of the acorn's expected landing noise, the blue-jay expresses frustration, and the story's conflict begins to build.

Ignorant people think it's the *noise* which fighting cats make that is so aggravating, but it ain't so; it's the sickening grammar they use. Now I've never heard a jay use bad grammar but very seldom; and when they do, they are as ashamed as a human; they shut right down and leave.

"When I first begun to understand jay language correctly, there was a little incident happened here. Seven years ago, the last man in this region but me, moved away. There stands his house,—been empty ever since; a log house, with a plank roof—just one big room, and no more; no ceiling—nothing between the rafters[1] and the floor. Well, one Sunday morning I was sitting out here in front of my cabin, with my cat, taking the sun, and looking at the blue hills, and listening to the leaves rustling so lonely in the trees, and thinking of the home away yonder in the States, that I hadn't heard from in thirteen years, when a blue-jay lit on that house, with an acorn in his mouth, and says, 'Hello, I reckon I've struck[2] something.' When he

---

1. **rafters:** roof beams.
2. **struck:** here, discovered.

98 *The Short Story*

spoke, the acorn dropped out of his mouth and rolled down the roof, of course, but he didn't care; his mind was all on the thing he had struck. It was a knot-hole in the roof. He cocked his head to one side, shut one eye and put the other one to the hole, like a 'possum looking down a jug; then he glanced up with his bright eyes, gave a wink or two with his wings—which signifies gratification, you understand,—and says, 'It looks like a hole, it's located like a hole,—blamed if I don't believe it *is* a hole!'

"Then he cocked his head down and took another look; he glances up perfectly joyful, this time; winks his wings and his tail both, and says, 'O, no, this ain't no fat thing, I reckon! If I ain't in luck!—why it's a perfectly elegant hole!' So he flew down and got that acorn, and fetched it up and dropped it in, and was just tilting his head back, with the heavenliest smile on his face, when all of a sudden he was paralyzed into a listening attitude and that smile faded gradually out of his countenance like breath off'n a razor, and the queerest look of surprise took its place. Then he says, 'Why I didn't hear it fall!' He cocked his eye at the hole again, and took a

---

GUIDED READING

LITERAL QUESTION

1a. What does the jay say after he drops the nut into the hole? (He says, "Why I didn't hear it fall.")

INFERENTIAL QUESTION

1b. Why does the jay not hear the nut fall? (The jay does not hear the nut fall because the floor of the empty house is a long way down.)

AT A GLANCE

■ The perplexed jay examines the hole, trying to understand why the nut did not make a noise.

1 THEME

In commenting on the jay's pre-occupation with the details of the hole, Twain is gently mocking the human tendency to focus too narrowly on problems.

long look; raised up and shook his head; stepped around to the other side of the hole and took another look from that side; shook **1** his head again. He studied a while, then he just went into the *details*—walked round and round the hole and spied into it from every point of the compass. No use. Now he took a thinking attitude on the comb[3] of the roof and scratched the back of his head with his right foot a minute, and finally says, 'Well, it's too many for *me*, that's certain; must be a mighty long hole; however, I ain't got no time to fool

---

3. **comb:** peak.

GUIDED READING

LITERAL QUESTION

1a. What does the jay do to try to solve the acorn's puzzling disappearance? (He looks at the hole from the other side and then walks around and around it.)

INFERENTIAL QUESTION

1b. What do we learn about the jay from this sequence of actions? (He analyzes the problem systematically but does not think to take an even broader view of the hole.)

- The jay fails to fill the hole with nuts.
- Other jays arrive and discuss the problem.
- One old jay discovers the door and solves the mystery.

1 VOCABULARY: DIALECT

Expressions such as *Consound it* and *fetched* and the substitution of *done* for *did* are examples of dialect that heighten the western flavor of the yarn.

2 HUMOR

The jay's pompous assumption that he has discovered a "totally new kind of a hole" is an example of bombast. Twain was a master at rendering this quality of boast, bluff, and blarney in the American character.

3 THEME

The jay is acting stubbornly and irrationally in the face of mystery. This behavior represents a common human foible, one of many that Twain mocks in this yarn.

4 EXAGGERATION

By saying the region " 'peared to have a blue flush about it" and citing the absurdly high figure of five thousand, Twain uses exaggeration to build to a humorous climax.

5 PLOT: CLIMAX

Baker's yarn climaxes with the boisterous whoop of the old jay, signaling the solution of the mystery.

---

around here, I got to 'tend to business; I reckon it's all right—chance it, anyway.'

"So he flew off and fetched another acorn and dropped it in, and tried to flirt his eye to the hole quick enough to see what become of it, but he was too late. He held his eye there as much as a minute; then he raised up and sighed, and says, 'Consound it, I don't seem to understand this thing, no way; however, I'll tackle her again.' He fetched another acorn, and done his level best to see what become of it, but he couldn't. He says, 'Well, *I* never struck no such a hole as this, before; I'm of the opinion it's a totally new kind of a hole.' Then he begun to get mad. He held in for a spell, walking up and down the comb of the roof and shaking his head and muttering to himself; but his feelings got the upper hand of him, presently. and he broke loose and cussed himself black in the face. I never see a bird take on so about a little thing. When he got through he walks to the hole and looks in again for half a minute; then he says, 'Well, you're a long hole, and a deep hole, and a mighty singular hole altogether—but I've started in to fill you, and I'm darned if I *don't* fill you, if it takes a hundred years!'

"And with that, away he went. You never see a bird work so since you was born. He laid into his work, and the way he hove[4] acorns into that hole for about two hours and a half was one of the most exciting and astonishing spectacles I ever struck. He never stopped to take a look any more—he just hove 'em in and went for more. Well at last he could hardly flop his wings, he was so tuckered out. He comes a-drooping down, once more, sweating like an ice-pitcher, drops his acorn in and says, '*Now* I guess I've got the bulge on you by this time!' So he bent down for a look. If you'll believe me, when his head come up again he was just pale with rage. He says, 'I've shoveled acorns enough in there to keep the family thirty years, and if I can see a sign of one of 'em I wish I may land in a museum with a belly full of sawdust in two minutes!'

"He just had strength enough to crawl up on to the comb and lean his back agin the chimbly, and then he collected his impressions and begun to free his mind.

"Another jay was going by, and stops to inquire what was up. The sufferer told him the whole circumstance, and says, 'Now yonder's the hole, and if you don't believe me, go and look for yourself.' So this fellow went and looked, and comes back and says, 'How many did you say you put in there?' 'Not any less than two tons,' says the sufferer. The other jay went and looked again. He couldn't seem to make it out, so he raised a yell, and three more jays come. They all examined the hole, they all made the sufferer tell it over again, then they all discussed it, and got off as many leather-headed opinions about it as an average crowd of humans could have done.

"They called in more jays; then more and more, till pretty soon this whole region 'peared to have a blue flush about it. There must have been five thousand of them; and such another jawing and disputing and ripping and cussing, you never heard. Every jay in the whole lot put his eye to the hole and delivered a more chuckle-headed opinion about the mystery than the jay that went there before him. They examined the house all over, too. The door was standing half open, and at last one old jay happened to go and light on it and look in. Of course that knocked the mystery galley-west[5] in a second. There lay the acorns, scattered all over the floor. He flopped his wings and raised a whoop. 'Come here!' he says, 'Come here, everybody; hang'd if this fool

---

4. **hove:** heaved, threw.

100   *The Short Story*

---

5. **knocked . . . galley-west:** put an end to the mystery.

GUIDED READING

LITERAL QUESTION

1a. What does every jay that comes to look at the hole do? (They all examine the hole, discuss it among themselves, and deliver "leather-headed opinions.")

INFERENTIAL QUESTION

1b. What human foible is Twain mocking by depicting the shortsighted method used by the jays to arrive at their opinions? (Twain is mocking the human tendency to form opinions without first searching for adequate evidence.)

hasn't been trying to fill up a house with acorns!' They all came a-swooping down like a blue cloud, and as each fellow lit on the door and took a glance, the whole absurdity of the contract that that first jay had tackled hit him home and he fell over backwards suffocating with laughter, and the next jay took his place and done the same.

"Well, sir, they roosted around here on the house-top and the trees for an hour, and guffawed[6] over that thing like human beings. It ain't any use to tell me a blue-jay hasn't got

a sense of humor, because I know better. And memory, too. They brought jays here from all over the United States to look down that hole, every summer for three years. Other birds too. And they could all see the point, except an owl that come from Nova Scotia[7] to visit the Yo Semite,[8] and he took this thing in on his way back. He said he couldn't see anything funny in it. But then he was a good deal disappointed about Yo Semite, too."

---

6. **guffawed** [gu fôd′]: laughed loudly.

7. **Nova Scotia** [nō′və skō′shə]: province in southeastern Canada.
8. **Yo Semite** [yō sem′i tē]: Yosemite National Park in east-central California.

STUDY QUESTIONS

Recalling

1. Who is Jim Baker? What is his unusual ability?
2. Name five ways in which blue-jays are superior, according to Jim Baker.
3. What does the blue-jay find on the roof of the house? What problem does he soon have?
4. What happens when more blue-jays examine the house?
5. What happens to the house during the next three years? What is the owl's opinion?

Interpreting

6. Name two personality traits for Jim Baker. Give examples from the story.
7. Why do you think the blue-jay never looks inside the door of the house?
8. Why do you think the other blue-jays enjoy visiting the house and laughing?

Extending

9. Think of someone you know who tells stories and jokes well. What qualities make this person a good storyteller?

READING AND LITERARY FOCUS

Effect of Setting on Plot and Character

In everyday life our surroundings can cause new developments. For example, moving to a different city may help a person find a job. Surroundings can also affect personality. For example, living in a mountain cabin may make someone more energetic and independent.

In stories, also, setting can affect plot and character. That is, setting can influence what happens in a story. For example, in "Gentleman of Río en Medio" Don Anselmo's land causes the disagreement between the new owners and the townspeople. Setting can also affect the personalities of characters. For example, Don Anselmo's family has farmed the same beautiful land for hundreds of years. As a result, Don Anselmo never hurries.

Thinking About Setting

1. According to the beginning of the story, in what ways has Jim Baker been affected by living in the wilderness without neighbors?
2. In what ways does the house cause the events of the story?

Jim Baker's Blue-jay Yarn 101

1. Standard
2. Dialect: use of word *reckon* to mean "think"
3. Standard
4. Dialect: words *agin* and *chimbly* are variations on standard pronunciations; *begun* is dialect for *began*.
5. Dialect: Two verbs in sentence have different tenses to indicate casual speech.

CHALLENGE

Students should
- explain the meaning of Charles Neider's comment
- show how it relates specifically to "Jim Baker's Blue-jay Yarn"

COMPARING STORIES

- "Crime on Mars": Setting strongly influences events in story; conditions in Martian colony described briefly but vividly; Gallery Three especially chilling. "Gentleman of Río en Medio": Land in valley is subject, barely described in first paragraph—farm land with a "small and wretched, but quaint" house, a little creek, and a "gnarled and beautiful" orchard.
- "Jim Baker's Blue-jay Yarn": Focus is on characters, but land in front of Jim Baker's cabin with its sunlit "blue hills" and "leaves rustling so lonely in the trees" is vivid and important; also, house in yard causes events of plot.

VOCABULARY

Dialect

Standard American English is the most used and recognized kind of English spoken and written in the United States. **Dialect** is a special kind of language that belongs to a particular group or region. For example, the language of the hill country of the South and of Boston, Massachusetts, are both regional dialects. Dialects differ from standard English because they contain words with different forms, sounds, and meanings.

Mark Twain was one of the first Americans to use realistic dialect in his writing. For example, "Jim Baker's Blue-jay Yarn" uses the dialect of the American West in the 1800s.

Which of the following sentences from the story do you think are regional dialect? Which are standard English? On a separate sheet write the number of each item. Next to each number mark the item *standard* or *dialect*. For each number that you mark *dialect,* tell why you made your decision.

1. According to Jim Baker, some animals have only a limited education. . . .
2. "I reckon I've struck something."
3. When he spoke, the acorn dropped out of his mouth and rolled down the roof. . . .
4. He just had strength enough to . . . lean his back agin the chimbly, and then he collected his impressions and begun to free his mind.
5. Another jay was going by, and stops to inquire what was up.

COMPOSITION

Writing About Conflict

■ Write about the conflict in "Jim Baker's Blue-jay Yarn." First tell whether the conflict is external or internal. Then tell what forces struggle in this conflict. Finally, tell how the conflict is solved. Be sure to use examples from the story to support your opinions.

Writing a Nonfiction Narrative

■ Write a true narrative about an experience in which someone tries to achieve an impossible goal. Tell how this experience taught you something about yourself or another person. *For help with this assignment, see Lesson 8 in the Writing About Literature Handbook at the back of this book.*

CHALLENGE

Literary Criticism

■ We can add to our enjoyment and understanding of literature by reading **literary criticism,** writing that analyzes a particular author's work. People who write literary criticism are experts on literature. Literary criticism helps us to understand literature and to form our own opinions of the works we read. The literary critic Charles Neider has written about Mark Twain's humorous work. He says that Twain's writing is funny because he sees

> that life, and not the least his own, is comical and barely rational [sane] at its very core.

In what ways does "Jim Baker's Blue-jay Yarn" show Twain's belief that life is comic?

COMPARING STORIES

■ Compare two or more of the following stories: "Crime on Mars," "Gentleman of Río en Medio," and "Jim Baker's Blue-jay Yarn." For each story identify an important setting. Then tell which story has a more vivid setting. Give details of setting from each story to support your opinion.

COMPOSITION: GUIDELINES FOR EVALUATION

WRITING ABOUT CONFLICT
Objective
To explain the conflict in a story

Guidelines for Evaluation
- suggested length: two to three paragraphs
- should tell whether conflict is internal or external and what forces struggle
- should explain how conflict is solved
- should use examples to support opinions

WRITING A NONFICTION NARRATIVE
Objective
To write a true narrative

Guidelines for Evaluation
- suggested length: three to four paragraphs
- should describe experience in which someone tries to achieve an impossible goal
- should explain what experience taught
- should use an informal style

POINT OF VIEW

Katherine Mansfield (1888–1923) was born and raised in New Zealand in the South Pacific. She attended college in London, England, and eventually settled there. Her first successful stories were based on her youth in New Zealand. Her work often concerns everyday events. However, these ordinary happenings cause her characters to realize important truths. In "Mary" a young girl must struggle with some very confusing emotions.

■ What are some of the things Kass feels?

Katherine Mansfield

Mary

On poetry afternoons Grandmother let Mary and me wear Mrs. Gardner's white hemstitched pinafores[1] because we had nothing to do with ink or pencil.

Triumphant and feeling unspeakably beautiful, we would fly along the road, swinging our kits and half chanting, half singing our new piece. I always knew my poetry, but Mary, who was a year and a half older, never knew hers. In fact, lessons of any sort worried her soul and body. She could never distinguish between "m" and "n."

"Now, Kass—turnip," she would say, wrinkling her nose, "t-o-u-r-*m*-i-p, isn't it?"

Also in words like "celery" or "gallery" she invariably said "cerely" and "garrely."

I was a strong, fat little child who burst my buttons and shot out of my shirts to Grandmother's entire satisfaction, but Mary was a "weed." She had a continual little cough. "Poor old Mary's bark," as Father called it.

Every spare moment of her time seemed to be occupied in journeying with Mother to the pantry and being forced to take something out of a spoon—cod-liver oil, Easton's syrup, malt extract. And though she had her nose held and a piece of barley sugar after, these sorties,[2] I am sure, told on her spirits.

"I can't bear lessons," she would say woefully. "I'm all tired in my elbows and my feet."

And yet, when she was well she was elfishly gay and bright—danced like a fairy and sang like a bird. And heroic! She would hold a rooster by the legs while Pat chopped his head off. She loved boys, and played with a fine sense of honor and purity. In fact, I think she loved everybody; and I, who did not, worshiped her. I suffered untold agonies when the girls laughed at her in class, and when she an-

---

1. **hemstitched pinafores:** sleeveless apronlike garments with decorative stitching along the bottom.

2. **sorties** [sôr'tēz]: trips.

Mary 103

GUIDED READING

LITERAL QUESTION

1a. What facts does Kass relate about her sister Mary? (She is older than Kass, not good at lessons, takes many medicines, dances and sings, is heroic, loves everybody, and plays fair.)

INFERENTIAL QUESTION

1b. Why do you think the girls laugh at Mary in class? (They probably laugh at her slowness, particularly her problems saying certain words.)

- Kass is always voted top of her poetry team. Mary is always at the bottom.
- Mary hopes to win this time, but she stumbles in her recitation.
- Kass succeeds in hers but asks Teacher to let Mary win.

1 CHARACTERIZATION

Kass's strong sense of family loyalty and love for Mary are evident as she defends Mary in class.

2 INTERNAL CONFLICT

Kass's great joy at her own success is clouded by her perception of Mary's failure. "Ignominiously" suggests just how humiliating Kass herself finds Mary's failure.

3 STYLE: WORD CHOICE

"I prayed viciously" suggests in a humorous way just how determined and single-minded Kass can be.

4 POINT OF VIEW

The first-person narrator reveals how sure she is of winning, making her sacrifice for Mary's sake all the more impressive.

---

1 swered wrongly I put up my hand and cried, "Please, Teacher, she means something quite different." Then I would turn to Mary and say, "You meant 'island' and not 'peninsula,' didn't you, dear?"

"Of course," she would say—"how very silly!"

But on poetry afternoons I could be of no help at all. The class was divided into two and ranged on both sides of the room. Two of us drew lots as to which side must begin, and when the first half had each in turn said their piece, they left the room while Teacher and the remaining ones voted for the best reciter. Time and again I was top of my side, and time 2 and again Mary was bottom. To stand before all those girls and Teacher, knowing my piece, loving it so much that I *went* in the knees and shivered all over, was joy; but she would stand twisting "Mrs. Gardner's white linen stitched," blundering and finally breaking down ignominiously.[3] There came a day when we had learned the whole of Thomas Hood's "I remember, I remember,"[4] and Teacher offered a prize for the best girl on each side. The prize for our side was a green-plush bracket[5] with a yellow china frog stuck on it. All the morning these treasures had stood on Teacher's table; all through playtime and the dinner hour we had talked of nothing else. It was agreed that it was bound to fall to me. I saw pictures of myself carrying it home to Grandmother—I saw it hanging on her wall—never doubting for one moment that she would think it the most desirable ornament in life. But as we ran to afternoon school, Mary's memory seemed weaker than ever before, and suddenly she stopped on the road.

"Kass," she said, "think what a s'prise if I got it after all; I believe Mother would go mad

---

3. **ignominiously** [ig'nə min′ē əs lē]: in shame.
4. **Thomas Hood's "I remember, I remember"**: poem by English poet Thomas Hood (1799–1845).
5. **green-plush bracket**: shelf covered with cloth.

104   *The Short Story*

---

with joy. I know I should. But then—I'm so stupid, I know."

She sighed, and we ran on. Oh, from that moment I longed that the prize might fall to Mary. I said the "piece" to her three times over as we ran up the last hill and across the playground. Sides were chosen. She and I, as our name began with "B," were the first to begin. And alas! that she was older, her turn was before mine.

3 The first verse went splendidly. I prayed viciously for another miracle.

"Oh please, God, dear, do be nice!—If you won't—"

The Almighty slumbered. Mary broke down. I saw her standing there all alone, her pale little freckled face flushed, her mouth quivering, and the thin fingers twisting and twisting at the unfortunate pinafore frill. She was helped, in a critical condition, to the very end. I saw Teacher's face smiling at me suddenly—the cold, shivering feeling came over me—and then I saw the house and "the little window where the sun came peeping in at morn."[6]

When it was over the girls clapped, and the look of pride and love on Mary's face decided me.

4 "Kass has got it; there's no good trying now," was the spirit on the rest of my side. Finally they left the room. I waited until the moment the door was shut. Then I went over to Teacher and whispered:

"If I've got it, put Mary's name. Don't tell anybody, and don't let the others tell her—oh, *please.*"

I shot out the last word at her, and Teacher looked astounded.

She shook her head at me in a way I could not understand. I ran out and joined the others. They were gathered in the passage,

---

6. **"the little window . . . at morn"**: lines from the Thomas Hood poem that the class is reciting.

GUIDED READING

LITERAL QUESTION

1a. What does Kass tell Teacher to do if Kass wins? (give the prize to Mary)

INFERENTIAL QUESTION

1b. Why do you think Teacher shakes her head at Kass? (Answers will vary. Possibilities: She may be shaking her head in wonder at Kass's sacrifice, or she may be indicating her own doubts about that sacrifice.)

AT A GLANCE
- Mary wins first prize, and Kass tries to keep from crying.
- Mary is made much of by the other students, who look at Kass with pitying contempt.

1 INTERNAL CONFLICT

Even before the prize is announced, Kass begins to regret her sacrifice. Her second thoughts suggest that her pride in her own achievement conflicts with her love for Mary.

2 THEME

Kass's sacrifice is all the more difficult for her because it earns her only pitying contempt, rather than admiration, from her classmates.

twittering like birds. Only Mary stood apart, clearing her throat and trying to hum a little tune. I knew she would cry if I talked to her, so I paid her no attention. I felt I would like to run out of school and never come back again. Trying not to be sorry for what I had done—trying not to think of that heavenly green bracket, which seemed big and beautiful enough now to give Queen Victoria—and longing for the voting to be over kept me busy. At last the door opened, and we trooped in. Teacher stood by the table. The girls were radiant. I shut my mouth hard and looked down at my slippers.

"The first prize," said Teacher, "is awarded to Mary Beetham." A great burst of clapping; but above it all I heard Mary's little cry of joy. For a moment I could not look up; but when I did, and saw her walking to the desk, so happy, so confident, so utterly unsuspecting, when I saw her going back to her place with that green-plush bracket in her hands, it needed all my wildest expostulations with the Deity[7] to keep back my tears. The rest of the afternoon passed like a dream; but when school broke up, Mary was the heroine of the hour. Boys and girls followed her—held the prize in their "own hands"—and all looked at me with pitying contempt, especially those

---

7. **expostulations** [iks pos′chə lā′shənz] **with the Deity** [dē′ə tē]: prayers to God.

Mary 105

GUIDED READING

LITERAL QUESTION

1a. How do the other students act when Mary wins? (They clap for her and later treat her as a heroine.)

INFERENTIAL QUESTION

1b. Why do you think the students applaud Mary? (They like Mary; perhaps they feel the prize makes up for the times they laughed at her.)

- Everyone is excited that Mary has won the poetry prize.
- The adults criticize Kass for sulking.
- Kass decides to tell Mary how she won but, touched by her vulnerability as she sleeps, kisses her.

1 THEME

For the first time Mary is the center of the family's attention for something other than illness.

2 POINT OF VIEW

Because the story is told from Kass's point of view, we experience intimately the sense of injustice she feels.

3 INTERNAL CONFLICT

The sentence "I stuffed a corner of the sheet into my mouth to stop me from shouting out the truth" shows the explosiveness of Kass's conflict.

4 PLOT: CLIMAX

The reader's emotional involvement reaches its peak as Kass tries to decide whether to tell her sister the truth.

5 PLOT: RESOLUTION

The tension is resolved only in the last sentence of the story, as Kass is moved by the image of her sleeping sister.

REFLECTING ON THE STORY

In what way do both Mary and Kass win in this story? (Mary receives confidence-boosting recognition; Kass grows up and responds to needs beyond her own.)

---

who were in on the secret and knew what I had done.

On the way home we passed the Karori bus going home from town full of businessmen. The driver gave us a lift, and we bundled in. We knew all the people.

"I've won a prize for po'try!" cried Mary, in a high, excited voice.

"Good old Mary!" they chorused.

Again she was the center of admiring popularity.

"Well, Kass, you needn't look so doleful," said Mr. England, laughing at me, "you aren't clever enough to win everything."

"I know," I answered, wishing I were dead and buried.

I did not go into the house when we reached home, but wandered down to the loft and watched Pat mixing the chicken food.

But the bell rang at last, and with slow steps I crept up to the nursery.

1 Mother and Grandmother were there with two callers. Alice had come up from the kitchen; Vera was sitting with her arms round Mary's neck.

"Well, that's wonderful, Mary," Mother was saying. "Such a lovely prize, too. Now, you see what you really can do, darling."

"That will be nice for you to show your little girls when you grow up," said Grandmother.

Slowly I slipped into my chair.

2 "Well, Kass, you don't look very pleased," cried one of the tactful callers.

Mother looked at me severely.

"Don't say you are going to be a sulky child about your sister," she said.

Even Mary's bright little face clouded.

"You are glad, aren't you?" she questioned.

"I'm frightfully glad," I said, holding on to the handle of my mug, and seeing all too plainly the glance of understanding that passed between the grownups.

We had the yellow frog for tea, we had the green-plush bracket for the entire evening

106   *The Short Story*

when Father came home, and even when Mary and I had been sent to bed she sang a little song made out of her own head:

> I got a yellow frog for a prize,
> An' it had china eyes.

But she tried to fit this to the tune of "Sun of My Soul," which Grandmother thought a little irreverent, and stopped.

Mary's bed was in the opposite corner of the room. I lay with my head pressed into the pillow. Then the tears came. I pulled the **3** clothes over my head. The sacrifice was too great. I stuffed a corner of the sheet into my mouth to stop me from shouting out the truth. Nobody loved me, nobody understood me, and they loved Mary without the frog, and now that she had it I decided they loved me less.

A long time seemed to pass. I got hot and stuffy, and came up to breathe. And the Devil entered into my soul. I decided to tell Mary the truth. From that moment I was happy and light again, but I felt savage. I sat up—then got out of bed. The linoleum was very cold. I crossed over to the other corner.

The moon shone through the window straight on to Mary's bed. She lay on her side, one hand against her cheek, soundly sleeping. Her little plait of hair stood straight up from her head; it was tied with a piece of pink wool. Very white was her small face, and the funny freckles I could see even in this light; she had thrown off half the bedclothes; one button of her nightdress was undone, showing her flannel chest protector.

4 I stood there for one moment, on one leg, watching her asleep. I looked at the green-plush bracket already hung on the wall above her head, at that perfect yellow frog with china eyes, and then again at Mary, who stirred and flung out one arm across the bed. **5** Suddenly I stooped and kissed her.

GUIDED READING

LITERAL QUESTIONS

1a. How does Kass's mother treat her that night? (She reprimands her for sulking.)

2a. How does Kass feel that night in bed as she is tempted to tell Mary the truth? (She feels that no one loves her or understands her.)

INFERENTIAL QUESTIONS

1b. Why do you think people treat Kass so roughly? (They probably realize how proud she is; they also know she is stronger than Mary and can take a little disappointment.)

2b. Why doesn't Kass tell Mary the truth? (Her love for her sister finally triumphs over her pride.)

STUDY QUESTIONS

Recalling

1. Find three important differences between Kass and Mary.
2. Tell what happens in the classroom on poetry afternoons.
3. From what moment does Kass wish that Mary would win?
4. After Kass recites, what does she ask the teacher to do? Who wins the contest?
5. List two things that people say to Kass after school.
6. At the end of the story, what does Kass decide to do? What does she do instead?

Interpreting

7. Why does Kass help Mary in the contest?
8. Give at least two reasons that Kass becomes upset after the contest.
9. Why do you think Kass feels that people love Mary more than they love her?

Extending

10. Do you agree with Kass's decision to help Mary in the contest? Why or why not?

READING AND LITERARY FOCUS

First-Person Point of View

Every story has a **narrator,** or a person who tells the story. Some narrators are characters in their stories. Others are not. For example, the narrator of "The Osage Orange Tree" (page 68) is the main character, the newspaper boy. On the other hand, the narrator of "A Game of Catch" (page 74) is not one of that story's three characters. In that story the narrator is the author.

Point of view is the relationship of the story-teller, or narrator, to the story. A story told from the **first-person point of view** is told by a character. This character speaks directly to us and refers to

himself or herself as "I." As a result, we learn about events from someone who lived them in the story. However, the first-person narrator can reveal only his or her own thoughts. This narrator cannot tell what others are thinking or what happens elsewhere. For example, the boy who narrates "The Osage Orange Tree" does not know how Evangeline pays for the newspaper. He does not know why she fails to appear at graduation.

Thinking About Point of View

1. Who is the narrator of "Mary"? What personal feelings does she reveal?
2. In what ways would the story be different if Mary were the narrator?

COMPOSITION

Writing About Character

■ Select either Kass or Mary, and tell whether she seems true-to-life. First state your opinion clearly. Then give reasons. You may want to include (a) the different traits she shows and (b) the motivations for her actions. Be sure to use examples from the story to support your opinions. *For help with this assignment, see Lesson 3 in the Writing About Literature Handbook at the back of this book.*

Writing a Story

■ Write a short story about someone who makes a sacrifice to help a brother or sister. Your story should have a plot that is a logical sequence of events. The plot should answer the following questions: What problem does the brother or sister have? What sacrifice does the main character make? What is the final result? Your story should also include descriptions of the two main characters and of the setting. *For help with this assignment, see Lesson 4 in the Writing About Literature Handbook at the back of this book.*

Mary 107

STUDY QUESTIONS

1. Kass is good at reciting poetry and schoolwork in general; Mary suffers over her lessons. Kass is strong, fat, healthy; Mary is skinny, sickly. Mary loves everyone; Kass does not.
2. Class is divided in two; after students on one team recite memorized poems, they leave room, and class votes for best reciter.
3. When Mary admits she would love to win prize, Kass truly realizes Mary has felt unworthy, left out.
4. Teacher should name Mary if Kass wins; Mary wins.
5. *Mr. England:* "Well, Kass, you needn't look so doleful . . . you aren't clever enough to win everything." *Mother:* "Don't say you are going to be a sulky child about your sister."
6. to tell Mary the truth; kisses her
7. understands Mary's longing to win
8. She is jealous of attention Mary gets; feels nobody loves or understands her; wants prize herself.
9. She knows she doesn't love everyone and realizes people may not love her; Kass needs to shine for own sense of self-worth. When attention is given Mary, Kass feels lost; Mary's poor health gains her sympathy.
10. Possible answers: *Yes,* Kass realizes Mary yearns to have something that comes easily to Kass; *no,* Mary probably knows that her recitation was inferior and that the prize was given out of pity

READING AND LITERARY FOCUS

1. Kass; she worships her sister and admires her bravery, fairness, acceptance of everyone; Kass is less accepting.
2. It would focus on Kass and Mary's feelings toward her; Mary couldn't tell reader how she won.

- The story is set in a Mississippi swamp near a small village.
- A young boy, Skeeter, and his Uncle Jesse are hunting an animal Skeeter has heard in the swamp.
- They see the animal and are surprised to hear it chuckle.

LITERARY OPTIONS

- point of view
- characterization
- internal conflict

THEMATIC OPTIONS

- growing up
- family life
- friendship and love

1 PLOT: SUSPENSE

The hushed creatures and brooding bog set a mood of tension and suspense as the gaunt man motions to the boy to be quiet.

2 CHARACTERIZATION

The dialogue contrasts the characters of the man and the boy: Skeeter is young and eager to catch the animal; Jesse is cautious and wary of the "thing."

3 POINT OF VIEW

The use of the third-person narrator allows Street to pause in his storytelling to reveal a characteristic of Jesse and Skeeter: They "never killed wantonly."

TEXAS ESSENTIAL ELEMENTS GRADE 8

3A plot development and character development
3B figurative language
3C setting and mood
3D literary genres
4B implied main idea
4E cause/effect
4F point of view
To locate treatment of an Element, see *Texas Teacher's Resources.*

James Street (1903–1954) was born and grew up in Mississippi. At fourteen he began to work part time as a newspaper reporter. Later he became a Baptist minister. Street also worked in several other fields, including law. When he decided to return to journalism, he moved to New York City. "Weep No More, My Lady" is about a boy who must make a difficult decision.

■ What influences help the boy to make his choice?

James Street

Weep No More, My Lady

1 The moonlight symphony of swamp creatures hushed abruptly, and the dismal bog was as peaceful as unborn time and seemed to brood in its silence. The gaunt man glanced back at the boy and motioned for him to be quiet, but it was too late. Their presence was discovered. A jumbo frog rumbled a warning, and the swamp squirmed into life as its denizens[1] scuttled to safety.

Fox fire[2] was glowing to the west and the bayou was slapping the cypress trees when suddenly a haunting laugh echoed through the wilderness, a strange chuckling yodel ending in a weird "*gro-o-o.*"

2 The boy's eyes were wide and staring. "That's it, Uncle Jess. Come on! Let's catch it!"

"Uh, oh." The man gripped his shotgun. "That ain't no animal. That's a thing."

They hurried noiselessly in the direction of the sound that Skeeter had been hearing for several nights. Swamp born and reared, they feared nothing they could shoot or outwit, so they slipped out of the morass and to the side of a ridge. Suddenly, Jesse put out his hand and stopped the child; then he pointed up the slope. The animal, clearly visible in the moonlight, was sitting on its haunches, its head cocked sideways as it chuckled. It was a merry and rather melodious little chuckle.

Skeeter grinned in spite of his surprise, then said, "Sh-h-h. It'll smell us."

Jesse said, "Can't nothing smell that far. Wonder what the durn thing is?" He peered up the ridge, studying the creature. He had **3** no intention of shooting unless attacked, for Jesse Tolliver and his nephew never killed wantonly.[3]

The animal, however, did smell them and

---

1. **denizens** [den'ə zənz]: inhabitants.
2. **Fox fire:** bluish light caused by gas from rotting wood.

---

3. **wantonly** [wont'ən lē]: carelessly, senselessly.

GUIDED READING

LITERAL QUESTION

1a. What does Jesse say after they hear the animal's haunting laugh? ("That ain't no animal. That's a thing.")

INFERENTIAL QUESTION

1b. What do you think he means? (The laugh does not resemble the sound of any earthly creature he knows; it sounds supernatural.)

whipped her nose into the wind, crouched, and braced. She was about sixteen inches high and weighed about twenty-two pounds. Her coat was red and silky, and there was a **1** blaze of white down her chest and a circle of white around her throat. Her face was wrinkled and sad, like a wise old man's.

Jesse shook his head. "Looks som'n like a mixture of bloodhound and terrier from here," he whispered. "It beats me—"

"It's a dog, all right," Skeeter said.

"Can't no dog laugh."

"That dog can." The boy began walking toward the animal, his right hand outstretched. "Heah, heah. I ain't gonna hurt you."

The dog, for she was a dog, cocked her head from one side to the other and watched Skeeter. She was trembling, but she didn't run. And when Skeeter knelt by her, she **2** stopped trembling, for the ways of a boy with a dog are mysterious. He stroked her, and the trim little creature looked up at him and blinked her big hazel eyes. Then she turned over, and Skeeter scratched her. She closed her eyes, stretched, and chuckled, a happy mixture of chortle and yodel. Jesse ambled up, and the dog leaped to her feet and sprang between the boy and the man.

Skeeter calmed her. "That's just Uncle Jess."

3 Jesse, still bewildered, shook his head again. "I still say that ain't no dog. She don't smell and she don't bark. Ain't natural. And look at her! Licking herself like a cat."

"Well, I'll be a catty wampus," Skeeter said. "Never saw a dog do that before." However, he was quick to defend any mannerism of his friend and said, "She likes to keep herself clean. She's a lady, and I'm gonna name her that, and she's mine 'cause I found her."

"Lady, huh?"

"No, sir. My Lady. If I name her just plain Lady, how folks gonna know she's mine?" He began stroking his dog again. "Gee m'netty, Uncle Jess, I ain't never had nothing like this before."

"It still don't make sense to me," Jesse said. But he didn't care, for he was happy because the child was happy.

4 Like most mysteries, there was no mystery at all about My Lady. She was a lady, all right, an aristocratic basenji,[4] one of those strange barkless dogs of Africa. Her ancestors were pets of the Pharaohs, and her line was well established when the now-proud races of men were wandering about Europe, begging handouts from nature. A bundle of nerves and muscles, she would fight anything and could scent game up to eighty yards. She had the gait of an antelope and was odorless, washing herself before and after meals. However, the only noises she could make were a piercing cry that sounded almost human and that chuckling little chortle. She could chuckle only when happy, and she had been happy in the woods. Now she was happy again.

As most men judge values, she was worth more than all the possessions of Jesse and his nephew. Several of the dogs had been shipped to New Orleans to avoid the dangerous upper route, thence by motor to a northern kennel. **5** While crossing Mississippi, My Lady had escaped from the station wagon. Her keeper had advertised in several papers, but Jesse and Skeeter never saw papers.

Skeeter said, "Come on, M'Lady. Let's go home."

The dog didn't hesitate, but walked proudly at the boy's side to a cabin on the bank of the bayou. Skeeter crumbled corn bread, wet it with potlikker,[5] and put it before her. She sniffed the food disdainfully at first,

---

4. **basenji** [bə sen′jē]: African breed of small dog that does not make a true barking sound.
5. **potlikker:** liquid remaining in a pot after meat and vegetables are cooked together.

Weep No More, My Lady   109

AT A GLANCE

- The animal is a dog that laughs and cleans herself like a cat.
- Skeeter calls her "My Lady."
- The narrator reveals facts the characters don't know: The dog is a valuable basenji of Africa. It escaped in transit to a kennel.

1 STYLE: SIMILE

Comparing the dog's sad face to a "wise old man's" seems to make it almost human. The dog is nearly a full-fledged character in the story.

2 THEME

This passage introduces the theme of friendship into the story. The boy and the dog seem to share an understanding that cannot be explained.

3 VOCABULARY: DIALECT

The use of *ain't* and *don't* (instead of *doesn't*) and the expression *I'll be a catty wampus* reflects the speech of the rural South. The generous use of such expressions gives the story a realistic flavor.

4 POINT OF VIEW

The third-person narrator fills in My Lady's background, thus allowing the reader to anticipate events in the story.

5 SETTING

The statement "but Jesse and Skeeter never saw papers" reveals the extent of their isolation in the remote swamp.

GUIDED READING

LITERAL QUESTIONS

1a. How does Skeeter react when Jesse talks about the dog licking herself like a cat? (Skeeter defends her.)

2a. Although Jesse knows nothing about the dog and where it comes from, why does he accept it? (to make Skeeter happy)

INFERENTIAL QUESTIONS

1b. What does Skeeter's defense of the dog show about him? (He is open to persons or things that are different; he is a good friend to have.)

2b. What problems might Skeeter's attachment cause later in the story? (If Skeeter becomes attached to the dog and later finds out the truth about her, he may be in conflict about what to do.)

- Jesse suggests that the dog may be worth two dollars but allows Skeeter to keep her.
- Skeeter, whose real name is Jonathan, is an orphan being raised by Jesse.
- The villagers consider Jesse shiftless.

1 IRONY

Because the reader has information the characters don't, the discussion of the dog's worth is ironic. To Jesse the dog itself is worthless. Only his nephew's love for it makes it precious and priceless.

2 CHARACTERIZATION

Skeeter's words suggest how thoughtful, loving, and generous Jesse is.

3 THEME

The account of Skeeter's birth and of how Jesse "took him to bring up" reveals Jesse's strong love for his family.

eating it only when she saw the boy fix a bowl for his uncle. She licked herself clean and explored the cabin, sniffing the brush brooms, the piles of wild pecans and hickory nuts, and then the cots. Satisfied at last, she jumped on Skeeter's bed, tucked her nose under her paws, and went to sleep.

"Acts like she owns the place," Jesse said.

"Where you reckon she came from?" The boy slipped his overall straps from his shoulders, flexed his stringy muscles, and yawned.

"Lord knows. Circus maybe." He looked at M'Lady quickly. "Say, maybe she's a freak and run off from some show. Bet they'd give us two dollars for her."

Skeeter's face got long. "You don't aim to get rid of her?"

The old man put his shotgun over the mantel and lit his pipe. "Skeets, if you want that thing, I wouldn't get shed of her for a piece of bottom land a mile long. Already plowed and planted."

110   *The Short Story*

"I reckoned you wouldn't, 'cause you like me so much. And I know how you like dogs, 'cause I saw you cry when yours got killed. But you can have part of mine."

Jesse sat down and leaned back, blowing smoke into the air to drive away mosquitoes. The boy got a brick and hammer and began cracking nuts, pounding the meat to pulp so his uncle could chew it. Skeeter's yellow hair hadn't been cut for months and was tangled. He had freckles, too. And his real name was Jonathan. His mother was Jesse's only sister and died when the child was born. No one thereabouts ever knew what happened to his father. Jesse, a leathery, toothless old man with faded blue eyes, took him to bring up and called him Skeeter because he was so little.

In the village, where Jesse seldom visited, folks wondered if he were fit'n to rear a little boy. They considered him shiftless and no-count. Jesse had lived all of his sixty years in

GUIDED READING

LITERAL QUESTION

1a. Why does Skeeter get a brick and hammer? (to crack nuts and pound the meat so toothless Jesse can chew it)

INFERENTIAL QUESTION

1b. What does this behavior suggest about Skeeter? (He is loving and considerate.)

the swamp, and his way of life was a torment to folks who believed life must be lived by rules. He earned a few dollars selling jumbo frogs and pelts, but mostly he just paddled around the swamp, watching things and teaching Skeeter about life.

The villagers might have tried to send Skeeter to an orphanage, but for Joe (Cash) Watson, the storekeeper. Cash was a hard man, but fair. He often hunted with Jesse, and the old man had trained Cash's dogs.

1 When there was talk of sending Skeeter away, Cash said, "You ain't gonna do it. You just don't take young'uns away from their folks." And that's all there was to it.

Jesse never coveted the "frills and furbelows[6] of durn-fool folks," and he yearned for only two things—a twenty-gauge shotgun for Skeeter and a set of Roebuckers for himself, as he called store-bought teeth. Cash had promised him the gun and the best false teeth in the catalog for forty-six dollars. Jesse had saved nine dollars and thirty-seven cents.

"Someday I'm gonna get them Roebuckers," he often told Skeeter. "Then I'm gonna eat me enough roastin' ears to kill a goat. Maybe I can get a set with a couple of gold teeth in 'em. I seen a man once with six gold teeth."

2 Once Skeeter asked him, "Why don't you get a job and make enough money to buy them Roebuckers?"

"I don't want 'em that bad," Jesse said.

So he was happy for Skeeter to have M'Lady, thinking the dog would sort of make up for the shotgun.

The boy cracked as many nuts as his uncle wanted, then put the hammer away. He was undressing when he glanced over at his dog.

---

6. **furbelows** [fur′bə lōz′]: showy, useless decorations.

"Gosh, Uncle Jess. I'm scared somebody'll come get her."

"I ain't heard of nobody losing no things around here. If'n they had, they'd been to me 'fo' now, being's I know all about dogs and the swamp."

3 "That's so," Skeeter said. "But you don't reckon she belonged to another fellow like me, do you? I know how I'd feel if I had a dog like her and she got lost."

Jesse said, "She didn't belong to another fellow like you. If'n she had, she wouldn't be so happy here."

Skeeter fed M'Lady biscuits and molasses for breakfast, and although the basenji ate it, she still was hungry when she went into the swamp with the boy. He was hoping he could find a bee tree or signs of wild hogs. They were at the edge of a clearing when M'Lady's chokebore[7] nose suddenly tilted and she froze to a flash point,[8] pausing only long enough to get set. Then she darted to the bayou, at least sixty yards away, dived into a clump of reeds, and snatched a water rat. She was eating it when Skeeter ran up.

"Don't do that," he scolded. "Ain't you got no more sense than to run into water after things? A snake or a gator might snatch you."

The basenji dropped the rat and tucked her head. She knew the boy was displeased, **4** and when she looked up at him, her eyes were filled, and a woebegone expression was on her face.

Skeeter tried to explain, "I didn't mean to hurt your feelings. Don't cry." He stepped back quickly and stared at her, at the tears in her eyes. "She *is* crying! By John Brown!" Skeeter

---

7. **chokebore:** narrow at the tip.
8. **flash point:** briefly held position in which a hunting dog points its head and body in the direction of hiding game.

Weep No More, My Lady 111

- The villagers wanted to send Skeeter to an orphanage, but Cash Watson protested.
- Jesse wants a shotgun for Skeeter and false teeth for himself.
- Skeeter fears someone will claim the dog. He begins training her.

1 THEME

Cash recognizes the value of family life and shows his friendship for Jesse as he protests the removal of "young'uns away from their folks."

2 READING SKILLS: INFERENCES

In very few words Jesse suggests his values. He will not take a job, even to earn money for something he clearly needs and longs for. His peace and freedom are more important to him than material things.

3 CHARACTERIZATION

Skeeter demonstrates his capacity to empathize with other people's feelings.

4 CHARACTERIZATION

Once more Street emphasizes the almost-human characteristics of the dog as he notes her "woebegone expression" and what appear to be tears.

GUIDED READING

LITERAL QUESTIONS

1a. What did the storekeeper Cash say when people wanted to send Skeeter to an orphanage? ("You don't take young'uns away from their folks.")

2a. What does Jesse say when Skeeter suggests he get a job so he can buy the Roebuckers? ("I don't want 'em that bad.")

INFERENTIAL QUESTIONS

1b. What does this incident suggest about Cash? (He has a strong sense of family; he is fair; he has strong principles and stands up for them; he is respected.)

2b. What does Jesse's comment suggest about him? (Possible answers: He is lazy; he is not materialistic and values freedom more than money.)

- Skeeter tells Jesse that M'Lady picked up a rat's scent sixty yards away.
- Jesse sees the dog pick up the scent of birds eighty yards away.
- Skeeter wants to train M'Lady as a bird dog.

1 PLOT: SUSPENSE

Jesse's realization that M'Lady has "been around folks" makes us wonder who the owner is and if the owner will later claim the dog.

2 STYLE: SIMILE

Skeeter's standing "as motionless as stone" indicates how amazed he is at the dog's accomplishment.

3 CHARACTERIZATION

Skeeter shows signs of growing up in his disagreement with Jesse over training M'Lady to be a bird dog. When Jesse says, "I know 'bout dogs," Skeeter responds, "Me too."

4 VOCABULARY: DIALECT

The dialect expression *a pure-D humdinger* (meaning "an excellent specimen") captures Skeeter's excitement and loyal appreciation of M'Lady.

---

called her and ran toward the cabin, where Jesse was cutting splinters.

"Uncle Jess! Guess what else my dog can do!"

"Whistle," the old man laughed.

"She can cry! I declare to goodness! Not out loud, but she can cry just the same."

Jesse knew that most dogs will get watery-eyed on occasion, but, not wanting to ridicule M'Lady's accomplishments, asked, "What made her cry?"

"Well, sir, we were walking along and all of a sudden she got a scent and flash-pointed and then . . ." Skeeter remembered something.

"Then what?"

Skeeter sat on the steps. "Uncle Jess," he said slowly, "we must have been fifty or sixty yards from that rat when she smelled it."

"What rat? What's eating you?"

The child told him the story, and Jesse couldn't believe it. For a dog to pick up the scent of a water rat at sixty yards simply isn't credible. Jesse reckoned Skeeter's love for M'Lady had led him to exaggerate.

Skeeter knew Jesse didn't believe the story, so he said, "Come on. I'll show you." He whistled for M'Lady.

1 The dog came up. "Hey," Jesse said. "That thing knows what a whistle means. Shows she's been around folks." He caught the dog's eye and commanded, "Heel!"

But M'Lady cocked her head quizzically. Then she turned to the boy and chuckled softly. She'd never heard the order before. That was obvious. Her nose came up into the breeze and she wheeled.

Her curved tail suddenly was still and her head was poised.

"Flash-pointing," Jesse said. "Well, I'll be a monkey's uncle!"

M'Lady held the strange point only for a second, though, then dashed toward a corn patch about eighty yards from the cabin.

112   *The Short Story*

Halfway to the patch, she broke her gait and began creeping. A whir of feathered lightning sounded in the corn, and a covey[9] of quail exploded almost under her nose. She sprang and snatched a bird.

"Partridges!" Jesse's jaw dropped.

2 The child was as motionless as stone, his face white and his eyes wide in amazement. Finally he found his voice, "She was right here when she smelled them birds. A good eighty yards."

"I know she ain't no dog now," Jesse said. "Can't no dog do that."

"She's fast as greased lightning and ain't scared of nothing." Skeeter still was under the spell of the adventure. "She's a hunting dog from way back."

"She ain't no dog a-tall, I'm telling you. It ain't human." Jesse walked toward M'Lady and told her to fetch the bird, but the dog didn't understand. Instead, she pawed it. "Well," Jesse said. "One thing's certain. She ain't no bird hunter."

"She can do anything," Skeeter said. "Even hunt birds. Maybe I can make a bird dog out'n her. Wouldn't that be som'n?"

3 "You're batty. Maybe a coon dog, but not a bird dog. I know 'bout dogs."

"Me too," said Skeeter. And he did. He'd seen Jesse train many dogs, even pointers, and had helped him train Big Boy, Cash Watson's prize gun dog.

Jesse eyed Skeeter and read his mind.

"It can't be done, Skeets."

"Maybe not, but I aim to try. Any dog can **4** run coons and rabbits, but it takes a pure-D humdinger to hunt birds. Ain't no sin in trying, is it?"

"Naw," Jesse said slowly. "But she'll flush[10] birds."

---

9. **covey:** small flock of birds, especially quail.
10. **flush:** drive from cover.

GUIDED READING

LITERAL QUESTIONS

1a. What does Jesse say when M'Lady smells birds at eighty yards? ("Can't no dog do that. . . . It ain't human.")

2a. What does Skeeter want to train M'Lady to do? (hunt birds)

INFERENTIAL QUESTIONS

1b. Do you think Jesse still considers M'Lady a worthless freak? (no)

2b. Why do you think Skeeter wants to do this? (to prove how special the dog is, because only the best hunting dogs can hunt birds; also, to prove himself to Jesse)

Jesse leaned against a tree and watched the fun.

Skeeter pointed toward a clump of sage. "She's pointing birds in that sage."

Cash couldn't restrain his mirth. "Boy, now that's what I call some pointing. Why, Skeeter, it's sixty or seventy yards to that sage."

Just then Big Boy flashed by M'Lady, his head high. He raced to the edge of the sage, caught the wind, then whipped around, freezing to a point. Cash called Jesse's attention to the point.

"That's M'Lady's point," Skeeter said. "She's got the same birds Big Boy has."

1 Jesse sauntered up. "The boy's right, Cash. I aimed to keep my mouth out'n this race, but M'Lady is pointing them birds. She can catch scents up to eighty yards."

Cash said, "Aw, go on. You're crazy." He walked over and flushed the birds.

Skeeter picked one off and ordered M'Lady to fetch. When she returned with the bird, the boy patted her, and she began chuckling.

Cash really studied her then for the first time. "Hey!" he said suddenly. "A basenji! That's a basenji!"

"A what?" Jesse asked.

2 "I should have known." Cash was very excited. "That's the dog that was lost by them rich Yankees. I saw about it in the paper." He happened to look at Skeeter then and wished he had cut out his tongue.

The boy's lips were compressed and his face was drawn and white. Jesse had closed his eyes and was rubbing his forehead.

Cash, trying to dismiss the subject, said, "Just 'cause it was in the paper don't make it so. I don't believe that's the same dog, come to think of it."

"Do you aim to tell 'em where the dog is?" Skeeter asked.

Cash looked at Jesse, then at the ground. "It ain't none of my business."

"How 'bout you, Uncle Jess?"

"I ain't telling nobody nothin'."

AT A GLANCE

Skeeter begins to train M'Lady to be a bird dog.

1 CHARACTERIZATION

Jesse bets against Skeeter and the dog, not because he lacks confidence in them, but because he wants to give Skeeter strong motivation for following through.

2 THEME

Skeeter's project will require all his patience and skill, but it is primarily a labor of love.

GUIDED READING

LITERAL QUESTION

1a. What does Skeeter tie around M'Lady's neck? (the rat she had killed)

INFERENTIAL QUESTION

1b. Why does Skeeter do this? (He's teaching M'Lady not to kill rats by making the consequences of doing so unpleasant for the dog.)

- Skeeter is patient and considerate in his training methods, and M'Lady is eager to please.
- The boy succeeds in making M'Lady a bird dog.
- Cash Watson arrives to give his dog, Big Boy, a workout.

1 POINT OF VIEW

The third-person narrator draws the reader further into the story by expressing even the dog's feelings: "a harsh word from the boy hurt more than a hickory limb."

2 THEME

Skeeter proves his budding maturity by deciding to use "his own system." Skeeter's initiative points to Street's theme that learning to make decisions is part of growing up.

3 THEME

While training his dog, Skeeter has matured. When Jesse congratulates him, Skeeter reminds him of their bet by responding confidently, "And you got yourself a job."

strange affinity between a boy and a dog, and the blind faith of a child.

M'Lady's devotion to Skeeter was so complete that she was anxious to do anything to earn a pat. It wasn't difficult to teach her to heel and follow at Skeeter's feet regardless of the urge to dash away and chase rabbits. The boy used a clothesline as a guide rope and made M'Lady follow him. The first time the dog tried to chase an animal, Skeeter pinched the rope around her neck just a bit and commanded "Heel!" And when she obeyed, Skeeter released the noose. It took M'Lady only a few hours to associate disobedience with disfavor.

The dog learned that when she chased and killed a rat or rabbit, the thing would be tied around her neck. The only things she could hunt without being disciplined were quail. Of course, she often mistook the scent of game chickens for quail and hunted them, but **1** Skeeter punished her by scolding. He never switched the dog, but to M'Lady a harsh word from the boy hurt more than a hickory limb.

Jesse watched the dog's progress and pretended not to be impressed. He never volunteered suggestions. M'Lady learned quickly, **2** but the task of teaching her to point birds seemed hopeless. Skeeter knew she'd never point as pointers do, so he worked with his own system. He taught her to stand motionless when he shouted "Hup!" One day she got a scent of birds, paused and pointed for a moment as most animals will, and was ready to spring away when Skeeter said "Hup!"

M'Lady was confused. Every instinct urged her to chase the birds, but her master had said stand still. She broke, however, and Skeeter scolded her. She pouted at first, then filled up, but the boy ignored her until she obeyed the next command, then he patted her and she chuckled.

The lessons continued for days and weeks,

and slowly and surely M'Lady learned her chores. She learned that the second she smelled birds she must stop and stand still until Skeeter flushed them; that she must not quiver when he shot.

Teaching her to fetch was easy, but teaching her to retrieve dead birds without damaging them was another matter. M'Lady had a hard mouth—that is, she sank her teeth into the birds. Skeeter used one of the oldest hunting tricks of the backwoods to break her.

He got a stick and wrapped it with wire and taught his dog to fetch it. Only once did M'Lady bite hard on the stick, and then the wire hurt her sensitive mouth. Soon she developed a habit of carrying the stick on her tongue and supporting it lightly with her teeth. Skeeter tied quail feathers on the stick, and soon M'Lady's education was complete.

Skeeter led Jesse into a field one day and turned his dog loose. She flashed to a point almost immediately. It was a funny point, and Jesse almost laughed. The dog's curved tail poked up over her back, she spraddled her front legs and sort of squatted, her nose pointing the birds, more than forty yards away. She remained rigid until the boy flushed and shot, then she leaped away, seeking and fetching dead birds.

3 Jesse was mighty proud. "Well, Skeets, looks like you got yourself a bird hunter."

"Yes, sir," Skeeter said. "And you got yourself a job." He pointed toward the kindling pile.

The swamp was dressing for winter when Cash Watson drove down that day to give his Big Boy a workout in the wild brush.

He fetched Jesse a couple of cans of smoking tobacco and Skeeter a bag of peppermint jawbreakers. He locked his fine pointer in the corncrib for the night and was warming him-

114   *The Short Story*

GUIDED READING

LITERAL QUESTIONS

1a. How does Jesse act as he watches the dog's progress? (He pretends not to be impressed; he doesn't volunteer suggestions; he doesn't laugh at M'Lady's point.)

2a. What does Skeeter tie on the stick wrapped with wire? (quail feathers)

INFERENTIAL QUESTIONS

1b. Why does Jesse act the way he does? (He doesn't want to baby Skeeter; he wants the success to be Skeeter's alone; he doesn't want to embarrass Skeeter by laughing.)

2b. What is Skeeter trying to do? (to condition M'Lady not to bite the quail, just carry it in her mouth) self in the cabin when he noticed M'Lady for the first time. She was sleeping in front of the fire.

"What's that?" he asked.

"My dog," said Skeeter. "Ain't she a beaut?"

"She sure is," Cash grinned at Jesse. Skeeter went out to the well, and Cash asked his old friend, "What the devil kind of mutt is that?"

"Search me," said Jesse. "Skeets found her in the swamp. I reckon she's got a trace of bloodhound in her and some terrier and a heap of just plain dog."

M'Lady cocked one ear and got up and stretched; then, apparently, not liking the company, she turned her tail toward Cash and strutted out, looking for Skeeter.

The men laughed. "Som'n wrong with her throat," Jesse said. "She can't bark. When she tries, she makes a funny sound, sort of a cackling, chuckling yodel. Sounds like she's laughing."

"Well," Cash said, "trust a young'un to love the orner'st dog he can find."

"Wait a minute," Jesse said. "She ain't no-count. She's a bird-hunting fool."

Just then Skeeter entered and Cash jestingly said, "Hear you got yourself a bird dog, son."

The boy clasped his hands behind him and rocked on the balls of his feet as he had seen the men do. "Well, now, I'll tell you, Mr. Cash. M'Lady does ever'thing except tote the gun."

"She must be fair to middling. Why not take her out with Big Boy tomorrow? Do my dog good to hunt in a brace."[11]

"Me and my dog don't want to show Big Boy up. He's a pretty good ol' dog."

"Whoa!" Cash was every inch a bird-dog man and nobody could challenge him without a showdown. Besides, Skeeter was shooting

---

11. **brace:** pair.

up and should be learning a few things about life. "Any old boiler can pop off steam." Cash winked at Jesse.

"Well, now, sir, if you're itching for a run, I'll just double-dog dare you to run your dog against mine. And anybody who'll take a dare will pull up young cotton and push a widow woman's ducks in the water."

Cash admired the boy's confidence. "All right, son, it's a deal. What are the stakes?"

Skeeter started to mention the twenty-gauge gun he wanted, but changed his mind quickly. He reached down and patted M'Lady, then looked up. "If my dog beats yours, then you get them Roebuckers for Uncle Jess."

Jesse's chest was suddenly tight. Cash glanced from the boy to the man, and he, too, was proud of Skeeter. "I wasn't aiming to go that high. But all right. What do I get if I win?"

"I'll cut you ten cords of stovewood."

"And a stack of splinters?"

"Yes, sir."

Cash offered his hand, and Skeeter took it. "It's a race," Cash said. "Jesse will be the judge."

The wind was rustling the sage and there was a nip in the early morning air when they took the dogs to a clearing and set them down. Skeeter snapped a belt around M'Lady's neck, and, at a word from Jesse, the dogs were released.

Big Boy bounded away and began circling, ranging into the brush. M'Lady tilted her nose into the wind and ripped away toward the sage, her bell tinkling. Cash said, "She sure covers ground." Skeeter made no effort to keep up with her, but waited until he couldn't hear the bell, then ran for a clearing where he had last heard it. And there was M'Lady on a point.

Cash laughed out loud. "That ain't no point, son. That's a squat."

"She's got birds."

"Where?"

Weep No More, My Lady 115

AT A GLANCE

- Cash makes fun of M'Lady to Jesse.
- Skeeter dares Cash to run his dog against M'Lady, and Cash accepts.
- The wager is settled: Cash gives the Roebuckers to Jesse, or Skeeter cuts wood for Cash.

1 CHARACTERIZATION

Cash is unimpressed with M'Lady but shows concern for Skeeter's feelings by not calling her a "mutt" until he is alone with Jesse.

2 THEME

Jesse shows his loyalty to his nephew Skeeter by describing M'Lady to Cash as "a bird-hunting fool."

3 CHARACTERIZATION

By assuming the pose of the backwoodsmen, Skeeter asserts that he is growing up and wishes to be taken seriously now.

4 THEME

Skeeter's love for Jesse is apparent in his decision to sacrifice the shotgun for Jesse's Roebuckers.

5 PLOT: SUSPENSE

The story reaches a suspenseful moment as Skeeter and Cash shake hands and Cash says, "It's a race." We wonder if M'Lady will prove equal to Skeeter's faith in her.

GUIDED READING

LITERAL QUESTION

1a. What old saying does Cash quote to Skeeter when Skeeter boasts about M'Lady? ("Any old boiler can pop off steam.")

INFERENTIAL QUESTION

1b. What do you think the saying means? (Anyone can talk; talk is cheap.)

- M'Lady wins the contest with Big Boy.
- Cash recognizes the dog as the basenji.
- Cash and Jesse assure Skeeter that they won't inform her owners of M'Lady's whereabouts.

1 THEME

Recognizing that Skeeter is growing up, Jesse tells Cash he "aimed to keep my mouth out'n this race." He speaks up only to support Skeeter's claim that M'Lady has won the contest.

2 PLOT: CONFLICT

Earlier Skeeter had experienced a feeling of conflict at the thought that M'Lady might have another owner. Now his conflict intensifies. The men feel torn between doing right and protecting Skeeter.

"I'll learn her not to."

"She won't hold no point. Any dog'll flash-point. And she'll hunt rats."

"I'm gonna learn her just to hunt birds. And I'm starting right now," Skeeter said. He started walking away, then turned. "I seen a man once train a razorback hawg to point birds. You know as good as me that if a dog's got pure-D hoss sense and a fellow's got bat brains, he can train the dog to hunt birds."

1 "Wanta bet?" Jesse issued the challenge in an effort to keep Skeeter's enthusiasm and determination at the high-water mark.

"Yes, sir. If I don't train my dog, then I'll cut all the splinters for a year. If I do, you cut 'em."

"It's a go," Jesse said.

Skeeter ran to the bayou and recovered the rat M'Lady had killed. He tied it round the dog's neck. The basenji was indignant and tried to claw off the hateful burden. Failing, she ran into the house and under a bed, but Skeeter made her come out. M'Lady filled up then, and her face assumed that don't-nobody-love-me look. The boy steeled himself, tapped M'Lady's nose with the rat, and left it around her neck.

"You done whittled out a job for yourself," Jesse said. "If'n you get her trained, you'll lose her in the brush. She's too fast and too little to keep up with."

"I'll bell her," Skeeter said. "I'm gonna learn her ever'thing. I got us a gun dog, Uncle Jess."

The old man sat on the porch and propped against the wall. "Bud, I don't know what that thing is. But you're a thoroughbred. John dog my hide!"

2 If Skeeter had loved M'Lady one bit less, his patience would have exploded during the ordeal of training the basenji. It takes judgment and infinite patience to train a bird dog properly, but to train a basenji, that'll hunt anything, to concentrate only on quail took something more than discipline and patience. It never could have been done except for that

GUIDED READING

LITERAL QUESTION

1a. What important information does Cash give Jesse and Skeeter? (that M'Lady is a basenji lost by some "rich Yankees")

INFERENTIAL QUESTION

1b. Why does Cash later say, "I don't believe that's the same dog, come to think of it"? (He sees how upset Skeeter is by the news and wants to make it easier for the boy to keep the dog.)

"I know she's the same dog," Skeeter said. "On account of I just know it. But she's mine now." His voice rose and trembled. "And ain't nobody gonna take her away from me." He ran into the swamp. M'Lady was at his heels.

Cash said, "Durn my lip. I'm sorry, Jesse. If I'd kept my big mouth shut he'd never known the difference."

"It can't be helped, now," Jesse said.

" 'Course she beat Big Boy. Them's the best hunting dogs in the world. And she's worth a mint of money."

They didn't feel up to hunting and returned to the cabin and sat on the porch. Neither had much to say, but kept glancing toward the swamp where Skeeter and M'Lady were walking along the bayou. "Don't you worry," he said tenderly, "ain't nobody gonna bother you."

He sat on a stump and M'Lady put her head on his knee. She wasn't worrying. Nothing could have been more contented than she was.

"I don't care if the sheriff comes down." Skeeter pulled her onto his lap and held her. "I don't give a whoop if the Governor comes down. Even the President of the United States! The whole shebang can come, but ain't nobody gonna mess with you."

His words gave him courage, and he felt better, but only for a minute. Then the tug of war between him and his conscience started.

"Once I found a Barlow knife and kept it, and it was all right," he mumbled.

"*But this is different.*"

"Finders, keepers; losers, weepers."

"*No, Skeeter.*"

"Well, I don't care. She's mine."

"*Remember what your Uncle Jess said.*"

"He said a heap of things."

"*Yes, but you remember one thing more than the rest. He said, 'Certain things are right and certain things are wrong. And nothing ain't gonna ever change that. When you*

learn that, then you're fit'n to be a man.' Remember, Skeeter?"

A feeling of despair and loneliness almost overwhelmed him. He fought off the tears as long as he could, but finally he gave in, and his sobs caused M'Lady to peer into his face and wonder why he was acting that way when she was so happy. He put his arms around her neck and pulled her to him. "My li'l old puppy dog. Poor li'l old puppy dog. But I got to do it."

He sniffed back his tears and got up and walked to the cabin. M'Lady curled up by the fire, and the boy sat down, watching the logs splutter for several minutes. Then he said, almost in a whisper, "Uncle Jess, if you keep som'n that ain't yours, it's the same as stealing, ain't it?"

Cash leaned against the mantel and stared into the fire.

Jesse puffed his pipe slowly. "Son, that's som'n you got to settle with yourself."

Skeeter stood and turned his back to the flames, warming his hands. "Mr. Cash," he said slowly, "when you get back to your store, please let them folks know their dog is here."

"If that's how it is—"

"That's how it is," Skeeter said.

The firelight dancing on Jesse's face revealed the old man's dejection, and Skeeter, seeing it, said quickly, "It's best for M'Lady. She's too good for the swamp. They'll give her a good home."

Jesse flinched, and Cash, catching the hurt look in his friend's eyes, said, "Your dog outhunted mine, Skeets. You win them Roe-buckers for your uncle."

"I don't want 'em," Jesse said, rather childishly. "I don't care if'n I never eat no roastin' ears." He got up quickly and hurried outside. Cash reckoned he'd better be going and left Skeeter by the fire, rubbing his dog.

Jesse came back in directly and pulled up a chair. Skeeter started to speak, but Jesse

- Skeeter runs into the swamp, M'Lady at his heels.
- Skeeter tells M'Lady that no one will take her away from him. Then he is conscience-stricken.
- He returns and tells Cash to inform the owners of M'Lady's whereabouts.

1 CHARACTERIZATION

By acknowledging that M'Lady is the lost dog, Skeeter takes responsibility for the decision to keep her. His growing maturity won't let him accept the men's attempts to protect him.

2 POINT OF VIEW

By attributing feelings to M'Lady, the third-person narrator intensifies the poignancy of the moment. The dog cannot know of Skeeter's struggle.

3 PLOT: CONFLICT

This dialogue dramatizes Skeeter's internal conflict as a "tug of war" with his conscience, an effective technique that builds suspense.

4 PLOT: CLIMAX

Skeeter's decision spoken to M'Lady marks the emotional high point of the story.

5 THEME

Jesse acknowledges Skeeter's ability to make his own decision about the dog. Skeeter adopts a grown-up stance at the fire when he speaks to Cash.

GUIDED READING

LITERAL QUESTIONS

1a. What does Cash say about what M'Lady is worth? ("And she's worth a mint of money.")

2a. What does Skeeter say to Jesse and Cash to defend his decision to return M'Lady? ("She's too good for the swamp. They'll give her a good home.")

INFERENTIAL QUESTIONS

1b. Why do you think Cash says this? (He may be suggesting that it's wrong to keep something so valuable; he may be hinting at a possible reward.)

2b. Why does Jesse flinch when Skeeter says that? (Skeeter seems to be criticizing the swamp and suggesting it's not a good home.)

- Jesse plans to send Skeeter to live in town. Skeeter rejects the idea.
- Jesse accepts the Roebuckers.
- Skeeter rejects a reward for returning M'Lady, but Cash accepts it for him.

1 PLOT: CONFLICT

Stung by Skeeter's seeming criticism of swamp life, Jesse offers to get a job and send the boy to town. The fact that he "dared not look at the boy" indicates that this is not really what he wants.

2 HUMOR

Jesse's attempt to "swap" for the dog is touching but comical. His haggling with the keeper indicates that he still has no real sense of the dog's actual value.

3 PLOT: CONFLICT

The dog's behavior severely tests Skeeter's resolve and creates one last moment of internal conflict before Skeeter helps get M'Lady into her cage.

---

spoke first. "I been doing a heap of thinking lately. You're sprouting up. The swamp ain't no place for you."

Skeeter forgot about his dog and faced his uncle, bewildered.

1 "I reckon you're too good for the swamp too," Jesse said. "I'm aiming to send you into town for a spell. I can make enough to keep you in fit'n clothes and all." He dared not look at the boy.

"Uncle Jess!" Skeeter said reproachfully. "You don't mean that. You're just saying that on account of what I said about M'Lady. I said it just to keep you from feeling so bad about our dog going away. Gee m'netty, Uncle Jess. I ain't ever gonna leave you." He buried his face in his uncle's shoulder. M'Lady put her head on Jesse's knee, and he patted the boy and rubbed the dog.

"Reckon I'll take them Roebuckers," he said at last. "I been wanting some for a long, long time."

Several days later Cash drove down and told them the man from the kennels was at his store. Skeeter didn't say a word, but called M'Lady and they got in Cash's car. All the way to town, the boy was silent. He held his dog's head in his lap.

The keeper took just one look at M'Lady and said, "That's she, all right. Miss Congo III." He turned to speak to Skeeter, but the boy was walking away. He got a glance at Skeeter's face, however. "I wish you fellows hadn't told me," he muttered. "I hate to take a dog away from a kid."

"He wanted you to know," Cash said.

2 "Mister"—Jesse closed his left eye and struck his swapping pose—"I'd like to swap you out'n that hound. Now, 'course she ain't much 'count. . . ."

The keeper smiled in spite of himself. "If she was mine, I'd give her to the kid. But she's not for sale. The owner wants to breed her and establish her line in this country. And if she was for sale, she'd cost more money than any of us will ever see." He called Skeeter and offered his hand. Skeeter shook it.

"You're a good kid. There's a reward for this dog."

"I don't want no reward." The boy's words tumbled out. "I don't want nothing, except to be left alone. You've got your dog, mister. Take her and go on. Please." He walked away again, fearing he would cry.

Cash said, "I'll take the reward and keep it for him. Someday he'll want it."

Jesse went out to the store porch to be with Skeeter. The keeper handed Cash the money. "It's tough, but the kid'll get over it. The dog never will."

"Is that a fact?"

"Yep. I know the breed. They never forget. That dog'll never laugh again. They never laugh unless they're happy."

He walked to the post where Skeeter had tied M'Lady. He untied the leash and started toward his station wagon. M'Lady braced her front feet and looked around for the boy. Seeing him on the porch, she jerked away from the keeper and ran to her master.

3 She rubbed against his legs. Skeeter tried to ignore her. The keeper reached for the leash again, and M'Lady crouched, baring her fangs. The keeper shrugged, a helpless gesture.

"Wild elephants couldn't pull that dog away from that boy," he said.

"That's all right, mister." Skeeter unsnapped the leash and tossed it to the keeper. Then he walked to the station wagon, opened the door of the cage, and called, "Heah, M'Lady!" She bounded to him. "Up!" he commanded. She didn't hesitate, but leaped into the cage. The keeper locked the door.

M'Lady, having obeyed a command, poked

GUIDED READING

LITERAL QUESTIONS

1a. How does Skeeter react to Jesse's plan to send Skeeter to live in town? (He says he'll never leave the swamp.)

2a. Does Skeeter accept a reward for returning M'Lady? (no)

INFERENTIAL QUESTIONS

1b. How do you think Skeeter and Jesse feel at this moment? (They're feeling close to each other but upset at the thought of having to give up M'Lady.)

2b. Why do you think Skeeter rejects the reward? (He doesn't measure M'Lady's value in material terms.)

her nose between the bars, expecting a pat. The boy rubbed her head. She tried to move closer to him, but the bars held her. She looked quizzically at the bars, then tried to nudge them aside. Then she clawed them. A look of fear suddenly came to her eyes, and she fastened them on Skeeter, wistfully at first, then pleadingly. She couldn't make a sound, for her unhappiness had sealed her throat. Slowly her eyes filled up.

"Don't cry no more, M'Lady. Ever'thing's gonna be all right." He reached out to pat her, but the station wagon moved off, leaving him standing there in the dust.

Back on the porch, Jesse lit his pipe and said to his friend, "Cash, the boy has lost his dog, and I've lost a boy."

"Aw, Jesse, Skeeter wouldn't leave you."

"That ain't what I mean. He's growed up, Cash. He don't look no older, but he is. He growed up that day in the swamp."

Skeeter walked into the store and Cash followed him. "I've got that reward for you, Jonathan."

It was the first time anyone ever had called him that, and it sounded like man talk.

"And that twenty-gauge is waiting for you," Cash said. "I'm gonna give it to you."

"Thank you, Mr. Cash." The boy bit his lower lip. "But I don't aim to do no more hunting. I don't never want no more dogs."

"Know how you feel. But if you change your mind, the gun's here for you."

Skeeter looked back toward the porch where Jesse was waiting, and said, "Tell you what, though. When you get them Roebuckers, get some with a couple of gold teeth in 'em. Take it out of the reward money."

"Sure, Jonathan."

Jesse joined them, and Skeeter said, "We better be getting back toward the house."

"I'll drive you down," Cash said. "But first I aim to treat you to some lemon pop and sardines."

"That's mighty nice of you," Jesse said, "but we better be gettin' on."

"What's the hurry?" Cash opened the pop.

"It's my time to cut splinters," Jesse said. "That's what I get for betting with a good man."

Weep No More, My Lady 119

1. red, silky coat; white markings; sad, wrinkled face; hazel eyes; licks herself like a cat and "laughs"

2. basenji; escaped from car when being sent from New Orleans

3. question Uncle Jesse's fitness to raise him—doesn't live by their rules; "You just don't take young'uns away from their folks."

4. ■ She scents water rat from fifty to sixty yards away and partridges from eighty.
   ■ To teach her to carry birds without damaging them, he wraps wire on a stick that she fetches; once she can carry it delicately, he attaches quail feathers.

5. believes keeping something not yours is like stealing; Skeeter has grown up, acted with integrity

6. Answers will vary. Possibilities: *considerate*—pounds nuts so uncle can eat them; *patient, thorough*—sees to every detail of his dog's training; *confident*—bets his dog can point birds better than Cash's; *deeply moral*—gives up dog even though he loves her

7. Possible answers: Bayou is too limited for person to develop fully; Skeeter would be less caring if he lived in town. All should agree Jesse is a good influence on the boy.

8. to show his respect for Skeeter's new maturity

9. Ties between young people and their pets are strong.

READING AND LITERARY FOCUS

1. Possible answers: "Skeeter knew Jesse didn't believe the story. . . ."; "Skeeter was still under the spell of the adventure."; "The boy steeled himself. . . ."

2. Possible answers: "In the village, where Jesse seldom visited, folks wondered if he were fit'n to rear a little boy"; ". . . to train a basenji . . . concentrate only on quail . . . never could have been done except for . . . the blind faith of a child."

STUDY QUESTIONS

Recalling

1. Describe My Lady. Why does Uncle Jesse think that she is not a dog?

2. What kind of dog is My Lady? Tell how she gets loose in the swamp.

3. Why do some people try to send Skeeter to an orphanage? What is Cash Watson's reaction to the plan?

4. Why does Skeeter think that My Lady is a hunting dog? Give one method he uses to train her.

5. Why does Skeeter decide to return My Lady to her owners? Why does Uncle Jesse say that he has lost a boy?

Interpreting

6. Name two character traits of Skeeter. Give an example from the story for each.

7. Do you think that Skeeter should have been raised in town? Why or why not?

8. At the end of the story, why does Cash Watson call Skeeter "Jonathan"?

Extending

9. Why do you think that people enjoy stories and movies about young people and their pets?

READING AND LITERARY FOCUS

Third-Person Point of View

A story told from the **third-person point of view** is told by the author. The author acts as a narrator, or storyteller, who stands outside the story. This narrator, who is not a character, refers to all the characters as "he" or "she."

A third-person narrator can tell the reader everything, including the thoughts and feelings of all the characters. For example, in the beginning of "Weep No More, My Lady," the narrator says that Uncle Jesse "had no intention of shooting unless attacked. . . ." Later the narrator says that Skeeter goes into the swamp "hoping he could find a bee tree or signs of wild hogs." The third-person narrator can even reveal to us things that the characters do not know. For example, the narrator of "Weep No More, My Lady" tells us that My Lady is a basenji before Cash Watson identifies the dog for Uncle Jesse and Skeeter.

Thinking About Point of View

1. Find two more examples in which the narrator reveals Skeeter's thoughts and feelings.

2. Find another example of information that the narrator gives the reader but that Uncle Jesse and Skeeter do not have.

CHALLENGE

Research Report

■ In your library, research at least three unusual breeds of dogs. Then prepare a report on your findings. Your report should give the following information for each breed of dog: size and appearance, behavior, native country, and ways in which humans have used it.

CHALLENGE

Students should
■ use resources at library to find out about at least three unusual breeds
■ discover size, appearance, native country, and uses of dog
■ relate information in a clear report

Ursula K. Le Guin (born 1929) is an American writer of science fiction. Her novels include *The Left Hand of Darkness*, *The Dispossessed*, and *The Earthsea Trilogy*. All of these contain imaginative descriptions of life on other planets. "The Rule of Names" takes place on the fictional planet of Earthsea.

■ What details about this surprising planet remind you of our own world?

AT A GLANCE

- The story is set on Earthsea, a fictional planet.
- Mr. Underhill is the incompetent wizard of Sattins Island.
- The villagers regard Mr. Underhill with "affectionate disdain."

LITERARY OPTIONS

- plot
- setting
- characterization

THEMATIC OPTIONS

- appearance and reality
- discoveries
- mystery and adventure

1 POINT OF VIEW

The third-person narrator seems amused by Mr. Underhill and charmed by life on Sattins Island. The humorous tone in the beginning of the story makes the surprise ending more dramatic.

2 SETTING

The power of a "careless adjective" on Sattins Island establishes it as a fairy-tale world where magical things happen; therefore, inhabitants must be prepared for surprises.

3 CHARACTERIZATION

Both Mr. Underhill's appearance and his incompetence are sources of the villagers' "affectionate disdain" for him.

Ursula K. Le Guin

The Rule of Names

1   Mr. Underhill came out from under his hill, smiling and breathing hard. Each breath shot out of his nostrils as a double puff of steam, snow-white in the morning sunshine. Mr. Underhill looked up at the bright December sky and smiled wider than ever, showing snow-white teeth. Then he went down to the village.

"Morning, Mr. Underhill," said the villagers as he passed them in the narrow street between houses with conical, overhanging roofs like the fat red caps of toadstools. "Morning, morning!" he replied to each. (It was of course bad luck to wish anyone a *good* morning; a 2 simple statement of the time of day was quite enough, in a place so permeated with[1] Influences as Sattins Island, where a careless adjective might change the weather for a week.) All of them spoke to him, some with affection, some with affectionate disdain. He was all the little island had in the way of a wizard, and

3 so deserved respect—but how could you respect a little fat man of fifty who waddled along with his toes turned in, breathing steam and smiling? He was no great shakes as a workman either. His fireworks were fairly elaborate but his elixirs[2] were weak. Warts he charmed off frequently reappeared after three days; tomatoes he enchanted grew no bigger than cantaloupes; and those rare times when a strange ship stopped at Sattins Harbor, Mr. Underhill always stayed under his hill—for fear, he explained, of the evil eye. He was, in other words, a wizard the way walleyed[3] Gan was a carpenter: by default. The villagers made do with badly-hung doors and inefficient spells, for this generation, and relieved their annoyance by treating Mr. Underhill quite familiarly, as a mere fellow villager. They even asked him to dinner. Once he asked

---

1. **permeated** [pur'mē ãt'id] **with:** full of.

2. **elixirs** [i lik'sərz]: magic cures.
3. **walleyed** [wôl'īd']: having eyes that turn outward.

The Rule of Names   121

GUIDED READING

LITERAL QUESTION

1a. What reason does Mr. Underhill give for staying under his hill when a strange ship arrives? (He is afraid "of the evil eye.")

INFERENTIAL QUESTION

1b. What do you think Mr. Underhill means by that? (He is afraid that some stranger will cast an evil spell on him.)

TEXAS ESSENTIAL ELEMENTS GRADE 8

3A plot development and character development
3C setting and mood
3D literary genres
4B implied main idea
4E cause/effect
4F point of view
4G prediction of outcomes
To locate treatment of an Element, see *Texas Teacher's Resources*.

- Mr. Underhill allows no one to visit his cave under the hill.
- Boys once tried to enter and were frightened away by the noise the wizard made.
- Mr. Underhill hears the schoolteacher telling the children about the Rule of Names.

1 PLOT: SUSPENSE

The wizard's refusal to let anyone enter his cave may suggest that there is something inside he wants to keep hidden.

2 PLOT: FORESHADOWING

The "huge hooting howling hissing horrible bellow" of which Mr. Underhill is capable hints at the possibility that his harmless appearance may disguise unexpected powers. The mysterious noise foreshadows the surprise ending of the story.

3 CHARACTERIZATION

Mr. Underhill's timidity and constant smiling suggest that he is nice. Nevertheless, there is something in his smiles that apparently makes the girls nervous.

4 SETTING

The fact that no one can read or write on Sattins Island means that there is no real learning and that people do not have the means to question the authority of the rules they are taught. Earthsea begins to seem a more sinister world.

some of them to dinner, and served a splendid repast, with silver, crystal, damask,[4] roast goose, and plum pudding with hard sauce; but he was so nervous all through the meal that it took the joy out of it, and besides, everybody was hungry again half an hour afterward. **He did not like anyone to visit his cave, not even the anteroom, beyond which in fact nobody had ever got. When he saw people** approaching the hill he always came trotting out to meet them. "Let's sit out here under the pine trees!" he would say, smiling and waving towards the fir grove, or if it was raining, "Let's go have a drink at the inn, eh?" though everybody knew he drank nothing stronger than well-water.

Some of the village children, teased by that locked cave, poked and pried and made raids while Mr. Underhill was away; but the small door that led into the inner chamber was spell-shut, and it seemed for once to be an effective spell. Once a couple of boys, thinking the wizard was over on the West Shore curing Mrs. Ruuna's sick donkey, brought a crowbar and a hatchet up there, but at the first whack of the hatchet on the door there came a roar of wrath from inside, and a cloud of purple steam. Mr. Underhill had got home early. The boys fled. He did not come out, and the boys **came to no harm, though they said you couldn't believe what a huge hooting howling hissing horrible bellow that little fat man could make unless you'd heard it.**

His business in town this day was three dozen fresh eggs and a pound of liver; also a stop at Seacaptain Fogeno's cottage to renew the seeing-charm on the old man's eyes (quite useless when applied to a case of detached retina,[5] but Mr. Underhill kept trying), and

finally a chat with old Goody[6] Guld, the concertina[7]-maker's widow. **Mr. Underhill's friends were mostly old people. He was timid with the strong young men of the village, and the girls were shy of him. "He makes me nervous, he smiles so much," they all said, pouting, twisting silky ringlets round a finger.** *Nervous* was a newfangled word, and their mothers all replied grimly, "Nervous my foot, *silliness* is the word for it. Mr. Underhill is a very respectable wizard!"

After leaving Goody Guld, Mr. Underhill passed by the school, which was being held **this day out on the common. Since no one on Sattins Island was literate, there were no books to learn to read from and no desks to carve initials on and no blackboards to erase,** and in fact no schoolhouse. On rainy days the children met in the loft of the Communal Barn, and got hay in their pants; on sunny days the schoolteacher, Palani, took them anywhere she felt like. Today, surrounded by thirty interested children under twelve and forty uninterested sheep under five, she was teaching an important item on the curriculum: the Rules of Names. Mr. Underhill, smiling shyly, paused to listen and watch. Palani, a plump, pretty girl of twenty, made a charming picture there in the wintry sunlight, sheep and children around her, a leafless oak above her, and behind her the dunes and sea and clear, pale sky. She spoke earnestly, her face flushed pink by wind and words. "Now you know the Rules of Names already, children. There are two, and they're the same on every island in the world. What's one of them?"

"It ain't polite to ask anybody what his name is," shouted a fat, quick boy, interrupted by a little girl shrieking, "You can't

---

4. **damask** [dam′əsk]: tablecloth and napkins made of damask, a fine fabric that has a design woven into it.
5. **detached retina** [ret′ən ə]: visual disorder produced by damaged nerve tissue in the eye.

6. **Goody:** short for "Goodwife," title once used for wives of working men.
7. **concertina:** musical instrument similar to a small accordion.

GUIDED READING

LITERAL QUESTIONS

1a. What do the boys discover about the spell that shuts the door to the inner chamber? (It is effective.)

2a. What surprising facts does the narrator reveal about the school on Sattins Island? (Since no one is literate, there are no books, desks, or blackboards.)

INFERENTIAL QUESTIONS

1b. What does the spell's effectiveness suggest about Mr. Underhill? (that sometimes he can be a good wizard)

2b. What would be the point of having a school in such a place? (The school on Sattins Island seems meant to teach obedience to the rules.)

never tell your own name to nobody, my ma says!"

"Yes, Suba. Yes, Popi dear, don't screech. **1** That's right. You never ask anybody his name. You never tell your own. Now think about that a minute and then tell me why we call our wizard Mr. Underhill." She smiled across the curly heads and the woolly backs at Mr. Underhill, who beamed, and nervously clutched his sack of eggs.

" 'Cause he lives under a hill!" said half the children.

"But is it his truename?"

"No!" said the fat boy, echoed by little Popi shrieking, "No!"

"How do you know it's not?"

2 " 'Cause he came here all alone and so there wasn't anybody knew his truename so they couldn't tell, and *he* couldn't—"

"Very good, Suba. Popi, don't shout. That's right. Even a wizard can't tell his truename. When you children are through school and go through the Passage, you'll leave your child-names behind and keep only your truenames, which you must never ask for and never give away. Why is that the rule?"

The children were silent. The sheep bleated gently. Mr. Underhill answered the question: "Because the name is the thing," he said in his shy, soft, husky voice, "and the

AT A GLANCE

- The Rules of Names are "You never ask anybody his name. You never tell your own."
- Mr. Underhill's truename is unknown. He is called Underhill because of where he lives.

1 THEME

A world in which people never reveal their "truenames" to each other is one in which people hide their true selves. It is a world of appearances in which people try to evade the power of the truth by disguising it.

2 STYLE: DIALOGUE

The dialogue between teacher and students reveals a crucial element of the plot: Mr. Underhill came to the island alone, so nothing is known of his past.

GUIDED READING

LITERAL QUESTION

1a. What is Mr. Underhill's truename? (No one knows.) How did he get the name Underhill? (He came to the island alone, and according to the Rules of Names, he could not reveal his truename; he was named after where he lives.)

INFERENTIAL QUESTION

1b. How do the Rules of Names protect someone with a secret past? (It is easy for individuals to disguise their identities because they never have to reveal their real names.)

- Mr. Underhill explains the reason for the rules.
- A boat from the Archipelago arrives with a sailor who carries a wizard's oaken stick.
- Everyone comes out to meet the boat except Mr. Underhill.
- They call the stranger Blackbeard.

1 RESPONSE JOURNAL

in their journals have students consider the statement, "To speak the name is to control the thing." In what ways does knowing the name of something or someone give us power over the thing or person?

2 SETTING

Sattins Island is apparently a very isolated part of the Earthsea world. This fact helps explain the character of its people and is also an important element of the plot.

3 THEME

There is a hint of mystery and adventure in Old Seacaptain Fogeno's reaction to the news that only one man is aboard the foreign boat.

4 CHARACTERIZATION

The voyager *seems* friendly, "like any sailor glad to have made port." In a world based solely on appearances, however, it is hard to gain a true reading of a person's character.

5 POINT OF VIEW

The third-person narrator reveals the characters' unexpressed suspicions of the stranger.

---

1 truename is the true thing. To speak the name is to control the thing. Am I right, Schoolmistress?"

She smiled and curtsied, evidently a little embarrassed by his participation. And he trotted off towards his hill, clutching his eggs to his bosom. Somehow the minute spent watching Palani and the children had made him very hungry. He locked his inner door behind him with a hasty incantation,[8] but there must have been a leak or two in the spell, for soon the bare anteroom of the cave was rich with the smell of frying eggs and sizzling liver.

The wind that day was light and fresh out of the west, and on it at noon a little boat came skimming the bright waves into Sattins Harbor. Even as it rounded the point a sharp-eyed boy spotted it, and knowing, like every child on the island, every sail and spar of the forty boats of the fishing fleet, he ran down the street calling out, "A foreign boat, a for- **2** eign boat!" Very seldom was the lonely isle visited by a boat from some equally lonely isle of the East Reach, or an adventurous trader from the Archipelago.[9] By the time the boat was at the pier half the village was there to greet it, and fishermen were following it homewards, and cowherds and clam-diggers and herb-hunters were puffing up and down all the rocky hills, heading towards the harbor.

But Mr. Underhill's door stayed shut.

3 There was only one man aboard the boat. Old Seacaptain Fogeno, when they told him that, drew down a bristle of white brows over his unseeing eyes. "There's only one kind of man," he said, "that sails the Outer Reach

---

8. **incantation:** chanting of magic words in order to cast a spell.
9. **Archipelago** [är′kə pel′ə gō′]: group of many islands; here, the name of an imaginary group of islands.

124 *The Short Story*

---

alone. A wizard, or a warlock, or a Mage. . . ."

So the villagers were breathless hoping to see for once in their lives a Mage, one of the mighty White Magicians of the rich, towered, crowded inner islands of the Archipelago. They were disappointed, for the voyager was **4** quite young, a handsome black-bearded fellow who hailed them cheerfully from his boat, and leaped ashore like any sailor glad to have made port. He introduced himself at once as a sea-peddler. But when they told Seacaptain Fogeno that he carried an oaken walking-stick around with him, the old man nodded. "Two wizards in one town," he said. "Bad!" And his mouth snapped shut like an old carp's.

As the stranger could not give them his name, they gave him one right away: Blackbeard. And they gave him plenty of attention. He had a small mixed cargo of cloth and sandals and piswi feathers for trimming cloaks and cheap incense and levity stones and fine herbs and great glass beads from Venway— the usual peddler's lot. Everyone on Sattins Island came to look, to chat with the voyager, and perhaps to buy something—"Just to remember him by!" cackled Goody Guld, who like all the women and girls of the village was smitten with Blackbeard's bold good looks. All the boys hung round him too, to hear him tell of his voyages to far, strange islands of the Reach or describe the great rich islands of the Archipelago, the Inner Lanes, the roadsteads white with ships, and the golden roofs of Hav- **5** nor. The men willingly listened to his tales; but some of them wondered why a trader should sail alone, and kept their eyes thoughtfully upon his oaken staff.

But all this time Mr. Underhill stayed under his hill.

"This is the first island I've ever seen that had no wizard," said Blackbeard one evening to Goody Guld, who had invited him and her nephew and Palani in for a cup of rushwash

---

GUIDED READING

LITERAL QUESTIONS

1a. Where is Mr. Underhill when the boat arrives? (inside his cave with the door shut) Does he come out to meet the stranger? (no)

2a. What kind of person do the villagers hope the stranger will be? (a mage, or White Magician) Why are they disappointed? (His cheerful appearance suggests he is merely an ordinary young sailor.)

INFERENTIAL QUESTIONS

1b. Why might the villagers not be surprised at Mr. Underhill's behavior? (He never comes out to meet strangers; he says he's afraid "of the evil eye.")

2b. How can you tell that appearances are very important on Sattins Island? (The inhabitants seem to base all their estimates of a person's character on appearances.)

tea. "What do you do when you get a tooth-ache, or the cow goes dry?"

"Why, we've got Mr. Underhill!" said the old woman.

"For what that's worth," muttered her nephew Birt, and then blushed purple and spilled his tea. Birt was a fisherman, a large, brave, wordless young man. He loved the schoolmistress, but the nearest he had come to telling her of his love was to give baskets of fresh mackerel to her father's cook.

1 "Oh, you do have a wizard?" Blackbeard asked. "Is he invisible?"

"No, he's just very shy," said Palani. "You've only been here a week, you know, and we see so few strangers here. . . ." She also blushed a little, but did not spill her tea.

Blackbeard smiled at her. "He's a good Sattinsman, then, eh?"

"No," said Goody Guld, "no more than you are. Another cup, nevvy?[10]—keep it in the cup this time. No, my dear, he came in a little bit of a boat, four years ago was it?—just a day after the end of the shad-run, I recall, for they

---

10. **nevvy**: dialect for *nephew.*

---

was taking up the nets over in East Creek, and Pondi Cowherd broke his leg that very morning—five years ago it must be. No, four. No, five it is, 'twas the year the garlic didn't 2 sprout. So he sails in on a bit of a sloop loaded full up with great chests and boxes and says to Seacaptain Fogeno, who wasn't blind then, though old enough goodness knows to be blind twice over, 'I hear tell,' he says, 'you've got no wizard nor warlock at all, might you be wanting one?' 'Indeed, if the magic's white!' says the Captain, and before you could say 'cuttlefish' Mr. Underhill had settled down in the cave under the hill and was charming the mange[11] off Goody Beltow's cat. Though the fur grew in gray, and 'twas an orange cat. Queer-looking thing it was after that. It died last winter in the cold spell. Goody Beltow took on so at that cat's death, poor thing, worse than when her man was drowned on the Long Banks, the year of the long herring-runs, when nevvy Birt here was but a babe in petticoats." Here Birt spilled his tea again, and Blackbeard grinned, but Goody Guld proceeded undismayed, and talked on till night-fall.

Next day Blackbeard was down at the pier, seeing after the sprung board in his boat which he seemed to take a long time fixing, and as usual drawing the taciturn[12] Sattinsmen into talk. "Now which of these is your wizard's craft?" he asked. "Or has he got one of those the Mages fold up into a walnut shell when they're not using it?"

3 "Nay," said a stolid fisherman. "She's oop in his cave, under hill."

"He carried the boat he came in up to his cave?"

"Aye. Clear oop. I helped. Heavier as lead she was. Full oop with great boxes, and they

---

11. **mange** [mānj]: skin disease in animals.
12. **taciturn** [tas′ə turn′]: not talkative.

The Rule of Names 125

AT A GLANCE

- Blackbeard asks questions about Mr. Underhill.
- Goody Guld tells Blackbeard how Mr. Underhill came to the island and about his wizardry.
- Blackbeard discovers that Underhill's boat is up in his cave.

1 CHARACTERIZATION

Blackbeard's pleasant appearance continues to deceive the villagers. Though his questions *appear* innocent, he is in reality cleverly drawing out information about Mr. Underhill. His question *Is he invisible?* suggests mocking humor.

2 PLOT: SUSPENSE

New information about Mr. Underhill's arrival creates suspense: What is in the "great chests and boxes" his ship carried?

3 PLOT: FORESHADOWING

Blackbeard's relentless questioning about Mr. Underhill suggests that he is tracking someone and that he believes Mr. Underhill is the one he is seeking.

GUIDED READING

LITERAL QUESTIONS

1a. What does Blackbeard ask when Goody Guld first mentions Mr. Underhill? ("Oh, you do have a wizard? . . . Is he invisible?")

2a. What does Blackbeard spend a long time doing at the pier? (fixing the sprung board in his boat)

INFERENTIAL QUESTIONS

1b. Why does Blackbeard say this? (He has been on the island a week and hasn't seen the wizard; he is looking for information about someone; he may be mocking Mr. Underhill and the villagers.)

2b. What is his real reason for being at the pier? (to get more information about Mr. Underhill)

1 VOCABULARY: CONNOTATIONS

The words *stolid*, *stolidly*, and *stolidity* not only indicate a lack of emotion but also connote dullness and stupidity. The villagers seem unable to make the connection between the loaded ship and Blackbeard's curiosity.

2 PLOT: FORESHADOWING

Blackbeard suggests that events are about to come to a head.

3 THEME

As Blackbeard tells of a priceless treasure and of innocent maidens pursued by an evil dragon, the gentle humor of the story gives way to elements of mystery and adventure.

4 PLOT: SUSPENSE

Mention of an "unknown wizard from somewhere" who slew the dragon and made off with the treasure creates suspense. We wonder if the mild-mannered Mr. Underhill could be that wizard.

---

1 full oop with books o' spells, he says. Heavier as lead she was." And the stolid fisherman turned his back, sighing stolidly. Goody Guld's nephew, mending a net nearby, looked up from his work and asked with equal stolidity.[13] "Would ye like to meet Mr. Underhill, maybe?"

Blackbeard returned Birt's look. Clever black eyes met candid blue ones for a long moment; then Blackbeard smiled and said, "Yes. Will you take me up to the hill, Birt?"

"Aye, when I'm done with this," said the fisherman. And when the net was mended, he and the Archipelagan set off up the village street towards the high green hill above it. But as they crossed the common, Blackbeard said, "Hold on awhile, friend Birt. I have a tale to tell you, before we meet your wizard."

"Tell away," says Birt, sitting down in the shade of a live oak.

2 "It's a story that started a hundred years ago, and isn't finished yet—though it soon will be, very soon. . . . In the very heart of the Archipelago, where the islands crowd thick as flies on honey, there's a little isle called Pendor. The sealords of Pendor were mighty men, in the old days of war before the League. Loot and ransom and tribute came pouring into Pendor, and they gathered a great treasure there, long ago. Then from somewhere away out in the West Reach, where dragons breed on the lava isles, came one day a very mighty dragon. Not one of those overgrown lizards most of you Outer Reach folk call dragons, but a big, black, winged, wise, cunning monster, full of strength and subtlety, and like all dragons loving gold and precious stones above all things. He killed the Sealord and his soldiers, and the people of Pendor fled in their ships by night. They all fled away and left the dragon coiled up in Pendor Towers. And there

---

13. **stolidity** [stə lid′ə tē]: lack of emotion.

3 he stayed for a hundred years, dragging his scaly belly over the emeralds and sapphires and coins of gold, coming forth only once in a year or two when he must eat. He'd raid nearby islands for his food. You know what dragons eat?"

Birt nodded and said in a whisper, "Maidens."

"Right," said Blackbeard. "Well, that couldn't be endured forever, nor the thought of his sitting on all that treasure. So after the League grew strong, and the Archipelago wasn't so busy with wars and piracy, it was decided to attack Pendor, drive out the dragon, and get the gold and jewels for the treasury of the League. They're forever wanting money, the League is. So a huge fleet gathered from fifty islands, and seven Mages stood in the prows of the seven strongest ships, and they sailed towards Pendor. . . . They got there. They landed. Nothing stirred. The houses all stood empty, the dishes on the tables full of a hundred years' dust. The bones of the old Sealord and his men lay about in the castle courts and on the stairs. And the Tower rooms reeked of dragon. But there was no dragon. And no treasure, not a diamond the size of a poppyseed, not a single silver bead. . . . Knowing that he couldn't stand up to seven Mages, the dragon had skipped out. They tracked him, and found he'd flown to a deserted island up north called Udrath; they followed his trail there, and what did they **4** find? Bones again. His bones—the dragon's. But no treasure. A wizard, some unknown wizard from somewhere, must have met him singlehanded, and defeated him—and then made off with the treasure, right under the League's nose!"

The fisherman listened, attentive and expressionless.

"Now that must have been a powerful wizard and a clever one, first to kill a dragon, and

---

GUIDED READING

LITERAL QUESTIONS

1a. How does the narrator describe Birt's eyes? (*candid blue*)

2a. How does Blackbeard describe what the Outer Reach folk call dragons? (*overgrown lizards*)

INFERENTIAL QUESTIONS

1b. Does Birt have any suspicions of Blackbeard? Explain. (No. Birt's candid eyes would give away his feelings.)

2b. How does Blackbeard seem to feel about the Outer Reach folk? (He seems to have contempt for them and their lack of knowledge about the real dangers in the world.)

second to get off without leaving a trace. The lords and Mages of the Archipelago couldn't track him at all, neither where he'd come from nor where he'd made off to. They were about to give up. That was last spring; I'd been off on a three-year voyage up in the North Reach, and got back about that time. And they asked me to help them find the unknown wizard. That was clever of them. Because I'm not only a wizard myself, as I think some of the oafs here have guessed, but I am also a descendant of the Lords of Pendor. That treasure is mine. It's mine, and knows that it's mine. Those fools of the League couldn't find it, because it's not theirs. It belongs to the House of Pendor, and the great emerald, the star of the hoard, Inalkil the Greenstone, knows its master. Behold!" Blackbeard raised his oaken staff and cried aloud, "Inalkil!" The tip of the staff began to glow green, a fiery green radiance, a dazzling haze the color of April grass, and at the same moment the staff tipped in the wizard's hand, leaning, slanting till it pointed straight at the side of the hill above them.

"It wasn't so bright a glow, far away in Havnor," Blackbeard murmured, "but the staff pointed true. Inalkil answered when I called. The jewel knows its master. And I know the thief, and I shall conquer him. He's a mighty wizard, who could overcome a dragon. But I am mightier. Do you want to know why, oaf? Because I know his name!"

As Blackbeard's tone got more arrogant, Birt had looked duller and duller, blanker and blanker; but at this he gave a twitch, shut his mouth, and stared at the Archipelagan. "How did you . . . learn it?" he asked very slowly.

Blackbeard grinned, and did not answer.

"Black magic?"

"How else?"

Birt looked pale, and said nothing.

"I am the Sealord of Pendor, oaf, and I will have the gold my fathers won, and the jewels my mothers wore, and the Greenstone! For they are mine. Now, you can tell your village boobies the whole story after I have defeated this wizard and gone. Wait here. Or you can come and watch, it you're not afraid. You'll never get the chance again to see a great wizard in all his power." Blackbeard turned, and without a backward glance strode off up the hill towards the entrance to the cave.

Very slowly, Birt followed. A good distance from the cave he stopped, sat down under a hawthorn tree, and watched. The Archipelagan had stopped; a stiff, dark figure alone on the green swell of the hill before the gaping cave-mouth, he stood perfectly still. All at once he swung his staff up over his head, and the emerald radiance shone about him as he shouted, "Thief, thief of the Hoard of Pendor, come forth!"

There was a crash, as of dropped crockery, from inside the cave, and a lot of dust came spewing out. Scared, Birt ducked. When he looked again he saw Blackbeard still standing motionless, and at the mouth of the cave, dusty and disheveled, stood Mr. Underhill. He looked small and pitiful, with his toes turned in as usual, and his little bowlegs in black tights, and no staff—he never had had one, Birt suddenly thought. Mr. Underhill spoke. "Who are you?" he said in his husky little voice.

"I am the Sealord of Pendor, thief, come to claim my treasure!"

At that, Mr. Underhill slowly turned pink, as he always did when people were rude to him. But he then turned something else. He turned yellow. His hair bristled out, he gave a coughing roar—and was a yellow lion leaping down the hill at Blackbeard, white fangs gleaming.

But Blackbeard no longer stood there. A gigantic tiger, color of night and lightning, bounded to meet the lion. . . .

The Rule of Names 127

AT A GLANCE
- Blackbeard identifies himself as the owner of the stolen treasure.
- His oaken staff points to Underhill's cave.
- Blackbeard demands that Underhill come forth with the treasure.
- Underhill emerges, and the men metamorphose into lion and tiger.

1 STYLE: REPETITION

The repetition of the word *mine* helps suggest the ferocity of Blackbeard's emotions.

2 PLOT: SUSPENSE

The magic staff seems to have indicated that Mr. Underhill is the "mighty wizard" who stole the treasure. But Blackbeard believes he himself is even mightier—because he knows Underhill's true name. Suspense increases about who will win out.

3 THEME

Mr. Underhill cleverly maintains his unassuming appearance until he is directly confronted by Blackbeard, who has finally revealed himself to be the Sealord of Pendor.

GUIDED READING

LITERAL QUESTIONS

1a. What words does Blackbeard use to refer to the villagers now? *(oafs, boobies)*

2a. What detail does Birt suddenly realize the villagers have overlooked about Mr. Underhill? (He is not holding a staff and had never had one.)

INFERENTIAL QUESTIONS

1b. Why does Blackbeard feel free to insult them now? (He doesn't need any more information from them.)

2b. What does this detail suggest? (Mr. Underhill is not a wizard.)

The lion was gone. Below the cave all of a sudden stood a high grove of trees, black in the winter sunshine. The tiger, checking himself in mid-leap just before he entered the shadow of the trees, caught fire in the air, became a tongue of flame lashing out at the dry black branches. . . .

But where the trees had stood a sudden cataract[14] leaped from the hillside, an arch of silvery crashing water, thundering down upon the fire. But the fire was gone. . . .

For just a moment before the fisherman's staring eyes two hills rose—the green one he knew, and a new one, a bare, brown hillock ready to drink up the rushing waterfall. That passed so quickly it made Birt blink, and after blinking he blinked again, and moaned, for what he saw now was a great deal worse. Where the cataract had been there hovered a dragon. Black wings darkened all the hill, steel claws reached groping, and from the dark, scaly, gaping lips fire and steam shot out.

Beneath the monstrous creature stood Blackbeard, laughing.

"Take any shape you please, little Mr. Underhill!" he taunted. "I can match you. But the game grows tiresome. I want to look upon **1** my treasure, upon Inalkil. Now, big dragon, little wizard, take your true shape. I command you by the power of your truename—Yevaud!"

Birt could not move at all, not even to blink. He cowered, staring whether he would or not. He saw the black dragon hang there in the air above Blackbeard. He saw the fire lick like many tongues from the scaly mouth, the steam jet from the red nostrils. He saw Blackbeard's face grow white, white as chalk, and the beard-fringed lips trembling.

"Your name is Yevaud!"

"Yes," said a great, husky, hissing voice.

---

14. **cataract** [kat′ə rakt′]: large waterfall.

2 "My truename is Yevaud, and my true shape is this shape."

"But the dragon was killed—they found dragon bones on Udrath Island—"

"That was another dragon," said the dragon, and then stooped like a hawk, talons outstretched. And Birt shut his eyes.

When he opened them the sky was clear, the hillside empty, except for a reddish-blackish trampled spot, and a few talonmarks in the grass.

Birt the fisherman got to his feet and ran. He ran across the common, scattering sheep to right and left, and straight down to the **3** village street to Palani's father's house. Palani was out in the garden weeding the nasturtiums. "Come with me!" Birt gasped. She stared. He grabbed her wrist and dragged her with him. She screeched a little, but did not resist. He ran with her straight to the pier, pushed her into his fishing sloop the *Queenie*, untied the painter,[15] took up the oars and set off rowing like a demon. The last that Sattins Island saw of him and Palani was the *Queenie*'s sail vanishing in the direction of the nearest island westward.

The villagers thought they would never stop talking about it, how Goody Guld's nephew Birt had lost his mind and sailed off with the schoolmistress on the very same day that the peddler Blackbeard disappeared without a trace, leaving all his feathers and beads behind. But they did stop talking about it, three days later. They had other things to talk about, when Mr. Underhill finally came out of his cave.

4 Mr. Underhill had decided that since his truename was no longer a secret, he might as well drop his disguise. Walking was a lot harder than flying, and besides, it was a long, long time since he had had a real meal.

---

15. **painter:** rope that ties a boat to a pier.

The Rule of Names 129

AT A GLANCE

- Underhill metamorphoses into a dragon.
- Blackbeard calls out Underhill's truename, Yevaud, and the dragon kills him.
- Birt sails away with Palani.
- Underhill remains a dragon—a very hungry dragon.

1 PLOT: CLIMAX

The story reaches its emotional high point as Blackbeard finally utters Mr. Underhill's truename—and we anxiously await the results.

2 SURPRISE ENDING

Little Mr. Underhill, who appeared so nice, timid, and inept, turns out to really be the mighty, merciless dragon who stole the treasure. He remains in his true shape even after his truename is said.

3 CHARACTERIZATION

The normally slow Birt grasps the danger: Dragons have a reputation for eating maidens. He escapes with Palani to another island.

4 THEME

The story ends on a note of grim humor as Underhill, or Yevaud, finally dispenses with appearances forever and brazenly lives out his true nature.

REFLECTING ON THE STORY

Why do you think the story is called "The Rule of Names"? (The story takes place in a world where a person cannot ask someone's truename or give one's own truename. The plot depends on this fact.)

GUIDED READING

LITERAL QUESTIONS

1a. What does Birt do when the dragon stretches out its talons? (shuts his eyes)

2a. What is Mr. Underhill's true identify? (He is Yevaud, the dragon who stole the treasure.)

INFERENTIAL QUESTIONS

1b. What would Birt have seen otherwise? (Blackbeard being killed by the dragon)

2b. Why has Yevaud pretended to be an inept wizard? (so that no one could come after him seeking the treasure)

1. wizard of Sattins Island; weak elixirs, reappearing warts, enchanted tomatoes no bigger than cantaloupes, inefficient spells, unsatisfying meals
2. ■ Never ask anybody's name; never tell your own.
   ■ "To speak the name is to control thing."
3. great, cunning dragon; dragon guarded it for a hundred years, League decided to attack, dragon and treasure disappeared
4. Tip glows, points to where Underhill lives. He knows wizard's truename.
5. huge, winged dragon; pretended to be weak, ineffective wizard
6. runs away with schoolmistress; decides to live in true shape
7. Underhill as dragon is too powerful for him; is probably devoured
8. Answers will vary. Possible answers: p. 122—"He [Underhill] did not like anyone to visit his cave"; p. 124—"So the villagers were breathless hoping to see for once in their lives a Mage. . . . They were disappointed."
9. Mr. Underhill looks weak and seems inefficient, but he is actually a villainous dragon with great powers.

READING AND LITERARY FOCUS

1. We are lead to believe Underhill is a poor, weak wizard and Blackbeard is the powerful one; the opposite is shown to be true.
2. shy, embarrassed, reclusive; has none of the assertiveness, confidence one might expect from dragon
3. Underhill carries fully loaded ship to cave; boys trying to break into his cave are amazed by bellowing.

VOCABULARY

1. (a) forfeit
2. (b) huddled in fear
3. (c) honest
4. (b) smelled of
5. (d) wide open

STUDY QUESTIONS

Recalling

1. What is Mr. Underhill's job? Give five examples of the poor quality of his work.
2. What are the two rules of names? Why are these rules important?
3. Who stole Blackbeard's treasure? What happened to the treasure after it was stolen?
4. After Blackbeard tells his tale, what happens to his staff? Why does he expect to defeat Underhill?
5. What is Underhill's true shape? In what way did he deceive Blackbeard?
6. What finally happens to Birt? To Underhill?

Interpreting

7. Why does Blackbeard's plan fail? What finally happens to him?
8. Find examples in which the third-person narrator reveals the thoughts of two characters.

Extending

9. Appearances are often misleading. Use the story as an example to explain this idea.

READING AND LITERARY FOCUS

Surprise Ending

Some stories have endings that are easy to predict. Others have surprise endings. In a story with a **surprise ending,** the conflict is solved in a way that most readers would not expect. Authors can create surprise endings by deliberately misleading the reader. However, the ending of a story develops logically from what goes before it. Therefore, the ending of a good story is never a complete surprise. In addition, **foreshadowing** often provides clues to a surprise ending. For example, in "Charles" (page 53) Laurie's tales about Charles mislead us. We think that Charles is a boy at school. Therefore, the ending is a surprise. However, Laurie's behavior during the story is a clue to the truth.

130   *The Short Story*

Thinking About the Surprise Ending

1. In what sense is the ending of "The Rule of Names" a surprise?
2. In what way does Underhill's personality mislead the reader?
3. Find two examples of foreshadowing.

VOCABULARY

Synonyms

A **synonym** is a word that has the same or nearly the same meaning as another word. *End* and *finish* are synonyms. The italicized words in the following numbered items are from "The Rule of Names." Choose the word that is nearest the meaning of the italicized word, *as the word is used in the story*. Write the number of each item and the letter of your choice on a separate sheet.

1. win by *default*
   (a) forfeit   (c) disdain
   (b) dishonesty   (d) talent
2. The mouse *cowered* in the corner.
   (a) ran wildly   (c) ate greedily
   (b) huddled in fear (d) lay down
3. a *candid* opinion
   (a) incomplete   (c) honest
   (b) delayed   (d) negative
4. *reeked of* onion
   (a) made from   (c) covered with
   (b) smelled of   (d) looked like
5. a *gaping* hole
   (a) filled in   (c) small
   (b) dangerous   (d) wide open

COMPARING STORIES

■ Compare two or more of the following stories: "Mary," "Weep No More, My Lady," and "The Rule of Names." Explain the secret in each story. Then tell which narrator gives the reader more information about the secret. Tell how your knowledge of the truth accounts for the story's impact on you.

COMPARING STORIES

■ "Mary": Kass arranges to have her prize given to Mary; all details of secret are given, so readers understand Kass's reaction to the praise Mary gets.

■ "Weep No More": Narrator reveals that a dog was lost in swamp and owners had run ads offering a reward for its return; Jesse and Skeeter never read papers—couldn't know about ads; dog's identity is not a primary concern; readers focus on characters.

■ "The Rule of Names": Narrator gives very few clues about secret; truth is surprising when revealed at end; narrators of other stories use secrets to involve rather than surprise readers.

Lucy Maude Montgomery (1874–1942) grew up on Prince Edward Island, which is off the east coast of Canada. Many of her stories and novels are set on the island. In "The Brother Who Failed" a large family gathers together for the first time in thirty years.

■ What do you think the story says about families, success, and failure?

L. M. Montgomery

¹ The Brother Who Failed

The Monroe family were holding a Christmas reunion at the old Prince Edward Island¹ homestead at White Sands. It was the first time they had all been together under one roof since the death of their mother, thirty years before. The idea of this Christmas reunion had originated with Edith Monroe the preceding spring, during her tedious convalescence from a bad attack of pneumonia among strangers in an American city, where she had not been able to fill her concert engagements, and had more spare time in which to feel the tug of old ties and the homesick longing for her own people than she had had for years. As a result, when she recovered, she wrote to her second brother, James Monroe, who lived on the homestead; and the consequence was this gathering of the Monroes under the old rooftree. Ralph Monroe for once laid aside the cares of his railroads, and the deceitfulness of his millions, in Toronto² and took the long-promised, long-deferred trip to the homeland. Malcolm Monroe journeyed from the far western university of which he was president. ² Edith came, flushed with the triumph of her latest and most successful concert tour. Mrs. Woodburn, who had been Margaret Monroe, came from the Nova Scotia³ town where she lived a busy, happy life as the wife of a rising young lawyer. James, prosperous and hearty, greeted them warmly at the old homestead whose fertile acres had well repaid his skillful management.

They were a merry party, casting aside their cares and years, and harking back to joyous boyhood and girlhood once more. James had a family of rosy lads and lasses;

_____
1. **Prince Edward Island:** island province off southeastern Canada.

2. **Toronto** [tə ron′tō]: large port city on Lake Ontario in southern Canada.
3. **Nova Scotia** [nō′və skō′shə]: province of southeastern Canada.

The Brother Who Failed   131

■ The story is set on Prince Edward Island, Canada.
■ The Monroe family, successful in their various fields, are holding a Christmas reunion, their first in thirty years.

LITERARY OPTIONS

■ characterization
■ point of view
■ title

THEMATIC OPTIONS

■ failure and success
■ family loyalty and love
■ justice

1 THEME

The title of the story alerts us immediately to the theme of failure and success.

2 POINT OF VIEW

The omniscient narrator can describe each character's history and feelings, enriching our sense of the complex relationships possible in a large family.

TEXAS ESSENTIAL ELEMENTS GRADE 8

1A writing process
1B purpose and audience
1C support for main idea
1E appropriate language
3A plot development and character development
3D literary genres
4E cause/effect
4F point of view
To locate treatment of an Element, see *Texas Teacher's Resources*.

GUIDED READING

LITERAL QUESTION

1a. How long has it been since the Monroe family have been together? (thirty years)

INFERENTIAL QUESTION

1b. What does this fact suggest about the brothers and sisters? (Answers will vary. Possibilities: They drifted apart after their mother's death; they lead busy lives.)

- Aunt Isabel is proud of her successful family.
- Robert, the only "failure" in the family, is largely ignored.
- He returns next day and sits in the yard to await the family's return from various activities.

1 CHARACTER

The description of Aunt Isabel as "talkative, clever, shrewd" suggests that she too had the ingredients for success, although she did not develop them. She identifies with her aggressive nieces' and nephews' successes.

2 POINT OF VIEW

The narrator intrudes briefly into the story as *I* to make a point: Robert is so easy to overlook that even the narrator has supposedly forgotten him for a moment.

3 CHARACTERIZATION

The description of Robert's sitting "back in a corner" without speaking and then slipping "noiselessly away" suggests that he may be partly responsible for being ignored.

4 PLOT: FORESHADOWING

The narrator seems to sympathize with the family's thoughtless treatment of Robert. Yet the reason for his early departure suggests a depth of character not previously suspected.

Margaret brought her two blue-eyed little girls; Ralph's dark, clever-looking son accompanied him, and Malcolm brought his, a young man with a resolute face, in which there was less of boyishness than in his father's, and the eye of a keen, perhaps a hard bargainer. The two cousins were the same age to a day, and it was a family joke among the Monroes that the stork must have mixed the babies, since Ralph's son was like Malcolm in face and brain, while Malcolm's boy was a second edition of his Uncle Ralph.

1 To crown all, Aunt Isabel came, too—a talkative, clever, shrewd old lady, as young at eight-five as she had been at thirty, thinking the Monroe stock the best in the world, and beamingly proud of her nephews and nieces, who had gone out from this humble, little farm to destinies of such brilliance and influence in the world beyond.

2 I have forgotten Robert. Robert Monroe was apt to be forgotten. Although he was the oldest of the family, White Sands people, in naming over the various members of the Monroe family, would add, "and Robert," in a tone of surprise over the remembrance of his existence.

He lived on a poor, sandy little farm down by the shore, but he had come up to James' place on the evening when the guests arrived; 3 they had all greeted him warmly and joyously, and then did not think about him again in their laughter and conversation. Robert sat back in a corner and listened with a smile, but he never spoke. Afterwards he had slipped noiselessly away and gone home, and nobody noticed his going. They were all gaily busy recalling what had happened in the old times and telling what had happened in the new.

Edith recounted the successes of her concert tours; Malcolm expatiated[4] proudly on his plans for developing his beloved college; Ralph described the country through which his new railroad ran, and the difficulties he had had to overcome in connection with it. James, aside, discussed his orchard and his crops with Margaret, who had not been long enough away from the farm to lose touch with its interests. Aunt Isabel knitted and smiled complacently[5] on all, talking now with one, now with the other, secretly quite proud of herself that she, an old woman of eighty-five, who had seldom been out of White Sands in her life, could discuss high finance with Ralph, and higher education with Malcolm, and hold her own with James in an argument on drainage.

The White Sands school teacher, an arch-eyed, red-mouthed bit of a girl—a Bell from Avonlea—who boarded with the James Monroes, amused herself with the boys. All were 4 enjoying themselves hugely, so it is not to be wondered at that they did not miss Robert, who had gone home early because his old housekeeper was nervous if left alone at night.

He came again the next afternoon. From James, in the barnyard, he learned that Malcolm and Ralph had driven to the harbor, that Margaret and Mrs. James had gone to call on friends in Avonlea, and that Edith was walking somewhere in the woods on the hill. There was nobody in the house except Aunt Isabel and the teacher.

"You'd better wait and stay the evening," said James indifferently. "They'll all be back soon."

Robert went across the yard and sat down on the rustic bench in the angle of the front porch. It was a fine December evening, as mild as autumn; there had been no snow, and the long fields, sloping down from the homestead, were brown and mellow. A quiet hush, hold-

---

4. **expatiated** [eks pā′shē āt′ed]: spoke in detail.

5. **complacently** [kəm plā′sənt lē]: with satisfaction.

GUIDED READING

LITERAL QUESTIONS

1a. How does the author describe Aunt Isabel? (She is talkative, clever, shrewd; she is proud of her nieces' and nephews' success and of her own ability to talk to them.)

2a. How does Robert act around his family? (He sits in a corner and is very quiet.)

INFERENTIAL QUESTIONS

1b. How do you think Aunt Isabel would feel about someone who was not successful? (She would probably not be understanding or sympathetic; she would judge harshly.)

2b. Why doesn't Robert join in the party? (He is naturally quiet and shy; perhaps aggressive people intimidate him.)

ing something of magic in it, rested like an unseen mantle on the dark forest, brooding field and the once flowering, fertile valley. The earth was like a tired old man patiently awaiting his well-earned sleep. Out to sea, a dull, red sunset faded out into somber clouds, and the soft sound of the waves breaking on the shore was wafted on the evening breeze.

Robert rested his chin on his hand and looked across the vales and hills, where the feathery gray of leafless hardwoods was mingled with the sturdy, unfailing green of the conebearers.[6] He was a tall, bent man, with thin, gray hair, a lined face, and deeply-set, gentle, brown eyes—the eyes of one who, looking through pain, sees rapture[7] beyond.

He felt very happy. He loved his family clannishly,[8] and he was rejoiced that they were all again near to him. He was proud of their success and fame. He was glad that James had prospered so well of late years. There was no canker[9] of envy or discontent in his soul.

He heard absently indistinct voices at the open hall window above the porch, where Aunt Isabel was talking to Kathleen Bell. Presently Aunt Isabel moved nearer to the window, and her words came down to Robert with startling clearness.

"Yes, I can assure you, Miss Bell, that I'm real proud of my nephews and nieces. They're a smart family. They've almost all done well, and they hadn't any of them much to begin with. Ralph had absolutely nothing and today he is a millionaire. Their father met with so many losses, what with his ill-health and the bank failing, that he couldn't help them any. But they've all succeeded, except poor Robert—and I must admit that he's a total failure."

"Oh, no, no," said the little teacher deprecatingly.[10]

"A total failure!" Aunt Isabel repeated her words emphatically.[11] She was not going to be contradicted by anybody, least of all a Bell from Avonlea. "He has been a failure since the time he was born. He is the first Monroe to disgrace the old stock that way. I'm sure his brothers and sisters must be dreadfully ashamed of him. He has lived sixty years and he hasn't done a thing worth while. He can't even make his farm pay. If he's kept out of debt it's as much as he's ever managed to do."

"Some men can't even do that," murmured the little school teacher. She was really so much in awe of this imperious,[12] clever old Aunt Isabel that it was positive heroism on her part to venture even this faint protest.

6. **conebearers:** evergreen trees that produce cones.
7. **rapture** [rap′chər]: joy.
8. **clannishly:** with the closeness of a family.
9. **canker:** infection that destroys.

10. **deprecatingly** [dep′ri kāt′ing lē]: with embarrassment.
11. **emphatically** [em fat′ik lē]: with force.
12. **imperious** [im pēr′ē əs]: behaving like a dictator.

The Brother Who Failed   133

AT A GLANCE

■ Robert is happy, rejoicing in his family's success.
■ He overhears Aunt Isabel call him a failure.

1 STYLE: SIMILE

"The earth was like a tired old man patiently awaiting his well-earned sleep" is a simile that suggests both the tranquility of the landscape and the close link between Robert and his surroundings.

2 POINT OF VIEW

The narrator gives an intimate look at Robert's feelings and motivations. Despite what we might expect, he feels no envy for his brothers and sisters.

3 STYLE: DIALOGUE

Aunt Isabel's overheard remarks about Robert's failure are central to the story. They motivate other characters' actions and become the focus of the story's developing plot and theme.

4 PLOT: CONFLICT

Aunt Isabel not only believes that Robert is a failure, but she is also aggressive in asserting it. Her certainty and smugness challenge the other characters.

5 TITLE

Based on the information we have about Robert thus far, we can reasonably assume that the value judgement expressed in the story's title belongs to Aunt Isabel.

GUIDED READING

LITERAL QUESTIONS

1a. What success has Robert achieved? (none)

2a. Whom does Aunt Isabel tell about Robert's failure? (the teacher, Miss Bell)

INFERENTIAL QUESTIONS

1b. What do you think Robert's contentment with his life suggests about him? (Answers will vary. Possibilities: He is not ambitious; he is more concerned about other people than himself; he doesn't need much to be happy.)

2b. Why do you think Aunt Isabel reveals her opinion to an outsider? (She thinks Robert's "failure" reflects badly on the family and wants to distance herself from it.)

- Robert is shattered by his aunt's remarks about his failure.
- His sister Edith overhears it too, sees how it affects Robert, and decides to do him justice.
- After Christmas dinner Malcolm leads off the speakers.

1 THEME

Robert is indifferent to the world's opinion of him, but his family's evaluation of his life is of critical importance.

2 READING SKILLS: CAUSE AND EFFECT

Robert's look of "deadly hurt" is both a cause and an effect in the story. It has been caused by Aunt Isabel's cruel words. His sister's awareness of his hurt will set in motion the rest of the plot.

3 PLOT: SUSPENSE

The brief dialogue signals a turning point in the story. We wonder how Edith will win justice for Robert.

4 RESPONSE JOURNAL

Have students respond to Robert's changed view of himself. Is it believable? Which is more important—how we ourselves evaluate our lives or how other people evaluate our lives?

"More is expected of a Monroe," said Aunt Isabel majestically. "Robert Monroe is a failure, and that is the only name for him."

Robert Monroe stood up below the window in a dizzy, uncertain fashion. Aunt Isabel had been speaking of him! He, Robert, was a failure, a disgrace to his blood, of whom his nearest and dearest were ashamed! Yes, it was true; he had never realized it before; he had known that he could never win power or accumulate riches, but he had not thought that **1** mattered much. Now, through Aunt Isabel's scornful eyes, he saw himself as the world saw him—as his brothers and sisters must see him. *There* lay the sting. What the world thought of him did not matter; but that his own should think him a failure and disgrace was agony. He moaned as he started to walk across the yard, only anxious to hide his pain and shame away from all human sight, and in his eyes was the look of a gentle animal which had been stricken by a cruel and unexpected blow.

Edith Monroe, who, unaware of Robert's proximity,[13] had been standing at the other side of the porch, saw that look, as he hurried past her, unseeing. A moment before her dark eyes had been flashing with anger at Aunt Isabel's words; now the anger was drowned in a sudden rush of tears.

2 She took a quick step after Robert, but checked the impulse. Not then—and not by her alone—could that deadly hurt be healed. Nay, more, Robert must never suspect that she knew of any hurt. She stood and watched him through her tears as he went away across the low-lying shore fields to hide his broken heart under his own humble roof. She yearned to hurry after him and comfort him, but she knew that comfort was not what Robert needed now. Justice, and justice only,

---

13. **proximity** [prok sim′ə te]: nearness.

134   *The Short Story*

---

could pluck out the sting, which otherwise must rankle[14] to the death.

3 Ralph and Malcolm were driving into the yard. Edith went over to them.

"Boys," she said resolutely, "I want to have a talk with you."

The Christmas dinner at the old homestead was a merry one. Mrs. James spread a feast that was fit for the halls of Lucullus.[15] Laughter, jest, and repartee[16] flew from lip to lip. Nobody appeared to notice that Robert ate little, said nothing, and sat with his form shrinking in his shabby "best" suit, his gray head bent even lower than usual, as if desirous of avoiding all observation. When the others spoke to him he answered deprecatingly, and shrank still further into himself.

Finally all had eaten all they could, and the remainder of the plum pudding was carried out. Robert gave a low sigh of relief. It was almost over. Soon he would be able to escape **4** and hide himself and his shame away from the mirthful eyes of these men and women who had earned the right to laugh at the world in which their success gave them power and influence. He—he—only—was a failure.

He wondered impatiently why Mrs. James did not rise. Mrs. James merely leaned comfortably back in her chair, with the righteous expression of one who has done her duty by her fellow creatures' palates, and looked at Malcolm.

Malcolm rose in his place. Silence fell on the company; everybody looked suddenly alert and expectant, except Robert. He still sat with bowed head, wrapped in his own bitterness.

"I have been told that I must lead off," said Malcolm, "because I am supposed to possess

---

14. **rankle**: cause long-lasting anger.
15. **Lucullus** [loo kul′əs]: ancient Roman general known for his great banquets.
16. **repartee** [rep′ər tē′]: fast, witty conversation.

GUIDED READING

LITERAL QUESTIONS

1a. What hurts Robert most about Aunt Isabel's words? (the idea that his own family considers him a failure and a disgrace)

2a. What does Edith yearn to do when she sees Robert's hurt face? (to comfort him)

INFERENTIAL QUESTIONS

1b. Why does Robert care so much about what his family thinks? (He loves them and is proud of them; to feel that they are ashamed of him isolates him.)

2b. Could Edith have made Robert feel better by comforting him at that moment? (Probably not; he might feel humiliated by her sympathy, and she alone could not convince him that Aunt Isabel was wrong.)

the gift of gab. But, if I do, I am not going to use it for any rhetorical[17] effect today. Simple, earnest words must express the deepest feelings of the heart in doing justice to its own. Brothers and sisters, we meet today under our own rooftree, surrounded by the benedictions[18] of the past years. Perhaps invisible guests are here—the spirits of those who founded this home and whose work on earth has long been finished. It is not amiss to hope that this is so and our family circle made indeed complete. To each one of us who are here in visible bodily presence some measure of success has fallen; but only one of us has been supremely successful in the only things that really count—the things that count for eternity as well as time—sympathy and unselfishness and self-sacrifice.

"I shall tell you my own story for the benefit of those who have not heard it. When I was a lad of sixteen I started to work out my own education. Some of you will remember that old Mr. Blair of Avonlea offered me a place in his store for the summer, at wages which would go far towards paying my expenses at the county academy the next winter. I went to work, eager and hopeful. All summer I tried to do my faithful best for my employer. In September the blow fell. A sum of money was missing from Mr. Blair's till. I was suspected and discharged in disgrace. All my neighbors believed me guilty; even some of my own family looked upon me with suspicion—nor could I blame them, for the circumstantial evidence was strongly against me."

Ralph and James looked ashamed; Edith and Margaret, who had not been born at the time referred to, lifted their faces innocently. Robert did not move or glance up. He hardly seemed to be listening.

---

17. **rhetorical** [ri tôr′i kəl]: using formal language.
18. **benedictions**: blessings.

"I was crushed in an agony of shame and despair," continued Malcolm. "I believed my career was ruined. I was bent on casting all my ambitions behind me, and going west to some place where nobody knew me or my disgrace. But there was one person who believed in my innocence, who said to me, 'You shall not give up—you shall not behave as if you were guilty. You are innocent, and in time your innocence will be proved. Meanwhile show yourself a man. You have nearly enough money to pay your way next winter at the Academy. I have a little I can give to help you out. Don't give in—never give in when you have done no wrong.'

"I listened and took his advice. I went to the Academy. My story was there as soon as I was, and I found myself sneered at and shunned. Many a time I would have given up in despair, had it not been for the encouragement of my counselor. He furnished the backbone for me. I was determined that his belief in me should be justified. I studied hard and came out at the head of my class. Then there seemed to be no chance of my earning any more money that summer. But a farmer at Newbridge, who cared nothing about the character of his help, if he could get the work out of them, offered to hire me. The prospect was distasteful but, urged by the man who believed in me, I took the place and endured the hardships. Another winter of lonely work passed at the Academy. I won the Farrell Scholarship the last year it was offered, and that meant an Arts course for me. I went to Redmond College. My story was not openly known there, but something of it got abroad, enough to taint my life there also with its suspicion. But the year I graduated, Mr. Blair's nephew, who, as you know, was the real culprit, confessed his guilt, and I was cleared before the world. Since then my career has been what is called a brilliant one. But"

The Brother Who Failed 135

- Malcolm says that he owes his success to Robert.
- Ralph, James, and Edith, in turn, tell how Robert made the crucial difference in their lives.

1 THEME

Robert is identified as the person whose love and family loyalty saved Malcolm. "It is his success—not mine" is a forceful expression of the theme the story is building.

2 CHARACTERIZATION

Ralph pays tribute to Robert's belief in truth and honor. Describing these virtues as "Monroe Traditions" links them with Robert's sense of family.

3 THEME

A cumulative sense of Robert's success in life begins to build as Ralph admits, "Robert really made every cent of my money."

4 CHARACTERIZATION

Edith's story reinforces our sense of Robert's love and capacity for self-sacrifice. Her statement that he made her take the tuition again suggests Robert's surprising forcefulness.

1 —Malcolm turned and laid his hand on Robert's thin shoulder—"all my success I owe to my brother Robert. It is his success—not mine—and here today, since we have agreed to say what is too often left to be said over a coffin lid, I thank him for all he did for me, and tell him that there is nothing I am more proud of and thankful for than such a brother."

Robert had looked up at last, amazed, bewildered, incredulous.[19] His face crimsoned as Malcolm sat down. But now Ralph was getting up.

"I am no orator as Malcolm is," he quoted gaily, "but I've got a story to tell, too, which only one of you knows. Forty years ago, when I started in life as a business man, money wasn't so plentiful with me as it may be today. And I needed it badly. A chance came my way to make a pile of it. It wasn't a clean chance. It was a dirty chance. It looked square on the surface; but, underneath, it meant trickery and roguery. I hadn't enough perception to see that, though—I was fool enough to think it was all right. I told Robert what I meant to do. And Robert saw clear through the outward sham to the real, hideous thing underneath.

2 He showed me what it meant and he gave me a preachment about a few Monroe Traditions of truth and honor. I saw what I had been about to do as he saw it—as all good men and true must see it. And I vowed then and there that I'd never go into anything that I wasn't sure was fair and square and clean through and through. I've kept that vow. I am a rich man, and not a dollar of my money is 'tainted'

3 money. But I didn't make it. Robert really made every cent of my money. If it hadn't been for him I'd have been a poor man today, or behind prison bars, as are the other men who went into that deal when I backed out. I've got

a son here. I hope he'll be as clever as his Uncle Malcolm; but I hope, still more earnestly, that he'll be as good and honorable a man as his Uncle Robert."

By this time Robert's head was bent again, and his face buried in his hands.

"My turn next," said James. "I haven't much to say—only this. After mother died I took typhoid fever. Here I was with no one to wait on me. Robert came and nursed me. He was the most faithful, tender, gentle nurse ever a man had. The doctor said Robert saved my life. I don't suppose any of the rest of us here can say we have saved a life."

Edith wiped away her tears and sprang up impulsively.

"Years ago," she said, "there was a poor, ambitious girl who had a voice. She wanted a musical education and her only apparent chance of obtaining it was to get a teacher's certificate and earn money enough to have her voice trained. She studied hard, but her brains, in mathematics at least, weren't as good as her voice, and the time was short. She failed. She was lost in disappointment and despair, for that was the last year in which it was possible to obtain a teacher's certificate without attending Queen's Academy, and she could not afford that. Then her oldest brother came to her and told her he could spare enough money to send her to the conservatory of music in Halifax[20] for a year.

4 He made her take it. She never knew till long afterwards that he had sold the beautiful horse which he loved like a human creature, to get the money. She went to the Halifax conservatory. She won a musical scholarship. She has had a happy life and a successful career. And she owes it all to her brother Robert—"

---

19. **incredulous** [in krej'ə ləs]: without believing.

20. **Halifax** [hal'ə faks]: port city and capital of Nova Scotia.

GUIDED READING

LITERAL QUESTIONS

1a. How does Robert look after Malcolm's tribute? (amazed, bewildered, incredulous)

2a. How does Robert look after Ralph's tribute? (His head is bent, and his face is buried in his hands.)

INFERENTIAL QUESTIONS

1b. Why do you think he reacts in this way? (He never expected such a tribute; he is confused because he had believed Aunt Isabel's words that the family was ashamed of him.)

2b. Why do you think he has buried his face in his hands? (He is probably crying, overcome with emotion.)

AT A GLANCE

- Margaret tells how Robert acted as her "father and mother."
- The schoolteacher says the people of White Sands love Robert.

1 THEME

Margaret's sobs suggest the emotion that all the brothers and sisters are feeling as the family finally celebrates Robert's love and generosity.

2 THEME

Robert's love extends to the community. The teacher feels determined to do him justice for his actions outside the family.

But Edith could go no further. Her voice failed her and she sat down in tears. Margaret did not try to stand up.

1 "I was only five when my mother died," she sobbed. "Robert was both father and mother to me. Never had child or girl so wise and loving a guardian as he was to me. I have never forgotten the lessons he taught me. Whatever there is of good in my life or character I owe to him. I was often headstrong and willful, but he never lost patience with me. I owe everything to Robert."

Suddenly the little teacher rose with wet eyes and crimson cheeks.

"I have something to say, too," she said resolutely. "You have spoken for yourselves. I 2 speak for the people of White Sands. There is a man in this settlement whom everybody loves. I shall tell you some of the things he has done.

"Last fall, in an October storm, the harbor

The Brother Who Failed   137

GUIDED READING

LITERAL QUESTION

1a. What person outside the family speaks in Robert's behalf? (the teacher)

INFERENTIAL QUESTION

1b. Why is it important that she add her tribute to the family's praise? (She shows that Robert's love extends beyond his family—and so does appreciation for him; she is the one whom Aunt Isabel told that Robert was a failure; the teacher defends him now.)

- The schoolteacher tells of Robert's kindnesses, even heroism.
- Robert accepts his family's adulation.
- Aunt Isabel acknowledges Robert's failure as the best success.

1 PLOT: RESOLUTION

Robert stands erect for the first time and is truly able to enjoy the honor that has been due him for so long.

2 TITLE

Since it was Aunt Isabel whose cruel statement prompted the outpouring of gratitude for Robert, it is fitting that she retract her opinion and that she explicitly state the theme of the story: "There's a kind of failure that's the best success."

REFLECTING ON THE STORY

Do you think Robert wasted his life by doing too much for other people? Explain your answer. (Answers will vary. Most students should see that Robert's heroic generosity has saved and advanced a number of other lives.)

STUDY QUESTIONS

1. Edith, concert singer; Ralph owns railroads; Malcolm, university president; Margaret, wife and mother; James manages the family farm; Robert, poor farmer
2. He's a total failure. He has not made money or become powerful.
3. sympathy, unselfishness, self-sacrifice
4. *Malcolm:* gave moral support when he was falsely accused; *Ralph:* dissuaded from dishonest deal; *James:* nursed back to health; *Edith:* paid for musical education; *Margaret:* raised
5. got doctor for lighthouse keeper during storm; took care of poor old woman; hired young man no one else trusted
6. feels first shy, then loved and

---

lighthouse flew a flag of distress. Only one man was brave enough to face the danger of sailing to the lighthouse to find out what the trouble was. That was Robert Monroe. He found the keeper alone with a broken leg; and he sailed back and made—yes, *made* the unwilling and terrified doctor go with him to the lighthouse. I saw him when he told the doctor he must go; and I tell you that no man living could have set his will against Robert Monroe's at that moment.

"Four years ago old Sarah Cooper was to be taken to the poorhouse. She was broken-hearted. One man took the poor, bed-ridden, fretful old creature into his home, paid for medical attendance, and waited on her himself, when his housekeeper couldn't endure her tantrums and temper. Sarah Cooper died two years afterwards, and her last breath was a benediction on Robert Monroe—the best man God ever made.

"Eight years ago Jack Blewett wanted a place. Nobody would hire him, because his father was in the penitentiary, and some people thought Jack ought to be there, too. Robert Monroe hired him—and helped him, and kept him straight, and got him started right—and Jack Blewett is a hard-working, respected

young man today, with every prospect of a useful and honorable life. There is hardly a man, woman, or child in White Sands who doesn't owe something to Robert Monroe!"

As Kathleen Bell sat down, Malcolm sprang up and held out his hands.

"Every one of us stand up and sing Auld Lang Syne,"[21] he cried.

1 Everybody stood up and joined hands, but one did not sing. Robert Monroe stood erect, with a great radiance on his face and in his eyes. His reproach had been taken away; for now his own people rose up as one to pay him honor and to call him blessed.

When the singing ceased Malcolm's stern-faced son reached over and shook Robert's hands.

"Uncle Rob," he said heartily, "I hope that when I'm sixty I'll be as successful a man as you."

2 "I guess," said Aunt Isabel, aside to the little school teacher, as she wiped the tears from her keen old eyes, "that there's a kind of failure that's the best success."

---

21. **Auld Lang Syne** [ōld′lang zīn′]: Scottish song sung on New Year's Eve; the title means "days long gone."

STUDY QUESTIONS

Recalling

1. List the six Monroe brothers and sisters. What does each one do for a living?
2. What is Aunt Isabel's opinion of Robert? Why?
3. According to Malcolm, what are the things "that count for eternity as well as time"?
4. Choose one of the other Monroes. Tell what kindness Robert did for him or her.

5. Give an example of Robert's kindness to the people of White Sands.
6. What is Robert's reaction to the stories told about him? What is Aunt Isabel's reaction?

Interpreting

7. At the beginning of the story, why do you think his family ignores Robert?
8. Why does Edith think that justice is the only cure for Robert's hurt?

---

respected; is chastened, admits Robert's success
7. They are busy telling each other about recent successes; Robert is a quiet type, easy to overlook.
8. He must hear that he is truly valued to undo Aunt Isabel's words.

9. In what way is Robert a failure? In what way is he a success?

Extending

10. Think of a person whom you consider successful. What qualities do you think make this person a success?

READING AND LITERARY FOCUS

Stated Theme

An author usually writes a story in order to communicate a message or theme. The **theme** is a general statement about life that is the main idea of a story. The plot of a story concerns one small group of people. On the other hand, the theme is a **generalization,** a broad statement that is true for most people. In a sense, what happens in the story is a specific example of the theme. For example, in "Christmas Day in the Morning" Robert's memories of his father's love remind him of his feelings for his wife. His realization can be made general to apply to people anywhere. This generalization is the story's theme: Only love can waken love. The theme of a story is usually expressed in a complete sentence.

A **stated theme** is a theme that is directly expressed in a story. This theme can be stated by the author or by a character, usually at the end of a story. For example, the theme of "Christmas Day in the Morning" is a stated theme that is expressed in Robert's thoughts.

Thinking About Stated Theme

1. In "The Brother Who Failed" what lesson does Aunt Isabel learn? What is the stated theme?
2. Tell how the theme is a generalization of what happens in the story.

Title

A story's **title,** or name, often sums up the story in a few words. Therefore, the title directs our at-
tention to what is important in a story. It can even help us to discover a story's theme, or main idea. For example, the title "Spring Victory" tells us that spring is a time for overcoming hardship, a time of new life. A title can also draw attention to one important character ("Mary") or to setting ("Crime on Mars"). As we read a story, we should be aware of its title. We should try to understand the clues it gives to the meaning of the story.

Thinking About Title

1. In what way does the title "The Brother Who Failed" draw attention to one character in the story?
2. In what way does its title give a clue to the theme of "The Brother Who Failed"?

COMPOSITION

Writing About Character

■ Do you think Robert Monroe is a lifelike character? Write an essay to explain your answer. First state your opinion clearly. Then give examples from the story to support your opinion. Your answer should include character traits, details, and motivation. *For help with this assignment, see Lesson 3 in the Writing About Literature Handbook at the back of this book.*

Writing a Fable

■ Write a **fable,** or very short story that teaches a lesson. Begin by choosing a famous **proverb,** or saying, as the lesson. Then tell a story in which a character learns from experience that the proverb is true. Finally, use the proverb as the last sentence of your story. You may want to use one of the following proverbs as your stated theme:
a. "A stitch in time saves nine."
b. "He who hesitates is lost."
c. "Do not count your chickens before they hatch."

The Brother Who Failed 139

Toshio Mori (1910–1980) grew up in San Leandro, California. His stories often display a great love of nature. They also reflect his heritage as a Japanese American. In the following story an uncle teaches a young boy to care for a garden.

■ What else is he trying to give the boy?

Toshio Mori

The Six Rows of Pompons[1]

When little Nephew Tatsuo[2] came to live with us he liked to do everything the adults were doing in the nursery, and although his little mind did not know it, everything he did was the opposite of adult conduct, unknowingly destructive and disturbing. So Uncle Hiroshi[3] after witnessing several weeks of rampage said, "This has got to stop, this sawing the side of a barn and nailing the doors to see if it would open. But we must not whip him. We must not crush his curiosity by any means."

And when Nephew Tatsuo, who was seven and in high second grade, got used to the place and began coming out into the fields and pestering us with difficult questions as "What are the plants here for? What is water? Why are the bugs made for? What are the birds and why do the birds sing?" and so on, I said to Uncle Hiroshi, "We must do something about this. We cannot answer questions all the time and we cannot be correct all the time and so we will do harm. But something must be done about this beyond a doubt."

"Let us take him in our hands," Uncle Hiroshi said.

So Uncle Hiroshi took little Nephew Tatsuo aside, and brought him out in the fields and showed him the many rows of pompons growing. "Do you know what these are?" Uncle Hiroshi said. "These things here?"

"Yes. Very valuable," Nephew Tatsuo said. "Plants."

"Do you know when these plants grow up and flower, we eat?" Uncle Hiroshi said.

Nephew Tatsuo nodded. "Yes," he said, "I knew that."

"All right. Uncle Hiroshi will give you six rows of pompons," Uncle Hiroshi said. "You own these six rows. You take care of them. Make them grow and flower like your uncles'."

---

1. **Pompons** [pom′ponz]: flowers with small rounded heads.
2. **Tatsuo** [tät soo′ō]
3. **Hiroshi** [hēr ō′shē]

140   *The Short Story*

GUIDED READING

LITERAL QUESTION

1a. What words does the narrator use to describe Tatsuo's behavior? *(destructive, disturbing, rampage, pestering)*

INFERENTIAL QUESTION

1b. Do you think the little boy's behavior actually does any harm to the family, or is it just annoying? (Answers will vary. Possibilities: The child's pestering only slightly interrupts the adults' work; his actions could hurt the family business.)

"Gee!" Nephew Tatsuo said.

"Do you want to do it?" Uncle Hiroshi said.

"Sure!" he said.

"Then jump right in and start working," Uncle Hiroshi said. "But first, let me tell you something. You cannot quit once you start. You must not let it die, you must make it grow and flower like your uncles'."

"All right," little Nephew Tatsuo said, "I will."

1 "Every day you must tend to your plants. Even after the school opens, rain or shine," Uncle Hiroshi said.

"All right," Nephew Tatsuo said. "You'll see!"

So the old folks once more began to work peacefully, undisturbed, and Nephew Tatsuo began to work on his plot. However, every now and then Nephew Tatsuo would run to Uncle Hiroshi with much excitement.

"Uncle Hiroshi, come!" he said. "There's bugs on my plants! Big bugs, green bugs with black dots and some brown bugs. What shall I do?"

"They're bad bugs," Uncle Hiroshi said. "Spray them."

"I have no spray," Nephew Tatsuo said excitedly.

2 "All right. I will spray them for you today," Uncle Hiroshi said. "Tomorrow I will get you a small hand spray. Then you must spray your own plants."

Several tall grasses shot above the pompons and Uncle Hiroshi noticed this. Also, he saw the beds beginning to fill with young weeds.

"Those grasses attract the bugs," he said. "Take them away. Keep the place clean."

It took nephew Tatsuo days to pick the weeds out of the six beds. And since the weeds were not picked cleanly, several weeks later it looked as if it was not touched at all. Uncle Hiroshi came around sometimes to feel the moisture in the soil. "Tatsuo," he said, "your plants need water. Give it plenty, it is summer. Soon it will be too late."

Nephew Tatsuo began watering his plants with the three-quarter hose.

"Don't hold the hose long in one place and short in another," Uncle Hiroshi said. "Keep it even and wash the leaves often."

In October Uncle Hiroshi's plants stood tall and straight and the buds began to appear. Nephew Tatsuo kept at it through summer and autumn, although at times he looked wearied and indifferent. And each time Nephew Tatsuo's enthusiasm lagged Uncle Hiroshi took him over to the six rows of pompons and appeared greatly surprised.

"Gosh," he said, "your plants are coming **3** up! It is growing rapidly; pretty soon the flowers will come."

"Do you think so?" Nephew Tatsuo said.

"Sure, can't you see it coming?" Uncle Hiroshi said. "You will have lots of flowers. When you have enough to make a bunch I will sell it for you at the flower market."

"Really?" Nephew Tatsuo said. "In the flower market?"

Uncle Hiroshi laughed. "Sure," he said. "That's where the plant business goes on, isn't it?"

One day Nephew Tatsuo wanted an awful lot to have us play catch with him with a tennis ball. It was at the time when the nursery was the busiest and even Sundays were all work.

"Nephew Tatsuo, don't you realize we are all men with responsibilities?" Uncle Hiroshi said. "Uncle Hiroshi has lots of work to do today. Now is the busiest time. You also, have lots of work to do in your beds. And this should be your busiest time. Do you know whether your pompons are dry or wet?"

"No, Uncle Hiroshi," he said. "I don't quite remember."

The Six Rows of Pompons 141

AT A GLANCE

- Hiroshi explains Tatsuo's duties, and Tatsuo accepts them.
- Tatsuo is a negligent gardener, but Hiroshi encourages him and promises to sell his pompons at the market.

1 CHARACTER

Hiroshi is matter-of-fact as he explains Tatsuo's responsibilities, "rain or shine." Tatsuo shows enthusiasm by answering, "All right. You'll see!"

2 THEME

Hiroshi teaches the boy responsibility gradually, adapting the work to the child's abilities. This approach underscores the implied theme that a child matures by being given tasks that are neither too overwhelming nor too simple.

3 CHARACTER

Hiroshi demonstrates an intuitive understanding of psychology. He offers the child praise and the promise of monetary rewards as encouragement for his good behavior.

GUIDED READING

LITERAL QUESTIONS

1a. What responsibilities of plant care does Hiroshi teach Tatsuo? (spraying bugs, weeding, watering)

2a. What does Hiroshi offer to do with Tatsuo's flowers? (sell them at the market)

INFERENTIAL QUESTIONS

1b. What general lesson is Tatsuo learning? (to take pride in and responsibility for what belongs to him)

2b. Why does Hiroshi make that offer? (He wants to give Tatsuo a concrete reason for tending his flowers.)

1 READING SKILLS: CAUSE AND EFFECT

The condition of Tatsuo's flowers is both an effect and a cause of actions in the story. First the plants die because Tatsuo does not care for them properly. Then the bugs in the dying plants threaten the nursery and cause conflict.

2 RESPONSE JOURNAL

In their journals have students comment on this external conflict and evaluate the contrasting viewpoints of Tatsuo's father and Hiroshi. What would students do in this situation?

3 READING SKILLS: CAUSE AND EFFECT

For the moment Hiroshi's faith in his nephew seems to have had the desired effect: Tatsuo takes great pride in his accomplishment.

"Then attend to it. Attend to it," Uncle Hiroshi said.

Nephew Tatsuo ran to the six rows of pompons to see if it was dry or wet. He came running back. "Uncle Hiroshi, it is still wet," he said.

"All right," Uncle Hiroshi said, "but did you see those holes in the ground with the piled-up mounds of earth?"

"Yes. They're gopher holes," Nephew Tatsuo said.

"Right," Uncle Hiroshi said. "Did you catch the gopher?"

"No," said Nephew Tatsuo.

"Then attend to it, attend to it right away," Uncle Hiroshi said.

One day in late October Uncle Hiroshi's pompons began to bloom. He began to cut and bunch and take them early in the morning to the flower market in Oakland.[4] And by this time Nephew Tatsuo was anxious to see his pompons bloom. He was anxious to see how it feels to cut the flowers of his plants. And by this time Nephew Tatsuo's six beds of pompons looked like a patch of tall weeds left uncut through the summer. Very few pompon buds stood out above the tangle.

1 Few plants survived out of the six rows. In some parts of the beds where the pompons had plenty of water and freedom, the stems grew strong and tall and the buds were big and round. Then there were parts where the plants looked shriveled and the leaves were wilted and brown. The majority of the plants were dead before the cool weather arrived. Some died by dryness, some by gophers or moles, and some were dwarfed by the great big grasses which covered the pompons altogether.

When Uncle Hiroshi's pompons began to

4. **Oakland:** city on San Francisco Bay in western California.

142   *The Short Story*

flower everywhere the older folks became worried.

2 "We must do something with Tatsuo's six beds. It is worthless and his bugs are coming over to our beds," Tatsuo's father said. "Let's cut it down and burn them today."

"No," said Uncle Hiroshi. "That will be a very bad thing to do. It will kill Nephew Tatsuo. Let the plants stay."

So the six beds of Nephew Tatsuo remained intact, the grasses, the gophers, the bugs, the buds and the plants and all. Soon after, the buds began to flower and Nephew Tatsuo began to run around calling Uncle Hiroshi. He said the flowers are coming. Big ones, good ones. He wanted to know when can he cut them.

"Today," Uncle Hiroshi said. "Cut it today and I will sell it for you at the market tomorrow."

Next day at the flower market Uncle Hiroshi sold the bunch of Nephew Tatsuo's pompons for twenty-five cents. When he came home Nephew Tatsuo ran to the car.

"Did you sell it, Uncle Hiroshi?" Nephew Tatsuo said.

"Sure. Why would it not sell?" Uncle Hiroshi said. "They are healthy, carefully cultured[5] pompons."

Nephew Tatsuo ran around excitedly. 3 First, he went to his father. "Papa!" he said, "someone bought my pompons!" Then he ran over to my side and said, "The bunch was sold! Uncle Hiroshi sold my pompons!"

At noontime, after the lunch was over, Uncle Hiroshi handed over the quarter to Nephew Tatsuo.

"What shall I do with this money?" asked Nephew Tatsuo, addressing all of us, with shining eyes.

5. **cultured:** grown; raised.

GUIDED READING

LITERAL QUESTIONS

1a. According to Hiroshi, what would burning Tatsuo's flower beds do to Tatsuo? (kill him)

2a. Is Hiroshi able to sell Tatsuo's flowers? (yes)

INFERENTIAL QUESTIONS

1b. What does Hiroshi mean by that? (perhaps that it would kill Tatsuo's enthusiasm, his pride in his accomplishment, or his budding self-respect)

2b. Why is it important for Tatsuo to earn money from his flowers? (The sale of his flowers makes him feel grown-up, since flower sales are how the family earns a living; the sale gives his work a purpose and a reward.)

Detail from *Chrysanthemums by a Stream,* a Japanese folding screen, Ogata Korin, 1658–1716.

The Six Rows of Pompons 143

- Tatsuo has a good time spending his quarter.
- His father has no confidence that Tatsuo will change, but Hiroshi expresses hope.

1 PLOT: CONFLICT

Tatsuo's father and Hiroshi again disagree. This external conflict reflects a fundamental difference in their understanding of human nature. Hiroshi's role in the family is such that his point of view wins out again.

2 THEME

Hiroshi maintains his firm belief in the power of love and responsibility. He will keep working with Tatsuo as long as it takes to make the boy a responsible member of the family.

REFLECTING ON THE STORY

Why do you think Tatsuo's father and Uncle Hiroshi see the boy so differently? (Some people are more easily discouraged than others; Hiroshi is unusually patient and kind, and the boy responds to him. Tatsuo's father may take the boy's failures personally.)

STUDY QUESTIONS

1. saws side of barn; nails barn doors; pesters adults with questions
2. six rows of pompons; tend them and make them flower
3. bugs, weeds, dryness; first helps him, then tells him he must attend to these problems himself
4. weeds; Uncle Hiroshi sells them for twenty-five cents
5. He enjoys praise and takes pride in success.
6. Answers will vary. Curiosity is a valuable characteristic: It leads people to find out more about things around them.

---

1 "Put it in your toy bank," said Tatsuo's father.

"No," said Uncle Hiroshi. "Let him do what he wants. Let him spend and have a taste of his money."

"Do you want to spend your quarter, Nephew Tatsuo?" I said.

"Yes," he said.

"Then do anything you wish with it," Uncle Hiroshi said. "Buy anything you want. Go and have a good time. It is your money."

On the following Sunday we did not see Nephew Tatsuo all day. When he came back late in the afternoon Uncle Hiroshi said, "Nephew Tatsuo, what did you do today?"

"I went to a show, then I bought an ice cream cone and then on my way home I watched the baseball game at the school, and then I bought a popcorn from the candy man. I have five cents left," Nephew Tatsuo said.

"Good," Uncle Hiroshi said. "That shows a good spirit."

Uncle Hiroshi, Tatsuo's father, and I sat in the shade. It was still hot in the late afternoon that day. We sat and watched Nephew Tatsuo riding around and around the yard on his red tricycle, making a furious dust.

"Next year he will forget what he is doing this year and will become a wild animal and go on a rampage again," the father of Tatsuo said.

"Next year is not yet here," said Uncle Hiroshi.

"Do you think he will be interested to raise pompons again?" the father said.

"He enjoys praise," replied Uncle Hiroshi, "and he takes pride in good work well done. We will see."

"He is beyond a doubt the worst gardener in the country," I said. "Probably he is the worst in the world."

"Probably," said Uncle Hiroshi.

"Tomorrow he will forget how he enjoyed spending his year's income," the father of Tatsuo said.

2 "Let him forget," Uncle Hiroshi said. "One year is nothing. We will keep this six rows of pompon business up till he comes to his senses."

We sat that night the whole family of us, Uncle Hiroshi, Nephew Tatsuo's father, I, Nephew Tatsuo, and the rest, at the table and ate, and talked about the year and the prospect of the flower business, about Uncle Hiroshi's pompon crop, and about Nephew Tatsuo's work and, also, his unfinished work in this world.

STUDY QUESTIONS

Recalling

1. From the beginning of the story, find two examples of Tatsuo's troublesome behavior.
2. What does Uncle Hiroshi give to Tatsuo? What must Tatsuo do?
3. Give one problem that Tatsuo has with his plants. What is Uncle Hiroshi's reaction?
4. At the end of the story, what do the majority of Tatsuo's plants look like? What happens to Tatsuo's good pompons?
5. According to Uncle Hiroshi, what two things does Tatsuo enjoy?

Interpreting

6. Why do you think Uncle Hiroshi does not want to crush Tatsuo's curiosity?

7. Do you think Tatsuo will want his own pompons again the next year? Why or why not?

Extending

8. Do you agree with Uncle Hiroshi's way of treating Tatsuo? Why or why not?

READING AND LITERARY FOCUS

Implied Theme

The **theme** is the main idea of a story. This idea is a general statement about life. An **implied theme** is not directly stated. Instead, it is gradually revealed by the other elements of the story. We can discover an implied theme by examining the following elements in a story:

- The title may tell us the author's opinion of what happens in the story.
- A character may learn a lesson about life.
- Personality traits of a character may tell us the author's ideas about people in general.
- Details of setting may tell us the author's ideas about the world in general.
- The choice of point of view may tell us how the author wants us to react to the story.

For example, "Mary" has an implied theme: Making sacrifices for others is difficult but rewarding. This idea is never stated in the story. Instead, we imply the theme from the lesson that Kass learns: She feels both sorrow and joy after she gives up the poetry prize for her sister.

Thinking About Implied Theme

1. What virtues does Tatsuo gain by caring for the plants? In what way will the experience change his behavior?
2. What is the story's implied theme? Your answer should be one sentence.

CHALLENGE

Research Report

■ Go to the library, and do research about some unusual flowers. Draw pictures of at least six different kinds of flower. Then give the following information for each flower: What is its Latin name and its popular name? Where does the flower grow in the wild? What conditions does it need in order to grow. What special properties or uses does the flower have?

The Six Rows of Pompons 145

7. Possible answers: *No,* he failed to raise marketable flowers and may want to try something new; *yes,* he will remember pleasure of spending his own money.
8. Some students may feel Hiroshi is too lenient with Tatsuo, that good farmland is wasted when left under the boy's care. Some may feel he is right to encourage the boy, praising his successes and ignoring his failures.

AT A GLANCE

- The story takes place in a small town in the United States during World War II.
- Timothy is on his way home from school on the first warm day of spring.

LITERARY OPTIONS

- characterization
- setting
- point of view

THEMATIC OPTIONS

- growing up
- discoveries
- hero worship

1 POINT OF VIEW

The third-person narrator fondly remembers the imaginative and superstitious games of late childhood, as well as its more serious conflicts. She takes us inside the mind of a good-natured boy.

2 CHARACTERIZATION

Timothy's determination to be "perfectly fair," while doing exactly what he wants, is presented in a humorous way that makes him seem very likable. The humor contrasts with the later mood of the story.

TEXAS ESSENTIAL ELEMENTS GRADE 8

3A plot development and character development
3C setting and mood
3D literary genres
4B implied main idea
4C fact vs. nonfact
4E cause/effect
4F point of view
4G prediction of outcomes
To locate treatment of an Element, see *Texas Teacher's Resources.*

Beatrice Joy Chute (1913–1987) is one of three sisters well known as writers. She grew up in Minnesota but lived in New York City. Chute wrote about the problems and the fun of being young. "Come of Age" shows us how one boy is affected by bad news.

■ How is the boy's behavior typical of an eleven-year-old?

B. J. Chute

Come of Age

Timothy crossed the road at the exact place where the tar ended and the dirt began, paused on the sidewalk, squinted up at the sun and gave a heave of satisfaction. He was too warm with his sweater on. He had known he was going to be too warm, and he had made a firm announcement to this effect to his mother before he left the house in the morning. Thousands of layers of woolly stuff, he had pointed out darkly, intimating[1] that a person might easily suffocate.

Having barely survived this fate so far, he now decided to make a test case out of it. If an automobile passed him on the road before he had counted up to ten, that meant it was really spring and too warm for sweaters. His own internal workings were positive on the subject, but he was amiably willing to put the whole thing on a sporting basis.

"One," said Timothy. After a while, he added, "Two." He then suspended his counting while he made a neat pile of his schoolbooks and lunch box, putting them carefully on a bare patch of ground, away from the few greenly white sprigs of grass that were struggling up into the sunlight. If the car came by, he would have to put the books on the ground anyhow, in order to take off his sweater, so it seemed wiser to do it ahead of time.

"Three," said Timothy, looking up the road. There was nothing in sight, so he closed his eyes, waited, said "Four" and opened them again. This time it worked. There was a car coming. Timothy put his hands to his sweater and stood pantingly prepared to jerk it over his head.

The car swished by with a friendly toot.

"Five-six-seven-eight-nine-ten," said Timothy rapidly, just to be perfectly fair about the whole thing, vanished momentarily into the sweater and reappeared with his hair standing on end and the expression of one who had

---

1. **intimating** [in′tə māt′ing]: hinting.

146   *The Short Story*

GUIDED READING

LITERAL QUESTION

1a. Why does Timothy count to ten and wait for a car to pass? (He has made up a game that if a car passes by before he counts to ten, he can take off his sweater.)

INFERENTIAL QUESTION

1b. Why does he have to make up a game before he can take off his sweater? (His mother made him wear it, and he feels conflict about disobeying her, so he makes up a game that will justify his actions.)

been saved from total collapse in the nick of time.

1 He turned the sweater virtuously right side to again, with his mother in mind, and tied its arms around his waist, allowing the rest of it to fall comfortably to the rear where it could flap without giving him any sense of responsibility. Then he tucked his school-books under one arm, picked up the lunch box and peered hopefully inside it. There were three cake crumbs and some orange peel. He licked his finger, collected the crumbs on the end of it and disposed of them tidily, then extracted a piece of the peel and took a thoughtful nibble.

It tasted vaguely like a Christmas tree, but rather leathery, so he put it back, felt a momentary dejection based on a sudden desperate need for a great deal of food, recovered rapidly, took another look at the sun and gave a pleased snort.

2 It was certainly spring, and for once it was starting on a Friday afternoon, which meant he would have the whole weekend to get used to it in. Also, by some great and good accident, his sixth-grade English teacher had forgotten to assign the weekly composition. This was almost incredibly gratifying, especially since the rumor had got around that she had been going to give them the dismal topic of What My Country Means to Me.

Timothy sighed with satisfaction over the narrow escape of the sixth-grade English class, knowing quite well the same topic would turn up again next week, but that next week was years away. Besides, she might change her mind and assign something else. One week she had told them to write what she referred to as a word portrait, called A Member of My Family. Timothy had enjoyed that one richly. He had written, inevitably, about his brother Bricky, and it was the longest composition he had ever achieved in his life. He

felt a great pity for his classmates, who didn't 3 have Bricky to write about, since Bricky was not only the most remarkable person in the world but he was also magnificently engaged in fighting the Japanese in the South Pacific. He was an Air Force pilot with silver wings and a bomber, and Timothy basked luxuriously in the warmth of his glory.

4 "Yoicks," said Timothy, addressing the spring and life in general. *Yoicks* was Bricky's favorite expression.

"Yoicks," he said again.

He was, at that moment, five blocks from home. The first block he used up in not stepping on the cracks in the sidewalk, which was not the mindless process it appeared to be. He was actually conducting an elaborate reconnaissance program,[2] and the cracks were vital supply lines. By the second block, however, his attitude on supplies had taken a more personal turn, and he spent the distance reflecting that this was the day his mother baked cookies. His imagination carried him willingly up the back steps, through the unlatched screen door and to the cooky jar, but there it gave up for lack of specific information on the type of cookies involved.

Besides, he was now at the third block, and the third block was important, consisting largely of a vacant lot with a run-down little shack lurching sideways in a corner of it. The old brown grass of last autumn and the matted tangle of vines and weeds were showing a faint stirring of greenness like a pale web.

At the edge of the lot, Timothy paused and his whole manner changed. He became alert and his eyes narrowed, shifting from left to right. He was listening intently. The only sound was the peevish chirp of a sparrow, but Timothy was a world away from it. What he

---

2. **reconnaissance** [ri kon'ə səns] **program**: spying mission over enemy territory.

Come of Age 147

- Timothy feels light and happy
- Timothy recalls writing a composition about his brother Bricky, an Air Force pilot fighting in the South Pacific.
- Timothy daydreams, pausing at a vacant lot.

1 **THEME**

Timothy seems to have found a nice balance in this minor conflict with his mother. He can behave "virtuously," for his mother's sake, without appearing to assume "any sense of responsibility." He seems a well-adjusted boy, though still immature.

2 **SETTING**

By setting the story on a Friday afternoon in spring, when there is no composition homework, the author evokes feelings in readers who remember their own sense of freedom and lightness at such a time.

3 **SETTING**

The reference to Bricky's military service reveals that the story takes place during World War II.

4 **CHARACTERIZATION**

Timothy's repetition of his older brother's favorite expression reflects his hero worship of Bricky.

GUIDED READING

LITERAL QUESTIONS

1a. What things is Timothy thinking about? (how to deal with the sweater, how hungry he is, how glad he is that it's a spring weekend with no composition to write, his brother, being on a spy mission, cookies)

2a. What is Timothy's brother doing? (fighting the war in the South Pacific)

INFERENTIAL QUESTIONS

1b. Do you think the narrator gives a convincing portrait of an eleven-year-old boy's thoughts? (Answers will vary. Possibilities: *Yes*—an eleven-year-old's thoughts jump all around, just like Timothy's; *no*—Timothy's unconnected thoughts make him seem younger.)

2b. Do you think Timothy is worried about his brother? (probably not, because he is—at this moment—basking "in the warmth" of his brother's glory.)

was listening for was the warning roar of revved-up motors.

1 In a moment now, from behind that shack, from beyond those tangled vines, Japanese planes would swarm upward viciously, in squadron attack.

Timothy put down the books and the lunch box, then he stepped back, holding himself steady. His hand moved, fingers curved knowingly, to control and throttle,[3] and from his parted lips there suddenly burst a chattering roar.

The Liberator surged forward gallantly to meet the attackers. Timothy's face became tense, and he interrupted the engine's explosive revolutions for a moment to warn himself grimly, "This is it. Watch yourselves, men." He then nodded soberly. It was a grave responsi-

bility for the pilot, knowing the crew trusted him to see them through.

2 The pilot, of course, was Bricky. It was Bricky who was holding the plane steady on its course, nerving himself for the final instant of action. The deadly swarm of Zeros swept forward, but the pilot's face remained impassive.

Z-z-z-zoom, they spread across the sky, their evil advance punctuated by the hail of machine-gun fire. The Liberator climbed, settling back on her tail in instant response to the pilot's sure hand. As she scaled the clouds, the bright silver of her name, painted along the side, shone defiantly—The Hornet. Bricky had at one time piloted a plane called The Hornet. It was the best name that Timothy knew.

After that, it was short and sharp. A Japanese fighter detached itself from the humming swarm. The Hornet rolled and the tail

---

3. **throttle:** valve that controls the flow of fuel to an engine and regulates speed.

148   *The Short Story*

GUIDED READING

LITERAL QUESTION

1a. What is Timothy's fantasy? (He imagines that he is his brother gallantly flying a bomber against the Japanese.)

INFERENTIAL QUESTION

1b. What qualities characterize Timothy's imaginary hero? (seriousness, reliability, steadiness, courage) gunner squeezed the triggers. The plane exploded in midair, disintegrated and streamered[4] to earth in flaming wreckage.

"Right on the nose," said the gunner with satisfaction.

The Hornet had their range now. Zero after Zero fluttered helplessly down out of the sky, **dissolving into the earth. The others turned and skittered for their home base, terrified before the invincibility[5] of American man and machine.**

A faint smile flickered across the face of The Hornet's pilot, and he permitted himself a nod. "Good show," he said.

Timothy sat down on the ground and drew a deep breath. Then he said "Gosh!" and scrambled back to his feet. At home, even now, there might be a letter waiting from Bricky, full of breathless and wonderful details that could be relayed to the fellows at school. A few of them, of course, had brothers of their own in the Air Force, but none of them had Bricky, and that made all the difference. He was quite sorry for them, but most willing **to share and to expound.[6]**

Gosh, he missed Bricky, but, gosh, it was worth it.

A dream crept across his mind. Maybe the war would last for years. Maybe some one of these days, a new pilot would stand before his commanding officer somewhere in Pacific territory and make a firm salute. "Lieutenant Baker reporting for duty, sir."

His commanding officer would look up quickly from his notes. "Timothy!" Bricky would say, holding it all back. They would shake hands.

For the entire next block toward home, Timothy shook hands with his brother, but on the last block spring got into his heels and

he raced the distance like a lunatic, yelling his jubilee. The porch steps he took in two leaps, crashed happily into the front hall and smacked his books and his lunch box down on the hall table. He then opened his mouth to shout for his mother, not because he wanted her for anything specific but because he simply needed to know her exact location.

His mouth, opened to "Hey, mom!" closed suddenly in surprise. His father's hat was **lying on the hall table. There was nothing to prepare him for his father's hat on the hall table at three-thirty in the afternoon. His father's hat kept regular hours. An unaccountable sense of formality descended on Timothy. He looked anxiously into the hall mirror and** made a gesture toward flattening the top lock of his hair. It sprang up again under his hand, and he compromised on untying the sleeves of his sweater from around his waist and putting it firmly down on top of his books. None of this had anything to do with his father, who maintained strict neutrality on the subject of his son's appearance. It was entirely a matter between Timothy, the time of day, and that unexpected gray felt hat on the hall table.

There were a dozen reasons for his father's having come home early. There was nothing to get excited about. Timothy turned his back on the hall table and went through into the living room. There was no one there, but he could hear his father's voice in the kitchen, and, because the kitchen was a reassuring place, he felt better. He went on into the kitchen, shoving the door only partly open and easing himself through it.

His mother was sitting on the kitchen chair beside the kitchen table. She was just sitting there, not doing anything. She never sat anywhere like that, doing nothing.

The formal pressed-down feeling returned to Timothy and stuck in his throat.

He looked toward his father appealingly, but his father was leaning against the sink,

---

4. **streamered:** fell in a wavy, rotating way.
5. **invincibility** [in vin′sə bil′ə tē]: inability to lose.
6. **expound:** explain in detail.

Come of Age 149

- Timothy finishes playacting and runs home, hoping for a letter from Bricky.
- His father is home early.
- He sees his parents in the kitchen and has a premonition of trouble.

1 THEME

Timothy will soon need to let go of his childish belief in the physical invincibility of those he loves, but he will also learn a certain invincibility of the spirit as he is forced to deal with bad news.

2 PLOT: CONFLICT

Timothy experiences internal conflict in missing his brother and enjoying having a hero in the family.

3 CHARACTERIZATION

Timothy childishly yearns for the war to last for years so that he can join his brother.

4 PLOT: FORESHADOWING

The unexpected break in family routine represented by his father's hat immediately makes Timothy anxious, hinting at the bad news to come.

GUIDED READING

LITERAL QUESTION

1a. What does Timothy see on the hall table? (his father's hat)

INFERENTIAL QUESTION

1b. What do you think has happened? (Timothy's parents may have received bad news about Bricky.)

- Timothy learns that Bricky is missing in action. He tells himself that his "invincible" brother must be safe.
- His mother begins to cry, and Timothy's secure world begins to crack.
- He leaves the house because it no longer feels safe.

1 THEME

In the face of bad news, Timothy clings desperately to his childish view of Bricky as invincible.

2 THEME

A crucial part of Timothy's growing up is realizing that those he has always counted on to protect him are subject to fear and weakness.

3 STYLE: SIMILE

The simile *He slid out of the room like a ghost* suggests both that Timothy feels invisible to his worried parents and that he feels as if his old self has ceased to exist.

4 READING SKILLS: MAKING INFERENCES

Timothy's reaction to his mother's tears suggests that he has always been sheltered from trouble.

---

with his hands behind him pressed against it, and staring down at the floor.

"Mom—" said Timothy.

They both looked at him then, but it was his father who answered. He answered right away, as if it had to be said very fast. "You'll have to know, Tim," he said, almost roughly. "It's Bricky. He's missing in action."

Missing in action. He had met the phrase so many times that it wasn't frightening. There was no possible connection in his mind between "Missing in action" and Bricky. . . . Missing in action. It was a picture on a movie **1** screen, nothing more. Bricky, the invincible, would have bailed out, perhaps somewhere in the jungle. Or he would have nursed his damaged crate down to earth in a fantastically cool exhibition of flying skill, his men trusting him to see them through.

A hot, fierce pride surged up in Timothy. He wanted to tell his mother and father not to look that way, to tell them that Bricky, wherever he was, was safe. He wanted to reassure them, so they would be smiling at him again and all the old cozy confidence would return to the kitchen.

His father was dragging words out, one by one. "The plane didn't come back," he said. "They were on a bombing mission, and they didn't come back. We just got the telegram."

An awful thing happened then. Timothy's **2** mother began to cry. He had never in his life seen her cry. It had never occurred to him that she was capable of it, and a monstrous chasm of insecurity yawned suddenly at his feet.

His father went over to her and got down on his knees on the kitchen linoleum, and he stayed there with his arm around her shoulders, murmuring, with his cheek against her hair, "Don't, Ellen. Don't, dearest."

Timothy stood there in the middle of the floor with his hands jammed stiffly into his pockets and his eyes turned away from his

father and mother. He was much more frightened by their sudden unfamiliarity than by what his father had told him. "Missing in action" was just words. His mother crying was a sheer impossibility, made visible before him.

He realized that he had to get out of the kitchen right away, because it was the place where he had always been safest, and now that made it unendurable. He couldn't do anything, anyway. Later, when his mother wasn't—when his mother felt better, he could **3** explain to her about Bricky being all right. He slid out of the room like a ghost, and, linked in their fear, neither of them even looked up.

In the front hall, he stopped for a moment. The spring sun outside was shining, bright and warm, on the street, and he knew exactly how the heat of it would feel slanting across his shoulders. But his mother had thought he ought to wear his sweater today. He wanted very badly to do something to make her feel better. He frowned and pulled the sweater on over his head, jamming his arms into the sleeves and resisting the temptation to push up the cuffs. It stretched them, his mother said.

He went slowly down the front steps, worrying about his mother. The words "missing in action" still meant exactly nothing to him. They were only another installment in the exciting war serial that was Bricky's Pacific adventures, and there was not the slightest shadow of doubt in his mind about Bricky's safe return, though he was eager for details. He guessed none of the other fellows at school had members of their family gallantly missing in action.

4 No, it wasn't Bricky that made him feel funny in the pit of his stomach. The thing was he hadn't known that grown-ups cried, and the discovery took a good deal of the stability out of his world.

His mother might go on being frightened

GUIDED READING

LITERAL QUESTIONS

1a. How does Timothy react to the phrase "missing in action"? (He connects it with the movies, not with his "invincible" brother.)

2a. What frightens Timothy the most about the way his parents are acting? (his mother's tears)

INFERENTIAL QUESTIONS

1b. Why do you think it had never occurred to Timothy that his brother might not come home from the war? (He is a happy, young child without any experience of anxiety or foreboding.)

2b. Why are Timothy's mother's tears so frightening to him? (He has never seen her cry before, and so he knows she must be very worried; she has always been his source of security, but she cannot comfort him or protect him now.)

for days ahead, until they heard that Bricky was all right, and he would be tiptoeing around her in his mind all the time to make things better for her, and what he would really be wanting would be for things to be again the way they had been before.

He didn't want to feel all unsettled inside. The way he felt now was the way he had felt the time they had been waiting to hear from his sister in California when the baby came. He had known quite well that Margaret would be fine and everything, but, just the same, the baby's coming had got into the house and filled it with uncertainties. Now it was the War Department. He was suddenly quite angry with the War Department. Bricky wasn't going to like it either, when he got back. He wouldn't like having his mother worried.

Timothy wished now he had stayed a little longer in the kitchen and asked a few questions. He would have liked to know what that War Department had said, and, as he went down the street without any particular aim or direction, he turned it over and over in his mind.

He had walked back, without meaning to, to the vacant lot with the old shack on it, and it occurred to him that, while he had been shooting down those planes in Bricky's Hornet, his mother and father had been there in the kitchen. Looking like that.

He left the sidewalk and walked into the grassy tangle, scuffing his shoes through last autumn's leaves. He would have liked some company, and he toyed for a moment with going over to Davy Peters' house and telling him that the War Department had sent them a telegram about Bricky, but decided against it.

He sat down on the grass with his back against the wall of the shack. He could feel the rough coolness of the brown boards even through his sweater, and the sun spilled warmth down his front. It was unthinkable that the shack should ever be more comforting than the kitchen at home, but this time it was.

He wished he knew just what the telegram had said. There was something, he thought, that they always put in. Something about "We regret to inform you," but maybe that was just for soldiers' families when the soldier had got killed. He had seen a movie with that in it once, and it had made quite an impression, because in the movie it was all tied up with not talking about the things you knew, and for days Timothy had gone around with a tightly shut mouth and the look of one who is giving no aid and comfort to the enemy. He had even torn the corners off all Bricky's letters and burned them up with a fine secret feeling of citizenship, and then he had regretted it afterwards, when he remembered it was only the United States APO[7] address and no good to anyone. It was too bad, in a way, because they would have made a good collection. On the other hand, he already had eighteen separate and distinct collections, and the shelf in his room, the corner of the second drawer down in the living-room desk, and the excellent location behind the laundry tub in the basement were all getting seriously overcrowded.

He wondered if maybe later he could have the telegram. He could start a good collection with the telegram, he thought. He would print on a piece of paper, "Things Relating to My Brother Bricky," and paste it onto a box. He even knew the box he would use. It held his father's golf shoes, but some kind of arrangement could be worked out for putting the shoes somewhere else. His father was very good about that sort of thing, once he understood boxes were really needed, and, later on,

---

7. **APO:** Army Post Office.

Come of Age 151

AT A GLANCE

- Timothy returns to the vacant lot and finds the shack more comforting than his home.
- He considers telling a friend about the telegram but decides not to.
- He thinks about the telegram and decides he will start a collection with it.

1 THEME

Timothy's wish "for things to be again the way they had been before" suggests his need to deny the bad news and the glimmerings of maturity it has already brought.

2 THEME

Timothy begins his search for comfort inside himself, rather than in his home and family. For now, his only comfort is escape.

3 POINT OF VIEW

The third-person narrator shows Timothy trying to make his wish "for things to be again the way they had been before" come true. Here, and in the next few paragraphs, he reverts to his old, immature view of war and his brother.

GUIDED READING

LITERAL QUESTIONS

1a. What does Timothy consider telling Davy Peters? (about the telegram from the War Department)

2a. How does Timothy feel at the vacant lot? (more comfortable than at home)

INFERENTIAL QUESTIONS

1b. Why does Timothy decide against it, do you think? (Perhaps he does not want to see Davy's reaction, which might force him to face the truth.)

2b. Why do you think he feels more comfortable there than at home? (He always goes to the lot to escape into his fantasies; he needs to escape now from the disturbing truth he has just learned at home.)

1 THEME

Timothy truly begins to mature, as the reality that his brother could be dead begins to sink in.

2 PLOT: CLIMAX

The story reaches its emotional high point as Timothy allows the full force of his new, mature awareness to wash over him: He is alive in a dangerous world where loneliness and loss are real.

3 THEME

Timothy is now more aware of the fragility of life than most boys of his age.

---

this one could hold all the souvenirs and medals and things Bricky would bring home.

The telegram, which maybe began "We regret to inform you," would fit neatly into the box without having to be folded. It would go on with something about "your son, Lieutenant Ronald Baker," and then there would be something more, not quite clear in his mind, about "He is reported missing in action over the South Pacific, having failed to return from an important bombing mission."

Timothy scowled at a sparrow. There was another part that went with the "missing in action" part. Missing, believed—Missing, believed killed.

1 That was when it hit him. That was the moment when he suddenly realized what had happened, when the thing that the telegram stood for took shape clearly before him, not as something that had frightened his mother and made his father hold her very tight, but as something real about Bricky.

Bricky, his brother. Bricky, with whom he had sat a hundred times in this exact place and talked and talked, Bricky who went fishing with him, who showed him how to tie a sheepshank,[8] who was going to help him build a radio when he came back.

"When he comes back," said Timothy aloud, licking his lips because they had unaccountably gone dry. But suppose now Bricky didn't come back? Suppose that telegram was the end of everything?

It was the vacant lot and the shack that weren't safe any more. In the kitchen, he had known, without questioning it, that Bricky was all right. It was here, out in the open, that fear had come crawling. Bricky was dead. He knew Bricky was dead, and he was dead thousands of miles from anywhere, and they wouldn't see him again ever.

Timothy sat there, and the pain in his stomach wasn't anything like the pain you got from eating too much or being hungry. He rocked back and forth, not very much, but enough to cradle the sharpness of it, being careful not to breathe, because if he breathed it went down too far inside and hurt too much. If he could just sit there, maybe, not breathing—

He couldn't. There came a time when his lungs took a deep gulp of air without his having anything to do with it, and when that time came there was no way of holding out any longer.

Bricky was dead. He gave a great strangled sob and rolled over on his face, sprawling **2** across the ground, and everything that was good and safe and beautiful quit the earth and left him with nothing to hold on to. He clung to the grass, shaking desperately with fear and pain and loss, and the immensity and the loneliness and the danger of being a human rolled over and over him in drowning waves.

Behind him, the shack, which only a little while ago had been a shelter for the sneak attack of Zero planes, was immobile and solid in the sunshine. It was only a shack in a vacant lot. The tumbled weeds and vines above which The Hornet had swooped and soared were weeds and vines, not a battleground for airborne knights.

It wasn't that way. It wasn't that way at all. It had nothing to do with a gallant plane, outnumbered but triumphant. It had nothing to do with the Bricky who had flown in his brother's dreams, as safe and invincible as Saint George.[9]

3 A plane was a thing that could be shot down out of the safe sky by murderous gunfire. Bricky was a man whose body could be thrown from the cockpit and spin senselessly down into cold water. It was a cheat. The whole thing was a cheat.

---

8. **sheepshank:** type of knot used to shorten a rope.

9. **Saint George:** legendary hero who slew a dragon.

GUIDED READING

LITERAL QUESTIONS

1a. Does the vacant lot still seem like a safe place to Timothy? (no)

2a. How does Timothy feel about his war fantasies now? (He doesn't want to have them any more; he feels that war is nothing like what he imagined.)

INFERENTIAL QUESTIONS

1b. Where do you think Timothy would feel safer? Explain. (He cannot hide from the fear of his brother's death anywhere because the fear is based on reality.)

2b. What does he mean when he says, "It was a cheat. The whole thing was a cheat"? (The images of war on which he had based his fantasies are not true; he is angry for having believed in them.)

AT A GLANCE

- Timothy faces up to what war is and how it has changed his life forever.
- He wishes he could have his old illusions of safety back.

1 POINT OF VIEW

The third-person narrator can summarize Timothy's feelings in a way that Timothy himself could not if he were telling the story.

2 PLOT: CONFLICT

Timothy struggles with an internal conflict: He realizes that there is no turning back from his mature realizations, but he still wishes he could go back to his old self.

1 The war—this vague big thing that moved in shadowy headlines, in a glorious pageantry of medals and flags and brave men shaking hands—wasn't that at all. He had thought it was something like the Holy Grail and King Arthur,[10] that it shone with beauty and was very high and proud.

And it wasn't. It was fear and this hollowed panic inside him, and it was not seeing Bricky again. Not seeing him again ever.

That was why his mother had cried. That was why his father's voice had been so rough and quick. And it wasn't to be endured. He breathed in shivering gasps, there with his face buried in cool-smelling grass and earth and the sun friendly and gentle on his shoulders that didn't feel it any more. It would go

on like this, day after day and week after week. Bricky was dead, and the place where Bricky had been would never be filled in.

That was what war was, and he knew about it now, and the knowledge was too awful and too immense to be borne. He wanted his mother. He wanted to run to her and to hold to her tightly and to cry his heart out with her arms around his shoulders and her reassuring voice in his ears.

2 But his mother felt like this, too, and his father. There was no safety anywhere. No one could help him, except himself, and he was eleven years old. He didn't want to know about all these things. He didn't want to know what war really was. He wanted it to be a picture on a movie screen again, with excitement and glory and men being brave. Not this immense, unendurable fear and emptiness. He couldn't even cry.

He was eleven years old, and he lay there

---

10. **the Holy . . . Arthur:** stories about King Arthur and the Knights of the Round Table. They searched for a legendary cup (the Holy Grail) in a series of colorful, heroic adventures.

Come of Age 153

GUIDED READING

LITERAL QUESTION

1a. How does Timothy feel about his new awareness of war? (He feels it is "too awful and too immense to be borne.")

INFERENTIAL QUESTION

1b. Do you think Timothy will ever be able to go back to his old way of thinking about war? Explain. (Once you know the truth about something, you cannot hide from it.)

AT A GLANCE

- Timothy realizes that the enemy are real people too.
- Timothy calms himself and finds the courage to return home and face reality.

1 THEME

The end of Timothy's innocence comes with the realization that the enemy are people too. No comfort is to be found in their deaths.

2 PLOT: RESOLUTION

The resolution of the story begins as Timothy, having comforted himself, accepts that he must go on living with his new understanding of life.

3 CHARACTERIZATION

Timothy's courage is evident as he faces up to what he must do and envisions his return home.

4 DIALOGUE

The brief dialogue shows a new Timothy, who speaks to his father calmly and with maturity.

face down in the grass, and he couldn't cry. He groped for anything to ease him, and he thought perhaps Bricky's plane hadn't been alone when it crashed to the flat blue water. He thought that other planes might have been blotted out with it—planes with big red suns[11] painted on them.

But even that didn't do any good. There were men in those planes with the suns on them. Not men like men he knew, not Americans, but real people just the same. No one had told him that he would one day know that the enemy were real people, no one had warned him against finding it out.

He pressed closer against the ground, trying to draw comfort up from it, but he kept shaking. "Now I lay me down to sleep," said Timothy into the grass. "Now I lay me down to sleep. Now I lay me—"

It was a long, long time before the shaking stopped. He was surprised, at the end of it, to find that he was still there on the ground. He pushed away from it and sat up, his head swimming. The sun was much lower now, and a little wind had sprung up to move the vines around him so they swayed against the shack. The sweater felt good around his shoulders, and it was the sweater that made him realize suddenly that he couldn't go on lying there waiting for the world to stop and end the pain.

The world wasn't going to stop. It was going right on, and Timothy Baker was still in it. He would go on being in it, and the thing inside him would go on being the thing inside him. He would have, somehow, to live with that too. He would have to go back to the house, to his mother and father, to school, to coming home and knowing that Bricky wouldn't be there.

---

11. **big red suns:** Japanese planes were decorated with red circles representing the rising sun, symbol of Japan.

Timothy looked around. He felt weak and dizzy, the way he'd felt once after a fever. The shack was there, with no Zeros behind it. The place where he had stood when he was being Bricky and The Hornet was just a piece of ground. His mouth drew in, with his teeth clipping his lower lip, while he stared. There wasn't any escape. He would have to go back—along the sidewalk, up the path, through the front door, into the hallway, into the living room, into the kitchen. There wasn't any escape from his mother's eyes or his father's voice. He knew all about it now, and he was stiff and sore from knowing about it.

He saw what he had to do. He had to go home and face that telegram. He got to his feet. He brushed off the dry bits of grass that clung to the blurred wool of his sweater, and he pulled the cuffs around straight so they wouldn't be stretched wrong. Then he walked across the grass, out of the lot and onto the sidewalk, holding himself very carefully against the pain.

He held himself that way all the distance back, and when he got to his own front yard he was able to walk quite directly and quickly up the path and up the steps. He turned the doorknob, and he went into the front hall. It was getting darker outdoors already, and the hall was dim. It was a moment before he realized that his father was standing in the hallway, waiting for him.

He stopped where he was, getting the pieces of himself together. He wasn't even shaking now, and some vague kind of pride stirred deep down inside him.

He said "Dad—" dragging the monosyllable out.

"Yes, Timmy."

"May I see the telegram, please?"

His father reached into his pocket and took out the brown leather wallet that he carried papers around in. The telegram was on top of

---

GUIDED READING

LITERAL QUESTIONS

1a. How does the sweater feel around Timothy's shoulders? (good)

2a. What does Timothy have to do? (read the telegram)

INFERENTIAL QUESTIONS

1b. What do you think the sweater reminds him of? (Answers will vary; possibilities: his mother and how much she loves him; how he had felt earlier that afternoon.)

2b. Earlier, Timothy wanted to put the telegram in a collection. How has his attitude toward it changed? (Before, Timothy was denying the painful truth of the telegram; now, he fully accepts it.)

some letters and bills, and it was strange to see it already so much a part of their living that it was jostled by business things.

Timothy took the yellow envelope and opened it carefully. There it was. "Lieutenant Ronald Baker, missing in action." The stiff formality of the printed words made it seem so final that he felt the coldness and the fear spreading through him again, the way it had **1** been at the shack. His mind wanted to drag away from the piece of paper, and he had to force it to think instead.

With careful stubbornness, he read the telegram again. It wasn't really very much that the War Department said—just that the plane had not returned and that the family would be advised of any further news. He read the last part once more. Any further news. That meant the War Department wasn't sure what had happened. Bricky might have bailed out somewhere. There had been stories in the newspaper about fliers who bailed out and were picked up later.

2 That was a hope. Timothy weighed it carefully in his mind, not letting himself clutch at it, and it was still a hope. It was a perfectly fair one that they were entitled to, he and his father and mother.

He held his thoughts steady on that for a moment, and then he made them go on logically and precisely. Another thing that could have happened was that Bricky had gone down somewhere over land that was held by the Japanese. If that was it, Bricky might be a prisoner of war. Prisoners of war came back. That was another hope, and it was a perfectly fair one too.

He had two hopes, then. They were reasonable hopes, and he had a right to hang on to them very tightly. The telegram didn't say "believed killed."

Frowning, he went through it in his head again, adding up as if it were an arithmetic

problem. There were three things that the telegram could mean. Two of them were on the side of Bricky's safety, and one was against it. Two chances to one was almost a promise.

Timothy drew a deep breath and handed the telegram back to his father. His father took it without saying anything, then he put his hand against the back of Timothy's neck and rubbed his fingers up through the stubbly hair. For just a moment, Timothy turned his head, pressing close against the buttons of his father's coat, then he pulled away.

3 "Can I go outdoors for a little while?" he said.

"Sure. I guess supper will be the usual time."

They nodded to each other, then Timothy turned and went out of the house. He went down the steps, his hands jammed in his pockets, and began to walk along the sidewalk, feeling still a little hollow, but perfectly steady.

His heart fitted him again. It had stopped pounding against the cage of his ribs, and it **4** didn't hurt any more. The old feeling of safety and comfort was beginning to come back, but now it wasn't a part of his home or of the day. It was inside himself and solid, so that he couldn't mislay it again ever. He pushed his hair away from his forehead, letting the wind get at it. The air was cooler now and felt good, and he had a vague moment of being hungry.

Then he looked around him. He was back at the vacant shack, and the shack had been waiting there for him to come. He eyed it gravely. **5** Behind the shack were the Zeros. They had been waiting for him too. He knew they were there and that their force was overwhelming. Timothy's fingers reached automatically for the controls of his plane. His jaw tightened and his eyes narrowed, and he opened his mouth to let out the roar of the motors.

Come of Age 155

GUIDED READING

LITERAL QUESTIONS

1a. What does Timothy do after his father rubs his fingers through Timothy's hair? (First he presses close to his father for a moment; then he pulls away.)

2a. What does Timothy imagine when he returns to the vacant lot? (the enemy planes waiting for him)

INFERENTIAL QUESTIONS

1b. How do you think Timothy is feeling at that moment? (He wants the old comfort his parents used to provide but realizes he can't count on it forever.)

2b. How is his war fantasy different now? (It is more serious; he knows the enemy planes are deadly, and he, not an invincible hero, is at the controls.)

And, suddenly, he stopped. His hand dropped down to his side and his mouth shut. He stood there quite quietly for a moment, as if he had lost something and was trying to remember what it was. Then he gave a sigh of relinquishment.[12]

His fingers curled firmly around air again

---

12. **relinquishment** [ri ling′kwish mənt]: surrender.

---

and closed, but this time they didn't close on the controls of a machine. They closed on dangling reins.

"Come on, Silver, old boy," said Timothy softly to the evening. "They've got the jump on us, but we can catch them yet."

He touched his spurs to his gallant pinto pony, and, wheeling, he loped away across the sunlit plain.

STUDY QUESTIONS

Recalling

1. Why does Timothy choose Bricky as the subject of his composition?
2. What news does Timothy receive from his father? What is his first reaction?
3. Why does Timothy think no one can help him?
4. After he reads the telegram, what three possibilities does Timothy see for Bricky?
5. At the end of the story, what does Timothy begin to play? What does he end up playing?

Interpreting

6. According to the title, what happens to Timothy during the story? What causes this change?
7. Give examples of this change in Timothy.
8. According to the story, what good can people gain from serious problems? Give the story's implied theme in one sentence.

Extending

9. Do you think many people react to bad news by at first not really believing that it is true? Why might this reaction be a common one?

VOCABULARY

Antonyms

Antonyms are words that have opposite or nearly opposite meanings. For example, *neat* and

sloppy are antonyms. The words in capitals are from "Come of Age." Choose the word that is *most nearly the opposite* of each word in capitals, *as the word is used in the story.*

1. DEJECTION: (a) joy (b) sadness (c) curiosity (d) friendship
2. DISMAL: (a) brown (b) gloomy (c) forceful (d) cheerful
3. IMPASSIVE: (a) quiet (b) emotional (c) unmoved (d) inactive
4. DETACHED: (a) not moving (b) active (c) creative (d) connected

COMPARING STORIES

1. In "The Brother Who Failed," "The Six Rows of Pompons," and "Come of Age," a bad experience has good results. Compare two or more stories. For each story identify the bad experience. Then give its good effect. Finally, tell which bad experience is more serious and which has a better result.
2. "The Brother Who Failed," "The Six Rows of Pompons," and "Come of Age" have different themes. However, each story has one character who is an example of its theme. Compare two or more stories. For each story give a theme. Then tell how one character is an example of that theme. Finally, tell which character is a better example of the theme and why.

THE TOTAL EFFECT

The most enjoyable way to read a short story is to enter completely into its world. Imagine yourself living the events of the plot. Picture the characters, and get to know them. Imagine the setting, and feel the mood it creates. Identify the storyteller. Think about the author's message, or theme. In other words, become part of the story.

To be this involved in a short story, you must be an active, alert reader. You should be aware of every element of the story. In addition to following the plot, you should notice information about character, setting, point of view, and theme. As a result, you will enjoy watching the story's elements work together to form a total effect.

Different people will notice different things in any story. However, an active reader will always think about the story's elements and their total effect. The following points can remind you of each element's role in a story.

Reminders for Active Reading of Short Stories

1. The **title** can help you to understand the story's theme.
2. The **plot** is built around a conflict. Suspense builds until the climax. The resolution is the final outcome.
3. Personalities of **characters** are revealed by what they do or say, by what others say about them, and by what the author says about them.
4. **Setting** can affect plot and character. Setting can also create atmosphere, or mood.
5. **Point of view** is the relationship of the storyteller to the story. A story can have a first-person narrator or a third-person narrator.
6. The **theme,** or main idea of a story, can be stated directly or implied by the other elements.

Model for Active Reading

On the following pages you will see how an alert reader used these reminders while reading "The Dog of Pompeii." Notations in the margin present the reader's observations about the work. Each notation gives a page reference for further information about the item in question. Read the selection first for your own enjoyment. Then read it again with the notations, and try to answer the questions in the notes. Afterward you can use the process followed in this model as you read any short story.

The Short Story   157

■ The story is set in Pompeii in A.D.79.
■ Tito, a blind teen-age orphan boy, lives on the streets with his dog, Bimbi.

LITERARY OPTIONS

■ setting
■ characterization
■ plot

THEMATIC OPTIONS

■ friendship and love
■ heroism
■ nature

The annotations that appear in the Teacher's Edition answer the questions asked in the Pupil's Edition sidenotes.

THE TITLE

The title suggests that the story concerns a dog and takes place in Pompeii, a city that met with disaster centuries ago. The dog and the disaster are probably related.

SETTING

Ancient Pompeii is an exciting place, with lively streets, crowded theaters, and numerous athletic events and sham battles in the stadium. When Caesar visits, there are days of fireworks and sacrifices in the Forum.

TEXAS ESSENTIAL ELEMENTS
GRADE 8

1A writing process
1B purpose and audience
1C support for main idea
1D evaluation of content and organization
1H grammatical conventions
3A plot development and character development
3C setting and mood
3D literary genres
4E cause/effect
4F point of view
To locate treatment of an Element, see *Texas Teacher's Resources.*

Louis Untermeyer (1885–1977) is best known as a literary critic and as an editor of poetry collections. The following story takes place in A.D. 79 in Pompeii, a Roman city in southern Italy. In that year Mount Vesuvius, a volcano near Pompeii, erupted. The city was completely buried. Today more than half of Pompeii has been uncovered.

■ As you read "The Dog of Pompeii," notice the mixture of fact and fiction.

Louis Untermeyer

The Dog of Pompeii[1]

Tito and his dog Bimbi lived (if you could call it living) under the wall[2] where it joined the inner gate. They really didn't live there; they just slept there. They lived anywhere. Pompeii was one of the gayest of the old Latin towns, but although Tito was never an unhappy boy, he was not exactly a merry one. The streets were always lively with shining chariots and bright red trappings; the open-air theaters rocked with laughing crowds; sham battles and athletic sports were free for the asking in the great stadium. Once a year the Caesar[3] visited the pleasure city and the fireworks lasted for days; the sacrifices in the Forum[4] were better than a show.

But Tito saw none of these things. He was blind—had been blind from birth. He was known to everyone in the poorer quarters. But no one could say how old he was, no one remembered his parents, no one could tell where he came from. Bimbi was another mystery. As long as people could remember seeing Tito— about twelve or thirteen years—they had seen Bimbi. Bimbi had

The **title** (p. 139) often directs attention to what is important in a story. As you read, ask yourself in what way the dog is related to the story's *theme.*

Setting (p. 92) is time and place. What details of setting are given here?

---

1. **Pompeii** [pom pā′]: ancient city in southwestern Italy.
2. **wall:** A wall with eight gates surrounded the entire city of Pompeii.
3. **Caesar** [sē′zər]: emperor of Rome.
4. **Forum:** open square and marketplace.

158　*The Short Story*

GUIDED READING

LITERAL QUESTION

1a. What handicap does Tito have? (blindness)

INFERENTIAL QUESTION

1b. Based on Tito's circumstances, what kind of relationship do you think he has with Bimbi? (a very close and dependent one, almost as if Bimbi were his family) never left his side. He was not only dog, but nurse, pillow, play-mate, mother and father to Tito.

Did I say Bimbi never left his master? (Perhaps I had better say comrade, for if anyone was the master, it was Bimbi.) I was wrong. Bimbi did trust Tito alone exactly three times a day. It was a fixed routine, a custom understood between boy and dog since the beginning of their friendship, and the way it worked was this: Early in the morning, shortly after dawn, while Tito was still dreaming, Bimbi would disappear. When Tito awoke, Bimbi would be sitting quietly at his side, his ears cocked, his stump of a tail tapping the ground, and a fresh-baked bread—more like a large round roll—at his feet. Tito would stretch him-self; Bimbi would yawn; then they would breakfast. At noon, no matter where they happened to be, Bimbi would put his paw on Tito's knee and the two of them would return to the inner gate. Tito would curl up in the corner (almost like a dog) and go to sleep, while Bimbi, looking quite important (almost like a boy), would disappear again. In half an hour he'd be back with their lunch. Sometimes it would be a piece of fruit or a scrap of meat, often it was nothing but a dry crust. But sometimes there would be one of those flat rich cakes, sprinkled with raisins and sugar, that Tito liked so much. At suppertime the same thing happened, although there was a little less of everything, for things were hard to snatch in the evening with the streets full of people. Besides, Bimbi didn't approve of too much food before going to sleep. A heavy supper made boys too restless and dogs too stodgy—and it was the business of a dog to sleep lightly with one ear open and muscles ready for action.

But, whether there was much or little, hot or cold, fresh or dry, food was always there. Tito never asked where it came from and Bimbi never told him. There was plenty of rain water in the hollows of soft stones; the old egg woman at the corner sometimes gave him a cupful of strong goat's milk; in the grape season the fat wine maker let him have drippings of the mild juice. So there was no danger of going hungry or thirsty. There was plenty of everything in Pompeii—if you knew where to find it—and if you had a dog like Bimbi.

As I said before, Tito was not the merriest boy in Pompeii. He could not romp with the other youngsters and play Hare-and-Hounds and I-Spy and Follow-Your-Master and Ball-Against-the-Building and Jackstones and Kings-and-Robbers with them. But that did not make him sorry for himself. If he could not see the sights that delighted the lads of Pompeii, he could hear and smell things they never noticed. He could really see more with his ears

Theme (pp. 139, 145) is the main idea of the story. What *generalization* about dogs can be made from details about Bimbi?

Plot (p. 41) is the sequence of events. Events in a plot are usually arranged in **chrono-logical order** (p. 47), the time order in which events natu-rally happen. What words show the chronological order in this paragraph?

Characterization (p. 85): The author may directly reveal the personality of a character. What traits of Tito are given here?

The Dog of Pompeii 159

- Bimbi is like a mother and fa-ther to Tito and brings him food.
- Pompeii is a city of abun-dance.
- Tito cannot play games with the other boys, but he does not feel sorry for himself

THEME

Bimbi is Tito's caretaker, play-mate, and comfort. Dogs can be more than pets and will do many things for the people they love.

PLOT

The phrases that show chrono-logical order are *Early in the morning, Shortly after dawn, At noon, In half an hour,* and *At sup-pertime.*

CHARACTERIZATION

Tito is "not the merriest boy in Pompeii," but he does not feel sorry for himself either. He can hear and smell things that sighted people never notice.

GUIDED READING

LITERAL QUESTIONS

1a. What does Tito look like when he is asleep? (al-most like a dog) How does Bimbi look asleep? (al-most like a boy)

2a. How does the narrator say that Bimbi feels about too much food before going to sleep? (He doesn't approve of it because it makes boys too restless and dogs too stodgy.)

INFERENTIAL QUESTIONS

1b. What do you think the narrator means to suggest by these comparisons? (that the boy and his dog are as close as any human being and animal could be)

2b. What does the narrator mean to suggest by cred-iting Bimbi with such human thoughts? (that the dog is always looking out for Tito and instinctively knows how to protect him)

AT A GLANCE

- Tito "sees" the world vividly through his senses of smell and hearing.
- The Forum, the marketplace of Pompeii, was rebuilt only twelve years before, after an earthquake.

CHARACTERIZATION

Tito is compassionate, but he also has a sense of humor.

FORESHADOWING

The clues in this section prepare us for the city's destruction.

and nose than they could with their eyes. When he and Bimbi went out walking, he knew just where they were going and exactly what was happening.

"Ah," he'd sniff and say, as they passed a handsome villa,[5] "Glaucus Pansa is giving a grand dinner tonight. They're going to have three kinds of bread, and roast pigling, and stuffed goose, and a great stew—I think bear stew—and a fig pie." And Bimbi would note that this would be a good place to visit tomorrow.

Or, "H'm," Tito would murmur, half through his lips, half through his nostrils. "The wife of Marcus Lucretius is expecting her mother. She's shaking out every piece of goods in the house; she's going to use the best clothes—the ones she's been keeping in pine needles and camphor—and there's an extra girl in the kitchen. Come, Bimbi, let's get out of the dust!"

Or, as they passed a small but elegant dwelling opposite the public baths, "Too bad! The tragic poet is ill again. It must be a bad fever this time, for they're trying smoke fumes instead of medicine. Whew! I'm glad I'm not a tragic poet!"

Or, as they neared the Forum, "Mm-m! What good things they have in the Macellum today!" (It really was a sort of butcher-grocer-market place, but Tito didn't know any better. He called it the Macellum.) "Dates from Africa, and salt oysters from sea caves, and cuttlefish, and new honey, and sweet onions, and—ugh!—water-buffalo steaks. Come, let's see what's what in the Forum." And Bimbi, just as curious as his comrade, hurried on. Being a dog, he trusted his ears and nose (like Tito) more than his eyes. And so the two of them entered the center of Pompeii.

The Forum was the part of the town to which everybody came at least once during the day. It was the Central Square, and everything happened here. There were no private houses; all was public—the chief temples, the gold and red bazaars, the silk shops, the town hall, the booths belonging to the weavers and jewel merchants, the wealthy woolen market, the shrine of the household gods. Everything glittered here. The buildings looked as if they were new—which, in a sense, they were. The earthquake of twelve years ago had brought down all the old structures and, since the citizens of Pompeii were ambitious to rival Naples[6] and even Rome,[7] they had seized the opportunity to rebuild the whole town. And they had done it all within a dozen years. There was scarcely a building that was older than Tito.

---

5. **villa:** large, expensive house.
6. **Naples** [nā′pəlz]: large port city in southwestern Italy.
7. **Rome** [rōm]: city in south central Italy, center of the ancient Roman civilization.

160   *The Short Story*

Characterization (p. 85): A character's words and actions may reveal his or her personality. What do Tito's words tell us about him?

Foreshadowing (p. 57) is the use of clues to prepare readers for upcoming events. For what does this section prepare us?

GUIDED READING

LITERAL QUESTION

1a. Why are the buildings in the Forum all new? (The citizens rebuilt them after an earthquake twelve years before.)

INFERENTIAL QUESTION

1b. What does the recent earthquake suggest about living in Pompeii? (that it can be a dangerous place in which to live)

Tito had heard a great deal about the earthquake, though being about a year old at the time, he could scarcely remember it. This particular quake had been a light one—as earthquakes go. The weaker houses had been shaken down, parts of the outworn wall had been wrecked; but there was little loss of life, and the brilliant new Pompeii had taken the place of the old. No one knew what caused these earthquakes. Records showed they had happened in the neighborhood since the beginning of time. Sailors said that it was to teach the lazy city folk a lesson and make them appreciate those who risked the dangers of the sea to bring them luxuries and protect their town from invaders. The priests said that the gods took this way of showing their anger to those who refused to worship properly and who failed to bring enough sacrifices to the altars and (though they didn't say it in so many words) presents to the priests. The tradesmen said that the foreign merchants had corrupted the ground and it was no longer safe to traffic in[8] imported goods that came from strange places and carried a curse with them. Everyone had a different explanation and everyone's explanation was louder and sillier than his neighbor's.

They were talking about it this afternoon as Tito and Bimbi came out of the side street into the public square. The Forum was the favorite promenade for rich and poor. What with the priests arguing with the politicians, servants doing the day's shopping, tradesmen crying their wares, women displaying the latest fashions from Greece and Egypt, children playing hide-and-seek among the marble columns, knots of soldiers, sailors, peasants from the provinces—to say nothing of those who merely came to lounge and look on—the square was crowded to its last inch. His ears even more than his nose guided Tito to the place where the talk was loudest. It was in front of the shrine of the household gods that, naturally enough, the householders were arguing.

"I tell you," rumbled a voice which Tito recognized as bath master Rufus', "there won't be another earthquake in my lifetime or yours. There may be a tremble or two, but earthquakes, like lightnings, never strike twice in the same place."

"Do they not?" asked a thin voice Tito had never heard. It had a high, sharp ring to it and Tito knew it as the accent of a stranger. "How about the two towns of Sicily[9] that have been ruined three times within fifteen years by the eruptions of Mount

---

8. **traffic in:** buy and sell.
9. **Sicily** [sis′ə lē]: island in the Mediterranean Sea, off the southwestern tip of Italy.

The Dog of Pompeii   161

AT A GLANCE

- Tito is too young to remember the earthquake.
- Earthquakes have always occurred in Pompeii. No one knows why.
- In the Forum Tito listens to talk about earthquakes. A stranger disagrees with a claim that they never strike twice in the same place.

GUIDED READING

LITERAL QUESTION

1a. What does bath master Rufus say about earthquakes? (that they never strike twice in the same place) Who disagrees with him? (a stranger)

INFERENTIAL QUESTION

1b. Which man is right? (the stranger) How do we know? (We have much more scientific information than the characters in the story do because they live in A.D. 79.)

Etna?[10] And were they not warned? And does that column of smoke above Vesuvius[11] mean nothing?"

"That?" Tito could hear the grunt with which one question answered another. "That's always there. We use it for our weather guide. When the smoke stands up straight, we know we'll have fair weather; when it flattens out, it's sure to be foggy; when it drifts to the east—"

"Yes, yes," cut in the edged voice. "I've heard about your mountain barometer. But the column of smoke seems hundreds of feet higher than usual and it's thickening and spreading like a shadowy tree. They say in Naples—"

"Oh, Naples!" Tito knew this voice by the little squeak that went with it. It was Attilio the cameo cutter. "They talk while we suffer. Little help we got from them last time. Naples commits the crimes and Pompeii pays the price. It's become a proverb with us. Let them mind their own business."

"Yes," grumbled Rufus, "and others', too."

"Very well, my confident friends," responded the thin voice which now sounded curiously flat. "We also have a proverb—and it is this: *Those who will not listen to men must be taught by the gods.* I say no more. But I leave a last warning. Remember the holy ones. Look to your temples. And when the smoke tree above Vesuvius grows to the shape of an umbrella pine, look to your lives."

Tito could hear the air whistle as the speaker drew his toga[12] about him and the quick shuffle of feet told him the stranger had gone.

"Now what," said the cameo cutter, "did he mean by that?"

"I wonder," grunted Rufus. "I wonder."

Tito wondered, too. And Bimbi, his head at a thoughtful angle, looked as if he had been doing a heavy piece of pondering. By nightfall the argument had been forgotten. If the smoke had increased, no one saw it in the dark. Besides, it was Caesar's birthday and the town was in a holiday mood. Tito and Bimbi were among the merrymakers, dodging the charioteers who shouted at them. A dozen times they almost upset baskets of sweets and jars of Vesuvian wine, said to be as fiery as the streams inside the volcano, and a dozen times they were cursed and cuffed. But Tito never missed his footing. He was thankful for

---

10. **Mount Etna** [et′nə]: volcano in eastern Sicily.
11. **Vesuvius** [vi soo′vē əs]: volcano in southern Italy; its base is about one mile from Pompeii.
12. **toga** [tō′gə]: ancient Roman item of clothing, a single piece of cloth that is draped over the body.

GUIDED READING

LITERAL QUESTIONS

1a. What has the stranger noticed about the column of smoke over Vesuvius? (It's hundreds of feet higher than usual, thickening, and spreading.)

2a. What proverb does the stranger quote to the Pompeians? ("Those who will not listen to men must be taught by the gods.")

INFERENTIAL QUESTIONS

1b. What does the stranger seem to hint that this sign means? (Mount Vesuvius is about to erupt.)

2b. What point is the stranger trying to make with the proverb? (If the people don't heed his warning, they'll learn the hard way by getting caught in the eruption.)

Left, House of the Golden Amoretti, Pompeii. *Above*, mosaic tile floor from the entrance to the House of the Tragic Poet, Pompeii. *Cave canem* is Latin for "Beware of the Dog."

his keen ears and quick instinct—most thankful of all for Bimbi.

They visited the uncovered theater and, though Tito could not see the faces of the actors, he could follow the play better than most of the audience, for their attention wandered—they were distracted by the scenery, the costumes, the byplay, even by themselves—while Tito's whole attention was centered in what he heard. Then to the city walls, where the people of Pompeii watched a mock naval battle in which the city was attacked by the sea and saved after thousands of flaming arrows had been exchanged and countless colored torches had been burned. Though the thrill of flaring ships and lighted skies was lost to Tito, the shouts and cheers excited him as much as any and he cried out with the loudest of them.

The next morning there were two of the beloved raisin and

The Dog of Pompeii   163

GUIDED READING

LITERAL QUESTION

1a. Why is Tito able to enjoy the play and the mock naval battle? (At the theater he can concentrate on the words and not be distracted.)

INFERENTIAL QUESTION

1b. What do you think that the author is trying to suggest about people with serious handicaps? (Their appreciation of life can be equal to or even greater than that of people without serious handicaps.)

AT A GLANCE

- The next morning the air is filled with thick fog and smoke.
- The morning after that Tito wakes to find Bimbi dragging him through hot, heavy air that stings his eyes and nose.
- The volcanic eruption and earthquake begin. Panic sets in.

SETTING

Mount Vesuvius is a crucial part of the setting of this story. Its eruption threatens Tito's life and makes Bimbi take action to save him. The volcano heats up the air and spews out ash that irritates Tito's nose and eyes. The volcano also makes noise, creates vibrations underfoot, and makes the ground move.

sugar cakes for his breakfast. Bimbi was unusually active and thumped his bit of a tail until Tito was afraid he would wear it out. The boy could not imagine whether Bimbi was urging him to some sort of game or was trying to tell something. After a while, he ceased to notice Bimbi. He felt drowsy. Last night's late hours had tired him. Besides, there was a heavy mist in the air— no, a thick fog rather than a mist—a fog that got into his throat and scraped it and made him cough. He walked as far as the marine gate to get a breath of the sea. But the blanket of haze had spread all over the bay and even the salt air seemed smoky.

He went to bed before dusk and slept. But he did not sleep well. He had too many dreams—dreams of ships lurching in the Forum, of losing his way in a screaming crowd, of armies marching across his chest, of being pulled over every rough pavement of Pompeii.

He woke early. Or, rather, he was pulled awake. Bimbi was doing the pulling. The dog had dragged Tito to his feet and was urging the boy along. Somewhere. Where, Tito did not know. His feet stumbled uncertainly; he was still half asleep. For a while he noticed nothing except the fact that it was hard to breathe. The air was hot. And heavy. So heavy that he could taste it. The air, it seemed, had turned to powder—a warm powder that stung his nostrils and burned his sightless eyes.

Then he began to hear sounds. Peculiar sounds. Like animals under the earth. Hissings and groanings and muffled cries that a dying creature might make dislodging the stones of his underground cave. There was no doubt of it now. The noises came from underneath. He not only heard them—he could feel them. The earth twitched; the twitching changed to an uneven shrugging of the soil. Then, as Bimbi half pulled, half coaxed him across, the ground jerked away from his feet and he was thrown against a stone fountain.

The water—hot water—splashing in his face revived him. He got to his feet, Bimbi steadying him, helping him on again. The noises grew louder; they came closer. The cries were even more animal-like than before, but now they came from human throats. A few people, quicker of foot and more hurried by fear, began to rush by. A family or two—then a section—then, it seemed, an army broken out of bounds. Tito, bewildered though he was, could recognize Rufus as he bellowed past him, like a water buffalo gone mad. Time was lost in a nightmare.

It was then the crashing began. First a sharp crackling, like a monstrous snapping of twigs; then a roar like the fall of a whole forest of trees; then an explosion that tore earth and sky. The

164   *The Short Story*

Setting (p. 101) can affect the plot of a story. In what way does setting make things happen here?

GUIDED READING

LITERAL QUESTIONS

1a. What does Tito dream of? (ships lurching in the Forum, losing his way in a screaming crowd, armies marching across his chest, being pulled over rough pavement)

2a. Whose perceptions of the disaster does the narrator present? (Tito's)

INFERENTIAL QUESTIONS

1b. What do Tito's dreams foretell? (They seem to foretell many of the things that happen the next day.)

2b. What limitations and advantages does this technique have? (Tito cannot see; he can only describe how the disaster feels and sounds. By the same token this limitation creates suspense and helps us identify with Tito.)

heavens, though Tito could not see them, were shot through with continual flickerings of fire. Lightnings above were answered by thunders beneath. A house fell. Then another. By a miracle the two companions had escaped the dangerous side streets and were in a more open space. It was the Forum. They rested here awhile—how long he did not know.

Tito had no idea of the time of day. He could feel it was black—an unnatural blackness. Something inside—perhaps the lack of breakfast and lunch—told him it was past noon. But it didn't matter. Nothing seemed to matter. He was getting drowsy, too drowsy to walk. But walk he must. He knew it. And Bimbi knew it; the sharp tugs told him so. Nor was it a moment too soon. The sacred ground of the Forum was safe no longer. It was beginning to rock, then to pitch, then to split. As they stumbled out of the square, the earth wriggled like a caught snake and all the columns of the temple of Jupiter came down. It was the end of the world—or so it seemed. To walk was not enough now. They must run. Tito was too frightened to know what to do or where to go. He had lost all sense of direction. He started to go back to the inner gate; but Bimbi, straining his back to the last inch, almost pulled his clothes from him. What did the creature want? Had the dog gone mad?

Then suddenly, he understood. Bimbi was telling him the way out—urging him there. The sea gate, of course. The sea gate—and then the sea. Far from falling buildings, heaving ground. He turned, Bimbi guiding him across open pits and dangerous pools of bubbling mud, away from buildings that had caught fire and were dropping their burning beams. Tito could no longer tell whether the noises were made by the shrieking sky or the agonized people. He and Bimbi ran on—the only silent beings in a howling world.

New dangers threatened. All Pompeii seemed to be thronging toward the marine gate and, squeezing among the crowds, there was the chance of being trampled to death. But the chance had to be taken. It was growing harder and harder to breathe. What air there was choked him. It was all dust now—dust and pebbles, pebbles as large as beans. They fell on his head, his hands—pumice stones from the black heart of Vesuvius. The mountain was turning itself inside out. Tito remembered a phrase that the stranger had said in the Forum two days ago: "Those who will not listen to men must be taught by the gods." The people of Pompeii had refused to heed the warnings; they were being taught now—if it was not too late.

Suddenly it seemed too late for Tito. The red-hot ashes blis-

Atmosphere (p. 92) is mood. What mood is created in this paragraph?

Conflict (p. 52) is struggle between opposing forces. What forces are in opposition in this story's main conflict?

The Dog of Pompeii   165

AT A GLANCE
- The buildings of Pompeii begin to collapse.
- Bimbi pulls Tito toward the sea. They fight their way through panicking crowds and air filled with choking dust and pebbles.

ATMOSPHERE

The mood is very dramatic and desperate. The passage is full of cracking, roaring, and exploding noises. The boy and the dog are running for their lives.

CONFLICT

The conflict is between the dog's desire to take care of the boy and the boy's panic, which makes him uncooperative.

GUIDED READING

LITERAL QUESTION

1a. What does Bimbi do when Tito loses his sense of direction? (Bimbi strains his back to the last inch and almost pulls off Tito's clothes in order to urge Tito toward the sea.)

INFERENTIAL QUESTION

1b. What does Bimbi's behavior suggest about him? (He is intelligent and absolutely dedicated to his master. He will go to any lengths to save Tito.)

AT A GLANCE

- Tito falls, and Bimbi is forced to bite him to get him up.
- Bimbi gets the weak, desperate boy out of the city. Tito faints.
- Tito wakes to find himself being put into a boat. Bimbi is gone.
- Eighteen hundred years later scientists are studying ruins of Pompeii.

CLIMAX

The boy has reached the shore and safety. We know this because someone is dashing sea water over him, and someone is carrying him to a boat.

---

tered his skin, the stinging vapors tore his throat. He could not go on. He staggered toward a small tree at the side of the road and fell. In a moment Bimbi was beside him. He coaxed. But there was no answer. He licked Tito's hands, his feet, his face. The boy did not stir. Then Bimbi did the last thing he could— the last thing he wanted to do. He bit his comrade, bit him deep in the arm. With a cry of pain, Tito jumped to his feet, Bimbi after him. Tito was in despair, but Bimbi was determined. He drove the boy on, snapping at his heels, worrying his way through the crowd; barking, baring his teeth, heedless of kicks or falling stones. Sick with hunger, half dead with fear and sulfur fumes, Tito pounded on, pursued by Bimbi. How long, he never knew. At last he staggered through the marine gate and felt soft sand under him. Then Tito fainted. . . .

Someone was dashing sea water over him. Someone was carrying him toward a boat.

"Bimbi," he called. And then louder, "Bimbi!" But Bimbi had disappeared.

Voices jarred against each other. "Hurry—hurry!" "To the boats!" "Can't you see the child's frightened and starving!" "He keeps calling for someone!" "Poor boy, he's out of his mind." "Here, child—take this!"

They tucked him in among them. The oarlocks creaked; the oars splashed; the boat rode over toppling waves. Tito was safe. But he wept continually.

"Bimbi!" he wailed. "Bimbi! Bimbi!"

He could not be comforted.

Eighteen hundred years passed. Scientists were restoring the ancient city; excavators were working their way through the stones and trash that had buried the entire town. Much had already been brought to light—statues, bronze instruments, bright mosaics, household articles; even delicate paintings had been preserved by the fall of ashes that had taken over two thousand lives. Columns were dug up, and the Forum was beginning to emerge.

It was at a place where the ruins lay deepest that the Director paused.

"Come here," he called to his assistant. "I think we've discovered the remains of a building in good shape. Here are four huge millstones[13] that were most likely turned by slaves or mules—and here is a whole wall standing with shelves inside it. Why! It must have been a bakery. And here's a curious thing. What do you

---

13. **millstones:** pair of circular stones used for grinding grain into flour.

166   *The Short Story*

Climax (p. 41) is the point of our highest interest. In what sense do we now know the solution to the conflict?

GUIDED READING

LITERAL QUESTION

1a. What finally happens to Tito and Bimbi? (Tito is put into a boat by strangers and is saved; we don't know what happens to Bimbi.)

INFERENTIAL QUESTION

1b. Why doesn't the author tell us about Bimbi at this point? (to create suspense, so that the resolution of the story will be a surprise) think I found under this heap where the ashes were thickest? The skeleton of a dog!"

"Amazing!" gasped his assistant. "You'd think a dog would have had sense enough to run away at the time. And what is that flat thing he's holding between his teeth? It can't be a stone."

"No. It must have come from this bakery. You know it looks to me like some sort of cake hardened with the years. And, bless me, if those little black pebbles aren't raisins. A raisin cake almost two thousand years old! I wonder what made him want it at such a moment?"

"I wonder," murmured the assistant.

Resolution (p. 41) is the final outcome. What finally happens to Bimbi?

STUDY QUESTIONS

Recalling

1. From the beginning, find two facts about Tito.
2. Why do the buildings of the forum look new? Describe the conversation that Tito overhears.
3. Give two details that Tito notices at the beginning of the eruption.
4. In what ways does Bimbi help Tito to escape the city? What finally happens to Tito?
5. Why are modern scientists surprised to find a dog in the ruins? What is the dog holding?

Interpreting

6. Why do you think the people of Pompeii do not heed warnings of the eruption?
7. Give at least two examples of foreshadowing. In what way does foreshadowing add suspense to the story?
8. Why did Bimbi not escape from the city?

COMPOSITION

Writing About Setting

■ Write about the change of setting in "The Dog of Pompeii." First tell in what way the setting changes. Then give details of the setting from before and after the change. Finally, tell how the change affects the characters. Be sure to use examples from the story to support your opinions.

Writing a Story

■ Write a story about a fictional person who lives through an important event of history. First describe your setting vividly. Then describe your fictional character clearly. Finally, tell what happens to your character during the historical event. You may want to use one of the following events: the building of a pyramid, the discovery of America, the first moon landing by Americans. *For help with this assignment, see Lesson 4 in the Writing About Literature Handbook at the back of this book.*

CHALLENGE

Research and Oral Report

■ Do research in a library. Then prepare an oral report on volcanoes. Your report should answer the following questions: What causes volcanic eruptions? What are some of the famous eruptions in history? Where was the most recent eruption? You may wish to bring to class pictures of volcanic eruptions or pictures of the ruins of Pompeii.

The Dog of Pompeii 167

COMPOSITION: GUIDELINES FOR EVALUATION

WRITING ABOUT SETTING

Objective

To describe the change of setting in the story

Guidelines for Evaluation

■ suggested length: 250–300 words
■ should describe change in setting, giving details before and after change
■ should tell how the change affects characters
■ should use examples to support opinions

WRITING A STORY

Objective

To create a fictional person who lives through an important historical event

Guidelines for Evaluation

■ suggested length: 300–500 words
■ should vividly describe setting, character
■ should tell what happens to character during the historical event

- The scientists find the skeleton of a dog buried in the ashes of an ancient bakery.
- The dog is holding what seems to have been a cake with raisins.

RESOLUTION

Bimbi returned to the bakery, where he was overcome by ash and smoke.

REFLECTING ON THE STORY

How is our reaction as readers different from the scientists' reaction to the discovery of the dog's skeleton? (The scientists are puzzled and amazed. We understand that Bimbi went to get the cake for Tito, and we are deeply touched by the dog's devotion.)

STUDY QUESTIONS

1. homeless; blind from birth
2. rebuilt after recent earthquake; talk about possible eruption
3. Bimbi thumps tail more than usual; thick fog irritates Tito's throat.
4. pulls him awake, drags him to beach, bites him; strangers carry him to a rowboat
5. wonder why he didn't have instinct to escape; a raisin cake
6. Possible answers: didn't expect disaster so soon after earthquake; became used to smoke column
7. explanation for new buildings; stranger's proverb; reader's knowledge of catastrophe adds tension and expectation
8. He returned to bakery to get sweet cake for Tito.

CHALLENGE

Students should

- find information about causes of volcanic eruptions, famous eruptions, and the most recent eruption
- prepare an outline of information
- present information orally

- The story is set in the village of Tarrytown in the Hudson River valley.
- Sleepy Hollow, nearby, is believed to be haunted.
- The most popular ghost of Sleepy Hollow is a headless horseman.

LITERARY OPTIONS

- plot
- point of view
- humor

THEMATIC OPTIONS

- superstition
- greed
- mystery and adventure

1 POINT OF VIEW

The third-person narrator's description of Sleepy Hollow reveals his strong affection for the area. The narrator's attitude gives the story a feeling of warmth and humor.

2 SETTING

The landscape of Sleepy Hollow seems to inspire superstitious stories, and the fact that Revolutionary War battles were fought nearby provides historical underpinnings for the ghost stories.

3 PLOT: FORESHADOWING

The narrator's detailed description of the headless horseman's supposed nightly habits suggests that they will play a central role in the plot.

TEXAS ESSENTIAL ELEMENTS GRADE 8

3A plot development and character development
3C setting and mood
3D literary genres
4B implied main idea
4C fact vs. nonfact
4E cause/effect
4F point of view
4G prediction of outcomes
4I use of parts of a book
To locate treatment of an Element, see *Texas Teacher's Resources*.

Washington Irving (1783–1859) was the first American author to win international fame. He was a lawyer who preferred to write. Today most people know his most famous stories, "Rip Van Winkle" and "The Legend of Sleepy Hollow." The setting of "The Legend of Sleepy Hollow" is the Hudson River valley north of New York City.

■ As you read the story, find examples of Irving's love for this region, its people, and its folklore.

Washington Irving

The Legend of Sleepy Hollow

In the bosom of one of those spacious coves which indent the eastern shore of the Hudson, there lies a small market town, which by some is called Greensburgh, but which is more generally and properly known by the name of Tarrytown. This name was given by the good housewives of the adjacent country, from the tendency of their husbands to linger about the village tavern on market days. Not far from this village, perhaps about two miles, there is a little valley among high hills, which is one of the quietest places in the whole world. A small brook glides through it, with just murmur enough to lull one to repose, and the occasional whistle of a quail, or tapping of a woodpecker, is almost the only sound that ever breaks in upon the uniform tranquillity.[1] This glen has long been known by the name of Sleepy Hollow.

A drowsy, dreamy influence seems to hang over the land. The whole neighborhood abounds with local tales, haunted spots, and twilight superstitions. The dominant spirit, however, that haunts this enchanted region is the apparition of a figure on horseback without a head. It is said by some to be the ghost of a Hessian trooper[2] whose head had been carried away by a cannonball, in some nameless battle during the Revolutionary War. His haunts are not confined to the valley, but extend at times to the adjacent roads, and especially to the vicinity of a church at no great distance. Certain historians of those parts claim that the body of the trooper having been buried in the churchyard, the ghost rides forth to the scene of battle in nightly quest of his head; and that the rushing speed with which he sometimes passes along the Hollow is owing to his being late, and in a

---

1. **tranquillity** [trang kwil'ə tē]: peace and quiet.

168   *The Short Story*

2. **Hessian** [hesh'ən] **trooper:** German soldier paid to fight for the British during the Revolutionary War.

GUIDED READING

LITERAL QUESTION

1a. What real places and what real event does the narrator mention? (the Hudson River, Tarrytown, the Revolutionary War)

INFERENTIAL QUESTION

1b. Why do you think the author begins a ghost story with detailed descriptions of actual places and events? (to make a fanciful story seem as if it could really have happened) hurry to get back to the churchyard before daybreak. The specter[3] is known, at all the country firesides, by the name of the Headless Horseman of Sleepy Hollow.

In this by-place of nature, there abode, some thirty years since,[4] a worthy fellow of the name of Ichabod Crane, who sojourned in Sleepy Hollow for the purpose of instructing the children of the vicinity. The name of Crane was not inapplicable to his person. He was tall, but exceedingly lank, with narrow shoulders, long arms and legs, hands that dangled a mile out of his sleeves, feet that might have served for shovels, and his whole frame most loosely hung together. To see him striding along the profile of a hill on a windy day, with his clothes bagging and fluttering about him, one might have mistaken him for the spirit of famine descending upon the earth, or some scarecrow eloped from a cornfield.

His schoolhouse was a low building of one large room, rudely constructed of logs. From here the low murmur of his pupils' voices might be heard in a drowsy summer's day, like the hum of a beehive; interrupted now and then by the authoritative voice of the master, in the tone of menace or command; or, perhaps, by the appalling sound of the birch,[5] as he urged some tardy loiterer along the flowery path of knowledge. Truth to say, he was a conscientious man, and ever bore in mind the golden maxim, "Spare the rod and spoil the child."—Ichabod Crane's scholars certainly were not spoiled.

The revenue arising from his school was small, and would have been scarcely sufficient to furnish him with daily bread, for he was a huge feeder. To help out his maintenance, he was, according to country custom in those parts, boarded and lodged at the houses of the farmers whose children he instructed. With these he lived successively a week at a time, thus going the rounds of the neighborhood, with all his worldly effects tied up in a cotton handkerchief. In addition, he was the singing master of the neighborhood, and picked up many bright shillings[6] by instructing the young folks in psalmody.[7] Thus, by various little makeshifts, the worthy pedagogue[8] got on tolerably enough, and was thought, by all who understood nothing of the labor of headwork, to have a wonderfully easy life of it.

The schoolmaster is generally a man of some importance in the female circle of a rural neighborhood, being considered of vastly superior taste and accomplishments to the rough country swains.[9] Our man was esteemed by the women as a man of great learning, for he had read several books quite through, and was a perfect master of Cotton Mather's *History of New England Witchcraft*,[10] in which, by the way, he most firmly believed. It was often his delight, after his school was dismissed in the afternoon, to stretch himself on the rich bed of clover bordering the little brook that whimpered by his schoolhouse, and there con over[11] old Mather's direful tales.

Another of his sources of fearful pleasure was to pass long winter evenings with the old Dutch wives and listen to their marvelous tales of ghosts and goblins, and haunted

---

6. **shillings:** coins. A shilling is worth one twentieth of a pound, the basic unit of British money; for a while pounds and shillings were used in America.
7. **psalmody** [sä′mə dē]: singing the psalms.
8. **pedagogue** [ped′ə gog′]: teacher.
9. **swains** [swānz]: young men.
10. **Cotton Mather's . . . Witchcraft:** imaginary book. Cotton Mather (1663–1728) was a preacher in colonial New England who wrote several books about witchcraft.
11. **con over:** study, memorize.

The Legend of Sleepy Hollow 169

---

3. **specter:** ghost.
4. **abode . . . since:** lived thirty years ago; actually, around the beginning of the 1800s.
5. **birch:** rod from a birch tree, used to punish slow or disobedient students.

AT A GLANCE

- Ichabod Crane is the schoolteacher of Sleepy Hollow.
- He is admired by the women of the area as refined and accomplished.
- He is very much interested in superstitions and witchcraft.

1 POINT OF VIEW

The narrator's use of exaggeration ("hands that dangled a mile out of his sleeve") to describe Crane's appearance suggests a cartoon figure. The narrator's attitude toward the teacher establishes the story's affectionately mocking tone.

2 CHARACTERIZATION

Crane appears to have a sinister side: He is an authoritarian taskmaster and does not hesitate to use physical punishment on his students.

3 HUMOR

The narrator mocks both Crane and the women who admire him by revealing that the women consider the teacher a "man of great learning" for simply having "read several books quite through."

4 PLOT: FORESHADOWING

Crane's fascination with the supernatural foreshadows a possible encounter with the Headless Horseman, who was mentioned earlier.

GUIDED READING

LITERAL QUESTIONS

1a. What does the narrator say Ichabod Crane looks like? (tall, exceedingly lank, with narrow shoulders, long arms and legs, hands dangling out of his sleeves, feet big as shovels) How does the narrator describe Crane's teaching style? (as authoritarian and punitive)

2a. According to the narrator, how do women in rural areas regard a schoolmaster? (as vastly superior to other local men)

INFERENTIAL QUESTIONS

1b. How do you think Crane's students regard him? (They probably consider him both ridiculous and cruel.)

2b. How do you think the local men regard Crane? (They probably both consider him ridiculous and resent his influence over the women.)

- Ichabod is terrified of riding through Sleepy Hollow at night.
- One of his students is Katrina Van Tassel, the daughter of a rich farmer.
- Ichabod decides to woo Katrina when he comprehends her father's wealth.

1 PLOT: FORESHADOWING

Crane's fearful imagination during his walks home is another hint at later developments in the plot.

2 THEME

The narrator's description of Crane's "soft and foolish heart" is ironic because the Crane he shows us is actually greedily attracted to Van Tassel's money rather than romantically attracted to Katrina.

3 HUMOR

Striking visual imagery humorously suggests that good food is the real passion of Crane's life and that he greedily yearns for affluence and comfort.

fields, and haunted brooks, and haunted bridges, and haunted houses, and particularly of the Headless Horseman, or Galloping Hessian of the Hollow, as they sometimes called him. He would delight them equally by his anecdotes of witchcraft, and would frighten them woefully with speculations upon comets and shooting stars, and with the alarming fact that the world did absolutely turn round, and that they were half the time topsy-turvy!

1 But if there was a pleasure in all this, it was dearly purchased by the terrors of his walk homewards later. What fearful shapes and shadows beset his path amidst the dim and ghastly glare of a snowy night! And how often was he thrown into complete dismay by some rushing blast, howling among the trees, in the idea that it was the Galloping Hessian on one of his nightly scourings![12]

Among the musical disciples who assembled, one evening in each week, to receive his instructions in psalmody was Katrina Van Tassel, the daughter and only child of a prosperous Dutch farmer. She was a blooming lass of fresh eighteen; plump as a partridge; ripe and melting and rosy-cheeked as one of her father's peaches; and universally famed, not merely as a beauty, but as an heiress. She was a little of a coquette,[13] as might be perceived even in her dress, which was a mixture of ancient and modern fashions, as most suited to set off her charms.

2 Ichabod Crane had a soft and foolish heart, and it is not to be wondered at that so tempting a morsel soon found favor in his eyes, more especially after he had visited her in her paternal mansion. Old Baltus Van Tassel was a perfect picture of a thriving, contented farmer. His stronghold was situated on the banks of the Hudson, in one of those green, sheltered, fertile nooks, in which the Dutch farmers are so fond of nestling. Close by the farmhouse was a vast barn that might have served for a church, every window and crevice of which seemed bursting forth with the treasures of the farm.

The pedagogue's mouth watered as he looked upon this sumptuous promise of luxurious winter fare. 3 In his devouring mind's eye he pictured to himself every roasting-pig running about him with a pudding in his belly, and an apple in his mouth. The pigeons were snugly put to bed in a comfortable pie, and tucked in with a coverlet of crust; the geese were swimming in their own gravy. Not a turkey but he beheld daintily trussed up, with its gizzard under its wing, and, perhaps, a necklace of savory sausages.

As the enraptured Ichabod fancied all this, and as he rolled his great green eyes over the fat meadowlands, his heart yearned after the damsel who was to inherit these domains.

When he entered the house, the conquest of his heart was complete. It was one of those spacious farmhouses, with high-ridged but lowly sloping roofs, built in the style handed down from the first Dutch settlers, the low, projecting eaves forming a piazza[14] along the front. From this piazza the wondering Ichabod entered the hall, which formed the center of the mansion. Here rows of resplendent pewter[15] ranged on a long dresser; a door left ajar gave him a peep into the best parlor, where the claw-footed chairs and dark mahogany tables shone like mirrors; and a corner cupboard, knowingly left open, displayed immense treasures of old silver and well-mended china.

---

12. **scourings:** rides to look for something.
13. **coquette** [kō ket′]: woman who flirts.

14. **projecting eaves . . . piazza** [pē az′ə]: The edges of the roof extend outward to form a porch.
15. **resplendent** [ri splen′dənt] **pewter** [pŭ′tər]: shiny utensils made from a silvery metal.

GUIDED READING

LITERAL QUESTIONS

1a. How does Crane feel as he rides home at night after hearing ghost stories? (terrified)

2a. According to the narrator, when is the "conquest" of Crane's heart complete? (when he enters the Van Tassel house and sees all the luxurious furnishings)

INFERENTIAL QUESTIONS

1b. What does the narrator mean by saying that Crane's pleasures that evening had been "dearly purchased"? (He has to pay a high price for his enjoyment of ghost stories—namely, by being terrified afterward.)

2b. What is ironic about the narrator's statement? (Usually the "conquest" of someone's heart refers to a romantic conquest, but Crane's heart seems won by Katrina's father's money.)

AT A GLANCE

- Ichabod wants to marry Katrina, but she has many admirers.
- Brom Van Brunt is her foremost suitor.

1 READING SKILLS: COMPARISON/CONTRAST

Katrina couldn't possibly have two more different suitors than Crane and Brom Van Brunt. Even Van Brunt's name suggests strength and earthiness. He is large, loud, fun-loving, and attractive—all the things that Crane is not.

2 PLOT: FORESHADOWING

Van Brunt's skill in horsemanship, his love of mischief, and his "waggish good humor" all hint at what this competitor for Katrina's affections might do to impede Crane's courtship.

From the moment that Ichabod laid his eyes upon these regions of delight, the peace of his mind was at an end, and his only study was how to gain the affections of the peerless daughter of Van Tassel. In this enterprise, however, he had to encounter a host of fearful adversaries of real flesh and blood, the numerous admirers who beset every portal to her heart, keeping a watchful and angry eye upon each other, but ready to fly out in the common cause against any new competitor.

1 Among these the most formidable was a burly, roaring, roistering blade,[16] of the name of Abraham, or, according to the Dutch abbreviation, Brom Van Brunt. He was broad-shouldered and double-jointed, with short, curly black hair, and a bluff but not unpleasant countenance, having a mingled air of fun and arrogance. From his Herculean[17] frame and great powers of limb, he had received the nickname of "Brom Bones," by which he was 2 universally known. He was famed for great knowledge and skill in horsemanship. He was foremost at all races. He was always ready for either a fight or a frolic, but had more mischief than ill will in his composition; and, with all his overbearing roughness, there was a strong dash of waggish[18] good humor at bottom. He had three or four boon compan-

---

16. **roistering** [rois′tər ing] **blade:** fun-loving, attractive young man.

17. **Herculean** [hur′kyə lē′ən]: large and powerful like Hercules, a hero in Greek mythology famous for his great strength.
18. **waggish:** playful.

The Legend of Sleepy Hollow 171

GUIDED READING

LITERAL QUESTION

1a. What does the narrator tell us about Brom Van Brunt? (He is burly, strong, fun-loving, and a good horseman who loves mischief.)

INFERENTIAL QUESTION

1b. What types of things would you expect Brom Bones to do in his competition with Crane? (Possible answers: He could show off his strength, play practical jokes, and make fun of Crane's appearance, weakness, and foolish superstitious fears.)

1 POINT OF VIEW

The narrator's characterization of Crane's nature as a "happy mixture of pliability and perseverance" sounds complimentary but is meant to be ironic. What the narrator is really suggesting is that Crane's "pliability" is really cowardice and that his "perseverance" stems from greed.

2 CHARACTER MOTIVATION

Brom Bones is much more straightforward than Crane and would prefer open *combat* for Katrina's hand. It is Crane's "obstinately pacific" and sneaky tactics that drive Brom Bones to "boorish practical jokes."

3 THEME

Ichabod does not realize that the disturbances are practical jokes. Because of his superstitious nature he believes witches are causing the mischief.

---

ions,[19] who regarded him as their model, and at the head of whom he scoured the country, attending every scene of feud or merriment for miles round.

This reckless hero had for some time singled out the blooming Katrina for the object of his gallantries, and it was whispered that she did not altogether discourage his hopes. Certain it is, his advances were signals for rival candidates to retire. When his horse was seen tied to Van Tassel's paling,[20] a sure sign that his master was courting within, all other suitors passed by in despair.

Such was the formidable rival with whom Ichabod Crane had to contend, and, considering all things, a stouter man than he would have shrunk from the competition, and a **1** wiser man would have despaired. He had, however, a happy mixture of pliability and perseverance[21] in his nature.

To have taken the field openly against his rivals would have been madness. Ichabod, therefore, made his advances in a quiet and gently insinuating[22] manner. Under cover of his character of singing master, he made frequent visits at the farmhouse.

I profess not to know how women's hearts are wooed and won. To me they have always been matters of riddle and admiration. He who wins a thousand common hearts is entitled to some renown; but he who keeps undisputed sway over the heart of a coquette is indeed a hero. Certain it is, this was not the case with the redoubtable[23] Brom Bones. From the moment Ichabod Crane made his advances, the interests of the former evidently declined. His horse was no longer seen tied at

---

19. **boon companions:** close friends.
20. **paling:** fence.
21. **pliability** [plī′ə bil′ə tē] **and perseverence** [pur′sə vēr′əns]: ability both to give in under pressure and to keep trying.
22. **insinuating** [in sin′ū āt′ing]: gradual and indirect.
23. **redoubtable** [ri dou′tə bəl]: causing fear.

172   *The Short Story*

---

the palings on Sunday nights, and a deadly feud gradually arose between him and the schoolmaster of Sleepy Hollow.

Brom, who had a degree of rough chivalry in his nature, would have carried matters to open warfare, and have settled their pretensions[24] to the lady according to the mode of the knights-errant of yore—by single combat; but Ichabod was too conscious of the superior might of his adversary to enter the lists[25] against him. He had overheard a boast of Bones, that he would "double the schoolmaster up, and lay him on a shelf of his own schoolhouse"; and he was too wary to give him an opportunity. There was something **2** extremely provoking[26] in this obstinately pacific[27] system; it left Brom no alternative but to play boorish practical jokes upon his rival. Ichabod became the object of whimsical persecution to Bones and his gang of rough-riders. They harried his hitherto peaceful domains; smoked out his singing school, by stopping up the chimney; broke into the schoolhouse at night and turned everything **3** topsy-turvy; so that the poor schoolmaster began to think all the witches in the country held their meetings there.

In this way matters went on for some time, without producing any material effect on the relative situation of the rivals. On a fine autumn afternoon, Ichabod, in pensive mood, sat enthroned on the lofty stool whence he usually watched all the concerns of his little literary realm. His scholars were all busily intent upon their books, or slyly whispering behind them with one eye kept upon the master; and a kind of buzzing stillness reigned throughout the schoolroom. It was suddenly

---

24. **pretensions:** claims.
25. **enter the lists:** agree to fight. Knights entered the field of battle to show their willingness to fight.
26. **provoking** [prə vōk′ing]: causing anger.
27. **obstinately pacific:** stubbornly peaceful.

GUIDED READING

LITERAL QUESTION

1a. Whom does Ichabod blame for all the practical jokes? (witches)

INFERENTIAL QUESTION

1b. What does his explanation show about the extent of Ichabod Crane's superstitiousness? (He is so foolishly superstitious that he does not investigate events for which there are reasonable explanations.)

---

interrupted by the appearance of a man who came clattering up to the school door with an invitation to Ichabod to attend a merrymaking, or "quilting frolic," to be held that evening at Mynheer[28] Van Tassel's.

All was now bustle and hubbub in the late quiet schoolroom. The scholars were hurried through their lessons; books were flung aside without being put away on the shelves; inkstands were overturned, benches thrown down; and the whole school was turned loose an hour before the usual time.

The gallant Ichabod now spent at least an extra half-hour brushing up his best and indeed only suit of rusty black, and arranging his locks by a bit of broken looking glass that hung up in the schoolhouse. That he might make his appearance before his mistress in the true style of a cavalier,[29] he borrowed a horse from the farmer with whom he was living and issued forth, like a knight-errant in quest of adventures. But it is proper that I should, in the true spirit of romantic story, give some account of the looks and equipment of my hero and his steed. The animal he bestrode was a broken-down plow horse that had outlived almost everything but his viciousness. He was gaunt and shaggy, with a thin neck and a head like a hammer; his rusty mane and tail were tangled and knotted with burrs. Still, he must have had fire in his day, if we may judge from the name he bore of Gunpowder.

Ichabod was a suitable figure for such a steed. He rode with short stirrups, which brought his knees nearly up to the pommel of the saddle; his sharp elbows stuck out like grasshoppers'. He carried his whip perpendicularly in his hand, and, as his horse jogged on, the motion of his arms was not unlike the flapping of a pair of wings.

It was toward evening that Ichabod arrived at the castle of the Heer Van Tassel, which he found thronged with the pride and flower of the adjacent country. Brom Bones, however, was a hero of the scene, having come to the gathering on his favorite steed, Daredevil, a creature, like himself, full of mettle[30] and mischief, which no one but himself could manage.

I pause to dwell upon the world of charms that burst upon the enraptured gaze of my hero as he entered the state parlor of Van Tassel's mansion. Not those of the lasses, but the ample charms of a genuine Dutch country tea table. There was the doughty doughnut, the tenderer olykoek,[31] and the crisp and crumbling cruller; sweet cakes and shortcakes, ginger cakes and honey cakes, and the whole family of cakes. And then there were apple pies and peach pies and pumpkin pies, besides slices of ham and smoked beef; not to mention broiled shad and roasted chickens.

I want breath and time to discuss this banquet as it deserves, and am too eager to get on with my story. Happily, Ichabod Crane was not in so great a hurry as his historian, but did ample justice to every dainty.

He could not help, too, rolling his large eyes round him as he ate, and chuckling with the possibility that he might one day be lord of all this scene of almost unimaginable luxury and splendor. Then, he thought, how soon he'd turn his back upon the old schoolhouse and kick any itinerant pedagogue out-of-doors that should dare to call him comrade!

And now the sound of the music from the common room, or hall, summoned to the dance. How could the flogger of urchins be

---

28. **Mynheer** [mīn hār′]: Dutch for "Mister" or "Sir."
29. **cavalier** [kav′ə lēr′]: brave and courteous gentleman devoted to a lady.

30. **mettle:** spirit.
31. **olykoek** [äl′ə kook′]: kind of doughnut.

The Legend of Sleepy Hollow 173

AT A GLANCE

- Ichabod is invited to a party at Mynheer Van Tassel's.
- He borrows a farm horse and rides to Van Tassel's farm.
- Brom Bones arrives on his fine horse Daredevil.

1 READING SKILLS: MAKING INFERENCES

Details about Crane's sudden, uncharacteristic speed and lack of discipline in the classroom suggest his eagerness to get to the Van Tassels' party.

2 HUMOR: WORD CHOICE

Crane, the unlikely "cavalier" and "knight-errant," sets out on his "steed." The narrator's careful choice of these mocking, ironic terms prepares us for the humorous adventure to follow.

3 PLOT: FORESHADOWING

The name and description of Brom Bones's horse—"Daredevil, a creature, like himself, full of mettle and mischief"—hint at trouble ahead for Crane and his broken-down plow horse.

4 STYLE: DETAILS

The narrator describes the food in loving detail to suggest how it appeared to the "enraptured gaze" of Crane, a comic hero who is more interested in food than in love.

5 POINT OF VIEW

The shift from third- to first-person narration here briefly draws attention to the teller behind the tale and contributes to the amusingly ironic tone of the story.

GUIDED READING

LITERAL QUESTIONS

1a. Whom does the narrator refer to as a "cavalier," a "knight-errant," and a "hero"? (Ichabod Crane)

2a. What "world of charms" does Crane turn his "enraptured gaze" to as he enters the party? (the food table)

INFERENTIAL QUESTIONS

1b. Why does the narrator use these words to describe Crane? (The narrator wants to make us laugh by suggesting an ironic contrast between the romantic association of the words and the comic reality of Crane.)

2b. Why is it ironic for our hero to be "enraptured" by a food table? (Romantic heros are supposed to be enraptured by ladies rather than by doughnuts and honey cakes.)

- Brom Bones is jealous of the attention Katrina shows Ichabod.
- The older people talk about the Headless Horseman of Sleepy Hollow, and Brom tells of racing this ghost.
- Ichabod speaks to Katrina, then leaves to ride home.

1 PLOT: SUSPENSE

Brom Bones's brooding jealousy suggests that he will soon take action against Crane. We wonder when he will strike and how.

2 THEME

Claims about the Headless Horseman's most recent activities prepare us for the adventure to come.

3 POINT OF VIEW

The narrator, who has been almost all-knowing until now, teases us here by claiming not to know what happens between Crane and Katrina. This device creates suspense, although Crane's "chopfallen" appearance indicates that he has received bad news.

4 PLOT: SUSPENSE

The setting and Crane's dread suggest that his encounter with the Headless Horseman may occur soon.

otherwise than animated and joyous? The lady of his heart was his partner in the dance, and smiling graciously in reply to all his amorous looks, while Brom Bones, sorely smitten with love and jealousy, sat brooding by himself in one corner.

When the dance was at an end, Ichabod was attracted to a knot of the sager folks, who, with old Van Tassel, sat smoking at one end of the piazza, gossiping over former times, and drawing out long stories about the war. But all these were nothing to the tales of ghosts and apparitions that succeeded. Many dismal tales were told about funeral trains and mourning cries and wailings heard and seen about the great tree where the unfortunate Major André[32] was taken, and which stood in the neighborhood. The chief part of the stories, however, turned upon the favorite specter of Sleepy Hollow, the Headless Horseman, who had been heard several times of late, patrolling the country, and, it was said, tethered his horse nightly among the graves in the churchyard.

The tale was told of old Brouwer, a disbeliever in ghosts, how he met the horseman returning from his foray[33] into Sleepy Hollow, and was obliged to get up behind him; how they galloped over bush and brake,[34] over hill and swamp, until they reached the bridge, when the horseman suddenly turned into a skeleton, threw old Brouwer into a brook, and sprang away over the treetops with a clap of thunder.

This story was immediately matched by a thrice-marvelous[35] adventure of Brom Bones, who made light of the Galloping Hessian as an arrant[36] jockey. He affirmed that, on re-

turning one night from the neighboring village of Sing Sing, he had been overtaken by this midnight trooper; that he had offered to race with him for a bowl of punch, and should have won it, too, for Daredevil beat the goblin horse all hollow, but, just as they came to the church bridge, the Hessian bolted, and vanished in a flash of fire.

All these tales sank deep in the mind of Ichabod. He repaid them in kind with large extracts from his invaluable author, Cotton Mather, and added many fearful sights which he had seen in his nightly walks about Sleepy Hollow.

The revel now gradually broke up. Ichabod only lingered behind, according to the custom of country lovers, to have a tête-à-tête[37] with the heiress, fully convinced that he was now on the high road to success. What passed at this interview I will not pretend to say, for in fact I do not know. Something, however, must have gone wrong, for he certainly sallied forth, after no very great interval, with an air quite desolate and chopfallen.[38] Without looking to the right or left to notice the scene of rural wealth on which he had so often gloated, he went straight to the stable, and with several hearty cuffs and kicks, roused his steed most uncourteously from the comfortable quarters.

It was the very witching time of night that Ichabod, heavy-hearted and crestfallen, pursued his travel homewards.

All the stories of ghosts and goblins that he had heard in the afternoon now came crowding upon his recollection. He had never felt so lonely and dismal. He was, moreover, approaching the very place where many of the scenes of the ghost stories had been laid. In the center of the road stood an enormous tulip

---

32. **Major André:** British officer during the Revolutionary War who was hanged as a spy in 1780.
33. **foray** [fôr′ā]: raid, attack.
34. **brake:** clump of bushes.
35. **thrice-marvelous:** three times as amazing.
36. **arrant** [ar′ənt]: notorious.

37. **tête-à-tête** [tāt′ə tāt]: French for "head-to-head," a private conversation.
38. **chopfallen:** open-mouthed with surprise and disappointment.

GUIDED READING

LITERAL QUESTIONS

1a. Who tells a story about racing the Headless Horseman for a bowl of punch? (Brom)

2a. How does Crane look and act after his talk with Katrina? (He looks desolate, no longer gloats over the Van Tassel estate, and treats his horse badly.)

INFERENTIAL QUESTIONS

1b. Why do you think he tells that story? (probably to frighten Ichabod, who has to go home by way of Sleepy Hollow)

2b. What do you think Katrina has just said to Crane? (that she is going to marry someone else) tree. It was connected with the tragical story of the unfortunate André, who had been taken prisoner close by, and was universally known by the name of Major André's Tree.

About two hundred yards from the tree a small brook crossed the road, and ran into a marshy and thickly wooded glen, known by the name of Wiley's Swamp. A few rough logs, laid side by side, served for a bridge over this stream. To pass this bridge was the severest trial. It was at this identical spot that the unfortunate André was captured. This has ever since been considered a haunted stream, and fearful are the feelings of the schoolboy who has to pass it alone after dark.

As he approached the stream his heart began to thump. He summoned up, however, all his resolution, gave his horse half a score of kicks in the ribs, and attempted to dash briskly across the bridge. But instead of starting forward, the perverse[39] old animal made a lateral movement, and ran broadside **1** against the fence. Ichabod, whose fears increased with the delay, jerked the reins on the other side and kicked lustily with the opposite foot. It was all in vain. His steed started, it is true, but it was only to plunge to the opposite side of the road into a thicket of brambles and alder bushes. Just at this moment a splashing step by the side of the bridge caught the sensitive ear of Ichabod. In the dark shadow of the grove, on the margin of the brook, he **2** beheld something huge, misshapen, black, and towering. It stirred not, but seemed gathered up in the gloom, like some gigantic monster ready to spring upon the traveler.

The hair of the affrighted pedagogue rose upon his head with terror. What was to be done? To turn and fly was now too late; and besides, what chance was there of escaping ghost or goblin, if such it was, which could

---

39. **perverse:** stubbornly doing the opposite of what is expected.

ride upon the wings of the wind? Summoning up, therefore, a show of courage, he demanded in stammering accents, "Who are you?" He received no reply. He repeated his demand in a still more agitated voice. Still there was no answer. Just then the shadowy object of alarm put itself in motion, and, with a scramble and a bound, stood at once in the middle of the road. Though the night was dark and dismal, yet the form of the unknown **3** might now in some degree be made out. He appeared to be a horseman of large dimensions, and mounted on a black horse of powerful frame. He made no offer of harm or sociability, but kept aloof on one side of the road, jogging along on the blind side of old Gunpowder, who had now got over his fright and waywardness.

Ichabod, who had no relish for this strange midnight companion, and bethought himself of the adventure of Brom Bones with the Galloping Hessian, now quickened his steed, in hopes of leaving him behind. The stranger, however, quickened his horse to an equal pace. Ichabod pulled up and fell into a walk, thinking to lag behind—the other did the same. There was something in the moody and dogged silence of this persistent companion that was mysterious and appalling. It was soon fearfully accounted for. On mounting a rising ground, which brought the figure of his **4** fellow traveler in relief against the sky, gigantic in height, and muffled in a cloak, Ichabod was horror-struck on perceiving that he was headless—but his horror was still more increased on observing that the head, which should have rested on his shoulders, was carried before him on the pommel of the saddle. His terror rose to desperation. He rained a shower of kicks and blows upon Gunpowder, hoping, by a sudden movement, to give his companion the slip—but the specter started full jump with him.

They had now reached the road which

The Legend of Sleepy Hollow 175

- Ichabod's saddle begins to slip, and the monster is close behind.
- Ichabod decides that safety lies across the bridge.
- They cross the bridge, and Ichabod looks back.

1 STYLE: DETAILS

Vivid details add to the humor of the scene by creating moment-by-moment images of Crane's comic predicament as it progressively worsens.

2 CHARACTERIZATION

Crane's reasoning that if he can just reach the church bridge he will be safe is a perfect example of superstitious thinking. Since Brom claims to have reached safety in this way, Crane assumes that it is a rule the "goblin" must obey.

turns off to Sleepy Hollow; but Gunpowder, who seemed possessed with a demon, instead of keeping on it, made an opposite turn, and plunged headlong downhill to the left. This road leads through a sandy hollow, and just beyond swells the green knoll on which stands the whitewashed church.

As yet the panic of the steed had given his unskillful rider an apparent advantage in the chase; but just as he had got halfway through **1** the hollow the girths of the saddle gave way, and he felt it slipping from under him. He seized it by the pommel, and endeavored to hold it firm, but in vain; and he had just time to save himself by clasping old Gunpowder round the neck, when the saddle fell to the earth, and he heard it trampled underfoot by his pursuer. The goblin was hard on his haunches; and (unskillful rider that he was!) he had much ado to maintain his seat, sometimes slipping on one side, sometimes on an-

other, and sometimes jolted on the high ridge of his horse's backbone, with a violence that he feared would cleave him asunder.[40]

An opening in the trees now cheered him **2** with the hopes that the church bridge was at hand. He recollected the place where Brom Bones's ghostly competitor had disappeared. "If I can but reach that bridge," thought Ichabod, "I am safe." Just then he heard the black steed panting and blowing close behind him; he even fancied that he felt his hot breath. Another convulsive[41] kick in the ribs, and old Gunpowder sprang upon the bridge; he thundered over the resounding planks; he gained the opposite side; and now Ichabod cast a look behind to see if his pursuer would vanish, according to the rule, in a flash of fire and brimstone. Just then he saw the goblin

---

40. **cleave him asunder:** split him in half.
41. **convulsive:** violent.

GUIDED READING

LITERAL QUESTION

1a. What happens to Crane just as he rides halfway through the hollow? (The girths of his saddle give way, it slips off, and Crane barely manages to stay on the horse by clasping it around the neck.)

INFERENTIAL QUESTION

1b. Do you think the author meant this scene to be suspenseful or comical? (The description causes most readers both to smile and to wonder what will happen next.)

AT A GLANCE

- The horseman hurls its head at Ichabod.
- The head hits Ichabod and hurls him to the ground.
- Ichabod disappears.

1 PLOT: CLIMAX

The story reaches its peak of emotional involvement as the horseman hurls his head at Crane, the head crashes into Crane's skull, and he tumbles "headlong into the dust."

2 STYLE: DETAILS

The detail of the shattered pumpkin—a clue to the mystery of the horseman's detached head—is offered to us in an offhand way. We can infer that a human rider carried the pumpkin as his "head."

3 POINT OF VIEW

The narrator's claim that the people of Sleepy Hollow "diligently considered" the cause of Crane's disappearance is ironic, since their thinking is superstitious. Their ultimate lack of concern for Crane—because he owed money to no one—is also ironic.

1 rising in his stirrups, and in the very act of hurling his head at him. Ichabod endeavored to dodge the horrible missile, but too late. It encountered his cranium with a tremendous crash—he was tumbled headlong into the dust, and Gunpowder, the black steed, and the goblin rider passed by like a whirlwind.

The next morning the old horse was found without his saddle, and with the bridle under his feet, soberly cropping the grass at his master's gate. Ichabod did not make his appearance at breakfast—dinner hour came, but no Ichabod. The boys assembled at the schoolhouse, and strolled idly about the banks of the brook, but no schoolmaster. An inquiry was set on foot, and after diligent investigation they came upon his traces. In one part of the road leading to the church was found the saddle trampled in the dirt. The tracks of horses' hoofs deeply dented in the road, and evidently at furious speed, were traced to the

2 bridge, beyond which, on the bank of a broad part of the brook, where the water ran deep and black, was found the hat of the unfortunate Ichabod, and close beside it a shattered pumpkin.

The brook was searched, but the body of the schoolmaster was not to be discovered. The mysterious event caused much speculation at the church on the following Sunday. Knots of gazers and gossips were collected in the churchyard, at the bridge, and at the spot where the hat and pumpkin had been found. The stories of Brouwer, of Bones, and a whole store of others, were called to mind; and when 3 they had diligently considered them all, and compared them with the symptoms of the present case, they shook their heads, and came to the conclusion that Ichabod had been carried off by the Galloping Hessian. As he was a bachelor, and in nobody's debt, nobody troubled his head any more about him. The

The Legend of Sleepy Hollow 177

GUIDED READING

LITERAL QUESTION

1a. What is found on the bank of the brook? (Crane's hat and a shattered pumpkin)

INFERENTIAL QUESTION

1b. How do you think the shattered pumpkin got there? (It is the "head" hurled at Crane by the mysterious horseman.)

■ Someone reports that Ichabod is still alive and living elsewhere.
■ Brom marries Katrina.
■ It is also reported that Ichabod haunts the bridge.

1 READING SKILLS: MAKING INFERENCES

Brom's behavior when the story of Crane is told confirms our earlier suspicions that he pretended to be the Headless Horseman.

2 PLOT: RESOLUTION

It is an amusingly fitting outcome for the superstitious Ichabod Crane to finally become, in other people's imaginations, a ghost himself.

REFLECTING ON THE STORY

Which elements in the story do you think have made it remain so popular? (possible answers: the narrator's gift for humorous detail, the memorable character of Ichabod Crane, the terrifying image of the Headless Horseman, the suspenseful plot)

STUDY QUESTIONS

1. Ghost of Hessian trooper patrols roads at night; can turn into skeleton; frightens locals.
2. *Looks:* tall, very thin, long arms and legs, feet like shovels, baggy clothes; *life style:* strict teacher, little money
3. Cotton Mather's *History of New England Witchcraft;* ghost stories
4. She is young, lovely, wealthy.
5. He is big, burly, athletic, skilled horseman, racer, mischief-maker; courts Katrina
6. He is huge, muffled in a cloak, carries his head; throws his head.
7. Crane's hat, shattered pumpkin; either spirited off or left Sleepy Hollow frightened and rejected
8. *Food:* Imagines all Van Tassel's livestock as delicious dishes; *comfortable home:* probably because he lives with students' families and has no home of his own

school was removed to a different quarter of the Hollow, and another pedagogue reigned in his stead.

It is true, an old farmer, who had been down to New York on a visit several years after, and from whom this account of the ghostly adventure was received, brought home word that Ichabod Crane was still alive; that he had left the neighborhood, partly through fear of the goblin and partly in mortification at having been suddenly dismissed by the heiress. Brom Bones, too, who shortly after his rival's disappearance conducted the blooming Katrina in triumph to the altar, was observed to look exceedingly knowing whenever the story of Ichabod was related, and always burst into a hearty laugh at the mention of the pumpkin,

which led some to suspect that he knew more about the matter than he chose to tell.

The old country wives, however, who are the best judges of these matters, maintain to this day that Ichabod was spirited away by supernatural means. The bridge became more than ever an object of superstitious awe; the schoolhouse, being deserted, soon fell to decay, and was reported to be haunted by the ghost of the unfortunate pedagogue; and the plowboy, loitering homeward of a still summer evening, has often fancied his voice at a distance, chanting a melancholy psalm tune among the tranquil solitudes[42] of Sleepy Hollow.

42. **solitudes:** lonely, quiet places.

STUDY QUESTIONS

Recalling

1. Who is the headless horseman thought to be? Describe his activities.
2. From the beginning of the story, give at least two details of Crane's appearance and two examples of the way he lives.
3. Name two things that give Ichabod Crane "fearful pleasure."
4. Give three reasons Crane wants to marry Katrina Van Tassel.
5. Give at least two pieces of information about Brom Bones and his activities. Why does he dislike Crane?
6. Describe the rider whom Crane meets after Van Tassel's party. What does he throw at Crane?
7. What is found near the bridge on the morning after the party? Give two different opinions of what finally happens to Crane.

178   *The Short Story*

Interpreting

8. What things in life does Crane consider most important? Give reasons for your opinion.
9. Compare and contrast Crane and Brom. In what ways are their names fitting?
10. What do you think actually happens to Crane after the party? Give at least two pieces of evidence from the story to support your opinion.

Extending

11. Why do you think that many people, like Crane, enjoy frightening stories?

READING AND LITERARY FOCUS

Total Effect

The **total effect** is the overall impact that a story has on a reader. For example, one story (like "Come of Age") may seem like a true-to-life experience. Another (like "The Rule of Names") may

9. *Crane:* thin, gangling, local intellectual; Ichabod Crane —good name for thin, bird-like teacher; *Brom:* strong, goodnatured, mischievous roughneck; Abraham Van Brunt, or "Brom Bones"— good name for threatening, hardy man

10. Answers will vary, but should suggest that Brom puts on cloak and carries pumpkin "head"—he is big, good horseman, wants to remove Crane as love rival.

11. People are fascinated with mysteries and the unknown.

be surprising and magical. Each of a story's major elements—plot, character, setting, point of view, and theme—contributes to this impact.

Thinking About the Total Effect

1. **Plot:** What is the main conflict of "The Legend of Sleepy Hollow"? What is the solution?
2. **Character:** In what way is Crane's trouble caused by his own personality?
3. **Setting:** What effect does the setting have on what happens in the story?
4. **Point of View:** Imagine that Brom is telling you about the events of the story. In what way do you think his version would be different from Irving's story?
5. **Theme:** What do you think is Irving's attitude toward superstition? Give the story's theme in one sentence.

VOCABULARY

The Thesaurus

A **synonym** is a word that has the same or nearly the same meaning as another word. For example, *afraid* and *frightened* are synonyms.

A **thesaurus** is a book that contains synonyms. Some thesauruses list key words in alphabetical order as dictionaries do. Each key word is followed by its synonyms. Another type of thesaurus, *Roget's Thesaurus,* organizes words with similar meanings into groups. Each group is listed by number. Therefore, guide numbers rather than guide words help you to find entries. An index of words in alphabetical order is located at the back of the book.

Suppose that you wanted to find a synonym for the word *age.* First find *age* in the index of *Roget's Thesaurus.* Then look at the group of words listed after *age.* Notice that a number follows each word. If you want to use *age* in the sense of "oldness," for example, you will look up number 124.

> **Sample from Index**
> **age,** period 108
> long time 110
> oldness 124
> advanced life 128

In the body of the book under number 124, you will find many words from which to choose the exact word that you need.

> **Sample Thesaurus Entry**
> 124. **OLDNESS.**—age, antiquity, maturity.

The following words are from "The Legend of Sleepy Hollow." Copy the words onto a separate sheet. Beside each word place a synonym that has the same meaning as the word has in the story. Use your library's thesaurus to do this exercise. Where possible, write down several synonyms for each word listed.

1. repose
2. beset
3. chivalry
4. pensive
5. awe

CHALLENGE

Literary Criticism

■ Critic Norman Foerster wrote about the respect that Washington Irving won both in the United States and in Europe:

> The respect in which he was held was partly owing to the man himself, with his warm friendliness of nature, [and] his good sense. . . .

In what ways does "The Legend of Sleepy Hollow" show Irving's warmth and good sense?

The Legend of Sleepy Hollow 179

1. between Brom and Ichabod, Katrina Van Tassel's two suitors; Crane's leaving Sleepy Hollow
2. His interest in the supernatural, benign acceptance of local legend, and timidity make him easy prey.
3. It is set in Hudson Valley, a site of Revolutionary War (basis of headless horseman legend); includes dark and shadowy locales appropriate for ghost stories.
4. He would present Crane as even more foolish; might gloat over success of his prank rather than leaving mystery unsolved.
5. ■ Irving seems to suggest that superstition is a natural extension of people's imaginations—a very human pleasure, entertainment; also it may lead believers to act foolishly.
   ■ Superstitious fears make people vulnerable.

VOCABULARY

1. *Repose:* rest, ease, relaxation, quiet, stillness
2. *Beset:* harass, annoy, torment, pester, plague, worry, vex, tease, persecute
3. *Chivalry:* courtesy, politeness, good manners
4. *Pensive:* thoughtful, meditative, reflective, contemplative, musing, thinking
5. *Awe:* wonder, astonishment, fascination

CHALLENGE

Students should
■ make a general statement about how Irving's narrator creates a warm, humorous tone in the story and maintains a rational perspective on superstition throughout
■ cite specific examples from the story showing these qualities

AT A GLANCE

- The first-person narrator calls attention to the death notice published for Philip Nolan.
- Known as "The Man Without a Country," Nolan was once a friend of Aaron Burr.

LITERARY OPTIONS

- irony
- dialogue
- point of view

THEMATIC OPTIONS

- patriotism
- American experiences
- communities

1 POINT OF VIEW

The first-person narrator introduces a death notice he saw in a particular newspaper on a specific date. This technique immediately gives the story a feeling of realism.

2 THEME

Although the idea of patriotism is not specifically mentioned here, it is hinted at. To be "A Man Without a Country" makes one a "poor creature."

3 IRONY

The title "His Excellency, Honorable Aaron Burr" is used ironically to describe a man who betrayed his country and tried to establish an empire.

TEXAS ESSENTIAL ELEMENTS GRADE 8

1A writing process
1B purpose and audience
1C support for main idea
1D evaluation of content and organization
3A plot development and character development
3B figurative language
3C setting and mood
3D literary genres
4E cause/effect
4F point of view
5B oral presentations
To locate treatment of an Element, see *Texas Teacher's Resources*.

Edward Everett Hale (1822–1909) was the grandnephew of Nathan Hale, the Revolutionary War hero. He was born in Boston, Massachusetts, and was a minister, writer, and magazine editor. His writing is often concerned with the ideals of peace and patriotism. "The Man Without a Country," his most famous story, was believed to be completely realistic when it was first published. In fact, many people did not realize that it was fiction.

■ What do you think gives the story its feeling of realism?

Edward Everett Hale

The Man Without a Country (abridged)

1 I suppose that very few readers of the New York *Herald* of August 13, 1863, observed in an obscure corner, among the "Deaths," the announcement:

NOLAN. Died on board the U.S. Corvette *Levant*, Lat.[1] 2° 11′ S., Long.[2] 131° W., on May 11, PHILIP NOLAN.

Hundreds of readers would have paused at that announcement, if it had read thus: "DIED, MAY 11, THE MAN WITHOUT A COUNTRY." For it was as "The Man Without a Country" that poor Philip Nolan had generally been known by the officers who had him in charge during some fifty years, as, indeed, by all the men who sailed under them.

2 Now the poor creature is dead, it seems to me worthwhile to tell a little of his story, by way of showing young Americans of today what it is to be "A Man Without a Country."

Philip Nolan was as fine a young officer as there was in the "Legion of the West," as the Western division of our army was then called. When Aaron Burr[3] made his first dashing expedition down to New Orleans in 1805, he met this gay, bright, young fellow. Burr marked him, talked to him, walked with him, took him a day or two's voyage in his flatboat, and, in short, fascinated him. For the next year, barrack life was very tame to poor Nolan. But 3 before long, His Excellency, Honorable Aaron Burr, appeared again under a very different aspect. There were rumors that he had an

---
1. **Lat.:** abbreviation for latitude, the distance north or south of the equator.
2. **Long.:** abbreviation for longitude, the distance east or west of the prime meridian, an imaginary line drawn around the earth at a right angle to the equator.

3. **Aaron Burr:** (1756–1836), vice-president of the United States, 1801–1805. In 1805 he traveled to New Orleans supposedly with secret plans to break from the United States and establish a new country. Burr was arrested and tried for treason.

180 *The Short Story*

GUIDED READING

LITERAL QUESTION

1a. What does the narrator call Philip Nolan? ("The man without a country")

INFERENTIAL QUESTION

1b. How does the narrator seem to feel about this man? (He refers to him as "the poor creature," pitying him.)

army behind him and an empire before him. At that time the youngsters all envied him. He asked Nolan if he could show him something of the great river and the plans for the new post. By the time the sail was over, Nolan was enlisted body and soul. From that time, though he did not yet know it, he lived as a man without a country.

1 | What Burr meant to do I know no more than you. It is none of our business just now. Only, when the grand catastrophe came, Burr's treason trial at Richmond,[4] Fort Adams got up a string of courts-martial[5] on the officers there. One and another of the colonels and majors were tried, and, to fill out the list, little Nolan, against whom there was evidence enough that he was sick of the service, had been willing to be false to it, and would have obeyed any order to march anywhere had the order been signed, "By command of his Exc. A. Burr." The courts dragged on. The big flies escaped—rightly for all I know. Nolan was proved guilty enough, yet you and I would never have heard of him but that, when the president of the court asked him at the close whether he wished to say anything to show that he had always been faithful to the United

2 | States, he cried out in a fit of frenzy: "Damn the United States! I wish I may never hear of the United States again!"

I suppose he did not know how the words shocked old Colonel Morgan, who was holding the court. Half the officers who sat in it had

3 | served through the Revolution,[6] and their lives had been risked for the very idea which he cursed in his madness. He, on his part, had grown up in the West of those days. He had spent half his youth with an older

---

4. **Richmond:** capital of Virginia.
5. **courts-martial:** trials of people in the military, conducted according to military law.
6. **Revolution:** American Revolutionary War, 1775–1783.

brother, hunting horses in Texas; and to him *United States* was scarcely a reality. I do not excuse Nolan; I only explain to the reader why he damned his country and wished he might never hear her name again.

From that moment, September 23, 1807, till the day he died, May 11, 1863, he never heard her name again. For that half-century and more, he was a man without a country.

Old Morgan, as I said, was terribly shocked. He called the court into his private room and returned in fifteen minutes, with a face like a sheet, to say: "Prisoner, hear the sentence of the court! The court decides that you never hear the name of the United States again."

Nolan laughed. But nobody else laughed.

4 | Old Morgan was too solemn, and the whole room was hushed dead as night for a minute. Even Nolan lost his swagger in a moment. Then Morgan added: "Mr. Marshal, take the prisoner to Orleans, in an armed boat, and deliver him to the naval commander there. Request him to order that no one shall mention the United States to the prisoner while he is on board ship. You will receive your written orders from the officer on duty here this evening. The court is adjourned."

5 | When I was second officer of the *Intrepid,* some thirty years after, I saw the original paper of instructions. It ran much in this way:

Washington [with a
date, which must have
been late in 1807]

Sir:

You will receive from Lieutenant Neale the person of Philip Nolan, late a lieutenant in the United States Army.

This person on trial by court-martial expressed, with an oath, the wish that he might "never hear of the United States again."

The Man Without a Country 181

Nolan is implicated when Burr is tried for treason. In response to a question from the judge, Nolan denounces his country, the United States. Nolan is sentenced never to hear of his country again.

1 **BACKGROUND**

Aaron Burr, who had been Vice-President under Thomas Jefferson, was tried for allegedly attempting to bring the western territories of the United States under the influence of Mexico.

2 **STYLE: DIALOGUE**

Philip Nolan's dialogue characterizes him as a hotheaded young man who does not consider the consequences of his words or actions.

3 **SETTING**

The story is set in the decades after the American Revolution. Nolan is too young to have served in the war and has grown up on the American frontier.

4 **STYLE: SIMILE**

The simile *hushed dead as night* vividly conveys the sense of shock in the courtroom as the sentence is announced.

5 **POINT OF VIEW**

The narrator explains how he came to know so much about Philip Nolan.

GUIDED READING

LITERAL QUESTION

1a. Upon what is Nolan's harsh sentence based? (his angry words against his country at his trial)

INFERENTIAL QUESTION

1b. Do you think the narrator feels that Nolan was treated fairly? (Answers will vary. Possibilities: No—he seems to suggest that Nolan was young and impetuous but not treasonous; yes—even though Nolan was young, his acts and words condemned him.)

1 IRONY

This description of Nolan's sentence points outs its irony: He is to be punished by having his own wish fulfilled.

2 THEME

This passage emphasizes the harshness of Nolan's punishment: Talk of home and country is precious to the community of men at sea, and being deprived of it is punishment for them.

3 POINT OF VIEW

The narrator reveals that he was one of Nolan's favorites. Therefore, we can expect an even closer look at Nolan's experiences.

4 CHARACTERIZATION

The fact that Nolan chooses to wear a regulation army uniform suggests his desire to remain a member of his community, the army, even if dishonored.

5 THEME

By describing the thoroughness with which Nolan's punishment is carried out, the narrator suggests just how painful it is to be cut off from one's homeland.

---

1 The court sentenced him to have his wish fulfilled.

You will take the prisoner on board your ship, and keep him there with such precautions as shall prevent his escape.

You will provide him with such quarters, rations, and clothing as would be proper for an officer of his late rank. He is to be exposed to no indignity of any kind, nor is he ever unnecessarily to be reminded that he is a prisoner.

But under no circumstances is he ever to hear of his country or to see any information regarding it; and you will especially caution all the officers under your command to take care that this rule, in which his punishment is involved, shall not be broken.

It is the intention of the government that he shall never again see the country which he has disowned. Before the end of your cruise, you will receive orders which will give effect to this intention.

Respectfully yours,
W. Southard,
for the Secretary of the Navy

The rule adopted on board the ships on which I have met "The Man Without a Country" was, I think, transmitted from the beginning. 2 No mess[7] liked to have him permanently, because his presence cut off all talk of home or of the prospect of return, of politics or letters, of peace or war—cut off more than half the talk men liked to have at sea. He was not permitted to talk with the men unless an officer was by. With officers he had unrestrained intercourse, as far as they and 3 he chose. But he grew shy, though he had favorites: I was one. Then the captain always asked him to dinner on Monday. Every mess

in succession took up the invitation in its turn.

According to the size of the ship, you had him at your mess more or less often at dinner. His breakfast he ate in his own stateroom. Sometimes, when the marines or sailors had any special jollification,[8] they were permitted to invite Plain Buttons, as they called him. Then Nolan was sent with some officer, and the men were forbidden to speak of home while he was there. They called him Plain But- 4 tons because, while he always chose to wear a regulation army uniform, he was not permitted to wear the army button, for the reason that it bore either the initials or the insignia of the country he had disowned.

I remember, soon after I joined the navy, I was on shore with some of the older officers from our ship, and some of the gentlemen fell to talking about Nolan, and someone told the system which was adopted from the first about his books and other reading. Everybody was permitted to lend him books, if they were not published in America and made no allu- 5 sion to it. He had almost all the foreign papers that came into the ship, sooner or later; only somebody must go over them first, and cut out any advertisement or stray paragraph that referred to America.

Phillips, who was of the party, told a story of something which happened at the Cape of Good Hope[9] on Nolan's first voyage.

They had touched at the Cape, paid their respects to the English admiral and the fleet, and then Phillips had borrowed a lot of English books from an officer. Among them was *The Lay of the Last Minstrel*,[10] which they had all of them heard of, but which most of them had never seen. Well, nobody thought there could be any risk of anything national

---

7. **mess:** group of people who eat meals together.

8. **jollification** (jol'ə fĭ kā'shən): merrymaking.
9. **Cape of Good Hope:** southern tip of Africa.
10. *The Lay . . . Minstrel:* long, romantic poem by the Scottish writer Sir Walter Scott (1771–1832).

GUIDED READING

LITERAL QUESTIONS

1a. What does the narrator say the men on Nolan's ships can never mention in his presence? (anything concerning the United States)

2a. What must be done to the foreign newspapers before Nolan can read them? (Any items referring to the United States must be cut out.)

INFERENTIAL QUESTIONS

1b. How do you think the sailors feel about Nolan? (Their feelings are probably mixed: They have reason both to pity him and to resent him; many may feel that his punishment is justified.)

2b. What effect do you think these cut-up newspapers have on Nolan? (The holes probably remind him of his punishment and probably make him even more curious about what is happening in his country.)

in that. So Nolan was permitted to join the circle one afternoon when a lot of them sat on deck smoking and reading aloud. In his turn, Nolan took the book and read to the others; and he read very well, as I know. Poor Nolan read steadily through the fifth canto,[11] stopped a minute and drank something, and then began, without a thought of what was coming:

Breathes there the man with soul so dead,
Who never to himself hath said . . .

It seems impossible to us that anybody ever heard this for the first time; but all these fellows did then, and poor Nolan himself went on, still unconsciously or mechanically:

This is my own, my native land!

Then they all saw that something was to pay; but he expected to get through, I suppose, turned a little pale, but plunged on:

Whose heart hath ne'er within him
    burned,
As home his footsteps he hath turned
From   wandering   on   a   foreign
    strand![12] . . .

Here the poor fellow choked, could not go on, but started up, swung the book into the sea, vanished into his stateroom, "And by Jove," said Phillips, "we did not see him for two months again. And I had to make up some story to that English surgeon why I did not return his Walter Scott to him."

That story shows about the time when Nolan's braggadocio[13] must have broken down. At first, they said, he took a very high tone,

considered his imprisonment a mere farce, affected to enjoy the voyage, and all that; but Phillips said that after he came out of his stateroom he never was the same man again. He was always shy afterward, when I knew him—very seldom spoke unless he was spoken to, except to a very few friends. He lighted up occasionally, but generally he had the nervous, tired look of a heart-wounded man.

When Captain Shaw was coming home, rather to the surprise of everybody they made one of the Windward Islands,[14] and lay off and on for nearly a week. After several days, the *Warren* came to the same rendezvous; they exchanged signals; she told them she was outward bound and took poor Nolan and his traps[15] on the boat to try his second cruise. He looked very blank when he was told to get ready to join her. He had known enough of the signs of the sky to know that till that moment he was going "home." But this was a distinct evidence of something he had not thought of, perhaps—that there was no going home for him, even to a prison. And this was the first of some twenty such transfers, which kept him all his life at least some hundred miles from the country he had hoped he might never hear of again.

It may have been on that second cruise that Mrs. Graff, the celebrated Southern beauty of those days, danced with him. The ship had been lying a long time in the Bay of Naples,[16] and the officers were very intimate in the English fleet, and there had been great festivities, and our men thought they must give a great ball on board the ship. They wanted to use Nolan's stateroom for something, and they hated to do it without asking him to the ball; so the captain said they might

---

11. **canto:** one of the main divisions of a long poem.
12. **strand:** land bordering a body of water.
13. **braggadocio** (brag′ə dō′shē ō′): false courage.

14. **Windward Islands:** group of islands off the northern coast of South America.
15. **traps:** belongings; baggage.
16. **Bay of Naples:** bay on the southwestern coast of Italy.

The Man Without a Country   183

AT A GLANCE

- Nolan reads aloud a poem about love of one's country, and he breaks down.
- The ship is headed for America, and so Nolan is transferred to another.
- His ship's officers plan a ball.

1 IRONY

Allowing Nolan to read aloud with the others is an act of kindness. Ironically, it intensifies his suffering once the patriotic subject matter of the new poem becomes obvious.

2 PLOT: CONFLICT

Nolan's extreme behavior shows the depth of his internal conflict. He is beginning to miss his country but has not let his feelings show until now.

3 POINT OF VIEW

The narrator begins to inject his own firsthand observations of Nolan to support what he has heard from others.

4 RESPONSE JOURNAL

Ask students to write about what Nolan must feel at this moment, when he realizes that there is "no going home for him."

GUIDED READING

LITERAL QUESTIONS

1a. What does Nolan do with the book? (swings it into the sea)

2a. Why is Nolan transferred from ship to ship? (to keep him from ever docking in the United States)

INFERENTIAL QUESTIONS

1b. Why does Nolan throw the book away? (He is overcome with grief and rage because the poem reminds him of how much he has lost.)

2b. In what way do you think that these transfers intensify his suffering? (Whenever he is transferred, he knows the ship must be close to America and that everyone else on board is going home.)

184   *The Short Story*

ask him, if they would be responsible that he did not talk with the wrong people, "who would give him intelligence."[17]

As the dancing went on, Nolan and our fellows all got at ease—so much that it seemed quite natural for him to bow to Mrs. Graff and say, "I hope you have not forgotten me, Miss Rutledge. Shall I have the honor of dancing?"

She laughed and said, "I am not Miss Rutledge any longer, Mr. Nolan; but I will dance all the same."

1   Nolan thought he had got his chance. He had known her at Philadelphia. He said boldly—a little pale, she said, as she told me the story years after—"And what do you hear from home, Mrs. Graff?"

"Home! Mr. Nolan! I thought you were the man who never wanted to hear of home again!"—and she walked directly up the deck to her husband and left poor Nolan alone. He did not dance again.

A happier story than either of these I have told is of the war.[18] That came along soon after. In one of the great frigate[19] duels with the English it happened that a round shot from the enemy entered one of our ports square[20] and took right down the officer of the gun himself and almost every man of the gun's crew. Now you may say what you choose about courage, but that is not a nice thing to

2   see. But, as the men who were not killed picked themselves up, and as they and the surgeon's people were carrying off the bodies, there appeared Nolan, in his shirtsleeves, with the rammer[21] in his hand, and, just as if he had been the officer, told them off with

---

17. **intelligence:** here, information.
18. **the war:** War of 1812 between the United States and England.
19. **frigate** [frig'it]: three-masted sailing warship.
20. **round shot . . . square:** cannon ball was fired through one of the openings in the ship's side.
21. **rammer:** block of wood at the end of a long pole, used to push ammunition into a cannon.

authority—who should go to the cockpit[22] with the wounded men, who should stay with him—perfectly cheery, and with that way which makes men feel sure all is right and is going to be right. And he finished loading the gun with his own hands, aimed it, and bade the men fire. And there he stayed, captain of that gun, keeping those fellows in spirits, till the enemy struck[23]—sitting on the carriage while the gun was cooling, though he was exposed all the time, showing them easier ways to handle heavy shot, making the raw hands laugh at their own blunders, and when the gun cooled again, getting it loaded and fired twice as often as any other gun on the ship. The captain walked forward by way of encouraging the men, and Nolan touched his hat and said, "I am showing them how we do this in the artillery, sir."

After the whole thing was over, and the commodore had the Englishman's sword,[24] in the midst of the state and ceremony of the quarter-deck, he said, "Where is Mr. Nolan? Ask Mr. Nolan to come here."

And when Nolan came, he said, "Mr. Nolan, we are all very grateful to you today; you are one of us today; you will be named in the dispatches."

And then the old man took off his own sword of ceremony, gave it to Nolan, and made him put it on. The man who told me this saw it. Nolan cried like a baby, and well he might. He had not worn a sword since that infernal day at Fort Adams. But always afterward on occasions of ceremony he wore that quaint old sword of the commodore.

The captain did mention him in the dispatches. It was always said he asked that No-

lan might be pardoned. He wrote a special letter to the Secretary of War, but nothing ever came of it.

My own acquaintance with Philip Nolan began six or eight years after the English war, on my first voyage after I was appointed a midshipman. From the time I joined, I believe I thought Nolan was a sort of lay chaplain—a chaplain with a blue coat. I never asked about him. Everything in the ship was strange to me. I knew it was green to ask questions, and I suppose I thought there was a Plain Buttons on every ship. We had him to dine in our mess once a week, and the caution was given that on that day nothing was to be said about home. But if they had told us not to say anything about the planet Mars or the Book of Deuteronomy,[25] I should not have asked why; there were a great many things which seemed to me to have as little reason. I first came to understand anything about "The Man Without a Country" one day when we overhauled a dirty little schooner which had slaves[26] on board. An officer named Vaughan was sent to take charge of her, and, after a few minutes, he sent back his boat to ask that someone might be sent who could speak Portuguese. None of the officers did; and just as the captain was sending forward to ask if any of the people could, Nolan stepped out and said he should be glad to interpret if the captain wished, as he understood the language.

When we got there, it was such a scene as you seldom see—and never want to. Nolan said he could speak Portuguese, and one or two Krumen[27] who had worked for the Portuguese on the coast were dragged out.

"Tell them they are free," said Vaughan.

---

22. **cockpit:** area below deck used for treating the wounded.
23. **struck:** lowered their national flag in order to surrender.
24. **the Englishman's sword:** military custom in which the defeated leader gives his sword to the victor.

25. **Book of Deuteronomy** (do͞o′tə ron′ə mē): fifth book of the Old Testament of the Bible.
26. **slaves:** people who were captured in Africa to be sold as slaves in America. In 1808 it became illegal to bring slaves into the United States.
27. **Krumen** (kro͞o′men): skillful sailors from Liberia in West Africa.

The Man Without a Country 185

1 READING SKILLS: MAKING INFERENCES

By the calm, authoritative, cheerful way Nolan takes command, we can infer that he would have made a fine officer and that his talents are being woefully wasted.

2 DIALOGUE

In the heat of the moment, Nolan uses the present tense. The strong sense of community he feels as he joins in the defense of the ship makes him forget that he no longer belongs to any group.

3 PLOT: CONFLICT

Nolan's pride in being presented with the commodore's sword is mixed with shame and grief. His internal conflict is so intense that he can only cry.

4 POINT OF VIEW

The story becomes more personal as the narrator shifts completely into his own memories of Nolan.

GUIDED READING

LITERAL QUESTIONS

1a. How does Nolan act while he is in charge of the gun? (perfectly cheery and confident)

2a. How does Nolan react when the commodore gives him his sword? (He cries like a baby.)

INFERENTIAL QUESTIONS

1b. Why do you think Nolan acts that way? (Answers will vary. Possibilities: He is doing the job he did in the army, and he is fighting the enemy; he is able to express his patriotism and sense of community; he is a natural leader.)

2b. Why do you think Nolan cries? (He is overcome with conflicting feelings—pride, shame, grief.)

- Nolan interprets the slaves' request to be taken home.
- Nolan expresses his regrets to the narrator and urges him to love his country as he does his own mother.
- They part, but the narrator hears about Nolan over the years and finally has a report of his death.

1 PLOT: CONFLICT

Nolan exhibits outward signs of his inner turmoil as he translates the slaves' pleas to be taken home.

2 THEME

Nolan's dialogue strongly suggests the story's theme: People belong to their countries in the same way they belong to their families.

3 PLOT: CLIMAX

Nolan's open admission of his mistake and his regret to the narrator marks the emotional high point of the story.

4 POINT OF VIEW

The narrator openly reveals his strong affection for "the dear old fellow" and hopes that in death Nolan has found a home.

Nolan explained it in such Portuguese as the Krumen could understand, and they in turn to such of the Negroes as could understand them. Then there was a yell of delight by way of spontaneous celebration.

"Tell them," said Vaughan, well pleased, "that I will take them all to Cape Palmas."[28]

This did not answer so well. Cape Palmas was practically as far from the homes of most of them as New Orleans or Rio de Janeiro was; that is, they would be eternally separated from home there. And their interpreters, as we could understand, instantly said, "*Ah, non Palmas*" and began to protest loudly. Vaughan was rather disappointed at this result of his liberality, and he asked Nolan eagerly what they said. The drops stood on poor Nolan's white forehead, as he hushed the men down, and said, "He says, 'Not Palmas.' He says, 'Take us home; take us to our own country; take us to our own house.' "

Vaughan always said Nolan grew gray himself while he struggled through this interpretation. As quick as he could get words, Vaughan said, "Tell them yes, yes, yes; tell them they shall go to the Mountains of the Moon,[29] if they will. If I sail the schooner through the Great White Desert,[30] they shall go home!"

And after some fashion, Nolan said so, and getting Vaughan to say he might go back, he beckoned me down into our boat. As we started back he said to me: "Youngster, let that show you what it is to be without a family, without a home, and without a country. Think of your home, boy; write and send and talk about it. Let it be nearer and nearer to your thought the farther you have to travel

---

28. **Cape Palmas:** port in West Africa.
29. **Mountains of the Moon:** mountain range in east central Africa.
30. **Great White Desert:** probably a reference to the Sahara Desert in northern Africa.

---

from it. Remember, boy, that behind all these men you have to do with, behind officers, and government, and people even, there is the Country herself, your Country, and that you belong to her as you belong to your own mother. Stand by her, boy, as you would stand by your mother!"

I was frightened to death by his calm, hard passion; but I blundered out that I would, by all that was holy, and that I had never thought of doing anything else. He hardly seemed to hear me; but he did, almost in a whisper, say, "Oh, if anybody had said so to me when I was of your age!"

I think it was this half-confidence of his, which I never abused, that afterward made us great friends. He was very kind to me. Often he sat up, or even got up, at night, to walk the deck with me when it was my watch. He explained to me a great deal of my mathematics, and I owe him my taste for mathematics. He lent me books and helped me about my reading. He never referred so directly to his story again; but from one and another officer, I have learned, in thirty years, what I am telling.

After that cruise I never saw Nolan again. The other men tell me that in those fifteen years he aged very fast, but he was still the same gentle, uncomplaining, silent sufferer that he ever was, bearing as best he could his self-appointed punishment. And now it seems that the dear old fellow is dead. He has found a home at last, and a country.

Since writing this I have received from Danforth, who is on board the *Levant*, a letter which gives an account of Nolan's last hours.

Here is the letter:

Dear Fred,

I try to find heart and life to tell you that it is all over with dear old Nolan. The doctor has been watching him very carefully, and yes-

---

GUIDED READING

LITERAL QUESTION

1a. What does Nolan speak of to the narrator in the boat? (home and country)

INFERENTIAL QUESTION

1b. Why does Nolan speak of home and country at this time? (The slaves' strong desire to go home reminds him that he no longer has a home.)

AT A GLANCE

- Nolan lies dying in his state-room, which he has made into a shrine to the United States.
- He asks the captain to tell him about America, now that he is dying.

1 IRONY

As a result of being forbidden to see or hear of the United States, the Man Without a Country has become the most devout of patriots.

2 THEME

The complete isolation of Nolan from American experiences is reflected in the outdated map on his wall.

terday morning he came to me and told me that Nolan was not so well and had not left his stateroom—a thing I never remember before. Do you remember the mysteries we boys used to invent about his room in the old *Intrepid* days? Well, I went in, and there, to be sure, the poor fellow lay in his berth, smiling pleasantly as he gave me his hand but looking very frail. I could not help a glance round, which showed me what a little shrine he had **1 made of the box he was lying in. The Stars and Stripes were draped up above and around a picture of Washington, and he had painted a majestic eagle, with lightnings blazing from** his beak. The dear old boy saw my glance, and said, with a sad smile, "Here, you see, I have a country!" Then he pointed to the foot of his bed, where I had not seen before a great map of the United States, as he had drawn it from memory, and which he had there to look upon as he lay. Quaint, queer old names were on it, **2 in large letters: "Indiana Territory," "Mississippi Territory," and "Louisiana Territory," as I suppose our fathers learned such things.**

"O Captain," he said, "I know I am dying. I cannot get home. Surely you will tell me something now? There cannot be a man who loves the old flag as I do, or prays for it as I do, or hopes for it as I do. There are thirty-four stars in it now, Danforth. I thank God for that, though I do not know what their

The Man Without a Country **187**

GUIDED READING

LITERAL QUESTION

1a. What words does the captain use to describe the names on Nolan's map of the United States? (*quaint* and *queer*)

INFERENTIAL QUESTION

1b. Why do the names seem so quaint to him? (Nolan had last seen a map of the United States about fifty years before; the nation has expanded and changed dramatically since then; the captain is considerably younger than Nolan.)

- Nolan begs for news of America and asks the captain to redraw his map, adding the names of new states.
- Nolan dies.
- His last wishes are to be buried at sea and have a memorial stone.

1 STYLE: SIMILE

The simile *how like a wretched night's dream* conveys the nightmarish consequences of Nolan's scorn of his country.

2 THEME

The reader feels the full impact of Nolan's deprivation as the captain reviews fifty years of change in America.

3 THEME

Nolan affirms his love for his country in his epitaph. He also claims his right, since his punishment has been carried out, to be a "Lieutenant in the Army of the United States" once more.

REFLECTING ON THE STORY

What effect does being kept uninformed about his country have on Nolan? (The more he is denied information about his country, the more he loves it.)

---

names are. There has never been one taken away; I know by that that there has never been any successful Burr. O Danforth," he sighed out, **"how like a wretched night's dream a boy's idea of personal fame or of separate sovereignty seems, when one looks back on it after such a life as mine! But tell me—tell me something—tell me everything, Danforth, before I die!"**

I swear to you that I felt like a monster because I had not told him everything before. "Mr. Nolan," said I, "I will tell you everything you ask about. Only, where shall I begin?"

Oh, the blessed smile that crept over his white face! He pressed my hand and said, "God bless you! Tell me their names," and he pointed to the stars on the flag. "The last I know is Ohio. My father lived in Kentucky. But I have guessed Michigan, and Indiana, and Mississippi—that is where Fort Adams was—they make twenty. But where are your other fourteen? You have not cut up any of the old ones, I hope?"

Well, I told him the names in as good order as I could, and he bade me take down his beautiful map and draw them in as I best could with my pencil. He was wild with delight about Texas, told me how his cousin died there; then he was delighted as he saw California and Oregon—that, he said, he had suspected partly, because he had never been permitted to land on that shore, though the ships were there so much. Then he settled down more quietly, and very happily, to hear me tell in an hour the history of fifty years.

I tell you, it was a hard thing to condense the history of half a century into that talk with a sick man. And I do not now know what I **told him—of emigration and the means of it— of steamboats, and railroads, and telegraphs—of inventions and books, and literature—of the colleges, and West Point, and the Naval School, but with the queerest interruptions** that ever you heard. You see it was Rob-

inson Crusoe[31] asking all the accumulated questions of fifty-six years!

And he drank it in and enjoyed it as I cannot tell you. He grew more and more silent. And then he said he would go to sleep, and he said, "Look in my Bible, Captain, when I am gone." And I went away.

But I had no thought it was the end. I thought he was tired and would sleep. I knew he was happy, and I wanted him to be alone.

But in an hour, when the doctor went in gently, he found Nolan had breathed his life away with a smile.

We looked in his Bible, and there was a slip of paper at the place where he had marked the text:

They desire a country, even a heavenly: where God is not ashamed to be called their God: for he hath prepared for them a city.[32]

On this slip of paper he had written this:

Bury me in the sea; it has been my home, and I love it. But will not someone set up a stone for my memory, that my disgrace may not be more than I ought to bear? Say on it:

In Memory of
PHILIP NOLAN
Lieutenant in the Army
of the United States

HE LOVED HIS COUNTRY
AS NO OTHER MAN HAS LOVED HER;
BUT NO MAN DESERVED LESS
AT HER HANDS.

---

31. **Robinson Crusoe:** The narrator is comparing Nolan to Robinson Crusoe, fictional hero who was shipwrecked on a deserted island for twenty-eight years.
32. **They desire . . . city:** Hebrews 11:16.

188   *The Short Story*

GUIDED READING

LITERAL QUESTIONS

1a. What character in fiction does the captain compare Nolan to? (Robinson Crusoe)

2a. What request does Nolan make of the captain? (to tell him about all the changes in the United States since he last saw it)

INFERENTIAL QUESTIONS

1b. In what way is Nolan like Robinson Crusoe? (Crusoe was stranded on an island for many years without knowledge of the outside world; Nolan is also "stranded," isolated from his country.)

2b. Why does the captain agree to Nolan's request? (He clearly feels that Nolan has already suffered too much for his youthful outburst and that Nolan's obvious love for his country entitles him to knowledge of it.)

STUDY QUESTIONS

Recalling

1. In what way does Nolan become involved with Aaron Burr? What is the result?
2. At his trial what wish does Nolan make about the United States? Why is the new country "scarcely a reality" to him?
3. In what year is Nolan's trial? His death?
4. What is Nolan's punishment? According to the official instructions, in what way will the sentence be carried out?
5. Give at least three examples of how Nolan is treated on the ships.
6. In what ways does Nolan help the Americans during the battle at sea? Give two ways in which the commodore rewards him.
7. After the incident with the slaves, what does Nolan tell the storyteller?
8. What favor does Nolan ask before he dies? What request does he leave in his Bible?

Interpreting

9. List three different character traits for Nolan. Give an example for each.
10. Why does Nolan become upset while reading Walter Scott's poem aloud?
11. Compare and contrast Nolan's situation with the situation of the Krumen slaves.
12. How does Nolan change during the story?

Extending

13. Do you think Nolan's punishment is fair? Why or why not?

READING AND LITERARY FOCUS

Irony

Irony exists when what actually happens is the opposite of what we expect to happen. For example, in "The Man Without a Country" Aaron Burr is accused of treason. However, he goes free. On the other hand, Nolan, who did not actually commit a crime, is punished.

Thinking About Irony

■ Tell how Nolan learns to love the United States. In what way is this ironic?

Dialogue

Dialogue is conversation between characters. Dialogue presents the exact words of the characters. As a result, we feel like eyewitnesses to what happens in the story. We also receive important information about characters from dialogue. We learn about their personalities and their opinions of other characters from what they say. In addition, a character sometimes states a story's theme. For example, at the end of "The Brother Who Failed" (page 131), Aunt Isabel states the theme.

Thinking About Dialogue

1. Cite two pieces of dialogue by Nolan. What do we learn about his personality from each?
2. Nolan speaks to the storyteller after the incident with the slaves. Find the story's stated theme in what he says.

COMPOSITION

Writing About the Total Effect

■ Write about the total effect of "The Man Without a Country." First describe the story's overall impact on you. Then tell how each of the following elements helped to achieve this impact: (a) plot, (b) character, (c) setting, (d) point of view, (e) theme. Give examples from the story to support what you say.

Writing a Scene

■ Write a short dramatic scene in which two strangers get to know each other. For example, they may be sitting beside each other on an airplane, or they may be waiting with their pets in a veterinarian's office. Your scene should include believable plot, characters, and setting. *For help with this assignment, see Lesson 10 in the Writing About Literature Handbook at the back of this book.*

The Man Without a Country 189

STUDY QUESTIONS

1. Burr enlists Nolan's aid; tried for treason along with Burr
2. that he might never hear of it again; had none of the experiences that made older men loyal to U.S.
3. 1807; 1863
4. will never hear of U.S. again; to be held prisoner on navy ships and denied information about the U.S.
5. moved from one mess to another so sailors could sometimes talk about home; can't wear buttons with U.S. insignia; can't read anything about America
6. takes charge when officer killed; mentions him in news dispatches; gives him his sword of ceremony
7. to stand by his country
8. to tell him news of U.S.; to be buried at sea and to have a stone marker acknowledging both his patriotism and his guilt
9. Possible answers: *bold, impetuous:* laughs, swears in court; *personable:* liked by all aboard ships; *brave:* faces death during battle on ship; *intelligent:* reads avidly
10. It concerns homesickness.
11. *Krumen:* set free to go home; *Nolan:* prisoner until death, can never return home
12. from a swaggering, bold, young man to a shy, emotional, patriotic man
13. Possible answers: *yes:* punishment suits crime; *no:* merciless to base lifelong sentence on outburst

READING AND LITERARY FOCUS

Thinking About Irony

by being kept away from it; growth of patriotism usually associated with positive experiences in country

Thinking About Dialogue

1. "Damn the United States! . . ."; hotheaded; "Stand by her, boy, . . .": intense patriotism
2. You belong to your country just as you belong to your own family.

COMPOSITION: GUIDELINES FOR EVALUATION

WRITING ABOUT THE TOTAL EFFECT

Objective

To describe the impact of the story

Guidelines for Evaluation

■ suggested length: 300–500 words
■ should describe story's overall impact on writer; tell how plot, character, setting, point of view, theme contribute
■ should support statements with examples

WRITING A SCENE

Objective

To illustrate how two strangers get to know each other

Guidelines for Evaluation

■ suggested length: five-minute presentation
■ should include believable plot, characters, and setting
■ should include dialogue for each character

- Charlie Gordon, a man of low intelligence, writes his first progress report for an experiment.
- He tells about himself and how much he wants to be smarter.

LITERARY OPTIONS

- point of view
- characterization
- plot

THEMATIC OPTIONS

- happiness and intelligence
- isolation
- friendship and love

1 POINT OF VIEW

The first-person narrator's child-like way of expressing himself shows that he is a man of very limited intelligence. His progress reports will offer an intimate look at the way he perceives himself and the world.

2 PLOT: CONFLICT

The story's chief conflict involves Charlie's struggles to understand the world, to become "smart," and to please others.

**TEXAS ESSENTIAL ELEMENTS
GRADE 8**

2E grammar, punctuation, spelling
2F pronoun agreement
2G subject-verb agreement
3A plot development and character development
3C setting and mood
3D literary genres
4B implied main idea
4E cause/effect
4F point of view
4G prediction of outcomes
To locate treatment of an Element, see *Texas Teacher's Resources.*

Daniel Keyes (born 1927) grew up in New York City. He has held a variety of jobs, including merchant seaman, editor, photographer, and English teacher in high school and college. "Flowers for Algernon" is his most famous work. Keyes has also written a longer, novel version of the story. In addition, television and movie versions have been made.

■ As you read the story, decide what gives this work of science fiction its wide appeal.

Daniel Keyes

Flowers for Algernon

progris riport—march 5 1965

Dr Strauss says I shud rite down what I think and evrey thing that happins to me from now on I dont know why but he says its importint so they will see if they will use me. I hope they use me. Miss Kinnian says maybe they can make me smart. I want to be smart. My name is Charlie Gordon. I am 37 years old and 2 weeks ago was my brithday. I have nuthing more to rite now so I will close for today.

progris riport 2—march 6

I had a test today I think I faled it and I think that maybe now they wont use me. What happind is a nice young man was in the room and he had some white cards with ink spillled all over them. He sed Charlie what do you see on this card. I was very skared even tho I had my rabits foot in my pockit because when I was a kid I always faled tests in school and I spillled ink to.

I told him I saw an inkblot. He said yes and it made me feel good. I thot that was all but when I got up to go he stopped me. He said now sit down Charlie we are not thru yet Then I dont remember so good but he wantid me to say what was in the ink. I dint see nuthing in the ink but he said there was picturs there other pepul saw some picturs. I coudnt see any picturs. I reely tried to see. I held the card close up and then far away. Then I said if I had my glases I could see better I usally only ware my glases in the movies or TV but I said they are in the closit in the hall. I got them. Then I said let me see that card agen I bet Ill find it now.

I tryed hard but I still coudnt find the picturs I only saw the ink. I told him maybe I need new glases. He rote somthing down on a paper and I got skared of faling the test. I told him it was a very nice inkblot with littel points all around the eges. He looked very sad so that wasnt it. I said please let me try agen.

GUIDED READING

LITERAL QUESTION

1a. What has Miss Kinnian told Charlie? ("that maybe they can make me smart")

INFERENTIAL QUESTION

1b. In what way is this evidence that this is a science fiction story? (We know of no way to increase intelligence scientifically.)

Ill get it in a few minits becaus Im not so fast somtimes. Im a slow reeder too in Miss Kinnians class for slow adults but I'm trying very hard.

He gave me a chance with another card that had 2 kinds of ink spilled on it red and blue.

He was very nice and talked slow like Miss Kinnian does and he explained to me that it was a *raw shok*.[1] He said pepul see things in the ink. I said show me where. He said think. I told him I think a inkblot but that wasnt rite eather. He said what does it remind you— pretend something. I closd my eyes for a long time to pretend. I told him I pretned a fowntan pen with ink leeking all over a table cloth. Then he got up and went out.

I dont think I passd the *raw shok* test.

progris riport 3—martch 7

Dr Strauss and Dr Nemur say it dont matter about the inkblots. I told them I dint spill the ink on the cards and I coudnt see anything in the ink. They said that maybe they will still use me. I said Miss Kinnian never gave me tests like that one only spelling and reading. They said Miss Kinnian told that I was her bestist pupil in the adult nite scool becaus I tryed the hardist and I reely wantid to lern. They said how come you went to the adult nite scool all by yourself Charlie. How did you find it. I said I askd pepul and sumbody told me where I shud go to lern to read and spell good. They said why did you want to. I told them becaus all my life I wantid to be smart and not dumb. But its very hard to be smart. They said you know it will probly be tempirery. I said yes. Miss Kinnian told me. I dont care if it herts.

---

1. **raw shok:** Charlie misspells *Rorschach* [rôr′shäk] test, a psychological test in which a subject describes a series of inkblots.

Later I had more crazy tests today. The nice lady who gave it me told me the name and I asked her how do you spellit so I can rite it in my progris riport. THEMATIC APPERCEPTION TEST.[2] I dont know the frist 2 words but I know what *test* means. You got to pass it or you get bad marks. This test lookd easy becaus I could see the picturs. Only this time she dint want me to tell her the picturs. That mixd me up. I said the man yesterday said I shoud tell him what I saw in the ink she said that dont make no difrence. She said make up storys about the pepul in the picturs.

I told her how can you tell storys about pepul you never met. I said why shud I make up lies. I never tell lies any more becaus I always get caut.

She told me this test and the other one the raw-shok was for getting personalty. I laffed so hard. I said how can you get that thing from inkblots and fotos. She got sore and put her picturs away. I dont care. It was sily. I gess I faled that test too.

Later some men in white coats took me to a difernt part of the hospitil and gave me a game to play. It was like a race with a white mouse. They called the mouse Algernon. Algernon was in a box with a lot of twists and turns like all kinds of walls and they gave me a pencil and a paper with lines and lots of boxes. On one side it said START and on the other end it said FINISH. They said it was *amazed*[3] and that Algernon and me had the same *amazed* to do. I dint see how we could have the same *amazed* if Algernon had a box and I had a paper but I dint say nothing. Anyway there wasnt time because the race started.

---

2. **THEMATIC** [thē mat′ik] **APPERCEPTION** [ap′ər sep′shən] **TEST:** personality test in which a subject creates stories to fit a series of pictures.
3. **amazed:** Charlie refers to a *maze*, a confusing series of paths. The intelligence of animals is often rated by how fast they can get through a maze.

Flowers for Algernon 191

- The Rorschach test stumps Charlie.
- He gives his reasons for going to night school.
- He fails another test.
- He meets Algernon and prepares to compete with the mouse on a maze test.

1 CHARACTERIZATION

Charlie's eagerness to learn is evidenced by his efforts in Miss Kinnian's class for slow adults.

2 PLOT: FORESHADOWING

Charlie seems to misunderstand the meaning of *temporary* when he responds "I don't care if it herts." However, his words hint at the mental anguish he will suffer as he becomes more intelligent.

3 PLOT: CONFLICT

Through Charlie's eyes the reader sees his frustration and internal conflict as he tries to apply the rules for one test to another— only to meet failure again.

4 SETTING

Charlie and the reader meet Algernon, the mouse of the story's title, in the story's main setting, a laboratory.

GUIDED READING

LITERAL QUESTIONS

1a. What does Charlie see when he closes his eyes and tries to "pretend" about the inkblot? (a fountain pen with ink leaking all over a tablecloth)

2a. When the second tester asks Charlie to make up stories about pictures, what does Charlie think she wants him to do? (make up lies)

INFERENTIAL QUESTIONS

1b. Why does the tester leave the room after Charlie gives his answer? (He is frustrated because Charlie is not intelligent enough to understand the test.)

2b. What confusion does Charlie demonstrate in the test given by the second tester? (He has trouble distinguishing between reality and imagination.)

- Algernon wins the maze race ten times.
- Charlie is accepted for the experiment, though Dr. Strauss and Dr. Nemur disagree about Charlie.
- Everyone in the lab wishes Charlie success.

1 PLOT: CONFLICT

The external conflict between Dr. Nemur and Dr. Strauss about the experiment hints that Charlie will have more than his own frustrations to deal with as the plot develops.

2 PLOT: SUSPENSE

Miss Kinnian's words to Charlie create suspense. We wonder if he really will grow more intelligent and what effects increased intelligence will have.

3 POINT OF VIEW

Because Charlie is of low intelligence, he has some limitations as a narrator. He cannot completely explain everything that is happening to him.

4 CHARACTERIZATION

The response of the nurses and testers to Charlie shows what a lovable person he is. Charlie reveals more details about his childlike clinging to superstition.

One of the men had a watch he was trying to hide so I woudnt see it so I tryed not to look and that made me nervus.

Anyway that test made me feel worser than all the others because they did it over 10 times with difernt *amazeds* and Algernon won every time. I dint know that mice were so smart. Maybe thats because Algernon is a white mouse. Maybe white mice are smarter then other mice.

progris riport 4—Mar 8

Their going to use me! Im so exited I can hardly write. Dr Nemur and Dr Strauss had a argament about it first. Dr Nemur was in the office when Dr Strauss brot me in. Dr Nemur was worryed about using me but Dr Strauss told him Miss Kinnian rekemmended me the best from all the people who she was teaching. I like Miss Kinnian becaus shes a very smart teacher. And she said Charlie your going to have a second chance. If you volenteer for this experament you mite get smart. They dont know if it will be perminint but theirs a chance. Thats why I said ok even when I was scared because she said it was an operashun. She said dont be scared Charlie you done so much with so little I think you deserv it most of all.

So I got scaird when Dr Nemur and Dr Strauss argud about it. Dr Strauss said I had something that was very good. He said I had a good *motor-vation*.[4] I never even knew I had that. I felt proud when he said that not every body with an eye-q[5] of 68 had that thing. I dont know what it is or where I got it but he said Algernon had it too. Algernons *motor-*

---

4. *motor-vation:* Charlie refers to *motivation*, the desire to work hard and be successful.
5. *eye-q:* Charlie refers to *I.Q.*, Intelligence Quotient, a measurement of a person's intelligence.

192   *The Short Story*

---

vation is the cheese they put in his box. But it cant be that because I didnt eat any cheese this week.

Then he told Dr Nemur something I dint understand so while they were talking I wrote down some of the words.

He said Dr Nemur I know Charlie is not what you had in mind as the first of your new brede of intelek** (coudnt get the word) superman. But most people of his low ment** are host** and uncoop** they are usualy dull apath** and hard to reach. He has a good natcher hes intristed and eager to please.

Dr Nemur said remember he will be the first human beeng ever to have his inteljence trippled by surgicle meens.

Dr Strauss said exakly. Look at how well hes lerned to read and write for his low mentel age its as grate an acheve** as you and I lerning einstines therey of **vity without help. That shows the intenss motor-vation. Its comparat** a tremen** achev** I say we use Charlie.

I dint get all the words and they were talking to fast but it sounded like Dr Strauss was on my side and like the other one wasnt.

Then Dr Nemur nodded he said all right maybe your right. We will use Charlie. When he said that I got so exited I jumped up and shook his hand for being so good to me. I told him thank you doc you wont be sorry for giving me a second chance. And I mean it like I told him. After the operashun Im gonna try to be smart. Im gonna try awful hard.

progris ript 5—Mar 10

Im skared. Lots of people who work here and the nurses and the people who gave me the tests came to bring me candy and wish me luck. I hope I have luck. I got my rabits foot and my lucky penny and my horse shoe. Only a black cat crossed me when I was com-

---

GUIDED READING

LITERAL QUESTIONS

1a. Which doctor wants Charlie on the experiment, and which doctor does not? (Dr. Strauss wants him; Dr. Nemur does not.)

2a. What is Charlie's I.Q. now? (68) How much do the doctors hope to increase it? (They hope to triple it.)

INFERENTIAL QUESTIONS

1b. How do you think this difference of opinion might affect the experiment? (Possible answers: Dr. Nemur might be more critical of Charlie and expect more from him; their arguments might interfere with the experiment or hurt Charlie.)

2b. Will Charlie's new I.Q. represent average or above-average intelligence? (Because the average I.Q. is 100, an I.Q. of 204 would make Charlie a genius.)

AT A GLANCE

- Charlie hopes to beat Algernon in the race after the operation.
- He has the operation but feels no different.

1 CHARACTERIZATION

Charlie wants to be intelligent like other people. He is also altruistic, wanting others to share the results of the experiment.

2 PLOT: FORESHADOWING

For the first time Charlie spells "progress report" correctly and exhibits some confidence: "I got to try and remember that." His gradual improvement in spelling hints at further progress to come.

ming to the hospitil. Dr Strauss says dont be supersitis Charlie this is sience. Anyway Im keeping my rabits foot with me.

I asked Dr Strauss if Ill beat Algernon in the race after the operashun and he said maybe. If the operashun works Ill show that mouse I can be as smart as he is. Maybe smarter. Then Ill be abel to read better and spell the words good and know lots of things **1** and be like other people. I want to be smart like other people. If it works perminint they will make everybody smart all over the wurld.

They dint give me anything to eat this morning. I dont know what that eating has to do with getting smart. Im very hungry and Dr Nemur took away my box of candy. That Dr Nemur is a grouch. Dr. Strauss says I can have it back after the operashun. You cant eat befor a operashun. . . .

Progress Report 6—Mar 15

The operashun dint hurt. He did it while I was sleeping. They took off the bandijis from my eyes and my head today so I can make a **2** PROGRESS REPORT. Dr Nemur who looked at some of my other ones says I spell PROGRESS wrong and he told me how to spell it and REPORT too. I got to try and remember that.

I have a very bad memary for spelling. Dr Strauss says its ok to tell about all the things that happin to me but he says I should tell more about what I feel and what I think. When I told him I dont know how to think he said try. All the time when the bandijis were on my eyes I tryed to think. Nothing happened. I dont know what to think about. Maybe if I ask him he will tell me how I can think now that Im suppose to get smart. What do smart peo-

Flowers for Algernon 193

GUIDED READING

LITERAL QUESTION

1a. What does Charlie ask Dr. Strauss? (if he will beat Algernon in the race after the operation)

INFERENTIAL QUESTION

1b. What does this question show about Charlie? (He has normal feelings of competition and self-respect.)

Flowers for Algernon   T-193

- Charlie is discouraged and hates Algernon.
- He returns to his factory job but will go to the lab each night.
- He recounts innocently his bad treatment at the factory.
- He is given a machine that will teach him while he sleeps.

1 PLOT: CONFLICT

Charlie's sense of frustration and internal conflict are expressed as anger at everyone around him. His less docile attitude may be an early sign of increased intelligence.

2 PLOT: FORESHADOWING

Charlie reveals that Algernon has also had an operation to increase his intelligence. Thus, changes in Algernon may help us predict changes to come in Charlie.

3 READING SKILLS: MAKING INFERENCES

Charlie's remarks about omitting the heading *Progress Report* to save time suggest that his ability to reason is improving.

4 THEME

Because of Charlie's low intelligence, he sees people as his friends as long as they are pleasant. He feels at home at the factory even when we know he is being treated cruelly.

5 POINT OF VIEW

The narrator reports incidents that readers can interpret but Charlie cannot, creating a sense of irony and suspense. We wonder how Charlie's perceptions will change as he grows more intelligent.

---

ple think about. Fancy things I suppose. I wish I knew some fancy things alredy.

Progress Report 7—mar 19

Nothing is happining. I had lots of tests and different kinds of races with Algernon. I hate that mouse. He always beats me. Dr Strauss said I got to play those games. And he said some time I got to take those tests over again. Those inkblots are stupid. And those pictures are stupid too. I like to draw a picture of a man and a woman but I wont make up lies about people.

I got a headache from trying to think so much. I thot Dr Strauss was my frend but he dont help me. He dont tell me what to think or when Ill get smart. Miss Kinnian dint come to see me. I think writing these progress reports are stupid too.

Progress Report 8—Mar 23

Im going back to work at the factery. They said it was better I shud go back to work but I cant tell anyone what the operashun was for and I have come to the hospitil for an hour evry night after work. They are gonna pay me mony every month for lerning to be smart.

Im glad Im going back to work because I miss my job and all my frends and all the fun we have there.

Dr Strauss says I shud keep writing things down but I dont have to do it every day just when I think of something or something speshul happins. He says dont get discoridged because it takes time and it happins slow. He says it took a long time with Algernon before he got 3 times smarter than he was before. Thats why Algernon beats me all the time because he had that operashun too. That makes me feel better. I could probly do that *amazed* faster than a reglar mouse. Maybe some day

194   *The Short Story*

Ill beat Algernon. Boy that would be something. So far Algernon looks like he mite be smart perminent.

Mar 25 (I dont have to write PROGRESS REPORT on top any more just when I hand it in once a week for Dr Nemur to read. I just have to put the date on. That saves time)

We had a lot of fun at the factery today. Joe Carp said hey look where Charlie had his operashun what did they do Charlie put some brains in. I was going to tell him but I remembered Dr Strauss said no. Then Frank Reilly said what did you do Charlie forget your key and open your door the hard way. That made me laff. Their really my friends and they like me.

Sometimes somebody will say hey look at Joe or Frank or George he really pulled a Charlie Gordon. I dont know why they say that but they always laff. This morning Amos Borg who is the 4 man at Donnegans used my name when he shouted at Ernie the office boy. Ernie lost a packige. He said Ernie what are you trying to be a Charlie Gordon. I dont understand why he said that. I never lost any packiges.

Mar 28   Dr Strauss came to my room tonight to see why I dint come in like I was suppose to. I told him I dont like to race with Algernon any more. He said I dont have to for a while but I shud come in. He had a present for me only it wasnt a present but just for lend. I thot it was a little television but it wasnt. He said I got to turn it on when I go to sleep. I said your kidding why shud I turn it on when Im going to sleep. Who ever herd of a thing like that. But he said if I want to get smart I got to do what he says. I told him I dint think I was going to get smart and he put his hand on my sholder and said Charlie you dont know it yet but your getting smarter all the time.

GUIDED READING

LITERAL QUESTION

1a. How does Charlie feel about his co-workers at the factory? (He thinks they are his friends.)

INFERENTIAL QUESTION

1b. Why does he think they are his friends? (He is not intelligent enough to know when he is being cruelly mocked.)

You wont notice for a while. I think he was just being nice to make me feel good because I dont look any smarter.

Oh yes I almost forgot. I asked him when I can go back to the class at Miss Kinnian's school. He said I wont go their. He said that soon Miss Kinnian will come to the hospital to start and teach me speshul. I was mad at her for not comming to see me when I got the operashun but I like her so maybe we will be frends again.

Mar 29   That crazy TV kept me up all night. How can I sleep with something yelling crazy things all night in my ears. And the nutty pictures. Wow. I dont know what it says when Im up so how am I going to know when Im sleeping.

Dr Strauss says its ok. He says my brains are lerning when I sleep and that will help me when Miss Kinnian starts my lessons in the hospitl (only I found out it isnt a hospitil its a labatory). I think its all crazy. If you can get smart when your sleeping why do people go to school. That thing I dont think will work.
1 I use to watch the late show and the late late show on TV all the time and it never made me smart. Maybe you have to sleep while you watch it.

PROGRESS REPORT 9—April 3

Dr Strauss showed me how to keep the TV turned low so now I can sleep. I dont hear a thing. And I still dont understand what it says. A few times I play it over in the morning to find out what I lerned when I was sleeping and I dont think so. Miss Kinnian says Maybe its another langwidge or something. But most times it sounds american. It talks so fast faster than even Miss Gold who was my teacher in 6 grade and I remember she talked so fast I couldnt understand her.

I told Dr Strauss what good is it to get smart in my sleep. I want to be smart when Im awake. He says its the same thing and I have two minds. Theres the *subconscious* and the *conscious* (thats how you spell it). And one dont tell the other one what its doing. They dont even talk to each other. Thats why I dream. And boy have I been having crazy dreams. Wow. Ever since that night TV. The late late late late late show.

I forgot to ask him if it was only me or if everybody had those two minds.

2 (I just looked up the word in the dictionary Dr Strauss gave me. The word is *subconscious. adj. Of the nature of mental operations yet not present in consciousness; as, subconscious conflict of desires.*) Theres more but I still don't know what it means. This isnt a very good dictionary for dumb people like me.

Anyway the headache is from the party. My frends from the factery Joe Carp and Frank Reilly invited me to go with them to Muggsys Saloon for some drinks. I dont like to drink but they said we will have lots of fun. I had a good time.

Joe Carp said I shoud show the girls how I mop out the toilet in the factory and he got me a mop. I showed them and everyone laffed when I told that Mr Donnegan said I was the best janiter he ever had because I like my job and do it good and never come late or miss a day except for my operashun.

I said Miss Kinnian always said Charlie be proud of your job because you do it good.

Everybody laffed and we had a good time and they gave me lots of drinks and Joe said
3 Charlie is a card. I dont know what that means but everybody likes me and we have fun. I cant wait to be smart like my best friends Joe Carp and Frank Reilly.

I dont remember how the party was over but I think I went out to buy a newspaper and

- Miss Kinnian is going to teach Charlie in the lab.
- Charlie's sleep machine is beginning to have an effect.
- The workers make a fool of Charlie at Muggsy's Saloon.

1 HUMOR

Charlie's puzzlement as he tries to use his growing intelligence to understand a confusing world has moments of humor. His attempts at explanations are touching, like those of a developing child.

2 CHARACTERIZATION

A different, more intelligent Charlie begins to emerge as he uses a dictionary for the first time.

3 PLOT: FORESHADOWING

Charlie's intelligence is increasing, and the reader suspects that soon he will see through the fun his co-workers have at his expense.

GUIDED READING

LITERAL QUESTIONS

1a. What puzzles Charlie about the idea of learning as he sleeps? (He wonders why people go to school if they could learn just as well while they sleep.)

2a. How smart does Charlie want to become? (as smart as his co-workers)

INFERENTIAL QUESTIONS

1b. What does his speculation show about how Charlie is changing? (He is beginning to use his reason to understand the world.)

2b. What do you think might happen if Charlie does become as smart as his co-workers? (He won't let them abuse him anymore; he may hate them and realize they've never been his friends; they might be scared and guilty.)

- Charlie's co-workers desert him at the bar.
- He beats Algernon for the first time and learns how the mouse is trained.
- He reads *Robinson Crusoe*.

1 CHARACTERIZATION

Charlie's innate goodness makes him concerned about Algernon, whom he has beaten in the test. He feels a strong sense of identification with the mouse, so his discovery that if Algernon "couldn't lern he would be hungry" is sad and terrifying.

2 IRONY

Charlie's statement "dont worry Miss Kinnian Im not smart yet" is ironic because by saying that he shows that he *is* smarter: He can tell that Miss Kinnian is worried and can infer what she is worried about.

3 THEME

Charlie takes an intellectual leap by making an inference about a picture. Significantly, his inference suggests his empathy for those who need friends.

4 CHARACTERIZATION

Miss Kinnian's concern as Charlie's intelligence grows is obvious as she tries to prepare him for a different view of his co-workers.

---

coffee for Joe and Frank and when I came back there was no one their. I looked for them all over till late. Then I dont remember so good but I think I got sleepy or sick. A nice cop brot me back home. Thats what my landlady Mrs Flynn says.

But I got a headache and a big lump on my head and black and blue all over. I think maybe I fell. Anyway I got a bad headache and Im sick and hurt all over. I dont think Ill drink anymore.

April 6 I beat Algernon! I dint even know I beat him until Burt the tester told me. Then the second time I lost because I got so exited I fell off the chair before I finished. But after that I beat him 8 more times. I must be getting smart to beat a smart mouse like Algernon. But I dont *feel* smarter.

I wanted to race Algernon some more but Burt said thats enough for one day. They let me hold him for a minit. Hes not so bad. Hes soft like a ball of cotton. He blinks and when he opens his eyes their black and pink on the eges.

I said can I feed him because I felt bad to beat him and I wanted to be nice and make frends. Burt said no Algernon is a very specshul mouse with an operashun like mine, and he was the first of all the animals to stay smart so long. He told me Algernon is so smart that every day he has to solve a test to get his food. Its a thing like a lock on a door that changes every time Algernon goes in to eat so he has to lern something new to get his food. That made me sad because if he couldnt lern he would be hungry.

I dont think its right to make you pass a test to eat. How woud Dr Nemur like it to have to pass a test every time he wants to eat. I think Ill be frends with Algernon.

April 9 Tonight after work Miss Kinnian was at the laboratory. She looked like she was glad

to see me but scared. I told her dont worry Miss Kinnian Im not smart yet and she laffed. She said I have confidence in you Charlie the way you struggled so hard to read and right better than all the others. At werst you will have it for a littel wile and your doing somthing for sience.

We are reading a very hard book. I never read such a hard book before. Its called *Robinson Crusoe*[6] about a man who gets merooned on a dessert Iland. Hes smart and figers out all kinds of things so he can have a house and food and hes a good swimmer. Only I feel sorry because hes all alone and has no frends. But I think their must be somebody else on the iland because theres a picture with his funny umbrella looking at footprints. I hope he gets a frend and not be lonly.

April 10 Miss Kinnian teaches me to spell better. She says look at a word and close your eyes and say it over and over until you remember. I have lots of truble with *through* that you say *threw* and *enough* and *tough* that you dont say *enew* and *tew*. You got to say *enuff* and *tuff*. Thats how I use to write it before I started to get smart. Im confused but Miss Kinnian says theres no reason in spelling.

Apr 14 Finished *Robinson Crusoe*. I want to find out more about what happens to him but Miss Kinnian says thats all there is. *Why*

Apr 15 Miss Kinnian says Im lerning fast. She read some of the Progress Reports and she looked at me kind of funny. She says Im a fine person and Ill show them all. I asked her why. She said never mind but I shouldnt feel bad if I find out that everybody isnt nice like I think. She said for a person who god gave so little to you done more then a lot of

---

6. **Robinson Crusoe** [krōō'sō]: novel by British author Daniel Defoe, written in 1719.

GUIDED READING

LITERAL QUESTIONS

1a. What does Charlie think of Algernon when he holds him? ("Hes not so bad.")

2a. How does Miss Kinnian look when she sees Charlie at the lab? (She is pleased to see him but "scared.")

INFERENTIAL QUESTIONS

1b. Why do you think Charlie is beginning to like Algernon? (The mouse is not a threat to him now that he has beaten it in the race.)

2b. Why do you think Miss Kinnian looks scared? (Answers will vary. Possibilities: She is not sure if the experiment is going to work; she is worried about how it will affect Charlie.)

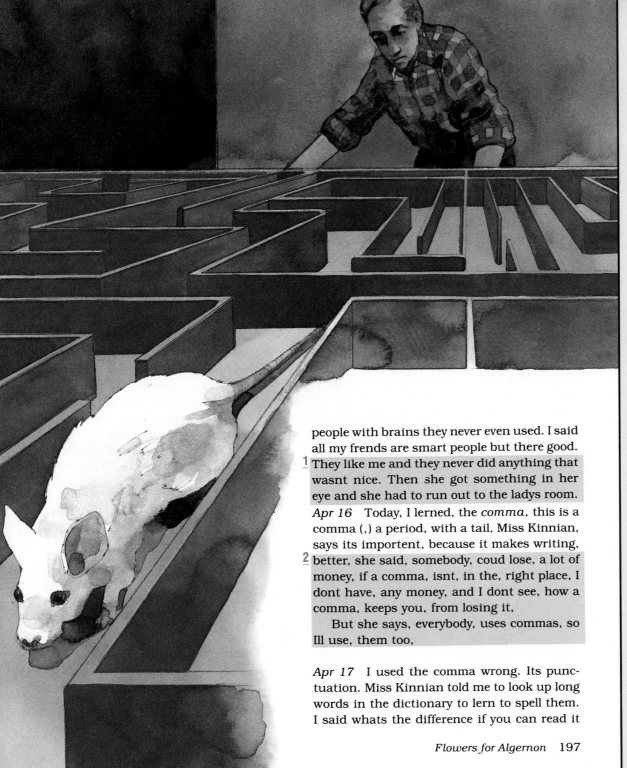

AT A GLANCE
- Charlie defends his co-workers to Miss Kinnian.
- He learns the use of the comma.

1 POINT OF VIEW

Though the narrator, Charlie, is getting smarter, he can still be fooled by polite excuses. We can infer from what he tells us, though, that Miss Kinnian has started to cry.

2 HUMOR

Charlie's enthusiastic experiments with the comma provide a moment of comic relief amid the growing suspense about his future.

people with brains they never even used. I said all my frends are smart people but there good. **1** They like me and they never did anything that wasnt nice. Then she got something in her eye and she had to run out to the ladys room.

Apr 16   Today, I lerned, the *comma*, this is a comma (,) a period, with a tail, Miss Kinnian, says its importent, because it makes writing, **2** better, she said, somebody, coud lose, a lot of money, if a comma, isnt, in the, right place, I dont have, any money, and I dont see, how a comma, keeps you, from losing it,

But she says, everybody, uses commas, so Ill use, them too,

Apr 17   I used the comma wrong. Its punctuation. Miss Kinnian told me to look up long words in the dictionary to lern to spell them. I said whats the difference if you can read it

Flowers for Algernon   197

GUIDED READING

LITERAL QUESTION

1a. What does Charlie say happens to Miss Kinnian? ("Then she got something in her eye and she had to run out to the ladys room.")

INFERENTIAL QUESTION

1b. What do you think really happens to Miss Kinnian? (Charlie's innocent and unfounded trust in his co-workers makes her cry.)

- Charlie learns more about punctuation.
- He reaches a learning plateau.
- He sees his co-workers for what they are.

1 CHARACTERIZATION

Charlie's growing intelligence shows in the way he can grasp ideas and use reference books.

2 POINT OF VIEW

The increasingly more intelligent narrator is now able to look back on his old self, as reflected in his earlier Progress Reports, in wonder. Charlie's access to written records of his progress adds poignancy to the story.

3 THEME

Charlie's increasing intelligence is already bringing him a new kind of psychological pain that he's never experienced before. He struggles to describe it in physical terms.

4 STYLE: DIALOGUE

The brief dialogue reveals Frank's callousness and Charlie's moment of truth.

5 READING SKILLS: COMPARISON/CONTRAST

Charlie suddenly sees people for what they are and realizes for the first time how exposed and vulnerable he's been. He has lost a crucial part of his old self: his innocent trust in other people.

---

anyway. She said its part of your education so now on Ill look up all the words Im not sure how to spell. It takes a long time to write that way but I think Im remembering. I only have to look up once and after that I get it right. Anyway thats how come I got the word *punctuation* right. (Its that way in the dictionary). Miss Kinnian says a period is punctuation too and there are lots of other marks to lern. I told her I thot all the periods had to have tails but she said no.

You got to mix them up, she showed? me" how to mix! them(up,. and now; I can! mix up all kinds" of punctuation, in! my writing? There, are lots! of rules? to lern; but Im gettin'g them in my head.

One thing I? like about, Dear Miss Kinnian: (thats the way it goes in a business letter if I ever go into business) is she, always gives me' a reason" when—I ask. She's a gen'ius! I wish! I cou'd be smart" like, her;

(Punctuation, is; fun!)

Apr 18 What a dope I am! I didn't even understand what she was talking about. I read the grammar book last night and it explanes the whole thing. Then I saw it was the same way as Miss Kinnian was trying to tell me, but I didn't get it. I got up in the middle of the night, and the whole thing straightened out in my mind.

Miss Kinnian said that the TV working in my sleep helped out. She said I reached a plateau. Thats like the flat top of a hill.

After I figgered out how punctuation worked, I read over all my old Progress Reports from the beginning. Boy, did I have crazy spelling and punctuation! I told Miss Kinnian I ought to go over the pages and fix all the mistakes but she said, "No, Charlie, Dr. Nemur wants them just as they are. That's why he let you keep them after they were photostated, to see your own progress. You're coming along fast, Charlie."

That made me feel good. After the lesson I went down and played with Algernon. We don't race any more.

April 20 I feel sick inside. Not sick like for a doctor, but inside my chest it feels empty like getting punched and a heartburn at the same time.

I wasn't going to write about it, but I guess I got to, because it's important. Today was the first time I ever stayed home from work.

Last night Joe Carp and Frank Reilly invited me to a party. There were lots of girls and some men from the factory. I remembered how sick I got last time I drank too much, so I told Joe I didn't want anything to drink. He gave me a plain Coke instead. It tasted funny, but I thought it was just a bad taste in my mouth.

We had a lot of fun for a while. Joe said I should dance with Ellen and she would teach me the steps. I fell a few times and I couldn't understand why because no one else was dancing besides Ellen and me. And all the time I was tripping because somebody's foot was always sticking out.

Then when I got up I saw the look on Joe's face and it gave me a funny feeling in my stomach. "He's a scream," one of the girls said. Everybody was laughing.

Frank said, "I ain't laughed so much since we sent him off for the newspaper that night at Muggsy's and ditched him."

"Look at him. His face is red."

"He's blushing. Charlie is blushing."

"Hey, Ellen, what'd you do to Charlie? I never saw him act like that before."

I didn't know what to do or where to turn. Everyone was looking at me and laughing and I felt naked. I wanted to hide myself. I ran out into the street and I threw up. Then I walked home. It's a funny thing I never knew that Joe and Frank and the others liked to have me around all the time to make fun of me.

GUIDED READING

LITERAL QUESTIONS

1a. What does Charlie learn from Frank? (what really happened at Muggsy's the night they got Charlie drunk)

2a. How does Charlie feel now when everyone starts laughing at him? (He feels naked and wants to hide.)

INFERENTIAL QUESTIONS

1b. Why doesn't Frank try to hide what happened? (He doesn't realize that Charlie is changing and becoming more intelligent.)

2b. What do you think Charlie means when he says he feels naked? (He realizes that he hasn't been able to protect himself from other people's cruelty; he feels deprived of dignity and self-respect.)

> Now I know what it means when they say "to pull a Charlie Gordon."
>
> I'm ashamed.

PROGRESS REPORT 10

April 21 Still didn't go into the factory. I told Mrs. Flynn my landlady to call and tell Mr. Donnegan I was sick. Mrs. Flynn looks at me very funny lately like she's scared of me.

I think it's a good thing about finding out how everybody laughs at me. I thought about it a lot. It's because I'm so dumb and I don't even know when I'm doing something dumb. People think it's funny when a dumb person can't do things the same way they can.

Anyway, now I know I'm getting smarter every day. I know punctuation and I can spell good. I like to look up all the hard words in the dictionary and I remember them. I'm reading a lot now, and Miss Kinnian says I read very fast. Sometimes I even understand what I'm reading about, and it stays in my mind. There are times when I can close my eyes and think of a page and it all comes back like a picture.

Besides history, geography, and arithmetic, Miss Kinnian said I should start to learn a few foreign languages. Dr. Strauss gave me some more tapes to play while I sleep. I still don't understand how that conscious and unconscious mind works, but Dr. Strauss says not to worry yet. He asked me to promise that when I start learning college subjects next week I wouldn't read any books on psychology—that is, until he gives me permission.

I feel a lot better today, but I guess I'm still a little angry that all the time people were laughing and making fun of me because I wasn't so smart. When I become intelligent like Dr. Strauss says, with three times my I.Q. of 68, then maybe I'll be like everyone else and people will like me and be friendly.

I'm not sure what an I.Q. is. Dr. Nemur said it was something that measured how intelligent you were—like a scale in the drugstore weighs pounds. But Dr. Strauss had a big argument with him and said an I.Q. didn't weigh intelligence at all. He said an I.Q. showed how much intelligence you could get, like the numbers on the outside of a measuring cup. You still had to fill the cup up with stuff.

Then when I asked Burt, who gives me my intelligence tests and works with Algernon, he said that both of them were wrong (only I had to promise not to tell them he said so). Burt says that the I.Q. measures a lot of different things including some of the things you learned already, and it really isn't any good at all.

So I still don't know what I.Q. is except that mine is going to be over 200 soon. I didn't want to say anything, but I don't see how if they don't know *what* it is, or *where* it is—I don't see how they know *how much* of it you've got.

Dr. Nemur says I have to take a *Rorschach Test* tomorrow. I wonder what *that* is.

April 22 I found out what a *Rorschach* is. It's the test I took before the operation—the one with the inkblots on the pieces of cardboard. The man who gave me the test was the same one.

I was scared to death of those inkblots. I knew he was going to ask me to find the pictures and I knew I wouldn't be able to. I was thinking to myself, if only there was some way of knowing what kind of pictures were hidden there. Maybe there weren't any pictures at all. Maybe it was just a trick to see if I was dumb enough to look for something that wasn't there. Just thinking about that made me sore at him.

"All right, Charlie," he said, "you've seen these cards before, remember?"

"Of course I remember."

Flowers for Algernon 199

AT A GLANCE

- Charlie understands what "to pull a Charlie Gordon" means.
- He knows he's becoming more intelligent and hopes it will make people like him.
- He faces the Rorschach Test again.

1 THEME

Charlie's increasing intelligence brings disillusionment: He understands what "to pull a Charlie Gordon" means and feels ashamed.

2 CHARACTERIZATION

Charlie's I.Q. is increasing rapidly, as he can visualize a whole page he has just read. Not only is he smarter, but now he *knows* he's getting smarter every day, and he takes pride in his intelligence.

3 IRONY

We realize what Charlie doesn't: He will only be "like everyone else" for a short time before his I.Q. becomes so high that he'll be different again, but in a new way. Charlie's simple need for friends will not be met.

4 CHARACTERIZATION

The tester, remembering the old Charlie, begins the session in a condescending way. But the new Charlie takes offense at his tone and replies angrily, "Of course I remember."

GUIDED READING

LITERAL QUESTION

1a. What does the tester say to Charlie before the Rorschach test? (He asks if Charlie remembers seeing the cards before.) What does Charlie reply? ("Of course I remember.")

INFERENTIAL QUESTION

2b. Why does Charlie answer the way he does? (He's angry because the tester has insulted him.)

- Charlie takes the Rorschach Test again, with vastly different results.
- He suggests a change at the factory that saves a great deal of money.
- His co-workers seem afraid of him. Dr. Nemur and Dr. Strauss argue about the experiment.

1 READING SKILLS: COMPARISON/CONTRAST

This time Charlie takes the test, he imagines "all sorts of things." He is also less trusting. Much of our enjoyment of the story comes from comparing and contrasting Charlie with his former self.

2 CHARACTERIZATION

Charlie's idea for saving the company money is the first hint that he's now becoming more intelligent than the average person.

3 THEME

Charlie's intelligence is bringing him a new sense of isolation, as people avoid him, fearful of the changes in him.

The way I said it, he knew I was angry, and he looked surprised. "Yes, of course. Now I want you to look at this one. What might this be? What do you see on this card? People see all sorts of things in these inkblots. Tell me what it might be for you—what it makes you think of."

I was shocked. That wasn't what I had expected him to say at all. 'You mean there are no pictures hidden in those inkblots?"

He frowned and took off his glasses. "What?"

"Pictures. Hidden in the inkblots. Last time you told me that everyone could see them and you wanted me to find them too."

He explained to me that the last time he had used almost the exact same words he was using now. I didn't believe it, and I still have the suspicion that he misled me at the time just for the fun of it. Unless—I don't know any more—could I have been *that* feeble-minded?

1 We went through the cards slowly. One of them looked like a pair of bats tugging at something. Another one looked like two men fencing with swords. I imagined all sorts of things. I guess I got carried away. But I didn't trust him any more, and I kept turning them around and even looking on the back to see if there was anything there I was supposed to catch. While he was making his notes, I peeked out of the corner of my eye to read it. But it was all in code that looked like this:

$$WF + A \quad DdF - Ad \ orig. \quad WF - A \quad SF + obj$$

The test still doesn't make sense to me. It seems to me that anyone could make up lies about things that they didn't really see. How could he know I wasn't making a fool of him by mentioning things that I didn't really imagine? Maybe I'll understand it when Dr. Strauss lets me read up on psychology.

April 25 I figured out a new way to line up

200 *The Short Story*

2 the machines in the factory, and Mr. Donnegan says it will save him ten thousand dollars a year in labor and increased production. He gave me a twenty-five-dollar bonus.

I wanted to take Joe Carp and Frank Reilly out to lunch to celebrate, but Joe said he had to buy some things for his wife, and Frank said he was meeting his cousin for lunch. I guess it'll take a little time for them to get used to the changes in me. Everybody seems to be frightened of me. When I went over to Amos Borg and tapped him on the shoulder, he jumped up in the air.

3 People don't talk to me much any more or kid around the way they used to. It makes the job kind of lonely.

April 27 I got up the nerve today to ask Miss Kinnian to have dinner with me tomorrow night to celebrate my bonus.

At first she wasn't sure it was right, but I asked Dr. Strauss and he said it was okay. Dr. Strauss and Dr. Nemur don't seem to be getting along so well. They're arguing all the time. This evening when I came in to ask Dr. Strauss about having dinner with Miss Kinnian, I heard them shouting. Dr. Nemur was saying that it was *his* experiment and *his* research, and Dr. Strauss was shouting back that he contributed just as much, because he found me through Miss Kinnian and he performed the operation. Dr. Strauss said that someday thousands of neurosurgeons[7] might be using his technique all over the world.

Dr. Nemur wanted to publish the results of the experiment at the end of this month. Dr. Strauss wanted to wait a while longer to be sure. Dr. Strauss said that Dr. Nemur was more interested in the Chair[8] of Psychology at Princeton than he was in the experiment. Dr.

---

7. **neurosurgeons** [noo′rō sur′jənz]: doctors who operate on parts of the nervous system, including the brain.
8. **Chair:** professorship.

GUIDED READING

LITERAL QUESTIONS

1a. What does Charlie want to do when he wins a bonus for his new idea? (take Joe Carp and Frank Reilly out to lunch)

2a. What reasons do Joe and Frank give for not going out to lunch with Charlie? (Joe says he has shopping to do; Frank says he's meeting his cousin.)

INFERENTIAL QUESTIONS

1b. What is surprising about what Charlie wants to do? (He still wants to be generous and share his success with the men, even though he now knows they've mistreated him.)

2b. What do you think is their real reason for refusing? (They're puzzled by his new intelligence and afraid he'll want revenge for their previous treatment of him.)

Nemur said that Dr. Strauss was nothing but an opportunist who was trying to ride to glory on *his* coattails.

When I left afterwards, I found myself trembling. I don't know why for sure, but it was as if I'd seen both men clearly for the first time. I remember hearing Burt say that Dr. Nemur had a wife who was pushing him all the time to get things published so that he could become famous. Burt said that the dream of her life was to have a big-shot husband.

Was Dr. Strauss really trying to ride on his coattails?

April 28   I don't understand why I never noticed how beautiful Miss Kinnian really is. She has brown eyes and feathery brown hair that comes to the top of her neck. She's only thirty-four! I think from the beginning I had the feeling that she was an unreachable genius—and very, very old. Now, every time I see her she grows younger and more lovely.

We had dinner and a long talk. When she said that I was coming along so fast that soon I'd be leaving her behind, I laughed.

"It's true, Charlie. You're already a better reader than I am. You can read a whole page at a glance while I can take in only a few lines at a time. And you remember every single thing you read. I'm lucky if I can recall the main thoughts and the general meaning."

"I don't feel intelligent. There are so many things I don't understand."

She took out a cigarette and I lit it for her. "You've got to be a *little* patient. You're accomplishing in days and weeks what it takes normal people to do in half a lifetime. That's what makes it so amazing. You're like a giant sponge now, soaking things in. Facts, figures, general knowledge. And soon you'll begin to connect them, too. You'll see how the different branches of learning are related. There are many levels, Charlie, like steps on a giant ladder that take you up higher and higher to see

AT A GLANCE

- Charlie sees his doctors objectively for the first time.
- He is falling in love with Miss Kinnian.
- She explains his intellectual progress.

1 CHARACTERIZATION

Charlie shows his intellectual growth as he judges his doctors objectively. He is "trembling" because what he perceives shakes his confidence in them.

2 READING SKILLS: COMPARISON/CONTRAST

Charlie has always been fond of Miss Kinnian, but in his childlike state he has seen all adults as being much older and wiser than himself. Now that he feels equal to Miss Kinnian, he has "grown up" and can fall in love.

3 STYLE: SIMILE

Miss Kinnian uses two similes to give Charlie a sense of his own progress. First she compares him to a "giant sponge" soaking up knowledge. Then she tells him he's reaching new levels of understanding, "like steps on a giant ladder."

GUIDED READING

LITERAL QUESTION

1a. What does Charlie notice about Miss Kinnian that he had not noticed before? (how young she is and how beautiful she is)

INFERENTIAL QUESTION

1b. Why do you think Charlie is recognizing these qualities now? (because he sees Miss Kinnian not as a teacher but as an equal, someone he can fall in love with)

- Miss Kinnian expresses concern about the outcome of the experiment.
- Charlie's co-workers petition to get him out of his job.
- He sees that his intelligence is isolating him from the people he once knew and loved.

1 PLOT: FORESHADOWING

Miss Kinnian continues the ladder simile to expand on her earlier statement that Charlie will soon be leaving her behind. Her figure of speech hints at the painful isolation Charlie will soon face.

2 CHARACTERIZATION

Charlie simultaneously displays both his new intellectual sophistication, as he infers what Miss Kinnian is thinking, and his clinging to old superstitious comforts in stressful moments, as he plays with his rabbit's foot.

3 THEME

Like Adam and Eve, Charlie has undergone a loss of innocence and has developed a sense of shame and a painful self-awareness as a result of acquiring knowledge.

4 RESPONSE JOURNAL

In their journals have students comment on this passage, explaining whether they think Charlie was better off in his ignorant bliss or whether he is fortunate to have a new self-awareness, even though it is painful.

---

more and more of the world around you.

1 "I can see only a little bit of that, Charlie, and I won't go much higher than I am now, but you'll keep climbing up and up, and see more and more, and each step will open new worlds that you never even knew existed." She frowned. "I hope . . . I just hope—"

"What?"

"Never mind, Charles. I just hope I wasn't wrong to advise you to go into this in the first place."

I laughed. "How could that be? It worked, didn't it? Even Algernon is still smart."

2 We sat there silently for a while and I knew what she was thinking about as she watched me toying with the chain of my rabbit's foot and my keys. I didn't want to think of that possibility any more than elderly people want to think of death. I *knew* that this was only the beginning. I knew what she meant about levels because I'd seen some of them already. The thought of leaving her behind made me sad.

I'm in love with Miss Kinnian.

PROGRESS REPORT 11

April 30 I've quit my job with Donnegan's Plastic Box Company. Mr. Donnegan insisted that it would be better for all concerned if I left. What did I do to make them hate me so?

The first I knew of it was when Mr. Donnegan showed me the petition. Eight hundred and forty names, everyone connected with the factory, except Fanny Girden. Scanning the list quickly, I saw at once that hers was the only missing name. All the rest demanded that I be fired.

Joe Carp and Frank Reilly wouldn't talk to me about it. No one else would either, except Fanny. She was one of the few people I'd known who set her mind to something and believed it no matter what the rest of the world proved, said, or did—and Fanny did not be-

202   *The Short Story*

lieve that I should have been fired. She had been against the petition on principle and despite the pressure and threats she'd held out.

"Which don't mean to say," she remarked, "that I don't think there's something mighty strange about you, Charlie. Them changes. I don't know. You used to be a good, dependable, ordinary man—not too bright maybe, but honest. Who knows what you done to yourself to get so smart all of a sudden. Like everybody around here's been saying, Charlie, it's not right."

"But how can you say that, Fanny? What's wrong with a man becoming intelligent and wanting to acquire knowledge and understanding of the world around him?"

She stared down at her work and I turned to leave. Without looking at me, she said: "It
3 was evil when Eve[9] listened to the snake and ate from the tree of knowledge. It was evil when she saw that she was naked. If not for that none of us would ever have to grow old and sick, and die."

4 Once again now I have the feeling of shame burning inside me. This intelligence has driven a wedge between me and all the people I once knew and loved. Before, they laughed at me and despised me for my ignorance and dullness; now, they hate me for my knowledge and understanding. What do they want of me?

They've driven me out of the factory. Now I'm more alone than ever before. . . .

May 15 Dr. Strauss is very angry at me for not having written any progress reports in two weeks. He's justified because the lab is now paying me a regular salary. I told him I was too busy thinking and reading. When I pointed out that writing was such a slow process that it made me impatient with my poor

---

9. **Eve** [ēv]: first woman in the Bible, in Genesis 2–3.

GUIDED READING

LITERAL QUESTIONS

1a. What hope does Miss Kinnian express to Charlie? (She hopes she was not wrong in advising him to try the experiment.)

2a. Why does Charlie lose his job? (His co-workers sign a petition demanding that he be fired because they are afraid of him and suspicious of his new intelligence.)

INFERENTIAL QUESTIONS

1b. What do you think Miss Kinnian is so worried about? (that Charlie will feel painfully isolated as he gets smarter, that the effects of the experiment may not last)

2b. Do you think the response of Charlie's co-workers is believable? (Possible answers: Yes—people tend to fear things they don't understand; no—Charlie is so lovable it is hard to imagine people turning against him.)

handwriting, he suggested that I learn to type. It's much easier to write now because I can type nearly seventy-five words a minute. Dr. Strauss continually reminds me of the need to speak and write simply so that people will be able to understand me.

I'll try to review all the things that happened to me during the last two weeks. Algernon and I were presented to the American Psychological Association sitting in convention with the World Psychological Association last Tuesday. We created quite a sensation. Dr. Nemur and Dr. Strauss were proud of us.

I suspect that Dr. Nemur, who is sixty—ten years older than Dr. Strauss—finds it necessary to see tangible results of his work. Undoubtedly the result of pressure by Mrs. Nemur.

Contrary to my earlier impressions of him I realize that Dr. Nemur is not at all a genius. He has a very good mind, but it struggles under the specter of self-doubt. He wants people to take him for a genius. Therefore, it is important for him to feel that his work is accepted by the world. I believe that Dr. Nemur was afraid of further delay because he worried that someone else might make a discovery along these lines and take the credit from him.

Dr. Strauss on the other hand might be called a genius, although I feel that his areas of knowledge are too limited. He was educated in the tradition of narrow specialization; the broader aspects of background were neglected far more than necessary—even for a neurosurgeon.

I was shocked to learn that the only ancient languages he could read were Latin, Greek, and Hebrew, and that he knows almost nothing of mathematics beyond the elementary levels of the calculus of variations. When he admitted this to me, I found myself almost annoyed. It was as if he'd hidden this part of himself in order to deceive me, pretending—

as do many people I've discovered—to be what he is not. No one I've ever known is what he appears to be on the surface.

Dr. Nemur appears to be uncomfortable around me. Sometimes when I try to talk to him, he just looks at me strangely and turns away. I was angry at first when Dr. Strauss told me I was giving Dr. Nemur an inferiority complex. I thought he was mocking me and I'm oversensitive at being made fun of.

How was I to know that a highly respected psychoexperimentalist like Nemur was unacquainted with Hindustani[10] and Chinese? It's absurd when you consider the work that is being done in India and China today in the very field of his study.

I asked Dr. Strauss how Nemur could refute Rahajamati's attack on his method and results if Nemur couldn't even read it in the first place. That strange look on Dr. Strauss's face can mean only one of two things. Either he doesn't want to tell Nemur what they're saying in India, or else—and this worries me—Dr. Strauss doesn't know either. I must be careful to speak and write clearly and simply so that people won't laugh.

May 18   I am very disturbed. I saw Miss Kinnian last night for the first time in over a week. I tried to avoid all discussions of intellectual concepts and to keep the conversation on a simple, everyday level, but she just stared at me blankly and asked me what I meant about the mathematical variance equivalent in Dobermann's Fifth Concerto.

When I tried to explain she stopped me and laughed. I guess I got angry, but I suspect I'm approaching her on the wrong level. No matter what I try to discuss with her, I am unable to communicate. I must review Vrostadt's equations on *Levels of Semantic Progression.* I

---

10. **Hindustani** [hin'doo stä'nē]: one language of northern India.

Flowers for Algernon   203

AT A GLANCE

- Charlie and Algernon are famous.
- Charlie becomes more critical of his doctors' intellect as his own increases rapidly.
- Charlie also finds Miss Kinnian's intellect lacking.

1 CHARACTERIZATION

Charlie's intellectual capacity now includes razor-sharp analyses of other people's motives—especially his doctors'.

2 THEME

The discovery that no one "is what he appears to be on the surface" is a very isolating, cynical result of Charlie's new powers.

3 IRONY

Before, people laughed at Charlie's ignorance. Now he fears they will laugh because they cannot comprehend his intelligence.

4 THEME

Charlie's intellect is now so advanced that he finds himself unable to communicate with the woman he first admired as a genius and later loved as an equal.

GUIDED READING

LITERAL QUESTIONS

1a. Why does Charlie feel "almost annoyed" with Dr. Strauss? (He feels that Dr. Strauss has deceived him by pretending to be more knowledgeable than he really is.)

2a. What does Miss Kinnian do when Charlie tries to explain a complicated mathematical problem? (laughs)

INFERENTIAL QUESTIONS

1b. What does Charlie's feeling toward Dr. Strauss indicate about his changing attitude toward people? (Before, he trusted everyone; now he seems to trust no one.)

2b. Why do you think Miss Kinnian reacts that way? (Charlie's vocabulary, knowledge, and reasoning are so advanced that his explanation probably sounds like total nonsense to her.)

1 THEME

Charlie reveals the full extent of his isolation: Books and music are his only companions now.

2 DIALOGUE

With this brief exchange the author portrays the careless cruelty of people to someone who is retarded. As a witness Charlie is forced to relive his past.

1 find that I don't communicate with people much any more. Thank God for books and music and things I can think about. I am alone in my apartment at Mrs. Flynn's boardinghouse most of the time and seldom speak to anyone.

May 20 I would not have noticed the new dishwasher, a boy of about sixteen, at the corner diner where I take my evening meals if not for the incident of the broken dishes.

They crashed to the floor, shattering and sending bits of white china under the tables. The boy stood there, dazed and frightened, holding the empty tray in his hand. The whistles and catcalls from the customers (the cries of "Hey, there go the profits!" . . . "*Mazel tov!*"[11] . . . and "Well, *he* didn't work here very long. . . ." which invariably seem to follow the breaking of glass or dishware in a public restaurant) all seemed to confuse him.

When the owner came to see what the excitement was about, the boy cowered as if he expected to be struck and threw up his arms as if to ward off the blow.

"All right! All right, you dope," shouted the owner, "don't just stand there! Get the broom and sweep that mess up. A broom . . . a broom, you idiot! It's in the kitchen. Sweep up all the pieces."

The boy saw that he was not going to be punished. His frightened expression disappeared and he smiled and hummed as he came back with the broom to sweep the floor. A few of the rowdier customers kept up the remarks, amusing themselves at his expense.

2 "Here, sonny, over here there's a nice piece behind you. . . ."

"C'mon, do it again. . . ."

"He's not so dumb. It's easier to break 'em than to wash 'em. . . ."

As his vacant eyes moved across the crowd

---

11. **Mazel tov!** [mä′zəl tōv]: Hebrew, "Congratulations!"

GUIDED READING

LITERAL QUESTION

1a. How does the boy act as the owner approaches him? (He cowers as if he expects to be hit and throws up his arms to ward off the blow.)

INFERENTIAL QUESTION

1b. What do the boy's actions suggest about his past experience? (that he has been beaten at other times) of amused onlookers, he slowly mirrored their smiles and finally broke into an uncertain grin at the joke which he obviously did not understand.

I felt sick inside as I looked at his dull, vacuous smile, the wide, bright eyes of a child, uncertain but eager to please. They were laughing at him because he was mentally retarded.

And I had been laughing at him too.

Suddenly, I was furious at myself and all those who were smirking at him. I jumped up **1** and shouted, "Shut up! Leave him alone! It's not his fault he can't understand! He can't help what he is! But . . . he's still a human being!"

The room grew silent. I cursed myself for losing control and creating a scene. I tried not to look at the boy as I paid my check and walked out without touching my food. I felt ashamed for both of us.

How strange it is that people of honest feelings and sensibility, who would not take advantage of a man born without arms or legs or eyes—how such people think nothing of abusing a man born with low intelligence. It infuriated me to think that not too long ago, I, like this boy, had foolishly played the clown.

And I had almost forgotten.

2 I'd hidden the picture of the old Charlie Gordon from myself because now that I was intelligent it was something that had to be pushed out of my mind. But today in looking at that boy, for the first time I saw what I had been. *I was just like him!*

Only a short time ago, I learned that people laughed at me. Now I can see that unknowingly I joined with them in laughing at myself. That hurts most of all.

I have often reread my progress reports and seen the illiteracy, the childish naiveté, **4** the mind of low intelligence peering from a dark room, through the keyhole, at the dazzling light outside. I see that even in my dull-

ness I knew that I was inferior, and that other people had something I lacked—something denied me. In my mental blindness, I thought that it was somehow connected with the ability to read and write, and I was sure that if I could get those skills I would automatically have intelligence too.

Even a feebleminded man wants to be like other men.

A child may not know how to feed itself, or what to eat, yet it knows of hunger.

This then is what I was like; I never knew. Even with my gift of intellectual awareness, I never really knew.

This day was good for me. Seeing the past more clearly, I have decided to use my knowledge and skills to work in the field of increas- **3** ing human intelligence levels. Who is better equipped for this work? Who else has lived in both worlds? These are my people. Let me use my gift to do something for them.

Tomorrow, I will discuss with Dr. Strauss the manner in which I can work in this area. I may be able to help him work out the problems of widespread use of the technique which was used on me. I have several good ideas of my own.

There is so much that might be done with this technique. If I could be made into a genius, what about thousands of others like myself? What fantastic levels might be achieved by using this technique on normal people? On *geniuses*?

There are so many doors to open. I am impatient to begin.

PROGRESS REPORT 12

May 23 It happened today. Algernon bit me. I visited the lab to see him as I do occasionally, **4** and when I took him out of his cage, he snapped at my hand. I put him back and watched him for a while. He was unusually disturbed and vicious.

Flowers for Algernon 205

AT A GLANCE

- Charlie berates the customers for laughing at the retarded boy.
- Charlie remembers that he was once like that boy.
- He decides to work to help others increase their intelligence.
- Algernon's behavior changes.

1 CHARACTERIZATION

Charlie's compassion forces him to defend the retarded boy against the customers' casual cruelty.

2 POINT OF VIEW

For Charlie, looking at the retarded boy is like looking at an image of his former self. We experience the narrator's shock of recognition intimately.

3 CHARACTERIZATION

Charlie's shock of recognition has re-ignited his compassionate, altruistic sentiments and quieted his cynicism. He has regained a valuable part of his old self.

4 PLOT: FORESHADOWING

Just as earlier parallels between Algernon's progress and Charlie's have been encouraging, so this slip in Algernon's behavior suggests ominous possibilities ahead for Charlie.

GUIDED READING

LITERAL QUESTIONS

1a. What had Charlie done with old pictures of himself? (hidden them)

2a. How does Algernon begin behaving? (He snaps at Charlie's hand and seems disturbed and vicious.)

INFERENTIAL QUESTIONS

1b. Why do you think Charlie has been hiding from images of his old self until now? (He is ashamed of his former self; he wants to forget his past.)

2b. Why is Algernon's behavior significant? (Charlie's operation was first tried on Algernon; changes in Algernon are usually followed by corresponding changes in Charlie.)

AT A GLANCE

- Algernon is changing, and everyone is upset about what it may mean.
- Charlie gets his own lab to do independent research.
- He completes his research, proving that the experiment is a failure.

1 READING SKILLS: COMPARISON/CONTRAST

Tension grows as Algernon refuses to perform the task that provides his food, in contrast to his former cooperation.

2 PLOT: CONFLICT

Charlie loses confidence in his doctors and takes responsibility for further research himself. Suspense builds because time is running out for him.

3 IRONY

Charlie, the subject of the experiment, must demonstrate to the doctors who planned it that it will fail. He apologizes for disproving their theory, when in fact it is they who should be apologizing to him.

May 24 Burt, who is in charge of the experimental animals, tells me that Algernon is changing. He is less cooperative; he refuses to run the maze any more; general motivation has decreased. And he hasn't been eating. Everyone is upset about what this may mean.

1 *May 25* They've been feeding Algernon, who now refuses to work the shifting-lock problem. Everyone identifies me with Algernon. In a way we're both the first of our kind. They're all pretending that Algernon's behavior is not necessarily significant for me. But it's hard to hide the fact that some of the other animals who were used in the experiment are showing strange behavior.

Dr. Strauss and Dr. Nemur have asked me not to come to the lab any more. I know what they're thinking but I can't accept it. I am going ahead with my plans to carry their re- **2** search forward. With all due respect to both of these fine scientists, I am well aware of their limitations. If there is an answer, I'll have to find it out for myself. Suddenly, time has become very important to me.

May 29 I have been given a lab of my own and permission to go ahead with the research. I'm on to something. Working day and night. I've had a cot moved into the lab. Most of my writing time is spent on the notes which I keep in a separate folder, but from time to time I feel it necessary to put down my moods and my thoughts out of sheer habit.

I find the *calculus of intelligence* to be a fascinating study. Here is the place for the application of all the knowledge I have acquired. In a sense it's the problem I've been concerned with all my life.

May 31 Dr. Strauss thinks I'm working too hard. Dr. Nemur says I'm trying to cram a lifetime of research and thought into a few weeks. I know I should rest, but I'm driven on

by something inside that won't let me stop. I've got to find the reason for the sharp regression[12] in Algernon. I've got to know *if* and *when* it will happen to me.

June 4

LETTER TO DR. STRAUSS (*copy*)

Dear Dr. Strauss:

Under separate cover I am sending you a copy of my report entitled "The Algernon-Gordon Effect: A Study of Structure and Function of Increased Intelligence," which I would like to have you read and have published.

As you see, my experiments are completed. I have included in my report all of my formulae, as well as mathematical analysis in the appendix. Of course, these should be verified.

Because of its importance to both you and **3** Dr. Nemur (and need I say to myself, too?) I have checked and rechecked my results a dozen times in the hope of finding an error. I am sorry to say the results must stand. Yet for the sake of science, I am grateful for the little bit that I here add to the knowledge of the function of the human mind and of the laws governing the artificial increase of human intelligence.

I recall your once saying to me that an experimental *failure* or the *disproving* of a theory was as important to the advancement of learning as a success would be. I know now that this is true. I am sorry, however, that my own contribution to the field must rest upon the ashes of the work of two men I regard so highly.

Yours truly,
Charles Gordon

June 5 I must not become emotional. The facts and the results of my experiments are

---

12. **regression** [ri gresh'ən]: going backwards.

GUIDED READING

LITERAL QUESTION

1a. What emotions does Charlie express in his letter to Dr. Strauss? (He says he is sorry to break the bad news and show that the experiment is a failure; he says he is grateful that he has been able to add to knowledge.)

INFERENTIAL QUESTION

1b. What else is Charlie probably feeling that he doesn't express in his letter? (anger, frustration, despair) clear, and the more sensational aspects of my own rapid climb cannot obscure the fact that **1** the tripling of intelligence by the surgical technique developed by Drs. Strauss and Nemur must be viewed as having little or no practical applicability (at the present time) to the increase of human intelligence.

As I review the records and data on Algernon, I see that although he is still in his physical infancy, he has regressed mentally. Motor activity[13] is impaired; there is a general reduction of glandular activity; there is an accelerated loss of coordination.

There are also strong indications of progressive amnesia.

As will be seen by my report, these and other physical and mental deterioration syndromes can be predicted with statistically significant results by the application of my formula.

The surgical stimulus to which we were both subjected has resulted in an intensification and acceleration of all mental processes. The unforeseen development, which I have taken the liberty of calling the "Algernon-Gordon Effect," is the logical extension of the entire intelligence speedup. The hypothesis here proven may be described simply in the following terms: Artificially increased intelligence deteriorates at a rate of time directly proportional to the quantity of the increase.

I feel that this, in itself, is an important discovery.

As long as I am able to write, I will continue to record my thoughts in these progress reports. It is one of my few pleasures. However, by all indications, my own mental deterioration will be very rapid.

2 I have already begun to notice signs of emotional instability and forgetfulness, the first symptoms of the burnout.

---

13. **Motor activity:** movement and coordination.

June 10 Deterioration progressing. I have become absent-minded. Algernon died two days ago. Dissection shows my predictions were right. His brain has decreased in weight and there was a general smoothing out of cerebral convolutions[14] as well as a deepening and broadening of brain fissures.[15]

3 I guess the same thing is or will soon be happening to me. Now that's it's definite, I don't want it to happen.

I put Algernon's body in a cheese box and buried him in the backyard. I cried.

June 15 Dr. Strauss came to see me again. I wouldn't open the door and I told him to go away. I want to be left to myself. I have become touchy and irritable. I feel the darkness closing in. I keep telling myself how important this introspective journal will be.

It's a strange sensation to pick up a book that you've read and enjoyed just a few months ago and discover that you don't remember it. I remembered how great I thought John Milton[16] was, but when I picked up *Paradise Lost* I couldn't understand it at all. I got so angry I threw the book across the room.

4 I've got to try to hold on to some of it. Some of the things I've learned. Oh, please don't take it all away.

June 19 Sometimes, at night, I go out for a walk. Last night I couldn't remember where I lived. A policeman took me home. I have the strange feeling that this has all happened to me before—a long time ago. I keep telling myself I'm the only person in the world who can describe what's happening to me.

June 21 Why can't I remember? I've got to fight. I lie in bed for days and I don't know who or where I am. Then it all comes back to

---

14. **cerebral** [ser′ə brəl] **convolutions** [kon′və lōo′shənz]: folds or ridges on the surface of the brain.
15. **fissures** [fish′ərz]: openings or splits.
16. **John Milton:** (1608–1674) English poet.

Flowers for Algernon 207

AT A GLANCE
- Charlie assesses the experiment and his own prospects.
- Algernon dies, and Charlie buries him, weeping.
- Charlie suffers an amnesia attack.

1 STYLE: WORD CHOICE

Charlie uses objective, academic language (*surgical technique, practical applicability*) to assess the failure of the experiment. The intellectual language helps him distance himself from the knowledge and deny its full emotional impact.

2 POINT OF VIEW

The first-person narrator, aware of what is happening to him, will now issue "progress reports" on his own intellectual decline. Just as we earlier shared his excitement and sense of discovery, so now we share his sense of dread and despair.

3 PLOT: CLIMAX

Now that Algernon has died and Charlie has dissected the animal's brain, the full emotional weight of what is happening to him hits Charlie at last, and he tries to fight it.

4 CHARACTERIZATION

Charlie is regressing. No longer the objective researcher, he begs, "Oh, please don't take it all away."

GUIDED READING

LITERAL QUESTIONS

1a. What does Charlie do when he buries Algernon? (he cries)

2a. What happens when Charlie gets lost? (A policeman takes him home.) How does Charlie feel then? (as if it has all happened before)

INFERENTIAL QUESTIONS

1b. Can you think of two reasons why Charlie acts that way? (Algernon's death means that Charlie will return to being retarded; the mouse had become Charlie's friend.)

2b. What previous incident might Charlie have a vague memory of? (the night his co-workers got him drunk when he was still retarded and a policeman had to bring him home)

1 PLOT: CONFLICT

The image of the boy in the restaurant drives Charlie to fight his own regression. The idea of being retarded again hurts even more because now he knows how others will regard him.

2 STYLE: SIMILE

The simile "like sand through my fingers" conveys the speed of Charlie's decline.

3 CHARACTERIZATION

Even in despair Charlie accepts responsibility for his own state: He knew what might happen. "But how it hurts" echoes his statement before the surgery: "I don't care if it herts."

4 POINT OF VIEW

As Charlie's intelligence slips, so does the writing style of his progress reports. Charlie's punctuation, which he was so proud to master, here begins to decline.

me in a flash. Fugues of amnesia.[17] Symptoms of senility—second childhood. I can watch them coming on. It's so cruelly logical. I learned so much and so fast. Now my mind is deteriorating rapidly. I won't let it happen. **I'll fight it. I can't help thinking of the boy in the restaurant, the blank expression, the silly smile, the people laughing at him. No— please—not that again . . .**

June 22 I'm forgetting things that I learned recently. It seems to be following the classic pattern—the last things learned are the first things forgotten. Or is that the pattern? I'd better look it up again. . . .

I reread my paper on the "Algernon-Gordon Effect" and I get the strange feeling that it was written by someone else. There are parts I don't even understand.

Motor activity impaired. I keep tripping over things, and it becomes increasingly difficult to type.

June 23 I've given up using the typewriter completely. My coordination is bad. I feel that I'm moving slower and slower. Had a terrible shock today. I picked up a copy of an article I used in my research, Krueger's "Über psychische Ganzheit," to see if it would help me understand what I had done. First I thought there was something wrong with my eyes. Then I realized I could no longer read German. I tested myself in other languages. All gone.

June 30 **A week since I dared to write again. It's slipping away like sand through my fingers. Most of the books I have are too hard for me now.** I get angry with them because I know that I read and understood them just a few weeks ago.

---

17. **Fugues** [fūgz] **of amnesia** [am nē′zhə]: periods during which a person loses memory.

208 *The Short Story*

I keep telling myself I must keep writing these reports so that somebody will know what is happening to me. But it gets harder to form the words and remember spellings. I have to look up even simple words in the dictionary now and it makes me impatient with myself.

Dr. Strauss comes around almost every day, but I told him I wouldn't see or speak to anybody. He feels guilty. They all do. But I don't blame anyone. I knew what might happen. But how it hurts.

July 7 I don't know where the week went. Todays Sunday I know becuase I can see through my window people going to church. I think I stayed in bed all week but I remember **Mrs. Flynn bringing food to me a few times. I keep saying over and over I've got to do something but then I forget or maybe its just easier not to do what I say Im going to do.**

I think of my mother and father a lot these days. I found a picture of them with me taken at a beach. My father has a big ball under his arm and my mother is holding me by the hand. I dont remember them the way they are in the picture. All I remember is my father arguing with mom about money. He never shaved much and he used to scratch my face when he hugged me. He said he was going to take me to see cows on a farm once but he never did. He never kept his promises . . .

July 10 My landlady Mrs Flynn is very worried about me. She said she doesnt like loafers. If Im sick its one thing, but if Im a loafer thats another thing and she wont have it. I told her I think Im sick.

I try to read a little bit every day, mostly stories, but sometimes I have to read the same thing over and over again because I dont know what it means. And its hard to write. I know I should look up all the words in the dictionary

GUIDED READING

LITERAL QUESTION

1a. Who can Charlie not help thinking about? (the retarded boy in the restaurant)

INFERENTIAL QUESTION

1b. Why can't Charlie stop thinking of him? (Charlie sees himself in the boy and knows he will be like him again soon.)

races together. He looked at me kind of funny like he thought I was crazy.

He smiled when I told him I used to be a genius. He talked to me like I was a baby and he winked at Mrs Flynn. I got mad and chased him out because he was making fun of me the way they all used to.

July 24 I have no money and Mrs Flynn says I got to go to work somewhere and pay the rent because I havent paid for over two months. I dont know any work but the job I used to have at Donnegans Plastic Box Company. I dont want to go back there because they all knew me when I was smart and maybe theyll laugh at me. But I dont know what else to do to get money.

July 25 I was looking at some of my old progress reports and its very funny but I cant read what I wrote. I can make out some of the words but they dont make sense.

Miss Kinnian came to the door but I said go away I dont want to see you. She cried and I cried too but I wouldnt let her in because I didnt want her to laugh at me. I told her I didnt like her any more. I told her I didnt want to be smart any more. Thats not true. I still love her and I still want to be smart but I had to say that so shed go away. She gave Mrs Flynn money to pay the rent. I dont want that. I got to get a job.

Please . . . please let me not forget how to read and write . . .

July 27 Mr Donnegan was very nice when I came back and asked him for my old job of janitor. First he was very suspicious but I told him what happened to me then he looked very sad and put his hand on my shoulder and said Charlie Gordon you got guts.

Everybody looked at me when I came downstairs and started working in the toilet sweep-

but its so hard and Im so tired all the time.

Then I got the idea that I would only use the easy words instead of the long hard ones. That saves time. I put flowers on Algernons grave about once a week. Mrs Flynn thinks Im crazy to put flowers on a mouses grave but I told her that Algernon was special.

July 14 Its sunday again. I dont have any thing to do to keep me busy now because my television set is broke and I dont have any money to get it fixed. (I think I lost this months check from the lab. I don't remember)

I get awful headaches and asperin doesnt help me much. Mrs Flynn knows Im really sick and she feels very sorry for me. Shes a wonderful woman whenever someone is sick.

July 22 Mrs Flynn called a strange doctor to see me. She was afraid I was going to die. I told the doctor I wasnt too sick and that I only forget sometimes. He asked me did I have any friends or relatives and I said no I dont have any. I told him I had a friend called Algernon once but he was a mouse and we used to run

Flowers for Algernon 209

AT A GLANCE

- Charlie has regressed even more and is friendless, penniless, and alone.
- Miss Kinnian comes to see him, but he sends her away.
- He returns to his job at the factory.

1 THEME

Charlie lost his old friends after the operation and his new friends when the experiment failed. The only friend he acknowledges is the dead mouse, Algernon.

2 PLOT: CONFLICT

Charlie's remaining pride and self-respect come up against the necessity of supporting himself and must give way.

3 THEME

Although he is still in love with Miss Kinnian, Charlie realizes the futility of his longing. He can no longer meet her on equal ground.

GUIDED READING

LITERAL QUESTION

1a. What does Mr. Donnegan tell Charlie when Charlie returns to work? ("Charlie Gordon you got guts.")

INFERENTIAL QUESTION

1b. Why does it take so much courage for Charlie to return to his old job? (It's a demeaning job for someone who used to be a genius; it takes courage to face his co-workers, who once mocked him and then turned against him.)

- Charlie's co-workers show that they are finally his friends.
- He forgets and returns to Miss Kinnian's class as before.
- He decides to go away and reconciles himself to being laughed at.

1 THEME

When he became smarter, Charlie discovered that people he thought were his friends really weren't. Now, when he expects nothing, he discovers that these people really have become his friends. His courage has earned him their respect.

2 IRONY

Charlie remains just smart enough to use his own name as an insult against himself, just smart enough so that he can't sink back into his old oblivious self—but not smart enough to do himself any good.

3 PLOT: RESOLUTION

It seems inevitable that Charlie has to move on. While his memory of the operation lasts, he cannot be around people who will compare the present Charlie to the genius he briefly was.

4 THEME

Charlie's observation that "It's easy to make friends if you let pepul laff at you" is part defeat, part survival technique, and part wisdom. As an intelligent person, he learned the importance of pride, but too much pride hinders friendship.

REFLECTING ON THE STORY

Do you think Charlie was happiest before he had the operation, after he became a genius, or after he returned to his former self? Why? (Answers will vary. Possibilities include: Before, because he didn't feel isolated; after, because he could enjoy the world of learning; after he returned to his former self, because he could have friends.)

ing it out like I used to. I told myself Charlie if they make fun of you dont get sore because you remember their not so smart as you once thot they were. And besides they were once your friends and if they laughed at you that doesnt mean anything because they liked you too.

One of the new men who came to work there after I went away made a nasty crack he said hey Charlie I hear your a very smart fella a real quiz kid. Say something intelligent. I felt bad but Joe Carp came over and grabbed him by the shirt and said leave him alone or Ill break your neck. I didnt expect Joe to take my part so I guess hes really my friend.

Later Frank Reilly came over and said Charlie if anybody bothers you or trys to take advantage you call me or Joe and we will set em straight. I said thanks Frank and I got choked up so I had to turn around and go into the supply room so he wouldnt see me cry. Its good to have friends.

July 28   I did a dumb thing today I forgot I wasnt in Miss Kinnians class at the adult center any more like I used to be. I went in and sat down in my old seat in the back of the room and she looked at me funny and she said Charles. I dint remember she ever called me that before only Charlie so I said hello Miss Kinnian Im redy for my lesin today only I lost my reader that we was using. She startid to cry and run out of the room and everybody looked at me and I saw they wasnt the same pepul who used to be in my class.

Then all of a suddin I remembered some things about the operashun and me getting smart and I said holy smoke I reely pulled a Charlie Gordon that time. I went away before she come back to the room.

Thats why Im going away from New York for good. I dont want to do nothing like that agen. I dont want Miss Kinnian to feel sorry

for me. Evry body feels sorry at the factery and I dont want that eather so Im going someplace where nobody knows that Charlie Gordon was once a genus and now he cant even reed a book or rite good.

Im taking a cuple of books along and even if I cant reed them Ill practise hard and maybe I wont forget every thing I lerned. If I try reel hard maybe Ill be a littel bit smarter then I was before the operashun. I got my rabits foot and my luky penny and maybe they will help me.

If you ever reed this Miss Kinnian dont be sorry for me Im glad I got a second chanse to be smart becaus I lerned a lot of things that I never even new were in this world and Im grateful that I saw it all for a littel bit. I dont know why Im dumb agen or what I did wrong maybe its becaus I dint try hard enuff. But if I try and practis very hard maybe Ill get a littl smarter and know what all the words are. I remember a littel bit how nice I had a feeling with the blue book that has the torn cover when I red it. Thats why Im gonna keep trying to get smart so I can have that feeling agen. Its a good feeling to know things and be smart. I wish I had it rite now if I did I would sit down and reed all the time. Anyway I bet Im the first dumb person in the world who ever found out somthing importent for sience. I remember I did somthing but I dont remember what. So I gess its like I did it for all the dumb pepul like me.

Good-by Miss Kinnian and Dr Strauss and evreybody. And P.S. please tell Dr Nemur not to be such a grouch when pepul laff at him and he woud have more frends. Its easy to make frends if you let pepul laff at you. Im going to have lots of frends where I go. P.P.S. Please if you get a chanse put some flowrs on Algernons grave in the bak yard . . .

GUIDED READING

LITERAL QUESTION

1a. Why is Charlie glad that, as he says, he "got a second chanse to be smart"? (He learned a great deal.)

INFERENTIAL QUESTION

1b. What lasting benefit does Charlie derive from this experience? (He develops self-respect and the respect of others.)

STUDY QUESTIONS

Recalling

1. Who is Miss Kinnian? What does she tell the doctors about Charlie?
2. According to progress report four, what is the experiment and operation that Charlie will undergo? What does Miss Kinnian warn Charlie about it?
3. Why does Charlie say that he hates Algernon? Why is Algernon not a normal mouse?
4. Give two examples of how the other factory workers treat Charlie. What does Charlie realize about them on April 20?
5. Why does Charlie quit his job?
6. What happens at the diner? As a result, what does Charlie realize about "the old Charlie"?
7. According to his report on May 20, in what way does Charlie decide to use his new intelligence?
8. On June 5 what happens to Algernon? What does this mean for Charlie?
9. When Charlie returns to his job, in what way do the other workers treat him?
10. At the end of the story, what does Charlie decide to keep trying? Why?

Interpreting

11. Why do you think the factory workers sign the petition against Charlie? Why do they change at the end of the story?
12. Why do you think Charlie cries after burying Algernon?
13. What parts of this story are science fiction? What parts are realistic?

READING AND LITERARY FOCUS

Total Effect

The **total effect** is a story's overall impact on the reader. It is created when a story's five elements work together. The elements are plot, character, setting, point of view, and theme.

Thinking About the Total Effect

1. **Plot:** What do you think is the main conflict of "Flowers for Algernon"? What is its solution?
2. **Character:** In what sense is Charlie chosen for the experiment because of his personality?
3. **Setting:** Settings for the story include the factory, the hospital, and Charlie's room. Tell how Charlie usually feels in each one.
4. **Point of View:** Who is the story's narrator? Why is this choice of narrator particularly effective?
5. **Theme:** When Charlie becomes smarter, why does he become more lonely? What is the theme of the story?

Comparison/Contrast

A **comparison** points out the similarities between two or more items. A **contrast** points out the differences. Authors sometimes describe characters or settings by using comparison/contrast. For example, in "The Dog of Pompeii" (page 158) we understand something about Bimbi's personality because the dog is compared to a nurse and playmate. In addition, we understand the effects of Tito's blindness because he is contrasted with other boys his age. Authors also use comparison/contrast to express ideas. For example, in "The Brother Who Failed" (page 131) Robert's success is contrasted with other types of success.

Thinking About Comparison/Contrast

■ Which of Charlie's personality traits remain the same during the story? Which traits change?

COMPARING STORIES

■ Imagine that movie versions of the following stories have been made: "The Dog of Pompeii," "The Legend of Sleepy Hollow," "The Man Without a Country," and "Flowers for Algernon." Choose two or more stories. Explain which story would make a more enjoyable movie. Be sure to include plot, character, setting, and theme for each story in your answer.

Flowers for Algernon 211

The activities in this lesson will teach students to use details in a story to see and hear the action, to make inferences, and to predict outcomes. Suggested responses to these activities are provided here. In addition, you will find among the materials for this unit in your *Teacher's Resource Book* the following related blackline masters: Interpreting Details in Short Stories; Making Inferences in Short Stories; Predicting Outcomes.

Active Reading

The Short Story

Interpreting Details

Just as authors use their imaginations to write stories, so you must use your imagination while reading them. By concentrating on the details in a story, you "see" in your mind the entire scene that an author creates. You picture the colors and shapes of the setting as well as the appearances and actions of the characters. Reading details carefully also enables you to "hear" the activity that takes place because you "listen" to sounds that accompany each movement. Being a good reader, then, means always using your imagination to see and hear the literature that you read.

Read the following passage from "Weep No More, My Lady." Try to picture and hear the scene as you read.

> The moonlight symphony of swamp creatures hushed abruptly, and the dismal bog was as peaceful as unborn time and seemed to brood in its silence. The gaunt man glanced back at the boy and motioned for him to be quiet, but it was too late. Their presence was discovered. A jumbo frog rumbled a warning, and the swamp squirmed into life as its denizens scuttled to safety.
>
> Fox fire was glowing to the west and the bayou was slapping the cypress trees when suddenly a haunting laugh echoed through the wilderness, a strange chuckling yodel ending in a weird *"gro-o-o."*

Activity 1 Study the following two pictures. Then answer each of the numbered items.

1. Which picture more accurately portrays the appearance of the man? Why?

2. Which picture more accurately depicts the bayou? Why?

3. Which picture indicates the correct time of day? Why?

4. Which picture has more appropriate trees? Why?

5. Identify at least two sounds mentioned in the passage.

Making Inferences About Stories

In a story the details are stated directly. Find the details that are stated directly in the following passage from "Weep No More, My Lady."

As most men judge values, she [My Lady] was worth more than all the possessions of Jesse and his nephew. Several of the dogs had been shipped to New Orleans to avoid the dangerous upper route, thence by motor to a northern kennel. While crossing Mississippi, My Lady had escaped from the station wagon. Her keeper had advertised in several papers, but Jesse and Skeeter never saw papers.

The passage includes several details. It tells you that My Lady was valuable. It also tells you that the dog had escaped and that the keeper had advertised in papers. The passage, however, does *not* say what the keeper advertised for. You must draw a conclusion, or inference, from the details. An *inference* is a conclusion based on details that are stated.

You might guess, for example, that the keeper advertised for a new dog or advertised that the other dogs were for sale. However, these inferences are not the most resonable to make from the details. You know that My Lady was valuable, and you know she escaped. Therefore, a reasonable inference to make is that the keeper advertised for My Lady's return.

The ability to make inferences will enhance your appreciation of literature. By making inferences as you read, you will naturally wish to continue the story to learn if your conclusions are correct. Eventually you may learn that your inferences were indeed accurate. However, even if your inferences are never confirmed, you can still consider them reasonable if you base them on details that are stated in the story.

The Short Story 213

Activity 2
1. d
2. b
3. d
4. a
5. d
6. c

Activity 2   Read the following passage. Then make inferences in order to complete each numbered sentence with the correct answer. Tell what details helped you make each inference.

Skeeter ran to the bayou and recovered the rat M'Lady had killed. He tied it round the dog's neck. The basenji was indignant and tried to claw off the hateful burden. Failing, she ran into the house and under a bed, but Skeeter made her come out. M'Lady filled up then, and her face assumed that don't-nobody-love-me look. The boy steeled himself, tapped M'Lady's nose with the rat, and left it around her neck.

1. Immediately after killing the rat M'Lady's face probably had a look of ____.
   a. pity   c. anger
   b. embarrassment   d. pride

2. Skeeter probably tied the rat to M'Lady in order to ____.
   a. carry it home easily   c. attract other rats
   b. teach M'Lady a lesson   d. reward M'Lady for bravery

3. M'Lady tried to claw off the rat because ____.
   a. she was hungry   c. her claws needed sharp-
   b. she wanted exercise   ening
                                        d. it bothered her

4. M'Lady probably ran under the bed in order to ____.
   a. escape from Skeeter   c. chase a rat
   b. take a nap   d. keep out of the rain

5. Skeeter probably made M'Lady come out from under the bed because he ____.
   a. needed to make the bed   c. wanted to walk her
   b. had a bone for her   d. wanted her to accept a
                                           punishment

6. Skeeter "steeled himself" in order to ____.
   a. lift up the dog   c. do something unpleasant
   b. move the bed   but necessary
                                        d. remain wide awake

Predicting Outcomes in Stories

You may make many types of inferences as you read stories. One type involves predicting outcomes. Naturally, you are not expected to guess the ending of every story you read. In fact, many stories have surprise endings that are meant to catch you unaware. Nevertheless, in any story you may predict the outcomes of individual conversations, actions, or events. In other words, you may anticipate what will happen next in the story. To be a good reader, you should use all the information about characters and events in a story to try to predict future developments.

For example, in "Weep No More, My Lady" Skeeter ultimately faces the decision of whether or not to return M'Lady to her rightful owner. After Skeeter battles with his conscience, the following passage appears in the story.

> A feeling of despair and loneliness almost overwhelmed him. He fought off the tears as long as he could, but finally he gave in, and his sobs caused M'Lady to peer into his face and wonder why he was acting that way when she was so happy. He put his arms around her neck and pulled her to him. "My li'l old puppy dog. Poor li'l old puppy dog. But I got to do it."

From the details in this passage you may be able to predict Skeeter's final decision. Skeeter's crying indicates that his choice has made him unhappy. Also, his words "I got to do it" further serve to imply that Skeeter has decided to give up the dog. However, until you actually learn this information later in the story, you are still left with an element of uncertainty.

Activity 3 Read each of the following situations and the three outcomes listed afterward. Choose the outcome you feel is most likely to occur, based on details in "Weep No More, My Lady." Then explain why you chose that particular outcome.

1. Suppose M'Lady runs away from her owner again and returns to Skeeter. What do you think Skeeter will do?
   a. He will keep M'Lady without telling anyone.
   b. He will contact the owner and inform him about M'Lady.
   c. He will say nothing unless the owner contacts him.

2. Suppose M'Lady has puppies and Skeeter is offered one by the owner. What do you think Skeeter will do?
   a. He will gladly accept the puppy.
   b. He will insist on keeping M'Lady as well as the puppy.
   c. He will refuse to keep the puppy under any condition.

3. Suppose M'Lady's owner asks Skeeter to watch the dog for two weeks each summer. What do you think Skeeter will do?
   a. He will turn down the offer.
   b. He will ask to keep M'Lady for eight weeks instead.
   c. He will accept the offer.

Activity 3
1. b; Skeeter has indicated his strong belief in honesty
2. a; Skeeter has shown his devotion toward animals, so he would probably keep a puppy
3. c; Skeeter's love for M'Lady would probably prompt him to accept the offer

Literary Skills Review

The Short Story

Guide for Reading the Short Story

As you read short stories, use this guide to understand how an author combines different techniques to create a fictional world.

Plot

1. What type of **conflict** does the main character face?
2. What is the **climax,** the point of our highest interest and involvement?
3. What is the **resolution,** or final outcome?
4. What events of the plot create **suspense**?

Character

1. Who are the most important **characters** in the story?
2. What **character traits** do the characters show?
3. What **motivations** do characters have for their actions?
4. What does the author **directly tell** about the characters?
5. What do the characters' **words and actions** reveal about their personalities?

Setting

1. **When and where** does the story take place?
2. What **details** describe the time and place of the story?
3. What **atmosphere,** or mood, does the setting create?
4. What effect does setting have on plot and character?

Point of View

1. Does the author use a character in the story as a **first-person narrator**?
2. Does the author tell the story, acting as a **third-person narrator**?

Theme

1. What is the story's **theme,** or main idea?
2. Is the theme directly **stated,** or is it **implied**?
3. In what sense is the theme a **generalization** of what happens in the story?
4. In what ways does the story's **title** point to its theme?

216   *The Short Story*

Themes Review

The Short Story

We find that certain general themes—for example, "friendship and love"—appear over and over in different literary works. However, each work has something very specific to say about these general themes. For example, consider what two different stories have to say about the general theme "love." The specific theme of "Christmas Day in the Morning" (page 59) is "Only love can waken love." The specific theme of "Mary" (page 103) is "Love sometimes requires painful sacrifice." Note that a general theme can be expressed as a word or phrase, such as "love," while a specific theme should be expressed as a complete sentence.

1. For two of the following stories, tell what point the author makes about the general theme "friendship and love."
   "The Osage Orange Tree"   "Then He Goes Free"
   "A Game of Catch"   "The Dog of Pompeii"

2. Choose two of the following stories, and tell what each says about the general theme "family life."
   "Fire!"   "Gentleman of Río en Medio"
   "Charles"   "The Brother Who Failed"
   "The Mixed-Up Feet and   "Christmas Day in the
      the Silly Bridegroom"   Morning"

3. Choose two of the following stories, and tell what specific point each makes about the general theme "American experiences."
   "Spring Victory"   "Jim Baker's Blue-jay Yarn"
   "The Legend of   "The Man Without a
      Sleepy Hollow"   Country"

4. For two of the following stories, tell what a major character learns from a mysterious situation.
   "Crime on Mars"   "Flowers for Algernon"
   "The Rule of Names"

5. From the following list choose one story and one other work. Then tell what specific view each work expresses about the general theme "discovery."
   Stories: "Thank You, M'am"   "The Six Rows of Pompons"
      "Come of Age"   "Weep No More, My Lady"
   Other: *Growing Up*   *The Miracle Worker*

THEMES REVIEW

The questions in the Themes Review for the Short Story unit recall the general themes portrayed in the selections in this unit. Suggested answers to these questions are presented here.

1. "The Osage Orange Tree," "Then He Goes Free," and "The Dog of Pompeii": Friendship often demands sacrifice. "A Game of Catch": People need the friendship of those their own age.

2. "Fire!" and "Gentleman of Rio": A family is a small community. "Charles": A family is often blind to the faults of its members. "The Mixed-Up Feet": Foolishness runs in families. "The Brother": Family members often make sacrifices for one another without expecting rewards. "Christmas Day": Family members often take love for granted.

3. "Spring Victory": Courage and hard work made America great. "Sleepy Hollow" and "Jim Baker's Blue-Jay Yarn": Folk tales and yarns are a great part of American culture. "The Man Without a Country": We often take love of country for granted.

4. "The Rule of Names": The real nature of things often remains a mystery. "Algernon": The mind remains a mystery.

5. "Thank You, M'am": We can discover truths about life through mistakes. "Come of Age" and "Weep No More": The most painful discoveries contribute to maturity. "Pompons": Discovering personal responsibility can lead to maturity. *Growing Up:* The discovery of talent can increase self-worth. *The Miracle Worker:* The discovery of language is a civilizing force.

For more information about the themes portrayed in these selections, see the Theme Index beginning on page 666.

Preview
Poetry

Did you ever have an emotion or a thought that you knew was important but that you could not quite put into words? Poetry is one kind of writing that can capture such emotions and thoughts, giving them shape.

A poet's purpose is different from that of other kinds of writers. Imagine a scientist writing about ice cream. The scientist may discuss the percentage of milk fat in the ice cream or the temperature at which it is made. A historian may write about how Marco Polo first brought the idea for the frozen dessert back from China. A businessperson may write about the number of gallons of ice cream sold per month. A poet, on the other hand, will try to stimulate the reader's senses, heighten awareness, arouse emotion, and create an "ice cream experience." A poet may "capture" the sounds of slurping, the crunching of a crisp cone, the tickle of cold on your tongue. A poet may suggest how ice cream is like or unlike other things. A poet may use ice cream to suggest an idea about cold or to tell something about a person who loves ice cream. A poet may simply want us to delight in a world that contains ice cream.

Poetry is a partnership. A poem is not just the work and joy of the poet. You, the reader, must actively participate. Your ear must pick up the poem's rhythms and hear its "music." Your eye must recognize its patterns on the page. Your mind must scan the poem for images and overall meaning and must "fill in" the leaps in logic that the poet takes.

In the following pages you will examine some of the basic elements that make a poem. You will explore the elements of *sound*, *language*, *form*, and *meaning* individually and finally look at how these elements work together to create a *total effect*. Take your time in reading the selections. Read each both silently and out loud. Consider the ideas and emotions that each spotlights, and enjoy yourself.

Poetry 219

PREVIEW

After students have read the Preview, ask them to discuss poems they have liked and disliked. As they give reasons for their feelings, list them on the board. You may find some of these reactions valuable because discussing feelings about poetry helps to overcome prejudices students sometimes form about the genre.

Then ask students to discuss the statement in the Preview—"Poetry is a partnership. A poem is not just the work and the joy of the poet. You, the reader, must actively participate." Point out that the reader's participation involves, among other things, a willingness to engage oneself in the poetic style of writing.

THE SOUND OF POETRY

When you read a poem aloud, its sound may surprise you. It may also relax you or make you laugh or remind you of something. A poem may sound like a roaring waterfall or the beat of a drum or almost anything at all. Sound is such a powerful part of a poem that you even "hear" the sound of a poem when you read silently. Each poem has its own "music," and as you read you can make that music come alive.

Edna St. Vincent Millay (1892–1950) was born in Maine. She became famous almost overnight and went on to write many emotion-packed, highly musical poems.

A counting-out rhyme is a poem used in a game. As the rhyme is recited, the player pointed to on the last word is "out."

■ Listen for the unusual sounds Millay creates as she plays with the names of trees such as beech, willow, popple (another word for poplar), and elder.

Robert Francis (born 1901) grew up in the Pennsylvania farm country and later was graduated from Harvard University. His poem "Preparation" shows his love of nature and his ability to picture a country scene in detail.

■ Why is the poem also considered a celebration of the music of language itself?

© Rollie McKenna

Sylvia Plath (1932–1963) studied at Smith College and later at Cambridge University in England, where she met and married poet Ted Hughes. Many of Plath's poems are intensely personal, but others, like "Mushrooms," are playful. Plath makes the mushrooms the speakers of this poem. The **speaker** is the person, object, or voice that presents the poem to the reader.

■ Notice how Plath lets the mushrooms themselves reveal their personalities.

220   *Poetry*

John Keats (1795–1821) was born in London, England, in the living quarters attached to the stable where his father worked. Keats apprenticed himself to a surgeon for seven years before deciding to write full time. His worldwide fame rests on the three volumes of poems that he wrote between the ages of twenty-two and twenty-five.

■ As you read "On the Grasshopper and the Cricket," listen for the sounds Keats calls "the poetry of earth."

Robert Frost (1874–1963) grew up in the New England country-side, where most of his poems are set. After working as a shoe-maker, a schoolteacher, and a farmer, he published his first book of poetry, *A Boy's Will*, in 1913.

■ Like many of Frost's poems, "Stopping by Woods on a Snowy Evening" presents a sensitive description of nature and raises important questions about people. Pay particular attention to line 14.

Alfred, Lord Tennyson (1809–1892) was England's Poet Laureate, or official poet, and he was the first writer ever to be knighted. A large part of his appeal was the music of his verse; in fact, Tennyson was said to be a poet with a heart "full of music." Tennyson wrote poems about historical events. He also wrote more personal poems, such as "Ring Out, Wild Bells."

■ As you read this New Year's Eve poem, listen for the rhythm of the bells.

William Jay Smith (born 1918) grew up in Louisiana and studied in Missouri, New York, England, France, and Italy. He has been poet-in-residence at many colleges and has written poems for both children and adults. Smith skillfully plays with sounds to create a keen sense of energy.

■ As you read "Seal," listen for the techniques of sound that Smith uses. Notice, too, how the poet makes the shape of the poem suggest its meaning.

Poetry 221

AT A GLANCE

As the speaker describes aspects of trees, she plays with the sounds of words.

LITERARY OPTIONS

- alliteration
- rhythm

THEMATIC OPTIONS

- nature
- playfulness

ALLITERATION

Alliteration of the *b*'s in *bark, beech,* and *birch* and of the *s*'s in *silver* and *sallow* contribute to the playful spirit of the poem (ll. 1–2).

SPEAKER

The repetition of sounds in *maple, apple,* and *popple* reflects the speaker's playful, childlike delight in nature (ll. 4–6).

IMAGERY

A simile is used to compare *popple* to a moonbeam (l. 7); Millay uses colors explicitly (*yellow, silver, green*) and implicitly (*leaf of apple*) (ll. 1–5).

VOCABULARY

A *hornbeam* is a small tree in the birch family (l. 9).

MAIN IDEA

The regular rhythm of the poem resembles a child's counting-out rhyme and reinforces the impression of playfulness (ll. 10–12).

REFLECTING ON THE POEM

How is the title appropriate? (The rhythms and repetitions of the poem suggest counting or listing, and the rhymes are the central feature in the poem.)

Edna St. Vincent Millay

Counting-Out Rhyme

Silver bark of beech, and sallow[1]
Bark of yellow birch and yellow
  Twig of willow.

Stripe of green in moosewood maple,
5 Color seen in leaf of apple,
  Bark of popple.

Wood of popple pale as moonbeam,
Wood of oak of yoke and barn-beam,
  Wood of hornbeam.

10 Silver bark of beech, and hollow
Stem of elder, tall and yellow
  Twig of willow.

---

1. **sallow:** pale yellow.

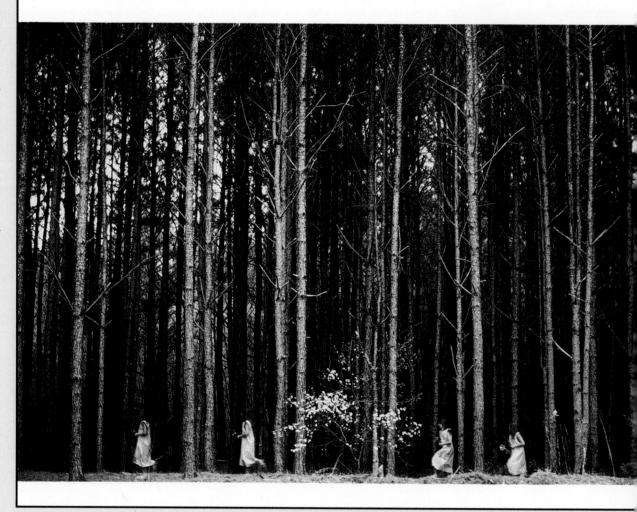

STUDY QUESTIONS

Recalling

1. Name five kinds of trees mentioned in the poem.
2. Name three colors that the poet uses to describe these trees.
3. Name three tree parts mentioned in the poem.

Interpreting

4. Tell which words in the poem sound *almost* like other words in the poem. Which letters does the poet change to turn one word into another?
5. Which do you think is more important in this poem—the fun of the sounds themselves or the meaning of the words? Why?

Extending

6. Do you think this poem would make a good song? Why or why not? How would you sing it?

READING AND LITERARY FOCUS

Wordplay

Everyone, at one time or another, has played with the sounds of words. We all know the fun of tongue twisters, nonsense words, or words that we simply like to pronounce. Poets capture that fun in poems. The skillful manipulation of words, often for humorous effect, is called **wordplay.**

Sometimes a poet uses repetition, or near repetition, as a kind of wordplay. Millay uses near repetition in "Counting-Out Rhyme." Listen, for example, to the words in the poem ending in *-llow*: *sallow, yellow, willow, hollow.*

A poet may also add unusual beginnings or endings to words or join two seemingly unrelated words. For example, one poet combined *telephone* and *elephant* and invented the *telephant.*

Wordplay can affect both sound and meaning.

A poet may play with a word pair that has the same sound but different spellings and meanings, like *hair* and *hare*. **Puns,** jokes based on the sound of words, show this kind of wordplay in action. For example, a famous pun asks, "What is black and white and *red* all over?" (A newspaper: It's black and white and *read* all over.)

Wordplay based on sound can be more than fun. It can hold a poem together, using sounds to create a feeling of unity in a poem from beginning to end.

Thinking About Wordplay

■ Find another example of near repetition in "Counting-Out Rhyme."

COMPOSITION

Writing About Wordplay

■ Write about the wordplay in "Counting-Out Rhyme." First define *wordplay* in your own words. Then point out wordplay in Millay's poem. End with a sentence about the effect the wordplay has on you.

Writing with Wordplay

■ Write a short poem that plays with the sounds of words. You may want to begin by starting each line with a letter of your name or nickname, for example:

K ____
A ____
T ____
E ____

Then, as you compose each line, change one letter of your name at a time (*Kate, late, lake, like, bike, bite, kite, Kate*), and build your poem with these words. Remember: A poem does not have to rhyme.

1. beech, birch, willow, maple, apple, popple, oak, hornbeam, elder
2. silver, sallow, yellow, green
3. bark, twig, leaf, wood, stem
4. ■ words at end of each line: sallow, yellow, willow; maple, apple, popple; moonbeam, barn-beam, hornbeam; hollow, willow, yellow
   ■ She changes beginning letters of simple words and first word in compound words.
5. fun of the sounds, because the sounds provide enjoyment and link the words in stanzas
6. Answers will vary. Possibilities: Sound and rhythm make it a good song. It would probably be sung with a simple melody repeated in each stanza.

READING AND LITERARY FOCUS

■ Stanza 2: words ending in *-ple—maple, apple, popple*
■ Stanza 3: words ending in *-beam—moonbeam, barn-beam, hornbeam*
■ Stanza 4: words ending in *-llow—hollow, yellow, willow*

COMPOSITION: GUIDELINES FOR EVALUATION

WRITING ABOUT WORDPLAY

Objective

To define and write about wordplay

Guidelines for Evaluation

■ suggested length: one paragraph
■ should define wordplay
■ should provide examples and describe the effect of wordplay

WRITING WITH WORDPLAY

Objective

To write a short poem

Guidelines for Evaluation

■ suggested length: three to six lines
■ should demonstrate wordplay involving near repetition
■ should create a feeling of unity using sounds

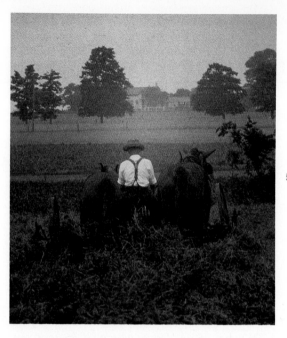

Robert Francis

Preparation

Last fall I saw the farmer follow
The plow that dug the long dark furrows[1]
Between the hillslope and the hollow.

All winter long the land lay fallow.[2]
5 The woodchuck slept within his burrow
And heard no hound or farm boy's hallow.[3]

Tonight the rain drives its dark arrows
Deep in the soil, down to its marrow.[4]
The arrows of the sun tomorrow.

---

1. **furrows:** grooves made in the soil by a plow.
2. **fallow:** plowed but not planted.
3. **hallow:** shout or call, "halloo."
4. **marrow:** innermost part.

STUDY QUESTIONS

Recalling

1. According to stanza 1, what did the speaker see the farmer follow? When did the farmer do this?
2. According to stanza 2, what "lay fallow," and what slept? What season does this stanza mention?
3. According to stanza 3, where does the rain drive its "arrows"?

Interpreting

4. In what season do you think the third stanza takes place? How do you know?
5. How do the farmer, the land, and the woodchuck make their "preparations"? What is each getting ready to do?
6. Read aloud the last word of each line. How are the words alike in sound?

224   *Poetry*

READING AND LITERARY FOCUS

Alliteration

One of the ways a poet can play with sound is to use alliteration. **Alliteration** is the repetition of consonant sounds, usually at the beginnings of words. The sound-related words are placed near each other in the poem, as in the line

The *l*one and *l*evel *s*ands *s*tretch far away.

As we read, we enjoy the repeated sounds, as if a bell were ringing throughout a line, a stanza, or an entire poem. Alliteration is one kind of poetic "music." It can also emphasize meaning or mood or unify a poem by connecting certain words with sound. For example, in the preceding line of poetry, the repeated *l* sounds emphasize the loneliness of the desert scene.

It is important to remember that words can be alliterative without having their initial consonant sounds spelled alike. For example, listen to the alliteration in this sentence:

The *f*riendly *f*armer lau*gh*ed on the old-*f*ashioned *ph*one.

Notice that the *f* sound is repeated within a word as well as at the beginnings of words.

Thinking About Alliteration
■ Find three examples of alliteration in "Preparation."

VOCABULARY

Words Often Confused
Many words in English are sometimes confused with other words. The confusion usually occurs because the words are similar or identical in sound. The words *lie* and *lay* and the words *its* and *it's* are two such frequently confused pairs. Francis uses *lay* and *its* in "Preparation."

The following chart shows the differences between the words of each pair.

Lie/Lay

Lie means "to recline."
Lay means "to put" or "place" something.

PRESENT TENSE	lie(s)	lay(s)
PAST TENSE	lay	laid

EXAMPLES
Now I *lie* on the floor.
Yesterday I *lay* on the floor.

Now I *lay* the book on the table.
Yesterday I *laid* the book on the table.

Its/It's

Its is a possessive pronoun.
It's is a contraction for *it is.*

EXAMPLES
The tiger licked *its* paws.
It's a beautiful day.

On a separate sheet of paper, copy the following sentences, choosing the appropriate word from those in parentheses to complete each thought.

1. He (lay, lie) down on the beach blanket to take a snooze.
2. The coach says that (its, it's) going to be a close game.
3. If you feel ill, you really ought to (lay, lie) down.
4. Yesterday the waitress (laid, lay) the plate of fried clams in front of me.
5. The editors say (its, it's) clear that she will be elected.

COMPOSITION

Writing About the Last Line of a Poem
■ Write one paragraph about the last line of "Preparation." In your paragraph answer the following questions: (1) Is the last line a sentence or a complete thought? (2) How is this line connected to the sentence before it? (3) How does it suggest something coming, something about to happen? (4) Why does it make a good ending to the poem?

Writing with Alliteration
■ Write five lines that describe the activities of various animals. Start each line with the name of the animal. Use alliteration in each line. For example, "Horses haul a heavy load of hay." Other animals to describe may include camels, dogs, elephants, pigs, or llamas.

CHALLENGE

Mapmaking
■ Make a weather map of the United States, showing temperatures, wind currents, and general conditions (rainy, sunny, snowy, cloudy) for a given day. Below the map summarize the specific ways in which the weather is different in different parts of the country and how it will change within one day.

Preparation 225

READING AND LITERARY FOCUS

- Line 1: fall, farmer, follow
- Line 4: long, land, lay, fallow
- Line 6: heard, hound, hallow
- Lines 7–8: drives, dark, deep, down

VOCABULARY

1. lay
2. it's
3. lie
4. laid
5. it's

COMPOSITION: GUIDELINES FOR EVALUATION

WRITING ABOUT THE LAST LINE OF A POEM
Objective
To tell how the last line relates to the poem

Guidelines for Evaluation
■ suggested length: one paragraph
■ should tell whether the last line is a sentence or complete thought
■ should tell how it connects to prior sentence
■ should tell how it suggests future activity
■ should tell why it is a good ending

WRITING WITH ALLITERATION
Objective
To write a verse that describes the activities of various animals and contains alliteration

Guidelines for Evaluation
■ suggested length: five lines
■ should start with the name of the animal
■ should describe various animals' activities
■ should contain alliteration in each line

Sylvia Plath

Mushrooms

Overnight, very
Whitely, discreetly,[1]
Very quietly

Our toes, our noses
5 Take hold on the loam,[2]
Acquire the air.

Nobody sees us,
Stops us, betrays us;
The small grains make room.

10 Soft fists insist on
Heaving the needles,
The leafy bedding,

Even the paving.
Our hammers, our rams,
15 Earless and eyeless,

Perfectly voiceless,
Widen the crannies,[3]
Shoulder through holes. We

Diet on water,
20 On crumbs of shadow,
Bland-mannered, asking

Little or nothing.
So many of us!
So many of us!

25 We are shelves, we are
Tables, we are meek,
We are edible,

Nudgers and shovers
In spite of ourselves.
30 Our kind multiplies:

We shall by morning
Inherit the earth.
Our foot's in the door.

---

1. **discreetly:** carefully.
2. **loam:** dark, rich soil.

---

3. **crannies:** narrow openings.

STUDY QUESTIONS

Recalling

1. What words in lines 1–3 describe how mushrooms grow? How long does it take for them to appear?
2. According to stanza 3, who sees them? Who stops them?
3. According to lines 14–18, what are the mushrooms doing?
4. Based on the information in stanza 7, what are the mushrooms doing?
5. What do the mushrooms call themselves in lines 25–26?
6. What do the speakers of the poem think they will inherit?

Interpreting

7. What words or phrases suggest the mushrooms' weakness? Their strength? Which of these qualities is emphasized at the end of the poem?
8. To what objects does Plath compare the mushrooms? Which of these comparisons do you find particularly unusual? Why?
9. Where in the poem does Plath use repetition? How does this repetition help to reinforce meaning?

READING AND LITERARY FOCUS

Assonance

Assonance is the repetition of similar vowel sounds. Like alliteration, assonance is a kind of repetition that helps to tie together the words of a poem.

Plath uses assonance in lines 4–5 of "Mushrooms": "Our *toes*, our *noses* / Take *hold* on the *loam*." The repeated long *o* sound has the effect of weaving together the words in the sentence. Notice, too, that the *o* sound is formed in different ways with different letter combinations. Like alliteration, assonance is a literary device that a poet can use to create music, mood, and meaning.

Thinking About Assonance

■ Find at least two other examples of assonance in "Mushrooms."

VOCABULARY

Sentence Completions

Each of the following sentences contains a blank with four possible choices for completing the sentence. All of the choices come from "Mushrooms." Choose the word that completes each sentence correctly and uses the word *as it is used in the poem*. Write the number of each item and the letter of your choice on a separate sheet of paper.

1. Quietly and ____ the man slipped out of the meeting before it was over.
   (a) spite   (c) discreetly
   (b) even   (d) whitely
2. At the fun house, he squeezed through the small ____.
   (a) cranny   (c) loam
   (b) paving   (d) bedding
3. She thought that she was too loud, but everyone else thought that she was ____.
   (a) insisting   (c) shoving
   (b) quietly   (d) meek
4. The boy wanted to eat the purple berry but was told that it was not ____.
   (a) acquired   (c) edible
   (b) multiplied   (d) inherited
5. The farmer planted the seeds in the deep ____.
   (a) paving   (c) loam
   (b) shelves   (d) spite

CHALLENGE

Research

■ Using a science book or an encyclopedia, gather scientific facts about different varieties of mushroom. Make a chart comparing the facts with statements made in Plath's poem. You may want to use these headings on your chart: Size, Color, Shape, Environment.

Mushrooms 227

1. *very whitely, discreetly, very quietly;* overnight
2. nobody; nobody
3. widening crannies and shouldering through holes with hammers and rams
4. subsisting on a diet of water and crumbs of shadow
5. "shelves" and "tables"
6. the earth
7. ■ weakness: *small grains; soft fists; bland-mannered; meek*
   ■ strength: *hammers; rams; shoulder through holes; nudgers and shovers*
   ■ Strengths are emphasized.
8. ■ creatures with noses and toes; workers using hammers and rams; creatures shouldering through holes; shelves and tables
   ■ Comparisons suggesting determination and strength—workers with hammers and rams—seem unusual, because mushrooms do not seem powerful.
9. ■ Stanza 8: "So many of us!"
   ■ Repetition underlines insistence and force of spreading mushrooms.

READING AND LITERARY FOCUS

■ Lines 1–3: over*ni*ght, wh*i*tely, qu*i*etly
■ Lines 10–13: h*ea*ving, n*ee*dles, l*ea*fy
■ Line 18: sh*ou*lder, h*o*les
■ Line 28: n*u*dgers, sh*o*vers
■ Lines 31–33: m*o*rning, d*oo*r

VOCABULARY

1. (c) discreetly
2. (a) cranny
3. (d) meek
4. (c) edible
5. (c) loam

CHALLENGE

Students should
■ gather information about mushrooms from outside sources
■ list the attributes given to mushrooms by Plath, using such categories as size, color, shape, environment
■ list objective outside information about mushrooms in these categories

- In summer the speaker enjoys the Grasshopper's song.
- In winter he hears the Cricket's song on the hearth and imagines it's the Grasshopper's.

LITERARY OPTIONS

- rhyme
- assonance

THEMATIC OPTIONS

- nature as poetry
- change vs. permanence

ASSONANCE

The repetition of long *o* sounds in *lone* and *stove* unifies the lines and suggests the blowing of winter wind (ll. 10–11).

RHYME SCHEME

The rhyme scheme is that of a sonnet: *abba, abba, cde, cde.* This most musical of forms is fitting in a poem devoted to the music of nature (ll. 1–14).

REFLECTING ON THE POEM

What part does imagination play in the poem? (The speaker seems to enjoy his imaginings more than the sounds themselves.)

STUDY QUESTIONS

1. poetry of the earth
2. a voice; the Grasshopper
3. the Cricket's song
4. the Grasshopper's song
5. sounds of the earth's creatures; no, exists in nature
6. ■ Each creates a musical or poetic sound.
   ■ the Grasshopper
   ■ the Cricket
7. Possible answers:
   ■ natural: waves crashing; thunder booming; mosquito buzzing
   ■ human: symphony music; movement of dancers; parade sounds
   ■ mechanical: motor revving; train whistle; foghorn

John Keats

On the Grasshopper and the Cricket

The poetry of earth is never dead:
  When all the birds are faint with the hot sun,
  And hide in cooling trees, a voice will run
From hedge to hedge about the new-mown mead;[1]
5 That is the Grasshopper's—he takes the lead
  In summer luxury—he has never done
  With his delights; for when tired out with fun
He rests at ease beneath some pleasant weed.
The poetry of earth is ceasing never:
10 On a lone winter evening, when the frost
    Has wrought[2] a silence, from the stove there shrills
The Cricket's song, in warmth increasing ever,
  And seems to one in drowsiness half lost,
    The Grasshopper's among some grassy hills.

---

1. **mead:** meadow.
2. **wrought:** made.

STUDY QUESTIONS

Recalling
1. What is "never dead"?
2. What will "run from hedge to hedge"? To whom does this belong?
3. What can you hear on a "long winter evening"?
4. According to the final two lines, of what does the cricket's song remind the poet?

Interpreting
5. What does Keats mean by the phrase "the poetry of earth"? Is this written poetry?
6. In what ways is each of the insects a "poet"? Which is the poet of summer? Of winter?

228 *Poetry*

Extending
7. Name some examples of "poetry" from the natural, human, or mechanical worlds that express beauty but do not rely on language to do so.

READING AND LITERARY FOCUS

Rhyme and Rhyme Scheme
Rhyme occurs when stressed vowel sounds and the consonants that come after them sound the same in two or more words. For example, the words *sweetly* and *neatly* rhyme because the stressed parts of the words and all the consonants that follow sound identical.

Poets also often use words that almost rhyme.

These are called **near rhymes,** or **approximate rhymes.** For example, the words *one* and *stone* are near rhymes because their end sounds are similar but not identical.

When rhyming words are placed at the ends of lines, they are called **end rhymes.** End rhymes often fall into a repeating pattern called a **rhyme scheme.** The rhyme scheme of a poem is indicated by assigning a different letter of the alphabet to each end rhyme. For example, the rhyme scheme of the following poem is *ababcb:*

It was many and many a year ago,
    In a kingdom by the sea,
That a maiden there lived whom you may know
    By the name of Annabel Lee;
And this maiden she lived with no other thought
    Than to love and be loved by me.

The rhyme scheme of a poem adds to its music and gives it structure. It can also link thoughts. For example, in the stanza above the rhymed words *sea* and *Lee* and *me* link the most important ideas in the poem. The poet uses rhyme to emphasize the oneness of himself and his beloved by the sea. Rhyme calls attention to the rhyming words and makes them stand out.

Thinking About Rhyme and Rhyme Scheme
1. On a separate sheet of paper, list all of Keats's end rhymes.
2. Assign letters of the alphabet to the identical and similar sounds, treating any approximate rhymes as full rhymes. What is the poet's rhyme scheme?

VOCABULARY

Homonyms
Homonyms, sometimes called **homophones,** are two words that are pronounced alike but that have different meanings. For example, the words *plane* and *plain* are homonyms.

One word in each of the homonym pairs below can be found in Keats's "On the Grasshopper and the Cricket." Select five of the numbered pairs, and on a separate sheet of paper, write five sentences. Each sentence should use both words from one pair. If you are not certain of the exact meanings, consult a dictionary.

1. sun/son	5. some/sum
2. all/awl	6. lone/loan
3. new/knew	7. there/their
4. mown/moan	8. seams/seems

COMPOSITION

Writing About Alliteration and Assonance
■ Write a description of Keats's use of alliteration and assonance in "On the Grasshopper and the Cricket." Give some examples of his use of alliteration, and point out how often he uses this literary device. Do the same for his use of assonance. Finally, discuss what these two sound techniques add to the poem.

Writing a Poem
■ Write a short unrhymed poem in which you describe vivid details of nature in summer and in winter. Begin your first line with the words "In summer . . . ," filling in the blank with a detail that you see, taste, touch, hear, or feel during this season. Begin the second line with the words "In winter . . . ," following the same format. Alternate these sentence beginnings in each line throughout the poem.

CHALLENGE

Description
■ Cut a picture of a nature scene out of a magazine. Write a prose description of the scene that is so accurate and filled with details that a friend can draw the scene by hearing your description. Now read your description, and ask your friend to draw what you describe.

On the Grasshopper and the Cricket 229

1. dead, mead; sun, run; lead, weed; done, fun; never, ever; frost, lost; shrills, hills
2. ■ *abba, abba, cde, cde*
   ■ Explain to students that a sonnet is a fourteen-line poem with a specific rhyming pattern that usually expresses a complete idea.

VOCABULARY
Answers will vary. Possible answers:
1. The *sun* shone on the couple's new *son.*
2. *All* the workers handled the *awl.*
3. I *knew* you'd get a *new* bike.
4. He gave a *moan* as he saw the new-*mown* hay.
5. *Some* students were unsure of the correct *sum.*
6. The *lone* man asked for a *loan.*
7. *Their* seats are over *there.*
8. It *seems* that the coat came apart at the *seams.*

CHALLENGE
Students should
■ cut out a picture of a natural scene
■ write a paragraph describing that scene in detail
■ ask someone who has not seen the picture to draw the scene described in the paragraph

---

COMPOSITION: GUIDELINES FOR EVALUATION

WRITING ABOUT ALLITERATION AND ASSONANCE

Objective
To describe the use of alliteration and assonance in the poem.

Guidelines for Evaluation
■ suggested length: two paragraphs
■ should offer examples of both devices
■ should tell how often they are used
■ should discuss what they add to the poem

WRITING A POEM

Objective
To write a nonrhyming poem describing summer and winter

Guidelines for Evaluation
■ suggested length: six to eight lines
■ should begin first line with, "In summer . . ."
■ should begin second line with, "In winter . . ."
■ should alternate seasons throughout
■ should tell how the seasons affect the senses

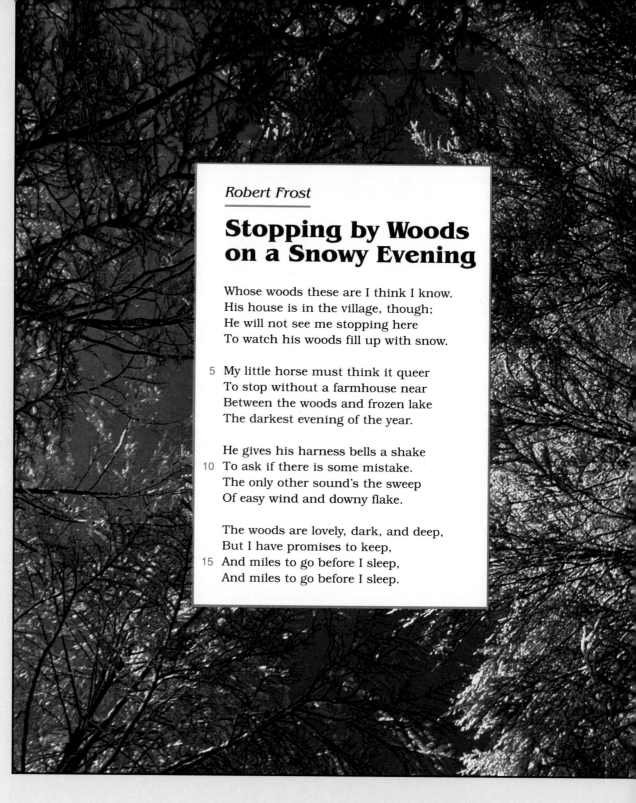

Robert Frost

Stopping by Woods on a Snowy Evening

Whose woods these are I think I know.
His house is in the village, though;
He will not see me stopping here
To watch his woods fill up with snow.

5 My little horse must think it queer
To stop without a farmhouse near
Between the woods and frozen lake
The darkest evening of the year.

He gives his harness bells a shake
10 To ask if there is some mistake.
The only other sound's the sweep
Of easy wind and downy flake.

The woods are lovely, dark, and deep,
But I have promises to keep,
15 And miles to go before I sleep,
And miles to go before I sleep.

STUDY QUESTIONS

Recalling

1. According to stanza 1, where does the speaker think the owner of the woods lives? What will the owner not see the speaker do?

2. According to stanza 2, what does the speaker suppose is his horse's reaction to stopping? Where exactly does the speaker stop? Which evening is it?

3. According to stanza 3, what does the horse do? What sound can be heard?

4. In the last stanza what three adjectives describe the woods? How far does the speaker still have to go?

Interpreting

5. Describe the weather in the poem. What qualities of the weather would make the speaker want to stop?

6. What does the speaker feel in the woods that an animal cannot understand?

7. What word in line 14 signals a sudden change in the speaker's thoughts? Describe that change in your own words.

8. What "promises" do you think the speaker would have to keep?

9. Poets often use ordinary events—like stopping in the woods—to say something about life itself. What might the speaker of this poem mean by "miles to go before I sleep"?

Extending

10. Why is it important for poets and artists to show us what they find in ordinary, everyday events?

READING AND LITERARY FOCUS

Rhythm

In poetry **rhythm** is the arrangement of stressed and unstressed syllables. When you speak your voice naturally rises and falls. You stress some syllables and do not stress others. In

poetry rhythm can be shown with stress marks (′) over stressed syllables and rounded marks (˘) over unstressed syllables. For example, in the word *poetry* the first syllable is stressed and the second two are not.

Sometimes the rhythm is as regular and predictable as the beat of a drum. In Millay's "Counting-Out Rhyme" (page 222), for example, the rhythm is regular:

> Silver bark of beech, and sallow
>
> Bark of yellow birch and yellow
>
> Twig of willow.

Sometimes the rhythm is irregular and less predictable, as it is in Keats's "On the Grasshopper and the Cricket" (page 228):

> That is the Grasshopper's—he takes the lead
>
> In summer luxury—he has never done
>
> With his delights

The rhythm of a poem often echoes the poem's meaning. For example, in a poem about a yo-yo, a poet might establish the pattern of a regular, up-and-down rhythm. In a poem about a seagull, a poet might choose a freer, more graceful, less predictable rhythm.

Thinking About Rhythm

■ Write out the last four lines of "Stopping by Woods on a Snowy Evening." Mark the stressed syllables.

CHALLENGE

Research

■ Find and read to the class the poem that Robert Frost read at the inauguration of President John F. Kennedy in 1961. Discuss the qualities that would make the poem appropriate for such a public occasion.

Stopping by Woods on a Snowy Evening 231

LITERARY OPTIONS

- repetition
- rhythm

THEMATIC OPTIONS

- hopes for change
- celebration

REPETITION

The repetition of *ring* unifies the structure and reinforces the main idea of the poem—the hope for a better world (ll. 5–8).

RHYTHM

The regular rhythm throughout the poem suggests the tolling of bells (ll. 1–20).

RHYME

The regular pattern of end rhymes creates its own music and highlights the strong rhythm of the bells (ll. 1–20).

REFLECTING ON THE POEM

Is it possible to change the things that Tennyson believes should be changed? (The poet deals with fundamental and universal problems; it is possible, though very difficult, to change them.)

STUDY QUESTIONS

1. *wild;* the year
2. the old and false; the new and true
3. grief that saps the mind, feud of rich and poor; false pride, civic slander, spite
4. peace
5. bring to an end; usher in
6. ■ *Ring out* begins every stanza.
   ■ Regular beat suggests bells pealing.

VOCABULARY

1. (d) controlled   4. (c) truce
2. (b) joy   5. (d) lovely
3. (a) strengthens

Alfred, Lord Tennyson

Ring Out, Wild Bells

Ring out, wild bells, to the wild sky,
　The flying cloud, the frosty light;
　The year is dying in the night;
Ring out, wild bells, and let him die.

5　Ring out the old, ring in the new,
　Ring, happy bells, across the snow:
　The year is going, let him go;
Ring out the false, ring in the true.

Ring out the grief that saps the mind,
10　For those that here we see no more;
　Ring out the feud of rich and poor,
Ring in redress[1] to all mankind.

Ring out false pride in place and blood,
　The civic slander[2] and the spite;
15　Ring in the love of truth and right,
Ring in the common love of good.

Ring out old shapes of foul disease;
　Ring out the narrowing lust of gold;
　Ring out the thousand wars of old,
20　Ring in the thousand years of peace.

---

2. **civil slander:** false and damaging statements about people of other nations.

1. **redress:** justice.

STUDY QUESTIONS

Recalling

1. In the first stanza what word does the speaker use to describe the bells? What is dying?
2. What does the speaker tell the bells to "ring out" in the second stanza? What should the bells "ring in"?
3. What does the speaker tell the bells to "ring out" in the third stanza? In the fourth stanza?
4. According to the last stanza, what should the next thousand years bring?

Interpreting

5. What does the speaker mean by the phrases "ring out" and "ring in"?
6. What does the speaker repeat in the poem to establish its rhythm? Describe the rhythm, and tell why it is appropriate to the poem's meaning.

232　*Poetry*

VOCABULARY

Antonyms

Antonyms are words that have opposite or nearly opposite meanings. *Happiness* and *sadness* are examples of antonyms. The words in capitals are from "Ring Out, Wild Bells." Choose the word that most nearly is the opposite of each of the words in capitals, *as it is used in the poem.* Write the number of each item and the letter of your answer on a separate sheet of paper.

1. WILD: (a) irresponsible (b) confusing (c) jungle (d) controlled
2. GRIEF: (a) sadness (b) joy (c) relief (d) death
3. SAPS: (a) strengthens (b) syrup (c) weakens (d) drinks
4. FEUD: (a) many (b) quarrel (c) truce (d) money
5. FOUL: (a) out (b) nasty (c) chicken (d) lovely

William Jay Smith

Seal

See how he dives
  From the rocks with a zoom!
  See how he darts
   Through his watery room
5   Past crabs and eels
    And green seaweed,
    Past fluffs of sandy
    Minnow feed!
  See how he swims
10   With a swerve and a twist,
  A flip of the flipper,
  A flick of the wrist!
  Quicksilver-quick,[1]
  Softer than spray,
15 Down he plunges
  And sweeps away;
  Before you can think,
  Before you can utter
  Words like "Dill pickle"
20 Or "Apple butter,"
  Back up he swims
   Past sting-ray and shark,
   Out with a zoom,
   A whoop, a bark;
25   Before you can say
    Whatever you wish,
     He plops at your side
     With a mouthful of fish!

---

1. **quicksilver-quick:** like mercury, slippery and changeable.

Seal 233

AT A GLANCE

The seal swims, dives, and catches fish.

LITERARY OPTIONS

- onomatopoeia
- concrete poem

THEMATIC OPTIONS

- playfulness
- animals

CONCRETE POEM

The visual curves of the poem suggest the sinuous motions and shape of the seal (ll. 1–28).

ONOMATOPOEIA

The sound of *zoom* suggests the word's meaning and helps readers visualize the seal's movement (l. 2).

IMAGERY

A metaphor compares the ocean to a *watery room,* allowing the reader to visualize and identify with the seal's environment (l. 4).

ALLITERATION

The repeated *fl* in *flip, flipper,* and *flick* helps the reader unify the two images (one animal, one human) and thus identify with the seal (ll. 11–12).

RHYTHM

The short lines of the poem establish a swift rhythm that reflects the movement of the seal (ll. 1–28).

REFLECTING ON THE POEM

What parts of the poem do you find humorous? How do they achieve humor? (Possible answers: the phrases *Dill pickle, Apple butter,* and the ending; each uses surprise.)

1. with a zoom
2. crabs, eels, seaweed, minnow feed
3. flips his flipper, plunges down
4. before you can think "dill pickle" or "apple butter"; fish
5. two stressed and varying unstressed syllables per line; yes, suggests a seal's motion
6. ■ 1, 3, 9: *See how;* 11: *flip;* 13: *quick;* 17, 18, 25: *Before*
   ■ 1–16: *s;* 1, 3: *d;* 11, 12: *fl*
   ■ 1–4: *oo* or *ou;* 8–13: *i*
   ■ imitate seal's playful motion
7. barks, dives, and splashes; graceful in water, clumsy on land
8. friendly, unafraid, playful; intelligence, playfulness, loyalty

READING AND LITERARY FOCUS
zoom, bark, whoop; zoom: quick movement; bark, whoop: seal's voice

COMPARING POEMS
1. ■ "Counting-Out Rhyme": near repetition, wordplay, alliteration
   ■ "Preparation": alliteration, rhythm
   ■ "Mushrooms": alliteration, assonance, short lines
   ■ "On the Grasshopper": alliteration, assonance, end rhymes
   ■ "Stopping by Woods on a Snowy Evening": rhythm, assonance, repetition
   ■ "Ring Out": assonance, repetition, lilting rhythm
   ■ "Seal": rhythm, assonance, onomatopoeia, alliteration
2. *Emotion:* "Preparation," "Stopping by Woods," "Ring Out"; *meaning:* "On the Grasshopper," "Counting-Out," "Mushrooms," "Seal"

STUDY QUESTIONS

Recalling
1. According to lines 1–2, how does the seal dive?
2. According to lines 5–8, past what things does the seal dart?
3. According to lines 10–16, what does the seal do as he swims?
4. According to lines 17–28, how quickly does the seal move up and out of the water? What does he bring with him?

Interpreting
5. Tap out the stressed words in the poem, and describe the rhythm. Is it an appropriate rhythm for a poem about a seal?
6. Identify the lines in which the poet uses (1) repetition, (2) alliteration, and (3) assonance. What do these sound techniques add to the playfulness of the poem?
7. Describe in your own words the poem's vivid picture of how a seal moves, sounds, looks, and eats.

Extending
8. What characteristics of the seal might make it someone's favorite animal? What characteristics of animals do you think are most appealing to people?

READING AND LITERARY FOCUS

Onomatopoeia
Onomatopoeia is the use of a word or phrase that actually imitates or suggests the sound of what it describes. For example, the words *whisper, snap, crackle,* and *splat* are all onomatopoetic.

Onomatopoeia is an effective way for the poet to reinforce meaning by making a poem's subject vivid and realistic. It also adds to the overall music of a poem.

Thinking About Onomatopoeia
■ Where in "Seal" does Smith use onomatopoeia? What actions do the sounds imitate?

COMPOSITION

Writing About the Shape of a Poem
■ Describe the shape of Smith's poem. Does the shape of the poem suggest both the shape and the motion of the animal? Describe any changes you would make in the poem's shape.

Writing with Onomatopoeia
■ Think of an object that produces different sounds, such as an automobile. Write a four-line poem that uses onomatopoeia to describe the sounds. Use the form "When the ____, the sound you hear is ____." For example:

When the doors slam, the sound you hear is wham!
When the tires skid, the sound you hear is screech!

Objects you may describe include a telephone, an alarm clock, and a typewriter.

COMPARING POEMS
1. Choose two or more of the poems from this section (pages 220–234), and compare their sounds. What techniques of sound (alliteration, assonance, rhyme scheme, rhythm, and onomatopoeia) does each use?
2. In which of the two poems does sound make the bigger contribution to the emotion of the poem? To the meaning of the poem?

COMPOSITION: GUIDELINES FOR EVALUATION

WRITING ABOUT THE SHAPE OF A POEM
Objective
To explain how the poem's shape suggests the seal's shape and motion

Guidelines for Evaluation
■ suggested length: one to two paragraphs
■ should describe the poem's shape and tell if it suggests the animal's shape and motion
■ should describe any changes student suggests

WRITING WITH ONOMATOPOEIA
Objective
To write a poem that uses onomatopoeia

Guidelines for Evaluation
■ suggested length: four lines
■ should use the form: "When the _____, the sound you hear is _____"
■ should mention an object and its sound
■ should identify each sound with onomatopoeia

THE LANGUAGE OF POETRY

TEXAS ESSENTIAL ELEMENTS
GRADE 8

1A writing process
1B purpose and audience
1C supporting main idea
1D evaluating content and organization
1E appropriate language
1I word choice
3B figurative language and sound devices
3C setting and mood
3D literary genres
4B implied main idea

To locate treatment of an Element, see *Texas Teacher's Resources*.

Poetry has been called "the best words in the best order." Poets choose words carefully and arrange them in particular relationships to one another. Like each colorful sliver of glass in a kaleidoscope, every word in a poem is an important part of an overall design.

Scientists choose words for their exactness in describing facts. Poets do too, but poets do not limit themselves to "facts." They try to describe other meanings and reach out to other experiences beyond the facts. The language of scientists is precise so that it can focus on one fact; the language of poets is precise so that it can open up the whole world of experience. A scientist may describe a space suit, for instance, in terms of its fiber and temperature resistance. A poet may remark that the suit "feels as cool as coins on a wintry day."

The language of poetry is a combination of exactness and imagination. In this section you will read poems that show how these two qualities constantly work together.

William Shakespeare's (1564–1616) plays—such as *Romeo and Juliet, Hamlet, Macbeth,* and *Julius Caesar*—are admired throughout the world. Shakespeare was born in Stratford-on-Avon, England. At about age twenty-two, however, he left his home town for London, where he wrote, acted, and produced plays. Shakespeare's plays included music, dances, and songs. "When Icicles Hang by the Wall" is a song from the comedy *Love's Labor's Lost.*

■ Notice how the poet uses vivid laguage to bring a scene to life.

The life of Edgar Allan Poe (1809–1849) was short and tragic. Often ill and depressed, Poe tried for years to lift himself out of poverty by means of his writing. A master of imagery, he wrote some of the best-known American poems, including "Annabel Lee," "The Bells," and "The Raven." "The Raven" tells the story of a visit from a large, mysterious bird.

■ As you read, notice that the power of the poem comes as much from its language as it does from the event it describes.

Poetry 235

Eve Merriam (born 1916) has written fiction, nonfiction, and song lyrics, but she is best known for her poems, particularly those for children. "Willow and Ginkgo" is characteristic of her poetry, which is playful and neatly structured. In it Merriam compares two kinds of trees: the willow, a tree with narrow leaves and a soft wood used to make baskets and furniture, and the ginkgo [ging′kō], a large shade tree with fan-shaped leaves.

■ Which tree do you prefer?

Evelyn Tooley Hunt began writing poetry when she was in school, but she waited many years before publishing her verse. Her book *Under the Baobob Tree* describes people and scenes from different parts of the world.

■ In "Mama Is a Sunrise" notice how Hunt uses language to make a personal statement and to celebrate the world around her.

James Stephens (1882–1950) was born in Dublin, Ireland, and first became famous for a book of Irish fairy tales. Later he gained wide recognition as a playwright, novelist, folklore expert, and poet. Stephens made tours during which he gave exciting presentations of Irish legends and poems to enthusiastic audiences.

■ What does the poem "The Wind" gain when it is read aloud?

Winter in the Country, A Cold Morning, Currier and Ives.

William Shakespeare

When Icicles Hang by the Wall

When icicles hang by the wall,
   And Dick the shepherd blows his nail,[1]
And Tom bears logs into the hall,
   And milk comes frozen home in pail,
5 When blood is nipped, and ways be foul,[2]
Then nightly sings the staring owl,
   Tu-whit,
Tu-who, a merry note,
While greasy Joan doth keel[3] the pot.

10 When all aloud the wind doth blow,
   And coughing drowns the parson's saw,[4]
And birds sit brooding in the snow,
   And Marian's nose looks red and raw,
When roasted crabs[5] hiss in the bowl,
15 Then nightly sings the staring owl,
   Tu-whit,
Tu-who, a merry note,
While greasy Joan doth keel the pot.

---

1. **blows his nail:** blows against his fingernails to warm his hands.
2. **ways be foul:** roads are muddy.
3. **keel:** cool by mixing.

4. **saw:** familiar wise saying.
5. **crabs:** crab apples.

1. Dick blows his nail, and Tom bears logs into the hall.
2. milk brought home in a pail
3. sings "Tu-whit, Tu-who"; nightly
4. keels the pot (cools the contents by mixing)
5. coughing
6. ■ *Lines 7–8:* "Tu-whit, Tu-who, a merry note"; *line 10:* "the wind doth blow"; *line 14:* "roasted crabs hiss in the bowl"
   ■ These sounds help reader "hear" life's actions during winter's stillness.
7. *Stanza 1:* icicles hanging by the wall, milk freezing in the pail, blood being nipped, muddy roads; *stanza 2:* wind blowing, birds sitting in the snow
8. ■ Stanza 1: makes picture vivid by telling in detail how cold affects people (e.g., Dick warms his hands by blowing on his nails)
   ■ Stanza 2: makes picture more vivid by describing Marion's red, raw nose and the hiss of roasting crabs
9. Answers will vary. Generally, the cold outside is unpleasant, but its severity makes the warmth inside more pleasant.

READING AND LITERARY FOCUS

1. "icicles hang by the wall," "Dick the shepherd blows his nail," "Tom bears logs into the hall," "milk comes frozen home in pail," "birds sit brooding in the snow"
2. "Dick the shepherd blows his nail," "milk comes frozen," "blood is nipped," "Ways be foul," "the wind doth blow"

STUDY QUESTIONS

Recalling

1. According to the first stanza, what do Dick and Tom do "when icicles hang by the wall"?
2. In addition to icicles, what else is frozen?
3. What sound does the owl make? When does he sing his "merry note"?
4. What does Joan do?
5. According to the second stanza, what drowns out the voice of the parson?

Interpreting

6. Identify at least two descriptions of sound in the poem. What do you think they add to the overall picture of winter that the poem presents?
7. What events in nature does Shakespeare use to draw this picture of winter in the first stanza? In the second stanza?
8. In stanza 1, what does Shakespeare add to the picture of winter by also telling what people do? What does he add in the second stanza?

Extending

9. Do you think the scene described in the poem is pleasant or unpleasant? Can it be both? Give details to support your opinion.

READING AND LITERARY FOCUS

Imagery

In literature an **image** is a picture created by words. **Imagery** is the collection of these images. A writer creates imagery by using **concrete language,** language that appeals to our senses. With vivid imagery poets appeal to our memories and our imaginations, helping us to see, hear, feel, taste, and smell the world described in poems.

"When Icicles Hang by the Wall" uses a wide variety of images to bring a winter scene to life. For example, the poet does not simply tell us that it is cold. He lets us see that "Marian's nose looks red and raw." By providing us with concrete images, the poet helps us to imagine the scene more vividly and understand the experience.

Visual imagery is the most common, but poets can put all of the senses to work. When the imagery in a poem is precise and genuine, we can more easily recognize in the poem our own vivid experience of the world.

Thinking About Imagery

1. Identify other images of sight in the poem.
2. What images of touch does Shakespeare use?

COMPOSITION

Writing About Imagery

■ Write about how "When Icicles Hang by the Wall" contrasts images of the inside with images of the outside. First identify the images Shakespeare creates to describe the indoor scene. Then identify the images Shakespeare creates to describe the outdoor scene. Finally, write a sentence about the contrast between the two sets of images.

Writing with Imagery

■ Write an eight-line poem that uses the language of the senses to describe a scene. First identify the scene in the poem's title, such as "The Airport" or "The Library." Then start each line with "I see," "I hear," "I taste," "I touch," or "I smell." For example, "I hear the deafening roar of jets." *For general help with writing poetry, see Lesson 6 in the Writing About Literature Handbook at the back of this book.*

COMPOSITION: GUIDELINES FOR EVALUATION

WRITING ABOUT IMAGERY

Objective

To demonstrate the contrast between interior and exterior images

Guidelines for Evaluation

■ suggested length: one to two paragraphs
■ should identify images describing interiors
■ should identify images describing exteriors
■ should contrast the two types of images

WRITING WITH IMAGERY

Objective

To write a poem that describes a scene

Guidelines for Evaluation

■ suggested length: eight lines
■ should have a title and identify its scene
■ should use sensory language
■ should start each line with *I see, I hear, I taste, I touch,* or *I smell*

Edgar Allan Poe

The Raven

Once upon a midnight dreary, while I pondered, weak and weary,
Over many a quaint and curious volume of forgotten lore[1]—
While I nodded, nearly napping, suddenly there came a tapping,
As of someone gently rapping, rapping at my chamber door—
5 "'Tis some visitor," I muttered, "tapping at my chamber door—
      Only this and nothing more."

Ah, distinctly I remember it was in the bleak December;
And each separate dying ember wrought its ghost upon the floor.
Eagerly I wished the morrow—vainly I had sought to borrow
10 From my books surcease[2] of sorrow—sorrow for the lost Lenore—
For the rare and radiant maiden whom the angels name Lenore—
      Nameless *here* for evermore.

And the silken, sad, uncertain rustling of each purple curtain
Thrilled me—filled me with fantastic terrors never felt before;
15 So that now, to still the beating of my heart, I stood repeating
"'Tis some visitor entreating entrance at my chamber door—
Some late visitor entreating entrance at my chamber door—
      This it is and nothing more."

Presently my soul grew stronger; hesitating then no longer,
20 "Sir," said I, "or Madam, truly your forgiveness I implore;
But the fact is I was napping, and so gently you came rapping,
And so faintly you came tapping, tapping at my chamber door,
That I scarce was sure I heard you"—here I opened wide the door—
      Darkness there and nothing more.

25 Deep into that darkness peering, long I stood there wondering, fearing,
Doubting, dreaming dreams no mortal ever dared to dream before;
But the silence was unbroken, and the stillness gave no token,[3]
And the only word there spoken was the whispered word, "Lenore?"
This I whispered, and an echo murmured back the word, "Lenore!"
30   Merely this and nothing more.

---

1. **lore:** learning.
2. **surcease:** end.
3. **token:** sign.

The Raven 239

AT A GLANCE

- The speaker is in his room when he hears a tap on the door.
- When he answers, no one is there.

LITERARY OPTIONS

- word choice
- atmosphere

THEMATIC OPTIONS

- grief
- love

SPEAKER

The speaker immediately depicts his psychological state with the evocative words *dreary, weak,* and *weary* (l. 1).

PLOT: CONFLICT

As we read a narrative poem, we can look for setting, characters, and plot. Here the speaker—also the main character in the poem—establishes the major external conflict: Someone or something knocks at the door and interrupts his solitude (l. 5).

ALLITERATION

Repeating the *s* sound—*silken, sad, uncertain, rustling*—creates the sound of the curtain. This intensifies our sense of suspense about who or what is behind the curtain (l. 13).

ATMOSPHERE

The predominant atmosphere of the poem is mysterious and nightmarish.

GUIDED READING

LITERAL QUESTIONS

1a. What name does the speaker call out? *(Lenore)*

2a. What two words end four of the stanzas on this page? *(nothing more)*

INFERENTIAL QUESTIONS

1b. Who do you think Lenore is? (probably someone the speaker loved and lost)

2b. What does repetion of these words add to the poem? (It creates a feeling of hopelessness and loss.)

- The speaker still hears the tapping and checks the window.
- A Raven enters and perches in the room.
- No matter what the speaker says, the bird answers only, "Nevermore."

WORD CHOICE

Obeisance and *mien,* rather than the more common *bow* and *face,* are examples of the many unusual word choices in the poem. These unusual, even exotic, words add to the rich, mysterious, formal, but highly emotional tone of the poem. (ll. 39–40).

ALLUSION

"Plutonian shore" is an allusion to the shore of the river going down into the Kingdom of Pluto, the Roman god of the dead. This reference to death contributes to the increasingly sad and somber tone of the poem (l. 47).

RHYME

Most of the end rhymes in the poem rhyme with the name *Lenore* and the word *Nevermore.* Regardless of the topic of a stanza, the woman's name and the finality of her death are never far from the speaker's or the reader's mind (ll. 49–54).

Back into the chamber turning, all my soul within me burning,
Soon again I heard a tapping somewhat louder than before.
"Surely," said I, "surely that is something at my window lattice;[4]
Let me see, then, what thereat[5] is, and this mystery explore—
35 Let my heart be still a moment and this mystery explore—
     'Tis the wind and nothing more!"

Open here I flung the shutter, when, with many a flirt and flutter,
In there stepped a stately Raven of the saintly days of yore.
Not the least obeisance[6] made he; not a minute stopped or stayed he;
40 But, with mien[7] of lord or lady, perched above my chamber door—
Perched upon a bust of Pallas[8] just above my chamber door—
     Perched, and sat, and nothing more.

Then this ebony bird beguiling my sad fancy into smiling,
By the grave and stern decorum of the countenance[9] it wore,
45 "Though thy crest be shorn and shaven, thou," I said, "art sure no craven,[10]
Ghastly grim and ancient Raven wandering from the Nightly shore—
Tell me what thy lordly name is on the Night's Plutonian[11] shore!"
     Quoth the Raven "Nevermore."

Much I marveled this ungainly fowl to hear discourse so plainly,
50 Though its answer little meaning—little relevancy bore;
For we cannot help agreeing that no living human being
Ever yet was blessed with seeing bird above his chamber door—
Bird or beast upon the sculptured bust above his chamber door,
     With such name as "Nevermore."

55 But the Raven, sitting lonely on the placid bust, spoke only
That one word, as if his soul in that one word he did outpour.
Nothing farther then he uttered—not a feather then he fluttered—
Till I scarcely more than muttered "Other friends have flown before—
On the morrow *he* will leave me, as my Hopes have flown before."
60   Then the bird said "Nevermore."

---

  4. **lattice** [lat′is]: strips of wood or metal forming a regular pattern across a window.
  5. **thereat:** there.
  6. **obeisance** [ō bā′səns]: gesture expressing obedience or respect.
  7. **mien** [mēn]: manner.
  8. **bust of Pallas** [pal′əs]: statue of the head and shoulders of Pallas Athena, ancient Greek goddess of wisdom and the arts.
  9. **countenance:** facial expression.
  10. **craven:** coward.
  11. **Plutonian** [plōō tō′nē ən] **shore:** shore of the river going down into the kingdom of Hades, or Pluto, god of the underworld.

240 *Poetry*

GUIDED READING

LITERAL QUESTIONS

1a. What look does the speaker say the Raven has on its countenance? (a look of "grave and stern decorum")

2a. In the last stanza what does the speaker say about friends? ("Other friends have flown before.")

INFERENTIAL QUESTIONS

1b. How do you think the speaker feels toward the Raven? (He finds the bird strange but is somehow amused by it.)

2b. What does the speaker mean by "Other friends have flown before"? (Other friends have died or have deserted him.)

Startled at the stillness broken by reply so aptly spoken,
"Doubtless," said I, "what it utters is its only stock and store
Caught from some unhappy master whom unmerciful Disaster
Followed fast and followed faster till his songs one burden[12] bore—
65 Till the dirges of his Hope that melancholy burden bore
      Of 'Never—nevermore.' "

But the Raven still beguiling my sad fancy[13] into smiling,
Straight I wheeled a cushioned seat in front of bird and bust and door;
Then, upon the velvet sinking, I betook myself to linking
70 Fancy unto fancy, thinking what this ominous[14] bird of yore—
What this grim, ungainly, ghastly, gaunt, and ominous bird of yore
      Meant in croaking "Nevermore."

This I sat engaged in guessing, but no syllable expressing
To the fowl whose fiery eyes now burned into my bosom's core;
75 This and more I sat divining,[15] with my head at ease reclining
On the cushion's velvet lining that the lamplight gloated o'er,
But whose velvet violet lining with the lamplight gloating o'er,
      She shall press, ah, nevermore!

Then, methought, the air grew denser, perfumed from an unseen censer[16]
80 Swung by seraphim[17] whose footfalls tinkled on the tufted floor.
"Wretch," I cried, "thy God hath lent thee—by these angels he hath sent thee
Respite[18]—respite and nepenthe[19] from thy memories of Lenore;
Quaff,[20] oh quaff this kind nepenthe and forget this lost Lenore!"
      Quoth the Raven "Nevermore."

---

12. **burden:** repeated message or meaning.
13. **fancy:** imagination.
14. **ominous:** like an evil omen, threatening.
15. **divining:** guessing, especially trying to penetrate something mysterious.
16. **censer:** container in which incense is burned.
17. **seraphim** [ser'ə fim]: angels.
18. **respite** [res'pit]: relief.
19. **nepenthe** [ni pen'thē]: drug believed by the ancient Greeks to cause forgetfulness of sorrow.
20. **Quaff** [kwaf]: drink.

The Raven   241

GUIDED READING

LITERAL QUESTIONS

1a. In lines 61–66 what reason does the speaker give as to why the Raven answers *Nevermore?* (He thinks the bird can say only one word, learned from an unhappy master, and that the word's appropriateness is simply coincidental.)

2a. What does the speaker think angels have sent him? ("respite and nepenthe" from his memories of Lenore)

INFERENTIAL QUESTIONS

1b. How do these thoughts reveal the speaker's state of mind? (He wants to find a way to explain the answer without admitting it might be true. His imaginings about the bird's master show how prone he is to gloomy thoughts.)

2b. Why might the speaker want to believe angels have sent him this "respite"? (He is haunted by Lenore's memory and would like to forget her and escape his misery.)

- The speaker asks the bird for reassurance that he will meet Lenore in the hereafter.
- The Raven repeats *Nevermore*.
- The speaker is angry and orders the Raven to leave, but the bird haunts him still.

MAIN IDEA

The speaker asks the central question of the poem: Will he ever be reunited with Lenore (ll. 93–94)?

WORD CHOICE

The powerful image in *Take thy beak from out my heart* allows the reader to feel the speaker's pain when the bird denies him any hope of ever seeing Lenore again (l. 101).

WORD CHOICE

Nevermore, the final word, concludes the poem on a note of hopelessness and grief. The effect of the word on the reader has intensified each time the poet has used it in the poem. Here it echoes in our ears again—like a death knell (l. 108).

REFLECTING ON THE POEM

What do you think the Raven represents in the poem? (Answers will vary. Possibilities: death, gloominess, mystery, fate, an oracle, hopelessness)

STUDY QUESTIONS

1. midnight; nodding, nearly napping over books he's reading
2. loss of Lenore
3. darkness; "Lenore"
4. the bird's name; "Nevermore"
5. only sound it knows, learned from a former, unhappy master

85 "Prophet!" said I, "thing of evil!—prophet still, if bird or devil!—
    Whether Tempter[21] sent, or whether tempest tossed thee here ashore,
    Desolate yet all undaunted, on this desert land enchanted—
    On this home by Horror haunted—tell me truly, I implore—
    Is there—*is* there balm in Gilead?[22]—tell me—tell me, I implore!"
90   Quoth the Raven "Nevermore."

 "Prophet!" said I, "thing of evil!—prophet still, if bird or devil!
    By that Heaven that bends above us—by that God we both adore—
    Tell this soul with sorrow laden if, within the distant Aidenn,[23]
    It shall clasp a sainted maiden whom the angels name Lenore—
95 Clasp a rare and radiant maiden whom the angels name Lenore."
      Quoth the Raven "Nevermore."

 "Be that word our sign of parting, bird or fiend!" I shrieked, upstarting—
    "Get thee back into the tempest and the Night's Plutonian shore!
    Leave no black plume as a token of that lie thy soul hath spoken!
100 Leave my loneliness unbroken!—quit the bust above my door!
    Take thy beak from out my heart and take thy form from off my door!"
      Quoth the Raven "Nevermore."

 And the Raven, never flitting, still is sitting, *still* is sitting
    On the pallid[24] bust of Pallas just above my chamber door;
105 And his eyes have all the seeming of a demon's that is dreaming,
    And the lamplight o'er him streaming throws his shadow on the floor;
    And my soul from out that shadow that lies floating on the floor
      Shall be lifted—nevermore!

---

21. **Tempter:** Satan.
22. **balm in Gilead** [gil′ē əd]: relief of suffering. In the Bible a special healing ointment, or *balm*, was made in Gilead, a region of ancient Palestine.
23. **Aidenn** [ād′ən]: Arabic word for "Eden," or paradise.
24. **pallid:** pale.

STUDY QUESTIONS

Recalling

1. Based on the first three lines, describe when the action occurs and what the speaker is doing when he hears tapping at his door.
2. According to lines 10–11, about what is the speaker feeling sorrow?

3. According to stanzas 4 and 5, when the speaker opens the door, what does he see and what does he whisper?
4. According to lines 43–48, what does the speaker demand to know? What is the bird's response?
5. What logical explanation for the raven's response does the speaker give in lines 62–65?

242 *Poetry*

6. In lines 88–89 what does the speaker beg the bird to tell him?
7. According to the second-to-last stanza, what does the speaker tell the bird to do?
8. According to the last stanza, where does the raven remain?

Interpreting

9. Describe in your own words the speaker's state of mind at the beginning of the poem.
10. What is the speaker's state of mind by the end of the poem? What has caused the change?
11. Describe in your own words the atmosphere created in the poem.
12. What do you think the raven comes to stand for in the speaker's mind?

Extending

13. Poe believed that the most important features of poetry were imagination, emotion, and beautiful sound. Do you think "The Raven" succeeds in emphasizing these elements? Why or why not?

READING AND LITERARY FOCUS

Word Choice

In literature **word choice** is the selection of the right word. Poets choose words carefully to fit the subject. The words should also convey clear images. For example, line 8 of "The Raven" presents a powerful image of a dying fire:

> And each separate dying ember wrought its
>   ghost upon the floor.

Notice, too, that even the choice of the word *separate* is important. It suggests the great sensitivity of a man who notices *individual* pieces of burning wood.

Poets also choose words for sound effects, as Poe often does. *Dreary* and *weary,* for example, do more than describe the night and the speaker in "The Raven." They make a memorable rhyme that adds to the poem's music.

Thinking About Word Choice

■ Choose another line of Poe's "Raven," and tell why the main words in the line are appropriate word choices. (1) Do they convey the meaning clearly? (2) Do they present a vivid image? (3) What do they suggest about the poet's or the speaker's attitude? (4) Are they formal or informal? (5) What sound effect do they create?

COMPOSITION

Writing About Plot

■ Analyze the plot of "The Raven" by discussing its major parts. For example, what is the conflict? Whom is the conflict between? What problems make it difficult for the speaker of "The Raven" to resolve the conflict? How does the poem conclude? *For help with this assignment, see Lesson 2 in the Writing About Literature Handbook at the back of this book.*

Writing a Dialogue

■ Write an eight-line poem that contains a dialogue between two people at the dinner table. You may rhyme each pair of lines if you wish. For example:

> Aunt Mabel asked, "Would you like peas?"
> Her nephew said, "They make me sneeze."

Begin each line with "Aunt Mabel asked" or "Her nephew said." Be sure to use correct punctuation in each line.

CHALLENGE

Diorama

■ A **diorama** is a three-dimensional scene that shows figures in a setting. Using a box as your diorama base, cut away one side. Decorate the other sides, showing the room, door, window, and furniture depicted in "The Raven." Use cardboard to make cutouts of the speaker and the raven. Secure these to the cardboard floor of your diorama so that they will stand up.

The Raven   243

6. "Is there balm in Gilead?" (relief for his suffering)
7. depart, return to the underworld, leave him alone
8. sitting on the bust of Pallas above the chamber door
9. grieving, mourning his lost love
10. anguished; convinced he will never see Lenore even in death
11. melancholic, then ominous, finally despairing
12. death
13. ■ Imagination is emphasized in the visit of the Raven, dialogue with the bird.
   ■ Emotion is emphasized in the speaker's changing states (grief for his lost love, fear of the mysterious raven, hope that he will see his love in death, despair that he will never again see Lenore).
   ■ Beautiful sound is created through repetition (of *-ore* and *-oor*), alliteration, and assonance.

COMPOSITION: GUIDELINES FOR EVALUATION

WRITING ABOUT PLOT

Objective

To analyze the plot of "The Raven"

Guidelines for Evaluation

■ suggested length: one–two paragraphs
■ should describe the conflict
■ should tell why it is difficult for the speaker to resolve his conflict
■ should tell how the poem concludes

WRITING A DIALOGUE

Objective

To write a poem that contains dialogue

Guidelines for Evaluation

■ suggested length: eight lines
■ should contain a dialogue between two people at the dinner table using correct punctuation
■ should begin each line with the speaker's name

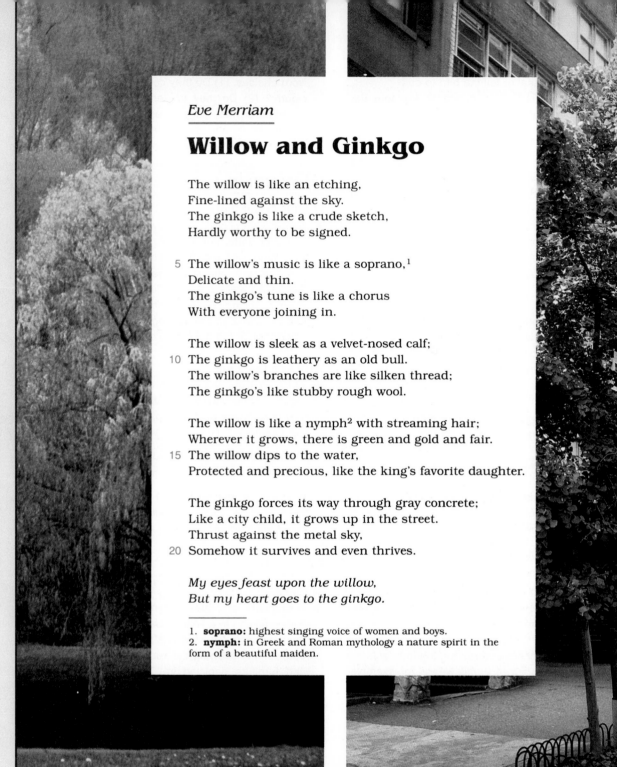

Eve Merriam

Willow and Ginkgo

The willow is like an etching,
Fine-lined against the sky.
The ginkgo is like a crude sketch,
Hardly worthy to be signed.

5 The willow's music is like a soprano,[1]
Delicate and thin.
The ginkgo's tune is like a chorus
With everyone joining in.

The willow is sleek as a velvet-nosed calf;
10 The ginkgo is leathery as an old bull.
The willow's branches are like silken thread;
The ginkgo's like stubby rough wool.

The willow is like a nymph[2] with streaming hair;
Wherever it grows, there is green and gold and fair.
15 The willow dips to the water,
Protected and precious, like the king's favorite daughter.

The ginkgo forces its way through gray concrete;
Like a city child, it grows up in the street.
Thrust against the metal sky,
20 Somehow it survives and even thrives.

My eyes feast upon the willow,
But my heart goes to the ginkgo.

---

1. **soprano:** highest singing voice of women and boys.
2. **nymph:** in Greek and Roman mythology a nature spirit in the form of a beautiful maiden.

STUDY QUESTIONS

Recalling

1. According to stanza 1, which tree is "fine-lined"? Which is "crude"?
2. According to stanza 2, which tree is "delicate"? Which one is not?
3. In stanza 3, to what animals are the trees compared? To what fabrics are they compared?
4. According to stanza 4, which tree "dips to the water"? According to stanza 5, which tree "survives" in the city?
5. According to lines 21–22, upon which tree do the poet's eyes "feast"? To which tree does her heart go?

Interpreting

6. How would you describe the character of each tree based on the poet's comparison?
7. What surprise is provided by the last two lines? Why does the poet place these lines in italics?
8. How does line 20 explain the feelings expressed in the last two lines?

Extending

9. To which of the two trees does your heart go out? Explain your opinion clearly.

READING AND LITERARY FOCUS

Figurative Language: Simile

Figurative language is imaginative language used for descriptive effect. It is not meant to be literally, or factually, true. Instead, figurative language—often called **figures of speech**—helps us to see in new ways what is true. The most common forms of figurative language are the imaginative comparisons called similes and metaphors.

A **simile** is a directly stated comparison that uses the words *like* or *as*. "She runs like a gazelle" and "He runs as fast as a gazelle" are both similes. In "Willow and Ginkgo" the first line is a simile.

Similes focus on the characteristics that two different things have in common. Similes help us to connect images and ideas within a poem. By creating sharp and unusual comparisons, similes also increase a poem's vividness.

Thinking About Similes

■ Identify another simile in "Willow and Ginkgo."

VOCABULARY

Suffixes

A **suffix** is a word element attached to the end of a root word or a base word. For example, the suffix *-dom* added to the base word *free* makes a new word, *freedom*, "the state of being free."

Many suffixes in English come from Latin, French, Greek, and other languages. Knowing exactly what a suffix means can clarify many vocabulary words that might at first look difficult.

Here are some of the most common suffixes:

Suffix	Meaning	Example
-able, -ible	able	visible (able to be seen)
-en	made of, like	golden (made of gold)
-ite	showing, marked by	united (marked by oneness)
-less	without	painless (without pain)
-y	result, action, quality	dusty (having the quality of dust)

All of the following words are taken from Merriam's "Willow and Ginkgo" and from Plath's "Mushrooms" (page 226). Copy them onto a separate sheet of paper. Underline each suffix. Give the meaning of the suffix and the meaning of the full word.

1. worthy
2. silken
3. favorite
4. leathery
5. voiceless
6. edible

Willow and Ginkgo 245

1. willow; ginkgo
2. willow; ginkgo
3. ■ willow: calf; ginkgo: bull
   ■ willow: silk; ginkgo: wool
4. willow; ginkgo
5. willow: ginkgo
6. ■ willow: fine, delicate, graceful, beautiful, protected and precious
   ■ ginkgo: rough, hardy, feisty
7. Poet prefers the ginkgo. Possible answer: She appreciates beauty but feels affection for things that struggle to survive.
8. It shows poet admires ginkgo for not only surviving, but thriving.
9. Answers will vary. Possible answers:
   ■ Gingko: because it is imperfect, unprotected, thriving despite the odds
   ■ Willow: because it is delicate, beautifully shaped, graceful

READING AND LITERARY FOCUS

■ "The willow is like an etching, . . .
The ginkgo is like a crude sketch."
■ "The willow's music is like a soprano, . . .
The ginkgo's tune is like a chorus."
■ "The willow is sleek as a . . . calf;
The ginkgo is leathery as an old bull."
■ "The willow's branches are like . . . thread;
The ginkgo's like . . . wool."
■ "The willow is like a nymph. . . ."
"The willow dips . . . like the King's favorite daughter."
■ "The ginkgo forces its way . . . like a city child."

VOCABULARY

1. *-y* (quality) having worth
2. *-en* (made of) made of silk
3. *-ite* (marked by) treated with favor
4. *-y* (quality) like leather
5. *-less* (without) without a voice
6. *-ible* (able) able to be eaten

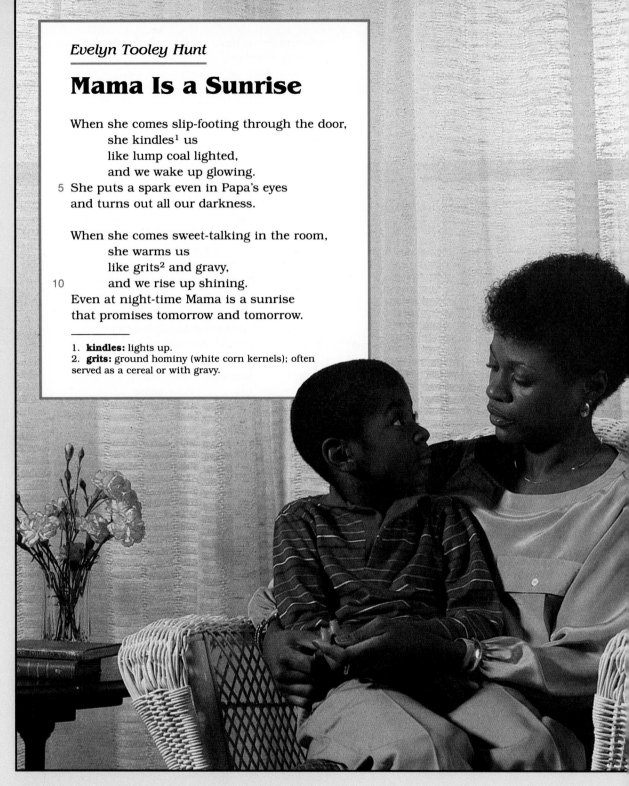

Evelyn Tooley Hunt

Mama Is a Sunrise

When she comes slip-footing through the door,
  she kindles[1] us
  like lump coal lighted,
  and we wake up glowing.
5 She puts a spark even in Papa's eyes
and turns out all our darkness.

When she comes sweet-talking in the room,
  she warms us
  like grits[2] and gravy,
10 and we rise up shining.
Even at night-time Mama is a sunrise
that promises tomorrow and tomorrow.

---

1. **kindles:** lights up.
2. **grits:** ground hominy (white corn kernels); often served as a cereal or with gravy.

STUDY QUESTIONS

Recalling

1. In the title what does Hunt say Mama is?
2. Name three things that Mama does in the first stanza when she comes through the door. Identify two reactions of those around her.
3. Recall three of Mama's actions in the second stanza. Identify the reactions of those around her.

Interpreting

4. Who are the "we" to which the speaker refers? Why do you think the speaker feels able to speak for more than one person?
5. Describe Mama's effect on those around her. What are the speaker's feelings for her?
6. On what time of day does the speaker focus? Where in the poem does the speaker suggest that Mama has a similar influence at other times?
7. What similes does the poet use? What do they add to the emotional force of the poem?

Extending

8. Offer examples to support the old saying, "It is in giving that we receive." How does this statement apply to Mama in Hunt's poem?

READING AND LITERARY FOCUS

Figurative Language: Metaphor

One of the most basic elements of poetry is **figurative language. Figurative language** is imaginative language used for descriptive effect. It is not meant to be taken literally, or word for word. Figurative language—often called **figures of speech**—is the imagination's way of seeing the world in a new light. The most common figures of speech are similes and metaphors.

A **metaphor** is a comparison that equates two seemingly different things. Unlike a simile, a metaphor does not use the words *like* or *as* to make its comparison. For example, "The dragonfly is like a delicate helicopter" is a simile. "The dragonfly is a delicate helicopter" is a metaphor.

Metaphors often make startling, unexpected connections in the world. Because they use language figuratively, making statements that are not literally true, they stretch our imaginations.

Thinking About Metaphor

1. Identify the central metaphor in "Mama Is a Sunrise."
2. What details throughout the poem support and clarify the metaphor?

COMPOSITION

Writing About Imagery

■ Write about the imagery of light in "Mama Is a Sunrise." First identify every word that helps to create an image of light (for example, *sunrise* and *kindles*). Then describe in your own words what these images add to the poem.

Writing with Metaphors

■ Write a four-line poem in which each line contains a metaphor. Have your metaphor compare a feeling to an object. Use the form "____ is ____." For example:

> Sadness is a flower that has wilted.
> Surprise is a birthday gift six months late.

Other feelings you may write about are happiness, embarrassment, confusion, and confidence. *For general help with writing poetry, see Lesson 6 in the Writing About Literature Handbook at the back of this book.*

CHALLENGE

Tribute

■ A **tribute** is a public statement that expresses admiration, love, or thanks. Find a tribute in a book, magazine, or newspaper. Read it to the class and identify the qualities that make the subject worthy of a tribute.

Mama Is a Sunrise 247

LITERARY OPTIONS

- personification
- rhyme

THEMATIC OPTIONS

- nature as a destructive force
- transformation of reality

PERSONIFICATION

Stephens brings the wind to life as a blustering bully who "gave a shout" and "whistled on his fingers" (ll. 1–2).

RHYME SCHEME

The rhyme scheme of the poem is *ab, ab, cc.* The final couplet ends the poem on a dramatic note (ll. 1–6).

REFLECTING ON THE POEM

Do you think the poet is trying to frighten us or make us laugh? (By personifying the wind as a bully, he both acknowledges its destructiveness and mocks it.)

STUDY QUESTIONS

1. stood up, gave a shout, whistle
2. kicks leaves, thumps branches
3. kill
4. hearing
5. harsh fall or winter
6. whatever is in his path
7. awe
8. Possible answers: power to sail vessels or to destroy homes

READING AND LITERARY FOCUS

1. " . . . stood up, and gave a shout"; "He whistled on his fingers"; "Kicked the withered leaves about, / And thumped the branches with his hand"; "And said he'd kill, . . ."
2. strength and vividness

James Stephens

The Wind

The wind stood up, and gave a shout;
He whistled on his fingers, and

Kicked the withered leaves about,
And thumped the branches with his hand,

5 And said he'd kill, and kill, and kill;
And so he will! And so he will!

STUDY QUESTIONS

Recalling

1. According to stanza 1, what actions does the wind perform?
2. According to stanza 2, what does the wind do to the leaves and branches?
3. At the end of the poem, what does the speaker say the wind will do?

Interpreting

4. In lines 1–2 on which of the five senses does the imagery focus?
5. What season is the speaker describing?
6. Who or what will the wind "kill"?
7. Describe in your own words the speaker's attitude toward the wind.

Extending

8. What specific properties of the wind do you think are the most fascinating to people?

READING AND LITERARY FOCUS

Personification

Personification is a figure of speech in which

248 *Poetry*

an animal, object, or idea is given the characteristics of a person. For example, when we use the expressions Mother Nature and Father Time we are using personifications.

Personification is another way that figurative language puts our imaginations to work. By giving human qualities to what is nonhuman, we enable ourselves to enjoy and understand the whole world more fully.

Thinking About Personification

1. Identify the words in "The Wind" that give human qualities to the wind.
2. What do you think is gained by describing the wind in this way?

COMPARING POEMS

- Choose any two poems from this section (pages 235–248), and compare their use of language. Describe how each poem uses vivid words, concrete imagery, and figures of speech (simile, metaphor, and personification). In each case, point out how the language fits the author's subject. Be sure to give examples to support your comparisons.

COMPARING POEMS

- "When Icicles": Vivid imagery contrasts the cold outdoors ("blood is nipped, and ways be foul" with the warm indoors).
- "The Raven": musical language ("lost Lenore") creates a haunting quality befitting a mysterious story.

- "Willow and Ginkgo": Similes contrast the trees and provide vivid images appropriate to each: "sleek as a velvet-nosed calf"; "leathery as an old bull."
- "Mama Is a Sunrise": Metaphors of light emphasize warm feelings about Mama: "She kindles us."

- "The Wind"; Vivid verbs like *kicked* and *thumped* suit this celebration of wind's power.

THE FORM OF POETRY

Like a painting or a statue, every poem has form. The **form** of a poem is its overall structure and organization. Form is created by patterns in a poem's sounds and images and ideas as well as by the way the words are placed on the page. At first we usually notice the sound of a poem or the language it uses. However, the form is a fundamental part of our experience of the whole poem.

Poems can have closed form or open form. Poems are said to be **closed** when they follow strict, traditional patterns of rhythm, rhyme, number of syllables, number of lines, length, and so on. Poems are said to be **open** when they have no formal groupings of lines; in these poems the poet has more freedom to create a new form that will fit the subject of the poem.

Poets who write in closed forms are like dancers who follow patterns of painted footprints on the floor but who also move naturally and gracefully. Poets who write in open forms are like dancers who create new movements to fit new moods and new music. In the following section you will see some of the ways poets give form to their words.

TEXAS ESSENTIAL ELEMENTS
GRADE 8
1A writing process
1B purpose and audience
1C supporting main idea
1I word choice
2C affixes to change words
3B figurative language and sound devices
3D literary genres
4C fact *vs.* nonfact
To locate treatment of an Element, see *Texas Teacher's Resources.*

William Stafford (born 1914) grew up in the American Midwest, where he worked on farms and for the United States Forest Service. Stafford's writing, however, is closely associated with the Pacific Northwest, where he has lived and taught for many years. In simple, songlike language Stafford describes the close relationship between nature and people.

■ As you read "Mouse Night," notice that only two lines of the poem end with full stops, or periods.

See page 221 for biographical information about Robert Frost. One writer said that Frost "has the good sense to speak naturally and to paint the thing, the thing as he sees it." In "A Minor Bird" Frost uses plain speech to paint a simple scene.

■ Notice that the form he uses is as simple as his subject.

Poetry 249

Theodore Roethke (1908–1963), a native of Michigan, taught English and coached tennis at several colleges. Roethke's poems often observe nature closely. His method is not surprising, since he spent much of his childhood observing the plants in the greenhouses where his father worked as a florist. Roethke is known for his strict control of form.

■ In "The Heron" notice how Roethke uses three separate groups of lines to show three aspects of this long-legged bird.

Lewis Carroll (1832–1898) was the pen name of Charles Lutwidge Dodgson. Dodgson was a professor of mathematics at Oxford University in England, where he wrote mathematics texts. He is best remembered, however, for his books *Alice in Wonderland* and *Through the Looking Glass.*

■ In "The Walrus and the Carpenter" notice that the poet uses a regular form to tell a very unusual, humorous tale.

■ As you read Edwin A. Hoey's "Foul Shot," notice how the poet has shaped the lines of the poem so that the form suggests what the poem is about.

William Stafford

Mouse Night: One of Our Games

We heard thunder. Nothing great—on high
ground rain began. Who ran through
that rain? I shrank, a fieldmouse, when
the thunder came—under grass with bombs
5 of water scything[1] stems. My tremendous
father cowered:[2] "Lions rushing make
that sound," he said; "we'll be brain-washed
for sure if head-size chunks of water hit us.
Duck and cover! It takes a man
10 to be a mouse this night," he said.

---

1. **scything** [sīth′ing]: cutting like a scythe, a long
curved blade used in harvesting grain.
2. **cowered:** bent low in fear.

LITERARY OPTIONS

- poetic form and meaning
- speaker

THEMATIC OPTIONS

- courage
- wisdom

FORM AND MEANING

The line breaks in the first two lines do not coincide with the punctuation. Readers should pause at punctuation rather than line breaks to clarify the poem's meaning and rhythm.

SPEAKER

The speaker is an adult describing a memorable night from his childhood. "My tremendous father" expresses a small boy's admiration of his father (ll. 3–6).

MAIN IDEA

These lines present the main idea: Sometimes true courage is admitting danger and having the wisdom to avoid it (ll. 9–10).

REFLECTING ON THE POEM

How does the title help us understand the poem? (The phrase *One of Our Games* alerts us that what we are reading a poem about is a playful childhood pastime.)

STUDY QUESTIONS

1. thunder
2. shrinks, pulls into himself
3. cowers
4. lions rushing
5. "Duck and cover!"
6. ■ *bombs, scything stems, Lions rushing make / that sound, Duck and cover!*
   ■ all of them
7. ■ a hiding game—field mice being chased by lions
   ■ close, to share an imaginary game
8. Most students will say that the poem praises the courage needed to face danger and the wisdom to know when to hide.
9. Answers will vary. Possible answers: Nursery rhymes teach children language; peekaboo teaches infants that people can go out of sight and reappear; games enable children to try out adult roles.

READING AND LITERARY FOCUS

1. Discuss the poet's use of punctuation in the middle or at the end of lines. Have students practice reading the poem aloud.
2. The meaning and music come from the description and dialogue, which are both clearer when the reader observes the punctuation.

CHALLENGE

Students should
■ choose a current or historical event in which someone displayed courage
■ gather information about this subject from outside sources
■ organize this information into a report to be presented in class

STUDY QUESTIONS

Recalling

1. As the poem begins, what does the speaker say he and his father heard?
2. According to lines 3–4, what does the speaker do when he hears the noise?
3. According to lines 5–6, what does the speaker's father do?
4. According to lines 6–7, to what does the father compare the noise?
5. As the poem ends, what advice does the father give?

Interpreting

6. Which words in the poem suggest danger? Which of these words are exaggerations?
7. What is the game that the father and son play? Based on this game, how would you describe their relationship?
8. Do you think this is a poem about courage? Cowardice? Wisdom? Explain your opinion fully.

Extending

9. Describe another game that has a serious purpose behind it.

READING AND LITERARY FOCUS

Reading a Line of Poetry

As you have seen, the "music" of a poem is an essential part of its meaning. However, that music can be easily lost if a reader does not pay close attention to the form of each line.

Some readers make the mistake of stopping at the end of each line whether or not there is a punctuation mark signaling them to do so. Some readers hardly stop at all, running each line into the next. The skillful reader, however, notices signs that the poet uses to show how the poem should be read.

Stop at the end of a line with a period, question mark, or exclamation point. Slow down if a line ends with a comma or a semicolon. These lines are called **end-stopped lines.**

If a line ends with no punctuation, the poet intends you to read without pausing, moving on smoothly to the next line. These lines are called **run-on lines.**

Sometimes the rhythm of a poem is so strong that it forces the reader to slow down or even stop at the end of every line. With this kind of poem—like Frost's "Stopping by Woods on a Snowy Evening" (page 230)—it is important to let the rhythm have its way without making the poem sound dull and singsong.

In general, read for the meaning in a poem. That is, read a poem in sentences. By doing so you will avoid the too-regular, singsong effect. You will also release more of a poem's natural music.

Thinking About Reading a Line of Poetry

1. Read "Mouse Night" aloud, stopping when the punctuation or meaning indicates you should. Read the run-on lines smoothly.
2. Tell how reading the poem in this way makes both the meaning and the music clearer.

CHALLENGE

Research and Oral Report

■ Research a real-life event from history or current events in which someone showed courage. Report to the class about the person's courageous actions and your reactions.

Robert Frost

A Minor Bird

I have wished a bird would fly away,
And not sing by my house all day;

Have clapped my hands at him from the door
When it seemed as if I could bear no more.

5 The fault must partly have been in me.
The bird was not to blame for his key.

And of course there must be something wrong
In wanting to silence any song.

STUDY QUESTIONS

Recalling

1. What two things has the speaker wished?
2. When did the speaker clap his hands?
3. For what is the bird not to blame?
4. What does the speaker think must be wrong?

Interpreting

5. What was the speaker's attitude toward the singing bird, according to lines 1–4? What is the speaker's attitude in lines 5–8?
6. Which meaning of the word *minor* do you think the poet intends?
7. What is the "something" the speaker thinks is "wrong"? Why does he think so?

READING AND LITERARY FOCUS

The Couplet

The most obvious aspect of form in a poem is the way its lines are grouped. One group is the **couplet,** two consecutive lines that usually rhyme.

The lines of a couplet usually rhyme, have the same length and rhythm, and combine to express a single, complete thought.

Thinking About the Couplet

■ Identify each of the couplets in "A Minor Bird." What complete thought does each express?

COMPOSITION

Writing About Rhythm

■ Write about the rhythm of "A Minor Bird." First tell whether the rhythm is regular or irregular. Then tell why the rhythm is appropriate in a poem that tries to teach a simple and memorable lesson.

Writing a Couplet

■ Write a couplet using the first two lines of "A Minor Bird" as a model. Begin the first line with "I have wished." Make the two lines rhyme, and have them combine to express a single complete thought.

A Minor Bird 253

LITERARY OPTIONS

- quatrain
- word choice

THEMATIC OPTIONS

- grace vs. awkwardness
- nature

QUATRAIN

The first four lines, describing a standing heron, form a quatrain. The quatrain is unified by the rhyme scheme *abab* and by a rhythm of five stressed syllables per line (ll. 1–4).

WORD CHOICE

"Antic grace" suggests both the gracefulness and awkwardness of the heron (l. 5).

SPEAKER

The speaker is a close observer and an admirer of nature. The speaker's observations and descriptions are careful and exact; for example, the phrase "bony lip" creates an immediate physical image of the bird's mouth.

REFLECTING ON THE POEM

In what way is this poem like a short movie? (Three different "scenes" portray the heron, each with a different type of action and mood. Those scenes create a sequence of images we can follow from beginning to end.)

Theodore Roethke

The Heron

The heron stands in water where the swamp
Has deepened to the blackness of a pool,
Or balances with one leg on a hump
Of marsh grass heaped above a muskrat[1] hole.

5　He walks the shallow with an antic[2] grace.
The great feet break the ridges of the sand,
The long eye notes the minnow's[3] hiding place.
His beak is quicker than a human hand.

He jerks a frog across his bony lip,
10　Then points his heavy bill above the wood.
The wide wings flap but once to lift him up.
A single ripple starts from where he stood.

---

1. **muskrat:** brown furry rodent often found near swamps.
2. **antic:** comical or clownish.
3. **minnow's:** A minnow is a very small fish.

254　*Poetry*

STUDY QUESTIONS

Recalling

1. According to stanza 1, where does the heron stand?
2. According to stanza 2, how does the heron walk? What do his feet and eyes do?
3. According to stanza 3, what does the heron do as he begins to fly? What remains "where he stood"?

Interpreting

4. Identify the heron's action described in each of the three stanzas of the poem.
5. Which words or images in the poem suggest the heron's size? Its skill? Its power?
6. What does the phrase "antic grace" tell about the bird? What balance of qualities in the bird does it describe?
7. What is the poet's attitude toward the heron? How can you tell?

Extending

8. What other animals demonstrate an unusual balance of qualities—for example, size and speed or beauty and awkwardness?

READING AND LITERARY FOCUS

The Quatrain

A **quatrain** is a group of four consecutive lines of poetry. The word *quatrain* comes from *quattuor,* the Latin word for "four."

Frequently, particularly in traditional poetry, the four lines of a quatrain are similar in length, rhythm, and end rhymes. Re-examine, for example, the first quatrain of Frost's "Stopping by Woods on a Snowy Evening":

> Whose woods these are I think I know.
> His house is in the village, though;
> He will not see me stopping here
> To watch his woods fill up with snow.

This quatrain, like the others in Frost's poem, has a definite pattern of rhyme, and there are four stressed syllables, or beats, per line. The lines are also similar in length.

Sometimes, however, the four lines of a quatrain do not share these similarities. Look at this quatrain from Merriam's "Willow and Ginkgo":

> The ginkgo forces its way through gray
>   concrete;
> Like a city child, it grows up in the street.
> Thrust against the metal sky,
> Somehow it survives and even thrives.

There are differences or irregularities in the end words, rhythms, and lengths of the four lines of this quatrain. What makes the line group a quatrain, then, is the fact that these four lines are "packaged" together apart from the rest of the poem.

Thinking About Quatrains

■ Locate each of Roethke's quatrains. How are they alike in line length, rhythm, or rhyme scheme? How are they different?

CHALLENGE

Illustration

■ A **triptych** is a set of three hinged panels with a picture on each panel. Make a triptych of Roethke's poem by bending a large piece of cardboard. Decorate each panel with an illustration of what happens in the poem. Do one panel for each stanza.

The Heron 255

STUDY QUESTIONS

1. in swamp water or on marsh grass above a muskrat hole
2. with antic (ludicrous) grace; feet break the sand's ridges, eyes note the minnow's hiding place
3. flaps wings once to lift up; a single ripple
4. ■ Stanza 1: stands
   ■ Stanza 2: walks, looks for food
   ■ Stanza 3: eats, flies away
5. ■ Size: *great feet, long eye, heavy bill, wide wings*
   ■ Skill: *notes the minnow's hiding place, His beak is quicker than a human hand*
   ■ Power: *He jerks a frog across his bony lip, The wide wings flap but once to lift him up.*
6. ■ Its beauty has a comic quality.
   ■ grace and awkwardness
7. ■ admiration
   ■ Description indicates detailed observation and includes primarily admirable traits.
8. Possible answers: Elephants have size and speed; Giraffes and tortoises are beautiful and awkward.

READING AND LITERARY FOCUS

■ Alike: line length, rhyme scheme: Lines 1 and 3 and lines 2 and 4 rhyme.
■ Different: rhythm: Stressed syllables per line vary.

CHALLENGE

Students should
■ bend a piece of cardboard into three equal segments
■ portray the heron in water on the first segment, then walking, then flying

Lewis Carroll

The Walrus and the Carpenter

The sun was shining on the sea,
  Shining with all his might:
He did his very best to make
  The billows smooth and bright—
5 And this was odd, because it was
  The middle of the night.

The moon was shining sulkily,
  Because she thought the sun
Had got no business to be there
10 After the day was done—
"It's very rude of him," she said,
  "To come and spoil the fun!"

The sea was wet as wet could be,
  The sands were dry as dry.
15 You could not see a cloud, because
  No cloud was in the sky:
No birds were flying overhead—
  There were no birds to fly.

The Walrus and the Carpenter
20 Were walking close at hand:
They wept like anything to see
  Such quantities of sand:
"If this were only cleared away,"
  They said, "it *would* be grand!"

25 "If seven maids with seven mops
  Swept it for half a year,
Do you suppose," the Walrus said,
  "That they could get it clear?"
"I doubt it," said the Carpenter,
30 And shed a bitter tear.

"O Oysters, come and walk with us!"
  The Walrus did beseech.
"A pleasant talk, a pleasant walk,
  Along the briny beach:
35 We cannot do with more than four,
  To give a hand to each."

The eldest Oyster winked his eye,
  But never a word he said.
The eldest Oyster winked his eye,
40 And shook his heavy head—
Meaning to say he did not choose
  To leave the oyster bed.

But four young Oysters hurried up,
  All eager for the treat:
45 Their coats were brushed, their faces washed,
  Their shoes were clean and neat—
And this was odd, because, you know,
  They hadn't any feet.

Four other Oysters followed them,
50 And yet another four;
And thick and fast they came at last,
  And more, and more, and more—
All hopping through the frothy waves,
  And scrambling to the shore.

55 The Walrus and the Carpenter
  Walked on a mile or so,
And then they rested on a rock
  Conveniently low:
And all the little oysters stood
60 And waited in a row.

256 *Poetry*

GUIDED READING

LITERAL QUESTION

1a. What did the eldest Oyster do when invited for a walk? (He winked his eye, didn't say anything, and shook his head.)

INFERENTIAL QUESTION

1b. What purpose does this scene serve in the poem? (The image of an oyster doing these things is humorous; these actions also foreshadow the coming events. They suggest that the eldest Oyster has wisely learned not to trust strangers.)

"The time has come," the Walrus said,
  "To talk of many things:
Of shoes—and ships—and sealing-wax—
  Of cabbages—and kings—
65 And why the sea is boiling hot—
  And whether pigs have wings."

"But wait a bit," the Oysters cried,
  "Before we have our chat;
For some of us are out of breath,
70   And all of us are fat!"
"No hurry!" said the Carpenter.
  They thanked him much for that.

"A loaf of bread," the Walrus said,
  "Is what we chiefly need:
75 Pepper and vinegar besides
  Are very good indeed—
Now if you're ready, Oysters dear,
  We can begin to feed."

"But not on us!" the Oysters cried,
80   Turning a little blue.
"After such kindness, that would be
  A dismal thing to do!"
"The night is fine," the Walrus said.
  "Do you admire the view?

85 "It was so kind of you to come!
  And you are very nice!"
The Carpenter said nothing but
  "Cut us another slice.
I wish you were not quite so deaf—
90   I've had to ask you twice!"

"It seems a shame," the Walrus said,
  "To play them such a trick,
After we've brought them out so far,
  And made them trot so quick!"
95 The Carpenter said nothing but
  "The butter's spread too thick!"

"I weep for you," the Walrus said:
  "I deeply sympathize."
With sobs and tears he sorted out
100   Those of the largest size,
Holding his pocket handkerchief
  Before his streaming eyes.

"O Oysters," said the Carpenter,
  "You've had a pleasant run!
105 Shall we be trotting home again?"
  But answer came there none—
And this was scarcely odd, because
  They'd eaten every one.

The Walrus and the Carpenter 257

1. along the briny beach
2. their shoes—they have no feet
3. shoes, ships, sealing wax, cabbages, kings, why the sea is boiling hot, whether pigs have wings
4. loaf of bread, pepper, vinegar
5. ■ "But not on us! . . . / After such kindness, that would be / A dismal thing to do!"
   ■ "It was so kind of you to come! / And you are very nice!"
6. "I weep for you, . . . / I deeply sympathize"; sobs, holds his handkerchief before his eyes, sorts out the largest oysters
7. They have all been eaten.
8. They become the Walrus and Carpenter's dinner after accepting their invitation to walk along the beach.
9. ■ emotional: cry easily; sly: tricked Oysters
   ■ Walrus
   ■ Carpenter, who complains about asking twice for bread and the thickness of butter on it
10. Possible answers:
    ■ Personification: The moon shone sulkily and complained about the sun.
    ■ Contradiction: Oysters wore shoes but had no feet.
    ■ Exaggeration: Sympathetic Walrus sobbed for the Oysters.
    ■ Insignificant or nonsensical details: "If seven maids with seven mops / Swept it for half a year, / Do you suppose, . . . / That they could get it clear?"
11. Answers will vary. Most will agree that people like to laugh at skillful, humorous works.

READING AND LITERARY FOCUS

- Rhyme scheme: lines 2, 4, and 6 of each stanza rhyme.
- Rhythm: lines 1, 3, and 5 of each stanza, four stressed beats; lines 2, 4, and 6, three

STUDY QUESTIONS

Recalling

1. According to lines 31–34, where does the Walrus ask the Oysters to walk?
2. Based on lines 43–48, what is "odd" about the young Oysters?
3. What do the Walrus and the Carpenter plan to talk about, according to lines 61–66?
4. What necessary items are mentioned in lines 73–76?
5. What do the Oysters cry out in lines 79–86? What does the Walrus reply?
6. What does the Walrus say in lines 97–98? What does he do in lines 99–102?
7. At the end of the poem, why is it "scarcely odd" that the Oysters do not reply?

Interpreting

8. Describe in your own words the trick played on the Oysters.
9. Describe the personalities of the Walrus and the Carpenter. Which one talks more? Which one seems more interested in food?
10. Carroll uses many different techniques to create the humorous, ridiculous effect of the poem. Find at least one example of each of the following methods used to create this effect: personification, contradiction, exaggeration, insignificant or nonsensical details.

Extending

11. Why do you think people enjoy poems, stories, and other works of art that are pure nonsense?

READING AND LITERARY FOCUS

The Stanza

A **stanza** is a group of lines forming a unit in a poem. It usually contains between two and eight lines, although there are traditional stanzas of up to sixteen lines. The couplet and the quatrain are types of stanzas.

Frequently the stanza has a definite rhyme scheme and similar rhythms in each of its lines. One stanza is separated from the others by a space before its first line and after its last line.

Sometimes the division between stanzas is made according to thought as well as form. In such cases stanzas serve the function that paragraphs do in prose, indicating changes in subject, focus, time, or speaker.

Thinking About Stanzas

■ Examine Carroll's stanzas in "The Walrus and the Carpenter." What similarities do you find in rhyme scheme and rhythm?

VOCABULARY

Roots

The **root** of a word is its core, or main part. It is the central portion of a word, to which either prefixes or suffixes may be attached. For example, the word *conductor* is made up of the central root *-duct-,* meaning "lead," plus the prefix *con-,* meaning "together," and the suffix *-or,* meaning "one who."

Here is a list of some common Greek and Latin roots now used in the English language:

Root	Meaning	Example
-agr-	field	agriculture
-aqu-	water	aquarium
-ben-	good	benefit
-mal-	evil	malice
-path-	feeling	pathetic
-tele-	distant	telephone
-ven-	gather, come	convention
-zo-	animal	zoo

■ Copy down the words *conveniently, dismal,* and *sympathize,* all of which appear in Carroll's "Walrus and the Carpenter." Underline the root of each word. Beside the word write both the meaning of the root and the meaning of the complete word.

VOCABULARY

- (-*ven,* come): easily done
- (-*mal,* evil): miserable
- (-*path,* feeling): feel compassion

Edwin A. Hoey

Foul Shot

With two 60's stuck on the scoreboard
And two seconds hanging on the clock,
The solemn boy in the center of eyes,
Squeezed by silence,
5 Seeks out the line with his feet,
Soothes his hands along his uniform,
Gently drums the ball against the floor,
Then measures the waiting net,
Raises the ball on his right hand,
10 Balances it with his left,
Calms it with fingertips,
Breathes,
Crouches,
Waits,
15 And then through a stretching of stillness,
Nudges it upward.

The ball
Slides up and out,
Lands,
20 Leans,
Wobbles,
Wavers,
Hesitates,
Exasperates,
25 Plays it coy
Until every face begs with unsounding screams—
And then

       And then

          And then,

30 Right before ROAR-UP,
Dives down and through.

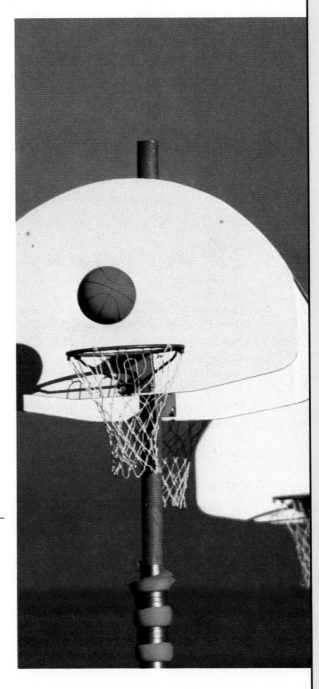

Foul Shot 259

AT A GLANCE

- The score of the basketball game is tied, and time is almost up.
- Tension mounts as a player prepares for a foul shot and finally throws the ball.
- He scores.

LITERARY OPTIONS

- free verse
- word choice
- repetition

THEMATIC OPTIONS

- competing and winning
- grace under pressure

MAIN IDEA

Contrasting images show the profile of a winner. The first three lines show a nervous boy; the next nine show how, despite nervousness, he has the control to function well (ll. 5–16).

FREE VERSE

Free verse allows Hoey to use lines of any length. In lines 19–24 he uses a series of one-word lines to create tiny but discrete spaces that heighten the tension and parallel the moment-by-moment actions of the ball.

WORD CHOICE

Logically impossible, "unsounding screams" nonetheless captures both the open-mouthed look on the faces of the spectators and their inner state (l. 26).

REPETITION

The repetition of lines creates suspense by delaying the outcome of the foul shot and adds to the mood of tension Hoey has sustained from the beginning (ll. 27–29).

REFLECTING ON THE POEM

Do you think the poem captures the feeling of a suspenseful basketball game? If so, how? (The poet creates suspense chiefly through the various line lengths; word choice helps too.)

1. tied at 60; two
2. drums it against the floor, raises it with his right hand, balances it with his left, calms it with his fingertips
3. breathes, crouches, waits
4. tense, anticipative
5. "ROAR-UP"
6. lines 5, 6, and 7; lines 8–16
7. He succeeds; his team wins.
8. *Squeezed by silence; a stretching of stillness; un-sounding screams*
9. The ball is personified as someone deciding where to land. The first two lines use near repetition and parallel structure.
10. Answers will vary. Students might use sports, political, and entertainment examples.

READING AND LITERARY FOCUS

1. One-word lines suggest speed of the boy and ball.
2. Word placement imitates the ball's movement as it circles the rim before going through the basket.

STUDY QUESTIONS

Recalling

1. At the beginning of the poem, what is the score of the game? How many seconds are left?
2. What does the boy do to the ball in lines 7–11?
3. According to lines 12–14, what does the boy do just before he shoots?
4. According to lines 24–26, how does the ball make the crowd feel?
5. What sound is heard just after the ball "dives down and through"?

Interpreting

6. Which lines in the poem suggest that the boy is nervous? Which lines suggest that he is controlled?
7. Does the boy succeed or fail at making the shot? What do you think is the outcome of the game?
8. Which words in lines 4, 15, and 26 describe the sound of the crowd before the "ROAR-UP"?
9. How does the poet use personification to add to the drama of the poem? How does the poet use repetition to add to the tension and suspense?

Extending

10. Do you think people perform better or worse under pressure? Give examples to support your answer.

READING AND LITERARY FOCUS

Free Verse

Free verse is poetry that has irregular rhythms and line lengths. It seldom rhymes and usually imitates the way we speak, without counting stressed and unstressed syllables.

A free-verse poem may combine quick rhythms and slow ones. It may have short stanzas, long

ones, a combination of the two, or no stanzas at all. Lines may be grouped in free verse, but a group does not have a fixed number of lines. They are grouped because of the natural breaks the poet wants to make in rhythm, imagery, form, or meaning.

Free verse allows a poet to fit sounds, rhythms, and line arrangements to the meaning of a poem. However, you should not think that free verse is easy to write. In fact, one great modern poet remarked, "No verse is free." The free-verse poet must create new forms instead of using traditional ones.

"Foul Shot" creates its own form to suggest the experience of a basketball game. Notice how in lines 1–16 each line focuses our attention on one single fact or action. Sometimes this requires several words:

Gently drums the ball against the floor.

Sometimes this focus needs only one word in a line, each followed by a pause:

Breathes,
Crouches,
Waits.

The result is tension and surprise. As we read the poem, we too breathe and crouch and wait. The form of the poem helps convey its meaning.

Thinking About Free Verse

1. Why does the poet use some one-word lines?
2. Why does he make lines 27–29 move forward and drop down across the page?

VOCABULARY

Word Origins

The origin and history of a word is called its **etymology.** You can locate the etymology of a word in the dictionary by looking for the information that appears in brackets—[ ]—just before or after its definition. For example, the word *coy,* which appears in "Foul Shot," has a history that is listed as follows in the dictionary:

coy (koi) *adj.* 1. shy; modest; bashful. 2. pretending to be shy; coquettishly modest or bashful. [Old French *coi,* earlier *quei* calm, quiet, going back to Latin *quiētus.* Doublet of QUIET.] **—coy′ly,** *adv.* **—coy′ness,** *n.*

—Scribner Dictionary

The bracketed information includes the facts that at an earlier time, in the Old French, the word *coy* had a somewhat different form. Earlier still the Latin form of the word was quite different from today's English word.

■ Use a good dictionary to look up the words *solemn, seek, hesitate,* and *exasperate,* all of which appear in Hoey's poem. On a separate sheet of paper, write down what you discover about the history of each. Include all of the languages, spellings, and meanings that your dictionary lists for each.

COMPOSITION

Writing About Free Verse

■ State your opinion of free verse. Begin by stating whether free verse is more enjoyable or less enjoyable to read than traditional poetry. Then support your opinion with examples from poems you have read.

Writing Free Verse

■ Think of a favorite place you like to visit. Write a description of the location and tell what you do there. Then arrange your sentences as a free-verse poem. For example, "The frothy ocean waves come crashing onto the beach" may be rewritten in free-verse form, as follows:

The frothy ocean waves
Come crashing
Onto the beach.

For general help with writing poetry, see Lesson 6 in the Writing About Literature Handbook at the back of this book.

CHALLENGE

Literary Criticism

■ Find a newspaper or magazine description of the actions of an athlete during a game or sport. Read the description to the class, and tell why it is effective or why it fails to capture the experience. You may want to consider the following questions: Is the description concrete? Is it detailed? Are the words vivid? Is the movement of the athlete clear?

COMPARING POEMS

■ Compare the form of any two poems in this section (pages 249–261). In your comparison, consider the following questions:

1. Which form is more strict?
2. What is the rhyme scheme of each poem?
3. Is the rhythm regular or irregular?
4. Which poem has the most dramatic visual impact on the page?
5. In which poem does form convey meaning more clearly?

VOCABULARY

- from Latin *sollemnis,* established, religious; from *sollus,* whole, + *annus,* year
- from Old English *secan,* to look for, ask for
- from Latin *haesitatus,* past participle of *haesitare,* to stick fast, be undecided; from *haerere,* to stick
- from Latin *exasperatus,* past participle of *exasperare,* to make rough, provoke; going back to *ex,* utterly, + *asper,* rough

COMPARING POEMS

- "Mouse Night: One of Our Games": open form, fitting for the recollection of a past event; no end rhymes; conversational rhythm
- "A Minor Bird": strict form, fitting for retelling of a simple moral tale; couplet; *aa bb cc dd* rhyme scheme; regular rhythm
- "The Heron": strict form—appropriate, as each stanza describes a new activity; *abab cdcd efef* rhyme scheme; regular rhythm
- "The Walrus and the Carpenter": lines 2, 4, and 6 in each stanza rhyme; regular rhythm; strict form to tell story clearly
- "Foul Shot": open form to fit the meaning; irregular rhythm, no rhyme scheme; dramatic visual impact to mimic the ball's path

CHALLENGE

Students should
- select a newspaper or magazine article describing an athlete's actions
- explain whether the description is concrete, detailed, vivid, and clear

COMPOSITION: GUIDELINES FOR EVALUATION

WRITING ABOUT FREE VERSE

Objective

To express an opinion about free verse

Guidelines for Evaluation
- suggested length: one to two paragraphs
- should state whether free verse is more or less enjoyable to read than traditional verse
- should support the opinion with examples from several poems

WRITING FREE VERSE

Objective

To write a poem in free verse

Guidelines for Evaluation
- suggested length: five to ten lines
- should describe a favorite place
- should tell what the writer does there
- should arrange lines in free verse form
- should include punctuation to guide readers

Foul Shot T-261

TEXAS ESSENTIAL ELEMENTS
GRADE 8

1A writing process
1B purpose and audience
1C support for main idea
1E appropriate language
1H grammatical conventions
1I word choice
2C affixes to change words
3A plot development
3B figurative language and sound devices
3C setting and mood
3D literary genres
4B implied main idea
4D sequential order
4F point of view
4K library references
To locate treatment of an Element, see *Texas Teacher's Resources.*

THE MEANING OF POETRY

The **meaning** of a poem is the idea it communicates. Sometimes the idea is stated as directly as the message on a greeting card. Sometimes the idea appears gradually as a poem unfolds. In such a poem the poet relies on you, the reader, to pay close attention to the details of the poem and to help bring out the meaning. In all poems, however, it is important to remember that the meaning may not be a message at all but rather a story, an expression of emotion, or some combination of the two.

E. V. Rieu [rē ū′] (1887–1972) was born in England and educated at Oxford University. In addition to writing poems of his own, Rieu became well known as a translator.

■ As you read "Night Thought of a Tortoise Suffering from Insomnia on a Lawn," think about the relationship between the title and the body of the poem. The word *insomnia* in the title means "the inability to fall asleep."

Henry Wadsworth Longfellow's (1807–1882) famous story-poems of America's past, such as "The Song of Hiawatha" and "Paul Revere's Ride," are still exciting to read. Paul Revere (1735–1818) was the American revolutionary hero who rode from Boston to Lexington and Concord to warn his fellow colonists that "the British are coming!"

■ As you read "Paul Revere's Ride," notice how the poet uses rhythm and rhyme while telling a story at the same time.

Sir Walter Scott (1771–1832) was born in Edinburgh, Scotland. Stricken with polio, he went to live with his grandfather in the Border country of Scotland, where Scotland and England meet. He grew up hearing romantic Scottish tales of castles, knights, and ladies. In his novels, such as *Ivanhoe*, and his poems, such as "Lochinvar," he demonstrates his love for past times.

■ Notice how the galloping rhythm of "Lochinvar" adds to its excitement.

Emily Brontë (1818–1848), the daughter of an Irish-born clergyman, grew up in Yorkshire, England. She is best known for her novel *Wuthering Heights*, though she also wrote many highly emotional poems.

■ Notice that the speaker of "Spellbound" does not tell a story but, rather, has an intense reaction.

Langston Hughes (1902–1967) was born in Missouri and raised in Kansas. He spent much of his life in New York City, where he wrote poems, plays, histories, and short stories. Hughes is best known, however, for adapting the rhythms of African and Afro-American music to poetry.

■ Notice the simplicity Hughes achieves in his lyric "The Dream Keeper," expressing strong emotion in the clearest words.

Mark Van Doren (1894–1972) was born in Illinois. After serving in the Army during World War I, he worked as a professor of English literature until 1959. In 1940 he was awarded the Pulitzer Prize for his *Collected Poems*.

■ As you read "The Story-Teller" by Van Doren, consider the general statement the poet is making about the story-teller and his amazing power.

■ As you read "I Am the Land. I Wait." by Mexican-American poet Marina de Bellagente, notice that its meaning depends on the voice that is speaking it.

Poetry 263

- title
- couplet
- rhythm

- communication
- discoveries

TITLE

The relatively lengthy title establishes the speaker, situation, and setting. The length and complexity of the title—especially when compared to the brevity of the poem itself—contribute to the humor.

RHYTHM

Ten of the poem's eleven words consist of a single syllable, creating a slow, ponderous rhythm that parallels the tortoise's thoughts and movements.

COUPLET

The poem's two lines form a couplet that is a complete thought. The matching rhythm of the lines adds unity to the couplet.

REFLECTING ON THE POEM

In what ways is the poem humorous? (The situation described in the title is intrinsically humorous. The tortoise's comment is amusing. There is humor in the first line, which is true only from the tortoise's perspective.)

E. V. Rieu

Night Thought of a Tortoise Suffering from Insomnia on a Lawn

The world is very flat—
There is no doubt of that.

STUDY QUESTIONS

Recalling

1. According to the title, when and where does the poem take place?
2. From what does the tortoise suffer?
3. Of what does the tortoise have no doubt?

Interpreting

4. What do you think a tortoise on a lawn would be able to see? What does the tortoise exaggerate in line 1?
5. Based on the tortoise's "night thought," how would you describe the tortoise's mood, or state of mind?
6. What is funny about the tortoise's conclusion?

READING AND LITERARY FOCUS

The Title as Part of the Poem

The **title** of a poem is its name. The word *title* comes from a Latin word meaning "label." The title of a poem is a kind of introduction that labels what is going to follow. It can give clues to meaning, introduce character or speaker, create imagery, set up the poem's emotions, or provide organization. Like the sign on the front of a movie theater, the title of a poem is what first grabs the attention and the eye of the reader.

A title may repeat a poem's first line, as in Shakespeare's "When Icicles Hang by the Wall" (page 237). It may state a poem's central idea, as in Robert Francis' "Preparation" (page 224), or it may pinpoint subject matter, as in Theodore Roethke's "The Heron" (page 254). A title may introduce or identify the poem's speaker, as in Sylvia Plath's "Mushrooms" (page 226), or tell something about a poem's sound, as in Edna St. Vincent Millay's "Counting-Out Rhyme" (page 222). Sometimes a title is figurative instead of literal, as in Evelyn Tooley Hunt's "Mama Is a Sunrise" (page 246). In such a case a title helps to create a picture and express emotion. A title may even tell how a poem will be organized, as in Eve Merriam's "Willow and Ginkgo" (page 244). Without their titles some poems would not make any sense at all. In those poems the title is like a large, central piece to a jigsaw puzzle without which the puzzle cannot be completed.

Thinking About the Title

1. Read Rieu's poem again. Now cover its title with your hand and reread only the body of the poem. Is the title needed to reveal the meaning of the poem? Why or why not?
2. In addition to providing information, what does Rieu's title add to the imagery, sound, and humor of the poem?

COMPOSITION

Writing About a Title

■ Write about the title of a poem or a short story in this book. First tell how the title would interest a reader who comes across the poem or story. Then tell what the title contributes to the meaning *after* the poem or story has been read.

Writing a Poem with a Vital Title

■ Write a two-line poem with a title that is absolutely necessary to understanding the poem's meaning. Make your title as long or as short as you wish. Using Rieu's poem as a model, include in your title the identity of the speaker, the time, the place, and a clue to the mood of the poem.

CHALLENGE

Research

■ Make a list of unusual titles of poems, books, and songs. Look through your own collections, and browse through the library. After each title add a comment of your own about why the title is a good one. Put the list on a poster so that members of the class can add to it.

Night Thought of a Tortoise . . . 265

COMPOSITION: GUIDELINES FOR EVALUATION

WRITING ABOUT A TITLE

Objective

To discuss the significance of a poem or short story title

Guidelines for Evaluation

■ suggested length: one–two paragraphs
■ should tell how the title interests a reader
■ should tell what the title contributes to the meaning of the work

WRITING A POEM WITH A VITAL TITLE

Objective

To write a two-line poem

Guidelines for Evaluation

■ suggested length: *poem*—two lines; *title*—any length
■ should have a title essential to understanding the poem
■ should have a title that gives the speaker's identity, the setting, and a clue to the mood

AT A GLANCE

- Paul Revere tells his friend to signal when the British begin to attack.
- The signal will be one lantern if the British attack by land and two if they attack by sea.
- He goes across the river to wait.
- His friend hears the British marching to their ship.

LITERARY OPTIONS

- narrative poem
- rhythm
- word choice

THEMATIC OPTIONS

- heroism
- adventure
- the American Revolution

NARRATIVE POEM

The first stanza announces a tale about a heroic individual whose deeds are important enough to be recorded in history.

RHYTHM

Most of the lines have 8–11 syllables with 4 beats in each line. Like line 2, many begin with 2 unstressed syllables, creating a fast rhythm suited to the galloping pace of the ride.

WORD CHOICE

The words "phantom," "prison bar," and "huge black hulk" (ll. 20–24) create a menacing atmosphere that reflects the political situation in which the colonists felt menaced by the British.

266 *Poetry*

Henry Wadsworth Longfellow

Paul Revere's Ride

Listen, my children, and you shall hear
Of the midnight ride of Paul Revere,
On the eighteenth of April, in seventy-five;
Hardly a man is now alive
5 Who remembers that famous day and year.

He said to his friend, "If the British march
By land or sea from the town tonight,
Hang a lantern aloft in the belfry[1] arch
Of the North Church tower, as a signal light—
10 One, if by land, and two, if by sea;
And I on the opposite shore will be,
Ready to ride and spread the alarm
Through every Middlesex[2] village and farm,
For the country folk to be up and to arm."

15 Then he said "Good night!" and with muffled oar
Silently rowed to the Charlestown[3] shore,
Just as the moon rose over the bay,
Where, swinging wide at her moorings, lay
The *Somerset*, British man-of-war:
20 A phantom[4] ship, with each mast and spar
Across the moon, like a prison bar,
And a huge black hulk, that was magnified
By its own reflection in the tide.

Meanwhile, his friend, through alley and street,
25 Wanders and watches with eager ears,
Till in the silence around him he hears
The muster[5] of men at the barrack door,
The sound of arms, and the tramp of feet,
And the measured tread of the grenadiers[6]
30 Marching down to their boats on the shore.

---

1. **belfry** [bel′frē]: bell tower.
2. **Middlesex:** county in Massachusetts.
3. **Charlestown:** city on Boston Harbor at the time of the American Revolution; now a part of Boston.
4. **phantom:** ghostly.
5. **muster:** gathering, assembly.
6. **grenadiers** [gren′ə dērz′]: regiment of the British Army.

GUIDED READING

LITERAL QUESTIONS

1a. To whom is the speaker telling the story? (children)

2a. What plan does Paul Revere set up with his friend? (His friend will go to the church tower and signal with a lantern: one if the British come by land, two if by sea. Revere will wait across the river to warn the people.)

INFERENTIAL QUESTIONS

1b. Why do you suppose the speaker focuses on children? (They were not living at the time of the events, and he does not want them to forget the heroism of their forebears.)

2b. Why was this a good plan? (In a day without electronic communications, a visual signal from a high point was both fast and undetectable by the enemy.)

Then he climbed the tower of the Old North Church
By the wooden stairs, with stealthy[7] tread,
To the belfry chamber overhead,
And startled the pigeons from their perch
35 On the somber rafters, that round him made
Masses and moving shapes of shade—
By the trembling ladder, steep and tall,
To the highest window in the wall,
Where he paused to listen and look down
40 A moment on the roofs of the town,
And the moonlight flowing over all.

Beneath, in the churchyard, lay the dead,
In their night encampment on the hill,
Wrapped in silence so deep and still
45 That he could hear, like a sentinel's[8] tread,
The watchful night wind, as it went
Creeping along from tent to tent,
And seeming to whisper, "All is well!"
A moment only he feels the spell
50 Of the place and the hour, the secret dread
Of the lonely belfry and the dead;
For suddenly all his thoughts are bent
On a shadowy something far away,
Where the river widens to meet the bay—
55 A line of black, that bends and floats
On the rising tide, like a bridge of boats.

Meanwhile, impatient to mount and ride,
Booted and spurred, with a heavy stride
On the opposite shore walked Paul Revere.
60 Now he patted his horse's side,
Now gazed at the landscape far and near,
Then, impetuous,[9] stamped the earth,
And turned and tightened his saddle girth;[10]
But mostly he watched with eager search
65 The belfry tower of the Old North Church,
As it rose above the graves on the hill,
Lonely and spectral[11] and somber and still.

---

7. **stealthy** [stel'thē]: secretive.
8. **sentinel's**: guard's.
9. **impetuous** [im pech'oo əs]: eager to rush ahead.
10. **girth**: strap.
11. **spectral**: ghostly.

Paul Revere's Ride 267

GUIDED READING

LITERAL QUESTIONS

1a. To what is the graveyard compared? (a soldier's encampment)

2a. What does Revere's friend suddenly notice? (a "line of black" in the river)

INFERENTIAL QUESTIONS

1b. How does this comparison link past, present, and future in the poem? (It recalls the colonial forbears who suffered and died to establish the colonies; it foreshadows the battles and deaths to come.)

2b. What is the significance of what he sees? (The British attack looks as if it will come from the water.)

- Paul Revere sees one and then two lights in the belfry.
- He quickly rides off to warn the people of Medford and Lexington.

IMAGERY AND METAPHOR

A spark from the pebbles becomes a metaphor: a spark that will ignite American patriots into action (ll. 75–80). The metaphor underscores the themes of heroism and patriotism.

MOOD

Tranquil images of nature contrast sharply with the tension and menace of the historical moment (ll. 82–84).

NARRATIVE POEM

Longfellow marks Revere's progress through the Massachusetts towns. The time device helps unify the action, in addition to building tension (ll. 87 and 93).

WORD CHOICE

The words "spectral," "aghast," and "bloody" foreshadow the coming war and help create the mood of the poem (ll. 98–100).

And lo! as he looks, on the belfry's height
A glimmer, and then a gleam of light.
70 He springs to the saddle, the bridle he turns,
But lingers and gazes, till full on his sight
A second lamp in the belfry burns!

A hurry of hoofs in a village street,
A shape in the moonlight, a bulk in the dark,
75 And beneath, from the pebbles, in passing, a spark
Struck out by a steed flying fearless and fleet:
That was all! And yet, through the gloom and the light,
The fate of a nation was riding that night;
And the spark struck out by that steed, in his flight,
80 Kindled the land into flame with its heat.

He has left the village and mounted the steep,
And beneath him, tranquil and broad and deep,
Is the Mystic,[12] meeting the ocean tides;
And under the alders[13] that skirt its edge,
85 Now soft on the sand, now loud on the ledge,
Is heard the tramp of his steed as he rides.

It was twelve by the village clock,
When he crossed the bridge into Medford town.
He heard the crowing of the cock,
90 And the barking of the farmer's dog,
And felt the damp of the river fog
That rises after the sun goes down.

It was one by the village clock,
When he galloped into Lexington.
95 He saw the gilded weathercock[14]
Swim in the moonlight as he passed,
And the meetinghouse windows, blank and bare,
Gaze at him with a spectral glare,
As if they already stood aghast[15]
100 At the bloody work they would look upon.

---

12. **Mystic:** river in northeastern United States.
13. **alders:** trees of the birch family.
14. **gilded weathercock:** gold-colored weathervane in the form of a rooster.
15. **aghast** [ə gast′]: amazed.

268   *Poetry*

GUIDED READING

LITERAL QUESTIONS

1a. What times do the village clocks say as Paul rides through? (twelve o'clock in Medford and one o'clock in Lexington)

2a. In lines 79–80 what metaphor is used to describe what happened to the nation? (The spark of the horse's hoofs caused it to burst into flame.)

INFERENTIAL QUESTIONS

1b. What purpose do the village clocks serve in this account? (They tell how much time is passing. They create tension; we wonder if Paul Revere will warn the villagers in time. They also increase our awareness of Revere's heroism: His ride is long.)

2b. What does this metaphor suggest about the mood of the colonies at that time? (They were ready for a fight; it took only a tiny spark to set them off.)

It was two by the village clock,
When he came to the bridge in Concord town.
He heard the bleating of the flock,
And the twitter of birds among the trees,
105 And felt the breath of the morning breeze
Blowing over the meadows brown.
And one was safe and asleep in his bed,
Who at the bridge would be first to fall,
Who that day would be lying dead,
110 Pierced by a British musket ball.

You know the rest. In the books you have read
How the British Regulars[16] fired and fled—
How the farmers gave them ball for ball,
From behind each fence and farmyard wall,
115 Chasing the redcoats[17] down the lane,
Then crossing the fields to emerge again
Under the trees at the turn of the road,
And only pausing to fire and load.

So through the night rode Paul Revere;
120 And so through the night went his cry of alarm
To every Middlesex village and farm—
A cry of defiance and not of fear—
A voice in the darkness, a knock at the door,
And a word that shall echo forevermore!
125 For, borne on the night wind of the past,
Through all our history, to the last,
In the hour of darkness and peril and need,
The people will waken and listen to hear
The hurrying hoofbeats of that steed,
130 And the midnight message of Paul Revere.

_____

16. **Regulars:** soldiers.
17. **redcoats:** British soldiers. who wore uniforms
with red coats.

Paul Revere's Ride 269

AT A GLANCE

- Paul Revere warns Concord.
- The speaker projects events into the future and describes the battle that followed the ride.
- Revere will be remembered and will inspire future generations with his heroism and patriotism.

SPEAKER

The speaker abandons his hour-by-hour account and jumps forward to the battle and then to the present day. This shift reflects his concern that each American remember the significance of Paul Revere's ride (l. 111).

MAIN IDEA

Not only was Paul Revere's ride of critical importance at the time, but it also serves to inspire future acts of heroism (ll. 125–130).

REFLECTING ON THE POEM

Do you think an individual can still have an impact on history? (Some may feel times are different, but some may cite figures such as Martin Luther King, Jr., who have changed modern history.)

GUIDED READING

LITERAL QUESTIONS

1a. How does the speaker say the two sides conducted themselves in the battle? (The British fired, then ran away. The farmers pursued them, firing. Then they crossed the fields and mounted a surprise attack on the British.)

2a. Why does the speaker say Paul Revere's ride was important? (He readied the villagers. His deed will be an inspiration to Americans whenever heroism is required.)

INFERENTIAL QUESTIONS

1b. In what way does this account of the battle show the speaker's nationality? (It is a frankly biased account that presents the Americans as heroic and the British as cowards.)

2b. Do you think the speaker is right about the ability of Paul Revere's ride to inspire us today? (Opinions will vary, but the poem's account of his ride is certainly exciting and inspiring.)

1. April 18, 1775
2. The British are coming by land. The British are coming by sea.
3. prison bars
4. He pats his horse, gazes at the landscape, stamps the earth, tightens the saddle, watches the tower, sees two lamps, mounts his horse, goes.
5. fate of a nation; land into flame (patriots stirred to act)
6. fired and fled; returned fire and chased the redcoats
7. hoofbeats, Paul Revere's message
8. He could see the lamps from across the river, enabling him to warn the colonists of the attack.
9. Prison bars convey an image of the British as jailers.
10. wooden stairs; startled pigeons; somber rafters' shadows; steep, tall, trembling ladder; highest window overlooking the town; graveyards beneath the tower; view of river and bay
11. the steed striking a spark that kindled the land into flame; the nation stirred into action
12. Americans will hear the echo of Revere's message of defiance in the nation's hours of peril.
13. Possible answers:
    - People want to show appreciation of heroes.
    - courage, sense of duty, strength, willingness to sacrifice

VOCABULARY

1. im / patient; im-, not; not patient, intolerant of delay
2. un / certain; un-, not; not certain, not surely known
3. out / pour; out-, forth; pour out
4. mid / night; mid-, in the middle of; in the middle of the night
5. un / merciful; un-, not; not merciful, cruel

STUDY QUESTIONS

Recalling

1. According to lines 1–3, on what date did Paul Revere make his ride?
2. According to lines 6–14, what will one lantern signal? What will two lanterns signal?
3. What are the masts of the *Somerset* like as they cross the moon in lines 18–23?
4. In lines 57–72 what does Revere see, and what does he do?
5. According to lines 78–80, what was riding that night? What was kindled?
6. In lines 111–115 what did the British Regulars do? What did the American farmers do?
7. According to lines 125–130, what will people continue to hear?

Interpreting

8. How successful was Paul Revere's signal system? Explain.
9. What does the image in lines 20–23 tell about the attitude of the colonists toward the British?
10. The day before writing this poem, Longfellow climbed the Old North Church tower. What details in lines 31–56 show the poet making his description as vivid and concrete as possible?
11. What image does the poet use in lines 75–80 to describe the mood of the nation?
12. What does the poet say in the last ten lines of the poem to suggest the lasting importance of Revere's cry?

Extending

13. Why do you think heroes are honored? What qualities make a person heroic? Give reasons to support your opinion.

VOCABULARY

Prefixes

A **prefix** is a word element attached to the beginning of a root, or base, word. For example,

270 *Poetry*

the prefix *un-* added to the base word *believable* makes a new word, *unbelievable*.

Here are some of the most common prefixes and their meanings:

Prefix	Meaning	Example
im-	not	impractical (not practical)
mid-	in the middle of	midday (middle of the day)
out-	forth; better	outrun (run better)
re-	back, again	rewrite (write again)
un-	not	unarmed (not armed)

All of the following words are taken from "Paul Revere's Ride" and from Poe's "Raven" (page 239). Copy them onto a separate sheet of paper. Divide each prefix from its base word with a slant line. Give the meaning of the prefix and the meaning of the full word.

1. impatient
2. uncertain
3. outpour
4. midnight
5. unmerciful

COMPOSITION

Writing About Character

■ Write about the character of Paul Revere in Longfellow's poem. Tell whether the character seems true to life. Give details from the selection to support your opinion. You might mention the character's physical appearance, actions, feelings, or motivations. *For help with this assignment, see Lesson 3 in the Writing About Literature Handbook at the back of this book.*

Writing About a Historical Event

■ Write about an event in American history. Be sure to identify clearly the characters, the setting, and the sequence of events. Whether you write prose or poetry, try to capture the excitement of the event by using vivid words.

COMPOSITION: GUIDELINES FOR EVALUATION

WRITING ABOUT CHARACTER

Objective
To analyze a character in a poem

Guidelines for Evaluation
- suggested length: one to two paragraphs
- should tell if Paul Revere seems real
- should support this opinion with details
- should include details about his physical appearance, actions, feelings, or motivations

WRITING ABOUT A HISTORICAL EVENT

Objective
To depict an event in American history

Guidelines for Evaluation
- suggested length: two to three paragraphs or a short poem
- should relate a historical event
- should clearly identify the characters, the setting, and the sequence of events
- should use vivid words to convey excitement

Sir Walter Scott

Lochinvar

Oh, young Lochinvar is come out of the west,
Through all the wide Border his steed was the best;
And, save his good broadsword, he weapons had none,
He rode all unarmed, and he rode all alone.
5 So faithful in love, and so dauntless in war,
There never was knight like the young Lochinvar.

He stayed not for brake,[1] and he stopped not for stone,
He swam the Eske River where ford there was none;
But ere he alighted at Netherby gate,
10 The bride had consented, the gallant came late:
For a laggard[2] in love, and a dastard[3] in war,
Was to wed the fair Ellen of brave Lochinvar.

So boldly he entered the Netherby Hall,
Among bridesmen,[4] and kinsmen, and brothers, and all.
15 Then spoke the bride's father, his hand on his sword
(For the poor craven[5] bridegroom said never a word),
"Oh, come ye in peace here, or come ye in war,
Or to dance at our bridal, young Lord Lochinvar?"

"I long wooed your daughter, my suit you denied—
20 Love swells like the Solway,[6] but ebbs like its tide—
And now I am come, with this lost love of mine,
To lead but one measure,[7] drink one cup of wine.
There are maidens in Scotland more lovely by far,
That would gladly be bride to the young Lochinvar."

---

1. **brake:** clump of brush or bushes.
2. **laggard:** slow person.
3. **dastard:** coward.
4. **bridesmen:** male members of a wedding party.
5. **craven:** cowardly.
6. **Solway:** inlet between England and Scotland.
7. **measure:** dance.

AT A GLANCE

- Lochinvar rides to Netherby Hall, where he finds the wedding party of his love, Ellen.
- Lochinvar says that he has come only for a drink and a dance.

LITERARY OPTIONS

- narrative poem
- rhyme scheme
- rhythm

THEMATIC OPTIONS

- thwarted love
- determination

RHYTHM

The poem uses an anapestic rhythm—two unstressed syllables followed by a stressed syllable. This rhythm creates a galloping effect appropriate to the rapid, exciting events of the poem.

MAIN IDEA

The main idea is stated in a few words: "So faithful in love, and so dauntless in war." In his journey to Netherby, Lochinvar sets out to prove both his faithfulness and his dauntlessness (l. 5).

NARRATIVE POEM: CONFLICT

The end of the second stanza states Lochinvar's conflict (ll. 10–12).

NARRATIVE POEM: DIALOGUE

Dialogue forwards the action of the poem by setting up the events to come (ll. 19–20).

IMAGERY

The image of the bride kissing the goblet before Lochinvar drinks reveals an important point: Ellen still loves Lochinvar (l. 25).

NARRATIVE POEM: CLIMAX

The swift departure of the lovers is the high point of the narrative (ll. 37–42).

VOCABULARY: DIALECT

"Scaur"—one of several examples of Scot's dialect—reinforces the setting and adds to the authenticity of the poem (l. 41).

RHYME SCHEME

The rhyme scheme is quite regular all through the poem—*aabbcc*, and so forth. The poem is made up of a series of rhyming couplets, each pair of lines expressing a complete thought.

REFLECTING ON THE POEM

Why might a hero from a different world, a Lochinvar, appeal to modern readers? (He offers romance, old-fashioned heroism, color and dash—often missing from our world today.)

25 The bride kissed the goblet; the knight took it up;
He quaffed off[8] the wine, and he threw down the cup.
She looked down to blush, and she looked up to sigh,
With a smile on her lips, and a tear in her eye.
He took her soft hand, ere her mother could bar—
30 "Now tread we a measure!" said young Lochinvar.

So stately his form, and so lovely her face,
That never a hall such a galliard[9] did grace;
While her mother did fret, and her father did fume,
And the bridegroom stood dangling his bonnet and plume,
35 And the bridesmaidens whispered, "'Twere better by far,
To have matched our fair cousin with young Lochinvar."

One touch to her hand, and one word to her ear,
When they reached the hall door, and the charger[10] stood near,
So light to the croup[11] the fair lady he swung,
40 So light to the saddle before her he sprung!
"She is won! we are gone, over bank, brush, and scaur;[12]
They'll have fleet steeds that follow," quoth young Lochinvar.

There was mounting 'mong Graemes of the Netherby clan;
Forsters, Fenwicks, and Musgraves, they rode and they ran.
45 There was racing and chasing on Cannobie Lee,[13]
But the lost bride of Netherby ne'er did they see.
So daring in love, and so dauntless in war,
Have ye e'er heard of gallant like young Lochinvar?

---

8. **quaffed** [kwäft] **off:** drank.
9. **galliard** [gal'yərd]: lively dance for two people.
10. **charger:** horse trained for battle.
11. **croup** [kroōp]: back of a horse, behind the saddle.
12. **scaur** [skär]: rocky hillside.
13. **Cannobie Lee:** meadow in Scotland.

STUDY QUESTIONS

Recalling

1. What adjectives are used to describe Lochinvar in stanza 1?
2. As Lochinvar arrives at Netherby in stanza 2, who intends to wed "the fair Ellen"?
3. What do the bride's father and Lochinvar say to each other in stanzas 3 and 4?
4. According to stanza 6, who favors the match between Ellen and Lochinvar?
5. As they dance near the hall door, what do Ellen and Lochinvar do?
6. According to the last stanza, do the kinsmen ever recover "the lost bride"?

Interpreting

7. Based on what the speaker tells us about Lochinvar, how would you describe the knight's character? What does the knight himself say to reinforce what the speaker says?
8. How does the speaker compare Lochinvar with the man Ellen is supposed to marry?
9. What details suggest that Ellen is happy to escape with Lochinvar?

Extending

10. Do you think Lochinvar's act is the act of a hero? Why or why not?

READING AND LITERARY FOCUS

Narrative Poetry

A **narrative poem** is a poem that tells a story. Thousands of years ago story-poems were recited and passed down from generation to generation by word of mouth. Eventually narrative poems came to be written down.

Like a short story, a narrative poem usually includes a setting, characters, dialogue, events, and conflict. Some narrative poems cover an entire series of events from beginning to end. However, other narrative poems focus on a few events.

Longfellow's "Paul Revere's Ride" (page 266), for example, focuses on the night of April 18, 1775. Its setting is the area near Boston during the American Revolution. Its characters are Paul Revere and his friend. Its dialogue includes Revere's signal, "One, if by land, and two, if by sea." The events in the story are Revere's night of waiting for the signal, his furious ride, and the colonists' victory. The conflict of the story is the Revolution itself, the Americans against the British.

It is important to remember that while a narrative poem tells a story, it is also a poem. In other words, it uses the devices of poetry to tell its story: repetition, rhythm, rhyme, alliteration, assonance, imagery, simile, metaphor, and poetic form. It combines the excitement of a tale with the delight of poetry.

Thinking About Narrative Poetry

1. Identify the setting and the characters of Scott's poem.
2. Summarize the plot of the poem.

COMPOSITION

Writing About Plot

■ Write about the conflict in the plot of "Lochinvar." As you write, consider the following questions: What is the problem the main character faces? Who is on his side? Who is against him? Are the two sides equally matched? What is the main character's reaction to the conflict? In what unexpected way is the conflict resolved? *For help with this assignment, see Lesson 2 in the Writing About Literature Handbook at the back of this book.*

Writing a Description

■ Write a description of Lochinvar himself, Ellen, the craven bridegroom, the castle, the countryside, the knight's horse, or any other object mentioned in the poem. Be very specific, giving your reader as many details as possible.

Lochinvar 273

STUDY QUESTIONS

1. *young, faithful in love, dauntless in war*
2. "a laggard in love, and a dastard in war"
3. ■ the father: "Oh, come ye in peace here, or come ye in war, / Or to dance at our bridal?"
   ■ Lochinvar: "I long wooed your daughter, my suit you denied . . . And now I am come, with this lost love of mine, / To lead but one measure, drink one cup of wine."
4. the bridesmaidens
5. ride off on Lochinvar's horse
6. no
7. ■ faithful, dauntless, stately, gallant
   ■ "There are maidens in Scotland more lovely by far, / That would gladly be bride to the young Lochinvar."
8. Speaker contrasts Lochinvar as "faithful in love, and so dauntless in war" with "a laggard in love, and a dastard in war."
9. She kissed Lochinvar's goblet, and "She looked down to blush, and she looked up to sigh."
10. Yes; he rescued Ellen from marriage to a man she did not love.

READING AND LITERARY FOCUS

1. Netherby Hall in Scotland and environs; Lochinvar, Ellen, Ellen's parents, the groom, the bridesmaidens, the guests
2. Ellen's father denies Lochinvar's suit to marry Ellen. She is wed to another. Lochinvar arrives too late to stop it, but they escape on his horse.

COMPOSITION: GUIDELINES FOR EVALUATION

WRITING ABOUT PLOT

Objective
To analyze the plot of a narrative poem

Guidelines for Evaluation
■ suggested length: one to two paragraphs
■ should identify the main character's problem
■ should identify his allies and enemies
■ should describe his reaction to the conflict
■ should tell how the conflict is resolved

WRITING A DESCRIPTION

Objective
To write a paragraph of description

Guidelines for Evaluation
■ suggested length: one paragraph
■ should describe a character, place or object mentioned in the poem
■ should include details to make the description specific

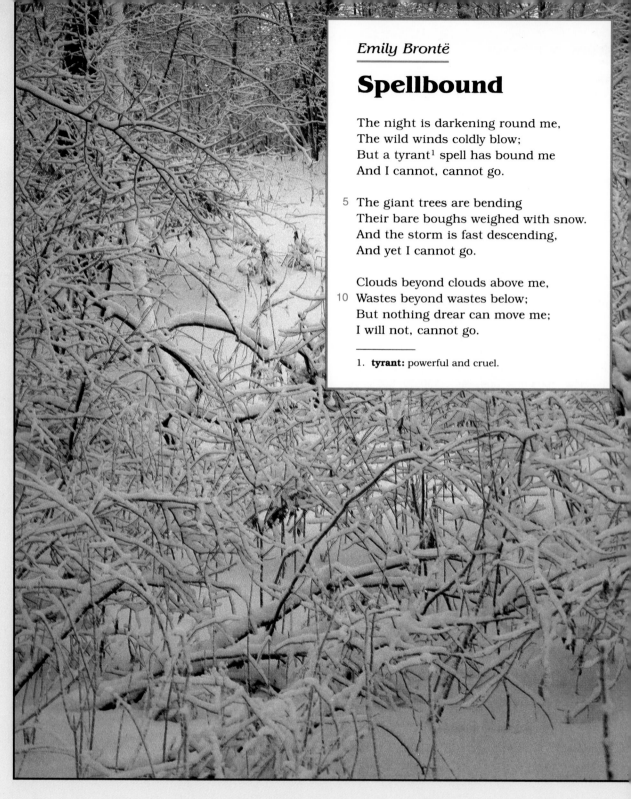

Emily Brontë

Spellbound

The night is darkening round me,
The wild winds coldly blow;
But a tyrant[1] spell has bound me
And I cannot, cannot go.

5 The giant trees are bending
Their bare boughs weighed with snow.
And the storm is fast descending,
And yet I cannot go.

Clouds beyond clouds above me,
10 Wastes beyond wastes below;
But nothing drear can move me;
I will not, cannot go.

---

1. **tyrant:** powerful and cruel.

STUDY QUESTIONS

Recalling

1. According to the speaker, what is the night doing? What has bound the speaker?
2. What details of the storm are given in stanza 2?
3. What is above the speaker? What is below the speaker?
4. What is the speaker's response at the end of each stanza?

Interpreting

5. Describe in your own words the effect of the weather on the speaker. What is unusual about this effect?
6. The speaker never directly tells us why she "cannot go." What do you think is the reason she cannot go?

Extending

7. Describe a situation in which being spellbound would be a positive experience. Describe one in which it would be negative. Which do you think it is in this poem? Explain.

READING AND LITERARY FOCUS

Lyrics—Poems That Express Emotion

Some poems, called narrative poems, tell stories. Other poems, called **lyrics,** express personal thoughts and emotions. In her lyric "Spellbound" Brontë expresses her emotions when she says, "I cannot, cannot go."

Lyrics are usually short and strive for a single, powerful effect. They are also highly musical, em-phasizing sound and language and the delight of the words themselves. In fact, a lyric was originally a poem sung to the music of a **lyre,** a small stringed instrument.

Most poems written today are lyrics. They vary widely in subject matter and style, but each one is an expression of personal thoughts and emotions.

Thinking About Lyrics

■ What central thought or emotion do you think the speaker of "Spellbound" is trying to express?

COMPOSITION

Writing About Repetition

■ Write about Brontë's use of repetition in "Spellbound." First identify the repeated words and phrases. Then tell why these repetitions are appropriate for someone who is spellbound.

Writing a Lyric Poem

■ Write a short lyric poem in which you describe someone's reaction to a scene, such as a thunderstorm or a city parade. You may want to follow this pattern: one line about the scene, followed by one line about the reaction. For example:

The parade passed by	(scene)
And I felt full of life.	(reaction)
The big drums beat	(scene)
And my heart beat with them.	(reaction)

For general help with writing poetry, see Lesson 6 in the Writing About Literature Handbook at the back of this book.

1. "darkening" around her; "a tyrant spell"
2. giant trees bending; bare boughs weighted with snow; storm quickly descending
3. "clouds beyond clouds;" "wastes beyond wastes"
4. She "cannot," "will not" go.
5. ■ She is bound by the storm's spell and cannot leave.
   ■ Storms usually drive people indoors, not hold them outdoors.
6. Possible answers: She is compelled to watch the storm. A tyrant spell has paralyzed her.
7. Possible answers:
   ■ watching a sunset or movie, listening to a concert, reading
   ■ seeing an accident, being frightened by a large animal
   ■ Most will agree it is negative and cite the repetition of "cannot go" and the storm's foreboding quality. However, the phrase *will not go* might suggest that she *chooses* to be "spellbound."

READING AND LITERARY FOCUS

Answers will vary. Most will agree it is helplessness. The poem describes the powerful mesmerizing effect that external events can create.

COMPOSITION: GUIDELINES FOR EVALUATION

WRITING ABOUT REPETITION

Objective
To analyze the use of repetition

Guidelines for Evaluation
■ suggested length: one paragraph
■ should identify the repeated words and phrases in "Spellbound"
■ should tell why these repetitions are appropriate

WRITING A LYRIC POEM

Objective
To write a lyric poem describing a reaction to a scene

Guidelines for Evaluation
■ suggested length: two lines
■ should describe a scene and the writer's reaction to it
■ should follow the following pattern: one line about the scene, then one line about the reaction

LITERARY OPTIONS

- theme
- repetition

THEMATIC OPTIONS

- friendship and loss
- faithfulness

THEME

The title prepares us for the poem's theme: a dream of friendship that did not remain a reality but is still remembered.

REPETITION

The poem ends as it begins. The repetition adds power by emphasizing the main idea: The speaker still loves his friend and keeps the dream of friendship alive (l. 6).

REFLECTING ON THE POEM

What does the word "soft" (l. 5) suggest about the emotions of the speaker? (It tells us that the speaker feels only gentle emotions about his friend—hurt, disappointment, love—but no harsh feeling such as anger, bitterness, or resentment.)

STUDY QUESTIONS

1. past tense: *loved*
2. went away
3. the poem
4. Line 6 repeats line 1.
5. feels a deep sense of loss since his friend went away
6. suggest the speaker is thinking more of his own loss than of his friend; that the speaker feels lost without his friend
7. the friendship
8. the speaker; the memory of a friendship
9. Possible answers:
   - Yes: The speaker must forgive his friend before he can make new friends.
   - No: Heartbreak is too intense to forget.

READING AND LITERARY FOCUS

- The loss of a friend leaves a painful void; indirectly.

Langston Hughes

The Dream Keeper

I loved my friend.
He went away from me.
There's nothing more to say.
The poem ends,
5 Soft as it began—
I loved my friend.

STUDY QUESTIONS

Recalling

1. In line 1 what tense of the verb *love* does the speaker use?
2. What does the speaker say his friend did?
3. According to line 4, what ends?
4. Which line does the poet repeat?

Interpreting

5. What does the tense of the verb in lines 1 and 6 suggest about the speaker's emotion?
6. In line 2 why are the last two words of the line important? What do they suggest about the speaker's emotion?
7. According to the whole poem, what has also ended besides the poem?
8. Who is "the dream keeper" of the title? Describe in your own words the dream that is kept.

Extending

9. Do you think the expression "forgive and forget" applies to Hughes's poem? Why or why not?

276 *Poetry*

READING AND LITERARY FOCUS

Theme

The **theme** of a literary work is its main idea. The theme usually makes some general statement or comment about life or human nature. For example, a poem's theme may be that people are basically good or that love can be painful.

The theme of a work should not be confused with the **topic,** or subject matter. The topic of a poem might be birds; the theme of that poem might be "People have always envied the grace and freedom of birds." As you see, the theme is usually an idea expressed in a complete sentence.

In some poems the theme is directly stated. In other poems the theme is not directly stated. If you have difficulty identifying the theme of a poem, restate the poem in your own words. Then ask yourself, "What general statement about life or human nature does this poem make?"

Thinking About Theme

- What is the theme of "The Dream Keeper"? Is it directly or indirectly stated in the poem?

Mark Van Doren

The Story-Teller

He talked, and as he talked
Wallpaper came alive;
Suddenly ghosts walked,
And four doors were five;

5 Calendars ran backward,
And maps had mouths;
Ships went tackward,[1]
In a great drowse;[2]

Trains climbed trees,
10 And soon dripped down
Like honey of bees
On the cold brick town.

He had wakened a worm
In the world's brain,
15 And nothing stood firm
Until day again.

---

1. **tackward:** against the wind and at an angle.
2. **drowse** [drouz]: state of sleepiness.

STUDY QUESTIONS

Recalling

1. According to the first stanza, what happened as the story-teller talked?
2. Based on stanzas 2 and 3, what impossible things happened as the story-teller talked?
3. According to stanza 4, what had wakened?
4. When did things stand firm again?

Interpreting

5. What images suggest that the story-teller gives life to things that do not have life? How is this possible?
6. What image suggests that the story-teller has power over time itself? How is this possible?
7. What does the story-teller cause people to do that they probably would not do without him?
8. Why is the title of the poem necessary to understanding its meaning?

Extending

9. What do you think is the greatest power of the imagination?

READING AND LITERARY FOCUS

Implied Theme

Sometimes the theme of a work is **implied.** In other words, instead of coming right out and stating the theme, the author uses all the devices of poetry to suggest the theme. The author expects us to read carefully enough to let the theme come through the language, the sound, and the images of the poem.

If you want to identify the theme of a poem, look first at the images. What do they have in common? For example, the images in "The Story-Teller" all suggest actions or events that are impossible in the real world. Then look at the language in the poem. Are there any unusual words or phrases that may suggest a general statement the poet is making? Consider the sound of the poem too. What overall sound effect is the poet trying to create?

Thinking About Implied Theme

■ Identify the theme of "The Story-Teller," and tell how you arrived at it.

The Story-Teller 277

LITERARY OPTIONS
- speaker
- personification

THEMATIC OPTIONS
- saving vs. abusing the environment
- nature and humanity

SPEAKER

The title and first line establish that the land is speaking for itself, thus personalizing the poet's message.

STYLE: FIGURATIVE LANGUAGE

Personifying the land ("I lie patient") dramatically shows that the land needs care. Personification also makes abuses of the environment seem more brutal ("chainlink necklace chokes me").

REPETITION AND MAIN IDEA

The repetition of the line adds emphasis to the main idea: The land, although mistreated, endures and can be renewed (l. 18).

REFLECTING ON THE POEM

What do you think the land is waiting for? (In one sense it waits to outlast people, for the renewing processes of nature are slow but inexorable. In another sense, it waits for humanity to learn how to treat its environment.)

Marina de Bellagente

I Am the Land. I Wait.

I am the land. I wait.
You say you own me.
I wait.

You shout. I lie patient.
5 You buy me. I wait.
With muddy holes and
car lot eyes I stare . . .

    Then someone
tickles me, plants life—fruit
10 grass—trees/children dance/someone
    Sings

You come with guns
A chainlink necklace
chokes me now

15 I wait.
YOU CANNOT PUT A FENCE
AROUND THE PLANET EARTH.
I am the land. I wait.

STUDY QUESTIONS

Recalling

1. According to lines 1–3, what does the land do?
2. What do people do to the land in lines 4–9?
3. According to lines 9–11, what happens after someone "plants life"?
4. In lines 12–14 what chokes the earth?
5. What statement does the land emphasize at the end of the poem?

Interpreting

6. Who is the "I" of the poem? Who is the "you"?
7. Do you think personification gives the poem greater emotional power? Why or why not?
8. What are the two different ways the land can be treated, according to the poem?
9. What do you think the land is waiting for?

Extending

10. How would you describe the attitude of the average person toward the land?

READING AND LITERARY FOCUS

Speaker

The **speaker** of a poem is the voice that delivers it. It is the voice that you "hear" when you read a poem.

Sometimes the speaker is the poet who directly states what he or she thinks, feels, or experiences. He or she can be deeply involved in the subject matter of the poem, like the speaker of Poe's "Raven" (page 239). The speaker can also be detached and less directly involved, like the speaker of "The Walrus and the Carpenter" (page 256). Sometimes the speaker of a poem is not the poet at all but a character or voice that the poet has created.

By creating a "mouthpiece" the poet can more freely explore attitudes and experiences different from his or her own. The poet may even make an inanimate, or nonliving, object the speaker of a poem. A talking whale, a lily, or a pile of laundry can present a unique point of view on a poet's behalf.

Thinking About the Speaker

1. Who is the speaker of de Bellagente's poem? Is it the poet? Another human being? An object?
2. Where in the poem do you first know who the speaker is? How does this help you with the poem's meaning?

COMPOSITION

Writing a Summary

■ Summarize the meaning of "I Am the Land. I Wait." First make a statement about the meaning of the title. Then write one sentence about each stanza of the poem. Conclude with a sentence about the overall meaning of the poem.

Writing a Lyric Poem

■ Write a short, nonrhyming lyric poem that clearly expresses one emotion. Using "I Am the Land. I Wait." as a model, begin and end your lyric with one simple statement. *For general help with writing poetry, see Lesson 6 in the Writing About Literature Handbook at the back of this book.*

COMPARING POEMS

■ Compare the poems in one of the following groups:

a. "Paul Revere's Ride" and "Lochinvar"
b. "Spellbound" and "I Am the Land. I Wait."
c. "The Dream Keeper" and "The Story-Teller"

State the theme of each poem you are comparing. What do the themes have in common? In what ways are they different? Which theme is more meaningful to you? Why?

I Am the Land. I Wait. 279

COMPOSITION: GUIDELINES FOR EVALUATION

WRITING A SUMMARY

Objective

To write a summary of a poem

Guidelines for Evaluation

■ suggested length: one paragraph of eight sentences
■ should begin with a sentence about the meaning of the poem's title and end with a sentence about the poem's overall meaning
■ should contain one sentence about each stanza

WRITING A LYRIC POEM

Objective

To express emotion in a nonrhyming lyric poem

Guidelines for Evaluation

■ suggested length: six lines
■ should express one emotion
■ should begin and end with a simple statement
■ should not rhyme
■ should imitate the form of "I Am the Land. I Wait"

THE TOTAL EFFECT

The **total effect** of a poem is your complete experience of the poem as a whole. It is the result of all the elements of sound, language, form, and meaning working together.

Walt Whitman (1819–1892) has been called the father of modern poetry. "O Captain! My Captain!" captures Whitman's emotion after the assassination of President Abraham Lincoln.

■ What is that emotion?

Alice Walker (born 1944) is a native of Eatonton, Georgia. She attended Spelman College in her home state and Sarah Lawrence College in New York. Later she lived in Kenya, Africa, where she was adopted by a local tribe. Her poetry, articles, essays, and fiction show her concern with racial equality. In 1983 Walker was awarded the Pulitzer Prize for her novel *The Color Purple.*

■ As you read "For My Sister Molly Who in the Fifties," listen for the warm and natural voice.

See page 221 for biographical information about Robert Frost. "The Road Not Taken" is one of the best-known American poems. Readers have praised it for its sound, imagery, form, and meaning—in other words, for its total effect.

■ What is the ordinary situation that Frost uses to make an important general statement about human nature?

Emily Dickinson (1830–1886) lived her entire life in Amherst, Massachusetts. A brilliantly imaginative poet, she withdrew from the world at the age of twenty-three. Her poems became the emotional focus of her life, though she did not publish them. She tied them up in small packets and stored them in a drawer.

■ In "Success Is Counted Sweetest" notice how Dickinson combines a simple, general statement and an intense, personal example to create the poem's total effect.

TEXAS ESSENTIAL ELEMENTS
GRADE 8

1A writing process
1B purpose and audience
1C supporting main idea
1E appropriate language
1H grammatical conventions
1I word choice
3B figurative language and sound devices
3D literary genres
4B implied main idea
4E perceiving cause/effect
4F author's purpose
To locate treatment of an Element, see *Texas Teacher's Resources.*

The Total Effect

As you have discovered, a poem works on many levels at once. Reading a poem means using your senses, your emotions, your mind, and your imagination. As you read, you see, hear, touch, taste, smell, feel, think, and imagine all at the same time.

To experience the total effect of a poem, first hear its sounds and see its images. Read it at least once aloud and then read it silently. Let the poem suggest its overall flavor or tell its story. Then take the poem apart, thinking about its elements.

Reminders for Active Reading of Poetry

1. The **title** of a poem will suggest the poem's main idea or focus.
2. The **speaker** is the person or thing whose voice presents the poem. It is important to determine who the speaker is and what his, her, or its attitudes are. **Word choice** helps to reveal what the speaker is like.
3. The **sound** of a poem (its wordplay, alliteration, assonance, rhyme scheme, rhythm, onomatopoeia, and repetition) should fit the poem's subject. The **music,** which these techniques create, should add to emotion and meaning.
4. The **imagery** and **figurative language** (simile, metaphor, personification) should stimulate the senses and help you to experience in fresh ways what is being described.
5. The **form** of a poem includes how its lines are grouped (couplets, quatrains, stanzas) and what visual effects the poem has on the page.
6. The central **meaning,** or **theme,** of a poem may be stated directly or indirectly. A poem may be a **narrative** poem, emphasizing story, or a **lyric** poem, emphasizing emotion.

After thinking about the separate elements, put the poem "back together again" for one more reading. The total effect of a poem depends on you. If you read actively, alertly, paying attention to the details the poet has created, you bring all the elements of a poem into action. The total effect is what *you* experience.

Model for Active Reading

With the following poem by Walt Whitman you can see how an active reader approaches poetry. First read the poem aloud, and then read it silently. Then read the notations in the margin. They show how a reader can actively question and answer while reading a poem. Finally read the poem again for its total effect.

LITERARY OPTIONS

- Total effect
- parallelism

THEMATIC OPTIONS

- American experiences
- heroism

The annotations that appear in the Teacher's Edition answer the questions asked in the Pupil's Edition sidenotes.

THE TITLE

We expect the poem to be an address to a beloved leader.

IMAGERY

The sounds are the ringing of bells and the exulting crowd of people. The color is the red of the drops of blood.

REPETITION AND ALLITERATION

Repetition appears in lines 5, 9–12, and the last lines of each stanza. Alliteration appears in lines 10, 11, 15–16, and 19.

FIGURATIVE LANGUAGE

The President is said to be a ship's captain and a father.

RHYTHM

The rhythm is regular.

THEME

The theme is that the speaker mourns for the loss of a great leader who led his country to peace.

REFLECTING ON THE POEM

In what ways can a President be like a captain? (He takes command and steers a course.) In what ways can a President be like a dear father? (He is a person of authority who can inspire love and respect.)

Walt Whitman

O Captain! My Captain!

O Captain! my Captain! our fearful trip is done,
The ship has weathered every rack,[1] the prize we sought is won,
The port is near, the bells I hear, the people all exulting,
While follow eyes the steady keel, the vessel grim and daring;
5   But O heart! heart! heart!
        O the bleeding drops of red,
          Where on the deck my Captain lies,
            Fallen cold and dead.

O Captain! my Captain! rise up and hear the bells;
10 Rise up—for you the flag is flung—for you the bugle trills,
For you bouquets and ribboned wreaths—for you the shores
    a-crowding,
For you they call, the swaying mass, their eager faces turning;
      Here Captain! dear father!
        This arm beneath your head!
15   It is some dream that on the deck
          You've fallen cold and dead.

My Captain does not answer, his lips are pale and still,
My father does not feel my arm, he has no pulse nor will,
The ship is anchored safe and sound, its voyage closed
    and done,
20 From fearful trip the victor ship comes in with object won;
      Exult O shores! and ring O bells!
        But I with mournful tread
          Walk the deck my Captain lies,
            Fallen cold and dead.

---

1. **rack:** hardship or strain, as that caused by bad weather.

282   *Poetry*

The **title** (p. 265) is the name of a poem and defines the poem's subject. What do you expect the subject of this poem to be?

Imagery (p. 238) presents vivid sense impressions. What sounds and colors are presented here?

Repetition and **alliteration** (repeated initial consonants, p. 224) are often used for musical and emotional effect. Which lines in this poem use repetition and alliteration?

Figurative language (p. 247), language not meant to be literally true, includes simile and metaphor. What metaphor does the poet use to describe President Lincoln?

Rhythm (p. 231) is the arrangement of stressed and unstressed syllables. Is the rhythm of this poem regular or irregular?

The **theme** (p. 276) is the main idea, usually expressed as a general statement about life or human nature. What is the theme of this poem?

STUDY QUESTIONS

Recalling

1. According to the first stanza, what has been won? What is the reaction of the people as the ship approaches?
2. Where does the Captain lie? What is his condition?
3. What does the speaker want the Captain to do in the second stanza?
4. In line 13 what other name does the speaker use to refer to the Captain?
5. What does the speaker say is a dream in lines 15–16?
6. According to the third stanza, what is the condition of the ship?
7. At the end of the poem, how does the speaker walk the deck?

Interpreting

8. The people of Whitman's time knew that the Captain of the poem was Lincoln. What is the storm the "ship has weathered"?
9. What words in lines 1–4 indicate the happiness of the people? What words in lines 9–12 show their happiness?

10. What does line 9 suggest about the emotional state of the speaker? What does line 15 also suggest about the speaker's state of mind?
11. What is the emotional effect of the word choice in line 13?
12. The first half of each stanza focuses on the crowd. On what does the second half of each stanza focus? Describe in your own words the emotional effect of this contrast.

Extending

13. What is the purpose of poems written about public events?

CHALLENGE

Further Reading

■ The assassination of President Lincoln inspired Walt Whitman to write at least two other poems about the leader's death—"When Lilacs Last in the Dooryard Bloom'd" and "The Carol of Death." Similarly, the assassination of President John F. Kennedy inspired poet W. H. Auden to write the poem "Elegy for J.F.K." Go to the library, and read one of these three poems. Report on the poem to the class.

O Captain! My Captain! 283

1. the prize we sought; exultation
2. on the deck; cold and dead
3. rise up and hear the bells
4. "dear father"
5. that the Captain has fallen cold and dead
6. "anchored safe and sound, its voyage closed and done"
7. "with mournful tread"
8. the Civil War
9. ■ *the bells I hear, the people all exulting*
   ■ *hear the bells; . . . for you the flag is flung—for you the bugle trills, / For you bouquets and ribboned wreaths—for you the shores a-crowding, / For you they call, the swaying mass, their eager faces turning*
10. ■ tries to deny the Captain is dead
    ■ wants to believe the Captain's death is a dream; still denies the death
11. conveys sorrow; makes the reader also feel sorrow
12. ■ the dead Captain
    ■ Answers will vary. Most will agree that the reader feels the speaker's sadness, which is intensified by contrasting it with the crowd's joy.
13. Answers will vary. Possible answers: to convey the emotions associated with the event; to depict significant events

CHALLENGE

Students should
■ read either the Auden poem on Kennedy or one of the other two Whitman poems on Lincoln
■ describe to the class the terms used to eulogize the subject in the poem
■ describe the poet's attitude toward his subject
■ indicate whether the poem is moving and why

LITERARY OPTIONS

- total effect
- title
- free verse

THEMATIC OPTIONS

- family relationships
- creativity
- leadership

TITLE

The title identifies the subject of the poem and establishes her relationship to the speaker.

FIGURATIVE LANGUAGE

Molly's storytelling abilities developed her sister's love of literature ("Waking up the story buds/like fruit"). The language in lines 38–39 makes Molly seem almost a force of nature, a giver of life.

TOTAL EFFECT

Walker repeatedly uses "WHO IN THE FIFTIES" as a launching point for a montage of scenes, a kind of spliced-together home movie. The refrain and the scenes portray Molly as a spirited, creative, liberated young woman.

FREE VERSE

The varying line lengths re-create the natural rhythm of colloquial speech, an effect that suits the images of the poem, which are taken from ordinary family life.

REFLECTING ON THE POEM

Why does Walker emphasize the time when Molly did all these things? (She reminds us that her sister behaved in this forceful, spirited way during a more conservative time.)

Alice Walker

For My Sister Molly Who in the Fifties

Once made a fairy rooster from
Mashed potatoes
Whose eyes I forget
But green onions were his tail
5 And his two legs were carrot sticks
A tomato slice his crown.
Who came home on vacation
When the sun was hot
and cooked
10 and cleaned
And minded least of all
The children's questions
A million or more
Pouring in on her
15 Who had been to school
And knew (and told us too) that certain
Words were no longer good
And taught me not to say us for we
No matter what "Sonny said" up the
20 road.

FOR MY SISTER MOLLY WHO IN THE FIFTIES
Knew Hamlet[1] well and read into the night
And coached me in my songs of Africa
A continent I never knew
25 But learned to love
Because "they" she said could carry
A tune
And spoke in accents never heard
in Eatonton.
30 Who read from *Prose and Poetry*
And loved to read "Sam McGee from Tennessee"[2]

On nights the fire was burning low
And Christmas wrapped in angel hair
And I for one prayed for snow.
35 WHO IN THE FIFTIES
Knew all the written things that made
Us laugh and stories by
The hour   Waking up the story buds
Like fruit. Who walked among the flowers
40 And brought them inside the house
And smelled as good as they
And looked as bright.
Who made dresses, braided
Hair. Moved chairs about
45 Hung things from walls
Ordered baths
Frowned on wasp bites
And seemed to know the endings
Of all the tales
50 I had forgot.

---

1. **Hamlet:** main character of the tragic play
Hamlet by William Shakespeare.
2. **"Sam McGee from Tennessee":** popular narrative poem by Robert W. Service.

284   *Poetry*

STUDY QUESTIONS

Recalling

1. According to the title, when did Molly do the things described in the poem?

2. What thing, described in lines 1–6, did Molly make?

3. According to lines 7–15, when did Molly come home? Where had she been?

4. What works of literature, named in lines 22–31, did Molly read? In what did she coach the speaker?

5. According to lines 36–39, what did Molly know?

6. According to lines 40–45, what did Molly do to brighten the house?

7. In the last three lines of the poem, what does the speaker say Molly knew?

Interpreting

8. What is unusual about the title and the first lines of the poem? How do you think they should be read?

9. Is the speaker older or younger than Molly? How do you know? What does this fact help to explain about the speaker's emotions?

10. What kind of person was Molly? Give specific examples to support your view.

11. Describe the overall emotion that the speaker feels for her sister. What quality of Molly's does the speaker seem to treasure most?

Extending

12. What do you think is the most important thing that older family members can give to younger ones?

READING AND LITERARY FOCUS

Total Effect

As you have seen, the **total effect** of a poem is the result of all the poem's elements working together. When you first read a poem, remember to try to experience it as a whole. Each reader will experience the poem differently. Relax with the poem. Let its sounds, images, and emotions carry you away.

When you begin to take the poem apart, focus on each element separately. You may want to look at the guidelines on page 281.

Finally, read the poem again. With the detailed thought you have given to the poem's separate elements, you will not only be able to experience the poem's total effect, but you will also understand how that total effect is created.

Thinking About the Total Effect

■ Choose one separate element of Alice Walker's poem, and describe in detail how Walker uses it. You might pick sound, language, form, or meaning, for example. Then tell what it contributes to the poem's total effect.

COMPOSITION

Writing About Poetry

■ Write about the total effect of Walker's poem. First describe the poem's overall impact on you. Then give examples of the sounds, imagery, and figurative language that help to create that effect. *For help with this assignment, see Lesson 5 in the Writing About Literature Handbook at the back of this book.*

Writing a Collage Poem

■ A **collage** is a picture made by patching together scraps of different materials. A collage poem is made by putting together images and phrases from different sources. Write a collage poem in which you present seemingly unrelated images to create an overall description of a person, object, or scene. You may want to write about one day in school, a journey, an athlete, or a city street.

For My Sister Molly Who in the Fifties   285

COMPOSITION: GUIDELINES FOR EVALUATION

WRITING ABOUT POETRY

Objective
To describe a poem's total effect

Guidelines for Evaluation
■ suggested length: one to two paragraphs
■ should describe the poem's overall impact on the reader
■ should cite examples of sounds, imagery, and figurative language that create that effect
■ should describe the writer's mood or attitude

WRITING A COLLAGE POEM

Objective
To write a collage poem that creates an overall impression of a person, object, or scene

Guidelines for Evaluation
■ suggested length: six lines or more
■ should create an overall description of the subject
■ should use vivid sensory language and images from different sources

The speaker stops at two diverging roads and takes the less-traveled one.

LITERARY OPTIONS

- symbol
- speaker and tone

THEMATIC OPTIONS

- choices and consequences
- nonconformity

SPEAKER AND TONE

The speaker begins to reveal his mixed feelings in the first person, creating the personal tone of the poem (l. 2).

SYMBOL

The final stanza clarifies the symbolic meaning of the two roads and the traveler's choice. The serious tone suggests that the choice of roads stands for an important life choice (ll. 16–20).

RHYME SCHEME

The rhyme scheme of the poem is *abaab*. This formal pattern balances the poem's personal tone and lends the poem a sense of structure.

REFLECTING ON THE POEM

Why do you think the speaker says he "will be telling this with a sigh"? (Possible answers include regret for the possible delights of the road not taken, acceptance of the difficulties of the road taken or of the limitations of human knowledge and choices.)

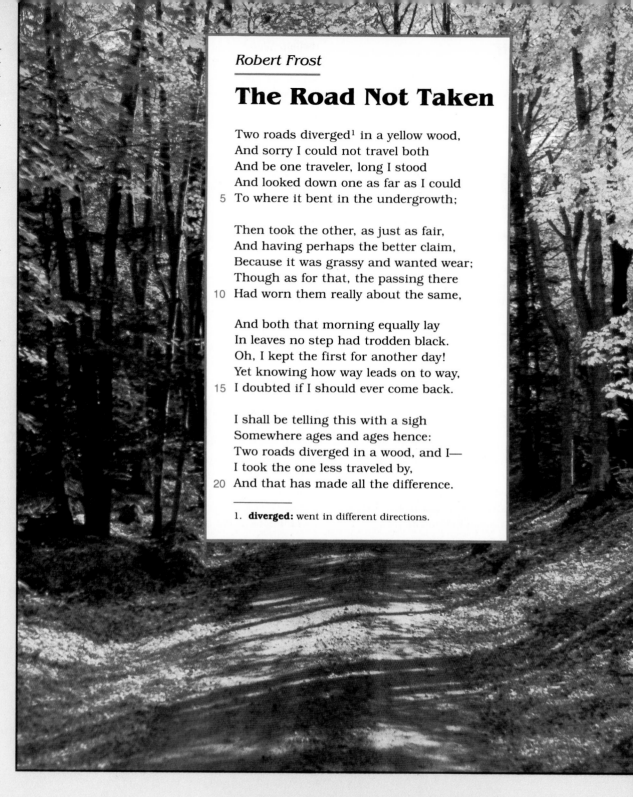

Robert Frost

The Road Not Taken

Two roads diverged[1] in a yellow wood,
And sorry I could not travel both
And be one traveler, long I stood
And looked down one as far as I could
5 To where it bent in the undergrowth;

Then took the other, as just as fair,
And having perhaps the better claim,
Because it was grassy and wanted wear;
Though as for that, the passing there
10 Had worn them really about the same,

And both that morning equally lay
In leaves no step had trodden black.
Oh, I kept the first for another day!
Yet knowing how way leads on to way,
15 I doubted if I should ever come back.

I shall be telling this with a sigh
Somewhere ages and ages hence:
Two roads diverged in a wood, and I—
I took the one less traveled by,
20 And that has made all the difference.

1. **diverged:** went in different directions.

STUDY QUESTIONS

Recalling

1. About what is the speaker sorry?
2. According to lines 6–8, what reasons does the speaker give for taking "the other" road?
3. According to lines 9–12, which road was more worn?
4. What does the speaker doubt in lines 14–15?
5. According to lines 16–17, where and when does the speaker imagine himself telling the story of the two roads?
6. At the end of the poem, what does the speaker say "has made all the difference"?

Interpreting

7. In the second stanza what two contradictory reasons does the speaker give for making the choice he did? What reason does he give in the third stanza?
8. Do you think the speaker feels he made the right choice? Why or why not?

Extending

9. What are some of the advantages and some of the disadvantages of not being able to reverse a decision?

READING AND LITERARY FOCUS

Paraphrasing a Poem

Paraphrasing a poem is restating its meaning in different words. When you paraphrase a poem you change its form and word choice but not its meaning. For example, the opening line of "The Raven,"

> Once upon a midnight dreary, while I pondered
> weak and weary

might be paraphrased in this way: "One gloomy night at twelve o'clock, while I was thinking, feeling very tired . . ."

The purpose of paraphrasing is to gain a clearer understanding of a poem's meaning. A paraphrase may be longer or shorter than the original poem. It may reduce figurative language to literal language. It may substitute different vocabulary, specify nouns instead of pronouns, and fill in any connecting ideas the poet has omitted.

Paraphrasing is a useful tool, a method you may want to use to clarify what a poem means. It is important to remember, however, that a paraphrase can never substitute for the experience of a poem itself. A paraphrase does not have the power of sound, language, images, form, and meaning working together.

Thinking About Paraphrasing a Poem

1. Paraphrase Frost's "Road Not Taken."
2. What is gained and what is lost by the paraphrase?

Symbol

A **symbol** is an object, person, place, or experience that means more than it is. For example, a young tree planted in someone's yard may be more than just a tree. To the person who planted it, the tree may also be a symbol of growth, of hope for the future, and of the power of nature itself.

Writers frequently use symbols in order to include as much meaning as possible in the literature that they create. Symbols expand our awareness. They help us to see that things around us may mean more than they seem. In "The Road Not Taken," for example, Frost makes an important decision. He decides to travel down one particular road and not to travel down another road. The road that he takes becomes for him a symbol of the course of his life. The road symbolizes the journey that the poet has taken through the years.

Thinking About Symbol

■ What do you think that the road *not* taken symbolizes?

The Road Not Taken 287

STUDY QUESTIONS

1. could not travel both paths
2. just as fair, grassy, wanted wear
3. They seemed equally worn.
4. that he will come back to try the other road
5. "Somewhere ages and ages hence"
6. taking the less-traveled road
7. ■ chose the road that "wanted wear"; "the passing there/Had worn them . . . the same"
   ■ kept the first path for another day
8. Possible answers:
   ■ wrong choice: line 16: "I shall be telling this with a sigh . . ."
   ■ right choice: lines 19–20: "I took the one less traveled by,/And that has made all the difference."
9. ■ Advantage: proceeding without hesitations, second thoughts
   ■ Disadvantage: living with the consequences without possibility of starting over

READING AND LITERARY FOCUS

Paraphrasing a Poem

1. Possible answer: I saw two roads that went through a wood. I was sorry I could not travel both. I tried to look down one path as far as I could. Then I took the other. It was just as attractive, but perhaps they were equally used. I hoped to explore the other path later, but I doubt that I will be able to. Someday I shall recall this decision with regret. I chose the less-traveled road. That has made all the difference in my life.
2. Most will agree: The paraphrase gains clarity but loses the poem's feeling; tone, language, imagery.

Symbol

the life the speaker did not lead

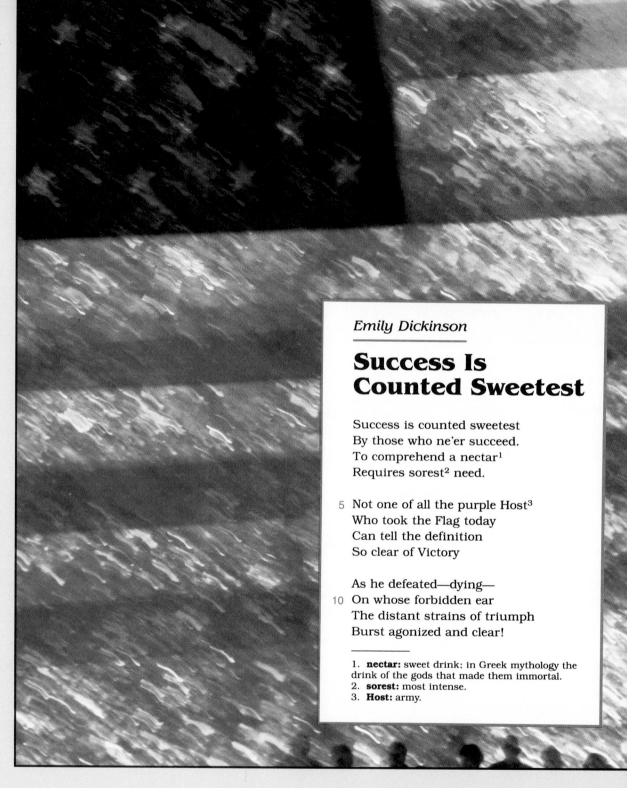

The speaker claims that only the unsuccessful can really appreciate success, citing the example of the effect of a battle on both the victorious and the defeated.

LITERARY OPTIONS

- imagery
- poetic form

THEMATIC OPTIONS

- success and failure
- confronting obstacles

MAIN IDEA AND PARADOX

The main idea is directly stated from the beginning. Paradoxically, those who fail put a higher value on success than those who succeed (ll. 1–2).

IMAGERY

Those who succeed are compared to a winning army taking the enemy's flag. Further, "purple" has connotations of royalty, high birth, pomp, and ceremony, which fit the idea of a victorious army (ll. 5–6).

POETIC FORM

A serious idea is compressed into a short poem of three stanzas. The short lines, simple rhythm, and rhyme scheme give the poem a songlike quality that contrasts with the often violent imagery.

REFLECTING ON THE POEM

Do you think the speaker counts herself among the successful or the defeated? Explain your answer. (The powerful imagery of the poem suggests the speaker has at some point tasted defeat.)

Emily Dickinson

Success Is Counted Sweetest

Success is counted sweetest
By those who ne'er succeed.
To comprehend a nectar[1]
Requires sorest[2] need.

5 Not one of all the purple Host[3]
Who took the Flag today
Can tell the definition
So clear of Victory

As he defeated—dying—
10 On whose forbidden ear
The distant strains of triumph
Burst agonized and clear!

---

1. **nectar:** sweet drink; in Greek mythology the drink of the gods that made them immortal.
2. **sorest:** most intense.
3. **Host:** army.

STUDY QUESTIONS

Recalling

1. According to stanza 1, by whom is success counted sweetest?
2. The second and third stanzas offer an example to illustrate the statement in the first stanza. In the example what did the purple host do? What is the purple host not able to do?
3. According to stanza 3, who *can* define "victory"?

Interpreting

4. Why do you think those who "took the Flag" cannot understand what victory means?
5. Why is the defeated person more sensitive to the real meaning of victory?
6. What attitude does the speaker have toward those who are defeated?

Extending

7. Do you agree with the poet's attitude toward defeat and victory? Why or why not?

COMPOSITION

Writing About Poetry

■ Write about the total effect of "Success Is Counted Sweetest." First describe the poem's overall impact on you. Then give examples of the sounds, imagery, and figurative language that help to create that effect. *For help with this assignment, see Lesson 5 in the Writing About Literature Handbook at the back of this book.*

Creating a Title

■ Emily Dickinson did not title her poems. Editors later began naming the poems based on the first line of each. Create a new title for the poem that begins "Success is counted sweetest." State your title, and explain why it is appropriate based on the poem's theme, imagery, and total effect.

CHALLENGE

Exhibit

■ With other members of your class, create a Poets' Hall of Fame. Each individual or small group should choose one poet from those whom you have studied in this unit and create a small exhibit about that person and his or her work. Each exhibit might include: (1) a drawing of the poet with his or her name and dates, (2) a list of important events and publications in the person's life, (3) one hand-copied poem by the poet *not* found in this textbook, (4) a quotation by the poet, and (5) statements, illustrations, or examples of the person's interests, hobbies, and influence on other poets.

COMPARING POEMS

Compare the total effects of the poems in one of the following pairs:

"O Captain! My Captain!" and "For My Sister Molly Who in the Fifties"
"The Road Not Taken" and "Success Is Counted Sweetest"

1. State the theme of each poem you are comparing. What do the themes have in common? In what way are they different?
2. Name the specific techniques of sound, language, imagery, and form used in each poem. What does each technique add to the total effect?
3. Which poem is more meaningful to you? Why?

STUDY QUESTIONS

1. by those who never achieve it
2. was victorious; define victory
3. one who was defeated
4. cannot know meaning of victory without experience of defeat
5. knows how the opposite feels
6. sympathy
7. students who agree may state that winners take success for granted, while the defeated know it from the contrast. Students who disagree may argue that winners know success through savoring it.

COMPARING POEMS

■ "O Captain! My Captain!": tribute to Lincoln; "For My Sister Molly Who in the Fifties": remembrance of a sister. Both praise a beloved person, but Whitman conveys a nation's feeling of loss for a public hero while Walker shares the warm memory of a family member. Whitman uses rhyme and regular rhythm and extended metaphor. Walker uses free verse and some repetition.

■ "The Road Not Taken": A person's choice of paths sets his life's course; "Success Is Counted Sweetest": The defeated understand success better than victors. Both poems discuss the consequences of actions, but Frost deals with choices, while Dickinson contrasts success and failure. Frost uses simple, everyday language, with assonance creating a musical effect. Dickinson uses alliteration, regular rhythm, and unusual, vivid language.

■ Students should cite reasons as to which poem is "most meaningful."

COMPOSITION: GUIDELINES FOR EVALUATION

WRITING ABOUT POETRY

Objective

To analyze a poem for its total effect

Guidelines for Evaluation

■ suggested length: one to two paragraphs
■ should begin with a description of the poem's overall impact and the writer's impressions
■ should give examples of sounds, imagery and figurative language that create the effect

CREATING A TITLE

Objective

To write a title for a poem and explain its appropriateness

Guidelines for Evaluation

■ suggested length: one to two paragraphs
■ should suggest an appropriate title
■ should capitalize its important words
■ should explain its appropriateness

CHALLENGE

Students should

■ choose one poet on whom to focus
■ find a drawing of the poet
■ list important events in the poet's life
■ copy one other poem by that poet along with a quotation and statements about the poet's interests.

The three activities in this lesson will teach students to see and hear details in a poem, to make inferences from those details, and to apply those inferences to the meaning of the poem. Suggested responses to those activities are provided here. In addition, you will find among the materials for this unit in your *Teacher's Resource Book* the following related blackline masters: Interpreting Details of Sound in Poetry; Interpreting Details of Language in Poetry; Interpreting Details of Meaning in Poetry.

Activity 1

1. The repetitiousness indicates that the speaker hears repeated raps at the door.

Active Reading

Poetry

Interpreting Details of Sound

When you read a poem aloud, the first element that captures your attention is the poem's sound. Even when you read silently, you enjoy the sound of the poem in your mind. The sound of the poem comes from the poet's careful choice and arrangement of words. By paying close attention to those words, you can enjoy the sound of poetry even more.

The sound of Edgar Allan Poe's poem "The Raven," for example, is one of its most important qualities. The sound creates a feeling that makes the events in the poem powerful and memorable. Read the following lines aloud.

> Deep into that darkness peering, long I stood there wondering, fearing,
> Doubting, dreaming dreams no mortal ever dared to dream before.

The poet repeats the sound of the letter *d* in these lines—*d*eep, *d*arkness, stoo*d*, won*d*ering, *d*oubting, *d*reaming, *d*reams, *d*ared, *d*ream. The repeated sound keeps our attention, like the intense beat of a drum. As we listen to the repeated sounds, we realize that the speaker is not calm. He is nervous and full of fear.

The lines also repeat another sound element. Notice how many words end in *-ing.* The repeated sounds build in intensity, suggesting that the speaker is growing more and more nervous.

Sound in poetry is often closely tied to meaning. Great poets use sound to communicate ideas and emotions, just as a composer will match the sounds of music to the emotion of a song. Listen carefully to the poems you read.

Activity 1 Read the following passages from "The Raven." Answer the question about repeated sounds after each passage.

1. While I nodded, nearly napping, suddenly there came a tapping,
   As of someone gently rapping, rapping at my chamber door

   What does the repetition of the word rapping *tell about the number of times the speaker hears sounds at his door?*

2. And the silken, sad, uncertain rustling of each purple curtain

   Identify the repeated s sounds in this line. What sound in the room is suggested by the repeated s sounds?

3. And the Raven, never flitting, still is sitting, still is sitting

   What are the repeated words in this line? What do they emphasize about the movement of the Raven?

Interpreting Details of Language

The poet chooses words both for what they mean directly and for what they suggest indirectly. The image we remember most clearly from "Paul Revere's Ride," for example, is the image of Paul Revere riding through the streets shouting, "The British are coming!" Certainly that part of the poem is powerful. However, that power is increased because of the long *quiet* part of the poem that comes before it. Look carefully at the italicized words in the following lines.

> Then he said "Good night!" and with *muffled* oar
> *Silently* rowed to the Charlestown shore

> Then he climbed the tower of the Old North Church
> By the wooden stairs, with *stealthy* tread

> The *watchful* night wind, as it went
> *Creeping* along from tent to tent,
> And seeming to *whisper,* "All is well!"

The language used to describe the events in this part of the poem emphasizes the silence that will be suddenly broken by the excitement of Paul Revere's ride.

Activity 2 Read the following passages from "Paul Revere's Ride." Answer the question after each passage.

1. A hurry of hoofs in a village street,
   A shape in the moonlight, a bulk in the dark,
   And beneath, from the pebbles, in passing, a spark
   Struck out by a steed flying fearless and fleet.

   Which words in the passage indicate the speed of Paul Revere's horse?

2. The repeated sounds are the s sound in "silken, sad, uncertain rustling." The repeated sounds suggest the sound of the moving curtain.
3. The repeated words are "still is sitting." They emphasize the fact that the raven does not move at all.

Activity 2
1. The speed of the horse is suggested by the words *hurry, passing, spark, flying,* and *fleet.*

2. The contrasting sounds are indicated by the words *soft* and *loud.*

3. The sound of Paul Revere's outcry is described by the words *alarm, defiance,* and *echo forevermore.*

2. Now soft on the sand, now loud on the ledge,
   Is heard the tramp of his steed as he rides.

   Which words in the passage indicate the contrasting sounds of the horse's hooves?

3. And so through the night went his cry of alarm
   To every Middlesex village and farm—
   A cry of defiance and not of fear—
   A voice in the darkness, a knock at the door,
   And a word that shall echo forevermore!

   Which words in the passage describe the sound of Paul Revere's outcry?

Interpreting Details of Meaning

One of the most useful ways to talk about the meaning of a poem is to identify its theme. A theme may be directly stated or it may be implied. In John Keats's poem "On the Grasshopper and the Cricket" the theme is stated directly in the first line.

The poetry of earth is never dead.

The other lines of the poem describe the musical voices of the grasshopper and the cricket. The poem as a whole describes the experiences and feelings that led the poet to the theme that he states in the first line.

Most poems, however, do not state a theme directly. Instead, they imply a theme. They present a great variety of details that enable you, the reader, to arrive at the theme. Read the last stanza of Robert Frost's "Stopping by Woods on a Snowy Evening."

The woods are lovely, dark, and deep,
But I have promises to keep,
And miles to go before I sleep,
And miles to go before I sleep.

These lines contain many clues to the theme of the poem. The speaker says that the woods are lovely, implying that he would like to enter them. However, they are also dark and deep. Perhaps he would never get out again.

The speaker then says that he has promises to keep. He does not say what those promises are or to whom he has made them. However, he feels a sense of responsibility. Then he says that he has miles to go, suggesting that he is going to continue on his journey. Finally he repeats his statement about the miles he has

292   *Poetry*

to go. The repetition may mean that he is forcing himself to go on. It may also mean that the woods have almost hypnotized him with their loveliness.

Putting all these clues together, you can arrive at the implied theme. One way to express the implied theme is as follows: "Though tempted to turn aside from our responsibilities, we face the tasks we must perform." How would you express the theme in your own words?

Activity 3 Read each of the following passages from poems in this unit. Answer the question about theme after each passage.

1. See how he dives
    From the rocks with a zoom!
      See how he darts
        Through his watery room
                                    —"Seal"

Name the details in this passage that suggest the following theme: The seal is a lively, delightful animal.

2. My eyes feast upon the willow,
    But my heart goes to the ginkgo.
                              —"Willow and Ginkgo"

What is the direct statement of theme in this passage?

3. Clouds beyond clouds above me.
    Wastes beyond wastes below;
    But nothing drear can move me;
    I will not, cannot go.
                              —"Spellbound"

Name the details in this passage that suggest the following theme: The power of nature can hold us spellbound.

Activity 3
1. The details that suggest the lively, delightful animal are his diving with a zoom and darting through the water.
2. The direct statement of theme is the two complete lines given.
3. The details that suggest the spellbinding power of nature are the suggestion of infinite clouds beyond nearer clouds, wastes stretching beyond nearer wastes, and the immobility of the speaker.

Literary Skills Review

Poetry

Guide for Reading Poetry

As you read poems, this guide will help you notice and appreciate the techniques poets use to appeal to our senses and emotions.

Sound

1. What examples can you find of **repetition, alliteration, assonance,** or **onomatopoeia**? What effect does each create?
2. Does the poem **rhyme**? What is the **rhyme scheme**?
3. What is the poem's **rhythm**? Is the rhythm appropriate to the subject matter of the poem?

Language

1. What **images** does the poem contain? To what sense do the images appeal?
2. What vivid **word choices** does the poet make?
3. What **similes** and **metaphors** does the poem contain?
4. What examples can you find of **personification**?

Form

1. What examples can you find of **couplets, quatrains,** or **stanzas**?
2. Is the poem written in **free verse**?

Meaning

1. What does the **title** tell about the poem's meaning?
2. What events in the poem form a **narrative**?
3. What thoughts and feelings does the poet share in a **lyric**?
4. What is the **theme** of the poem? Is it directly or indirectly stated?

Themes Review

Poetry

Writers throughout history have communicated fascination with the natural world. However, each writer who focuses on the general theme "nature" presents a different specific idea about it. For example, the poem "Stopping by Woods on a Snowy Evening" (page 230) expresses the following specific view of the general theme "nature": "The beauty of nature can draw us away from the human world." On the other hand, "When Icicles Hang by the Wall" (page 237) expresses a different view of nature: "The harshness of nature often intrudes into the human world."

1. Choose two of the following poems, and tell what each says about the general theme "nature."

   "Mushrooms" "Spellbound" "The Heron"
   "Seal" "The Grasshopper "Counting-Out
   "The Wind"   and the Cricket" Rhyme"

2. Choose two of the following poems, and tell what specific theme each expresses about the general theme "ideals."

   "I Am the Land" "The Road Not "Foul Shot"
   "The Dream   Taken" "Ring Out,
   Keeper" "Success . . ." Wild Bells"

3. Choose two of the following poems, and tell what each poem says about the general theme "discoveries."

   "Preparation" "For My Sister "Willow and
   "A Minor Bird" Molly" Ginkgo"
   "Mouse Night" "Night Thought of "The Walrus and
    a Tortoise . . ." the Carpenter"

4. Choose one poem and one story from the following list, and explain what each says about "love and friendship."

   Poems: "Mama Is a Sunrise" "The Raven"
   Stories: "Then He Goes "The Osage Orange
    Free" Tree"

5. Choose one poem and one other work from the following list, and explain how each treats the general theme "heroism."

   Poems: "Paul Revere's Ride" "O Captain!
    "Lochinvar" My Captain!"
   Other: *The Miracle* "The Dog of Pom-
    Worker peii"

THEMES REVIEW

The questions in the Themes Review for the Poetry unit recall the general themes portrayed in the selections in this unit. Suggested answers to these questions are presented here.

1. "Mushrooms": Nature is unstoppable. "Wind": Nature destroys and creates. "Counting-Out": Nature offers great variety. "Grasshopper": Nature has its own poetry. "Seal": We delight in natural creatures. "Heron": Nature offers moments of great beauty. "Spellbound": The spectacle of nature can overwhelm.

2. "I Am": The lands awaits its ideal use. "Foul Shot": Persevering, we may reach our goals. "The Road Not Taken": Our goals are changed by everyday choices. "Success": Failure makes us understand ideals more keenly. "Dream Keeper": Despite ideals of friendship, people change. "Ring Out": With each new year, we renew our ideals.

3. "Preparation": Each season offers discoveries. "Minor Bird": "Minor" events can offer great discoveries. "Mouse Night": We discover much about ourselves through relationships with our parents. "For My Sister Molly": Looking back, we rediscover precious moments. "Night Thoughts": Situation and mood often determine what we discover. "Willow": We discover much about nature and ourselves through contrasts. "Walrus": Surprise and delight often accompany discovery.

4. "Mama": Parental love is life-giving. "The Raven": A lost love can give unending pain. "Then He Goes Free" and "Osage Orange Tree": Friendship often leads to sacrifices.

5. "Paul Revere": Heroes often awaken courage in others. "The Story-Teller": Poets may be heroes of the imagination. "Lochinvar": Romantic heroes are proud and courageous. "O Captain!": We mourn our greatest heroes. *Miracle Worker:* Some heroic victories are won on private battlefields. "Pompeii": A hero may put the welfare of others first.

For more information about the themes portrayed in these selections, see the Theme Index beginning on page 666.

Preview Nonfiction

Nonfiction is factual prose writing. Unlike fiction, nonfiction concerns people who really lived and events that really happened. A work of nonfiction, however, does more than present facts. It interprets these facts.

Two pieces of nonfiction about the same subject will be different because each writer has selected, organized, and interpreted the facts in a unique way. For example, two writers describing the same baseball game may write very different pieces of nonfiction. One writer may write a serious, detailed study of the game for people who know a great deal about baseball, while the other may write a humorous account to be read by people who know nothing about the game.

These accounts of the same baseball game will differ largely because each author writes for a different purpose and audience. A writer's **purpose** may be to inform, entertain, or persuade the audience, or to express an idea about life in general. The **audience** is the reader for whom the work is intended. The author who writes for experts on baseball will choose different information and write in a different style from the author who writes for people who know little about the subject.

The following nonfiction selections include autobiography, biography, and essays. An **autobiography** is the story of a person's life written by that person. A **biography** is the story of a person's life written by someone else. An **essay** is a short nonfiction work that can deal with any subject. Essays may be narrative, descriptive, expository, or persuasive. Narrative essays tell true stories, while descriptive essays create pictures of their subjects. Expository essays present facts or explain ideas, and persuasive essays try to convince readers to accept an opinion or take action. As you read each of the following selections, decide for what purpose and audience the work was written.

Nonfiction 297

After students have read the Preview, you might compare nonfiction and short stories. At its best nonfiction is a demanding art that requires as much control of language as a short story does. In fact, nonfiction uses most of the elements of the short story: events, people, places, and ideas. Make sure, however, that students understand the difference between nonfiction and fiction: Nonfiction deals with "verifiable facts" and fiction is a work of the imagination. To check, ask students to name examples of nonfiction that they have read. Use a newspaper to introduce the types of nonfiction. Human-interest stories can be descriptive or narrative; reviews and editorials can be persuasive; how-to articles are expository; interviews often contain biographical sketches.

© Arnold Newman

Agnes De Mille (born 1908) is an influential American choreographer, or creator of dances. The niece of the film producer Cecil B. De Mille, she grew up in Hollywood. When she was twelve, she saw a performance by the great Russian ballerina Anna Pavlova and decided to become a dancer. After a long struggle she succeeded. De Mille became known as a creator of dances that portray American subjects. Her inventive choreography for the musical play *Oklahoma!* (1943) was a major advance in the theater.

In the following excerpt from her autobiography *Dance to the Piper* (1952), De Mille recalls her early struggles at the school run by the Russian dancing teacher Theodore Kosloff.

■ What qualities enable her to overcome her shortcomings?

Agnes De Mille

from Dance to the Piper

1 Kosloff agreed to take us as pupils and out of courtesy to Uncle Cecil[1] he took us free without pay of any sort for as long or as often as we wished to go to his school.

We went down for our audition on a summer morning. The studio was an enormous bare room with folding chairs pushed against the white walls for the mothers to sit on while they watched their daughters sweat. Across one end of the hall hung a large mirror. Around the other three sides stretched the traditional barre.[2] I gave my audition in a bathing suit. Kosloff himself put me through the **2** test. He did not say how talented I was or how naturally graceful. He said my knees were weak, my spine curved, that I was heavy for my age and had "no juice." By this he meant, I came to learn, that my muscles were dry, stubborn and unresilient. He said I was a bit old to start training; I was at the time thirteen. I looked at him in mild surprise. I hardly **3** knew what emotion to give way to, the astonishment of hurt vanity or gratitude for professional help. I was sent off (I keep saying "I"—my sister of course was with me but from the start I took for granted that these lessons were mine. She just came along). We were sent off to buy blocked toe slippers, fitted right to the very ends of our toes, and to prepare proper practice dresses.

1. **Uncle Cecil:** Cecil B. De Mille (1881–1959), famous film producer.
2. **barre** [bär]: long horizontal pole attached to a wall; used by dancers to steady themselves during exercises.

298 *Nonfiction*

GUIDED READING

LITERAL QUESTION

1a. Which of Agnes' physical traits does Kosloff call attention to at the audition? (He says that she has weak knees, a curved spine, an overweight body, and unresilient muscles; in addition, she is a bit old to begin training.)

INFERENTIAL QUESTION

1b. Based on Kosloff's opinions, how would you rate Agnes' chances for success in ballet? (With a body that seems so unsuitable for ballet, she would seem to have little chance for success.)

The first lesson was a private one conducted by Miss Fredova. Miss Fredova was born Winifred Edwards and had received her training in London from Anna Pavlova.[3] She was as slim as a sapling and always wore white like a trained nurse. She parted her dark hair in the center and drew it to the nape of her neck in glossy wings, Russian style. She was shod in low-heeled sandals. She taught standing erect as a guardsman, and beat time with a long pole. First she picked up a watering can and sprinkled water on the floor in a sunny corner by the barre. This she explained was so that we should not slip. Then she placed our hands on the barre and showed us how to turn out our feet ninety degrees from their normal walking stance into first position.[4] Then she told us to *plier*[5] or bend our knees deeply, keeping our heels as long as possible on the floor. I naturally stuck out behind. I found the pole placed rigidly against my spine. I naturally pressed forward on my insteps. Her leg and knee planted against my foot curbed this tendency. "I can't move," I said, laughing with winning helplessness.

"Don't talk," she said. "Down-ee, two-ee, three-ee, four-ee. Down the heels, don't rock on your feet."

At the end of ten minutes the sweat stuck in beads on my forehead. "May I sit down?" I asked.

1 "You must never sit during practice. It ruins the thigh muscles. If you sit down you may not continue with class." I of course would have submitted to a beating with whips rather than stop. I was taking the first steps into the promised land. The path might be thorny but it led straight to Paradise. "Down-

---

3. **Anna Pavlova** [päv lō'və] (1881–1931): Russian ballerina and perhaps the best-known dancer of all time.
4. **first position:** first of the five basic ballet stances.
5. *plier* [plē'ā]: French for "bend."

---

ee, two-ee, three-ee, four-ee. *Nuca.*[6] Give me this fourth position. Repeat the exercise."

2 So she began every lesson. So I have begun every practice period since. It is part of the inviolable ritual of ballet dancing. Every ballet student that has ever trained in the classic technique in any part of the world begins just this way, never any other. They were dreary exercises and I was very bad at them but these were the exercises that built Taglioni's leg.[7] These repeated stretches and pulls gave Pavlova her magic foot and Legnani hers and Kchessinska[8] hers. This was the very secret of how to dance, the tradition handed down from teacher to pupil for three hundred years. A king had patterned the style and named the steps, the king who built Versailles.[9] Here was an ancient and enduring art whose technique stood like the rules of harmony. All other kinds of performance in our Western theater had faded or changed. What were movies to this? Or Broadway plays?

3 I, a complacent child, who had been flattered into believing I could do without what had gone before, now inherited the labor of centuries. I had come into my birthright. I was fourteen, and I had found my life's work. I felt superior to other adolescents as I stood beside the adults serene and strong, reassured by my vision.

I bent to the discipline. I learned to relax with my head between my knees when I felt sick or faint. I learned how to rest my insteps

---

6. *Nuca:* informal Russian expression, urging the listener on to the next activity; similar in meaning to "Come on."
7. **Taglioni's** [tä lyō'nēz] **leg:** Maria Taglioni (1804–1884) was an Italian ballerina.
8. **Legnani** [lā nyä'nē] **. . . Kchessinska** [che sēn'skä]: Pierina Legnani (1863–1923) was an Italian ballerina famous for her technical skill; Mathilda Kchessinska (1872–1956) was a Polish ballerina.
9. **king . . . Versailles** [vār sī']: King Louis XIV (1638–1715), who ruled France from 1643 to 1715, built a magnificent palace in the city of Versailles near Paris.

Dance to the Piper 299

GUIDED READING

LITERAL QUESTION

1a. With what exercise do all classic ballet lessons begin? (Every ballet lesson begins with the practice of the five basic foot positions.)

INFERENTIAL QUESTION

1b. The author thought the opening exercise was dreary, and she did it badly. Why then was it important? (For over 300 years the exercises had helped dancers build their muscles and master the techniques of their art.)

- Agnes makes ballet practice the most important part of her life.
- Lacking physical traits desirable for success, Agnes compensates with extra determination and effort.
- Later in life she discovers that she is built for endurance and can outperform better "technicians."

1 VOCABULARY: DICTION

De Mille's word choices—*arbitrary, effort, long and relentless, painful, grueling*—emphasize the artist's challenge in achieving her goal.

2 AUTOBIOGRAPHY

De Mille shares with us a perception about herself that has been gained with the passing of time.

3 READING SKILLS: COMPARISON/CONTRAST

The author contrasts her body point by point with that of the ideal dancer's body described at the beginning of this paragraph. Through the mustang simile, De Mille suggests that she shares independence and self-reliance.

---

by lying on my back with my feet vertically up against the wall. I learned how to bind up my toes so that they would not bleed through the satin shoes. But I never sat down. I learned the first and all-important dictate of ballet dancing—never to miss the daily practice, hell or high water, sickness or health, never to miss the barre practice; to miss meals, sleep, rehearsals even but not the practice, not for one day ever under any circumstances, except on Sundays.

I seemed, however, to have little aptitude for the business. What had all this talk about God-given talent amounted to? It was like trying to wiggle my ears. I strained and strained. Nothing perceptible happened. A terrible sense of frustration drove me to striving with masochistic[10] frenzy. Twice I fainted in class. My calves used to ache until tears stuck in my eyes. I learned every possible manipulation of the shoe to ease the aching tendons of my insteps. I used to get abominable stitches in my sides from attempting continuous jumps. But I never sat down. I learned to cool my forehead against the plaster of the walls. I licked the perspiration off from around my mouth. I breathed through my nose though my eyes bugged. But I did not sit and I did not stop.

1 Ballet technique is arbitrary and very difficult. It never becomes easy; it becomes possible. The effort involved in making a dancer's body is so long and relentless, in many instances so painful, the effort to maintain the technique so grueling that unless a certain satisfaction is derived from the disciplining and punishing, the pace could not be maintained. Most dancers are to an extent masochists. "What a good pain! What a profitable

pain!" said Miss Fredova as she stretched her insteps in her two strong hands. "I have practiced for three hours. I am exhausted, and I feel wonderful."

The ideal ballet body is long limbed with a small compact torso. This makes for beauty of line; the longer the arms and legs the more exciting the body line. The ideal ballet foot has a high taut instep and a wide stretch in the Achilles' tendon.[11] This tendon is the spring on which a dancer pushes for his jump, the hinge on which he takes the shock of landing. If there is one tendon in a dancer's body more important than any other, it is this tendon. It is, I should say, the prerequisite for all great technique. When the heel does not stretch easily and softly like a cat's, as mine did not, almost to the point of malformation, the shock of running or jumping must be taken somewhere in the spine by sticking out behind, for instance, in a sitting posture after every jump. I seemed to be all rusty wire and 2 safety pins. My torso was long with unusually broad hips, my legs and arms abnormally short, my hands and feet broad and short. I was besides fat. What I did not know was that I was constructed for endurance and that I developed through effort alone a capacity for outperforming far, far better technicians. Be-3 cause I was built like a mustang,[12] stocky, mettlesome and sturdy, I became a good jumper, growing special compensating muscles up the front of my shins for the lack of a helpful heel. But the long, cool, serene classic line was forever denied me.

And at first, of course, the compensations and adjustments were neither present nor indicated. Every dancer makes his own body. He is born only with certain physical tendencies.

---

10. **masochistic** [mas′ə kis′tik]: typical of those who enjoy pain.

11. **Achilles' tendon:** cord of tissue connecting the calf muscles to the heel.
12. **mustang:** small wild horse of the American West.

GUIDED READING

LITERAL QUESTIONS

1a. What discomfort and pain did De Mille suffer during practice? (She fainted from the exertion; her calves and foot tendons ached until she cried; she got abominable stitches in her side.)

2a. How did Agnes De Mille's body differ from the ideal? (Ideally, a dancer has a short torso and long arms and legs. De Mille had a long, heavy torso and unusually short arms and legs.)

INFERENTIAL QUESTIONS

1b. When her teacher exclaims, "What a profitable pain!" what do you think she means? (The discomfort is not wasted. It will build a strong ballet body.)

2b. How does Agnes feel about having a less-than-ideal body for ballet? (She regrets that she lacks the cool, serene, classic line yet is proud of herself for using her strength to develop compensating qualities.)

Agnes De Mille rehearsing in 1929.

1 This making of a ballet leg takes approximately ten years and the initial stages are almost entirely discouraging, for even the best look awkward and paralyzed at the beginning.

My predicament was intensified by the fact that Mother and Father had no intention of permitting me to slight my other studies for this new enthusiasm. I was allowed one private lesson a week (forty-five minutes) and one class lesson (one hour). In between times I practiced at home alone, something no dancer, pupil or professional, ever does. One needs company to overcome the almost irresistible tendency to flag. One needs someone else's eye on awkward parts impossible to see. It is an unnatural and unprofitable strain for **2** a child to practice without supervision. I practiced in Mother's bathroom where she had a little barre fitted for me. The floor was slippery and there was no mirror. And I hated to prac-

tice there. I flagellated[13] myself into the daily **3** grind. Mother thought I was overworking and forbade me to practice more than forty-five minutes. When I showed signs of resisting, she persuaded Kosloff to order me not to exceed this limit. All the other children practiced one hour a day in the studio and had a daily class lesson besides. They practically lived at the studio, practicing in the morning, taking lessons in the afternoon, sewing costumes and talking dancing in between times.

Since I could not practice long, obviously I must practice harder. I strained and strained. Between the Monday lesson and the Thursday lesson, I developed and matured rigid bad habits. Every week I developed a new bad habit.

---

13. **flagellated** [flaj′ə lāt′əd]: whipped; drove to an extreme degree.

Dance to the Piper 301

AT A GLANCE

- Fearing Agnes is overworking, Mrs. De Mille limits her daughter's lessons and practice.
- Agnes practices harder but alone, developing bad habits.

1 READING SKILLS: TOPIC SENTENCE

While this topic sentence appears at the end of the paragraph, it expresses the main idea of the entire page—the "making of a ballet leg."

2 SETTING

The bathroom setting, inadequate—event treacherous—for practice, presents yet another obstacle. It contrasts with Kosloff's well-equipped studio, where the other students practice.

3 THEME

The young Agnes perceives her mother's concern for her general well-being as another stumbling block in achieving her ideal.

GUIDED READING

LITERAL QUESTION

1a. Why don't ballet dancers usually practice alone? (Dancers need supervision to make sure their body parts are in the correct position. They also need company so as not to flag, or tire.)

INFERENTIAL QUESTION

1b. Agnes De Mille did practice alone. What does this tell you about her? (Her desire to dance was so strong that she didn't need others to encourage her to work hard. However, since her solo practice encouraged her to develop bad habits, her insistence on practicing this way suggests her headstrong immaturity.)

- Despite her efforts, Agnes is the worst pupil in the class.
- Kosloff's emphasis on technique instead of expressiveness does not suit Agnes' ability.

1 MAIN IDEA

Agnes' vision of herself as "destined to be great" motivates her during difficult and unpromising periods of her training.

2 IRONY

This contrast between Agnes' performance in class and her visions of greatness is ironic. Time has added another irony: De Mille actually achieved greatness, despite the early contrast.

3 TONE

Humorous phrases such as "muscle-locking gut-busters" and "hell-bent for beauty" convey both the desperate determination of the young pupil and the wry amusement of the mature author.

Two views of Agnes De Mille. *Above:* choreographing *Oklahoma!* in 1943. *Below:* at work in the 1960s.

1 The plain truth is I was the worst pupil in the class. Having grown into adolescence feeling that I was remarkably gifted and destined to be great (I remember a friend asking Mother, "But do you want her to be a professional dancer?" and Mother's cool reply, "If she can be a Pavlova—not otherwise"), I now found I could not hold my own with any of the **2** girls standing on the floor beside me. So I crept about at the rear of the group, found matters wrong with my shoes, with my knees, with my hair, resorted to any device to get away from the dreadful exposure.

Furthermore, the Kosloff method of teaching rather accentuated my dilemma. The accent was placed on force and duration instead of harmony. He was intent on disciplining the feet and legs, and paid almost no attention to the co-ordination of arms and facial expression. The girls grew as vigorous as Cossacks,[14] leaping prodigiously, whirling without cease, flailing and thrashing as they went and contorting their necks and faces in a hideous effort to show the master how altogether **3** hell-bent for beauty they were. The exercises he devised were little miracles of perverse difficulty, muscle-locking gut-busters, all of them. I have never since seen healthy girls faint in class, but in Kosloff's class they went down quite regularly and were dragged off with their heels bumping on the floor behind them. Kosloff barely stopped counting. He used to sit in a great armchair facing the room, stamping and roaring, whacking a cane in measure to the music. In the corner sat the man with the balalaika[15] barely audible through the noise. All the girls adored the master and gladly fainted for him. It was Miss Fredova, however, who gave me my private lessons, quietly, patiently, kindly. Kosloff oc-

---

14. **Cossacks:** group of people in southeastern Russia, known for their skill on horseback and in combat.
15. **balalaika** [bal'ə li'kə]: Russian stringed musical instrument, similar to a guitar.

GUIDED READING

LITERAL QUESTION

1a. What did Agnes do when she was unable to "hold her own" in the class? (She crept about at the rear of the group, found something wrong with her shoes or knees or hair.)

INFERENTIAL QUESTION

1b. Why do you think Agnes continued dance lessons when she could not seem to hold her own in class? (Agnes had such a strong desire to be a great dancer that she was able to overcome her feelings of embarrassment.)

casionally walked in, looked for a minute, said, "No juice, no juice. More *plié*. Do you know? More expression, more sowl,"[16] grinned suddenly with Tartar[17] glee and lost interest. "Don't be discouraged," said the angel Fredova, "I wish though you could practice more regularly."

I was always late for class. We had a piano lesson before the dancing lesson and the traveling between required at least forty minutes and getting into practice clothes another ten. Mother allowed twenty minutes exactly from keyboard to barre and in three years she refused to adjust her timetable, always hoping that geography would somehow give way. As a consequence I always missed the preliminary warming-up exercises and started every class half through, cold and unprepared. I was not permitted ever to make the trip into town alone so I could not better the situation. Mother gave up two afternoons a week, a noteworthy sacrifice in a busy life, to driving us downtown. She never put off one class in three years, but she also was never on time.

Only once did I have a small bit of my share of success. On a single occasion Kosloff gave exercises in pantomime.[18] He suddenly stopped the class and called me out from my position in the back of the room. I demonstrated the exercise to a hushed and watching group. I did, of course, the best I could, trembling a little. They applauded. Kosloff beamed on me. He told Uncle Cecil that I showed the finest talent for pantomime of any pupil he had ever taught. This remark was naturally not repeated to me until long after.

Ah but there was a glory in that room! Each day's class was important and a little frightening. When the master praised a pupil we shivered with envy and excitement. When he roared and denounced we blanched. When he made jokes we laughed although we rarely understood what he was saying—it nearly always had to do with teasing some wretch. When he talked about expression and "sowl" I, for one, wept. When he talked about fame, galas, "applows," and *réclame*,[19] I slept poorly for nights after. We curtsied formally at the end of class. We were never late—that is, the others never were, I always was. When he talked of his triumphs with Diaghilev[20] in Paris and how the pupils practice in Moscow with butter on the floor to make it harder, and how as a young man he could easily turn twenty pirouettes[21] with a single push, we listened round-eyed, grabbing the chance to get our breaths before the next frantic series of jumps.

At Christmas there was a table covered with gifts, photographs for the first year pupils, gold pins for the second year, and pins with additional diamonds and wreaths and bars for the veterans. We were called out singly by name and given our gift. We then made a reverence,[22] said "thank you" in Russian and retired. Kosloff kept open house on Christmas with magnificent Russian food and boundless Russian welcome.

My weeks were divided into two sections, the three days I prepared for the class lesson, and the three days I prepared for the private lesson. I woke on Monday saying happily, "Today I have a lesson, today I need not practice alone." I woke most blissfully on Thursday saying, "Today I have a lesson with Miss Fredova." Friday entailed disappointment since it introduced a whole week before the next pri-

---

16. **sowl:** Kosloff's pronunciation of *soul*.
17. **Tartar:** characteristic of a fierce tribe that migrated from Turkey to parts of Russia and central Asia.
18. **pantomime:** communication through gestures rather than words.

19. *réclame* [rā kläm′]: French for "publicity."
20. **Diaghilev** [dyä′gi lef]: Sergei Pavlovich Diaghilev (1872–1929), famous Russian choreographer and producer.
21. **pirouettes** [pir′oo etz′]: rapid turns made on the tips of the toes.
22. **reverence:** bow or curtsy.

Dance to the Piper 303

AT A GLANCE

■ Agnes is always late for class.
■ She shows promise in pantomime.
■ Kosloff's stories and parties give the pupils a taste of the glamour and history of ballet.
■ Agnes looks forward to her lessons and rues the loneliness of the preparation days.

1 STYLE: DIALOGUE

Through dialogue, De Mille contrasts the impetuous, critical Kosloff with the patient, understanding Fredova.

2 BACKGROUND

Irony: Agnes gets praise from Kosloff for pantomime when she has been working so hard at ballet. Later, as a choreographer, she gained fame for dances that conveyed themes—an outgrowth of pantomime.

3 READING SKILLS: CAUSE AND EFFECT

The paragraph is organized by cause and effect and shows shifts of mood. Each of Kosloff's actions prompts a reaction among the students. When he praises, the students shiver; when he denounces, they pale.

4 ANECDOTE

De Mille's anecdote adds color and shows Kosloff's generous side along with the intoxicating glamour of the sophisticated, European world he made accessible to these raw young Americans.

GUIDED READING

LITERAL QUESTIONS

1a. Why was Agnes always late for class? (Her mother did not leave enough time to drive between her piano lesson and her dance lesson.)

2a. How do the students react to Theodore Kosloff's praise, denouncements, and jokes? (They shiver at his praise, blanch at his denouncements, and laugh at his jokes, even when they don't understand them.)

INFERENTIAL QUESTIONS

1b. What effect did Agnes' constant lateness probably have on her standing in the class? (Since she missed warming up, her lateness could have contributed to her poor performance.)

2b. What did Kosloff bring into his pupils' lives that made them admire him so much? (He made his unsophisticated American pupils feel as if they were connected to an exotic world.)

1 TOPIC SENTENCE

By telling the other girls that she has a "use" for her feet, De Mille sums up the combination of yearning and budding sense of accomplishment she experienced as a result of her ballet classes.

REFLECTING ON THE SELECTION

"Ah but there was a glory in that room!" exclaims the author, speaking of Kosloff's school. How was glory there? (Agnes' enthusiasm for ballet, Kosloff's spirited teaching, and the students' sense of shared purpose all imparted glory.)

STUDY QUESTIONS

1. "no juice": dry, stubborn, unresilient muscles
2. must not miss daily practice
3. ■ nonideal body; Achilles' tendon lacks wide stretch; overweight
   ■ She is strong-willed and hard-driving. Her body is strong, enabling her to outperform better technicians.
4. rigorous training, little praise or encouragement, excitement
5. dream of becoming a great dancer
6. Desire can overcome obstacles.
7. Answers will vary. Possible answers: Determination cannot achieve unrealistic goals; strong-willed desire enables people to test limits and succeed.

vate lesson. Three times during the first winter, Miss Fredova said "very good" and I recorded the event duly in my diary. On those nights I drove home with a singing heart and stood in the bedroom in the dark gripping the edge of my desk in excitement, so in love with dancing. "Oh God," I prayed, "let me be like her. Let me be a fine dancer." I took to wearing sandals because she did, even to parties, and when my schoolmates teased, I scoffed at their fashionably distorted toes and said proudly, "I have a use for *my* feet."

My well-filled curriculum—classes, homework, tennis, piano, editing—was ordered with just one thought: to make room for the dance practice. I rose at six-thirty and I studied and practiced at breakneck concentration until six in the evening when I was at last free to put on dancing dress and walk—to Mother's bathroom.

All through the lonely, drab exercises beside Mother's tub, without music or beat, proper floor or mirror, I had the joy of looking forward to dinner with Father, to hearing him talk about his scenarios[23] and what was going on at the studio. Sometimes he talked about music and literature. Once he said he thought I was an artist. Sometimes after dinner he sang and I accompanied him. These evenings my cup ran over. I went to bed early planning next day's practice, praying to do better in class. And as I lay waiting for sleep, breathing in the moist garden smells with my fox terrier slowly pressing me from the comfortable center of the bed, I used to dream about dancing on the stage with Pavlova, dancing until I dropped in a faint at her feet so that she would notice me and say, "That girl has talent."

---

23. **scenarios** [si när′ē ōz′]: outlines or rough scripts for movie plots. De Mille's father was a screenwriter during the early years of the film industry.

STUDY QUESTIONS

Recalling

1. What is Kosloff's verdict at Agnes' audition?
2. According to De Mille, what is "the first and all-important dictate of ballet dancing"?
3. List three of the shortcomings De Mille faces as a dancer. List two things that she learns at the school.

Interpreting

4. What picture of the Kosloff School does De Mille create?
5. What do you think keeps Agnes from becoming demoralized at the Kosloff School?
6. What lesson about life might De Mille's struggle to become a dancer teach all of us?

304   *Nonfiction*

Extending

7. Do you think a strong will can always overcome a person's shortcomings?

READING AND LITERARY FOCUS

Purpose in Autobiography

An **autobiography** is the story of a person's life written by that person. Like any other author of nonfiction, the autobiographer writes for a particular **purpose.** Authors write autobiographies, for example, in order to inform us about their own successes and failures or persuade us to appreciate their actions or to entertain us with stories from their past. An autobiographer may also combine some of these purposes or may write for an entirely different purpose.

Many authors write autobiographies in order to share the insights that they have gained with the passage of time. For example, in *Dance to the Piper* Agnes De Mille recalls how she strove as a girl to overcome her physical limitations. She then shares with us what she has come to realize only after years of hard work: "What I did not know was that I was constructed for endurance and that I developed through effort alone a capacity for out-performing far, far better technicians."

Thinking About Purpose in Autobiography

1. Find one more comment by De Mille that shows an adult's understanding rather than the girl's viewpoint.
2. For what specific purpose do you think De Mille wrote about the Kosloff School?

Topic Sentences

A **topic sentence** of a paragraph is the sentence that expresses the main idea of the paragraph. Usually the topic sentence is placed early in the paragraph; the remaining sentences develop and support this sentence with specific facts, examples, incidents, and opinions. For example, on page 300 Agnes De Mille writes of her difficulties at the Kosloff School: "I seemed, however, to have little aptitude for the business." The remaining sentences present specific examples of how De Mille struggled to learn the business of dancing.

Thinking About Topic Sentences

■ From this selection choose another paragraph that contains more than one sentence, and point out the topic sentence. Explain how the other sentences in the paragraph develop the idea expressed in this topic sentence.

VOCABULARY

Technical Terms

Many activities have their own vocabulary of **technical terms.** In *Dance to the Piper* Agnes De Mille uses a number of words that refer to the discipline of dance—for example, *barre, first position,* and *pirouettes.*

■ Using a dictionary when necessary, identify the performing arts to which the following terms apply: (1) aria, (2) timpani, (3) tenor, (4) farce, (5) arabesque, (6) dissolve.

COMPOSITION

Writing About Autobiography

■ Any work of nonfiction has a central idea. This idea may be a particular point about the subject or an insight about life in general. Explain what you think is Agnes De Mille's central idea in writing about the Kosloff School. Cite examples of facts, incidents, and details that she uses to support her idea. *For help with this assignment, see Lesson 7 in the Writing About Literature Handbook at the back of this book.*

Writing a Nonfiction Narrative

■ Write a narrative in which you relate an experience in which you learned something about yourself. Begin by telling when the experience occurred and what the circumstances of your life were. Then give specific facts and details about the experience. End by saying what you learned about yourself and why you learned it. *For help with this assignment, see Lesson 8 in the Writing About Literature Handbook at the back of this book.*

Dance to the Piper 305

COMPOSITION: GUIDELINES FOR EVALUATION

AT A GLANCE

- The piece opens with a description of a bloody Civil War battle in which Tubman participated.
- Tubman is born into slavery in Maryland, about 1820.

LITERARY OPTIONS

- biography
- anecdote
- characterization

THEMATIC OPTIONS

- confronting obstacles
- heroism

1 STYLE: METAPHOR

The metaphors of *lightning, thunder, rain,* and *crops* prepare us to understand Tubman's elemental view of her times and her motivation to engage in the struggle for freedom.

2 BIOGRAPHY

Tubman's childhood rebellion against slavery foreshadows the events of her later life.

TEXAS ESSENTIAL ELEMENTS GRADE 8

1E appropriate language
1I word choice
3B figurative language
3C setting and mood
3E types of nonfiction
4E perceiving cause/effect
4F author's purpose
To locate treatment of an Element, see *Texas Teacher's Resources.*

Langston Hughes (1902–1967) was born in Joplin, Missouri. He attended public school in Kansas and Ohio and later entered Columbia University in New York. As a young man, while he was working in a hotel in Washington, D.C., Hughes met the famous poet Vachel Lindsay. Hughes showed Lindsay some poems he had written, and the older poet was so impressed that he included some of them in a public reading. The following selection comes from Hughes's book of biographies of famous black Americans. Here he surveys the life of Harriet Tubman, who led many slaves to freedom before the Civil War.

Moses was the Old Testament prophet who led the Jews from Egypt, where they were enslaved, to Israel.

■ Why do you think Hughes calls Tubman "the Moses of her people"?

Langston Hughes

Harriet Tubman: The Moses of Her People

1 "Then we saw the lightning, and that was the guns; and then we heard the thunder, and that was the big guns; and then we heard the rain falling, and that was the drops of blood falling; and when we came to get in the crops, it was dead men that we reaped." So the escaped slave, Harriet Tubman, described one of the battles of the War between the North and South[1] in which she took part, for she was in the thick of the fighting. Before the War, like Frederick Douglass,[2] Harriet Tubman devoted her life to the cause of freedom,

and after the War to the advancement of her people.

Like Douglass she was born in Maryland a slave, one of eleven sons and daughters. No one kept a record of her birth, so the exact year is not known. But she lived so long and so much was written about her that most of the other facts of her life are accurately re- **2** corded. She was a homely child, morose, willful, wild, and constantly in rebellion against slavery. Unlike Phillis Wheatley[3] or Douglass, Harriet had no teaching of any sort, except the whip. As a little girl, on the very first day

---

1. **War . . . South:** that is, the Civil War (1861–1865) between the Union, or Northern, states and the Confederate, or Southern, states.
2. **Frederick Douglass** (1817–1895): black American leader, orator, and journalist.

3. **Phillis Wheatley** (1754?–1784): black poet who was born in Africa. Captured as a slave at the age of eight, Wheatley was purchased by a Boston family who taught her to read and write.

306 *Nonfiction*

GUIDED READING

LITERAL QUESTION

1a. To what two goals did Harriet Tubman devote her life? (the cause of freedom and the advancement of her people)

INFERENTIAL QUESTION

1b. Why do the circumstances of Harriet's birth and childhood represent an unlikely beginning for a life that achieved so much? (She was born a slave, with no record of her birth; she was a homely, unpleasant child who had no education.)

that she was sent to work in the Big House,[4] her mistress whipped her four times. Once she ran away and hid in a pig sty for five days, eating the scraps thrown to the pigs. "There were good masters and mistresses, so I've heard tell," she once said, "but I didn't happen to come across any of them."

1 Harriet never liked to work as a servant in the house, so perhaps because of her rebellious nature, she was soon ordered to the fields. One day when she was in her early teens something happened that affected her whole life. It was evening and a young slave had, without permission, gone to a country store. The overseer followed him to whip him. He ordered Harriet to help tie him up. As Harriet refused, the slave ran. The overseer picked up a heavy iron weight from the scales 2 and threw it. But he did not hit the fellow. He struck Harriet's head, almost crushing her skull, and leaving a deep scar forever. Unconscious, the girl lingered between life and death for days. When at last she was able to work again, Harriet still suffered fits of unconsciousness. These lasted all her life. They would come upon her at any time, any place, and it would seem as if she had suddenly fallen asleep. Sometimes in the fields, sometimes leaning against a fence, sometimes in church, she would "go to sleep" and no one could wake her until the seizure had passed. When she was awake, this did not affect her 3 thinking. But her master thought the blow had made her half-witted. Harriet continued to let him believe this. Meanwhile, she prayed God to deliver her from bondage.

When she was about twenty-four years old, she married a jolly, carefree fellow named Tubman, who did not share her concern for leaving the slave country. A few years later, when her old master died, Harriet heard that she

---

4. **Big House:** slaveowner's house.

and two of her brothers were to be sold, so they decided to run away, together. It was dangerous to tell anyone. Harriet had no chance to let even her mother know directly. But on the evening that she was leaving, she went about the fields and the slaves' quarters singing:

"When that old chariot comes
I'm gwine to leave you.
I'm bound for the Promised Land. . . ."

4 And the way she sang that song let her friends and kinfolks know that to Harriet the Promised Land right then meant the North, not heaven. That night she left the Brodas Plantation on the Big Buckwater River never to return. Before dawn her brothers became frightened and went back to the slave huts before their absence was discovered. But Harriet went on alone through the woods by night, hiding by day, having no map, unable to read or write, but trusting God, instinct, and the North star[5] to guide her. By some miracle she eventually got to Philadelphia, found work there, and was never again a slave.

But Harriet could not be happy while all her family were slaves. She kept thinking about them. So, some months later, she went back to Maryland, hoping to persuade her husband to come North with her. He said he did not wish to go. She led others Northward, however, and, within two years of her own escape, she had secretly returned to the South three times to rescue two brothers, a sister and her children, and a dozen more slaves. The Fugitive Slave Law of 1850[6] now made it

---

5. **North star:** bright star directly above the North Pole, used as a guide by travelers.
6. **Fugitive . . . 1850:** strengthened version of a 1793 law allowing slaveowners with proof of ownership to recapture runaway slaves.

Harriet Tubman: The Moses of Her People 307

AT A GLANCE

- Harriet receives a brutal blow from her master, which causes seizures throughout her life.
- Harriet runs away from the Maryland plantation to freedom in Philadelphia. She signals her escape to friends and family by singing about going to the Promised Land.
- By 1850 she has returned to Maryland three times to lead relatives and other slaves to freedom.

1 BACKGROUND

The work of house slaves was less strenuous and included more benefits than that of field slaves. Sending a house slave to the fields was a form of punishment.

2 SYMBOLISM

The injury and scar inflicted by the cruel master symbolize the deep and enduring damage caused by the system of slavery on an entire people.

3 CHARACTERIZATION

Allowing the master to believe she is half-witted shows Harriet to be wily. A master would not expect a half-witted slave to try to escape.

4 ANECDOTE

This anecdote shows the young Tubman in action, again cleverly outwitting a slaveowner. The lines of the song also develop Tubman's likeness to Moses, who led his people to the Promised Land.

GUIDED READING

LITERAL QUESTION

1a. Why didn't Harriet's brothers escape with her from the plantation? (They became frightened and returned before they were missed.)

INFERENTIAL QUESTION

1b. How do you think Harriet was different from her brothers? (She was braver and more determined; she may have had a stronger desire for freedom.)

- As Tubman's fame spreads, slaveowners offer rewards for her capture.
- Leading runaways northward, she uses a gun to prevent them from returning home out of fear.
- She becomes a daring "conductor" on the Underground Railroad.

1 CHARACTERIZATION

The description of Tubman's use of a pistol underlines her seriousness of purpose. A responsible leader, she is resolved to succeed at her dangerous mission.

2 BIOGRAPHY

To appreciate the events of a life, it is necessary to identify the influences of individuals and organizations. The author shows how the Underground Railroad and Anti-Slavery Society encouraged Tubman.

3 ANECDOTE

This anecdote adds depth and humor to the biography. The contrast between Josiah Bailey's fear and Harriet's casual acceptance of danger becomes apparent when she teases him.

4 READING SKILLS: DETAILS

Details of character lead us to infer that Tubman did not allow her limitations to interfere with her goals.

---

dangerous for runaways to stop anywhere in the United States, so Harriet led her followers to Canada where she spent a winter begging, cooking, and praying for them. Then she returned to Maryland to rescue nine more Negroes.

During the first years of her own freedom, Harriet spent most of her time showing others how to follow in her footsteps. Her fame as a fearless leader of "freedom bands" spread rapidly. Shortly large rewards were offered by the slaveholders for her capture. But she was never captured, and she never lost any of her followers to the slave catchers. One reason for this was that once a slave made up his mind to go with her and started out, Harriet did not permit any turning back. Perhaps her experience with her two brothers when she first ran away accounted for this insistence. Her method of preventing frightened or weak travelers on the freedom road from returning to slavery, and perhaps being whipped into betraying the others, was simple. Harriet Tub-

1 man carried a pistol. When anyone said he could not, or would not go on, Harriet pulled her gun from the folds of her dress and said, "You *will* go on—or you'll die." The strength or the courage to continue was always forthcoming when her faltering companions looked into the muzzle of Harriet's gun. Through swamp and thicket, rain and cold, they went on toward the North. Thus everyone who started out with Harriet Tubman lived to thank her for freedom.

Long before the War between the States came, so many slaves were escaping, and so many white people in the North were helping them, that the routes to freedom became known as the "Underground Railroad." Secret "stations" where escaping slaves might be hidden, warmed, and fed were established in homes, barns, and sometimes even churches along the way. The Quakers were especially

2 helpful and active in this regard. And a strong Anti-Slavery Society supported such activities. Slave owners were losing thousands of dollars worth of slaves by escape every year. Harriet Tubman became known as a "conductor" on the Underground Railroad. She was not the only "conductor" but she was the most famous, and one of the most daring. Once she brought as many as twenty-five slaves in a single band to freedom.

Another time she had in her party of runaways a big strong slave worth $1500. His name was Josiah Bailey and the Maryland countryside was plastered with posters offering a reward for his capture. There were ads in the papers for his return. On the way through New York City a friend of freedom recognized Bailey from the description in the papers and said, "I'm glad to meet a man whose head is worth fifteen hundred dollars!" Josiah was so shocked at being recognized and so afraid that he would be captured that a mood of deep despair descended upon him and he would not speak the rest of the trip. When the train was carrying the runaways across the bridge at Buffalo into Canada, Bailey would not even look at the wonder of Ni-

3 agara Falls.[7] But when they got on free soil and he was finally safe, he burst into song, and nobody could stop him from singing. He cried that at last, thanks to God, he was in Heaven! Harriet Tubman said, "Well, you old fool, you! You might at least have looked at Niagara Falls on the way to Heaven."

Harriet had a great sense of humor. She enjoyed telling the story on herself of how, not

4 being able to read, she once sat down and went to sleep on a park bench right under a sign offering a big reward for her capture. When she began to make speeches to raise

---

7. **Niagara Falls:** large waterfall on the Niagara River between northwestern New York State and Canada.

GUIDED READING

LITERAL QUESTIONS

1a. What did Harriet Tubman do whenever a runaway was too frightened to go on? (She took out a pistol and threatened to kill the slave if he or she did not go on.)

2a. What was the Underground Railroad? (The Underground Railroad was a secret network of people and organizations that fed and housed runaway slaves during their flight to freedom.)

INFERENTIAL QUESTIONS

1b. Do you think Tubman was right to threaten people who had already suffered a great deal? (Some students may feel that she was too harsh; others may note that she needed to be firm.)

2b. How do you think the Underground Railroad made Harriet Tubman's work easier? (She did not have to worry constantly about finding food and shelter. She could stay at a "station" until conditions were right to travel onward.)

money for the cause of freedom, she often told jokes, sang, and sometimes even danced. She might have been a great actress, people said, because without makeup she could hollow out her cheeks and wrinkle her brow to seem like a very old woman. She would make her body shrink and cause her legs to totter when she chose to so disguise herself. Once, making a trip to Maryland to rescue some relatives, she had to pass through a village where she was known. She bought two hens, tied them by their feet and hung them heads down around her neck, then went tottering along. Sure enough, a slave catcher came up the street who might, she thought, recognize her, tot-

1 tering or not. So she unloosed the squalling chickens in the middle of the street and dived after them, purposely not catching them so she could run down the road in pursuit and out of the slave catcher's sight, while all the passers-by laughed.

Sometimes, knowing that her band of fugitives was pursued by angry masters, she would get on a train headed South—because nobody would suspect that runaway slaves would be going South. Sometimes she would disguise the women in her party and herself as men. Babies would be given a sleeping medicine to keep them quiet and then wrapped up like bundles. Sometimes she would wade for hours up a stream to throw

2 the hounds off scent. In the dark of night when there was no North star, she would feel the trunks of trees for the moss that grows on the northern side, and that would serve as a guide toward freedom. Often when all seemed hopeless—although she never told her followers she had such feelings—Harriet would pray. One of her favorite prayers was, "Lord, you've been with me through six troubles. Be with me in the seventh." Some people thought that Harriet Tubman led a charmed life because, within twelve years, she made

Harriet Tubman.

3 nineteen dangerous trips into the South rescuing slaves. She herself said, "I never run my train off the track, and I never lost a passenger."

Her father and mother were both over seventy years of age when she rescued them and brought her parents North to a home she had begun to buy in Auburn, New York. At first they stayed in St. Catharines, Canada, where

Harriet Tubman: The Moses of Her People 309

AT A GLANCE

- Tubman uses disguises and other tricks to escape slave-catchers.
- In times of hopelessness, Harriet prays for help.
- Tubman rescues her seventy-year-old parents.

1 ANECDOTE

With this amusing anecdote, the author entertains the reader while making the point that the shrewd Tubman lived by her wits.

2 SETTING

The foreboding setting reminds us of the obstacles Tubman had to contend with and that, time and time again, her resourcefulness stood between life and death for herself and her "passengers."

3 STYLE: METAPHOR

Members of the Underground Railroad used railroad metaphors as a code to conceal their illegal work. Hughes employs them, as direct quotes, to reflect Tubman's pride in a job well done.

GUIDED READING

LITERAL QUESTION

1a. When did Harriet Tubman pray? (She prayed when all else seemed hopeless.)

INFERENTIAL QUESTION

1b. Why do you think she didn't reveal her feelings of hopelessness to others? (She probably didn't want her followers to worry about how hopeless she felt since she was often their only source of hope.)

1 PARAPHRASING THIS PASSAGE

Although she appeared rather ordinary, she had great ability as a leader.

2 BIOGRAPHY

Biographers rely on a variety of primary sources for facts. Contemporary eyewitness accounts, such as Brown's, are particularly valuable.

3 AUTHOR'S PURPOSE

The author cites evidence to persuade us that Harriet Tubman was treated unfairly by the government she had served so bravely.

escaped slaves were safe, since, in 1833, Queen Victoria[8] had declared all slavery illegal. But it was too cold for the old folks there. And Harriet's work was not on foreign soil. She herself seemed to have no fear of being captured. She came and went about the United States as she chose. And became so famous that, although she never sought the spotlight, it was hard for her not to be recognized wherever she was. Once at a great woman's suffrage meeting where her old head wound had caused her to go sound asleep in the audience, she was recognized, and awoke to find herself on the platform. Her speech for women's rights was roundly applauded. In those days neither Negroes nor women could vote. Harriet believed both should, so, like Frederick Douglass, she followed the woman's suffrage movement closely.

1 In appearance "a more ordinary specimen of humanity could hardly be found," but there was no one with a greater capacity for leadership than she had. Among the slaves, where she walked in secret, Harriet began to be known as Moses. And at the great public meetings of the North, as the Negro historian **2** William Wells Brown wrote in 1854, "all who frequented anti-slavery conventions, lectures, picnics, and fairs, could not fail to have seen a black woman of medium size, upper front teeth gone, smiling countenance, attired in coarse but neat apparel, with an old-fashioned reticule[9] or bag suspended by her side, who, on taking her seat, would at once drop off into a sound sleep. . . . No fugitive was ever captured who had Moses for a leader." She was very independent. Between rescue trips or speeches, she would work as a cook

or a scrubwoman. She might borrow, but she never begged money for herself. All contributions went toward the cause of freedom in one way or another, as did most of what she earned.

But when the War between the States began and she became a nurse for the Union Armies, and then a military scout and an invaluable intelligence agent behind the Rebel lines, she was promised some compensation. Technically she was not a registered nurse, and being a woman, she could not be a soldier. **3** Yet she carried a Union pass, traveled on government transports, did dangerous missions in Confederate territory, and gave advice to chiefs of staffs. But she never got paid for this, although she had been promised $1800 for certain assignments. To Harriet this made no difference until, after the War, she badly needed money to care for her aged parents. Petitions were sent to the War Department and to Congress to try to get the $1800 due her. But it was never granted.

Harriet Tubman's war activities were amazing. She served under General Stevens at Beaufort, South Carolina. She was sent to Florida to nurse those ill of dysentery, small pox, and yellow fever.[10] She was with Colonel Robert Gould Shaw at Fort Wagner. She organized a group of nine Negro scouts and river pilots and, with Colonel Montgomery, led a Union raiding contingent of three gunboats[11] and about 150 Negro troops up the Combahee River.[12] As reported by the Boston *Commonwealth*, for July 10, 1863, they "under the guidance of a black woman, dashed into the enemy's country, struck a bold and effective

---

8. **Queen Victoria** (1819–1901): queen of Great Britain and Ireland from 1837 to 1901. Canada was ruled by Britain until 1867.
9. **reticule** [ret′ə kūl′]: small purse.

10. **dysentery** [dis′ən ter′ē] . . . **fever:** dangerous, often deadly diseases that were widespread in wartime.
11. **gunboats:** small armed ships used to patrol rivers and harbors.
12. **Combahee River:** river in southeastern South Carolina.

GUIDED READING

LITERAL QUESTIONS

1a. In addition to leading slaves to freedom, how else did Harriet help her people? (She gave speeches at antislavery meetings.)

2a. What dangerous work did Tubman do during the Civil War? (She was a military scout and intelligence agent behind Rebel lines.)

INFERENTIAL QUESTIONS

1b. Do you think Tubman was effective at this activity? (Yes. Her speeches must have been effective since she soon became famous even though she did not seek the spotlight.)

2b. How do you think her experience as a leader of runaways helped her in this new work? (She was familiar with Southern territory and hiding places; she was used to traveling secretly.)

blow, destroying millions of dollars worth of commissary stores, cotton and lordly dwellings, and striking terror into the heart of rebeldom, brought off near 800 slaves and thousands of dollars worth of property." Concerning Harriet Tubman, it continued, "Many and many times she has penetrated the enemy's lines and discovered their situation and condition, and escaped without injury, but not without extreme hazard."

One of the songs Harriet sang during the War was:

"Of all the whole creation in the East or in the West,
The glorious Yankee nation is the greatest and the best.
Come along! Come along! Don't be alarmed,
Uncle Sam is rich enough to give you all a farm."

But Harriet Tubman never had a farm of her own. Her generous nature caused her to give away almost all the money she ever got her hands on. There were always fugitives, or relatives, or causes, or friends in need. She was over forty years old when Abraham Lincoln signed the Emancipation Proclamation,[13] making legal for all the freedom she had struggled to secure. She lived for almost fifty years after the War was over. Some people thought she was a hundred years old when she died in 1913. Certainly she was over ninety.

A number of books have been written about her. The first one, *Scenes in the Life of Harriet Tubman,* by Sarah H. Bradford, appeared in 1869, and the proceeds from its sale helped Harriet pay for her cottage. She wrote

---

13. **Emancipation Proclamation:** law signed by President Lincoln stating that, as of January 1, 1863, all slaves in the United States were to be free.

her friend, Frederick Douglass, who had hidden her and her runaway slaves more than once in his home in Rochester, for a letter about her book. In his reply he compared their two careers:

"The difference between us is very marked. Most that I have done and suffered in the service of our cause has been in public, and I have received much encouragement at every step of the way. You, on the other hand, have labored in a private way. I have wrought in the day—you in the night. I have had the applause of the crowd and the satisfaction that comes of being approved by the multitude, while the most that you have done has been witnessed by a few trembling, scared and footsore bondsmen and women, whom you have led out of the house of bondage, and whose heartfelt, *God bless you,* has been your only reward. The midnight sky and the silent stars have been the witnesses of your devotion to freedom and of your heroism."

When years later, in her old age, a reporter for *The New York Herald Tribune* came to interview her one afternoon at her home in Auburn, he wrote that, as he was leaving, Harriet looked toward an orchard nearby and said, "Do you like apples?"

On being assured that the young man liked them, she asked, "Did you ever plant any apples?"

The writer confessed that he had not.

"No," said the old woman, "but somebody else planted them. I liked apples when I was young. And I said, 'Some day I'll plant apples myself for other young folks to eat.' And I guess I did."

Her apples were the apples of freedom. Harriet Tubman lived to see the harvest. Her home in Auburn, New York, is preserved as a memorial to her planting.

Harriet Tubman: The Moses of Her People 311

AT A GLANCE

- Harriet Tubman is cited for her brave actions during the Civil War.
- Harriet lives to be over ninety and dies in 1913.
- Frederick Douglass honors Tubman for her devotion to freedom.

1 THEME

In addition to being a hero to runaway slaves, Tubman behaved heroically as a military spy and leader during the Civil War, when she was probably in her forties.

2 IRONY

It is ironic that during the war Harriet sings about the riches of "Uncle Sam," while after the war she learns she will not be paid, as promised, for her dangerous work.

3 READING SKILLS: COMPARISON AND CONTRAST

In another primary source, Frederick Douglass uses a point by point method to compare and contrast his efforts for freedom with those of Harriet Tubman.

4 ANECDOTE

This concluding anecdote gives us a different view of Tubman. We see a contented Tubman looking back with satisfaction on a job well done.

5 BIOGRAPHY

The author eulogizes Tubman through a fitting metaphor—"apples of freedom"—which parallels and contrasts with Tubman's opening metaphors about the "harvest" of war.

REFLECTING ON THE SELECTION

In what different ways did Harriet Tubman plant the "apples of freedom"? (She led runaway slaves to freedom; she made speeches against slavery; during the Civil War, she fought against states that allowed slavery.)

GUIDED READING

LITERAL QUESTIONS

1a. How long did Harriet Tubman live after her people had gained their freedom? (almost fifty years; until 1913)

2a. At the end of the story, what does the author compare with freedom? (Tubman's apples)

INFERENTIAL QUESTIONS

1b. How do you think Tubman spent these years? (She probably continued to show concern for her people by helping them to improve the conditions of their everyday life.)

2b. In what ways is this a good comparison? (Growing apple trees—like getting freedom—takes time, patience, hard work. Sometimes trees—or the struggle for freedom—do not bear fruit right away.)

1. ■ wildness, willfulness, rebelliousness toward slavery
   ■ ran away after a whipping; refused to tie up another slave
2. She and her two brothers planned to escape. They turned back, so she went to Philadelphia alone.
3. a network of people who hid escaping slaves before the Civil War; led slaves northward through the Railroad's "stations"
4. "apples of freedom"
5. Possible answers: desire to be free, fearlessness, cleverness, persistence
6. He admires her strength, humor, liveliness, skillfulness, willingness to work without acclaim.

READING AND LITERARY FOCUS

■ While trying to rescue some relatives, she was approached by a slave catcher in a town where she was known. She set loose the hens she was carrying and chased them to take his attention from identifying her.
■ She was clever and well prepared.

VOCABULARY

1. (b) gloomy
2. (a) ability
3. (d) face
4. (c) dressed
5. (b) priceless

CHALLENGE

After reading other biographical works, students could report on these works in class.

STUDY QUESTIONS

Recalling

1. What qualities does Hughes associate with Harriet Tubman as a girl? Relate two incidents from her early life as a slave.
2. Describe Tubman's own escape from slavery.
3. What was the Underground Railroad? What was Tubman's part in it?
4. What does Hughes say that Tubman planted?

Interpreting

5. What qualities do you think helped Harriet Tubman to triumph?
6. What is Hughes's opinion of Tubman?

READING AND LITERARY FOCUS

Biography and Anecdote

A **biography** is the story of a person's life written by someone other than that person. A biography may be as short as a few pages or as long as several books. Whatever its length, a good biography both relates the facts about its subject's life and presents the writer's attitude toward the subject.

The skilled biographer uses details, incidents, examples, and quotations to help us understand the subject's personality. In particular, a good biographer includes **anecdotes,** brief accounts of true events, to add depth and color to a biography. Anecdotes help us see the subject's personality in action. For example, in the preceding biography Hughes tells us that Tubman teased Josiah Bailey for refusing to look at Niagara Falls on his way to freedom. This anecdote gives us a vivid picture of Tubman's personality—her earthiness, her sense of humor, and, most important, her fearlessness.

Thinking About Anecdotes

■ Relate the anecdote about Tubman's use of hens to confuse the slave catcher. Tell what that anecdote shows about Tubman.

VOCABULARY

Synonyms

A **synonym** is a word that has the same or nearly the same meaning as another word. For example, *love* and *worship* are synonyms. The italicized words in the following numbered items are from "Harriet Tubman: The Moses of Her People." From the four choices that follow each numbered item, choose the word that is nearest the meaning of the italicized word, *as the word is used in the selection.* Write the number of each item and the letter of your choice on a separate sheet.

1. a *morose* nature
   (a) joking   (c) evil
   (b) gloomy   (d) saintly
2. a great *capacity* for invention
   (a) ability   (c) disregard
   (b) affection   (d) resentment
3. a friendly *countenance*
   (a) laugh   (c) invitation
   (b) handshake   (d) face
4. *attired* handsomely
   (a) walking   (c) dressed
   (b) weary   (d) dancing
5. an *invaluable* assistant
   (a) worthless   (c) courteous
   (b) priceless   (d) difficult

CHALLENGE

Further Reading

■ You may enjoy reading other biographies or biographical essays, such as the following:
   ● *Helen and Teacher* by Joseph Lash, a study of Helen Keller, who was blind and deaf from infancy, and her teacher, Annie Sullivan.
   ● *Abraham Lincoln: The Prairie Years and the War Years* by Carl Sandburg, a prize-winning account of the life of the sixteenth President.

ESSAY

Edward Abbey (born 1927) grew up in Pennsylvania and now lives in Arizona. He worked as a ranger and a fire lookout for the National Park Service. The following narrative comes from one of Abbey's best-known books, *Desert Solitaire* (1968). He recalls a nearly fatal detour that he once took while wandering through the canyons of Arizona.

■ As you read, try to put yourself in Abbey's position. What do you think you would have done in his circumstances?

AT A GLANCE

- Abbey explores the Havasu Canyon in the Arizona desert.
- To reach his camp before dark, he searches for a short route back.
- Equipped only with his walking stick, he starts down a narrow pass.

LITERARY OPTIONS

- narration
- cause and effect
- imagery

THEMATIC OPTIONS

- discoveries
- responding to nature
- adventure

Edward Abbey

Havasu[1]

Most of my wandering in the desert I've done alone. Not so much from choice as from necessity—I generally prefer to go into places where no one else wants to go. I find that in contemplating the natural world my pleasure is greater if there are not too many others contemplating it with me, at the same time. However, there are special hazards in traveling alone. Your chances of dying, in case of sickness or accident, are much improved, simply because there is no one around to go for help.

Exploring a side canyon off Havasu Canyon one day, I was unable to resist the temptation to climb up out of it onto what corresponds in that region to the Tonto Bench.[2] Late in the afternoon I realized that I would not have enough time to get back to my camp before dark, unless I could find a much shorter route than the one by which I had come. I looked for a shortcut.

Nearby was another little side canyon which appeared to lead down into Havasu Canyon. It was a steep, shadowy, extremely narrow defile[3] with the usual meandering course and overhanging walls; from where I stood, near its head, I could not tell if the route was feasible[4] all the way down to the floor of the main canyon. I had no rope with me—only my walking stick. But I was hungry and thirsty, as always. I started down.

For a while everything went well. The floor of the little canyon began as a bed of dry sand, scattered with rocks. Farther down a few boulders were wedged between the walls; I climbed over and under them. Then the canyon took on the slickrock character—smooth, sheer,

---

1. **Havasu** [hä′vä sōō]: canyon in Arizona.
2. **Tonto Bench:** A bench is any elevated ridge of land along the bank of a body of water.

3. **defile** [di fīl′]: narrow pass in a mountain or valley.
4. **feasible** [fē′zə bəl]: possible.

Havasu 313

1 READING SKILLS: CAUSE AND EFFECT

As the story teller expresses his thoughts and feelings, he also relates the specific circumstances that set the narrative in motion.

2 THEME

The author hints that this adventure involves a life-threatening situation.

3 READING SKILLS: CAUSE AND EFFECT

Hunger and thirst prompt Abbey to try the unfamiliar route, even though he has no rope.

TEXAS ESSENTIAL ELEMENTS GRADE 8

3A plot and character development
3B figurative language
3C setting and mood
3E types of nonfiction
4B implied main idea
4D sequential order
4E perceiving cause/effect
4G predicting outcomes
To locate treatment of an Element, see *Texas Teacher's Resources*.

GUIDED READING

LITERAL QUESTION

1a. What does the author do in order to reach his camp before dark? (He decides to climb down an unfamiliar side canyon, hoping it will be a shortcut to his camp.)

INFERENTIAL QUESTION

1b. What does this course of action tell you about the author? (Answers will vary. He feels confident of his ability as a hiker; he likes variety and adventure; he overrides his sense of caution.)

Havasu **T-313**

- Abbey jumps off a ledge and lands in a pool of stagnant water twelve feet below.
- Unable to turn back, he slides down a steep cliff to another ledge.
- He discovers himself trapped on a ledge cut into an eighty-foot cliff.
- With no hope of being rescued, he concludes he will starve.

1 SETTING

The sheer stone and stagnant water reinforce the sense of an unfriendly environment, on the one hand, and point to the possibilities for adventure, on the other.

2 AUDIENCE

By presenting a contrast between what would be expected or sensible (turning back) and what he actually does (continue downward), Abbey makes sure that his audience understands the foolhardiness of his decision.

3 IMAGERY

To help us imagine his passage through this disgusting water, Abbey appeals to our senses of smell and touch.

4 NARRATIVE HOOK

Abbey abruptly halts the reader here, in a parallel to the physical impasse he faces. Now the *potential* for danger becomes an actual, life-threatening situation.

5 READING SKILLS: CAUSE AND EFFECT

The author uses cause and effect to accentuate his helplessness. He couldn't scream for help because no one would hear. He couldn't weave a rope because he didn't have enough material. He couldn't light a signal fire because he lacked fuel.

---

slippery sandstone carved by erosion into a series of scoops and potholes which got bigger as I descended. In some of these basins there was a little water left over from the last flood, warm and fetid[5] water under an oily-looking scum, condensed by prolonged evaporation to a sort of broth, rich in dead and dying organisms. My canteen was empty and I was very thirsty but I felt that I could wait.

1 I came to a lip on the canyon floor which overhung by twelve feet the largest so far of these stagnant pools. On each side rose the canyon walls, roughly perpendicular. There was no way to continue except by dropping into the pool. I hesitated. Beyond this point there could hardly be any returning, yet the **2** main canyon was still not visible below. Obviously the only sensible thing to do was to turn back. I edged over the lip of stone and dropped feet first into the water.

Deeper than I expected. The warm, thick fluid came up and closed over my head as my feet touched the muck at the bottom. I had to swim to the farther side. And here I found myself on the verge of another drop-off, with one more huge bowl of green soup below.

This drop-off was about the same height as the one before, but not overhanging. It resembled a children's playground slide, concave and S-curved, only steeper, wider, with a vertical pitch[6] in the middle. It did not lead directly into the water but ended in a series of steplike ledges above the pool. Beyond the pool lay another edge, another drop-off into an unknown depth. Again I paused, and for a much longer time. But I no longer had the option of turning around and going back. I eased myself into the chute[7] and let go of everything—except my faithful stick.

---

5. **fetid** [fet′id]: bad-smelling.
6. **vertical pitch:** straight drop.
7. **chute** [shoot]: downward passageway.

3 I hit rock bottom hard, but without any physical injury. I swam the stinking pond dog-paddle style, pushing the heavy scum away from my face, and crawled out on the far side to see what my fate was going to be.

4 Fatal. Death by starvation, slow and tedious. For I was looking straight down an overhanging cliff to a rubble pile of broken rocks eighty feet below.

After the first wave of utter panic had passed I began to try to think. First of all I was not going to die immediately, unless another flash flood came down the gorge; there was the pond of stagnant water on hand to save me from thirst and a man can live, they say, for thirty days or more without food. My sun-bleached bones, dramatically sprawled at the bottom of the chasm, would provide the diversion of the picturesque for future wanderers—if any man ever came this way again.

My second thought was to scream for help, although I knew very well there could be no other human being within miles. I even tried it but the sound of that anxious shout, cut short in the dead air within the canyon walls, was so inhuman, so detached as it seemed from myself, that it terrified me and I didn't attempt it again.

I thought of tearing my clothes into strips and plaiting a rope. But what was I wearing?—boots, socks, a pair of old and ragged blue jeans, a flimsy T-shirt, an ancient and **5** rotten sombrero[8] of straw. Not a chance of weaving such a wardrobe into a rope eighty feet long, or even twenty feet long.

How about a signal fire? There was nothing to burn but my clothes; not a tree, not a shrub, not even a weed grew in this stony cul-de-sac.[9] Even if I burned my clothing the

---

8. **sombrero** [səm brār′ō]: broad-brimmed hat.
9. **cul-de-sac** [kul′də sak′]: dead end; place from which there is no escape.

GUIDED READING

LITERAL QUESTIONS

1a. Why does the author hesitate before dropping the twelve feet into the first pool? (He cannot see the main canyon below, so he still is not sure the route is feasible; if he drops down, he will not be able to climb back.)

2a. After realizing he is trapped, what plans does Abbey consider but reject as impractical? (He considers screaming for help, weaving his clothes into a rope, and building a signal fire.)

INFERENTIAL QUESTIONS

1b. Why do you think the author finally decides to drop? (He likes the idea of doing something adventurous; he enjoys flirting with danger; he needs to return to camp before sundown.)

2a. Abbey lives to tell his story. How do you think he will save himself? (Students may suggest that he will climb back up the way he came down.)

¹chances of the smoke being seen by some Hualapai Indian[10] high on the south rim were very small; and if he did see the smoke, what then? He'd shrug his shoulders. Furthermore, without clothes, the sun would soon bake me to death.

There was only one thing I could do. I had a tiny notebook in my hip pocket and a stub of pencil. When these dried out I could at least record my final thoughts. I would have plenty of time to write not only my epitaph but my ²own elegy.[11]

But not yet.

There were a few loose stones scattered about the edge of the pool. Taking the biggest first, I swam with it back to the foot of the slickrock chute and placed it there. One by one I brought the others and made a shaky little pile about two feet high leaning against the chute. Hopeless, of course, but there was nothing else to do. I stood on the top of the pile and stretched upward, straining my arms to their utmost limit and groped with fingers and fingernails for a hold on something firm. ³There was nothing. I crept back down. I began to cry. It was easy. All alone, I didn't have to be brave.

Through the tears I noticed my old walking stick lying nearby. I took it and stood it on the most solid stone in the pile, behind the two topmost stones. I took off my boots, tied them together and hung them around my neck, on my back. I got up on the little pile again and lifted one leg and set my big toe on the top of the stick. This could never work. Slowly and painfully, leaning as much of my weight as I

---

10. **Hualapai** [wä′lə pī] **Indian:** member of a tribe of Indians living in the Colorado River valley in Arizona. Also known as Walapai.
11. **epitaph** [ep′ə taf′] . . . **elegy** [el′ə jē]: An epitaph is an inscription on a tombstone. An elegy is a formal poem in honor of the dead person.

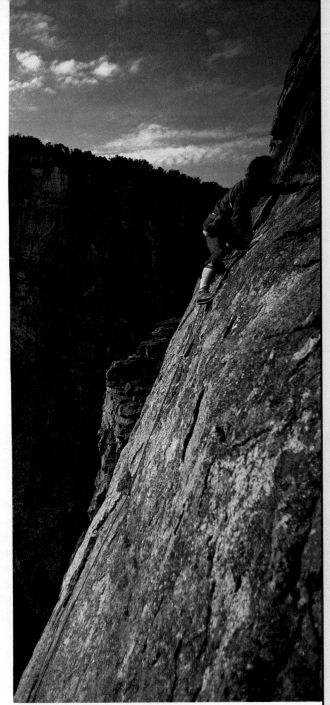

A climber scaling a cliff in Colorado.

Havasu 315

AT A GLANCE

- The author contemplates writing his final thoughts in a notebook.
- Standing on a pile of stones, he unsuccessfully searches for a handhold on the sheer rock chute.
- To raise himself higher, he stands atop his walking stick.

1 SETTING

The barren and isolated setting blocks every possibility of rescue.

2 NARRATION

The three-word paragraph, "But not yet," at the middle of the essay marks a turning point in the narrative: The first half describes entrapment and realization that rescue is unlikely. The second half details efforts to save himself.

3 MOOD

A mood of helplessness overcomes the author. The short sentences here add to his sense of being at the end of his resources.

GUIDED READING

LITERAL QUESTION

1a. How does the author try to escape from the rocky ledge? (He piles up stones and stands on them, searching for a handhold on the cliff wall. When that fails, he stands on his walking stick to reach higher.)

INFERENTIAL QUESTION

1b. Explain why the author has mixed feelings about this escape attempt. (He feels the attempt is "hopeless" and "could never work." At the same time, it is his only chance, and he desperately wants it to work.)

AT A GLANCE

- The walking stick raises Abbey high enough to allow him to inch his way up the chute.
- At the top, he faces his next obstacle, the twelve-foot high overhanging spout.

1 NARRATION

The author quickly refutes the pessimistic ending of one paragraph with the optimistic opening of the next. He increases suspense.

2 STYLE: IMAGERY

The simile of the slug suggests that Abbey's desperate situation has reduced him to a primitive life form in which the survival instinct is all-important.

3 STYLE: IMAGERY

The use of the words *slogged,* *floundered,* and *scrabbling* emphasize the image of Abbey as a trapped beast desperate to escape.

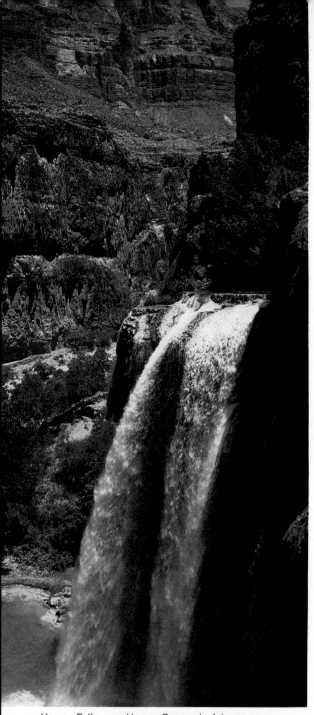

Havasu Falls, near Havasu Canyon in Arizona.

316 *Nonfiction*

could against the sandstone slide, I applied more and more pressure to the stick, pushing my body upward until I was again stretched out full length above it. Again I felt about for a fingerhold. There was none. The chute was smooth as polished marble.

No, not quite that smooth. This was sandstone, soft and porous, not marble, and between it and my wet body and wet clothing a certain friction was created. In addition, the stick had enabled me to reach a higher section of the S-curved chute, where the angle was more favorable. I discovered that I could move upward, inch by inch, through adhesion[12] and with the help of the leveling tendency of the curve. I gave an extra little push with my big toe—the stones collapsed below, the stick clattered down—and crawled rather like a snail or slug, oozing slime, up over the rounded summit of the slide.

The next obstacle, the overhanging spout twelve feet above a deep plunge pool, looked impossible. It *was* impossible, but with the blind faith of despair I slogged into the water and swam underneath the drop-off and floundered around for a while, scrabbling[13] at the slippery rock until my nerves and tiring muscles convinced my numbed brain that *this was not the way.* I swam back to solid ground and lay down to rest and die in comfort.

Far above I could see the sky, an irregular strip of blue between the dark, hard-edged canyon walls that seemed to lean toward each other as they towered above me. Across that narrow opening a small white cloud was passing, so lovely and precious and delicate and forever inaccessible that it broke the heart and made me weep like a woman, like a child.

---

12. **adhesion** [ad hē′zhən]: force that causes surfaces to stick together.
13. **scrabbling** [skrab′ling]: scraping or pawing.

GUIDED READING

LITERAL QUESTION

1a. What is the author's reaction when he sees a cloud pass over the gap in the canyon walls? (He begins to weep.)

INFERENTIAL QUESTION

1b. Why do you think he has such a reaction? (Strong emotional reactions often occur when someone is under stress. The cloud's beauty has made him realize that all beautiful things in life will be denied him if he cannot escape.)

In all my life I had never seen anything so beautiful.

The walls that rose on either side of the drop-off were literally perpendicular. Eroded by weathering, however, and not by the corrasion[14] of rushing floodwater, they had a rough surface, chipped, broken, cracked. Where the walls joined the face of the overhang they formed almost a square corner, with a number of minute crevices and inch-wide shelves on either side. It might, after all, be possible. What did I have to lose?

When I had regained some measure of nerve and steadiness I got up off my back and tried the wall beside the pond, clinging to the rock with bare toes and fingertips and inching my way crabwise toward the corner. The water-soaked, heavy boots dangling from my neck, swinging back and forth with my every movement, threw me off balance and I fell into the pool. I swam out to the bank, unslung the boots and threw them up over the drop-off, out of sight. They'd be there if I ever needed them again. Once more I attached myself to the wall, tenderly, sensitively, like a limpet,[15] and very slowly, very cautiously, worked my way into the corner. Here I was able to climb upward, a few centimeters at a time, by bracing myself against the opposite sides and finding sufficient niches for fingers and toes. As I neared the top and the overhang became noticeable I prepared for a slip, planning to push myself away from the rock so as to fall into the center of the pool where the water was deepest. But it wasn't necessary. Somehow, with a skill and tenacity I could never

1 have found in myself under ordinary circumstances, I managed to creep straight up that gloomy cliff and over the brink of the drop-off and into the flower of safety. My boots were floating under the surface of the little puddle above. As I poured the stinking water out of them and pulled them on and laced them up I discovered myself bawling again for the third time in three hours, the hot delicious tears of victory. And up above the clouds replied—thunder.

2 I emerged from that treacherous little canyon at sundown, with an enormous fire in the western sky and lightning overhead. Through sweet twilight and the sudden dazzling flare of lightning I hiked back along the Tonto Bench, bellowing the *Ode to Joy*.[16] Long before I reached the place where I could descend safely to the main canyon and my camp, however, darkness set in, the clouds opened their bays and the rain poured down. I took shelter under a ledge in a shallow cave about three

3 feet high—hardly room to sit up in. I had some matches with me, sealed in paraffin[17] (the prudent explorer); I scraped together the handiest twigs and built a little fire and waited for the rain to stop.

It didn't stop. The rain came down for hours in alternate waves of storm and drizzle and I very soon had burnt up all the fuel

4 within reach. No matter. I stretched out in the coyote den, pillowed my head on my arm and suffered through the long long night, wet, cold, aching, hungry, wretched, dreaming claustrophobic[18] nightmares. It was one of the happiest nights of my life.

---

14. **corrasion** [côr ā′zhən]: wearing away of land by running water that contains pebbles, sand, and other matter.
15. **limpet** [lim′pit]: a kind of shellfish with a low, round shell and a thick, fleshy foot that enables it to cling to wood and rock.

16. **Ode to Joy:** final, choral movement of the *Ninth Symphony* by the German composer Ludwig van Beethoven (1770–1827).
17. **paraffin** [par′ə fin]: substance similar to wax.
18. **claustrophobic** [klôs′trə fō′bik]: marked by deep fear of small, enclosed spaces.

Havasu 317

AT A GLANCE

- Bracing himself against opposite walls, Abbey inches his way up.
- He hikes back toward his camp, but darkness overtakes him.
- He spends an uncomfortable but happy night in a shallow cave.

1 **MAIN IDEA**

By describing his goal as a flower, Abbey suggests the beauty, sweetness, and fragility of life. He affirms that his will to survive really *did* make him find strengths within himself.

2 **IMAGERY**

The dazzling lightning and loud thunder are like fireworks celebrating Abbey's triumphant return. Nature reflects the author's own excitement.

3 **IRONY**

Abbey's rash descent and near death in the unknown canyon contrast with the "prudent explorer" who carries waterproof matches.

4 **SETTING**

The setting—cold, dark and uncomfortable—has no power to diminish his joy. It is as if he has conquered the elements.

REFLECTING ON THE SELECTION

Abbey found himself crying three times. What different emotions caused his tears? (despair; sorrow at the contrast between beauty and misery; joy at his escape)

GUIDED READING

LITERAL QUESTIONS

1a. How does Abbey successfully climb the steep drop-off? (He braces himself against two opposite walls and uses tiny niches to inch his way upward.)

2a. Describe the physical conditions in which Abbey had to sleep. (Cold, wet, and hungry, he spent an uncomfortable night in a shallow cave.)

INFERENTIAL QUESTIONS

1b. As he makes the difficult climb, what detail shows that Abbey's mind is alert? (He realizes he might slip and so prepares himself to fall into the pool not onto the rock.)

2b. Why do you think this was the happiest night of Abbey's life? (He was filled with joy to be alive and well, after narrowly escaping a horrible death.)

1. fatalities from sickness or accident because there is no help
2. ■ looking for a shortcut to camp;
   ■ through a sandy canyon bed, over boulders, through potholes, over a twelve-foot cliff, into a stagnant pool, through a chute, into a "stinking pond"
3. will die of starvation
4. piles stones at the base; pushes, with his bare foot, off his walking stick wedged in the stones; inches up
5. ■ inches crabwise, bracing himself against the opposite wall;
   ■ hikes; then takes shelter in a cave from a rainstorm
6. ■ Yes, he is hungry and thirsty and needs a shortcut to reach camp before dark. However, he goes on at the twelve-foot drop, knowing he should turn back.
   ■ People often make crucial decisions without thinking.
7. People will try anything to live.
8. Answers will vary. Possible answers: No, I've had enough of those risks; yes, exploring and taking risks is part of my character.

READING AND LITERARY FOCUS

Answers will vary. Possible answers:
■ The account of the decisions that led him to the eighty-foot cliff follows cause-and-effect order.
■ The account of how he climbed the twelve-foot drop follows cause-effect order.

VOCABULARY

1. from American Spanish *canon,* probably a variation of obsolete Spanish *callon,* street; from the Latin *callis,* footpath; a deep, narrow valley with steep sides
2. French from the Old French *cheoir,* to fall, from the Latin *cadere;* fall, a quick descent
3. Middle French from the Latin *concavus, com + cavus,* hollow; hollowed or rounded inward like a bowl

---

STUDY QUESTIONS

Recalling

1. What are the "special hazards" in traveling alone in the desert?
2. Why does Abbey venture into the little side canyon? Trace the steps that lead him to the cliff.
3. What is his first opinion about his chances?
4. Describe how Abbey climbs up the smooth sandstone chute.
5. How does he climb the twelve-foot drop-off? How does he end the day?

Interpreting

6. Does Abbey have a good reason for going into the canyon? What might he be saying about the way in which we often make decisions?
7. What might Abbey's essay show about the will to survive?

Extending

8. If you were Abbey, would you ever venture into another unknown canyon again?

READING AND LITERARY FOCUS

Narration and Cause and Effect

Narration is the type of writing that tells a story. Autobiographies, biographies, narrative essays, short stories, and novels are forms of narration.

Most narratives are organized in **chronological order,** the order in which events actually take place. Usually the events in a narrative are also related by **cause and effect.** That is, certain events lead logically to certain other events. For example, in "Havasu" Edward Abbey shows how he inches up the smooth sandstone chute by standing on his walking stick:

> I applied more and more pressure to the stick, pushing my body upward until I was again stretched out full length above it. . . . This was sandstone . . . and between it and my wet body

---

and wet clothing a certain friction was created. In addition, the stick had enabled me to reach a higher section of the S-curved chute, where the angle was more favorable. I discovered that I could move upward, inch by inch. . . .

In a gripping narrative like "Havasu," the events form a chain of causes and effects, as one thing causes another that causes another, and so on. This chain of events creates **suspense,** or great interest in the final outcome.

Thinking About Narration and Cause and Effect

■ Choose another suspenseful passage from "Havasu." Point out the cause-and-effect relationships between the events in the passage.

VOCABULARY

Word Origins

You can find the origin and history of a word in a dictionary. This information usually appears in brackets—[ ]—just before or just after the definitions for the word. For example, one dictionary gives the origin and history of the word *desert* as follows:

des-ert[1] (dez′ərt) *n.* [Old French *desert* wilderness, from Late Latin *dēsertum* waste, from Latin *dēserere* to abandon.]

—Scribner Dictionary

The entry tells us that the word came to English from Old French—an early form of today's French language—and that the Old French word itself derived from two words from different periods of the Latin language.

■ The following words are from "Havasu." Look them up in a dictionary, and write down the origin and history for each, as well as the first definition given for each word: (1) canyon, (2) chute, (3) concave, (4) chasm, (5) coyotes.

---

4. Latin *chasma,* from Greek; akin to Latin *hiare,* to yawn; a deep cleft in the earth
5. Mexican Spanish from Nahuatl *coyotl;* small wolf native to Western America

James Herriot (born 1916) grew up in Scotland but has spent most of his life in England. Since 1940 he has worked as a veterinarian, or animal doctor, in Yorkshire, a largely rural area in the northern part of England. Herriot is also a world-famous author, best known for a series of books on the life of a country veterinarian. These autobiographical works include *All Creatures Great and Small* (1972), *All Things Bright and Beautiful* (1974), and *All Things Wise and Wonderful* (1977). The books are filled with funny and touching anecdotes. The following excerpt from *All Things Bright and Beautiful* is an affectionate character sketch of Jock, a farm dog.

■ What are the most striking traits of Jock's personality?

James Herriot

from **All Things Bright and Beautiful**

1 The injured foal[1] was at Robert Corner's farm and I hadn't been there long before I spotted Jock, his sheep dog. And I began to watch the dog because behind a vet's daily chore of treating his patients there is always the fascinating kaleidoscope[2] of animal personality and Jock was an interesting case.

A lot of farm dogs are partial to a little light relief from their work. They like to play and one of their favorite games is chasing cars off the premises. Often I drove off with a hairy form galloping alongside and the dog would usually give a final defiant bark after a few

---

1. **foal:** young horse.
2. **kaleidoscope** [kə lī′də skōp′]: literally, a tube containing many pieces of colored glass that form changing patterns; here, a thing that shows great variety.

2 hundred yards to speed me on my way. But Jock was different.

He was really dedicated. Car chasing to him was a deadly serious art which he practiced daily without a trace of levity. Corner's farm was at the end of a long track, twisting for nearly a mile between its stone walls down through the gently sloping fields to the road 3 below and Jock didn't consider he had done his job properly until he had escorted his chosen vehicle right to the very foot. So his hobby was an exacting one.

I watched him now as I finished stitching the foal's leg and began to tie on a bandage. He was slinking about the buildings, a skinny little creature who without his mass of black and white hair would have been an almost

All Things Bright and Beautiful 319

AT A GLANCE

- As Herriot prepares to leave the farm, Jock gets ready to follow.
- Jock easily keeps up with Herriot's fast-moving car.

1 DESCRIPTION

Trained as a veterinarian, Herriot is skillful at noticing animal behavior. In an engaging manner he characterizes Jock as a bad actor, since he gives away his real intentions.

2 READING SKILLS: CAUSE AND EFFECT

The paragraphs on this page are organized by cause and effect. Each of the author's actions causes a reaction in Jock.

3 STYLE: WORD CHOICE

Herriot uses a variety of vivid words—"sailed," "streaked," "blur," "zooming"—to create an overall impression of great speed and high energy. The passage is an example of Herriot's purposely cultivated entertaining style.

Two views of James Herriot's Yorkshire.

1 invisible mite, and he was playing out a transparent charade of pretending he was taking no notice of me—wasn't the least bit interested in my presence, in fact. But his furtive glances in the direction of the stable, his repeated criss-crossing of my line of vision gave him away. He was waiting for his big moment.

When I was putting on my shoes and throwing my wellingtons[3] into the boot[4] I saw him again. Or rather part of him; just a long nose and one eye protruding from beneath a 2 broken door. It wasn't till I had started the engine and begun to move off that he finally declared himself, stealing out from his hiding place, body low, tail trailing, eyes fixed intently on the car's front wheels, and as I gathered speed and headed down the track he

---

3. **wellingtons:** high boots.
4. **boot:** British term for the trunk of a car.

320   *Nonfiction*

broke into an effortless lope.

I had been through this before and was always afraid he might run in front of me so I put my foot down and began to hurtle downhill. This was where Jock came into his own. I often wondered how he'd fare against a racing greyhound because by golly he could run. That sparse frame housed a perfect physical machine and the slender limbs reached and flew again and again, devouring the stony ground beneath, keeping up with the speeding car with joyful ease.

3 There was a sharp bend about half way down and here Jock invariably sailed over the wall and streaked across the turf, a little dark blur against the green, and having craftily cut off the corner he reappeared like a missile zooming over the gray stones lower down. This put him into a nice position for the run to the road and when he finally saw me on to

---

GUIDED READING

LITERAL QUESTION

1a. How does Jock behave as Herriot finishes up his work at the farm? (Jock tries to pretend he takes no notice of the veterinarian, but his furtive glances and repeated crisscrossing of Herriot's line of vision showed he was waiting for his big moment.)

INFERENTIAL QUESTION

1b. What does Herriot's description of Jock's behavior tell you about the veterinarian? (He is a keen observer of animals; he is interested in why animals act as they do, and he appreciates their personalities.)

AT A GLANCE

Corner purchases a female sheep dog to breed with Jock. They have seven puppies.

1 BACKGROUND

At trials sheep dogs must follow commands to move sheep in a given direction or through a series of gates. They must also separate a designated sheep from the flock and hold it.

2 AUDIENCE

Herriot purposely uses endearing terms ("fluffy," "tumbling," "indulgently") that appeal to his animal-loving audience.

3 NARRATION

In telling the story, the narrator establishes the chronology of events with transitions that mark the passage of time—in this case, "ten months."

the tarmac[5] my last view of him was of a happy, panting face looking after me. Clearly he considered it was a job well done and he would wander contentedly back up to the farm to await the next session, perhaps with the postman or the baker's van.

And there was another side to Jock. He was an outstanding performer at the sheep-dog trials and Mr. Corner had won many trophies with him. In fact the farmer could have sold the little animal for a lot of money but couldn't be persuaded to part with him. Instead he purchased a scrawny little female counterpart of Jock and a trial winner in her own right. With this combination Mr. Corner thought he could breed some world-beating types for sale. On my visits to the farm she joined in the car-chasing but it seemed as

though she was doing it more or less to humor her new mate and she always gave up at the first bend leaving Jock in command. You could see her heart wasn't in it.

When the pups arrived, seven fluffy black balls tumbling about the yard and getting under everybody's feet, Jock watched indulgently as they tried to follow him in his pursuit of my vehicle and you could almost see him laughing as they fell over their feet and were left trailing far behind.

It happened that I didn't have to go there for about ten months but I saw Robert Corner in the market occasionally and he told me he was training the pups and they were shaping well. Not that they needed much training; it was in their blood and he said they had tried to round up the cattle and sheep nearly as soon as they could walk. When I finally saw them they were like seven Jocks—meager,

---

5. **tarmac:** paved road.

All Things Bright and Beautiful 321

GUIDED READING

LITERAL QUESTIONS

1a. Why is Jock worth "a lot of money"? (He is an excellent sheep dog and wins many trials.)

2a. How is the new female dog like Jock? (She is an excellent sheep dog; her scrawny appearance is similar to Jock's.)

INFERENTIAL QUESTIONS

1b. Why do you think Robert Corner couldn't be persuaded to sell Jock? (He probably loved the dog too much to sell him.)

2b. Despite these similarities, why does the author seem less interested in her than Jock? (It is Jock's dedication to car chasing that interests the author. The female cares little about car chasing.)

AT A GLANCE

- The pups, now a year old, join Jock in chasing the author's car.
- Only with great difficulty can Jock outrace them.
- Two months later all the puppies are sold, and Jock remains top dog.

1 READING SKILL:
PREDICTING OUTCOMES

Herriot tells us enough to suggest that Jock is going to have strong competition in his favorite game.

2 MAIN IDEA

The desire to win in a competition is shared by animals and humans alike.

3 CHARACTERIZATION

To help us appreciate Jock's plight, the author attributes to him various human thoughts and feelings.

4 NARRATION

The narrator not only tells the events of the story, he also describes his feelings.

5 VOCABULARY: DIALECT

In the Yorkshire dialect, *aye* means "yes" and *t'awd* means "the old." The Yorkshire speech adds authenticity and color to the sketch.

---

1 darting little creatures flitting noiselessly about the buildings—and it didn't take me long to find out that they had learned more than sheep herding from their father. There was something very evocative[6] about the way they began to prowl around in the background as I prepared to get into my car, peeping furtively from behind straw bales, slinking with elaborate nonchalance into favorable positions for a quick getaway. And as I settled in my seat I could sense they were all crouched in readiness for the off.

I revved my engine, let in the clutch with a bump and shot across the yard and in a second the immediate vicinity erupted in a mass of hairy forms. I roared on to the track and put my foot down and on either side of me the little animals pelted along shoulder to shoulder, their faces all wearing the intent fanatical expression I knew so well. When Jock cleared the wall the seven pups went with him and when they reappeared and entered the home straight[7] I noticed something different. On past occasions Jock had always had one eye on the car—this was what he considered his opponent; but now on that last quarter mile as he hurtled along at the head of a shaggy phalanx[8] he was glancing at the pups on either side as though they were the main opposition.

And there was no doubt he was in trouble. Superbly fit though he was, these stringy bundles of bone and sinew which he had fathered had all his speed plus the newly minted **2** energy of youth and it was taking every shred of his power to keep up with them. Indeed there was one terrible moment when he stumbled and was engulfed by the bounding creatures around him; it seemed that all was lost but there was a core of steel in Jock. Eyes

popping, nostrils dilated, he fought his way through the pack until by the time we reached the road he was once more in the lead.

But it had taken its toll. I slowed down before driving away and looked down at the little animal standing with lolling tongue and heaving flanks on the grass verge. It must have been like this with all the other vehicles and it wasn't a merry game any more. I suppose it sounds silly to say you could read a dog's thoughts but everything in his posture betrayed the mounting apprehension that his days of supremacy were numbered. Just **3** round the corner lay the unthinkable ignominy[9] of being left trailing in the rear of that litter of young upstarts and as I drew away Jock looked after me and his expression was eloquent.

"How long can I keep this up?"

4 I felt for the little dog and on my next visit to the farm about two months later I wasn't looking forward to witnessing the final degradation[10] which I felt was inevitable. But when I drove into the yard I found the place strangely unpopulated.

Robert Corner was forking hay into the cow's racks in the byre.[11] He turned as I came in.

"Where are all your dogs?" I asked.

5 He put down his fork. "All gone. By gaw, there's a market for good workin' sheep dogs. I've done right well out of t'job."

"But you've still got Jock?"

"Oh aye, ah couldn't part with t'awd lad. He's over there."

And so he was, creeping around as of old, pretending he wasn't watching me. And when the happy time finally arrived and I drove

---

6. **evocative** [i vok′ə tiv]: hauntingly familiar.
7. **home straight:** home stretch, or final part of a race.
8. **phalanx** [fā′langks]: group massed for battle.

9. **ignominy** [ig′nə min′ē]: shame.
10. **degradation** [deg′rə dā′shən]: humiliating defeat.
11. **byre** [bīr]: British word for cow barn.

GUIDED READING

LITERAL QUESTIONS

1a. What is the outcome of the race when the seven pups join Jock to chase the car? (With great difficulty Jock manages to win.)

2a. What does Herriot notice is different about the farm on the last visit there? (The puppies are gone, having been sold as sheep dogs to other farmers.)

INFERENTIAL QUESTIONS

1b. What role does Jock's "core of steel" have in this outcome? (After stumbling and being overtaken by the others, Jock's core of steel gives him the strength and desire to fight his way back to the lead position.)

2b. How and why does this change affect the author? (He is probably happy and greatly relieved that he will not have to see Jock lose the car-chasing race to a younger dog.)

away it was like it used to be with the lean little animal haring along by the side of the car, but relaxed, enjoying the game, winging effortlessly over the wall and beating the car down to the tarmac with no trouble at all.

I think I was as relieved as he was that he was left alone with his supremacy unchallenged; that he was still top dog.

REFLECTING ON THE SELECTION

In what senses is Jock "top dog"? (He is the best car chaser; he is a trophy-winning sheep dog; he also shows tremendous strength and willpower.)

STUDY QUESTIONS

Recalling

1. According to Herriot, how does Jock differ from other dogs that chase cars?
2. What eventually replaces the car as Jock's "main opposition"?
3. Who wins the race? What does Jock seem to be saying as Herriot leaves?
4. What finally happens to the pups? What term does Herriot use to describe Jock at the end of the essay?

Interpreting

5. What character traits do you see in Jock?
6. What point about the relationships between generations might the story of Jock make?

READING AND LITERARY FOCUS

Description

Description is the type of writing that creates a clear, vivid picture of its subject—a person, animal, object, or place, for example. Every literary work includes some description.

Good description is made up of **details**—specific pictures, colors, shapes, movements, sounds, smells, textures, and tastes. These details should give the reader an **overall impression** of that subject, as in this passage:

I revved my engine, let in the clutch with a bump and shot across the yard and in a second the immediate vicinity erupted in a mass of hairy forms. I roared on to the track and put my foot down and on either side of me the little animals pelted along shoulder to shoulder. . . .

Thinking About Description

1. Identify the details in another descriptive passage from the selection.
2. What overall impression is created?

COMPOSITION

Writing About Description

▩ Explain what you think James Herriot's central idea is in writing his description of Jock. Begin with a statement about what you take to be Herriot's central idea in this essay. Then use specific facts, incidents, examples, and details to support your opinion. *For help with this assignment, see Lesson 7 in the Writing About Literature Handbook at the back of this book.*

Writing a Description

▩ Write a clear, vivid description of a person, animal, or thing in motion. Begin your description by identifying your subject and explaining why it is in motion. Then describe as exactly and vividly as you can what it looks and sounds like.

STUDY QUESTIONS

1. dedicated to car chasing; practices it like an art
2. his pups
3. Jock, but he's exhausted; "How long can I keep this up?"
4. sold as working sheep dogs; "top dog"
5. Possible answers: enthusiasm, playfulness, speed, competitiveness, determination
6. Possible answers: Youngsters challenge elders with their strength and talent; parents are relieved but proud when children go off on their own.

READING AND LITERARY FOCUS

1. ■ "And there was no doubt he was in trouble . . ." Details contrast the pups' strength with Jock's struggle to keep up and outdo them.
   ■ "And when the happy time finally arrived . . ." Uses vivid verbs to describe the "lean little animal": *haring, winging*.
2. First passage: intense competition; second passage: relaxed pleasure, satisfaction

COMPOSITION: GUIDELINES FOR EVALUATION

WRITING ABOUT DESCRIPTION

Objective

To explain the central idea in writing descriptively about a dog

Guidelines for Evaluation

■ suggested length: two to three paragraphs
■ should begin by stating the essay's main idea
■ should show how it is developed with facts, incidents, examples, details, and statements

WRITING A DESCRIPTION

Objective

To describe a person, animal, or thing in motion

Guidelines for Evaluation

■ suggested length: 100–150 words
■ should begin by identifying the subject
■ should explain why it is in motion
■ should use vivid details to describe how it looks and sounds as it moves

Lorraine Hansberry (1930–1965) won the 1959 New York Drama Critics Circle award for *A Raisin in the Sun,* a play about a black family's struggle to make a better life. She followed this moving and highly successful work with another play in 1964, *The Sign in Sidney Brustein's Window.* Hansberry's great promise was cut short by her death from cancer in 1965. In the following autobiographical selection, Hansberry tells us how her feelings about the season of summer changed over the course of her life.

■ What impression of herself does she give you in "On Summer"?

Lorraine Hansberry

On Summer

1 It has taken me a good number of years to come to any measure of respect for summer. I was, being May-born, literally an "infant of the spring" and, during the later childhood years, tended, for some reason or other, to rather worship the cold aloofness of winter. Adolescence, admittedly lingering still, brought the traditional passionate commitment to melancholy autumn—and all that. For the longest kind of time I simply thought that *summer* was a mistake.

2 In fact, my earliest memory of anything at all is of waking up in a darkened room where I had been put to bed for a nap on a summer's afternoon, and feeling very, very hot. I acutely disliked the feeling then and retained the bias for years. It had originally been a matter of

the heat but, over the years, I came actively to associate displeasure with most of the usually celebrated natural features and social by-products of the season: **3** the too-grainy texture of sand; the too-cold coldness of the various waters we constantly try to escape into, and the icky-perspiry feeling of bathing caps.

It also seemed to me, aesthetically speaking, that nature had got inexcusably carried away on the summer question and let the whole thing get to be rather much. By duration alone, for instance, a summer's day seemed maddeningly excessive; an utter overstatement. Except for those few hours at either end of it, objects always appeared in too sharp a relief against backgrounds; shadows too pronounced and light too blinding. It al-

324   *Nonfiction*

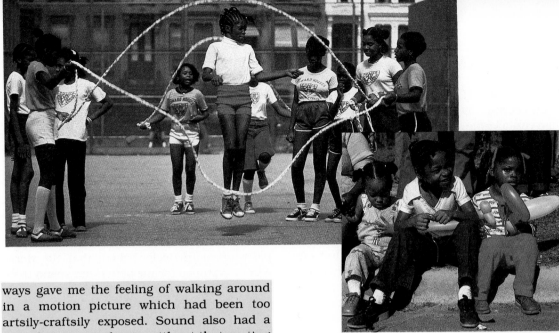

AT A GLANCE

- The author recalls summer street games and rhymes from her childhood.
- She lovingly recounts how her family sometimes passed very hot nights at a local park.

1 STYLE: IMAGERY

Sight and sound images capture the season's jarring effects and support the view that summer was both "too stark" and "too intimate."

2 RESPONSE JOURNAL

Ask students to jot down a few rhymes they remember from *their* childhood. What associations do they have with the rhymes?

3 THEME

The pleasant memories of the park are Hansberry's first positive associations with summer. They signal the beginning of a shift in her perceptions of and feelings about the season.

1 ways gave me the feeling of walking around in a motion picture which had been too artsily-craftsily exposed. Sound also had a way of coming to the ear without that muting influence, marvelously common to winter, across patios or beaches or through the woods. I suppose I found it too stark and yet too intimate a season.

My childhood Southside[1] summers were the ordinary city kind, full of the street games which other rememberers have turned into fine ballets these days and rhymes that anticipated what some people insist on calling modern poetry:

2
Oh, Mary Mack, Mack, Mack
All dressed in black, black, black
With the silver buttons, buttons, buttons
All down her back, back, back
She asked her mother, mother, mother
For fifteen cents, cents, cents
To see the elephant, elephant, elephant
Jump the fence, fence, fence
Well, he jumped so high, high, high
'Til he touched the sky, sky, sky
And he didn't come back, back, back
'Til the Fourth of Ju-ly, ly, ly!

---

1. **Southside:** neighborhood in Chicago.

Evenings were spent mainly on the back porches where screen doors slammed in the darkness with those really very special summertime sounds. And, sometimes, when Chicago nights got too steamy, the whole family got into the car and went to the park and slept out in the open on blankets. Those were, of course, the best times of all because the grownups were invariably reminded of having been children in rural parts of the country **3** and told the best stories then. And it was also cool and sweet to be on the grass and there was usually the scent of freshly cut lemons or melons in the air. And Daddy would lie on his back, as fathers must, and explain about how men thought the stars above us came to be and how far away they were. I never did learn to believe that anything could be as far away as *that*. Especially the stars.

My mother first took us south to visit her Tennessee birthplace one summer when I was seven or eight, I think. I woke up on the back

On Summer 325

GUIDED READING

LITERAL QUESTIONS

1a. How does the author describe the light and sounds of summer? (Like "walking around in a motion picture which had been too . . . exposed"; sound was "without that muting influence.")

2a. What especially pleasant summer memories does the author recall? (She recalls enjoying the summer nights that her family spent in the park, eating, storytelling and stargazing.)

INFERENTIAL QUESTIONS

1b. What do these descriptions suggest about Hansberry's skill as a writer? (These descriptions show she is keenly aware of sensory impressions.)

2b. How do these memories compare with the opinions of summer that she stated earlier? (They seem to contradict the opinions that summer was "a mistake," "rather much," and "excessive.")

1 seat of the car while we were still driving through some place called Kentucky and my mother was pointing out to the beautiful hills on both sides of the highway and telling my brothers and my sister about how her father had run away and hidden from his master in those very hills when he was a little boy. She said that his mother had wandered among the wooded slopes in the moonlight and left food 2 for him in secret places. They were very beautiful hills and I looked out at them for miles and miles after that wondering who and what a *master* might be.

I remember being startled when I first saw my grandmother rocking away on her porch. All my life I had heard that she was a great beauty and no one had ever remarked that they meant a half century before. The woman that I met was as wrinkled as a prune and could hardly hear and barely see and always seemed to be thinking of other times. But she could still rock and talk and even make wonderful cupcakes which were like cornbread, only sweet. She was captivated by automobiles and, even though it was well into the Thirties, I don't think she had ever been in one before we came down and took her driving. She was a little afraid of them and could not seem to negotiate the windows, but she loved driving. She died the next summer and that is all that I remember about her, except that she was born in slavery and had memories of it and they didn't sound anything like *Gone with the Wind.*[2]

Like everyone else, I have spent whole or bits of summers in many different kinds of places since then: camps and resorts in the Middle West and New York State; on an island; in a tiny Mexican village; Cape Cod, perched

atop the Truro bluffs at Longnook Beach that Millay[3] wrote about; or simply strolling the streets of Provincetown[4] before the hours when the parties begin.

3 And, lastly, I do not think that I will forget days spent, a few summers ago, at a beautiful lodge built right into the rocky cliffs of a bay on the Maine coast. We met a woman there who had lived a purposeful and courageous life and who was then dying of cancer. She had, characteristically, just written a book and taken up painting. She had also been of radical viewpoint all her life; one of those people who energetically believe that the world *can* be changed for the better and spend their lives trying to do just that. And that was the way she thought of cancer; she absolutely refused to award it the stature of tragedy, a devastating instance of the brooding doom and inexplicability[5] of the absurdity of human destiny, etc., etc. The kind of characterization given, lately, as we all know, to far less formidable foes in life than cancer.

But for this remarkable woman it was a matter of nature in imperfection, implying, as always, work for man to do. It was an *enemy*, but a palpable[6] one with shape and effect and source; and if it existed, it could be destroyed. She saluted it accordingly, without despondency, but with a lively, beautiful and delightfully ribald[7] anger. There was one thing, she felt, which would prove equal to its relentless ravages and that was the genius of man. Not his mysticism, but man with tubes and slides and the stubborn human notion that the

2. *Gone with the Wind:* popular 1936 novel by Margaret Mitchell, made into a film in 1939. It offered a sympathetic portrait of the South during and after the Civil War.

326 *Nonfiction*

3. **Millay:** Edna St. Vincent Millay (1892–1950), American poet.
4. **Provincetown:** summer resort on Cape Cod in Massachusetts.
5. **inexplicability** [in'iks plik'ə bil'ə tē]: quality of being impossible to explain.
6. **palpable** [pal'pə bəl]: capable of being touched or felt.
7. **ribald** [rib'əld]: earthy.

stars are very much within our reach.

The last time I saw her she was sitting surrounded by her paintings with her manuscript laid out for me to read, because, she said, she wanted to know what a *young person* would think of her thinking; one must always keep up with what *young people* thought about things because, after all, they were *change*.

Every now and then her jaw set in anger as we spoke of things people should be angry about. And then, for relief, she would look out at the lovely bay at a mellow sunset settling on the water. Her face softened with love of all that beauty and, watching her, I wished with all my power what I knew that she was wishing: that she might live to see at least one more *summer*. Through her eyes I finally gained the sense of what it might mean: more than the coming autumn with its pretentious melancholy; more than an austere and silent winter which must shut dying people in for precious months; more even than the frivolous spring, too full of too many false promises, would be the gift of another summer with its stark and intimate assertion of neither birth nor death but life at the apex;[8] with the gentlest nights and, above all, the longest days.

I heard later that she did live to see another summer. And I have retained my respect for the noblest of the seasons.

_____

8. **apex** [ā′peks]: highest point.

STUDY QUESTIONS

Recalling

1. In her first sentence what does Hansberry say of her feelings about summer?
2. Name two things that Hansberry did not like about summer when she was young.
3. What happy memories does Hansberry have about summers in Chicago? What does she remember about the summer visit to her grandmother?
4. From her friendship with the woman who is ill, what does Hansberry see as summer's special advantages?

Interpreting

5. What do you think Hansberry means when she says that life is "at the apex" in summer?
6. In telling about her own changing feelings toward summer, what do you think Hansberry might be saying about the changes that we go through in life?

Extending

7. What are your own opinions of each season?

READING AND LITERARY FOCUS

Exposition and Thesis Statement

Exposition is the type of writing that presents information or explains an idea. The author of an expository essay often sets forth the central idea that the essay will develop in a **thesis statement,** a sentence or two that clearly states the central thought of the work. The thesis statement usually appears near the beginning of a piece and is then developed and supported throughout the rest of the work with specific facts, incidents, examples, and details. Often an author restates the thesis in fresh terms near the end of the piece, thereby adding new impact to the central idea of the work.

For example, in "On Summer" Lorraine Hansberry states her thesis in her first sentence: "It has taken me a good number of years to come to any measure of respect for summer." She then explains

On Summer 327

1. waking from a nap feeling hot and uncomfortable; days being too long, bright, and noisy
2. next-to-last paragraph: recalls the dying woman loving the sunset, and realizes she loves summer's "stark and intimate assertion of . . . life at the apex"

VOCABULARY

1. (c) dedication
2. (a) purpose
3. (b) power
4. (d) depth

---

with examples and incidents why she once disliked summer but then came gradually to appreciate it.

Thinking About Exposition

1. Give two of the examples or incidents Hansberry uses to develop her idea about summer.
2. Where near the end of her essay does Hansberry restate her ideas about summer?

VOCABULARY

Analogies

Analogies are comparisons that are stated as double relationships—for example, *A* is to *B* as *C* is to *D*. On tests analogies are written as two pairs of words, *A* : *B* :: *C* : *D*. You may be given one pair and asked to find or complete a second pair that has the same kind of relationship as the first. For example, in the analogy SUMMER : HOT :: WINTER : COLD the first word in each pair names a season, and the second word describes the weather of that season.

The following numbered items are analogies that need to be completed. The third word in each item comes from "On Summer." Decide how the first two words in each item are related. Then from the four choices that follow each numbered item choose the word that best completes the second pair. Write the number of each item and the letter of your choice on a separate sheet.

1. OPTIMISM : HOPE :: COMMITMENT :
   (a) pessimism   (c) dedication
   (b) commit   (d) neglect
2. FASCINATING : FASCINATION :: PURPOSEFUL :
   (a) purpose   (c) propose
   (b) committed   (d) interesting
3. RAPID : SPEED :: FORMIDABLE :
   (a) slowness   (c) powerful
   (b) power   (d) weakness

4. ABYSS : HEIGHT :: APEX :
   (a) happy   (c) climax
   (b) highest   (d) depth

COMPOSITION

Writing About Exposition

■ Explain what you think Lorraine Hansberry's central idea was in writing "On Summer." Begin with a statement of what you think Hansberry wants us to understand about summer and her feelings for it. Then use specific quotations, examples, and details from the piece to support your opinion about its central idea. *For help with this assignment, see Lesson 7 in the Writing About Literature Handbook at the back of this book.*

Writing Exposition

■ Write a composition in which you identify your favorite time of year and explain why you prefer it. Be sure to support your main points with examples and anecdotes. You may want to use vivid description and interesting narration in your composition, as Hansberry does in "On Summer." Conclude with one or two sentences singling out what you consider to be the best quality of this season.

CHALLENGE

Outline

■ A good way to review and to remember an expository essay is to outline it. Write an outline of "On Summer." Begin by identifying the thesis, or central idea, of the essay with the Roman numeral *I*. Then indicate all the supporting ideas with capital letters (*A, B, C,* etc.). Note any examples within supporting ideas by using Arabic numerals (*1, 2, 3,* etc.).

COMPOSITION: GUIDELINES FOR EVALUATION

WRITING ABOUT EXPOSITION

Objective
To explain the essay's central idea

Guidelines for Evaluation
■ suggested length: three to four paragraphs
■ should begin with a thesis statement expressing Hansberry's thoughts about summer
■ should support the thesis with quotations, examples, and details from the essay
■ should tell how each element conveys the idea

WRITING EXPOSITION

Objective
To support an opinion with examples

Guidelines for Evaluation
■ suggested length: three paragraphs
■ should identify a favorite season
■ should give reasons for the preference and support them with examples and anecdotes
■ should end stating the season's best quality

Abraham Lincoln (1809–1865), the sixteenth President of the United States, was born in Kentucky and grew up in Indiana. As an adult he moved to Illinois where he practiced law and became involved in politics. Shortly after he became President in 1861, the Civil War between the North and the South began. Five days after the fighting stopped in April 1865, Lincoln was shot by John Wilkes Booth.

Lincoln was an extraordinary speaker. He delivered his greatest speech on November 19, 1863, at the dedication of a national cemetery in Gettysburg, Pennsylvania, where the Northern troops had recently won an important but costly victory. As Lincoln rode the train to Pennsylvania, he jotted down ten sentences on the back of an envelope.

■ Why do you think these ten sentences have become the most enduring statement of the ideals on which this country was founded?

Abraham Lincoln

The Gettysburg Address

1 Four score and seven years ago our fathers brought forth on this continent, a new nation, conceived in Liberty, and dedicated to the proposition that all men are created equal.

Now we are engaged in a great civil war, testing whether that nation, or any nation so conceived and so dedicated, can long endure. We are met on a great battlefield of that war. We have come to dedicate a portion of that field, as a final resting place for those who here gave their lives that that nation might live. It is altogether fitting and proper that we should do this.

2 But, in a larger sense, we can not dedicate—we can not consecrate—we can not hallow—this ground. The brave men, living and dead, who struggled here, have consecrated it, far above our poor power to add or detract. The world will little note, nor long remember what we say here, but it can never forget what they did here. It is for us the living, rather, to be dedicated here to the unfinished work which they who fought here have thus far so nobly advanced. **3** It is rather for us to be here dedicated to the great task remaining before us—that from these honored dead we take increased devotion to that cause for which they gave the last full measure of devotion—that we here highly resolve that these dead shall not have died in vain—that this nation, under God, shall have a new birth of freedom—and that government of the people, by the people, for the people, shall not perish from the earth.

The Gettysburg Address 329

LITERARY OPTIONS

- persuasion
- repetition

THEMATIC OPTIONS

- American experiences
- ideals and visions

1 STYLE: WORD CHOICE

"Four score and seven" instead of "eighty-seven" sets a dignified tone that is appropriate for a serious subject.

2 ORATORY: REPETITION

By repeating "we can not" and, later, "It is for us," Lincoln urges his listeners to insure that liberty survives.

3 PERSUASION

Lincoln becomes more persuasive by characterizing the nation as a living being. It is "conceived" and "brought forth." It shall have "a new birth" and "shall not perish." Just as a person breathes to live, our country needs the breath of liberty.

REFLECTING ON THE SELECTION

What makes Lincoln's speech memorable? (possible answers: unusual opening phrase, effective use of repetition, moving description of the country's history, wartime setting)

TEXAS ESSENTIAL ELEMENTS GRADE 8

1A writing process
1B purpose and audience
1E appropriate language
3E types of nonfiction
4F author's purpose
To locate treatment of an Element, see *Texas Teacher's Resources*.

GUIDED READING

LITERAL QUESTION

1a. In addition to honoring soldiers who died at Gettysburg, what other purpose did Lincoln have for giving this address? (He wanted to persuade the living to continue to work to advance the cause of freedom and equality.)

INFERENTIAL QUESTION

1b. Was Lincoln successful in this purpose? Explain. (Union soldiers continued to fight for Lincoln's ideas; people then and now view the speech as a moving statement of American ideals; our country continues to extend freedom and equality to its people.)

1. The Declaration of Independence was adopted.
2. "conceived in liberty," "brought forth": words describing a birth
3. the nation and democracy
4. The living must dedicate themselves to their cause: preserving freedom.
5. to consider the soldiers' cause and valor; to resolve to fight for the nation and democracy
6. Possible answers: liberty, equality, democracy, willingness to fight for such principles
7. Possible answers:
   - Yes: We must protect democracy and the ideal of equality.
   - No: U.S. is a world power, and today's weapons make diplomacy a better way to solve problems.

READING AND LITERARY FOCUS

1.
   - Paragraph 1: America has always been dedicated to equality.
   - Paragraph 2: Today we set aside part of this battlefield as a cemetery for soldiers who died for the nation.
   - Paragraph 3: The men who died here consecrated the land; we must dedicate ourselves to their cause: protecting democracy.
2.
   - mostly Union sympathizers: soldiers' families, Union military officials, local people
   - pride of their loved ones and as Americans; determination to fight for freedom and democracy

CHALLENGE

Students should be able to repeat the final paragraph of the Gettysburg Address. Students might help each other memorize the paragraph.

STUDY QUESTIONS

Recalling

1. What great event happened four score and seven years before Lincoln's speech?
2. What words does Lincoln use to describe America at that time?
3. According to the second paragraph, what is being tested?
4. According to Lincoln, what must happen if those who gave their lives for the country "shall not have died in vain"?

Interpreting

5. Tell in your own words what you think Lincoln is urging his audience to do.
6. What features or values in American life does Lincoln seem to feel are most worthy?

Extending

7. Do you think what Lincoln says still applies to the United States today? Why or why not?

READING AND LITERARY FOCUS

Persuasion

Persuasion attempts to convince people to accept an opinion or to take action of some kind. Persuasion is used in such different types of expression as editorials, advertisements, and speeches. Of all the forms of persuasion, the **speech** is the most direct, since the speaker presents opinions directly to a group of listeners. The best speeches appeal both to their listeners' intellects and to their emotions.

Persuasive speakers, like persuasive writers, should appeal to the intellects of their audiences by presenting **evidence, examples,** and **logical arguments** in favor of their opinions. In addition, a persuasive speech should present arguments that are logically connected in a clear, simple structure that listeners can follow easily.

Because a speaker addresses an audience di-

330   *Nonfiction*

rectly, a persuasive speech can touch its audience's emotions in a way that few pieces of writing can. Effective speakers—like Abraham Lincoln—understand that if their listeners can be moved to feel compassion, pride, anger, or determination, then they are also more likely to agree with the speaker's opinions.

Thinking About Persuasion

1. Lincoln's speech is divided into three paragraphs. What is the main idea of each paragraph? What is the connection between these paragraphs and their main ideas?
2. What particular audience did Lincoln address? To what emotions did he appeal?

COMPOSITION

Writing a Paraphrase

■ Write a composition in which you paraphrase, or summarize in your own words, Lincoln's Gettysburg Address. Prepare to write by making sure that you understand what every word of the Gettysburg Address means. In addition, decide how each sentence is connected to the one that precedes it. Organize your composition into three paragraphs that follow Lincoln's own organization of his speech.

Writing a Persuasive Speech

■ Choose a subject about which you are concerned. Write a short speech in which you try to convince others to accept your opinion on this subject. Be sure to state your opinion clearly and to back it up with convincing evidence and logical arguments.

CHALLENGE

Memorizing

■ Memorize the third paragraph of the Gettysburg Address. Be prepared to write it down from memory or to recite it aloud.

COMPOSITION: GUIDELINES FOR EVALUATION

WRITING A PARAPHRASE
Objective
To summarize a famous speech

Guidelines for Evaluation
- suggested length: three paragraphs
- should recap the Gettysburg Address's main points in one's own words
- should present the points in the same order
- should use an informal style

WRITING A PERSUASIVE SPEECH
Objective
To write a short persuasive speech

Guidelines for Evaluation
- suggested length: three to four paragraphs
- should state an opinion clearly
- should support the opinion with evidence, examples, and arguments in logical order
- should appeal to the listeners' intellect and emotions

THE TOTAL EFFECT

The most effective way to approach nonfiction is to read it actively and attentively. Keep in mind that a work of nonfiction, while factual, represents only one author's version of the truth, written for a particular purpose and audience. When you actively look for clues about the author's intentions, you will increase your ability to understand and judge what the author is saying. You will also find more pleasure in reading nonfiction if you notice the facts, details, and language that the author uses to accomplish his or her purpose. The following reminders will help you to think about the various elements of nonfiction so that you will experience the **total effect** of the work.

Reminders for Active Reading of Nonfiction

1. The **title** often announces the author's purpose.
2. The writer of **autobiography** shares both memories and insights about past events.
3. The writer of **biography** presents the facts about a person's life and reveals the subject's personality.
4. The writer of any type of nonfiction—autobiography, biography, or essay—uses various elements and techniques, including the following:

   - a **thesis statement** or clearly implied main idea
   - **facts, incidents,** and **examples** supporting this idea
   - **topic sentences** to alert the reader to the main idea in each paragraph
   - **chronological order, cause-and-effect order,** or some other clear organization
   - **anecdotes** to reveal character
   - **descriptive details** to create vivid pictures

5. The writer of any piece of nonfiction has a **purpose** in mind. The reader should uncover that purpose.

Model for Active Reading

On the following pages you will see how an alert reader kept in mind these reminders while reading a selection from *Kon-Tiki.* Notes in the margins present the reader's observations about the work. Each notation gives a page reference for further information about the item. Read the selection first for your own enjoyment, and then read it along with the notations. Later you can use the process followed in this model with any nonfiction work.

Nonfiction 331

- Heyerdahl describes the variety of fish the men see during their first three days alone at sea.
- A flying fish lands on board, and they use it as bait.

LITERARY OPTIONS

- main idea
- purpose
- audience

THEMATIC OPTIONS

- nature
- adventure
- observation

The annotations that appear in the Teacher's Edition answer the questions asked in Pupil's Edition sidenotes.

NARRATION

On the first day out the crew barely notice the fish around the raft. On the second day the raft goes through a school of sardines and meets a shark. On the third day they are visited by tunnies, bonitos, dolphins, and a flying fish that lands on deck.

TEXAS ESSENTIAL ELEMENTS
GRADE 8

3A plot development
3D literary genres
3E types of nonfiction
4E cause/effect
4F author's purpose
4H generalizations
To locate treatment of an Element, see *Texas Teacher's Resources.*

Thor Heyerdahl [hī'ər däl] (born 1914) is a Norwegian ethnologist—a person who studies and compares different cultures throughout the world. Heyerdahl became famous in 1947 when he and five companions sailed a balsa-wood raft, named the *Kon-Tiki,* more than four thousand miles across the Pacific Ocean, from Peru in South America to the Polynesian islands. Heyerdahl made this trip to test his idea that Polynesia might actually have been settled centuries ago by South American Indians. Heyerdahl narrates the story of his remarkable adventure in his book *Kon-Tiki* (1950).

■ Of the strange creatures seen by the crew of the *Kon-Tiki,* which do you find the most memorable?

Thor Heyerdahl

from Kon-Tiki

The very first day we were left alone on the sea we had noticed fish round the raft, but we were too much occupied with the steering to think of fishing. The second day we went right into a thick shoal[1] of sardines, and soon afterward an eight-foot blue shark came along and rolled over with its white belly uppermost as it rubbed against the raft's stern,[2] where Herman and Bengt stood barelegged in the seas, steering. It played round us for a while but disappeared when we got the hand harpoon ready for action.

Next day we were visited by tunnies, bonitos,[3] and dolphins, and when a big flying fish thudded on board we used it as bait and at once pulled in two large dolphins (dorados) weighing from twenty to thirty-five pounds each. This was food for several days. On steering watch we could see many fish we did not even know, and one day we came into a school of porpoises which seemed quite endless. The black backs tumbled about, packed close to-

Narration (p. 318) tells a story. A narrative is usually organized in **chronological order** (p. 47), the order in which events actually occur. What happens during the first three days at sea?

---

1. **shoal:** school of fish.
2. **stern:** back end of a boat, raft, or other sailing craft.
3. **tunnies, bonitos:** types of tuna.

332   *Nonfiction*

GUIDED READING

LITERAL QUESTION

1a. Describe the appearance and location of Herman and Bengt when the blue shark comes along. (They are standing barelegged in the seas, steering.)

INFERENTIAL QUESTION

1b. Why do you think that Heyerdahl points out that the men are barelegged? (to indicate how unprotected and vulnerable they are) gether, right in to the side of the raft, and sprang up here and there all over the sea as far as we could see from the masthead. And the nearer we came to the Equator, and the farther from the coast, the commoner flying fish became. When at last we came out into the blue water where the sea rolled by majestically, sunlit and serene, ruffled by gusts of wind, we could see them glittering like a rain of projectiles[4] which shot from the water and flew in a straight line till their power of flight was exhausted and they vanished beneath the surface.

If we set the little paraffin[5] lamp out at night, flying fish were attracted by the light and, large and small, shot over the raft. They often struck the bamboo cabin or the sail and tumbled helpless on the deck. Unable to get a take-off by swimming through the water, they just remained lying and kicking helplessly, like large-eyed herrings with long breast fins. It sometimes happened that we heard an outburst of strong language from a man on deck when a cold flying fish came unexpectedly, at a good speed, slap into his face. They always came at a good pace and snout first, and if they caught one full in the face they made it burn and tingle. But the unprovoked attack was quickly forgiven by the injured party, for, with all its drawbacks, we were in a maritime land of enchantment where delicious fish dishes came hurling through the air. We used to fry them for breakfast, and whether it was the fish, the cook, or our appetites, they reminded us of fried troutlings once we had scraped the scales off.

The cook's first duty, when he got up in the morning, was to go out on deck and collect all the flying fish that had landed on board in the course of the night. There were usually half a dozen or more, and once we found twenty-six fat flying fish on the raft. Knut[6] was much upset one morning because, when he was standing operating with the frying pan, a flying fish struck him on the hand instead of landing right in the cooking fat.

Our neighborly intimacy with the sea was not fully realized by Torstein till he woke one morning and found a sardine on his pillow. There was so little room in the cabin that Torstein had to lie with his head in the doorway, and, if anyone inadvertently[7] trod on his face when going out at night, he bit him in the leg. He grasped the sardine by the tail and confided to it understand-

Descriptive details (p. 323) create a sharp picture. What details help you to see these fish?

An **anecdote** (p. 312) is a brief account of a true event. It is usually used to illustrate a point that the author is making. What idea is illustrated by this anecdote?

---

4. **projectiles** [prə jek′tīlz]: objects that can be thrown or shot forth, as if from a gun.
5. **paraffin** [par′ə fin]: substance similar to wax.
6. **Knut** [kə nōōt′]
7. **inadvertently** [in′ad vurt′ənt lē]: accidentally.

Kon-Tiki 333

AT A GLANCE

- Heyerdahl describes the sea as a "land of enchantment," where flying fish drop on deck to become the men's food.
- He begins a humorous anecdote to show the full extent of their "neighborly intimacy" with the sea.

DESCRIPTIVE DETAILS

The creature was "over three feet long, as slender as a snake, with dull black eyes and a long snout with a greedy jaw full of long sharp teeth" that folded back into the mouth. "The snakefish's thin skin was bluish violet on the back and steel blue underneath, and it came loose in flakes" when the crew handled the fish.

ANECDOTE

The *Kon-Tiki*'s "intimacy" with the sea is illustrated.

GUIDED READING

LITERAL QUESTION

1a. What does Heyerdahl say that Torstein finds on his pillow? (a sardine)

INFERENTIAL QUESTION

1b. How does the sardine on the pillow demonstrate the men's "neighborly intimacy with the sea"? (The men have encounters with fish not only during the day on deck but even at night while they are asleep in the cabin.)

AT A GLANCE

- Torstein sympathizes with crowded sardines.
- Torstein is wakened when something cold and wet lands on his head.
- The men gaze in wonder and fear at a *Gempylus*, a snake-like fish with long, sharp teeth.

ingly that all sardines had his entire sympathy. We conscientiously drew in our legs so that Torstein should have more room the next night, but then something happened which caused Torstein to find himself a sleeping place on top of all the kitchen utensils in the radio corner.

It was a few nights later. It was overcast and pitch dark, and Torstein had placed the paraffin lamp close by his head, so that the night watches could see where they were treading when they crept in and out over his head. About four o'clock Torstein was awakened by the lamp tumbling over and something cold and wet flapping about his ears. "Flying fish," he thought and felt for it in the darkness to throw it away. He caught hold of something long and wet, which wriggled like a snake, and let go as if he had burned himself. The unseen visitor twisted itself away and over to Herman, while Torstein tried to get the lamp lighted again. Herman started up, too, and this made me wake, thinking of the octopus which came up at night in these waters.

When we got the lamp lighted, Herman was sitting in triumph with his hand gripping the neck of a long thin fish which wriggled in his hands like an eel. The fish was over three feet long, as slender as a snake, with dull black eyes and a long snout with a greedy jaw full of long sharp teeth. The teeth were as sharp as knives and could be folded back into the roof of the mouth to make way for what was swallowed. Under Herman's grip a large-eyed white fish, about eight inches long, was suddenly thrown up from the stomach and out of the mouth of the predatory fish, and soon after up came another like it. These were clearly two deep-water fish, much torn by the snakefish's teeth. The snakefish's thin skin was bluish violet on the back and steel blue underneath, and it came loose in flakes when we took hold of it.

Bengt too was awakened at last by all the noise, and we held the lamp and the long fish under his nose. He sat up drowsily in his sleeping bag and said solemnly:

"No, fish like that don't exist."

With which he turned over quietly and fell asleep again.

Bengt was not far wrong. It appeared later that we six sitting round the lamp in the bamboo cabin were the first men to have seen this fish alive. Only the skeleton of a fish like this one had been found a few times on the coast of South America and the Galapagos Islands;[8] ichthyologists[9] called it *Gempylus*, or snake

Two dolphins.

---

8. **Galapagos** [gə lä′pə gōs′] Islands: group of islands in the eastern Pacific, along the equator.
9. **ichthyologists** [ik′thē ol′ə jists]: scholars who study fish.

334   *Nonfiction*

GUIDED READING

LITERAL QUESTION

1a. What does Torstein confide understandingly to a sardine? (that all sardines have his entire sympathy)

INFERENTIAL QUESTION

1b. What does Torstein mean? (Because the sleeping quarters on board are so cramped, he now understands what it is like to be crowded like sardines in a tin.)

mackerel, and thought it lived at the bottom of the sea at a great depth because no one had ever seen it alive. But, if it lived at a great depth, it must have done so by day when the sun blinded its big eyes. For on dark nights *Gempylus* was abroad high over the surface of the sea; we on the raft had experience of that.

A week after the rare fish had landed on Torstein's sleeping bag, we had another visit. Again it was four in the morning, and the new moon had set so that it was dark but the stars were shining. The raft was steering easily, and when my watch was over I took a turn along the edge of the raft to see if everything was shipshape for the new watch. I had a rope round my waist, as the watch always had, and, with the paraffin lamp in my hand, I was walking carefully along the outermost log to get round the mast. The log was wet and slippery, and I was furious when someone quite unexpectedly caught hold of the rope behind me and jerked till I nearly lost my balance. I turned round wrathfully with the lantern, but not a soul was to be seen. There came a new tug at the rope, and I saw something shiny lying writhing on the deck. It was a fresh *Gempylus*, and this time it had got its teeth so deep into the rope that several of them broke before I got the rope loose. Presumably the light of the lantern had flashed along the curving white rope, and our visitor from the depths of the sea had caught hold in the hope of jumping up and snatching an extra long and tasty tidbit. It ended its days in a jar of Formalin.[10]

The sea contains many surprises for him who has his floor on a level with the surface and drifts along slowly and noiselessly. A sportsman who breaks his way through the woods may come back and say that no wild life is to be seen. Another may sit down on a stump and wait, and often rustlings and cracklings will begin and curious eyes peer out. So it is on the sea, too. We usually plow across it with roaring engines and piston strokes, with the water foaming round our bow. Then we come back and say that there is nothing to see far out on the ocean.

Not a day passed but we, as we sat floating on the surface of the sea, were visited by inquisitive guests which wriggled and waggled about us, and a few of them, such as dolphins and pilot fish, grew so familiar that they accompanied the raft across the sea and kept round us day and night.

When night had fallen and the stars were twinkling in the

---

10. **Formalin** [fôr′mə lin]: solution of water and formaldehyde used to disinfect and preserve specimens.

The **topic sentence** (p. 305) announces the main idea to be developed in a paragraph. How does the rest of this paragraph develop the idea in this sentence?

The **thesis statement** (p. 327) expresses the central idea to be developed in an essay. What is the idea expressed in this sentence? How does the rest of the selection develop this idea?

AT A GLANCE

- A week later another *Gempylus* appears. Heyerdahl kills it and preserves the skeleton.
- Heyerdahl explains that the sea contains many wonderful surprises for those who are quiet and patient enough to wait for them.

TOPIC SENTENCE

The sentence tells that the crew had another visit from a *Gempylus*, and the rest of the paragraph describes the circumstances of that visit.

THESIS STATEMENT

The idea is that someone who drifts quietly, with a deck level with the surface of the water, will see all sorts of surprising creatures. The selection develops this idea by describing the many different sea creatures that visit the raft.

GUIDED READING

LITERAL QUESTION

1a. Where does the second *Gempylus* end up? (in a jar of Formalin)

INFERENTIAL QUESTION

1b. Why does Heyerdahl put the fish in a jar of Formalin? (He wants a specimen for later study and to show others because no one had ever seen the fish before.)

AT A GLANCE

- Heyerdahl describes various types of phosphorescent ocean creatures that create a magical effect on dark tropical nights.
- He describes the crew's fascination with mysterious new creatures that make a ghostly appearance one night.

A

dark tropical sky, a phosphorescence[11] flashed around us in rivalry with the stars, and single glowing plankton[12] resembled round live coals so vividly that we involuntarily drew in our bare legs when the glowing pellets were washed up round our feet at the raft's stern. When we caught them, we saw that they were little brightly shining species of shrimp. On such nights we were sometimes scared when two round shining eyes suddenly rose out of the sea right alongside the raft and glared at us with an unblinking hypnotic stare. The visitors were often big squids which came up and floated on the surface with their devilish green eyes shining in the dark like phosphorus. But sometimes the shining eyes were those of deep-water fish which came up only at night and lay staring, fascinated by the glimmer of light before them. Several times, when the sea was calm, the black water round the raft was suddenly full of round heads two or three feet in diameter, lying motionless and staring at us with great glowing eyes. On other nights balls of light three feet and more in diameter would be visible down in the water, flashing at irregular intervals like electric lights turned on for a moment.

We gradually grew accustomed to having these subterranean or submarine creatures under the floor, but nevertheless we were just as surprised every time a new species appeared. About two o'clock on a cloudy night, when the man at the helm[13] had difficulty in disinguishing black water from black sky, he caught sight of a faint illumination down in the water which slowly took the shape of a large animal. It was impossible to say whether it was plankton shining on its body, or whether the animal itself had a phosphorescent surface, but the glimmer down in the black water gave the ghostly creature obscure, wavering outlines. Sometimes it was roundish, sometimes oval, or triangular, and suddenly it split into two parts which swam to and fro under the raft independently of each other. Finally there were three of these large shining phantoms wandering round in slow circles under us.

B

They were real monsters, for the visible parts alone were some five fathoms[14] long, and we all quickly collected on deck and followed the ghost dance. It went on for hour after hour, following the course of the raft. Mysterious and noiseless, our shining

D

---

11. **phosphorescence** [fos'fə res'əns]: glowing light coming from a substance that has absorbed heat or light.
12. **plankton** [plangk'tən]: microscopic animal and plant life found in the ocean.
13. **helm:** steering mechanism.
14. **five fathoms:** thirty feet. A fathom is a unit of measure equal to six feet.

336   *Nonfiction*

GUIDED READING

LITERAL QUESTION

1a. What supernatural images does Heyerdahl use to describe the three large shining creatures that circle the raft? *(ghostly, phantoms, monsters, ghost dance)*

INFERENTIAL QUESTION

1b. Why do you think Heyerdahl uses such images to describe these fish? (They are silent, mysterious, and unidentifiable; they seem to change shape and suddenly split; there seems no reasonable explanation for them.)

Pages 336–337: (A) a shark; (B) an octopus; (C) the deck of the *Kon-Tiki*, showing the sail with the head of Kon-Tiki, an ancient chieftain; (D) a snake mackerel; (E) a sea snake.

Kon-Tiki 337

companions kept a good way beneath the surface, mostly on the starboard side where the light was, but often they were right under the raft or appeared on the port side.[15] The glimmer of light on their backs revealed that the beasts were bigger than elephants but they were not whales, for they never came up to breathe. Were they giant ray fish which changed shape when they turned over on their sides? They took no notice at all if we held the light right down on the surface to lure them up, so that we might see what kind of creatures they were. And, like all proper goblins and ghosts, they had sunk into the depths when the dawn began to break.

We never got a proper explanation of this nocturnal visit from the three shining monsters, unless the solution was afforded by another visit we received a day and a half later in the full midday sunshine. It was May 24, and we were lying drifting on a leisurely swell in exactly 95° west by 7° south. It was about noon, and we had thrown overboard the guts of two big dolphins we had caught earlier in the morning. I was having a refreshing plunge overboard at the bow,[16] lying in the water but keeping a good lookout and hanging on to a rope end, when I caught sight of a thick brown fish, six feet long, which came swimming inquisitively toward me through the crystal-clear sea water. I hopped quickly up on to the edge of the raft and sat in the hot sun looking at the fish as it passed quietly, when I heard a wild war whoop from Knut, who was sitting aft behind the bamboo cabin. He bellowed "Shark!" till his voice cracked in a falsetto,[17] and, as we had sharks swimming alongside the raft almost daily without creating such excitement, we all realized that this must be something extraspecial and flocked astern to Knut's assistance.

Knut had been squatting there, washing his pants in the swell, and when he looked up for a moment he was staring straight into the biggest and ugliest face any of us had ever seen in the whole of our lives. It was the head of a veritable sea monster, so huge and so hideous that, if the Old Man of the Sea[18] himself had come up, he could not have made such an impression on us. The head was broad and flat like a frog's, with two small eyes right at the sides, and a toadlike jaw which was four or five feet wide and had long fringes drooping from the corners of the

---

15. **starboard side . . . port side:** The starboard side is the right-hand side of a sailing craft; the port side is the left-hand side.
16. **bow** [bou]: front end of a sailing craft.
17. **falsetto** [fol set'ō]: unnaturally high-pitched voice.
18. **Old Man of the Sea:** in classical mythology a kindly old god who lived at the bottom of the sea and rose out of the water to give advice to sailors.

338 *Nonfiction*

GUIDED READING

LITERAL QUESTION

1a. To what does Heyerdahl compare the impression that the shark makes on the men? (He says the Old Man of the Sea himself could not have created more of an impression.)

INFERENTIAL QUESTION

1b. How does this comparison suggest how the men feel? (as amazed and terrified as they would have felt at seeing a mythological character) mouth. Behind the head was an enormous body ending in a long thin tail with a pointed tail fin which stood straight up and showed that this sea monster was not any kind of whale. The body looked brownish under the water, but both head and body were thickly covered with small white spots.

The monster came quietly, lazily swimming after us from astern. It grinned like a bulldog and lashed gently with its tail. The large round dorsal fin[19] projected clear of the water and sometimes the tail fin as well, and, when the creature was in the trough of the swell, the water flowed about the broad back as though washing round a submerged reef. In front of the broad jaws swam a whole crowd of zebra-striped pilot fish in fan formation, and large remora fish and other parasites sat firmly attached to the huge body and traveled with it through the water, so that the whole thing looked like a curious zoological collection crowded round something that resembled a floating deep-water reef.

A twenty-five-pound dolphin, attached to six of our largest fishhooks, was hanging behind the raft as bait for sharks, and a swarm of the pilot fish shot straight off, nosed the dolphin without touching it, and then hurried back to their lord and master, the sea king. Like a mechanical monster it set its machinery going and came gliding at leisure toward the dolphin which lay, a beggarly trifle, before its jaws. We tried to pull the dolphin in, and the sea monster followed slowly, right up to the side of the raft. It did not open its mouth but just let the dolphin bump against it, as if to throw open the whole door for such an insignificant scrap was not worth while. When the giant came close up to the raft, it rubbed its back against the heavy steering oar, which was just lifted up out of the water, and now we had ample opportunity of studying the monster at the closest quarters—at such close quarters that I thought we had all gone mad, for we roared stupidly with laughter and shouted overexcitedly at the completely fantastic sight we saw. Walt Disney himself, with all his powers of imagination, could not have created a more hair-raising sea monster than that which thus suddenly lay with its terrific jaws along the raft's side.

The monster was a whale shark, the largest shark and the largest fish known in the world today. It is exceedingly rare, but scattered specimens are observed here and there in the tropical oceans. The whale shark has an average length of fifty feet, and according to zoologists it weighs fifteen tons. It is said that large

---

19. **dorsal fin:** fin on the back.

AT A GLANCE

■ Heyerdahl further describes the appearance and movements of the whale shark. It seems to regard the dolphin bait as an "insignificant scrap."

■ The men laugh in hysterical fear and amazement when they see the jaws of the shark up close.

GUIDED READING

LITERAL QUESTIONS

1a. How does Heyerdahl describe the movements of the shark? (It "came quietly, lazily swimming"; it "lashed gently with its tail"; it "came gliding at leisure.")

2a. How do the men react when they see the shark up close? (They roar "stupidly with laughter.")

INFERENTIAL QUESTIONS

1b. What effect do these images of gentleness create? (They create a suspenseful effect as we feel the great creature holding back its enormous strength, and we wonder how long it will continue to do so.)

2b. Why do you think they laugh? (They are so scared and amazed that they are hysterical.)

EXPOSITION

The whale shark is the largest shark and the largest fish known in the world today. Specimens are rare. Whale sharks average fifty feet in length and weigh about fifteen tons.

SUSPENSE

The whale shark circles round and under the raft. The men realize how huge and strong it is. They are helpless and can only wonder what the creature will do next.

specimens can attain a length of sixty feet; one harpooned baby had a liver weighing six hundred pounds and a collection of three thousand teeth in each of its broad jaws.

Our monster was so large that, when it began to swim in circles round us and under the raft, its head was visible on one side while the whole of its tail stuck out on the other. And so incredibly grotesque, inert, and stupid did it appear when seen full-face that we could not help shouting with laughter, although we realized that it had strength enough in its tail to smash both balsa logs and ropes to pieces if it attacked us. Again and again it described narrower and narrower circles just under the raft, while all we could do was to wait and see what might happen. When it appeared on the other side, it glided amiably under the steering oar and lifted it up in the air, while the oar blade slid along the creature's back.

We stood round the raft with hand harpoons ready for action, but they seemed to us like toothpicks in relation to the mammoth beast we had to deal with. There was no indication that the whale shark ever thought of leaving us again; it circled round us and followed like a faithful dog, close up to the raft. None of us had ever experienced or thought we should experience anything like it; the whole adventure, with the sea monster swimming behind and under the raft, seemed to us so completely unnatural that we could not really take it seriously.

In reality the whale shark went on encircling us for barely an hour, but to us the visit seemed to last a whole day. At last it became too exciting for Erik, who was standing at a corner of the raft with an eight-foot hand harpoon, and, encouraged by ill-considered shouts, he raised the harpoon above his head. As the whale shark came gliding slowly toward him and its broad head moved right under the corner of the raft, Erik thrust the harpoon with all his giant strength down between his legs and deep into the whale shark's gristly[20] head. It was a second or two before the giant understood properly what was happening. Then in a flash the placid half-wit was transformed into a mountain of steel muscles.

We heard a swishing noise as the harpoon line rushed over the edge of the raft and saw a cascade of water as the giant stood on its head and plunged down into the depths. The three men who were standing nearest were flung about the place, head over heels, and two of them were flayed[21] and burned by the line as it

20. **gristly** [grisʹlē]: tough, bony, and elastic.
21. **flayed** [flād]: whipped.

Exposition (p. 327) presents facts or explains an idea. What facts are given here?

Suspense (p. 318) is rising interest in the outcome of a narrative. What happens in this passage? Why is it suspenseful?

GUIDED READING

LITERAL QUESTION

1a. How long does the whale shark circle the raft and how long does it seem to the men? (The whale shark circles for about an hour; it seems like a whole day.)

INFERENTIAL QUESTION

1b. Why does it seem like a whole day? (The men are so afraid of what the shark might do that their feelings of suspense make time seem to slow down.)

rushed through the air. The thick line, strong enough to hold a boat, was caught up on the side of the raft but snapped at once like a piece of twine, and a few seconds later a broken-off harpoon shaft came up to the surface two hundred yards away. A shoal of frightened pilot fish shot off through the water in a desperate attempt to keep up with their old lord and master. We waited a long time for the monster to come racing back like an infuriated submarine, but we never saw anything more of him.

Events in a narrative can be connected in a **cause-and-effect** relationship (p. 318). What cause-and-effect relationship is shown here?

STUDY QUESTIONS

Recalling

1. Describe the unusual long fish that Torstein discovers one night. What does this creature turn out to be?

2. For what sort of traveler does the sea have "many surprises," according to Heyerdahl?

3. One night one of the crew saw a large glowing shape circling under the raft. Why does this shape puzzle the men on the *Kon-Tiki*?

4. Describe the whale shark that Knut sees. List three facts that zoologists know about this creature.

5. What does the crew do during the encounter with the whale shark?

Interpreting

6. From Heyerdahl's descriptions what is your overall impression of the sea and the life it contains?

7. What is your impression of the general attitude of the author and his crew toward the sea and its various forms of life?

8. What do you think is Heyerdahl's purpose in telling us about the various creatures that he sees?

Extending

9. Heyerdahl says that we see more of life when we move slowly or even "sit and wait." Prove this idea with specific examples of your own.

COMPARING NONFICTION

1. Edward Abbey's "Havasu," Lorraine Hansberry's "On Summer," and Thor Heyerdahl's *Kon-Tiki* are all concerned with the relationship between human beings and nature. Choose two or more of these selections, and show how their views of this relationship differ.

2. Langston Hughes's "Harriet Tubman: The Moses of Her People" and Abraham Lincoln's Gettysburg Address deal with America's past. What period do these selections concern? On what features of that period does each focus?

3. Agnes De Mille's *Dance to the Piper,* Langston Hughes's "Harriet Tubman: The Moses of Her People," Edward Abbey's "Havasu," and James Herriot's *All Things Bright and Beautiful* all present people or creatures who succeed through sheer determination. Choose two or more of these selections, and tell what obstacles or opposition the main character faces and how he or she overcomes it.

Kon-Tiki 341

The three activities in this lesson will teach students to distinguish between fact and opinion in an essay, to recognize facts that support an opinion, and to identify persuasive language. Suggested responses to these activities are provided here. In addition, you will find among the materials for this unit in your *Teacher's Resource Book* the following related blackline masters: Distinguishing Fact from Opinion; Evaluating Opinions; Recognizing Persuasive Techniques.

Activity 1
1. Fact. This fact and the other facts below could be verified in a book about Harriet Tubman.
2. Fact
3. Opinion
4. Opinion
5. Fact
6. Opinion
7. Opinion
8. Fact

Active Reading

Nonfiction

Distinguishing Fact from Opinion

Nonfiction is literature that describes real people and events. Nevertheless, writers of nonfiction may report more than mere facts. They may also express their personal opinions on the subject matter. In order to evaluate nonfiction effectively, you must first be able to distinguish between fact and opinion.

A *fact* is a statement that can be proven true or false. You may prove it by checking a reference source or by using personal observation. An *opinion* is a statement that expresses an individual's personal belief. Unlike a fact, an opinion cannot be proven true or false.

Read the following two passages about Harriet Tubman from the nonfiction piece "Harriet Tubman: The Moses of Her People."

> . . . she was born in Maryland a slave, one of eleven sons and daughters.
>
> She was a homely child.

The first passage states a fact. You can prove it by checking historical records. The second passage offers an opinion. You cannot prove whether or not someone is "homely." It is a matter of personal taste.

Activity 1   On a separate piece of paper, write whether each of the following sentences about Harriet Tubman states a fact or an opinion. If it states a fact, tell how you could prove the statement.

1. Harriet left the Brodas Plantation on the Big Buckwater River and never returned.

2. Harriet had fits of unconsciousness that lasted all her life.

3. Harriet was the most ordinary specimen of humanity ever to be found.

4. Harriet Tubman led a charmed life.

5. Harriet got married when she was twenty-four years old.

6. No one had a greater capacity for leadership than Harriet.

7. Harriet was a very wise woman.

8. She lived for almost fifty years after the Civil War ended.

9. A number of books have been written about Harriet Tubman.

10. Harriet Tubman was a fearless leader.

Evaluating Opinions

Nonfiction writers often express personal opinions in their work. Even though their opinions cannot be proven, the writers still offer evidence to support their beliefs. As a careful reader of nonfiction, you should always search for facts that help support an author's opinion. After you consider these facts, you may then decide whether or not you agree with the opinion that is stated. In some cases you may conclude that the facts are too weak to support the author's belief. In other cases you may discover that the author has actually provided no facts at all to support an opinion.

Read the following description of Harriet Tubman by Langston Hughes.

> Harriet had a great sense of humor. She enjoyed telling the story on herself of how, not being able to read, she once sat down and went to sleep on a park bench right under a sign offering a big reward for her capture. When she began to make speeches to raise money for the cause of freedom, she often told jokes, sang, and sometimes even danced.

The author states his opinion that Harriet had a great sense of humor. He offers several facts as supporting evidence. For one thing, Harriet often told people the funny story about sleeping under her "wanted" poster. Also, she often told jokes. These facts help to support Hughes's opinion that Harriet had a great sense of humor.

Activity 2 Identify the facts and opinions that are stated in each of the following passages about Harriet Tubman. Tell whether you think the facts help to support the opinion in each passage.

1. Harriet Tubman became known as a "conductor" on the Underground Railroad. She was not the only "conductor" but she was the most famous, and one of the most daring. Once she brought as many as twenty-five slaves in a single band to freedom.

2. She might have been a great actress . . . because without makeup she could hollow out her cheeks and wrinkle her brow to seem like a very old woman. She would make her body

9. Fact (verify in a library)
10. Opinion

Activity 2
1. Opinion: She was most famous and daring. Facts: She was a "conductor"; she brought as many as twenty-five slaves to free land (supports opinion about Tubman's daring).
2. Opinion: She could have been an actress. Facts: All other details are factual and support the opinion.

shrink and cause her legs to totter when she chose to so disguise herself.

3. Harriet Tubman led a charmed life because, within twelve years, she made nineteen dangerous trips into the South rescuing slaves.

4. She was very independent. Between rescue trips or speeches, she would work as a cook or a scrubwoman. She might borrow, but she never begged money for herself.

5. Harriet Tubman's war activities were amazing. She served under General Stevens at Beaufort, South Carolina. She was sent to Florida to nurse those ill of dysentery, smallpox, and yellow fever. She was with Colonel Robert Gould Shaw at Fort Wagner. She organized a group of nine Negro scouts and river pilots and, with Colonel Montgomery, led a Union raiding contingent of three gunboats and about 150 Negro troops up the Combahee River.

Recognizing Persuasive Techniques

Usually, nonfiction writers hope that readers will agree with their opinions. In her essay, for example, Agnes De Mille wants to convince readers that ballet technique "never becomes easy; it becomes possible." Similarly, Lorraine Hansberry wishes us to respect summer for "its stark and intimate assertion of neither birth nor death but life at the apex." In his essay about Havasu Canyon, Edward Abbey explains why "there are special hazards in traveling alone." Regardless of the type of essay—narrative, descriptive expository, or persuasive—the author tries to persuade us to accept his or her personal belief.

Authors attempt to persuade readers in two ways. The first way involves *what* the authors say. They present facts as supporting evidence for their opinions. The second way involves *how* they express their ideas. Writers may use emotion-packed words, or slanted language, that is intended to create a positive or negative picture in the reader's mind.

For example, in the selection about Harriet Tubman, Langston Hughes describes Harriet as having a "rebellious nature." He could have simply called her a "troublemaker," but that expression creates a negative impression. The phrase "rebellious nature," on the other hand, presents a more positive picture. Langston Hughes uses this expression to help persuade readers that Harriet was an admirable individual fighting for a noble cause.

344 *Nonfiction*

Activity 3 Read each pair of sentences below. One sentence contains a phrase taken from the selection about Harriet Tubman. The other sentence states a similar idea but in a different way. Indentify the sentence that creates a more *positive* picture.

1. a. Harriet married a jolly, carefree fellow.
   b. Harriet married a silly, unconcerned fellow.

2. a. He did not dare think about running from home.
   b. He did not share her concern for leaving the slave country.

3. a. Her brothers became frightened and went back.
   b. Her brothers became timid and scampered back.

4. a. Any cowards were threatened if they didn't continue.
   b. Any faltering companions found strength to continue.

5. a. Her earlier experience accounted for this insistence.
   b. Her earlier experience accounted for this bossiness.

6. a. Her generous nature made her give away all her money.
   b. She did not handle her own finances well.

7. a. She always owed people money but eventually paid it back.
   b. She might borrow, but she never begged money for herself.

8. a. She was very independent.
   b. She refused to listen to anyone else's advice.

9. a. She never came across any good masters.
   b. All her masters were cruel and mean.

10. a. Through no skill of her own she finally got to Philadelphia.
    b. By some miracle she eventually got to Philadelphia.

11. a. Her petitions for past payments were never granted.
    b. She never got money that was owed to her.

12. a. She was a sneaky spy.
    b. She became an invaluable intelligence agent.

Activity 3
1. a
2. b
3. a
4. b
5. a
6. a
7. b
8. a
9. a
10. b
11. a
12. b

Literary Skills Review

Nonfiction

Guide for Reading Nonfiction

As you read nonfiction, use the following guide to help you notice and appreciate the ways that nonfiction writers communicate their ideas.

Autobiography

1. What seems to be the author's **purpose** in writing this autobiography? That is, does the author want to inform, entertain, or persuade the reader, or does the author want to express an idea about life?
2. About what main **events** and **people** has the author written? Why are these events and people important?
3. What understanding about life or what impression of himself or herself does the author present?

Biography

1. What seems to be the author's **purpose** in writing this biography?
2. About what major **events** of the subject's life has the author written? Why?
3. What **opinion** of the subject or **idea** about people in general does the author communicate?
4. What **anecdotes** reveal the subject's human qualities?

Essay

1. What is the **central idea** of the essay—that is, what information, idea, or opinion is the author presenting?
2. For what **purpose** and **audience** has the essay been written?
3. If the essay is **narrative,** what major events does it relate? What is the outcome?
4. If the essay is **descriptive,** what impression of the subject does it create? What details does it present?
5. If the essay is **expository**, what is the **thesis statement**? How does the rest of the essay develop and support the thesis?
6. If the essay is **persuasive,** what opinion does the author present? What facts, examples, and reasons back up this opinion? To what emotions does the author appeal?

Themes Review

Nonfiction

Because people share many of the same problems and needs, many writers deal with the same general themes. For example, many stories, poems, essays, plays, and other works are concerned with the general theme "ideals." However, each author has something unique to say about this general theme. For instance, "Harriet Tubman: The Moses of Her People" (page 306) communicates the following specific theme about ideals: "Living for an ideal can lift us above concern for ourselves to brave and unselfish acts." *Dance to the Piper* (page 298) makes a different specific point about ideals: "Dedicating one's life to an artistic ideal is both frustrating and fulfilling." Note that the general theme can be a word or phrase, while the specific theme can be stated in a complete sentence.

1. In the Gettysburg Address what does Abraham Lincoln tell his audience about the value of ideals?

2. The following works present discoveries that the authors made about themselves or the world. Tell what two of these works say about the general theme "discovery."
   "On Summer"   *Dance to the Piper*   "Havasu"

3. Choose two works below, and explain what each says about the general theme "nature."
   "Havasu"   *Kon-Tiki*   *All Things Bright and Beautiful*

4. Choose one nonfiction selection and one story, and tell what specific point each makes about "communities."
   Nonfiction: *Kon-Tiki*   *Dance to the Piper*
   Stories: "Gentleman of Río en Medio"   "Fire!"

5. Choose one nonfiction selection and one other work from the following lists, and explain the view that each author presents of uniquely American experiences or values.
   Nonfiction: The Gettysburg Address   "Harriet Tubman"
   Stories: "The Man Without a Country"   ". . . Sleepy Hollow"
   Poems: "O Captain! My Captain!"   "Paul Revere's Ride"

The questions in the Themes Review for the Nonfiction unit recall the general themes portrayed in the selections in this unit. Suggested answers to these questions are presented here.

1. "The Gettysburg Address" proclaims that the ideals of freedom and democracy on which the U.S. was founded have ennobled the country and made it endure.

2. "On Summer": Hansberry discovers that summer has the special appeal of life at its peak. "Dance to the Piper": DeMille discovers that she must give up delusions and discipline herself. "Havasu": Abbey discovers reserves of strength and ingenuity.

3. "Havasu": Nature is fascinating but an adversary. *Kon-Tiki:* Nature teems with exotic creatures that coexist with us. *All Things Bright:* Natural creatures can show human qualities.

4. *Kon-Tiki:* The crew forms a community by sharing unique experiences. *Dance:* The students are drawn into a community by devotion to a demanding art. "A Gentleman": The closest community is an extended family. "Fire!": Individuals are responsible for the good of their communities.

5. "Harriet Tubman": Hughes portrays a hero who embodies the American ideals of freedom, justice, and equality. Gettysburg Address: Lincoln celebrates the heroism of thousands of Americans. "O Captain!": Whitman laments an American tragedy—the death of Abraham Lincoln. "Paul Revere": Love of freedom made this country independent. "The Man Without a Country": Love of our country should not be taken for granted. "Sleepy Hollow": A famous American folk tale portrays life in a rural, less sophisticated America.

For more information about the themes portrayed in these selections, see the Theme Index beginning on page 666.

348   *Drama*

Preview
Drama

Drama presents stories to be performed for an audience. The origins of drama go back thousands of years, to a time when all literature was *oral*—spoken aloud rather than written down. Every community included a storyteller, who entertained and inspired the group with exciting tales. As years went by, the storyteller was joined by other people who acted out different roles in the story. Gradually these actors took over, and the single voice of the storyteller broke into many voices.

Drama keeps alive its oral beginnings. We still enjoy dramatic performances, just as people did thousands of years ago. However, today we can also read plays and screenplays. Seeing a performance brings a work to life before our eyes because of the **staging,** which includes the acting, costumes, sets, lighting, and sound effects. Reading a play, on the other hand, allows us to reread and think over the writer's words—an opportunity that we do not have when we watch a performance. The written script for any dramatic work consists of two parts: **dialogue,** which refers to the speeches of the characters, and **stage directions,** which describe the sets, characters, and actions.

In the following pages you will read a **one-act play** and a **full-length play.** The one-act play, *The Romancers*, is a **comedy,** a play that makes light of human problems. Written a century ago, *The Romancers* takes us into a make-believe world in which wishes come true. The full-length play, *The Diary of Anne Frank*, consists of two acts, each with several scenes. It is based on a diary actually kept by a German girl who lived during a tragic period of recent history. As recent as it is, this play also reminds us of the very beginnings of drama. For in addition to seeing different characters acting out scenes, we also hear Anne's voice—like the voice of the ancient storyteller—reading from her diary and telling us the story of her short life.

Drama   349

PREVIEW

Ask students if they have acted in a play or seen one performed. Discuss how seeing a performance of a play is different from reading a story. Emphasize that in drama the plot is developed through speeches of the characters. Then have students read the Preview. Help them to understand the difference between the two parts of a script—the dialogue and the stage directions. Ask students what kind of information they would expect to learn from each.

THE ROMANCERS

Edmond Rostand

The French playwright Edmond Rostand (1869–1918) was born into a well-to-do family in Marseilles [mär sā'], a city in southern France. He moved to Paris as a young man to study law. Once in Paris he was drawn to the excitement of the theater. In 1894, while Rostand was still working at his law studies, his first play was produced. It was a light comedy called *Les Roman-esques*, translated as *The Romancers*. The play was so popular that Rostand decided to give up law and continue writing.

Rostand's career as a dramatist met early success. In 1897 Rostand wrote his masterpiece, *Cyrano de Bergerac* [sē'rə nō də bur'zhə räk']. Both witty and moving, this play was a spectacular success in Paris and has since been performed many times.

The Romancers

The Romancers is a **comedy,** a type of play that treats human problems lightly. *The Romancers* has pleased audiences for nearly a century. It has also been turned into an extremely popular musical comedy, called *The Fantasticks*, which has been playing continuously in New York City since 1960.

The Romancers pokes gentle fun at the fantasies of young love. Its title is appropriate because the word *romance* means both "love" and "a fanciful story." The play's hero is a starry-eyed young man named Percinet [pur sē nā']. Its heroine is his next-door neighbor, Sylvette [sēl vet']. These young lovers are called romancers because they see their lives through a romantic haze of poetry and fiction. Percinet and Sylvette are kept apart by an old wall and by an even greater barrier. Their fathers have forbidden them to speak to each other, claiming that their two families are enemies.

As the play opens, we see Percinet and Sylvette reading from William Shakespeare's play *Romeo and Juliet*. Percinet and Sylvette identify with the young lovers in Shakespeare's play since the parents of Romeo and Juliet are also enemies. But Shakespeare's play is a **tragedy,** a serious play that ends sadly—his young lovers eventually die. Rostand's play, on the other hand, is a comedy with a happy ending. Although a wall may separate Sylvette and Percinet at the start of *The Romancers*, the two young people must triumph in the end.

■ How will the barrier between them be removed?

350 *Drama*

Key Ideas in *The Romancers*

As you read *The Romancers*, think about the following topics. If you keep track of what the play says about each topic, you will begin to understand the most important themes of the work.

- The difference between fantasy and reality
- Love and friendship
- Relationships between parents and children

Scenes from a production of *The Fantasticks*, which is the musical version of *The Romancers*.

Edmond Rostand

The Romancers

CHARACTERS

PERCINET [pur sē nä′]: romantic young man
SYLVETTE [sēl vet′]: romantic young woman
BERGAMIN [bur gä maɴ′]: Percinet's father
PASQUINOT [päs kē nō′]: Sylvette's father
STRAFOREL [strä fôr el′]: entertainer; hired swordsman

The Romancers 351

AT A GLANCE

- Percinet reads to Sylvette from *Romeo and Juliet.*
- Sylvette bemoans the fate of Romeo and Juliet.

LITERARY OPTIONS

- a one-act play
- dialogue
- irony

THEMATIC OPTIONS

- fantasy and reality
- love and friendship
- families

1 SETTING

This one-act play takes place in a garden. The whimsical note about time *(It can occur at any time)* prepares us for a light play, one in which realism is not that important.

2 STAGE DIRECTIONS

The wall allows the young lovers to meet in secret but in full view of the audience. The wall plays an important part in the plot of the play.

3 DIALOGUE

The opening lines of dialogue reveal that Sylvette and Percinet are romantics caught up in the love story of Romeo and Juliet.

---

1 **Scene**   The action takes place in a garden. It can occur at any time.

2 [*Dividing the stage in the center is a picturesque wall. On the left side is the garden of* BERGAMIN,[1] *and on the right is the garden of* PASQUINOT.[2] *There is a bench against the wall on each side.* PERCINET[3] *is discovered sitting on the left side of the wall, holding a book of verse. He is young and romantic. He is reading to* SYLVETTE,[4] *who sits gracefully on the bench on the right side of the wall. She listens in rapture.*]

3 SYLVETTE. [*Sighs.*] Ah, Percinet! How beautiful it is!

PERCINET. Is it not? Listen to Romeo's answer.[5] [*Reads with passion.*]

> "It was the lark, the herald of the morn;
> No nightingale. Look, love, what envious streaks
> Do lace the severing[6] clouds in yonder East.
> Night's candles are burnt out, and jocund[7] day
> Stands tiptoe on the misty mountaintops.
> I must be gone—"

SYLVETTE. [*Rises, interrupting.*] Sh! Someone is coming! [*Goes to right, looks nervously.*]

PERCINET. [*Looks anxiously to left.*] No one. [*Motions her back to bench. She sits, looking fondly at him.*] Now you must not be frightened like a startled bird, who at the slightest noise flies off the branch. Listen to what the immortal lovers say to each other. [*Reads, dramatically.*]

> Romeo. "Let me be ta'en,[8] let me be put to death.
> I am content, so thou wilt have it so.
> I'll say, yon gray is not the morning's eye,
> 'Tis but the pale reflex of Cynthia's brow;[9]
> Nor that is not the lark whose notes do beat
> The vaulty heaven so high above our heads.
> I have more care to stay than will to go.
> Come, death, and welcome. . . ."

SYLVETTE. Oh, no! I do not wish him to speak of death. No . . . I shall cry.

PERCINET. Then we will close our book until tomorrow. Since you wish it, we will let Romeo live! [*Shuts book, looks at gardens.*] What a lovely spot. It seems to me it was made especially to cradle the beautiful verses of the great Shakespeare.

SYLVETTE. Oh, the verses are beautiful . . . and the gardens are beautiful . . . but what makes it more beautiful to me is the music of your voice.

PERCINET. Flatterer.

4 SYLVETTE. [*Rises and walks to right.*] Poor lovers. How cruel their fate. How sad for them. Ah, I think that Romeo and Juliet—

PERCINET. [*Leaning far over the wall toward her.*] Yes?

SYLVETTE. [*Turns away shyly.*] Nothing.

PERCINET. Yes. Something which suddenly made you blush.

---

1. **Bergamin** [bur gä maɴ']
2. **Pasquinot** [päs kē nō']
3. **Percinet** [pur sē nä']
4. **Sylvette** [sēl vet']
5. **Romeo's answer:** Percinet is reading from William Shakespeare's tragedy *Romeo and Juliet.* Shakespeare's play concerns two young people, Romeo Montague and Juliet Capulet, who fall in love but die tragically because of the violent feud between their families. In the passage Percinet is reading, Romeo is parting from Juliet on the morning after their secret wedding.
6. **severing:** parting.
7. **jocund** [jok'ənd]: cheery.

8. **ta'en** [tān]: taken.
9. **reflex . . . brow:** reflection of the moon's forehead. Cynthia is another name for the Roman goddess of the moon.

GUIDED READING

LITERAL QUESTIONS

1a. Whose speech does Percinet read to Sylvette? (He reads Romeo's speech.)

2a. Why does Percinet stop reading? (Sylvette does not wish to hear about death.)

INFERENTIAL QUESTIONS

1b. What does his appreciation of Romeo's lines reveal about Percinet? (He is imaginative and romantic.)

2b. Why is Sylvette so saddened at the fate of Romeo and Juliet? (She may be comparing the famous lovers with Percinet and herself.)

SYLVETTE. Nothing.

PERCINET. You cannot deceive me. Your eyes are too transparent. Ah, I understand! I see what you meant. You are thinking of us . . . of our families.

SYLVETTE. Perhaps.

PERCINET. Of your father . . . of my father . . . of the hate they have for each other.

SYLVETTE. Oh, yes! That is what grieves me. That is what makes me cry . . . often . . . when I'm alone. I remember last month, when I returned from the convent,[10] my father showed me your father's park and said to me, "My child, you see there the domain of my mortal enemy, Bergamin. Never let your path cross that of his or of his rascal son, Percinet. Promise me that, or else, I shall disavow you as an enemy. Their family has always hated yours!"

[*Weakly.*]

I promised.

[*Runs to wall and to him.*]

But you see how I keep my word.

PERCINET. And did not I also promise my father to hate you always, Sylvette? But . . . I love you.

SYLVETTE. [*Nods happily.*] Yes . . . [*Then naively fearful.*] and it is so sinful.

PERCINET. Yes. But what can we do?

[*They sigh and gaze at each other.*]

The greater the barriers to love, the stronger the desire. Sylvette, kiss me!

SYLVETTE. Never!

PERCINET. But you do love me?

---

10. **convent:** boarding school run by nuns.

SYLVETTE. [*To herself, pleased.*] What does he say?

PERCINET. I am saying only what you yourself said a short while ago. Yes, you yourself, Sylvette, compared Romeo and Juliet with us . . . here.

SYLVETTE. But I didn't say—

PERCINET. But you did! And it is true! My father and your father are Juliet's father and Romeo's father—and we are Romeo and Juliet! Yes, and that is why we are so recklessly in love, and I dare to face the terrible hatred of Pasquinot-Capulet and Bergamin-Montague![11]

SYLVETTE. Then, we are in love? But, Percinet, how has it happened so quickly?

PERCINET. Love is born, one knows not how, because it must be born. I often saw you pass my window . . .

SYLVETTE. I, too . . .

PERCINET. And our eyes spoke secretly.

SYLVETTE. One day, near the wall, by chance I was gathering flowers . . .

PERCINET. By chance I was reading Shakespeare. And—see how everything has conspired to unite two hearts.

SYLVETTE. And then the wind whisked my scarf—whoosh—over to you.

PERCINET. And I climbed the wall to return it . . .

SYLVETTE. And I, too, climbed the wall . . .

PERCINET. And since then, I have waited for you each day, and each day my heart beats

---

11. **Pasquinot-Capulet and Bergamin-Montague:** Percinet identifies Sylvette's father, Pasquinot, with Juliet's father, Capulet; he identifies his own father, Bergamin, with Romeo's father, Montague.

The Romancers 353

AT A GLANCE
- Sylvette and Percinet discuss their fathers' feud.
- They declare their love, comparing themselves to Romeo and Juliet.

1 PLOT: CONFLICT

Sylvette states the major conflict in the play: Their fathers are apparently enemies, and Sylvette's father has forbidden her to associate with Percinet's family.

2 THEME

Percinet romantically believes that obstacles make love grow stronger. This idea is developed throughout the play.

3 READING SKILLS: ANALOGY

Percinet feels that he and Sylvette are in the same tragic situation as Romeo and Juliet.

4 THEME

The play gently lampoons young love. Here the lovers begin to reflect in an exaggeratedly romantic way on the birth of their secret love.

GUIDED READING

LITERAL QUESTIONS

1a. What promise did Sylvette make to her father? (that she would never associate with Bergamin's son Percinet)

2a. To whom does Percinet compare Sylvette and himself? (to Romeo and Juliet)

INFERENTIAL QUESTIONS

1b. How does Sylvette feel about breaking the promise she made? (guilty, helpless, confused)

2b. How does this comparison enhance their romance in their own eyes? (The comparison with Romeo and Juliet makes their romance seem more poetic and tragic.)

Sylvette details possible plans to unite Percinet and herself.

1 STAGE DIRECTIONS

Just as they are about to kiss, Sylvette pulls back, reminding Percinet of their problem. The staging of this sequence would probably be stylized and exaggerated to point up its humor.

2 CHARACTERIZATION

Sylvette's naive reference to romantic novels as a source of solutions to their problem shows youthful confusion of fantasy (literature) and reality (everyday life).

354 *Drama*

faster until finally from behind the wall, I hear your soft gentle laugh and then your head appears and you are here.

1 [*Face to face over the wall they are close enough to kiss.*]

SYLVETTE. [*Pulls away.*] But our fathers forbid us to see each other. If only their hatred would end.

PERCINET. I doubt that it will.

SYLVETTE. [*Walks to right.*] I have faith in the future. I have already thought of five or six possible things which could happen . . . very possible.

PERCINET. [*As far as he can get over the wall toward her.*] Really? What are they?

SYLVETTE. [*Excitedly acts each scene for*
2 *him.*] Now just suppose . . . I've read in more than one novel of a similar occurrence . . . suppose the reigning Prince happened to be passing one day . . . I run . . . I appeal to him . . . I tell him of our love . . . and how our fathers harbor an ancient hatred. The Prince summons my father and your father, and they are reconciled!

PERCINET. And he gives me your hand!

SYLVETTE. [*Runs to him.*] Yes!

[*Again they are close enough to kiss. She turns away, and dramatizes the next scene.*]

Or else . . . it can be arranged as it was in another novel. You languish . . . become pale and ill . . . and the doctor says you will surely die . . .

PERCINET. My father asks me, "What is your last desire?"

SYLVETTE. And you answer, "Sylvette." [*She runs to him.*]

GUIDED READING

LITERAL QUESTIONS

1a. Where did Sylvette learn about the plans she suggests to Percinet? (She read about them in novels.)

2a. How does Percinet respond to Sylvette's ideas? (He receives each idea enthusiastically.)

INFERENTIAL QUESTIONS

1b. What does this fact reveal about Sylvette? (She is a romantic, not a practical person; she confuses fantasy and reality.)

2b. What does this response tell you about Percinet? (He is as much a romantic as Sylvette.)

PERCINET. And his stubborn pride is forced to yield.

[*He almost kisses her, but she turns away.*]

SYLVETTE. Or else . . . [*Goes to right, acting the scene.*] this adventure could happen: an old duke, having seen my portrait, falls in love with me and offers to make me his duchess.

PERCINET. [*Jealously.*] And you answer, "NO!"

SYLVETTE. [*Nods.*] He is offended! One night, late on a dark path in the park where I have gone to meditate, I am kidnapped! I cry out!

1 **PERCINET.** And I lose not a second in leaping to your side. Dagger in hand, I fight the assassins like a lion!

SYLVETTE. You put to chase three or four men! My father runs out, takes you in his arms. You identify yourself. His hatred melts. He gives me to my rescuer. And your father, proud of your courage, gives his consent. [*Goes to him.*]

PERCINET. And we live forever and ever, happily together.

2 [*So close together that their lips meet, but* PERCINET *suddenly pulls away.*]

Someone is coming!

[*They look toward their houses, then speak quickly to each other.*]

This evening again? Here? At the hour of eight. You will come? Tell me you will.

SYLVETTE. I can't. No.

PERCINET. You must. Yes.

SYLVETTE. [*Nods. Then points.*] Your father!

[*They each ad-lib[12] "At eight . . . this eve-*

_____
12. **ad-lib:** say or do something not in the script.

ning . . . Yes . . . etc.," and quickly sit on a bench, each on his side of the wall, SYLVETTE *trying to listen,* PERCINET *innocently reading his book.* BERGAMIN *enters from left. He is an elderly gentleman. He sees his son and shouts to him.*]

BERGAMIN. Aha! Here I find you . . . alone . . . dreaming . . . in this corner of the park.

PERCINET. Father, I adore this corner of the park. I love sitting on this bench which is sheltered by this drooping vine. See how gracefully it falls. [*Inhales romantically.*] Ah, the air is purer here.

BERGAMIN. [*Inhales vigorously.*] By *this* wall?

3 **PERCINET.** [*Looks adoringly toward wall.*] I have fallen in love—[SYLVETTE *sighs on the other side of the wall.*] with it.

BERGAMIN. I see nothing lovable about it!

SYLVETTE. [*To the audience.*] He can't see why!

PERCINET. But it *is* lovely . . . this ancient wall, topped with greenery and scarlet vines . . . with honeysuckle which peeping through each crack and cranny . . . like eyes . . . is kissed by the warm sun.

BERGAMIN. Eyes? Does the wall have eyes?

4 **PERCINET.** Ah, what lovely eyes . . . soft azure smiles, gentle blue wonders, you are my delight, and if ever tears bedim them, I shall dispatch them with a single kiss.

[*Blows a kiss toward wall.* SYLVETTE *shivers with delight.*]

SYLVETTE. How clever.

BERGAMIN. How stupid. Ah, but now I see what has made you lose your senses. You come here to read in secret. [*Takes book from* PERCINET.] And drama! In verse! That is why

The Romancers 355

- Sylvette suggests a scenario in which Percinet is her rescuer.
- Bergamin confronts his son in the park, and Sylvette withdraws.
- Percinet tells Bergamin why he loves the wall.

1 CHARACTERIZATION

Percinet sees himself responding to danger as a hero out of books might respond. He, too, confuses fantasy and reality.

2 PLOT: SUSPENSE

The lovers' kiss is interrupted when Percinet hears someone coming. Rostand uses this moment of tension to create light-hearted suspense.

3 IRONY

The audience knows that Percinet is actually declaring his love for Sylvette, who is sitting on the other side of the wall, but Bergamin supposedly does not.

4 STYLE: METAPHOR

Percinet calls Sylvette's eyes "soft azure smiles" and further reveals his romantic personality through his use of language.

GUIDED READING

LITERAL QUESTION

1a. How does Bergamin regard his son? (as a dreamer who reads too much)

INFERENTIAL QUESTION

1b. What does this judgment suggest about Bergamin? (He is a shrewd judge of character and seems to delight in being hard-nosed and practical.)

1 PLOT: CONFLICT

Bergamin's announcement that he wants Percinet to marry presents yet another obstacle to the love of Sylvette and Percinet.

2 IRONY

Bergamin could be describing Percinet's true love, Sylvette, and yet Percinet rejects the idea of marrying a lady who is "a pearl" because the suggestion comes from Bergamin.

3 STYLE: DIALOGUE

In this humorous dialogue Rostand contrasts Bergamin, the practical father, and Percinet, the romantic son.

you dream and talk of honeysuckle and a wall with blue eyes! Poetry! [*He throws the book away.*] A wall, my son, is meant for protection, not beauty. Protection from our neighbor's spying eyes! [*Studies the wall.*] I am going to rebuild this wall, re-lay the bricks. I want a white wall, very tidy, very high. No vines or honeysuckle. Instead we shall decorate the top with pieces of sharp, broken glass.

PERCINET. Oh, pity!

BERGAMIN. No pity. [*Gleefully.*] I will sprinkle glass all along the top.

PERCINET and **SYLVETTE.** Oh!

BERGAMIN. Now I want to talk with you, my son. I have something important to say to you. [*Starts to speak, stops, looks at wall, and whispers.*] If the wall doesn't have eyes, it may have ears.

[SYLVETTE, *eavesdropping, reacts.*]

See if some curious listener is listening.

PERCINENT. [*Stands on bench and looks over wall, whispers to* SYLVETTE.] Until tonight.

SYLVETTE. I will come as the chimes strike eight.

BERGAMIN. Well?

PERCINET. [*Turns, innocently.*] No one.

1 BERGAMIN. Good. This, my son, is what I have to tell you. I wish you to marry.

[SYLVETTE *gives a startled cry.*]

What was that?

PERCINET. Nothing.

BERGAMIN. Someone cried out.

PERCINET. [*Looking tragically toward wall.*] Perhaps . . . a wounded bird.

356 *Drama*

SYLVETTE. Alas!

PERCINET. . . . In the branches.

BERGAMIN. Now to continue our discussion. After some lengthy reflection, I have chosen you a wife.

[*Startled,* PERCINET *begins to whistle and walks away.* BERGAMIN *follows him.*]

I am firmly resolved in this.

[*Louder whistling.*]

I tell you I shall force you.

[*Loudest whistling.*]

2 Will you stop that idiotic whistling! The lady is still young and very rich . . . a pearl!

PERCINET. And what if I do not want your pearl?

BERGAMIN. You will. Just wait. I'll show you!

PERCINET. [*He walks, romantically reciting.* BERGAMIN *follows, fuming and threatening.*] Spring has filled the trees with sounds of wings, and the brooklets murmur with the birds cooing to each other.

3 BERGAMIN. You scallywag![13]

PERCINET. All laugh and sing farewell to April. The butterflies . . .

BERGAMIN. Rascal!

PERCINET. . . . skim across the meadows to the flowers they adore! Love . . .

BERGAMIN. Scamp!

PERCINET. . . . makes all hearts open. [*Turns on* BERGAMIN.] And you wish to make a marriage of convenience!

BERGAMIN. Certainly I do.

———————

13. **scallywag:** rascal.

GUIDED READING

LITERAL QUESTIONS

1a. What does Bergamin say is the purpose of the wall? (He says it is for protection from their neighbor's spying eyes.)

2a. What news does Bergamin have for his son? (Bergamin tells Percinet that he has chosen a wife for him.)

INFERENTIAL QUESTIONS

1b. Why is this explanation especially funny at the moment? (It is funny because Sylvette is actually spying from the other side of the wall.)

2b. Why does Percinet recite poetry as Bergamin tries to talk to him about marriage? (Percinet refuses to accept the reality of the idea.)

PERCINET. Then my answer is no, no, no, father. I swear . . . by this wall which hears me I hope . . . that I shall not marry one of your choice.

BERGAMIN. Yes, you will!

PERCINET. I will marry only the one of *my* choice. [*Starts to exit left.*]

BERGAMIN. [*After him with raised fist.*] Villain!

PERCINET. My own bright, dazzling, beautiful jewel. [*Exits.*]

BERGAMIN. Wait until I catch you! You knave! Scoundrel! Scallywag! [*Exits after him.*]

SYLVETTE. Now I can truly understand my father's hate for that miserable man.

[*PASQUINOT enters from right. He, too, is an elderly gentleman. He sees his daughter.*]

PASQUINOT. Ah! What are you doing here, young lady?

SYLVETTE. [*Too innocently.*] Nothing. Walking in the garden.

PASQUINOT. Here! Alone! But foolish girl, aren't you afraid?

SYLVETTE. I am not easily frightened.

1 PASQUINOT. But alone near this wall! Remember, I forbid you to come near this wall! My child, take a good look at that park. Over there you see the estate of my ancient mortal enemy.

SYLVETTE. I know, father, you have told me often enough.

PASQUINOT. And still you come to expose yourself to insults. Heaven knows what those two are capable of! If that rascal, or his son, knew that my daughter comes here alone—oh-oh! [*Shivers.*] Just thinking about it makes me shudder! [*Looks at wall and has an idea.*]

Ah, I have an idea! I shall rebuild the wall. Make it higher! And on the top put sharp steel spikes!

SYLVETTE. [*To the audience.*] He will never do it. It would cost too much.

PASQUINOT. And now, my dear, go into the house. At once! Away from this wall. Quick . . . quick . . . quick.

[*He watches her hurry off right, then looks left at the wall, and with excited anticipation goes to it and calls cheerfully.*]

2 Bergamin . . . Bergamin!

[*Looks over the wall.* BERGAMIN *enters from left, also excited and happy.*]

BERGAMIN. Pasquinot! [*Hurries to the wall, climbs upon the bench with difficulty.*]

PASQUINOT. My dear friend.

[*They embrace over the wall, kissing each other on one cheek.*]

BERGAMIN. My old friend.

[*They embrace again, and kiss each other on the other cheek.*]

PASQUINOT. How are you?

BERGAMIN. Not bad.

PASQUINOT. How's your gout?[14]

BERGAMIN. Better. And how is your cold?

PASQUINOT. Still in my head.

3 BERGAMIN. Well, my dear friend, I have news for you, about our children. It is all settled. The wedding will be soon.

PASQUINOT. Wedding?

BERGAMIN. I heard them talking while I was

---

14. **gout:** swelling of the joints.

The Romancers 357

AT A GLANCE

- Percinet and his father leave.
- Pasquinot appears and sends Sylvette inside.
- Bergamin and Pasquinot greet each other as old friends.
- Bergamin reveals that their children's wedding will take place soon.

1 PLOT: CONFLICT

Paralleling Bergamin's warning to his son, Sylvette's father reminds her that Bergamin is his enemy.

2 IRONY

Unknown to Percinet, Sylvette, and the audience up to this point, Bergamin and Pasquinot are really old friends.

3 PLOT: RISING ACTION

The audience is further surprised to learn that Bergamin wants the two lovers to marry. This series of sudden reversals heightens the comic tone of the play.

GUIDED READING

LITERAL QUESTION

1a. What news does Bergamin give his old friend Pasquinot? (He tells him that the wedding will be soon.)

INFERENTIAL QUESTION

1b. What seems to be Bergamin's attitude regarding this news? (He seems satisfied that it is all settled.)

1 PLOT: CONFLICT

Bergamin and Pasquinot reveal the real conflict of the play: their desire to merge their estates through the marriage of children who would not agree to a marriage of convenience.

2 IRONY

The arranged marriage that would be spurned by the young romantics has been skillfully engineered to seem unarranged.

3 IRONY

In discussing how to manipulate their parents, the lovers have suggested a plan that their parents can use to manipulate *them*.

4 HUMOR

The exaggerated character of Straforel adds a new dimension to the play's humor—an absurd theatricality. Straforel lives in a world of his own; he is constantly "on stage."

5 DIALOGUE

The rapid exchange between Bergamin and Straforel contributes to a whimsical suspense about the plan and its workability.

---

hidden by the foliage. [*He, too, is a romantic.*] They adore each other!

PASQUINOT. Bravo! Bravo!

BERGAMIN. The time has come to bring matters to a head. What has always been our one goal?

PASQUINOT. To remove this wall . . .

BERGAMIN. In order that we may live together . . .

PASQUINOT. And merge our two estates!

BERGAMIN. And how is this going to be accomplished?

PASQUINOT. By marrying our two children.

BERGAMIN. But arranged marriages are never tempting to poetic young lovers. So my scheme has worked admirably. Percinet, home from college, and Sylvette home from the convent, when forbidden never to speak to each other, have, of course, sought each other out and fallen in love. Now we have only to say, "Yes" to them.

PASQUINOT. Agreed! But how can we give our consent without telling them of the trick? I have called you "scoundrel" . . . and "idiot" . . .

BERGAMIN. Idiot? Scoundrel was enough!

PASQUINOT. But what pretext can we give for suddenly becoming friends?

BERGAMIN. Your daughter herself has just given us the perfect strategy. While she was talking to Percinet, she described the very plan I was considering. This evening, they will meet here by the wall at eight. Percinet will come first. Then just as Sylvette appears, some dangerous characters leap from a hiding place and seize her! She cries out! Then my young hero leaps over the wall on to the ravishers. Swords meet swords! The kidnappers

358 *Drama*

---

flee. You appear. I arrive. Your daughter and her honor are saved. Your joy is unbounding. You give your blessing to them both, dropping a few appropriate tears. I am equally touched by the heroic rescue and give my consent. Embraces. End of scene.

PASQUINOT. Ah, you are a genius!

BERGAMIN. Yes, I think it is rather good. Sh! [*Points off left.*] Look! You see who is coming? It is Straforel, the bravado whom I sent a note to about this plot. Yes, if this is going to be an abduction with style, he is the one to do it.

[STRAFOREL *struts in from left, an overly dressed, theatrical swordsman.* BERGAMIN *goes to him and bows.*]

BERGAMIN. Monsieur.[15]

STRAFOREL. [*Bows with a great flourish.*] Monsieur.

BERGAMIN. Allow me to introduce you to my friend Pasquinot.

STRAFOREL. [*Bows with a flourish.*] Monsieur. [*But sees he has bowed to no one.*]

BERGAMIN. No, no. There—on the wall. [*Points to* PASQUINOT *whose head appears over the wall.*]

STRAFOREL. Ah. [*Walks to wall and bows elaborately.*] Monsieur.

PASQUINOT. [*Bows with even a greater flourish.*] Monsieur.

BERGAMIN. You have read my note in which I explained my plan? How does it impress you?

STRAFOREL. It is—elementary.

BERGAMIN. You will act quickly. . . .

STRAFOREL. And be discreet!

---

15. *Monsieur* [mə syœ′]: French for "sir."

GUIDED READING

LITERAL QUESTIONS

1a. Why have Bergamin and Pasquinot pretended to be enemies? (They hoped that by forbidding contact between their children, they would make Percinet and Sylvette fall in love.)

2a. Whose plan does Bergamin want to use to unite the two lovers? (He wants to use Sylvette's plan, which is similar to one of his own.)

INFERENTIAL QUESTIONS

1b. Why don't Bergamin and Pasquinot tell their children about the trick? (Perhaps they fear the children may then refuse to marry.)

2b. Do you think this strategy will succeed with the lovers? Why? (Yes. They are romantics, and they will be delighted to enact their fantasies.)

BERGAMIN. A pretended kidnapping . . . a make-believe sword fight . . .

STRAFOREL. I understand exactly.

BERGAMIN. Make sure you have skilled swordsmen, so that they do not harm my boy. I love him. He is my only child.

STRAFOREL. I will duel with him myself.

BERGAMIN. Excellent. In that case, I will have no fears.

PASQUINOT. [*Motions for* BERGAMIN, *who comes to wall.*] Psst! Psst! Ask him how much it will cost.

BERGAMIN. What do you charge, Maestro, for an abduction?

STRAFOREL. That depends, *Monsieur*, on what one is willing to pay. There are abductions at every price. But, in this case, if I understand correctly, money is no object, so if I were you, I would have a first-class abduction.

BERGAMIN. You have several classes?

STRAFOREL. Numerous! There is the common abduction by cab with two sinister characters—that is hardly ever used. A midnight abduction, a daylight abduction, the pompous abduction in a court carriage with servants—wigs are extra. The post-chaise abduction[16] with two, three, four, five horses—one plays the number by ear. The discreet abduction in a little carriage—which is a bit dreary. The droll abduction in a sack. The romantic one by boat—but one needs a lake for that. The Venetian[17] abduction by gondola[18]—one, of course, would need a lagoon! The sinister ab-

duction with combat. The brutal abduction; the polite abduction; the abduction by torch-light—very pretty. The classical abduction with masks. The gallant abduction with music. But the gayest, the newest, and the most distinguished of all is the full-moon abduction!

BERGAMIN. [*Eagerly to* PASQUINOT.] What do you think?

PASQUINOT. [*Eagerly to* BERGAMIN.] What do you?

BERGAMIN. [*Excited.*] I think we should have the best—spare no expense! Let us give our young fantasists something they will long remember. Let us have masks, music, torches, and a full moon!

STRAFOREL. A first-class abduction—with all the trimmings!

BERGAMIN. Bravo! Bravo!

STRAFOREL. I shall return. Remember, *Monsieur*, you must leave the park gate open.

PASQUINOT. It will be open.

STRAFOREL. My compliments. [*Bows profusely.*]

PASQUINOT. *Monsieur.* [*Bows, almost falling off bench.*]

STRAFOREL. [*Bows to* BERGAMIN.] *Au revoir.*[19]

BERGAMIN. *Monsieur.* [*Out-bowing* STRAFOREL.]

STRAFOREL. [*Crosses to left.*] One first-class abduction with all the extras! [*Exits grandly.*]

PASQUINOT. The honest man, he went without setting a price.

BERGAMIN. [*Almost dancing with joy.*] Ah, it

---

16. **post-chaise** [shāz] **abduction:** that is, one using a very fast, four-wheeled coach.
17. **Venetian** [vĭ nē′shən]: relating to Venice, an Italian city of many canals through which people often travel by boat.
18. **gondola** [gŏn′də lə]: a long, narrow boat used on the canals in Venice.

---

19. *Au revoir* [ō′rə vwär′]: French for "until we meet again."

The Romancers 359

- Bergamin describes to Straforel his requirements for a bogus kidnapping.
- Straforel itemizes the various classes of abductions.
- Bergamin opts for a first-class abduction.

1 DIALOGUE

This humorous dialogue advances the plot by quickly detailing the requirements for the abduction.

2 CHARACTERIZATION

Straforel lists the types of abductions as if they were items in a mail-order catalogue.

3 IRONY

The fathers talk about the abduction as they would discuss wedding plans.

GUIDED READING

LITERAL QUESTION

1a. What kind of abduction does Straforel recommend to the two men? (Straforel recommends a first-class abduction.)

INFERENTIAL QUESTION

1b. Why do Bergamin and Pasquinot choose a first-class abduction? (They want the best for their children; they want the children to enjoy it and have fond memories of it.)

AT A GLANCE

- Sylvette sees Pasquinot and Bergamin at the wall.
- The two men stage a fight.
- Sylvette and Percinet separate their fathers.

1 PLOT: SUSPENSE

The fathers' friendship is almost discovered, threatening to spoil the plan.

2 IRONY

The two men, who are playing at fighting, suddenly feel real anger.

is all settled. Soon we will demolish the wall. Our wishes are about to be fulfilled!

PASQUINOT. We will grow old together.

BERGAMIN. Your daughter is provided for.

PASQUINOT. Your son, too!

BERGAMIN. [*With difficulty climbs on bench by the wall.*] Ah! My dear old Pasquinot.

PASQUINOT. Ah! My dear old Bergamin.

BERGAMIN. Dear friend. [*They embrace, kissing on one cheek.*]

PASQUINOT. Old friend. [*They embrace again, kissing on the other cheek.*]

SYLVETTE. [*Enters at right, sees the men at the wall. She is startled.*] Oh!

1 **BERGAMIN.** [*In a panic to* PASQUINOT.] Your daughter!

PERCINET. [*Enters at left, sees the men at the wall. He is startled.*] Oh!

PASQUINOT. [*In a panic to* BERGAMIN.] Your son!

BERGAMIN. Quick! We must pretend we are fighting. [*Starts shouting and hitting.*] You— you rogue!

PASQUINOT. [*Takes up the fight.*] You scoundrel!

BERGAMIN. Rascal!

PASQUINOT. Fool!

SYLVETTE. [*Runs to father and pulls at his coat.*] Papa!

PERCINET. [*Runs to father and pulls at his coat.*] Papa!

BERGAMIN. Leave us alone!

PASQUINOT. He insulted me!

BERGAMIN. He struck me!

360 *Drama*

PASQUINOT. Coward!

SYLVETTE. Papa!

BERGAMIN. Thief!

PERCINET. Papa!

PASQUINOT. Bandit!

SYLVETTE. Papa!

PERCINET. Come home. It is late!

2 **BERGAMIN.** Let me go! Let me at him! [*He winds up, swings, and hits* PASQUINOT *unexpectedly hard.*]

PASQUINOT. [*Surprised, then dangerously swings an uppercut.[20]*] I'll kill him!

---

20. **uppercut:** punch from below, aimed at the chin.

GUIDED READING

LITERAL QUESTIONS

1a. Why do Bergamin and Pasquinot want the wall to be demolished? (They want to grow old together and to provide for their children.)

2a. What happens when Sylvette and Percinet find their fathers at the wall? (The two men quickly pretend they are fighting.)

INFERENTIAL QUESTIONS

1b. How do you think Bergamin and Pasquinot feel just before their children arrive? (They probably feel satisfied and pleased with their cleverness.)

2b. Why do they begin fighting in earnest? (Bergamin seems to hit Pasquinot a bit too hard, and Pasquinot becomes angry.)

[BERGAMIN *is knocked off the bench, falling into* PERCINET's *arms.*]

1 **SYLVETTE.** [*Pulls her father off the bench.*] Please, Papa. Come! The air is getting cooler. Remember your rheumatism.

BERGAMIN. [*As* PERCINET *guides him off left.*] Fool!

PASQUINOT. [*As* SYLVETTE *pushes him off right.*] Scoundrel!

BERGAMIN. [*Shouts offstage.*] Villain!

PASQUINOT. [*Shouts offstage*] Idiot!

SYLVETTE. [*Following him off.*] Papa.

PERCINET. [*Following him off.*] Papa.

2 [*Slowly the stage becomes darker, until it*

---

is a beautiful romantic evening. STRAFOREL *enters right, creeping mysteriously.*]

STRAFOREL. Ah! One star already brightens the evening sky. Day is dying.

[*Motions to his men.* SWORDSMEN, TORCH-BEARERS, *and* MUSICIANS *enter in the shadows. Like an artist, he sets the stage.*]

You—there. You—there. And you—there.

[*Satisfied, he enjoys the romantic scene.*]

Ah, the hour is near. When the chimes sound eight, a girl will appear—there. Then I will whistle—

[*Whistles loudly. The large moon in the back suddenly lights up.*]

The moon . . . perfect! Everything is ready.

[*Inspects their attire.*]

3 Spread your capes—excellent. Turn up your collar a bit more. Stand here—in the shadow. Ah, the swordsmen are not bad! Torches! You do not appear until my signal. Musicians—there! Down more in the back. Now—oh, some grace, please.

[*Shows them a graceful pose, which they all imitate.*]

No, no! Vary your poses. Stand straight, mandolin![21] Sit, alto! This is a first-class abduction.

[*Turns suddenly.*]

First masked man—what are you doing? No, no! A desperado never waddles! Come—show some character! A dangerous, villainous walk! Good. Now, instruments, tune up. *Sol . . . mi*

---

21. **mandolin** [mand'əl in']: small stringed musical instrument. In this case Straforel is actually using the term to address the musician who is playing the mandolin.

The Romancers 361

AT A GLANCE

- Sylvette and Percinet lead their fathers offstage.
- Straforel checks the staging of the abduction, giving instructions to the musicians and desperadoes.

1 THEME

The two lovers take on the role of adults and guide their fathers home. This role reversal elaborates on one of Rostand's themes: the complex relationship between parents and children.

2 ONE-ACT PLAY

The play is set in the same place during the course of a single day. Lighting changes indicate the passage of time.

GUIDED READING

LITERAL QUESTIONS

1a. What do Sylvette and Percinet do when they discover their fathers fighting? (They lead them home.)

2a. What theatrical elements does Straforel provide? (He provides a moon, swordsmen, torches, musicians, and masked men.)

INFERENTIAL QUESTIONS

1b. In what way are the roles of parent and child reversed? (The children are giving guidance to their father.)

2b. Why is this performance appropriate for Sylvette and Percinet? (They live in a world of fantasy, not reality.)

- The two lovers go out to meet each other by the wall.
- Sylvette is "abducted," and Percinet attacks her "abductors."
- Percinet wounds Straforel.

1 HUMOR

Rostand pokes fun at the conventions of a play when Percinet accepts the music without questioning where it comes from.

2 DRAMATIC IRONY

Sylvette believes she is really being abducted. The audience is aware of the plot and can be amused at Sylvette's temporary distress.

3 THEME

Percinet has his chance to fulfill his image of the romantic hero.

4 PLOT: CLIMAX

In this make-believe duel the action of the play reaches its emotional high point.

5 READING SKILLS: SEQUENCE

It is important to read carefully any sequence of actions given in the stage directions for a play. Here, Percinet and Straforel struggle, and Straforel is supposedly wounded.

. . . si. . . .[22] Ah. Listen. . . . Quick! Someone comes.

[STRAFOREL *waves his arms in a wild dramatic signal. All his helpers hurry to a hiding place.* STRAFOREL *tiptoes down right and hides his face behind his cape. All is silent.* PERCINET *enters from the left.*]

PERCINET. My father is calmer now. I can slip away. [*Romantically.*] It is the end of the day. The scent of the elders[23] intoxicates my senses. The flowers sleep in the gray shadows . . .

STRAFOREL. [*Quietly leads musicians.*] Music!

PERCINET. I am trembling like a reed. What can be wrong with me? Ah, I shall soon see her again.

STRAFOREL. [*As musicians play softly, he gets carried away with romance.*] Amoroso![24]

PERCINET. Our first evening meeting. I can scarcely believe it. The breeze sounds like the rustle of her gown . . . one can no longer see the flowers . . . but their scent grows sweeter. And this old tree with a star at its top. . . . Music . . . ah, there is music, too. . . . Night has come. . . . Oh, gentle night . . . with its twinkling lights . . . there and there . . . one by one they come in the deep blue sky . . . sparkling sapphire and diamond. . . . Oh, stars, I thought you dazzling until I met Sylvette. Now her eyes outshine you a thousand times . . . oh, poor poor little stars . . .

[*The chimes strike eight.* SYLVETTE *appears at right.*]

22. **Sol . . . mi . . . si:** notes in the musical scale.
23. **elders:** shrubs with red or purple berries.
24. **Amoroso** [äm´ôr ō´zō]: Italian word meaning "tender" or "romantic." Straforel is directing the musicians to play tenderly.

362   *Drama*

SYLVETTE. The chimes have struck eight. He must be waiting by the wall.

SYLVETTE *starts toward wall.* STRAFOREL *whistles and motions to men who seize her. She struggles and calls.*]

SYLVETTE. Help! Help! Save me!

PERCINET. Good heavens!

SYLVETTE. Percinet, help! They are carrying me away. I am being abducted!

PERCINET. Fear not! I am coming! [*Leaps to the top of the wall.*] I will save you!

STRAFOREL. [*To the* MUSICIANS *who play fast and exciting music.*] Tremolo![25]

[PERCINET *with sword drawn attacks the* MEN *who hold* SYLVETTE. *They are quickly overcome and flee.*]

PERCINET. Take that! And that! And that!

[*Only* STRAFOREL *stands in the way.*]

Ah!

[*They stand in formal position for dueling, then begin a fast and furious duel.* SYLVETTE *trembles and gasps as* PERCINET *is pushed backwards and almost stumbles. Then she cries with joy when* PERCINET *forces* STRAFOREL *back. They circle.* STRAFOREL *moves desperately. Finally he is forced back to the bench. He jumps upon it, making a last stand.* PERCINET *gives one mighty thrust.* STRAFOREL *groans, drops his sword, and clutches his heart.*]

STRAFOREL. Oh! Oh, oh! I am mortally wounded! [*With many last gasps, he strug-*

25. **Tremolo** [trem´ə lō´]: vibrating musical sound. Straforel is directing the musicians to produce such a sound.

GUIDED READING

LITERAL QUESTIONS

1a. Who seizes Sylvette? (Straforel's men)

2a. How does Percinet respond to Sylvette's cry for help? (He promises to save her.)

INFERENTIAL QUESTIONS

1b. Why isn't she really in trouble? (Bergamin and Pasquinot have hired Straforel to stage an abduction.)

2b. How do you think Percinet feels at that moment? (He probably feels heroic.)

gles, and then falls limp, draped over the wall.]

PERCINET. [*Rushes to* SYLVETTE.] Sylvette. [*Kneels and takes her hand.*]

PASQUINOT. [*Appears at right.*] What is going on?

1 **SYLVETTE.** My hero! You saved my life!

PASQUINOT. What? Bergamin's son—saved your life?

SYLVETTE. Oh, yes!

PASQUINOT. [*Loud and clearly.*] I give you to him.

PERCINET and **SYLVETTE.** [*Together.*] Heavens!

PASQUINOT. [*Calls, and* BERGAMIN *appears at left immediately, as if waiting.*] Bergamin! Your son is a hero. He has saved my daughter.

BERGAMIN. [*Hurrying to the wall and with his usual difficulty, climbs upon the bench.*] Bravo! Bravo!

PASQUINOT. Let us forgive and forget—and make them happy.

BERGAMIN. My hate has left me!

PERCINET. Did you hear, Sylvette? We must be dreaming!

2 **BERGAMIN.** The hatred of our two families will end with this marriage. Let peace come with the demolishing of the wall!

PERCINET. Who would have believed my father would change so!

3 **SYLVETTE.** I told you everything would turn out happily.

[*The lovers stand facing each, in eternal happiness.* PASQUINOT *stands by them gazing on them with fond blessings.* STRAFOREL *rises from the "dead," and hands* BERGAMIN *a slip of paper.*]

STRAFOREL. Psst! Psst!

BERGAMIN. Yes?

STRAFOREL. Your signature.

BERGAMIN. My signature? What is it?

STRAFOREL. It is my bill!

[STRAFOREL *falls "dead" on the wall again. Tableau.*[26]]

---

26. **Tableau** [tab lō´]: dramatic term for a striking stage picture, created by actors posing motionless and silent.

The Romancers 363

STUDY QUESTIONS

1. They are both pairs of lovers whose parents are mortal enemies.
2. ■ The reigning prince could bring about their marriage by settling their fathers' dispute.
   ■ His father could consent when Percinet feigns illness and asks to wed her as a last wish.
   ■ Sylvette's father could give Percinet her hand in gratitude after he rescues her from the spurned suitor who kidnaps her.
3. to break down the wall and unite their estates; through the marriage of their children
4. They feel the children will do the opposite of what they say.
5. stage Sylvette's abduction, so Percinet can rescue her; to reconcile their families
6. ■ impractical: do not reflect how things work in the real world
   ■ They are romantic, naive, and sheltered.
7. old friends; love them very much
8. because he loves and believes in happy endings; Sylvette, Percinet, and Pasquinot
9. ■ It makes life an interesting and enjoyable experience.
   ■ Trusting people may be taken advantage of by cynical people.

READING AND LITERARY FOCUS

The One-Act Play

1. ■ five: Sylvette, Percinet, Bergamin, Pasquinot, and Straforel
   ■ No in-depth portraits: Straforel is motivated by money, the others are romantic. Percinet and Sylvette are in love; the parents want them happily wed.
2. the parents' garden divided by a picturesque wall; suited to the happy ending in marriage and the theme of love and friendship

STUDY QUESTIONS

Recalling

1. For what reason do Percinet and Sylvette compare themselves with Romeo and Juliet?
2. According to Sylvette, what three things that she has read about in novels might solve the lovers' problem?
3. What is the goal of Bergamin and Pasquinot? In what way do they plan to accomplish it?
4. What is the real reason that Bergamin and Pasquinot order their children not to speak to each other?
5. What do the two fathers hire Straforel to do? Why?

Interpreting

6. How practical do *you* find Sylvette's proposed solutions to the lovers' problem? What does their belief in these solutions show about Percinet and Sylvette?
7. Describe Bergamin's and Pasquinot's feelings toward each other and toward their children.
8. One stage direction says of Bergamin that "he too is a romantic." Why is Bergamin called a romantic, and what other characters in the play are also romantics?

Extending

9. What might be appealing about a romantic view of life? What might be dangerous about it?

READING AND LITERARY FOCUS

The One-Act Play

A **full-length play** is made up of two or more acts and takes several hours to perform. On the other hand, a **one-act play** contains only a single act and can be performed in a short time. A one-act play usually focuses on a few characters and takes place on a single set. It usually presents a situation that can be resolved in a short time. For

example, *The Romancers* concerns two young lovers who think that their fathers are enemies. However, the fathers turn out to be old friends who want their children to marry. They stage an abduction that quickly ends their "feud" and makes everyone's wishes come true.

Most one-act plays portray life in simpler terms than full-length plays do. One-act plays usually focus on a single **theme,** or idea about life. They present this theme in a few vivid strokes. For example, *The Romancers,* with its vanishing feud and happy ending, shows us life not as it is, but as we might, in our fondest dreams, imagine it to be.

Thinking About the One-Act Play

1. How many characters do we meet in *The Romancers*? How much do we know about them?
2. What is the stage set of *The Romancers*? Why might this particular set be appropriate to the play's outcome and its theme?

Dialogue

Dialogue is the conversation between characters in a literary work. Short stories, novels, and some poems and nonfiction pieces include dialogue, but dialogue is most important in drama. Usually the only words spoken in a play or film are the characters' speeches. The dialogue moves the action forward and tells the audience what the characters are like. For example, *The Romancers* opens with these lines:

SYLVETTE. Ah, Percinet! How beautiful it is!
PERCINET. Is it not? Listen to Romeo's answer.

From this bit of dialogue we learn a great deal about Percinet and Sylvette. We notice that they speak very differently from us and that they sound a little old-fashioned and starry-eyed ("Ah"; "How beautiful"; "Is it not?"). We learn that they love literature. Most important, their interest in Romeo, a famous literary lover, suggests that these two young people may be in love themselves.

364 *Drama*

Thinking About Dialogue

■ What surprising fact do Bergamin and Pasquinot reveal in their first bit of dialogue?

VOCABULARY

Context Clues

You can often discover a word's general meaning from its **context,** or the words around it. For example, in the following sentence from *The Romancers,* the context provides clues to the meaning of the word *languish*:

> You *languish* . . . become pale and ill . . . and the doctor says you will surely die.

The passage connects the word *languish* with the idea of becoming pale and ill and possibly dying. Therefore, *languish* means something like "grow very sick or weak."

Each of the following passages comes from *The Romancers.* Find the meaning of each of the italicized words in these passages by studying its context. Check your answer in the Glossary at the back of the book or in a dictionary. Then use the word in a sentence of your own. Make sure that your sentence uses the word in the same way *as it is used in the play.*

1. . . . my father showed me your father's park and said to me, "You see there the *domain* of my mortal enemy. . . ."
2. Ah, what lovely eyes . . . soft *azure* smiles, gentle blue wonders . . .
3. No, no! A *desperado* never waddles! Come—show some character! A dangerous, villainous walk!
4. Percinet, help! They are carrying me away. I am being *abducted*!

COMPOSITION

Writing About Character

■ Describe the character of Straforel. Begin your composition by briefly explaining who Straforel is and how he is related to the main action of the play. Then describe his personality, using specific examples of his words and actions.

Writing an Advertisement

■ Create a television advertisement in which Straforel sells his services to the public. You might begin by getting viewers' attention with a remark like "Perk up your life and be a hero! Stage a first-class abduction and rescue someone you love!" Then describe in glowing terms the various types of abduction that Straforel can arrange. End with a list of prices or special rates for his services.

CHALLENGE

Staging

■ **Staging** refers to the scenery, lighting, sounds, costumes, and acting that bring a playwright's words to life on stage in front of an audience. With other students stage one short scene from *The Romancers.* Plan and decorate your set— a garden divided by a wall. Choose the character you will play, and bring in any costumes or props that might make you more believable or interesting.

CHALLENGE

Students should
- choose one scene from *The Romancers*
- create a set suggesting a garden divided by a wall
- assign roles
- bring in appropriate props and costumes
- act out the scene

The Romancers 365

COMPOSITION: GUIDELINES FOR EVALUATION

WRITING ABOUT CHARACTER

Objective
To describe Straforel's character

Guidelines for Evaluation
- suggested length: two to three paragraphs
- should tell who Straforel is and how he relates to the main action of the play
- should describe his personality using his words and actions as examples

WRITING AN ADVERTISEMENT

Objective
To write a television commercial in which Straforel sells his services

Guidelines for Evaluation
- suggested length: 100–200 words
- should briefly state the service provided
- should describe the abductions available
- should give a list of prices or special rates

THE DIARY OF ANNE FRANK

Frances Goodrich and Albert Hackett

Frances Goodrich (1890–1984) and her husband Albert Hackett (born 1900), began their careers in the theater as actors. Together they have written screenplays for many successful movies. Their most famous work is *The Diary of Anne Frank,* a play first performed in 1955. *The Diary of Anne Frank* was later made into both a film and a television drama.

The Diary of Anne Frank

The Diary of Anne Frank is based on a real-life diary kept for two years by Anne Frank, a young girl born in Germany in 1929. Not long after Anne's birth, Adolf Hitler and the Nazi party came to power in Germany. Germany was suffering from great economic problems at the time, and Hitler blamed these on the Jewish people. Anne Frank's family was Jewish. To escape the cruel treatment of Hitler and the Nazis, the Franks, like many other Jews, moved to Holland. There, in Amsterdam, Anne and her older sister, Margot, grew up in the 1930s and early 1940s.

As a present for her thirteenth birthday, on June 12, 1942, Anne received a diary. Within a month she wrote in it, "So much has happened, it is just as if the whole world had turned upside down." For by then World War II was raging, and Hitler had conquered Holland. The Nazi terror had followed the Franks to their new homeland. The Nazis soon began rounding up Jews to send them to concentration camps in central Europe. Eventually millions of Jews died in these camps.

To escape that fate, the Franks went into hiding. Dutch friends helped establish the family in a "secret annex," several attic rooms above a warehouse in Amsterdam. In that small space the Franks and a few friends lived secretly for more than two years—specifically, for seven hundred and fifty-nine days and nights from July 6, 1942, to August 4, 1944. During that time Anne continued to write in her diary.

By the summer of 1944, the Americans, British, and other Allied forces had begun to win the war against Nazi Germany. However, not long before the Allies freed Holland from the Nazis, the annex where the Franks were hiding was discovered. Police broke into the apartment, arrested the Franks and their friends, and sent them to distant concentration camps. Anne Frank died in the camp at Belsen in March 1945, shortly before the British freed it. She was not yet sixteen years old.

366 *Drama*

Anne Frank, 1929–1945.

Of the people who hid in the secret attic, all but Anne's father died. After the war Mr. Frank returned to Amsterdam. He revisited the rooms in which his family had hidden so courageously for so long. Among the rubbish that had been left behind, he found his daughter's precious diary.

■ As you read the play that was based on this diary, imagine the conditions under which Anne Frank lived and wrote. What do you think it would be like to live in secret for several years in a few rooms without going outdoors?

Key Ideas in *The Diary of Anne Frank*

As you read *The Diary of Anne Frank*, think about the following topics. If you keep track of what the play says about each topic, you will begin to understand the most important themes of *The Diary of Anne Frank*.

- Relationships among members of a community
- Relationships between family members
- Love and friendship
- The process of becoming more mature
- Courage and fear in the face of danger
- The belief in goodness in the face of evil
- The importance of hope

The set for the original production of *The Diary of Anne Frank*.

Anne.

Mr. Frank.

Peter.

Frances Goodrich and Albert Hackett

The Diary of Anne Frank

CHARACTERS

ANNE FRANK: German girl; thirteen years old
MR. FRANK: her father
MRS. FRANK: her mother
MARGOT FRANK: her older sister; eighteen years old
MR. VAN DAAN: Dutch businessman
MRS. VAN DAAN: his wife
PETER VAN DAAN: their son; sixteen years old
DUSSEL [doo′səl]: Dutch dentist
MIEP GIES [mēp′gēs′]: young Dutchwoman in the anti-Nazi underground
MR. KRALER [krä′ler]: member of the anti-Nazi underground

Scene: *Amsterdam, Holland. July 1942 to November 1945.*

368 *Drama*

ACT I

Scene 1

Amsterdam, Holland. November 1945.

[*The scene remains the same throughout the play. It is the top floor of a warehouse and office building in Amsterdam, Holland. The sharply peaked roof of the building is outlined against a sea of other rooftops, stretching away into the distance. Nearby is the belfry of a church tower, the Westertoren, whose carillon[1] rings out the hours. Occasionally faint sounds float up from below: the voices of children playing in the street, the tramp of marching feet, a boat whistle from the canal.*

The three rooms of the top floor and a small attic space above are exposed to our view. The largest of the rooms is in the center, with two small rooms, slightly raised on either side. On the right is a bathroom, out of sight. A narrow, steep flight of stairs at the back leads up to the attic. The rooms are sparsely furnished with a few chairs, cots, a table or two. The windows are painted over, or covered with makeshift blackout curtains. In the main room there is a sink, a gas ring for cooking, and a wood-burning stove for warmth.

1 *The room on the left is hardly more than a closet. There is a skylight in the sloping ceiling. Directly under this room is a small steep stairwell, with steps leading down to a door. This is the only entrance from the building below. When the door is opened we see that it has been concealed on the outer side by a bookcase attached to it.*

The curtain rises on an empty stage. It is late afternoon, November 1945.

---

1. **carillon** [kar′ə lon′]: set of bells on which melodies can be played, usually located in a tower.

The rooms are dusty, the curtains in rags. Chairs and tables are overturned.

The door at the foot of the small stairwell **2** *swings open.* MR. FRANK *comes up the steps into view. He is a gentle, cultured European in his middle years. There is still a trace of a German accent in his speech.*

He stands looking slowly around, making a supreme effort at self-control. He is weak, ill. His clothes are threadbare.

After a second he drops his rucksack on the couch and moves slowly about. He opens the door to one of the smaller rooms and then abruptly closes it again, turning away. He goes to the window at the back, looking off at the Westertoren as its carillon strikes the hour of six; then he moves restlessly on.

From the street below we hear the sound of a barrel organ and children's voices at play. There is a many-colored scarf hanging from a nail. MR. FRANK *takes it, putting it around his neck. As he starts back for his rucksack, his eye is caught by something lying on the floor. It is a woman's white glove. He holds it in his hand and suddenly all of his self-control is gone. He breaks down, crying.*

We hear footsteps on the stairs. MIEP GIES[2] *comes up, looking for* MR. FRANK. MIEP *is a Dutch girl of about twenty-two. She wears a coat and hat, ready to go home. She is pregnant. Her attitude toward* MR. FRANK *is protective, compassionate.*]

3 **MIEP.** Are you all right, Mr. Frank?

MR. FRANK [*Quickly controlling himself.*] Yes, Miep, yes.

MIEP. Everyone in the office has gone home.

---

2. **Miep Gies** [mēp′gēs′]

The Diary of Anne Frank, Act I 369

AT A GLANCE

- *Act I, Scene 1:* The stage directions describe the set: the top floor (attic) of a warehouse and office building in Amsterdam, Holland, November 1945.
- Mr. Frank appears in the attic.
- Miep, a young Dutch woman, enters the attic.

LITERARY OPTIONS

- characterization
- plot
- setting

THEMATIC OPTIONS

- friendship and love
- family and love
- ideals and visions

1 SETTING

The details of the setting are important because the play is based on a true story and a real setting.

2 CHARACTERIZATION

Mr. Frank is described in the stage directions before he speaks. His tears show that this room holds sad memories for him.

3 STYLE: DIALOGUE

Miep reveals her concern for Mr. Frank, alerting the audience that something is wrong. She helps to establish an ominous mood.

GUIDED READING

LITERAL QUESTIONS

1a. When and where does the first scene of the play take place? (the top floor of a warehouse and office building in Amsterdam, Holland, in November 1945)

2a. What reaction does Mr. Frank have to the white glove? (He breaks down and cries when he holds it in his hand.)

INFERENTIAL QUESTIONS

1b. How do you know Mr. Frank has been in the room before? (The way he looks around, struggles for self-control, and moves about the room show that the room is not unfamiliar to him.)

2b. Why do you suppose he cries? (The glove probably belonged to someone he loved.)

- *Scene 1 (continued):* Mr. Frank is going to leave Amsterdam.
- He asks Miep to burn old papers.
- Miep shows him Anne's diary.

1 DIALOGUE

Mr. Frank's explanation about leaving shows the impact of past events on his life.

2 CHARACTERIZATION

Mr. Frank shows himself to be empathetic in spite of his own obvious suffering.

3 STAGE DIRECTIONS

The actor playing Mr. Frank is to begin reading Anne's diary aloud. In a play, unlike a book or a movie, the audience cannot read the diary for themselves.

. . . It's after six. [*Then pleading.*] Don't stay up here, Mr. Frank. What's the use of torturing yourself like this?

MR. FRANK. I've come to say goodbye. . . . I'm leaving here, Miep.

MIEP. What do you mean? Where are you going? Where?

MR. FRANK. I don't know yet, I haven't decided.

MIEP. Mr. Frank, you can't leave here! This is your home! Amsterdam is your home. Your business is here, waiting for you. . . . You're needed here. . . . Now that the war is over, there are things that . . .

1 MR. FRANK. I can't stay in Amsterdam, Miep. It has too many memories for me. Everywhere there's something . . . the house we lived in . . . the school . . . that street organ playing out there. . . . I'm not the person you used to know, Miep. I'm a bitter old man. [*Breaking off.*] Forgive me. I shouldn't speak to you like this . . . after all that you did for us . . . the suffering . . .

MIEP. No. No. It wasn't suffering. You can't say we suffered. [*As she speaks, she straightens a chair that is overturned.*]

2 MR. FRANK. I know what you went through, you and Mr. Kraler.[3] I'll remember it as long as I live. [*He gives one last look around.*] Come, Miep. [*He starts for the steps, then remembers his rucksack, going back to get it.*]

MIEP. [*Hurrying up to a cupboard.*] Mr. Frank, did you see? There are some of your papers here. [*She brings a bundle of papers to him.*] We found them in a heap of rubbish on the floor after . . . after you left.

MR. FRANK. Burn them. [*He opens his rucksack to put the glove in it.*]

---

3. **Kraler** [krä′ler]

MIEP. But, Mr. Frank, there are letters, notes . . .

MR. FRANK. Burn them. All of them.

MIEP. Burn *this?* [*She hands him a paper-bound notebook.*]

3 MR. FRANK. [*Quietly.*] Anne's diary. [*He opens the diary and begins to read.*] "Monday, the sixth of July, nineteen forty-two." [*To* MIEP.] Nineteen forty-two. Is it possible, Miep? . . . Only three years ago. [*As he continues his reading, he sits down on the couch.*] "Dear Diary, since you and I are going to be great friends, I will start by telling you about myself. My name is Anne Frank. I am thirteen years old. I was born in Germany the twelfth of June, nineteen twenty-nine. As my family is

---

GUIDED READING

LITERAL QUESTION

1a. What does Mr. Frank tell Miep to do with the papers she finds? (burn them)

INFERENTIAL QUESTION

1b. Why do you think he asks her to destroy these letters? (These notes and letters are probably full of painful memories of the family that he lost.)

Jewish, we emigrated to Holland when Hitler came to power."

[*As* MR. FRANK *reads on, another voice joins his, as if coming from the air. It is* ANNE's *voice.*]

1 MR. FRANK *and* ANNE. "My father started a business, importing spice and herbs. Things went well for us until nineteen forty. Then the war came, and the Dutch capitulation,[4] followed by the arrival of the Germans. Then things got very bad for the Jews."

[MR. FRANK's *voice dies out.* ANNE's *voice continues alone. The lights dim slowly to darkness. The curtain falls on the scene.*]

2 ANNE's VOICE. You could not do this and you could not do that. They forced Father out of his business. We had to wear yellow stars.[5] I had to turn in my bike. I couldn't go to a Dutch school any more. I couldn't go to the movies, or ride in an automobile, or even on a streetcar, and a million other things. But somehow we children still managed to have fun. Yesterday Father told me we were going into hiding. Where, he wouldn't say. At five o'clock this morning Mother woke me and told me to hurry and get dressed. I was to put on as many clothes as I could. It would look too suspicious if we walked along carrying suitcases. It wasn't until we were on our way that I learned where we were going. Our hiding place was to be upstairs in the building where Father used to have his business. Three other people were coming with us . . . the Van Daans

---

4. **capitulation** [kə pich'ə lā'shən]: surrender. The Netherlands surrendered to the Nazis in May 1940, although the Dutch underground continued to fight the Nazis and to aid Jews and other refugees hunted by the Nazis.

5. **yellow stars:** The Nazis ordered all Jews in German-occupied countries to wear yellow six-pointed stars on their clothing so that they could be readily recognized. The six-pointed Star of David symbolizes the Jewish faith.

---

and their son Peter. . . . Father knew the Van Daans but we had never met them. . . .

[*During the last lines the curtain rises on the scene. The lights dim on.* ANNE's *voice fades out.*]

Scene 2

3 It is early morning, July 1942. The rooms are bare, as before, but they are now clean and orderly.

[MR. VAN DAAN, *a tall, portly man in his late* 4 *forties, is in the main room, pacing up and down. His clothes and overcoat are expensive and well cut.*

MRS. VAN DAAN *sits on the couch, clutching her possessions—a hatbox, bags, etc. She is a pretty woman in her early forties. She wears a fur coat over her other clothes.*

PETER VAN DAAN *is standing at the window of the room on the right, looking down at the street below. He is a shy, awkward boy of sixteen. He wears a cap, a raincoat, and long Dutch trousers, like "plus fours."[6] At his feet is a black case, a carrier for his cat.*

The yellow Star of David is conspicuous on all of their clothes.]

5 MRS. VAN DAAN. [*Rising, nervous, excited.*] Something's happened to them! I know it!

MR. VAN DAAN. Now Kerli!

MRS. VAN DAAN. Mr. Frank said they'd be here at seven o'clock. He said . . .

MR. VAN DAAN. They have two miles to walk. You can't expect . . .

MRS. VAN DAAN. They've been picked up. That's what's happened. They've been taken. . . .

---

6. **"plus fours":** loose-fitting trousers gathered just below the knees.

The Diary of Anne Frank, Act I 371

AT A GLANCE

■ *Scene 1 (continued):* Anne's voice is introduced.
■ The restrictions imposed on Jews are enumerated.
■ *Scene 2:* The next scene is a flashback to the same attic in 1942.

1 **DIALOGUE**

Anne's enthusiastic, young voice contrasts with Mr. Frank's sad, older voice as they read together.

2 **CHARACTERIZATION**

Anne's innocence and optimism are revealed in the way she enumerates the severe restrictions matter-of-factly, as if they were regulations at school or rules for a game.

3 **PLOT: FLASHBACK**

In the flashback the setting changes. The orderly appearance of the annex contrasts with the disorder of the first scene.

4 **STAGE DIRECTIONS**

The stage directions help develop characterization by describing appearance and actions. The Van Daans' nervousness is revealed in their "pacing" and "clutching."

5 **CHARACTERIZATION**

Mr. Van Daan's attempts to be calm and rational contrast with Mrs. Van Daan's agitation.

GUIDED READING

LITERAL QUESTIONS

1a. Whose voice joins Mr. Frank's voice in reading the diary? (Anne's)

2a. How does Mrs. Van Daan behave? (She is nervous and excited because she is afraid.)

INFERENTIAL QUESTIONS

1b. What effect does this have? (Possible answers: It helps explain why Mr. Frank is probably so sad; it makes us eager to meet Anne.)

2b. Do Mrs. Van Daan's fears seem reasonable? (Her husband offers plausible explanations for the Franks' delay, but her fears still seem reasonable, given the persecution of the Jews.)

- *Scene 2 (continued)*: Anne is described in stage directions.
- Mr. Frank introduces his family to the Van Daans.
- Miep starts to go out for ration books.

1 READING SKILLS: COMPARISON AND CONTRAST

Mr. Frank's younger appearance and brisk, confident manner are in dramatic contrast to the earlier description of him as a defeated, sad man.

2 STAGE DIRECTIONS

Before Anne speaks a word, we have a strong sense of her youthful enthusiasm from the stage directions.

3 CHARACTERIZATION

Anne's curiosity makes the trip to the attic seem like a happy adventure.

4 PLOT: CONFLICT

The war's effects extend to such vital daily matters as eating. Talk of ration books further agitates Mrs. Van Daan.

[MR. VAN DAAN *indicates that he hears someone coming.*]

MR. VAN DAAN. You see?

[PETER *takes up his carrier and his schoolbag, etc., and goes into the main room as* MR. FRANK *comes up the stairwell from below.* MR. FRANK *looks much younger now. His movements are brisk, his manner confident. He wears an overcoat and carries his hat and a small cardboard box. He crosses to the* VAN DAANS, *shaking hands with each of them.*]

MR. FRANK. Mrs. Van Daan, Mr. Van Daan, Peter. [*Then, in explanation of their lateness.*] There were too many of the Green Police[7] on the streets. . . . We had to take the long way around.

[*Up the steps come* MARGOT FRANK, MRS. FRANK, MIEP (*not pregnant now*), *and* MR. KRALER. *All of them carry bags, packages, and so forth. The Star of David is conspicuous on all of the* FRANKS' *clothing.* MARGOT *is eighteen, beautiful, quiet, shy.* MRS. FRANK *is a young mother, gently bred, reserved. She, like* MR. FRANK, *has a slight German accent.* MR. KRALER *is a Dutchman, dependable, kindly.*

As MR. KRALER *and* MIEP *go upstage to put down their parcels,* MRS. FRANK *turns back to call* ANNE.]

MRS. FRANK. Anne?

[ANNE *comes running up the stairs. She is thirteen, quick in her movements, interested in everything, mercurial[8] in her emotions. She wears a cape, long wool socks, and carries a schoolbag.*]

---

7. **Green Police:** Nazi police, who wore green uniforms.
8. **mercurial** [mər kū′rē əl]: changeable; lively.

372 *Drama*

MR. FRANK [*Introducing them.*] My wife, Edith. Mr. and Mrs. Van Daan . . .

[MRS. FRANK *hurries over, shaking hands with them.*]

. . . their son, Peter . . . my daughters, Margot and Anne.

[ANNE *gives a polite little curtsy as she shakes* MR. VAN DAAN's *hand. Then she immediately starts off on a tour of investigation of her new home, going upstairs to the attic room.*

MIEP *and* MR. KRALER *are putting the various things they have brought on the shelves.*]

MR. KRALER. I'm sorry there is still so much confusion.

MR. FRANK. Please. Don't think of it. After all, we'll have plenty of leisure to arrange everything ourselves.

MIEP [*To* MRS. FRANK.] We put the stores of food you sent in here. Your drugs are here . . . soap, linen here.

MRS. FRANK. Thank you, Miep.

MIEP. I made up the beds . . . the way Mr. Frank and Mr. Kraler said. [*She starts out.*] Forgive me. I have to hurry. I've got to go to the other side of town to get some ration books[9] for you.

MRS. VAN DAAN. Ration books? If they see our names on ration books, they'll know we're here.

---

9. **ration books:** During the war ration coupons or stamps were required for the purchase of food, clothing, and other necessities to make sure that such items would be evenly distributed to all citizens. Each month the government issued new books of these stamps to the population. Without them many essential goods could not be obtained.

GUIDED READING

LITERAL QUESTIONS

1a. Whom does Mr. Frank introduce? (He introduces his wife and daughters to Mr. and Mrs. Van Daan and their son, Peter.)

2a. What is the first thing Anne does after meeting the Van Daans? (She goes on a tour of her new home.)

INFERENTIAL QUESTIONS

1b. What feelings do the characters share? (They probably share apprehension about living together and fear of the Green Police.)

2b. How do you think Anne's response differs from that of the other people in the attic? (She seems more enthusiastic, more interested in exploring, than the others.)

MR. KRALER. There isn't anything—

MIEP. Don't worry. Your names
won't be on them. [*As she hurries out.*] I'll be up later.

[*Together.*]

MR. FRANK. Thank you, Miep.

1 **MRS. FRANK** [*To* MR. KRALER.] It's illegal, then,
the ration books? We've never done anything
illegal.

MR. FRANK. We won't be living here exactly
according to regulations.

[*As* MR. KRALER *reassures* MRS. FRANK, *he
takes various small things, such as
matches, soap, etc., from his pockets,
handing them to her.*]

MR. KRALER. This isn't the black market,[10]
Mrs. Frank. This is what we call the white
market . . . helping all of the hundreds and
hundreds who are hiding out in Amsterdam.

2 [*The carillon is heard playing the quarter-
hour before eight.* MR. KRALER *looks at his
watch.* ANNE *stops at the window as she
comes down the stairs.*]

ANNE. It's the Westertoren!

MR. KRALER. I must go. I must be out of here
and downstairs in the office before the workmen get here. [*He starts for the stairs leading
3 out.*] Miep or I or both of us, will be up each
day to bring you food and news and find out
what your needs are. Tomorrow I'll get you a
better bolt for the door at the foot of the stairs.
It needs a bolt that you can throw yourself
and open only at our signal. [*To* MR. FRANK.]
Oh . . . You'll tell them about the noise?

MR. FRANK. I'll tell them.

---

10. **black market:** illegal means of buying and selling
goods outside the official rationing system.

MR. KRALER. Goodbye then for the moment.
I'll come up again after the workmen leave.

MR. FRANK. Goodbye, Mr. Kraler.

MRS. FRANK. [*Shaking his hand.*] How can we
thank you?

[*The others murmur their goodbyes.*]

MR. KRALER. I never thought I'd live to see the
day when a man like Mr. Frank would have to
go into hiding. When you think—

[*He breaks off, going out.* MR. FRANK *follows
him down the steps, bolting the door after
him. In the interval before he returns,* PE-
TER *goes over to* MARGOT, *shaking hands
with her. As* MR. FRANK *comes back up the
steps,* MRS. FRANK *questions him anxiously.*]

MRS. FRANK. What did he mean about the
noise?

MR. FRANK. First let us take off some of these
clothes.

4 [*They all start to take off garment after garment. On each of their coats, sweaters,
blouses, suits, dresses, is another yellow
Star of David.* MR. *and* MRS. FRANK *are un-
derdressed quite simply. The others wear
several things—sweaters, extra dresses,
bathrobes, aprons, nightgowns, etc.*]

MR. VAN DAAN. It's a wonder we weren't arrested, walking along the streets . . . Petronella with a fur coat in July . . . and that cat
of Peter's crying all the way.

ANNE. A cat?

[*Finally, as they have all removed their
surplus clothes, they look to* MR. FRANK,
waiting for him to speak.]

MR. FRANK. Now. About the noise. While the
men are in the building below, we must have
complete quiet. Every sound can be heard

The Diary of Anne Frank, Act I   373

GUIDED READING

LITERAL QUESTIONS

1a. How does Mrs. Frank react to the fact that they will
have illegal ration books? (She says they've never
done anything illegal.)

2a. What made Mr. Van Daan fearful that they would
be arrested? (His wife was wearing a fur coat in
July, and the cat was crying.)

INFERENTIAL QUESTIONS

1b. Why is this response ironic? (It is illegal for them
even to live in hiding.)

2b. What do their possessions tell you about their lives
before they came to live in the attic? (They were
fairly well-off financially.)

- *Scene 2 (continued):* Mr. Frank lists the restrictions they must follow.
- Marching feet are heard outside.
- Mr. Frank describes his debt to Mr. Van Daan.

1 PLOT: SUSPENSE

This enumeration of cautions creates suspense, making us wonder if the families can really remain so quiet for such a long time each day.

2 PLOT: CONFLICT

The characters' response to street sounds indicates that they always feel in danger of being discovered and taken away.

3 THEME

The group will live together as a family. Even in desperate times the routines of family life preserve a sense of order.

4 THEME

Mr. Frank's indebtedness to and feelings of friendship for Mr. Van Daan help explain why he has included them in this secret undertaking.

---

1 down there, not only in the workrooms, but in the offices too. The men come at about eight thirty, and leave at about five thirty. So, to be perfectly safe, from eight in the morning until six in the evening we must move only when it is necessary, and then in stockinged feet. We must not speak above a whisper. We must not run any water. We cannot use the sink, or even, forgive me, the w.c.[11] The pipes 2 go down through the workrooms. It would be heard. No trash . . . [MR. FRANK *stops abruptly as he hears the sound of marching feet from the street below. Everyone is motionless, paralyzed with fear.* MR. FRANK *goes quietly into the room on the right to look down out of the window.* ANNE *runs after him, peering out with him. The tramping feet pass without stopping. The tension is relieved.* MR. FRANK, *followed by* ANNE, *returns to the main room and resumes his instructions to the group.*] . . . No trash must ever be thrown out which might reveal that someone is living up here . . . not even a potato paring. We must burn everything in the stove at night. This is the way we must live until it is over, if we are to survive.

[*There is silence for a second.*]

3 **MRS. FRANK.** Until it is over.

MR. FRANK [*Reassuringly.*] After six we can move about . . . we can talk and laugh and have our supper and read and play games . . . just as we would at home. [*He looks at his watch.*] And now I think it would be wise if we all went to our rooms, and were settled before eight o'clock. Mrs. Van Daan, you and your husband will be upstairs. I regret that there's no place up there for Peter. But he will be here, near us. This will be our common room, where we'll meet to talk and eat and read, like one family.

---

11. **w.c.:** water closet, or toilet.

374 *Drama*

MR. VAN DAAN. And where do you and Mrs. Frank sleep?

MR. FRANK. This room is also our bedroom.

MRS. VAN DAAN. That isn't right. We'll sleep here and you take the room upstairs. ⎫
⎬ [*Together.*]
MR. VAN DAAN. It's your place. ⎭

MR. FRANK. Please. I've thought this out for weeks. It's the best arrangement. The only arrangement.

4 **MRS. VAN DAAN.** [*To* MR. FRANK.] Never, never can we thank you. [*Then, to* MRS. FRANK.] I don't know what would have happened to us, if it hadn't been for Mr. Frank.

MR. FRANK. You don't know how your husband helped me when I came to this country . . . knowing no one . . . not able to speak the language. I can never repay him for that. [*Going to* MR. VAN DAAN.] May I help you with your things?

MR. VAN DAAN. No. No. [*To* MRS. VAN DAAN.] Come along, *liefje.*[12]

MRS. VAN DAAN. You'll be all right, Peter? You're not afraid?

PETER. [*Embarrassed.*] Please, Mother.

[*They start up the stairs to the attic room above.* MR. FRANK *turns to* MRS. FRANK.]

MR. FRANK. You too must have some rest, Edith. You didn't close your eyes last night. Nor you, Margot.

ANNE. I slept, Father. Wasn't that funny? I knew it was the last night in my own bed, and yet I slept soundly.

MR. FRANK. I'm glad, Anne. Now you'll be able

---

12. *liefje* [lēf'hyə]: Dutch for "little one."

GUIDED READING

LITERAL QUESTIONS

1a. Why must the group live under the restrictions Mr. Frank lists? (to prevent the workers below from suspecting that anyone is upstairs)

2a. Why is Mr. Frank indebted to Mr. Van Daan? (Mr. Van Daan helped him when he came to the country.)

INFERENTIAL QUESTIONS

1b. How do you think they feel about the restrictions? (They probably feel resentful but resigned.)

2b. How is Mr. Frank repaying the debt? (He is providing the Van Daans with a place to hide.)

to help me straighten things in here. [*To* MRS. FRANK *and* MARGOT.] Come with me. . . . You and Margot rest in this room for the time being. [*He picks up their clothes, starting for the room on the right.*]

MRS. FRANK. You're sure . . . ? I could help. . . . And Anne hasn't had her milk. . . .

MR. FRANK. I'll give it to her. [*To* ANNE *and* PETER.] Anne, Peter . . . it's best that you take off your shoes now, before you forget. [*He leads the way to the room, followed by* MARGOT.]

MRS. FRANK. You're sure you're not tired, Anne?

ANNE. I feel fine. I'm going to help Father.

MRS. FRANK. Peter, I'm glad you are to be with us.

PETER. Yes, Mrs. Frank.

[MRS. FRANK *goes to join* MR. FRANK *and* MARGOT.

During the following scene MR. FRANK *helps* MARGOT *and* MRS. FRANK *to hang up their clothes. Then he persuades them both to lie down and rest. The* VAN DAANS *in their room above settle themselves. In the main room* ANNE *and* PETER *remove their shoes.* PETER *takes his cat out of the carrier.*]

ANNE. What's your cat's name?

PETER. Mouschi.

ANNE. Mouschi! Mouschi! Mouschi! [*She picks up the cat, walking away with it. To* PETER.] I love cats. I have one . . . a darling little cat. But they made me leave her behind. I left some food and a note for the neighbors to take care of her. . . . I'm going to miss her terribly. What is yours? A him or a her?

PETER. He's a tom. He doesn't like strangers. [*He takes the cat from her, putting it back in its carrier.*]

ANNE. [*Unabashed.*] Then I'll have to stop being a stranger, won't I? Where did you go to school?

PETER. Jewish Secondary.

ANNE. But that's where Margot and I go! I never saw you around.

PETER. I used to see you . . . sometimes . . .

ANNE. You did?

PETER. . . . in the schoolyard. You were always in the middle of a bunch of kids. [*He takes a penknife from his pocket.*]

ANNE. Why didn't you ever come over?

PETER. I'm sort of a lone wolf. [*He starts to rip off his Star of David.*]

ANNE. What are you doing?

PETER. Taking it off.

ANNE. But you can't do that. They'll arrest you if you go out without your Star. [*He tosses his knife on the table.*]

PETER. Who's going out?

ANNE. Why, of course! You're right! Of course we don't need them any more. [*She picks up his knife and starts to take her Star off.*] I wonder what our friends will think when we don't show up today?

PETER. I didn't have any dates with anyone.

ANNE. Oh, I did. I had a date with Jopie to go and play ping-pong at her house. Do you know Jopie deWaal?[13]

PETER. No.

---

13. **Jopie deWaal** [yō′pē də väl′]

The Diary of Anne Frank, Act I 375

AT A GLANCE

- *Scene 2 (continued):* Mr. Frank helps Margot and Mrs. Frank get settled.
- Peter shows Anne his cat.
- Peter rips the Star of David off his clothes.

1 STYLE: DIALOGUE

In this dialogue with Anne and Peter, Mrs. Frank reveals her gentle nature as she makes a special effort to communicate with the young people.

2 STAGE DIRECTIONS

These stage directions poignantly show that remaining motionless and quiet will be easier for the older characters than for the younger ones.

3 CHARACTERIZATION

Peter's abrupt speech does not daunt Anne. She characteristically has a confident and ready answer for Peter's snub.

GUIDED READING

LITERAL QUESTION

1a. What does Peter say to Anne to explain why he never socialized? ("I'm sort of a lone wolf.")

INFERENTIAL QUESTION

1b. What does their first conversation show about the difference between Peter and Anne? (He is withdrawn; she is outgoing, friendly, and outspoken.)

- *Scene 2 (continued):* Anne and Peter talk about the Star of David they wear.
- Mr. Frank helps Peter get settled.
- Anne opens her box of possessions.

1 THEME

How Anne's best friend will react to her disappearance underscores one of the plays themes: how the war affects love and friendship.

2 CHARACTERIZATION

Anne's reluctance to throw away the yellow symbols reveals her respect for her religion, since the Star of David is an important symbol in Judaism.

3 CHARACTERIZATION

Mr. Frank helps Peter to care for his cat because he recognizes that Peter's feelings for Mouschi will help him through the difficult times they face.

4 CHARACTERIZATION

When Anne calls Peter "awfully shy," Mr. Frank reveals his fatherly, optimistic nature by encouraging Anne to believe she will eventually get along with the boy.

5 THEME

Anne's decision to think of their experience as a kind of summer vacation demonstrates her touchingly youthful optimism and idealism.

---

1 **ANNE.** Jopie's my best friend. I wonder what she'll think when she telephones and there's no answer? . . . Probably she'll go over to the house. . . . I wonder what she'll think . . . we left everything as if we'd suddenly been called away . . . breakfast dishes in the sink . . . beds not made. . . . [*As she pulls off her Star the cloth underneath shows clearly the color and form of the Star.*] Look! It's still there! [PETER *goes over the stove with his Star.*] What're you going to do with yours?

PETER. Burn it.

2 **ANNE.** [*She starts to throw hers in, and cannot.*] It's funny, I can't throw mine away. I don't know why.

PETER. You can't throw . . . ? Something they branded you with . . . ? That they made you wear so they could spit on you?

ANNE. I know. I know. But after all, it *is* the Star of David, isn't it?

[*In the bedroom, right,* MARGOT *and* MRS. FRANK *are lying down.* MR. FRANK *starts quietly out.*]

PETER. Maybe it's different for a girl.

[MR. FRANK *comes into the main room.*]

3 **MR. FRANK.** Forgive me, Peter. Now let me see. We must find a bed for your cat. [*He goes to a cupboard.*] I'm glad you brought your cat. Anne was feeling so badly about hers. [*Getting a used small washtub.*] Here we are. Will it be comfortable in that?

PETER. [*Gathering up his things.*] Thanks.

MR. FRANK. [*Opening the door of the room on the left*]. And here is your room. But I warn you, Peter, you can't grow any more. Not an inch, or you'll have to sleep with your feet out of the skylight. Are you hungry?

PETER. No.

MR. FRANK. We have some bread and butter.

PETER. No, thank you.

MR. FRANK. You can have it for luncheon then. And tonight we will have a real supper . . . our first supper together.

PETER. Thanks. Thanks. [*He goes into his room. During the following scene he arranges his possessions in the new room.*]

MR. FRANK. That's a nice boy, Peter.

4 **ANNE.** He's awfully shy, isn't he?

MR. FRANK. You'll like him, I know.

ANNE. I certainly hope so, since he's the only boy I'm likely to see for months and months.

[MR. FRANK *sits down, taking off his shoes.*]

MR. FRANK. Annele,[14] there's a box there. Will you open it?

[*He indicates a carton on the couch.* ANNE *brings it to the center table. In the street below there is the sound of children playing.*]

5 **ANNE.** [*As she opens the carton.*] You know the way I'm going to think of it here? I'm going to think of it as a boardinghouse. A very peculiar summer boardinghouse, like the one that we—[*She breaks off as she pulls out some photographs.*] Father! My movie stars! I was wondering where they were! I was looking for them this morning . . . and Queen Wilhelmina![15] How wonderful!

MR. FRANK. There's something more. Go on. Look further. [*He goes over to the sink, pouring a glass of milk from a thermos bottle.*]

ANNE [*Pulling out a pasteboard-bound book.*]

---

14. **Annele** [än′ə lə]: Yiddish nickname for Anne.
15. **Queen Wilhelmina** [wil′hel mē′nə] (1880–1962): queen of the Netherlands from 1890 to 1948.

GUIDED READING

LITERAL QUESTIONS

1a. What does Anne say about her star? (She cannot throw it away.)

2a. What did Mr. Frank save for Anne? (her pictures of movie stars and Queen Wilhelmina)

INFERENTIAL QUESTIONS

1b. What does this reaction reveal about Anne? (She has strong feelings about her religion.)

2b. What does this action indicate about Mr. Frank? (He understands his daughter and wants her to be happy.)

A diary. [*She throws her arms around her father.*] I've never had a diary. And I've always longed for one. [*She looks around the room.*] Pencil, pencil, pencil, pencil. [*She starts down the stairs.*] I'm going down to the office to get a pencil.

MR. FRANK. Anne! No! [*He goes after her, catching her by the arm and pulling her back.*]

ANNE. [*Startled.*] But there's no one in the building now.

MR. FRANK. It doesn't matter. I don't want you ever to go beyond that door.

ANNE. [*Sobered.*] Never . . . ? Not even at night-time, when everyone is gone? Or on Sundays? Can't I go down to listen to the radio?

MR. FRANK. Never, I am sorry, Anneke.[16] It isn't safe. No, you must never go beyond that door.

[*For the first time* ANNE *realizes what "going into hiding" means.*]

ANNE. I see.

MR. FRANK. It'll be hard, I know. But always remember this, Anneke. There are no walls, there are no bolts, no locks that anyone can put on your mind. Miep will bring us books. We will read history, poetry, mythology. [*He gives her the glass of milk.*] Here's your milk. [*With his arm about her, they go over to the couch, sitting down side by side.*] As a matter of fact, between us, Anne, being here has certain advantages for you. For instance, you remember the battle you had with your mother the other day on the subject of overshoes? You said you'd rather die than wear overshoes? But in the end you had to wear them? Well now, you see, for as long as we are here you will never have to wear overshoes! Isn't that

---

16. **Anneke** [än′ə kə]: German nickname for Anne.

good? And the coat that you inherited from Margot, you won't have to wear that any more. And the piano! You won't have to practice on the piano. I tell you, this is going to be a fine life for you!

[ANNE'*s panic is gone.* PETER *appears in the doorway of his room, with a saucer in his hand. He is carrying his cat.*]

PETER. I . . . I . . . I thought I'd better get some water for Mouschi before . . .

MR. FRANK. Of course.

[*As he starts toward the sink the carillon begins to chime the hour of eight. He tip-toes to the window at the back and looks down at the street below. He turns to* PETER,

---

AT A GLANCE

- *Scene 2 (continued):* Anne opens her new diary.
- Mr. Frank lists the "advantages" of their life in hiding.
- The carillon chimes eight.

1 CHARACTERIZATION

Anne demonstrates her enthusiastic affection for her father and her youthful exuberance over the prospect of keeping a diary.

2 THEME

Mr. Frank assures Anne that she can remain free by maintaining her ideals and by opening her mind to ideas they will read about.

3 HUMOR

In the face of government persecution, Mr. Frank provides poignantly humorous reassurance by suggesting that their life in hiding has advantages.

GUIDED READING

LITERAL QUESTIONS

1a. Why does Mr. Frank tell Anne she cannot go to the office to get a pencil? (She must never go beyond the door.)

2a. What humorous consolation does Mr. Frank give Anne? (She won't have to wear overshoes or Margot's old coat or practice the piano.)

INFERENTIAL QUESTIONS

1b. Why does this restriction surprise Anne? (She thought she would have some freedom at night or on Sundays when the workers were at home.)

2b. What do these comments reveal about Mr. Frank? (He is a thoughtful, loving man and father who is trying to keep morale high.)

- Scene 2 (continued): Anne shares her milk with Peter's cat.
- Anne describes her feelings about being in hiding.
- Scene 3: Two months later. The group is together in the main room.

1 CHARACTERIZATION

Anne's gesture in sharing her milk with Peter's cat is an overture Peter can accept without embarrassment.

2 THEME

Even in hiding, the couples share private moments together to show their concern for each other.

3 PLOT: SUSPENSE

Anne's diary is a reminder that however much the families adjust to life in the attic, danger lurks just outside.

4 THEME

War and oppression can create heroes who risk their own safety to protect others.

5 CONFLICT

Anne expresses a common adolescent complaint. Even in such dire circumstances, the conflict between mother and daughter continues.

---

indicating in pantomime[17] that it is too late. PETER *starts back for his room. He steps on a creaking board. The three of them are frozen for a minute in fear. As* **1** PETER *starts away again,* ANNE *tiptoes over to him and pours some of the milk from her glass into the saucer for the cat.* PETER *squats on the floor, putting the milk before the cat.* MR. FRANK *gives* ANNE *his fountain pen and then goes into the room at the right. For a second* ANNE *watches the cat; then she goes over to the center table and opens her diary.*

In the room at the right, MRS. FRANK *has sat up quickly at the sound of the carillon.* MR. FRANK *comes in and sits down beside her on the settee,[18] his arm comfortingly around her.*

2 *Upstairs, in the attic room,* MR. *and* MRS. VAN DAAN *have hung their clothes in the closet and are now seated on the iron bed.* MRS. VAN DAAN *leans back exhausted.* MR. VAN DAAN *fans her with a newspaper.*

ANNE *starts to write in her diary. The lights dim out; the curtain falls.*

In the darkness ANNE's *voice comes to us again, faintly at first, and then with growing strength.]*

ANNE'S VOICE. I expect I should be describing what it feels like to go into hiding. But I really don't know yet myself. I only know it's funny never to be able to go outdoors . . . never to breathe fresh air . . . never to run and shout **3** and jump. It's the silence in the nights that frightens me most. Every time I hear a creak in the house, or a step on the street outside, I'm sure they're coming for us. The days aren't so bad. At least we know that Miep and Mr. Kraler are down there below us in the office.

---

17. **pantomime:** communication by means of gestures rather than words.
18. **settee** [se tē′]: medium-sized sofa.

378 *Drama*

---

4 Our protectors, we call them. I asked Father what would happen to them if the Nazis found out they were hiding us. Pim said that they would suffer the same fate that we would. . . . Imagine! They know this, and yet when they come up here, they're always cheerful and gay as if there were nothing in the world to bother them. . . . Friday, the twenty-first of August, nineteen forty-two. Today I'm going to tell you **5** our general news. Mother is unbearable. She insists on treating me like a baby, which I loathe. Otherwise things are going better. The weather is . . .

[As ANNE's *voice is fading out, the curtain rises on the scene.]*

Scene 3

It is a little after six o'clock in the evening, two months later.

*[*MARGOT *is in the bedroom at the right, studying.* MR. VAN DAAN *is lying down in the attic room above.*

The rest of the "family" is in the main room. ANNE *and* PETER *sit opposite each other at the center table, where they have been doing their lessons.* MRS. FRANK *is on the couch.* MRS. VAN DAAN *is seated with her fur coat, on which she has been sewing, in her lap. None of them are wearing their shoes.*

Their eyes are on MR. FRANK, *waiting for him to give them the signal which will release them from their day-long quiet.* MR. FRANK, *his shoes in his hand, stands looking down out of the window at the back, watching to be sure that all of the workmen have left the building below.*

After a few seconds of motionless silence, MR. FRANK *turns from the window.]*

MR. FRANK. [*Quietly, to the group.*] It's safe now. The last workman has left.

GUIDED READING

LITERAL QUESTIONS

1a. What does Anne give to Peter's cat? (some of her milk)

2a. What name does the group give to Miep and Mr. Kraler? (The group calls them "our protectors.")

INFERENTIAL QUESTIONS

1b. What does this gesture show about Anne? (She is compassionate and loves animals; she wants to make friends with Peter.)

2b. How do you think the group feels toward their protectors? (They probably feel gratitude and respect for them and fear for their safety.)

[*There is an immediate stir of relief.*]

ANNE. [*Her pent-up energy explodes.*] WHEE!

MRS. FRANK. [*Startled, amused.*] Anne!

MRS. VAN DAAN. I'm first for the w.c.

[*She hurries off to the bathroom.* MRS. FRANK *puts on her shoes and starts up to the sink to prepare supper.* ANNE *sneaks* PETER'S *shoes from under the table and hides them behind her back.* MR. FRANK *goes into* MAR-GOT'S *room.*]

MR. FRANK. [*To* MARGOT.] Six o'clock. School's over.

[MARGOT *gets up, stretching.* MR. FRANK *sits down to put on his shoes. In the main room* PETER *tries to find his.*]

1 **PETER.** [*To* ANNE.] Have you seen my shoes?

ANNE. [*Innocently.*] Your shoes?

PETER. You've taken them, haven't you?

ANNE. I don't know what you're talking about.

PETER. You're going to be sorry!

ANNE. Am I?

[PETER *goes after her.* ANNE, *with his shoes in her hand, runs from him, dodging behind her mother.*]

MRS. FRANK. [*Protesting.*] Anne, dear!

PETER. Wait till I get you!

ANNE. I'm waiting! [PETER *makes a lunge for her. They both fall to the floor.* PETER *pins her down, wrestling with her to get the shoes.*] Don't! Don't! Peter, stop it. Ouch!

MRS. FRANK. Anne! . . . Peter!

[*Suddenly* PETER *becomes self-conscious. He grabs his shoes roughly and starts for his room.*]

ANNE. [*Following him.*] Peter, where are you going? Come dance with me.

PETER. I tell you I don't know how.

ANNE. I'll teach you.

2 **PETER.** I'm going to give Mouschi his dinner.

ANNE. Can I watch?

PETER. He doesn't like people around while he eats.

ANNE. Peter, please.

PETER. No!

[*He goes into his room.* ANNE *slams his door after him.*]

MRS. FRANK. Anne, dear, I think you shouldn't play like that with Peter. It's not dignified.

ANNE. Who cares if it's dignified? I don't want to be dignified.

[MR. FRANK *and* MARGOT *come from the room on the right.* MARGOT *goes to help her mother.* MR. FRANK *starts for the center table to correct* MARGOT'S *school papers.*]

MRS. FRANK. [*To* ANNE.] You complain that I don't treat you like a grown-up. But when I do, you resent it.

3 **ANNE.** I only want some fun . . . someone to laugh and clown with. . . . After you've sat still all day and hardly moved, you've got to have some fun. I don't know what's the matter with that boy.

MR. FRANK. He isn't used to girls. Give him a little time.

ANNE. Time? Isn't two months time? I could cry. [*Catching hold of* MARGOT.] Come on, Margot . . . dance with me. Come on, please.

MARGOT. I have to help with supper.

The Diary of Anne Frank, Act I 379

AT A GLANCE

- *Scene 3 (continued):* Anne hides Peter's shoes and teases him.
- Peter becomes self-conscious when they wrestle.
- Mrs. Frank admonishes Anne.

1 **STYLE: DIALOGUE**

This dialogue reveals Anne's youthful flirtatiousness. She teases Peter to force him to notice her.

2 **CHARACTERIZATION**

Peter's sudden feelings of self-consciousness contrast with his earlier playfulness with Anne.

3 **SETTING**

Anne's speech reminds us of the toll their confinement is taking on her.

GUIDED READING

LITERAL QUESTIONS

1a. What does Anne hide from Peter? (his shoes)

2a. How does Peter react? (First he wrestles playfully with her; then he becomes self-conscious when Mrs. Frank intervenes.)

INFERENTIAL QUESTIONS

1b. What do you think Anne's feelings are toward Peter? (She likes him—perhaps even has a crush on him—but doesn't understand him.)

2b. How do you think Peter feels when Anne teases him? (He probably feels annoyed, embarrassed, and perhaps a little pleased.)

- *Scene 3 (continued):* Peter returns to his lessons, and Anne feeds Mouschi.
- Mrs. Van Daan teases Peter about Anne.
- A car stops outside and then pulls away.

1 CHARACTERIZATION

Anne's hopefulness is in poignant contrast to the desperateness of their situation.

2 THEME

Peter's mother is apparently insensitive to his private nature. Family members continue to interact as they would at home.

3 CHARACTERIZATION

By changing the subject Mrs. Frank tries to protect her own privacy from the overbearing Mrs. Van Daan.

4 IRONY

The sounds from the street below point out the grim irony of the petty squabbles of the previous few minutes.

---

1 **ANNE.** You know we're going to forget how to dance. . . . When we get out we won't remember a thing.

[*She starts to sing and dance by herself.* MR. FRANK *takes her in his arms, waltzing with her.* MRS. VAN DAAN *comes in from the bathroom.*]

MRS. VAN DAAN. Next? [*She looks around as she starts putting on her shoes.*] Where's Peter?

ANNE. [*As they are dancing.*] Where would he be!

MRS. VAN DAAN. He hasn't finished his lessons, has he? His father'll kill him if he catches him in there with that cat and his work not done. [MR. FRANK *and* ANNE *finish their dance. They bow to each other with extravagant formality.*] Anne, get him out of there, will you?

ANNE. [*At* PETER's *door.*] Peter? Peter?

PETER. [*Opening the door a crack.*] What is it?

ANNE. Your mother says to come out.

PETER. I'm giving Mouschi his dinner.

MRS. VAN DAAN. You know what your father says. [*She sits on the couch sewing on the lining of her fur coat.*]

PETER. For heaven's sake, I haven't even looked at him since lunch.

MRS. VAN DAAN. I'm just telling you, that's all.

ANNE. I'll feed him.

PETER. I don't want you in there.

MRS. VAN DAAN. Peter!

PETER. [*To* ANNE.] Then give him his dinner and come right out, you hear?

[*He comes back to the table.* ANNE *shuts the*

380   Drama

---

door of PETER's *room after her and disappears behind the curtain covering his closet.*]

2 **MRS. VAN DAAN.** [*To* PETER.] Now is that any way to talk to your little girlfriend?

PETER. Mother . . . for heaven's sake . . . will you please stop saying that?

MRS. VAN DAAN. Look at him blush! Look at him!

PETER. Please! I'm not . . . anyway . . . let me alone, will you?

MRS. VAN DAAN. He acts like it was something to be ashamed of. It's nothing to be ashamed of, to have a little girlfriend.

PETER. You're crazy. She's only thirteen.

MRS. VAN DAAN. So what? And you're sixteen. Just perfect. Your father's ten years older than I am. [*To* MR. FRANK.] I warn you, Mr. Frank, if this war lasts much longer, we're going to be related and then . . .

MR. FRANK. *Mazel tov!*[19]

3 **MRS. FRANK.** [*Deliberately changing the conversation.*] I wonder where Miep is. She's usually so prompt.

[*Suddenly everything else is forgotten as they hear the sound of an automobile coming to a screeching stop in the street below.* **4** *They are tense, motionless in their terror. The car starts away. A wave of relief sweeps over them. They pick up their occupations again.* ANNE *flings open the door of* PETER's *room, making a dramatic entrance. She is dressed in* PETER's *clothes.* PETER *looks at her in fury. The others are amused.*]

---

19. *Mazel tov!* [mä′zəl tôf′]: Hebrew for "Congratulations."

GUIDED READING

LITERAL QUESTION

1a. What sound interrupts the banter? (the sound of an automobile screeching to a halt)

INFERENTIAL QUESTION

1b. Why does this sound terrify the group? (It could be police coming to find them.)

AT A GLANCE

- *Scene 3 (continued):* Anne teases Peter.
- Peter calls her Mrs. Quack Quack.
- Anne trips Peter as he passes.

1 CHARACTERIZATION

Anne's actions increase our understanding of her personality: She is an extrovert and a tease; she is insensitive to Peter's adolescent insecurity.

2 CHARACTERIZATION

Peter's angry retaliation shows he is willing and able to fight back: He reveals that Anne had a reputation as an incessant talker at school.

3 CONFLICT

This dialogue sums up the stormy relationship between Anne and Peter, which is made more difficult by their living together in the small attic.

1 **ANNE.** Good evening, everyone. Forgive me if I don't stay. [*She jumps up on a chair.*] I have a friend waiting for me in there. My friend Tom. Tom Cat. Some people say that we look alike. But Tom has the most beautiful whiskers, and I have only a little fuzz. I am hoping . . . in time . . .

PETER. All right, Mrs. Quack Quack!

ANNE. [*Outraged—jumping down.*] Peter!

2 **PETER.** I heard about you. . . . How you talked so much in class they called you Mrs. Quack Quack. How Mr. Smitter made you write a composition . . . " 'Quack, quack,' said Mrs. Quack Quack."

ANNE. Well, go on. Tell them the rest. How it was so good that he read it out loud to the class and then read it to all his other classes!

PETER. Quack! Quack! Quack . . . Quack . . . Quack . . .

[ANNE *pulls off the coat and trousers.*]

ANNE. You are the most intolerable, insufferable boy I've ever met!

[*She throws the clothes down the stairwell.* PETER *goes down after them.*]

PETER. Quack, quack, quack!

MRS. VAN DAAN. [*To* ANNE.] That's right, Anneke! Give it to him!

3 **ANNE.** With all the boys in the world . . . Why I had to get locked up with one like you! . . .

PETER. Quack, quack, quack, and from now on stay out of my room!

[*As* PETER *passes her,* ANNE *puts out her foot,*

The Diary of Anne Frank, Act I   381

GUIDED READING

LITERAL QUESTION

1a. What does Anne tease Peter about? (She teases Peter about his small amount of facial hair.)

INFERENTIAL QUESTION

1b. Why does Anne bait Peter? (She really wants them to be friends.)

- *Scene 3 (continued):* Mrs. Frank shows concern for Anne's health.
- The sounds of bombers are heard from outside.
- Mr. Van Daan chides Peter: Mrs. Van Daan defends him.

1 SETTING

A doctor can never be called to their hiding place.

2 THEME

Trivial problems are exacerbated because there is no escape for the group from their day-to-day interactions.

3 STAGING

The sound effects help keep the audience aware of the constant presence of the war.

4 CONFLICT

Conflict between Mr. and Mrs. Van Daan flares again as Mr. Van Daan criticizes Peter for his apparent lack of concern for his studies and Mrs. Van Daan immediately comes to her son's defense.

5 CHARACTERIZATION

Mr. Frank uses praise to guide and motivate his daughter in contrast to Mr. Van Daan's impatient criticism of Peter.

---

tripping him. He picks himself up and goes on into his room.]

MRS. FRANK. [*Quietly.*] Anne, dear . . . your hair. [*She feels* ANNE's *forehead.*] You're warm. Are you feeling all right?

ANNE. Please, Mother. [*She goes over to the center table, slipping into her shoes.*]

MRS. FRANK [*Following her.*] You haven't a fever, have you?

ANNE. [*Pulling away*]. No. No.

1 **MRS. FRANK.** You know we can't call a doctor here, ever. There's only one thing to do . . . watch carefully. Prevent an illness before it comes. Let me see your tongue.

ANNE. Mother, this is perfectly absurd.

MRS. FRANK. Anne, dear, don't be such a baby. Let me see your tongue. [*As* ANNE *refuses,* MRS. FRANK *appeals to* MR. FRANK.] Otto . . . ?

MR. FRANK. You hear your mother, Anne.

[ANNE *flicks out her tongue for a second, then turns away.*]

MRS. FRANK. Come on—open up! [*As* ANNE *opens her mouth very wide.*] You seem all right . . . but perhaps an aspirin . . .

2 **MRS. VAN DAAN.** For heavens sake, don't give that child any pills. I waited for fifteen minutes this morning for her to come out of the w.c.

ANNE. I was washing my hair!

MRS. FRANK. I think there's nothing the matter with our Anne that a ride on her bike or a visit with her friend Jopie deWaal wouldn't cure. Isn't that so, Anne?

[MR. VAN DAAN *comes down into the room. From outside we hear faint sounds of*

382   *Drama*

---

3 *bombers going over and a burst of ack-ack.*[20]]

MR. VAN DAAN. Miep not come yet?

MRS. VAN DAAN. The workmen just left, a little while ago.

MR. VAN DAAN. What's for dinner tonight?

MRS. VAN DAAN. Beans.

MR. VAN DAAN. Not again!

MRS. VAN DAAN. Poor Putti! I know. But what can we do? That's all that Miep brought us.

[MR. VAN DAAN *starts to pace, his hands behind his back.* ANNE *follows behind him, imitating him.*]

ANNE. We are now in what is known as the "bean cycle." Beans boiled, beans *en casserole,* beans with strings, beans without strings . . .

[PETER *has come out of his room. He slides into his place at the table, becoming immediately absorbed in his studies.*]

4 **MR. VAN DAAN.** [*To* PETER.] I saw you . . . in there, playing with your cat.

MRS. VAN DAAN. He just went in for a second, putting his coat away. He's been out here all the time, doing his lessons.

MR. FRANK. [*Looking up from the paper.*] Anne, you got an excellent in your history paper today . . . and very good in Latin.

ANNE. [*Sitting beside him.*] How about algebra?

5 **MR. FRANK.** I'll have to make a confession. Up until now I've managed to stay ahead of you in algebra. Today you caught up with me. We'll leave it to Margot to correct.

20. **ack-ack:** antiaircraft fire.

GUIDED READING

LITERAL QUESTIONS

1a. Why is Mrs. Frank concerned about Anne? (Mrs. Frank is afraid that Anne is getting sick.)

2a. How does Anne refer to the meals they will be having? (She calls them the "bean cycle.")

INFERENTIAL QUESTIONS

1b. Why does Anne refuse to cooperate with her mother? (She is probably embarrassed at being treated like a child.)

2b. What does this tell you about the meals the group eats? (The meals are monotonous because the food supply is limited.)

ANNE. Isn't algebra *vile*, Pim!

MR. FRANK. Vile!

1
MARGOT. [*To* MR. FRANK.] How did I do?

ANNE. [*Getting up.*] Excellent, excellent, excellent, excellent.

MR. FRANK. [*To* MARGOT.] You should have used the subjunctive[21] here.

MARGOT. Should I? . . . I thought . . . look here . . . I didn't use it here.

[*The two become absorbed in the papers.*]

ANNE. Mrs. Van Daan, may I try on your coat?

MRS. FRANK. No, Anne.

2
MRS. VAN DAAN. [*Giving it to* ANNE.] It's all right . . . but careful with it. [ANNE *puts it on and struts with it.*] My father gave me that the year before he died. He always bought the best that money could buy.

ANNE. Mrs. Van Daan, did you have a lot of boyfriends before you were married?

MRS. FRANK. Anne, that's a personal question. It's not courteous to ask personal questions.

MRS. VAN DAAN. Oh, I don't mind. [*To* ANNE.] Our house was always swarming with boys. When I was a girl we had . . .

3
MR. VAN DAAN. Not again!

MRS. VAN DAAN. [*Good-humored.*] Shut up! [*Without a pause, to* ANNE. MR. VAN DAAN *mimics* MRS. VAN DAAN, *speaking the first few words in unison with her.*] One summer we had a big house in Hilversum.[22] The boys came buzzing round like bees around a jam pot. And when I was sixteen! . . . We were

---

21. **subjunctive:** particular verb form.
22. **Hilversum:** city in west-central Netherlands.

---

wearing our skirts very short those days and I had good-looking legs. [*She pulls up her skirt, going to* MR. FRANK.] I still have 'em. I may not be as pretty as I used to be, but I still have my legs. How about it, Mr. Frank?

MR. VAN DAAN. All right. All right. We see them.

MRS. VAN DAAN. I'm not asking you. I'm asking Mr. Frank.

PETER. Mother, for heaven's sake.

MRS. VAN DAAN. Oh, I embarrass you, do I? Well, I just hope the girl you marry has as good. [*Then, to* ANNE.] My father used to worry about me, with so many boys hanging round. He told me, if any of them gets fresh, you say to him . . . "Remember, Mr. So-and-So, remember I'm a lady."

ANNE. "Remember, Mr. So-and-So, remember I'm a lady." [*She gives* MRS. VAN DAAN *her coat.*]

MR. VAN DAAN. Look at you, talking that way in front of her! Don't you know she puts it all down in that diary?

MRS. VAN DAAN. So, if she does? I'm only telling the truth!

[ANNE *stretches out, putting her ear to the floor, listening to what is going on below. The sound of the bombers fades away.*]

MRS. FRANK. [*Setting the table.*] Would you mind, Peter, if I moved you over to the couch?

ANNE. [*Listening.*] Miep must have the radio on.

[PETER *picks up his papers, going over to the couch beside* MRS. VAN DAAN.]

MR. VAN DAAN. [*Accusingly, to* PETER.] Haven't you finished yet?

PETER. No.

The Diary of Anne Frank, Act I 383

AT A GLANCE

- *Scene 3 (continued):* Anne tries on Mrs. Van Daan's coat.
- Mrs. Van Daan tells the group about her boyfriends and flirts with Mr. Frank.

1 CHARACTERIZATION

Anne is resentful of Margot's conscientiousness and excellent work.

2 THEME

Mrs. Van Daan treasures memories of her family and her girlhood. Her reminiscences make a sad contrast to the confined life of Anne, Margot, and Peter.

3 DIALOGUE

Mrs. Van Daan's popularity seems to be an old topic in their family. Mr. Van Daan is characteristically embarrassed and impatient at his wife's display.

GUIDED READING

LITERAL QUESTIONS

1a. What comment does Anne make when Margot asks her father about her work? (Anne interrupts with, "Excellent, excellent, excellent, excellent.")

2a. What does Mr. Van Daan say as a caution to his wife about what she says in front of Anne? (He says that Anne writes about everything in her diary.)

INFERENTIAL QUESTIONS

1b. What does this reveal about Anne's feelings? (She seems to resent Margot's being such a good student.)

2b. How does Mr. Van Daan feel about the diary? (He seems to feel that it is intrusive.)

- *Scene 3 (continued):* Mr. Frank agrees to tutor Peter.
- Mrs. Van Daan and Mr. Van Daan argue about his smoking.
- Mrs. Frank tries to keep the peace.

1 CONFLICT

The Van Daans' conflict over Peter's studies is apparently a familiar one.

2 PLOT: CONFLICT

Otherwise minor quarrels are magnified because they are aired outside the privacy of the family and, in this situation, absorbed by the ever-curious Anne.

3 CHARACTERIZATION

In contrast to Anne's curiosity, Mrs. Frank is pained when there is open confrontation in the group. She tries to change the subject to something uncontroversial.

---

1 **MR. VAN DAAN.** You ought to be ashamed of yourself.

PETER. All right. All right. I'm a dunce. I'm a hopeless case. Why do I go on?

MRS. VAN DAAN. You're not hopeless. Don't talk that way. It's just that you haven't anyone to help you, like the girls have. [*To* MR. FRANK.] Maybe you could help him, Mr. Frank?

MR. FRANK. I'm sure that his father . . . ?

MR. VAN DAAN. Not me. I can't do anything with him. He won't listen to me. You go ahead . . . if you want.

MR. FRANK. [*Going to* PETER.] What about it, Peter? Shall we make our school coeducational?

MRS. VAN DAAN. [*Kissing* MR. FRANK.] You're an angel, Mr. Frank. An angel. I don't know why I didn't meet you before I met that one there. Here, sit down, Mr. Frank. . . . [*She forces him down on the couch beside* PETER.] Now, Peter, you listen to Mr. Frank.

MR. FRANK. It might be better for us to go into Peter's room.

MRS. VAN DAAN. That's right. You go in there, Peter. You listen to Mr. Frank. Mr. Frank is a highly educated man.

[*As* MR. FRANK *is about to follow* PETER *into his room,* MRS. FRANK *stops him and wipes the lipstick from his lips. Then she closes the door after them.*]

ANNE. [*On the floor, listening.*] Shh! I can hear a man's voice talking.

MR. VAN DAAN. [*To* ANNE.] Isn't it bad enough here without your sprawling all over the place?

[ANNE *sits up.*]

MRS. VAN DAAN. [*To* MR. VAN DAAN.] If you didn't

smoke so much, you wouldn't be so bad-tempered.

MR. VAN DAAN. Am I smoking? Do you see me smoking?

MRS. VAN DAAN. Don't tell me you've used up all those cigarettes.

MR. VAN DAAN. One package. Miep only bought me one package.

MRS. VAN DAAN. It's a filthy habit anyway. It's a good time to break yourself.

MR. VAN DAAN. Oh, stop it, please.

MRS. VAN DAAN. You're smoking up all our money. You know that, don't you?

2 **MR. VAN DAAN.** Will you shut up? [*During this,* MRS. FRANK *and* MARGOT *have studiously kept their eyes down. But* ANNE, *seated on the floor, has been following the discussion interestedly.* MR. VAN DAAN *turns to see her staring up at him.*] And what are you staring at?

ANNE. I never heard grown-ups quarrel before. I thought only children quarreled.

MR. VAN DAAN. This isn't a quarrel! It's a discussion. And I never heard children so rude before.

ANNE. [*Rising, indignantly.*] I, rude!

MR. VAN DAAN. Yes!

3 **MRS. FRANK.** [*Quickly.*] Anne, will you get me my knitting? [ANNE *goes to get it.*] I must remember, when Miep comes, to ask her to bring me some more wool.

MARGOT. [*Going to her room.*] I need some hairpins and some soap. I made a list. [*She goes into her bedroom to get the list.*]

MRS. FRANK. [*To* ANNE.] Have you some library books for Miep when she comes?

ANNE. It's a wonder that Miep has a life of her

GUIDED READING

LITERAL QUESTIONS

1a. With whom does Mr. Van Daan argue? (He argues with Peter, Mrs. Van Daan, and Anne.)

2a. How does Anne react when the Van Daans quarrel? How do Margot and her mother react? (Anne watches intently; Margot and her mother look down.)

INFERENTIAL QUESTIONS

1b. Why do you think Mr. Van Daan is arguing? (He is probably frustrated with their cramped quarters.)

2b. What differences in temperament do these reactions demonstrate? (Margot and her mother are proper and demure; Anne is open and curious.)

own, the way we make her run errands for us. Please, Miep, get me some starch. Please take my hair out and have it cut. Tell me all the latest news, Miep. [*She goes over, kneeling on the couch beside* MRS. VAN DAAN.] Did you know she was engaged? His name is Dirk, and Miep's afraid the Nazis will ship him off to Germany to work in one of their war plants. That's what they're doing with some of the young Dutchmen . . . they pick them up off the streets—

MR. VAN DAAN. [*Interrupting.*] Don't you ever get tired of talking? Suppose you try keeping still for five minutes. Just five minutes.

[*He starts to pace again. Again* ANNE *follows him, mimicking him.* MRS. FRANK *jumps up and takes her by the arm up to the sink and gives her a glass of milk.*]

MRS. FRANK. Come here, Anne. It's time for your glass of milk.

MR. VAN DAAN. Talk, talk, talk. I never heard such a child. Where is my . . . ? Every evening it's the same, talk, talk, talk. [*He looks around.*] Where is my . . . ?

MRS. VAN DAAN. What're you looking for?

MR. VAN DAAN. My pipe. Have you seen my pipe?

MRS. VAN DAAN. What good's a pipe? You haven't got any tobacco.

MR. VAN DAAN. At least I'll have something to hold in my mouth! [*Opening* MARGOT's *bedroom door.*] Margot, have you seen my pipe?

MARGOT. It was on the table last night.

[ANNE *puts her glass of milk on the table and picks up his pipe, hiding it behind her back.*]

MR. VAN DAAN. I know, I know. Anne, did you see my pipe? . . . Anne!

MRS. FRANK. Anne, Mr. Van Daan is speaking to you.

ANNE. Am I allowed to talk now?

MR. VAN DAAN. You're the most aggravating . . . The trouble with you is, you've been spoiled. What you need is a good old-fashioned spanking.

ANNE. [*Mimicking* MRS. VAN DAAN.] "Remember, Mr. So-an-So, remember I'm a lady." [*She thrusts the pipe into his mouth, then picks up her glass of milk.*]

MR. VAN DAAN. [*Restraining himself with difficulty.*] Why aren't you nice and quiet like your sister Margot? Why do you have to show off all the time? Let me give you a little advice, young lady. Men don't like that kind of thing in a girl. You know that? A man likes a girl who'll listen to him once in a while . . . a domestic girl, who'll keep her house shining for her husband . . . who loves to cook and sew and . . .

ANNE. I'd cut my throat first! I'd open my veins! I'm going to be remarkable! I'm going to Paris . . .

MR. VAN DAAN. [*Scoffingly.*] Paris!

ANNE. . . . to study music and art.

MR. VAN DAAN. Yeah! Yeah!

ANNE. I'm going to be a famous dancer or singer . . . or something wonderful.

[*She makes a wide gesture, spilling the glass of milk on the fur coat in* MRS. VAN DAAN's *lap.* MARGOT *rushes quickly over with a towel.* ANNE *tries to brush the milk off with her skirt.*]

MRS. VAN DAAN. Now look what you've done . . . you clumsy little fool! My beautiful fur coat my father gave me . . .

ANNE. I'm so sorry.

The Diary of Anne Frank, Act I 385

GUIDED READING

LITERAL QUESTIONS

1a. What complaint does Mr. Van Daan make about Anne? (He complains that she talks all the time.)

2a. What dream does Anne have for her future? (She wants to be a famous dancer or singer or something "remarkable.")

INFERENTIAL QUESTIONS

1b. Why do you suppose this trait is especially annoying to Mr. Van Daan? (He and his son are quiet. The close quarters exaggerate slight annoyances.)

2b. What do these ambitions tell you about Anne? (She is self-confident and hopeful about the future, despite the horrors of the present.)

- *Scene 3 (continued):* Mrs. Van Daan storms out of the room.
- Mrs. Frank tells Anne she should be more like Margot.
- Mrs. Frank bemoans the tension and the bickering.

1 THEME

As family life continues to be strained, Mrs. Frank holds Margot up as a role model for Anne. Anne rejects Margot's behavior as too passive.

2 PLOT: CONFLICT

Anne finally lashes out at being constantly compared unfavorably with Margot, who is so unlike her.

3 PLOT: SUSPENSE

Mrs. Frank's revelation that she had not been in favor of including the Van Daans increases suspense: We wonder if and how the two families can coexist.

MRS. VAN DAAN. What do you care? It isn't yours. . . . So go on, ruin it! Do you know what that coat cost? Do you? And now look at it! Look at it!

ANNE. I'm very, very sorry.

[MRS. VAN DAAN *goes up the stairs, clutching the coat.* MR. VAN DAAN *starts after her.*]

MR. VAN DAAN. Petronella . . . *liefje! Leifje!* . . . Come back . . . the supper . . . come back!

MRS. FRANK. Anne, you must not behave in that way.

ANNE. It was an accident. Anyone can have an accident.

MRS. FRANK. I don't mean that. I mean the answering back. You must not answer back. They are our guests. We must always show the greatest courtesy to them. We're all living under terrible tension. [*She stops as* MARGOT *indicates that* MR. VAN DAAN *can hear. When he is gone, she continues.*] That's why we **1** must control ourselves. . . . You don't hear Margot getting into arguments with them, do you? Watch Margot. She's always courteous with them. Never familiar. She keeps her distance. And they respect her for it. Try to be like Margot.

ANNE. And have them walk all over me, the way they do her? No, thanks!

MRS. FRANK. I'm not afraid that anyone is going to walk all over you, Anne. I'm afraid for other people, that you'll walk on them. I don't know what happens to you, Anne. You are wild, self-willed. If I had ever talked to my mother as you talk to me . . .

ANNE. Things have changed. People aren't like that any more. "Yes, Mother." "No, Mother." "Anything you say, Mother." I've got to fight things out for myself! Make something of myself!

386   *Drama*

MRS. FRANK. It isn't necessary to fight to do it. Margot doesn't fight, and isn't she . . . ?

2 ANNE. [*Violently, rebellious.*] Margot! Margot! Margot! That's all I hear from everyone . . . how wonderful Margot is . . . "Why aren't you like Margot?"

MARGOT. [*Protesting.*] Oh, come on, Anne, don't be so . . .

ANNE. [*Paying no attention.*] Everything she does is right, and everything I do is wrong! I'm the goat around here! . . . You're all against me! . . . And you worst of all!

[*She rushes off into her room and throws herself down on the settee, stifling her sobs.* MRS. FRANK *sighs and starts toward the stove.*]

MRS. FRANK. [*To* MARGOT.] Let's put the soup on the stove . . . if there's anyone who cares to eat. Margot, will you take the bread out? [MARGOT *gets the bread from the cupboard.*] I don't know how we can go on living this way . . . I can't say a word to Anne . . . she flies at me. . . .

MARGOT. You know Anne. In half an hour she'll be out here, laughing and joking.

3 MRS. FRANK. And . . . [*She makes a motion upwards, indicating the* VAN DAANS.] I told your father it wouldn't work . . . but no . . . no . . . he had to ask them, he said . . . he owed it to him, he said. Well, he knows now that I was right! These quarrels! . . . This bickering!

MARGOT. [*With a warning look.*] Shush. Shush.

[*The buzzer for the door sounds.* MRS. FRANK *gasps, startled.*]

MRS. FRANK. Every time I hear that sound, my heart stops!

MARGOT. [*Starting for* PETER'S *door.*] It's Miep.

GUIDED READING

LITERAL QUESTIONS

1a. How does Anne react when her mother suggests she be more like Margot? (She reacts violently and rebelliously.)

2a. What does Mrs. Frank say she felt about Mr. Frank's plan to invite the Van Daans to their attic? (that it wouldn't work)

INFERENTIAL QUESTIONS

1b. Why do you think Anne's reaction is so strong? (Anne and Margot are very different, and Anne has no doubt been compared unfavorably with Margot in the past.)

2b. Why do you think Mr. Frank acted contrary to his wife's advice? (because of his generosity and feeling of indebtedness to Mr. Van Daan)

1 [She knocks at the door.] Father?

[MR. FRANK comes quickly from PETER's room.]

MR. FRANK. Thank you, Margot. [As he goes down the steps to open the outer door.] Has everyone his list?

MARGOT. I'll get my books. [Giving her mother a list.] Here's your list. [MARGOT goes into her and ANNE's bedroom on the right. ANNE sits up, hiding her tears as MARGOT comes in.] Miep's here.

[MARGOT picks up her books and goes back. ANNE hurries over to the mirror smoothing her hair.]

MR. VAN DAAN. [Coming down the stairs.] Is it Miep?

MARGOT. Yes. Father's gone down to let her in.

2 MRS. FRANK. [To MR. VAN DAAN.] I can't tell you how unhappy I am about Mrs. Van Daan's coat. Anne should never have touched it.

MR. VAN DAAN. She'll be all right.

MRS. FRANK. Is there anything I can do?

MR. VAN DAAN. Don't worry.

[He turns to meet MIEP. But it is not MIEP who comes up the steps. It is MR. KRALER, followed by MR. FRANK. Their faces are grave. ANNE comes from the bedroom. PETER comes from his room.]

3

MRS. FRANK. Mr. Kraler!

MR. VAN DAAN. How are you, Mr. Kraler?

MARGOT. This is a surprise.

MRS. FRANK. When Mr. Kraler comes, the sun begins to shine.

MR. VAN DAAN. Miep is coming?

MR. KRALER. Not tonight. [MR. KRALER goes to MARGOT and MRS. FRANK and ANNE, shaking hands with them.]

MRS. FRANK. Wouldn't you like a cup of coffee? . . . Or, better still, will you have supper with us?

MR. FRANK. Mr. Kraler has something to talk over with us. Something has happened, he says, which demands an immediate decision.

MRS. FRANK. [Fearful.] What is it?

[MR. KRALER sits down on the couch. As he talks he takes bread, cabbages, milk, etc., from his briefcase, giving them to MARGOT and ANNE to put away.]

MR. KRALER. Usually, when I come up here, I try to bring you some bit of good news. What's the use of telling you the bad news when there's nothing that you can do about it? But today something has happened. . . . Dirk . . . Miep's Dirk, you know, came to me just now.
4 He tells me that he has a Jewish friend living near him. A dentist. He says he's in trouble. He begged me, could I do anything for this man? Could I find him a hiding place? . . . So I've come to you. . . . I know it's a terrible thing to ask of you, living as you are, but would you take him in with you?

MR. FRANK. Of course we will.

MR. KRALER. [Rising.] It'll be just for a night or two . . . until I find some other place. This happened so suddenly that I didn't know where to turn.

MR. FRANK. Where is he?

MR. KRALER. Downstairs in the office.

MR. FRANK. Good. Bring him up.

MR. KRALER. His name is Dussel[23] . . . Jan Dussel.

---

23. **Dussel** [doo'səl]

The Diary of Anne Frank, Act I 387

■ *Scene 3 (continued):* Mrs. Frank apologizes to Mr. Van Daan.
■ Mr. Kraler comes to the attic in Miep's place.
■ He asks the group to make room for Jan Dussel, a friend of Miep's fiancé.

1 STAGE DIRECTIONS

The nonchalant manner in which the characters go about this sequence of actions reveals that this routine is now familiar.

2 PLOT: CONFLICT

Mrs. Frank apologizes to Mr. Van Daan. The conflict between Anne and Mr. Van Daan appears resolved. However, our knowledge of the characters makes us doubt that the conflict is over.

3 STAGING

If we were viewing the play, the grave faces of Mr. Kraler and Mr. Frank described here would prepare us for a new obstacle, even before they speak.

4 SETTING

The request to accept another person into a space that is already too crowded increases tension and suspense.

GUIDED READING

LITERAL QUESTIONS

1a. Who comes to the attic instead of Miep? (Mr. Kraler)

2a. What problem does Mr. Kraler bring to the group? (He must find a hiding place for a Jewish dentist.)

INFERENTIAL QUESTIONS

1b. What indication is given before Mr. Kraler speaks that he has bad news? (Both Mr. Frank and Mr. Kraler enter with grave faces.)

2b. Why is this a bad time to make such a request? (The day's quarrels show that, after two months in close quarters, the members of the group are not getting along well.)

- *Scene 3 (continued):* Mr. Frank apologizes for not consulting the others.
- Mr. Van Daan expresses concern over the food supply.
- It is decided that Anne will share her room with Mr. Dussel.

1 PLOT: CONFLICT

Mr. Van Daan's concern is typical of his self-centered attitude—a trait that embarrasses Peter. Van Daan's concern foreshadows what could be a source of major conflict.

2 CHARACTERIZATION

This short exchange points out Anne's naiveté concerning propriety. It also reconfirms that Mrs. Frank still regards Anne as a child.

3 THEME

Mr. Frank's wish to toast Mr. Dussel's arrival is an expression of the theme that love and friendship can flourish in the most dire circumstances.

4 CHARACTERIZATION

Mr. and Mrs. Van Daans' unhappiness at sharing their crowded hiding place is in sharp contrast to Mr. Frank's generosity.

MR. FRANK. Dussel . . . I think I know him.

MR. KRALER. I'll get him.

[*He goes quickly down the steps and out.* MR. FRANK *suddenly becomes conscious of the others.*]

MR. FRANK. Forgive me. I spoke without consulting you. But I knew you'd feel as I do.

1 MR. VAN DAAN. There's no reason for you to consult anyone. This is your place. You have a right to do exactly as you please. The only thing I feel . . . there's so little food as it is . . . and to take in another person . . .

[PETER *turns away, ashamed of his father.*]

MR. FRANK. We can stretch the food a little. It's only for a few days.

MR. VAN DAAN. You want to make a bet?

MRS. FRANK. I think it's fine to have him. But, Otto, where are you going to put him? Where?

PETER. He can have my bed. I can sleep on the floor. I wouldn't mind.

MR. FRANK. That's good of you, Peter. But your room's too small . . . even for *you.*

ANNE. I have a much better idea. I'll come in here with you and Mother, and Margot can take Peter's room, and Peter can go in our room with Mr. Dussel.

MARGOT. That's right. We could do that.

MR. FRANK. No, Margot. You mustn't sleep in that room . . . neither your nor Anne. Mouschi has caught some rats in there. Peter's brave. He doesn't mind.

ANNE. Then how about *this?* I'll come in here with you and Mother, and Mr. Dussel can have my bed.

MRS. FRANK. No. No. *No!* Margot will come in here with us and he can have her bed. It's the

388 *Drama*

---

only way. Margot, bring your things in here. Help her, Anne.

[MARGOT *hurries into her room to get her things.*]

2 ANNE. [*To her mother.*] Why Margot? Why can't I come in here?

MRS. FRANK. Because it wouldn't be proper . . . Please, Anne. Don't argue. Please.

[ANNE *starts slowly away.*]

MR. FRANK. [*To* ANNE.] You don't mind sharing your room with Mr. Dussel, do you, Anne?

ANNE. No. No, of course not.

MR. FRANK. Good. [ANNE *goes off into her bedroom, helping* MARGOT. MR. FRANK *starts to search in the cupboards.*] Where's the cognac?

MRS. FRANK. It's there. But, Otto, I was saving it in case of illness.

3 MR. FRANK. I think we couldn't find a better time to use it. Peter, will you get five glasses for me?

[PETER *goes for the glasses.* MARGOT *comes out of her bedroom, carrying her possessions, which she hangs behind a curtain in the main room.* MR. FRANK *finds the cognac and pours it into the five glasses that* PETER *brings him.* MR. VAN DAAN *stands looking on sourly.* MRS. VAN DAAN *comes downstairs and looks around at all of the bustle.*]

4 MRS. VAN DAAN. What's happening? What's going on?

MR. VAN DAAN. Someone's moving in with us.

MRS. VAN DAAN. In here? You're joking.

MARGOT. It's only for a night or two . . . until Mr. Kraler finds him another place.

GUIDED READING

LITERAL QUESTIONS

1a. What problem does Mr. Van Daan mention? (There is so little food even now.)

2a. What does Mr. Frank want to serve in honor of Mr. Dussel's arrival? (cognac)

INFERENTIAL QUESTIONS

1b. Why is Peter ashamed of his father's remark? (Peter doesn't want his father to act selfishly or greedily in front of the others.)

2b. What does Mrs. Frank's objection reveal about her? (She is frugal and practical; she wants to be prepared for an emergency.)

MR. VAN DAAN. Yeah! Yeah!

[MR. FRANK *hurries over as* MR. KRALER *and* DUSSEL *come up.* DUSSEL *is a man in his late fifties, meticulous, finicky . . . bewildered now. He wears a raincoat. He carries a briefcase, stuffed full, and a small medicine case.*]

MR. FRANK. Come in, Mr. Dussel.

MR. KRALER. This is Mr. Frank.

DUSSEL. Mr. Otto Frank?

MR. FRANK. Yes. Let me take your things. [*He takes the hat and briefcase, but* DUSSEL *clings to his medicine case.*] This is my wife Edith . . . Mr. and Mrs. Van Daan . . . their son, Peter . . . and my daughters, Margot and Anne.

[DUSSEL *shakes hands with everyone.*]

MR. KRALER. Thank you, Mr. Frank. Thank you all. Mr. Dussel, I leave you in good hands. Oh . . . Dirk's coat.

[DUSSEL *hurriedly takes off the raincoat, giving it to* MR. KRALER. *Underneath is his white dentist's jacket, with a yellow Star of David on it.*]

DUSSEL. [*To* MR. KRALER.] What can I say to thank you . . . ?

MRS. FRANK. [*To* DUSSEL.] Mr. Kraler and Miep . . . They're our lifeline. Without them we couldn't live.

MR. KRALER. Please, please. You make us seem very heroic. It isn't that at all. We simply don't like the Nazis. [*To* MR. FRANK, *who offers him a drink.*] No, thanks. [*Then going on.*] We don't like their methods. We don't like . . .

MR. FRANK. [*Smiling.*] I know. I know. "No one's going to tell us Dutchmen what to do with our Jews!"

MR. KRALER. [*To* DUSSEL.] Pay no attention to Mr. Frank. I'll be up tomorrow to see that they're treating you right. [*To* MR. FRANK.] Don't trouble to come down again. Peter will bolt the door after me, won't you, Peter?

PETER. Yes, sir.

MR. FRANK. Thank you, Peter. I'll do it.

MR. KRALER. Good night. Good night.

GROUP. Good night, Mr. Kraler. We'll see you tomorrow, *etc. etc.*

[MR. KRALER *goes out with* MR. FRANK. MRS. FRANK *gives each one of the "grown-ups" a glass of cognac.*]

MRS. FRANK. Please, Mr. Dussel, sit down.

[MR. DUSSEL *sinks into a chair.* MRS. FRANK *gives him a glass of cognac.*]

DUSSEL. I'm dreaming. I know it. I can't believe my eyes. Mr. Otto Frank here! [*To* MRS. FRANK.] You're not in Switzerland then? A woman told me . . . She said she'd gone to your house . . . the door was open, everything was in disorder, dishes in the sink. She said she found a piece of paper in the wastebasket with an address scribbled on it . . . an address in Zurich. She said you must have escaped to Zurich.[24]

ANNE. Father put that there purposely . . . just so people would think that very thing!

DUSSEL. And you've been *here* all the time?

MRS. FRANK. All the time . . . ever since July.

[ANNE *speaks to her father as he comes back.*]

ANNE. It worked, Pim . . . the address you left! Mr. Dussel says that people believe we escaped to Switzerland.

---

24. **Zurich** [zoor′ik]: largest city in Switzerland, a neutral country and safe home for many refugees.

The Diary of Anne Frank, Act I 389

AT A GLANCE

- *Scene 3 (continued):* Mr. Dussel is introduced to the group.
- He expresses his gratitude.
- The Franks learn that people think they escaped to Zurich.

1 STAGE DIRECTIONS

The stage directions develop a character. Dussel is described as meticulous and finicky. This provides a warning that he may be difficult to live with.

2 THEME

Mr. Kraler and Miep do not consider themselves to be heroes but rather ordinary citizens. Nevertheless, by living up to their own ideals, Mr. Kraler and Miep do seem heroic.

3 CHARACTERIZATION

This information helps characterize Mr. Frank as clever and resourceful.

GUIDED READING

LITERAL QUESTIONS

1a. What does Mr. Kraler say when Mrs. Frank praises them? (He says he does not think he and Miep are being heroic.)

2a. Why is Mr. Dussel surprised to find the Franks in the attic? (He thought they had escaped to Zurich.)

INFERENTIAL QUESTIONS

1b. What does this tell you about Mr. Kraler? (He is modest and truly a hero; he is motivated by a sense of justice and outraged by Nazi terrors.)

2b. Why is Anne so elated at Mr. Dussel's surprise? (She probably believes that because the plan has worked so far they will be safe.)

- *Scene 3 (continued):* The group drinks a toast to Mr. Dussel.
- Mr. Dussel tells them about the call-up notices, searches, and deportations.
- Anne learns that her friend Jopie is gone.

1 CHARACTERIZATION

When Mr. Dussel bolts his drink, he reveals the nervous strain that he has been under.

2 PLOT: CONFLICT

The group learns for the first time how severely the war has escalated.

3 DIALOGUE

In a few sentences Mr. Dussel describes the horrors of the seizure and deportation of the Jews in Amsterdam.

4 THEME

The awful news about her friend Jopie brings the horrors of deportation from a general level to a personal one for Anne.

---

1 **MR. FRANK.** I'm glad. . . . And now let's have a little drink to welcome Mr. Dussel. [*Before they can drink,* DUSSEL *bolts his drink.* MR. FRANK *smiles and raises his glass.*] To Mr. Dussel. Welcome. We're very honored to have you with us.

MRS. FRANK. To Mr. Dussel, welcome.

[*The* VAN DAANS *murmur a welcome. The "grown-ups" drink.*]

MRS. VAN DAAN. Um. That was good.

MR. VAN DAAN. Did Mr. Kraler warn you that you won't get much to eat here? You can imagine . . . three ration books among the seven of us . . . and now you make eight.

[PETER *walks away, humiliated. Outside a street organ is heard dimly.*]

2 **DUSSEL.** [*Rising.*] Mr. Van Daan, you don't realize what is happening outside that you should warn me of a thing like that. You don't realize what's going on. . . . [*As* MR. VAN DAAN *starts his characteristic pacing,* DUSSEL *turns to speak to the others.*] Right here in Amsterdam every day hundreds of Jews disappear. . . . They surround a block and search house by house. Children come home from school to find their parents gone. Hundreds are being deported . . . people that you and I know . . . the Hallensteins . . . the Wessels . . .

MRS. FRANK. [*In tears.*] Oh, no. No!

DUSSEL. They get their call-up notice . . . come to the Jewish theater on such and such a day and hour . . . bring only what you can carry 3 in a rucksack. And if you refuse the call-up notice, then they come and drag you from your home and ship you off to Mauthausen. The death camp!

MRS. FRANK. We didn't know that things had got so much worse.

390 *Drama*

DUSSEL. Forgive me for speaking so.

4 **ANNE.** [*Coming to* DUSSEL.] Do you know the deWaals? . . . What's become of them? Their daughter Jopie and I are in the same class. Jopie's my best friend.

DUSSEL. They are gone.

ANNE. Gone?

DUSSEL. With all the others.

ANNE. Oh, no. Not Jopie!

[*She turns away, in tears.* MRS. FRANK *motions to* MARGOT *to comfort her.* MARGOT *goes to* ANNE, *putting her arms comfortingly around her.*]

MRS. VAN DAAN. There were some people called Wagner. They lived near us . . . ?

MR. FRANK. [*Interrupting with a glance at* ANNE.] I think we should put this off until later. We all have many questions we want to ask. . . . But I'm sure that Mr. Dussel would like to get settled before supper.

DUSSEL. Thank you. I would. I brought very little with me.

MR. FRANK. [*Giving him his hat and briefcase.*] I'm sorry we can't give you a room alone. But I hope you won't be too uncomfortable. We've had to make strict rules here . . . a schedule of hours. . . . We'll tell you after supper. Anne, would you like to take Mr. Dussel to his room?

ANNE. [*Controlling her tears.*] If you'll come with me, Mr. Dussel? [*She starts for her room.*]

DUSSEL. [*Shaking hands with each in turn.*] Forgive me if I haven't really expressed my gratitude to all of you. This has been such a shock to me. I'd always thought of myself as

---

GUIDED READING

LITERAL QUESTIONS

1a. What is the first thing Mr. Van Daan tells Mr. Dussel about life in the attic? (Mr. Van Daan tells Dussel that he won't get much to eat.)

2a. Whom does Anne inquire about? (She inquires about her best friend, Jopie deWaals.)

INFERENTIAL QUESTIONS

1b. Why does Mr. Dussel think this is of little importance? (Because Mr. Dussel has seen Jews disappear, food seems less important to him.)

2b. What does Anne seem to be discovering as she hears about Jopie's disappearance? (For the first time in the play, she seems to realize the horrors of the world outside.)

AT A GLANCE

- *Scene 3 (continued):* Dussel says he has always considered himself Dutch.
- Dussel warns Anne that he will have trouble living with other people.

1 READING SKILLS: INFERENCES

We can infer that Mr. Kraler does not want the group to be upset by outside events.

2 PLOT: FORESHADOWING

Dussel warns Anne that he may be very difficult to live with. This provides yet another possibility for future conflict.

3 CHARACTERIZATION

Anne's concern for Dussel's loneliness is genuine and typical of her generous spirit.

Dutch. I was born in Holland. My father was born in Holland, and my grandfather. And now . . . after all these years . . . [*He breaks off.*] If you'll excuse me.

[DUSSEL *gives a little bow and hurries off after* ANNE. MR. FRANK *and the others are subdued.*]

ANNE. [*Turning on the light.*] Well, here we are.

[DUSSEL *looks around the room. In the main room* MARGOT *speaks to her mother.*]

1 MARGOT. The news sounds pretty bad, doesn't it? It's so different from what Mr. Kraler tells us. Mr. Kraler says things are improving.

MR. VAN DAAN. I like it better the way Kraler tells it.

[*They resume their occupations, quietly.* PETER *goes off into his room. In* ANNE's *room,* ANNE *turns to* DUSSEL.]

ANNE. You're going to share the room with me.

2 DUSSEL. I'm a man who's always lived alone. I haven't had to adjust myself to others. I hope you'll bear with me until I learn.

ANNE. Let me help you. [*She takes his briefcase.*] Do you always live all alone? Have you no family at all?

DUSSEL. No one. [*He opens his medicine case and spreads his bottles on the dressing table.*]

3 ANNE. How dreadful. You must be terribly lonely.

The Diary of Anne Frank, Act I 391

GUIDED READING

LITERAL QUESTIONS

1a. What does Dussel tell about his family? (He and his father and grandfather were all born in Holland.)

2a. What does Dussel tell Anne about himself? (He tells her that he has always lived alone.)

INFERENTIAL QUESTIONS

1b. Why is his Dutch birth so significant to Dussel? (He thinks he is Dutch and, therefore, should not be deported because he is Jewish.)

2b. Why is Anne's response so characteristic of her? (Because she cares about everyone, she worries that he must be lonely.)

- *Scene 3 (continued):* Dussel tells Anne that he is allergic to fur-bearing animals.
- Dussel tells her he gets along well with children.

1 PLOT: CONFLICT

Dussel's allergy to fur-bearing animals is further indication of the difficulty he will probably have adjusting to life in the attic.

2 THEME

Anne shows interest in another family and expresses worries about the baby's safety. Anne has strong feelings of love and concern for others.

3 CHARACTERIZATION

Anne shows her desire to get along with Dussel by adjusting the schedule to fit his needs.

4 STAGING

The change in lighting provides a smooth transition from a scene with characters talking to a moment when Anne reads from her diary.

DUSSEL. I'm used to it.

ANNE. I don't think I could ever get used to it. Didn't you even have a pet? A cat, or a dog?

1 **DUSSEL.** I have an allergy for fur-bearing animals. They give me asthma.

ANNE. Oh, dear. Peter has a cat.

DUSSEL. Here? He has it here?

ANNE. Yes. But we hardly ever see it. He keeps it in his room all the time. I'm sure it will be all right.

DUSSEL. Let us hope so. [*He takes some pills to fortify himself.*]

ANNE. That's Margot's bed, where you're going to sleep. I sleep on the sofa there. [*Indicating the clothes hooks on the wall.*] We cleared these off for your things. [*She goes over to the window.*] The best part about this room . . .

2 you can look down and see a bit of the street and the canal. There's a houseboat . . . you can see the end of it . . . a bargeman lives there with his family. . . . They have a baby and he's just beginning to walk and I'm so afraid he's going to fall into the canal some day. I watch him. . . .

DUSSEL. [*Interrupting.*] Your father spoke of a schedule.

ANNE. [*Coming away from the window.*] Oh, yes. It's mostly about the times we have to be quiet. And times for the w.c. You can use it now if you like.

DUSSEL. [*Stiffly.*] No, thank you.

ANNE. I suppose you think it's awful, my talking about a thing like that. But you don't know how important it can get to be, especially when you're frightened. . . . About this room, the way Margot and I did . . . she had it to herself in the afternoons for studying, reading . . . lessons, you know . . . and I took

392 *Drama*

---

the mornings. Would that be all right with you?

3 **DUSSEL.** I'm not at my best in the morning.

ANNE. You stay in here in the mornings then. I'll take the room in the afternoons.

DUSSEL. Tell me, when you're in here, what happens to me? Where am I spending my time? In there, with all the people?

ANNE. Yes.

DUSSEL. I see. I see.

ANNE. We have supper at half past six.

DUSSEL. [*Going over to the sofa.*] Then, if you don't mind . . . I like to lie down quietly for ten minutes before eating. I find it helps the digestion.

ANNE. Of course. I hope I'm not going to be too much of a bother to you. I seem to be able to get everyone's back up.

[DUSSEL *lies down on the sofa, curled up, his back to her.*]

DUSSEL. I always get along very well with children. My patients all bring their children to me, because they know I get on well with them. So don't you worry about that.

[ANNE *leans over him, taking his hand and shaking it gratefully.*]

ANNE. Thank you. Thank you, Mr. Dussel.

4 [*The lights dim to darkness. The curtain falls on the scene.* ANNE'S *voice comes to us faintly at first, and then with increasing power.*]

ANNE'S VOICE. . . . And yesterday I finished Cissy Van Marxvelt's latest book. I think she is a first-class writer. I shall definitely let my children read her. Monday, the twenty-first of September, nineteen forty-two. Mr. Dussel and I had another battle yesterday. Yes, Mr.

GUIDED READING

LITERAL QUESTION

1a. What single piece of hopeful information does Dussel tell Anne about himself? (He tells her that he has always gotten along well with children.)

INFERENTIAL QUESTION

1b. Why does this information soon seem ironic? (In her next diary entry Anne tells about having "another battle" with Mr. Dussel.)

Dussel! According to him, nothing, I repeat . . . nothing, is right about me . . . my appearance, my character, my manners. While he was going on at me I thought . . . sometime I'll give you such a smack that you'll fly right up to the ceiling! Why is it that every grownup thinks he knows the way to bring up children? Particularly the grown-ups that never had any. I keep wishing that Peter was a girl instead of a boy. Then I would have someone to talk to. Margot's a darling, but she takes everything too seriously. To pause for a moment on the subject of Mrs. Van Daan. I must tell you that her attempts to flirt with Father are getting her nowhere. Pim, thank goodness, won't play.

[*As she is saying the last lines, the curtain rises on the darkened scene.* ANNE's *voice fades out.*]

STUDY QUESTIONS

Recalling

1. In what year does the play begin? Why does Mr. Frank want to leave Amsterdam?
2. From Anne's diary list three rules that the Nazis imposed on the Jews.
3. When does Scene 2 begin? What words in the stage directions describe Anne when she first appears in Scene 2?
4. List five restrictions on life in the annex that Mr. Frank announces to the group.
5. When does Anne realize for the first time what "going into hiding" means? What cannot be locked up, according to Mr. Frank?
6. Tell how Anne irritates, in turn, Peter, Mr. Van Daan, and Mrs. Van Daan in Scene 3.
7. About what do Anne and her mother disagree?
8. What request does Mr. Kraler make of the group in Scene 3? What is Mr. Frank's answer, and how does Mr. Van Daan react to it?

Interpreting

9. Give several examples of Anne's words or actions in these three scenes that bear out the description of her on her first entrance. From what you have seen of Anne so far, what qualities would *you* add to this description?
10. Who is the leader of the group in the attic? What qualities make this person the leader?

Extending

11. What future problems do you foresee for the group in the attic?

VOCABULARY

Using a Pronunciation Key

The Diary of Anne Frank contains a number of foreign words and names for which pronunciations are given in the footnotes. The phonetic symbols in these footnotes are explained in the **pronunciation key** in the Glossary at the back of this book. For example, in the footnote explaining how to pronounce *Annele*, the first *a* is written as *ä*. If you look in the pronunciation key in the Glossary, you will see that this sound is to be pronounced like the *a* in *car*.

Using the footnotes and the pronunciation key in the Glossary, answer the following questions.

1. Is the *i* in *Miep* to be pronounced like the *i* in *it*, the *i* in *ice*, or the *e* in *me*?
2. Is the *w* in *deWaal* to be pronounced like the *v* in *very*, the *w* in *white*, or the *w* in *wet*?
3. Is the first *e* in *Anneke* to be pronounced like the *e* in *me*, the *a* in *ago*, or the *e* in *taken*?
4. Is the *v* in *Mazel tov* to be pronounced like the *w* in *wet*, the *v* in *very*, or the *f* in *five*?
5. Is the *ch* in *Zurich* to be pronounced like the *ch* in *chin*, the *k* in *kit*, or the *sh* in *shoe*?

The Diary of Anne Frank, Act I 393

AT A GLANCE

- *Scene 3 (continued):* Anne expresses to her diary her resentment of Dussel.
- She shows affection for Margot.
- She reveals her indignation at Mrs. Van Daan's flirting.

1 THEME

Anne resents the criticism she receives from Dussel and other adults and expresses her longing for a friend to confide in.

REFLECTING ON SCENES 1–3

Which member of the group seems most responsible for the friction in the annex? Why? (Some students may choose Anne, whose pent-up spirits have irritated nearly everyone. Others may point to Mr. Van Daan, citing his irritability and selfishness.)

STUDY QUESTIONS

1. 1945; holds too many memories of the past and his family
2. cannot attend Dutch schools, go to the movies, ride in autos or streetcars; must wear yellow stars and turn in their bikes; forced out of business
3. 1942; thirteen years old, curious, quick, mercurial
4. must burn their trash; 8 A.M.–6 P.M.: must whisper and move only if necessary; cannot wear shoes or use any water
5. when she cannot get a pencil; the mind
6. hides Peter's socks; mimics Mr. Van Daan and hides his pipe; spills milk on Mrs. Van Daan's fur coat
7. behavior toward the Van Daans

8. ■ to take in Mr. Dussel
   ■ agrees; doesn't want to share the food and tight quarters
9. ■ *quick in movement:* tours the home upon meeting the Van Daans; *interested in everything:* eager to befriend Peter: wants to feed his cat, listens to the Van Daans' "discussions"; observes life outside; *mercurial:* reacts vociferously when Mr. Van Daan suggests that men like domestic girls; sobs when Mrs. Frank compares her unfavorably with Margot
   ■ bright, popular, direct, fun-loving, and affectionate
10. Mr. Frank; well-educated, respected, organized, confident
11. less space, food, and privacy for Anne; more quarreling

VOCABULARY

1. *e* in *me*
2. *v* in *very*
3. *a* in *ago*
4. *f* in *five*
5. *k* in *kit*

- *Scene 4:* Mr. Van Daan goes secretly to the food cupboard.
- Anne screams out in a nightmare.
- Mrs. Frank tries to comfort Anne.

1 STAGE DIRECTIONS

The stage directions indicate that several months have passed since the previous scene. To create the sense that it is the middle of the night, the stage directions call for a nearly dark stage.

2 MOOD

Off-stage sound effects of night life and the sound of airplanes establish the mood of Amsterdam, where everyday, commonplace events and grim wartime maneuvers occur simultaneously.

3 CHARACTERIZATION

Anne's fears are revealed as she screams out in a nightmare. This hysteria is a dramatic change from Anne the exuberant optimist.

4 THEME

This exchange briefly shows a different relationship between Anne and her mother. Rather than rejecting her mother's attention, Anne welcomes it.

5 CHARACTERIZATION

Mr. Dussel's lack of sympathy for Anne is characteristic of his self-centered behavior.

Scene 4

1 *It is the middle of the night, several months later. The stage is dark except for a little light which comes through the skylight in* PETER's *room.*

[Everyone is in bed. MR. *and* MRS. FRANK *lie on the couch in the main room, which has been pulled out to serve as a makeshift double bed.*

MARGOT *is sleeping on a mattress on the floor in the main room behind a curtain stretched across for privacy. The others are all in their accustomed rooms.*

2 *From outside we hear two drunken soldiers singing "Lili Marlene." A girl's high giggle is heard. The sound of running feet is heard coming closer and then fading in the distance. Throughout the scene there is the distant sound of airplanes passing overhead.*

A match suddenly flares up in the attic. We dimly see MR. VAN DAAN. *He is getting his bearings. He comes quickly down the stairs and goes to the cupboard where the food is stored. Again the match flares up, and is as quickly blown out. The dim figure is seen to steal back up the stairs.*

There is quiet for a second or two, broken only by the sound of airplanes, and running feet on the street below.

Suddenly out of the silence and the dark we hear ANNE *scream.]*

3 **ANNE.** [*Screaming.*] No! No! Don't . . . don't take me!

[She moans, tossing and crying in her sleep. The other people wake, terrified. DUSSEL *sits up in bed, furious.]*

DUSSEL. Shush! Anne! Anne, shush!

ANNE. [*Still in her nightmare.*] Save me! Save me!

394   Drama

[She screams and screams. DUSSEL *gets out of bed, going over to her, trying to wake her.]*

DUSSEL. Quiet! Quiet! You want someone to hear?

[In the main room MRS. FRANK *grabs a shawl and pulls it around her. She rushes in to* ANNE, *taking her in her arms.* MR. FRANK *hurriedly gets up, putting on his overcoat.* MARGOT *sits up, terrified.* PETER's *light goes on in his room.]*

4 **MRS. FRANK.** [*To* ANNE, *in her room.*] Hush, darling, hush. It's all right. It's all right. [*Over her shoulder to* DUSSEL.] Will you be kind enough to turn on the light, Mr. Dussel? [*Back to* ANNE.] It's nothing, my darling. It was just a dream.

*[*DUSSEL *turns on the light in the bedroom.* MRS. FRANK *holds* ANNE *in her arms. Gradually* ANNE *comes out of her nightmare, still trembling with horror.* MR. FRANK *comes into the room and goes quickly to the window, looking out to be sure that no one outside has heard* ANNE's *screams.* MRS. FRANK *holds* ANNE, *talking softly to her. In the main room* MARGOT *stands on a chair, turning on the center hanging lamp. A light goes on in the* VAN DAANS' *room overhead.* PETER *puts his robe on, coming out of his room.]*

DUSSEL. [*To* MRS. FRANK, *blowing his nose.*] Something must be done about that child, Mrs. Frank. Yelling like that! Who knows but there's somebody on the streets? She's endangering all our lives.

5 **MRS. FRANK.** Anne, darling.

DUSSEL. Every night she twists and turns. I don't sleep. I spend half my night shushing her. And now it's nightmares!

*[*MARGOT *comes to the door of* ANNE's *room,*

GUIDED READING

LITERAL QUESTIONS

1a. What does Mr. Van Daan do? (He sneaks downstairs to where the food is kept.)

2a. What causes Anne to cry out? (She is having a nightmare.)

INFERENTIAL QUESTIONS

1b. Why does he sneak to the cupboard? (probably to steal food)

2b. What does Anne's nightmare suggest about her cheerful daytime behavior? (She may be pushing anxieties to the back of her mind; they emerge only when she is unconscious.)

followed by PETER. MR. FRANK *goes to them, indicating that everything is all right.* PETER *takes* MARGOT *back.*]

MRS. FRANK. [*To* ANNE.] You're here, safe, you see? Nothing has happened. [*To* DUSSEL.] Please, Mr. Dussel, go back to bed. She'll be herself in a minute or two. Won't you, Anne?

DUSSEL. [*Picking up a book and a pillow.*] Thank you, but I'm going to the w.c. The one place where there's peace!

[*He stalks out.* MR. VAN DAAN, *in underwear and trousers, comes down the stairs.*]

MR. VAN DAAN. [*To* DUSSEL.] What is it? What happened?

1 **DUSSEL.** A nightmare. She was having a nightmare!

MR. VAN DAAN. I thought someone was murdering her.

DUSSEL. Unfortunately, no.

[*He goes into the bathroom.* MR. VAN DAAN *goes back up the stairs.* MR. FRANK, *in the main room, sends* PETER *back to his own bedroom.*]

2 **MR. FRANK.** Thank you, Peter. Go back to bed.

[PETER *goes back to his room.* MR. FRANK *follows him, turning out the light and looking out the window. Then he goes back to the main room and gets up on a chair, turning out the center hanging lamp.*]

MRS. FRANK. [*To* ANNE.] Would you like some water? [ANNE *shakes her head.*] Was it a very bad dream? Perhaps if you told me . . . ?

ANNE. I'd rather not talk about it.

MRS. FRANK. Poor darling. Try to sleep then. I'll sit right here beside you until you fall asleep. [*She brings a stool over, sitting there.*]

ANNE. You don't have to.

MRS. FRANK. But I'd like to stay with you . . . very much. Really.

3 **ANNE.** I'd rather you didn't.

MRS. FRANK. Good night, then. [*She leans down to kiss* ANNE. ANNE *throws her arm up over her face, turning away.* MRS. FRANK, *hiding her hurt, kisses* ANNE's *arm.*] You'll be all right? There's nothing that you want?

ANNE. Will you please ask Father to come.

MRS. FRANK. [*After a second.*] Of course, Anne dear. [*She hurries out into the other room.* MR. FRANK *comes to her as she comes in.*] *Sie verlangt nach Dir!*[25]

4 **MR. FRANK.** [*Sensing her hurt.*] *Edith, Liebe, schau . . .*[26]

MRS. FRANK. *Es macht nichts! Ich danke dem lieben Herrgott, dass sie sich wenigstens an Dich wendet, wenn sie Trost braucht! Geh hinein, Otto, sie ist ganz hysterisch vor Angst.*[27] [*As* MR. FRANK *hesitates.*] *Geh zu ihr.*[28]

[*He looks at her for a second and then goes to get a cup of water for* ANNE. MRS. FRANK *sinks down on the bed, her face in her hands, trying to keep from sobbing aloud.* MARGOT *comes over to her, putting her arms around her.*]

She wants nothing of me. She pulled away when I leaned down to kiss her.

5 **MARGOT.** It's a phase . . . You heard Father. . . . Most girls go through it . . . they turn to their fathers at this age . . . they give all their love to their fathers.

---

25. *Sie . . . Dir!:* She's asking for you!
26. *Liebe, schau . . . :* Dear, look . . .
27. *Es macht . . . Angst:* It doesn't matter. I thank the blessed Lord that at least she turns to you when she needs comfort. Go in to see her, Otto, she's completely hysterical with fear.
28. *Geh zu ihr:* Go to her.

The Diary of Anne Frank, Act I 395

AT A GLANCE

- *Scene 4 (continued):* Anne refuses to have her mother stay but asks for her father.
- Mrs. Frank sends her husband in to Anne and then tries to stifle her sobs at being rejected.

1 STYLE: DIALOGUE

Dussel's sarcastic answer to Mr. Van Daan's question reveals his increasingly uncontrollable impatience with Anne.

2 CHARACTERIZATION

The stage directions help define Mr. Frank's leadership role by describing his actions as he tries to restore order to the hiding place.

3 THEME

In a return to their former strained relationship, Anne refuses to accept her mother's comfort.

4 THEME

Mr. Frank always the diplomat, wants to comfort his wife as much as he wants to comfort his daughter.

5 DIALOGUE

Margot understands her mother's distress and tries to become her mother's comforter. This exchange underscores the theme of family life, in which parents and children sometimes exchange roles.

GUIDED READING

LITERAL QUESTIONS

1a. What question does Mr. Van Daan ask Dussel? ("What is it? What happened?")

2a. How does Anne respond to her mother's offer to stay with her? (Anne sends her mother away; she asks for her father.)

INFERENTIAL QUESTIONS

1b. What fear does Mr. Van Daan probably have? (He is probably afraid that someone saw him sneak down to the food cupboard.)

2b. Why do you think Mrs. Frank speaks German to her husband at this point? (Under stress she probably reverts to German, the language she knows best; also, Anne may not speak German well and Mrs. Frank may not want her to understand what she says.)

- *Scene 4 (continued):* Margot comforts Mrs. Frank, as Mr. Frank comforts Anne.
- Anne describes her nightmare to her father.
- She reveals her inner conflict over her treatment of her mother.

1 STAGE DIRECTIONS

The parallel actions (Margot sitting with her mother and Mr. Frank sitting with Anne) described in the stage directions create a strong visual image of the rift between Anne and her mother.

2 CHARACTERIZATION

Speaking to her father, Anne describes herself more honestly than she can with anyone else.

3 PLOT: CONFLICT

Anne reveals her inner conflict as she struggles to deal with the feelings she has about her mother.

MRS. FRANK. You weren't like this. You didn't shut me out.

MARGOT. She'll get over it. . . .

1 [*She smooths the bed for* MRS. FRANK *and sits beside her a moment as* MRS. FRANK *lies down. In* ANNE'S *room* MR. FRANK *comes in, sitting down by* ANNE. ANNE *flings her arms around him, clinging to him. In the distance we hear the sound of ack-ack.*]

ANNE. Oh, Pim. I dreamed that they came to get us! The Green Police! They broke down the door and grabbed me and started to drag me out the way they did Jopie.

MR. FRANK. I want you to take this pill.

ANNE. What is it?

MR. FRANK. Something to quiet you.

[*She takes it and drinks the water. In the main room* MARGOT *turns out the light and goes back to her room.*]

MR. FRANK. [*To* ANNE.] Do you want me to read to you for a while?

ANNE. No. Just sit with me for a minute. Was I awful? Did I yell terribly loud? Do you think anyone outside could have heard?

MR. FRANK. No. No. Lie quietly now. Try to sleep.

2 ANNE. I'm a terrible coward. I'm so disappointed in myself. I think I've conquered my fear . . . I think I'm really grown-up . . . and then something happens . . . and I run to you like a baby. . . . I love you, Father. I don't love anyone but you.

MR. FRANK. [*Reproachfully.*] Annele!

ANNE. It's true. I've been thinking about it for a long time. You're the only one I love.

MR. FRANK. It's fine to hear you tell me that you love me. But I'd be happier if you said you loved your mother as well. . . . She needs your help so much . . . your love . . .

ANNE. We have nothing in common. She doesn't understand me. Whenever I try to explain my views on life to her she asks me if I'm constipated.

MR. FRANK. You hurt her very much now. She's crying. She's in there crying.

3 ANNE. I can't help it. I only told the truth. I didn't want her here. . . . [*Then, with sudden change.*] Oh, Pim, I was horrible, wasn't I? And the worst of it is, I can stand off and look at myself doing it and know it's cruel and yet I can't stop doing it. What's the matter with me? Tell me. Don't say it's just a phase! Help me.

MR. FRANK. There is so little that we parents

GUIDED READING

LITERAL QUESTION

1a. In describing her feelings for her mother, what does Anne say is the "worst of it"? (that she can stand off and watch her own cruelty)

INFERENTIAL QUESTION

1b. What does Anne mean? (She means she is aware of what she is doing and knows it is wrong even as she is doing it.)

can do to help our children. We can only try to set a good example . . . point the way. The rest you must do yourself. You must build your own character.

ANNE. I'm trying. Really I am. Every night I think back over all of the things I did that day that were wrong . . . like putting the wet mop in Mr. Dussel's bed . . . and this thing now with Mother. I say to myself, that was wrong. I make up my mind. I'm never going to do that again. Never! Of course I may do something worse . . . but at least I'll never do *that* again! . . . I have a nicer side, Father . . . a sweeter, nicer side. But I'm scared to show it. I'm afraid that people are going to laugh at me if I'm serious. So the mean Anne comes to the outside and the good Anne stays on the inside, and I keep on trying to switch them around and have the good Anne outside and the bad Anne inside and be what I'd like to be . . . and might be . . . if only . . . only . . .

[*She is asleep.* MR. FRANK *watches her for a moment and then turns off the light and starts out. The lights dim out. The curtain falls on the scene.* ANNE'*s voice is heard dimly at first, and then with growing strength.*]

ANNE'S VOICE. . . . The air raids are getting worse. They come over day and night. The noise is terrifying. Pim says it should be music to our ears. The more planes, the sooner will come the end of the war. Mrs. Van Daan pretends to be a fatalist. What will be, will be. But when the planes come over, who is the most frightened? No one else but Petronella! . . . Monday, the ninth of November, nineteen forty-two. Wonderful news! The Allies[29] have

landed in Africa. Pim says that we can look for an early finish to the war. Just for fun he asked each of us what was the first thing we wanted to do when we got out of here. Mrs. Van Daan longs to be home with her own things, her needlepoint chairs, the Beckstein piano her father gave her . . . the best that money could buy. Peter would like to go to a movie. Mr. Dussel wants to get back to his dentist's drill. He's afraid he is losing his touch. For myself, there are so many things . . . to ride a bike again . . . to laugh till my belly aches . . . to have new clothes from the skin out . . . to have a hot tub filled to overflowing and wallow in it for hours . . . to be back in school with my friends . . .

[*As the last lines are being said, the curtain rises on the scene. The lights dim on as* ANNE'*s voice fades away.*]

Scene 5

December, 1942.

[*It is the first night of the Hanukkah*[30] *celebration.* MR. FRANK *is standing at the head of the table, on which is the* menorah.[31] *He lights the* shamas, *or servant candle, and holds it as he says the blessing. Seated listening is all of the "family," dressed in their best. The men wear hats;* PETER *wears his cap.*]

MR. FRANK. [*Reading from a prayer book.*] "Praised be Thou, O Lord our God, Ruler of the universe, who hast sanctified us with Thy

---

29. **Allies:** group of nations, including the United States, France, Britain, and Russia, that fought against Germany, Italy, and Japan in World War II. In 1942 an Allied army landed in Africa, recovering territory that had been taken by Italy.

30. **Hanukkah** [hä′nə kə]: joyous eight-day Jewish holiday celebrating religious freedom. Hanukkah commemorates a rebellion in 165 B.C. in which the Jews, led by the Macabee brothers, won their independence from the Syrians, who had forced them to place statues of Greek gods in their Temple in Jerusalem.
31. *menorah* [mə nô′rə]: candleholder. A Hanukkah *menorah* holds eight candles and the *shamas* [shä′məs], or central candle, which is used to light the others.

The Diary of Anne Frank, Act I 397

AT A GLANCE

- *Scene 4 (continued):* Anne describes her inner conflict.
- The air raids are getting worse.
- *Scene 5:* The "family" celebrates the first night of Hanukkah.

1 PLOT: CONFLICT

Anne poignantly reveals her adolescent identity problems as she describes her inner conflicts to her father.

2 MOOD

Anne's diary entry read aloud helps indicate a time change and creates a momentary mood of exuberance as we hear how the characters look forward to the end of the war.

3 CHARACTERIZATION

Anne typically cannot identify only one thing she will do. In her enthusiasm she describes many of the little things that she misses.

4 SETTING

The stage directions indicate the passage of time to the ritual celebration of Hanukkah. The atmosphere is momentarily one of happy festivity—as if life were being lived under normal conditions.

GUIDED READING

LITERAL QUESTIONS

1a. Why is Anne afraid to show her nicer side? (She is afraid people will laugh at her.)

2a. What does Anne say she will do when the war is over? (She will ride a bike, laugh, have new clothes, wallow in a tub, be with friends.)

INFERENTIAL QUESTIONS

1b. Who among the characters might laugh at Anne? (Mr. and Mrs. Van Daan and Mr. Dussel might laugh at Anne's thoughts.)

2b. Why is Anne's answer characteristic of her? (In her enthusiasm she identifies five things, not one.)

AT A GLANCE

- *Scene 5 (continued):* Mr. Frank reads a traditional prayer and lights one candle of the Hanukkah menorah.
- Mrs. Frank continues the reading.
- Margot and Mrs. Frank prepare to serve dinner.

1 IRONY

The prayer Mr. Frank reads praises God and identifies Hanukkah as a happy season. The irony of the group's present situation is thus highlighted.

2 THEME

The historical reference to the Maccabees, who fought against tyranny, is a strong parallel to the characters' present situation. In the face of oppression, they attempt to hold fast to their ideals and visions.

3 THEME

The prayer of faith and trust Mrs. Frank reads reflects her own true faith in the power of love.

1 commandments and bidden us kindle the Hanukkah lights. Praised be Thou, O Lord our God, Ruler of the universe, who hast wrought wondrous deliverances for our fathers in days of old. Praised be Thou, O Lord our God, Ruler of the universe, that Thou hast given us life and sustenance and brought us to this happy season." [MR. FRANK *lights the one candle of the* menorah *as he continues.*] "We kindle this Hanukkah light to celebrate the great and wonderful deeds wrought through the zeal with which God filled the hearts of the heroic 2 Maccabees, two thousand years ago. They fought against indifference, against tyranny and oppression, and they restored our Temple to us. May these lights remind us that we should ever look to God, whence cometh our help." Amen. [*Pronounced "O-mayn."*]

ALL. Amen.

[MR. FRANK *hands* MRS. FRANK *the prayer book.*]

398 *Drama*

3 **MRS. FRANK.** [*Reading.*] "I lift up mine eyes unto the mountains, from whence cometh my help. My help cometh from the Lord who made heaven and earth. He will not suffer thy foot to be moved. He that keepeth thee will not slumber. He that keepeth Israel doth neither slumber nor sleep. The Lord is thy keeper. The Lord is thy shade upon thy right hand. The sun shall not smite thee by day, nor the moon by night. The Lord shall keep thee from all evil. He shall keep thy soul. The Lord shall guard thy going out and thy coming in, from this time forth and forevermore." Amen.

ALL. Amen.

[MRS. FRANK *puts down the prayer book and goes to get the food and wine.* MARGOT *helps her.* MR. FRANK *takes the men's hats and puts them aside.*]

DUSSEL. [*Rising.*] That was very moving.

ANNE. [*Pulling him back.*] It isn't over yet!

GUIDED READING

LITERAL QUESTIONS

1a. What adjective describes the season in the prayer recited by Mr. Frank? (happy)

2a. What promise is made in the last line of the prayer read by Mrs. Frank? ("The Lord shall guard thy going out and thy coming in, from this time forth and forevermore.")

INFERENTIAL QUESTIONS

1b. Is this a happy season for those living in the attic? (The season may bring with it happy memories, and the families are still alive and well, but their circumstances are in no way happy.)

2b. What message does this prayer have for the group in hiding? (It offers a message of hope that they may one day be safe.)

MRS. VAN DAAN. Sit down! Sit down!

ANNE. There's a lot more, songs and presents.

DUSSEL. Presents?

MRS. FRANK. Not this year, unfortunately.

MRS. VAN DAAN. But always on Hanukkah everyone gives presents . . . everyone!

DUSSEL. Like our St. Nicholas' Day.[32]

[*There is a chorus of no's from the group.*]

MRS. VAN DAAN. No! Not like St. Nicholas! What kind of a Jew are you that you don't know Hanukkah?

MRS. FRANK. [*As she brings the food.*] I remember particularly the candles. . . . First one, as we have tonight. Then the second night you light two candles, the next night three . . . and so on until you have eight candles burning. When there are eight candles it is truly beautiful.

MRS. VAN DAAN. And the potato pancakes.

MR. VAN DAAN. Don't talk about them!

MRS. VAN DAAN. I make the best *latkes*[33] you ever tasted!

MRS. FRANK. Invite us all next year . . . in your own home.

MR. FRANK. God willing!

MRS. VAN DAAN. God willing.

MARGOT. What I remember best is the presents we used to get when we were little . . . eight days of presents . . . and each day they got better and better.

---

32. **St. Nicholas' Day:** Christian holiday on December 6 celebrated in the Netherlands with gift-giving. Mr. Dussel knows this holiday rather than Hanukkah because he had been raised as a Christian. However, since his ancestry is Jewish, he is considered a Jew by the Nazis.

33. *latkes* [lät′kēz]: potato pancakes, a traditional Hanukkah dish.

MRS. FRANK. [*Sitting down.*] We are all here, alive. That is present enough.

ANNE. No, it isn't. I've got something. . . .

[*She rushes into her room, hurriedly puts on a little hat improvised from the lampshade, grabs a satchel bulging with parcels and comes running back.*]

MRS. FRANK. What is it?

ANNE. Presents!

MRS. VAN DAAN. Presents!

DUSSEL. Look!

MR. VAN DAAN. What's she got on her head?

PETER. A lampshade!

ANNE. [*She picks out one at random.*] This is for Margot. [*She hands it to* MARGOT, *pulling her to her feet.*] Read it out loud.

MARGOT. [*Reading.*]
"You have never lost your temper.
You never will, I fear,
You are so good.
But if you should,
Put all your cross words here."

[*She tears open the package.*]

A new crossword puzzle book! Where did you get it?

ANNE. It isn't new. It's one that you've done. But I rubbed it all out, and if you wait a little and forget, you can do it all over again.

MARGOT. [*Sitting.*] It's wonderful, Anne. Thank you. You'd never know it wasn't new.

[*From outside we hear the sound of a streetcar passing.*]

ANNE. [*With another gift.*] Mrs. Van Daan.

MRS. VAN DAAN. [*Taking it.*] This is awful. . . . I haven't anything for anyone. . . . I never thought . . .

The Diary of Anne Frank, Act I 399

AT A GLANCE

- Characters describe Hanukkah traditions.
- Anne brings out the presents she has prepared.

1 CHARACTERIZATION

It is appropriate that Anne, the youngest member of the group, should be the first to mention presents. We later learn she has another reson for bringing up the subject.

2 CHARACTERIZATION

Anne reveals the generous side of her nature to people who have usually seen her only as a nuisance.

3 MOOD

In a rare moment of fun among the group, Anne shows her desire and ability to make others laugh.

4 THEME

Anne reveals her affection for Margot in her gentle characterization of her sister.

GUIDED READING

LITERAL QUESTIONS

1a. What does Mrs. Van Daan remember about Hanukkah celebrations? (She recalls the potato pancakes.)

2a. What does Anne do that surprises everyone? (She comes out of her room with a satchel of presents.)

INFERENTIAL QUESTIONS

1b. How does Mrs. Frank add a hopeful note to the conversation? (She asks Mrs. Van Daan to invite them all to her home next year.)

2b. Why is this action characteristic of Anne? (She is sharing her enthusiasm for Hanukkah with everyone; she is expressing her generosity.)

- *Scene 5 (continued):* Anne gives shampoo to Mrs. Van Daan and cigarettes to Mr. Van Daan.
- Mrs. Frank receives an IOU and Mr. Frank a muffler.
- Anne gives Peter a ball for Mouschi.

1 CHARACTERIZATION

Anne's gift shows she understands Mrs. Van Daan's vanity and desire to have nice things.

2 MOOD

The stage directions describe a moment of visual humor when Mr. Van Daan becomes the center of attention.

3 THEME

Mrs. Frank is touched by Anne's promise and takes the opportunity to embrace her daughter. For the moment strong family affection overrides any mother-daughter conflict.

DRAMATIC IRONY

This is a stirring moment of irony. Mr. Frank is grateful for his gift and touched by Anne's thoughtfulness—but he does not know something the audience knows: This is the scarf that will be a sad token to him after the war.

MR. FRANK. This is all Anne's idea.

1 MRS. VAN DAAN. [*Holding up a bottle.*] What is it?

ANNE. It's hair shampoo. I took all the odds and ends of soap and mixed them with the last of my toilet water.

MRS. VAN DAAN. Oh, Anneke!

ANNE. I wanted to write a poem for all of them, but I didn't have time. [*Offering a large box to* MR. VAN DAAN.] Yours, Mr. Van Daan, is *really* something . . . something you want more than anything. [*As she waits for him to open it.*] Look! Cigarettes!

MR. VAN DAAN. Cigarettes!

ANNE. Two of them! Pim found some old pipe tobacco in the pocket lining of his coat . . . and we made them . . . or rather, Pim did.

MRS. VAN DAAN. Let me see. . . . Well, look at that! Light it, Putti! Light it.

[MR. VAN DAAN *hesitates.*]

ANNE. It's tobacco, really it is! There's a little fluff in it, but not much.

2 [*Everyone watches as* MR. VAN DAAN *cautiously lights it. The cigarette flares up. Everyone laughs.*]

PETER. It works!

MRS. VAN DAAN. Look at him.

MR. VAN DAAN. [*Spluttering.*] Thank you, Anne. Thank you.

[ANNE *rushes back to her satchel for another present.*]

ANNE. [*Handing her mother a piece of paper.*] For Mother, Hanukkah greeting. [*She pulls her mother to her feet.*]

MRS. FRANK. [*She reads.*]

400 *Drama*

---

3 "Here's an IOU that I promise to pay.
Ten hours of doing whatever you say.
Signed, Anne Frank."

[MRS. FRANK, *touched, takes* ANNE *in her arms, holding her close.*]

DUSSEL. [*To* ANNE.] Ten hours of doing what you're told? *Anything* you're told?

ANNE. That's right.

DUSSEL. You wouldn't want to sell that, Mrs. Frank?

MRS. FRANK. Never! This is the most precious gift I've ever had!

[*She sits, showing her present to the others.* ANNE *hurries back to the satchel and pulls out a scarf, the scarf that* MR. FRANK *found in the first scene.*]

ANNE. [*Offering it to her father.*] For Pim.

MR. FRANK. Anneke . . . I wasn't supposed to have a present! [*He takes it, unfolding it and showing it to the others.*]

ANNE. It's a muffler . . . to put round your neck . . . like an ascot, you know. I made it myself out of odds and ends. . . . I knitted it in the dark each night, after I'd gone to bed. I'm afraid it looks better in the dark!

MR. FRANK. [*Putting it on.*] It's fine. It fits me perfectly. Thank you, Annele.

[ANNE *hands* PETER *a ball of paper, with a string attached to it.*]

ANNE. That's for Mouschi.

PETER. [*Rising to bow.*] On behalf of Mouschi, I thank you.

ANNE. [*Hesitant, handing him a gift.*] And . . . this is yours . . . from Mrs. Quack Quack. [*As he holds it gingerly in his hands.*] Well . . . open it . . . Aren't you going to open it?

GUIDED READING

LITERAL QUESTION

1a. What gifts did Anne give to the Van Daans? (She gave Mrs. Van Daan shampoo and Mr. Van Daan cigarettes.)

INFERENTIAL QUESTION

1b. What do these gifts reveal about Anne? (The gifts show that she understands what people like and that she wants to make them happy.)

PETER. I'm scared to. I know something's going to jump out and hit me.

ANNE. No. It's nothing like that, really.

MRS. VAN DAAN. [*As he is opening it.*] What is it, Peter? Go on. Show it.

ANNE. [*Excitedly.*] It's a safety razor!

DUSSEL. A what?

ANNE. A razor!

MRS. VAN DAAN. [*Looking at it.*] You didn't make that out of odds and ends.

1 **ANNE.** [*To* PETER.] Miep got it for me. It's not new. It's secondhand. But you really do need a razor now.

DUSSEL. For what?

ANNE. Look on his upper lip . . . you can see the beginning of a mustache.

DUSSEL. He wants to get rid of that? Put a little milk on it and let the cat lick it off.

2 **PETER.** [*Starting for his room.*] Think you're funny, don't you.

DUSSEL. Look! He can't wait! He's going to try it!

PETER. I'm going to give Mouschi his present! [*He goes into his room, slamming the door behind him.*]

MR. VAN DAAN. [*Disgustedly.*] Mouschi, Mouschi, Mouschi.

[*In the distance we hear a dog persistently barking.* ANNE *brings a gift to* DUSSEL.]

ANNE. And last but never least, my roommate, Mr. Dussel.

DUSSEL. For me? You have something for me? [*He opens the small box she gives him.*]

ANNE. I made them myself.

DUSSEL. [*Puzzled.*] Capsules! Two capsules!

ANNE. They're earplugs!

3 **DUSSEL.** Earplugs?

ANNE. To put in your ears so you won't hear me when I thrash around at night. I saw them advertised in a magazine. They're not real ones. . . . I made them out of cotton and candle wax. Try them. . . . See if they don't work . . . see if you can hear me talk. . . .

DUSSEL. [*Putting them in his ears.*] Wait now until I get them in . . . so.

ANNE. Are you ready?

DUSSEL. Huh?

ANNE. Are you ready?

DUSSEL. They've gone inside! I can't get them out! [*They laugh as* DUSSEL *jumps about, trying to shake the plugs out of his ears. Finally he gets them out. Putting them away.*] Thank you, Anne! Thank you!

MR. VAN DAAN. A real Hanukkah!

MRS. VAN DAAN. Wasn't it cute of her?

MRS. FRANK. I don't know when she did it.

MARGOT. I love my present.

[*Together.*]

ANNE. [*Sitting at the table.*] And now let's have the song, Father . . . please. . . . [*To* DUSSEL.] Have you heard the Hanukkah song, Mr. Dussel? The song is the whole thing! [*She sings.*]
   "Oh, Hanukkah! Oh, Hanukkah!
   The sweet celebration. . . ."

4 **MR. FRANK.** [*Quieting her.*] I'm afraid, Anne, we shouldn't sing that song tonight. [*To* DUSSEL.] It's a song of jubilation, of rejoicing. One is apt to become too enthusiastic.

The Diary of Anne Frank, Act I   401

AT A GLANCE

- Anne gives Peter a razor.
- Dussel receives earplugs.
- Anne requests the Hanukkah song.

1 THEME

Anne shows her sympathetic understanding of Peter's needs and feelings when she tells him he needs a razor.

2 DIALOGUE

This exchange of dialogue further defines Peter's shyness and Dussel's insensitivity to adolescent feelings.

3 CHARACTERIZATION

Anne's gift for Dussel shows that she understands his annoyance with her and that she is willing to make fun of herself.

4 PLOT: CONFLICT

Mr. Frank reluctantly quiets Anne in her enthusiasm for the traditional Hanukkah song, bringing the group back to the reality of their grim situation.

GUIDED READING

LITERAL QUESTIONS

1a. What does Anne give to Peter? (a razor)

2a. What does Anne want after the presents? (She wants to sing the Hanukkah song.)

INFERENTIAL QUESTIONS

1b. How do you think Peter feels about his gift? (He is probably pleased by it until Mr. Dussel embarrasses him.)

2b. How does Mr. Frank feel when he says they shouldn't sing the song? (He probably regrets spoiling Anne's celebration.)

- Dussel falsely accuses Peter of bringing his cat into the room.
- Mr. Van Daan resolves to get rid of the cat.
- A crash from below frightens everyone into silence.

1 THEME

Mr. Frank protectively guides Anne to help her enjoy the Hanukkah celebration.

2 DIALOGUE

Dussel's accusation creates a further rift between Mr. Van Daan and Peter.

3 CHARACTERIZATION

Mr. Van Daan's characteristic obsession with food is growing as the days go on and the food supply dwindles.

4 STAGE DIRECTIONS

The stage directions indicate a sudden and serious change in mood. With the sound of a crash, fear dominates and everyone is silent. The tension mounts as Peter loses his balance.

---

1 **ANNE.** Oh, please, please. Let's sing the song. I promise not to shout!

MR. FRANK. Very well. But quietly now . . . I'll keep an eye on you and when . . .

[*As* ANNE *starts to sing, she is interrupted by* DUSSEL, *who is snorting and wheezing.*]

DUSSEL. [*Pointing to* PETER.] You . . . you! [PETER *is coming from his bedroom, ostentatiously holding a bulge in his coat as if he were holding his cat, and dangling* ANNE's *present before it.*] How many times . . . I told you . . . Out! Out!

2 **MR. VAN DAAN.** [*Going to* PETER.] What's the matter with you? Haven't you any sense? Get that cat out of here.

PETER. [*Innocently.*] Cat?

MR. VAN DAAN. You heard me. Get it out of here!

PETER. I have no cat.

[*Delighted with his joke, he opens his coat and pulls out a bath towel. The group at the table laugh, enjoying the joke.*]

DUSSEL. [*Still wheezing.*] It doesn't need to be the cat . . . his clothes are enough . . . when he comes out of that room. . . .

MR. VAN DAAN. Don't worry. You won't be bothered any more. We're getting rid of it.

DUSSEL. At last you listen to me. [*He goes off into his bedroom.*]

3 **MR. VAN DAAN.** [*Calling after him.*] I'm not doing it for you. That's all in your mind . . . all of it! [*He starts back to his place at the table.*] I'm doing it because I'm sick of seeing that cat eat all our food.

PETER. That's not true! I only give him bones . . . scraps . . .

402 *Drama*

MR. VAN DAAN. Don't tell me! He gets fatter every day! Cat looks better than any of us. Out he goes tonight!

PETER. No! No!

ANNE. Mr. Van Daan, you can't do that! That's Peter's cat. Peter loves that cat.

MRS. FRANK. [*Quietly.*] Anne.

PETER. [*To* MR. VAN DAAN.] If he goes, I go.

MR. VAN DAAN. Go! Go!

MRS. VAN DAAN. You're not going and the cat's not going! Now please . . . this is Hanukkah . . . Hanukkah . . . this is the time to celebrate. . . . What's the matter with all of you? Come on, Anne. Let's have the song.

ANNE. [*Singing.*]
"Oh, Hanukkah! Oh, Hanukkah!
The sweet celebration."

MR. FRANK. [*Rising.*] I think we should first blow out the candle . . . then we'll have something for tomorrow night.

MARGOT. But, Father, you're supposed to let it burn itself out.

MR. FRANK. I'm sure that God understands shortages. [*Before blowing it out.*] "Praised be Thou, O Lord our God, who hast sustained us and permitted us to celebrate this joyous festival."

4 [*He is about to blow out the candle when suddenly there is a crash of something falling below. They all freeze in horror, motionless. For a few seconds there is complete silence.* MR. FRANK *slips off his shoes. The others noiselessly follow his example.* MR. FRANK *turns out a light near him. He motions to* PETER *to turn off the center lamp.* PETER *tries to reach it, realizes he cannot and gets up on a chair. Just as he is touching the lamp he loses his balance.*

GUIDED READING

LITERAL QUESTION

1a. What frightens everyone? (the crash of something falling below)

INFERENTIAL QUESTION

1b. Why do you think the crash is so frightening? (Everyone is fearful that whoever is below will discover their presence.)

AT A GLANCE

- The chair falls, and the lamp-shade crashes to the floor.
- Steps are heard as someone runs down the stairs.
- As the characters argue about what to do, Anne faints.

1 PLOT: SUSPENSE

Peter's fall is a terrifying moment in the play. It is the first time a noise from the attic may have revealed the characters' presence. The light of the Hanukkah candle, which once symbolized hope, now casts an eerie glow on the proceedings.

2 PLOT: CONFLICT

Anne's fainting creates yet another external conflict among the tense and hostile characters.

1 *The chair goes out from under him. He falls. The iron lampshade crashes to the floor. There is a sound of feet below, running down the stairs. The only light left comes from the Hanukkah candle.* DUSSEL *comes from his room.* MR. FRANK *creeps over to the stairwell and stands listening. The dog is heard barking excitedly.*]

MR. VAN DAAN. Do you hear anything?

MR. FRANK. [*In a whisper.*] No. I think they've gone.

MRS. VAN DAAN. It's the Green Police. They've found us.

MR. FRANK. If they had, they wouldn't have left. They'd be up here by now.

MRS. VAN DAAN. I know it's the Green Police. They've gone to get help. That's all, they'll be back.

MR. VAN DAAN. Or it may have been the Gestapo,[34] looking for papers. . . .

---

34. **Gestapo** [gə stä′pō]: Nazi secret police. Mr. Van Daan fears that the Gestapo suspect Mr. Kraler.

MR. FRANK. [*Interrupting.*] Or a thief, looking for money.

MRS. VAN DAAN. We've got to do something. . . . Quick! Quick! Before they come back.

MR. VAN DAAN. There isn't anything to do. Just wait.

[MR. FRANK *holds up his hand for them to be quiet. He is listening intently. There is complete silence as they all strain to hear any sound from below. Suddenly* ANNE *begins to sway. With a low cry she falls to the floor in a faint.* MRS. FRANK *goes to her quickly, sitting beside her on the floor and taking her in her arms.*]

2 **MRS. FRANK.** Get some water, please! Get some water!

[MARGOT *starts for the sink.*]

MR. VAN DAAN. [*Grabbing* MARGOT.] No! No! No one's going to run water!

MR. FRANK. If they've found us, they've found us. Get the water. [MARGOT *starts again for the sink.* MR. FRANK, *getting a flashlight.*] I'm going down.

The Diary of Anne Frank, Act I **403**

GUIDED READING

LITERAL QUESTION

1a. Who do the characters fear may be downstairs? (They think it is the Green Police, the Gestapo, or a thief.)

INFERENTIAL QUESTION

1b. Which possibility is the least threatening to them? Why? (a thief, because it is unlikely that the thief would reveal their presence)

- Mr. Frank goes downstairs in spite of Margot's protests.
- Mrs. Van Daan wants to get money to pay off the Green Police.
- Mr. Frank reports that a thief was scared away by the noise.

1 THEME

Margot fears for her father, but Mrs. Frank remains calm and quiet and reassures her as Mr. Frank slips downstairs.

2 DIALOGUE

Mrs. Van Daan's fear prompts her to blame her husband for his inaction. He brushes her request aside as he physically pushes her aside.

3 PLOT: CONFLICT

The level of hostility between Mr. Van Daan and Peter escalates. The increased tension causes Mr. Van Daan to denigrate his son. Peter's guilt prompts him to retaliate, but he stops himself in guilt and misery.

4 THEME

The religious faith expressed in the psalm helps sustain the Franks in their fear and suffering.

5 PLOT: SUSPENSE

The thief who heard the noise knows that someone is living above the warehouse. The hiding place is now known to at least one more person.

[MARGOT *rushes to him, clinging to him.* ANNE *struggles to consciousness.*]

MARGOT. No, Father, no! There may be someone there, waiting. . . . It may be a trap!

MR. FRANK. This is Saturday. There is no way for us to know what has happened until Miep or Mr. Kraler comes on Monday morning. We cannot live with this uncertainty.

1 MARGOT. Don't go, Father!

MRS. FRANK. Hush, darling, hush. [MR. FRANK *slips quietly out, down the steps and out through the door below.*] Margot! Stay close to me.

[MARGOT *goes to her mother.*]

MR. VAN DAAN. Shush! Shush!

[MRS. FRANK *whispers to* MARGOT *to get the water.* MARGOT *goes for it.*]

MRS. VAN DAAN. Putti, where's our money? Get our money. I hear you can buy the Green Police off, so much a head. Go upstairs quick! Get the money!

MR. VAN DAAN. Keep still!

2 MRS. VAN DAAN. [*Kneeling before him, pleading.*] Do you want to be dragged off to a concentration camp? Are you going to stand there and wait for them to come up and get you? Do something, I tell you!

MR. VAN DAAN. [*Pushing her aside.*] Will you keep still!

[*He goes over to the stairwell to listen.* PETER *goes to his mother, helping her up onto the sofa. There is a second of silence. Then* ANNE *can stand it no longer.*]

ANNE. Someone go after Father! Make Father come back!

PETER. [*Starting for the door.*] I'll go.

404 *Drama*

MR. VAN DAAN. Haven't you done enough?

3 [*He pushes* PETER *roughly away. In his anger against his father* PETER *grabs a chair as if to hit him with it, then puts it down, burying his face in his hands.* MRS. FRANK *begins to pray softly.*]

ANNE. Please, please, Mr. Van Daan. Get Father.

MR. VAN DAAN. Quiet! Quiet!

[ANNE *is shocked into silence.* MRS. FRANK *pulls her closer, holding her protectively in her arms.*]

4 MRS. FRANK. [*Softly, praying.*] "I lift up mine eyes unto the mountains, from whence cometh my help. My help cometh from the Lord who made heaven and earth. He will not suffer thy foot to be moved. . . . He that keepeth thee will not slumber. . . ."

[*She stops as she hears someone coming. They all watch the door tensely.* MR. FRANK *comes quietly in.* ANNE *rushes to him, holding him tight.*]

MR. FRANK. It was a thief. That noise must have scared him away.

MRS. VAN DAAN. Thank God.

5 MR. FRANK. He took the cashbox. And the radio. He ran away in such a hurry that he didn't stop to shut the street door. It was swinging wide open. [*A breath of relief sweeps over them.*] I think it would be good to have some light.

MARGOT. Are you sure it's all right?

MR. FRANK. The danger has passed. [MARGOT *goes to light the small lamp.*] Don't be so terrified, Anne. We're safe.

DUSSEL. Who says the danger has passed? Don't you realize we are in greater danger than ever?

GUIDED READING

LITERAL QUESTIONS

1a. Why does Mr. Frank insist on going downstairs? (He knows the group cannot live with the uncertainty until Monday when Miep or Mr. Kraler will arrive.)

2a. Who does Mr. Frank say has been downstairs? (a thief)

INFERENTIAL QUESTIONS

1b. Why do you think this is a wise decision? (Answers will vary. Possibilities: There is already too much tension among the group; perhaps they can escape if it's something serious.)

2b. What danger could a thief pose to the group in hiding? (The thief could reveal the information to an unsympathetic person who might turn in the group to the authorities.)

MR. FRANK. Mr. Dussel, will you be still! [MR. FRANK *takes* ANNE *back to the table, making her sit down with him, trying to calm her.*]

DUSSEL. [*Pointing to* PETER.] Thanks to this clumsy fool, there's someone now who knows we're up here! Someone now knows we're up here, hiding!

MRS. VAN DAAN. [*Going to* DUSSEL.] Someone knows we're here, yes. But who is the someone? A thief! A thief! You think a thief is going to go to the Green Police and say . . . I was robbing a place the other night and I heard a noise up over my head? You think a thief is going to do that?

DUSSEL. Yes. I think he will.

MRS. VAN DAAN. [*Hysterically.*] You're crazy!

[*She stumbles back to her seat at the table.* PETER *follows protectively, pushing* DUSSEL *aside.*]

1 **DUSSEL.** I think someday he'll be caught and then he'll make a bargain with the Green Police . . . if they'll let him off, he'll tell them where some Jews are hiding!

[*He goes off into the bedroom. There is a second of appalled silence.*]

MR. VAN DAAN. He's right.

ANNE. Father, let's get out of here! We can't stay here now. . . . Let's go. . . .

MR. VAN DAAN. Go! Where?

MRS. FRANK. [*Sinking into her chair at the table.*] Yes. Where?

2 **MR. FRANK.** [*Rising, to them all.*] Have we lost all faith? All courage? A moment ago we thought that they'd come for us. We were sure it was the end. But it wasn't the end. We're alive, safe. [MR. VAN DAAN *goes to the table and sits.* MR. FRANK *prays.*] "We thank Thee, O Lord our God, that in Thy infinite mercy Thou hast again seen fit to spare us." [*He blows out the candle, then turns to* ANNE.] Come on, Anne. The song! Let's have the song!

[*He starts to sing.* ANNE *finally starts falteringly to sing as* MR. FRANK *urges her on. Her voice is hardly audible at first.*]

ANNE. [*Singing.*]
"Oh, Hanukkah! Oh, Hanukkah!
The sweet . . . celebration. . . ."

[*As she goes on singing, the others gradually join in, their voices still shaking with fear.* MRS. VAN DAAN *sobs as she sings.*]

GROUP.
"Around the feast . . . we . . . gather
In complete . . . jubilation. . . .
Happiest of sea . . . sons
Now is here.
Many are the reasons for good cheer.

[DUSSEL *comes from the bedroom. He comes over to the table, standing beside* MARGOT, *listening to them as they sing.*]

"Together
We'll weather
Whatever tomorrow may bring.

[*As they sing on with growing courage, the lights start to dim.*]

"So hear us rejoicing
And merrily voicing
The Hanukkah song that we sing.
Hoy!

3 [*The lights are out. The curtain starts slowly to fall.*]

"Hear us rejoicing
And merrily voicing
The Hanukkah song that we sing."

[*They are still singing as the curtain falls.*]

The Diary of Anne Frank, Act I   405

AT A GLANCE

- Dussel accuses Peter of endangering the group.
- Mr. Frank calls for a renewal of courage.
- The group comes together again to sing the Hanukkah song.

1 PLOT: FORESHADOWING

The playwright has Dussel speak a terrifying truth that foreshadows events to come.

2 THEME

Mr. Frank calls for faith and courage as the group recovers from the awful threat of exposure.

3 IRONY

Singing after learning about the threat of exposure by the thief creates a mood of ironic celebration. When the curtain falls on Act I, we sense impending doom as the characters poignantly struggle to keep up their spirits.

REFLECTING ON ACT I

Which of the characters tend to be sympathetic peacemakers and which tend to be less sympathetic troublemakers? (peacemakers: Mr. and Mrs. Frank, Margot, and usually Anne; troublemakers: Mr. and Mrs. Van Daan and Dussel; sometimes Peter and Anne)

GUIDED READING

LITERAL QUESTIONS

1a. Why does Mrs. Van Daan believe that the thief will not reveal their hiding place? (She thinks that a thief will not go to the police.)

2a. How does Mr. Frank rally the group? (He calls on them to show faith and courage now that they are still alive and safe.)

INFERENTIAL QUESTIONS

1b. Why is there sudden silence when Dussel disagrees with Mr. Van Daan? (Everyone realizes there is truth in what he says.)

2b. Why is the Hanukkah song appropriate now? (It is a song of rejoicing, and the characters have lived through a difficult moment.)

1. the Green Police have come
2. unable to conquer her fear; her good and mean sides compete
3. Margot—a crossword puzzle; Mrs. Van Daan—shampoo; Mr. Van Daan—cigarettes; Mrs. Frank—ten hours of her time; Mr. Frank—a scarf; Mouschi—a ball of paper; Peter—a safety razor; Mr. Dussel—earplugs
4. a burglary downstairs; he falls trying to turn off the lamp
5. fears the thief will inform on them when caught
6. The group sings a Hanukkah song to try to regain their hope.
7. her seriousness, vulnerability, and anxiety
8. She is perceptive and knows and cares about each group member.
9. Possible answers:
   - best qualities: politeness and respect for each other's needs; try to lead normal lives with school and reading; Franks' unselfishness toward each other and Mr. Dussel
   - worst qualities: Anne's meanness to her mother; Mr. Dussel's complaining self-centeredness; the Van Daans' bickering; Peter's sulkiness
10. reminds them of happier times, gives hope; reaffirms their identity as Jews

READING AND LITERARY FOCUS

1. ■ Scene 4: She regrets rejecting her mother after openly confiding in her father.
   ■ Scene 5: She becomes an insecure little girl during the burglary after being happy and adult when presenting Hanukkah gifts.
2. ■ Anne and Mr. Frank: warmth and honesty
   ■ Van Daans: actions and words conflict; Mr. Dussel: self-centered and rigid

STUDY QUESTIONS

Recalling

1. What is Anne's nightmare about in Scene 4?
2. In Scene 4 why is Anne disappointed with herself? What split in herself does she describe?
3. What Hanukkah presents does Anne give each member of the group in Scene 5?
4. What frightening incident interrupts the Hanukkah celebration? How does Peter make the situation worse?
5. According to Mr. Dussel, what new danger threatens the group as a result of this incident?
6. What happens at the end of Act I?

Interpreting

7. What side of herself does Anne show in her nightmare and in her confession to her father?
8. What do we learn about Anne from the Hanukkah gifts she gives?
9. Give an example of how life in the attic brings out the best in the characters and an example of how it brings out the worst.

Extending

10. Why do you think it might be important for a group like those in the attic to celebrate an event like Hanukkah, even though they have few "reasons for good cheer"?

READING AND LITERARY FOCUS

Characterization in Drama

We learn about **characters** in drama from what they do and say and what other characters say about them. However, we cannot always take characters' words and actions at face value. We must interpret this information and draw our own **inferences,** or conclusions, about it.

We must draw our own inferences about characters in drama for a number of reasons. A character in a play may be insincere and may not always mean what he or she says. For example, in Act I, Scene 3, of *The Diary of Anne Frank,* Mr. Van Daan says that Mr. Frank has a right to invite Mr. Dussel to move in. However, Mr. Van Daan keeps complaining about the lack of food, and we soon realize that he did not really mean what he had said. On the other hand, a character may shift from one sincere emotion to another, as Anne does in this same scene. We must decide for ourselves that Anne, an excitable young girl, does not fake these different feelings—she simply changes her mood quickly. Finally, two characters may express different opinions about a third character, as Mrs. Frank and Margot do about Anne in Scene 3. It is up to us to decide which opinion, or which part of each opinion, rings true.

Thinking About Characterization in Drama

1. Point out two examples of Anne's rapid changes in behavior in either Scene 4 or Scene 5.
2. Which characters seem most sincere? That is, which characters are you more likely to believe or trust? Which ones seem least sincere? Explain.

CHALLENGE

Literary Criticism

■ In his opening night review of *The Diary of Anne Frank,* theater critic Walter Kerr said that the essential quality of the play is

> the quality of glowing . . . life—life in its warmth, its wonder, its . . . anguish, and its wild and flaring humor.

From Act I of *The Diary of Anne Frank,* find examples of two of the four traits that Kerr mentions in this comment.

Students should point to specific moments in Act I creating warmth (Mr. Frank's tenderness toward Anne); wonder (the Hanukkah celebration); anguish (Anne's nightmare); and humor (Anne's teasing of Peter).

ACT II

Scene 1   *January 1944.*

[*In the darkness we hear* ANNE's *voice, again reading from the diary.*]

ANNE'S VOICE. Saturday, the first of January, nineteen forty-four. Another new year has begun and we find ourselves still in our hiding place. We have been here now for one year, five months and twenty-five days. It seems that our life is at a standstill.

1 [*The curtain rises on the scene. It is late afternoon. Everyone is bundled up against the cold. In the main room* MRS. FRANK *is taking down the laundry, which is hung across the back.* MR. FRANK *sits in the chair down left, reading.* MARGOT *is lying on the couch with a blanket over her and the many-colored knitted scarf around her throat.* ANNE *is seated at the center table, writing in her diary.* PETER, MR. *and* MRS. VAN DAAN, *and* DUSSEL *are all in their own rooms, reading or lying down.*

As the lights dim on, ANNE's *voice continues, without a break.*]

ANNE'S VOICE. We are all a little thinner. The Van Daans' "discussions" are as violent as ever. Mother still does not understand me. But then I don't understand her either. There is one great change, however. A change in myself. I read somewhere that girls of my age don't feel quite certain of themselves. . . .

2 [*We hear the chimes and then a hymn being played on the carillon outside.*

The buzzer of the door below suddenly sounds. Everyone is startled: MR. FRANK *tiptoes cautiously to the top of the steps and listens. Again the buzzer sounds, in* MIEP's *V-for-Victory signal.*[1]]

---

1. **V-for-Victory signal:** three short rings and one long ring, Morse code for the letter *V.*

MR. FRANK. It's Miep!

[*He goes quickly down the steps to unbolt the door.* MRS. FRANK *calls upstairs to the* VAN DAANS *and then to* PETER.]

MRS. FRANK. Wake up, everyone! Miep is here! [ANNE *quickly puts her diary away.* MARGOT *sits up, pulling the blanket around her shoulders.* DUSSEL *sits on the edge of his bed, listening, disgruntled.* MIEP *comes up the steps, followed by* MR. KRALER. *They bring flowers, books, newspapers, etc.* ANNE *rushes to* MIEP, *throwing her arms affectionately around her.*] Miep . . . and Mr. Kraler . . . What a delightful surprise!

MR. KRALER. We came to bring you New Year's greetings.

3 **MRS. FRANK.** You shouldn't . . . you should have at least one day to yourselves. [*She goes quickly to the stove and brings down teacups and tea for all of them.*]

ANNE. Don't say that, it's so wonderful to see them! [*Sniffing at* MIEP's *coat.*] I can smell the wind and the cold on your clothes.

MIEP. [*Giving her the flowers.*] There you are. [*Then, to* MARGOT, *feeling her forehead.*] How are you, Margot? . . . Feeling any better?

MARGOT. I'm all right.

ANNE. We filled her full of every kind of pill so she won't cough and make a noise.

[*She runs into her room to put the flowers in water.* MR. *and* MRS. VAN DAAN *come from upstairs. Outside there is the sound of a band playing.*]

MRS. VAN DAAN. Well, hello, Miep. Mr. Kraler.

MR. KRALER. [*Giving a bouquet of flowers to*

The Diary of Anne Frank, Act II   **407**

AT A GLANCE

- *Act II, Scene 1:* It is New Year's Day, 1944.
- Margot lies sick on the couch.
- Mr. Kraler and Miep come with gifts and greetings.

LITERARY OPTIONS

- characterization
- plot
- setting

THEMATIC OPTIONS

- friendship and love
- family life
- ideals

1 **SETTING**

The action takes place in the same setting as Act I; however, the cold weather makes the attic an even more forbidding environment.

2 **STAGE DIRECTIONS**

The familiar carillon and then Miep's sounding of the buzzer are reminders of the audience that the group's fate is in the hands of those on the outside.

3 **CHARACTERIZATION**

Anne's candid welcome is played against her mother's reserve and thoughtfulness.

GUIDED READING

LITERAL QUESTIONS

1a. How do we learn the time of year at the beginning of Act II? (from Anne's diary)

2a. What change in herself does Anne note? (increased uncertainty)

INFERENTIAL QUESTIONS

1b. What does Anne's phrase "We are all a little thinner" suggest? (The phrase suggests that their food supply has been insufficient.)

2b. What do you think Anne means? (She may be growing more self-conscious as she becomes less of a child and more of a woman.)

- Peter asks Miep about Mouschi.
- Miep offers a cake.
- Dussel and the Van Daans argue about the cutting of the cake.

1 READING SKILLS: MAKING INFERENCES

Mouschi apparently has disappeared from the attic. Miep has looked for the cat, but to no avail.

2 THEME

The characters' responses reflect their feelings of gratitude to Miep for what would ordinarily be considered an unremarkable gift. In time of severe rationing, a cake is a significant gift.

3 IRONY

This reference to the cake Miep brought a year ago ironically underscores their unfulfilled hope for peace in 1943 and reminds us of the passage of time.

4 PLOT: CONFLICT

Dussel speaks the truth about the larger portions Mrs. Van Daan serves her husband. Dussel's words are a reminder of an ongoing conflict among the group.

MRS. VAN DAAN.] With my hope for peace in the New Year.

1 PETER. [*Anxiously.*] Miep, have you seen Mouschi? Have you seen him anywhere around?

MIEP. I'm sorry, Peter. I asked everyone in the neighborhood had they seen a gray cat. But they said no.

[MRS. FRANK *gives* MIEP *a cup of tea.* MR. FRANK *comes up the steps carrying a small cake on a plate.*]

2 MR. FRANK. Look what Miep's brought for us!

MRS. FRANK. [*Taking it.*] A cake!

MR. VAN DAAN. A cake! [*He pinches* MIEP's *cheeks gaily and hurries up to the cupboard.*] I'll get some plates.

[DUSSEL, *in his room, hastily puts a coat on and starts out to join the others.*]

MRS. FRANK. Thank you, Miepia. You shouldn't have done it. You must have used all of your sugar ration for weeks. [*Giving it to* MRS. VAN DAAN.] It's beautiful, isn't it?

MRS. VAN DAAN. It's been ages since I even saw a cake. Not since you brought us one last year.

3 [*Without looking at the cake, to* MIEP.] Remember? Don't you remember, you gave us one on New Year's Day? Just this time last year? I'll never forget it because you had "Peace in nineteen forty-three" on it. [*She looks at the cake and reads.*] "Peace in nineteen forty-four!"

MIEP. Well, it has to come sometime, you know. [*As* DUSSEL *comes from his room.*] Hello, Mr. Dussel.

MR. KRALER. How are you?

MR. VAN DAAN. [*Bringing plates and a knife.*] Here's the knife, *liefje*. Now, how many of us are there?

408   *Drama*

MIEP. None for me, thank you.

MR. FRANK. Oh, please. You must.

MIEP. I couldn't.

MR. VAN DAAN. Good! That leaves one . . . two . . . three . . . seven of us.

DUSSEL. Eight! Eight! It's the same number as it always is!

MR. VAN DAAN. I left Margot out. I take it for granted Margot won't eat any.

ANNE. Why wouldn't she!

MRS. FRANK. I think it won't harm her.

MR. VAN DAAN. All right! All right! I just didn't want her to start coughing again, that's all.

DUSSEL. And please, Mrs. Frank should cut the cake.

MR. VAN DAAN. What's the difference?

MRS. VAN DAAN. It's not Mrs. Frank's cake, is it, Miep? It's for all of us.   } [*Together.*]

DUSSEL. Mrs. Frank divides things better.

MRS. VAN DAAN. [*Going to* DUSSEL.] What are you trying to say?

MR. VAN DAAN. Oh, come on! Stop wasting time!   } [*Together.*]

MRS. VAN DAAN. [*To* DUSSEL.] Don't I always give everybody exactly the same? Don't I?

MR. VAN DAAN. Forget it, Kerli.

MRS. VAN DAAN. No. I want an answer! Don't I?

4 DUSSEL. Yes. Yes. Everybody gets exactly the same . . . except Mr. Van Daan always gets a little bit more.

GUIDED READING

LITERAL QUESTION

1a. Why does Dussel want Mrs. Frank to cut the cake instead of Mrs. Van Daan? (He says Mrs. Frank divides things better.)

INFERENTIAL QUESTION

1b. How does Dussel feel about Mr. Van Daan's larger portions? (He probably feels angry, resentful, and envious.)

[MR. VAN DAAN *advances on* DUSSEL, *the knife still in his hand.*]

MR. VAN DAAN. That's a lie!

[DUSSEL *retreats before the onslaught of the* VAN DAANS.]

MR. FRANK. Please, please! [*Then, to* MIEP.] You see what a little sugar cake does to us? It goes right to our heads!

MR. VAN DAAN. [*Handing* MRS. FRANK *the knife.*] Here you are, Mrs. Frank.

MRS. FRANK. Thank you. [*Then, to* MIEP *as she goes to the table to cut the cake.*] Are you sure you won't have some?

MIEP. [*Drinking her tea.*] No, really, I have to go in a minute.

[*The sound of the band fades out in the distance.*]

PETER. [*To* MIEP.] Maybe Mouschi went back to our house . . . they say that cats . . . Do you ever get over there . . . ? I mean . . . do you suppose you could . . . ?

MIEP. I'll try, Peter. The first minute I get I'll try. But I'm afraid, with him gone a week . . .

DUSSEL. Make up your mind, already someone has had a nice big dinner from that cat!

[PETER *is furious, inarticulate. He starts toward* DUSSEL *as if to hit him.* MR. FRANK *stops him.* MRS. FRANK *speaks quickly to ease the situation.*]

MRS. FRANK. [*To* MIEP.] This is delicious, Miep!

MRS. VAN DAAN. [*Eating hers.*] Delicious!

MR. VAN DAAN. [*Finishing it in one gulp.*] Dirk's in luck to get a girl who can bake like this!

MIEP. [*Putting down her empty teacup.*] I have to run. Dirk's taking me to a party tonight.

1 **ANNE.** How heavenly! Remember now what everyone is wearing, and what you have to eat and everything, so you can tell us tomorrow.

MIEP. I'll give you a full report! Goodbye, everyone!

MR. VAN DAAN. [*To* MIEP.] Just a minute. There's something I'd like you to do for me. [*He hurries off up the stairs to his room.*]

MRS. VAN DAAN. [*Sharply.*] Putti, where are you going? [*She rushes up the stairs after him, calling hysterically.*] What do you want? Putti, what are you going to do?

MIEP. [*To* PETER.] What's wrong?

PETER. [*His sympathy is with his mother.*] Father says he's going to sell her fur coat. She's crazy about that old fur coat.

DUSSEL. Is it possible? Is it possible that anyone is so silly as to worry about a fur coat in times like this?

2 **PETER.** It's none of your darn business . . . and if you say one more thing . . . I'll, I'll take you and I'll . . . I mean it . . . I'll . . .

[*There is a piercing scream from* MRS. VAN DAAN *above. She grabs at the fur coat as* MR. VAN DAAN *is starting downstairs with it.*]

3 **MRS. VAN DAAN.** No! No! No! Don't you dare take that! You hear? It's mine. [*Downstairs* PETER *turns away, embarrassed, miserable.*] My father gave me that! You didn't give it to me. You have no right. Let go of it . . . you hear?

[MR. VAN DAAN *pulls the coat from her hands and hurries downstairs.* MRS. VAN DAAN *sinks to the floor, sobbing. As* MR. VAN DAAN *comes into the main room the others look away, embarrassed for him.*]

MR. VAN DAAN. [*To* MR. KRALER.] Just a little—discussion over the advisability of selling this

The Diary of Anne Frank, Act II 409

AT A GLANCE

- Mrs. Frank cuts the cake.
- Dussel tells Peter his cat has probably been eaten.
- Mr. Van Daan gives Miep his wife's fur coat to sell.

1 CHARACTERIZATION

Even after more than a year in hiding Anne becomes excited at the thought of a party. She will take vicarious pleasure in Miep's description of the clothing and the food.

2 THEME

Peter's strong loyalty to his family, which is not often expressed, prompts him to threaten Dussel for his insensitive remarks.

3 PLOT: CONFLICT

Mrs. Van Daan's protests are especially poignant and pathetic in light of all the losses the characters have endured.

GUIDED READING

LITERAL QUESTIONS

1a. How does Mr. Frank explain the argument between Dussel and Mr. Van Daan to Miep? (He says that a little sugar cake goes right to their heads.)

2a. About what do the Van Daans quarrel? (the selling of her fur coat)

INFERENTIAL QUESTIONS

1b. How do you think he feels? (He probably feels embarrassed that Miep sees the petty argument.)

2b. Why does her fur coat mean so much when she must stay indoors all the time? (Mrs. Van Daan is especially fond of her possessions; the coat was a gift from her father, and she has a sentimental attachment to it.)

- Mr. Van Daan gives Miep the coat and asks for cigarettes.
- Mr. Kraler asks to speak privately to Mr. Frank.
- Mr. Kraler recounts his conversation with an employee.

1 CHARACTERIZATION

From Mr. Van Daan's request for cigarettes, his selfish motive for selling his wife's coat becomes apparent.

2 HUMOR

Mr. Kraler's joke about the doctor is typical of the kind of humor that develops during difficult times.

3 CHARACTERIZATION

Mr. Frank's response to Mr. Kraler's request shows his wisdom as a leader. Margot's fears underscore the wisdom of her father's choice to share the problem with everyone.

4 READING SKILLS: MAKING PREDICTIONS

Carl's reported questioning about the Franks leads us to infer that he knows more than he is saying. We begin to make tentative predictions that Carl may cause problems for the group in hiding. Ultimately these predictions prove incorrect.

---

1 coat. As I have often reminded Mrs. Van Daan, it's very selfish of her to keep it when people outside are in such desperate need of clothing. . . . [*He gives the coat to* MIEP.] So if you will please to sell it for us? It should fetch a good price. And by the way, will you get me cigarettes. I don't care what kind they are . . . get all you can.

MIEP. It's terribly difficult to get them, Mr. Van Daan. But I'll try. Goodbye.

[*She goes.* MR. FRANK *follows her down the steps to bolt the door after her.* MRS. FRANK *gives* MR. KRALER *a cup of tea.*]

MRS. FRANK. Are you sure you won't have some cake, Mr. Kraler?

MR. KRALER. I'd better not.

MR. VAN DAAN. You're still feeling badly? What does your doctor say?

MR. KRALER. I haven't been to him.

MRS. FRANK. Now, Mr. Kraler! . . .

2 MR. KRALER. [*Sitting at the table.*] Oh, I tried. But you can't get near a doctor these days . . . they're so busy. After weeks I finally managed to get one on the telephone. I told him I'd like an appointment . . . I wasn't feeling very well. You know what he answers . . . over the telephone . . . Stick out your tongue! [*They laugh. He turns to* MR. FRANK *as* MR. FRANK *comes back.*] I have some contracts here. . . . I wonder if you'd look over them with me. . . .

MR. FRANK. [*Putting out his hand.*] Of course.

MR. KRALER. [*He rises.*] If we could go downstairs . . . [MR. FRANK *starts ahead;* MR. KRALER *speaks to the others.*] Will you forgive us? I won't keep him but a minute. [*He starts to follow* MR. FRANK *down the steps.*]

MARGOT. [*With sudden foreboding.*] What's

410 *Drama*

happened? Something's happened! Hasn't it, Mr. Kraler?

[MR. KRALER *stops and comes back, trying to reassure* MARGOT *with a pretense of casualness.*]

3 MR. KRALER. No, really. I want your father's advice. . . .

MARGOT. Something's gone wrong! I know it!

MR. FRANK. [*Coming back, to* MR. KRALER.] If it's something that concerns us here, it's better that we all hear it.

MR. KRALER. [*Turning to him, quietly.*] But . . . the children . . . ?

MR. FRANK. What they'd imagine would be worse than any reality.

[*As* MR. KRALER *speaks, they all listen with intense apprehension.* MRS. VAN DAAN *comes down the stairs and sits on the bottom step.*]

MR. KRALER. It's a man in the storeroom. . . . I don't know whether or not you remember him . . . Carl, about fifty, heavyset, nearsighted . . . He came with us just before you left.

MR. FRANK. He was from Utrecht?[2]

MR. KRALER. That's the man. A couple of weeks ago, when I was in the storeroom, he 4 closed the door and asked me . . . how's Mr. Frank? What do you hear from Mr. Frank? I told him I only knew there was a rumor that you were in Switzerland. He said he'd heard that rumor too, but he thought I might know something more. I didn't pay any attention to it . . . but then a thing happened yesterday. . . . He'd brought some invoices to the office for me to sign. As I was going through them,

---

2. **Utrecht** [ū′trekt]: city in central Netherlands.

GUIDED READING

LITERAL QUESTIONS

1a. What reason does Mr. Van Daan give for selling the coat? (He says it is selfish of Mrs. Van Daan to keep it when people need clothes.)

2a. What reason does Mr. Kraler give for asking Mr. Frank to go downstairs? (Mr. Kraler wants Mr. Frank to look at some contracts.)

INFERENTIAL QUESTIONS

1b. Why does he really want to sell the coat? (He wants to have the money for cigarettes.)

2b. What is Mr. Kraler's real reason? (He wants to spare the others any worry that his news will bring.)

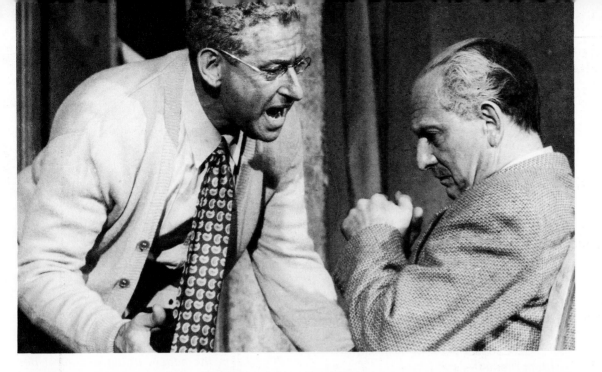

AT A GLANCE

- *Scene 1 (continued):* Mr. Kraler reveals that the employee asked for more money.
- He asks Mr. Frank's advice.
- Mr. Frank suggests offering him half of what he asked.

1 PLOT: SUSPENSE

The suspense builds as Mr. Kraler reveals that the employee has referred to a door that used to lead up to the loft—and is, in fact, now the hidden entrance to the loft.

2 DIALOGUE

The dialogue between Mr. Kraler and Dussel points up the extreme vulnerability of the group in hiding. By covering up their whereabouts, Mr. Kraler is also vulnerable.

3 CHARACTERIZATION

The contrast between Mr. Frank and Dussel is apparent as Mr. Frank steps back to assess the situation and Dussel oversimplifies the case in his eagerness to resolve it.

1 I looked up. He was standing staring at the bookcase . . . your bookcase. He said he thought he remembered a door there. . . . Wasn't there a door there that used to go up to the loft? Then he told me he wanted more money. Twenty guilders[3] more a week.

MR. VAN DAAN. Blackmail!

MR. FRANK. Twenty guilders? Very modest blackmail.

MR. VAN DAAN. That's just the beginning.

DUSSEL. [*Coming to* MR. FRANK.] You know what I think? He was the thief who was down there that night. That's how he knows we're here.

MR. FRANK. [*To* MR. KRALER.] How was it left? What did you tell him?

---

3. **Twenty guilders:** Dutch currency worth about five dollars at the time.

2 **MR. KRALER.** I said I had to think about it. What shall I do? Pay him the money? . . . Take a chance on firing him . . . or what? I don't know.

DUSSEL. [*Frantic.*] Don't fire him! Pay him what he asks . . . keep him here where you can have your eye on him.

MR. FRANK. Is it so much that he's asking? What are they paying nowadays?

MR. KRALER. He could get it in a war plant. But this isn't a war plant. Mind you, I don't know if he really knows . . . or if he doesn't know.

3 **MR. FRANK.** Offer him half. Then we'll soon find out if it's blackmail or not.

DUSSEL. And if it is? We've got to pay it, haven't we? Anything he asks we've got to pay!

MR. FRANK. Let's decide that when the time comes.

The Diary of Anne Frank, Act II **411**

GUIDED READING

LITERAL QUESTIONS

1a. What does Mr. Kraler say the employee asked for? (twenty guilders more a week)

2a. What is Mr. Frank's advice? (to offer him half)

INFERENTIAL QUESTIONS

1b. Why does Mr. Kraler suspect blackmail? (Before he mentioned money, the man asked about Mr. Frank and remembered a door behind the bookcase.)

2b. Why is this good advice? (It may keep the man quiet for a while and give Mr. Kraler time to assess how much the man knows.)

- *Scene 1 (continued):* Mr. Kraler leaves, promising to offer the man half the amount.
- Margot reveals her desire for the ordeal to be over.
- Anne argues with her mother.

1 PLOT: CONFLICT

Dussel exhibits a characteristic of many people under stress: looking for a scapegoat.

2 CHARACTERIZATION

The good, quiet Margot reveals the depth of her depression in her wish to have the ordeal of waiting end—even if it means being sent to a concentration camp.

3 PLOT: FORESHADOWING

Mrs. Frank's response to Margot outlines not only the fate of others but the eventual fate of those hiding in the attic.

4 THEME

In her outrage Anne stresses her need for hope at a time when everything she cares about is being destroyed.

5 THEME

When Peter brings the cake to Anne, he is bringing an offer of friendship as well.

MR. KRALER. This may be all imagination. You get to a point, these days, where you suspect everyone and everything. Again and again . . . on some simple look or word, I've found myself . . .

[*The telephone rings in the office below.*]

MRS. VAN DAAN. [*Hurrying to* MR. KRALER.] There's the telephone! What does that mean, the telephone ringing on a holiday?

MR. KRALER. That's my wife. I told her I had to go over some papers in my office . . . to call me there when she got out of church. [*He starts out.*] I'll offer him half then. Goodbye . . . we'll hope for the best!

[*The group call their goodbyes halfheartedly.* MR. FRANK *follows* MR. KRALER, *to bolt the door below. During the following scene,* MR. FRANK *comes back up and stands listening, disturbed.*]

1 DUSSEL. [*To* MR. VAN DAAN.] You can thank your son for this . . . smashing the light! I tell you, it's just a question of time now. [*He goes to the window at the back and stands looking out.*]

2 MARGOT. Sometimes I wish the end would come . . . whatever it is.

MRS. FRANK. [*Shocked.*] Margot!

[ANNE *goes to* MARGOT, *sitting beside her on the couch with her arms around her.*]

3 MARGOT. Then at least we'd know where we were.

MRS. FRANK. You should be ashamed of yourself! Talking that way! Think how lucky we are! Think of the thousands dying in the war, every day. Think of the people in concentration camps.

ANNE. [*Interrupting.*] What's the good of that?

412   *Drama*

What's the good of thinking of misery when you're already miserable? That's stupid!

MRS. FRANK. Anne!

[*As* ANNE *goes on raging at her mother,* MRS. FRANK *tries to break in, in an effort to quiet her.*]

4 ANNE. We're young. Margot and Peter and I! You grown-ups have had your chance! But look at us. . . . If we begin thinking of all the horror in the world, we're lost! We're trying to hold on to some kinds of ideals . . . when everything . . . ideals, hopes . . . everything, are being destroyed! It isn't our fault that the world is in such a mess! We weren't around when all this started! So don't try to take it out on us! [*She rushes off to her room, slamming the door after her. She picks up a brush from the chest and hurls it to the floor. Then she sits on the settee, trying to control her anger.*]

MR. VAN DAAN. She talks as if we started the war! Did we start the war?

[*He spots* ANNE's *cake. As he starts to take it,* PETER *anticipates him.*]

PETER. She left her cake. [*He starts for* ANNE's *room with the cake. There is silence in the main room.* MRS. VAN DAAN *goes up to her room, followed by* MR. VAN DAAN. DUSSEL *stays looking out the window.* MR. FRANK *brings* MRS. FRANK *her cake. She eats it slowly, without relish.* MR. FRANK *takes his cake to* MARGOT **5** *and sits quietly on the sofa beside her.* PETER *stands in the doorway of* ANNE's *darkened room, looking at her, then makes a little movement to let her know he is there.* ANNE *sits up, quickly, trying to hide the signs of her tears.* PETER *holds out the cake to her.*] You left this.

ANNE. [*Dully.*] Thanks.

GUIDED READING

LITERAL QUESTIONS

1a. What does Margot say she wishes? (She wishes the end would come.)

2a. What does Anne say she, Margot, and Peter are trying to hold on to? (some kinds of ideals)

INFERENTIAL QUESTIONS

1b. What does this reveal about Margot? (She is deeply depressed, for she is saying that even death is preferable to a life of terror.)

2b. Why do you think Anne says they must hold on to their ideals? (She believes they need ideals to help them endure the horrors of the war and persecution.)

[PETER *starts to go out, then comes back.*]

1 **PETER.** I thought you were fine just now. You know just how to talk to them. You know just how to say it. I'm no good . . . I never can think . . . especially when I'm mad. . . . That Dussel . . . when he said that about Mouschi . . . someone eating him . . . all I could think is . . . I wanted to hit him. I wanted to give him such a . . . a . . . that he'd . . . That's what I used to do when there was an argument at school. . . . That's the way I . . . but here . . . And an old man like that . . . it wouldn't be so good.

ANNE. You're making a big mistake about me. I do it all wrong. I say too much. I go too far. I hurt people's feelings. . . .

[DUSSEL *leaves the window, going to his room.*]

2 **PETER.** I think you're just fine. . . . What I want to say . . . if it wasn't for you around here, I don't know. What I mean . . .

[PETER *is interrupted by* DUSSEL'S *turning on the light.* DUSSEL *stands in the doorway, startled to see* PETER. PETER *advances toward him forbiddingly.* DUSSEL *backs out of the room.* PETER *closes the door on him.*]

3 **ANNE.** Do you mean it, Peter? Do you really mean it?

PETER. I said it, didn't I?

ANNE. Thank you, Peter!

[*In the main room* MR. *and* MRS. FRANK *collect the dishes and take them to the sink, washing them.* MARGOT *lies down again on the couch.* DUSSEL, *lost, wanders into* PETER's *room and takes up a book, starting to read.*]

PETER. [*Looking at the photographs on the wall.*] You've got quite a collection.

ANNE. Wouldn't you like some in your room? I could give you some. Heaven knows you spend enough time in there . . . doing heaven knows what. . . .

PETER. It's easier. A fight starts, or an argument . . . I duck in there.

ANNE. You're lucky, having a room to go to. His Lordship is always here. . . . I hardly ever get a minute alone. When they start in on me, I can't duck away. I have to stand there and take it.

PETER. You gave some of it back just now.

4 **ANNE.** I get so mad. They've formed their opinions . . . about everything . . . but we . . . we're still trying to find out. . . . We have problems here that no other people our age have ever had. And just as you think you've solved them, something comes along and bang! You have to start all over again.

PETER. At least you've got someone you can talk to.

5 **ANNE.** Not really. Mother . . . I never discuss anything serious with her. She doesn't understand. Father's all right. We can talk about everything . . . everything but one thing. Mother. He simply won't talk about her. I don't think you can be really intimate with anyone if he holds something back, do you?

PETER. I think your father's fine.

ANNE. Oh, he is, Peter! He is! He's the only one who's ever given me the feeling that I have any sense. But anyway, nothing can take the place of school and play and friends of your own age . . . or near your age . . . can it?

PETER. I suppose you miss your friends and all.

ANNE. It isn't just . . . [*She breaks off, staring up at him for a second.*] Isn't it funny, you

The Diary of Anne Frank, Act II 413

AT A GLANCE

- *Scene 1 (continued):* Peter praises Anne for speaking out.
- Anne describes her inner struggles and tells Peter about her relationship with her parents.

1 READING SKILLS: COMPARISON AND CONTRAST

Peter contrasts Anne's ability to speak out with his own struggle to articulate his feelings.

2 DIALOGUE

Peter finally expresses how much Anne's presence in the attic has meant to him.

3 CHARACTERIZATION

When Anne finally receives an expression of friendship from the usually shy and aloof Peter, she is unable to believe what she is hearing.

4 THEME

Anne articulates her struggle to resolve her doubts and find out what she truly believes in.

5 THEME

The theme of family relationships surfaces here. Anne explains she has a difficult relationship with her mother and a good relationship with her father. But she has begun to be disappointed in her father—a change since Act I.

GUIDED READING

LITERAL QUESTIONS

1a. How does Peter say he behaved when there was an argument at school? (He hit people.)

2a. What does Anne say about friends "of your own age . . . or near your age"? (Nothing can take their place.)

INFERENTIAL QUESTIONS

1b. Why do you think Peter fought at school? (He never knew what to say when he was angry and so he got into fights.)

2b. What is Anne trying to ask Peter? (She is inviting him to be her friend.)

- *Scene 1 (continued)*: Peter invites Anne to come to his room whenever she wishes.
- Anne describes the lack of food.
- *Scene 2:* Peter prepares for a visit from Anne.

1 THEME

Anne expresses her need for friendship.

2 CHARACTERIZATION

Since Peter is far less demonstrative than Anne, his invitation to her marks an important change in his character.

3 SETTING

Although Dussel is not a very sympathetic character, his isolation and inability to find comfort in the setting are poignantly amusing.

4 TONE

The shifts in tone in Anne's diary—from serious to whimsical to yearning—portray her mercurial character.

5 STAGE DIRECTIONS

The stage directions describe Peter's preparation for a visit from Anne. These preparations for a "date" could be taking place in normal times under normal circumstances.

---

1 and I? Here we've been seeing each other every minute for almost a year and a half, and this is the first time we've ever really talked. It helps a lot to have someone to talk to, don't you think? It helps you to let off steam.

PETER. [*Going to the door.*] Well, any time you want to let off steam, you can come into my room.

2 ANNE. [*Following him.*] I can get up an awful lot of steam. You'll have to be careful how you say that.

PETER. It's all right with me.

ANNE. Do you really mean it?

PETER. I said it, didn't I?

[*He goes out.* ANNE *stands in her doorway looking after him. As* PETER *gets to his door, he stands for a minute looking back at her.* 3 *Then he goes into his room.* DUSSEL *rises as he comes in, and quickly passes him, going out. He starts across for his room.* ANNE *sees him coming and pulls her door shut.* DUSSEL *turns back toward* PETER's *room.* PETER *pulls his door shut.* DUSSEL *stands there, bewildered, forlorn.*

The scene slowly dims out. The curtain falls on the scene. ANNE's *voice comes over in the darkness . . . faintly at first, and then with growing strength.*]

ANNE'S VOICE. We've had bad news. The people from whom Miep got our ration books have been arrested. So we have had to cut down on our food. Our stomachs are so empty that they rumble and make strange noises, all in different keys. Mr. Van Daan's is deep and low, like a bass fiddle. Mine is high, whistling like a flute. As we all sit around waiting for supper, it's like an orchestra tuning up. It only needs Toscanini[4] to raise his baton and we'd be off

in the "Ride of the Valkyries."[5] Monday, the sixth of March, nineteen forty-four. Mr. Kraler is in the hospital. It seems he has ulcers. Pim says we are his ulcers. Miep has to run the business and us too. The Americans have landed on the southern tip of Italy. Father looks for a quick finish to the war. Mr. Dussel is waiting every day for the warehouseman to 4 demand more money. Have I been skipping too much from one subject to another? I can't help it. I feel that spring is coming. I feel it in my whole body and soul. I feel utterly confused. I am longing . . . so longing . . . for everything . . . for friends . . . for someone to talk to . . . someone who understands . . . someone young, who feels as I do. . . .

[*As these last lines are being said, the curtain rises on the scene. The lights dim on.* ANNE's *voice fades out.*]

Scene 2

It is evening, after supper.

[*From the outside we hear the sound of children playing. The "grown-ups," with the exception of* MR. VAN DAAN, *are all in the main room.* MRS. FRANK *is doing some mending.* MRS. VAN DAAN *is reading a fashion magazine.* MR. FRANK *is going over business accounts.* DUSSEL, *in his dentist's jacket, is pacing up and down, impatient to get into his bedroom.* MR. VAN DAAN *is upstairs working on a piece of embroidery in an embroidery frame.*

5 *In his room* PETER *is sitting before the mirror, smoothing his hair. As the scene goes on, he puts on his tie, brushes his coat and puts it on, preparing himself meticulously for a visit from* ANNE. *On his wall are now hung some of* ANNE's *motion-picture stars.*

---

4. **Toscanini** [tôs′kə nē′nē]: Arturo Toscanini (1867–1957), famous Italian orchestra conductor.

5. **"Ride of the Valkyries"** [val kēr′ēz]: exciting music by the German composer Richard Wagner.

GUIDED READING

LITERAL QUESTION

1a. What invitation does Peter give to Anne? (She can come to his room to let off steam.)

INFERENTIAL QUESTION

1b. Why do you think this invitation means so much to Anne? (She wants a friend, and Peter is offering to be that friend.)

1 *In her room* ANNE *too is getting dressed. She stands before the mirror in her slip, trying various ways of dressing her hair.* MARGOT *is seated on the sofa, hemming a skirt for* ANNE *to wear.*]

In the main room DUSSEL *can stand it no longer. He comes over, rapping sharply on the door of his and* ANNE'S *bedroom.*]

ANNE. [*Calling to him.*] No, no, Mr. Dussel! I am not dressed yet. [DUSSEL *walks away, furious, sitting down and burying his head in his hands.* ANNE *turns to* MARGOT.] How is that? How does that look?

MARGOT. [*Glancing at her briefly.*] Fine.

ANNE. You didn't even look.

2 **MARGOT.** Of course I did. It's fine.

ANNE. Margot, tell me, am I terribly ugly?

MARGOT. Oh, stop fishing.

ANNE. No. No. Tell me.

MARGOT. Of course you're not. You've got nice eyes . . . and a lot of animation, and . . .

ANNE. A little vague, aren't you?

[*Outside,* MRS. FRANK, *feeling sorry for* DUSSEL, *comes over, knocking at the girls' door.*]

MRS. FRANK. [*Outside.*] May I come in?

MARGOT. Come in, Mother.

MRS. FRANK. [*Shutting the door behind her.*] Mr. Dussel's impatient to get in here.

ANNE. Heavens, he takes the room for himself the entire day.

MRS. FRANK. [*Gently.*] Anne, dear, you're not going in again tonight to see Peter?

ANNE. [*Dignified.*] That is my intention.

MRS. FRANK. But you've already spent a great deal of time in there today.

ANNE. I was in there exactly twice. Once to get the dictionary, and then three quarters of an hour before supper.

MRS. FRANK. Aren't you afraid you're disturbing him?

ANNE. Mother, I have some intuition.

MRS. FRANK. Then may I ask you this much, Anne. Please don't shut the door when you go in.

ANNE. You sound like Mrs. Van Daan!

MRS. FRANK. No. No. I don't mean to suggest anything wrong. I only wish that you wouldn't expose yourself to criticism . . . that you wouldn't give Mrs. Van Daan the opportunity to be unpleasant.

ANNE. Mrs. Van Daan doesn't need an opportunity to be unpleasant!

MRS. FRANK. Everyone's on edge, worried about Mr. Kraler. This is one more thing. . . .

ANNE. I'm sorry, Mother. I'm going to Peter's room. I'm not going to let Petronella Van Daan spoil our friendship.

3 [MRS. FRANK *hesitates for a second, then goes out, closing the door after her. She gets a pack of playing cards and sits at the center table playing solitaire. In* ANNE'S *room* MARGOT *hands the finished skirt to* ANNE. *As* ANNE *is putting it on,* MARGOT *takes off her high-heeled shoes and stuffs paper in the toes so that* ANNE *can wear them.*]

4 **MARGOT.** [*To* ANNE.] Why don't you two talk in the main room? It'd save a lot of trouble. It's hard on Mother, having to listen to those remarks from Mrs. Van Daan and not say a word.

ANNE. Why doesn't she say a word? I think it's ridiculous to take it and take it.

MARGOT. You don't understand Mother at all,

The Diary of Anne Frank, Act II 415

AT A GLANCE

- *Scene 2 (continued):* Anne prepares for her visit to Peter's room.
- Anne looks to Margot for reassurance.
- Mrs. Frank urges Anne to use discretion.

1 STAGE DIRECTIONS

Anne's actions in her room parallel, in a sweetly humorous way, Peter's actions in his. The audience sees into both rooms at the same time.

2 DIALOGUE

In an exchange that could occur between two teen-age girls almost anywhere, Anne reveals her insecurity about her appearance to Margot, who does her best to be honest and bolster Anne's self-esteem.

3 STAGE DIRECTIONS

Mrs. Frank's isolation from her two daughters is dramatized as she plays solitaire while Anne and Margot continue their preparations.

4 CHARACTERIZATION

Margot tries to mediate between Anne and her mother in their new conflict.

GUIDED READING

LITERAL QUESTION

1a. Why does Mrs. Frank ask Anne not to shut the door when she goes to Peter's room? (Mrs. Frank does not want Anne to expose herself to criticism.)

INFERENTIAL QUESTION

1b. Why do you think Margot involves herself in the conflict between Anne and her mother? (Margot probably wants to save her mother some discomfort, and she thinks that Anne will listen to her.)

AT A GLANCE

- *Scene 2 (continued):* Anne expresses her concern for Margot.
- Mrs. Van Daan expresses her disapproval of Anne's visiting Peter.

1 READING SKILLS: CONTRAST

Anne shows real concern for Margot. In Act I she had envied Margot; now, Anne feels sorry for her talented, pretty elder sister.

2 CHARACTERIZATION

Margot, always contained and unselfish, has responded to the ordeal by withdrawing and losing hope.

3 CONFLICT

Mrs. Van Daan's love for her son is expressed in her frustration that he is not more demonstrative in his love for her. Instead of telling Peter of her love, she tells him he needs his sleep.

do you? She can't talk back. She's not like you. It's just not in her nature to fight back.

1 ANNE. Anyway . . . the only one I worry about is you. I feel awfully guilty about you. [*She sits on the stool near* MARGOT, *putting on* MARGOT'*s high-heeled shoes.*]

MARGOT. What about?

ANNE. I mean, every time I go into Peter's room, I have a feeling I may be hurting you. [MARGOT *shakes her head.*] I know if it were me, I'd be wild. I'd be desperately jealous, if it were me.

MARGOT. Well, I'm not.

ANNE. You don't feel badly? Really? Truly? You're not jealous?

2 MARGOT. Of course I'm jealous . . . jealous that you've got something to get up in the morning for. . . . But jealous of you and Peter? No.

[ANNE *goes back to the mirror.*]

ANNE. Maybe there's nothing to be jealous of. Maybe he doesn't really like me. Maybe I'm just taking the place of his cat. . . . [*She picks up a pair of short, white gloves, putting them on.*] Wouldn't you like to come in with us?

MARGOT. I have a book.

[*The sound of the children playing outside fades out. In the main room* DUSSEL *can stand it no longer. He jumps up, going to the bedroom door and knocking sharply.*]

DUSSEL. Will you please let me in my room!

ANNE. Just a minute, dear, dear Mr. Dussel. [*She picks up her mother's pink stole and adjusts it elegantly over her shoulders, then gives a last look in the mirror.*] Well, here I go . . . to run the gantlet.[6] [*She starts out, followed by* MARGOT.]

---

6. **to run the gantlet** [gont′lit]: to run between rows of attackers without striking back.

416 *Drama*

DUSSEL. [*As she appears—sarcastic.*] Thank you so much.

[DUSSEL *goes into his room.* ANNE *goes toward* PETER'*s room passing* MRS. VAN DAAN *and her parents at the center table.*]

MRS. VAN DAAN. Look at her! [ANNE *pays no attention. She knocks at* PETER'*s door.*] I don't know what good it is to have a son. I never see him. He wouldn't care if I killed myself. [PETER *opens the door and stands aside for* ANNE *to come in.*] Just a minute, Anne. [*She goes to them at the door.*] I'd like to say a few words to my son. Do you mind? [PETER *and* ANNE *stand waiting.*] Peter, I don't want you staying up till all hours tonight. You've got to have some sleep. You're a growing boy. You hear?

MRS. FRANK. Anne won't stay late. She's going to bed promptly at nine. Aren't you, Anne?

ANNE. Yes, Mother . . . [*To* MRS. VAN DAAN.] May we go now?

MRS. VAN DAAN. Are you asking me? I didn't know I had anything to say about it.

MRS. FRANK. Listen for the chimes, Anne dear.

[*The two young people go off into* PETER'*s room, shutting the door after them.*]

MRS. VAN DAAN. [*To* MRS. FRANK.] In my day it was the boys who called on the girls. Not the girls on the boys.

MRS. FRANK. You know how young people like to feel that they have secrets. Peter's room is the only place where they can talk.

MRS. VAN DAAN. Talk? That's not what they called it when I was young.

[MRS. VAN DAAN *goes off to the bathroom.* MARGOT *settles down to read her book.* MR. FRANK *puts his papers away and brings a chess game to the center table. He and* MRS. FRANK *start to play. In* PETER'*s room,*

GUIDED READING

LITERAL QUESTION

1a. Why does Anne worry about Margot? (She fears that when she visits Peter, Margot is jealous.)

INFERENTIAL QUESTION

1b. What does Margot's answer reveal? (She is not jealous of Anne and Peter, but wishes for something that would give her as much joy as Anne gains from her friendship with Peter.)

ANNE *speaks to* PETER, *indignant, humiliated.*]

ANNE. Aren't they awful? Aren't they impossible? Treating us as if we were still in the nursery.

[*She sits on the cot.* PETER *gets a bottle of pop and two glasses.*]

PETER. Don't let it bother you. It doesn't bother me.

ANNE. I suppose you can't really blame them . . . they think back to what *they* were like at our age. They don't realize how much more advanced we are. . . . When you think what wonderful discussions we've had! . . . Oh, I forgot. I was going to bring you some more pictures.

PETER. Oh, these are fine, thanks.

ANNE. Don't you want some more? Miep just brought me some new ones.

PETER. Maybe later. [*He gives her a glass of pop and, taking some for himself, sits down facing her.*]

ANNE. [*Looking up at one of the photographs.*] I remember when I got that. . . . I won it. I bet Jopie that I could eat five ice-cream cones. We'd all been playing ping-pong. . . . We used to have heavenly times . . . we'd finish up with ice cream at the Delphi, or the Oasis, where Jews were allowed . . . there'd always be a lot of boys . . . we'd laugh and joke. . . . I'd like to go back to it for a few days or a week. But after that I know I'd be bored to death. I think more seriously about life now. I want to be a journalist . . . or something. I love to write. What do you want to do?

PETER. I thought I might go off someplace . . . work on a farm or something . . . some job that doesn't take much brains.

ANNE. You shouldn't talk that way. You've got the most awful inferiority complex.

PETER. I know I'm not smart.

ANNE. That isn't true. You're much better than I am in dozens of things . . . arithmetic and algebra and . . . well, you're a million times better than I am in algebra. [*With sudden directness.*] You like Margot, don't you? Right from the start you liked her, liked her much better than me.

PETER. [*Uncomfortably.*] Oh, I don't know.

[*In the main room* MRS. VAN DAAN *comes from the bathroom and goes over to the sink, polishing a coffeepot.*]

ANNE. It's all right. Everyone feels that way. Margot's so good. She's sweet and bright and beautiful and I'm not.

PETER. I wouldn't say that.

The Diary of Anne Frank, Act II 417

AT A GLANCE

- *Scene 2 (continued):* Anne says she would like to become a writer.
- Peter says he will look for a job that doesn't take much intelligence.
- Anne asks Peter whether he likes Margot better than her.

1 CHARACTERIZATION

In a self-analysis Anne recalls her longing for former happier times and reveals her more serious ambitions.

2 DIALOGUE

Anne's conversation goes exuberantly in all directions. She presses Peter to reveal how he compares her and Margot.

GUIDED READING

LITERAL QUESTIONS

1a. Why does Anne think she would be bored if she returned to her former life? (She says she thinks more seriously about life now.)

2a. What does Anne ask Peter about Margot? (She asks him whether he liked Margot better than her.)

INFERENTIAL QUESTIONS

1b. What experiences do you think have changed Anne? (She has lived confined in an attic; her best friend was sent to a concentration camp; she has lived in fear for her life.)

2b. Why do you think Anne asks Peter about his feelings about Margot? (Anne seems to think that everyone likes Margot better than her; she is testing Peter's attraction to her.)

- Peter tells Anne how she's changed.
- Peter tells Anne he has no friends.
- Anne asks Peter if he has ever kissed a girl.

1 THEME

Anne's protests reveal her adolescent uncertainty about her identity.

2 DIALOGUE

In an exchange typical of teenagers, Anne is trying to lead Peter to say something positive about her.

3 CHARACTERIZATION

Peter has always thought of himself as a loner, but Anne's ebullience has melted his reserve.

4 THEME

Anne and Peter exchange confidences. Their youthful concerns contrast with the dire circumstances that have brought them together.

---

1 **ANNE.** Oh, no, I'm not. I know that. I know quite well that I'm not a beauty. I never have been and never shall be.

PETER. I don't agree at all. I think you're pretty.

ANNE. That's not true!

PETER. And another thing. You've changed . . . from at first, I mean.

ANNE. I have?

PETER. I used to think you were awful noisy.

ANNE. And what do you think now, Peter? How have I changed?

PETER. Well . . . er . . . you're . . . quieter.

[*In his room* DUSSEL *takes his pajamas and toilet articles and goes into the bathroom to change.*]

2 **ANNE.** I'm glad you don't just hate me.

PETER. I never said that.

ANNE. I bet when you get out of here you'll never think of me again.

PETER. That's crazy.

ANNE. When you get back with all of your friends, you're going to say . . . now what did I ever see in that Mrs. Quack Quack.

PETER. I haven't got any friends.

ANNE. Oh, Peter, of course you have. Everyone has friends.

3 **PETER.** Not me. I don't want any. I get along all right without them.

ANNE. Does that mean you can get along without me? I think of myself as your friend.

PETER. No. If they were all like you, it'd be different.

[*He takes the glasses and the bottle and*

418   *Drama*

---

puts them away. There is a second's silence and then ANNE *speaks, hesitantly, shyly.*]

ANNE. Peter, did you ever kiss a girl?

PETER. Yes. Once.

ANNE. [*To cover her feelings.*] That picture's crooked. [PETER *goes over, straightening the* **4** *photograph.*] Was she pretty?

PETER. Huh?

ANNE. The girl that you kissed.

PETER. I don't know. I was blindfolded. [*He comes back and sits down again.*] It was at a party. One of those kissing games.

ANNE. [*Relieved.*] Oh, I don't suppose that really counts, does it?

PETER. It didn't with me.

ANNE. I've been kissed twice. Once a man I'd never seen before kissed me on the cheek when he picked me up off the ice and I was crying. And the other was Mr. Koophuis, a friend of Father's who kissed my hand. You wouldn't say those counted, would you?

PETER. I wouldn't say so.

ANNE. I know almost for certain that Margot would never kiss anyone unless she was engaged to them. And I'm sure too that Mother never touched a man before Pim. But I don't know . . . things are so different now. . . . What do you think? Do you think a girl shouldn't kiss anyone except if she's engaged or something? It's so hard to try to think what to do, when here we are with the whole world falling around our ears and you think . . . well . . . you don't know what's going to happen tomorrow and . . . What do you think?

PETER. I suppose it'd depend on the girl. Some

GUIDED READING

LITERAL QUESTIONS

1a. What does Peter say about friends? (He says he doesn't have or want friends, and that he gets along without them.)

2a. How does Anne react when Peter says he kissed a girl? (First she refers to a crooked picture to hide her feelings; then she asks if the girl was pretty.)

INFERENTIAL QUESTIONS

1b. How do you think Peter feels when Anne says she thinks of herself as his friend? (He seems gruffly grateful that she considers him her friend.)

2b. Why is Peter's answer important to Anne? (She is trying to find out whether Peter had a girlfriend and whether he still prefers her to Anne.)

girls, anything they do's wrong. But others . . . well . . . it wouldn't necessarily be wrong with them. [*The carillon starts to strike nine o'clock.*] I've always thought that when two people . . .

ANNE. Nine o'clock. I have to go.

PETER. That's right.

1 **ANNE.** [*Without moving.*] Good night.

[*There is a second's pause; then* PETER *gets up and moves toward the door.*]

PETER. You won't let them stop you coming?

2 **ANNE.** No. [*She rises and starts for the door.*] Sometime I might bring my diary. There are so many things in it that I want to talk over with you. There's a lot about you.

PETER. What kind of things?

ANNE. I wouldn't want you to see some of it. I thought you were a nothing, just the way you thought about me.

PETER. Did you change your mind, the way I changed my mind about you?

ANNE. Well . . . You'll see. . . .

AT A GLANCE

- *Scene 2 (continued):* The carillon strikes nine o'clock.
- Anne assures Peter she will come back.
- Anne says she may bring her diary for Peter to read.

1 CHARACTERIZATION

Calling for a partnership between themselves, Peter wants Anne's reassurance that she will continue their friendship. He is beginning to come out of his shell.

2 THEME

Anne's offer to bring her diary is a further overture of friendship toward Peter.

GUIDED READING

LITERAL QUESTION

1a. What question does Peter ask before Anne leaves? ("You won't let them stop you coming?")

INFERENTIAL QUESTION

1b. Why does Peter ask this question? (He knows she is under pressure to stop, and her visits mean a lot to him.)

AT A GLANCE

- *Scene 2 (continued):* Peter kisses Anne good night.
- *Scene 3:* Mrs. Frank awakens when Mr. Van Daan takes bread from the food safe.

1 **IRONY**

Peter's kiss has so moved Anne that she offers her friendship to Mrs. Van Daan. Ironically, this gesture of friendship confirms the woman's suspicions.

2 **PLOT: CONFLICT**

External events are encouraging, but the group still lives in fear and confinement.

3 **THEME**

Anne's friendship with Peter has transformed her experience of living in hiding. She has a reason for living and hoping for the future.

4 **SETTING**

The refugees cannot hide anything from one another for long. Here is just one more example of how the attic setting itself contributes to conflicts among the characters.

[*For a second* ANNE *stands looking up at* PETER, *longing for him to kiss her. As he makes no move she turns away. Then suddenly* PETER *grabs her awkwardly in his arms, kissing her on the cheek.* ANNE *walks out dazed. She stands for a minute, her back to the people in the main room. As she regains her poise she goes to her mother and father and* MARGOT, *silently kissing them. They murmur their goodnights to her. As she is about to open her bedroom door, she catches sight of* MRS. VAN

1 DAAN. *She goes quickly to her, taking her face in her hands and kissing her first on one cheek and then on the other. Then she hurries off into her room.* MRS. VAN DAAN *looks after her and then looks over at* PETER's *room. Her suspicions are confirmed.*]

MRS. VAN DAAN. [*She knows.*] Ah hah!

[*The lights dim out. The curtain falls on the scene. In the darkness* ANNE's *voice comes faintly at first, and then with growing strength.*]

ANNE'S VOICE. By this time we all know each other so well that if anyone starts to tell a story, the rest can finish it for him. We're having to cut down still further on our meals. What makes it worse, the rats have been at work again. They've carried off some of our precious food. Even Mr. Dussel wishes now

2 that Mouschi were here. Thursday, the twentieth of April, nineteen forty-four. Invasion fever is mounting every day. Miep tells us that people outside talk of nothing else. For myself, life has become much more pleasant. I often go to Peter's room after supper. Oh, don't think I'm in love, because I'm not. But it does make life more bearable to have someone with whom you can exchange views. No more tonight. P.S. . . . I must be honest. I must confess that I actually live for the next meeting.

420 *Drama*

3 Is there anything lovelier than to sit under the skylight and feel the sun on your cheeks and have a darling boy in your arms? I admit now that I'm glad the Van Daans had a son and not a daughter. I've outgrown another dress. That's the third. I'm having to wear Margot's clothes after all. I'm working hard on my French and am now reading *La Belle Nivernaise.*[7]

[*As she is saying the last lines, the curtain rises on the scene. The lights dim on as* ANNE's *voice fades out.*]

Scene 3

It is night, a few weeks later.

[*Everyone is in bed. There is complete quiet. In the* VAN DAANS' *room a match flares up for a moment and then is quickly put out.* MR. VAN DAAN, *in bare feet, dressed in underwear and trousers, is dimly seen coming stealthily down the stairs and into the main room, where* MR. *and* MRS. FRANK *and* MARGOT *are

4 sleeping. He goes to the food safe and again lights a match. Then he cautiously opens the safe, taking out a half-loaf of bread. As he closes the safe, it creaks. He stands rigid.* MRS. FRANK *sits up in bed. She sees him.*]

MRS. FRANK. [*Screaming.*] Otto! Otto! Komme schnell![8]

[*The rest of the people wake, hurriedly getting up.*]

MR. FRANK. Was ist los? Was ist passiert?[9]

[DUSSEL, *followed by* ANNE, *comes from his room.*]

---

7. *La Belle Nivernaise* [nē ver nez´]: novel by French author Alphonse Daudet (1867–1942).
8. *Komme schnell!:* Come quickly!
9. *Was . . . passiert?:* What is the matter? What is happening?

GUIDED READING

LITERAL QUESTIONS

1a. What does Anne do after Peter kisses her? (After she regains her poise, she kisses her family and then Mrs. Van Daan.)

2a. What awakens Mrs. Frank? (She is awakened by the creaking of the food safe as it is closed.)

INFERENTIAL QUESTIONS

1b. Why does Anne kiss her enemy, Mrs. Van Daan? (Her relationship with Peter makes her feel very loving, even toward Mrs. Van Daan.)

2b. What do you think her reaction will be? (She will be shocked, angry, or distressed.)

MRS. FRANK. [*As she rushes over to* MR. VAN DAAN.] *Er stiehlt das Essen!*[10]

DUSSEL. [*Grabbing* MR. VAN DAAN.] You! You! Give me that.

MRS. VAN DAAN. [*Coming down the stairs.*] Putti . . . Putti . . . what is it?

DUSSEL. [*His hands on* VAN DAAN'*s neck.*] You dirty thief . . . stealing food . . . you good-for-nothing . . .

MR. FRANK. Mr. Dussel! Help me, Peter!

[PETER *comes over, trying, with* MR. FRANK, *to separate the two struggling men.*]

PETER. Let him go! Let go!

[DUSSEL *drops* MR. VAN DAAN, *pushing him away. He shows them the end of a loaf of bread that he has taken from* MR. VAN DAAN.]

DUSSEL. You greedy, selfish . . .

[MARGOT *turns on the lights.*]

MRS. VAN DAAN. Putti . . . what is it?

[*All of* MRS. FRANK'*s gentleness, her self-control, is gone. She is outraged, in a frenzy of indignation.*]

MRS. FRANK. The bread! He was stealing the bread!

DUSSEL. It was you, and all the time we thought it was the rats!

MR. FRANK. Mr. Van Daan, how could you!

MR. VAN DAAN. I'm hungry.

MRS. FRANK. We're all of us hungry! I see the children getting thinner and thinner. Your own son Peter . . . I've heard him moan in his sleep, he's so hungry. And you come in the

---

10. *Er . . . Essen!:* He is stealing the food!

night and steal food that should go to them . . . to the children!

MRS. VAN DAAN. [*Going to* MR. VAN DAAN *protectively.*] He needs more food than the rest of us. He's used to more. He's a big man.

[MR. VAN DAAN *breaks away, going over and sitting on the couch.*]

MRS. FRANK. [*Turning on* MRS. VAN DAAN.] And you . . . you're worse than he is! You're a mother, and yet you sacrifice your child to this man . . . this . . . this . . .

MR. FRANK. Edith! Edith!

[MARGOT *picks up the pink woolen stole, putting it over her mother's shoulders.*]

MRS. FRANK. [*Paying no attention, going on to* MRS. VAN DAAN.] Don't think I haven't seen you! Always saving the choicest bits for him! I've watched you day after day and I've held my tongue. But not any longer! Not after this! Now I want him to go! I want him to get out of here!

MR. FRANK. Edith!

MR. VAN DAAN. Get out of here? } [*Together.*]

MRS. VAN DAAN. What do you mean?

MRS. FRANK. Just that! Take your things and get out!

MR. FRANK. [*To* MRS. FRANK.] You're speaking in anger. You cannot mean what you are saying.

MRS. FRANK. I mean exactly that!

[MRS. VAN DAAN *takes a cover from the* FRANKS' *bed, pulling it about her.*]

MR. FRANK. For two long years we have lived here, side by side. We have respected each other's rights . . . we have managed to live in

The Diary of Anne Frank, Act II 421

- *Scene 3 (continued):* Mrs. Frank announces that Mr. Van Daan was stealing food.
- Dussel struggles with Mr. Van Daan, but Mrs. Van Daan defends her husband.
- Mrs. Frank says that Mr. Van Daan must go.

1 READING SKILLS: CAUSE AND EFFECT

Mr. Vann Daan's greed has caused the worst conflict so far among the group.

2 THEME

Mrs. Frank voices her concern for the children, including Peter. The act of stealing, she suggests, is more heinous when it takes away from one's own children.

3 CHARACTERIZATION

Mrs. Frank's rage is out of character for her. Living in fear and deprivation has worn away her gentleness and reticence.

GUIDED READING

LITERAL QUESTIONS

1a. What does Dussel do when he enters the room? (He grabs Mr. Van Daan and demands that he give back the bread.)

2a. How does Mrs. Frank want to resolve the crisis? (She wants Mr. Van Daan to leave.)

INFERENTIAL QUESTIONS

1b. Why is everyone so angry with Mr. Van Daan? (They are all hungry, and Mr. Van Daan has betrayed the group by stealing food.)

2b. Why does this shock everyone? (Everyone is shocked because the desire for revenge is so unlike Mrs. Frank and because Mr. Van Daan would almost certainly be captured.)

■ *Scene 3 (continued):* Mr. Frank pleads for calm to talk the situation out.

■ Mrs. Van Daan reminds Mr. Frank of his debt to her husband.

■ Peter says he'd have to leave if his father leaves, and Anne begs her mother to change her mind.

1 CHARACTERIZATION

Mr. Frank again assumes the role of the leader who must work things out for everyone's benefit.

2 DIALOGUE

When Mrs. Van Daan reminds Mr. Frank of the debt he claimed to owe Mr. Van Daan, Mrs. Frank remains unmoved because of her pent-up anger.

3 PLOT: CONFLICT

The external conflict of the war is mirrored in the conflict that takes place within the small group.

4 THEME

Although his father has often angered him, Peter expresses loyalty to his family in this crisis.

5 CHARACTERIZATION

Anne's affection for Peter and her resentment of her mother combine here.

---

peace. Are we now going to throw it all away? I know this will never happen again, will it, Mr. Van Daan?

MR. VAN DAAN. No. No.

MRS. FRANK. He steals once! He'll steal again!

[MR. VAN DAAN, *holding his stomach, starts for the bathroom.* ANNE *puts her arms around him, helping him up the step.*]

1 MR. FRANK. Edith, please. Let us be calm. We'll all go to our rooms . . . and afterwards we'll sit down quietly and talk this out . . . we'll find some way . . .

MRS. FRANK. No! No! No more talk! I want them to leave!

MRS. VAN DAAN. You'd put us out, on the streets?

MRS. FRANK. There are other hiding placcs.

MRS. VAN DAAN. A cellar . . . a closet. I know. And we have no money left even to pay for that.

MRS. FRANK. I'll give you money. Out of my own pocket I'll give it gladly. [*She gets her purse from a shelf and comes back with it.*]

2 MRS. VAN DAAN. Mr. Frank, you told Putti you'd never forget what he'd done for you when you came to Amsterdam. You said you could never repay him, that you . . .

MRS. FRANK. [*Counting out money.*] If my husband had any obligation to you, he's paid it, over and over.

MR. FRANK. Edith, I've never seen you like this before. I don't know you.

MRS. FRANK. I should have spoken out long ago.

DUSSEL. You can't be nice to some people.

MRS. VAN DAAN. [*Turning on* DUSSEL.] There

422 *Drama*

would have been plenty for all of us, if *you* hadn't come in here!

3 MR. FRANK. We don't need the Nazis to destroy us. We're destroying ourselves.

[*He sits down, with his head in his hands.* MRS. FRANK *goes to* MRS. VAN DAAN.]

MRS. FRANK. [*Giving* MRS. VAN DAAN *some money.*] Give this to Miep. She'll find you a place.

ANNE. Mother, you're not putting *Peter* out. Peter hasn't done anything.

MRS. FRANK. He'll stay, of course. When I say I must protect the children, I mean Peter too.

4 [PETER *rises from the steps where he has been sitting.*]

PETER. I'd have to go if Father goes.

[MR. VAN DAAN *comes from the bathroom.* MRS. VAN DAAN *hurries to him and takes him to the couch. Then she gets water from the sink to bathe his face.*]

MRS. FRANK. [*While this is going on.*] He's no father to you . . . that man! He doesn't know what it is to be a father!

PETER. [*Starting for his room.*] I wouldn't feel right. I couldn't stay.

MRS. FRANK. Very well, then. I'm sorry.

5 ANNE. [*Rushing over to* PETER.] No, Peter! No! [PETER *goes into his room, closing the door after him.* ANNE *turns back to her mother, crying.*] I don't care about the food. They can have mine! I don't want it! Only don't send them away. It'll be daylight soon. They'll be caught. . . .

MARGOT. [*Putting her arms comfortingly around* ANNE.] Please, Mother!

MRS. FRANK. They're not going now. They'll

GUIDED READING

LITERAL QUESTIONS

1a. What does Mr. Frank say about the threat posed by the Nazis? (He says the group doesn't need the Nazis—they are destroying themselves.)

2a. What does Peter say when it is clear that he will be allowed to stay? (He says that he will have to go if his father goes.)

INFERENTIAL QUESTIONS

1b. What does he mean? (The group's only hope is cooperation.)

2b. Why is Peter's loyalty significant? (His father has often angered and berated him.)

stay here until Miep finds them a place. [*To* MRS. VAN DAAN.] But one thing I insist on! He must never come down here again! He must never come to this room where the food is stored! We'll divide what we have . . . an equal share for each! [DUSSEL *hurries over to get a sack of potatoes from the food safe.* MRS. FRANK *goes on, to* MRS. VAN DAAN.] You can cook it here and take it up to him.

[DUSSEL *brings the sack of potatoes back to the center table.*]

1 **MARGOT.** On, no. No. We haven't sunk so far that we're going to fight over a handful of rotten potatoes.

DUSSEL. [*Dividing the potatoes into piles.*] Mrs. Frank, Mr. Frank, Margot, Anne, Peter, Mrs. Van Daan, Mr. Van Daan, myself . . . Mrs. Frank . . .

[*The buzzer sounds in* MIEP's *signal.*]

MR. FRANK. It's Miep! [*He hurries over, getting his overcoat and putting it on.*]

MARGOT. At this hour?

MRS. FRANK. It is trouble.

2 **MR. FRANK.** [*As he starts down to unbolt the door.*] I beg you, don't let her see a thing like this!

MR. DUSSEL. [*Counting without stopping.*] . . . Anne, Peter, Mrs. Van Daan, Mr. Van Daan, myself . . .

MARGOT. [*To* DUSSEL.] Stop it! Stop it!

DUSSEL. . . . Mr. Frank, Margot, Anne, Peter, Mrs. Van Daan, Mr. Van Daan, myself, Mrs. Frank . . .

MRS. VAN DAAN. You're keeping the big ones for yourself! All the big ones . . . Look at the size of that! . . . And that! . . .

[DUSSEL *continues on with his dividing.* PE-

TER, *with his shirt and trousers on, comes from his room*]

MARGOT. Stop it! Stop it!

[*We hear* MIEP's *excited voice speaking to* MR. FRANK *below.*]

3 **MIEP.** Mr. Frank . . . the most wonderful news! . . . The invasion has begun!

MR. FRANK. Go on, tell them! Tell them!

[MIEP *comes running up the steps, ahead of* MR. FRANK. *She has a man's raincoat on over her nightclothes and a bunch of orange-colored flowers in her hand.*]

MIEP. Did you hear that, everybody? Did you hear what I said? The invasion has begun! The invasion!

[*They all stare at* MIEP, *unable to grasp what she is telling them.* PETER *is the first to recover his wits.*]

PETER. Where?

MRS. VAN DAAN. When? When, Miep?

MIEP. It began early this morning. . . .

4 [*As she talks on, the realization of what she has said begins to dawn on them. Everyone goes crazy. A wild demonstration takes place.* MRS. FRANK *hugs* MR. VAN DAAN.]

MRS. FRANK. Oh, Mr. Van Daan, did you hear that?

[DUSSEL *embraces* MRS. VAN DAAN. PETER *grabs a frying pan and parades around the room, beating on it, singing the Dutch national anthem.* ANNE *and* MARGOT *follow him, singing, weaving in and out among the excited grown-ups.* MARGOT *breaks away to take the flowers from* MIEP *and distribute them to everyone. While this pandemonium is going on* MRS. FRANK *tries*

The Diary of Anne Frank, Act II 423

AT A GLANCE

- *Scene 3 (continued):* Dussel counts out the potatoes.
- Miep brings news that the invasion has begun.
- A celebration begins in the attic.

1 CHARACTERIZATION

The sight of Dussel dividing up the potatoes drives the clearly distraught Margot to this uncharacteristic outburst.

2 DIALOGUE

As Miep is about to enter, the tension continues. Mr. Frank implores the others not to reveal their sordid quarrel to Miep, a plea ignored by the insensitive Dussel.

3 PLOT: CONFLICT

Just as the conflict among the group has pushed them to a breaking point, the external conflict of the war is building to a climax.

4 MOOD

In their exuberance the characters forget their earlier hostility. The mood of celebration overrides every other emotion, including Mrs. Frank's anger at Mr. Van Daan.

GUIDED READING

LITERAL QUESTIONS

1a. Why does Margot object when Dussel begins to count out the potatoes? (She is appalled that they would fight over something so petty.)

2a. What happens to interrupt the argument? (Miep comes with news of the invasion.)

INFERENTIAL QUESTIONS

1b. How has Margot changed during the course of the play? (She has begun to speak out rather than remaining silent.)

2b. Why is the group at first unable to grasp what Miep is telling them? (They have been waiting so long for this news that it is hard to believe. They are also still distraught from the quarrel.)

- *Scene 3 (continued):* Miep relays the B.B.C. report of the landing in Normandy.
- Mr. Van Daan is so ashamed of himself that he sobs.
- Mr. Frank calls for them all to celebrate.
- Mrs. Frank bursts into tears of remorse.

1 MOOD

The mood of happiness that accompanies the news of victory reminds Mr. Van Daan of his earlier transgression and shames him all the more.

2 CHARACTERIZATION

Anne's confession signifies the resolution of her conflict with her mother.

3 MOOD

Suddenly the mood is somber again. The violent mood swings in these moments are evidence of the intense pressure building in the characters.

---

to make herself heard above the excitement.]

MRS. FRANK. [*To* MIEP.] How do you know?

MIEP. The radio . . . The B.B.C.[11] They said they landed on the coast of Normandy![12]

PETER. The British?

MIEP. British, Americans, French, Dutch, Poles, Norwegians . . . all of them! More than four thousand ships! Churchill[13] spoke, and General Eisenhower![14] D-Day they call it!

MR. FRANK. Thank God, it's come!

MRS. VAN DAAN. At last!

MIEP. [*Starting out.*] I'm going to tell Mr. Kraler. This'll be better than any blood transfusion.

MR. FRANK. [*Stopping her.*] What part of Normandy did they land, did they say?

MIEP. Normandy . . . that's all I know now. . . . I'll be up the minute I hear some more! [*She goes hurriedly out.*]

MR. FRANK. [*To* MRS. FRANK.] What did I tell you? What did I tell you?

[MRS. FRANK *indicates that he has forgotten to bolt the door after* MIEP. *He hurries down the steps.* MR. VAN DAAN, *sitting on the couch, suddenly breaks into a convulsive sob. Everybody looks at him, bewildered.*]

1 **MRS. VAN DAAN.** [*Hurrying to him.*] Putti! Putti! What is it? What happened?

MR. VAN DAAN. Please. I'm so ashamed.

---

11. **B.B.C.:** British Broadcasting Corporation.
12. **Normandy:** region of northern France; the point at which Allied troops invaded northern Europe on June 6, 1944.
13. **Churchill:** Sir Winston Churchill (1871–1965), British Prime Minister at the time.
14. **General Eisenhower:** Dwight D. Eisenhower (1890–1969), who commanded the Allied troops in Europe during World War II and served as President of the United States from 1953 to 1961.

424   *Drama*

[MR. FRANK *comes back up the steps.*]

MRS. VAN DAAN. Don't, Putti.

MARGOT. It doesn't matter now!

MR. FRANK. [*Going to* MR. VAN DAAN.] Didn't you hear what Miep said? The invasion has come! We're going to be liberated! This is a time to celebrate. [*He embraces* MRS. FRANK *and then hurries to the cupboard and gets the cognac and a glass.*]

MR. VAN DAAN. To steal bread from children!

2 **MRS. FRANK.** We've all done things that we're ashamed of.

ANNE. Look at me, the way I've treated Mother . . . so mean and horrid to her.

MRS. FRANK. No, Anneke, no.

[ANNE *runs to her mother, putting her arms around her.*]

ANNE. Oh, Mother, I was. I was awful.

MR. VAN DAAN. Not like me. No one is as bad as me!

DUSSEL. [*To* MR. VAN DAAN.] Stop it now! Let's be happy!

MR. FRANK. [*Giving* MR. VAN DAAN *a glass of cognac.*] Here! Here! Schnapps! L'chaim![15]

[MR. VAN DAAN *takes the cognac. They all watch him. He gives them a feeble smile.* ANNE *puts up her fingers in a V-for-Victory sign. As* MR. VAN DAAN *gives an answering*
3 *V-sign, they are startled to hear a loud sob from behind them. It is* MRS. FRANK, *stricken with remorse. She is sitting on the other side of the room.*]

MRS. FRANK. [*Through her sobs.*] When I think of the terrible things I said . . .

---

15. **L'chaim!** [lə KHä′yim]: Hebrew toast meaning "To life!"

GUIDED READING

LITERAL QUESTIONS

1a. Where does Miep say she has learned about the invasion? (She heard on the radio that the landing has occurred on the coast of Normandy.)

2a. Which characters express shame for their actions? (Mr. Van Daan, Anne, and Mrs. Frank)

INFERENTIAL QUESTIONS

1b. What do the members of the group seem to assume after hearing Miep's news? (that they will soon be free)

2b. Why do you think they are remorseful at this time of celebration? (In a time of hope for a return to a normal life, their actions seem especially regrettable and petty.)

[MR. FRANK, ANNE *and* MARGOT *hurry to her, trying to comfort her.* MR. VAN DAAN *brings her his glass of cognac.*]

MR. VAN DAAN. No! No! You were right!

MRS. FRANK. That I should speak that way to you! . . . Our friends! . . . Our guests! [*She starts to cry again.*]

DUSSEL. Stop it, you're spoiling the whole invasion!

[*As they are comforting her, the lights dim out. The curtain falls.*]

ANNE'S VOICE. [*Faintly at first, and then with growing strength.*] We're all in much better spirits these days. There's still excellent news of the invasion. The best part about it is that I have a feeling that friends are coming. Who knows? Maybe I'll be back in school by fall.

Ha, ha! The joke is on us! The warehouseman doesn't know a thing and we are paying him all that money! . . . Wednesday, the second of July, nineteen forty-four. The invasion seems temporarily to be bogged down. Mr. Kraler has to have an operation, which looks bad. The Gestapo have found the radio that was stolen. Mr. Dussel says they'll trace it back and back to the thief, and then, it's just a matter of time till they get to us. Everyone is low. Even poor Pim can't raise their spirits. I have often been downcast myself . . . but never in despair. I can shake off everything if I write. But . . . and that is the great question . . . will I ever be able to write well? I want to so much. I want to go on living even after my death. Another birthday has gone by, so now I am fifteen. Already I know what I want. I have a goal, an opinion.

[*As this is being said, the curtain rises on the scene, the lights dim on, and* ANNE's *voice fades out.*]

Scene 4

It is an afternoon a few weeks later. . . . Everyone but MARGOT is in the main room. There is a sense of great tension.

[*Both* MRS. FRANK *and* MR. VAN DAAN *are nervously pacing back and forth;* DUSSEL *is standing at the window, looking down fixedly at the street below.* PETER *is at the center table, trying to do his lessons.* ANNE *sits opposite him, writing in her diary.* MRS. VAN DAAN *is seated on the couch, her eyes on* MR. FRANK *as he sits reading.*

The sound of a telephone ringing comes from the office below. They all are rigid, listening tensely. DUSSEL rushes down to MR. FRANK.]

DUSSEL. There it goes again, the telephone! Mr. Frank, do you hear?

The Diary of Anne Frank, Act II 425

AT A GLANCE

- *Scene 3 (continued):* News of the invasion makes everyone optimistic.
- When the invasion bogs down, events make everyone low.
- *Scene 4:* Tension has increased because the office telephone downstairs keeps on ringing.

PLOT: SUSPENSE

The temporary halt of the invasion and Mr. Kraler's impending surgery bode poorly for the group. Dussel's earlier prediction that the thief would give them away becomes more likely.

2 RESPONSE JOURNAL

Ask students to respond to Anne's thoughts in this diary entry. Encourage them to consider the ways in which Anne Frank has lived on after her death.

3 STAGE DIRECTIONS

The actions, described in detail by the stage directions, communicate the tension in the room. Only Mr. Frank seems determined to remain calm.

GUIDED READING

LITERAL QUESTIONS

1a. What bad news follows after the invasion? (The invasion bogs down, Mr. Kraler has to have an operation, and the Gestapo has found the radio that had been stolen.)

2a. What is the mood at the opening of Scene 4? (one of great tension)

INFERENTIAL QUESTIONS

1b. Why is the bad news especially difficult for the group to take after the excitement of the invasion? (In their hopeful state they had assumed that all trouble had passed.)

2b. Why might the ringing telephone make everyone more anxious? (They are probably not used to hearing the telephone ring when the office is empty.)

1 PLOT: SUSPENSE

Dussel's theory about the ringing phone seems to make sense. Suspense builds as the terrible logic of the explanation sinks in.

2 CHARACTERIZATION

Peter's loyalty to Mr. Frank's leadership intensifies his father's anger and reopens old wounds.

3 STAGE DIRECTIONS

For the first time in the play, someone seriously challenges Mr. Frank's leadership. Dussel's action reveals the growing desperation of the group.

4 THEME

The Van Daans' family disputes are both poignant and pointless in the light of the tragedy they face.

MR. FRANK. [*Quietly.*] Yes. I hear.

DUSSEL. [*Pleading, insistent.*] But this is the third time, Mr. Frank! The third time in quick succession! It's a signal! I tell you it's Miep, trying to get us! For some reason she can't come to us and she's trying to warn us of something!

MR. FRANK. Please. Please.

MR. VAN DAAN. [*To* DUSSEL.] You're wasting your breath.

1 DUSSEL. Something has happened, Mr. Frank. For three days now Miep hasn't been to see us! And today not a man has come to work. There hasn't been a sound in the building!

MRS. FRANK. Perhaps it's Sunday. We may have lost track of the days.

MR. VAN DAAN. [*To* ANNE.] You with the diary there. What day is it?

DUSSEL. [*Going to* MRS. FRANK.] I don't lose track of the days! I know exactly what day it is! It's Friday, the fourth of August. Friday, and not a man at work. [*He rushes back to* MR. FRANK, *pleading with him, almost in tears.*] I tell you Mr. Kraler's dead. That's the only explanation. He's dead and they've closed down the building, and Miep's trying to tell us!

MR. FRANK. She'd never telephone us.

DUSSEL. [*Frantic.*] Mr. Frank, answer that! I beg you, answer it!

MR. FRANK. No.

MR. VAN DAAN. Just pick it up and listen. You don't have to speak. Just listen and see if it's Miep.

DUSSEL. [*Speaking at the same time.*] I ask you—

426 *Drama*

---

2 MR. FRANK. No. I've told you, no. I'll do nothing that might let anyone know we're in the building.

PETER. Mr. Frank's right.

MR. VAN DAAN. There's no need to tell us what side you're on.

MR. FRANK. If we wait patiently, quietly, I believe that help will come.

[*There is silence for a minute as they all listen to the telephone ringing.*]

3 DUSSEL. I'm going down. [*He rushes down the steps.* MR. FRANK *tries ineffectually to hold him.* DUSSEL *runs to the lower door, unbolting it. The telephone stops ringing.* DUSSEL *bolts the door and comes slowly back up the steps.*] Too late.

[MR. FRANK *goes to* MARGOT *in* ANNE's *bedroom.*]

MR. VAN DAAN. So we just wait here until we die.

MRS. VAN DAAN. [*Hysterically.*] I can't stand it. I'll kill myself! I'll kill myself!

MR. VAN DAAN. Stop it!

[*In the distance, a German military band is heard playing a Viennese waltz.*]

MRS. VAN DAAN. I think you'd be glad if I did! I think you want me to die!

4 MR. VAN DAAN. Whose fault is it we're here? [MRS. VAN DAAN *starts for her room. He follows, talking at her.*] We could've been safe somewhere . . . in America or Switzerland. But no! No! You wouldn't leave when I wanted to. You couldn't leave your things. You couldn't leave your precious furniture.

MRS. VAN DAAN. Don't touch me!

[*She hurries up the stairs, followed by* MR.

GUIDED READING

LITERAL QUESTION

1a. Why does Dussel want Mr. Frank to answer the telephone? (He thinks Miep is calling to warn them of danger.)

INFERENTIAL QUESTION

1b. Why can Mr. Frank not stop Dussel? (In this crisis Mr. Frank's word does not rule, his role as leader is now uncertain.)

VAN DAAN. PETER, *unable to bear it, goes to his room.* ANNE *looks after him, deeply concerned.* DUSSEL *returns to his post at the window.* MR. FRANK *comes back into the main room and takes a book, trying to read.* MRS. FRANK *sits near the sink, starting to peel some potatoes.* ANNE *quietly goes to* PETER's *room, closing the door after her.* PETER *is lying face down on the cot.* ANNE *leans over him, holding him in her arms, trying to bring him out of his despair.*]

ANNE. Look, Peter, the sky. [*She looks up through the skylight.*] What a lovely, lovely day! Aren't the clouds beautiful? You know what I do when it seems as if I couldn't stand being cooped up for one more minute? I *think* myself out. I think myself on a walk in the park where I used to go with Pim. Where the jonquils and the crocuses and violets grow down the slopes. You know the most wonderful part about *thinking* yourself out? You can have it any way you like. You can have roses and violets and chrysanthemums all blooming at the same time. . . . It's funny . . . I used to take it all for granted . . . and now I've gone crazy about everything to do with nature. Haven't you?

PETER. I've just gone crazy. I think if something doesn't happen soon . . . if we don't get out of here . . . I can't stand much more of it!

ANNE. [*Softly.*] I wish you had a religion, Peter.

PETER. No, thanks! Not me!

ANNE. Oh, I don't mean you have to be Orthodox[16] . . . or believe in heaven and hell and purgatory and things . . . I just mean some religion . . . it doesn't matter what. Just to believe in something! When I think of all

---

16. **Orthodox:** Orthodox Judaism requires strict attention to the traditional laws of the faith.

that's out there . . . the trees . . . the flowers . . . and sea gulls . . . when I think of the dearness of you, Peter . . . and the goodness of the people we know . . . Mr. Kraler, Miep, Dirk, the vegetable man, all risking their lives for us every day . . . When I think of these good things, I'm not afraid any more . . . I find myself, and God, and I . . .

[PETER *interrupts, getting up and walking away.*]

PETER. That's fine! But when I begin to think, I get mad! Look at us, hiding out for two years. Not able to move! Caught here like . . . waiting for them to come and get us . . . and all for what?

ANNE. We're not the only people that've had to suffer. There've always been people that've had to . . . sometimes one race . . . sometimes another . . . and yet . . .

PETER. That doesn't make me feel any better!

ANNE. [*Going to him.*] I know it's terrible, trying to have any faith . . . when people are doing such horrible . . . But you know what I sometimes think? I think the world may be going through a phase, the way I was with Mother. It'll pass, maybe not for hundreds of years, but someday. . . . I still believe, in spite of everything, that people are really good at heart.

PETER. I want to see something now. . . . Not a thousand years from now!

[*He goes over, sitting down again on the cot.*]

ANNE. But, Peter, if you'd only look at it as part of a great pattern . . . that we're just a little minute in the life . . . [*She breaks off.*] Listen to us, going at each other like a couple of stupid grown-ups! Look at the sky now. Isn't it lovely? [*She holds out her hand to*

The Diary of Anne Frank, Act II **427**

- *Scene 4 (continued):* The sound of cars coming to the building is heard.
- Voices are heard from below.
- Anne seeks to reassure her parents.

1 STAGE DIRECTIONS

Sound effects move the action forward as it becomes clear that cars are converging on the warehouse.

2 THEME

Mr. Frank finds reason to hope even in this moment of despair.

3 CHARACTERIZATION

Anne, who has matured during the play, reassures her father and mother even as they face danger.

---

him. PETER *takes it and rises, standing with her at the window looking out, his arms around her.*] Someday, when we're outside again, I'm going to . . .

1 [*She breaks off as she hears the sound of a car, its brakes squealing as it comes to a sudden stop. The people in the other rooms also become aware of the sound. They listen tensely. Another car roars up to a screeching stop.* ANNE *and* PETER *come from* PETER'*s room.* MR. *and* MRS. VAN DAAN *creep down the stairs.* DUSSEL *comes out from his room. Everyone is listening, hardly breathing. A doorbell clangs again and again in the building below.* MR. FRANK *starts quietly down the steps to the door.* DUSSEL *and* PETER *follow him. The others stand rigid, waiting, terrified.*

In a few seconds DUSSEL *comes stumbling back up the steps. He shakes off* PETER'*s help and goes to his room.* MR. FRANK *bolts the door below and comes slowly back up the steps. Their eyes are all on him as he stands there for a minute. They realize that what they feared has happened.* MRS. VAN DAAN *starts to whimper.* MR. VAN DAAN *puts her gently in a chair, and then hurries off up the stairs to their room to collect their things.* PETER *goes to comfort his mother. There is a sound of violent pounding on a door below.*]

2 MR. FRANK. [*Quietly.*] For the past two years we have lived in fear. Now we can live in hope.

[*The pounding below becomes more insistent. There are muffled sounds of voices, shouting commands.*]

MEN'S VOICES. *Aufmachen! Da drinnen! Aufmachen! Schnell! Schnell! Schnell!*[17] etc., etc.

---

17. *Aufmachen! . . . Schnell!:* Open up! You in there! Open up! Quickly! Quickly! Quickly!

428 *Drama*

[*The street door below is forced open. We hear the heavy tread of footsteps coming up.* MR. FRANK *gets two schoolbags from the shelves and gives one to* ANNE *and the other to* MARGOT. *He goes to get a bag for* MRS. FRANK. *The sound of feet coming up grows louder.* PETER *comes to* ANNE, *kissing her goodbye; then he goes to his room to collect his things. The buzzer of their door starts to ring.* MR. FRANK *brings* MRS. FRANK *a bag. They stand together, waiting. We hear the thud of gun butts on the door, trying to break it down.*

3 ANNE *stands, holding her school satchel, looking over at her father and mother with a soft, reassuring smile. She*

GUIDED READING

LITERAL QUESTIONS

1a. What sounds do the characters hear from outside? (They hear the sound of cars and squealing brakes; a clanging doorbell; pounding on a door; and the muffled sound of voices.)

2a. What does Mr. Frank say to comfort everyone? (He says that now they can live in hope.)

INFERENTIAL QUESTIONS

1b. What thought is on everyone's mind? (They all fear that the police have come for them.)

2b. What hope can they have? (They can hope that the war will end, and they will be saved.)

is no longer a child, but a woman with courage to meet whatever lies ahead.

The lights dim out. The curtain falls on the scene. We hear a mighty crash as the door is shattered. After a second ANNE's *voice is heard.*]

1 **ANNE'S VOICE.** And so it seems our stay is over. They are waiting for us now. They've allowed us five minutes to get our things. We can each take a bag and whatever it will hold of clothing. Nothing else. So, dear Diary, that means I must leave you behind. Goodbye for a while. P.S. Please, please, Miep, or Mr. Kraler, or anyone else. If you should find this diary, will you please keep it safe for me, because someday I hope . . .

[*Her voice stops abruptly. There is silence. After a second the curtain rises.*]

Scene 5

2 *It is again the afternoon in November 1945.*

[*The rooms are as we saw them in the first scene.* MR. KRALER *has joined* MIEP *and* MR. FRANK. *There are coffee cups on the table. We see a great change in* MR. FRANK. *He is calm now. His bitterness is gone. He slowly turns a few pages of the diary. They are blank.*]

MR. FRANK. No more. [*He closes the diary and puts it down on the couch beside him.*]

MIEP. I'd gone to the country to find food. When I got back the block was surrounded by police. . . .

MR. KRALER. We made it our business to learn how they knew. It was the thief . . . the thief who told them.

[MIEP *goes up to the gas burner, bringing back a pot of coffee.*]

MR. FRANK. [*After a pause.*] It seems strange

to say this, that anyone could be happy in a concentration camp. But Anne was happy in the camp in Holland where they first took us. After two years of being shut up in these rooms, she could be out . . . out in the sunshine and the fresh air that she loved.

MIEP. [*Offering the coffee to* MR. FRANK.] A little more?

MR. FRANK. [*Holding out his cup to her.*] The news of the war was good. The British and Americans were sweeping through France. We felt sure that they would get to us in time. In September we were told that we were to be shipped to Poland. . . . The men to one camp. The women to another. I was sent to Auschwitz. They went to Belsen. In January we were freed, the few of us who were left. The war wasn't yet over, so it took us a long time to get home. We'd be sent here and there behind the lines where we'd be safe. Each time our train would stop . . . at a siding, or a crossing . . . we'd all get out and go from group to group. . . . Where were you? Were you at Belsen? At Buchenwald? At Mauthausen? Is it possible that you knew my wife? Did you ever **3** see my husband? My son? My daughter? That's how I found out about my wife's death . . . of Margot, the Van Daans . . . Dussel. But Anne . . . I still hoped . . . Yesterday I went to Rotterdam. I'd heard of a woman there. . . . She'd been in Belsen with Anne. . . . I know now.

[*He picks up the diary again and turns the pages back to find a certain passage. As he finds it we hear* ANNE's *voice.*]

4 **ANNE'S VOICE.** In spite of everything, I still believe that people are really good at heart.

[MR. FRANK *slowly closes the diary.*]

MR. FRANK. She puts me to shame.

[*They are silent. The curtain falls.*]

The Diary of Anne Frank, Act II 429

AT A GLANCE

- *Scene 4 (continued):* The door below is shattered, and Anne reads her last diary entry.
- *Scene 5:* The scene shifts to the time of the play's opening.
- Mr. Kraler reports that the thief told the police about the refugees.
- Mr. Frank explains about his internment and the deaths of all the others, including Anne.

1 **PLOT: CLIMAX**

The moment everyone has feared has come, and Anne records it in her diary.

2 **SETTING**

The appearance of the stage shows that the play has moved again to the time when Mr. Frank returns to the attic after the war.

3 **PLOT: RESOLUTION**

Mr. Frank brings Anne's story to a close as he explains about the deaths of his wife, Margot, the Van Daans, Dussel, and—finally—Anne.

4 **THEME**

Mr. Frank finds comfort in Anne's diary because he knows now that her life had meaning. Her undying hope has put his despair to shame.

REFLECTING ON THE PLAY

How does Anne change over the course of the play? (She matures in her relationship with people; her natural exuberance develops an inner strength; she becomes more selfless, trying to comfort and protect others without demanding much for herself.)

GUIDED READING

LITERAL QUESTIONS

1a. What plea does Anne make in her dairy? (She asks that her diary be kept safe for her.)

2a. What does Mr. Frank say after reading Anne's diary? ("She puts me to shame.")

INFERENTIAL QUESTIONS

1b. Why is this request touching? (Her hopes of returning and reclaiming her diary were never realized.)

2b. What does he mean? (He means that if a young girl—his daughter, Anne—could be so hopeful in the face of desperate circumstances, he should be able to be brave now himself.)

STUDY QUESTIONS

1. a year; that a worker may know they are living in the attic
2. ability to stand up to others and express her feelings
3. fixes hair, wears Margot's heels and her mother's stole; quieter
4. steals bread; that he leave; the group itself
5. ■ The world is going through a phase.
   ■ People are good at heart.
6. The Green Police break in, tipped off by the Hanukkah thief.
7. November, 1945, in the warehouse attic; calmer, not bitter
8. ■ happy she could be outside
   ■ Anne was alive; she is dead.
9. ■ Act I: loud, unable to control feelings and moods, undirected; Act II: brave, idealistic adult, aspiring writer
   ■ Yes: maturer; stronger
10. ■ boy to talk to and fantasize about
    ■ Anne cheers, comforts, and opens him up.
11. ■ Hunger leads to bitter fights: Mr. Van Daan tries to take Margot's cake and steal bread.
    ■ Mr. Van Daan and Mrs. Frank regret their fight; group unites to celebrate D-Day; Anne wishes Margot had a friend and reassures her parents about her strength.
12. ■ Anne's hope moves him; he was unable to hope in the face of horror and inhumanity.
13. Yes—her diary tells of her life, re-creates her spirit.

READING AND LITERARY FOCUS

1. ■ group's struggle to survive
   ■ relationship between Anne and Peter, which helps them to find hope; hostility between Mr. Van Daan and Mr. Dussel, which weakens the group
2. Act I, Scene 2: from 1945 to 1942
3. Green Police arrest everyone.

STUDY QUESTIONS

Recalling

1. How much time passes between Act I and Act II? What alarming news does Mr. Kraler bring in Act II, Scene 1?
2. In Act II, Scene 1, what quality does Peter say he admires in Anne?
3. Describe Anne's preparations for her visit to Peter in Scene 2. According to Peter, how has Anne changed in the past year?
4. What does Mr. Van Daan do to anger Mrs. Frank in Scene 3, and what does she demand? What does Mr. Frank say is destroying the group?
5. How does Anne explain to Peter the horrible events in the world? What does she "still believe, in spite of everything"?
6. Tell how and why the group leaves the attic.
7. When and where does Act II, Scene 5, take place? According to the stage directions, how has Mr. Frank changed from Act I, Scene 1?
8. What does Mr. Frank say about Anne's attitude in the concentration camp? What hope had he clung to, and what does he "know now"?

Intepreting

9. Explain in your own words how Anne changes from Act I to Act II. Do you think that she changes for the better? Explain.
10. What do you think Anne's friendship with Peter means to her? What might she mean to him?
11. Use examples of human weakness from Act II to show how life among the group has grown worse. Nonetheless, what signs of humanity and courage do we still see?
12. Why might Mr. Frank be different in the play's final scene from the way he was in Act I, Scene 1? Why might he say of Anne, "She puts me to shame"?

Extending

13. Anne says that she wants to go on living even after her death. Has she? Explain.

READING AND LITERARY FOCUS

The Total Effect of a Full-Length Play

When we watch a full-length play being performed, we see it as a **total effect**—a combination of a number of elements: plot, character, setting, and theme.

The **plot** of a full-length play includes a number of incidents, which develop several **conflicts.** Some of these conflicts may be presented in **subplots,** or secondary but related plots within the main story. The action of the play moves forward to a **climax,** the point at which we know how the conflicts will be resolved. A full-length play can cover a long span of time. As in *The Diary of Anne Frank,* chronological order might be varied to include **flashbacks,** or scenes about earlier events.

A full-length play also introduces a number of **characters** and gives us much information about them. We usually see many different sides to these characters. We also see them change and grow. In *The Diary of Anne Frank* we see a group of characters changing as they live together under great pressure for two years.

Many full-length plays involve more than one **setting.** *The Diary of Anne Frank* is unusual because it does not move from the rooms of the attic. The play builds tension and power by showing us the effect of such confined living on a group of people over a long time.

Finally, a full-length play develops several **themes,** or ideas about life. By showing us how a specific group of people lived through a terrible time, the play shows us both the greatness and the weakness of the human spirit.

Thinking About Plot

1. What would you say is the main plot and central conflict of *The Diary of Anne Frank*? Identify one subplot, and explain how that subplot is related to the main plot.
2. At what point does the action of the play shift back in time?
3. What is the climax of this play?

Thinking About Character

4. Which characters in the play grow? Which seem to crumble under pressure?

Thinking About Setting

5. In a play that has only one set, minor changes take on greater impact. What might be the effect of seeing the bare attic in the final scene?

Thinking About Theme

6. What character traits does the play suggest help a person to endure an ordeal like that of life in the attic?

7. Anne says "I still believe that people are really good at heart." Do you agree? Explain.

COMPOSITION

Writing a Drama Review

■ Write a review of *The Diary of Anne Frank.* Begin by relating the most important facts about Anne Frank and the play. Then go on to describe the main characters and to summarize the plot of the play. End by giving your opinion of the play and backing up this opinion with logical arguments and specific examples and quotations from the play. *For help with this assignment, see Lesson 9 in the Writing About Literature Handbook at the back of this book.*

Writing a Scene

■ Use the following excerpt from Anne's actual diary as the basis for a brief scene to be included in Act I. As you write, follow the format used in the play. Be sure to indicate where the scene takes place and who is speaking. Add stage directions where you feel they are necessary. *For help with this assignment, see Lesson 10 in the Writing About Literature Handbook at the back of this book.*

If I take a small helping of some vegetable I detest and make up with potatoes, the Van Daans, and Mrs. Van Daan in particular, can't get over it, that any child should be so spoiled.

"Come along, Anne, have a few more vegetables," she says straight away.

"No, thank you, Mrs. Van Daan," I answer, "I have plenty of potatoes."

"Vegetables are good for you, your mother says so too. Have a few more," she says, pressing them on me until Daddy comes to my rescue.

Then we have from Mrs. Van Daan—"You ought to have been in our home, we were properly brought up. It's absurd that Anne's so frightfully spoiled. I wouldn't put up with it if Anne were my daughter." . . .

There was a deadly silence after Mrs. Van Daan had finished speaking yesterday. Then Daddy said, "I think Anne is extremely well brought up; she has learned one thing anyway, and that is to make no reply to your long sermons. As to vegetables, look at your own plate." Mrs. Van Daan was beaten, well and truly beaten. She had taken a minute helping of vegetables herself. But *she* is not spoiled!

COMPARING PLAYS

1. *The Romancers* is a light, fanciful comedy about young love. *The Diary of Anne Frank* is a serious, powerful drama about actual tragic events in our century. Yet both plays portray relationships between neighbors, between parents and children, and between young men and young women. Point out some of the specific ways in which the plays differ in their portrayal of these relationships.

2. Which play would you rather see on stage? Why?

The Diary of Anne Frank 431

4. ■ Anne and Peter mature.
   ■ the Van Daans and Dussel
5. conveys feeling of loss; symbolizes the group's lives
6. courage, ideals, ability to express oneself, sense of humor
7. Answers will vary. Students who agree may cite Anne herself or the heroism of Miep and Mr. Kraler. Those who disagree may cite the Holocaust itself.

COMPARING PLAYS

1. *The Romancers:* one-dimensional, idealistic, static relationships and contrived conflicts; *The Diary of Anne Frank:* multidimensional, real, evolving relationships and real conflicts
2. Answers will vary. Students' answers will reflect their preference for comedy or tragedy, romance or realism.

COMPOSITION: GUIDELINES FOR EVALUATION

WRITING A DRAMA REVIEW

Objective

To write a review of a play

Guidelines for Evaluation

■ suggested length: three to five paragraphs
■ should relate facts about Anne and the play
■ should describe the main characters
■ should summarize the plot
■ should state an opinion and support it with examples, quotations, and logic

WRITING A SCENE

Objective

To write a scene using a *Diary* excerpt

Guidelines for Evaluation

■ suggested length: shorter than five minutes
■ should give the setting and stage directions
■ should assign a speaker for each piece of dialogue
■ should include the excerpt's main elements

Active Reading

Drama

Interpreting Stage Directions

Hundreds of years ago people did not say that they were going "to see a play." They said that they were going "to hear a play." In those days players performed with little or no scenery and very few props. They relied on the *words* of the play—the spoken dialogue—to tell the audience how to visualize the scene. The imagination of the audience was important then, and it is still important now.

When you read a play, you are the audience. However, as you read, you are also providing the performance. You create a theater in your imagination. You rely on the stage directions to imagine the stage, the costumes, the props, and the way the characters move on stage. You bring the play to life by paying attention to the many details written into the stage directions, just as a good actor or a good director does.

Activity 1 Read the following lines from the opening stage directions of *The Diary of Anne Frank*. Then, based on the details in the stage directions, answer each question. Be prepared to give reasons for your choices.

[*The scene remains the same throughout the play. It is the top floor of a warehouse and office building in Amsterdam, Holland. The sharply peaked roof of the building is outlined against a sea of other rooftops, stretching away into the distance. Nearby is the belfry of a church tower, the Westertoren, whose carillon rings out the hours. Occasionally faint sounds float up from below: the voices of children playing in the street, the tramp of marching feet, a boat whistle from the canal.*

The three rooms of the top floor and a small attic space above are exposed to our view. The largest of the rooms is in the center, with two small rooms, slightly raised on either side. On the right is a bathroom, out of sight. A narrow, steep flight of stairs at the back leads up to the attic. The rooms are sparsely furnished with a few chairs, cots, a table or two. The windows are painted over, or covered with makeshift blackout curtains. In the main room there is a sink, a gas ring for cooking, and a wood-burning stove for warmth.]

1. How many different stage sets are there in the play?
   a. one
   b. two
   c. three
   d. four

2. In what kind of building does the play take place?
   a. a church
   b. a factory
   c. a warehouse
   d. a private home

3. What sound occurs each hour during the play?
   a. a siren
   b. a carillon
   c. a slamming door
   d. an elevator

4. What sound does *not* float up from below?
   a. children's voices
   b. a train whistle
   c. marching feet
   d. a boat whistle

5. Where is the largest room on the stage?
   a. at the left
   b. at the right
   c. at the back
   d. at the center

6. What piece of furniture is *not* on the stage?
   a. a cot
   b. a desk
   c. a chair
   d. a table

7. What can you see through the windows?
   a. rooftops
   b. the sea
   c. the sky
   d. nothing

8. What is the overall effect of the stage set?
   a. modern and new
   b. old and abandoned
   c. old and elegant
   d. large and roomy

Interpreting Dialogue in Drama

To appreciate fully a drama that you are reading, you need to pay close attention to the dialogue. Just as you use the stage directions to picture the stage, you use both the stage directions and the dialogue to bring the characters to life. The stage directions and the dialogue help you picture the characters' facial expressions and gestures as well as the sound of their voices. By hearing the lines as they would be spoken, you will better understand the emotions and motivations of the characters.

Read the following excerpt of a conversation between Anne and Mr. Frank in *The Diary of Anne Frank:*

ANNE. [*Pulling out a pasteboard-bound book.*] A diary! [*She throws her arms around her father.*] I've never had a diary.

Drama 433

And I've always longed for one. [*She looks around the room.*] Pencil, pencil, pencil, pencil. [*She starts down the stairs.*] I'm going down to the office to get a pencil.

MR. FRANK. Anne! No! [*He goes after her, catching her by the arm and pulling her back.*]

ANNE. [*Startled.*] But there's no one in the building now.

MR. FRANK. It doesn't matter. I don't want you ever to go beyond that door.

ANNE. [*Sobered.*] Never . . . ? Not even at nighttime, when everyone is gone? Or on Sundays? Can't I go down to listen to the radio?

MR. FRANK. Never, I am sorry, Anneke. It isn't safe. No, you must never go beyond that door.

[*For the first time* ANNE *realizes what "going into hiding" means.*]

When Anne finds the diary, she throws her arms around her father. This action, given in the stage direction, suggests the strong emotion that accompanies her exclamation in the dialogue. Then she repeats the word *pencil* several times. These repetitions, given only in the dialogue, indicate that Anne is searching around the room, trying to find a pencil. Here the dialogue alone indicates the action of the character.

When Mr. Frank pulls Anne by the arm, the stage direction tells you that she is startled. She would probably deliver her next line in a slightly confused and surprised manner, perhaps hesitating between some of the words: "But there's no one in the building now." Anne's next speech consists entirely of four questions. These questions emphasize her disbelief as she learns what "going into hiding" really means. By paying close attention to the dialogue and by using the clues given in the stage directions, you can arrive at a more complete understanding of what is happening in the minds and hearts of the characters in a play.

Activity 2 Read the following excerpt from Act II, Scene 2, of *The Diary of Anne Frank*, a conversation between Anne and her sister, Margot. Then answer each numbered question. Be prepared to give reasons for your answer.

ANNE. Anyway . . . the only one I worry about is you. I feel

434 *Drama*

awfully guilty about you. [*She sits on the stool near* MARGOT, *putting on* MARGOT's *high-heeled shoes.*]

MARGOT. What about?

ANNE. I mean, every time I go into Peter's room, I have a feeling I may be hurting you. [MARGOT *shakes her head.*] I know if it were me, I'd be wild. I'd be desperately jealous, if it were me.

MARGOT. Well, I'm not.

ANNE. You don't feel badly? Really? Truly? You're not jealous?

MARGOT. Of course I'm jealous . . . jealous that you've got something to get up in the morning for. . . . But jealous of you and Peter? No.

[ANNE *goes back to the mirror.*]

ANNE. Maybe there's nothing to be jealous of. Maybe he doesn't really like me. Maybe I'm just taking the place of his cat. . . . [*She picks up a pair of short, white gloves, putting them on.*] Wouldn't you like to come in with us?

MARGOT. I have a book.

1. Why does Anne feel guilty about her relationship with Peter? What action of Margot's indicates that Anne should not worry?

2. What two different kinds of jealousy does Margot identify?

3. In her last speech in this passage, Anne begins three sentences with the word *maybe*. What is Anne trying to make Margot feel as she suggests these other possibilities?

4. As Anne talks with Margot in this passage, the stage directions indicate three actions she performs. What are the actions? How do you think Margot reacts as Anne performs these actions?

Literary Skills Review

Drama

Guide for Reading Drama

Watching a play or film can make us feel almost as if we are witnessing life itself. However, a play or screenplay is also a work of literature. Drama adds the unique excitement of live action to literary features such as plot, character, setting, and theme. Review the following questions when you read or see a dramatic work. In helping you understand how drama creates its special impact, this guide will add to your enjoyment of any play or film.

1. Is the work a **one-act play** or a **full-length play**? Is the work serious or comic?
2. What central **conflict** does the **plot** present?
3. Does the drama move forward in normal **chronological order,** or does it include **flashbacks** to earlier times? What event is the **climax** of the drama?
4. Who are the main **characters** of the work? What does the **dialogue** reveal about the personalities of these characters? Do any characters change, and, if so, how?
5. What is the **setting,** or time and place, of the work? How do the **stage directions** help us to see the details of the setting?
6. What **themes,** or ideas about life, does the work present? How do the plot, characters, and setting help reveal these themes?
7. In what way could **staging**—scenery, props, lighting, costumes, and acting—bring the writer's words to life?

436   *Drama*

Themes Review

Drama

Many works of literature have in common certain general themes—problems and situations shared by many people. For example, many stories, poems, essays, and plays deal with the general theme "family life." However, each writer has something specific and original to say about families.

Noticing what different literary works say about the same general theme can add to our enjoyment of these works. For example, both *The Romancers* (page 351) and *The Diary of Anne Frank* (page 368) deal with family life, but each play communicates a different specific view of this general theme. *The Romancers* makes the following specific point about families: "Parents and children are often more alike than they may recognize." On the other hand, *The Diary of Anne Frank* conveys this idea about family life: "Extraordinary situations deepen the bonds and the divisions that exist within families."

1. What specific theme about families is suggested by the fact that *The Diary of Anne Frank* occasionally refers to the entire group living in the annex as "the family"?

2. Tell what specific points *The Romancers* and *The Diary of Anne Frank* make about the general theme "confronting obstacles."

3. What specific views about the general theme "love" are presented in *The Romancers* and *The Diary of Anne Frank*?

4. Choose one play and one other work, and explain the specific view each presents of the general theme "heroism."

Drama:	*The Romancers*	*The Diary of Anne Frank*
Nonfiction:	"Harriet Tubman"	"On Summer"
Stories:	"Spring Victory"	"The Brother Who Failed"

5. What specific ideas about the general theme "communication" are presented in *The Diary of Anne Frank* and one of the works listed below?

Stories:	"Charles"	"Flowers for Algernon"
Poems:	"Spellbound"	"The Story-Teller"
Drama:	*The Miracle Worker*	

Drama 437

THEMES REVIEW

The questions in the Themes Review for the Drama unit recall the general themes portrayed in the selections in this unit. Suggested answers to these questions are presented here.

1. *The Diary of Anne Frank* shows how the refugees' life together knits them into a family.

2. *The Romancers:* Obstacles are illusions of the young lovers and are eliminated through another illusion—the abduction. *Diary of Anne Frank:* The characters confront real and great obstacles, sometimes bravely and sometimes badly.

3. *The Romancers:* People can be encouraged, even induced, to "fall" in love. *The Diary of Anne Frank:* Love is a source of consolation amid suffering.

4. *The Romancers:* The staged abduction mocks heroism gently by making it an illusion. *The Diary of Anne Frank:* Life in the annex portrays the real, everyday heroism of people living under great pressure. "Spring Victory": A family works together heroically to survive. "The Brother Who Failed": many acts of unselfishness can make someone an unsung hero. "Harriet Tubman": A gifted person can surmount difficult circumstances and be a hero. "On Summer": A woman displays heroism by facing death bravely.

5. *The Diary of Anne Frank:* By communicating to us through her diary, Anne lives on beyond her death. "Charles": People do not always communicate the whole truth to one another. "Spellbound": Nature's nonverbal communication is powerful. "The Story-Teller": Verbal communication can cast a spell over external reality. *The Miracle Worker:* Human existence is not possible without language.

For more information about the themes portrayed in these selections, see the Theme Index beginning on page 666.

Preview
Greek Myths and American Folk Tales

Point out to students that the telling of stories about both real and fictional characters and events is one of the earliest forms of entertainment and communication. Explain that as such stories were told and passed on, they were often embellished and exaggerated to make their telling more lively and appealing. Then have students read the Preview. Emphasize to students that as they read the selections in this unit, they should bear in mind the role imagination played in their creation and in the enjoyment and believability of them.

People have been telling stories for thousands of years. Long before writing was invented, stories were told around crackling campfires and at family meetings. They often formed part of important community ceremonies and public gatherings. As time passed, these stories were sung by wandering minstrels who knew them by heart and recited them with musical accompaniment. The earliest of these stories are called myths.

The word *myth* comes from *mythos*, a Greek word meaning "story." A myth is a special kind of story, usually about a culture's gods and goddesses and their experiences with human beings. For the people who invented myths, the stories told how nature works and why people do what they do. They tell, for example, how the sun rises, why the seasons change, why some people make foolish mistakes, and why other people become great heroes. No one knows exactly when the Greek myths began. However, they were already old and familiar when the Greek writer Homer used them in his poems about 850 B.C.

The myths of the Greeks have had more importance for our literature than the myths of any other people. Their stories are exciting, their characters unforgettable. Through their power of imagination, the Greek myths still speak to us across the ages. The adventures of the ancient Greek heroes can be easily compared to the great deeds of our modern heroes.

Like the Greek myths, the folk tales of America are one of our richest imaginative treasures. No one knows who invented these tales. Like myths, they were told and retold by many different people over many generations. Unlike myths, they do not tell of gods and goddesses, but many of them do describe the adventures of great heroes. As you read, you will notice many ways in which the folk tales of America share the same imaginative power as the ancient myths.

Greek Myths and American Folk Tales   439

GREEK MYTHS

A **myth** is an ancient anonymous story, usually involving gods and goddesses, that conveys the beliefs and ideals of a culture. Myths are more than entertaining stories. They tell the history of a people—who their kings were, what great battles they won and lost, and how their culture was founded.

The five Greek myths in this unit will take you on five different heroic adventures. The first myth is the story of Theseus, one of the greatest heroes of mythology. His story includes all of the ingredients of a heroic tale: the hero's youth, his quest, his battles, and his return to claim his kingdom.

The stories of Phaethon and of Daedalus and Icarus show what happens when high spirits are not balanced by equally heroic intelligence and wisdom. Orpheus is heroic in a different way: His weapon is music; his motivation is love; his challenge is to conquer death itself. Finally, the story of the heroine Alcestis shows that character is the real source of heroism.

Gods and Goddesses of Greece and Rome

When the ancient Romans conquered Greece in the second century B.C., they took many Greek myths home to Rome, but they substituted Roman names for the gods.

Greek Name	Roman Name	Description
Cronus [krō′nəs]	Saturn	ruler of the Titans
Zeus [zoos]	Jupiter	king of the gods
Hera [hēr′ə]	Juno	queen of the gods
Poseidon [pō sī′dən]	Neptune	god of the sea
Hades [hā′dēz]	Pluto	god of the underworld
Ares [ār′ēz]	Mars	god of war
Apollo [ə pol′ō]	Apollo	god of the sun
Artemis [är′tə mis]	Diana	goddess of the moon
Athena [ə thē′nə]	Minerva	goddess of wisdom
Aphrodite [af′rə dī′tē]	Venus	goddess of love
Eros [er′os]	Cupid	god of love
Hephaestus [hi fes′təs]	Vulcan	god of fire
Hermes [hur′mēz]	Mercury	messenger of the gods
Demeter [di mē′tər]	Ceres	goddess of agriculture
Dionysus [dī′ə nī′səs]	Bacchus	god of the vine

Theseus [thē′sē əs] was honored as the official hero of the city of Athens. Although there is no proof that Theseus was a real person, some experts on myths believe that he was an ancient warrior-king. The story of Theseus has been told and retold many times. This version is related by one of America's master storytellers, the nineteenth-century novelist Nathaniel Hawthorne.

■ What details in the story of Theseus show his leadership?

Drawing of a labyrinth, or maze.

Retold by
Nathaniel Hawthorne

Theseus

In the old city of Troezene,[1] at the foot of a lofty mountain, there lived long ago a boy named Theseus. His grandfather, King Pittheus,[2] was the sovereign of that country. His mother's name was Aethra.[3] As for his father, the boy had never seen him. But from his earliest remembrance, Aethra used to go with Theseus into a wood and sit upon a moss-grown rock which was deeply sunken into the earth. Here she often talked with her son about his father. She said that he was called Aegeus[4] and that he was a great king and ruled over Attica[5] and dwelt at Athens, which was as famous a city as any in the world.

1   "Mother," asked the boy, "why cannot I go to Athens and tell King Aegeus that I am his son?"

---

1. **Troezene** [trō′ə zēn]
2. **Pittheus** [pit′thē əs]
3. **Aethra** [ēth′rə]
4. **Aegeus** [ē′jē əs]
5. **Attica** [at′i kə]: ancient region in east-central Greece.

"That may happen by and by," said Aethra. "You are not yet big and strong enough to set out on such an errand."

"And how soon shall I be strong enough?"

2   "You are but a boy," replied his mother. "When you can lift this rock and show me what is hidden beneath it, I promise you my permission to depart."

Often after this did Theseus ask his mother whether it was yet time for him to go to Athens. Still his mother pointed to the rock and told him that for years to come he could not be strong enough to move it. Again and again the boy would tug and strain at the huge mass of stone. Meanwhile the rock seemed to be sinking farther and farther into the ground. The moss grew over it thicker and thicker.

3   But difficult as the matter looked, Theseus was now growing up to be such a vigorous youth that, in his own opinion, the time would quickly come when he might hope to get the upper hand of the lump of stone.

Theseus   441

- Theseus moves the stone and finds a chest containing a sword with a golden hilt and sandals.
- He prepares to seek his father in Athens.
- His grandfather, Pittheus, suggests that he travel by sea to avoid robbers.

1 THEME

The time comes for Theseus to embark on his quest. He has reached manhood and must now prove himself.

2 CHARACTERIZATION

Epithets such as "the *wise* King Pittheus" reveal character traits. These were a favorite device of Greek myth makers.

3 HEROES

Theseus, in true heroic style, has courage that supersedes his caution.

"Mother, I do believe it has started!"[6] cried he after one of his attempts.

"No, no!" his mother hastily answered. "It is not possible you can have moved it."

It was not more than a year afterwards when they were again sitting on the moss-covered stone. Aethra had once more told him the story of his father.

"Mother," he exclaimed, "I never felt half so strong as now! I feel myself a man! It is now time to make one earnest trial to remove the stone."

Then Theseus bent himself in good earnest to the task and strained every sinew. The great rock stirred! Yes, it was raised slowly from the bedded moss and earth and was turned upon its side. While taking breath, he looked at his mother, and she smiled upon him.

1 "Yes, Theseus," she said, "the time has come, and you must stay no longer at my side. See what King Aegeus left for you."

Theseus looked and saw that the rock had been placed over another slab of stone that somewhat resembled a roughly made chest.

Within lay a sword with a golden hilt and a pair of sandals.

"That was your father's sword," said Aethra, "and those were his sandals. When he went to be king of Athens, he bade me treat you as a child until you should prove yourself a man by lifting his heavy stone. That task being accomplished, you are to put on his sandals in order to follow in your father's footsteps and to gird on his sword."

2 When his grandfather, the wise King Pittheus, heard that Theseus intended to present himself at his father's palace, he earnestly advised him to go by sea.

"The roads are very bad by land," said the venerable[7] king, "and they are infested with robbers and monsters. Let him go by sea!"

3 But when Theseus heard of robbers and monsters, he was eager to take the road along

---

6. **started:** moved.

7. **venerable** [ven′ər ə bəl]: old and respected.

GUIDED READING

LITERAL QUESTIONS

1a. What does Theseus find under the stone? (He finds a chest containing his father's sword and sandals.)

2a. Why does King Pittheus advise traveling by sea? (There are robbers along the roads.)

INFERENTIAL QUESTIONS

1b. What do these articles represent for Theseus? (They represent his growth into manhood and his developing readiness to take his father's place.)

2b. When Theseus ignores this advice, what do we learn about him? (He is headstrong and brave.)

which they were to be met with. Therefore, he bade a respectful farewell to his grandfather, thanking him for all his kindness, and after affectionately embracing his mother, he set forth.

Many adventures befell Theseus on the road to Athens. He quite cleared that part of the country of the robbers about whom King Pittheus had been so much alarmed. One of these was named Procrustes,[8] and he was indeed a terrible fellow. In his cavern he had a bed on which, with great pretense[9] of hospitality, he invited his guest to lie down. But if they happened to be shorter than the bed, this wicked villain stretched them out by main force. Or if they were too long, he lopped off their heads or feet. Thus, however weary a man might be, he never liked to lie in the bed of Procrustes. Another of these robbers, named Scinis,[10] must likewise have been a great scoundrel. He was in the habit of flinging his victims off a high cliff into the sea. Theseus tossed him off the very same place.

Thus by the time he reached his journey's end, Theseus had done many valiant feats with his father's golden-hilted sword and had gained the renown of being one of the bravest young men of the day. His fame traveled faster than he did and reached Athens before him. As he entered the city, he heard the inhabitants talking at the street corners and saying that Theseus, the son of their own king, would turn out as great a hero as the best of them.

He little suspected, innocent youth that he was, that here in this very Athens a greater danger awaited him than any which he had encountered on the road. The father of Theseus was almost worn out with the cares of government and had thus grown aged before his time. His nephews intended to get all the power of the kingdom into their own hands. Thus these nephews of King Aegeus, who were the cousins of Theseus, became his enemies. A still more dangerous enemy was Medea,[11] the wicked enchantress, for she wanted to give the kingdom to her son Medus.[12]

It so happened that the king's nephews met Theseus and found out who he was just as he reached the entrance of the royal palace. They pretended to be his friends. They proposed that he should come into the king's presence as a stranger to try whether Aegeus would recognize him. Theseus consented, but while he waited at the door, the nephews ran and told the king that a young man had arrived who intended to get possession of his crown.

"Aha!" cried the old king. "What would you advise me to do with him?"

"Leave that to me, your Majesty," replied Medea. "Invite him to drink a goblet of wine. Let me put a single drop of this powerful medicine into the goblet."

King Aegeus, like most other kings, thought any punishment mild enough for a person who was plotting against his life and therefore gave orders that the young stranger should be admitted into his presence. The goblet was set on a table beside the king's throne.

Advancing to the foot of the throne, Theseus attempted to make a little speech, but he was almost choked by the tender feelings that swelled into his throat.

"Young man," said the king, "you are welcome! Do me the favor to drink the contents of this goblet."

So saying, King Aegeus took the golden

---

8. **Procrustes** [prō krus′tēz]
9. **pretense** [prē′tens]: false show.
10. **Scinis** [sin′əs]

11. **Medea** [mi dē′ə]
12. **Medus** [me′dūs]

Theseus 443

AT A GLANCE
- Theseus travels by land and vanquishes the robbers. His fame spreads.
- Danger awaits him in Athens in the person of Medea, who wants the kingdom for her son, Medus.

1 VOCABULARY: ETYMOLOGY

A *procrustean bed* now refers to a scheme into which someone is forced arbitrarily. To behave in a *procrustean* manner is to act with ruthless disregard for individual differences.

2 THEME

In ridding the countryside of villains and thus protecting the public, Theseus shows his people that he is indeed the ideal hero.

3 BACKGROUND

Medea appears in earlier myths as the wife of Jason of the golden fleece. By the time she weds Aegeus, she has already murdered her half-brother and her own two children by Jason. She is the focus of many dramas and operas.

4 READING SKILLS: INFERENCE

Given Medea's enmity toward Theseus, we can surmise that the "medicine" Medea puts in his goblet is actually poison.

5 CHARACTERIZATION

Theseus is overwhelmed with joy at the sight of his father. This joy heightens the sense of impending tragedy should Theseus drink the wine.

GUIDED READING

LITERAL QUESTIONS

1a. What adventures does Theseus undergo on the way to Athens? (He fights many robbers, including Procrustes and Scinis.)

2a. Why does Medea feel threatened by Theseus? (She wants the kingdom for her own son.)

INFERENTIAL QUESTIONS

1b. What do these adventures suggest about Theseus' development? (He is growing in strength and displaying his heroic nature more and more.)

2b. What do you think Medea plans to do to end the threat? (She plans to poison Theseus.)

■ Medea's trickery is foiled when Aegeus recognizes Theseus' sword; the men are reconciled.

■ Aegeus tells the story of the Minotaur.

■ Theseus vows to kill the Minotaur.

1 **MYTH PLOT**

A traditional development in the plot of a myth is the revelation of the hero, who has been disguised or unrecognized up to this point.

2 **SUBPLOT**

The standard mythic plot moves from adventure to adventure. Usually, only the presence of the hero unifies the story. Hawthorne modifies the myth somewhat so that Theseus' quest for the throne remains the goal throughout.

3 **BACKGROUND**

The god Poseidon sent a bull to prove Minos' right to rule Crete. When Minos failed to sacrifice the bull to him, Poseidon caused Minos' wife to bear a creature part bull and part man, the Minotaur.

4 **PLOT: CONFLICT**

Once again, Theseus' heroic resolve supersedes his caution and the warnings of his elders. In his youthful idealism he is stronger than the once-powerful king and so is on his way to achieving the right to rule.

---

goblet from the table and offered it to Theseus. Theseus held out his hand to take the wine. But before he touched it, King Aegeus trembled. His eyes had fallen on the gold-hilted sword that hung at the young man's side. He drew back the goblet.

"That sword!" he cried. "How came you by it?"

"It was my father's sword," replied Theseus, with a tremulous[13] voice. "These were his sandals. It is only a month since I grew strong enough to lift the heavy stone and take the sword and sandals and come to Athens to seek my father."

1   "My son! My son!" cried King Aegeus, flinging away the fatal goblet. "Yes, these are Aethra's eyes. It is my son."

And now Prince Theseus was taken into great favor by his royal father. The old king was never weary of hearing him tell about his childhood and his many efforts to lift the stone.

2   One morning when Prince Theseus awoke, he fancied that he must have had a sorrowful dream. For it appeared as if the air was full of a melancholy wail. And when he listened more attentively, he could hear sobs and groans. He put on his clothes quickly, and hastening to the king, inquired what it all meant.

"Alas! My son," said King Aegeus, heaving a long sigh, "this is the woefullest anniversary in the whole year. It is the day when we annually draw lots to see which of the youths and maidens of Athens shall go to be devoured by the horrible Minotaur."[14]

"The Minotaur!" exclaimed Prince Theseus. "What kind of a monster may that be? Is it not possible to slay him?"

But King Aegeus shook his venerable head and gave him an explanation of the whole af-

---

3   fair. It seems that in the island of Crete[15] there lived a certain dreadful monster called a Minotaur, which was shaped partly like a man and partly like a bull and was altogether a hideous sort of a creature. King Minos,[16] who reigned over Crete, laid out a vast deal of money in building a habitation for the Minotaur and took great care of his health and comfort merely for mischief's sake. A few years before this time, there had been a war between Athens and Crete in which the Athenians were beaten and compelled to beg for peace. No peace could they obtain, however, except on condition that they should send seven young men and seven maidens every year to be devoured by the pet monster of the cruel King Minos. For three years past this grievous calamity had been borne.[17] And now the fatal day had come again.

When Theseus heard the story, he straightened himself up so that he seemed taller than ever before.

"Let the people of Athens this year draw lots for only six young men instead of seven," said he. "I will myself be the seventh. Let the Minotaur devour me, if he can!"

4   The old king shed tears and begged Theseus not to leave him desolate in his old age. Theseus, however, felt that he was in the right and would not give up his resolution. But he assured his father that if the Minotaur devoured him, it should not be without a battle for his dinner. So a vessel was got ready and rigged with black sails. Theseus, with six other young men and seven maidens, came down to the harbor to embark.

Just as Theseus was going on board his father thought of one last word to say.

"My beloved son," said he, "the sails of this

---

13. **tremulous** [trem′yə ləs]: trembling.
14. **Minotaur** [min′ə tôr′]

15. **Crete** [krēt]: island southeast of Greece.
16. **Minos** [mī′nəs]
17. **borne:** endured.

GUIDED READING

LITERAL QUESTIONS

1a. What is the Minotaur? (It is a beast, part bull and part man, that eats Athenians and dwells on Crete.)

2a. What does Theseus say when he hears the story about the Minotaur? (He volunteers to be counted as the seventh man and challenges the Minotaur.)

INFERENTIAL QUESTIONS

1b. What might the part-man, part-bull Minotaur represent? (Some students may note that he could represent the evil in humanity, just as the heroic Theseus represents the good.)

2b. Does his father believe that Theseus will succeed? How can you tell? (No; he sheds tears and tries to convince Theseus to stay.)

vessel are black, since it goes on a voyage of sorrow and despair. I shall creep daily to the top of yonder cliff to watch if there be a sail upon the sea. And if by some happy chance you should escape the jaws of the Minotaur, then tear down those dismal sails and hoist others that shall be bright as the sunshine. Then I will know that you are coming back victorious."

Theseus promised that he would do so. Then the mariners trimmed[18] the vessel's black sails to the wind, which blew faintly off the shore. But by and by when they had got fairly out to sea, there came a stiff breeze from the northwest that drove them along merrily.

1 Soon the high blue mountains of Crete began to show themselves among the far-off clouds. The vessel went bounding onward until it glided between the headlands of the port. No sooner had they entered the harbor than a party of the guards of King Minos came down to the waterside and took charge of the fourteen young men and damsels. Surrounded by these armed warriors, Theseus and his companions were led to the king's palace and ushered into his presence. Now Minos was a stern and pitiless king. When his eyes rested on Theseus, the king looked at him attentively because his face was calm and brave.

"Young man," asked he with his stern voice, "are you not appalled at the certainty of being devoured by this terrible Minotaur?"

2 "I have offered my life in a good cause," answered Theseus, "and therefore I give it freely and gladly. But thou, King Minos, art thou not thyself appalled who hast committed this dreadful wrong year after year? I tell thee to thy face that thou art a more hideous monster than the Minotaur himself!"

"Aha! Do you think me so?" cried the king, laughing in his cruel way. "Tomorrow at breakfast time you shall have an opportunity of judging which is the greater monster, the Minotaur or the king! Take them away, guards, and let this free-spoken youth be the Minotaur's first morsel!"

3 Near the king's throne stood his daughter Ariadne.[19] She was a beautiful and tender-hearted maiden and looked at these poor doomed captives with very different feelings from those of the iron-breasted King Minos. And when she beheld the brave, spirited figure of Theseus bearing himself so calmly in his terrible peril, she flung herself at the king's feet and begged him to set all the captives free, especially this one young man.

But the king would hear not a word in their favor. The prisoners were led away and clapped into a dungeon. The seven maidens and six of the young men soon fell asleep, but **4** Theseus was not like them. He felt conscious that he was wiser and braver and stronger than his companions. Therefore he had the responsibility of all their lives upon him and must consider whether there was no way to save them. So he kept himself awake and paced to and fro across the gloomy dungeon in which they were shut up.

Just before midnight the door was softly unbarred, and the gentle Ariadne showed herself, with a torch in her hand.

"Are you awake, Theseus?" she whispered.

"Yes," answered Theseus. "With so little time to live, I do not choose to waste any of it in sleep."

"Then follow me," said Ariadne.

Ariadne opened all the doors and led him forth from the darksome prison into the pleasant moonlight.

"Theseus," said the maiden, "you can now get on board your vessel and sail away for Athens."

---

18. **trimmed:** adjusted.

---

19. **Ariadne** [ar′ē ad′nē]

Theseus 445

AT A GLANCE

- Aegeus sends Theseus off in a vessel with black sails, asking him to exchange the sails for bright ones if he returns victorious.
- Theseus and his companions travel to Crete and are cast into Minos' prison.
- Ariadne, Minos' daughter, is attracted to Theseus and helps him escape.

1 SETTING

The pleasant view of the island contrasts with the grim fate awaiting the travelers.

2 THEME

While summarizing the conflict in this subplot, Theseus' speech to Minos shows idealism, a heroic trait.

3 CHARACTERIZATION

The epithet *iron-breasted* contrasts Minos with his "tender-hearted" daughter. Epithets are a common descriptive device in myths.

4 HEROES

A true hero who is a defender of society, Theseus will use his strengths to protect his weaker companions. This decision also advances his quest to conquer the Minotaur.

GUIDED READING

LITERAL QUESTIONS

1a. What words are used to describe Minos? (stern, pitiless, cruel, iron-breasted)

2a. Who attempts to rescue Theseus? (Ariadne, Minos' daughter, helps him escape.)

INFERENTIAL QUESTIONS

1b. How does this description contrast with the depiction of Theseus? (Theseus is calm and brave; he thinks of his companions before himself.)

2b. Would it be in character for Theseus to accept Ariadne's offer to help him escape from the Minotaur? Why or why not? (No; Theseus always puts honor before his own safety.)

AT A GLANCE

- Theseus refuses to leave without killing the Minotaur.
- Ariadne leads him to the Minotaur's labyrinth.
- Holding one end of a silken string, Theseus vanishes into the labyrinth.
- Theseus and the Minotaur begin a raging battle.

1 SETTING

The description of the path to the labyrinth emphasizes its mysterious, forbidding nature.

2 BACKGROUND

Daedalus was the greatest architect and sculptor of his time. Minos commissioned him to design the labyrinth so that the Minotaur could not escape.

3 POINT OF VIEW

We experience the labyrinth through Theseus' senses. In this passage the narrator moves closer than usual to Theseus' point of view, heightening the narrative's excitement and suspense.

4 IMAGERY

In a powerful auditory image Hawthorne reveals the anger and terrible confusion of the half-man, half-bull Minotaur.

"No," answered the young man. "I will never leave Crete unless I can first slay the Minotaur and save my poor companions and deliver Athens from this cruel tribute."

"I knew that this would be your resolution," said Ariadne. "Come then with me. Here is your own sword, which the guards deprived you of."

1 Then she led Theseus along until they came to a dark, shadowy grove, where the moonlight wasted itself on the tops of the trees without shedding so much as a glimmering beam upon their pathway. After going a good way, they reached a high marble wall which was overgrown with creeping plants. The wall seemed to have no door but rose up, lofty and massive and mysterious. Nevertheless, Ariadne pressed her finger against a particular block of marble, and it yielded, disclosing an entrance just wide enough to admit them. They crept through, and the marble stone swung back into place.

"We are now," said Ariadne, "in the famous labyrinth[20] which Daedalus[21] built. That Daedalus was a very cunning workman, but of all his artful contrivances,[22] this labyrinth is the most wondrous. Were we to take but a few steps from the doorway, we might wander about all our lifetime and never find it again. In the center of this labyrinth is the Minotaur, and, Theseus, you must go to seek him."

Just then, they heard a rough and disagreeable roar, which greatly resembled the lowing of a fierce bull, but yet had some sort of sound like the human voice.

2 "That is the Minotaur's noise," whispered Ariadne. "You must follow that sound through the labyrinth and you will find him. Take the end of this silken string. I will hold the other

---

20. **labyrinth** [lab'ə rinth']: maze.
21. **Daedalus** [ded'əl əs]
22. **contrivances** [kən trī'vəns əz]: inventions.

446 *Greek Myths and American Folk Tales*

---

end, and then if you win the victory, it will lead you again to this spot. Farewell, brave Theseus."

So the young man took the end of the silken string in his left hand and his gold-hilted sword in the other and trod boldly into the labyrinth. Theseus had not taken five steps before he lost sight of Ariadne. But still **3** he went on, now creeping through a low arch, now ascending a flight of steps, now in one crooked passage and now in another, with here a door opening before him, and there one banging behind, until it really seemed as if the walls spun round and whirled him round along with them. And all the while through these hollow avenues, now nearer, now farther off again, resounded the cry of the Minotaur, which now grew louder and louder and finally so loud that Theseus expected to come upon him at every new zigzag of the path. At last in an open space at the very center of the labyrinth, he did discern the hideous creature.

What an ugly monster it was! Only his horned head belonged to a bull, and yet somehow or other, he looked like a bull all over. He kept striding to and fro in a solitary frenzy of rage, continually emitting a hoarse roar. Now the Minotaur, turning suddenly about, caught sight of Theseus and instantly lowered his horribly sharp horns exactly as a mad bull does when he means to rush against an en- **4** emy. At the same time he belched forth a tremendous roar in which there was something like the words of human language, but all disjointed[23] and shaken to pieces by passing through the gullet of a miserably enraged brute.

There ensued[24] the most awful fight that ever happened beneath the sun or moon. The

---

23. **disjointed:** mixed up.
24. **ensued:** took place.

GUIDED READING

LITERAL QUESTIONS

1a. What is the labyrinth like? (It is a maze that seems to wind back in on itself.)

1b. Why might the labyrinth be more challenging than any difficulty Theseus has faced so far? (It is confusing as well as dangerous.)

INFERENTIAL QUESTIONS

2a. In what terms does Hawthorne describe the Minotaur's cry when he sees Theseus? (a tremendous roar that sounded something like disjointed human speech)

2b. Is the Minotaur more frightening or less frightening because it is part human? Why? (Some students might find the unnatural combination of man and beast especially terrifying.)

- Theseus kills the Minotaur.
- Ariadne's string guides Theseus out of the labyrinth.
- He sets the captives free, and they sail for Athens, forgetting to change the sails.
- Aegeus sees the black sails and leaps from a cliff to his death. Theseus becomes king.

1 PLOT: CLIMAX

Theseus slays the Minotaur, completing his quest and his rite of passage.

2 DIALOGUE

Ariadne expresses her awe at Theseus' heroism, and he gallantly credits her aid, revealing another facet of his heroic nature: generosity.

3 RESPONSE JOURNAL

Ask students to discuss in their response journals whether Ariadne's daughterly devotion to King Minos is justified or not.

4 PLOT: RESOLUTION

Aegeus' death darkens Theseus' triumph, but it also allows Theseus to ascend the throne, the position for which he was born. Therefore, this event is essential to the resolution of the narrative.

monster, in his first headlong rush against Theseus, missed him by a hair's breadth and broke one of his horns short off against the stone wall. After this, the two antagonists fought sword to horn for a long while. At last the Minotaur made a run at Theseus, grazed his left side, and flung him down. He opened his bull mouth from ear to ear and prepared to snap the young man's head off. But Theseus leaped up and caught the monster off his **1** guard. With all his force, he hit the Minotaur upon the neck and made his bull head skip from his human body, which fell down upon the ground.

So now the battle was ended. Immediately the moon shone out as brightly as if all the troubles of the world and all the wickedness and the ugliness that infest human life were past and gone forever. And Theseus, as he leaned on his sword, taking breath, felt a twitch of the silken cord. Eager to let Ariadne know of his success, he followed the guidance of the thread and soon found himself at the entrance of the labyrinth.

2 "Thou hast slain the monster," cried Ariadne, clasping her hands.

"Thanks to thee," answered Theseus, "I return victorious."

"Then," said Ariadne, "we must quickly summon thy friends and get them and thyself on board the vessel. If morning finds thee here, my father will avenge the Minotaur."

The captives were awakened and were told of what Theseus had done. Hastening down to the vessel, they all clambered on board except Theseus, who lingered behind, holding Ariadne's hand clasped in his own.

"Thou wilt surely go with us," said he. "Thou art too gentle and sweet for such an iron-hearted father as King Minos. Come with us, then, for he will be very angry when he knows what thou hast done."

3 "No, Theseus," the maiden said, "I cannot go with you. My father is old and has nobody but myself to love him. At first King Minos will be angry, but he will soon forgive his only child. Farewell!"

Nothing remained for Theseus, therefore, but to bid Ariadne an affectionate farewell and go on board the vessel and set sail. In a few moments the white foam was boiling up before their prow as Prince Theseus and his companions sailed out of the harbor with a whistling breeze behind them. In due season they came within sight of the coast of Attica, which was their native country. But here happened a sad misfortune.

King Aegeus had asked Theseus to hoist sunshine sails instead of black ones in case he should overcome the Minotaur and return victorious. In the joy of their success, however, these young people never once thought whether their sails were black, white, or rainbow colored. Thus the vessel returned, like a raven, with the same sable wings that had wafted her away. But poor King Aegeus, day after day, infirm as he was, had clambered to the summit of a cliff that overhung the sea and there sat watching for Theseus, homeward bound. No sooner did he behold the fatal blackness of the sails than he concluded that his dear son whom he loved so much and felt so proud of had been eaten by the Minotaur.

4 He could not bear the thought of living any longer, so King Aegeus stooped forward and fell headlong over the cliff and was drowned in the waves that foamed at its base.

This was melancholy news for Prince Theseus, who when he stepped ashore found himself king of all the country. However, he sent for his mother to Athens, and by taking her advice in matters of state, became a very excellent monarch and was greatly beloved by his people.

448 *Greek Myths and American Folk Tales*

GUIDED READING

LITERAL QUESTIONS

1a. What happens on Crete immediately after Theseus kills the Minotaur? (The moon shines out with sudden brightness.)

2a. How does King Aegeus die? (Theseus forgets to signal his father by changing the sails of his boat, so Aegeus believes that his son has been killed by the Minotaur. Aegeus loses his will to live and plunges into the sea.)

INFERENTIAL QUESTIONS

1b. Why is this development a fitting one? (Having killed the Minotaur, Theseus has removed an evil force from Crete and thereby "brightened" life there.)

2b. How much should Theseus be blamed for the death of his father? (Answers may vary. Some students may feel it was understandable to forget about the sails. Others may say that Theseus should not have forgotten Aegeus' request.)

STUDY QUESTIONS

Recalling

1. Where does Theseus intend to go as he sets out on his journey?
2. What did Procrustes do to his visitors?
3. For what reason did Aegeus' nephews and Medea want to destroy Theseus?
4. What does Aegeus notice as Theseus is about to drink from the goblet?
5. For what reason must Athens send young men and women to Crete each year? What happens to them there?
6. What is the labyrinth? What does Ariadne do to help Theseus?
7. What does Theseus become at the end of the myth?

Interpreting

8. Describe Theseus' character in your own words. Support your opinions with examples from the myth.
9. What does Theseus believe is his mission in life? What events in the story demonstrate his belief?

Extending

10. What similarities can you find between modern adventure stories and the myth of Theseus?

READING AND LITERARY FOCUS

Heroes and Mythological Heroes

The **hero** of a story is the central character. In modern stories heroes are people like ourselves and the people that we know. **Mythological heroes**, however, are often the special children of gods and usually have some supernatural and superhuman abilities.

Often the hero goes on a journey, usually in search of something. The hero sets out to reach a goal, answer a question, fulfill a desire, keep a promise, or solve a problem. Theseus, for example, sets forth to claim his kingdom. Along the way the hero is tested and often suffers. However, by meeting challenges, the hero usually triumphs.

The mythological hero is often fortunate enough to have the help and advice of a supernatural being. However, the main reasons for the true hero's success are personal strength, courage, nobility, and leadership.

Thinking About Heroes

■ What do you think is Theseus' most heroic act?

VOCABULARY

Antonyms

Antonyms are words that have opposite or nearly opposite meanings. *Hot* and *cold* are antonyms. The words in capitals are from "Theseus." Choose the word that is most nearly the opposite of each word in capitals.

1. HOIST: (a) tear (b) rob (c) turn (d) lower
2. CALAMITY: (a) accident (b) monstrosity (c) disaster (d) accomplishment
3. SABLE: (a) white (b) silk (c) expensive (d) heavy
4. PERIL: (a) liquid (b) anger (c) safety (d) surprise

COMPOSITION

Writing About Character

■ Identify one villain, or evil character, in the story of Theseus. First describe the character. Then tell what quality leads to the villian's defeat. Finally, tell what admirable quality the villain brings out in the hero Theseus.

Writing a Speech

■ Imagine that you are Theseus and that you have just returned to Athens from your adventures in Crete. Write a speech that will convince the people of the city that you are worthy of becoming their king. First describe what you have done. Then tell what you plan to do.

Theseus 449

COMPOSITION: GUIDELINES FOR EVALUATION

WRITING ABOUT CHARACTER

Objective

To describe relationship between villain, hero

Guidelines for Evaluation

■ suggested length: one to two paragraphs
■ should identify a villain or evil character
■ should describe the character in detail
■ should tell what quality leads to defeat
■ should tell what admirable quality the character brings out in the hero, Theseus

WRITING A SPEECH

Objective

To write a persuasive speech

Guidelines for Evaluation

■ suggested length: one to three paragraphs
■ should be written from Theseus' point of view
■ should describe what Theseus did
■ should tell what he would plan to do as king
■ should tell why he would be a great king

- Phaethon enters the palace of the Sun on Mount Olympus.
- He asks whether the Sun is truly his father.
- The Sun admits that he is and promises to give Phaethon proof.

LITERARY OPTIONS

- allusion
- characterization
- imagery

THEMATIC OPTIONS

- the effects of pride
- confronting obstacles
- heroism

1 STYLE: SENSORY LANGUAGE

Words such as *radiant, shone, flashed,* and *glowed* reveal the palace of the Sun in its dazzling splendor.

2 THEME

Phaethon's understandable fear and awe at approaching a god is overruled by his urgent purpose and his pride.

3 CHARACTERIZATION

Phaethon is bold enough to endure the blindingly brilliant light and to address the Sun.

TEXAS ESSENTIAL ELEMENTS GRADE 8

1A writing process
1C support for main idea
1I word choice
3A character development
3B figurative language
3D literary genres
4B implied main idea
4G prediction of outcomes
4H generalizations
To locate treatment of an Element, see *Texas Teacher's Resources.*

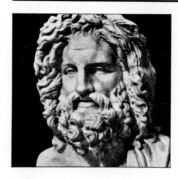

How does the sun move across the sky? Why are the mountaintops bare and the deserts barren? In an age before science, these questions were answered by the story of Phaethon (fā′ə thon′), the reckless son of the sun god.

■ Can you find the answers to these questions as you read?

Statue of Zeus, king of the gods.

Retold by Edith Hamilton

Phaethon

1   The palace of the Sun was a radiant place. It shone with gold and gleamed with ivory and sparkled with jewels. Everything without and within flashed and glowed and glittered. It was always high noon there. Shadowy twilight never dimmed the brightness. Darkness and night were unknown. Few among mortals could have long endured that unchanging brilliancy of light, but few had ever found their way thither.

    Nevertheless, one day a youth, mortal on **2** his mother's side, dared to approach. Often he had to pause and clear his dazzled eyes, but the errand which had brought him was so urgent that his purpose held fast and he pressed on, up to the palace, through the burnished[1] doors, and into the throne room where surrounded by a blinding, blazing splendor the sun god sat. There the lad was forced to halt. He could bear no more.

    Nothing escapes the eyes of the Sun. He saw the boy instantly and he looked at him very kindly. "What brought you here?" he asked.

3   "I have come," the other answered boldly, "to find out if you are my father or not. My mother said you were, but the boys at school laugh when I tell them I am your son. They will not believe me. I told my mother and she said I had better go and ask you."

    Smiling, the Sun took off his crown of burning light so that the lad could look at him without distress. "Come here, Phaethon," he said. "You are my son. Clymene[2] told you the truth. I expect you will not doubt my word too? But I will give you a proof. Ask anything you want of me and you shall have it. I call the Styx[3] to be witness to my promise, the river of the oath of the gods."

1. **burnished:** polished.

450   *Greek Myths and American Folk Tales*

2. **Clymene** [klim′ə nē]
3. **Styx** [stiks]: river surrounding the underworld.

GUIDED READING

LITERAL QUESTION

1a. What is Phaethon's "urgent errand"? (He wants to find out if the Sun is truly his father.)

INFERENTIAL QUESTION

1b. Why is it so important for him to know? (His friends think he is lying and mock him, and this mocking hurts his pride.)

No doubt Phaethon had often watched the Sun riding through the heavens and had told himself with a feeling, half awe, half excitement, "It is my father up there." And then he would wonder what it would be like to be in that chariot, guiding the steeds along that dizzy course, giving light to the world. Now at his father's words this wild dream had become possible. Instantly he cried, "I choose to take your place, Father. That is the only thing I want. Just for a day, a single day, let me have your car[4] to drive."

The Sun realized his own folly. Why had he taken that fatal oath and bound himself to give in to anything that happened to enter a boy's rash young head? "Dear lad," he said, "this is the only thing I would have refused you. I know I cannot refuse. I have sworn by the Styx. I must yield if you persist. But I do not believe you will. Listen while I tell you what this is you want. You are Clymene's son as well as mine. You are mortal and no mortal could drive my chariot. Indeed, no god except myself can do that. The ruler of the gods cannot. Consider the road. It rises up from the sea so steeply that the horses can hardly climb it, fresh though they are in the early morning. In midheaven it is so high that even I do not like to look down. Worst of all is the descent, so precipitous[5] that the sea gods waiting to receive me wonder how I can avoid falling headlong. To guide the horses, too, is a perpetual struggle. Their fiery spirits grow hotter as they climb and they scarcely suffer[6] my control. What would they do with you?

"Are you fancying that there are all sorts of wonders up there, cities of the gods full of beautiful things? Nothing of the kind. You will have to pass beasts, fierce beasts of prey,

and they are all that you will see. The Bull, the Lion, the Scorpion, the great Crab,[7] each will try to harm you. Be persuaded. Look around you. See all the goods the rich world holds. Choose from them your heart's desire and it shall be yours. If what you want is to be proved my son, my fears for you are proof enough that I am your father."

But none of all this wise talk meant anything to the boy. A glorious prospect[8] opened before him. He saw himself proudly standing in that wondrous car, his hands triumphantly guiding those steeds which Zeus himself could not master. He did not give a thought to the dangers his father detailed. He felt not a quiver of fear, not a doubt of his own powers. At last the Sun gave up trying to dissuade him.[9] It was hopeless, as he saw. Besides, there was no time. The moment for starting was at hand. Already the gates of the east glowed purple, and Dawn had opened her courts full of rosy light. The stars were leaving

---

4. **car:** chariot.
5. **precipitous** [pri sip′ə təs]: steep.
6. **suffer:** allow.

7. **Bull . . . Crab:** constellations, or groups, of stars forming the animal figures of the zodiac.
8. **prospect:** mental view.
9. **dissuade** [di swād′] **him:** change his mind.

Phaethon   451

AT A GLANCE

- Phaethon, a mortal, asks to drive the immortal Sun's chariot.
- The Sun regrets his promise and tries to dissuade Phaethon by describing the dangers he faces, but the boy is extremely proud and will not be swayed.

1 PLOT: FORESHADOWING

The phrase *fatal oath* suggests that Phaethon's request will lead to tragedy.

2 ALLUSION

This vision of sunrise is the basis of many subsequent literary references. For example, Shakespeare's *Cymbeline* contains this reference to the Sun's chariot: "Hark! hark! the lark at heaven's gate sings, / And Phoebus 'gins arise, / His steeds to water at those springs. . . ." (II, iii, 22–24)

3 CHARACTERIZATION

The pride Phaethon feels at the vision of himself as a god deafens him to his father's words. This pride, the Greek *hubris*, was nearly always fatal.

GUIDED READING

LITERAL QUESTIONS

1a. What does Phaethon demand of the Sun? (He asks to drive the chariot.)

2a. What does the Sun say to dissuade him? (The Sun says that no mortal and, in fact, no other god can manage the horses on the treacherous road.)

INFERENTIAL QUESTIONS

1b. What is foolish about Phaethon's request? What might be admirable about it? (Phaethon is foolish to try to be something he is not, but he is admirable for his daring.)

2b. Who do you think will prove to be right, Phaethon or his father? Why? (Students may point out that the Sun's arguments are so forceful that no mortal, no matter how brave, can succeed in driving his chariot.)

AT A GLANCE

- Phaethon mounts the chariot and drives off.
- He is unable to control the horses.
- The horses set the world on fire, and Earth cries to Zeus to save her.
- Zeus strikes down Phaethon with a thunderbolt; his sisters mourn Phaethon.

1 STYLE: IMAGERY

Vivid sensory description of the ride sharpens our awareness of Phaethon's exhilaration.

2 BACKGROUND

In ancient times the Greeks believed in a flat, circular Earth with high mountains brushing the sky. The central, tallest mountain was Olympus, home of the gods.

3 THEME

This epitaph summarizes Phaethon's character and his flawed sense of greatness.

REFLECTING ON THE STORY

Does Phaethon's punishment fit his crime? (Possible answers: yes, he set himself up as a god, and the only fit punishment is death; no, he learned his lesson, and the Sun should have saved him.)

---

the sky; even the lingering morning star was dim.

There was need for haste, but all was ready. The Seasons, the gatekeepers of Olympus, stood waiting to fling the doors wide. The horses had been bridled and yoked to the car. Proudly and joyously Phaethon mounted it and they were off. He had made his choice. Whatever came of it he could not change now. Not that he wanted to in that first exhilarating rush through the air, so swift that the East Wind was outstripped and left far behind. The horses' flying feet went through the low-banked clouds near the ocean as through a thin sea mist and then up and up in the clear air, climbing the height of heaven. For a few ecstatic moments Phaethon felt himself the lord of the sky. But suddenly there was a change. The chariot was swinging wildly to and fro; the pace was faster; he had lost control. Not he, but the horses were directing the course. That light weight in the car, those feeble hands clutching the reins, had told them their own driver was not there. They were the masters then. No one else could command them. They left the road and rushed where they chose, up, down, to the right, to the left. They nearly wrecked the chariot against the Scorpion; they brought up short and almost ran into the Crab. By this time the poor charioteer was half fainting with terror, and he let the reins fall.

That was the signal for still more mad and reckless running. The horses soared up to the very top of the sky and then, plunging headlong down, they set the world on fire. The highest mountains were the first to burn, Ida and Helicon, where the Muses dwell, Parnassus, and heaven-piercing Olympus. Down their slopes the flame ran to the low-lying valleys and the dark forest lands, until all things everywhere were ablaze. The springs turned

into steam; the rivers shrank. It is said that it was then the Nile fled and hid his head, which still is hidden.

In the car Phaethon, hardly keeping his place there, was wrapped in thick smoke and heat as if from a fiery furnace. He wanted nothing except to have this torment and terror ended. He would have welcomed death. Mother Earth, too, could bear no more. She uttered a great cry which reached up to the gods. Looking down from Olympus they saw that they must act quickly if the world was to be saved. Zeus seized his thunderbolt and hurled it at the rash, repentant driver. It struck him dead, shattered the chariot, and made the maddened horses rush down into the sea.

Phaethon all on fire fell from the car through the air to the earth. The mysterious river Eridanus,[10] which no mortal eyes have ever seen, received him and put out the flames and cooled the body. The naiads,[11] in pity for him, so bold and so young to die, buried him and carved upon the tomb:

> Here Phaethon lies who drove the sun god's car.
> Greatly he failed, but he had greatly dared.

His sisters, the Heliades,[12] the daughters of Helios,[13] the Sun, came to his grave to mourn for him. There they were turned into poplar trees, on the bank of the Eridanus,

> Where sorrowing they weep into the stream forever.
> And each tear as it falls shines in the water
> A glistening drop of amber.

---

10. **Eridanus** [i rid'ə nəs]
11. **naiads** [nā'adz]: water nymphs, or spirits.
12. **Heliades** [hē lē'ə dēz]
13. **Helios** [hē'lē os']

GUIDED READING

LITERAL QUESTION

1a. What saves the world from destruction? (Zeus hurls a thunderbolt that kills Phaethon, and the horses drown in the sea.)

INFERENTIAL QUESTION

1b. What events at the end of the story imply that Phaethon is forgiven? (Although he is killed, the river cools him, and the naiads refer to his deed as daring.)

STUDY QUESTIONS

Recalling

1. For what reason does Phaethon go the the palace of the Sun?
2. What request does Phaethon make of the Sun? Why does he make this request?
3. Give three reasons why the Sun's daily journey is difficult.
4. What do the horses do during Phaethon's ride?
5. What does Zeus do to save the world? What happens to Phaethon?

Interpreting

6. Is Phaethon's fearlessness heroic or foolish? Give reasons to support you answer.
7. Explain the words written on Phaethon's tomb. Do the words pity him, scold him, or praise him?
8. What qualities of a hero does Phaethon have? What heroic qualities does he lack?

Extending

9. Under what circumstances should people heed the advice of those with experience?

READING AND LITERARY FOCUS

Allusion

An **allusion** is a reference to a person, place, or event from literature. Writers who use allusions expect their audiences to recognize the original source of the reference. For example, a writer would expect readers to apply their knowledge of Greek mythology as they read this sentence: "Margo, like Phaethon, would not listen to her father's warnings." Readers who know of Phaethon can assume that Margo sees the excitement but not the danger in what she wants to do.

Thinking About Allusions

■ Tell what mythical event the italicized words refer to in the following sentences. You may want to check the words in a dictionary.

1. I feel like *Theseus* trying to find my way in these corridors.
2. She certainly has *the Midas touch.*
3. His brand new car was *as bright as Phaethon's chariot.*

VOCABULARY

Shades of Meaning

Writers often use several closely related words to describe something. For example, the words *red, rosy, scarlet,* and *crimson* may all refer to the same flower. Writers do this to suggest shades of meaning. **Shades of meaning** are the slightly different meanings of words used to convey the same basic idea.

In the story of Phaethon, the palace of the Sun is described as a place filled with light. The words used to describe the palace's special quality of light are *radiant, shone, sparkled, flashed, glowed, glittered, brightness, brilliancy, dazzled, burnished, blinding,* and *blazing.*

■ Using a dictionary or a thesaurus, list as many words as you can to describe darkness.

COMPOSITION

Writing About Details

■ Write about the effectiveness of the description of Phaethon's journey. First quote several details that make you see what is happening, and explain why these details are effective. Then quote several details that make you feel Phaethon's emotions, and explain why these details are effective.

Writing with Details

■ Write a description of a single action, such as a leaf falling or a moth circling a flame. Use many specific details to convey the action precisely. First tell what you see when you watch the action. Then tell what you hear and smell and feel during the action.

Phaethon 453

STUDY QUESTIONS

1. to find out if the Sun is his father
2. to drive his chariot; must have watched the sun riding through the heavens
3. steep road; frightening height of midheaven; precipitous descent to earth; fierce beasts in the sky
4. They leave the road, rush where they choose; nearly wreck the chariot against constellations.
5. ■ hurls thunderbolt at Phaethon, killing him; chariot shatters
   ■ Phaethon falls to earth afire; lands in the river Eridanus; buried by naiads, mourned by his sisters
6. Foolish—the sun had explained that no mortal could drive the chariot and had offered his own father's fears as proof of his paternity.
7. identify him as the one who drove the sun's car and attempted a great deed but failed; praise
8. fearlessness, imagination; wisdom, humility
9. Most will agree that advice should be heeded when the situation is critical or the consequences severe.

READING AND LITERARY FOCUS

1. Theseus' difficulty finding his way through the labyrinth suggests that the corridors are a complex maze.
2. The power given to King Midas to turn everything into gold suggests the ability to acquire wealth with apparent ease.
3. The sun's belongings glitter, suggesting that the car is shiny.

VOCABULARY

Possible answers: dim, dusky, gloomy, murky, dull, unilluminated, shadowy, shady, pitch-black

COMPOSITION: GUIDELINES FOR EVALUATION

WRITING ABOUT DETAILS

Objective

To analyze the use of details

Guidelines for Evaluation

■ suggested length: two to three paragraphs
■ should quote details about journey showing actions, details conveying emotion, show why these details are effective
■ should conclude by identifying the most important detail, explaining its importance

WRITING WITH DETAILS

Objective

To write a description of an action

Guidelines for Evaluation

■ suggested length: one to two paragraphs
■ should describe a single action
■ should use specific details to convey action
■ should tell what is seen during the action
■ should tell what is heard, smelled, and felt during the action

It is common in mythology for a character in one myth to appear in others as well. You may recall Daedalus [ded'əl əs] from the myth of Theseus (page 441). Daedalus was the architect of the labyrinth, where the Minotaur was kept. The following myth tells how Daedalus came to build the labyrinth for King Minos and how he and his son Icarus [ik'ər əs] escaped from Crete.

■ What weakness in Icarus causes his terrible mistake?

Depiction of Icarus.

Retold by
Anne Terry White

Daedalus and Icarus

In the days when King Minos ruled Crete,[1] and his mighty navy ranged the seas, there lived in Athens a man by the name of Daedalus. And his name was known as far and wide as that of Minos. For Daedalus was the greatest architect and sculptor of his time. There was nothing his ingenious mind could not design or his skillful hands execute. And his statues were so real that people said they lived. It seemed that any moment they might move a hand or take a step or open their lips and speak.

His young nephew, Talus, also had clever hands and a creative mind. So his mother placed him with her brother that the boy might learn his marvelous skills. But Talus had a genius of his own and even more imagination. Walking on the shore one day, he picked up the backbone of a fish. Idly he drew the strong, sharp spines forward and back

across a piece of driftwood. They cut deep into the wood. He went home and notched a metal blade all along one edge—and he had a saw. Another time he fixed two iron rods together at the tip. He held one firmly upright against the earth and moved the other slowly around. It made a perfect circle—he had invented the compass.

Talus was a pupil to make any teacher excited and proud. But not Daedalus. Instead of being pleased, he was frightened and sorely jealous.

"Talus will soon surpass me!" he thought.

He could not bear the idea of a rival, and came to hate the boy. And one day, when they stood together on a height, Daedalus pushed Talus off to his death.

He had not planned the deed. It had been a sudden, crazy impulse. The next instant, horrified at what he had done, he rushed down to the boy. But it was too late. Talus was dead, and not all the wonderful skills of

---

1. **Crete:** island southeast of Greece.

454   *Greek Myths and American Folk Tales*

Daedalus could call him back. Clearly, if Daedalus wished to save his own life, he must flee. So he left Athens and wandered miserably from place to place, until at last he left Greece altogether and crossed the sea to Crete.

King Minos was delighted to have the Athenian in his realm. The King had something in mind that called for the genius of Daedalus. Minos possessed a fearful monster, with the head and shoulders of a bull and the legs and trunk of a man. The creature was called the Minotaur—that is, the Bull of Minos. The King wanted a suitable place to keep the Minotaur. The building must be such that neither the monster himself nor any victim sent in to be devoured by him could possibly escape from it.

So, at the King's command, Daedalus designed the labyrinth. The building was a bewildering maze of passages. They turned back upon themselves, crisscrossed, and went round and round without leading anywhere. Once inside the labyrinth, it was all but impossible to find the way out again. Even Daedalus himself was once nearly lost.

King Minos was delighted with Daedalus' work and held him in highest favor. Yet Daedalus was less than pleased, for he felt himself to be no better than a prisoner in Crete. The King was so afraid Daedalus would reveal the secret of the labyrinth that he would not let him leave the island. And for that very reason Daedalus yearned to go. With what envy he watched the birds winging their way through the sky!

One day, as his eyes followed the graceful sea birds cleaving² the ocean of air, an idea came to him.

"King Minos may shut my way out by land

---

2. **cleaving:** dividing and moving through.

---

and by sea," he thought, "but he does not control the air."

And he began to study the flight of birds and to observe how their wings are fashioned. He watched the little song birds fold and unfold their wings, watched how they rose from the ground, flew down from the trees, and went to and fro. He also watched the herons slowly flapping their great wings. He watched the eagles soar and swoop. He saw, too, how their feathers overlapped one another—where they were large and where they were small.

When he thought he understood the secrets of flight, Daedalus went to a nesting place he knew of and gathered feathers of various sizes. And in a chamber close to the roof he began to build wings. First he laid down a row of the tiniest feathers, then a row of larger ones overlapping them, and yet larger ones beyond these. He fastened the feathers together in the middle with thread and at the bottom with wax. And when he had built on enough rows, he bent them around into a gentle curve to look like real birds' wings.

His young son Icarus stood by and watched his father work. Laughing, the boy caught the feathers when they blew away in the wind. He pressed his thumb into the yellow wax to soften it for his father, hindering more than he helped.

When Daedalus had finished the pair of wings, he put them on. He raised himself in the air and hovered there. He moved the wings just as he had seen birds do, and lo! he could fly. Icarus clapped his hands together in delight.

"Make me a pair of wings, too, father!" he cried.

Then Daedalus made a second pair of wings and prepared his son to fly.

"Now I warn you, Icarus," Daedalus said, "not to be reckless. Be wise, not bold. Take a

Daedalus and Icarus 455

AT A GLANCE

- Daedalus leaves in disgrace and wanders until he comes to Crete.
- He builds the Minotaur's labyrinth for Minos and is imprisoned lest he give away its secret.
- While watching the birds fly, Daedalus thinks of a plan to escape.
- Under the eyes of his son, Icarus, he fashions wings of feathers and wax.

1 SETTING

The island of Crete marks the southern part of the Aegean Sea, some two hundred miles from Athens. Its distance and relative isolation help explain Daedalus' desire to leave.

2 RESPONSE JOURNAL

Have students compare the portrayal of Minos, the Minotaur, and the labyrinth in this selection to Hawthorne's description of them in "Theseus."

3 CHARACTERIZATION

Daedalus is an acute observer of the natural world and can put these observations to ingenious use. As his foolish indulgence of Icarus shows later, Daedalus is not so acute in his observation of and response to human behavior.

4 FORESHADOWING

Icarus is presented as a happy-go-lucky, somewhat careless child. These qualities, combined with Daedalus' poor judgment, will lead to tragedy for both.

GUIDED READING

LITERAL QUESTIONS

1a. What plan for leaving Crete does Daedalus devise? What does Icarus do as Daedalus works? (Daedalus plans to construct a pair of wings and fly away. Icarus plays and hinders his work.)

2a. What request does Icarus make to his father? What is Daedalus' response? (Icarus asks for his own pair of wings, and Daedalus consents.)

INFERENTIAL QUESTIONS

1b. How does Icarus' behavior contrast with that of his father? (Daedalus is serious and purposeful; Icarus is frivolous and playful.)

2b. Do you think Daedalus shows good judgment? Why or why not? (No; Icarus is too young and irresponsible to understand the dangers of flight.)

1 FORESHADOWING

Daedalus' warning to Icarus presents the potential disasters that may befall him.

2 STYLE: SIMILE

In his concern for his son, Daedalus is compared to a mother bird, and Icarus to a fledgling testing his wings. This simile adds a tender, parental element to our picture of Daedalus. It prepares us for his later grief.

The flight of Daedalus and Icarus, as depicted on woodcut, 1493.

1 course midway between heaven and earth. For if you fly too high, the sun will scorch your feathers. And if you fly too low, the sea will wet them. Take me for your guide. Follow me and you will be safe."

All the time he was speaking, Daedalus was fastening the wings to his son's shoulders. His hands trembled as he thought of the great adventure before them. At the same time, he was worried about the boy. He did not know whether he could quite trust Icarus

to obey. As he adjusted his own wings and kissed the excited child, tears ran down Daedalus' face.

"Remember," he repeated for the last time. "Heed my words and stay close to me!"

Then he rose on his wings and flew from the housetop. Icarus followed.

2 Daedalus kept a watchful eye on the boy, even as a mother bird does when she has brought a fledgling out of its nest in the treetops and launched it in the air. It was early

456 *Greek Myths and American Folk Tales*

GUIDED READING

LITERAL QUESTION

1a. Why is Daedalus worried about Icarus? (He does not trust him to obey.)

INFERENTIAL QUESTION

1b. What can we surmise about Daedalus' feelings for Icarus from the fact that tears run down his cheek as he prepares his son for flight? (that Daedalus loves his son deeply)

morning. Few people were about. But here and there a plowman in the field or a fisherman tending his nets caught sight of them.

"They must be gods!" the simple toilers[3] cried, and they bent their bodies in reverent worship.

Father and son flew far out over the sea. Daedalus was no longer worried about Icarus, who managed his wings as easily as a bird. Already the islands of Delos and Paros were behind them. Calymne,[4] rich in honey, was on their right hand. But now Icarus began to yield to the full delight of his new-found powers. He wanted to soar and swoop. How thrilling it was to rise to a height, close his wings, and speed down, down, like a thunderbolt, then turn and rise again!

Time after time Icarus tried it, each time daring greater heights. Then, forgetting his father's warning, he soared higher still, far up into the cloudless sky.

"Not even the eagle soars as high as this!" the boy thought. "I am like the gods that keep the wide heaven."

As the words crossed his mind, he felt a warm stream flow over his shoulders. He had come too close to the blazing sun, and the sweet-smelling wax that bound the feathers was melting. With a shock of terror he felt

---

3. **toilers:** workers.
4. **Calymne** [kal′əm nē]

himself hurtling downward. His wings, broken in a thousand parts, were hurtling downward, too. In vain Icarus moved his arms up and down—he could get no hold on the air.

"Father!" he shrieked. "Father! Help! I am falling."

Even as he cried, the deep blue water of the sea—that ever since has been called Icarian[5]—closed over him.

"Icarus! Icarus! Where are you?" Daedalus cried, turning in every direction and searching the air behind, above, and all around. Then his eyes fell on the sea. Tufts of feathers were floating on the crest of the waves.

Too well he understood their meaning. Folding his great wings, he came to earth on the nearest island and fixed his streaming eyes upon the sea. He beat his breast. Wildly he clutched his hair.

"O Icarus, my son!" he wailed. "Even so fell Talus whom my envy slew![6] The gods have avenged him." He ripped off his glorious wings and stamped upon them. "Cursed be the skill that wrought my son's destruction!" he cried.

Days afterwards, the body of Icarus washed to the shore. There, on the lonely island which bears the boy's name, Daedalus buried his only son.

---

5. **Icarian** [i ker′ē ən]: ancient name of the Aegean Sea.
6. **slew** [slōō]: killed; past tense of *slay*.

STUDY QUESTIONS

Recalling

1. According to the first paragraph, for what is Daedalus famous?
2. Why is Daedalus jealous of Talus?
3. What does Daedalus make to help him escape?
4. What does Icarus want when he sees his father's invention?
5. What warning does Daedalus give Icarus?
6. What happens to Icarus?

Daedalus and Icarus 457

Interpreting

7. Describe the character of Daedalus in your own words. What do you think is his greatest mistake?

8. Describe the character of Icarus in your own words. Tell what his last words reveal about his character: "I am like the gods that keep the wide heavens."

9. Who do you think is most to blame for Icarus' death—Daedalus, Icarus, or the gods? Support your opinion with evidence from the myth.

Extending

10. "Be wise, not bold. Take a course midway between heaven and earth." To what situations other than flying may these words apply?

READING AND LITERARY FOCUS

Foreshadowing

Foreshadowing is the use of clues by an author to prepare readers for events that will happen later in the story. For example, in "Phaethon" after the boy asks to drive the chariot, we are immediately told that the Sun regrets his "fatal oath." This detail foreshadows the boy's eventual tragedy. It also increases our curiosity by building suspense.

Thinking About Foreshadowing

■ What words and thoughts of Daedalus alert readers to the likelihood of danger for Icarus?

VOCABULARY

Context Clues

You can often discover a word's general meaning from its **context**, or the words and sentences that surround it. For example, in the following passage from "Daedalus and Icarus," the context gives clues to the meaning of the word *ingenious:*

For Daedalus was the greatest architect and sculptor of his time. There was nothing his *ingenious* mind could not design or his skillful hands execute.

The passage connects *ingenious* with *greatest architect, design,* and *skillful.* Based on these context clues, you would be correct in thinking that *ingenious* means "very clever" or "inventive."

The following passages come from "Daedalus and Icarus." Choose the best meaning for each italicized word by studying its context. That is, examine the ideas found in the sentence in which the word appears or in surrounding sentences. Write the number of each item and the letter of your choice on a separate sheet.

1. He had not planned the deed. It had been a sudden, crazy *impulse.*
   (a) urge   (c) design
   (b) intention   (d) heartbeat

2. He also watched the *herons* slowly flapping their great wings.
   (a) airplanes   (c) birds
   (b) buildings   (d) heroes

3. There was nothing his ingenious mind could not design or his skillful hands *execute.*
   (a) remember   (c) worry
   (b) produce   (d) exercise

4. Daedalus kept a watchful eye on the boy, even as a mother bird does when she has brought a *fledgling* out of its nest in the treetops and launched it in the air.
   (a) flower   (c) feather
   (b) young boy   (d) young bird

CHALLENGE

Research

■ Scientists today use labyrinths, or mazes, to study how animals learn. Some famous garden designs have mazes of shrubs to amuse visitors. Use your library to find examples of mazes. Copy a maze you find puzzling, and see if you and your class can solve it.

458   *Greek Myths and American Folk Tales*

Orpheus [ôr′fē əs] was a very different kind of hero. He was not a warrior who led armies or a king who slew fierce monsters. According to the myth, the power of Orpheus was in his music and poetry, the most beautiful sounds ever made by a mortal. His love for Eurydice [yoo rid′ə sē] brought about the greatest test of his marvelous musical power.

■ What tragic mistake does Orpheus make?

Relief sculpture of Orpheus and Eurydice.

*Retold by
Padraic Colum*

Orpheus and Eurydice

Many were the minstrels who, in the early days of the world, went amongst men, telling them stories of the gods, of their wars and their births, and of the beginning of things. Of all these minstrels none was so famous as Orpheus; none could tell truer things about the gods; he himself was half divine, and there were some who said that he was in truth Apollo's son.

But a great grief came to Orpheus, a grief that stopped his singing and his playing upon the lyre.[1] His young wife, Eurydice, was taken from him. One day, walking in the garden, she was bitten on the heel by a serpent; straightway[2] she went down to the World of the Dead.

Then everything in this world was dark and bitter for the minstrel of the gods; sleep would not come to him, and for him food had no taste. Then Orpheus said, "I will do that which no mortal has ever done before; I will do that which even the Immortals might shrink from doing; I will go down into the World of the Dead, and I will bring back to the living and to the light my bride, Eurydice."

Then Orpheus went on his way to the cavern which goes down, down to the World of the Dead—the Cavern Tainaron.[3] The trees showed him the way. As he went on, Orpheus played upon his lyre and sang; the three heard his song and were moved by his grief, and with their arms and their heads they showed him the way to the deep, deep cavern named Tainaron.

Down, down, down by a winding path Orpheus went. He came at last to the great gate

---

1. **lyre** [līr]: stringed musical instrument that looks like a miniature harp.
2. **straightway:** immediately.

3. **Tainaron** [tī′när ọn]

Orpheus and Eurydice 459

AT A GLANCE

- Orpheus, the minstrel of the gods, is grief-stricken at the death of his bride, Eurydice.
- He descends into the World of the Dead in search of her, playing his lyre to lure the guards into showing him the way.

LITERARY OPTIONS

- character motivation
- theme

THEMATIC OPTIONS

- the power of art
- the power of love

1 BACKGROUND

Phoebus Apollo, the Sun, is also the god of music. Orpheus' almost godlike skill enables him to bargain with the gods.

2 THEME

Art, especially when inspired by love, becomes a powerful force in this myth.

**TEXAS ESSENTIAL ELEMENTS
GRADE 8**

1A writing process
1C support for main idea
1D evaluation of content and organization
1K dictionary skills
3A character development
3C setting and mood
3D literary genres
4B implied main idea
4E cause/effect
4G prediction of outcomes
To locate treatment of an Element, see *Texas Teacher's Resources*.

GUIDED READING

LITERAL QUESTION

1a. What causes Orpheus' grief? (His young wife is killed by a serpent.)

INFERENTIAL QUESTION

1b. How does his grief aid him in reaching the World of the Dead? (His sad music is so touching that it moves the trees to guide him to the cavern.)

- Hades and Persephone, Rulers of the Dead, are moved by Orpheus' sad song.
- Orpheus is allowed to return with Eurydice as long as neither one of them looks back.
- Orpheus and Eurydice climb up toward the World of the Living.

1 CHARACTER MOTIVATION

Orpheus has made his journey with one purpose in mind. His musical skill translates this single-mindedness into beautiful song that, in turn, motivates others to help him.

2 BACKGROUND

When Hades stole Persephone, her mother, goddess of agriculture, sought her the world over. The Earth lay barren until Demeter found Persephone and persuaded Hades to allow Persephone to return to her for six months each year.

3 VOCABULARY: ETYMOLOGY

From Tantalus comes our word *tantalize*, meaning "torment by presenting something desirable but keeping it always out of reach."

4 SETTING

The World of the Dead is known for its never-ending punishments. This fact alone demonstrates the extraordinariness of the offer Hades is about to make.

that opens upon the World of the Dead. And the silent guards who keep watch there for the Rulers of the Dead were astonished when they saw a living being coming towards them, and they would not let Orpheus approach the gate.

The minstrel took the lyre in his hands and played upon it. As he played, the silent watchers gathered around him, leaving the gate unguarded. And as he played, the Rulers of the Dead came forth, Hades and Persephone, and listened to the words of the living man.

1 "The cause of my coming through the dark and fearful ways," sang Orpheus, "is to strive to gain a fairer fate for Eurydice, my bride. All that is above must come down to you at last, O Rulers of the most lasting World. But before her time has Eurydice been brought here. I have desired strength to endure her loss, but I cannot endure it. And I have come before you, Hades and Persephone, brought here by love."

When Orpheus said the name of love, Persephone, the queen of the dead, bowed her young head, and bearded Hades, the king, **2** bowed his head also. Persephone remembered how Demeter, her mother, had sought her all through the world, and she remembered the touch of her mother's tears upon her face. And Hades remembered how his love for Persephone had led him to carry her away from the valley where she had been gathering flowers. He and Persephone stood aside, and Orpheus went through the gate and came amongst the dead.

Still upon his lyre he played. Tantalus—who for his crime had been condemned to stand up to his neck in water and yet never **3** be able to assuage his thirst—Tantalus heard, and for a while did not strive to put his lips towards the water that ever flowed away from him; Sisyphus—who had been condemned to

460 *Greek Myths and American Folk Tales*

roll up a hill a stone that ever rolled back— **4** Sisyphus heard the music that Orpheus played, and for a while he sat still upon his stone. Ixion, bound to a wheel, stopped its turning for a while; the vultures abandoned their torment of Tityus; the daughters of Danaus ceased to fill their jars; even those dread ones, the Furies, who bring to the dead the memories of all their crimes and all their faults, had their cheeks wet with tears.

In the throng of the newly-come dead Orpheus saw Eurydice. She looked upon her husband, but she had not the power to come near him. But slowly she came when Hades, the king, called her. Then with joy Orpheus took her hands.

It would be granted them—no mortal ever gained such privilege before—to leave, both together, the World of the Dead, and to abide for another space in the World of the Living. One condition there would be—that on their way up neither Orpheus nor Eurydice should look back.

They went through the gate and came out amongst the watchers that are around the portals. These showed them the path that went up to the World of the Living. That way they went, Orpheus and Eurydice, he going before her.

Up and through the darkened ways they went, Orpheus knowing that Eurydice was behind him, but never looking back upon her. As he went his heart was filled with things to tell her—how the trees were blossoming in the garden she had left; how the water was sparkling in the fountain; how the doors of the house stood open; how they, sitting together, would watch the sunlight on the laurel bushes. All these things were in his heart to tell her who came behind him, silent and unseen.

And now they were nearing the place where

GUIDED READING

LITERAL QUESTIONS

1a. What do Hades and Persephone think of when Orpheus sings his plea? (They recall their own experience of love, and Persephone remembers her grieving mother.)

2a. What condition is set for the lovers' departure? (They must not look back.)

INFERENTIAL QUESTIONS

1b. Why do you think Hades allows Orpheus to take Eurydice away? (Probably the power of Orpheus' lovestruck song so moves Hades that he consents.)

2b. Why might this condition be difficult to meet? (Orpheus loves Eurydice so much that he may want to look back at her; also, the way is steep, and he may fear her falling behind.)

the cavern opened on the world of the living. Orpheus looked up towards the light from the sky. Out of the opening of the cavern he went; he saw a white-winged bird fly by. He turned around and cried, "O Eurydice, look upon the world I have won you back to!"

He turned to say this to her. He saw her with her long dark hair and pale face. He held out his arms to clasp her. But in that instant she slipped back into the gloom of the cavern. And all he heard spoken was a single word, "Farewell!" Long, long had it taken Eurydice to climb so far, but in the moment of his turning around she had fallen back to her place amongst the dead. For Orpheus had looked back.

Back through the cavern Orpheus went again. Again he came before the watchers of the gate. But now he was not looked at nor listened to; hopeless, he had to return to the World of the Living.

The birds were his friends now, and the trees and the stones. The birds flew around him and mourned with him; the trees and stones often followed him, moved by the music of his lyre. But a savage band slew Orpheus and threw his severed head and his lyre into the River Hebrus.[4] It is said by the poets that while they floated in midstream the lyre gave out some mournful notes, and the head of Orpheus answered the notes with song.

And now that he was no longer to be counted with the living, Orpheus went down to the World of the Dead, going down straightway. The silent watchers let him pass; he went amongst the dead, and he saw his Eurydice in the throng. Again they were together, Orpheus and Eurydice, and them the Furies could not torment with memories of crimes and faults.

---

4. **Hebrus** [hē′brəs]

Orpheus and Eurydice 461

Orpheus and Eurydice, Anselm Feuerbach (1829–1880).

AT A GLANCE

- As Orpheus reaches the World of the Living, he is moved by its beauty and turns back to Eurydice.
- Eurydice slips back into the World of the Dead.
- Orpheus mourns in isolation; eventually he is slain and joins Eurydice in the World of the Dead.

1 CHARACTER MOTIVATION

Just as his love of his wife inspired music that nearly rescued Eurydice, so this same love makes Orpheus disobey Hades and lose Eurydice again.

2 THEME

Orpheus' art is powerful but not powerful enough to overrule Hades. Only his own death can reunite the lovers now.

REFLECTING ON THE STORY

Some myths were meant to instruct or explain the laws of nature. What might this tale tell people about death? (It might tell them that death cannot be overruled; it might console them by implying that they can be reunited with their loved ones in death.)

GUIDED READING

LITERAL QUESTION

1a. How does Orpheus finally die? (He is killed by a savage band.)

INFERENTIAL QUESTION

1b. How can you tell that his return to the World of the Dead, despite its violent cause, is a happy occasion? (Orpheus was no longer happy in the World of the Living; now he is reunited with Eurydice, and "them the Fates could not torment with memories of crimes and faults.")

1. ■ famous minstrel, told true stories of gods, their wars, births, the beginning of things
   ■ half divine, said to be Apollo's son
2. A serpent bit her.
3. goes into the World of the Dead; plays lyre, makes Furies cry
4. On their way up, neither Orpheus nor Eurydice may look back.
5. As they near opening to land of living, Orpheus sees a bird, turns to say, "look upon the world I have won you back to"; because he looks back, Eurydice cannot leave the Underworld.
6. He is slain by a savage band, his head and lyre thrown into the Hebrus.
7. ■ courage to go into World of Dead, talent to play so well
   ■ pride in pointing out the world he had brought Eurydice back to
8. Those who believe Orpheus a hero should cite his courage and musical skill. Those who do not find him heroic should point out that he causes his mission to fail.
9. Answers will vary. An artist can inspire others to think, feel, and act. A heroic leader has a direct, tangible effect on people and history that the artist does not.

Possible answers: great love for Eurydice; pride in rescuing her; joy in having her back, relief in success of mission

STUDY QUESTIONS

Recalling

1. According to the first paragraph, why was Orpheus famous? What might have accounted for his great talent?
2. How does Eurydice die?
3. Where does Orpheus go to win Eurydice's release? What does he do there?
4. What does Hades make Orpheus promise in return for Eurydice?
5. What prevents Eurydice's leaving the underworld with Orpheus?
6. How does Orpheus die?

Interpreting

7. What personal qualities enabled Orpheus to almost succeed in his task? What quality caused him to fail?
8. Do you think Orpheus ranks as a hero? Support you opinion with reasons.

Extending

9. Do you think the power of an artist can be as great as the power of a heroic leader? Why or why not?

READING AND LITERARY FOCUS

Character Motivation

Motivation is the idea, emotion, or goal that causes a character to act. Like real people, characters in a story should have clear motivations for their actions. For example, Orpheus goes down into the underworld because he loves Eurydice very much. When motivation in a story is effective, the reader feels that the characters are genuine.

Sometimes a character's motivation is clearly stated, like the love of Orpheus for his wife. Sometimes, however, a character's motivation is suggested by his or her words or actions. For example, when Hades warns Orpheus not to look back, we are not given a reason for the god's behavior. We can guess, however, that he intends to test Orpheus' strength of will.

Thinking About Character Motivation

■ What motivates Orpheus to look back?

COMPOSITION

Answering an Essay Question

■ Answer the following essay question: "Why is Orpheus unable to release Eurydice from the underworld a *second* time?" First rephrase the question as the first sentence of your answer. Then support your opinion with details from the selection. Finally, describe what this myth says about the relationship of the gods to mortals. *For help with this assigment, see Lesson 1 in the Writing About Literature Handbook at the back of this book.*

Writing a Description of Sounds

■ Write a description of the music of Orpheus, music so beautiful that it moved rocks and trees. First tell what such music would sound like. Then tell how it would be similar to and different from today's music. Finally, tell how today's listener would react to it.

COMPOSITION: GUIDELINES FOR EVALUATION

ANSWERING AN ESSAY QUESTION
Objective
To compose an answer for an essay question

Guidelines for Evaluation
■ suggested length: one paragraph
■ should begin by rephrasing the question
■ should cite details from the selection that support the writer's opinion
■ should conclude by describing the myth's view of the relationship between gods and mortals

WRITING A DESCRIPTION OF SOUNDS
Objective
To write a description of music

Guidelines for Evaluation
■ suggested length: one to two paragraphs
■ should tell what Orpheus' music would sound like
■ should compare and contrast this music's sound with today's music
■ should tell how today's listener would react

The story of Alcestis [al ses′tis] and her husband Admetus [ad mēt′əs] is admired today as in ancient times for the lessons it teaches about selfishness, love, and loyalty.

■ Who do you think is the real hero of this myth?

Statue of Apollo, god of the sun.

*Retold by
Olivia Coolidge*

Alcestis

1   Admetus, king of Pherae[1] in Thessaly,[2] was thought by many to be among the luckiest of men. He was young, strong, and handsome, the only son of a father who had given up the kingdom to him as soon as he came of age. Admetus was an affectionate son, and the old people felt proud and pleased that, though they had given him all their power, he still paid them every attention which could make their old age a happy one. Nor was this all. The wealth of the king lay largely in his immense flocks and herds, for which he had the good fortune to obtain a marvelous herdsman.

Apollo himself had been condemned to spend a year on earth in the form of a servant as a punishment for an offense he had committed in anger against Zeus. He came in this way to to Admetus, and since the young king was a just master, the year was a good one for them both. Admetus saw much of his chief herdsman and came to respect him, while Apollo mightily increased the flocks of the **2** king in return for his upright dealing. When the year came to an end, Admetus learned that not only was he a much richer man than before, but he had also acquired a powerful friend and protector. One of the first uses he made of Apollo's friendship was to gain himself a wife whom any prince in Greece would have been proud to marry.

Pelias,[3] ruler of another Thessalian kingdom which he had seized by force from his cousin, had several daughters, but Alcestis was by far the loveliest. Not only was she beautiful, but she was skilled in all the arts of women. She was a notable spinner and maker of cloth, a good housewife, and performed everything with a charm which really came from a gentle, affectionate, and honorable nature. Even her dark and sinister father was fond of her and by no means anxious to let her marry and go to live in some other land.

---

1. **Pherae** [fē′rē]
2. **Thessaly** [thes′ə lē]: region in northern Greece.

3. **Pelias** [pē′lē əs]

Alcestis   463

GUIDED READING

LITERAL QUESTION

1a. How does Apollo help Admetus? (He increases his flocks and makes him wealthy.)

INFERENTIAL QUESTION

1b. How does Admetus' own character help lead to his good fortune? (His just and upright behavior impresses Apollo.)

- Apollo helps Admetus win Alcestis. They live happily.
- Apollo tells Admetus that the Fates have called for his death, unless someone else agrees to take his place.
- Admetus cannot bear the thought of death and hopes that someone will take his place.

1 FORESHADOWING

The words *nothing seemed to be lacking* and *did not know what misfortune meant* suggests a happiness too great to last. These words hint that Admetus' fortune will change.

2 THEME

Happiness cannot last forever, even for those who seem blessed by the gods. Apollo explicitly states the lesson taught by this myth: Everyone will experience both good and bad fortune.

3 THEME

Apollo's offer encourages Admetus to believe that he can bargain with Fate. It does not occur to him that it would be unfair to expect someone else to take on his burden.

4 CONFLICT

Admetus is a beloved king, but his people's desire to live conflicts with their loyalty, just as Admetus' desire to live conflicts with his pride, and, more important, with his prescribed fate.

Nevertheless from the first moment she was old enough Pelias had been bothered by suitors for Alcestis. Every young man who saw her and a great many who only heard of her asked her father for her hand. At last Pelias became weary of the business and let it be known that he would marry his daughter only to the prince who could come to ask for her in a chariot drawn by a wild boar and a lion. Of course, no man could do this without help from the gods, so Pelias thought it most likely that he would be able to keep his daughter. But when Admetus accomplished the feat with Apollo's aid, Pelias at least could be satisfied that she was marrying a prosperous king who had the help of a powerful protector. He made the best of it, therefore, and the wedding was held with much rejoicing.

For several years after this Admetus was even happier than before. His parents thoroughly approved of his bride, who treated them with loving respect. Alcestis was a gentle, dignified queen, a beloved mistress of the household, and an affectionate mother. Towards her husband, even though she had not chosen him herself, she showed all the love **1** he could desire. Nothing seemed to be lacking. Admetus' face was radiant as he moved among his people; everything he did, he enjoyed. Men would mention him in conversation as an example of one who did not know what misfortune meant.

Meanwhile Apollo had not forgotten his friend, and loved to appear in human form from time to time and talk with him. But at last one day he came with a very grave face. "Admetus, my friend," he said seriously, "the Fates[4] will spin out lasting happiness for no **2** man. Each must have fortune and misfortune too, and so it is with you. It is decreed that in this very year your luck shall change. Within twelve months it is your fate to die."

The "fortunate" king went pale as ashes. His legs failed beneath him so that he sat down heavily, his hands limp at his sides. Then in a moment he leapt up and began to beg and implore Apollo. "You are powerful," he said desperately. "Save me from this. I am young. I am strong, no man enjoys life as I do. Why should I die? Life is full and rich for me; I enjoy every moment. Why, they say I even smile in sleep, and my dreams are glad ones. People point at me in the streets, 'There goes a happy man,' they say. And it is true. Why should I die when so many live who are weary of life, who are old, poor, sick, or lonely? Why should I die?"

3 "It is not possible to alter Fate," said Apollo gravely, "that is, not entirely. What I could do I have done. Someone, at least, must die, but I have won for you the promise that if another will die instead of you when the time comes, you may live." And with that hope the king was forced to be content.

From that time on nobody pointed to Admetus in the streets and called him the fortunate king. Indeed he made no secret of his misfortune, hoping always that someone who was tired of life would offer to change with him. But time went forward, and no one came. Other people who had envied his luck did not see why a less happy man should take on his load now that it was his turn to suffer. **4** The year went on, and in all his kingdom no one offered the service that Admetus was too proud to ask. He found himself wandering past mean hovels,[5] casting imploring glances at poor or crippled people. He fancied they

---

4. **Fates:** the three daughters of Necessity, who controlled human destiny: One Fate spun the thread of life, the second measured it, the third cut it off.

5. **hovels** [huv′əls]: miserable huts.

GUIDED READING

LITERAL QUESTION

1a. What possibility of escape does Apollo offer Admetus? (Admetus will not die if he can find someone else to take his place.)

INFERENTIAL QUESTION

1b. Do you think Admetus should try to escape his fate? Why or why not? (Some students may say that it is cowardly and unfair of Admetus to hope that someone else will take his place; others may say that anyone will try to avoid death.)

understood what he wanted of them and that they looked at him mockingly. At last he could bear the city no longer and went out to manage his estate as he had been used. But the bleating of the countless lambs and the lowing of the cows in his great milking sheds only drove him to desperation. Finally his courage failed him, and as the long year came to an end, he went to see his father.

1 His father was outraged at the proposition Admetus put before him. "How dare you suggest such a thing?" he shouted. "I have ten more good years of life and it is my own. I earned it and I shall enjoy it. Nobody ever called me the fortunate king. I toiled hard all my life for what I had. And now you, who have had everything given you and made no effort, want my last years of peace and happiness as well. What do you think a father is for, my son? Do you expect him always to give what you need? Oh no, I have given already and far too much. A father should receive—receive respect and affection and obedience from his children as the gods have ordained it. And this is all you offer: respect when it takes no trouble, affection when it is the easiest way. Get out of my sight."

2 "Selfish old man," answered Admetus, beside himself with fury at the direct refusal. "Now I know how much your own son is worth to you, not even a few miserable, toothless years of life."

"Get out of my sight," yelled the old man.

"I will," shouted Admetus, "and gladly, for you are no true parent of mine. At least I have a mother."

Admetus' mother was no more willing than her husband. "Look after yourself," she said indignantly.[6] "You are not a baby any more. As long as you were one, I watched over you,

fed you, dressed you, and sat up with you. You owe your life to me in any case. I never asked you as a baby to look after me. Now it is your turn."

3 "Now may you be cursed," retorted Admetus in a passion. "May the gods remember you as an unworthy mother, a hard, unfeeling woman. What use was it to give me life and nurse me up for this? A fine gift you gave! May you die unwept and unhonored."

"May Hera, the great queen mother, and Leto[7] hear me," screamed the old woman. "They know what it is to have children. May they . . ." But Admetus turned away without hearing, for he felt that his time was come.

Admetus lay down on his couch and groaned aloud in bitter despair as he hid his face and waited for the coming of death. Meanwhile in her inner chamber the queen Alcestis quietly arose, kissed her two children, and gave them to her attendants. Then she bathed herself and put on fresh, white garments and went to the sacrifice. There she prayed the gods to take her life. Then as faintness came over her, she lay down on a couch and died quietly, while the groaning Admetus felt health surging back again and sat suddenly bolt upright. It was the miracle! His luck had saved him; he was not to die!

Even as he felt sure of this, he heard wails of women from the inner chamber and, rushing in, beheld the body of his wife. Admetus fell on his knees beside the corpse and kissed it, tears running down his cheeks. It had never occurred to him to ask Alcestis. He loved her, and she was so young. Everybody was so fond of her. She had as much to look forward to as he; there was no possible reason why she should die. Then as the greatness of the queen's sacrifice became clear to him, he saw

---

6. **indignantly** [in dig′nənt lē]: with restrained anger.

7. **Leto** [lē′tō]: mother of Apollo and Artemis.

Alcestis 465

GUIDED READING

LITERAL QUESTIONS

1a. How do Admetus' parents react to his suggestion that they die in his place? (They are outraged.)

2a. Who dies for Admetus? (Alcestis)

INFERENTIAL QUESTIONS

1b. What does Admetus' behavior toward them say about his changing character? (He has become selfish and cruel in his desperation.)

2b. In what sense is Alcestis' action heroic? (Alcestis' selflessness and quiet acceptance of the fate her husband has been fleeing is heroic.)

AT A GLANCE

- Admetus recognizes his own selfishness.
- Heracles arrives for a visit, and Admetus attends to him without mentioning his own troubles.

1 PLOT: CLIMAX

Admetus has a revelation about his own selfishness and the pain it has caused others.

2 THEME

Despite his own misery, Admetus refuses to impose any more selfish behavior on those around him. He is regaining his former nobility.

1 for the first time how selfish he had been. Of course, he should shoulder his own misfortunes just like everybody else. What right had he running to his parents? He had had more luck than other people in any case. Why should it not be his turn? Admetus groaned again and would gladly have died if by so doing he could have brought his Alcestis to life, but it was too late.

An attendant touched him timidly on the shoulder. There was a stranger shouting for him in the great hall. It was Heracles,[8] the mighty hero, returned from one of his deeds of strength and bursting to celebrate his achievement. He could not have come at a worse time, but he had to be met, so Admetus roused himself to go out and explain to him that this was a house of mourning. On the way, however, he thought better of it. Why

---

8. **Heracles** [her′ə klēz′]: a mortal son of Zeus, known for his tremendous strength.

should the happiness of Heracles be spoiled? **2** Admetus had brought this sorrow on himself, and it was fitting he should bear it alone. He was utterly tired of his own selfishness. He stopped and gave orders to his servants to prepare a feast. He spoke firmly to them and they went obediently at last, muttering among themselves. Admetus went out to see his guest and made himself smile as he welcomed him.

The great, good-humored Heracles was not a sensitive man, and just now he was in an excited mood. He noticed nothing curious about Admetus or the servants; he was bent only on having a good time. And Admetus gave him a good time with wine, and song, and feasting. There was much laughter and a lot of noise. The disapproving servants, who had loved their mistress far more than they did Admetus, looked as gloomy as they dared. They grouped together in corners muttering, but for a long time Heracles noticed nothing

---

GUIDED READING

LITERAL QUESTION

1a. How does Admetus greet Heracles? (He presents him with a feast and music and laughter.)

INFERENTIAL QUESTION

1b. What change in Admetus does this action suggest? (It suggests that Admetus accepts his fate and is at last able to take sole responsibility for his sorrow. He is regaining the generous spirit that won Apollo's favor.)

at all. When finally the revelry[9] was dying down and the excitement was nearly over, Heracles perceived their disapproval and, not liking it, called loudly for more wine. It was brought to him, but with an air of reluctance which made him strike his fist on the table and demand indignantly why they could not serve him better. Admetus was out of the room, and there was no one to restrain the anger of the servants at what was going on. They told him exactly what was the matter in the plainest terms.

Heracles was appalled[10] at the trouble he had caused, but he was also touched by Admetus. Never, he felt, had he been entertained in so princely a fashion before. It was like a great prince to put aside his grief and celebrate with a guest, even while his beloved wife lay dead within his halls. Heracles questioned the servants as to how long ago the queen had died, for he knew the way to Hades well and **1** he had a plan. He had been down to Hades, and so great was his strength that not all the monsters of that place had availed to keep him there. He had bound the mighty Cerberus[11] and brought him up to earth alive. In fact, there was no feat that Heracles was not equal to, for he was half divine and, though he was a man now, he would be a god in time. It might be possible to pursue Death and wrestle with him for the spirit of Alcestis as they went hand in hand down the steep path to the underworld. He said nothing to Admetus as yet and told the servants to keep silence, but he took up his great club from the corner where he laid it, threw his lionskin over his shoulders, and strode off in the direction of the dreadful path he had trodden once before.

---

9. **revelry** [rev′əl rē]: celebration.
10. **appalled** [ə pôld′]: shocked.
11. **Cerberus** [sur′bər əs]: monstrous three-headed dog of Hades, god of the underworld.

It was early morning when Heracles came back, and with him walked a muffled figure. Admetus, summoned haggard and sleepless from his chamber, came, much tried but still courteous, to answer his guest's unreasonable demands. Heracles put back the cloak, and Alcestis looked at her husband as though she were just waking from sleep. As he ran forward and clasped her, he felt her come to life in his arms.

2 Alcestis and Admetus lived long after that time, happy yet generous to the poor and ailing. Admetus had learned both seriousness and sympathy. Though he was as prosperous as before, he had found that there were qualities more admirable than good luck, and he never cared again to be known by the title of "the fortunate king."

SHELLEY FRESHMAN

GUIDED READING

LITERAL QUESTION

1a. To whom are the reunited Alcestis and Admetus generous? (the poor and ailing)

INFERENTIAL QUESTION

1b. How does this generosity show a change in Admetus' character? (Once he thought that such people should be eager to die in his place; now he sees that everyone has a right to live a good life.)

1. young, strong, handsome, only son of generous father; immense flocks, marvelous herdsman
2. treats him well, respects him
3. goes to Pelius' palace in chariot drawn by boar and lion
4. In twelve months Admetus will die; wins promise that if someone will die in his place, Admetus will be spared.
5. offers her life to the gods
6. does not want Heracles to suffer for Admetus' grief
7. ■ touched by Admetus' hospitality in the face of grief
   ■ pursues Death, wrestles with him for Alcestis; brings her back to Admetus
8. affectionate son, pays parents every attention to please them
9. Sample answer: It is impossible to avoid fate without disaster.
10. *king:* successful, generous, hospitable; *husband:* considerate, good provider; *son:* respectful, caring, grateful; *wife:* gentle, dignified, kind, affectionate, loving
11. It takes great generosity to make sacrifices without regret.

READING AND LITERARY FOCUS

learns to bear sorrows; sympathetic to poor, ailing; has acquired qualities more admirable than good luck

COMPARING MYTHS

1. ■ "Theseus": determined, brave, respectful, prudent
   ■ "Phaethon": bold, daring, reckless, imprudent
   ■ "Orpheus": brave, skillful, not prudent
2. ■ "Daedalus": Mortals are not like gods; gods avenge wrongdoing.
   ■ "Orpheus": Gods require obedience.
   ■ "Alcestis": Those who sacrifice themselves are rewarded.

STUDY QUESTIONS

Recalling

1. According to the first paragraph, why is Admetus thought to be lucky?
2. What does Admetus do to win Apollo's friendship?
3. What does Admetus do to win Alcestis in marriage?
4. What sad news does Apollo bring Admetus? In what way does Apollo try to solve Admetus' problem?
5. What does Alcestis do for her husband that no one else would do?
6. For what reason does Admetus order a feast for Heracles on the very day of Alcestis' death?
7. Why does Heracles decide to help Admetus? What unusual help does Heracles give?

Interpreting

8. What evidence at the beginning of the story suggests that Admetus has not been spoiled by his great wealth?
9. What do you think this myth suggests about the possibility of avoiding fate?
10. According to this myth, what qualities did the Greeks admire in a king? A husband? A son? A wife?

Extending

11. Why do you think people honor and respect someone who is selfless and willing to make sacrifices for others?

READING AND LITERARY FOCUS

Characters that Change

Some characters remain the same throughout a story. Alcestis, for example, is loyal and loving from beginning to end. Other characters, however, change during the course of a story. As in real life, the events cause the character to change attitudes, emotions, and sometimes behavior. For example,

in "Orpheus and Eurydice" Orpheus' mood changes from grief to joy to grief again.

Thinking About Characters that Change

■ How is Admetus' attitude toward his family and his people different by the end of the story? Support your answer with evidence from the story.

COMPOSITION

Writing About Character

■ Write about one of the minor characters in "Alcestis," such as the father, the mother, Heracles, Apollo, or one of the servants. Tell whether the character's actions are consistent and believable and why. End with your own opinion of the character.

Writing a Dialogue

■ Admetus and his parents exchange harsh words in the myth. Write a dialogue in which the parents and son make amends. First tell what Admetus says when he first sees his parents again. Then give his parents' responses. Have each character speak at least twice.

CHALLENGE

Further Reading

■ The Greek myths tell of many other heroes, including Heracles, Perseus, Jason, and Bellerophon. Read another heroic tale in a collection of myths, and summarize it for the class.

COMPARING MYTHS

1. Compare the heroes of two or more of the following myths: "Theseus," "Phaethon," and "Orpheus." Tell how the heroes are like and unlike one another.
2. Compare the lessons that seem to be taught by two or more of the following myths: "Daedalus and Icarus," "Orpheus," and "Alcestis."

COMPOSITION: GUIDELINES FOR EVALUATION

WRITING ABOUT CHARACTER

Objective
To analyze the behavior of a character

Guidelines for Evaluation
■ suggested length: one to two paragraphs
■ should identify a minor character in myth
■ should tell whether the character's actions are consistent and believable and why
■ should end with an opinion of the character

WRITING A DIALOGUE

Objective
To write a dialogue showing change in character

Guidelines for Evaluation
■ suggested length: six or more speeches
■ should tell what Admetus says to his parents
■ should give his parents' responses
■ should show how Admetus has changed
■ should contain at least two pieces of dialogue for each character

AMERICAN FOLK TALES

The American land has always played an important part in the imagination of the American people. Mountains and coasts, plains and valleys, cities and countryside have all provided the settings for exciting American stories. The great variety of the land itself and the experiences of the people who lived on it contributed to the great variety of American folk tales.

Folk tales are anonymous stories passed down by word of mouth generation after generation. Many folk tales originally had some basis in fact and grew out of the lives of real people. With folk tales, *grew* is an important word. As the tales were told over and over, they often grew as fast as Paul Bunyan's pumpkin vine. They took on new aspects and added new characters and episodes. They became more humorous and more unbelievable as one storyteller would try to outdo another.

Folk tales usually reflect the beliefs and goals of the people who invent the tales. For example, folk tales may glorify the greatness of the land or the cleverness and independence of the people. The tales are a source of pride, telling of the heroes who cut paths across the continent, worked the land, built the towns, and gave the country its personality. They reflect the vitality of a great, new people. The characters are often larger than life, achieving what others only dream of achieving. In this way the tales encourage people to do more and work harder.

In the centuries before the television and telephone, even before printed books were common, Americans entertained themselves with tales like the ones on the following pages. The amazing family of Davy Crockett, the feats of Paul Bunyan and Pecos Bill, the mystery of Strong Wind, and the challenge of John Henry have long been part of the American folk tradition. These characters and incidents continue to live not only because they are retold here by modern writers but also because they live in our own imagination.

American Folk Tales 469

AT A GLANCE

- A seemingly ordinary family from the early Tennessee frontier is, in fact, unusual.
- Davy Crockett's mother and father have incredible talents.
- Davy himself can sink posts for piers with his feet and swim without getting wet.

LITERARY OPTIONS

- tall tales
- style

THEMATIC OPTIONS

- Heroic accomplishments
- American experiences

1 TALL TALE

In a serious manner the narrator presents the Crocketts as humble, down-to-earth folks who have extraordinary talents. Incredible events, wit, and a homespun style announce the presence of a tall tale.

2 STYLE: IMAGERY

Vivid and hilarious images such as this one are traditional devices of the tall tale.

3 THEME

Juxtaposed with the ridiculous notion that Davy can pound in posts by jumping on them, the line *and what's more, got his feet wet* makes a person who actually lived larger than life.

TEXAS ESSENTIAL ELEMENTS GRADE 8

3B figurative language
3D literary genres
4B implied main idea
4C fact *vs.* nonfact
To locate treatment of an Element, see *Texas Teacher's Resources.*

Davy Crockett.

Davy Crockett (1786–1836) was an actual Tennessee frontiersman. His own stories and the stories that other people told about him turned his adventures into heroic American folk tales. He became famous for his hunting ability and his sense of humor. He was even said to be able to "grin a raccoon right out of a tree." As the stories about Davy grew, his whole family became part of the legend.

■ What do you think was the most "amazing" thing a Crockett could do?

Retold by
Walter Blair

The Amazing Crockett Family

The Crockett family ate about the way everybody else did. To cut things up, they used hunting knives. For dishes, they used wooden bowls, trenchers[1] and noggins,[2] and such home-made affairs.

All this, you might say, was as common as an old shoe.

But as a matter of fact the Crocketts weren't ordinary people— far from it. They had great talents, and they lived in a great place.

Davy Crockett's father could grin a hailstorm into sunshine, and could look the sun square in the face without sneezing.

Davy Crockett's mother, even when she was an old woman and had lost a good part of her spryness, could do these things:

1. Jump a seven-rail fence backwards;
2. Dance a hole through a double oak floor;
3. Spin more wool than a steam mill; and

4. Cut down a gum tree ten feet around, and sail it across the Nolachucky River,[3] using her apron for a sail. . . .

If people wanted to sink tree posts into the bed of the Nolachucky River or the brown Mississippi for bridge piers, all they had to do was lower them down into the mud and then ask Davy to jump on them. He'd step from post to post all the way across the river, making the tallest posts pop down quick as half a wink. He'd have to swim back, of course, because if he stepped on the posts twice, he sank them clear out of sight, and what's more, got his feet wet.

Swimming back was easy enough for Davy, though, because even at this age he was a ripsnorter[4] of a swimmer. He could swim faster, dive deeper, and come up dryer than half the men in all creation. . . .

---

1. **trenchers:** wooden boards on which meat was carved and served.
2. **noggins:** small mugs.

3. **Nolachucky** [nō′lə chu′kē] **River:** river in northeastern Tennessee; also spelled *Nolichuckey.*
4. **ripsnorter:** person who is strikingly active, wild, and exciting.

470 *Greek Myths and American Folk Tales*

GUIDED READING

LITERAL QUESTION

1a. The storyteller describes some of the Crocketts' special abilities. What does he say to introduce their feats? ("They had great talents, and they lived in a great place.")

INFERENTIAL QUESTION

1b. What real traits of the Crockett family are most likely being extolled in this tale? (speed, strength, energy, helpfulness)

1　Davy's wife, Sally Ann Thunder Ann Whirlwind Crockett, was a streak of lightning set up edgeways and buttered with quicksilver.[5] She could laugh the bark off a pine tree, blow out the moonlight, and sing a wolf to sleep.

The children were worthy of such a father as Davy and such a mother as Sally Ann Thunder Ann Whirlwind Crockett. They could outrun, outjump, and outscream almost any creature in creation. They could also outfight a middling-sized thunderstorm.

---

5. **quicksilver:** silvery liquid substance characterized by quick, unpredictable movement; mercury.

STUDY QUESTIONS

Recalling

1. What made the Crocketts different from "ordinary people"?
2. How would Davy's mother cross the Nolachucky River?
3. How would the local people sink tree posts for their bridges?
4. What could Davy's children do to "almost any creature in creation"?

Interpreting

5. Suggest three adjectives that describe the amazing Crockett family.
6. Which actions of the Crocketts do you think are absolutely impossible? Which actions *might* be possible?
7. Do you think the narrator intends you to believe everything about the Crocketts? Why or why not?

Extending

8. Why do you think people would enjoy hearing about such amazing people?

READING AND LITERARY FOCUS

Folk Tales and Tall Tales

Folk tales are anonymous stories passed down by word of mouth generation after generation. They often concern very strong or clever people who come from humble backgrounds. These people usually triumph over their opponents because of their wit and their sheer energy. Folk tales are both down-to-earth and highly imaginative.

Many folk tales—like those about Davy Crockett—originally had some basis in fact and grew out of the lives of real people. They changed, however, as they were told and retold. A man might once have fought a bear, for example, and the tales told about him might make him into the greatest bear fighter who ever lived. Through the power of imagination, folk tales can turn real people into heroes.

Many American folk tales are also **tall tales**—stories of unbelievable events told with perfect seriousness. For example, the narrator of "The Amazing Crockett Family" would not crack a smile while assuring you that Sally Ann Crockett could "laugh the bark off a pine tree." A tall tale, in other words, is a story in which the truth has been stretched.

A culture's anonymous myths, folk tales, legends, fables, songs, and proverbs are an important part of its literature. By reading and listening to folk tales, we may gain important insights into the true values, beliefs, and goals of the people.

Thinking About Folk Tales and Tall Tales

■ What beliefs and goals of the American people seem to be shown by the tale of the amazing Crockett family?

The Amazing Crockett Family 471

Building America was a big job, calling for people with big ideas and tremendous energy to match. In our national folk tales perhaps the biggest character of them all was Paul Bunyan, a lumberjack famous for oversized deeds. As the tales tell it, no task was too large for Paul, even though his size and strength sometimes caused problems.

■ What problems were caused by Paul's cornstalk and pumpkin vine?

Paul Bunyan, lumberjack.

Retold by
Harold Courlander

Paul Bunyan's Cornstalk

1 Paul Bunyan was the fellow who invented the ax with two edges so a man could stand between two trees and chop them both down at the same time. As it turned out, Paul was the only man who could do that trick, but the other lumberjacks used the double-bitted ax anyway, because they didn't have to sharpen the blades so often. Paul Bunyan also had other tricks. Most lumberjacks used to cut off the tops of the pines before they felled them. But when Paul was in a hurry, he'd wait till a tree started falling; then he'd get set with his ax and lop off the top of the tree as it came down.

2 Nothing Paul Bunyan ever did was small. He had an ox named Babe, who used to help him with his logging work. Babe was just about the most phenomenal ox in Michigan. His color was blue, and he stood ninety hands[1] high. If you happened to hang on the tip of one horn, it's doubtful if you could have seen the tip of the other, even on a clear day. One day when Paul had Babe out plowing, the ox was stung by a Michigan deerfly about the size of a bushel basket. Babe took off across the country dragging the plow behind him, right across Indiana, Illinois, and Missouri, with the deerfly bringing up the rear. After a while Babe veered south and didn't stop till **3** he got to the Rio Grande.[2] The plow that Babe was hitched to dug a furrow four miles wide and two hundred miles long. You can check it in your own geography book. They call it Grand Canyon nowadays.

Even the storms that Paul was in were big. The biggest of all was the one they call the Big Blue Snow. It snowed for two months straight, and the way the drifts piled up only the tops of the tallest pines were showing.

----
1. **ninety hands:** thirty feet.

2. **Rio Grande** [rē′ō grand′]: river flowing from southwestern Colorado into the Gulf of Mexico.

472   *Greek Myths and American Folk Tales*

GUIDED READING

LITERAL QUESTION

1a. What is unusual about Babe? (his color, size, and strength)

INFERENTIAL QUESTION

1b. What does Paul's ownership of such an animal say about Paul? (Only a big man could control so huge an ox; Paul could probably do more work than anyone else with Babe's help.)

AT A GLANCE

- During the storm Babe's tail freezes, and its weight pulls Babe's hide so hard it forces his eyes to remain open all winter.
- Paul grows huge corn and pumpkins in his vegetable garden.
- One of the cornstalks grows as big as a fifty-year-old pine.

1 PLOT: EPISODIC STRUCTURE

As in Greek myths, tall tales often move from episode to episode. Only the presence of the hero connects the stories.

2 STYLE: SIMILE

The cornstalk is compared to a house and a pine tree to show its incredible rate of growth.

3 AUDIENCE AND SETTING

Listeners to tall tales would recognize homey references to animals and plants specific to their regions. Such homey details help establish the credibility of this yarn.

Lumberjacks went out that winter on their snowshoes and cut off all the pine tops. It saved them a lot of time when spring came around. Babe the blue ox didn't get a wink of sleep, though, from December till the first of March. It seems that standing out there in the weather the way he was, the snow that fell on his back melted and ran down his tail, and once it got there it froze into ice. Babe's tail kept getting heavier and heavier, and it drew on his hide so hard it just pulled his eyelids wide open and kept them that way. Babe never did get his eyes closed until the spring thaw came and melted the ice off his tail.

1 But the Big Blue Snow wasn't anything compared to the big drought that started in Saginaw County[3] and spread out as far as the Alleghenies[4] in the East and the Rockies in the West. It all started with Paul Bunyan's vegetable garden. Paul planted some corn and some pumpkins. One of those cornstalks was six feet high before the others had sprouted. **2** In two weeks it was tall as a house and growing like crazy. About the time it was as big as a fifty-year-old pine, people began to come in from all over the county to see it. It was growing out of the ground so fast it was pulling up stones that even the frost couldn't heave out. Same kind of thing, more or less, happened **3** to one of the pumpkin vines. It grew so fast it just darted around like a Massauga rattlesnake.[5] It climbed into any place where there

---

3. **Saginaw** [sag'ə nô'] **County:** county in east-central Michigan.

4. **Alleghenies** [al'ə gā'nēz]: mountain range extending from north-central Pennsylvania to western Virginia.
5. **Massauga rattlesnake:** massasauga [mas'ə sô'gə], small rattlesnake found in swampy areas of the eastern and southern United States.

Paul Bunyan's Cornstalk 473

GUIDED READING

LITERAL QUESTION

1a. Why doesn't Babe sleep during the winter of the Big Blue Snow? (Ice on his tail is so heavy it pulls his hide and keeps his eyes open.)

INFERENTIAL QUESTION

1b. Why would tales of impossibly hard winters appeal to early audiences of this tale? (They are probably used to hard winters themselves. Such details help them identify with the experiences of their folk heroes.)

- Paul's outsize plants soak up all the water in the Midwest.
- Paul uses Babe to pull up the pumpkin vine and climbs the cornstalk to top it off.
- Once the plants are dead, life returns to "normal."

1 STYLE: SIMILE

The image of barrel-sized pumpkins whipping around like "crabapples on a string" is a humorous one meant to emphasize the astonishing size of everything Paul Bunyan touches.

2 THEME

Again a natural phenomenon—a drought—is supposedly caused by unbelievable circumstances. This belief sets up conditions under which an American hero can demonstrate extraordinary abilities that are comforting to frontier settlers.

3 SETTING

The tale takes place primarily in Michigan: A heroic Babe must run to the easternmost of the Great Lakes (at least three hundred miles) in order to uproot the pumpkin vine.

4 BACKGROUND

Many settlers in the timberland of the Midwest were Scandinavian immigrants. The three names cited here are comic versions of Scandinavian names.

5 READING SKILLS: INFERENCE

The implication is that the top has fallen for three days without landing. The cornstalk's height is exaggerated even further with this detail.

REFLECTING ON THE STORY

Which of Paul's traits were probably vital for real lumberjacks? (humor, strength, resourcefulness)

---

was an opening. People had to keep their windows closed. The ones that didn't had to cut their way out of their beds with a brush knife. Sometimes that vine would grow into one window and out another between sunset and sunrise. Things weren't too bad until the vine **blossomed and the pumpkins came out. They were about the size of hogsheads[6]—the *little* pumpkins, that is—and when the vine whipped back and forth looking for someplace to grow it just snapped the pumpkins around like crab apples on a string. People had to be mighty alert to keep from getting hit by those pumpkins.** One man lost a team of horses that way, and half a dozen good barns and one silo were stove[7] in.

But the real problem started when the corn and pumpkin roots began to soak up all the water out of the ground. Farms for sixty miles around went dry—fields, springs, and wells. The pine woods turned yellow from lack of moisture. The Au Sable River[8] just turned into a trickle, and pretty soon there wasn't anything there but dry mud. The next thing that happened was that the water in the Great Lakes began to go down. It went down so fast in Lake Huron it left the fish hanging in the air. When things began to look real bad, folks came and told Paul Bunyan he'd just have to get rid of his corn and pumpkins. Paul was reasonable about it. First he went after the pumpkin vine. He spent four hours racing around trying to catch hold of the end, and finally did it by trapping it in a barn. He

---

6. **hogsheads:** large barrels holding from 63 to 140 gallons of liquid.
7. **stove:** smashed, broken.
8. **Au Sable** [ô sä′bəl] **River:** river in the northern part of Michigan's Lower Peninsula.

---

474   *Greek Myths and American Folk Tales*

---

hitched Babe up to the end of the vine, but **as fast as Babe pulled the vine grew. Babe ran faster and faster, and he was near Lake Ontario before he had the vine tight enough to pull it out.**

Then Paul sized up his cornstalk. He figured he'd have to chop it down. He sharpened up his ax and spit on his hands. He made a good deep cut in that stalk, but before he could chip out a wedge the stalk grew up six feet, cut and all. Every time he made a cut it would shoot up out of reach before he could swing his ax again. Pretty soon he saw there wasn't any use going on this way. "Only way to kill this stalk is to cut off the top," he said. He hung his ax in his belt and started climbing. In about two hours he was completely out of sight. People just stood around and waited. They stood around two and a half days **without any sight of Paul. Lars Larson called, "Paul!" but there was no answer. Erik Erikson and Hans Hanson called, "Paul!" But there wasn't any word from Paul Bunyan.** So they waited some more. Two more days went by. No word from Paul. They decided that if everyone yelled at once maybe the sound would carry. So all together the two thousand eight hundred men and boys hollered, "Paul!" And sure enough, they heard his faint voice from up above.

"When you going to top that cornstalk?" they yelled back at him.

"Hasn't that top come down yet?" Paul hollered back. "I cut it off three days ago!"

And it was the truth, too. The stalk stopped growing, the water in the Great Lakes stopped falling, the Au Sable River began to run, the springs began to flow again, and things came back to normal. But it was a narrow escape.

GUIDED READING

LITERAL QUESTIONS

1a. What happened when Paul's corn and pumpkin roots soak all the water out of the ground? (Farms for sixty miles around go dry; the pine woods and the Au Sable River go dry.)

2a. What does Paul do to help during the drought? (He pulls out the vine, tops the cornstalk, and saves the Midwest.)

INFERENTIAL QUESTIONS

1b. What would a drought mean to the local population? (lost crops and possible starvation)

2b. Why don't Paul's neighbors pull the vine and top the cornstalk themselves? (In true tall-tale fashion only Paul has the ability to deal with such massive problems.)

STUDY QUESTIONS

Recalling

1. For what reason did Paul invent the ax with two edges?
2. How did Babe make the Grand Canyon?
3. What kept Babe awake during the Big Blue Snow?
4. What did Paul and Babe do to stop the pumpkin vine from growing?
5. What did Paul do to stop the cornstalk from growing?

Interpreting

6. Describe Paul's skills in your own words. Why was he a valuable worker?
7. Why was Babe a perfect match for Paul?
8. At the end of the tale, Paul says, "Hasn't that top come down yet? . . . I cut it off three days ago!" What do his words suggest about the cornstalk?

Extending

9. In what ways are some of today's comic-strip superheroes like Paul Bunyan?

READING AND LITERARY FOCUS

Humor and Exaggeration

The humor in many American folk tales is the result of exaggeration. **Exaggeration** is saying that something is much greater than it actually is. In many American folk tales the actions or events are so unbelievable that they are funny. For example, consider the humor in the story of the drought that caused the water in Lake Huron to go down so fast "it left the fish hanging in the air."

Exaggeration is funny because it makes us see a surprising contrast between the possible and the impossible. We laugh at exaggerations because we know they are impossible, even though the narrator of a tale assures us that the exaggerations are really true.

Thinking About Humor and Exaggeration

▓ Identify one other example of humorous exaggeration in the tale of Paul Bunyan.

COMPOSITION

Writing About a Folk Tale

▓ Write about "Paul Bunyan's Cornstalk," telling what characteristics of a folk tale it possesses. First name the characteristics of folk tales. Then cite examples that show how Paul Bunyan's tale demonstrates those characteristics. Finally, give your opinion of this folk tale.

Writing with Exaggeration

▓ Write a brief description of an event in which you exaggerate what happens. For example, you may want to complete this sentence: *The weather was so hot that . . .* First make a statement so unbelievable that your reader will know you are being humorous. Then expand the statement with "proof" that it really happened. Finally, assure the reader that you are completely serious.

1. to chop down two trees at once
2. stung by fly while plowing; took off, dragging plow behind him; furrow became the Grand Canyon
3. The ice on his tail pulled his hide so hard that it kept his eyelids open.
4. caught the vine's end in a barn, stretched it tight, and pulled it out of ground
5. He climbed to the top, chopped top off with his axe. The stalk was so tall that the top took several days to land.
6. Possible answers: strength, determination, inventiveness
7. big, unusual, strong, capable of great tasks
8. It's so tall that the top takes over three days to fall to earth.
9. Possible answers: They are larger than life, face superhuman tasks, are unaffected by obstacles that stop ordinary people.

READING AND LITERARY FOCUS

Possible answers: Babe's size; Babe's being stung by a fly "the size of a bushel basket"; Babe's staying awake through the Big Blue Snow; Paul's pumpkin vine and cornstalk

COMPOSITION: GUIDELINES FOR EVALUATION

WRITING ABOUT A FOLK TALE

Objective

To write an analysis of a folk tale

Guidelines for Evaluation

- suggested length: one to two paragraphs
- should name characteristics of folk tales
- should show how Paul Bunyan's tale demonstrates those characteristics
- should end with an opinion of this folk tale

WRITING WITH EXAGGERATION

Objective

To write a description using exaggeration

Guidelines for Evaluation

- suggested length: one to two paragraphs
- should begin with a humorous exaggeration, such as "The weather was so hot that . . ."
- should provide details "proving" statement
- should conclude with assurance of seriousness
- should include vivid description

- Bill is born to a large family near the Pecos River in Texas.
- When he is two weeks old, he trains a bear cub and keeps it as a pet.

LITERARY OPTIONS

- exaggeration
- setting
- characterization

THEMATIC OPTIONS

- resourcefulness
- heroism
- American experiences

1 SETTING

The tale takes place on the prairies of Texas in some unspecified long-ago time.

2 CHARACTERIZATION

Bill is introduced at once as an extraordinary character.

3 EXAGGERATION

The image of a two-week-old boy wrestling a bear cub and winning is an example of the impossible feats that heroes in American tall tales often perform, their foils being the wild animals, geographic features, and weather of the American landscape.

TEXAS ESSENTIAL ELEMENTS
GRADE 8

1K dictionary skills
3A plot development and character development
3B figurative language
3C setting and mood
3D literary genres
4B implied main idea
4C fact vs. nonfact
To locate treatment of an Element, see *Texas Teacher's Resources.*

The American West has contributed many heroes to our folk literature. None, however, is as spectacular as Pecos Bill. Bill is a kind of Paul Bunyan of the West. His reputation among cowboys matches Paul's reputation among lumberjacks. Like Paul, Bill seems to have grown up with the land itself. He seems as naturally at home in the West as a cactus or a coyote.

■ What unusual event gave Bill the nickname "coyote cowboy"?

Pecos Bill, Coyote Cowboy.

Retold by
Adrien Stoutenburg

Pecos Bill, Coyote Cowboy

1 There aren't as many coyotes in Texas now as there were when Pecos Bill was born. But the ones that there are still do plenty of howling at night, sitting out under the sagebrush like thin, gray shadows, and pointing their noses at the moon.

Some of the cowboys around the Pecos River[1] country claim that the oldest coyotes remember the time when Bill lived with them and are howling because they are lonesome for him. It's not often that coyotes have a boy grow up with them like one of their own family.

2 Bill had over a dozen older brothers and sisters for playmates, but they were ordinary boys and girls and no match for him. When Bill was two weeks old, his father found a half-grown bear and brought the bear home.

"You treat this bear nice, now," Bill's father said.

3 The bear didn't feel friendly and threatened to take a bite out of Bill. Bill wrestled the bear and tossed it around until the bear put its paws over its head and begged for mercy. Bill couldn't talk yet, but he patted the bear to show that he didn't have any hard feelings. After that, the bear followed Bill around like a big, flat-footed puppy.

Pecos Bill's father was one of the first settlers in the West. There was lots of room in Texas, with so much sky that it seemed as if there couldn't be any sky left over for the rest of the United States. There weren't many people, and it was lonesome country, especially on nights when the wind came galloping over the land, rattling the bear grass and the yucca plants[2] and carrying the tangy smell of greasewood.[3] However, Bill didn't feel lonely often, with all the raccoons, badgers, and jack rab-

---

1. **Pecos River:** river flowing from northern Mexico through southeast Texas.

2. **bear grass . . . yucca plants:** flowering desert plants with stiff, sword like leaves.
3. **greasewood:** spiny evergreen shrub.

476   *Greek Myths and American Folk Tales*

GUIDED READING

LITERAL QUESTION

1a. How does Bill train his bear cub? (He wrestles it until it begs for mercy.)

INFERENTIAL QUESTION

1b. What does this choice of a pet tell you about young Bill? (He is an unusually strong and fearless child.)

bits he had for friends. Once he made the mistake of trying to pet a skunk. The skunk sprayed Bill with its strongest scent. Bill's mother had to hang Bill on the clothesline for a week to let the smell blow off him.

Bill was a little over one year old when another family of pioneers moved into the country. The new family settled about fifty miles from where Bill's folks had built their homestead.

"The country's getting too crowded," said Bill's father. "We've got to move farther west."

So the family scrambled back into their big wagon and set out, the oxen puffing and snorting as they pulled the wagon toward the Pecos River. Bill was sitting in the rear of the wagon when it hit some rocks in a dry stream bed. There was a jolt, and Bill went flying out of the wagon. He landed so hard that the wind was knocked out of him and he couldn't even cry out to let his folks know. It might not have made any difference if he had, because all his brothers and sisters were making such a racket and the wagon wheels were creaking so loudly that no one could have heard him. In fact, with so many other children in the family besides Bill, it was four weeks before Bill's folks even missed him. Then, of course, it was too late to find him.

Young Bill sat there in the dry stream bed awhile, wondering what to do. Wherever he looked there was only the prairie and the sky, completely empty except for a sharp-shinned hawk floating overhead. Bill felt more lonely than he ever had in his life. Then, suddenly, he saw a pack of coyotes off in the distance, eating the remains of a dead deer. The coyotes looked at Bill and Bill looked at them. These coyotes had never seen a human baby before, and they didn't know quite what to think. Apparently, they decided Bill was some new kind of hairless animal, for one of the female coyotes took a hunk of deer meat in her teeth

and trotted over to Bill with it. She put it in front of him and stood back, waiting for him to eat it.

Bill had not eaten much raw meat before, but he knew that the female coyote meant well, and he didn't want to hurt her feelings. So he picked the meat up and began chewing. It tasted so good that he walked over and joined the other coyotes.

From that time on, Bill lived with the coyotes, going wherever they went, joining in their hunts, and even learning their language. Those years he lived with the coyotes were happy ones. He ran with them through the moonlit nights, curled up with them in their shady dens, and howled with them when they sang to the stars.

By the time Bill was ten years old, he could outrun and outhowl any coyote in the Southwest. And since he had not seen any other human beings in all that time, he thought he was a coyote himself.

He might have gone on believing this forever if one day a cowboy hadn't come riding through the sagebrush. The cowboy stopped, stared, and rubbed his eyes, because he could scarcely believe what he saw. There in front of him stood a ten-year-old boy wrestling with a giant grizzly bear. Nearby sat a dozen coyotes, their tongues hanging out. Before the cowboy could say, "Yipee yi-yo!" or plain "Yipee!" the boy had hugged the bear to death.

When Pecos Bill saw the cowboy, he snarled like a coyote and put his head down between his shoulders, ready to fight.

"What's your name?" the cowboy asked. "What are you doing out here?"

Since Bill didn't know anything but coyote talk, he naturally didn't understand a word.

The cowboy tossed Bill a plug of tobacco. Bill ate it and decided it tasted pretty good, so when the cowboy came up close, Bill didn't bite him.

Pecos Bill, Coyote Cowboy   477

AT A GLANCE

- Bill's family moves farther west when Bill is one year old.
- Their wagon hits a rock; Bill is flung out and stranded on the prairie.
- He is adopted by a coyote family and grows up as a coyote pup.
- Bill is ten years old when he next sees a human—a cowboy.

1 EXAGGERATION

The idea that one family living fifty miles away makes the country "too crowded" exaggerates the settlers' desire for privacy.

2 PLOT: SUSPENSE

The listener / reader does not know how the wild animals will react to the small child. In a realistic story, they might attack him.

3 THEME

Bill shows his resourcefulness by adapting easily to his new life as a coyote.

4 VOCABULARY: REGIONALISM

The phrase *Yipee yi-yo* often appears in the choruses of cowboy songs. It is a meaningless phrase that may be meant to imitate the call of the coyote.

5 RESPONSE JOURNAL

Ask students to expand a bit on this moment, describing the scene from either Bill's or the cowboy's point of view.

GUIDED READING

LITERAL QUESTIONS

1a. Why does Bill's family move? (They think the country is getting too crowded when another family settles fifty miles away.)

2a. Why does Bill think he is a coyote? (After he is adopted by the coyotes, he sees no people for years.)

INFERENTIAL QUESTIONS

1b. In what way is this attitude an exaggeration? In what sense true to life? (Fifty miles between families is too great a distance to make the country seem crowded. But this exaggeration conveys the Westerner's hunger for open spaces.)

2b. How does Bill prove that he is as extraordinary a coyote as he is a person? (He outruns and outhowls any coyote around; he wrestles grizzly bears, natural enemies of coyotes.)

- The cowboy convinces Bill that he is human.
- Bill mounts his mountain lion and follows the cowboy to his ranch.
- On the way he captures a rattlesnake and invents the lasso.
- He is made ranch boss and teaches the cowboys to round up cattle.

1 EXAGGERATION

Bill's strength and fearlessness are so awesome that he has tamed a ferocious mountain lion.

2 SETTING

Bill's easy mastery of the animals of the American Southwest, creatures familiar to settlers, localizes him as a hero of that particular region.

3 THEME

Bill's resourcefulness leads to the invention of the lasso—only one of the many innovations he brings to the world of ranching.

4 AUDIENCE

Early listeners to this tale would know that no such cattle trap ever existed. They would probably be highly amused at the image of a rancher ambushing a cow.

5 DIALOGUE AND CHARACTERIZATION

This brief humorous exchange is typical of the terseness of cowboy speech. The exchange further establishes Bill's prowess: His heroic stature is immediately clear, even at age ten, to the ranch boss.

The cowboy stayed there for three days, teaching Bill to talk like a human. Then he tried to prove to Bill that Bill wasn't a coyote.

"I must be a coyote," Bill said. "I've got fleas, haven't I? And I can howl the moon out of the sky. And I can run a deer to death."

The cowboy said, "In order to be a true coyote, you have to have a bushy tail."

Bill looked around and realized for the first time that he didn't have a nice bushy, waving tail like his coyote friends. "Maybe I lost it somewhere."

"No siree," the cowboy said. "You're a human being, sure as shooting. You'd better come along with me."

Being human was a hard thing for Bill to face up to, but he realized that the cowboy must be right. He told his coyote friends good-by and thanked them for all that they had

1 taught him. Then he straddled a mountain lion he had tamed and rode with the cowboy toward the cowboy's ranch. On the way to the ranch, a big rattlesnake reared up in front of them. The cowboy galloped off, but Bill jumped from his mount and faced the snake.

"I'll let you have the first three bites, Mister Rattler, just to be fair. Then I'm going to beat the poison out of you until you behave yourself!"

2 That is just what Bill did. He whipped the snake around until it stretched out like a thirty-foot rope. Bill looped the rattler-rope in one hand, got back on his lion, and caught up with the cowboy. To entertain himself, he made a loop out of the snake and tossed it over the head of an armadillo[4] plodding along through the cactus. Next, he lassoed several Gila monsters.[5]

---

4. **armadillo** [är′mə dil′ō]: insect-eating mammal with a shell made of bony plates, a long snout, sharp claws, and a long tail.
5. **Gila** [hē′lə] **monsters:** large, poisonous lizards.

478   *Greek Myths and American Folk Tales*

---

3 "I never saw anybody do anything like that before," said the cowboy.

"That's because nobody invented the lasso before," said Pecos Bill.

Before Pecos Bill came along, cowboys didn't know much about their job. They didn't know anything about rounding up cattle, or branding them, or even about ten-gallon

4 hats.[6] The only way they knew to catch a steer was to hide behind a bush, lay a looped rope on the ground, and wait for the steer to step into the loop.

Pecos Bill changed all that the minute he reached the Dusty Dipper Ranch. He slid off his mountain lion and marched up to the biggest cowboy there.

5 "Who's the boss here?" he asked.

The man took one look at Bill's lion and at the rattlesnake-rope, and said, "I *was*."

Young though he was, Bill took over. At the Dusty Dipper and at other ranches, Bill taught the cowboys almost everything they know today. He invented spurs for them to wear on their boots. He taught them how to round up the cattle and drive the herds to railroad stations where they could be shipped to market. One of the finest things Bill did was to teach the cowboys to sing cowboy songs.

Bill made himself a guitar. On a night when the moon was as reddish-yellow as a ripe peach, though fifty times as large, he led some of the fellows at the ranch out to the corral and set himself down on the top rail.

"I don't want to brag," he told the cowhands, "but I learned my singing from the coyotes, and that's about the best singing there is."

He sang a tune the coyotes had taught him, and made up his own words:

---

6. **ten-gallon hats:** high, wide-brimmed felt hats, especially popular in Texas.

GUIDED READING

LITERAL QUESTION

1a. How does Bill invent the lasso? (He uses a rattlesnake to rope an armadillo and some lizards.)

INFERENTIAL QUESTION

1b. How does Bill show his resourcefulness at the ranch? (He invents equipment for the cowboys, shows them how to do their jobs better, and teaches them to sing.)

1 "My seat is in the saddle, and my saddle's
  in the sky,
  And I'll quit punchin' cows[7] in the sweet
  by and by."

He made up many more verses and sang
many other songs. When Bill was through, the
roughest cowboy of all, Hardnose Hal, sat wip-
ing tears from his eyes because of the beauty
of Bill's singing. Lefty Lightning, the smallest
cowboy, put his head down on his arms and
2 wept. All the cowboys there vowed they would
learn to sing and make up songs. And they
did make up hundreds of songs about the lone
prairie, and the Texas sky, and the wind blow-

---
7. **punchin' cows:** driving cattle to market.

ing over the plains. That's why we have so
many cowboy songs today. . . .

3 One of the most exciting things Bill did
was to find himself the wildest, strongest,
most beautiful horse that ever kicked up the
Texas dust. He was a mighty, golden mustang, and even Bill couldn't outrun that
horse. To catch the mustang, Bill had the
cowboys rig up a huge slingshot and shoot
him high over the cactus and greasewood.
When Bill landed in front of the mustang, the
horse was so surprised he stopped short,
thrusting out his front legs stiff as rifle barrels. The mustang had been going so fast that
his hoofs drove into the ground, and he was
stuck. Bill leaped on the animal's back,
yanked on his golden mane, and pulled him
free. The mustang was so thankful for being
pulled from the trap that he swung his head

AT A GLANCE

- All the cowboys decide to sing songs like Bill's.
- Bill catches and tames the wildest horse in Texas.

1 VOCABULARY: REGIONALISM

Punchin' cows, a western idiom, refers to tasks cowboys tradition-ally performed. *The sweet by and by* is sometimes a euphemism for death; *by and by* simply means "before too long."

2 SETTING

American cowboys created a particular form of expression known as the "cowboy ballad." These ballads tell stories about the experiences of settlers of the Great Plains and the Southwest.

3 HEROES

Typically, heroes must have mounts that equal them in spirit. Thus Paul Bunyan has his blue ox, the Long Ranger has Silver, and Pecos Bill has "the wildest, strongest, most beautiful horse that ever kicked up the Texas dust."

GUIDED READING

LITERAL QUESTION

1a. How does Bill catch his horse? (Bill is shot over the horse's back with a slingshot.)

INFERENTIAL QUESTION

1b. Why is the golden mustang the perfect horse for Bill? (He is the wildest horse around; even Bill can't outrun him; he is as extraordinary a horse as Bill is a man.)

- A drought parches Texas, and ranchers ask Bill for help.
- Bill rides around on his mustang, looking for a way to make rain.
- He locates a cyclone over Oklahoma.
- He rides a bolt of lightning up into the cyclone and wrestles it until it sends down rain.

1 STYLE: SIMILE

The teller of the tale chooses a homey comparison: Bill's horse is compared to "a soft wind in a thatch of jimson weed." The juxtaposition of pleasant and vile images shows that the horse retains some wild characteristics, as does the horse's nickname, "Widow-Maker."

2 CHARACTERIZATION

Bill's fame has spread. Everyone now comes to him for help.

3 SETTING

Vivid descriptions of drought are mixed with exaggerated details to paint a picture of the harshness of frontier life.

4 VOCABULARY: REGIONALISM

Giddap, a slurred version of the words *get up*, is used to command a horse to go forward.

5 STYLE: PERSONIFICATION

The cyclone is given human characteristics that make its battle with Bill more vivid.

---

around and gave Pecos Bill a smacking kiss. From then on, the horse was as gentle as a soft wind in a thatch of jimson weed.[8]

No one else could ride him, however. Most of the cowboys who tried ended up with broken necks. That's why Bill called his mustang Widow-Maker.

Bill and Widow-Maker traveled all over the western range, starting new ranches and helping out in the long cattle drives. In stormy weather they often holed up with a band of coyotes. Bill would strum his guitar and the coyotes would sing with him.

Then came the year of the Terrible Drought. The land shriveled for lack of water, and the droves of cattle stood panting with thirst.

The cowboys and the ranch bosses from all around came to Bill, saying, "The whole country's going to dry up and blow away, Bill, unless you can figure out some way to bring us rain."

"I'm figuring," Bill told them. "But I've never tried making rain before, so I'll have to think a little."

While Bill thought, the country grew so dry it seemed that there would be nothing but bones and rocks left. Even cactus plants, which could stand a lot of dryness, began to turn brown. The pools where the cattle drank dried up and turned to cracked mud. All the snakes hid under the ground in order to keep from frying. Even the coyotes stopped howling, because their throats were too dry for them to make any sound.

Bill rode around on Widow-Maker, watching the clear, burning sky and hoping for the sight of a rain cloud. All he saw were whirls of dust, called dust devils, spinning up from the yellowing earth. Then, toward noon one day, he spied something over in Oklahoma

---

8. **jimson weed:** poisonous, foul-smelling weed.

480   *Greek Myths and American Folk Tales*

---

which looked like a tall whirling tower of black bees. Widow-Maker reared up on his hind legs, his eyes rolling.

"It's just a cyclone," Pecos Bill told his horse, patting the golden neck.

But Widow-Maker was scared and began bucking around so hard that even Bill had a time staying in the saddle.

"Whoa there!" Bill commanded. "I could ride that cyclone as easy as I can ride you, the way you're carrying on."

That's when Bill had an idea. There might be rain mixed up in that cyclone tower. He nudged Widow-Maker with his spurs and yelled, "Giddap!"

What Bill planned to do was leap from his horse and grab the cyclone by the neck. But as he came near and saw how high the top of the whirling tower was, he knew he would have to do something better than that. Just as he and Widow-Maker came close enough to the cyclone to feel its hot breath, a knife of lightning streaked down into the ground. It struck there, quivering, just long enough for Bill to reach out and grab it. As the lightning bolt whipped back up into the sky, Bill held on. When he was as high as the top of the cyclone, he jumped and landed astraddle its black, spinning shoulders.

By then, everyone in Texas, New Mexico, Arizona, and Oklahoma was watching. They saw Bill grab hold of that cyclone's shoulders and haul them back. They saw him wrap his legs around the cyclone's belly and squeeze so hard the cyclone started to pant. Then Bill got out his lasso and slung it around the cyclone's neck. He pulled it tighter and tighter until the cyclone started to choke, spitting out rocks and dust. All the rain that was mixed up in it started to fall.

Down below, the cattle and the coyotes, the jack rabbits and the horned toads, stuck out their tongues and caught the sweet, blue, fall-

---

GUIDED READING

LITERAL QUESTIONS

1a. Why do the cowboys need help from Bill? (They hope he can bring rain to the dry land.)

2a. What words describe the cyclone as Bill wrestles it? (*hot breath, shoulders, belly, pant, neck, choke*)

INFERENTIAL QUESTIONS

1b. Why would a drought be bad for ranchers? (Cattle would die for lack of water and food.)

2b. Why might the cyclone be given human qualities? (Possible answers: to create a clearer picture of the fight with Bill; to exaggerate its actions; to provide a humorous image) ing rain. Cowboys on the ranches and people in town ran around whooping and cheering, holding out pans and kettles to catch the raindrops.

Bill rode the cyclone across three states. By the time the cyclone reached California, it was all out of steam, and out of rain, too. It gave a big sigh, trembled weakly, and sank to **1** earth. Bill didn't have time to jump off. He fell hard, scooping out a few thousand acres of sand and rock and leaving a big basin below sea level. That was what made Death Valley.[9]

Bill was a greater hero than ever after that. Yet at times, he felt almost as lonely as on the day when he had bounced out of his folks' wagon and found himself sitting alone under the empty sky. Widow-Maker was good company most of the time, but Bill felt there was something missing in his life.

One day, he wandered down to the Rio Grande[10] and stood watching the brown river flow slowly past. Suddenly, he saw a catfish as big as a whale jumping around on top of the water, its whiskers shining like broomsticks. On top of the catfish was a brown-eyed, brown-haired girl.

2 Somebody beside Bill exclaimed, "Look at Slue-Foot[11] Sue ride that fish!"

Pecos Bill felt his heart thump and tingle in a way it had never done before. "That's the girl I want to marry!" he said. He waded out into the Rio Grande, poked the catfish in the nose, and carried Slue-Foot Sue to a church. "You're going to be my bride," he said.

"That's fine with me," said Sue, looking Pecos Bill over and seeing that he was the biggest, boldest, smartest cowboy who had

---

9. **Death Valley:** hottest, driest place in the United States, 282 feet below sea level.
10. **Rio Grande** [rē′ō grand′]: river flowing from southwestern Colorado into the Gulf of Mexico. It forms the border between Texas and New Mexico.
11. **Slue-Foot:** having large, ungraceful feet.

---

ever happened to come along beside the Rio Grande.

That was the beginning of a very happy life for Bill. He and Sue raised a large family. All of the boys grew up to be fine cowboys, and the girls grew up to be cowgirls. The only time Bill and Sue had any trouble was when Bill wanted to adopt a batch of baby coyotes who were orphans.

"We're human beings," Sue said, "and we can't be raising a bunch of varmints."[12]

"I was a varmint once myself," said Bill. He argued so much that Sue agreed to take the coyotes in and raise them as members of the **3** family. The coyotes grew to be so human that two of them were elected to the House of Representatives.

Pecos Bill grew old, as everyone and everything does in time. Even so, there wasn't a bronco he couldn't bust, or a steer he couldn't rope, or a bear he couldn't hug to death faster and better than anyone else.

4 No one knows, for sure, how he died, or even if he did die. Some say that he mixed barbed wire in his coffee to make it strong enough for his taste, and that the wire rusted in his stomach and poisoned him. Others say that one day he met a dude[13] cowboy, all dressed up in fancy clothes, who didn't know the front end of a cow from the side of a boxcar. The dude asked so many silly questions about cowpunching that Pecos Bill lay down in the dust and laughed himself to death.

5 But the cowboys back in the Pecos River country say that every once in a while, when the moon is full and puffing its white cheeks out and the wind is crooning softly through the bear grass, Pecos Bill himself comes along and sits on his haunches and sings right along with the coyotes.

---

12. **varmints** [vär′mənts]: troublesome animals.
13. **dude:** inexperienced.

Pecos Bill, Coyote Cowboy 481

- The cyclone sinks to earth, and Bill carves out Death Valley as he falls.
- One day Bill sees a girl riding a catfish down the Rio Grande.
- He punches the fish, seizes the girl, and marries her.
- Bill and Sue raise children and a few coyotes.
- The legend of Pecos Bill lives on.

1 EXAGGERATION

Absurd circumstances are used to explain a natural geographic phenomenon: Death Valley.

2 CHARACTERIZATION

Her name indicates that Slue-Foot Sue is not beautiful. Bill is intrigued by her skill and daring rather than by her looks.

3 HUMOR

In this line the taleteller satirizes politicians and amuses his audience while doing so.

4 HEROES

Pecos Bill attains mythic proportions because "no one knows, for sure, how he died." As with many legendary heroes, the implication is that he may still be alive.

5 SETTING

This final image of Bill singing with the coyotes further incorporates the hero into his regional setting. Just as Paul Bunyan is associated with northern timberland, Pecos Bill is associated with the Southwest.

REFLECTING ON THE STORY

Why would cowboys invent a hero like Pecos Bill? (He embodies the qualities of an ideal cowboy: He can break in horses, round up cattle, and sing songs better than anyone. His nononsense attitude and resourcefulness were probably valued characteristics.)

GUIDED READING

LITERAL QUESTIONS

1a. What is Bill's wife doing when they first meet? (riding on a catfish)

2a. Why has Pecos Bill possibly "laughed himself to death"? (Some say he met a dude who asked silly questions about cowpunching.)

INFERENTIAL QUESTIONS

1b. In what ways are Bill and Sue well matched? (Both are unusually resourceful and daring.)

2b. How might this description of his death appeal to an early audience? (Real ranch hands would know how ridiculous a dude could be; they would appreciate Bill's laughter and laugh with him.)

1. ■ His father brought a bear home; Bill wrestled and beat it.
   ■ thrown from wagon as a baby; not missed for four weeks
2. A cowboy taught Bill human language, convinced him he wasn't a coyote. He rode a mountain lion swinging a rattlesnake rope.
3. to wear spurs, to round up cattle, to sing cowboy songs
4. He rode a cyclone, squeezed it, choked out rain with a lasso.
5. on the Rio Grande; riding a catfish
6. He mixed barbed wire in his coffee, rusting his stomach; he laughed to death at an ignorant dude cowboy.
7. ■ bold, fearless, strong, loving
   ■ skill in roping steers, busting broncos, riding
8. Old boss resigned immediately, acknowledging Bill's superiority.
9. both wild, strong; both bold, daring, unconventional
10. Possible answers: resourcefulness, cleverness, initiative, friendliness

VOCABULARY

1. coyote: from Spanish *coyote,* from Nahuatl *coyotl*
2. jack rabbit: *jack*(ass) from its long ears + *rabbit*
3. sagebrush: from Old French *sau(l)ge,* the plant; from Latin *salvia,* literally the healing plant and from *salvus,* unharmed, well
4. homestead: land provided for by the Homestead Act

CHALLENGE

Students should
■ find American folk songs in the library
■ identify songs from different areas
■ bring songs to class

STUDY QUESTIONS

Recalling

1. What experience did Bill have with a bear when he was two weeks old? How was he separated from his family?
2. What happened to make Bill decide to leave the coyotes? How did he arrive at the Dusty Dipper Ranch?
3. Name three things Bill taught the cowboys.
4. What did Bill do to end the drought?
5. Where did Bill meet Slue-Foot Sue? What was she doing at the time?
6. Give two explanations for Bill's death.

Interpreting

7. Describe the character of Pecos Bill in your own words. What qualities made him such a great cowboy?
8. Why did Bill immediately become the new boss of the Dusty Dipper Ranch?
9. Why was Bill's horse a perfect match for Bill's personality? In what ways were Bill and Sue perfectly matched?

Extending

10. What qualities of the American people do you think are demonstrated by the folk tale of Pecos Bill?

VOCABULARY

Using the Dictionary: Americanisms

Many American folk tales contain Americanisms. An **Americanism** is a word or phrase that was invented in America. Americans created many new words to express the experiences they had while settling the continent. Common sources of Americanisms are new scientific terms, dialect, and words adapted from other languages. For example, Pecos Bill adapts a word from the Spanish language to name his useful invention, the *lasso.*

Use a dictionary to look up each of the following Americanisms from "Pecos Bill, Coyote Cowboy." Identify the background of each word.

1. coyote
2. jack rabbit
3. sagebrush
4. homestead

COMPOSITION

Writing About Setting

■ Write about the setting of "Pecos Bill, Coyote Cowboy." First identify the setting. Then name at least four details that help create a vivid picture of the setting. Finally, tell what those details reveal about the part of America in which the tale was created.

Writing a Description of a Setting

■ Describe an outdoor setting that is familiar to you. For example, you might describe a beach or a street. First tell what you see in this setting. Then tell what you hear and smell. Finally, tell which details of the setting make it most appealing to you.

CHALLENGE

Folk Songs

■ According to the folk tale, Pecos Bill made up many cowboy songs and encouraged other cowboys to do so too. Use your library to find some American folk songs, such as "The Old Chisholm Trail" and "Shenandoah." Find songs from several different parts of the country, and bring the songs into class.

COMPOSITION: GUIDELINES FOR EVALUATION

WRITING ABOUT SETTING

Objective
To describe the significance of setting

Guidelines for Evaluation
■ suggested length: one to two paragraphs
■ should identify the setting
■ should name at least four details that create a vivid picture of the setting
■ should tell what those details reveal about the West

WRITING A DESCRIPTION OF A SETTING

Objective
To describe a familiar outdoor setting

Guidelines for Evaluation
■ suggested length: one to two paragraphs
■ should identify a setting
■ should tell what is seen in the setting
■ should describe sounds, odors
■ should identify the details of the setting that make it most appealing to the writer

The Algonquians are the members of a large group of North American Indian tribes who spoke similar languages. They probably came from Alaska about 3000 B.C. Eventually the Algonquians spread into what is now Canada, the northeastern United States, and the Great Plains. "Strong Wind, the Invisible" is a tale of mystery. Like many myths and folk tales, however, it also teaches a lesson.

■ What mystery is solved by the Chief's youngest daughter?

American Indian drawing of a god of storm and thunder.

Retold by
Cyrus Macmillan

Strong Wind, the Invisible

1   On the shores of a wide bay on the Atlantic coast there dwelt in old times a great Indian warrior. He had a very wonderful and strange power: He could make himself invisible. He could thus mingle unseen with his enemies and listen to their plots. He was known among the people as Strong Wind, the Invisible. He dwelt with his sister in a tent near the sea, and his sister helped him greatly in his work.

  Many maidens would have been glad to marry him, and he was much sought after because of his mighty deeds. It was known that Strong Wind would marry the first maiden who could see him as he came home at night. Many made the trial, but it was a long time before one succeeded.

2   Strong Wind used a clever trick to test the truthfulness of all who sought to win him. Each evening his sister walked on the beach with any girl who wished to make the trial. His sister could always see him, but no one else could see him. And as he came home from

work in the twilight, his sister would ask the girl who sought him, "Do you see him?"

  And each girl would falsely answer, "Yes."

  And his sister would ask, "With what does he draw his sled?"

  And each girl would answer, "With the hide of a moose," or "With a pole," or "With a great cord."

  And then his sister would know that they all had lied. And many tried and lied and failed, for Strong Wind would not marry any who were untruthful.

  There lived in the village a great Chief who had three daughters. Their mother had long been dead. One of these was much younger

3 than the others. She was very beautiful and gentle and well beloved by all. For that reason her older sisters were very jealous of her charms and treated her very cruelly.

  They clothed her in rags that she might be ugly. They cut off her long black hair. They burned her face with coals from the fire that

Strong Wind, the Invisible 483

AT A GLANCE

- An Indian warrior named Strong Wind can make himself invisible.
- He promises to marry the first maiden who can see him.
- Many maidens pretend to see him but are found out.

LITERARY OPTIONS

- audience
- characterization
- plot

THEMATIC OPTIONS

- truthfulness
- heroism

1 AUDIENCE

This warrior with unusual powers was an intriguing hero to the Algonquians. They would have heard versions of this story many times.

2 PLOT AND THEME

Strong Wind's test is a crucial plot element in the tale. The test also underscores the importance of truthfulness to him and to the Algonquians.

3 CHARACTERIZATION

The suggestion is that the gentle one will become Strong Wind's bride. Her situation parallels the story of Cinderella: the mistreated, beautiful daughter who is the youngest of the three.

TEXAS ESSENTIAL ELEMENTS GRADE 8

3A plot development and character development
3D literary genres
4B implied main idea
4E cause/effect
4G prediction of outcomes
To locate treatment of an Element, see *Texas Teacher's Resources.*

GUIDED READING

LITERAL QUESTIONS

1a. What is known about the maiden Strong Wind will marry? (He will marry the first maiden who can see him as he comes home at night.)

2a. What set the Chief's youngest daughter apart from her sisters? (She was beautiful, gentle, and loved by all.)

INFERENTIAL QUESTIONS

1b. Why does he need to test the maidens who seek to win him? (He knows that some will lie and say they see him in order to marry him at any cost.)

2b. What do you think will happen to this maiden? (Students should be able to predict that she will probably pass the test and marry Strong Wind.)

she might be scarred and disfigured. And they lied to their father, telling him that she had done these things herself.

1 But the young girl kept her gentle heart and went gladly about her work.

Like other girls, the Chief's two oldest daughters tried to win Strong Wind. One evening they walked on the shore with Strong Wind's sister and waited for his coming. Soon he came home from his day's work, drawing his sled.

And his sister asked as usual, "Do you see him?"

And each one, lying, answered, "Yes."

And she asked, "Of what is his shoulder strap made?"

And each, guessing, said, "Of rawhide."

Then they entered the tent, where they hoped to see Strong Wind eating his supper. They saw nothing. Strong Wind knew that they had lied. He kept himself from their sight, and they went home.

2 One day the Chief's youngest daughter with her rags and her burnt face resolved to seek Strong Wind. She patched her clothes and went forth to try to see the Invisible One as all the other girls of the village had done before. And her sisters laughed at her and called her "fool." As she passed along the road, all the people laughed at her, but silently she went her way.

Strong Wind's sister received the little girl kindly, and at twilight she took her to the beach. Soon Strong Wind came home drawing his sled.

3 And his sister asked, "Do you see him?"
And the girl answered, "No."

His sister wondered greatly. And again she asked, "Do you see him now?"

And the girl answered, "Yes, and he is very wonderful."

4 And the sister asked, "With what does he draw his sled?"

And the girl answered, "With the rainbow."

And the sister asked further, "Of what is his bowstring?"

And the girl answered, "His bowstring is the Milky Way."[1]

Then Strong Wind's sister knew that because the girl had spoken the truth at first, her brother had made himself visible to her. And she said, "Truly, you have seen him."

And she took her home and bathed her, and all the scars disappeared from her face and body. Her hair grew long and black again like the raven's wing. She gave her fine clothes to wear and many rich ornaments. Then she bade her take the wife's seat in the tent.

Soon Strong Wind entered and sat beside her and called her his bride. The very next day she became his wife, and ever afterwards she helped him to do great deeds.

The girl's two elder sisters wondered greatly at what had taken place. But Strong Wind resolved to punish them. Using his great power, he changed them both into aspen trees and rooted them in the earth. And since that day the leaves of the aspen have always trem-**5**bled. They shiver in fear at the approach of Strong Wind. They are still mindful of his great power and anger because of their lies and their cruelty to their sister long ago.

---

1. **Milky Way:** vast group of stars appearing as a path.

Strong Wind, the Invisible 485

AT A GLANCE

- The Chief's two oldest daughters fail to win Strong Wind—because they lie.
- The youngest daughter is truthful and sees Strong Wind.
- Strong Wind marries the youngest daughter and turns her sisters into aspen trees.

1 CHARACTERIZATION

The youngest daughter distinguishes herself by maintaining her gentleness in the face of her sisters' lies.

2 PLOT: SUSPENSE

The ridicule that the youngest daughter receives heightens suspense and our uncertain hopes that she will succeed.

3 PLOT: RISING ACTION

Unlike the other maidens, the youngest daughter answers truthfully that she does not see Strong Wind. This honesty will soon be rewarded.

4 FOLK TALE

The legend paints Strong Wind in almost godlike terms, associating him with the heavenly rainbow and Milky Way. Like other cultures the Algonquians often attributed superhuman qualities to their heroes.

5 THEME

The one-dimensional quality of the characters and the simple system of rewards and punishment enable this tale to teach its lesson about the importance of truthfulness.

REFLECTING ON THE SELECTION

What qualities were valued by the people who told this tale? (truthfulness, gentleness, heroism)

GUIDED READING

LITERAL QUESTIONS

1a. How do her sisters and others treat the youngest daughter when she goes to seek Strong Wind? (They laugh at her and call her "fool.")

2a. How does the girl's appearance change when Strong Wind's sister takes her home? (Her scars disappear, and her hair grows long and black again.)

INFERENTIAL QUESTIONS

1b. Why do you think she stays silent when they laugh? (Their opinion is not important to her; she is also gentle and uncomplaining and knows she is *not* a fool.)

2b. Why do you think this change occurs? (Strong Wind allows her inner goodness to be reflected in her outward appearance, just as he turns the inhumane sisters into inhuman aspen trees.)

STUDY QUESTIONS

1. He can make himself invisible.
2. will marry the first woman who can see him as he comes home; tests truthfulness by making himself invisible
3. She is beautiful, gentle, well beloved; they are jealous.
4. She first admits she does not see him. After he reveals himself, she says he draws his sled with the rainbow; his bowstring is the Milky Way.
5. changed to aspen trees; always tremble in fear at Strong Wind's approach
6. wants to marry someone truthful; probably believes other good qualities are associated with truthfulness
7. ■ beautiful, gentle, kindly
   ■ She may fear that her father will not believe her or does not want sisters punished.
8. Kindness, gentleness, and truthfulness win out in the end.
9. Both tales involve a younger sister mistreated by older sisters; the mistreated sister is rewarded for her goodness by marriage to a hero.

READING AND LITERARY FOCUS

Answers will vary. It is reassuring to hear familiar stories in which characters have become known to listeners; stories are easier to follow when their plots or characters are familiar; when stories deal with basic human emotions and desires, each retelling provides new insights into familiar themes.

CHALLENGE

Students should
■ go to the library and locate Native American recordings
■ choose one that tells an interesting story and share it with the class

STUDY QUESTIONS

Recalling

1. What special power does Strong Wind possess?
2. By what method does Strong Wind plan to choose a bride?
3. Why do the Chief's two older daughters treat their sister cruelly?
4. What answers does the youngest daughter give to solve the mystery?
5. What is the final fate of the two older sisters?

Interpreting

6. Why do you think Strong Wind designs this particular test for his bride?
7. Describe the character of the Chief's youngest daughter. Why do you think she does not tell her father the truth about her sisters' actions?
8. What do you think is the lesson this tale attempts to teach?

Extending

9. In what ways are the characters and plot of this story similar to those in the story of Cinderella?

READING AND LITERARY FOCUS

Audience

One of the most important abilities of a good storyteller is the ability to fit the story to the audience. The **audience** is the group of people to whom the story is told. Like most groups of people, audiences vary in age, background, interests, and experiences.

Folk tales were told aloud to generations of listeners. The listening audiences were often already familiar with the characters of a tale because the same characters appeared in many different stories. Sometimes the audience even knew the plot of a story because they had heard it before.

The audience of a folk tale was also familiar with the background, the customs, and the way of life described in the tale. The audience of "Strong Wind, the Invisible," for example, was a group of North American Indians who hunted and fished for a living. They easily recognized the setting and the objects talked about in the story: a village near the shore, a bowstring, a sled, a moose hide. They felt familiar with the tale and felt that the tale had grown out of their own lives.

This familiarity added to the audience's enjoyment of the tale. It also enabled people to pay close attention to the way each particular storyteller told the story. Each storyteller, therefore, had the confidence of the audience but still had to be as entertaining as possible.

Thinking About Audience

■ Why do you think audiences like to hear the same types of stories over and over again?

CHALLENGE

Native American Recordings

■ Many Native American tribes have made recordings of their folk tales, songs, and dance music. Use your library to locate one of these recordings. Play for the class one recording that tells an especially entertaining tale.

486   *Greek Myths and American Folk Tales*

During the nineteenth century thousands of strong workers built great railroad lines that connected distant parts of America. This giant task produced the story of the railroad worker John Henry, just as the giant task of clearing the forests had produced the tale of Paul Bunyan. John Henry, however, is a hero who had to face an obstacle no American hero had ever faced before. He did not have to ride a cyclone as Pecos Bill did or chop down a cornstalk as Paul Bunyan did.

■ What is John Henry's opponent?

*Retold by
Adrien Stoutenburg*

Hammerman

1 People down South still tell stories about John Henry, how strong he was, and how he could whirl a big sledge[1] so lightning-fast you could hear thunder behind it. They even say he was born with a hammer in his hand. John Henry himself said it, but he probably didn't mean it exactly as it sounded.

2 The story seems to be that when John Henry was a baby, the first thing he reached out for was a hammer, which was hung nearby on the cabin wall.

John Henry's father put his arm around his wife's shoulder. "He's going to grow up to be a steel-driving man. I can see it plain as rows of cotton running uphill."

As John Henry grew a bit older, he practiced swinging the hammer, not hitting things, but just enjoying the feel of it whooshing against the air. When he was old enough

to talk, he told everyone, "I was born with a hammer in my hand."

John Henry was still a boy when the Civil War started, but he was a big, hard-muscled boy, and he could outwork and outplay all the other boys on the plantation.

"You're going to be a mighty man, John Henry," his father told him.

"A man ain't nothing but a man," young John Henry said. "And I'm a natural man, born to swing a hammer in my hand."

At night, lying on a straw bed on the floor, John Henry listened to a far-off train whistling through the darkness. . . .

3 John Henry thought to himself, there's a big hammer waiting for me somewhere, because I know I'm a steel-driving man. All I have to do is hunt till I find it.

That night he told his folks about a dream he had had.

"I dreamed I was working on a railroad somewhere," he said, "a big new railroad

---

1. **sledge:** heavy hammer with a long handle, usually held with both hands.

Hammerman 487

- John Henry reports his dream that he will die working for a railroad.
- John Henry asks for a job building a railroad.
- He claims he can drive a steel spike by himself.

1 PLOT: FORESHADOWING

As in many legends John Henry's dream foreshadows the outcome of the tale.

2 CHARACTERIZATION

In this passage the details *heart beat in rhythm with the falling hammers* and *fingers ached* reveal John Henry's passion about his work. The hammer seems a part of his "natural" body.

3 THEME

The folk tale emphasizes John Henry's striving to fulfill a vision, no matter what.

called the C.&O., and I had a mighty hammer in my hand. Every time I swung it, it made a whirling flash around my shoulder. And every time my hammer hit a spike,[2] the sky lit up from the sparks."

"I believe it," his father said. "You were born to drive steel."

1 "That ain't all of the dream," John Henry said. "I dreamed that the railroad was going to be the end of me, and I'd die with the hammer in my hand."

The next morning John Henry bundled up some food in a red bandanna handkerchief, told his parents good-by, and set off into the world. He walked until he heard the clang-

---

2. **spike:** large, heavy nail used for splitting rock.

488   *Greek Myths and American Folk Tales*

---

clang of hammers in the distance. He followed the sound to a place where gangs of men were building a railroad. John Henry watched the men driving steel spikes down into the crossties[3] to hold the rails in place. Three men would stand around a spike, then each, in turn, would swing a long hammer.

2 John Henry's heart beat in rhythm with the falling hammers. His fingers ached for the feel of a hammer in his own hands. He walked over to the foreman.

"I'm a natural steel-driving man," he said. "And I'm looking for a job."

"How much steel-driving have you done?" the foreman asked.

"I was born knowing how," John Henry said.

The foreman shook his head. "That ain't good enough. I can't take any chances. Steel-driving's dangerous work, and you might hit somebody."

"I wouldn't hit anybody," John Henry said, "because I can drive one of those spikes all by myself."

The foreman said sharply, "The one kind of man I don't need in this outfit is a bragger. Stop wasting my time."

3 John Henry didn't move. He got a stubborn look around his jaw. "You loan me a hammer, mister, and if somebody will hold a spike for me, I'll prove what I can do."

The three men who had just finished driving in a spike looked toward him and laughed. One of them said, "Anybody who would hold a spike for a greenhorn[4] don't want to live long."

"I'll hold it," a fourth man said.

John Henry saw that the speaker was a small, darkskinned fellow about his own age.

---

3. **crossties:** crosswise beams supporting the rails of a railroad track.
4. **greenhorn:** inexperienced person.

GUIDED READING

LITERAL QUESTIONS

1a. How does John Henry's dream end? (He dies with the hammer in his hand.)

2a. Why is the foreman reluctant to hire an inexperienced man? (He is afraid the man might hit somebody.)

INFERENTIAL QUESTIONS

1b. Do you think John Henry's dream will come true? Why? (Answers will vary. Possibilities: *Yes*, John Henry seems doomed; *no*, John Henry is too powerful.)

2b. Do you think John Henry will change the foreman's mind? (He probably will because John Henry has heroic power and determination.)

The foreman asked the small man, "D'you aim to get yourself killed, Li'l Willie?"

1 Li'l Willie didn't answer. He knelt and set a spike down through the rail on the crosstie. "Come on, big boy," he said.

John Henry picked up one of the sheep-nose hammers lying in the cinders. He hefted it and decided it was too light. He picked up a larger one, which weighed twelve pounds. The handle was lean and limber and greased with tallow[5] to make it smooth.

Everyone was quiet, watching, as he stepped over to the spike. John Henry swung the hammer over his shoulder so far that the hammerhead hung down against the backs of his knees. He felt a thrill run through his arms and chest.

"Tap it down gentle, first," said Li'l Willie.

2 But John Henry had already started to swing. He brought the hammer flashing down, banging the spike squarely on the head. Before the other men could draw a breath of surprise, the hammer flashed again, whirring through the air like a giant hummingbird. One more swing and the spike was down, its steel head smoking from the force of the blow.

The foreman blinked, swallowed, and blinked again. "Man," he told John Henry, "you're hired!"

That's the way John Henry started steel-driving. From then on, Li'l Willie was always with him, setting the spikes or placing the drills[6] that John Henry drove with his hammer. There wasn't another steel-driving man in the world who could touch John Henry for **3** speed and power. He could hammer every which way, up or down or sidewise. He could drive for ten hours at a stretch and never miss a stroke.

---

5. **tallow:** solid fat from cattle or sheep.
6. **drills:** pointed tools used for making holes in stone.

After he'd been at the work for a few years, he started using a twenty-pound hammer in each hand. It took six men, working fast, to carry fresh drills to him. People would come for miles around to watch John Henry.

Whenever John Henry worked, he sang. Li'l Willie sang with him, chanting the rhythm of the clanging hammer strokes.

4 Those were happy days for John Henry. One of the happiest days came when he met a black-eyed, curly-haired girl called Polly Ann. And on the day that Polly Ann said she would marry him, John Henry almost burst his throat with singing.

Every now and then, John Henry would remember the strange dream he had had years before, about the C.&O. Railroad and dying with a hammer in his hand. One night, he had the dream again. The next morning when he arrived at work, the steel gang gathered round him, hopping with excitement.

"The Chesapeake and Ohio Railroad wants men to drive a tunnel through a mountain in West Virginia!" they said.

"The C.&O. wants the best hammermen there are!" they said. "And they'll pay twice as much as anybody else."

Li'l Willie looked at John Henry. "If they want the best, John Henry, they're goin' to need you."

John Henry looked back at his friend. "They're going to need you, too, Li'l Willie. I ain't going without you." He stood a minute, **5** looking at the sky. There was a black thundercloud way off, with sunlight flashing behind it. John Henry felt a small chill between his shoulder blades. He shook himself, put his hammer over his shoulder, and said, "Let's go, Willie!"

When they reached Summers County where the Big Bend Tunnel was to be built, John Henry sized up the mountain standing in the way. It was almost solid rock.

Hammerman 489

AT A GLANCE

- John Henry proves himself and is hired, working in a team with Li'l Willie.
- John Henry marries Polly Ann.
- The C.&O. looks for the best hammermen to build a tunnel.

1 THEME

Li'l Willie believes in John Henry's ability to confront this challenge and succeed.

2 STYLE: SIMILE

The simile *like a giant humming-bird* conveys how quickly John Henry can raise and lower the hammer.

3 FOLK HERO

John Henry is larger than life and possesses powers that far surpass those of an ordinary human being.

4 CHARACTERIZATION

Almost burst his throat with singing indicates that John Henry has not only great physical power but also strong emotions.

5 PLOT: FORESHADOWING

The look of the sky makes John Henry recall the dream he had about dying.

GUIDED READING

LITERAL QUESTIONS

1a. When he proves himself to the foreman, how many blows does John Henry use to drive the spike? (three)

2a. What does the Chesapeake and Ohio Railroad want to do? (They want to drive a tunnel through a mountain in West Virginia.)

INFERENTIAL QUESTIONS

1b. Why are the men so impressed with John Henry's ability? (It usually requires a team of men working together to drive a spike.)

2b. Why does John Henry feel a chill between his shoulder blades when he decides to go? (The C.&O. Railroad was the railroad in the dream he had about his death.)

- Polly Ann goes with John Henry and Li'l Willie to West Virginia.
- A stranger tries to sell a steam drill to Cap'n Tommy, the tunnel boss.
- John Henry agrees to race against the steam drill.

1 FOLK TALE

John Henry's speed is exaggerated by this colorful image.

2 CHARACTERIZATION

John Henry believes a man is better than a machine and expresses his heroic willingness to confront to prove his point.

3 THEME

John Henry describes his greatest strength, his heart, and states a major theme of the tale: People, with their minds and hearts, are superior to machines.

4 INTERPRETATION

John Henry's statements *I feel like a bird ready to burst out of a nest egg* and *I feel powerful free* suggest that he is about to meet his destiny. At last he has met a challenge that will "free" every bit of strength he has.

"Looks soft," said John Henry. "Hold a drill up there, Li'l Willie."

Li'l Willie did. John Henry took a seventy-pound hammer and drove the drill in with one mountain-cracking stroke. Then he settled down to working the regular way, pounding in the drills with four or five strokes of a twenty-pound sledge. He worked so fast that his helpers had to keep buckets of water ready to pour on his hammers so they wouldn't catch fire.

Polly Ann, who had decided to come along to West Virginia, sat and watched and cheered him on. She sang along with him, clapping her hands to the rhythm of his hammer, and the sound echoed around the mountains. The songs blended with the rumble of dynamite where the blasting crews were at work. For every time John Henry drilled a hole in the mountain's face, other men poked dynamite and black powder into the hole and then lighted a fuse to blow the rock apart.

One day the tunnel boss, Cap'n Tommy Walters, was standing watching John Henry when a stranger in city clothes walked up to him.

"Howdy, Cap'n Tommy," said the stranger. "I'd like to talk to you about a steam engine[7] I've got for sale. My engine can drive a drill through rock so fast that not even a crew of your best men can keep up with it."

"I don't need any machine," Cap'n Tommy said proudly. "My man John Henry can outdrill any machine ever built."

"I'll place a bet with you, Cap'n," said the salesman. "You race your man against my machine for a full day. If he wins, I'll give you the steam engine free."

Cap'n Tommy thought it over. "That sounds fair enough, but I'll have to talk to

---

7. **steam engine:** here, a machine that uses steam power to drive a drill.

490   *Greek Myths and American Folk Tales*

John Henry first." He told John Henry what the stranger said. "Are you willing to race a steam drill?" Cap'n Tommy asked.

John Henry ran his big hands over the handle of his hammer, feeling the strength in the wood and in his own great muscles.

"A man's a man," he said, "but a machine ain't nothing but a machine. I'll beat that steam drill, or I'll die with my hammer in my hand!"

"All right, then," Cap'n Tommy said. "We'll set a day for the contest."

Polly Ann looked worried when John Henry told her what he had promised to do.

"Don't you worry, honey," John Henry said. It was the end of the workday, with the sunset burning across the mountain, and the sky shining like copper. He tapped his chest. "I've got a man's heart in here. All a machine has is a metal engine." He smiled and picked Polly Ann up in his arms, as if she were no heavier than a blade of grass.

On the morning of the contest, the slopes around the tunnel were crowded with people. At one side stood the steam engine, its gears and valves and mechanical drill gleaming. Its operators rushed around, giving it final spurts of grease and oil and shoving fresh pine knots into the fire that fed the steam boiler.

John Henry stood leaning on his hammer, as still as the mountain rock, his shoulders shining in the rising sun.

"How do you feel, John Henry?" asked Li'l Willie. Li'l Willie's hands trembled a bit as he held the drill ready.

"I feel like a bird ready to bust out of a nest egg," John Henry said. "I feel like a rooster ready to crow. I feel pride hammering at my heart, and I can hardly wait to get started against that machine." He sucked in the mountain air. "I feel powerful free, Li'l Willie."

Cap'n Tommy held up the starting gun.

GUIDED READING

LITERAL QUESTIONS

1a. What does the stranger want to sell to Cap'n Tommy? (He wants to sell him a steam drill.)

2a. Why does John Henry believe that he would beat the machine? (He says a machine with a metal engine is no match for a man with a heart.)

INFERENTIAL QUESTIONS

1b. Why does the stranger suggest a contest between the hammerman and his engine? (He is confident that no man can beat his machine.)

2b. Why would having a heart make a man superior to a machine in a contest like this? (A man's desire to win can drive him beyond his normal capabilities while a machine can never be more than the sum of its mechanical parts.)

For a second everything was as silent as the dust in a drill hole. Then the gun barked, making a yelp that bounced against mountain and sky.

John Henry swung his hammer, and it rang against the drill. At the same time, the steam engine gave a roar and a hiss. Steam whistled through its escape valve. Its drill crashed down, gnawing into the granite.

John Henry paid no attention to anything except his hammer, not to any sound except the steady pumping of his heart. At the end of an hour, he paused long enough to ask, "How are we doing, Li'l Willie?"

1 Willie licked his lips. His face was pale with rock dust and with fear. "The machine's ahead, John Henry."

John Henry tossed his smoking hammer aside and called to another helper, "Bring me two hammers! I'm only getting warmed up."

2 He began swinging a hammer in each hand. Sparks flew so fast and hot they singed his face. The hammers heated up until they glowed like torches.

"How're we doing now, Li'l Willie?" John Henry asked at the end of another hour.

Li'l Willie grinned. "The machine's drill busted. They have to take time to fix up a new one. You're almost even now, John Henry! How're you feeling?"

"I'm feeling like sunrise," John Henry took time to say before he flashed one of his hammers down against the drill. "Clean out the hole, Willie, and we'll drive right down to China."

Above the clash of his hammers, he heard the chug and hiss of the steam engine starting up again and the whine of its rotary drill biting into rock. The sound hurt John Henry's ears.

"Sing me a song, Li'l Willie!" he gasped. "Sing me a natural song for my hammers to sing along with."

Hammerman 491

GUIDED READING

LITERAL QUESTIONS

1a. What does John Henry say when the machine is ahead in the early part of the race? ("Bring me two hammers! I'm only getting warmed up.")

2a. What kind of song does John Henry ask Li'l Willie to sing? ("a natural song for my hammers to sing along with")

INFERENTIAL QUESTIONS

1b. How does John Henry feel at this point? (He feels fresh and confident.)

2b. Why do you think he asks for this kind of song? (He wants to hear something other than the sound of the machine, which hurts his ears and throws off his concentration. Also, the rhythm of Willie's song will help John Henry drive himself harder.)

AT A GLANCE

- Cap'n Tommy signals the end of the contest.
- John Henry beats the steam engine by four feet.
- John Henry dies.

1 FORESHADOWING

The setting sun foreshadows John Henry's death.

2 THEME

With the challenge of the steam drill successfully confronted, John Henry dies a hero's death. His final words show he feels no regret, only satisfaction at having fulfilled his destiny.

REFLECTING ON THE SELECTION

Was John Henry really superior to the steam drill? (Possibilities: yes, because he won the contest with power and determination; no, because although he won the contest, he died.)

Li'l Willie sang, and John Henry kept his hammers going in time. Hour after hour, he kept driving, sweat sliding from his forehead and chest.

The sun rolled past noon.

"How're you feeling, John Henry?" Li'l Willie asked.

"I ain't tired yet," said John Henry and stood back, gasping, while Willie put a freshly sharpened drill into the rock wall. "Only, I have a kind of roaring in my ears."

"That's only the steam engine," Li'l Willie said, but he wet his lips again. "You're gaining on it, John Henry, if you can keep on drivin'!"

John Henry ground his teeth together and tried not to hear the roar in his ears or the racing thunder of his heart. "I'll go until I drop," he gasped. "I'm a steel-driving man and I'm bound to win, because a machine ain't nothing but a machine."

The sun slid lower. The shadows of the crowd grew long and purple.

"John Henry can't keep it up," someone said.

"The machine can't keep it up," another said.

Polly Ann twisted her hands together and waited for Cap'n Tommy to fire the gun to mark the end of the contest.

"Who's winning?" a voice cried.

"Wait and see," another voice answered.

There were only ten minutes left.

"How're you feeling, John Henry?" Li'l Willie whispered, sweat dripping down his own face.

John Henry didn't answer. He just kept slamming his hammers against the drill, his mouth open.

Li'l Willie tried to go on singing. "Flash that hammer—uh! Wham that drill—uh!" he croaked.

Out beside the railroad tracks, Polly beat her hands together in time until they were numb.

1 The sun flashed an instant, then died behind the mountain. Cap'n Tommy's gun cracked. The judges ran forward to measure the depth of the holes drilled by the steam engine and by John Henry. At last the judges came walking back and said something to Cap'n Tommy before they turned to announce their findings to the crowd.

Cap'n Tommy walked over to John Henry, who stood leaning against the face of the mountain.

"John Henry," he said, "you beat that steam engine by four feet!" He held out his hand and smiled.

John Henry heard a distant cheering. He held his own hand out, and then he staggered. He fell and lay on his back, staring up at the mountain and the sky, and then he saw Polly Ann and Li'l Willie leaning over him.

"Oh, how do you feel, John Henry?" Polly Ann asked.

"I feel a bit tuckered out," said John Henry.

"Do you want me to sing to you?" Li'l Willie asked.

2 "I got a song in my own heart, thank you, Li'l Willie," John Henry said. He raised up on his elbow and looked at all the people and the last sunset light gleaming like the edge of a golden trumpet. "I was a steel-driving man," he said, and lay back and closed his eyes forever.

Down South, and in the North, too, people still talk about John Henry and how he beat the steam engine at the Big Bend Tunnel. They said if John Henry were alive today he could beat almost every other kind of machine, too.

Maybe so. At least John Henry would die trying.

492 *Greek Myths and American Folk Tales*

GUIDED READING

LITERAL QUESTIONS

1a. Who wins the contest? (John Henry beat the machine by four feet.)

2a. How do people still talk about John Henry? (They still talk about how he beat the steam drill at the Big Bend Tunnel and how he could beat any machine today.)

INFERENTIAL QUESTIONS

1b. In what way can it be said that the machine wins the contest? (The machine survived the effort, but John Henry died.)

2b. Why is John Henry a hero? (He is a hero because he had the heart to challenge the steam engine and the strength to beat it by four feet.)

STUDY QUESTIONS

Recalling

1. According to the tale, how does John Henry's father know that his son will be "a steel-driving man"?
2. What does John Henry dream?
3. What does John Henry do to get his first job?
4. Why do John Henry and Li'l Willie go off to work for the C.&O. Railroad?
5. Who wins the race? What happens to John Henry after the race?

Interpreting

6. Describe the character of John Henry in your own words. What does his pursuit of his dream tell about his character?
7. What do you think John Henry means when he says, "A man's a man, but a machine ain't nothing but a machine"?

Extending

8. What do you think are the qualities required of a modern hero?

VOCABULARY

Compound Words

A **compound word** is a word made up of two or more words joined together. Some compounds are written as one word (*railroad*), some with a hyphen (*steel-driving*), and some as two words (*steam drill*).

Match each numbered word in the left column with a lettered word from the right column to form a compound. Write the correct compounds. Each compound appears in "Hammerman."

1. thunder	a. light
2. steam	b. where
3. sun	c. cloud
4. near	d. engine
5. some	e. bird
6. humming	f. by

COMPOSITION

Writing About a Description

■ Write about the detailed description of John Henry at work, telling which details you think are most vivid. First comment on the description of how John Henry prepares to use the hammer. Then talk about the description of how he swings the hammer and how he hits the spike. Finally, give your overall opinion of the effectiveness of the description.

Writing a Description

■ Write a description of a person or a machine at work. For example, you may describe a person running or a crane lifting a heavy weight. First identify the work to be performed. Then outline each detail of the process from beginning to end. Conclude by describing the end result.

CHALLENGE

Further Reading

■ Use your library to find a collection of American folk tales. Read one folk tale about a hero from your area of the country and one tale about a hero from another area of the country.

COMPARING FOLK TALES

1. Compare the heroes of two or more of the following American folk tales: "The Amazing Crockett Family," "Paul Bunyan," and "Pecos Bill, Coyote Cowboy." Tell how the heroes are like and unlike one another.
2. Compare the lessons that seem to be taught by two or more of the following American folk tales: "Pecos Bill, Coyote Cowboy," "Strong Wind, the Invisible," and "Hammerman." First tell what events are similar in each plot. Then identify the lessons that the folk tales seem to teach. Next tell how the lessons are like and unlike one another.

Hammerman 493

Active Reading

Greek Myths and American Folk Tales

Identifying Causes and Effects

The Greeks, like many ancient peoples, invented myths in order to explain the world around them. The Greeks invented the chariot of the sun god, for example, to explain why the sun traveled across the sky every day. Myths are works of imaginative literature. Many of them, however, are based on the desire to identify causes and effects.

A *cause* is a reason something happens. An *effect* is a result, or what happens. Read this passage from "Phaethon."

> For a few ecstatic moments Phaethon felt himself the lord of the sky. But suddenly there was a change. The chariot was swinging wildly to and fro; the pace was faster; he had lost control. Not he, but the horses were directing the course. That light weight in the car, those feeble hands clutching the reins, had told them their own driver was not there. They were the masters then.

This passage describes an effect and its cause. The effect, or result, is the wild swinging and fast pace of the chariot. The cause is Phaethon's light weight and feeble hands on the reins.

The swinging, however, is not the end of the story. The effect of one cause can be the cause of another effect. As Phaethon continues his ride, the wild swinging of the chariot causes even more terror in the boy and makes him drop the reins. In other words, the swinging of the chariot then becomes a *cause.* It creates another *effect*—dropping the reins. This is the way the action of most narratives moves forward: Each effect causes something further to happen. One event leads to another.

As the story continues, Phaethon's dropping the reins then creates an effect on the horses:

> That was the signal for still more mad and reckless running.

In this sentence, the words *that was the signal* clearly indicate a cause and an effect. As you read, be on the lookout for other words and phrases that indicate causes and effects, including *because, so that, therefore, since, in order that, for this reason,* and *as a result.* By recognizing causes and effects as you read, you can follow the action of a story more easily and better appreciate the flow of events.

Activity 1 Read each of the following passages from "Phaethon." Answer the question that follows each passage.

1. No doubt Phaethon had often watched the Sun riding through the heavens and had told himself with a feeling, half awe, half excitement, "It is my father up there." And then he would wonder what it would be like to be in that chariot, guiding the steeds along that dizzy course, giving light to the world. *According to the myth, what was the cause of the world's sunlight?*

2. At last the Sun gave up trying to dissuade him [Phaethon]. It was hopeless, as he saw. Besides, there was no time. The moment for starting was at hand. *What two things caused the Sun to give up trying to dissuade Phaethon?*

3. Zeus seized his thunderbolt and hurled it at the rash, repentant driver [Phaethon]. It struck him dead, shattered the chariot, and made the maddened horses rush down into the sea. *What was the cause of Phaethon's death?*

Understanding Character Motivation

Characters in literature, just like people in real life, do things for particular reasons, or motivations. *Motivation* is a feeling or goal that causes a character to act. We can consider character motivations and actions as a specific kind of cause and effect. For example, Theseus eagerly awaited the opportunity to travel to Athens. What caused him to make that trip? What was his motivation? It was his strong desire to meet his father.

Sometimes a character's motivation is stated directly, and you do not have to infer it. To infer something is to reach a conclusion about it from other facts or details that are known. When the cause for a particular action is not stated directly, you must infer the motivation. For example, when Theseus first thinks he has moved the great stone, Aethra exclaims, "No, no! It is not possible you can have moved it." You can infer that Aethra does not want her son to set off on his dangerous journey. She knows that he is not yet strong enough. What is the cause of her outcry? What is her motivation? It is her love for her son.

In order to appreciate fully the characters you meet in literature, it is important to understand why they act as they do. When you understand a character's motivations, you feel more deeply involved in what happens to the character.

Myths and Folk Tales 495

Activity 1
1. the journey of the sun across the sky, pulled by the chariot and horses of the sun god
2. Phaethon's stubbornness and the fact that time had run out
3. Zeus's thunderbolt

1. The motivation must be inferred. The king wants Theseus to travel by sea because the land journey is too dangerous.
2. The motivation is stated directly. The father of Theseus had grown aged because of the cares of government.
3. The motivation is stated directly. The cousins became Theseus' enemies because they wanted power over the kingdom.
4. The motivation is stated directly. Medea became an enemy because she wanted to give the kingdom to Medus.
5. The motivation must be inferred. Ariadne begged for the life of Theseus because she admired his bravery and bearing.

Activity 2 Read each of the following passages from "Theseus." Answer the question about motivation that follows each passage. Tell whether the motivation is stated directly or if you must infer it. If you infer it, tell what details in the passage help you identify the motive.

1. "The roads are very bad by land," said the venerable king, "and they are infested with robbers and monsters. Let him [Theseus] go by sea!"
   Why did the king want Theseus to travel by sea?

2. The father of Theseus was almost worn out with the cares of government and had thus grown aged before his time.
   Why had the father of Theseus grown aged before his time?

3. His [Aegeus'] nephews intended to get all the power of the kingdom into their own hands. Thus these nephews of King Aegeus, who were the cousins of Theseus, became his enemies.
   Why did the cousins of Theseus become his enemies?

4. A still more dangerous enemy was Medea, the wicked enchantress, for she wanted to give the kingdom to her son Medus.
   Why did Medea become a dangerous enemy of Theseus?

5. And when she [Ariadne] beheld the brave, spirited figure of Theseus bearing himself so calmly in his terrible peril, she flung herself at the king's feet and begged him to set all the captives free, especially this one young man.
   Why did Ariadne beg for the life of Theseus?

Evaluating Characters in Myths and Folk Tales

Characters in stories, myths, and folk tales all grow out of the human imagination. Some characters, however, are more realistic than others. Realistic characters, like those in most modern short stories, are believable and lifelike characters who say and do ordinary things in the everyday world. Most characters in myths and folk tales, however, are larger-than-life characters who meet with unbelievable adventures and have superhuman powers.

Do the amazing Crocketts, for example, seem like a real American family? Not at all. Can anyone actually change a hailstorm into sunshine simply by the power of his grin? Davy Crockett's father could perform that great feat, but Mr. Crockett is not a realistic character. No matter how hard you might try, you would never find a person able to do what Mr. Crockett could do.

Realistic characters live their lives with the qualities and abilities that people really possess. You admire them for their good qualities, such as intelligence, courage, and patience. You sympathize with them because they face the problems and challenges that people really face, such as fear and uncertainty.

On the other hand, superhuman characters offer wonders that realistic characters do not. They may have some realistic qualities, but they can also fly through the air, slay monsters, lift huge boulders, and even defeat death itself. You admire them not because they are like everyone else but because they are like no one else in the world. They are fantastic, and they are one of literature's greatest delights.

Activity 3 Read each of the following passages. Tell whether the character described in each passage is realistic or imaginary. Give reasons for your answers.

1. Steven trudged home through the deep snow, bravely fighting the fierce storm.

2. Laura arrived at the edge of the earth and found the tree on which grew apples made of gold.

3. They were face to face with the chimera, a creature with the head of a lion, the body of a goat, and the tail of a serpent.

4. As the crowd roared, Jason picked up the golden trophy and held it high over his head.

5. As the crowd roared, Jason mounted his flying horse and rode off into the sunset.

Activity 3
1. realistic; a true-to-life scene
2. imaginary; the earth's edge and golden apples
3. imaginary; a fabulous beast
4. realistic; a true-to-life scene
5. imaginary; a flying horse

The Literary Skills Review for the unit on Greek Myths and American Folk Tales serves as a summary of the literary skills taught in the unit. You may also encourage students to try to answer the questions in the Guide for Reading Myths and Folk Tales when they read any myth or folk tale. These questions appear with write-on lines, in blackline master form, among the materials for this unit in your *Teacher's Resource Book.*

Literary Skills Review

Greek Myths and American Folk Tales

Guide for Reading Myths and Folk Tales

As you read myths and folk tales, use this guide to help you understand and appreciate the way these tellers related their tales.

Greek Myths

1. What event or belief did the **myth** explain as it was passed down through **oral tradition**?
2. Which **gods** and **goddesses** appear in the myth? What are their roles and responsibilities?
3. What ideals does the mythological **hero** represent?
4. Which **character traits** do the main characters show? What changes do the characters undergo?
5. What **conflict** takes place in the myth? Which events in the myth are **foreshadowed**?
6. What **allusions** can be explained by the myth?
7. What is the **theme,** or main idea, of the myth?

American Folk Tales

1. What values and characteristics of the American people does the **folk tale** reveal?
2. What examples of **humor** and **exaggeration** can you find in the **tall tale**?
3. What are the qualities of the **hero** of the American folk tale? What **conflict** or ordeal does the hero face? What qualities enable the hero to triumph?
4. What is the **theme,** or main idea, of the folk tale?

Themes Review

Greek Myths and American Folk Tales

Throughout literature, certain general themes occur over and over again. The theme "heroism," for example, appears in many myths and folk tales. However, each myth or tale that explores this general theme says something very specific about it. For example, "Orpheus and Eurydice" (page 459) expresses this specific view of heroism: "A hero may follow a vision of true love through the greatest dangers." "Hammerman" (page 487) expresses a different view of heroism: "Strong determination may lead a hero to great accomplishments."

1. Choose two selections below, and tell what each says about the general theme "heroism."
   Myths: "Theseus"   "Daedalus and Icarus"
   Folk Tales: "Strong Wind"   "Paul Bunyan's Cornstalk"

2. Choose two selections below, and tell what each says about the general theme "ideals and visions."
   Myths: "Phaethon"   "Theseus"
   Folk Tales: "Hammerman"   "Strong Wind"

3. Choose one myth or folk tale and one other work from the following list, and tell what each says about the general theme "friendship and love."
   Myths: "Alcestis"   "Orpheus and Eurydice"
   Folk Tales: "Pecos Bill . . ."   "Hammerman"
   Stories: "Christmas Day in the Morning"   "Then He Goes Free"
   Drama: *The Romancers*   *Anne Frank*

4. Choose one folk tale and one other work from the following list, and tell what each says about the theme "American experiences."
   Folk Tales: "Hammerman"   "Pecos Bill . . ."
   "Paul Bunyan's Cornstalk"   "The Amazing Crockett Family"
   Stories: "The Man Without a Country"   "Jim Baker's Blue-jay Yarn"
   Poems: "Paul Revere's Ride"   "O Captain! My Captain!"
   Nonfiction: "Harriet Tubman"   The Gettysburg Address

1. "Theseus": The hero's courage and perseverance enable him to overcome monsters, rescue the innocent, and regain his rightful kingdom. "Daedalus and Icarus": The hero without prudence fails and is destroyed. "Strong Wind": The hero needs to be truthful in order to succeed. "Bunyan": The hero is larger than life and accomplishes the extraordinary.
2. "Phaethon": A vision of oneself as mature and powerful must be tempered with prudence. "Theseus": Courage and perseverance can make a vision of peace and harmony come true. "Hammerman": A hero must follow a personal vision, wherever it leads. "Strong Wind": Truthfulness makes an ideal a reality.
3. "Alcestis": Love makes great sacrifices possible. "Orpheus": Love makes great victories possible. "Pecos Bill": Perfectly matched people may fall in love at first sight. "Hammerman": Love and friendship are the strongest of bonds. "Christmas Day": Only love can awaken love. "Then He Goes Free": Friendship may demand great sacrifices.
4. "Hammerman": Building railroads united the American continent. "Pecos Bill," "Bunyan," and "Crockett": The settling of our continent required extraordinary people and deeds. "The Man Without a Country": America should not be taken for granted. "Baker": American humor is found in yarns and folk tales. "Revere": The American Revolution was won by heroic individuals. "O Captain!": America lamented the loss of a great leader. "Tubman": Many Americans had to struggle for freedom. "Gettysburg": We must not forget the price paid for peace and freedom.

For more information abut the themes portrayed in these selections, see the Theme Index beginning on page 666.

Preview
The Novel

A **novel** is a long work of narrative fiction written in prose. A novel, like a short story, is not a real-life account but the product of an author's imagination. The novel's greater length, however, allows the author to develop a larger vision of the world and to involve us more deeply in it.

A novel contains the same elements as a short story: plot, character, setting, point of view, and theme. Unlike a short story, however, a novel often presents a variety of settings and themes as well as more fully developed characters. Also, a novel usually has at least one subplot in addition to the main plot. A **subplot** is a less important plot that is related to the main action of the novel.

Novels reflect the societies in which they are written. In many ways they are records of the world's changing ideas and customs. Through novels we can learn about life at a particular time and place. In *The Hound of the Baskervilles*, for example, Sir Arthur Conan Doyle describes English country life of the late 1800s during the course of presenting another adventure of his famous detective Sherlock Holmes. Novels can help us to understand ourselves and our present world, too. *The Hound of the Baskervilles* has meaning for us today. We may not be confronted by monstrous hounds, but each of us must face important challenges. Conan Doyle's detective shows us how to do so by careful observation and reasoning.

The Novel 501

THE HOUND OF THE BASKERVILLES

Sir Arthur Conan Doyle (1859–1930) is remembered today mainly as the creator of the famous detective character, Sherlock Holmes, who has been called "the most famous man who never lived." Like Dr. Watson, the narrator of *The Hound of the Baskervilles,* Conan Doyle was a medical doctor. When his practice failed to provide him with sufficient income, he turned to writing detective stories. Sherlock Holmes, whom he modeled after one of his medical professors, brought Conan Doyle both fortune and fame. Between 1887 and 1927 Conan Doyle wrote fifty-six short stories and four novels about the adventures of his brilliant detective.

Because readers have always found the character appealing, many other authors have written tales about Holmes. His popularity is evident in films, too. According to *The Encyclopedia of Mystery and Detection,* over a hundred films have been made about Holmes, the first in 1903. The character is so real to some people that every year the London post office receives large numbers of letters addressed to Holmes at 221B Baker Street, the detective's fictional address.

Most critics agree that *The Hound of the Baskervilles* (1902) is Conan Coyle's masterpiece. It contains all the ingredients that readers have come to expect in detective fiction: a baffling crime, suspects, clues, suspenseful action, surprising twists, and a logical solution to the mystery. What helps make *The Hound of the Baskervilles* memorable, however, is Conan Doyle's talent as a novelist. The plot centers on a legendary hound that preys on the Baskerville family. The events of the novel pit reason against superstition and good against evil. Conan Doyle's characters—such as Holmes, Dr. Watson, and Sir Henry Baskerville—are people whom we want to know. The novel's settings are realistic but mysterious and dangerous as well.

Key Ideas in *The Hound of the Baskervilles*

As you read *The Hound of the Baskervilles,* think about the following topics. Keep track of what the novel says about each one. You will then be able to determine the major themes of *The Hound of the Baskervilles.*

- Observation and deduction
- Ambition and greed
- Friendship and loyalty
- Common sense and superstition

502   *The Novel*

As the novel begins, Holmes and his friend Dr. Watson try to determine a visitor's identity from a walking stick that the visitor has left behind. Notice in these first chapters the methods Holmes uses to solve problems.

■ *What qualities make him the world's greatest detective?*

Sir Arthur Conan Doyle

The Hound of the Baskervilles (abridged)

1 Mr. Sherlock Holmes

Mr. Sherlock Holmes, who was usually very late in the mornings, save upon those not infrequent occasions when he was up all night, was seated at the breakfast table. I stood upon the hearth rug[1] and picked up the stick[2] which our visitor had left behind him the night before. It was a fine, thick piece of wood, bulbous-headed, of the sort which is known as a "Penang lawyer." Just under the head was a broad silver band, nearly an inch across. "To James Mortimer, M.R.C.S.,[3] from his friends of the C.C.H." was engraved upon it, with the date "1884." It was just such a stick as the old-fashioned family practitioner used to carry—dignified, solid, and reassuring.

"Well, Watson, what do you make of it?"

Holmes was sitting with his back to me.

"How did you know what I was doing? I believe you have eyes in the back of your head."

"I have, at least, a well-polished, silver-plated coffeepot in front of me," said he. "But, tell me, Watson, what do you make of our visitor's stick? Since we have been so unfortunate as to miss him and have no notion of his errand, this accidental souvenir becomes of importance. Let me hear you reconstruct the man by an examination of it."

"I think," said I, following as far as I could the methods of my companion, "that Dr. Mortimer is a successful elderly medical man, well esteemed, since those who know him give him this mark of their appreciation."

"Good!" said Holmes. "Excellent!"

"I think also that the probability is in favor

---

1. **hearth rug:** rug in front of a fireplace.
2. **stick:** walking stick, or cane.
3. **M.R.C.S.:** Member of the Royal College of Surgeons.

The Hound of the Baskervilles 503

- Watson suggests Dr. Mortimer is an elderly and established country physician.
- Holmes points out fallacies in Watson's deductions, concluding Mortimer is young and unambitious.

1 CHARACTERIZATION

Holmes's frank comparison of himself and Watson is typical of their relationship. Holmes, the genius, is the leader; the good-natured Watson, in awe of Holmes's brainpower, follows and does not seem to mind such comparisons.

2 THEME

Holmes urges Watson to apply Holmes's successful methods: close observation of the known followed by careful reasoning about what the known suggests.

3 BACKGROUND

Holmes's extensive knowledge of the medical profession reflects Doyle's own experience as a doctor. The author based the character Holmes on Dr. Joseph Bell, a professor of medicine at Edinburgh University.

of his being a country practitioner who does a great deal of his visiting on foot."

"Why so?"

"Because this stick, though originally a very handsome one, has been so knocked about that I can hardly imagine a town practitioner carrying it. The thick iron ferrule is worn down, so it is evident that he has done a great amount of walking with it."

"Perfectly sound!" said Holmes.

"And then again, there is the 'friends of the C.C.H.' I should guess that to be the Something Hunt, the local hunt,[4] which has made him a small presentation."

"Really, Watson, you excel yourself," said Holmes, pushing back his chair. "Some people without possessing genius have a remarkable power of stimulating it. I confess that I am very much in your debt."

He now took the stick from my hands and examined it for a few minutes. Carrying the cane to the window, he looked over it again with a convex lens.

"Interesting, though elementary," said he, as he returned to his favorite corner of the settee. "There are certainly one or two indications upon the stick. It gives us the basis for several deductions."

"Has anything escaped me?" I asked with some self-importance.

1 "I am afraid, my dear Watson, that most of your conclusions were erroneous. When I said that you stimulated me I meant, to be frank, that in noting your fallacies I was occasionally guided toward the truth. Not that you are entirely wrong in this instance. The man is certainly a country practitioner. And he walks a good deal."

"Then I was right."

"To that extent."

"But that was all."

"No, no, my dear Watson, not all—by no

means all. I would suggest, for example, that a presentation to a doctor is more likely to come from a hospital than from a hunt, and that when the initials 'C.C.' are placed before that hospital the words 'Charing Cross'[5] very naturally suggest themselves."

2 "You may be right. Well, then, supposing that 'C.C.H.' does stand for 'Charing Cross Hospital,' what further inferences may we draw?"

"Do none suggest themselves? You know my methods. Apply them!"

"I can only think of the obvious conclusion that the man has practiced in town before going to the country."

"I think that we might venture a little farther than this. Look at it in this light. On what occasion would it be most probable that such a presentation would be made? Obviously at the moment when Dr. Mortimer withdrew from the service of the hospital in order to start in practice for himself. We know there has been a presentation. We believe there has been a change from a town hospital to a country practice. Is it, then, stretching our inference too far to say that the presentation was on the occasion of the change?"

"It certainly seems probable."

3 "Now, you will observe that he could not have been on the *staff* of the hospital, since only a man well established in a London practice could hold such a position, and such a one would not drift into the country. What was he, then? If he was in the hospital and yet not on the staff he could only have been a house surgeon or a house physician—little more than a senior student. And he left five years ago—the date is on the stick. So your grave, middle-aged family practitioner vanishes into thin air, my dear Watson, and there emerges a young fellow under thirty, amiable, unambitious, absent-minded, and the posses-

---

4. **local hunt:** neighborhood group of fox hunters.

504   *The Novel*

---

5. **Charing Cross:** busy area of central London.

GUIDED READING

LITERAL QUESTION

1a. How does Sherlock Holmes describe Watson's effect on him? (He says that Watson, although not possessing genius himself, stimulates Holmes's own genius through his fallacious reasoning.)

INFERENTIAL QUESTION

1b. What does Holmes's description of Watson reveal about Holmes himself? (He is proud, perhaps arrogant, about his intellect; he is comfortable enough with Dr. Watson to speak frankly.)

sor of a favorite dog, which I should describe roughly as being larger than a terrier and smaller than a mastiff."

I laughed incredulously as Sherlock Holmes leaned back in his settee.

"As to the latter part, I have no means of checking you," said I, "but at least it is not difficult to find out a few particulars about the man's age and professional career." From my small medical shelf I took down the Medical Directory and turned up the name. There were several Mortimers, but only one who could be our visitor. I read his record aloud.

"Mortimer, James, M.R.C.S., 1882, Grimpen, Dartmoor, Devon.[6] House surgeon, from 1882 to 1884, at Charing Cross Hospital. Winner of the Jackson prize for Comparative Pathology,[7] with essay entitled 'Is Disease a Reversion?' Medical Officer for the parishes of Grimpen, Thorsley, and High Barrow."

"No mention of that local hunt, Watson," said Holmes with a mischievous smile, "but a country doctor, as you very astutely observed. I think that I am fairly justified in my inferences. As to the adjectives, I said, if I remember right, amiable, unambitious, and absentminded. It is my experience that it is only an amiable man in this world who receives testimonials, only an unambitious one who abandons a London career for the country, and only an absent-minded one who leaves his stick and not his visiting card after waiting an hour in your room."

1 "And the dog?"

"Has been in the habit of carrying this stick behind his master. Being a heavy stick the dog has held it tightly by the middle, and

---

6. **Grimpen, Dartmoor, Devon:** Grimpen is a town in the district of Dartmoor, in the county of Devon, located in southwest England.
7. **Comparative Pathology:** area of medicine that compares and examines the nature, causes, and symptoms of disease.

---

the marks of his teeth are very plainly visible. **2** The dog's jaw, as shown in the space between these marks, is too broad in my opinion for a terrier and not broad enough for a mastiff. It may have been—yes, by Jove, it *is* a curly-haired spaniel."

He had risen and paced the room as he spoke. Now he halted in the recess of the window. There was such a ring of conviction in his voice that I glanced up in surprise.

"My dear fellow, how can you possibly be so sure of that?"

"For the very simple reason that I see the dog himself on our very doorstep, and there is the ring of its owner. Don't move, I beg you, Watson. He is a professional brother of yours, and your presence may be of assistance to me. **3** Now is the dramatic moment of fate, Watson, when you hear a step upon the stair which is walking into your life, and you know not whether for good or ill. What does Dr. James Mortimer, the man of science, ask of Sherlock Holmes, the specialist in crime? Come in!"

The appearance of our visitor was a surprise to me, since I had expected a typical country practitioner. **4** He was a very tall, thin man, with a long nose like a beak, which jutted out between two keen, gray eyes, set closely together and sparkling brightly from behind a pair of gold-rimmed glasses. He was clad in a professional but rather slovenly fashion, for his frock coat was dingy and his trousers frayed. Though young, his long back was already bowed, and he walked with a forward thrust of his head. As he entered his eyes fell upon the stick in Holmes's hand, and he ran toward it with an exclamation of joy. "I am so very glad," said he. "I was not sure whether I had left it here or in the Shipping Office.[8] I would not lose that stick for the world."

"A presentation, I see," said Holmes.

---

8. **Shipping Office:** office that packs and ships out goods.

The Hound of the Baskervilles 505

AT A GLANCE

- Watson checks Mortimer's biography in a medical directory, verifying Holmes's deductions.
- Dr. Mortimer arrives.

1 STYLE: DIALOGUE

Watson's subordinate role to Holmes is made evident here. Watson's role in the conversation is largely limited to asking questions or stating his agreement.

2 CHARACTERIZATION

One of Holmes's memorable traits is his encyclopedic mind. He possesses an endless store of detailed information on such obscure topics as the relative width of the jaws of various breeds of dogs.

3 PLOT: EXPOSITION

The author has the luxury of spending several pages to introduce his two main characters and describe their special methods of detection. Now, with the arrival of Dr. Mortimer, the events of the story begin in earnest.

4 STYLE: DETAILS

Through the use of details, Mortimer is portrayed as a birdlike creature, careless about his appearance, unsuccessful at his profession, and seemingly aged prematurely.

GUIDED READING

LITERAL QUESTION

1a. What does the narrator, Watson, tell us about Dr. Mortimer's appearance? (He is tall and thin and has a long nose and keen gray eyes set close together. His clothes are slovenly, and he seems prematurely aged.)

INFERENTIAL QUESTION

1b. Do you think Watson is a good observer of human beings? (He may not be the genius that Holmes is, but he appears to be quite perceptive nonetheless.)

- Mortimer enters and reclaims his stick.
- He relocated to the country after his marriage.
- The doctor requires Holmes's services for an extraordinary problem.

1 STYLE: HUMOR

Holmes's one-track mind, still intent on testing his deductions, leads him to comment humorously "That's bad" upon hearing that Mortimer received the gift for his marriage rather than as a going-away present.

2 CHARACTERIZATION

Holmes is proud and conscious of his reputation. His use of the word *asperity* shows that Holmes responds severely to the suggestion that there is a greater expert than him.

3 STYLE: REALISM

Holmes is ranked with Bertillon, an actual nineteenth-century French criminologist. This detail furthers the illusion that Holmes is a real person.

"Yes, sir."

"From Charing Cross Hospital?"

1 "From one or two friends there on the occasion of my marriage."

"Dear, dear, that's bad!" said Holmes, shaking his head.

Dr. Mortimer blinked through his glasses in mild astonishment.

"Why was it bad?"

"Only that you have disarranged our little deductions. Your marriage, you say?"

"Yes, sir. I married, and so left the hospital, and with it all hopes of a consulting practice. It was necessary to make a home of my own."

"Come, come, we are not so far wrong after all," said Holmes. "And now, Dr. James Mortimer—"

"Mister, sir, Mister—a humble M.R.C.S."

"And a man of precise mind, evidently."

"A dabbler in science, Mr. Holmes, a picker up of shells on the shores of the great unknown ocean. I presume that it is Mr. Sherlock Holmes whom I am addressing and not—"

"No, this is my friend Dr. Watson."

"Glad to meet you, sir. I have heard your name mentioned in connection with that of your friend. You interest me very much, Mr. Holmes. I came to you because I recognized that I am myself an unpractical man and because I am suddenly confronted with a most 2 serious and extraordinary problem. Recognizing, as I do, that you are the second highest expert in Europe—"

"Indeed, sir! May I inquire who has the honor to be the first?" asked Holmes, with some asperity.

"To the man of precisely scientific mind 3 the work of Monsieur Bertillon[9] must always appeal strongly."

"Then had you not better consult him?"

"I said, sir, to the precisely scientific mind. But as a practical man of affairs it is acknowledged that you stand alone. I trust, sir, that I have not inadvertently—"

"Just a little," said Holmes. "I think, Dr. Mortimer, you would do wisely if without more ado you would kindly tell me plainly what the exact nature of the problem is in which you demand my assistance."

---

9. **Monsieur Bertillon** [mə syœ′ ber tē yōn′]: Alphonse Bertillon invented the first scientific system of criminal identification, based on photographs and the measurement of the skeleton.

506 *The Novel*

GUIDED READING

LITERAL QUESTION

1a. How does Dr. Mortimer first describe Sherlock Holmes's reputation? (He describes Holmes as the second-highest expert in Europe.)

INFERENTIAL QUESTION

1b. How do you think he expects Holmes to react to this description? (He probably expects Holmes to be flattered by it.)

2 The Curse of the Baskervilles

"I have in my pocket a manuscript," said Dr. James Mortimer.

"I observed it as you entered the room," said Holmes.

"It is an old manuscript."

"Early eighteenth century, unless it is a forgery."

"How can you say that, sir?"

"You have presented an inch or two of it to my examination all the time that you have been talking. It would be a poor expert who would not give the date of a document within a decade or so. I put that at 1730."

"The exact date is 1742." Dr. Mortimer drew it from his breast pocket. "This family paper was committed to my care by Sir Charles Baskerville, whose sudden and tragic death some three months ago created so much excitement in Devonshire. I may say that I was his personal friend as well as his medical attendant. He was a strong-minded man, sir, shrewd, practical, and as unimaginative as I am myself. Yet he took this document very seriously, and his mind was prepared for just such an end as did eventually overtake him."

Holmes stretched out his hand for the manuscript and flattened it upon his knee.

I looked over his shoulder at the yellow paper and the faded script. At the head was written: "Baskerville Hall," and below, in large, scrawling figures: "1742."

"It appears to be a statement of some sort."

"Yes, it is a statement of a certain legend which runs in the Baskerville family."

"But I understand that it is something more modern and practical upon which you wish to consult me?"

"Most modern. A most practical, pressing matter, which must be decided within twenty-four hours. But the manuscript is short and is intimately connected with the affair. With your permission I will read it to you."

Holmes leaned back in his chair, placed his finger tips together, and closed his eyes, with an air of resignation. Dr. Mortimer turned the manuscript to the light and read in a high, crackling voice the following curious, old-world narrative:

"Of the origin of the Hound of the Baskervilles there have been many statements, yet as I come in a direct line from Hugo Baskerville, I had the story from my father, who also had it from his.

"Know then that in the time of the Great Rebellion[1] this Manor of Baskerville was held by Hugo of that name. There was in him a certain cruel humor which made his name a byword through the west. It chanced that this Hugo came to love the daughter of a yeoman who held lands near the Baskerville estate. But the young maiden would ever avoid him, for she feared his evil name. So it came to pass that one Michaelmas[2] this Hugo, with five or six of his idle and wicked companions, stole down upon the farm and carried off the maiden, her father and brothers being from home, as he well knew. When they had brought her to the Hall the maiden was placed in an upper chamber, while Hugo and his friends sat down to a long carouse,[3] as was their nightly custom. Now, the poor lass upstairs was like to have her wits turned at the terrible noise which came up to her from below. At last in the stress of her fear she did that which might have daunted the bravest or most active man, for by the aid of the

---

1. **Great Rebellion:** refers to the Puritan revolution (1642–1651), a civil war in England.
2. **Michaelmas:** Christian holiday in honor of the archangel Michael, celebrated, mainly in England, on September 29.
3. **carouse:** noisy feast.

The Hound of the Baskervilles 507

- Mortimer produces a copy of a legend dating from 1742.
- He claims that the legend has a bearing on his present problem and on the recent death of Sir Charles Baskerville.
- The legend describes the cruel Hugo Baskerville, who in the mid-1600s kidnapped a local maiden and brought her to the Baskerville manor house.

1 PLOT: SUSPENSE

Dr. Mortimer's allusion to a recent tragic death that is somehow related to an old document creates a sense of suspense about the document.

2 THEME

The sense of mystery and adventure is heightened by the suggestion that an old legend could somehow affect events in the present.

3 STYLE: ARCHAIC LANGUAGE

The legend contains archaic words and phrases such as *yeoman* and *it came to pass,* which heighten its authenticity to modern readers.

GUIDED READING

LITERAL QUESTIONS

1a. What does Holmes observe about the manuscript in Mortimer's pocket? (He determines it is from the early eighteenth century—about 1730.)

2a. How does Dr. Mortimer characterize the late Sir Charles Baskerville? (He says he was shrewd, practical, and unimaginative.)

INFERENTIAL QUESTIONS

1b. What does this tell you about Holmes as a detective? (He is very alert and observant; he is an expert in many areas, such as the dating of manuscripts.)

2b. Why do you think he mentions these particular qualities before reading the legend? (He wants to suggest that Sir Charles was not ordinarily the type to believe in legends.)

- The legend continues with the maiden's escape onto the nearby moor.
- Hugo rides after the maiden.
- A fearsome hound overtakes Hugo and kills him, and the maiden dies of fright.
- The legend ends with the warning that this hound will plague the Baskervilles down through history.

1 BACKGROUND

Doyle claimed that an actual legend from the West Country of England, similar to the one presented here, gave him the idea for *The Hound of the Baskervilles*. In fact the novel is dedicated to a friend of Doyle's who showed him the legend.

2 SETTING

The moor, an open wasteland, surrounds the Baskerville manor house; at night this is an especially eerie setting.

3 IMAGERY

By describing the hound's gigantic size, strangely blazing eyes, and dripping mouth, Doyle appeals mainly to our sense of sight to create an image of an awesome beast.

4 THEME

The superstitious idea that Hugo's evil deed would affect his descendants is placed in contrast to Holmes's reason and common sense.

---

growth of ivy which covered (and still covers) the south wall she came down from under the eaves, and so homeward across the moor, there being three leagues betwixt the Hall and her father's farm.

1 "It chanced that some little time later Hugo left his guests to carry food to his captive, and so found the cage empty and the bird escaped. Then, as it would seem, he became as one that hath a devil, for, rushing down the stairs into the dining hall, he sprang upon the great table, flagons[4] and trenchers[5] flying before him, and he cried aloud before all the company that he would that very night render his body and soul to the Powers of Evil if he might but overtake the maid. And while the revelers stood aghast at the fury of the man, one more wicked than the rest cried out that they should put the hounds upon her. Whereat Hugo ran from the house, crying to his grooms that they should saddle his mare and unkennel the pack, and giving the hounds a **2** kerchief of the maid's, he swung them to the line, and so off full cry in the moonlight over the moor.

"Now, for some space the revelers stood agape, unable to understand all that had been done in such haste. But at length some sense came back to their crazed minds, and the whole of them, thirteen in number, took horse and started in pursuit. The moon shone clear above them, and they rode swiftly abreast, taking that course which the maid must needs have taken if she were to reach her own home.

"They had gone a mile or two when they passed one of the night shepherds upon the moorlands, and they cried to him to know if

---

4. **flagons:** containers for liquids, having handles, spouts, and usually lids.
5. **trenchers:** wooden boards on which meat is carved and served.

508   *The Novel*

---

he had seen the hunt. And the man, as the story goes, was so crazed with fear that he could scarce speak, but at last he said that he had indeed seen the unhappy maiden, with the hounds upon her track. 'But I have seen more than that,' said he, 'for Hugo Baskerville passed me upon his black mare, and there ran mute behind him such a hound as heaven forbid should ever be at my heels.' So the squires rode onward. But soon their skins turned cold, for there came a galloping across the moor, and the black mare, dabbled with white froth, went past with trailing bridle and empty saddle. Then the revelers rode close together.

"The moon was shining bright upon the clearing, and there in the center lay the unhappy maid where she had fallen, dead of fear and of fatigue. But it was not the sight of her body, nor yet was it that of the body of Hugo Baskerville lying near her, which raised the hair upon the heads of these daredevil roisterers, but it was that, standing over Hugo, **3** and plucking at his throat, there stood a foul thing, a great, black beast, shaped like a hound, yet larger than any hound that ever mortal eye has rested upon. And even as they looked the thing tore the throat out of Hugo Baskerville, on which, as it turned its blazing eyes and dripping jaws upon them, they shrieked with fear and rode for dear life, still screaming, across the moor.

"Such is the tale, my sons, of the coming **4** of the hound which is said to have plagued the family so sorely ever since. It cannot be denied that many of our family have been unhappy in their deaths, which have been sudden, bloody, and mysterious. I hereby counsel you by way of caution to forbear from crossing the moor in those dark hours when the powers of evil are exalted.

"[This from Hugo Baskerville to his sons

GUIDED READING

LITERAL QUESTIONS

1a. What method does Hugo use to track down the escaped maiden? (He uses his hounds to follow her scent.)

2a. Besides telling about their ancestor Hugo, why is this legend of special importance to the Baskerville family? (The hound is said to plague family members and perhaps cause their deaths.)

INFERENTIAL QUESTIONS

1b. Considering how Henry tracked the maiden, why is there a kind of justice in the way he meets his own death? (He too is tracked down by a hound.)

2b. How do you think the legend affected the Baskerville family down through the years? (They may have feared to go out onto the moor.)

AT A GLANCE
- The legend evokes little interest from Sherlock Holmes.
- Dr. Mortimer begins to read the recent obituary of Sir Charles Baskerville.
- Sir Charles died suddenly after returning to Baskerville Hall.

1 CHARACTERIZATION

Holmes's boredom in the face of such a fascinating tale clearly and humorously characterizes him as extremely rational and totally unsuperstitious.

2 NOVEL

Doyle uses first a legend and now a newspaper obituary to provide background information in an interesting fashion. A novel's length allows an author to use various techniques to develop the plot.

3 PLOT: CLUES

Sir Charles Baskerville was rich, generous with his money, and childless—three clues that may prove useful in solving his murder.

Rodger and John, with instructions that they say nothing thereof to their sister Elizabeth.]"

When Dr. Mortimer had finished reading this singular narrative he pushed his spectacles up on his forehead and stared across at Mr. Sherlock Holmes. The latter yawned.

"Well?" said he.

"Do you not find it interesting?"

"To a collector of fairy tales."

Dr. Mortimer drew a folded newspaper out of his pocket.

"Now, Mr. Holmes, we will give you something a little more recent. This is the *Devon County Chronicle* of May fourteenth of this year. It is a short account of the facts elicited at the death of Sir Charles Baskerville which occurred a few days before that date."

My friend leaned a little forward and his expression became intent. Our visitor readjusted his glasses and began:

"The recent sudden death of Sir Charles Baskerville, whose name has been mentioned as the probable Liberal[6] candidate for Mid-Devon at the next election, has cast a gloom over the county. Though Sir Charles had resided at Baskerville Hall for a comparatively short period his amiability of character and extreme generosity had won the affection and respect of all who had been brought into contact with him. Sir Charles, as is well known, made large sums of money in South African speculation.[7] He realized his gains and returned to England with them. Being himself childless, it was his openly expressed desire that the whole countryside should, within his own lifetime, profit by his good fortune, and many will bewail his untimely end. His generous donations to local and county charities have been frequently chronicled in these columns.

"The circumstances connected with the

---

6. **Liberal:** In the 1880s the Liberal party was a strong political party in favor of reform, abolition of slavery, and religious freedom.
7. **speculation:** practice of buying and selling something at a risk, with the hope of making huge profits.

The Hound of the Baskervilles 509

GUIDED READING

LITERAL QUESTIONS

1a. How does Sherlock Holmes react to the legend? (He yawns and suggests it would be interesting only to a collector of fairy tales.)

2a. What does Dr. Mortimer next read to Holmes and Watson? (He reads them a newspaper account of the death of Sir Charles Baskerville.)

INFERENTIAL QUESTIONS

1b. What does Holmes's reaction tell you about him? (He is a rational, practical man who has little use for fantasy; he is not superstitious.)

2b. What connection is there between the legend and the obituary? (Both concern a sudden death in the Baskerville family; the legend mentions a curse on that family.)

- The newspaper article explains that Sir Charles had been in poor health and was attended by Dr. Mortimer.
- Sir Charles was outside near the moor when he died; his face was marked by great distortion.
- A nephew, Mr. Henry Baskerville, was the sole survivor.

1 MOOD

The description of Sir Charles's physical and emotional condition helps to create the morbid, uneasy mood of the novel.

2 PLOT: EXPOSITION

Normally a newspaper account of a death would not go into such fine detail. But Doyle's purpose is to lay out facts for his detective and his readers alike.

3 PLOT: CLUES

The mysterious footprints are among many clues in the article, clues that Holmes (and readers) must sift through to solve the mystery.

4 PLOT: FORESHADOWING

The mention of Henry Baskerville in the article foreshadows his appearance in the story and his impending conflicts at Baskerville Hall.

death of Sir Charles cannot be said to have been entirely cleared up by the inquest, but at least enough has been done to dispose of those rumors to which local superstition has given rise. There is no reason whatever to suspect foul play, or to imagine that death could be from any but natural causes. Sir Charles was a widower, and a man who may be said to have been in some ways of an eccentric habit of mind. In spite of his considerable wealth he was simple in his personal tastes, and his indoor servants at Baskerville Hall consisted of a married couple named Barrymore, the husband acting as butler and the wife as housekeeper. Their evidence, corroborated by that of several friends, tends to **1** show that Sir Charles's health has for some time been impaired, and points especially to some affection of the heart, manifesting itself in changes of color, breathlessness, and acute attacks of nervous depression. Dr. James Mortimer, the friend and medical attendant of the deceased, has given evidence to the same effect.

2 "The facts of the case are simple. Sir Charles Baskerville was in the habit every night before going to bed of walking down the famous yew alley[8] of Baskerville Hall. The evidence of the Barrymores shows that this had been his custom. On the fourth of May Sir Charles had declared his intention of starting next day for London, and had ordered Barrymore to prepare his luggage. That night he went out as usual for his nocturnal walk. He never returned. At twelve o'clock Barrymore, finding the hall door still open, became alarmed, and, lighting a lantern, went in search of his master. The day had been wet, and Sir Charles's footmarks were easily traced down the alley. Halfway down this walk there

is a gate which leads out on to the moor. There were indications that Sir Charles had stood for some little time here. He then proceeded down the alley, and it was at the far end of it **3** that his body was discovered. One fact which has not been explained is the statement of Barrymore that his master's footprints altered from the time that he passed the moor gate,[9] and that he appeared from thence onward to have been walking upon his toes.

"No signs of violence were to be discovered upon Sir Charles's person, and though the doctor's evidence pointed to an almost incredible facial distortion—so great that Dr. Mortimer refused at first to believe that it was indeed his friend and patient who lay before him—it was explained that that is a symptom which is not unusual in cases of dyspnea[10] and death from cardiac exhaustion. This explanation was borne out by the post-mortem examination, which showed longstanding organic disease, and the coroner's jury returned a verdict in accordance with the medical evidence. It is well that this is so, for it is obviously of the utmost importance that Sir Charles's heir should settle at the Hall and continue the good work which has been so **4** sadly interrupted. Had the prosaic finding of the coroner not finally put an end to the romantic stories which have been whispered in connection with the affair, it might have been difficult to find a tenant for Baskerville Hall. It is understood that the next of kin is Mr. Henry Baskerville, if he be still alive, the son of Sir Charles Baskerville's younger brother. The young man when last heard of was in America, and inquiries are being instituted with a view to informing him of his good fortune."

---

8. **yew alley:** passage between two rows of yews, which are dark evergreen trees.

9. **moor gate:** gate separating farms or gardens from the moor, an open, marshy wasteland.
10. **dyspnea** [disp'nē ə]: difficult or painful breathing.

510   *The Novel*

GUIDED READING

LITERAL QUESTIONS

1a. What does the coroner determine as the cause of Baskerville's death? (He died of heart failure and the difficult breathing it caused.)

2a. How does Sir Charles look when he is found? What is the explanation for this? (His features are distorted; it resulted from his difficult breathing.)

INFERENTIAL QUESTIONS

1b. What do you think were the "romantic stories" that this finding supposedly put to rest? (stories about the legend of the hound and its possible connection to the death)

2b. What else might have caused a person's features to be so distorted? (extreme emotion, such as fear)

Dr. Mortimer refolded his paper and replaced it in his pocket.

"Those are the public facts, Mr. Holmes, in connection with the death of Sir Charles Baskerville."

"I must thank you," said Sherlock Holmes, "for calling my attention to a case which certainly presents some features of interest. This article, you say, contains all the public facts?"

"It does."

"Then let me have the private ones." He leaned back, put his finger tips together, and assumed his most impassive and judicial expression.

"In doing so," said Dr. Mortimer, who had begun to show signs of some strong emotion, "I am telling that which I have not confided to anyone.

1 "The moor is very sparsely inhabited, and those who live near each other are thrown very much together. For this reason I saw a good deal of Sir Charles Baskerville. With the exception of Mr. Frankland, of Lafter Hall, and Mr. Stapleton, the naturalist, there are no other men of education within many miles. Sir Charles was a retiring man, but the chance of his illness brought us together, and a community of interests in science kept us so.

"Within the last few months it became increasingly plain to me that Sir Charles's nervous system was strained to the breaking point. He had taken this legend which I have read you exceedingly to heart—so much so that, although he would walk in his own grounds, nothing would induce him to go out upon the moor at night. Incredible as it may appear to you, Mr. Holmes, he was honestly convinced that a dreadful fate overhung his family. The idea of some ghastly presence constantly haunted him, and on more than one occasion he asked me whether I had on my medical journeys at night ever seen any 2 strange creature or heard the baying of a hound.

"It was at my advice that Sir Charles was about to go to London. His heart was, I knew, affected, and the constant anxiety in which he lived was evidently having a serious effect upon his health. I thought that a few months among the distractions of town would send him back a new man. Mr. Stapleton, a mutual friend who was much concerned at his state of health, was of the same opinion.

"On the night of Sir Charles's death Barrymore the butler, who made the discovery, sent Perkins the groom on horseback to me, and as I was sitting up late I was able to reach Baskerville Hall within an hour of the event. I followed the footsteps down the yew alley, I saw the spot at the moor gate where he seemed to have waited, I remarked the change in the shape of the prints after that point, I noted that there were no other footsteps save those of Barrymore on the soft gravel, and finally I carefully examined the body, which had not been touched until my arrival. Sir Charles lay on his face, his arms out, his fingers dug into the ground, and his features convulsed with some strong emotion to such an extent that I could hardly have sworn to his identity. There was certainly no physical injury of any kind. But one false statement was made by Barrymore at the inquest. He said that there were no traces upon the ground round the body. He did not observe any. But I did—some little distance off, but fresh and clear."

"Footprints?"

"Footprints."

"A man's or a woman's?"

3 Dr. Mortimer looked strangely at us for an instant, and his voice sank almost to a whisper as he answered:

"Mr. Holmes, they were the footprints of a gigantic hound!"

The Hound of the Baskervilles 511

GUIDED READING

LITERAL QUESTIONS

1a. According to Dr. Mortimer, what is the cause of Sir Charles Baskerville's poor health? (His fear of the legendary hound caused such anxiety that his nerves and heart were affected.)

2a. What important clue found near the body does Dr. Mortimer not mention at the inquest? (He does not mention the footprints of a gigantic hound.)

INFERENTIAL QUESTIONS

1b. Do you think Sir Charles's fears had any basis in reality, or was he suffering from an emotional disorder? (Answers will vary, but the hound's footprints suggest his fears had some basis in reality.)

2b. Why do you think Mortimer withholds this evidence? (probably because he does not want to encourage rumors and fears about the legend)

- Mortimer's revelation about the hound tracks excites Holmes.
- Holmes questions Mortimer closely about the scene of Sir Charles's death.

1 POINT OF VIEW

The first-person narrator, Watson, resumes an active role, describing his impressions and emotions.

2 STYLE: DIALOGUE

Holmes's rapid-fire interrogation of Mortimer not only presents the facts of the case but also helps characterize Holmes as quick-witted and penetrating, rapidly mastering the details of the situation.

3 SETTING

In a mystery the details of a setting that might have been the scene of a crime are particularly important. These details suggest how a criminal might have approached or left the yew alley.

4 CHARACTERIZATION

From Holmes's remarks and reactions the reader can tell that Holmes is impatient and easily frustrated by those less thorough than he.

3 The Problem

1 I confess that at these words a shudder passed through me. There was a thrill in the doctor's voice which showed that he was himself deeply moved by that which he told us. Holmes leaned forward in his excitement and his eyes had the hard, dry glitter which shot from them when he was keenly interested.

"You saw this?"

"As clearly as I see you."

"How was it that no one else saw it?"

"The marks were some twenty yards from the body and no one gave them a thought. I don't suppose I should have done so had I not known this legend."

2 "There are many sheep dogs on the moor?"

"No doubt, but this was no sheep dog."

"You say it was large?"

"Enormous."

"But it had not approached the body?"

"No."

"What sort of night was it?"

"Damp and raw."

"But not actually raining?"

"No."

"What is the alley like?"

"There are two lines of old yew hedge, twelve feet high and impenetrable. The walk in the center is about eight feet across."

"Is there anything between the hedges and the walk?"

512   *The Novel*

3 "Yes, there is a strip of grass about six feet broad on either side."

"I understand that the yew hedge is penetrated at one point by a gate?"

"Yes, the wicket gate which leads on to the moor."

"Is there any other opening?"

"None."

"So that to reach the yew alley one either has to come down it from the house or else to enter it by the moor gate?"

"There is an exit through a summerhouse at the far end."

"Had Sir Charles reached this?"

"No; he lay about fifty yards from it."

"Now, tell me, Dr. Mortimer—and this is important—the marks which you saw were on the path and not on the grass?"

"No marks could show on the grass."

"Were they on the same side of the path as the moor gate?"

"Yes; they were on the edge of the path on the same side as the moor gate."

"You interest me exceedingly. Another point. Was the wicket gate closed?"

"Closed and padlocked."

"How high was it?"

"About four feet high."

"Then anyone could have got over it?"

"Yes."

"And what marks did you see by the wicket gate?"

"None in particular."

"Good heaven! Did no one examine?"

"Yes, I examined, myself."

"And found nothing?"

"It was all very confused."

"But the marks?"

"Sir Charles had left his own marks all over that small patch of gravel. I could discern no others."

4 Sherlock Holmes struck his hand against his knee with an impatient gesture.

GUIDED READING

LITERAL QUESTIONS

1a. What area does Holmes ask Dr. Mortimer to describe in great detail? (the yew alley just outside the house, where Sir Charles's body was found)

2a. How does Holmes react when Dr. Mortimer explains that he found only Sir Charles's marks by the wicket gate? (He is impatient.)

INFERENTIAL QUESTIONS

1b. Why do you think Holmes is so interested in this area? (He wants to establish how Sir Charles or a possible criminal might have entered or left the area.)

2b. Why do you think Holmes reacts this way? (He is certain that he would have found other meaningful clues. He is frustrated that these clues are lost.)

"If I had only been there!" he cried. "It is evidently a case of extraordinary interest, and one which presented immense opportunities to the scientific expert."

"I could not call you in, Mr. Holmes, without disclosing these facts to the world. Besides, besides—"

"Why do you hesitate?"

"There is a realm in which the most acute and most experienced of detectives is helpless."

"You mean that the thing is supernatural?"

"I did not positively say so."

"No, but you evidently think it."

1 "Since the tragedy, Mr. Holmes, there have come to my ears several incidents which are hard to reconcile with the settled order of nature."

"For example?"

"I find that before the terrible event occurred several people had seen a creature upon the moor which corresponds with this Baskerville demon, and which could not possibly be any animal known to science. They all agreed that it was a huge creature, luminous, ghastly, and spectral, exactly corresponding to the hound of the legend. I assure you that there is a reign of terror in the district and that it is a hardy man who will cross the moor at night."

"And you, a trained man of science, believe it to be supernatural?"

"I do not know what to believe."

Holmes shrugged his shoulders.

"The original hound was material enough to tug a man's throat out, and yet he was diabolical as well."

"I see that you have quite gone over to the supernaturalists. But now, Dr. Mortimer, tell me this. How can I assist you?"

"By advising me as to what I should do with Sir Henry Baskerville, who arrives at Waterloo Station"—Dr. Mortimer looked at his watch—"in exactly one hour and a quarter."

"He being the heir?"

"Yes. On the death of Sir Charles we inquired for this young gentleman, and found **2** that he had been farming in Canada. From the accounts which have reached us he is an excellent fellow in every way."

"There is no other claimant, I presume?"

"None. The only other kinsman whom we have been able to trace was Rodger Baskerville, the youngest of the three brothers of whom poor Sir Charles was the elder. The second brother, who died young, is the father of this lad Henry. The third, Rodger, was the black sheep of the family. He came of the old masterful Baskerville strain, and was the very image, they tell me, of the family picture of **3** old Hugo. He made England too hot to hold him, fled to Central America, and died there in 1876 of yellow fever. Henry is the last of the Baskervilles. In one hour and five minutes I meet him at Waterloo Station. Now, Mr. Holmes, what would you advise me to do with him?"

"Why should he not go to the home of his fathers?"

"It seems natural, does it not? And yet, consider that every Baskerville who goes there meets with an evil fate."

Holmes considered for a little time.

4 "Put into plain words, the matter is this," said he. "In your opinion there is a diabolical agency which makes Dartmoor an unsafe abode for a Baskerville—that is your opinion?"

"At least I might go the length of saying that there is some evidence that this may be so."

"Exactly. But surely, if your supernatural theory be correct, it could work the young man evil in London as easily as in Devonshire."

The Hound of the Baskervilles 513

AT A GLANCE

- Mortimer admits his suspicion that there may be a supernatural hound.
- Mortimer explains that Sir Henry Baskerville, heir to Sir Charles's estate, will arrive shortly.
- The men discuss whether young Baskerville is in danger.

1 CHARACTERIZATION

As a man of science, Mortimer tries to understand the natural world in a rational way. When his reason cannot explain certain phenomena, he finds supernatural explanations tempting.

2 CHARACTERIZATION

Sir Henry Baskerville, the heir to the Baskerville estate, is described initially as a good and honorable person.

3 PLOT: SUSPENSE

The information that Sir Henry is "the last of the Baskervilles" may be an important clue; there is a suggestion that someone may be trying to eliminate all claimants to the Baskerville estate.

4 READING SKILL: FACT AND OPINION

The footprints on the moor, the baying sounds, and the sightings of a huge creature are all facts. Mortimer's belief that Dartmoor is unsafe for all Baskervilles because of supernatural forces is an opinion: It can't be proved or disproved.

GUIDED READING

LITERAL QUESTIONS

1a. What assistance does Dr. Mortimer ask Holmes to give him? (to advise him about whether Sir Henry should go to Baskerville Hall)

2a. What information does the reader learn about Sir Henry Baskerville on this page? (He is said to be "an excellent fellow in every way"; he is the last of the Baskervilles.)

INFERENTIAL QUESTIONS

1b. Why do you think Dr. Mortimer has chosen Holmes to assist him in this matter? (Mortimer knows his own mind is clouded with superstitious fears; he is counting on the unsuperstitious Holmes to think clearly about the matter.)

2b. Why might this information about Sir Henry be significant? (The fact that he is the last member of a rich old family might be a motive for his murder.)

1 CHARACTERIZATION

The loyal Watson accepts that his presence would be inappropriate when Holmes wants to think deeply about the case. Watson is a sort of assistant, a "right-hand man" who gladly carries out Holmes's orders.

2 SETTING

The place name *Foulmire* and the existence of a large prison on the moor help create an ominous, unpleasant feeling about the moor.

3 PLOT: EXPOSITION

Holmes's two questions neatly summarize the problem he and Watson face. Their efforts to solve the problem will set in motion a series of events that further the plot.

"Your advice, then, Mr. Holmes, is that the young man will be as safe in Devonshire as in London. He comes in fifty minutes. What would you recommend?"

"I recommend, sir, that you take a cab and proceed to Waterloo to meet Sir Henry Baskerville."

"And then?"

"And then you will say nothing to him at all until I have made up my mind about the matter."

"How long will it take you to make up your mind?"

"Twenty-four hours. At ten o'clock tomorrow, Dr. Mortimer, call upon me here, and bring Sir Henry Baskerville with you."

"I will do so, Mr. Holmes."

"Thank you. Good morning."

Holmes returned to his seat with that quiet look of inward satisfaction which meant that he had a congenial task before him.

1 "Going out, Watson?"

"Unless I can help you."

"No, my dear fellow, it is at the hour of action that I turn to you for aid. But this is splendid, really unique from some points of view. It would be as well if you could make it convenient not to return before evening. Then I should be very glad to compare impressions as to this most interesting problem which has been submitted to us this morning."

I spent the day at my club and did not return to Baker Street until evening. It was nearly nine o'clock when I found myself in the sitting room once more.

"I have been to Devonshire," Holmes said.

"In spirit?"

"Exactly. My body has remained in this armchair. After you left I sent down to Stamford's for the Ordnance map[1] of this portion

---

1. **Ordnance map:** official survey map of Great Britain, showing shape, area, and boundaries.

514 *The Novel*

of the moor, and my spirit has hovered over it all day. I flatter myself that I could find my way about."

"A large-scale map, I presume?"

"Very large." He unrolled one section and held it over his knee. "Here you have the particular district which concerns us. That is Baskerville Hall in the middle."

"With a wood round it?"

"Exactly. I fancy the yew alley, though not marked under that name, must stretch along this line, with the moor, as you perceive, upon the right of it. This small clump of buildings here is the hamlet of Grimpen, where our friend Dr. Mortimer has his headquarters. Within a radius of five miles there are, as you see, only a very few scattered dwellings. Here is Lafter Hall, which was mentioned in the narrative. There is a house indicated here which may be the residence of the naturalist—Stapleton, if I remember right, was his

2 name. Here are two moorland farmhouses, High Tor and Foulmire. Then fourteen miles away the great convict prison of Princetown. Between and around these scattered points extends the desolate, lifeless moor."

"It must be a wild place."

"Yes, the setting is a worthy one. If the devil did desire to have a hand in the affairs of men—"

"Then you are yourself inclining to the supernatural explanation."

3 "The devil's agents may be of flesh and blood, may they not? There are two questions waiting for us at the outset. The one is whether any crime has been committed at all; the second is, what is the crime and how was it committed? What do you make of it?"

"It is very bewildering."

"It has certainly a character of its own. There are points of distinction about it. That change in the footprints, for example. What do you make of that?"

GUIDED READING

LITERAL QUESTION

1a. What is the first question that Holmes and Watson must answer? (They must decide whether a crime has been committed.)

INFERENTIAL QUESTION

1b. Based on what Holmes says on this page, what do you think will be his answer to this question? (By saying "The devil's agents may be flesh and blood," Holmes suggests a crime was committed by a human being.)

"Mortimer said that the man had walked on tiptoe down that portion of the alley."

"He only repeated what some fool had said at the inquest. Why should a man walk on tiptoe down the alley?"

"What then?"

1 "He was running, Watson—running desperately, running for his life, running until he burst his heart and fell dead upon his face."

"Running from what?"

"There lies our problem. There are indications that the man was crazed with fear before ever he began to run."

"How can you say that?"

"I am presuming that the cause of his fears came to him across the moor. If that were so, and it seems most probable, only a man who has lost his wits would have run *from* the house instead of toward it, in the direction where help was least likely to be. Then, again, whom was he waiting for that night, and why was he waiting for him in the yew alley rather than in his own house?"

"You think that he was waiting for someone?"

"The man was elderly and infirm. We can understand his taking an evening stroll, but the ground was damp and the night inclement. Is it natural that he should stand for five or ten minutes? The evidence is that he avoided the moor. That night he waited there. It was the night before he made his departure for London. The thing takes shape, Watson. It becomes coherent. Might I ask you to hand me my violin, and we will postpone all further thought upon this business until we have had the advantage of meeting Dr. Mortimer and Sir Henry Baskerville in the morning."

STUDY QUESTIONS

Recalling

1. What object are Holmes and Watson discussing as the novel begins? What does each man conclude about Dr. Mortimer from this object?

2. What is the curse of the Baskervilles, as described in Chapter 2? Briefly tell what Hugo Baskerville did to bring about the curse.

3. What facts concerning Sir Charles Baskerville's death were reported in the newspaper? What details did Dr. Mortimer withhold from the coroner's inquiry?

4. According to Chapter 3, describe the creature that several people reported seeing before Sir Charles's death.

5. What does Holmes conclude about Sir Charles's footprints and his actions on the night of his death?

Interpreting

6. Basing your answer on the opening scene, explain Holmes's method of reaching conclusions. Why do Holmes and Watson, using the same method, arrive at opposing conclusions?

7. How accurate is Holmes's method of deduction? Support your answer with examples.

8. What is the main force against which Sherlock Holmes is struggling? Is the conflict internal or external? Why?

9. Holmes asks himself what the crime is and how it was committed. Try to answer these questions based on the facts that you have learned in Chapters 1–3.

Extending

10. Do you think that there are any detectives today, fictional or real, who are as talented as Holmes?

The Hound of the Baskervilles 515

- Holmes believes that Sir Charles was crazed with fear and running wildly at the time of his death.
- The detective suggests that Sir Charles went outside on the night of his death in order to meet someone.

1 STYLE: DIALOGUE

The dialogue contrasts the two friends. Holmes has spent the day using the few clues available to reach conclusions; Watson reports no insights and is limited to exploring Holmes's ideas with questions.

REFLECTING ON CHAPTERS 1–3

Why is this case intriguing to Holmes? (it appears to be unexplainable—full of mystery and supernatural events. Yet he finds several clues that will challenge his ability to illuminate the facts of the situation.)

STUDY QUESTIONS

1. ■ walking stick
   ■ Watson: elderly, presented stick by hunt; Holmes: young, once at Charing Cross Hospital
2. death by hound; abducted maiden, who escaped—gave himself to the Powers of Evil
3. heart failure, died in yew alley; footprints of hound
4. huge, luminous, ghastly
5. waiting, saw something coming from the moor, ran, had a heart attack
6. inference from evidence; Holmes more attentive, scientific
7. very accurate; Mortimer's dog
8. evil; external
9. Most students will suggest murder.
10. Holmes is the most famous fictional detective.

AT A GLANCE

- Dr. Mortimer and Sir Henry Baskerville arrive at Holmes's rooms the next morning.
- Sir Henry announces that he received a curious note.
- Holmes asks who might have known where Sir Henry was staying.

LITERARY OPTIONS

- characterization
- setting
- style

THEMATIC OPTIONS

- observation and deduction
- ambition and greed
- mystery and adventure

1 CHARACTERIZATION

Saying that Henry Baskerville was a "gentleman" indicates that he came from a respected and socially prominent family. Details about his physical appearance characterize him as a strong, capable man.

2 SETTING

The author uses actual locations in London, such as Charing Cross Station and the Northumberland Hotel, adding to the realism of the novel.

As Holmes and Watson continue their investigation, the clues begin to multiply.

■ *Try using Holmes's method to solve the deepening mystery: Is the anonymous letter a friendly warning or a threat? Who is the cunning stranger in the cab? What does an escaped convict have to do with the death of Sir Charles? Who is the woman heard crying in the night?*

4 Sir Henry Baskerville

Our breakfast table was cleared early, and Holmes waited in his dressing gown for the promised interview. Our clients were punctual to their appointment, for the clock had just struck ten when Dr. Mortimer was shown up, followed by the young baronet.[1] The latter 1 was a small, alert, dark-eyed man about thirty years of age, very sturdily built, with thick black eyebrows and a strong, pugnacious face. There was something in his steady eye and the quiet assurance of his bearing which indicated the gentleman.

"This is Sir Henry Baskerville," said Dr. Mortimer.

"Why, yes," said he, "and the strange thing is, Mr. Sherlock Holmes, that if my friend here had not proposed coming round to you this morning I should have come on my own account. I understand that you think out little puzzles, and I've had one this morning which wants more thinking out than I am able to give it."

---

1. **baronet:** lowest rank of honor that can be inherited in Great Britain. A baronet is addressed as *Sir* even though he is not a nobleman.

516 *The Novel*

"Pray take a seat, Sir Henry. Do I understand you to say that you have yourself had some remarkable experience since you arrived in London?"

"Nothing of much importance, Mr. Holmes. Only a joke, as like as not. It was this letter, if you can call it a letter, which reached me this morning."

He laid an envelope upon the table, and we all bent over it. It was of common quality, 2 grayish in color. The address, "Sir Henry Baskerville, Northumberland Hotel," was printed in rough characters; the postmark "Charing Cross," and the date of posting the preceding evening.

"Who knew that you were going to the Northumberland Hotel?" asked Holmes, glancing keenly across at our visitor.

"No one could have known. We only decided after I met Dr. Mortimer."

"But Dr. Mortimer was no doubt already stopping there?"

"No, I had been staying with a friend," said the doctor. "There was no possible indication that we intended to go to this hotel."

"Hum! Someone seems to be very deeply

GUIDED READING

LITERAL QUESTION

1a. Why is Sir Henry surprised to receive a letter at his hotel? (He says no one knows his whereabouts.)

INFERENTIAL QUESTION

1b. What does the arrival of the letter suggest to you? (Answers will vary. Students might suggest that some unknown person is following Sir Henry.)

interested in your movements." Out of the envelope he took a half sheet of foolscap paper[2] folded into four. This he opened and spread flat upon the table. Across the middle of it a single sentence had been formed by the expedient of pasting printed words upon it. It ran: "As you value your life or your reason keep away from the moor." The word "moor" only was printed in ink.

"Now," said Sir Henry Baskerville, "perhaps you will tell me, Mr. Holmes, what in thunder is the meaning of that, and who it is that takes so much interest in my affairs?"

"What do you make of it, Dr. Mortimer? You must allow that there is nothing supernatural about this, at any rate?"

"No, sir, but it might very well come from someone who was convinced that the business is supernatural."

"What business?" asked Sir Henry sharply. "It seems to me that all you gentlemen know a great deal more than I do about my own affairs."

"You shall share our knowledge before you leave this room, Sir Henry. I promise you that," said Sherlock Holmes. "We will confine ourselves for the present with your permission to this very interesting document, which must have been put together and posted yesterday evening. Have you yesterday's *Times*, Watson?"

"It is here in the corner."

"Might I trouble you for it—the inside page, please, with the leading articles?" He glanced swiftly over it, running his eyes up and down the columns. "Capital article, this, on free trade. Permit me to give you an extract from it. 'You may be cajoled into imagining that your own special trade or your own industry will be encouraged by a protective tar-

iff, but it stands to reason that such legislation must in the long run keep away wealth from the country, diminish the value of our imports, and lower the general conditions of life in this island.' What do you think of that, Watson?" cried Holmes, in high glee, rubbing his hands together with satisfaction. "Don't you think that is an admirable sentiment?"

Dr. Mortimer look at Holmes with an air of professional interest, and Sir Henry Baskerville turned a pair of puzzled dark eyes upon me.

"I don't know much about the tariff and things of that kind," said he, "but it seems to me we've got a bit off the trail so far as that note is concerned."

"On the contrary, I think we are particularly hot upon the trail. There is so very close a connection that the one is extracted out of the other. 'You,' 'your,' 'your,' 'life,' 'reason,' 'value,' 'keep away,' 'from the.' Don't you see now whence these words have been taken?"

"By thunder, you're right! Well, if that isn't smart!" cried Sir Henry.

"If any possible doubt remained it is settled by the fact that 'keep away' and 'from the' are cut out in one piece."

"Well, now—so it is!"

"Really, Mr. Holmes, this exceeds anything which I could have imagined," said Dr. Mortimer, gazing at my friend in amazement. "How did you do it?"

"This is my special hobby. There is much difference to my eyes between the leaded bourgeois type[3] of a *Times* article and the slovenly print of an evening halfpenny paper. A *Times* leader is entirely distinctive, and these words could have been taken from nothing else. As it was done yesterday the strong probability

---

2. **foolscap paper:** large sheet of paper measuring about thirteen by sixteen inches.

---

3. **leaded bourgeois** [boor zhwä´] **type:** distinguished printing type. *Bourgeois* refers to the size of the letters, about nine-tenths of an inch high.

The Hound of the Baskervilles   517

AT A GLANCE
- The anonymous note solemnly warns Sir Henry to stay away from the moor.
- Holmes demonstrates that most of the words in the note were cut from a newspaper article.

1 PLOT: RISING ACTION

With the arrival of Sir Henry Baskerville and the appearance of the ominous note, the mystery is both complicated and enriched.

2 CHARACTERIZATION

Holmes, usually presented as a formal and serious character, shows a lighter, playful side as he teases the others by reading an article that *seems* to have nothing to do with the case.

3 STYLE: HUMOR

Watson's dry sense of humor is evident as he implies (by reporting that attention was drawn to the two physicians) that the two strangers view Holmes's outburst as irrational.

4 THEME

Holmes's knowledge of newspaper type underscores the importance his keen powers of observation and deductive ability play in his work.

GUIDED READING

LITERAL QUESTIONS

1a. What is unusual about the words that formed the note to Sir Henry? (Most of the words have been cut out of a newspaper and pasted down on paper to form the message.)

2a. What is the message in the note? ("As you value your life or your reason keep away from the moor.")

INFERENTIAL QUESTIONS

1b. Why does the sender of the note choose this unusual way of writing? (The sender does not want to be identified. A detective might have been able to trace the sender's handwriting.)

2b. What do those words suggest might happen if Sir Henry goes to Baskerville Hall? (He might be murdered or driven mad.)

- Holmes deduces that the writer was educated and feared having his or her handwriting identified by Sir Henry.
- Holmes deduces that the note was composed hurriedly in a hotel.
- Sir Henry reports that one of his new boots was stolen.

1 BACKGROUND

Some aspects of this detective novel, such as the words cut from newspaper to make an anonymous communication, may seem hackneyed to modern readers. In 1902, however, when the novel appeared, the device was original and effective.

2 RESPONSE JOURNAL

Have students keep a list of clues that will help them sort out the suspects that appear later in the novel. For example, students might note that the writer of the note is educated and that his or her writing might be known to Sir Henry.

3 VOCABULARY: SLANG

Dime novels were the "pulp" fiction of the period—melodramatic or sensational with little literary merit. By saying he has "walked into a dime novel," Sir Henry shows skepticism about the depth and tone of Holmes's inquiry.

---

was that we should find the words in yesterday's issue."

"So far as I can follow you, then, Mr. Holmes," said Sir Henry Baskerville, "someone cut out this message with scissors and pasted it to the paper. But I want to know why the word 'moor' should have been written?"

1 "Because he could not find it in print. The other words were all simple and might be found in any issue, but 'moor' would be less common."

"Why, of course, that would explain it. Have you read anything else in this message, Mr. Holmes?"

"There are one or two indications, and yet the utmost pains have been taken to remove all clues. The address, you observe, is printed in rough characters. But the *Times* is a paper which is seldom found in any hands but those 2 of the highly educated. We may take it, therefore, that the letter was composed by an educated man who wished to pose as an uneducated one, and his effort to conceal his own writing suggests that that writing might be known, or come to be known, by you. Again, you will observe that the words are not gummed on in an accurate line, but that some are much higher than others. That may point to hurry upon the part of the cutter. Did the composer fear an interruption?"

"We are coming now rather into the region of guesswork," said Dr. Mortimer.

"Say, rather, into the region where we balance probabilities and choose the most likely. It is the scientific use of the imagination. Now, you would call it a guess, no doubt, but I am almost certain that this address has been written in a hotel."

"How in the world can you say that?"

"If you examine it carefully you will see that both the pen and the ink have given the writer trouble. The pen has spluttered twice in a single word and has run dry three times in a short address, showing that there was very

little ink in the bottle. Now, a private pen or ink bottle is seldom allowed to be in such a state, and the combination of the two must be quite rare. But you know the hotel ink and the hotel pen, where it is rare to get anything else. Yes, I have very little hesitation in saying that could we examine the wastepaper baskets of the hotels round Charing Cross until we found the remains of the mutilated *Times* leader we could lay our hands straight upon the person who sent this singular message.

"I think we have drawn as much as we can from this curious letter; and now, Sir Henry, has anything else of interest happened to you since you have been in London?"

"Why, no, Mr. Holmes. I think not."

"You have not observed anyone follow or watch you?"

3 "I seem to have walked right into the thick of a dime novel," said our visitor. "Why in thunder should anyone follow or watch me?"

"We are coming to that. You have nothing else to report to us before we go into this matter?"

"Well, it depends upon what you think worth reporting."

"I think anything out of the ordinary routine of life well worth reporting."

Sir Henry smiled.

"I don't know much of British life yet, for I have spent nearly all my time in the States and in Canada. But I hope that to lose one of your boots is not part of the ordinary routine of life over here."

"You have lost one of your boots?"

"Well, mislaid it, anyhow. I put them both outside my door last night, and there was only one in the morning. I could get no sense out of the chap who cleans them. The worst of it is that I only bought the pair last night in the Strand,[4] and I have never had them on."

---

4. **the Strand:** famous London street with theaters, hotels, and businesses.

518   *The Novel*

GUIDED READING

LITERAL QUESTIONS

1a. When Dr. Mortimer says that Holmes's questions require guesswork, what does Holmes say they require? (the "scientific use of the imagination")

2a. Besides getting the strange letter, what other unusual event occurs at Sir Henry's hotel? (One of his new boots is lost or stolen.)

INFERENTIAL QUESTIONS

1b. In what way is Holmes's method scientific? In what way is it imaginative? (It is based on observation and logical deduction; he is able to imagine other people's circumstances, reasoning, and motivations.)

2b. Why might someone have stolen Sir Henry's boot? (to make him feel that he is in imminent danger)

"If you have never worn them, why did you put them out to be cleaned?"

"They were tan boots and had never been varnished. That was why I put them out."

"Then I understand that on your arrival in London yesterday you went out at once and bought a pair of boots?"

"I did a good deal of shopping. Dr. Mortimer here went round with me. I bought these brown boots—gave six dollars for them[5]—and had one stolen before ever I had them on my feet."

"It seems a singularly useless thing to steal," said Sherlock Holmes. "It will not be long before the missing boot is found."

"And, now, gentlemen," said the baronet, with decision, "it seems to me that I have spoken quite enough about the little that I know. It is time that you kept your promise and gave me a full account of what we are all driving at."

"Your request is a very reasonable one," Holmes answered. "Dr. Mortimer, I think you could not do better than to tell your story as you told it to us."

Thus encouraged, our scientific friend drew his papers from his pocket and presented the whole case as he had done upon the morning before. Sir Henry Baskerville listened with the deepest attention and with an occasional exclamation of surprise.

"Well, I seem to have come into an inheritance with a vengeance," said he when the long narrative was finished. "Of course, I've heard of the hound ever since I was in the nursery. It's the pet story of the family, though I never thought of taking it seriously before. But as to my uncle's death—well, it all seems boiling up in my head, and I can't get it clear yet. You don't seem quite to have made up

_____
5. **gave . . . for them:** The boots were expensive for that time.

your mind whether it's a case for a policeman or a clergyman."

"Precisely."

"And now there's this affair of the letter to me at the hotel. I suppose that fits into its place."

"It seems to show that someone knows more than we do about what goes on upon the moor," said Dr. Mortimer.

1 "And also," said Holmes, "that someone is not ill-disposed toward you, since they warn you of danger."

"Or it may be that they wish, for their own purposes, to scare me away."

"Well, of course, that is possible also. I am very much indebted to you, Dr. Mortimer. But the practical point which we now have to decide, Sir Henry, is whether it is or is not advisable for you to go to Baskerville Hall."

"Why should I not go?"

"There seems to be danger."

"Do you mean danger from this family fiend or do you mean danger from human beings?"

"Well, that is what we have to find out."

2 "Whichever it is, my answer is fixed. There is no man upon earth who can prevent me from going to the home of my own people, and you may take that to be my final answer." His dark brows knitted and his face flushed to a dusky red as he spoke. "Meanwhile," said he, "I have hardly had time to think over all that you have told me. Suppose you and your friend, Dr. Watson, come round and lunch with us at two. I'll be able to tell you more clearly then how this thing strikes me."

"Is that convenient to you, Watson?"

"Perfectly."

"Then you may expect us. Shall I have a cab called?"

3 "I'd prefer to walk, for this affair has flurried me rather."

"I'll join you in a walk, with pleasure," said his companion.

The Hound of the Baskervilles 519

AT A GLANCE
- Dr. Mortimer presents the whole case to Sir Henry, who is both surprised and confused.
- Regardless of danger, Sir Henry vows to go to Baskerville Hall.
- Sir Henry and Dr. Mortimer leave after agreeing to meet Holmes and Watson later for lunch.

1 CHARACTERIZATION

In mysteries the motivations of a character's actions are crucial: The sender of the letter may or may not be a suspect, depending on *why* the letter was sent.

2 CHARACTERIZATION

Sir Henry's bold statement and flash of anger show that—unlike Sir Charles—he will not be easily frightened.

3 PLOT: RISING ACTION

A novelist carefully paces the many events that make up the plot. Here, after a lengthy discussion of the case, there is an interruption in order to change the scene and actively introduce new clues.

GUIDED READING

LITERAL QUESTIONS

1a. How has Sir Henry always viewed the legend about the Baskerville hound? (It was a "pet" story, told often but not taken seriously.)

2a. How do the facts of the case affect Sir Henry's plan to move into Baskerville Hall? (not at all; if anything, he seems more resolved to go "to the home of my own people")

INFERENTIAL QUESTIONS

1b. How do you predict Sir Henry's attitude toward the tale might change? (Now that he knows a terrible hound may have had a role in his uncle's death, he might take the tale more seriously.)

2b. What does this tell you about Sir Henry? (He is resolute, perhaps reckless; he is not easily deterred once he has made up his mind.)

"Then we meet again at two o'clock. Au revoir,[6] and good morning!"

We heard the steps of our visitors descend the stair and the bang of the front door. In an instant Holmes had changed from the languid dreamer to the man of action.

"Your hat and boots, Watson, quick! Not a moment to lose!" He rushed into his room in his dressing gown and was back again in a few seconds in a frock coat. We hurried together down the stairs and into the street. Dr. Mortimer and Baskerville were still visible about two hundred yards ahead of us in the direction of Oxford Street.

"Shall I run on and stop them?"

"Not for the world, my dear Watson. I am perfectly satisfied with your company if you will tolerate mine."

He quickened his pace until we had decreased the distance which divided us by about half. Then, still keeping a hundred yards behind, we followed into Oxford Street and so down Regent Street. Once our friends stopped and stared into a shop window, upon which Holmes did the same. An instant afterwards he gave a little cry of satisfaction, and, following the direction of his eager eyes, I saw that a hansom cab with a man inside which had halted on the other side of the street was now walking slowly onward again.

"There's our man, Watson! Come! We'll have a good look at him, if we can do no more."

At that instant I was aware of a bushy black beard and a pair of piercing eyes turned upon us through the side window of the cab. Instantly the trapdoor at the top flew up, something was screamed to the driver, and the cab flew madly off down Regent Street. Holmes looked eagerly round for another, but no empty one was in sight. Then he dashed in wild pursuit amid the stream of the traffic,

---

6. **Au revoir** [ō rə vwär']: French for "until we meet again."

520   *The Novel*

but the start was too great, and already the cab was out of sight.

"There now!" said Holmes bitterly as he emerged panting and white with vexation from the tide of vehicles. "Was ever such bad luck and such bad management, too? Watson, Watson, if you are an honest man you will record this also and set it against my successes!"

"Who was the man?"

"I have not an idea."

"A spy?"

"Well, it was evident from what we have heard that Baskerville has been very closely shadowed by someone since he has been in town. How else could it be known so quickly

GUIDED READING

LITERAL QUESTION

1a. What two factors does Holmes give as reasons for his failure to follow the man with the beard? (bad luck and bad management)

INFERENTIAL QUESTION

1b. What does this explanation for the failure tell you about Holmes as a person? (He is willing to admit and accept responsibility for what he views as his shortcomings.)

that it was the Northumberland Hotel which he had chosen? We are dealing with a clever man, Watson. So wily was he that he had not trusted himself upon foot, but he had availed himself of a cab so that he could loiter behind or dash past them and so escape their notice. His method had the additional advantage that if they were to take a cab he was all ready to follow them. It has, however, one obvious disadvantage."

"It puts him in the power of the cabman."

"Exactly."

"What a pity we did not get the number!"

¹"My dear Watson, clumsy as I have been, you surely do not seriously imagine that I neglected to get the number? No. 2704 is our man. But that is no use to us for the moment."

"I fail to see how you could have done more."

"On observing the cab I should have instantly turned and walked in the other direction. I should then at my leisure have hired a second cab and followed the first at a respectful distance, or, better still, have driven to the Northumberland Hotel and waited there. There is no object in our following them," said Holmes. ²"The shadow has departed and will not return. We must see what further cards we have in our hands and play them with decision. Could you swear to that man's face within the cab?"

"I could swear only to the beard."

"And so could I—from which I gather that in all probability it was a false one. A clever man upon so delicate an errand has no use for a beard save to conceal his features. Come in here, Watson!"

³He turned into one of the district messenger offices, where he was warmly greeted by the manager.

"Ah, Wilson, I see you have not forgotten the little case in which I had the good fortune to help you?"

"No, sir, indeed I have not. You saved my good name, and perhaps my life."

"My dear fellow, you exaggerate. I have some recollection, Wilson, that you had among your boys a lad named Cartwright, who showed some ability during the investigation."

"Yes, sir, he is still with us."

"Could you ring him up? Thank you! And I should be glad to have change of this five-pound note."[7]

A lad of fourteen, with a bright, keen face, had obeyed the summons of the manager. He

---

7. **five-pound note:** The pound is the basic monetary unit in Great Britain. At the time of the story, five pounds was worth about twenty-five dollars.

The Hound of the Baskervilles 521

AT A GLANCE

- Holmes has managed to get the number of the escaping cab.
- Holmes speculates on how he might have trailed the cab more effectively.
- The detective enlists the aid of a district messenger office in tracking down leads in the case.

1 CHARACTERIZATION

Holmes acknowledges his previous "clumsy" failure but quickly affirms that he is back in command of the situation, revealing himself to be someone who does not dwell on past mistakes.

2 STYLE: METAPHOR

This is the first of a series of metaphors that Holmes uses to describe his work. Here he compares the solution of the mystery to a card game.

3 SETTING

Holmes's success in ridding London of various criminals has created good will toward the detective. As a result he is able to call informally upon various individuals and institutions for aid.

GUIDED READING

LITERAL QUESTION

1a. What clue has the incident with the cab provided to Holmes? (He has learned the number of the cab driver—2704.)

INFERENTIAL QUESTION

1b. In what way might this clue be useful to Holmes? (He will be able to locate and question the cab driver about his passenger.)

- Holmes employs a messenger, Cartwright, to search hotel trash for the cut-up *Times*.
- Holmes and Watson arrive at Sir Henry's hotel.
- Holmes cunningly determines that the person following Sir Henry is not a guest at the hotel.

1 CHARACTERIZATION

A novel often has many characters. Major characters, such as Holmes, Watson, and Sir Henry, are developed in great detail; minor characters, such as Cartwright, are simpler and less developed.

2 CHARACTERIZATION

This incident points out two more of Holmes's character traits: He is thorough and realistic. Although the odds are "enormously against him," he still painstakingly follows up every clue.

3 STYLE: METAPHOR

In the chapter title Doyle uses a metaphor to foreshadow the unsuccessful results of Holmes's initial efforts. The three threads are the three clues—the cut-up newspaper, cab driver 2704, and the man with the black beard.

4 CHARACTERIZATION

Holmes's cunning line of questioning points to a creative ability to improvise. From the unwitting clerk he draws out information that should be kept confidential.

5 READING SKILLS: INFERENCE

Holmes has deduced an important clue: Sir Henry's "shadow" does not want to be seen. From this the reader may further infer that Sir Henry may know the person.

---

stood now gazing with great reverence at the famous detective.

"Let me have the Hotel Directory," said Holmes. "Thank you! Now, Cartwright, there are the names of twenty-three hotels here, all in the immediate neighborhood of Charing Cross. Do you see?"

"Yes, sir."

"You will visit each of these in turn."

"Yes, sir."

"You will begin in each case by giving the outside porter one shilling.[8] Here are twenty-three shillings."

"Yes, sir."

"You will tell him that you want to see the wastepaper of yesterday. You will say that an important telegram has miscarried and that you are looking for it. You understand?"

"Yes, sir."

"But what you are really looking for is the center page of the *Times* with some holes cut in it with scissors. Here is a copy of the *Times*. It is this page. You could easily recognize it, could you not?"

"Yes, sir."

"In each case the outside porter will send for the hall porter, to whom also you will give a shilling. Here are twenty-three shillings. You will then learn in possibly twenty cases out of the twenty-three that the waste of the day before has been burned or removed. In the three other cases you will be shown a heap of paper and you will look for this page of the *Times* among it. The odds are enormously against your finding it. There are ten shillings over in case of emergencies. Let me have a report by wire at Baker Street before evening.

"And now, Watson, it only remains for us to find out by wire the identity of the cabman, No. 2704, and then we will drop into one of the Bond Street picture galleries and fill in the time until we are due at the hotel."

---

8. **shilling:** British coin then worth about a quarter.

522   *The Novel*

---

3   5   Three Broken Threads

We soon found ourselves at the Northumberland Hotel.

"Sir Henry Baskerville is upstairs expecting you," said the clerk. "He asked me to show you up at once when you came."

"Have you any objection to my looking at your register?" said Holmes.

"Not in the least."

The book showed that two names had been added after that of Baskerville. One was Theophilus Johnson and family, of Newcastle; the other Mrs. Oldmore and maid, of High Lodge, Alton.

"Surely that must be the same Johnson whom I used to know," said Holmes to the porter. "A lawyer, is he not, gray-headed, and walks with a limp?"

"No, sir, this is Mr. Johnson, the coal owner, a very active gentleman, not older than yourself."

"Surely you are mistaken about his trade?"

"No, sir; he has used this hotel for many years, and he is very well known to us."

"Ah, that settles it. Mrs. Oldmore, too; I seem to remember the name. Excuse my curiosity, but often in calling upon one friend one finds another."

"She is an invalid lady, sir. Her husband was once Mayor of Gloucester. She always comes to us when she is in town."

"Thank you; I am afraid I cannot claim her acquaintance. We have established a most important fact by these questions, Watson," he continued, in a low voice, as we went upstairs together. "We know now that the people who are so interested in our friend have not settled down in his own hotel. That means that while they are, as we have seen, very anxious to watch him they are equally anxious that he should not see them. Now, this is a most suggestive fact."

GUIDED READING

LITERAL QUESTION

1a. What does Holmes want Cartwright, the messenger, to find? (the copy of the *Times* from which the words of the message to Sir Henry were cut)

INFERENTIAL QUESTION

1b. If Cartwright finds this object, of what use will it be to Holmes? (If the paper is found, Holmes will know where the sender stayed and might be able to find out his or her name.)

"What does it suggest?"

"It suggests—halloa, my dear fellow, what on earth is the matter?"

As we came round the top of the stairs we had run up against Sir Henry Baskerville himself. His face was flushed with anger, and he held an old and dusty boot in one of his hands.

1 "Seems to me they are playing me for a sucker in this hotel," he cried. "They'll find they've started in to monkey with the wrong man unless they are careful. By thunder, if that chap can't find my missing boot there will be trouble. I can take a joke with the best, Mr. Holmes, but they've got a bit over the mark this time."

"Still looking for your boot?"

"Yes, sir, and mean to find it."

"But, surely, you said that it was a new brown boot?"

"So it was, sir. And now it's an old black one."

"What! you don't mean to say—?"

"That's just what I do mean to say. I only had three pairs in the world—the new brown, the old black, and the patent leathers, which I am wearing. Last night they took one of my brown ones, and today they have sneaked one of the black. Well, have you got it? Speak out, man, and don't stand staring!"

An agitated German waiter had appeared upon the scene.

"No, sir; I have made inquiry all over the hotel, but I can hear no word of it."

"Well, either that boot comes back before sundown or I'll see the manager and tell him that I go right straight out of this hotel."

"It shall be found, sir—I promise you that if you will have a little patience it will be found."

"Mind it is, for it's the last thing of mine that I'll lose in this den of thieves. Well, well, Mr. Holmes, you'll excuse my troubling you about such a trifle—"

"I think it's well worth troubling about."

"Why, you look very serious over it."

"How do you explain it?"

2 "I just don't attempt to explain it. It seems the very maddest, oddest thing that ever happened to me."

"The oddest perhaps—" said Holmes thoughtfully.

"What do you make of it yourself?"

"Well, I don't profess to understand it yet. This case of yours is very complex, Sir Henry. **3** But we hold several threads in our hands, and the odds are that one or another of them guides us to the truth."

We had a pleasant luncheon in which little was said of the business which had brought us together. It was in the private sitting room to which we afterwards repaired that Holmes asked Baskerville what were his intentions.

"To go to Baskerville Hall."

"And when?"

"At the end of the week."

"On the whole," said Holmes, "I think that **4** your decision is a wise one. I have ample evidence that you are being dogged in London, and amid the millions of this great city it is difficult to discover who these people are or what their object can be. If their intentions are evil they might do you a mischief, and we should be powerless to prevent it. You did not know, Dr. Mortimer, that you were followed this morning from my house?"

Dr. Mortimer started violently.

"Followed! By whom?"

"That, unfortunately, is what I cannot tell you. Have you among your neighbors or acquaintances on Dartmoor any man with a black, full beard?"

"No—or, let me see—why, yes. Barrymore, Sir Charles's butler, is a man with a full, black beard."

"Ha! Where is Barrymore?"

"He is in charge of the Hall."

"We had best ascertain if he is really there,

The Hound of the Baskervilles 523

- Holmes sends a telegram to Barrymore to make sure the butler is at Baskerville Hall.
- Holmes learns that Barrymore, Dr. Mortimer, and others received inheritances from Sir Charles.
- If Sir Henry dies without a will, the estate goes to James Desmond, an elderly clergyman.

1 BACKGROUND

The telephone, invented before the novel's publication in 1901, was nonetheless not in widespread use and rarely found in rural areas. Holmes's use of a telegram attests to the historical accuracy of details of setting in the novel.

2 CHARACTERIZATION

Dr. Mortimer helps build the case against Barrymore beyond the circumstantial evidence of the dark beard. The Barrymores had a motivation to kill Sir Charles: an inheritance and an easier life at the hall.

3 PLOT: RISING ACTION

Holmes suggests an explanation for the odd incidents involving Sir Henry as well as a reason why people are following him: to kill him and somehow benefit from his estate.

4 CHARACTERIZATION

The characterization of Desmond as a saintly clergyman who refused money from Sir Charles seems to eliminate him as a possible suspect in the case, even though he would have a strong motive.

---

or if by any possibility he might be in London."

"How can you do that?"

1 "Give me a telegraph form. 'Is all ready for Sir Henry?' That will do. Address to Mr. Barrymore, Baskerville Hall. What is the nearest telegraph office? Grimpen. Very good, we will send a second wire to the postmaster, Grimpen: 'Telegram to Mr. Barrymore to be delivered into his own hand. If absent, please return wire to Sir Henry Baskerville, Northumberland Hotel.' That should let us know before evening whether Barrymore is at his post in Devonshire or not."

"That's so," said Baskerville. "By the way, Dr. Mortimer, who is this Barrymore, anyhow?"

"He is the son of the old caretaker, who is dead. They have looked after the Hall for four generations now. So far as I know, he and his wife are as respectable a couple as any in the county."

"At the same time," said Baskerville, "it's clear enough that so long as there are none of the family at the Hall these people have a mighty fine home and nothing to do."

"That is true."

2 "Did Barrymore profit at all by Sir Charles's will?" asked Holmes.

"He and his wife had five hundred pounds each."

"Ha! Did they know that they would receive this?"

"Yes; Sir Charles was very fond of talking about the provisions of his will."

"That is very interesting."

"I hope," said Dr. Mortimer, "that you do not look with suspicious eyes upon everyone who received a legacy from Sir Charles, for I also had a thousand pounds left to me."

"Indeed! And anyone else?"

"There were many insignificant sums to individuals, and a large number of public charities. The residue all went to Sir Henry."

524   *The Novel*

"And how much was the residue?"

"Seven hundred and forty thousand pounds."

Holmes raised his eyebrows in surprise. "I had no idea that so gigantic a sum was involved," said he.

"Sir Charles had the reputation of being rich, but we did not know how very rich he was until we came to examine his securities. The total value of the estate was close on to a million."

3 "Dear me! It is a stake for which a man might well play a desperate game. And one more question, Dr. Mortimer. Supposing that anything happened to our young friend here—you will forgive the unpleasant hypothesis!—who would inherit the estate?"

"Since Rodger Baskerville, Sir Charles's younger brother, died unmarried, the estate would descend to the Desmonds, who are distant cousins. James Desmond is an elderly clergyman in Westmorland."

"Thank you. These details are all of great interest. Have you met Mr. James Desmond?"

4 "Yes; he once came down to visit Sir Charles. He is a man of venerable appearance and of saintly life. I remember that he refused to accept any settlement from Sir Charles, though he pressed it upon him."

"And this man of simple tastes would be the heir to Sir Charles's thousands."

"He would be the heir to the estate because that is entailed.[1] He would also be the heir to the money unless it were willed otherwise by the present owner, who can, of course, do what he likes with it."

"And have you made your will, Sir Henry?"

"No, Mr. Holmes, I have not. I've had no time, for it was only yesterday that I learned how matters stood."

"Quite so. Well, Sir Henry, I am of one mind

---

1. **entailed:** property inheritance limited by law to a certain group of heirs.

GUIDED READING

LITERAL QUESTIONS

1a. How does Holmes hope to determine whether Barrymore is home at Baskerville Hall? (He sends a telegram to be delivered into the butler's own hands; if Barrymore is not there, the wire will be returned.)

2a. Who will inherit the Baskerville fortune if Sir Henry dies without a will? (Mr. James Desmond)

INFERENTIAL QUESTIONS

1b. Why is Holmes so interested in establishing Barrymore's whereabouts? (Barrymore has a full dark beard like the man in the cab; he could have been the man following Sir Henry.)

2b. Is Desmond a likely suspect in the case? Why or why not? (No, Desmond is old, has lived a saintly life, and previously refused money from Sir Charles.)

with you as to the advisability of your going down to Devonshire without delay. There is only one provision which I must make. You certainly must not go alone."

"Dr. Mortimer returns with me."

"But Dr. Mortimer has his practice to attend to, and his house is miles away from yours. With all the good will in the world, he may be unable to help you. No, Sir Henry, you must take with you someone, a trusty man, who will be always by your side."

"Is it possible that you could come yourself, Mr. Holmes?"

1 "If matters came to a crisis I should endeavor to be present in person; but you can understand that, with my extensive consulting practice and with the constant appeals which reach me from many quarters, it is impossible for me to be absent from London for an indefinite time."

"Whom would you recommend, then?"

Holmes laid his hand upon my arm.

"If my friend would undertake it there is no man who is better worth having at your side when you are in a tight place. No one can say so more confidently than I."

2 The proposition took me completely by surprise, but before I had time to answer, Baskerville seized me by the hand and wrung it heartily.

"Well, now, that is real kind of you, Dr. Watson," said he.

The promise of adventure had always a fascination for me, and I was complimented by the words of Holmes.

"I will come, with pleasure," said I. "I do not know how I could employ my time better."

3 "And you will report very carefully to me," said Holmes. "When a crisis comes, as it will, I will direct how you shall act. I suppose that by Saturday all might be ready?"

"Would that suit Dr. Watson?"

"Perfectly."

"Then on Saturday, unless you hear to the contrary, we shall meet at the ten-thirty train from Paddington."

We had risen to depart when Baskerville gave a cry of triumph, and diving into one of the corners of the room he drew a brown boot from under a cabinet.

"My missing boot!" he cried.

"May all our difficulties vanish as easily!" said Sherlock Holmes.

"But it is a very singular thing," Dr. Mortimer remarked. "I searched this room carefully before lunch."

"And so did I," said Baskerville. "Every inch of it."

"There was certainly no boot in it then."

"In that case the waiter must have placed it there while we were lunching."

The German was sent for, but professed to know nothing of the matter, nor could any 4 inquiry clear it up. Another item had been added to that constant and apparently purposeless series of small mysteries which had succeeded each other so rapidly. Holmes sat in silence in the cab as we drove back to Baker Street. All afternoon and late into the evening he sat lost in thought.

The Hound of the Baskervilles 525

AT A GLANCE

- Since Holmes is busy in London, he proposes that Watson go with Sir Henry to Devonshire.
- The first of Sir Henry's lost boots reappears in his room.

1 PLOT: RISING ACTION

Holmes, whose greatest enjoyment is a good case, is especially intrigued by this one. Yet instead of heading to Devonshire with the others, he stays in London to attend to routine responsibilities.

2 THEME

This passage emphasizes Watson's loyal friendship for Holmes. Holmes has not even consulted Watson before he announces the plan; he assumes Watson will do whatever is necessary.

3 CHARACTERIZATION

Holmes is seen to be the mastermind who is able to predict the future; Watson is the loyal foot soldier, ready and willing to follow orders.

4 MOOD

The "constant and apparently purposeless series of small mysteries" have created a somber yet intense mood. Even Holmes seems unable to fathom the peculiar details of this case.

GUIDED READING

LITERAL QUESTIONS

1a. Why does Holmes decide not to go to Devonshire with Sir Henry Baskerville? (He says his practice in London is too busy for him to leave.)

2a. What does Sir Henry suddenly find in his hotel room? (He finds the new brown boot that had been missing.)

INFERENTIAL QUESTIONS

1b. Why does this decision seem slightly surprising? (Holmes is the main character of the story and seems intrigued by the case. One would expect him to go to Baskerville Hall to follow up clues.)

2b. Why might someone steal one of Sir Henry's boots and then return it? (Answers will vary. Possibilities: to unnerve him, to warn him of danger)

- Sir Henry reports that Barrymore is at Baskerville Hall.
- Cartwright reports that he could not find the cut-up *Times*.
- Cabman 2704 says his passenger's name was Sherlock Holmes.

1 STYLE: IMAGERY

Holmes, unlike a hound, is not easily discouraged. The image of Holmes casting "round for another scent" suggests a curiously apt and intriguing parallel in the novel.

2 STYLE: DIALECT

The cabman's rhythm of speech reflects British working-class speech of the time.

3 IRONY

Holmes, as confident and sarcastic as the reader has yet seen him, seems about to discover the suspect's name; ironically, he learns only that the suspect has ingeniously used Holmes's name as his own.

4 STYLE: METAPHOR

Holmes earlier likened the case to a card game; here he describes it as a fencing match.

Just before dinner two telegrams were handed in. The first ran:

"Have just heard that Barrymore is at the Hall.—BASKERVILLE."

The second:

"Visited twenty-three hotels as directed, but sorry to report unable to trace cut sheet of *Times*.—CARTWRIGHT."

1 "There go two of my threads, Watson. There is nothing more stimulating than a case where everything goes against you. We must cast round for another scent."

"We have still the cabman who drove the spy."

"Exactly. I have wired to get his name and address from the Official Registry. I should not be surprised if this were an answer to my question."

The ring at the bell proved to be something even more satisfactory than an answer, however, for the door opened and a rough-looking fellow entered who was evidently the man himself.

"I got a message from the head office that a gent at this address had been inquiring for No. 2704," said he. "I've driven my cab this seven years and never a word of complaint. I came here straight from the yard[2] to ask you to your face what you had against me."

"I have nothing in the world against you, my good man," said Holmes. "On the contrary, I have half a sovereign[3] for you if you will give me a clear answer to my questions."

2 "Well, I've had a good day and no mistake," said the cabman, with a grin. "What was it you wanted to ask, sir?"

"First of all your name and address."

"John Clayton, 3, Turpey Street, the Borough."

---

2. **yard:** area where cabs are parked.
3. **sovereign** [sov'rən]: former British gold coin worth one pound.

"Now, Clayton, tell me all about the fare who came and watched this house at ten o'clock this morning and afterwards followed the two gentlemen down Regent Street."

The man looked surprised and a little embarrassed. "Why, there's no good my telling you things, for you seem to know as much as I do already," said he. "The truth is that the gentleman told me that he was a detective and that I was to say nothing about him to anyone."

"My good fellow, this is a very serious business, and you may find yourself in a pretty bad position if you try to hide anything from me. You say that your fare told you that he was a detective?"

"Yes, he did."

"Did he say anything more?"

"He mentioned his name."

3 Holmes cast a swift glance of triumph at me. "Oh, he mentioned his name, did he? That was imprudent. What was the name that he mentioned?"

"His name," said the cabman, "was Mr. Sherlock Holmes."

Never have I seen my friend more completely taken aback than by the cabman's reply. For an instant he sat in silent amazement. Then he burst into a hearty laugh.

4 "A touch, Watson—an undeniable touch!" said he. "I feel a foil as quick and supple as my own. He got home upon me very prettily that time. So his name was Sherlock Holmes, was it?"

"Yes, sir, that was the gentleman's name."

"Excellent! Tell me where you picked him up and all that occurred."

"He hailed me at half past nine in Trafalgar Square. He said that he was a detective, and he offered me two guineas[4] if I would do ex-

---

4. **guineas** [gin'ēz]: former British coins. One guinea was worth slightly more than a pound.

GUIDED READING

LITERAL QUESTIONS

1a. How do the first two of Sherlock Holmes's threads break? (Baskerville learns by telegram that Barrymore is at the hall; Cartwright cannot trace the cut-up *Times* used in the strange message.)

2a. What most surprising piece of information does the cabman give Holmes? (He tells Holmes that his passenger, the man with the beard who followed Sir Henry, gave his name as "Sherlock Holmes.")

INFERENTIAL QUESTIONS

1b. In what way is Holmes's reaction to the breaking of these threads somewhat surprising? (One would expect him to be discouraged; instead he claims to be stimulated.)

2b. What does this piece of information tell you about the cabman's passenger? (Answers will vary. Possibilities: He was clever to realize who Holmes was and to know that the detective would soon question the cabman; he has a sense of humor.)

actly what he wanted all day and ask no questions. I was glad enough to agree. First we drove down to the Northumberland Hotel and waited there until two gentlemen came out and took a cab from the rank. We followed their cab until it pulled up somewhere near here."

"This very door," said Holmes.

"Well, I couldn't be sure of that, but I daresay my fare knew all about it. We pulled up halfway down the street and waited an hour and a half. Then the two gentlemen passed us, walking, and we followed down Baker Street and along—"

"I know," said Holmes.

"Until we got three-quarters down Regent Street. Then my gentleman threw up the trap, and he cried that I should drive right away to Waterloo Station as hard as I could go. I whipped up the mare and we were there under the ten minutes. Then he paid up his two guineas, like a good one, and away he went into the station. Only just as he was leaving he turned round and he said: 'It might interest you to know that you have been driving Mr. Sherlock Holmes.' That's how I come to know the name."

"And how would you describe Mr. Sherlock Holmes?"

The cabman scratched his head. "Well, he wasn't altogether such an easy gentleman to **1** describe. I'd put him at forty years of age, and he was of a middle height, two or three inches shorter than you, sir. He was dressed like a toff, and he had a black beard, cut square at the end, and a pale face."

"Nothing more that you can remember?"

"No, sir; nothing."

"Well, then, here is your half sovereign. There's another one waiting for you if you can bring any more information. Good night!"

"Good night, sir, and thank you!"

John Clayton departed chuckling, and Holmes turned to me with a shrug of the shoulders and a rueful smile.

"Snap goes our third thread, and we end **2** where we began," said he. "I tell you, Watson, this time we have got a foeman who is worthy of our steel. I've been checkmated in London. I can only wish you better luck in Devonshire. But I'm not easy in my mind about it."

"About what?"

3 "About sending you. It's an ugly business, Watson, an ugly, dangerous business, and the more I see of it the less I like it."

6 Baskerville Hall

Sir Henry Baskerville and Dr. Mortimer were ready upon the appointed day, and we started as arranged for Devonshire. Mr. Sherlock Holmes drove with me to the station and gave me his last parting injunctions and advice.

"I will not bias your mind by suggesting theories or suspicions, Watson," said he; "I wish you simply to report facts in the fullest possible manner to me, and you can leave me to do the theorizing."

"What sort of facts?" I asked.

"Anything which may seem to have a bearing however indirect upon the case, and especially the relations between young Baskerville and his neighbors or any fresh particulars concerning the death of Sir Charles."

"Would it not be well in the first place to get rid of this Barrymore couple?"

"By no means. You could not make a greater mistake. If they are innocent it would be a cruel injustice, and if they are guilty we should be giving up all chance of bringing it home to them. No, no, we will preserve them upon our list of suspects. Then there is a groom at the Hall, if I remember right. There

The Hound of the Baskervilles 527

1 STYLE: DETAILS

Although the cabman says the passenger isn't easy to describe, he does establish the suspect's age, height, and complexion. The word *toff* is British slang for a well-dressed upper-class gentleman.

2 STYLE: METAPHOR

Earlier, Holmes described his contest with the unknown suspect as a card game and as a fencing match. Now it is a chess match—one in which Holmes has been "checkmated."

3 PLOT: SUSPENSE

Holmes's parting appraisal heightens suspense. The reader wonders about the fate of Watson and Baskerville as they prepare to enter what even Holmes calls an "ugly, dangerous business."

GUIDED READING

LITERAL QUESTIONS

1a. According to the cabman, where did the passenger ask to be taken after following the two gentlemen down Baker and Regent streets? (Waterloo Station)

2a. Why doesn't Holmes want to get rid of the Barrymores right away? (It would be unjust to do so if they are innocent; their departure would make the case against them hard to prove if they are guilty.)

INFERENTIAL QUESTIONS

1b. What does this destination suggest about the man? (He was about to leave London for another location.)

2b. What does Holmes's attitude toward the Barrymores tell you about him? (He has a keen sense of justice; he is also wily, realizing that guilty persons can be used to entrap themselves.)

- Holmes says good-bye to his friends and warns them to be careful.
- Watson, Mortimer, and Baskerville enjoy an uneventful journey.
- Baskerville explains that he has never seen Baskerville Hall.

1 PLOT: EXPOSITION

In giving Watson instructions Holmes introduces the cast of minor characters who will appear later in the novel and who are all possible suspects.

2 PLOT: SUSPENSE

Holmes's insistence that something will happen to Sir Henry if he goes about alone heightens the reader's anticipation that Sir Henry may be in grave danger.

3 SETTING

With the images in this brief paragraph, the author neatly marks the transition from the city to the countryside.

4 VOCABULARY: BRITISH TERMS

A *cob* is a short-legged, stout variety of horse. A *wagonette* is a four-wheeled carriage with a bench on each side facing inward.

---

1 are two moorland farmers. There is our friend Dr. Mortimer, whom I believe to be entirely honest, and there is his wife, of whom we know nothing. There is this naturalist Stapleton, and there is his sister, who is said to be a young lady of attractions. There is Mr. Frankland, of Lafter Hall, who is also an unknown factor, and there are one or two other neighbors. These are the folk who must be your very special study."

"I will do my best."

"You have arms, I suppose?"

"Yes, I thought it as well to take them."

"Most certainly. Keep your revolver near you night and day, and never relax your precautions."

Our friends had already secured a first-class carriage, and were waiting for us upon the platform.

"No, we have no news of any kind," said Dr. Mortimer, in answer to my friend's questions.

2 "I beg, Sir Henry, that you will not go about alone," said Holmes. "Some great misfortune will befall you if you do. Did you get your other boot?"

"No, sir, it is gone forever."

"Indeed. That is very interesting. Well, good-bye." he added, as the train began to glide down the platform. "Bear in mind, Sir Henry, one of the phrases in that queer old legend which Dr. Mortimer has read to us and avoid the moor in those hours of darkness when the powers of evil are exalted."

I looked back at the platform when we had left it far behind and saw the tall, austere figure of Holmes standing motionless and gazing after us.

3 The journey was a swift and pleasant one. In a very few hours the brown earth had become ruddy, the brick had changed to granite, and red cows grazed in well-hedged fields.

"You were very young when you last saw Baskerville Hall, were you not?" said Dr. Mortimer.

"I was a boy in my teens at the time of my father's death," he said, "and have never seen Baskerville Hall, for he lived in a little cottage on the South Coast. Thence I went straight to a friend in America. I tell you it is all as new to me as it is to Dr. Watson, and I'm as keen as possible to see the moor."

"Are you? Then your wish is easily granted, for there is your first sight of the moor," said Dr. Mortimer, pointing out of the carriage window.

Over the green squares of the fields and the low curve of a wood there rose in the distance a gray, melancholy hill, with a strange jagged summit, dim and vague in the distance, like some fantastic landscape in a dream. Baskerville sat for a long time, his eyes fixed upon it.

The train pulled up at a small wayside station and we all descended. Outside, beyond 4 the low, white fence, a wagonette with a pair of cobs was waiting. Our coming was evi-

528   *The Novel*

GUIDED READING

LITERAL QUESTION

1a. What simile does the author use to describe the moor? (It is "like some fantastic landscape in a dream.")

INFERENTIAL QUESTION

1b. What atmosphere does this simile help to create? (It creates an eerie, unreal atmosphere.)

statue upon its pedestal, was a mounted soldier, dark and stern, his rifle poised ready over his forearm. He was watching the road along which we traveled.

"What is this, Perkins?" asked Dr. Mortimer.

Our driver half turned in his seat.

2 "There's a convict escaped from Princetown, sir. He's been out three days now, and the warders[1] watch every road and every station, but they've had no sight of him yet. The farmers about here don't like it, sir, and that's a fact."

"Well, I understand that they get five pounds if they can give information."

"Yes, sir, but the chance of five pounds is but a poor thing compared to the chance of having your throat cut. You see, it isn't like any ordinary convict. This is a man that would stick at nothing."

3 "Who is he, then?"

"It is Selden, the Notting Hill murderer."

I remembered the case well, for it was one in which Holmes had taken an interest. The commutation of the assassin's death sentence had been due to some doubts as to his complete sanity.

Our wagonette had topped a rise and in front of us rose the huge expanse of the moor, mottled with gnarled and craggy cairns[2] and tors.[3] A cold wind swept down from it and set **4** us shivering. Somewhere there, on that desolate plain, was lurking this fiendish man, hiding in a burrow like a wild beast. Even Baskerville fell silent and pulled his overcoat more closely around him.

Suddenly we looked down into a cuplike depression, patched with stunted oaks and firs which had been twisted and bent by the

dently a great event, for stationmaster and porters clustered round us to carry out our **1** luggage. It was a sweet, simple country spot, but I was surprised to observe that by the gate there stood two soldierly men in dark uniforms who leaned upon their short rifles and glanced keenly at us as we passed. The coachman, a hard-faced, gnarled little fellow, saluted Sir Henry Baskerville, and in a few minutes we were flying swiftly down the broad, white road. Rolling pasturelands curved upward on either side of us, and old gabled houses peeped out from amid the thick green foliage, but behind the peaceful and sunlit countryside there rose ever, dark against the evening sky, the long, gloomy curve of the moor.

At every turning Baskerville gave an exclamation of delight.

"Halloa!" cried Dr. Mortimer, "what is this?"

A steep curve of heath-clad land, an outlying spur of the moor, lay in front of us. On the summit, hard and clear like an equestrian

---

1. **warders:** prison guards.
2. **cairns** [kărnz]: ancient rounded or cone-shaped piles of stones.
3. **tors:** high rocky hills.

The Hound of the Baskervilles 529

GUIDED READING

LITERAL QUESTION

1a. Who and where is the man named Selden? (Selden, a vicious murderer who has escaped from the nearby prison, is hiding on the moor.)

INFERENTIAL QUESTION

1b. How do you think the news about Selden will affect Watson's and Sir Henry's feelings about the moor? (Having a dangerous criminal lurking there will make the moor seem even more dangerous and frightening.)

1 STYLE: SIMILE

By comparing the house to a glimmering ghost, the author reminds us that supernatural occurences are said to have occurred here.

2 STYLE: DETAILS

The details of this description of Barrymore (*square black beard and pale, distinguished features*) seem to match the cabman's description of his passenger.

3 PLOT: RISING ACTION

The Barrymore's intent to leave throws further suspicion on them, and the unspecified "emotion" the butler exhibits also heightens the reader's interest.

---

fury of years of storm. Two high, narrow towers rose over the trees. The driver pointed with his whip.

"Baskerville Hall," said he.

Its master had risen and was staring with flushed cheeks and shining eyes. A few minutes later we had reached the lodge gates. The lodge was a ruin of black granite and bared ribs of rafters.

1 Baskerville shuddered as he looked up the long, dark drive to where the house glimmered like a ghost at the farther end.

"Was it here?" he asked in a low voice.

"No, no, the yew alley is on the other side."

The young heir glanced round with a gloomy face.

"It's no wonder my uncle felt as if trouble were coming on him in such a place as this," said he. "It's enough to scare any man. I'll have a row of electric lamps up here inside of six months, and you won't know it again, with a thousand candle-power Swan and Edison[4] right here in front of the hall door."

"Welcome, Sir Henry! Welcome, to Baskerville Hall!"

A tall man had stepped from the shadow of the porch to open the door of the wagonette. The figure of a woman was silhouetted against the yellow light of the hall.

"You don't mind my driving straight home, Sir Henry?" said Dr. Mortimer. "My wife is expecting me."

"Surely you will stay and have some dinner?"

"No, I must go. I shall probably find some work awaiting me. Good-bye, and never hesitate night or day to send for me if I can be of service."

The wheels died away down the drive while Sir Henry and I turned into the hall, and the door clanged heavily behind us. It was a fine apartment in which we found ourselves, large,

---

4. **Swan and Edison:** powerful lamp or light fixture.

530 *The Novel*

---

lofty, and heavily raftered with huge balks of age-blackened oak. In the great old-fashioned fireplace behind the high iron dogs a log fire crackled and snapped. Sir Henry and I held out our hands to it, for we were numb from our long drive.

"It's just as I imagined it," said Sir Henry. "Is it not the very picture of an old family home?"

Barrymore had returned from taking our luggage to our rooms. He stood in front of us now with the subdued manner of a well-**2** trained servant. He was a remarkable-looking man, tall, handsome, with a square black beard and pale, distinguished features.

"Would you wish dinner to be served at once, sir?"

"Is it ready?"

"In a very few minutes, sir. You will find hot water in your rooms. My wife and I will be happy, Sir Henry, to stay with you until you have made your fresh arrangements, but you will understand that under the new conditions this house will require a considerable staff."

"What new conditions?"

"I only meant, sir, that Sir Charles led a very retired life, and we were able to look after his wants. You would, naturally, wish to have more company, and so you will need changes in your household."

"Do you mean that your wife and you wish to leave?"

"Only when it is quite convenient to you, sir."

3 "But your family have been with us for several generations, have they not? I should be sorry to begin my life here by breaking an old family connection."

I seemed to discern some signs of emotion upon the butler's white face.

"I feel that also, sir, and so does my wife. But to tell the truth, sir, we were both very much attached to Sir Charles, and his death

---

GUIDED READING

LITERAL QUESTIONS

1a. What is the first change that Sir Henry proposes to make in his new home? (install a row of electric lights outside the house)

2a. What unexpected news does Barrymore give Sir Henry shortly after meeting him? (He and his wife plan to leave their jobs soon.)

INFERENTIAL QUESTIONS

1b. What does this change suggest about Sir Henry's plans for the hall? (He wants to modernize the house and to dispel its gloomy appearance.)

2b. Why might this news make Watson suspicious? (Barrymore is a suspect in the case; by leaving he might be attempting to avoid having his role in the crime proved.)

gave us a shock and made these surroundings very painful to us. I fear that we shall never again be easy in our minds at Baskerville Hall."

"But what do you intend to do?"

"I have no doubt, sir, that we shall succeed in establishing ourselves in some business. Sir Charles's generosity has given us the means to do so. And now, sir, perhaps I had best show you to your rooms."

A square balustraded gallery ran round the top of the old hall, approached by a double stair. From this central point two long corridors extended the whole length of the building, from which all the bedrooms opened. My own was in the same wing as Baskerville's and almost next door to it. These rooms appeared to be much more modern than the central part of the house.

But the dining room which opened out of the hall was a place of shadow and gloom. I for one was glad when the meal was over and we were able to retire.

I drew aside my curtains before I went to bed and looked out from my window. It opened upon the grassy space which lay in front of the hall door. Beyond, two copses of trees moaned and swung in a rising wind. A half-moon broke through the rifts of racing clouds. In its cold light I saw beyond the trees a broken fringe of rocks, and the long, low curve of the melancholy moor.

I found myself weary and yet wakeful, tossing restlessly from side to side, seeking for the sleep which would not come. Far away a chiming clock struck out the quarters of the hours, but otherwise a deathly silence lay upon the old house. And then suddenly, in the very dead of the night, there came a sound to my ears, clear, resonant, and unmistakable. It was the sob of a woman, the muffled, strangling gasp of one who is torn by an uncontrollable sorrow. I sat up in bed and listened intently. The noise could not have been far away and was certainly in the house. For half an hour I waited with every nerve on the alert, but there came no other sound save the chiming clock and the rustle of the ivy on the wall.

STUDY QUESTIONS

Recalling

1. According to Chapter 4, describe the letter that Sir Henry Baskerville received at his hotel. What does Holmes conclude about the source of the letter and the person who sent it?

2. According to Chapter 4, describe what happens to one of Sir Henry's boots. What happens to a different boot at the beginning of Chapter 5?

3. What are the three threads referred to in the title of Chapter 5? Explain why Holmes considers each one to be broken.

4. Whom does Holmes tell Watson to study carefully in Devonshire? Whom does Holmes eliminate as suspects?

5. What noise does Watson hear at the end of Chapter 6?

Interpreting

6. Describe the personality of Sir Henry. What qualities are revealed by his decision to go to Baskerville Hall?

7. Do you think that the person who sent the letter to Sir Henry and the person who followed him are the same? Why or why not?

8. What connection might there be between the disappearance of Sir Henry's boots and the mystery of the hound of the Baskervilles?

9. Whom do you think should be Holmes's prime suspect? Base your opinion on events of the novel.

The Hound of the Baskervilles 531

What is your theory at this point regarding the mysterious hound? (Answers will vary. The creature may well be an actual hound, since someone may be using Sir Henry's boots to train it. It seems as if the hound is being used to further someone's revenge on the Baskervilles or designs on their fortune.)

STUDY QUESTIONS

1. warning, words cut from newspaper; at the hotel, hurried, educated

2. new boot stolen; old boot stolen

3. leads to identity of person shadowing Sir Henry; letter, Barrymore, number of cab; Holmes exhausted each lead fruitlessly

4. ■ The two Barrymores, a groom, farmers, Mortimer's wife, the Stapletons, Frankland, neighbors
   ■ Mortimer, Mr. Desmond

5. woman's muffled sob

6. alert, amiable, energetic, strong; pride, courage, temper

7. *Agree:* Both knew where Sir Henry was staying and were anonymous. *Disagree:* Letter tries to warn; spy is more threatening.

8. Preference for old boot suggests a real hound is involved: scent

9. Possible answers: Barrymore (beard, inherited money); Stapleton or Frankland (would need disguises)

- The following morning Watson learns that Sir Henry also heard the woman's sobs.
- The butler, Barrymore, claims he has no knowledge of a woman crying.
- Watson spies Mrs. Barrymore in a corridor, her eyes red from weeping.

THEMATIC OPTIONS

- observation and deduction
- common sense and superstition
- friendship and loyalty

LITERARY OPTIONS

- point of view
- setting
- plot

1 SETTING

The time of day affects the moods of the characters in Baskerville Hall. All is well in the bright sunshine; at night, though, fearful superstitions prey upon their minds.

2 PLOT: RISING ACTION

The case against Barrymore seems to grow ever stronger: In addition to having a motive and matching the description of the man in the carriage, he has now been caught lying.

3 POINT OF VIEW

In Holmes's absence it is the narrator, Dr. Watson, who must observe details and deduce important information from them.

In Devonshire Watson carries out Holmes's orders to report on the people who surround Sir Henry.

■ *As you read about Watson's observations, pay careful attention to everything each suspect says and does.*

7   The Stapletons of Merripit House

1   The fresh beauty of the following morning did something to efface from our minds the grim and gray impression which had been left upon both of us by our first experience of Baskerville Hall. As Sir Henry and I sat at breakfast the sunlight flooded in through the huge mullioned windows, and it was hard to realize that this was indeed the chamber which had struck such a gloom into our souls upon the evening before.

"I guess it is ourselves and not the house that we have to blame!" said the baronet. "We were tired with our journey and chilled by our drive, so we took a gray view of the place. Now we are fresh and well, so it is all cheerful once more."

"And yet it was not entirely a question of imagination," I answered. "Did you, for example, happen to hear someone, a woman I think, sobbing in the night?"

"That is curious, for I did when I was half-asleep fancy that I heard something of the sort. I waited quite a time, but there was no more of it, so I concluded that it was all a dream."

"I heard it distinctly, and I am sure that it was really the sob of a woman."

"We must ask about this right away." He rang the bell and asked Barrymore whether he could account for our experience. It seemed to me that the pallid features of the butler turned a shade paler still as he listened to his master's question.

"There are only two women in the house, Sir Henry," he answered. "One is the scullery maid, who sleeps in the other wing. The other is my wife, and I can answer for it that the sound could not have come from her."

And yet he lied as he said it, for it chanced that after breakfast I met Mrs. Barrymore in the long corridor with the sun full upon her face. She was a large, impassive, heavy-featured woman with a stern set expression of mouth. But her telltale eyes were red and glanced at me from between swollen lids. It was she, then, who wept in the night, and if she did so her husband must know it. Yet he had taken the obvious risk of discovery in declaring that it was not so. Why had he done this? And why did she weep so bitterly?

532   *The Novel*

GUIDED READING

LITERAL QUESTION

1a. What lie does Barrymore tell Watson? (He tells Watson that his wife was not the woman who had been heard crying.)

INFERENTIAL QUESTION

1b. Why do you think Barrymore told this lie to Watson? (Answers will vary. Possibilities: He is trying to hide information; he is embarrassed.)

1 Already round this pale-faced, handsome, black-bearded man there was gathering an atmosphere of mystery and of gloom. It was he who had been the first to discover the body of Sir Charles, and we had only his word for all the circumstances which led up to the old man's death. Was it possible that it was Barrymore, after all, whom we had seen in the cab in Regent Street? The beard might well have been the same. The cabman had described a somewhat shorter man, but such an impression might easily have been erroneous. How could I settle the point forever? Obviously the first thing to do was to see the Grimpen postmaster and find whether the test telegram had really been placed in Barrymore's own hands. Be the answer what it might, I should at least have something to report to Sherlock Holmes.

It was a pleasant walk of four miles along the edge of the moor, leading me at last to a small gray hamlet. The postmaster, who was also the village grocer, had a clear recollection of the telegram.

"Certainly, sir," said he, "I had the telegram delivered to Mr. Barrymore exactly as directed."

"Who delivered it?"

"My boy here. James, you delivered that telegram to Mr. Barrymore at the Hall last week, did you not?"

"Yes, father, I delivered it."

"Into his own hands?" I asked.

"Well, he was up in the loft at the time, so that I could not put it into his own hands, but I gave it into Mrs. Barrymore's hands, and she promised to deliver it at once."

"Did you see Mr. Barrymore?"

"No, sir; I tell you he was in the loft."

"If you didn't see him, how do you know he was in the loft?"

"Well, surely his own wife ought to know where he is," said the postmaster testily. "Didn't he get the telegram? If there is any

mistake it is for Mr. Barrymore himself to complain."

It seemed hopeless to pursue the inquiry any farther, but it was clear that in spite of Holmes's ruse we had no proof that Barrymore had not been in London all the time. Suppose that it were so—suppose that the same man had been the last who had seen Sir Charles alive, and the first to dog the new heir when he returned to England. What then? Was he **2** the agent of others or had he some sinister design of his own? What interest could he have in persecuting the Baskerville family? I thought of the strange warning clipped out of the leading article of the *Times*. Was that his work or was it possibly the doing of someone who was bent upon counteracting his schemes? The only conceivable motive was that which had been suggested by Sir Henry, that if the family could be scared away a comfortable and permanent home would be secured for the Barrymores. As I walked back along the gray, lonely road, suddenly my thoughts were interrupted by the sound of running feet behind me and by a voice which called me by name. I turned, expecting to see Dr. Mortimer, but to my surprise it was a stranger who was pursuing me.

3 He was a small, slim, clean shaven, prim-faced man, flaxen-haired and lean-jawed, between thirty and forty years of age, dressed in a gray suit and wearing a straw hat. A tin box for botanical specimens hung over his shoulder and he carried a green butterfly net in one of his hands.

"You will, I am sure, excuse my presumption, Dr. Watson," said he as he came panting up to where I stood. "Here on the moor we are homely folk and do not wait for formal introductions. You may possibly have heard my name from our mutual friend, Mortimer. I am Stapleton, of Merripit House."

"Your net and box would have told me as much," said I, "for I knew that Mr. Stapleton

The Hound of the Baskervilles 533

AT A GLANCE

- Watson goes to the post office, where he learns that the test telegram was given to Mrs. Barrymore, since her husband was unavailable.
- Mr. Stapleton, the naturalist, introduces himself to Watson.

1 PLOT: SUSPENSE

Watson's growing suspicions of Barrymore create suspense. The reader wonders if Watson is right to suspect the butler—or if there is some other explanation for the "atmosphere of mystery and of gloom" that surrounds Barrymore.

2 POINT OF VIEW

Watson's musings, a kind of internal monologue, serve to review the various clues and prompt the reader to ask questions that might lead ultimately to the solution.

3 STYLE: DETAILS

Watson provides a detailed description of Stapleton. In a mystery novel closely observed details are likely to be important clues.

GUIDED READING

LITERAL QUESTIONS

1a. What interesting information does Watson learn from the village postmaster? (The telegram was not handed directly to Barrymore.)

2a. What does Stapleton look like? (He is "small, slim, clean shaven, prim-faced . . . flaxen-haired and lean-jawed, between thirty and forty. . . ." He is well-dressed.)

INFERENTIAL QUESTIONS

1b. What effect does this information have on the case Watson is building against Barrymore? (It makes his case stronger; the butler may have been in London.)

2b. Does Stapleton appear to be mysterious or out of the ordinary in any way? (Answers will vary. Possibilities: *No*, he seems average in every way; *yes*, it seems odd for him to be "pursuing" Dr. Watson.)

1 STYLE: WORD CHOICE

By asking why Sir Henry would want to "bury himself" by the moor, Stapleton implies that the place is isolated. But his words also contain ominous overtones of death.

2 CHARACTERIZATION

Stapleton is presented as being aggressive and nosy. He seems overly interested in matters that seem not to concern him.

3 CONFLICT

Holmes has given Watson conflicting instructions. The doctor is to guard Sir Henry, yet he is also to investigate the neighbors.

was a naturalist. But how did you know me?"

"I have been calling on Mortimer, and he pointed you out to me from the window of his surgery as you passed. As our road lay the same way I thought that I would overtake you and introduce myself. I trust that Sir Henry is none the worse for his journey?"

"He is very well, thank you."

"We were all rather afraid that after the sad death of Sir Charles the new baronet might **1** refuse to live here. It is asking much of a wealthy man to come down and bury himself in a place of this kind, but I need not tell you that it means a very great deal to the country-side. Sir Henry has, I suppose, no supersti-tious fears in the matter?"

"I do not think that it is likely."

"Of course you know the legend of the fiend dog which haunts the family?"

"I have heard it."

"The story took a great hold upon the imagination of Sir Charles, and I have no doubt that it led to his tragic end."

"But how?"

"His nerves were so worked up that the appearance of any dog might have had a fatal effect upon his diseased heart. I fancy that he really did see something of the kind upon that last night in the yew alley."

"You think, then, that some dog pursued Sir Charles, and that he died of fright in con-sequence?"

"Have you any better explanation?"

"I have not come to any conclusion."

"Has Mr. Sherlock Holmes?"

The words took away my breath for an in-stant, but a glance at the placid face and steadfast eyes of my companion showed that no surprise was intended.

"It is useless for us to pretend that we do not know you, Dr. Watson," said he. "The rec-ords of your detective have reached us here, and you could not celebrate him without

534   *The Novel*

2 being known yourself. When Mortimer told me your name he could not deny your identity. If you are here, then it follows that Mr. Sherlock Holmes is interesting himself in the matter, and I am naturally curious to know what view he may take."

"I am afraid that I cannot answer that question."

"May I ask if he is going to honor us with a visit himself?"

"He cannot leave town at present. He has other cases which engage his attention."

"What a pity! He might throw some light on that which is so dark to us. But as to your own researches, if there is any possible way in which I can be of service to you I trust that you will command me."

We had come to a point where a narrow grassy path struck off from the road and wound away across the moor. A steep, boul-der-sprinkled hill lay upon the right which had in bygone days been cut into a granite quarry. From over a distant rise there floated a gray plume of smoke.

"A moderate walk along this moor path brings us to Merripit House," said he. "Per-haps you will spare an hour that I may have the pleasure of introducing you to my sister."

3 My first thought was that I should be by Sir Henry's side. But then I remembered the pile of papers and bills with which his study table was littered. It was certain that I could not help him with those. And Holmes had expressly said that I should study the neigh-bors upon the moor. I accepted Stapleton's invitation, and we turned together down the path.

"It is a wonderful place, the moor," said he. "It is so vast, and so barren, and so mysteri-ous."

"You know it well, then?"

"I have only been here two years. The res-idents would call me a newcomer. We came

GUIDED READING

LITERAL QUESTIONS

1a. What explanation does Stapleton give for Sir Charles's death? (The legend of the fiend dog caused Sir Charles great fear. Mistaking a real dog for the legend, he died of fright.)

2a. What information does Stapleton attempt to get from Dr. Watson? (Sherlock Holmes's views on the case)

INFERENTIAL QUESTIONS

1b. What clues in the novel so far suggest that he is right? (the expression on Sir Charles's face when he was found, the paw print found near the body by Dr. Mortimer)

2b. Why do you think Watson doesn't give this infor-mation to Stapleton? (because Stapleton is a sus-pect in the case)

shortly after Sir Charles settled. But my tastes led me to explore every part of the country round, and I should think that there are few men who know it better than I do."

"Is it hard to know?"

"Very hard. You see, for example, this great plain to the north here, with the queer hills breaking out of it. Do you observe anything remarkable about that?"

"It would be a rare place for a gallop."

"You would naturally think so and the thought has cost several their lives before now. You notice those bright green spots scattered thickly over it?"

"Yes, they seem more fertile than the rest."

Stapleton laughed.

"That is the great Grimpen Mire," said he. "A false step yonder means death to man or beast. Only yesterday I saw one of the moor ponies wander into it. He never came out. I saw his head for quite a long time craning out of the bog hole, but it sucked him down at last. Even in dry seasons it is a danger to cross it, but after these autumn rains it is an awful place. And yet I can find my way to the very heart of it and return alive. By George, there is another of those miserable ponies!"

Something brown was rolling and tossing among the green sedges. Then a long, agonized, writhing neck shot upward and a __1__ dreadful cry echoed over the moor. It turned me cold with horror, but my companion's nerves seemed to be stronger than mine.

"It's gone!" said he. "The mire has him. Two in two days, and many more, perhaps, for they get in the way of going there in the dry weather, and never know the difference until the mire has them in its clutch. It's a bad place, the great Grimpen Mire."

"And you say you can penetrate it?"

"Yes, there are one or two paths which a very active man can take. I have found them out."

"But why should you wish to go into so horrible a place?"

"Well, you see the hills beyond? That is where the rare plants and butterflies are, if you have the wit to reach them."

"I shall try my luck some day."

He looked at me with a surprised face.

"For heaven's sake put such an idea out of your mind," said he. "Your blood would be upon my head. I assure you that there would not be the least chance of your coming back alive. It is only by remembering certain complex landmarks that I am able to do it."

"Halloa!" I cried. "What is that?"

__2__ A long, low moan, indescribably sad, swept over the moor. It filled the whole air, and yet it was impossible to say whence it came. From a dull murmur it swelled into a deep roar, and then sank back into a melancholy, throbbing murmur once again. Stapleton looked at me with a curious expression in his face.

"Queer place, the moor!" said he.

"But what is it?"

"The peasants say it is the Hound of the Baskervilles calling for its prey. I've heard it once or twice before, but never quite so loud."

I looked round, with a chill of fear in my heart, at the huge swelling plain, mottled with the green patches of rushes. Nothing stirred over the vast expanse save a pair of ravens, which croaked loudly from a tor behind us.

"You are an educated man. You don't believe such nonsense as that?" said I. "What do you think is the cause of so strange a sound?"

__3__ "Bogs make queer noises sometimes. It's the mud settling, or the water rising, or something."

"No, no, that was a living voice."

"Well, perhaps it was."

"It's the weirdest, strangest thing that ever I heard in my life."

"Yes, it's rather an uncanny place alto-

The Hound of the Baskervilles 535

AT A GLANCE

- Stapleton points out unusual features of the moor to Watson.
- They watch a pony drown in a mire.
- A low moan fills the air, causing Watson to wonder if he has heard the legendary hound.

1 CHARACTERIZATION

Stapleton's unemotional response to the pony's death suggests that he is either unfeeling or accustomed to such sights.

2 STYLE: IMAGERY

Doyle uses a string of images to evoke the chilling sound and to prolong the moment's suspense. A "dull murmur" progresses to a "deep roar" and then back to a "melancholy, throbbing murmur."

3 PLOT: SUSPENSE

Stapleton's explanation for the sound is obviously inadequate. The fact that two men of science seem to be at such a loss for explanations is unsettling.

GUIDED READING

LITERAL QUESTION

1a. What dangerous feature of the moor does Watson witness firsthand? (a mire, or bog hole, which drowns a pony)

INFERENTIAL QUESTION

1b. Do you think people's fears of the moor are based on fact or on superstition? (Answers will vary. Possibilities: The moor has real dangers, which intensify the eerie feelings inspired by its appearance; the moor seems dangerous only to superstitious people.)

AT A GLANCE

- Stapleton points out the remains of stone houses where prehistoric people once lived.
- As the naturalist races off to chase a rare butterfly, Miss Stapleton approaches Dr. Watson.

1 SETTING

The prehistoric huts add a gothic touch to the desolate setting. Seemingly unchanged since the Stone Age, the huts suggest that time stands still on the moor and that primitive human emotions are still at work there.

2 CHARACTERIZATION

Stapleton's words suggest that he is well-educated and that he enjoys educating others. His references to "bronze sword" and "stone axe" seem oddly violent.

gether. Look at the hillside yonder. What do you make of those?"

The whole steep slope was covered with gray circular rings of stone, a score of them at least.

"What are they? Sheep pens?"

1 "No, they are the homes of our worthy ancestors. Prehistoric man lived thickly on the moor, and as no one in particular has lived there since, we find all his little arrangements exactly as he left them. These are his wigwams with the roofs off. You can even see his hearth and his couch if you have the curiosity to go inside."

"But it is quite a town. When was it inhabited?"

"Neolithic man[1]—no date."

"What did he do?"

"He grazed his cattle on these slopes, and

---

1. **Neolithic man:** referring to people of the last part of the Stone Age (8000–3000 B.C.); they developed polished stone tools and weapons.

536   *The Novel*

2 he learned to dig for tin when the bronze sword began to supersede the stone axe. Look at the great trench in the opposite hill. That is his mark. Yes, you will find some very singular points about the moor, Dr. Watson. Oh, excuse me an instant! It is surely Cyclopides."

A small fly or moth had fluttered across our path, and in an instant Stapleton was rushing with extraordinary energy and speed in pursuit of it.

I was standing watching his pursuit with admiration when I heard the sound of steps, and, turning round, found a woman near me upon the path. She had come from the direction in which the plume of smoke indicated the position of Merripit House, but the dip of the moor had hid her until she was quite close.

I could not doubt that this was the Miss Stapleton of whom I had been told, since ladies of any sort must be few upon the moor, and I remembered that I had heard someone describe her as being a beauty. The woman

GUIDED READING

LITERAL QUESTION

1a. What are the circular rings of stone Watson sees on a hillside? (the remains of prehistoric houses)

INFERENTIAL QUESTION

1b. What do these houses add to the mood of the novel? (Answers will vary. Possibilities: The moor seems increasingly a mysterious place where the past lives on and a person is likely to encounter the unexpected; the moor seems to be a place of violent, primitive emotions that are as old as these houses.)

who approached me was certainly that, and of a most uncommon type.

There could not have been a greater contrast between brother and sister, for Stapleton was neutral tinted, with light hair and gray eyes, while she was darker than any brunette whom I have seen in England—slim, elegant, and tall. I was about to make some explanatory remark when her own words turned all my thoughts into a new channel.

"Go back!" she said. "Go straight back to London, instantly."

I could only stare at her in stupid surprise. Her eyes blazed at me, and she tapped the ground impatiently with her foot.

"Why should I go back?" I asked.

"I cannot explain." She spoke in a low, eager voice, with a curious lisp in her utterance. "But for heaven's sake do what I ask you. Go back and never set foot upon the moor again."

"But I have only just come."

"Man, man!" she cried. "Can you not tell when a warning is for your own good? Go back to London! Start tonight! Get away from this place at all costs! Hush, my brother is coming! Not a word of what I have said. Would you mind getting that orchid for me among the mare's-tails yonder? We are very rich in orchids on the moor, though, of course, you are rather late to see the beauties of the place."

Stapleton had abandoned the chase and came back to us breathing hard and flushed with his exertions.

"Halloa, Beryl!" said he, and it seemed to me that the tone of his greeting was not altogether a cordial one.

"Well, Jack, you are very hot."

"Yes, I was chasing a Cyclopides." He spoke unconcernedly, but his small light eyes glanced incessantly from the girl to me.

"You have introduced yourselves, I can see."

"Yes. I was telling Sir Henry that it was rather late for him to see the true beauties of the moor."

"Why, who do you think this is?"

"I imagine that it must be Sir Henry Baskerville."

"No, no," said I. "Only a humble commoner, but his friend. My name is Dr. Watson."

A flush of vexation passed over her expressive face. "We have been talking at cross-purposes," said she.

"Why, you had not very much time for talk," her brother remarked, with the same questioning eyes.

"I talked as if Dr. Watson were a resident instead of being merely a visitor," said she. "It cannot much matter to him whether it is early or late for the orchids. But you will come on, will you not, and see Merripit House?"

A short walk brought us to it, a bleak moorland house, once the farm of some grazier in the old prosperous days, but now put into repair and turned into a modern dwelling. An orchard surrounded it, but the trees, as is usual upon the moor, were stunted and nipped, and the effect of the whole place was mean and melancholy. As I looked from their windows at the moor I could not but marvel at what could have brought this highly educated man and this beautiful woman to live in such a place.

"Queer spot to choose, is it not?" said he, as if in answer to my thought. "And yet we manage to make ourselves fairly happy, do we not, Beryl?"

"Quite happy," said she, but there was no ring of conviction in her words.

"I had a school," said Stapleton. "It was in the north country. A serious epidemic broke out in the school and three of the boys died. It never recovered from the blow, and my capital was irretrievably swallowed up."

"It certainly did cross my mind that it

The Hound of the Baskervilles 537

1 READING SKILLS: COMPARISON AND CONTRAST

The sharp contrast between the features of Mr. Stapleton and his sister seems unusual for two people so closely related.

2 CHARACTERIZATION

After giving her warning in a wildly emotional manner, Miss Stapleton asks a total stranger to keep the warning secret from her own brother. Her behavior suggests that she is deeply troubled.

3 POINT OF VIEW

Watson provides keen observations of Stapleton's tone of voice and facial expression. From these observations we can deduce that Stapleton does not trust his sister.

4 STYLE: WORD CHOICE

Like so much about the moor, the name *Merripit* presents a mixed image. The first part of the word suggests bright happiness, but *pit* suggests something dark and unpleasant. The description of Merripit reinforces the contrast.

GUIDED READING

LITERAL QUESTION

1a. What warning does Miss Stapleton give to Watson? What does she tell Watson as Stapleton returns? (to leave the moor and go back to London at once; not to tell her brother what she's said)

INFERENTIAL QUESTION

1b. Why do you think Miss Stapleton does not want her brother to know she has warned Watson? (Answers will vary. Possibilities: Her brother is involved in the crime, and she is afraid of what he might do; she is trying to protect her brother from knowledge she has.)

- Eager to return to Baskerville Hall, Watson leaves Merripit House.
- Miss Stapleton overtakes him and apologizes for her strange warning.
- She insists it was merely a whim based on her belief in the legend of the hound.

1 SETTING

The eerie moor and the weird events that occur there have infected Watson with fear and sadness.

2 POINT OF VIEW

The narrator, Watson, is not only observant but is becoming more confident about the implications of what he has observed and more forceful in insisting on the truth. Here he challenges Miss Stapleton's feeble explanation for her emotional warning.

3 THEME

This passage focuses on the conflict between Watson's rationality and Miss Stapleton's belief in the supernatural.

4 PLOT: CONFLICT

Watson says that it is Sir Henry's nature to confront, if not court, danger. So the stage is set for conflict between Baskerville and the forces of evil on the moor.

might be a little dull—less for you, perhaps, than for your sister."

"No, no, I am never dull," said she quickly.

"We have books, we have our studies, and we have interesting neighbors. Dr. Mortimer is a most learned man in his own line. Poor Sir Charles was also an admirable companion. We knew him well, and miss him more than I can tell. Do you think that I should intrude if I were to call this afternoon and make the acquaintance of Sir Henry?"

"I am sure that he would be delighted."

"Then perhaps you would mention that I propose to do so."

1 I was eager to get back to my charge. The melancholy of the moor, the death of the unfortunate pony, the weird sound which had been associated with the grim legend of the Baskervilles, all these things tinged my thoughts with sadness. Then on top of these more or less vague impressions there had come the definite and distinct warning of Miss Stapleton. I could not doubt that some grave and deep reason lay behind it. I resisted all pressure to stay for lunch, and I set off at once upon my return journey, taking the grass-grown path by which we had come.

It seems, however, that there must have been some shortcut for those who knew it, for before I had reached the road I was astounded to see Miss Stapleton sitting upon a rock by the side of the track. Her face was beautifully flushed with her exertions, and she held her hand to her side.

"I have run all the way in order to cut you off, Dr. Watson," said she. "I had not even time to put on my hat. I must not stop, or my brother may miss me. I wanted to say to you how sorry I am about the stupid mistake I made in thinking that you were Sir Henry. Please forget the words I said, which have no application whatever to you."

"But I can't forget them, Miss Stapleton," said I. "I am Sir Henry's friend, and his wel-

fare is a very close concern of mine. Tell me why it was that you were so eager that Sir Henry should return to London."

"A woman's whim, Dr. Watson. When you know me better you will understand that I cannot always give reasons for what I say or do."

2 "No, no. I remember the thrill in your voice. I remember the look in your eyes. Please, please, be frank with me, Miss Stapleton."

An expression of irresolution passed for an instant over her face, but her eyes had hardened again when she answered me.

"You make too much of it, Dr. Watson," said she. "My brother and I were very much shocked by the death of Sir Charles. We knew him very intimately, for his favorite walk was over the moor to our house. He was deeply impressed with the curse which hung over his family, and when this tragedy came I naturally felt that there must be some grounds for the fears which he had expressed. I was distressed therefore when another member of the family came down to live here, and I felt that he should be warned of the danger which he will run. That was all which I intended to convey."

3 "But what is the danger?"

"You know the story of the hound?"

"I do not believe in such nonsense."

"But I do. If you have any influence with Sir Henry, take him away from a place which has always been fatal to his family. The world is wide. Why should he wish to live at the place of danger?"

4 "Because it is the place of danger. That is Sir Henry's nature. I fear that unless you can give me some more definite information than this it would be impossible to get him to move."

"I cannot say anything definite, for I do not know anything definite."

"I would ask you one more question, Miss

GUIDED READING

LITERAL QUESTION

1a. What explanation does Miss Stapleton give when Watson asks her to be frank? (She claims that she believes the legend of the hound and therefore feels Sir Henry is in danger.)

INFERENTIAL QUESTION

1b. How would you describe Watson's reaction to this explanation? (Although he thinks the legend of the hound is nonsense, he seems to accept that Miss Stapleton's belief in it might be why she acted as she did.)

Stapleton. If you meant no more than this when you first spoke to me, why should you not wish your brother to overhear what you said? There is nothing to which he, or anyone else, could object."

"My brother is very anxious to have the Hall inhabited, for he thinks that it is for the good of the poor folk upon the moor. He would be very angry if he knew that I had said anything which might induce Sir Henry to go away. But I have done my duty now and I will say no more. I must get back, or he will miss me and suspect that I have seen you. Good-bye!" She turned, and had disappeared in a few minutes among the scattered boulders, while I, with my soul full of vague fears, pursued my way to Baskerville Hall.

8 First Report of Dr. Watson

1 From this point onward I will follow the course of events by transcribing my own letters to Mr. Sherlock Holmes which lie before me on the table.

Baskerville Hall, October 13

2 My Dear Holmes:

My previous letters and telegrams have kept you pretty well up to date as to all that has occurred in this most forsaken corner of the world.

If you have not had any report within the last few days it is because up to today there was nothing of importance to relate. Then a very surprising circumstance occurred, which I shall tell you in due course. But, first of all, I must keep you in touch with some of the other factors in the situation.

One of these, concerning which I have said little, is the escaped convict upon the moor. There is strong reason now to believe that he has got right away, which is a considerable relief to the lonely householders of this dis-3 trict. A fortnight has passed since his flight, during which he has not been seen and nothing has been heard of him. It is surely inconceivable that he could have held out upon the moor during all that time. Of course, so far as his concealment goes there is no difficulty at all. Any one of the stone huts would give him a hiding place. But there is nothing to eat unless he were to catch and slaughter one of the moor sheep. We think, therefore, that he has gone, and the outlying farmers sleep the better in consequence.

We are four able-bodied men in this household, so that we could take good care of ourselves, but I confess that I have had uneasy moments when I have thought of the Stapletons. They live miles from any help. There are one maid, an old manservant, the sister, and the brother, the latter not a very strong man. They would be helpless in the hands of a desperate fellow like this Notting Hill criminal if he could once effect an entrance. Both Sir Henry and I were concerned at their situation.

The fact is that our friend, the baronet, begins to display a considerable interest in our fair neighbor. It is not to be wondered at, for time hangs heavily in this lonely spot to an active man like him, and she is a very fascinating and beautiful woman. There is something tropical and exotic about her which forms a singular contrast to her cool and unemotional brother. Yet he also gives the idea of hidden fires. He has certainly a very marked influence over her, for I have seen her continually glance at him as she talked as if seeking approbation for what she said. I trust 4 that he is kind to her. There is a dry glitter in his eyes and a firm set of his thin lips, which goes with a positive and possibly a harsh nature. You would find him an interesting study.

He came over to call upon Baskerville on that first day, and the very next morning he took us both to show us the spot where the

The Hound of the Baskervilles 539

AT A GLANCE

- Miss Stapleton says her brother would be angry if he knew she had tried to warn Sir Henry.
- In a letter to Holmes, Watson reports that the convict seems to have gone away and that Sir Henry has begun a friendship with Miss Stapleton.

1 THE NOVEL

Earlier Doyle used a legend and a newspaper article to help tell his story. Now he turns to letters. Novelists introduce such changes of format to vary the pace of long narratives.

2 POINT OF VIEW

The narrator, in effect, puts us in Holmes's place as we read the great detective's mail. However, we can only guess what is going through Holmes's mind as he reads.

3 PLOT: SUBPLOT

The subplot involving Selden, the escaped convict, continues. If Selden were truly gone, as Watson supposes, the author would not develop the subplot. We wonder, then, where Selden is and what role will he play in events.

4 CHARACTERIZATION

Watson believes that the "dry glitter" in Stapleton's eyes betrays a harsh nature. This belief is in keeping with Stapleton's reaction to the death of the pony earlier.

GUIDED READING

LITERAL QUESTIONS

1a. What reason does Miss Stapleton give for not wanting her brother to know about her warning to Watson? (She says Stapleton would be angry; he wants the hall inhabited for the good of the poor.)

2a. What reason does Watson give for thinking that the convict Selden has left the area? (He says the convict could not have survived because there is so little food on the moor.)

INFERENTIAL QUESTIONS

1b. What does this explanation tell you about the relationship between Stapleton and his sister? (Miss Stapleton is afraid of her brother's anger.)

2b. Do you agree with Watson's reasoning? (Answers will vary. Possibilities: Selden could have found someone to help him; it is unlikely the author would introduce a subplot and then drop it.)

- Watson describes the location where Hugo Baskerville met his fate.
- Stapleton seems unhappy about his sister's interest in Sir Henry.
- Dr. Mortimer shows where Sir Charles died.

1 STYLE: SIMILE

This memorable image compares a feature of the landscape to the deadly fangs of a fearful hound. Perhaps Watson is suggesting that the unusual appearance of this rock formation actually gave rise to the legend.

2 PLOT: CONFLICT

A new cause of external conflict emerges. Stapleton is jealous of Sir Henry. His negative reaction to the possibility of a "brilliant marriage" for his sister makes us focus on the Stapletons' relationship.

legend of the wicked Hugo is supposed to have had its origin. It was an excursion of some miles across the moor to a place which is so dismal that it might have suggested the story. We found a short valley between rugged tors which led to an open, grassy space flecked over with the white cotton grass. In the middle of it rose two great stones, worn and sharpened at the upper end until they looked like the huge corroding fangs of some monstrous beast. In every way it corresponded with the scene of the old tragedy.

On our way back we stayed for lunch at Merripit House, and it was there that Sir Henry made the acquaintance of Miss Stapleton. From the first moment he saw her he appeared to be strongly attracted by her, and I am much mistaken if the feeling was not mutual. He referred to her again and again on our walk home, and since then hardly a day has passed that we have not seen something of the brother and sister. They dine here tonight, and there is some talk of our going to them next week. One would imagine that such a match would be very welcome to Stapleton, and yet I have more than once caught a look of the strongest disapprobation in his face when Sir Henry has been paying some attention to his sister. He is much attached to her, no doubt, and would lead a lonely life without her, but it would seem the height of selfishness if he were to stand in the way of her making so brilliant a marriage.

The other day—Thursday, to be more exact—Dr. Mortimer lunched with us. The Stapletons came in afterward, and the good doctor took us all to the yew alley, at Sir Henry's request, to show us exactly how everything occurred upon that fatal night. It is a long, dismal walk, the yew alley, between two high walls of clipped hedge, with a narrow band of grass upon either side. At the far end is an old tumbledown summerhouse. Halfway down is the moor gate. It is a white wooden

GUIDED READING

LITERAL QUESTION

1a. How does Stapleton react to the relationship that is developing between his sister and Sir Henry? (with disapproval)

INFERENTIAL QUESTION

1b. Why is his reaction to the romance surprising? (Sir Henry is handsome, kind, and wealthy; one would think Stapleton would welcome Sir Henry's interest in his sister.)

gate with a latch. Beyond it lies the wide moor. I remembered your theory of the affair and tried to picture all that had occurred. As the old man stood there he saw something coming across the moor, something which terrified him so that he lost his wits and ran and ran until he died of sheer horror and exhaustion. There was the long, gloomy tunnel down which he fled. And from what? A sheep dog of the moor? Or a spectral hound, black, silent, and monstrous? Was there a human agency in the matter? Did the pale, watchful Barrymore know more than he cared to say? It was all dim and vague, but always there is the dark shadow of crime behind it.

One other neighbor I have met since I wrote last. This is Mr. Frankland, of Lafter Hall, who lives some four miles to the south of us. He is an elderly man, red-faced, white-haired, and choleric. His passion is for the British law, and he has spent a large fortune in litigation.

He seems a kindly, good-natured person, and I only mention him because you were particular that I should send some description of the people who surround us. He is curiously employed at present, for, being an amateur astronomer, he has an excellent telescope, with which he lies upon the roof of his own house and sweeps the moor all day in the hope of catching a glimpse of the escaped convict.

And now, let me end on that which is most important and tell you more about the Barrymores, and especially about the surprising development of last night.

First of all about the test telegram, which you sent from London in order to make sure that Barrymore was really here. I have already explained that the testimony of the postmaster shows that the test was worthless and that we have no proof one way or the other. I told Sir Henry how the matter stood, and he at once, in his downright fashion, had Barry-

more up and asked him whether he had received the telegram himself. Barrymore said that he had.

"Did the boy deliver it into your own hands?" asked Sir Henry.

Barrymore looked surprised, and considered for a little time.

"No," said he, "I was in the box room at the time, and my wife brought it up to me."

"Did you answer it yourself?"

"No; I told my wife what to answer and she went down to write it."

In the evening he recurred to the subject of his own accord.

"I could not quite understand the object of your questions this morning, Sir Henry," said he. "I trust that they do not mean that I have done anything to forfeit your confidence?"

Sir Henry had to assure him that it was not so and pacify him by giving him a considerable part of his old wardrobe, the London outfit having now all arrived.

Mrs. Barrymore is of interest to me. She is a heavy, solid person, very limited, intensely respectable, and inclined to be puritanical. You could hardly conceive a less emotional subject. Yet I have told you how, on the first night here, I heard her sobbing bitterly, and since then I have more than once observed traces of tears upon her face. Some deep sorrow gnaws ever at her heart. Sometimes I wonder if she has a guilty memory which haunts her.

And yet it may seem a small matter in itself. You are aware that I am not a very sound sleeper, and since I have been on guard in this house my slumbers have been lighter than ever. Last night, about two in the morning, I was aroused by a stealthy step passing my room. I rose, opened my door, and peeped out. A long black shadow was trailing down the corridor. It was thrown by a man who walked softly down the passage with a candle

The Hound of the Baskervilles 541

AT A GLANCE

- Continuing his letter, Watson describes his reaction upon viewing the site of Sir Charles's death.
- An amateur astronomer has a telescope aimed at the moor.
- Watson and Sir Henry confront Barrymore about the test telegram.

1 POINT OF VIEW

Watson's reflections focus attention back on the central questions of the mystery: What frightened Sir Charles to death? Was a crime committed? If so, who was behind it?

2 PLOT: FORESHADOWING

The presence of an amateur astronomer who "sweeps the moor all day" with his telescope hints at future plot developments.

3 THEME

Another aspect of the theme of friendship and loyalty is shown here. Barrymore seems genuinely hurt by the insinuation that he is not to be trusted.

GUIDED READING

LITERAL QUESTIONS

1a. How does Barrymore react after Sir Henry questions him about the test telegram? (He says he's confused and asks if Sir Henry still trusts him.)

2a. What reasons does Watson suggest for Mrs. Barrymore's frequent weeping? (He suggests that she has some deep sorrow or guilty memory.)

INFERENTIAL QUESTIONS

1b. Does Barrymore's reaction change your opinion of him as a likely suspect? (Answers will vary. Possibilities: Yes, his reaction seems that of an innocent and loyal man; no, he is only pretending.)

2b. Why does Watson concern himself with Mrs. Barrymore's tears? (Answers will vary. Possibilities: The Barrymores are still suspects; her tears could result from guilt.)

- Awakened by Barrymore's footsteps, Watson follows him.
- Barrymore holds a candle to the window and looks out at the moor.
- Watson tells Sir Henry of this. They plan to follow Barrymore.

1 SETTING

The empty rooms in the house create an eerie mood and call to mind the empty stone huts on the hillside. The entire moor seems inhospitable to human habitation.

2 READING SKILLS: INFERENCES

Barrymore's groan and impatient gestures suggest that he is not pleased with what he sees.

3 POINT OF VIEW

Watson allows only one day to pass between letters to Holmes; he is anxious to give a full account of the case. Lacking return letters from Holmes, Watson and the reader must try to solve the case themselves.

4 THEME

This passage indicates the value of close observation and reasoning. Watson observes the window and room carefully and deduces the purpose for which Barrymore chose it.

---

held in his hand. He was in shirt and trousers, with no covering to his feet. I could merely see the outline, but his height told me that it was Barrymore.

I followed him. When I came round the balcony he had reached the end of the farther corridor, and I could see from the glimmer of light through an open door that he had entered one of the rooms. Now, all these rooms are unfurnished and unoccupied, so that his expedition became more mysterious than ever. The light shone steadily as if he were standing motionless. I crept down the passage as noiselessly as I could and peeped round the corner of the door.

Barrymore was crouching at the window with the candle held against the glass. His profile was half turned toward me, and his face seemed to be rigid with expectation as he stared out into the blackness of the moor. For some minutes he stood watching intently. Then he gave a deep groan and with an impatient gesture he put out the light. Instantly I made my way back to my room, and very shortly came the stealthy steps passing once more upon their return journey. Long afterward when I had fallen into a light sleep I heard a key turn somewhere in a lock, but I could not tell whence the sound came. What it all means I cannot guess, but there is some secret business going on in this house of gloom.

9 Second Report of Dr. Watson The Light Upon the Moor

Baskerville Hall, October 15

My Dear Holmes:

In my last report I ended upon my top note with Barrymore at the window.

Before breakfast on the morning following my adventure I went down the corridor and examined the room in which Barrymore had been on the night before. The western window through which he had stared so intently has, I noticed, one peculiarity above all other windows in the house—it commands the nearest outlook on to the moor. It follows, therefore, that Barrymore, since only this window would serve his purpose, must have been looking out for something or somebody upon the moor.

Whatever the true explanation of Barrymore's movements might be, I felt that the responsibility of keeping them to myself until I could explain them was more than I could bear. I had an interview with the baronet in his study after breakfast, and I told him all that I had seen. He was less surprised than I had expected.

"I knew that Barrymore walked about nights, and I had a mind to speak to him about it," said he. "Two or three times I have heard his steps in the passage, coming and going, just about the hour you name."

"Perhaps then he pays a visit every night to that particular window," I suggested.

"Perhaps he does. If so, we should be able to shadow him and see what it is that he is after. I wonder what your friend Holmes would do if he were here."

"I believe that he would do exactly what you now suggest," said I. "He would follow Barrymore and see what he did."

"Then we shall do it together."

"But surely he would hear us."

"The man is rather deaf, and in any case we must take our chance of that. We'll sit up in my room tonight and wait until he passes."

The baronet has been in communication with the architect who prepared the plans for Sir Charles, and with a contractor from London, so that we may expect great changes to begin here soon. All that he will need will be a wife to make it complete. Between ourselves

542   *The Novel*

GUIDED READING

LITERAL QUESTIONS

1a. After following Barrymore down the hall, what does Watson watch the butler do? (Watson watches Barrymore enter an empty room, hold his candle up to the window, and stare out at the moor.)

2a. Later, as he enters a light sleep, what sound does Watson hear? (Watson hears a key turning in a lock.)

INFERENTIAL QUESTIONS

1b. What explanation can you give for the butler's behavior? (Barrymore seems to be signaling with the candle to someone who is outside on the moor.)

2b. What connection might this sound have with Barrymore's action at the window? (Perhaps as a result of the signal, someone seems to be entering or leaving the house.)

there are pretty clear signs that this will not be wanting if the lady is willing, for I have seldom seen a man more infatuated with a woman than he is with our beautiful neighbor, Miss Stapleton. And yet the course of true love does not run quite as smoothly as one would under the circumstances expect. Today, for example, its surface was broken by a very unexpected ripple, which has caused our friend considerable perplexity and annoyance.

After the conversation which I have quoted about Barrymore Sir Henry put on his hat and prepared to go out. As a matter of course I did the same.

"What, are *you* coming, Watson?" he asked, looking at me in a curious way.

"That depends on whether you are going on the moor," said I.

"Yes, I am."

"Well, you know what my instructions are. I am sorry to intrude, but you heard how earnestly Holmes insisted that I should not leave you, and especially that you should not go alone upon the moor."

Sir Henry put his hand upon my shoulder, with a pleasant smile.

"My dear fellow," said he, "Holmes, with all his wisdom, did not foresee some things which have happened since I have been on the moor. You understand me? I am sure that you are the last man in the world who would wish to be a spoilsport. I must go out alone."

It put me in a most awkward position. I was at a loss what to say or what to do, and before I had made up my mind he picked up his cane and was gone.

But when I came to think the matter over my conscience reproached me bitterly for having on any pretext allowed him to go out of my sight, so I set off at once in the direction of Merripit House.

I hurried along the road at the top of my speed without seeing anything of Sir Henry,

until I came to the point where the moor path branches off. There, fearing that perhaps I had come in the wrong direction after all, I mounted a hill from which I could command a view—the same hill which is cut into the dark quarry. Thence I saw him at once. He was on the moor path, about a quarter of a mile off, and a lady was by his side who could only be Miss Stapleton. It was clear that there was already an understanding between them and that they had met by appointment. They were walking slowly along in deep conversation, and I saw her making quick little movements of her hands as if she were very earnest in what she was saying, while he listened intently, and once or twice shook his head in strong dissent. I stood among the rocks watching them, very much puzzled as to what I should do next.

Our friend, Sir Henry, and the lady had halted on the path and were standing deeply absorbed in their conversation when I was suddenly aware that I was not the only witness of their interview. A wisp of green floating in the air caught my eye, and another glance showed me that it was carried on a stick by a man who was moving along the broken ground. It was Stapleton with his butterfly net. He was very much closer to the pair than I was, and he appeared to be moving in their direction. At this instant Sir Henry suddenly drew Miss Stapleton to his side. His arm was round her, but it seemed to me that she was straining away from him with her face averted. He stooped his head to hers, and she raised one hand as if in protest. Next moment I saw them spring apart and turn hurriedly around. Stapleton was the cause of the interruption. He was running wildly toward them, his absurd net dangling behind him. He gesticulated and almost danced with excitement in front of the lovers. What the scene meant I could not imagine, but it seemed to me that

The Hound of the Baskervilles 543

AT A GLANCE

- Sir Henry rushes off to meet Miss Stapleton on the moor. Watson follows.
- From a distance Watson sees Sir Henry try to hug Miss Stapleton—only to be angrily interrupted by her brother.

1 PLOT: FORESHADOWING

With these introductory sentences Watson foreshadows the events of this page.

2 PLOT: CONFLICT

By courting the sister of a possible suspect in the case, Sir Henry may be putting himself in danger. To make matters worse, the lovers' desire for privacy conflicts with Watson's instructions to guard Sir Henry at all times.

3 CHARACTERIZATION

Watson, a former military officer, takes his orders seriously. He is conscientious about his duty and does not make excuses for himself.

4 READING SKILLS: INFERENCES

Miss Stapleton's earnest gestures suggest she is warning Sir Henry or breaking off their relationship. Sir Henry's gesture of "strong dissent" suggests that he will not go away.

5 POINT OF VIEW

Because he cannot hear what is being said, Watson's narration is almost more vivid than it would be if he had recorded any dialogue here. He has to concentrate on Stapleton's body movements, which seem almost maniacal.

GUIDED READING

LITERAL QUESTIONS

1a. What special request does Sir Henry make of Watson? (He asks the doctor to stay at home while he goes out onto the moor to speak privately with Miss Stapleton.)

2a. How does Stapleton act when he discovers Sir Henry and Miss Stapleton together on the moor? (He runs wildly toward them, gesticulates wildly, and dances in excitement.)

INFERENTIAL QUESTIONS

1b. Why does this request put Watson in "a most awkward position"? (As Sir Henry's friend, Watson wants to honor his request for privacy. Yet he has orders and feels personally obligated to protect Sir Henry.)

2b. What do Stapleton's actions suggest? (He is uncontrollably angry and perhaps jealous as well.)

- Watson confesses to Sir Henry that he has witnessed the entire scene.
- Sir Henry says Miss Stapleton had urged him to leave the moor. He had proposed marriage.
- Later in the day Stapleton apologizes for his behavior.

1 CHARACTERIZATION

Watson risks Sir Henry's anger by being candid about observing him. His honesty has a soothing effect on Sir Henry, and their friendship seems to deepen.

2 IRONY

Sir Henry has chosen what he thought to be a private place. Ironically, there were two interested onlookers. Baskerville sees the humor in the situation when he likens the event to a theater performance ("Where had you engaged a seat?").

3 CHARACTERIZATION

Miss Stapleton warns Sir Henry of danger, much as she had warned Watson earlier. She shows a consistency of purpose that is hard to credit to mere whim or superstition.

4 CHARACTERIZATION

Baskerville and Watson show a lack of imagination in their inability to suggest motives for Stapleton's behavior. Later they show themselves to be almost gullible in the ease with which they accept Stapleton's explanation.

Stapleton was abusing Sir Henry, who offered explanations, which became more angry as the other refused to accept them. The lady stood by in haughty silence. Finally Stapleton turned upon his heel and beckoned in a peremptory way to his sister, who, after an irresolute glance at Sir Henry, walked off by the side of her brother. The naturalist's angry gestures showed that the lady was included in his displeasure. The baronet stood for a minute looking after them, and then he walked slowly back the way that he had come, his head hanging, the very picture of dejection.

What all this meant I could not imagine, but I was deeply ashamed to have witnessed so intimate a scene without my friend's knowledge. I ran down the hill therefore and met the baronet at the bottom. His face was flushed with anger and his brows were wrinkled, like one who is at his wits' ends what to do.

"Halloa, Watson! Where have you dropped from?" said he. "You don't mean to say that you came after me in spite of all?"

1 I explained everything to him. For an instant his eyes blazed at me, but my frankness disarmed his anger, and he broke at last into a rather rueful laugh.

"You would have thought the middle of that prairie a fairly safe place for a man to be private," said he, "but, by thunder, the whole **2** countryside seems to have been out to see me do my wooing—and a mighty poor wooing at that! Where had you engaged a seat?"

"I was on that hill."

"Quite in the back row, eh? But her brother was well up to the front. Did you see him come out on us?"

"Yes, I did."

"Did he ever strike you as being crazy—this brother of hers?"

"I can't say that he ever did."

"I dare say not. I always thought him sane enough until today, but you can take it from me that either he or I ought to be in a strait-jacket. What's the matter with me, anyhow? You've lived near me for some weeks, Watson. Tell me straight, now! Is there anything that would prevent me from making a good husband to a woman that I loved?"

"I should say not."

"He can't object to my worldly position, so it must be myself that he has this down on. What has he against me? I tell you, Watson, I've only known her these few weeks, but from the first I just felt that she was made for me, and she, too—she was happy when she was with me, and that I'll swear. But it was only today for the first time that I saw a chance of having a few words with her alone. She was glad to meet me, but when she did it was not love that she would talk about, and she wouldn't have let me talk about it either if she **3** could have stopped it. She kept coming back to it that this was a place of danger, and that she would never be happy until I had left it. I told her that since I had seen her I was in no hurry to leave it, and that if she really wanted me to go, the only way to work it was for her to arrange to go with me.

"With that I offered in as many words to marry her, but before she could answer, down came this brother of hers, running at us with **4** a face on him like a madman. Just tell me what it all means, Watson, and I'll owe you more than ever I can hope to pay."

I tried one or two explanations, but, indeed, I was completely puzzled myself. However, our conjectures were set at rest by a visit from Stapleton himself that very afternoon. He had come to offer apologies for his rudeness of the morning, and after a long private interview with Sir Henry in his study, the upshot of their conversation was that the breach is quite healed, and that we are to dine at Merripit House next Friday as a sign of it.

"I don't say now that he isn't a crazy man," said Sir Henry; "I can't forget the look in his

---

GUIDED READING

LITERAL QUESTION

1a. What feelings does Sir Henry try to express to Miss Stapleton? (He tries to express the love he feels toward her.)

INFERENTIAL QUESTION

1b. Does Miss Stapleton seem to share these feelings? Explain your answer. (Answers will vary. Possibilities: It is difficult to say; she is giving Sir Henry mixed signals; her warning is difficult to interpret—it *could* mean she cares for him.)

eyes when he ran at me this morning, but I must allow that no man could make a more handsome apology than he has done."

"Did he give any explanation of his conduct?"

"His sister is everything in his life, he says. That is natural enough, and I am glad that he should understand her value. They have always been together, and according to his account he has been a very lonely man with only her as a companion, so that the thought of losing her was really terrible to him. He had not understood, he said, that I was becoming attached to her, but when he saw with his own eyes that it was really so, and that she might be taken away from him, it gave him such a shock that for a time he was not responsible for what he said or did. He was very sorry for all that had passed."

So there is one of our small mysteries cleared up. Now I pass on to another thread which I have extricated out of the tangled skein, the mystery of the sobs in the night, of the tear-stained face of Mrs. Barrymore, of the secret journey of the butler to the western lattice window. Congratulate me, my dear Holmes. All these things have by one night's work been thoroughly cleared.

I have said "by one night's work," but, in truth, it was by two nights' work, for on the first we drew entirely blank. Fortunately we were not discouraged, and we determined to try again. The next night we lowered the lamp and sat without making the least sound. It was incredible how slowly the hours crawled by. One struck, and two, and we had almost for the second time given it up in despair when in an instant we both sat bolt upright in our chairs, with all our weary senses keenly on the alert once more. We had heard the creak of a step in the passage.

Very stealthily we heard it pass along until it died away in the distance. Then the baronet gently opened his door and we set out in pursuit. Already our man had gone round the gallery, and the corridor was all in darkness. Softly we stole along until we had come into the other wing. We were just in time to catch a glimpse of the tall, black-bearded figure, his shoulders rounded, as he tiptoed down the passage. Then he passed through the same door as before, and the light of the candle framed it in the darkness and shot one single yellow beam across the gloom of the corridor. We shuffled cautiously toward it, trying every plank before we dared to put our whole weight upon it. When at last we reached the door and peeped through we found him crouching at the window, candle in hand, his white, intent face pressed against the pane, exactly as I had seen him two nights before.

We had arranged no plan of campaign, but the baronet is a man to whom the most direct way is always the most natural. He walked into the room, and as he did so Barrymore sprang up from the window with a sharp hiss of his breath, and stood, livid and trembling, before us. His dark eyes, glaring out of the white mask of his face, were full of horror and astonishment as he gazed from Sir Henry to me.

"What are you doing here, Barrymore?"

"Nothing, sir." His agitation was so great that he could hardly speak, and the shadows sprang up and down from the shaking of his candle. "It was the window, sir. I go round at night to see that they are fastened."

"On the second floor?"

"Yes, sir, all the windows."

"Look here, Barrymore," said Sir Henry sternly, "we have made up our minds to have the truth out of you, so it will save you trouble to tell it sooner rather than later. Come, now! No lies! What were you doing at that window?"

"Don't ask me, Sir Henry—don't ask me! I give you my word, sir, that it is not my secret, and that I cannot tell it. If it concerned no one but myself I would not try to keep it from you."

The Hound of the Baskervilles 545

AT A GLANCE
- Stapleton apologizes for his behavior on the moor.
- The following night Watson and Sir Henry follow Barrymore to the empty room.
- They confront him and demand that he explain his actions.

1 STYLE: METAPHOR

This metaphor compares the case to a skein of tangled yarn and recalls Holmes's mention of the "three broken threads" in Chapter 5. Both detectives view the case as something that can be "untangled" by patiently following each clue.

2 POINT OF VIEW

Watson is proud of his progress and interrupts the narrative briefly to pat himself on the back. As always, he wants Holmes's approval as well.

3 MOOD

This suspenseful description uses classic elements of mystery and horror fiction.

4 STYLE: IMAGERY

The shadows flickering in rhythm with Barrymore's nervous shaking create a strong visual image that emphasizes the butler's fear.

5 PLOT: CONFLICT

Sir Henry dismisses Barrymore's first explanation as totally implausible. The baronet makes it clear that he intends to discover the butler's real motive. Barrymore's response deepens the mystery.

GUIDED READING

LITERAL QUESTIONS

1a. As he apologizes to Sir Henry, how does Stapleton explain his wild behavior? (He claims that realizing his sister might leave him for Sir Henry caused him such a shock that he lost all self-control.)

2a. How does Barrymore react when Sir Henry and Watson confront him in the empty room? (He shows horror and astonishment.)

INFERENTIAL QUESTIONS

1b. Why might Sir Henry's feelings for Miss Stapleton cause him to accept this explanation? (Since Sir Henry wants to marry Miss Stapleton, he might want to smooth over the unpleasantness.)

2b. What does this reaction suggest? (It seems to indicate that Barrymore is doing something wrong or illegal. He is terrified that his secret will be uncovered.)

Watson decides that Barrymore is using the candle to signal someone on the moor. He holds the candle in the window, and someone seems to answer him.

1 CHARACTERIZATION

Watson shows himself capable of a sudden flash of creative intuition at a time when it is most needed.

2 STYLE: IMAGERY

The "pinpoint of yellow light" out on the dark moor represents the first breakthrough, however small, that Watson has made in the complicated, perplexing case.

1 A sudden idea occurred to me, and I took the candle from the hand of the butler.

"He must have been holding it as a signal," said I. "Let us see if there is any answer." I held it as he had done, and stared out into the darkness of the night. Vaguely I could discern the black bank of the trees and the lighter expanse of the moor, for the moon was behind the clouds. And then I gave a cry of exultation, for a tiny pinpoint of yellow light glowed steadily in the center of the black square framed by the window.

"There it is!" I cried.

"No, no, sir, it is nothing—nothing at all!" the butler broke in; "I assure you, sir—"

"Move your light across the window, Wat-

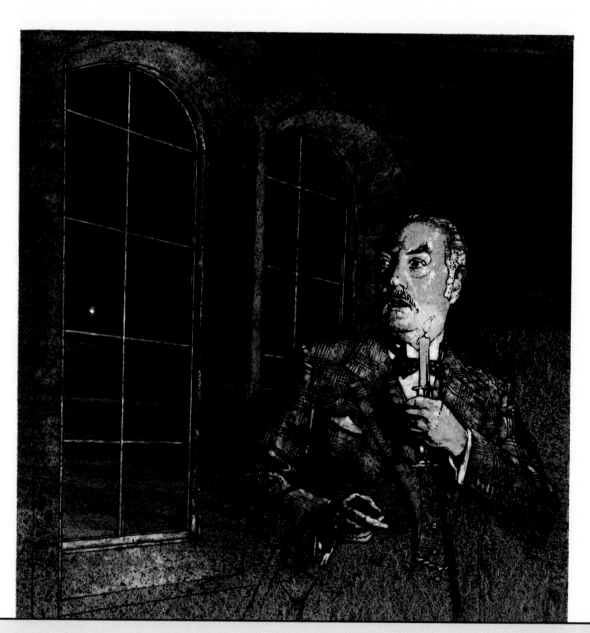

GUIDED READING

LITERAL QUESTION

1a. What does Watson discover about the reason for Barrymore's late-night walks? (The butler is using his candle to signal to someone out on the moor.)

INFERENTIAL QUESTION

1b. What does this discovery indicate about Barrymore's secret? (Barrymore has a partner of some sort in his secret activity; the partner is on the moor.)

son!" cried the baronet. "See, the other moves also! Now, you rascal, do you deny that it is a signal? Come, speak up! Who is your confederate out yonder, and what is this conspiracy that is going on?"

The man's face became openly defiant.

"It is my business, not yours. I will not tell."

"Then you leave my employment right away."

"Very good, sir. If I must I must."

"And you go in disgrace. By thunder, you may well be ashamed of yourself. Your family has lived with mine for over a hundred years **1** under this roof, and here I find you deep in some dark plot against me."

"No, no, sir; no, not against you!" It was a woman's voice, and Mrs. Barrymore, paler and more horror-struck than her husband, was standing at the door.

"Oh, John, John, have I brought you to this? It is my doing, Sir Henry—all mine. He has done nothing except for my sake, and because I asked him."

"Speak out, then! What does it mean?"

"My unhappy brother is starving on the moor. We cannot let him perish at our very gates. The light is a signal to him that food is ready for him, and his light out yonder is to show the spot to which to bring it."

2 "Then you brother is—"

"The escaped convict, sir—Selden, the criminal."

This, then, was the explanation of the stealthy expeditions at night and the light at the window. Sir Henry and I both stared at the woman in amazement. Was it possible that this stolidly respectable person was of the same blood as one of the most notorious criminals in the country?

"Yes, sir, my name was Selden, and he is my younger brother. We humored him too much when he was a lad and gave him his own way in everything until he came to think that the world was made for his pleasure, and that he could do what he liked in it. Then, as he grew older, he met wicked companions, and he broke my mother's heart and dragged our name in the dirt. He knew that I was here and that we could not refuse to help him.

"When he dragged himself here one night, weary and starving, with the warders hard at his heels, what could we do? We took him in and fed him and cared for him. Then you returned, sir, and my brother thought he would be safer on the moor than anywhere else until the hue and cry was over, so he lay in hiding there. But every second night we made sure if he was still there by putting a light in the window, and if there was an answer my husband took out some bread and meat to him. Every day we hoped that he was gone, but as long as he was there we could not desert him. That is the whole truth."

"Is this true, Barrymore?"

"Yes, Sir Henry. Every word of it."

"Well, I cannot blame you for standing by your own wife. Forget what I have said. Go to your room, you two, and we shall talk further about this matter in the morning."

When they were gone we looked out of the window again. Sir Henry had flung it open, and the cold night wind beat in upon our faces. Far away in the black distance there still glowed that one tiny point of yellow light.

"I wonder he dares," said Sir Henry.

"It may be so placed as to be only visible from here."

"Very likely. How far do you think it is?"

"Out by the Cleft Tor, I think."

"Not more than a mile or two off."

"Hardly that."

3 "Well, it cannot be far if Barrymore had to carry out the food to it. And he is waiting, this villain, beside that candle. By thunder, Watson, I am going out to take that man!"

The same thought had crossed my own mind. It was not as if the Barrymores had taken us into their confidence. Their secret

The Hound of the Baskervilles 547

AT A GLANCE

■ Barrymore agrees to resign rather than reveal his secret.

■ Mrs. Barrymore enters and explains that her husband is signaling to her brother, the escaped convict.

■ Sir Henry and Watson decide to try to capture the convict.

1 THEME

This passage portrays one type of loyalty, one of the novel's primary values. In the end the servants' loyalty to their master is stronger than their desire to protect their relative.

2 SUBPLOT: CLIMAX

Like the main plot the subplot has a climax, or point of highest interest and emotional involvement. We reach this point as we discover the Barrymores' relationship to Selden, and we understand their suspicious behavior.

3 CHARACTERIZATION

The strong-willed Sir Henry shows a bold, impetuous side. He decides to go out onto the moor at night to capture a dangerous murderer who may be armed.

GUIDED READING

LITERAL QUESTIONS

1a. What is the Barrymores' secret? (Mrs. Barrymore's brother is the escaped convict, Selden. The Barrymores have been signaling to him on the moor and feeding him.)

2a. What do Sir Henry and Watson resolve to do about Selden? (They decide to go out onto the moor and capture him.)

INFERENTIAL QUESTIONS

1b. Are the Barrymores likely to remain suspects now that their secret has been revealed? (No. The revelation clears up the reason for their mysterious behavior.)

2b. What does this decision tell you about Sir Henry and Watson? (They are brave; they have a taste for adventure.)

- Watson and Sir Henry hurry out onto the moor to catch Selden.
- They hear the eerie moan of a hound.
- Watson explains that it is said to be the Hound of the Baskervilles.
- Despite the fearful cry the two men continue on.

1 CHARACTERIZATION

Holmes is a sort of role model to both Sir Henry and Watson. From time to time, they make decisions and take actions based on what they believe Holmes would do or say.

2 PLOT: CONFLICT

The cry of the hound punctures Sir Henry's self-confidence. The possibility of real danger on the moor tempers the baronet's behavior for the remainder of the novel.

3 THEME

This passage reopens the debate over the validity of supernatural events. The sound on the moor is so eerie that even a man as unsuperstitious as Sir Henry cannot deny the legend of the supernatural hound.

---

had been forced from them. The man was a danger to the community.

"I will come," said I.

"Then get your revolver and put on your boots. The sooner we start the better, as the fellow may put out his light and be off."

In five minutes we were outside the door, starting upon our expedition. We hurried through the dark shrubbery, amid the dull moaning of the autumn wind and the rustle of the falling leaves.

"Are you armed?" I asked.

"I have a hunting crop."

"We must close in on him rapidly, for he is said to be a desperate fellow. We shall take him by surprise and have him at our mercy before he can resist."

1 "I say, Watson," said the baronet, "what would Holmes say to this?"

2 As if in answer to his words there rose suddenly out of the vast gloom of the moor that strange cry which I had already heard upon the borders of the great Grimpen Mire. It came with the wind through the silence of the night, a long, deep mutter, then a rising howl, and then the sad moan in which it died away. Again and again it sounded, the whole air throbbing with it, strident, wild, and menacing. The baronet caught my sleeve and his face glimmered white through the darkness.

"What's that, Watson?"

"I don't know. It's a sound they have on the moor. I heard it once before."

It died away, and an absolute silence closed in upon us. We stood straining our ears, but nothing came.

"Watson," said the baronet, "it was the cry of a hound."

My blood ran cold in my veins, for there was a break in his voice which told of the sudden horror which had seized him.

"What do they call this sound?" he asked.

"Who?"

"The folk on the countryside?"

"Oh, they are ignorant people. Why should you mind what they call it?"

"Tell me, Watson. What do they say of it?"

I hesitated, but could not escape the question.

"They say it is the cry of the Hound of the Baskervilles."

He groaned, and was silent.

"A hound it was," he said at last, "but it seemed to come from miles away, over yonder, I think."

"It was hard to say whence it came."

"It rose and fell with the wind. Isn't that the direction of the great Grimpen Mire?"

"Yes, it is."

"Well, it was up there. Come now, Watson, didn't you think yourself that it was the cry of a hound? I am not a child. You need not fear to speak the truth."

"It might be the calling of a strange bird."

3 "No, no, it was a hound. Can there be some truth in all these stories? Is it possible that I am really in danger from so dark a cause? You don't believe it, do you, Watson?"

"No, no."

"And yet it was one thing to laugh about it in London, and it is another to stand out here in the darkness of the moor and to hear such a cry as that. And my uncle! There was the footprint of the hound beside him as he lay. It all fits together. I don't think that I am a coward, Watson, but that sound seemed to freeze my very blood. Feel my hand!"

It was as cold as a block of marble.

"Shall we turn back?"

"No, by thunder; we have come out to get our man, and we will do it."

We stumbled slowly along in the darkness, with the black loom of the craggy hills around us, and the yellow speck of light burning steadily in front. At last we could see whence it came, and then we knew that we were indeed very close. A guttering candle was stuck

---

GUIDED READING

LITERAL QUESTION

1a. What fearful sound do Watson and Sir Henry hear as they cross the moor in search of Selden? (They hear the moan of a hound.)

INFERENTIAL QUESTION

1b. Why is Sir Henry more frightened by the sound than Watson? (Watson had heard the hound earlier; Sir Henry had not. Also, if it is the legendary hound, it would be after Sir Henry Baskerville, not Watson.)

in the crevice of the rocks which flanked it on each side so as to keep the wind from it and also to prevent it from being visible, save in the direction of Baskerville Hall. A boulder of granite concealed our approach, and crouching behind it we gazed over it at the light.

"What shall we do now?" whispered Sir Henry.

"Wait here. We must be near his light. Let us see if we can get a glimpse of him."

The words were hardly out of my mouth when we both saw him. Over the rocks, in the crevice of which the candle burned, there was thrust out an evil yellow face.

Something had evidently aroused his suspicions. It may have been that Barrymore had some private signal which we had neglected to give, or the fellow may have had some other reason for thinking that all was not well, but I could read his fears upon his wicked face. Any instant he might dash out the light and vanish in the darkness. I sprang forward therefore, and Sir Henry did the same. At the some moment the convict screamed out a curse at us and hurled a rock which splintered up against the boulder which had sheltered us. I caught one glimpse of his short, squat, strongly built figure as he sprang to his feet and turned to run. At the same moment by a lucky chance the moon broke through the clouds. We rushed over the brow of the hill, and there was our man running with great speed down the other side, springing over the stones in his way with the activity **1** of a mountain goat. A lucky long shot of my revolver might have crippled him, but I had brought it only to defend myself if attacked and not to shoot an unarmed man who was running away.

We were both swift runners and in fairly good training, but we soon found that we had no chance of overtaking him. We ran and ran until we were completely out of breath, but the space between us grew ever wider. Finally we stopped and sat panting on two rocks, while we watched him disappearing in the distance.

And it was at this moment that there occurred a most strange and unexpected thing. We had risen from our rocks and were turning to go home, having abandoned the hopeless **2** chase. The moon was low upon the right, and the jagged pinnacle of a granite tor stood up against the lower curve of its silver disc. There, outlined as black as an ebony statue on that shining background, I saw the figure of a man upon the tor. As far as I could judge, the figure was that of a tall, thin man. It was not the convict. This man was far from the place where the latter had disappeared. Besides, he was a much taller man. With a cry of surprise I pointed him out to the baronet, but in the instant during which I had turned to grasp his arm the man was gone.

I wished to go in that direction and to search the tor, but it was some distance away. The baronet's nerves were still quivering from that cry, which recalled the dark story of his family, and he was not in the mood for fresh **3** adventures. He had not seen this lonely man upon the tor and could not feel the thrill which his strange presence and his commanding attitude had given to me. "A warder, no doubt," said he. "The moor has been thick with them since this fellow escaped." Well, perhaps his explanation may be the right one, but I should like to have some further proof of it. Today we mean to communicate to the Princetown people where they should look for their missing man, but it is hard lines[1] that we have not actually had the triumph of bringing him back as our own prisoner. Such are the adventures of last night. You must acknowledge, my dear Holmes, that I have done you very well in the matter of a report.

---

1. **hard lines:** regrettable, unfortunate.

The Hound of the Baskervilles 549

AT A GLANCE

- Watson and Sir Henry chase the convict Selden, but he escapes.
- Watson briefly spots a mysterious tall stranger, who also disappears.

1 CHARACTERIZATION

Watson's inherent sense of fair play and compassion extends even to escaped murderers. Also, as a physician, he would find it repugnant to cripple a man.

2 STYLE: IMAGERY

The unknown man is described in majestic terms—"an ebony statue" framed in silver moonlight and jagged granite. Whoever he is, this imposing figure is surely important.

3 PLOT: SUSPENSE

The sighting of the tall, thin stranger adds a new twist to the plot. His description does not match that of any of the neighbors. We wonder who he is and what he is doing.

REFLECTING ON CHAPTERS 7–9

How does the outcome of the subplot about Selden change your opinions about the suspects in the case? (The Barrymores are no longer likely suspects.)

GUIDED READING

LITERAL QUESTIONS

1a. What happens when Watson and Sir Henry chase Selden? (The convict outruns them, and Watson is unwilling to use his gun.)

2a. What identity does Sir Henry suggest for the mysterious tall, thin man? (Sir Henry thinks he may be a warder, or guard.)

INFERENTIAL QUESTIONS

1b. What does this outcome suggest about the subplot about Selden? (Selden is still out on the moor, and we will probably hear from him again.)

2b. Do you think Sir Henry's explanation is probably right? (His explanation is probably not right because a warder would have helped pursue Selden or would have approached the men to find out why they were on the moor.)

1. lied to Sir Henry about his wife's crying, devious about telegram, nervous; learns that Holmes's telegram to Barrymore was delivered to his wife
2. Grimpen Mire, plain with hills, dangerous bog holes; noise of bogs or bittern booming
3. return to London and never come to moor again; Sir Henry
4. creeps to the window with a candle, stares at the moor, departs
5. ■ Sir Henry and Miss Stapleton talk; he embraces her; her brother runs wildly up, abuses Sir Henry; Stapletons depart.
   ■ fear of losing his sister to Sir Henry, being left alone
6. The escaped criminal, Selden, is Mrs. Barrymore's brother. They have been feeding him.
7. ■ Possible answers: hound, animal caught in mire, convict
   ■ probably
8. Possible answers: Yes—Stapleton made the first move to heal breach, and jealousy is powerful. No—Watson has made previous errors; also, Stapleton's crazed behavior seems to go beyond brotherly possessiveness.
9. Possible answers: a warder or a new suspect in the murder
10. ■ quality of being faithful, steadfast in time of need or danger
    ■ Mrs. Barrymore's loyalty to her brother, Dr. Mortimer's loyalty to Sir Charles, Watson's loyalty to Holmes

1. He is conscientious in reporting events, conversations, and facts but is less adept at figuring out the meaning of his observations.
2. Holmes would reveal information more quickly; revelation of evidence at slower pace increases suspense.

STUDY QUESTIONS

Recalling

1. Why does Watson consider Barrymore mysterious? What investigation by Watson in Chapter 7 adds to the mystery surrounding Barrymore?
2. Describe the danger on the moor that Stapleton points out to Watson. How does Stapleton explain the long, low moan that Watson hears?
3. What warning does Miss Stapleton give Watson? For whom does she mistake him?
4. What surprising development concerning Barrymore does Watson report at the end of Chapter 8?
5. Describe the scene that Watson witnesses in Chapter 9 when he follows Sir Henry onto the moor. What excuse does Stapleton later make for his behavior?
6. What secret do Sir Henry and Watson learn after they catch Barrymore with the candle?

Interpreting

7. What might have made the long, low moan that Watson and Stapleton heard on the moor? Do you think the sound was made by something living?
8. Watson finds Stapleton's apology to Sir Henry convincing. Do you? Give reasons for your opinion.
9. Who do you think the "lonely man upon the tor" may be? Give reasons for your opinion.

Extending

10. How would you define *loyalty*? What examples of loyalty can you find in the novel so far?

READING AND LITERARY FOCUS

Point of View

Point of view refers to the relationship of the narrator, or storyteller, to the story. A story told from the **first-person point of view** is told by one of the characters, who refers to himself or herself as "I." The narrator of *The Hound of the Baskervilles* is one of the characters, Dr. Watson. He tells the story from the first-person point of view and refers to himself as "I." First-person point of view helps to make the novel especially lifelike since we imagine that the narrator is a real person speaking directly to us about events that actually happened.

Because we learn everything in *The Hound of the Baskervilles* through Watson, we cannot know what he himself does not know. What puzzles him puzzles us. When he is sure that he has solved a problem, he may be mistaken. What he leads us to think is true may not be true at all.

A story told from the **third-person point of view** is told by the author, who is the narrator and who stands outside the story. The narrator speaks of the characters as "he" or "she." A third-person narrator can tell the reader everything, including the thoughts and feelings of all the characters. "Then He Goes Free" (page 78) is told from the third-person point of view.

Thinking About Point of View

1. Do you think Watson is a helpful narrator? How well can Watson figure out the meaning of what he observes? Give evidence to support your answers.
2. Why do you think Conan Doyle makes Watson the narrator instead of Holmes?

The man upon the tor poses another baffling mystery for Watson.

■ *By the end of Chapter 12, however, you will discover not only his identity but that of Sir Charles's murderer as well.*

10 Extract from the Diary of Dr. Watson

October 16. A dull and foggy day with a drizzle of rain. The house is banked in with rolling clouds, which rise now and then to show the dreary curves of the moor. It is melancholy outside and in. The baronet is in a black reaction after the excitements of the night. I am conscious myself of a weight at my heart and a feeling of impending danger—ever present danger, which is the more terrible because I am unable to define it.

And have I not cause for such a feeling? A stranger is still dogging us, just as a stranger dogged us in London. We have never shaken him off. If I could lay my hands upon that man, then at last we might find ourselves at the end of all our difficulties. To this one purpose I must now devote all my energies.

My first impulse was to tell Sir Henry all my plans. My second and wisest one is to play my own game and speak as little as possible to anyone. He is silent and distrait. His nerves have been strangely shaken by that sound upon the moor. I will say nothing to add to his anxieties, but I will take my own steps to attain my own end.

We had a small scene this morning after breakfast. Barrymore asked leave to speak with Sir Henry, and they were closeted in his study some little time. Sitting in the billiard room I more than once heard the sound of voices raised, and I had a pretty good idea what the point was which was under discussion. After a time the baronet opened his door and called for me.

"Barrymore considers that he has a grievance," he said. "He thinks that it was unfair on our part to hunt his brother-in-law down when he, of his own free will, had told us the secret."

The butler was standing very pale but very collected before us.

"I may have spoken too warmly, sir," said he, "and if I have, I am sure that I beg your pardon. At the same time, I was very much surprised when I heard you two gentlemen come back this morning and learned that you had been chasing Selden. The poor fellow has enough to fight against without my putting more upon his track."

"The man is a public danger. There are lonely houses scattered over the moor, and he is a fellow who would stick at nothing. You only want to get a glimpse of his face to see that. Look at Mr. Stapleton's house, for ex-

The Hound of the Baskervilles   551

GUIDED READING

LITERAL QUESTIONS

1a. How does Watson plan to change his methods? (He plans to operate independently in order not to further burden the already anxious baronet.)

2a. What grievance does Barrymore express to Sir Henry? (Barrymore is annoyed that Sir Henry and Watson tried to catch Selden, his brother-in-law. He feels the poor criminal has had enough trouble already.)

INFERENTIAL QUESTIONS

1b. Why might this change be a little dangerous? (To keep his activities secret, Watson might have to spend more time away from Sir Henry, making Sir Henry more vulnerable.)

2b. Do you think this is a valid grievance? (Answers will vary. Possibilities: *yes*, Sir Henry and Watson should empathize with Selden's situation; *no*, the butler cannot expect Sir Henry to help shield a dangerous murderer.)

- Sir Henry seems to agree not to try to catch Selden again.
- In return Barrymore offers a clue about Sir Charles's death.
- From a letter Barrymore learned that a woman with the initials *L. L.* was to see Sir Charles shortly before his death.

1 PLOT: SUSPENSE

The fact that the police have given up on Selden invalidates Sir Henry's suggestion the previous night that the tall, thin man on the moor was in all likelihood a warder searching for Selden. Suspense about the man's identity builds.

2 PLOT: RISING ACTION

By the end of Chapter 3, Holmes had already deduced that Sir Charles was meeting someone on the night of his death. Now there is finally evidence to support his deduction.

3 PLOT: SUSPENSE

Is the woman L. L. a possible suspect in the case? Asking that the letter be burned suggests that L. L. wants her involvement with Sir Charles to remain secret.

4 THEME

The Barrymores' loyalty to Sir Charles parallels Watson's loyalty to Holmes.

---

ample, with no one but himself to defend it. There's no safety for anyone until he is under lock and key."

"He'll break into no house, sir. I give you my solemn word upon that. But he will never trouble anyone in this country again. I assure you, Sir Henry, that in a very few days the necessary arrangements will have been made and he will be on his way to South America.
1 For heaven's sake, sir, I beg of you not to let the police know that he is still on the moor. They have given up the chase there, and he can lie quiet until the ship is ready for him. You can't tell on him without getting my wife and me into trouble. I beg you, sir, to say nothing to the police."

"Well, Barrymore—"

"God bless you, sir, and thank you from my heart! It would have killed my poor wife had he been taken again."

With a few broken words of gratitude the man turned, but he hesitated and then came back.

"You've been so kind to us, sir, that I should like to do the best I can for you in return. I know something, Sir Henry, and perhaps I should have said it before, but it was long after the inquest that I found it out. I've never breathed a word about it yet to mortal man. It's about poor Sir Charles's death."

The baronet and I were both upon our feet. "Do you know how he died?"

"No, sir, I don't know that."

"What then?"

2 "I know why he was at the gate at that hour. It was to meet a woman."

"To meet a woman! He?"

"Yes, sir."

"And the woman's name?"

"I can't give you the name, sir, but I can give you the initials. Her initials were L. L."

"How do you know this, Barrymore?"

"Well, Sir Henry, your uncle had a letter that morning. He had usually a great many letters, for he was a public man and well known for his kind heart, so that everyone who was in trouble was glad to turn to him. But that morning, as it chanced, there was only this one letter, so I took the more notice of it. It was from Coombe Tracey, and it was addressed in a woman's hand."

"Well?"

"Well, sir, I thought no more of the matter, and never would have done had it not been for my wife. Only a few weeks ago she was cleaning out Sir Charles's study—it had never been touched since his death—and she found the ashes of a burned letter in the back of the grate. The greater part of it was charred to pieces, but one little slip, the end of a page, hung together, and the writing could still be read, though it was gray on a black ground. It seemed to us to be a postscript at the end
3 of the letter, and it said: 'Please, please, as you are a gentleman, burn this letter, and be at the gate by ten o'clock.' Beneath it were signed the initials L. L."

"Have you got that slip?"

"No, sir, it crumbled all to bits after we moved it."

"And you have no idea who L. L. is?"

"No, sir. No more than you have. But I expect if we could lay our hands upon that lady we should know more about Sir Charles's death."

"I cannot understand, Barrymore, how you came to conceal this important information."

"Well, sir, it was immediately after that our
4 own trouble came to us. And then again, sir, we were both of us very fond of Sir Charles, as we well might be considering all that he has done for us. To rake this up couldn't help our poor master, and it's well to go carefully when there's a lady in the case. Even the best of us—"

"You thought it might injure his reputation?"

"Well, sir, I thought no good could come of

GUIDED READING

LITERAL QUESTIONS

1a. What request does Barrymore make of Sir Henry? (He requests that Sir Henry not tell the authorities about Selden's whereabouts.)

2a. What important clue does Barrymore give Sir Henry and Watson? (He says that Sir Charles had a letter on the day of his death from a woman with the initials L. L.)

INFERENTIAL QUESTIONS

1b. Does Sir Henry agree to Barrymore's request? (It is not clear because Barrymore interrupts before Sir Henry can answer. However, Sir Henry does not object when Barrymore jumps to this conclusion.)

2b. Why does Barrymore not make this clue public earlier? (Barrymore wants to protect Sir Charles's good name; meeting a woman at night might ruin the man's reputation.)

it. But now you have been kind to us, and I feel as if it would be treating you unfairly not to tell you all that I know about the matter."

"Very good, Barrymore; you can go." When the butler had left us Sir Henry turned to me. **1** "Well, Watson, what do you think of this new light?"

"It seems to leave the darkness rather blacker than before."

"So I think. But if we can only trace L. L. it should clear up the whole business. We have gained that much. We know that there is someone who has the facts if we can only find her. What do you think we should do?"

"Let Holmes know all about it at once. It will give him the clue for which he has been seeking. I am much mistaken if it does not bring him down."

2 I went at once to my room and drew up my report of the morning's conversation for Holmes.

October 17.   All day today the rain poured down, rustling on the ivy and dripping from the eaves. I thought of the convict out upon the bleak, cold, shelterless moor. Poor devil! Whatever his crimes, he has suffered something to atone for them. And then I thought of that other one—the face in the cab, the figure against the moon. Was he also out in that deluge—the unseen watcher, the man of darkness? In the evening I put on my waterproof and I walked far upon the sodden moor, full of dark imaginings, the rain beating upon my face and the wind whistling about my **3** ears. God help those who wander into the great mire now, for even the firm uplands are becoming a morass. I found the black tor upon which I had seen the solitary watcher, and from its craggy summit I looked out myself across the melancholy downs. Nowhere was there any trace of that lonely man whom I had seen on the same spot two nights before.

As I walked back I was overtaken by Dr.

Mortimer driving in his dogcart[1] over a rough moorland track which led from the outlying farmhouse of Foulmire. He has been very attentive to us, and hardly a day has passed that he has not called at the Hall to see how we were getting on. He insisted upon my climbing into his dogcart, and he gave me a lift homeward.

"By the way, Mortimer," said I, as we jolted along the rough road, "I suppose there are few people living within driving distance whom you do not know?"

"Hardly any, I think."

"Can you, then, tell me the name of any woman whose initials are L.L.?"

He thought for a few minutes.

"No," said he. "There are a few gypsies and laboring folk for whom I can't answer, but among the farmers or gentry there is no one whose initials are those. Wait a bit though," he added after a pause. "There is Laura Lyons—her initials are L. L.—but she lives in Coombe Tracey."

4 "Who is she?" I asked.

"She is Frankland's daughter."

"What! Old Frankland the crank?"

"Exactly. She married an artist named Lyons, who came sketching on the moor. He proved to be a blackguard and deserted her."

"How does she live?"

"I fancy old Frankland allows her a pittance, but it cannot be more, for his own affairs are considerably involved. Whatever she may have deserved one could not allow her to go hopelessly to the bad. Her story got about, and several of the people here did something to enable her to earn an honest living. Stapleton did for one, and Sir Charles for another. I gave a trifle myself. It was to set her up in a typewriting business."

---

1. **dogcart:** small, light, open, one-horse carriage with two seats. It originally had a space for dogs under the rear seat.

The Hound of the Baskervilles   553

1 STYLE: METAPHOR

Like Holmes earlier in the novel, Watson uses the metaphor of a card game to describe the case. Watson's description of the cards he holds suggests he is becoming more confident of winning the game.

2 SUBPLOT

The subplot concerning Selden still has not reached its resolution. We are still unsure about what has happened to the escapee.

3 PLOT: FORESHADOWING

These details hint at the identity of the man on the moor. We shall soon know his name.

4 POINT OF VIEW

The narrator is staring through "a blurred pane" that represents the limited nature of first-person narration. We know no more than Watson. If his assumptions about the man on the moor are wrong, we can be easily misled.

He wanted to know the object of my inquiries, but I managed to satisfy his curiosity without telling him too much, for there is no reason why we should take anyone into our confidence. Tomorrow morning I shall find my way to Coombe Tracey and see this Mrs. Laura Lyons.

I have only one other incident to record upon this tempestuous and melancholy day. 1 This was my conversation with Barrymore just now, which gives me one more strong card which I can play in due time.

Mortimer had stayed to dinner, and he and the baronet played écarté[2] afterwards. The butler brought me my coffee into the library, and I took the chance to ask him a few questions.

"Well," said I, "has this precious relation of yours departed, or is he still lurking out yonder?"

2 "I don't know, sir. I hope to heaven that he has gone, for he has brought nothing but trouble here! I've not heard of him since I left out food for him last, and that was three days ago."

"Did you see him then?"

"No, sir, but the food was gone when next I went that way."

"Then he was certainly there?"

"So you would think, sir, unless it was the other man who took it."

I sat with my coffee cup halfway to my lips and stared at Barrymore.

"You know that there is another man then?"

"Yes, sir; there is another man upon the moor."

"Have you seen him?"

"No, sir."

"How do you know of him then?"

_____
2. **écarté** [ā′kär tā′]: two-person card game.

554   *The Novel*

"Selden told me of him, sir, a week ago or more. He's in hiding, too, but he's not a convict as far as I can make out."

"Can you tell me anything about him? What did Selden say? Did he find out where he hid, or what he was doing?"

3 "He saw him once or twice, but he is a deep one and gives nothing away. At first he thought that he was the police, but soon he found that he had some job of his own. A kind of gentleman he was, as far as he could see, but what he was doing he could not make out."

"And where did he say that he lived?"

"Among the old houses on the hillside—the stone huts where the old folk used to live."

"But how about his food?"

"Selden found out that he has got a lad who works for him and brings him all he needs. I dare say he goes to Coombe Tracey for what he wants."

"Very good, Barrymore. We may talk further of this some other time." When the butler had gone 4 I walked over to the black window, and I looked through a blurred pane at the driving clouds and at the tossing outline of the wind-swept trees. It is a wild night indoors, and what must it be in a stone hut upon the moor. What passion of hatred can it be which leads a man to lurk in such a place at such a time!

11   The Man on the Tor

The extract from my private diary which forms the last chapter has brought my narrative up to the eighteenth of October. I start then from the day which succeeded that upon which I had established two facts of great importance, the one that Mrs. Laura Lyons of Coombe Tracey had written to Sir Charles Baskerville and made an appointment with him at the very place and hour that he met

---

GUIDED READING

LITERAL QUESTIONS

1a. What fact that Watson already suspected does Barrymore confirm? (There is another man besides Selden living on the moor.)

2a. In what way does the man on the moor get food and supplies? (A boy brings them up to him from the village of Coombe Tracey.)

INFERENTIAL QUESTIONS

1b. What do you think this other man on the moor is doing there? (Answers will vary. Possibilities: The man has some connection with the mysterious sound heard on the moor; the man has an interest in Sir Henry.)

2b. How could this information be useful to Watson? (Watson could watch for the boy in the small village and then question him or follow him.)

his death, the other that the lurking man upon the moor was to be found among the stone huts upon the hillside.

I had no opportunity to tell the baronet what I had learned about Mrs. Lyons upon the evening before, for Dr. Mortimer remained with him at cards until it was very late. At breakfast, however, I informed him about my discovery, and asked him whether he would care to accompany me to Coombe Tracey. On second thought it seemed to both of us that if I went alone the results might be better. The more formal we made the visit the less information we might obtain.

When I reached Coombe Tracey I told Perkins to put up the horses, and I made inquiries for the lady whom I had come to interrogate. I had no difficulty in finding her rooms, which were central and well appointed. A maid showed me in without ceremony, and as I entered the sitting room a lady, who was sitting before a Remington typewriter, sprang up with a pleasant smile of welcome. Her face fell, however, when she saw that I was a stranger, and she sat down again and asked me the object of my visit.

1 "I have the pleasure," said I, "of knowing your father."

It was a clumsy introduction, and the lady made me feel it.

"There is nothing in common between my father and me," she said. "I owe him nothing, and his friends are not mine. If it were not for the late Sir Charles Baskerville and some other kind hearts I might have starved for all that my father cared."

"It was about the late Sir Charles Baskerville that I have come here to see you."

2 The freckles started out on the lady's face.

"What can I tell you about him?" she asked, and her fingers played nervously over the stops of her typewriter.

"You knew him, did you not?"

"I have already said that I owe a great deal to his kindness. If I am able to support myself it is largely due to the interest which he took in my unhappy situation."

"Did you correspond with him?"

The lady looked quickly up with an angry gleam in her hazel eyes.

"What is the object of these questions?" she asked sharply.

"The object is to avoid a public scandal. It is better that I should ask them here than that the matter should pass outside our control."

She was silent and her face was still very pale. At last she looked up with something reckless and defiant in her manner.

"Well, I'll answer," she said. "What are your questions?"

"Did you correspond with Sir Charles?"

"I certainly wrote to him once or twice to acknowledge his delicacy and his generosity."

"Have you the dates of those letters?"

"No."

"Have you ever met him?"

"Yes, once or twice, when he came into Coombe Tracey. He was a very retiring man."

"But if you saw him so seldom and wrote so seldom, how did he know enough about your affairs to be able to help you, as you say that he has done?"

She met my difficulty with the utmost readiness.

3 "There were several gentlemen who knew my sad history and united to help me. One was Mr. Stapleton, a neighbor and intimate friend of Sir Charles's. He was exceedingly kind, and it was through him that Sir Charles learned about my affairs."

"Did you ever write to Sir Charles asking him to meet you?" I continued.

Mrs. Lyons flushed with anger again.

"Really, sir, this is a very extraordinary question."

The Hound of the Baskervilles 555

1 CHARACTERIZATION

Watson has a tendency to be clumsy and dense at times; that he readily acknowledges this aspect of his personality is endearing.

2 READING SKILLS: INFERENCES

Mrs. Lyons' nervous fidgeting at the mention of Sir Charles suggests that she has information about the man or his death that she has not made public.

3 PLOT: FORESHADOWING

The murky outline of a triangle emerges. Did Stapleton interest Sir Charles in the "sad history" of Laura Lyons for purely noble reasons? Or did he have an ulterior motive?

GUIDED READING

LITERAL QUESTION

1a. When Mrs. Lyons reacts angrily to Watson's questions, what warning does the doctor make? (He warns Mrs. Lyons that there might be a public scandal if she doesn't cooperate.)

INFERENTIAL QUESTION

1b. What do you think Watson means? (The news that Mrs. Lyons asked to meet a murder victim may sound suspicious to the police.)

1 CHARACTERIZATION

The dialogue reveals the determination and rationality of Watson: He does not allow the lady's emotional turmoil to distract him for an instant.

2 STYLE: METAPHOR

The fact that Mrs. Lyons is "pouring out her soul in a torrent of words" indicates that what she is telling Watson is the truth. At this point she is so upset that she is unable to fabricate lies or excuses.

3 BACKGROUND

Doyle was a social activist who worked for reforms in a variety of areas. He believed that laws concerning marriage and divorce were unfair to women. Here he takes the opportunity to persuade readers of this opinion.

4 PLOT: SUSPENSE

The information about Mrs. Lyons' other source of help would establish the truth of her story. The reason she keeps it secret may have some bearing on the case.

"I am sorry, madam, but I must repeat it."

"Then I answer, certainly not."

"Not on the very day of Sir Charles's death?"

1 The flush had faded in an instant, and a deathly face was before me. Her dry lips could not speak the "No" which I saw rather than heard.

"Surely your memory deceives you," said I. "I could even quote a passage of your letter. It ran 'Please, please, as you are a gentleman, burn this letter, and be at the gate by ten o'clock.' "

I thought that she had fainted, but she recovered herself by a supreme effort.

"Is there no such thing as a gentleman?" she gasped.

"You do Sir Charles an injustice. He *did* burn the letter. But sometimes a letter may be legible even when burned. You acknowledge now that you wrote it?"

2 "Yes, I did write it," she cried, pouring out her soul in a torrent of words. "I did write it. Why should I deny it? I have no reason to be ashamed of it. I wished him to help me. I believed that if I had an interview I could gain his help, so I asked him to meet me."

"But why at such an hour?"

"Because I had only just learned that he was going to London next day and might be away for months. There were reasons why I could not get there earlier."

"But why a rendezvous in the garden instead of a visit to the house?"

"Do you think a woman could go alone at that hour to a bachelor's house?"

"Well, what happened when you did get there?"

"I never went."

"Mrs. Lyons!"

"No, I swear it to you on all I hold sacred. I never went. Something intervened to prevent my going."

"What was that?"

"That is a private matter. I cannot tell it."

"Mrs. Lyons," I said, "you are taking a very great responsibility and putting yourself in a very false position by not making an absolutely clean breast of all that you know. I ask you once again why it was that you were so pressing that Sir Charles should destroy this letter which he received on the day of his death."

"The matter is a very private one."

"The more reason why you should avoid a public investigation."

"I will tell you, then. If you have heard anything of my unhappy history you will know that I made a rash marriage and had reason to regret it."

"I have heard so much."

3 "My life has been one incessant persecution from a husband whom I abhor. The law is upon his side, and every day I am faced by the possibility that he may force me to live with him. At the time that I wrote this letter to Sir Charles I had learned that there was a prospect of my regaining my freedom if certain expenses could be met. It meant everything to me—peace of mind, happiness, self-respect—everything. I knew Sir Charles's generosity, and I thought that if he heard the story from my own lips he would help me."

4 "Then how is it that you did not go?"

"Because I received help in the interval from another source."

"Why, then, did you not write to Sir Charles and explain this?"

"So I should have done had I not seen his death in the paper next morning."

The woman's story hung coherently together, and all my questions were unable to shake it. I could only check it by finding if she had, indeed, instituted divorce proceedings against her husband at or about the time of the tragedy.

GUIDED READING

LITERAL QUESTIONS

1a. What lie does Mrs. Lyons tell Watson? (At first she insists that she did not write to Sir Charles requesting a meeting. At last she admits it.)

2a. What help did Mrs. Lyons plan to ask Sir Charles for? (She planned to ask him for money to pay the expenses of getting a divorce.)

INFERENTIAL QUESTIONS

1b. Why does this lie tend to make Mrs. Lyons a suspect in the case? (Lying about asking Sir Charles to meet her on the night he died suggests she has something to hide.)

2b. From what other source do you think Mrs. Lyons got this help? (Stapleton probably helped her, since he was the only other individual to whom she seemed grateful.)

I came away baffled and disheartened. Once again I had reached that dead wall which seemed to be built across every path by which I tried to get at the object of my mission. And yet the more I thought of the lady's face and of her manner the more I felt that something was being held back from me. Surely the explanation of all this could not be as innocent as she would have me believe. For the moment I could proceed no farther in that direction, but must turn back to that other clue which was to be sought for among the stone huts upon the moor.

Luck had been against us again and again in this inquiry, but now at last it came to my aid. And the messenger of good fortune was none other than Mr. Frankland, who was standing, gray-whiskered and red-faced, outside the gate of his garden, which opened on to the high road along which I traveled.

"Good-day, Dr. Watson," cried he with unwonted good humor, "you must really give your horses a rest, and come in to congratulate me."

My feelings toward him were far from being friendly after what I had heard of his treatment of his daughter, but I followed Frankland into his dining room.

"It is a great day for me, sir—one of the red-letter days of my life," he cried with many chuckles. "I have brought off a double event. I mean to teach them in these parts that law is law, and that there is a man here who does not fear to invoke it. I've closed the wood where the Fernworthy folk used to picnic."

"I have no doubt that the Fernworthy people will burn me in effigy tonight. I told the police last time they did it that they should stop these disgraceful exhibitions. The County Constabulary is in a scandalous state, sir, and it has not afforded me the protection to which I am entitled. The case of Frankland *v.* Regina will bring the matter before the attention of the public. I told them that they would have occasion to regret their treatment of me, and already my words have come true."

"How so?" I asked.

The old man put on a very knowing expression.

"Because I could tell them what they are dying to know; but nothing would induce me to help the rascals in any way."

I had been casting round for some excuse by which I could get away from his gossip, but now I began to wish to hear more of it.

"Some poaching case, no doubt?" said I with an indifferent manner.

"Ha, ha, my boy, a very much more important matter than that! What about the convict on the moor?"

I started. "You don't mean that you know where he is?" said I.

"I may not know exactly where he is, but I am quite sure that I could help the police to lay their hands on him. Has it never struck you that the way to catch that man was to find out where he got his food and so trace it to him?"

He certainly seemed to be getting uncomfortably near the truth. "No doubt," said I; "but how do you know he is on the moor?"

"I know it because I have seen with my own eyes the messenger who takes him his food."

My heart sank for Barrymore. It was a serious thing to be in the power of this spiteful old busybody. But his next remark took a weight from my mind.

"You'll be surprised to hear that his food is taken to him by a child. I see him every day through my telescope upon the roof. He passes along the same path at the same hour, and to whom should he be going except to the convict?"

Here was luck indeed! And yet I suppressed all appearance of interest. A child! Barrymore had said that our unknown was supplied by

The Hound of the Baskervilles 557

AT A GLANCE
- Watson stops to speak with Mr. Frankland, Mrs. Lyons' father.
- The old man announces that he has used his telescope to watch a child bringing supplies to a man on the moor. Frankland believes the man is Selden.

1 PLOT: FORESHADOWING

Watson's musings suggest that there is another explanation for Mrs. Lyons' behavior the night of Sir Charles's death. The true explanation will soon be revealed.

2 CHARACTERIZATION

The portrayal of Frankland as the village busybody adds humor and local color. However, the main purpose of this minor character is to advance the plot toward its climax.

3 CHARACTERIZATION

Watson exhibits a cunning streak, cleverly leading Frankland to reveal more about his secret discovery by appearing uninterested.

GUIDED READING

LITERAL QUESTIONS

1a. What does Frankland claim to have seen on the moor? (He says he has watched a boy bring supplies to someone on the moor.)

2a. How does Watson react as Frankland talks about his sightings? (He tries to appear uninterested.)

INFERENTIAL QUESTIONS

1b. What mistaken conclusion does Frankland make, based on this sighting? (Frankland assumes the boy is bringing food to the convict, but from Barrymore we know the boy is bringing food to the other man on the moor.)

2b. Why does Watson react this way? (He knows Frankland will tell him more if he appears uninterested.)

1 a boy. It was on his track, and not upon the convict's, that Frankland had stumbled. If I could get his knowledge it might save me a long and weary hunt.

"I should say that it was much more likely that it was the son of one of the moorland shepherds taking out his father's dinner."

2 The last appearance of opposition struck fire out of the old autocrat. His eyes looked malignantly at me, and his gray whiskers bristled like those of an angry cat.

"Indeed, sir!" said he, pointing out over the wide-stretching moor. "Do you see that Black Tor over yonder? Well, do you see the low hill beyond with the thornbrush upon it? It is the stoniest part of the whole moor. Is that a place where a shepherd would be likely to take his station? Your suggestion, sir, is a most absurd one."

I meekly answered that I had spoken without knowing all the facts. My submission pleased him.

"But wait a moment, Dr. Watson. Do my eyes deceive me, or is there at the present moment something moving upon that hillside?"

3 It was several miles off, but I could distinctly see a small dark dot against the dull green and gray.

"Come, sir, come!" cried Frankland, rushing upstairs. "You will see with your own eyes and judge for yourself."

The telescope, a formidable instrument mounted upon a tripod, stood upon the flat leads of the house. Frankland clapped his eye to it and gave a cry of satisfaction.

"Quick, Dr. Watson, quick, before he passes over the hill!"

There he was, sure enough, a small urchin with a little bundle upon his shoulder, toiling slowly up the hill. When he reached the crest I saw the ragged uncouth figure outlined for an instant against the cold blue sky. He looked round him with a furtive and stealthy air, as one who dreads pursuit. Then he vanished over the hill.

GUIDED QUESTIONS

LITERAL QUESTION

1a. What further information does Frankland give about the man hiding on the moor? (He reveals his hiding spot, a low hill beyond the Black Tor.)

INFERENTIAL QUESTION

1b. How does Watson cleverly get him to reveal this additional information? (Watson purposely angers Frankland by suggesting the boy is bringing food to a shepherd. To prove Watson wrong, Frankland reveals the hiding spot.)

"Well! Am I right?"

"Certainly, there is a boy who seems to have some secret errand."

"And what the errand is even a county constable could guess. But not one word shall they have from me, and I bind you to secrecy also, Dr. Watson. Not a word! You understand!"

"Just as you wish."

I succeeded in dissuading him from his announced intention of walking home with me. I kept the road as long as his eye was on me, and then I struck off across the moor and made for the stony hill over which the boy had disappeared.

The sun was already sinking when I reached the summit of the hill, and the long slopes beneath me were all golden-green on one side and gray shadow on the other.

The boy was nowhere to be seen. But down beneath me in a cleft of the hills there was a circle of the old stone huts, and in the middle of them there was one which retained sufficient roof to act as a screen against the weather. My heart leaped within me as I saw it. This must be the burrow where the stranger lurked. At last my foot was on the threshold of his hiding place—his secret was within my grasp.

As I approached the hut, walking as warily as Stapleton would do when with poised net he drew near the settled butterfly, I satisfied myself that the place had indeed been used as a habitation. A vague pathway among the boulders led to the dilapidated opening which served as a door. All was silent within. The unknown might be lurking there, or he might **1** be prowling on the moor. My nerves tingled with the sense of adventure. I closed my hand upon the butt of my revolver and, walking swiftly up to the door, I looked in. The place was empty.

In the middle of the hut a flat stone served the purpose of a table, and upon this stood a small cloth bundle—the same, no doubt, which I had seen through the telescope upon the shoulder of the boy. After having exam**2** ined it, my heart leaped to see that beneath it there lay a sheet of paper with writing upon it. I raised it, and this was what I read, roughly scrawled in pencil:

"Dr. Watson has gone to Coombe Tracey."

For a minute I stood there with the paper in my hands thinking out the meaning of this curt message. It was I, then, and not Sir Henry, who was being dogged by this secret man. He had not followed me himself, but he had set an agent—the boy, perhaps—upon my track, and this was his report. Possibly I had taken no step since I had been upon the moor which had not been observed and reported.

I could not discover any sign which might indicate the character or intentions of the **3** man who lived in this singular place. Was he our malignant enemy, or was he by chance our guardian angel? I swore that I would not leave the hut until I knew. Outside the sun was sinking low and the west was blazing with scarlet and gold. I sat in the dark recess of the hut and waited with somber patience for the coming of its tenant.

And then at last I heard him. Far away came the sharp clink of a boot striking upon a stone. Then another, and yet another, coming nearer and nearer. I shrank back into the darkest corner and cocked the pistol in my pocket, determined not to discover[1] myself until I had an opportunity of seeing some**4** thing of the stranger. There was a long pause which showed that he had stopped. Then once more the footsteps approached and a shadow fell across the opening of the hut.

"It is a lovely evening, my dear Watson," said a well-known voice. "I really think that you will be more comfortable outside than in."

---

1. **discover:** show; reveal.

The Hound of the Baskervilles 559

AT A GLANCE

- Watson leaves Frankland and heads out onto the moor.
- The doctor finds the stone hut where the man is hiding.
- Inside, a note refers to Watson's trip to Coombe Tracey.
- Outside, a familiar voice welcomes him.

1 PLOT: SUSPENSE

Watson's tingling nerves and ready revolver build suspense. He seems about to trap the stranger and finally crack the case.

2 IRONY

Watson expects the note to help clear up the identity of the man in the hut and his intentions toward Sir Henry. Ironically Watson learns that *his* movements have been observed.

3 PLOT: FORESHADOWING

Watson suggests that the man in the hut might be a "guardian angel." For the first time he imagines a benevolent purpose for the man's presence, foreshadowing the man's identity.

4 PLOT: SUSPENSE

Again suspense mounts. Surprisingly, the mysterious "stranger" seems to be none other than Watson's best friend, Sherlock Holmes.

GUIDED READING

LITERAL QUESTIONS

1a. What does Watson conclude after reading the message left on the table in the hut? (Watson concludes that it has been he, not Sir Henry, who has been followed all along.)

2a. What fact does the author give about the person who finally greets Watson at the hut? (This person had a voice that Watson knew well.)

INFERENTIAL QUESTIONS

1b. How do you think Watson feels about this new piece of information? (He doesn't appear to be afraid—only more curious and determined.)

2b. Who do you think the person is? (From the speech pattern and the words *my dear Watson,* we can deduce it is Sherlock Holmes.)

- Watson is overjoyed to see Holmes.
- Holmes deduces how Watson found his hiding place.
- Watson is annoyed that Holmes did not share his plan of hiding on the moor while investigating the case.

1 PLOT: FORESHADOWING

The chapter title foreshadows the main event of the chapter. It hints at this content without giving away the details. We know there will be a death, but we do not know whose.

2 READING SKILLS: INFERENCES

The details of Holmes's appearance suggest that he has been living in the open on the moor for some time, perhaps for as long as Watson has been at Baskerville Hall.

3 THEME

Holmes's return to the narrative reminds us of the powerful combination of logic and observation. Holmes makes three deductions: Watson saw him on the night of the convict hunt; Frankland spotted the boy; Watson went to see Mrs. Lyons.

4 CHARACTERIZATION

Understandably, Watson is angry and hurt that his close friend chose not to reveal the plan. The loyal doctor's worst fear is that Holmes does not trust him.

1 **12 Death on the Moor**

For a moment or two I sat breathless, hardly able to believe my ears. Then my senses and my voice came back to me, while a crushing weight of responsibility seemed in an instant to be lifted from my soul. That cold, incisive, ironical voice could belong to but one man in all the world.

"Holmes!" I cried—"Holmes!"

"Come out," said he, "and please be careful with the revolver."

I stood under the rude lintel, and there he sat upon a stone outside, his gray eyes dancing with amusement as they fell upon my as-

560 *The Novel*

2 tonished features. He was thin and worn, but clear and alert, his keen face bronzed by the sun and roughened by the wind.

"I never was more glad to see anyone in my life," said I as I wrung him by the hand.

"Or more astonished, eh?"

"Well, I must confess to it."

"So you actually thought that I was the criminal?"

"I did not know who you were, but I was determined to find out."

3 "Excellent, Watson! And how did you localize me? You saw me, perhaps, on the night of the convict hunt, when I was so imprudent as to allow the moon to rise behind me?"

"Yes, I saw you then."

"And have no doubt searched all the huts until you came to this one?"

"No, your boy had been observed, and that gave me a guide where to look."

"The old gentleman with the telescope, no doubt. I could not make it out when first I saw the light flashing upon the lens." He rose and peeped into the hut. "Ha, I see that Cartwright has brought up some supplies. What's this paper? So you have been to Coombe Tracey, have you?"

"Yes."

"To see Mrs. Laura Lyons?"

"Exactly."

"Well done! Our researches have evidently been running on parallel lines, and when we unite our results I expect we shall have a fairly full knowledge of the case."

"Well, I am glad from my heart that you are here, for indeed the responsibility and the mystery were both becoming too much for my nerves. But how in the name of wonder did you come here, and what have you been doing? I thought that you were in Baker Street."

4 "That was what I wished you to think."

"Then you use me, and yet do not trust me!" I cried with some bitterness. "I think

---

GUIDED READING

LITERAL QUESTIONS

1a. What words does the author use to describe Sherlock Holmes's appearance? (He is *thin and worn;* his face is *bronzed by the sun and roughened by the wind.*)

2a. How does Holmes compare his investigation of the case with Watson's "researches"? (Holmes says that they have "been running on parallel lines.")

INFERENTIAL QUESTIONS

1b. What does this description suggest about Holmes's activities in recent days? (He has been out on the moor for some time now; he has been walking about a great deal, probably investigating the case.)

2b. What does Holmes mean by this comparison? (that the investigations of both men are leading to the same conclusions in the case)

that I have deserved better at your hands, Holmes."

"My dear fellow, you have been invaluable to me in this as in many other cases, and I beg that you will forgive me if I have seemed to play a trick upon you. Had I been with Sir Henry and you, my presence would have warned our very formidable opponents to be on their guard. As it is, I have been able to get about as I could not possibly have done had I been living in the Hall, and I remain an unknown factor in the business."

"But why keep me in the dark?"

"For you to know might possibly have led to my discovery. You would have wished to tell me something, or in your kindness you would have brought me out some comfort or other, and so an unnecessary risk would be run. I brought Cartwright down with me—you remember the little chap at the express office—and he has seen after my simple wants: a loaf of bread and a clean collar."

1 "Then my reports have all been wasted!"— My voice trembled as I recalled the pains and the pride with which I had composed them.

Holmes took a bundle of papers from his pocket.

"Here are your reports, my dear fellow, and very well thumbed, I assure you. I made excellent arrangements, and they are only delayed one day upon their way. I must compliment you exceedingly upon the zeal and the intelligence which you have shown over an extraordinarily difficult case."

2 The warmth of Holmes's praise drove my anger from my mind. I felt also in my heart that he was right in what he said and that it was really best for our purpose that I should not have known that he was upon the moor.

"That's better," said he, seeing the shadow rise from my face. "And now tell me the result of your visit to Mrs. Laura Lyons—it was not difficult for me to guess that it was to see her that you had gone, for I am already aware that

she is the one person in Coombe Tracey who might be of service to us in the matter. In fact, if you had not gone today it is exceedingly probable that I should have gone tomorrow."

I told Holmes of my conversation with the lady. So interested was he that I had to repeat some of it twice before he was satisfied.

"This is most important," said he when I had concluded. "It fills up a gap which I had been unable to bridge in this most complex affair. You are aware, perhaps, that a close intimacy exists between this lady and the man Stapleton?"

"I did not know of a close intimacy."

"There can be no doubt about the matter. They meet, they write, there is a complete understanding between them. Now, this puts a **3** very powerful weapon into our hands. If I could only use it to detach his wife—"

"His wife?"

"I am giving you some information now, in return for all that you have given me. The lady who has passed here as Miss Stapleton is in reality his wife."

"Good heavens, Holmes! Are you sure of what you say? How could he have permitted Sir Henry to fall in love with her?"

"Sir Henry's falling in love could do no harm to anyone except Sir Henry. I repeat that the lady is his wife and not his sister."

"But why this elaborate deception?"

"Because he foresaw that she would be very much more useful to him in the character of a free woman."

All my unspoken instincts, my vague suspicions, suddenly took shape and centered upon the naturalist. In that impassive, colorless man, with his straw hat and his butterfly net, I seemed to see something terrible—a creature of infinite patience and craft, with a smiling face and a murderous heart.

"It is he, then, who is our enemy—it is he who dogged us in London?"

"So I read the riddle."

The Hound of the Baskervilles 561

- Holmes has traced the Stapletons' real identities and background.
- According to Holmes, Stapleton's plan is to murder Sir Henry.
- The detectives are suddenly interrupted by a human scream and the wail of the horrible hound.

1 STYLE: METAPHOR

Much of the mystery has been cleared up by Holmes's information about Stapleton. Still "hidden by the shadows," however, are Stapleton's motive and methods.

2 SETTING

A haunting and colorful picture of nightfall on the moor, these lines also remind us that the darkness has come, the time when the powers of evil are loose on the moor.

3 PLOT: CONFLICT

The conflict between Holmes and Stapleton is now clearly delineated. Holmes closes his nets on Stapleton by gathering evidence; meanwhile, Stapleton closes in on Sir Henry.

4 PLOT: FORESHADOWING

Holmes's misgivings about leaving Sir Henry alone foreshadow the possibility that the human cries heard in the next paragraphs are those of Sir Henry.

5 CHARACTERIZATION

Not only Watson's nerves have been affected by the case. Holmes, the "man of iron," displays a rare moment of emotional distress.

"And the warning—it must have come from her!"

"Exactly."

"But are you sure of this, Holmes? How do you know that the woman is his wife?"

"Because he so far forgot himself as to tell you a true piece of autobiography upon the occasion when he first met you, and I dare say he has many a time regretted it since. He *was* once a schoolmaster in the north of England. Now, there is no one more easy to trace than a schoolmaster. A little investigation showed me that a school had come to grief under atrocious circumstances, and that the man who had owned it—the name was different—had disappeared with his wife. The descriptions agreed. When I learned that the missing man was devoted to entomology the identification was complete."

1 The darkness was rising, but much was still hidden by the shadows.

"If this woman is in truth his wife, where does Mrs. Laura Lyons come in?" I asked.

"That is one of the points upon which your own researches have shed a light. Your interview with the lady has cleared the situation very much. I did not know about a projected divorce between herself and her husband. In that case, regarding Stapleton as an unmarried man, she counted no doubt upon becoming his wife."

"And when she is undeceived?"

"Why, then we may find the lady useful. It must be our first duty to see her—both of us—tomorrow. Don't you think, Watson, that you are away from your charge rather long? Your place should be at Baskerville Hall."

2 The last red streaks had faded away in the west and night had settled upon the moor. A few faint stars were gleaming in a violet sky.

"One last question, Holmes," I said as I rose. "Surely there is no need of secrecy between you and me. What is the meaning of it all? What is he after?"

Holmes's voice sank as he answered:

"It is murder, Watson—refined, cold-blooded, deliberate murder. Do not ask me for particulars. My nets are closing upon him, even as his are upon Sir Henry, and with your help he is already almost at my mercy. There is but one danger which can threaten us. It is that he should strike before we are ready to do so. Another day—two at the most—and I have my case complete, but until then guard your charge as closely as ever a fond mother watched her ailing child. Your mission today has justified itself, and yet I could almost wish that you had not left his side. Hark!"

A terrible scream—a prolonged yell of horror and anguish burst out of the silence of the moor. That frightful cry turned the blood to ice in my veins.

I gasped. "What is it? What does it mean?"

"Where is it?" Holmes whispered; and I knew from the thrill of his voice that he, the man of iron, was shaken to the soul. "Where is it, Watson?"

"There, I think." I pointed into the darkness.

"No, there!"

Again the agonized cry swept through the silent night, louder and much nearer than ever. And a new sound mingled with it, a deep, muttered rumble, musical and yet menacing, rising and falling like the low, constant murmur of the sea.

"The hound!" cried Holmes. "Come, Watson, come! Great heavens, if we are too late!"

He had started running swiftly over the moor, and I had followed at his heels. But now from somewhere among the broken ground immediately in front of us there came one last despairing yell, and then a dull, heavy thud. We halted and listened. Not another sound broke the heavy silence of the windless night.

5 I saw Holmes put his hand to his forehead like a man distracted. He stamped his feet upon the ground.

GUIDED READING

LITERAL QUESTIONS

1a. In what way is Stapleton deceiving Mrs. Laura Lyons? (He is claiming to be single and is leading her to believe that they might marry one day.)

2a. What frightening sounds do Holmes and Watson suddenly hear? (They hear a human scream followed closely by a hound's deep roar.)

INFERENTIAL QUESTIONS

1b. Why do you think Mrs. Lyons will be useful to Holmes when she learns the truth? (She will be furious with Stapleton and likely to cooperate with Holmes's investigations.)

2b. Upon hearing these sounds, why does the frightened Holmes fear they might be "too late"? (The hound is clearly chasing someone, and it is probably Sir Henry; they may have failed to protect him.)

"He has beaten us, Watson. We are too late."

"No, no, surely not!"

"Fool that I was to hold my hand.[1] And you, Watson, see what comes of abandoning your charge! But, by heavens, if the worst has happened, we'll avenge him!"

Blindly we ran through the gloom, blundering against boulders, forcing our way through gorse bushes, panting up hills and rushing down slopes, heading in the direction whence those dreadful sounds had come.

"Can you see anything?"

"Nothing."

"But, hark, what is that?"

A low moan had fallen upon our ears. There it was again upon our left! On that side a ridge of rocks ended in a sheer cliff which overlooked a stone-strewn slope. On its jagged face was spread-eagled some dark, irregular object. As we ran toward it the vague outline hardened into a definite shape. It was a prostrate man face downward upon the ground, the head doubled under him at a horrible angle, the shoulders rounded and the body hunched together as if in the act of throwing a somersault.

Holmes laid his hand upon him and held it up again with an exclamation of horror. The gleam of the match which he struck shone upon his clotted fingers and upon the ghastly pool which widened slowly from the crushed skull of the victim. And it shone upon something else which turned our hearts sick and faint within us—the body of Sir Henry Baskerville!

There was no chance of either of us forgetting that peculiar ruddy tweed suit—the very one which he had worn on the first morning that we had seen him in Baker Street. We caught the one clear glimpse of it, and then

---

1. **hold my hand:** not take action until all the elements of the case were clear.

the match flickered and went out, even as the hope had gone out of our souls. Holmes groaned, and his face glimmered white through the darkness.

"The brute! the brute!" I cried, with clenched hands. "Oh, Holmes, I shall never forgive myself for having left him to his fate."

"I am more to blame than you, Watson. In order to have my case well rounded and complete, I have thrown away the life of my client. It is the greatest blow which has befallen me in my career. But how could I know—how *could* I know—that he would risk his life alone upon the moor in the face of all my warnings?"

"That we should have heard his screams—those screams!—and yet have been unable to save him! Where is this brute of a hound which drove him to his death? It may be lurking among these rocks at this instant. And Stapleton, where is he? He shall answer for this deed."

"He shall. I will see to that. Uncle and nephew have been murdered—the one frightened to death by the very sight of a beast which he thought to be supernatural, the other driven to his end in his wild flight to escape from it. But now we have to prove the connection between the man and the beast. Save from what we heard, we cannot even swear to the existence of the latter, since Sir Henry has evidently died from the fall. But, by heavens, cunning as he is, the fellow shall be in my power before another day is past!"

"What can we do?"

"There will be plenty for us to do tomorrow. Tonight we can only perform the last offices to our poor friend."

"We must send for help, Holmes! We cannot carry him all the way to the Hall. Good heavens, are you mad?"

He had uttered a cry and bent over the body. Now he was dancing and laughing and wringing my hand. Could this be my stern,

The Hound of the Baskervilles 563

GUIDED READING

LITERAL QUESTIONS

1a. In what way does Holmes blame himself for the death of the man on the cliff? (He blames himself for ignoring the safety of Sir Henry while building a perfect case against Stapleton.)

2a. What does Holmes do that surprises Watson? (After bending over the body, Holmes begins to laugh and dance.)

INFERENTIAL QUESTIONS

1b. Do you think Holmes's guilty feelings are justified? (No, not really; he had warned Sir Henry to stay off the moor at night; Watson was sent to protect Sir Henry; Holmes needed evidence to stop Stapleton.)

2b. How do you account for his behavior? (Holmes must have seen something that indicated that the victim is not Sir Henry.)

- The detectives discover that the dead man is Selden, not Sir Henry.
- Selden had been wearing the castoff suit of Sir Henry.
- Stapleton approaches from across the moor. He seems amazed and perhaps disappointed that it is Selden who is dead.

1 SUBPLOT

With the death of Selden, the subplot finally reaches its resolution.

2 PLOT

The peculiar mystery of the missing boots is finally resolved here. The boots were stolen as a source of Sir Henry's scent so that he could be tracked by the hound.

3 DIALOGUE

Holmes is certain about his reconstruction of the crime. The curt way in which he interrupts Watson indicates that he is annoyed by the suggestion that their understanding of the case is based on presumption rather than certain knowledge.

4 POINT OF VIEW

Thanks to Holmes, Watson is now aware of Stapleton's guilt. This knowledge enables him to interpret Stapleton's actions.

---

self-contained friend? These were hidden fires, indeed!

"A beard! A beard! The man has a beard!"

"A beard?"

"It is not the baronet—it is—why, it is my neighbor, the convict!"

With feverish haste we had turned the body over, and that dripping beard was pointing up to the cold, clear moon. There could be no doubt about the beetling forehead, the sunken animal eyes. It was indeed the same **face which had glared upon me in the light of the candle from over the rock—the face of Selden, the criminal.**

Then in an instant it was all clear to me. I remembered how the baronet had told me that he had handed his old wardrobe to Barrymore. Barrymore had passed it on in order to help Selden in his escape.

"Then the clothes have been the poor devil's death," said Holmes. "It is clear enough that the hound has been laid on from some **article of Sir Henry's—the boot which was abstracted in the hotel, in all probability—and so ran this man down. There is one very singular** thing, however: How came Selden, in the darkness, to know that the hound was on his trail?"

"He heard him."

"To hear a hound upon the moor would not work a hard man like this convict into such a paroxysm of terror that he would risk recapture by screaming wildly for help. By his cries he must have run a long way after he knew the animal was on his track. How did he know?"

"A greater mystery to me is why this hound, presuming that all our conjectures are correct—"

"I presume nothing."

"Well, then, why this hound should be loose tonight. I suppose that it does not always run loose upon the moor. Stapleton

would not let it go unless he had reason to think that Sir Henry would be there."

"My difficulty is the more formidable of the two, for I think that we shall very shortly get an explanation of yours, while mine may remain forever a mystery. The question now is, what shall we do with this poor wretch's body? We cannot leave it here to the foxes and the ravens."

"I suggest that we put it in one of the huts until we can communicate with the police."

"Exactly. I have no doubt that you and I could carry it so far. Halloa, Watson, what's this? It's the man himself, by all that's wonderful and audacious! Not a word to show your suspicions—not a word, or my plans crumble to the ground."

A figure was approaching us over the moor. The moon shone upon him, and I could distinguish the dapper shape and jaunty walk of the naturalist. He stopped when he saw us, and then came on again.

"Why, Dr. Watson, that's not you, is it? You are the last man that I should have expected to see out on the moor at this time of night. But, dear me, what's this? Somebody hurt? Not—don't tell me that it is our friend Sir Henry!" He hurried past me and stooped over the dead man. I heard a sharp intake of his breath.

"Who—who's this?" he stammered.

"It is Selden, the man who escaped from Princetown."

Stapleton turned a ghastly face upon us, but by a supreme effort he had overcome his amazement and his disappointment. He looked sharply from Holmes to me.

"Dear me! What a very shocking affair! How did he die?"

"He appears to have broken his neck by falling over these rocks. My friend and I were strolling on the moor when we heard a cry."

"I heard a cry also. That was what brought

GUIDED READING

LITERAL QUESTIONS

1a. Why is Selden wearing Sir Henry's clothes? (Sir Henry had given his old clothes to Barrymore, and he passed them along to Selden.)

2a. What does Holmes warn Watson as Stapleton approaches from across the moor? (He warns the doctor not to say a word that reveals their suspicion.)

INFERENTIAL QUESTIONS

1b. What role do the clothes play in Selden's death? (By putting on Sir Henry's clothes, Selden unwittingly becomes the hound's object of pursuit.)

2b. Why does Holmes say that his plan will "crumble to the ground" if Watson ignores this warning? (If Stapleton learns that Holmes suspects him, he will be on his guard.)

me out. I was uneasy about Sir Henry."

"Why about Sir Henry in particular?" I could not help asking.

"Because I had suggested that he should come over. When he did not come I was surprised, and I naturally became alarmed for his safety when I heard cries upon the moor. By **1** the way"—his eyes darted again from my face to Holmes's—"did you hear anything else besides a cry?"

"No," said Holmes; "did you?"

"No."

"What do you mean, then?"

"Oh, you know the stories that the peasants tell about a phantom hound, and so on. It is said to be heard at night upon the moor. I was wondering if there were any evidence of such a sound tonight."

"We heard nothing of the kind," said I.

"And what is your theory of this poor fellow's death?"

"I have no doubt that anxiety and exposure have driven him off his head. He has rushed about the moor in a crazy state and eventually fallen over here and broken his neck."

"That seems the most reasonable theory," said Stapleton, and he gave a sigh which I **2** took to indicate his relief. "What do you think about it, Mr. Sherlock Holmes?"

My friend bowed his compliments.

"You are quick at identification," said he.

"We have been expecting you in these parts since Dr. Watson came down. You are in time to see a tragedy."

"Yes, indeed. I have no doubt that my **3** friend's explanation will cover the facts. I will take an unpleasant remembrance back to London with me tomorrow."

"Oh, you return tomorrow?"

"That is my intention."

"I hope your visit has cast some light upon those occurrences which have puzzled us?"

AT A GLANCE

- Stapleton says he was worried about Sir Henry, who was coming to visit.
- In answer to Stapleton, the detectives say they heard no hound.
- Holmes pretends to believe that Selden's death was accidental. He maintains that he will return to London on the following day.

1 CHARACTERIZATION

The author accentuates Stapleton's guilt by having his eyes dart from Holmes to Watson. It is as if he cannot look either detective in the eye for very long.

2 READING SKILLS: INFERENCES

That Stapleton easily recognizes Holmes without an introduction suggests that he might have been the man who watched Holmes from the carriage in London.

3 CHARACTERIZATION

Both Watson and Holmes show themselves to be quick thinkers and good actors. Watson coolly improvises a false explanation for Selden's death. Holmes smoothly falsifies his own plans. They offer Stapleton a false sense of reassurance.

GUIDED READING

LITERAL QUESTIONS

1a. What theory of Selden's death does Watson give Stapleton? (Watson suggests that the convict had gone crazy on the moor and eventually fell of the cliff.)

2a. What does Holmes tell Stapleton about his plans for the following day? (He says he will return to London.)

INFERENTIAL QUESTIONS

1b. Why does Watson relate this theory? (He wants Stapleton to think that he is not suspected in the case.)

2b. What do you think Holmes will really do on the following day? (He will probably be on the moor actively investigating Stapleton's role in the murders.)

- Holmes continues to lull Stapleton into a false sense of security.
- Stapleton returns home. Holmes and Watson walk to Baskerville Hall.

1 READING SKILLS: INFERENCES

The fact that Stapleton "looked hard" at Holmes suggests that he is not totally persuaded that Holmes is telling the truth.

REFLECTING ON CHAPTERS 10–12

What do Watson and Holmes learn about the relationship between Stapleton and Miss Stapleton and between Stapleton and Laura Lyons? (Stapleton and Miss Stapleton are actually man and wife; Laura Lyons is probably expecting to marry Stapleton.)

STUDY QUESTIONS

1. to meet a woman with initials L. L.; remains of burned letter
2. He is a gentleman, lives among huts, has a boy bring supplies from Coombe Tracey.
3. help with legal expenses for her divorce; received help elsewhere
4. ■ sees boy bringing supplies
   ■ evidence of a dweller, a paper with a message about himself, and, finally, Sherlock Holmes
5. married, posing as siblings; to persuade Mrs. Lyons to tell him about Stapleton
6. chased and killed by hound; Sir Henry; wearing Sir Henry's discarded clothes
7. gentleman, deep, not one of Sir Henry's neighbors, tall, thin
8. It was probably wise: Watson might have unintentionally warned Stapleton.
9. Stapleton: living under false identity; passing wife as sister; newcomer, yet knows moor; neighbor of Sir Henry's; lied to and used Laura Lyons against Sir Charles

---

Holmes shrugged his shoulders.

"One cannot always have the success for which one hopes. An investigator needs facts and not legends or rumors. It has not been a satisfactory case."

1   My friend spoke in his frankest and most unconcerned manner. Stapleton still looked hard at him. Then he turned to me.

"I would suggest carrying this poor fellow to my house, but it would give my sister such a fright that I do not feel justified in doing it.

I think that if we put something over his face he will be safe until morning."

And so it was arranged. Resisting Stapleton's offer of hospitality, Holmes and I set off to Baskerville Hall, leaving the naturalist to return alone. Looking back we saw the figure moving slowly away over the broad moor, and behind him that one black smudge on the silvered slope which showed where the man was lying who had come so horribly to his end.

STUDY QUESTIONS

Recalling

1. According to Barrymore, why was Sir Charles at the moor gate on the night of his death? What evidence does he cite for his opinion?
2. At the end of Chapter 10, what information does Barrymore give Watson about the man on the tor?
3. According to Chapter 11, why did Mrs. Lyons ask for a secret meeting with Sir Charles? Why did she not keep the appointment?
4. What discovery leads Watson to the stone hut? Explain what he finds there.
5. What secret does Holmes reveal about the Stapletons in Chapter 12? How does he intend to use this information?
6. Describe the manner in which Selden dies. For whom do Holmes and Watson at first mistake him and why?

Interpreting

7. What clues in the various descriptions of the man on the tor might have led you to guess that he was Holmes?
8. Do you think Holmes was right to keep his presence a secret from Watson?
9. Who is the main suspect in the mystery? List the evidence that points to this person.

READING AND LITERARY FOCUS

Major and Minor Characters

Because a novel is longer than a short story, a novelist is able to show us many aspects of a character's personality. Characters with well-developed, complex personalities are called **major characters.** Less well developed, simpler characters, such as Dr. Mortimer, are called **minor characters.**

Thinking About Major and Minor Characters

■ Find an example of a minor character (other than Dr. Mortimer), and give reasons for labeling the character a minor character.

Foreshadowing and Predicting Outcomes

Many authors use clues or hints known as **foreshadowing** to help their readers predict future developments of plot. For example, the real identity of Beryl Stapleton is not what we might have expected. Yet several hints, including the physical description of her in Chapter 7, help us to predict the outcome of this future development.

Thinking About Foreshadowing and Predicting Outcomes

■ What hints does Conan Doyle use to help us predict the true identity of "the man on the tor"?

Major and Minor Characters
Sample answer: Cartwright, the boy who helps Holmes in London; for assistance to Holmes

Foreshadowing
described as "gentleman," "deep"; has boy who helps him—Holmes has used Cartwright before and so might enlist him again; tall, thin; not one of Sir Henry's neighbors

Holmes knows who the murderer is, but does he know the murderer's motive? Once Holmes determines the motive, he will be ready to trick the culprit into revealing himself—as well as revealing the terrifying hound of the Baskervilles.

■ *What accident of nature almost spoils his attempts?*

13 Fixing the Nets

"We're at close grips at last," said Holmes as we walked together across the moor. "What a nerve the fellow has! How he pulled himself together in the face of what must have been a paralyzing shock when he found that the wrong man had fallen a victim to his plot."

"Why should we not arrest him at once?"

"My dear Watson, we could prove nothing against him. There's the devilish cunning of it! If he were acting through a human agent we could get some evidence, but if we were to drag this great dog to the light of day it would not help us in putting a rope round the neck of its master."

"Surely we have a case."

"Not a shadow of one. We should be laughed out of court if we came with such a story and such evidence."

"There is Sir Charles's death."

"Found dead without a mark upon him. You and I know that he died of sheer fright, and we know also what frightened him; but how are we to get twelve stolid jurymen to know it? What signs are there of a hound? Where are the marks of its fangs? Of course we know that a hound does not bite a dead

body and that Sir Charles was dead before ever the brute overtook him. But we have to *prove* all this, and we are not in a position to do it."

"Well, then, tonight?"

"We are not much better off tonight. Again, there was no direct connection between the hound and the man's death. We never saw the hound. We heard it, but we could not prove that it was running upon this man's trail. There is a complete absence of motive."

I could draw nothing further from him, and he walked, lost in thought, as far as the Baskerville gates.

"Are you coming up?"

"Yes; I see no reason for further concealment. But one last word, Watson. Say nothing of the hound to Sir Henry. Let him think that Selden's death was as Stapleton would have us believe. He will have a better nerve for the ordeal which he will have to undergo tomorrow, when he is engaged, if I remember your report aright, to dine with these people."

"And so am I."

"Then you must excuse yourself and he must go alone. That will be easily arranged.

The Hound of the Baskervilles 567

AT A GLANCE

- Holmes reasserts that he must find Stapleton's motive for wanting to kill Sir Henry and prove the man's connection with the hound.
- Holmes decides not to mention the hound to Sir Henry and to allow him to go to the Stapletons' house alone the following evening.

LITERARY OPTIONS

- plot
- characterization
- point of view

THEMATIC OPTIONS

- observation and deduction
- common sense and superstition
- ambition and greed

1 STYLE: METAPHOR

The chapter's title suggests that it will deal primarily with Holmes's attempts to trap Stapleton. The metaphor of nets is apt for Stapleton, who seems to spend so much time netting butterflies.

2 POINT OF VIEW

Now that Holmes is back on the scene, Watson's role as narrator is once again limited largely to reporting Holmes's analysis of the case.

3 PLOT: FORESHADOWING

By suggesting that Sir Henry will have to undergo an "ordeal," Holmes hints at the climax of the plot. Given Holmes's previous statement of his objectives, the ordeal is likely to involve Stapleton and the dreaded hound.

GUIDED READING

LITERAL QUESTION

1a. What must Holmes and Watson do to prove that Stapleton was guilty of bringing about Sir Charles's death? (They must prove that there is a deadly hound and that Stapleton controls it.)

INFERENTIAL QUESTION

1b. How might the detectives do this? (They might catch Stapleton with the hound, ideally as he attempted to frighten or kill Sir Henry.)

- Holmes and Watson tell Sir Henry and the Barrymores about the fate of Selden.
- Holmes promises Sir Henry that the case will soon be cleared up.
- Holmes's attention is riveted upon a portrait of Sir Hugo Baskerville.

1 CHARACTERIZATION

Holmes's secrecy here and earlier with Watson demonstrates both his caution and his need to orchestrate events.

2 IRONY

Holmes uses the word *lively* ironically, for he knows that if Sir Henry had kept his engagement with Stapleton, his "lively" evening would have ended in death.

3 STYLE: METAPHOR

By likening Holmes to a "clear-cut classical statue," the author conveys the detective's amazing powers of concentration. Holmes's gaze is so intent that he is as motionless as a statue.

4 PLOT: FORESHADOWING

This description of Sir Hugo parallels that of another character in the story who is very much on Holmes's mind at the moment: Stapleton.

And now, if we are too late for dinner, I think that we are both ready for our suppers."[1]

Sir Henry was more pleased than surprised to see Sherlock Holmes, for he had for some days been expecting that recent events would bring him down from London. He did raise his eyebrows, however, when he found that my friend had neither any luggage nor any explanations for its absence. Between us we **1** soon supplied his wants, and then over a belated supper we explained to the baronet as much of our experience as it seemed desirable that he should know. But first I had the unpleasant duty of breaking the news to Barrymore and his wife. To him it may have been a relief, but she wept bitterly.

"I've been moping in the house all day since Watson went off in the morning," said the baronet. "I guess I should have some **2** credit, for I have kept my promise. If I hadn't sworn not to go about alone I might have had a more lively evening, for I had a message from Stapleton asking me over there."

"I have no doubt that you would have had a more lively evening," said Holmes dryly. "By the way, I don't suppose you appreciate that we have been mourning over you as having broken your neck?"

Sir Henry opened his eyes. "How was that?"

"This poor wretch was dressed in your clothes."

"But how about the case?" asked the baronet. "Have you made anything out of the tangle?"

"I think that I shall be in a position to make the situation rather more clear to you before long."

He stopped suddenly and stared fixedly up over my head into the air. The lamp beat upon

---

1. **dinner . . . suppers:** Dinner in Britain is eaten in the evening; supper is a late-night snack.

568   *The Novel*

---

3 his face, and so intent was it and so still that it might have been that of a clear-cut classical statue.

"What is it?" we both cried.

I could see as he looked down that he was repressing some internal emotion.

"Excuse the admiration of a connoisseur," said he as he waved his hand toward the line of portraits which covered the opposite wall. These are a really very fine series of portraits."

"Well, I'm glad to hear you say so," said Sir Henry, glancing with some surprise at my friend. "I don't pretend to know much about these things."

"I know what is good when I see it, and I see it now. They are all family portraits, I presume?"

"Every one."

"Do you know the names?"

"Barrymore has been coaching me in them, and I think I can say my lessons fairly well."

"Who is this Cavalier opposite to me—the one with the black velvet and the lace?"

"Ah, you have a right to know about him. That is the cause of all the mischief, the wicked Hugo, who started the Hound of the Baskervilles. We're not likely to forget him."

I gazed with interest and some surprise upon the portrait.

4 "Dear me!" said Holmes, "he seems a quiet, meek-mannered man enough, but I dare say that there was a lurking devil in his eyes."

Holmes said little more, but the picture of the old roisterer seemed to have a fascination for him, and his eyes were continually fixed upon it during supper. It was not until later, when Sir Henry had gone to his room, that I was able to follow the trend of his thoughts. He led me back into the banqueting hall, his bedroom candle in one hand, and he held it up against the time-stained portrait on the wall.

GUIDED READING

LITERAL QUESTIONS

1a. What information do Holmes and Watson keep from Sir Henry? (They do not tell him about the role of the hound in Selden's death; they do not inform him that they suspect Stapleton will attempt to murder him.)

2a. What object strikes Holme's attention during supper at Baskerville Hall? (a portrait of Hugo Baskerville, who gave rise to the legend of the hound)

INFERENTIAL QUESTIONS

1b. Why do you think they withhold this information from Sir Henry? (They do not wish to worry him needlessly; they hope to use Sir Henry as bait in the trap they are setting.)

2b. Why do you think Holmes is so struck by the portrait? (Answers will vary. Possibilities: He sees in the portrait a resemblance to someone; it gives him an idea about how to catch Stapleton.)

1 STYLE: DETAILS

Many of the adjectives here have been used earlier to describe Stapleton. The details give readers another chance to guess Stapleton's identity before Watson does.

2 THEME

The phrase *one of our most obvious missing links* refers to Stapleton's motive for the murder. The fact that he is a Baskerville suggests that his motive was probably ambition and greed, an important theme in the novel.

3 STYLE: SIMILE

Sir Henry's simile is instructive. For the rest of the novel, Holmes is very much in charge of the situation, marshaling his forces for a climactic battle with the enemy, Stapleton.

---

right arm over the broad hat and round the long ringlets.

"Good heavens!" I cried in amazement.

The face of Stapleton had sprung out of the canvas.

"Ha, you see it now. My eyes have been trained to examine faces and not their trimmings. It is the first quality of a criminal investigator that he should see through a disguise."

"But this is marvelous. It might be his portrait."

"Yes, the fellow is a Baskerville—that is evident."

"With designs upon the succession."

2 "Exactly. This chance of the picture has supplied us with one of our most obvious missing links. We have him, Watson, we have him, and I dare swear that before tomorrow night he will be fluttering in our net as helpless as one of his own butterflies."

I was up betimes in the morning, but Holmes was afoot earlier still, for I saw him as I dressed, coming up the drive.

"Have you been on the moor already?"

"I have sent a report from Grimpen to Princetown as to the death of Selden," he remarked. "And I have also communicated with my faithful Cartwright."

"What is the next move?"

"To see Sir Henry. Ah, here he is!"

3 "Good morning, Holmes," said the baronet. "You look like a general who is planning a battle with his chief of the staff."

"That is the exact situation. Watson was asking for orders."

"And so do I."

"Very good. You are engaged, as I understand, to dine with our friends the Stapletons tonight."

"I hope that you will come also. They are very hospitable people, and I am sure that they would be very glad to see you."

The Hound of the Baskervilles 569

"Do you see anything there?"

I looked at the broad plumed hat, the curling love-locks, the white lace collar, and the straight, severe face which was framed between them. It was not a brutal countenance, but it was prim, hard, and stern, with a firm-set, thin-lipped mouth, and a coldly intolerant eye.

"There is something of Sir Henry about the jaw."

"Just a suggestion, perhaps. But wait an instant!" He stood upon a chair, and, holding up the light in his left hand, he curved his

---

GUIDED READING

LITERAL QUESTION

1a. What conclusion does Sherlock Holmes base on the portrait of Hugo Baskerville? (Based on Stapleton's striking resemblance to Sir Hugo, Holmes concludes that Stapleton is a Baskerville.)

INFERENTIAL QUESTION

1b. How does this conclusion supply one of the missing links in the case? (The conclusion establishes Stapleton's motive: Killing Sir Charles and Sir Henry puts Stapleton in line to inherit the Baskerville fortune.)

- To keep their plans secret, Holmes and Watson tell Sir Henry that they are going to London.
- Holmes arranges for the police to be present at Dartmoor.
- The detectives interview Mrs. Lyons more closely.

1 VOCABULARY: DENOTATION

A *trap* is a light, two-wheeled carriage with heavy springs for riding on rough terrain.

2 PLOT: FORESHADOWING

Holmes's warning suggests that he expects something important to happen that evening on the straight path between Merripit House and Grimpen Road.

3 CHARACTERIZATION

Holmes is so sure of his plan's success that he has called in Inspector Lestrade of Scotland Yard to arrest Stapleton.

4 POINT OF VIEW

Here Watson sums up Holmes's plan for the benefit of those readers who may not have picked up earlier hints of it.

5 CHARACTERIZATION

Holmes brusquely puts Mrs. Lyons on the defensive. He is impatient to reach his goal and has no time to waste on pleasantries.

"I fear that Watson and I must go to London."

"To London?"

"Yes, I think that we should be more useful there at the present juncture."

The baronet's face perceptibly lengthened.

"I hoped that you were going to see me through this business. The Hall and the moor are not very pleasant places when one is alone."

"My dear fellow, you must trust me implicitly and do exactly what I tell you. You can tell your friends that we should have been happy to have come with you, but that urgent business required us to be in town. We hope very soon to return to Devonshire. Will you remember to give them that message?"

"If you insist upon it."

1 "One more direction! I wish you to drive to Merripit House. Send back your trap, however, and let them know that you intend to walk home."

"To walk across the moor?"

"Yes."

"But that is the very thing which you have so often cautioned me not to do."

"This time you may do it with safety. If I had not every confidence in your nerve and courage I would not suggest it, but it is essential that you should do it."

"Then I will do it."

2 "And as you value your life do not go across the moor in any direction save along the straight path which leads from Merripit House to the Grimpen Road, and is your natural way home."

"I will do just what you say."

"Very good. I should be glad to get away as soon after breakfast as possible, so as to reach London in the afternoon."

A small boy was waiting upon the platform.

"Any orders, sir?"

"You will take this train to town, Cartwright. The moment you arrive you will send a wire to Sir Henry Baskerville, in my name, to say that if he finds the pocketbook which I have dropped he is to send it by registered post to Baker Street."

"Yes, sir."

"And ask at the station office if there is a message for me."

The boy returned with a telegram, which 3 Holmes handed to me. It ran: "Wire received. Coming down with unsigned warrant. Arrive five-forty. LESTRADE."

"That is in answer to mine of this morning. He is the best of the professionals, I think, and we may need his assistance. Now, Watson, I think that we cannot employ our time better than by calling upon your acquaintance, Mrs. Laura Lyons."

4 His plan of campaign was beginning to be evident. He would use the baronet in order to convince the Stapletons that we were really gone, while we should actually return at the instant when we were likely to be needed. That telegram from London, if mentioned by Sir Henry to the Stapletons, must remove the last suspicions from their minds. Already I seemed to see our nets drawing closer round that lean-jawed pike.

Mrs. Laura Lyons was in her office, and Sherlock Holmes opened his interview with a frankness and directness which considerably amazed her.

"I am investigating the circumstances which attended the death of the late Sir 5 Charles Baskerville," said he. "My friend here, Dr. Watson, has informed me of what you have communicated, and also of what you have withheld in connection with that matter."

"What have I withheld?" she asked defiantly.

"You have confessed that you asked Sir Charles to be at the gate at ten o'clock. We

570   *The Novel*

GUIDED READING

LITERAL QUESTIONS

1a. What dangerous act does Holmes ask Sir Henry to perform? (walk across the moor alone at night)

2a. Instead of going to London, whom do Watson and Holmes visit? (They visit Mrs. Laura Lyons at her home.)

INFERENTIAL QUESTIONS

1b. Why do you think he asks Sir Henry to do this? (He wants to give Stapleton an opportunity to try to kill Sir Henry; of course, Holmes plans to interrupt the murder attempt and prove Stapleton's guilt.)

2b. What could they reveal to her about Stapleton that would surprise her? (They could reveal that Stapleton lied to her about being unmarried; as a result, she may feel betrayed and cooperate with Holmes.)

know that that was the place and hour of his death. You have withheld what the connection is between these events."

"There is no connection."

"In that case the coincidence must indeed be an extraordinary one. But I think that we shall succeed in establishing a connection after all. I wish to be perfectly frank with you, Mrs. Lyons. We regard this case as one of murder, and the evidence may implicate not only your friend Mr. Stapleton, but his wife as well."

The lady sprang from her chair.

"His wife!" she cried.

"The fact is no longer a secret. The person who has passed for his sister is really his wife."

Mrs. Lyons had resumed her seat. Her hands were grasping the arms of her chair, and I saw that the pink nails had turned white with the pressure of her grip.

"His wife!" she said again. "His wife! He is not a married man."

Sherlock Holmes shrugged his shoulders.

"Prove it to me! Prove it to me! And if you can do so—!" The fierce flash of her eyes said more than any words.

"I have come prepared to do so," said Holmes, drawing several papers from his pocket. "Here is a photograph of the couple taken in York four years ago. It is endorsed 'Mr. and Mrs. Vandeleur,' but you will have no difficulty in recognizing him, and her also, if you know her by sight."

She glanced at them, and then looked up at us with the set, rigid face of a desperate woman.

"Mr. Holmes," she said, "this man had offered me marriage on condition that I could get a divorce from my husband. Not one word of truth has he ever told me. And why—why? I imagined that all was for my own sake. But now I see that I was never anything but a tool

in his hands. Why should I try to shield him from the consequences of his own wicked acts? Ask me what you like, and there is nothing which I shall hold back. One thing I swear to you, and that is that when I wrote the letter I never dreamed of any harm to the old gentleman, who had been my kindest friend."

"I entirely believe you, madam," said Sherlock Holmes. "Perhaps it will make it easier if I tell you what occurred, and you can check me if I make any material mistake. The sending of this letter was suggested to you by Stapleton?"

"He dictated it."

"I presume that the reason he gave was that you would receive help from Sir Charles for the legal expenses connected with your divorce?"

"Exactly."

"And then after you had sent the letter he dissuaded you from keeping the appointment?"

"He told me that it would hurt his self-respect that any other man should find the money for such an object, and that though he was a poor man himself he would devote his last penny to removing the obstacles which divided us."

"And then you heard nothing until you read the reports of the death in the paper?"

"No."

"And he made you swear to say nothing about your appointment with Sir Charles?"

"He did. He said that the death was a very mysterious one, and that I should certainly be suspected if the facts came out. He frightened me into remaining silent."

"I think that on the whole you have had a fortunate escape," said Sherlock Holmes. "You have had him in your power and he knew it, and yet you are alive. We must wish you good morning now, Mrs. Lyons, and it is probable that you will very shortly hear from us again."

The Hound of the Baskervilles 571

GUIDED READING

LITERAL QUESTIONS

1a. What information had Mrs. Lyons withheld from Dr. Watson earlier? (Stapleton's role in Mrs. Lyons' missed rendezvous with Sir Charles)

2a. What reason does Mrs. Lyons say Stapleton gave when he asked her to break her appointment with Sir Charles? (She says that Stapleton told her that a request for money from Charles would hurt his [Stapleton's] self-respect.)

INFERENTIAL QUESTIONS

1b. Why do you think Mrs. Lyons didn't reveal this information earlier? (She wanted to protect both Stapleton, whom she hoped to marry, and herself from becoming suspects.)

2b. What do you think was the real reason Stapleton told her not to keep the appointment? (He wanted to keep Sir Charles waiting alone on the moor so that he could frighten him to death.)

- Holmes, Watson, and Lestrade arrange an ambush outside Merripit House, where Sir Henry is dining with Stapleton.
- A fog rolls in, threatening to thwart Holmes's plans.

1 PLOT: FORESHADOWING

The chapter title hints that the climax of the novel is near. Holmes's confrontation with the hound will mark the high point of the plot.

2 PLOT: SUSPENSE

The talk of guns suggests that violence is a real possibility before the events of the evening reach their conclusion. Suspense mounts as we wonder about the final confrontation with the hound and Stapleton.

3 STYLE: IMAGERY

Hiding in the darkness, Watson relies largely on his sense of hearing. The sounds he hears build suspense: the creak of a door, the crunch of boots, the clink of a key in a lock, and an ominous scuffling sound.

4 CHARACTERIZATION

The role of Beryl Stapleton in the mystery remains puzzling. We wonder if she is her husband's accomplice. The fact that she tried to warn Sir Henry earlier and is not now at the party suggests that she is not a willing collaborator.

The London express came roaring into the station, and a small, wiry bulldog of a man had sprung from a first-class carriage. We all three shook hands.

"Anything good?" he asked.

"The biggest thing for years," said Holmes. "We have two hours before we need think of starting. I think we might employ it in getting some dinner, and then, Lestrade, we will take the London fog out of your throat by giving you a breath of the pure night air of Dartmoor. Never been there? Ah, well, I don't suppose you will forget your first visit."

1 | **14** | **The Hound of the Baskervilles**

"Are you armed, Lestrade?"

The little detective smiled.

2 "As long as I have my trousers I have a hip pocket, and as long as I have my hip pocket I have something in it."

"Good! My friend and I are also ready for emergencies."

"You're mighty close about this affair, Mr. Holmes. What's the game now?"

"A waiting game."

"My word, it does not seem a very cheerful place," said the detective with a shiver, glancing round him at the gloomy slopes of the hill and at the huge lake of fog which lay over the Grimpen Mire. "I see the lights of a house ahead of us."

"That is Merripit House and the end of our journey. I must request you to walk on tiptoe and not to talk above a whisper."

We moved cautiously along the track as if we were bound for the house, but Holmes halted us when we were about two hundred yards from it.

"This will do," said he. "These rocks upon the right make an admirable screen."

"We are to wait here?"

572   *The Novel*

"Yes, we shall make our little ambush here. Get into this hollow, Lestrade. You have been inside the house, have you not, Watson? Can you tell the position of the rooms? What are those latticed windows at this end?"

"I think they are the kitchen windows."

"And the one beyond, which shines so brightly?"

"That is certainly the dining room."

"The blinds are up. You know the lie of the land best. Creep forward quietly and see what they are doing—but for heaven's sake don't let them know that they are watched!"

There were only two men in the room, Sir Henry and Stapleton. They sat with their profiles toward me on either side of the round table.

As I watched them Stapleton rose and left the room, while Sir Henry leaned back in his **3** chair. I heard the creak of a door and the crisp sound of boots upon gravel. The steps passed along the path on the other side of the wall under which I crouched. Looking over, I saw the naturalist pause at the door of a shed in the corner of the orchard. A key turned in a lock, and as he passed in there was a curious scuffling noise from within. He was only a minute or so inside, and then I heard the key turn once more and he passed me and reentered the house. I saw him rejoin his guest, and I crept quietly back to where my companions were waiting to tell them what I had seen.

4 "You say, Watson, that the lady is not there?" Holmes asked when I had finished my report.

"No."

"Where can she be, then, since there is no light in any other room except the kitchen?"

"I cannot think where she is."

I have said that over the great Grimpen Mire there hung a dense, white fog. It was drifting slowly in our direction and banked itself up like a wall on that side of us, low but thick and well defined. The moon shone on

---

GUIDED READING

LITERAL QUESTIONS

1a. How does Holmes describe the men's purpose in hiding behind some rocks? (He says they are about to "make our little ambush.")

2a. What natural occurrence do the men observe as they wait? (A dense, white fog slowly drifts in the men's direction from Grimpen Mire.)

INFERENTIAL QUESTIONS

1b. What exactly do you think he plans to do? (He hopes to surprise Stapleton in the act of attempting to kill Sir Henry.)

2b. Why might this occurrence concern Sherlock Holmes? (A thick fog will cut down on visibility; Holmes's plan to catch Stapleton in the act and protect Sir Henry might be thwarted.)

it, and it looked like a great shimmering ice field, with the heads of the distant tors as rocks borne upon its surface. Holmes's face was turned toward it, and he muttered impatiently as he watched its sluggish drift.

"It's moving toward us, Watson."

"Is that serious?"

"Very serious, indeed—the one thing upon earth which could have disarranged my plans. He can't be very long, now. It is already ten o'clock. Our success and even his life may depend upon his coming out before the fog is over the path. If he isn't out in a quarter of an hour the path will be covered. In half an hour we won't be able to see our hands in front of us."

"Shall we move farther back upon higher grounds?"

"Yes, I think it would be as well."

So as the fog bank flowed onward we fell back before it until we were half a mile from the house, and still that dense white sea, with the moon silvering its upper edge, swept slowly and inexorably on.

"We are going too far," said Holmes. "We dare not take the chance of his being overtaken before he can reach us. At all costs we must hold our ground where we are." He dropped on his knees and clapped his ear to the ground. "Thank God, I think that I hear him coming."

A sound of quick steps broke the silence of the moor. Crouching among the stones, we stared intently at the silver-tipped bank in front of us. The steps grew louder, and through the fog, as through a curtain, there stepped the man whom we were awaiting. He looked round him in surprise as he emerged into the clear, starlit night. Then he came swiftly along the path, passed close to where we lay, and went on up the long slope behind us. As he walked he glanced continually over either shoulder, like a man who is ill at ease.

"Hist!" cried Holmes, and I heard the sharp click of a cocking pistol. "Look out! It's coming!"

There was a thin, crisp, continuous patter from somewhere in the heart of that crawling bank. The cloud was within fifty yards of where we lay, and we glared at it, all three, uncertain what horror was about to break from the heart of it. I was at Holmes's elbow, and I glanced for an instant at his face. It was pale and exultant, his eyes shining brightly in the moonlight. But suddenly they started forward in a rigid, fixed stare, and his lips parted in amazement. At the same instant Lestrade gave a yell of terror and threw himself face downward upon the ground. I sprang to my feet, my inert hand grasping my pistol, my mind paralyzed by the dreadful shape which had sprung out upon us from the shadows of the fog. A hound it was, an enormous coal-black hound, but not such a hound as mortal eyes have ever seen. Fire burst from its open mouth, its eyes glowed with a smoldering glare, its muzzle and hackles and dewlap were outlined in flickering flame. Never in the delirious dream of a disordered brain could anything more savage, more appalling, more fiendish be conceived than that dark form and savage face which broke upon us out of the wall of fog.

With long bounds the huge black creature was leaping down the track, following hard upon the footsteps of our friend. So paralyzed were we by the apparition that we allowed him to pass before we had recovered our nerve. Then Holmes and I both fired together, and the creature gave a hideous howl, which showed that one at least had hit him. He did not pause, however, but bounded onward. Far away on the path we saw Sir Henry looking back, his face white in the moonlight, his hands raised in horror, glaring helplessly at the frightful thing which was hunting him down.

But the cry of pain from the hound had

The Hound of the Baskervilles 573

- The fast-approaching fog threatens to disrupt Holmes's plans by obscuring the path Sir Henry will travel.
- Sir Henry leaves Merripit House and starts up the path.
- The detectives suddenly spot an enormous hound, its body outlined in flame, pursuing Sir Henry.

1 PLOT: SUSPENSE

The suspense mounts as Holmes spells out the disaster that will ensue if Sir Henry does not soon start on his homeward trek.

2 SETTING

The thick white fog that shrouds the moor heightens the atmosphere of mystery and danger.

3 STYLE: IMAGERY

The hound is described as if it were supernatural. In addition to using the imagery of fire, the author describes the fiendish beast as being beyond what "mortal eyes have ever seen."

4 READING SKILLS: MAKING INFERENCES

Surprisingly, even the intrepid Holmes is "paralyzed" by the apparition and takes a while to recover his nerve. The beast must be horrible indeed.

GUIDED READING

LITERAL QUESTION

1a. What seems unnatural about the hound's appearance? (Fire flows from the hound's mouth and eyes; parts of its body are also outlined with flame.)

INFERENTIAL QUESTION

1b. What superstitious possibility is this aspect of the dog's appearance likely to suggest to those who see it? (The fire suggests that the hound is not a mortal creature but some sort of evil spirit.)

- Holmes and Watson race after the hound to see it hurl Sir Henry to the ground.
- Holmes shoots the dog before it can hurt Sir Henry.
- Watson touches the hound's glowing muzzle, and something gleaming rubs off on his fingers.

1 PLOT: CLIMAX

With the hound's attack on Sir Henry, the novel reaches its high point of emotional involvement.

2 CHARACTERIZATION

Holmes might well be grateful. The plan to use Sir Henry as live bait showed a bold if not reckless aspect of the detective's character. Holmes's tremendous confidence in his ability to pull off the clever trap has been justified—but only barely.

3 THEME

Holmes has used reason to track down a human murderer; he has "laid to rest the family ghost" by proving the supernatural legend false.

blown all our fears to the winds. If he was vulnerable he was mortal, and if we could wound him we could kill him. Never have I seen a man run as Holmes ran that night. In front of us as we flew up the track we heard scream after scream from Sir Henry and the **1** deep roar of the hound. I was in time to see the beast spring upon its victim, hurl him to the ground, and worry at his throat. But the next instant Holmes had emptied five barrels of his revolver into the creature's flank. With a last howl of agony and a vicious snap in the air, it rolled upon its back, four feet pawing furiously, and then fell limp upon its side. I stooped, panting, and pressed my pistol to the dreadful, shimmering head, but it was useless to press the trigger. The giant hound was dead.

2 Sir Henry lay insensible where he had fallen. We tore away his collar, and Holmes breathed a prayer of gratitude when we saw

574 *The Novel*

that there was no sign of a wound and that the rescue had been in time. Already our friend's eyelids shivered and he made a feeble effort to move.

"What was it?" he whispered. "What, in heaven's name, was it?"

3 "It's dead, whatever it is," said Holmes. "We've laid to rest the family ghost once and forever."

In mere size and strength it was a terrible creature which was lying stretched before us. It was not a pure bloodhound and it was not a pure mastiff; but it appeared to be a combination of the two—gaunt, savage, and as large as a small lioness. Even now, in the stillness of death, the huge jaws seemed to be dripping with a bluish flame and the small, deep-set, cruel eyes were ringed with fire. I placed my hand upon the glowing muzzle, and as I held them up my own fingers smoldered and gleamed in the darkness.

GUIDED READING

LITERAL QUESTION

1a. What does Holmes say after he kills the hound? ("We've laid to rest the family ghost once and forever.")

INFERENTIAL QUESTION

1b. What does he mean by "laid to rest the family ghost"? (He's killed a real hound that was used by a human murderer, and thereby he has proved that the supernatural legend was nonsense.)

"Phosphorus,"[1] I said.

"A cunning preparation of it," said Holmes, sniffing at the dead animal. "There is no smell which might have interfered with his power of scent. We owe you a deep apology, Sir Henry, for having exposed you to this fright. I was prepared for a hound, but not for such a creature as this. And the fog gave us little time to receive him."

"You have saved my life."

"Having first endangered it. Are you strong enough to stand?"

"Yes, if you will help me up. What do you propose to do?"

"To leave you here. You are not fit for further adventures tonight. If you will wait, one or the other of us will go back with you to the Hall."

He tried to stagger to his feet; but he was still ghastly pale and trembling in every limb. We helped him to a rock, where he sat shivering with his face buried in his hands.

"We must leave you now," said Holmes. "The rest of our work must be done, and every moment is of importance. We have our case, and now we only want our man.

"It's a thousand to one against our finding him at the house," he continued as we retraced our steps swiftly down the path. "Those shots must have told him that the game was up."

The front door was open, so we rushed in and hurried from room to room, to the amazement of a doddering old manservant, who met us in the passage.

"There's someone in here," cried Lestrade. "I can hear a movement. Open this door!"

A faint moaning and rustling came from within. Holmes struck the door just over the lock with the flat of his foot and it flew open.

---

1. **Phosphorus** [fos′fər əs]: nonmetallic chemical that glows in the dark.

Pistol in hand, we all three rushed into the room.

But there was no sign within it of that desperate and defiant villain whom we expected to see. Instead we were faced by an object so strange and so unexpected that we stood for a moment staring at it in amazement.

The room had been fashioned into a small museum, and the walls were lined by a number of glass-topped cases full of that collection of butterflies and moths the formation of which had been the relaxation of this complex and dangerous man. In the center of this room there was an upright beam. To this post a figure was tied, so swathed and muffled in the sheets which had been used to secure it that one could not for the moment tell whether it was that of a man or a woman. One towel passed round the throat and was secured at the back of the pillar. Another covered the lower part of the face, and over it two dark eyes—eyes full of grief and shame and a dreadful questioning—stared back at us. In a minute we had torn off the gag, unswathed the bonds, and Mrs. Stapleton sank upon the floor in front of us. Her beautiful head fell upon her chest.

"The brute!" cried Holmes. "Here, Lestrade, put her in the chair! She has fainted from exhaustion."

She opened her eyes again.

"Is he safe?" she asked. "Has he escaped?"

"He cannot escape us, madam."

"No, no, I did not mean my husband. Sir Henry? Is he safe?"

"Yes."

"And the hound?"

"It is dead."

She gave a long sigh of satisfaction.

"Thank God! Thank God! Oh, this villain! I could endure it all, ill-usage, solitude, a life of deception, everything, as long as I could

The Hound of the Baskervilles 575

- Watson determines that phosphorus gave the dog its fiery appearance.
- At Merripit House the detectives find no sign of Stapleton.
- They do find Mrs. Stapleton there, tied up and gagged by her husband.

1 STYLE: DETAILS

Details vividly suggest the grave effect that the events of the evening have had on Sir Henry. Normally rough and ready, he is now staggering, "shivering," "trembling," and "ghastly pale."

2 STYLE: IMAGERY

The image of Beryl Stapleton rendered immobile in the butterfly museum strongly suggests that she is just another specimen in his collection.

3 DIALOGUE

The brief dialogue effectively establishes Mrs. Stapleton's innocence.

GUIDED READING

LITERAL QUESTIONS

1a. What preparation does Watson find on the hound? (phosphorus)

2a. What did Holmes and Watson find in the museum room at Merripit House? (They found Beryl Stapleton tied up and gagged.)

INFERENTIAL QUESTIONS

1b. What does this discovery explain? (The phosphorus made the hound gleam and appear fiery in the dark.)

2b. What does this discovery suggest about the Stapletons? (They have not been working together. Beryl Stapleton obviously objected strongly to her husband's plan to kill Sir Henry, or he would not have had to tie her up.)

- Beryl Stapleton surmises that her husband has fled to the mire.
- Sir Henry's nerves are shattered by the facts about the Stapletons.
- The next morning Holmes and Watson enter the mire and search for Stapleton.

1 STYLE: IMAGERY

The description of Beryl Stapleton's "fierce merriment" at her husband's plight reveals the depth of the emotional stress she has experienced.

2 POINT OF VIEW

The narrator, Watson, steps out of the background to formally announce that the end of the novel is near. As a new day dawns and the fog lifts, he and Holmes will rapidly tie up the remaining loose ends of the case.

3 STYLE: IMAGERY

The imagery of death and decay in the mire hints that Stapleton met his end there the previous night. After all, even in broad daylight, Holmes and Watson narrowly miss being sucked into the seemingly bottomless pit.

---

still cling to the hope that I had his love, but now I know that in this also I have been his dupe and his tool." She broke into passionate sobbing as she spoke.

"You bear him no good will, madam," said Holmes. "Tell us then where we shall find him. If you have ever aided him in evil, help us now and so atone."

"There is but one place where he can have fled," she answered. "There is an old tin mine on an island in the heart of the mire. It was there that he kept his hound and there also he had made preparations so that he might have a refuge. That is where he would fly."

The fog bank lay like white wool against the window. Holmes held the lamp toward it.

"See," said he. "No one could find his way into the Grimpen Mire tonight."

1 She laughed and clapped her hands. Her eyes and teeth gleamed with fierce merriment.

"He may find his way in, but never out," she cried. "How can he see the guiding wands tonight? We planted them together, he and I, to mark the pathway through the mire. Oh, if I could only have plucked them out today. Then indeed you would have had him at your mercy!"

It was evident to us that all pursuit was in vain until the fog had lifted. Meanwhile we left Lestrade in possession of the house while Holmes and I went back with the baronet to Baskerville Hall. The story of the Stapletons could no longer be withheld from him, but he took the blow bravely when he learned the truth about the woman whom he had loved. But the shock of the night's adventures had shattered his nerves, and before morning he lay delirious in a high fever, under the care of Dr. Mortimer.

2 And now I come rapidly to the conclusion of this singular narrative, in which I have tried to make the reader share those dark

fears and vague surmises which clouded our lives so long and ended in so tragic a manner. On the morning after the death of the hound the fog had lifted and we were guided by Mrs. Stapleton to the point where they had found a pathway through the bog. It helped us to realize the horror of this woman's life when we saw the eagerness and joy with which she laid us on her husband's track. We left her standing upon the thin peninsula of firm, peaty soil which tapered out into the widespread bog. From the end of it a small wand planted here and there showed where the path zigzagged from tuft to tuft of rushes among those green-scummed pits and foul quagmires which barred the way to the stranger.

3 Rank reeds and lush, slimy waterplants sent an odor of decay and a heavy miasmatic vapor[2] onto our faces, while a false step plunged us more than once thigh-deep into the dark, quivering mire. Once only we saw a trace that someone had passed that perilous way before us. From amid a tuft of cotton grass which bore it up out of the slime some dark thing was projecting. Holmes sank to his waist as he stepped from the path to seize it, and had we not been there to drag him out he could never have set his foot upon firm land again. He held an old black boot in the air. "Meyers, Toronto," was printed on the leather inside.

"It is worth a mud bath," said he. "It is our friend Sir Henry's missing boot."

"Thrown there by Stapleton in his flight."

"Exactly. He retained it in his hand after using it to set the hound upon the track. He fled when he knew the game was up, still clutching it. And he hurled it away at this point of his flight. We know at least that he came so far in safety."

---

2. **miasmatic** [mī az mat′ik] **vapor:** foul-smelling mist from swamps.

576   *The Novel*

GUIDED READING

LITERAL QUESTIONS

1a. How does Beryl Stapleton help Holmes and Watson in their efforts to conclude the case? (She tells them about Stapleton's hiding place and shows them the path of wands that will lead them there.)

2a. What is the Grimpen Mire like? (dark, quivering, slimy, and dangerous)

INFERENTIAL QUESTIONS

1b. Why do you think Beryl Stapleton helps Holmes and Watson? (She wants her husband to pay for the crimes he has committed; she wants the whole horrible business to end.)

2b. Do you think Holmes and Watson will find Stapleton there? (Answers will vary. Possibilities: *Yes,* he will be at his hiding place; *no,* he probably died trying to get to the hiding place.)

But more than that we were never destined to know. If the earth told a true story, then Stapleton never reached that island of refuge toward which he struggled through the fog upon that last night. Somewhere in the heart of the great Grimpen Mire, down in the foul slime of the huge morass which had sucked him in, this cold and cruel-hearted man is forever buried.

Many traces we found of him in the boggy island where he had hidden his savage ally. A huge driving wheel and a shaft half-filled with rubbish showed the position of an abandoned mine. A quantity of gnawed bones showed where the animal had been confined.

"Well," said Holmes, "I do not know that this place contains any secret which we have not already fathomed. He could hide his hound, but he could not hush its voice, and hence came those cries which even in daylight were not pleasant to hear. On an emergency he could keep the hound in the shed at Merripit, but it was always a risk, and it was only on the supreme day, which he regarded as the end of all his efforts, that he dared do it.

"This paste in the tin is no doubt the luminous mixture with which the creature was daubed. It was suggested, of course, by the story of the family hound, and by the desire to frighten old Sir Charles to death. No wonder the poor devil of a convict ran and screamed, even as our friend did, when he saw such a creature bounding through the darkness of the moor upon his track."

1 | **15   A Retrospection**

2 | It was the end of November, and Holmes and I sat, upon a raw and foggy night, on either side of a blazing fire in our sitting room in Baker Street. Sir Henry and Dr. Mortimer were in London, on their way to a long voyage which had been recommended for the resto-

ration of his shattered nerves. They had called upon us that very afternoon, so that it was natural that the subject should come up for discussion.

"The whole course of events," said Holmes, "from the point of view of the man who called himself Stapleton was simple and direct, although to us, who had no means in the beginning of knowing the motives of his actions and could only learn part of the facts, it all appeared exceedingly complex.

3 | "Perhaps you would kindly give me a sketch of the course of events from memory."

"My inquiries show beyond all question that the family portrait did not lie," Holmes said, "and that this fellow was indeed a Baskerville. He was a son of that Rodger Baskerville, the younger brother of Sir Charles, who fled with a sinister reputation to South America, where he was said to have died unmarried. He did, as a matter of fact, marry, and had one child, this fellow, whose real name is the same as his father's. He married Beryl Garcia, one of the beauties of Costa Rica, and, having purloined a considerable sum of public money, he changed his name to Vandeleur and fled to England, where he established a school in the east of Yorkshire.

"The fellow had evidently made inquiry, and found that only two lives intervened between him and a valuable estate. When he went to Devonshire his plans were, I believe, exceedingly hazy. He meant in the end to have the estate, and he was ready to use any tool or run any risk for that end. His first act was to establish himself as near to his ancestral home as he could, and his second was to cultivate a friendship with Sir Charles Baskerville and with the neighbors.

"The baronet himself told him about the family hound, and so prepared the way for his own death. Stapleton, as I will continue to call him, knew that the old man's heart was weak

The Hound of the Baskervilles   577

AT A GLANCE
- Holmes and Watson find Stapleton's hiding place, but the mire seems to have swallowed up the criminal.
- Back in London Holmes reviews the case, revealing that Stapleton was the son of Sir Charles's brother, Rodger, who had emigrated to South America.

1 PLOT: RESOLUTION

This last chapter is the novel's official resolution. We may expect any points that still puzzle us to be cleared up shortly.

2 SETTING

We are back to the setting in which the novel opened. The familiar and cozy sitting room on London's Baker Street is just the place for two friends to sum up the case they have so cleverly solved.

3 POINT OF VIEW

Watson asks Holmes to review everything he now knows about the case. Watson represents all those readers whose powers of deduction and recall are not as sharp as Holmes's.

GUIDED READING

LITERAL QUESTIONS

1a. What do Watson and Holmes conclude happened to Stapleton? (They believe he was sucked into the mire.)

2a. What does Holmes say was Stapleton's relationship to Sir Charles Baskerville? (Stapleton was Sir Charles's nephew.)

INFERENTIAL QUESTIONS

1b. Why might this conclusion be valid? (Holmes and Watson know that Stapleton went into the mire because they found the boot used to set the hound on Sir Henry, yet there are no other signs of Stapleton.)

2b. Why do you think Sir Charles didn't know about his brother's son? (The family was widely scattered.)

1 CHARACTERIZATION

Through details such as the name of the animal dealer who sold the dog to Stapleton, we see how thorough Holmes's investigation has been.

2 THEME

Having committed murder, Stapleton must have been bitterly disappointed to learn that the inheritance would not be his. His greed and ambition were such, however, that he did not hesitate to plan quickly a second murder.

3 READING SKILLS: MAKING INFERENCES

From the fact that Beryl Stapleton was in London with her husband, we can infer that it was she who composed the original warning to Sir Henry in London.

---

and that a shock would kill him. So much he had learned from Dr. Mortimer. The dog he bought in London from Ross and Mangles, the dealers in Fulham Road. It was the strongest and most savage in their possession. He brought it down by the North Devon line and walked a great distance over the moor so as to get it home without exciting any remarks.

"He had hoped that his wife might lure Sir Charles to his ruin, but here she proved un-<u>1</u>expectedly independent. She would not endeavor to entangle the old gentleman in a sentimental attachment which might deliver him over to his enemy. Threats refused to move her. She would have nothing to do with it, and for a time Stapleton was at a deadlock.

"His plans were suddenly brought to a head by his knowledge that Sir Charles was about to leave the Hall on the advice of Dr. Mortimer, with whose opinion he himself pretended to coincide. He must act at once, or his victim might get beyond his power. He therefore put pressure upon Mrs. Lyons to write this letter, imploring the old man to give her an interview on the evening before his departure for London. He then, by a specious argument, prevented her from going, and so had the chance for which he had waited.

"Driving back in the evening from Coombe Tracey he was in time to get his hound, to treat it with his infernal paint, and to bring the beast round to the gate at which he had reason to expect that he would find the old gentleman waiting. The dog, incited by its master, sprang over the wicket gate and pursued the unfortunate baronet, who fled screaming down the yew alley. In that gloomy tunnel it must indeed have been a dreadful sight to see that huge black creature, with its flaming jaws and blazing eyes, bounding after its victim. He fell dead at the end of the alley from heart disease and terror.

"The hound had kept upon the grassy bor-

578   *The Novel*

der while the baronet had run down the path, so that no track but the man's was visible. On seeing him lying still the creature had probably approached to sniff at him, but finding him dead had turned away again. It was then that it left the print which was actually observed by Dr. Mortimer. The hound was called off and hurried away to its lair in the Grimpen Mire, and a mystery was left which puzzled the authorities, alarmed the countryside, and finally brought the case within the scope of our observation.

"So much for the death of Sir Charles Baskerville. You perceive the devilish cunning of it, for really it would be almost impossible to make a case against the real murderer. His only accomplice was one who could never give him away.

"It is possible that Stapleton did not know of the existence of an heir in Canada. In any case he would very soon learn it from his friend Dr. Mortimer, and he was told by the latter all details about the arrival of Henry Baskerville.

<u>2</u> "Stapleton's first idea was that this young stranger from Canada might possibly be done to death in London without coming down to Devonshire at all. He distrusted his wife ever since she had refused to help him in laying a trap for the old man, and he dared not leave <u>3</u> her long out of his sight for fear he should lose his influence over her. It was for this reason that he took her to London with him.

"It was very essential for Stapleton to get some article of Sir Henry's attire so that, in case he was driven to use the dog, he might always have the means of setting him upon his track. He set about this at once, and we cannot doubt that the boots[1] or chambermaid of the hotel was well bribed to help him in his

---

1. **boots:** servant who polishes boots.

GUIDED READING

LITERAL QUESTION

1a. What did Stapleton ask both his wife and Laura Lyons to do? (Stapleton asked his wife and, later, Mrs. Lyons to set up a meeting with Sir Charles Baskerville.)

INFERENTIAL QUESTION

1b. What does Mrs. Stapleton's refusal to do what her husband requested suggest? (She was aware of her husband's evil plans and wanted no part of them; she is basically a decent person.)

design. By chance, however, the first boot which was procured for him was a new one and, therefore, useless for his purpose. He then had it returned and obtained another— a most instructive incident, since it proved conclusively to my mind that we were dealing with a real hound, as no other supposition could explain this anxiety to obtain an old boot and this indifference to a new one."

"One moment!" said I. "You have, no doubt, described the sequence of events correctly, but there is one point which you have left unexplained. What became of the hound when its master was in London?"

"I have given some attention to this matter and it is undoubtedly of importance. There can be no question that Stapleton had a confidant, though it is unlikely that he ever placed himself in his power by sharing all his plans with him. There was an old manservant at Merripit House, whose name was Anthony. His connection with the Stapletons can be traced for several years, as far back as the schoolmastering days, so that he must have been aware that his master and mistress were really husband and wife. This man has disappeared and has escaped from the country. I have myself seen this old man cross the Grimpen Mire by the path which Stapleton had marked out. It is very probable, therefore, that in the absence of his master it was he who cared for the hound, though he may never have known the purpose for which the beast was used.

"The Stapletons then went down to Devonshire, whither they were soon followed by Sir Henry and you. It was my game to watch Stapleton. It was evident, however, that I could not do this if I were with you, since he would be keenly on his guard. I deceived everybody, therefore, yourself included, and I came down secretly when I was supposed to be in London. When I was watching Stapleton, Cartwright was frequently watching you, so that I was able to keep my hand upon all the strings.

AT A GLANCE

- Holmes points out that the new boot was returned and an old one stolen to give the hound the necessary scent.
- Stapleton's servant was his confidant, caring for the hound when Stapleton was away.
- Holmes evidently suspected Stapleton from the beginning.

1 THEME

Holmes had to deduce the purpose for which the boot might be used before he could conclude that he was dealing with a real hound.

2 STYLE: METAPHOR

By describing his role in the case as keeping his "hand upon all the strings," Holmes suggests that he sees himself as a puppeteer. Other people are the puppets; he manipulates them toward an end that he determines.

GUIDED READING

LITERAL QUESTION

1a. What explanation does Holmes give for his secret presence in Devonshire? (He says he wanted to keep an eye on Stapleton without Stapleton's suspecting.)

INFERENTIAL QUESTION

1b. Do you think Holmes's plan was wise? (Answers will vary. Some students may note that the plan ultimately worked and so was wise. Others may insist that Watson, at least, should have known of Holmes's true whereabouts.)

1 CHARACTERIZATION

The urbane Holmes takes advantage of London's rich cultural offerings both to relax and to refine further his thoughts and feelings. Once a case has been solved to his satisfaction, he immediately moves on to something else.

REFLECTING ON THE NOVEL

Compare Holmes's and Watson's contributions to solving the mystery. (Watson was good at carrying out orders and observing and reporting on events. Holmes excelled at developing strategies and drawing conclusions.)

STUDY QUESTIONS

1. that Stapleton is a Baskerville, resembles Hugo; to inherit estate
2. to drive to Stapletons, send back the trap, say Holmes and Watson are in London, and walk home; to London
3. ■ They will wait in ambush for Sir Henry to pass and then intercept the hound as it comes after him.
   ■ thick fog
4. enormous, black, outlined in flame; phosphorus

"By the time that you discovered me upon the moor I had a complete knowledge of the whole business, but I had not a case which could go to a jury. Even Stapleton's attempt upon Sir Henry that night which ended in the death of the unfortunate convict did not help us much in proving murder against our man. There seemed to be no alternative but to catch him red-handed, and to do so we had to use Sir Henry, alone and apparently unprotected, as a bait.

"We succeeded in our object at a cost which Dr. Mortimer assures me will be a temporary one. A long journey may enable our friend to recover not only from his shattered nerves but also from his wounded feelings. His love for the lady was deep and sincere, and to him the saddest part of all this black business was that he should have been deceived by her.

"There can be no doubt that Stapleton exercised an influence over her. At his command she consented to pass as his sister, though he found the limits of his power over her when he endeavored to make her the direct accessory to murder. She was ready to warn Sir Henry so far as she could without implicating her husband, and again and again she tried to do so.

"On the day of the crisis, however, his wife turned suddenly against him. She had learned something of the death of the convict, and she knew that the hound was being kept in the shed on the evening that Sir Henry was coming to dinner. She taxed her husband with his intended crime, and a furious scene followed in which he showed her for the first time that she had a rival in his love. Her fidelity turned in an instant to bitter hatred and he saw that she would betray him."

"There only remains one difficulty. If Stapleton came into the succession, how could he explain that fact that he, the heir, had been living unannounced under another name so close to the property? How could he claim it without causing suspicion and inquiry?"

"There were three possible courses. He might claim the property from South America, or he might adopt an elaborate disguise during the short time that he need be in London; or, again, he might furnish an accomplice with the proofs and papers, putting him in as heir, and retaining a claim upon some proportion of his income.

1 "And now, my dear Watson, we have had some weeks of severe work, and for one evening, I think, we may turn our thoughts into more pleasant channels. I have a box for *Les Hugenots.* Have you heard the de Reszkes?"[2]

---

2. *Les Huguenots* [läz ū′gə nō′] . . . **de Reszkes** [də rezh′kez]: French grand opera by Giacomo Meyerbeer, in which the de Reszkes, famous opera singers of the time, were appearing.

STUDY QUESTIONS

Recalling

1. In Chapter 13 what does Holmes discover from the portrait of Sir Hugo Baskerville? What motive does Holmes conclude Stapleton has for wanting to kill Sir Henry?

2. What instructions does Holmes give Sir Henry in Chapter 14? Where does Sir Henry think Holmes and Watson are going?

3. What is Holmes's plan for trapping Stapleton? What natural event on the moor threatens his plan?

4. Describe the hound that chases Sir Henry.

What does Watson discover is the cause of its terrifying appearance?

5. What do Holmes, Watson, and Lestrade discover in Stapleton's house? How does Stapleton die?

6. List four new facts about the mystery that are revealed in Chapter 15.

Interpreting

7. Choose a word or phrase to describe the personality of Stapleton. Find three actions that support the word or phrase you have chosen.

8. Evaluate Holmes's plan to trap Stapleton. Do you think Holmes took unnecessary risks with Sir Henry's life?

9. Do you think that Holmes could have solved this case without the help of Watson? Give reasons for your opinion.

Extending

10. Why do you think detective stories are so popular? Give examples from *The Hound of the Baskervilles* to support your answer.

READING AND LITERARY FOCUS

The Total Effect

Sir Arthur Conan Doyle's tales about Sherlock Holmes maintain their worldwide popularity because of their fascinating plots, vivid characterization, effective settings, and the endearing point of view of Dr. Watson. Together these elements help Conan Doyle present his themes. In turn, all of these elements of fiction—plot, character, setting, point of view, and theme—interact and create a total effect, or impact, on the reader.

Thinking About Plot

1. What is the climax of the novel, the point of our highest interest and greatest emotional involvement in the story?

2. What exactly is the main conflict, and what is its outcome?

Thinking About Character

3. In what ways is Holmes made to appear almost superhuman?

4. In what ways does Watson prove his friendship for Sir Henry?

Thinking About Setting

5. What does the fog in Chapter 14 add to the mood of the novel? In what way does it contribute to the climax?

Thinking About Point of View

6. What are the advantages of seeing the events of the novel through the eyes of Dr. Watson? What are the disadvantages?

Thinking About Theme

7. Consider the various friendships in *The Hound of the Baskervilles,* especially the friendship of Holmes and Watson and of Sir Henry and Watson. What is Conan Doyle suggesting are the qualities of a good friend?

8. In what ways is Stapleton greedy? What theme might Conan Doyle be suggesting about the relationship between greed and crime?

9. Think about the relationship in the novel between common sense or reason and superstition. Which is considered a good force, and which is associated with evil? What theme regarding good and evil might Conan Doyle be suggesting?

VOCABULARY

Context Clues

Context clues allow us to solve the mystery of unfamiliar words, just as Sherlock Holmes used clues to solve the mystery of the Baskerville family. By finding clues in the sentence or sentences surrounding an unknown word, we can often find out its meaning. Consider the following example from one of Watson's letters to Holmes:

You are aware that I am not a very sound

The Hound of the Baskervilles 581

1. (d) untidy
2. (d) regarded highly
3. (a) able to speak
4. (c) pale
5. (d) great skill or cunning

CHALLENGE

Students should
- list five questions about this case to ask Sherlock Holmes
- select another student to act as Holmes
- conduct the interview, following up on "Holmes's" answers, when appropriate

---

sleeper, and since I have been on guard in this house my *slumbers* have been lighter than ever. . . .

From Watson's remarks we learn that he is not a heavy sleeper and that his *slumbers* are now "lighter than ever." *Slumber* must mean "sleep."

Choose the best meaning for each italicized word in the following sentences by studying its *context.* Examine the ideas found in the sentence in which the word appears or in adjoining sentences. Write your answers on a separate sheet.

1. He was clad in a professional but rather *slovenly* fashion, for his frockcoat was dingy and his trousers frayed.
   (a) neat   (c) uninteresting
   (b) clean   (d) untidy

2. Dr. Mortimer is a successful elderly medical man, well *esteemed,* since those who know him give him this mark of their appreciation.
   (a) educated   (c) relaxed
   (b) blessed   (d) regarded highly

3. So furious was he that he was hardly *articulate,* and when he did speak it was in a much broader and more Western dialect than any which we had heard from him in the morning.
   (a) able to speak (c) alive
   (b) awake   (d) serious

4. It seemed to me that the *pallid* features of the butler turned a shade paler still as he listened to his master's question.
   (a) healthy   (c) pale
   (b) royal   (d) lively

5. Having conceived the idea he proceeded to carry it out with considerable *finesse.* An ordinary schemer would have been content with a savage hound. The use of artificial means to make the creature diabolical was a flash of genius upon his part.
   (a) inability   (c) hard work
   (b) humor   (d) great skill or cunning

COMPOSITION

Writing a Book Review

■ Write a book review of *The Hound of the Baskervilles.* Begin with general information about Sir Arthur Conan Doyle. Then describe the setting of the novel and the main characters. Next summarize the plot. Conclude by giving your opinion of the book, backed by supporting details from the story. *For help with this assignment, see Lesson 9 in the Writing About Literature Handbook at the back of this book.*

Writing a Diary Entry

■ Imagine that you are Watson writing in your diary the day after the case of the hound of the Baskervilles has ended. Write about the following topics: what you think about the role you played in solving the mystery; your opinion of the events that have occurred; and what you and Holmes will undertake in the future. Base your response on your knowledge of Watson's personality.

CHALLENGE

Interview

■ Imagine that you are a reporter who is assigned to interview Sherlock Holmes about his case involving the hound of the Baskervilles. First make a list of at least five questions to ask. For example, you might ask what the most difficult part of the case was or at what point Holmes discovered the identity of the murderer. Then ask a classmate to play the part of Holmes. Conduct your interview before the rest of the class.

COMPOSITION: GUIDELINES FOR EVALUATION

WRITING A BOOK REVIEW
Objective
To write a review of a book

Guidelines for Evaluation
- suggested length: five to seven paragraphs
- should relate facts about Conan Doyle
- should describe plot, main characters, and setting of the novel
- should state and support the writer's opinion about novel

WRITING A DIARY ENTRY
Objective
To write a diary entry from Watson's viewpoint

Guidelines for Evaluation
- suggested length: three to four paragraphs
- should describe role played in mystery
- should state opinion of events
- should indicate what Watson and Holmes will undertake in the future
- should show understanding of Watson

Active Reading

The Novel

Understanding Deductive Reasoning

In *The Hound of the Baskervilles* Sherlock Holmes draws conclusions about James Mortimer based on his walking stick. To arrive at these conclusions, Holmes uses deductive reasoning. *Deductive reasoning* is reasoning that starts with a general rule or assumption in order to reach a specific conclusion.

Holmes concludes that Doctor Mortimer works in the country, not in the city. He bases this conclusion on the general assumption that worn-down walking sticks belong to country doctors, who walk more than city doctors. Since Mortimer's walking stick is worn down, Holmes concludes that Mortimer must work in the country.

Holmes's deductive reasoning may be summarized in the format outlined below. Here the *major premise* is the general assumption. The *minor premise* is a piece of evidence related to that assumption. The *conclusion* is the result of the major and minor premise.

MAJOR PREMISE: Worn-down walking sticks belong to country doctors.

MINOR PREMISE: Doctor Mortimer owns a worn-down walking stick.

CONCLUSION: Therefore Doctor Mortimer is a country doctor.

The following drawings may help you understand the reasoning more easily.

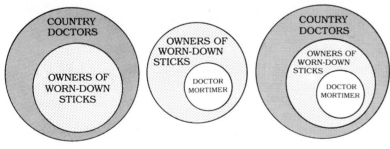

MAJOR PREMISE: Worn-down walking sticks belong to country doctors.

MINOR PREMISE: Doctor Mortimer owns a worn-down walking stick.

CONCLUSION: Therefore Doctor Mortimer is a country doctor.

ACTIVE READING

The two activities in this lesson will teach students to understand deductive reasoning and to recognize fallacies in reasoning. Suggested responses to these activities are provided here. In addition, you will find among the materials for this unit in your *Teacher's Resource Book* the following related blackline masters: Understanding Deductive Reasoning; Recognizing Fallacies in Reasoning.

Activity 1 Read each of the following examples of a *major premise* and *minor premise.* Then choose the correct *conclusion.*

1. MAJOR PREMISE: All people who receive gifts are well liked.
   MINOR PREMISE: Doctor Mortimer receives gifts.
   CONCLUSION:
   a. Therefore Doctor Mortimer likes his gifts.
   b. Therefore Doctor Mortimer is well liked.
   c. Therefore Doctor Mortimer likes to give gifts.

2. MAJOR PREMISE: All country doctors are unambitious.
   MINOR PREMISE: Doctor Mortimer is a country doctor.
   CONCLUSION:
   a. Therefore Doctor Mortimer is unambitious.
   b. Therefore Doctor Mortimer is ambitious.
   c. Therefore Doctor Mortimer is a city doctor.

3. MAJOR PREMISE: All student surgeons are under thirty.
   MINOR PREMISE: Doctor Mortimer is a student surgeon.
   CONCLUSION:
   a. Therefore Doctor Mortimer teaches surgeons.
   b. Therefore Doctor Mortimer is over thirty.
   c. Therefore Doctor Mortimer is under thirty.

Recognizing Fallacies in Reasoning

In the novel each of Holmes's conclusions about Mortimer turns out to be true. That is because every general assumption, or major premise, that Holmes makes is a reliable one. In deductive reasoning *the truth of the conclusion depends on the reliability of the major premise it is based upon.*

For example, consider the following case of reasoning.

MAJOR PREMISE: All doctors study medicine.
MINOR PREMISE: James Mortimer is a doctor.
CONCLUSION: Therefore James Mortimer studies medicine.

The conclusion is true because it is based upon a reliable major premise. It is reasonable to believe that all doctors study medicine. Therefore it must be true that James Mortimer, being a doctor, also studies medicine.

However, now consider this case of reasoning.

MAJOR PREMISE: All doctors are women.
MINOR PREMISE: James Mortimer is a doctor.
CONCLUSION: Therefore James Mortimer is a woman.

584   *The Novel*

In this example the conclusion is obviously not true. It is based upon an unreliable major premise—that all doctors are women. Since the assumption is unreliable, it leads us to a false conclusion. This conclusion, however, still remains valid. A conclusion is *valid* if the reasoning is correct, even though the major premise is unreliable. Here is another example.

MAJOR PREMISE: All doctors are detectives.
MINOR PREMISE: James Mortimer is a doctor.
CONCLUSION: Therefore James Mortimer is a detective.

This conclusion, like the previous one, is false. It is based upon the unreliable assumption that all doctors are detectives. However, the conclusion has been reasoned correctly from the assumption that is given. Therefore the conclusion is valid, even though it is not true.

To determine whether a conclusion is true or valid, keep the following two points in mind.

1. A conclusion is *true* only if it has been reasoned correctly from a reliable major premise.
2. A conclusion is *valid* if it has been reasoned correctly, even if the major premise is unreliable.

Activity 2 For each of the following examples of deductive reasoning, tell whether the conclusion is *true* or merely *valid*.

1. MAJOR PREMISE: All hospitals have doctors.
   MINOR PREMISE: Charing Cross Hospital is a hospital.
   CONCLUSION: Therefore Charing Cross Hospital has doctors.

2. MAJOR PREMISE: All doctors are over eighty years old.
   MINOR PREMISE: James Mortimer is a doctor.
   CONCLUSION: Therefore James Mortimer is over eighty years old.

3. MAJOR PREMISE: All doctors attended medical school.
   MINOR PREMISE: James Mortimer is a doctor.
   CONCLUSION: Therefore James Mortimer attended medical school.

4. MAJOR PREMISE: All detectives live in Paris.
   MINOR PREMISE: Sherlock Holmes is a detective.
   CONCLUSION: Therefore Sherlock Holmes lives in Paris.

The Novel 585

Activity 1
1. (b) Therefore Doctor Mortimer is well liked.
2. (a) Therefore Doctor Mortimer is unambitious.
3. (c) Therefore Doctor Mortimer is under thirty.

Activity 2
1. True
2. Valid
3. True
4. Valid

Literary Skills Review

The Novel

Guide for Reading the Novel

As you read novels, use this guide to help you notice and appreciate the way authors create fictional worlds.

Plot

1. What is the main **plot** and main **conflict** of the novel?
2. Does the novel have **subplots** that are related to the main plot?
3. Does **foreshadowing** help you to predict future plot developments?

Character

1. Who are the **major characters** of the novel?
2. Who are the **minor characters** of the novel?
3. What aspects in the characters' personalities does the author reveal directly?
4. What aspects of the characters' personalities does the author reveal indirectly through the characters' own words and actions?

Setting

1. **When and where** does the novel take place? Does the setting change?
2. What **atmosphere,** or mood, is created by the setting?

Point of View

1. Does the author use the **first-person point of view,** making a character the storyteller?
2. Does the author tell the story, using the **third-person point of view**?
3. What are the advantages and disadvantages of the author's choice of narrator?

Theme

1. What is the novel's **theme,** or main idea? Does the novel have more than one theme?
2. What themes are stated directly by the author or by characters?
3. What themes are implied in the novel?

Themes Review

The Novel

Time and again authors have written about such general themes as friendship, nature, heroism, and overcoming obstacles. These general themes represent aspects of life that concern all people. For instance, many works of literature focus on individuals who confront obstacles. Yet each writer says something special about the general theme "confronting obstacles." For example, *The Hound of the Baskervilles* (page 503) communicates the following specific view of confronting obstacles: "Determination, ingenuity, and courage can enable a person to confront many different kinds of obstacles." On the other hand, *The Miracle Worker* (page 12) presents a different specific view of this theme: "We often need the love and strength of other people to help us confront the greatest obstacles."

1. In *The Hound of the Baskervilles* what point about confronting obstacles is made by Watson's helping Holmes?

2. For *The Hound of the Baskervilles* and one of the following selections, explain each work's specific view of the general theme "heroism."
   Stories: "The Dog of Pompeii"   "Spring Victory"
   Folk Tales: "Pecos Bill . . ."   "Paul Bunyan's Cornstalk"

3. For *The Hound of the Baskervilles* and one of the following selections, explain the point made about mysteries.
   Stories: "Crime on Mars"   "The Rule of Names"
   Poems: "The Raven"   "Stopping by Woods on a Snowy Evening"

4. For *The Hound of the Baskervilles* and one other work below, explain the specific point made about friendship or love.
   Stories: "Then He Goes Free"   "The Osage Orange Tree"
   Poems: "The Raven"   "Mama Is a Sunrise"
   Nonfiction: "On Summer"   *Kon-Tiki*
   Drama: *The Romancers*   *Anne Frank*
   Myths: "Alcestis"   "Orpheus and Eurydice"

A major goal of the *Scribner Literature Series* is to help students become active, independent learners. Resources on the following pages are designed to help students develop and refine the skills that mature learners use constantly as they interact with literature. Such learners know how to *manage* their assignments by applying these skills:

- speaking and listening skills
- thinking skills
- reading and study skills
- writing skills

Students will be able to refer to these pages throughout the term—not just in connection with a single literary selection. In other words, students can use this easy-to-find reference and practice guide continually, as they experience all the literature they read. With outstanding literature, on the one hand, and a comprehensive resource guide, on the other, the *Scribner Literature Series* provides the means for you and your students to deal with both *ideas* and *skills*.

In addition, these pages also include the following elements, designed for successful teaching and learning:

- Reading and Literary Terms Handbook
- Glossary
- Vocabulary Review
- Index of Titles by Theme
- Index of Skills
- Index of Authors and Titles

STUDENT'S RESOURCES
LESSONS IN ACTIVE LEARNING

SPEAKING AND LISTENING HANDBOOK

THINKING SKILLS HANDBOOK

READING AND STUDY SKILLS HANDBOOK

WRITING ABOUT
LITERATURE HANDBOOK

READING AND LITERARY
TERMS HANDBOOK

This handbook enables students to practice and improve their speaking and listening skills while studying literature. The four lessons in the handbook cover a wide range of interrelated speaking and listening skills:

- public speaking
- listening/discussion
- oral interpretation of literature
- collaborative learning

Each literature-based lesson is set up in a step-by-step format so that students can easily work on the skill on their own. The final step in each lesson is a transfer activity in which the student is directed to apply the skill to a variety of selections in the anthology. In other words, the lessons are designed to be used or referred to many times—as often as you wish your students to work with a particular speaking or listening skill.

In addition to this handbook, speaking and listening skills are practiced in the Challenge strand of this textbook and in the Additional Projects listed in the *Teacher's Resource Book*. The Listening to a Speech and Evaluating a Speech blackline masters in the *Teacher's Resource Book* will prove helpful as your students work with the lessons in this handbook.

Lesson 1

The first lesson gives students an opportunity to work with public speaking—perhaps the activity they most often associate with speaking and listening. Here students practice techniques of preparing and delivering a speech and, at the same time, examine literature from new perspectives.

SPEAKING AND LISTENING HANDBOOK

LESSON 1: *An Informative Speech About an Author*

OVERVIEW

You will select an author who is represented in the anthology and do research to learn more about the author. Then you will organize your information into a brief informative speech to present to the class.

PREPARING THE SPEECH

1. Get research underway.

The first step is to select an author who appears in this book and about whom you want to learn more.

- Select an author whose literary work you enjoyed a great deal.
- Select an author whose biographical note (before the selection) intrigued you. Might there be other unusual things that you would enjoy learning about the author?

If the author wrote a long time ago or is quite famous, you will probably find some information about him or her in an encyclopedia, but you may not find enough information there. In any event, it is always a good idea to consult more than one source—to go beyond an encyclopedia. Here is a brief list of other reference materials that you may find in your school or local library.

- *Current Biography*
- *Who's Who* and *Who Was Who*
- *Dictionary of American Biography*
- *Dictionary of National Biography*
- *Webster's Biographical Dictionary*

Sometimes you will find that these sources provide only cut-and-dried information about your author. For richer information you may have to use the library's catalog to find a book about the author and the *Readers' Guide to Periodical Literature* to identify magazine articles.

2. Take notes.

As you read the reference books or other sources, look for information that answers questions such as your classmates will want you to answer in your speech:

- How did family influence the writer?
- How did youthful experiences influence the writer?
- What social conditions or current events concern the writer?
- What particularly unusual facts can I uncover about the writer?

With these questions—and others like them—in mind, begin to take notes from your sources. *Remember that you must use your own words to summarize or retell what the source states. (Keep track of which source says what because you may have to hand in this information.)*

3. Form an overall impression or central idea.

Looking over your sources and your notes, you must form some general picture of the author. You will present a better speech if you leave your audience with a main idea about the author rather than just miscellaneous facts.

ORGANIZING YOUR IDEAS

Consider one of the following organizations:

- *Chronological:* Begin with facts or anecdotes about the author's youth, and then provide information about the later years.
- *Order of importance:* Save the most unusual piece of information for last.

You will also need to decide how to begin and end your speech.

- You may begin by giving the audience an idea of what to expect from you.
- You may end by telling your audience what works by the author you are now thinking of reading.

Use an outline to place all your ideas in the order in which you will present them.

SAMPLE SPEECH

Let us assume that you enjoyed "The Legend of Sleepy Hollow" (page 168) so much that you want to find out more about the author who wrote it. Here is an outline based on notes we will assume you took from the *World Book Encyclopedia* and the *Oxford Companion to American Literature.*

I. Opening
I want to show you that the author of the unusual tale "Legend of Sleepy Hollow" was himself unusual in some ways.

II. Body
   A. Education and early interest in writing
   B. Pseudonyms
      1. Strange for someone so interested in writing?
      2. Knickerbocker (*World Book*); Crayon (*Oxford*)
   C. Reputation as writer: Not always great
   D. Romance
      1. Fiancée died
      2. May have been infatuated with Mary Shelley, author of *Frankenstein* (*Oxford*)
   E. Most interesting to me: Other careers and almost careers
      1. Trained as lawyer (textbook)
      2. Worked in family hardware business (*World Book*)
      3. Offered nomination as mayor of New York and appointment as Secretary of Navy (*Oxford*)
      4. Diplomat to Spain and England (*Oxford*)

III. Closing
I want to read *Knickerbocker's History of New York.* Will I find it as amusing today as readers did in the early 1800s?

DELIVERING THE SPEECH

1. Be clear and interesting. You will want to stand where you can be seen by everyone; you will want to speak up so that you can be heard by everyone. You will want to speak clearly and vary your voice and pacing.

2. Your speech will be extemporaneous. (In an **extemporaneous** speech you prepare your thoughts and write down the key words and phrases but select the specific language spontaneously as you speak to the audience.)

ASSIGNMENT

Here are suggestions from this book of other authors you might enjoy researching:

- Ernest Hemingway: How did his life in Spain influence him as a writer?
- I. B. Singer: How did his life in Poland influence him?
- Mark Twain: What did life on the Mississippi do for him as a writer?
- Alice Walker: Did her visit to Africa have any impact on her writing?

LESSON 2: *An Interview About Literature*

▬ OVERVIEW

An innovative way to practice your speaking and listening skills as they relate to literature is to conduct an interview. One student will interview another about reactions to a selection in this anthology. The interview will take place in front of the rest of the class, and so the participants must remember to speak up loudly and clearly to assure that everyone can hear. The interviewer and the interviewee will sit in the front of the class, partly facing each other and partly facing the audience.

The overall interview can be as short as ten minutes:

- one-minute introduction by interviewer
- six-minute interview
- three-minute audience question period

▬ GUIDELINES FOR INTERVIEWER

To ask good questions, the interviewer must be familiar with the work. The purpose of the questions is to probe the interviewee's understanding of the work in order to help the entire class.

1. The interviewer should plan to ask a variety of questions.

   a. *Primary or secondary questions.* Primary questions introduce brand-new topics and move the discussion into a new phase. Secondary questions are follow-up questions designed to elicit further information after a primary question has been answered. One kind of secondary question seeks to clarify the meaning of the interviewee's answer by asking, "Did you mean by that. . .?"

   b. *Planned or spontaneous.* Most of the primary questions should be planned and considered well in advance of the interview. Secondary, or follow-up, questions can often be spontaneous; they may depend on the interviewee's answer to the primary question. Some questions simply occur to the interviewer on the spur of the moment.

   c. *Leading or straight.* A leading question tries to get the interviewee to agree with the interviewer. An interviewer can use a leading question effectively when he or she suspects the interviewee is having trouble expressing a particular opinion. A straight question simply probes for an honest answer.

   d. *Open or closed.* An open question encourages a longer answer and a more complex response than simply *yes* or *no*. It usually begins with a word such as *Why, How,* or *What.* A closed question can be answered in one word or a short phrase and attempts to establish facts and cover ground quickly: "What is the author's name?" "What period are we talking about?" "Did you like the work?" Both questions have their place in an interview. For example, the closed question "Did you like this work?" might precede the open question "How would you explain why you didn't like this work?"

   e. *Imaginative.* Questions such as the following get the interviewee to think intently about the literary work and reactions to it: "What other kind of ending might this selection have had?"

592 *Speaking and Listening Handbook*

2. The interviewer should structure the questions so that the interview has an easy-to-follow structure with a beginning, a middle, and an end. However, not every interview should follow exactly the same structure, or the audience will soon become bored. Some interviewers may ask very early whether or not the interviewee enjoyed the work; other interviewers may hold that question until the end of the interview. Here's one possible structure:

a. The interviewer may begin with simple questions to establish the basic facts of the work. There are many questions to ask about the formal elements of the work—its plot, characters, setting, for example.

b. Then the interviewer may move on to more complex or subtle matters concerning, say, the climax, the imagery, the author's choice of words. The interviewer may even read a particular passage aloud and ask the interviewee to comment on it.

c. Finally, the interviewer can ask about the work's theme or for an overall impression of the work.

GUIDELINES FOR INTERVIEWEE

1. To prepare, the interviewee should read the work several times and think about it in many different ways. The interviewee should be able to anticipate the topics that the interviewer will want to cover but should realize that the interview must be free and spontaneous, not "staged."

2. The interviewee must listen very carefully to the questions and ask for clarification if necessary. The interviewee should let the interviewer lead; the interviewee should cooperate but should not hesitate to set forth his or her opinions.

3. The interviewee should give simple, straightforward answers, allowing the interviewer to go on to follow-up or other primary questions.

4. The interviewee may pause for a moment to consider a question. By doing so the interviewee may ultimately give a better answer.

5. The interviewee may refer to the selection and even quote from it as part of an answer.

6. It is all right if occasionally the interviewee chooses not to answer a particular question.

ASSIGNMENTS

1. Any single selection in this anthology lends itself to an interview setup as described here, but you may want to explore the following suggestions in particular:

- Conduct an interview based on all *four* of the Frost poems: "A Time to Talk," "Stopping by Woods on a Snowy Evening," "A Minor Bird," and "The Road Not Taken."
- Conduct an interview based on the Langston Hughes story "Thank You, M'am," the Hughes poem "The Dream Keeper," and the Hughes biography "Harriet Tubman: The Moses of Her People."

2. Consider a variation on the interview: Interview an "author." The interviewee would be a student dressed up to represent one of the famous authors in this anthology—for example, Mark Twain. The student playing the role of the author will have to be extremely well prepared.

Speaking and Listening Handbook 593

Oral interpretation—the performance of literature—is gaining increased attention as another avenue to the understanding and appreciation of literature. As students work on their oral presentations of poems, short stories, and so forth, they find themselves reading more closely and thinking about literature more critically than ever before.

LESSON 3:   *Images in Oral Interpretation*

OVERVIEW

You will put special emphasis on highlighting sensory appeals and imagery as you read a piece of literature to the class. Your reading will be an oral interpretation of the work of literature.

PREPARING AN ORAL INTERPRETATION

1. Select a literary work.

Most of the selections in this anthology make appeals to the senses. For the purpose of this assignment, you might stay away from the more abstract pieces, however. Select a work that you particularly like.

2. Think about the work of literature.

Notice how the author works with various senses, concentrating now on one, now on another.

Examples

- SIGHT: Anne in *The Diary of Anne Frank* looking out of her room at the bargeman and his family (page 392); the "I" in a Frost poem looking down the road to where it bends in the undergrowth (page 286).
- SOUND: in "The Osage Orange Tree" the wind through the branches (page 70), the hallway of the school described as "quiet" and "echoey" (page 71), the growling dog (page 72)
- TOUCH, MOVEMENT: the cold wind (page 69) and the flipping of the newspaper (page 72) in "The Osage Orange Tree"; the extreme heat of summer in "On Summer" (page 324); the contrasting textures of trees in "Willow and Ginkgo" (page 244); the heron jerking the frog (page 254); the lady shaking

the boy in "Thank You, M'am" (page 64); the boy's gaze relaxing slowly in "A Day's Wait" (page 4)
- SMELL: the smell of flowers and of the sister in Alice Walker's poem (page 284)
- TASTE: the Walrus and the Carpenter's oyster dinner (page 257)

3. Adjust the work to your time allotment.

The piece of literature you intend to read to the class should take no more than five minutes to read—including a brief introduction in your own words. These guidelines will help you meet that schedule.

a. If you are working with a long piece of literature, cut it so that you can give your oral interpretation in the time specified. Find a beginning and ending for a section of the work. Alternatively, read one part of the work, stop and explain in your own words what happens next, and then pick up your oral interpretation later on in the selection.

b. If you are working with a short poem, you may find that you need to pair it with another poem or two in order to have a long enough presentation.

4. Prepare a manuscript.

Type or print the selection double-spaced. During rehearsal (see below) you can mark where to pause, which words to emphasize, where and how to change your tone and pacing.

5. Rehearse.

As you rehearse, follow these steps:

a. Identify the appeals that the author makes to each of your senses. Find the particular words that the author uses to make those appeals.

b. Make the images come alive for yourself. See, hear, touch, taste, smell what the author is describing for you. Then try to feel what the character or narrator of the selection feels about these sights, sounds, feelings, tastes, and smells.

c. Try to share those feelings with the audience through tone of voice, pacing, emphasis.

6. Prepare an introduction.

Give the facts about the literary work: What is its title? Who wrote it? When? Then briefly tell the audience why you chose this work of literature to present orally.

▥ SAMPLE ORAL INTERPRETATION

Consider the following notes for a performance of the Lorraine Hansberry essay "On Summer" (page 324).

1. Analysis

"Summer" (page 324) lends itself to oral interpretation with an emphasis on sensory details. In this piece Hansberry recalls summers, which she did not like, during her childhood in Chicago. By the end of the essay, she shows that she has changed her mind about summer.

This essay uses many sensory appeals. First, she feels the tremendous heat: She woke up "feeling very, very hot." She describes the negative associations she has with summer and the sense of touch ("the too-grainy texture of sand; the too-cold coldness of the various waters . . . the icky-perspiry feeling of bathing caps"); with the sense of sight ("shadows too pronounced and light too blinding"); with sound

(too stark). Of course, she also acknowledges positive associations with sensory images.

2. Performance

a. Approach the front of the room slowly. Pause for a moment, and look at the audience. Either hold the script in your hands, or lay it on a table or lectern.

b. Give your introduction informally and extemporaneously, using your notes for reference if necessary.

c. Make a clear transition from your introduction to the literature that you are going to read.

d. Concentrate on the images that you have been thinking about.

e. Speak loudly and clearly so that everyone can hear you and understand you.

f. Speak expressively. Use variety in your voice to make the images come alive. That is, vary pitch, intonation, rhythm, rate, and volume. Pause to convey emphasis.

g. End your reading firmly. Keep your attention on the final image for a moment after you stop speaking. Then relax, close your manuscript, and return to your seat.

▥ ASSIGNMENT

Selections that have very strong images and lend themselves to oral interpretation include:

- "The Osage Orange Tree" (page 68)
- "Foul Shot" (page 259)
- "Paul Revere's Ride" (page 266)
- "The Story-Teller" (page 277)
- "The Heron" (page 254)
- "Mouse Night" (page 251)
- "Havasu" (page 313)

LESSON 4:   *Group Playreading*

▬ OVERVIEW

You will work with one to five other students on an oral interpretation of a scene from *The Diary of Anne Frank*. You will *not* fully stage the play; you will do only a reading—with scripts and with one student sometimes playing more than one character or one character divided among several students. The reading should last five to eight minutes. This activity will help you gain more insights into the play, and, in turn, your audience will profit.

Suggested scenes

1. Scene for three males and three females: Act I, Scene 3. Begin page 389 with Mrs. Frank's line "Please, Mr. Dussel, sit down." End page 391 with Mr. Dussel's line "If you'll excuse me."
   1 male—Mr. Dussel   1 female—Mrs. Frank
   1 male—Mr. Frank   1 female—Anne
   1 male—Mr. Van   1 female—Mrs. Van
      Daan   Daan and Margot

2. Scene for four males and two females: Act II, Scene 3.
   1 male—Mr. Frank   1 female—Mrs. Frank
   1 male—Mr. Dussel   1 female—Mrs. Van
   1 male—Mr. Van   Daan and Anne
      Daan   [Drop Margot's line.]
   1 male—Peter and
      stage directions

3. Scene for two males and one female: Act I, Scene 2. Begin page 375 with Anne's line "What's your cat's name?" End with end of scene.
   1 male—Peter   1 female—Anne
   1 male—Mr. Frank

4. Scenes for three females:
   ● Act I, Scene 3. Begin page 386 with Mrs. Frank's line "You must not behave that way."
   ● Act II, Scene 2. Begin page 415 with Anne's line, "No, no, Mr. Dussel!"

5. Scenes for one male and one female: pages 375, 412, 417, 427

▬ PREPARING AN ORAL INTERPRETATION

1. **Analyze the scene and assign roles.**
   As your group reads the scene, discuss its meaning. What is the scene trying to show?

   Example: The point of the scene in which Mr. Van Daan is caught stealing food shows both the shortage of food and the problems that develop among people who must share a small space for a long time.

   Decide who in your group will read which role. You may have to read the scene several times, having different people try the same role, and then decide who is best suited to it.

2. **Develop characterization.**
   Each reader must discover the outstanding traits of his or her character and find ways to reveal these traits to the audience through voice.

   Examples: Mr. Frank's compassion might be shown by soft, quick speech as he comforts Anne after a nightmare. His strength might be shown by slow, firm speech as he commands the group to be still when he hears noise downstairs.

   Think also of body movements. Does the character, for example, stand straight or slouch?

596   *Speaking and Listening Handbook*

Select two or three gestures that you think would be typical of your character.

3. Incorporate stage directions.

As you read the play, you will actually follow some stage directions—such as those referring to voice. Other stage directions—such as those referring to props or scenery or major movements (e.g., a character throwing herself on a couch)—will have to be read to the audience rather than performed by the reader. All such stage directions can be read by one student or shared by the group. Regarding exiting as indicated in stage directions: Consider turning your back on the audience to indicate an exit, and then turn back to face the audience for an entrance.

4. Select positions.

Even though your reading is not a full-scale theatrical production, how you position yourselves while reading is important. You might place major characters in the center and minor characters to the sides. You can sit or stand as appropriate.

5. Pace the scene.

You must be able to pick up your cue—the last thing the character before you says—because you do not want to have an unnecessarily long pause between speeches. Be ready to begin your speech right after the preceding character ends.

Slow down or speed up the tempo of a scene according to what is happening.

Example: The Hanukkah scene (Act I, Scene 5) might begin slowly with the reading from the prayer book, speed up considerably as Anne presents the gifts, and then contain a long, significant pause with all freezing as they hear the crash downstairs.

6. Prepare a manuscript for your role.

It is a good idea for you to prepare a script of your cues, your lines, and notes about all the matters covered in the preceding five points.

PERFORMING THE PLAYREADING

In addition to speaking loudly and clearly enough to be heard by everyone in the audience and positioning yourself so that you can be seen, pay attention to these points:

1. Concentration

You must give all your attention to your character and to the playreading. Remain very still when you are not speaking so that you will not distract other readers.

2. Familiarity with the script

If you rehearse enough, you will gain a familiarity with the script and with your role in particular. You will then be able to speak some of your lines "by heart," spontaneously and meaningfully. You will then be able to use your eyes to suggest that you are addressing another character. Another advantage to being able to look up rather than burying your eyes in the script is that the audience will be able to see the expressions on your face.

ASSIGNMENT

You can work on any of the scenes suggested earlier in this lesson or on any other scene of your own choice from *The Diary of Anne Frank*. In addition, you may decide to select a scene from *The Romancers*.

Speaking and Listening Handbook **597**

Each of the six lessons in this handbook serves to integrate a particular thinking skill with the experience of literature. Each lesson is literature-based and demonstrates to the student that the active reader is a thinking reader, that the results of thinking are both understanding and enjoyment. The step-by-step format of each lesson allows for either teacher involvement or student independence. Gradually, as students continue to use the procedures shown in the lessons, they can grow more and more independent as thinkers about literature and as confident, thinking young adults.

Each lesson is structured in the following way:

- DEFINITION—A clear, jargon-free definition that expresses the thinking skill in a student's own terms
- EXAMPLE—A model of the thinking skill being applied in a literature-based situation. Each example emphasizes the student's own experience in using the skill.
- EXPLANATION—A detailed "walk-through" of the example, demonstrating and discussing each individual step in the application of the thinking skill.
- PROCEDURES—A list and summary of the individual steps used in the example and the explanation. Identifying procedures is an essential step in thinking about thinking and developing independence.
- ACTIVITIES—All activities are literature-based. Those activities keyed to specific literary selections give the student an opportunity to follow the correct procedures in thinking about some aspect of the selection. Those activities not keyed to specific literary selections provide the opportunity to transfer the thinking skill to a new literary situation.

THINKING SKILLS HANDBOOK

LESSON 1: *Representation*

DEFINITION

Representation involves changing the way that you perceive information. If the information is in words, making pictures or diagrams is a different way of representing that information. This is called *graphic* representation. If the information is given in some type of picture or diagram, thinking about its meaning in words is another way of representing that information. In making graphic representations, different shapes may be used to represent different ideas. Graphic representations make it easier to *select* what is important, *integrate* and *organize* the different parts, and *summarize*.

EXAMPLE

Comparison charts may be used to compare and contrast two or more of anything: characters, authors, periods of time, short stories, and so on. These charts may be used before, during, and after reading to guide reading, note taking, and writing a composition. For example, Bobbie Jo was asked to compare and contrast the use of suspense in three stories in the Short Story unit— "Spring Victory" (page 32), "The Mixed-Up Feet and the Silly Bridegroom" (page 42), and "Fire!" (page 48).

EXPLANATION

To help organize her thoughts, Bobbie Jo constructed a comparison chart. The names of the three stories were column headings. The elements in the story that lead to the sense of suspense were row headings. Her comparison chart looked like the one at the bottom of the page.

She used this chart to guide her note taking as she reread and reconsidered parts of each story. Then, when she finished her note taking, she used the chart to help organize her composition. Basically she used the information in the column and row headings for her introductory paragraph. Then she used the information in each row for three middle paragraphs: one on the effects of setting on suspense, one on how the events created suspense, and one on how the characterization led to suspense.

PROCEDURES

1. **Identify the things to be compared**, and place them as column headings in a chart like the one above.

2. **Decide on the points of comparison**, and place them as row headings.

3. Use the chart to **take notes** by filling in as

Elements for suspense	"Spring Victory"	"Mixed-Up Feet"	"Fire!"
Setting			
Events			
Characters			

598   *Thinking Skills Handbook*

many cells as you can. Sometimes you will end up with some empty cells. For each empty cell, ask yourself whether you could have skipped some relevant information. If you have, go back and fill in the cell. If not, you may be able to use the fact that the cell is empty in your composition. For example, you may be able to say that the author does not use the setting to create suspense.

4. Analyze the information in the comparison chart as follows:

   a. *Analyze the row information.* Ask yourself whether the items in the cells for row 1 are basically similar or different. This means you will read each row from left to right. Look for underlying patterns in each row.

   b. *Analyze the column information.* Skim the information in each column. This means you will read each column from top to bottom. Ask yourself whether there are more similarities than differences among the columns. Look for underlying patterns.

5. Use the chart to **organize your compare-and-contrast compositon**.

   a. *In the introductory paragraph.* In a sentence or two identify the column headings (the names of the authors, characters, and so on) to be compared. Also identify the points of comparison in the row headings.

   b. *In each middle paragraph.* Make a generalization about the similarities or differences among items in each row. This will be your topic sentence. Support your topic sentence by using the information in the cells for each row.

   c. *For the conclusion.* Make a general statement from your column analysis. That is, state whether the things compared are basically similar or different considering the information in each of the rows.

▦ ACTIVITY I. REPRESENTING INFORMATION ABOUT SHORT STORIES

Construct a comparison chart for one of the following:

1. Compare the elements of suspense in "Spring Victory," "The Mixed-Up Feet and the Silly Bridegroom," and "Fire!" using Bobbie Jo's chart in the example.

2. Compare the conflicts in "Spring Victory," "Charles" (page 53), and "Christmas Day in the Morning" (page 59). (Hint: Brainstorm with your teacher or your classmate to decide which conflicts in each story you will choose as row headings.)

▦ ACTIVITY II. USING REPRESENTATION TO ORGANIZE A COMPOSITION

Compare the problems faced by characters in any two short stories you have read. Hint: For this chart you will have two *sets* of traits—the various behaviors that make up the problem (fear, ignorance, pride, and so on) and the solutions that each person finds for the problem.

Use the following chart to organize a comparison composition. The first paragraph identifies what is being compared (the column headings) and the points of comparison (the row headings). You will have two middle paragraphs: one on the problems and one on the solutions. In the conclusion you may want to compare the two characters in terms of which solution was the most effective and why it was effective.

	Character 1	Character 2
Problem behaviors	1. 2.	1. 2.
Solutions	1. 2.	1. 2.

Thinking Skills Handbook 599

The detailed lessons in this handbook are not the only application of thinking skills in the *Scribner Literature Series.* Throughout each book students also practice and reinforce thinking skills through the following features:
- Purpose-setting questions
- Study Questions divided into Recalling, Interpreting, and Extending categories
- Thinking About . . . questions within Reading and Literary Focuses
- Models for Active Reading

LESSON 2:   Problem Solving

▮▮ DEFINITION

Problem solving is a way of thinking. It involves identifying a goal, the obstacles to that goal, and methods for getting through or around those obstacles. Problem solving involves thinking in an orderly fashion. No matter what you are thinking about, if you can define the problem, you can also use your problem-solving skills to solve it. Poetry, for example, does not usually present its ideas in an orderly fashion. But reading and understanding poetry can sometimes be made easier if you approach it as a problem solver.

▮▮ EXAMPLE

Three students are assigned to read and report to the class on a poem about an event in the American Revolution. In their report the group is to include a discussion of the poem's language, historical background, and form. After reading the poem several times both silently and aloud, the group does not understand certain parts of the poem and is unable to plan the report.

▮▮ EXPLANATION

1. **Goal**—what you want
   The goal in this example is to report on the language, historical background, and form of a particular poem, according to the directions of the teacher. Providing this information will solve your problem.

2. **Givens**—what you start with
   The members of the group have read many poems before. They have also studied American history. They have read the particular poem about the revolution.

3. **Obstacles**—things that get in the way of a solution
   - The poem uses some vocabulary words the students have never seen before.

- The poem describes a particular event the students have never read about.
- The poem is in a form the students have never seen before.

4. **Methods**—how things will be done
   The group "brainstorms" to come up with a variety of ideas. By considering each obstacle, the students identify the methods they will use to solve the problem.
   - The students agree that they will divide the report into three parts and that each of them will do one part.
   - The student working on the language of the poem will identify each unfamiliar word, look it up in a dictionary, and provide the other students in the group with the definitions.
   - The student working on the background of the poem will look up the American Revolution in an encyclopedia and in a history book and provide the other students with the historical background that will help to clarify the poem.
   - The student working on the form of the poem will ask the librarian for help in finding a book about poetic forms. If necessary, the student will also show the poem to an older friend who is studying American poetry.

5. **Carrying out the plan**
   Each student found the necessary information and shared it with the other students. The group found that they were able to help each other as they each solved part of the problem. For example, some of the vocabulary words had special meanings in the time of the American Revolution and helped make the historical background of the poem clearer. The group reported its findings to the class.

600   *Thinking Skills Handbook*

6. Checking the results

The teacher rated the report on content, equal participation, clear organization, and length. The teacher, the three reporters, and the class audience were pleased.

▨ PROCEDURES

1. State a goal.

If you can say clearly what the goal is, you can usually also define the problem clearly.

2. List the givens.

What information is available to you as you start to think about the problem?

3. List the obstacles.

Obstacles are those things that prevent a solution. If there are no obstacles, there probably is no problem. Obstacles may be easy to see and clearly stated. They may also be unstated or hidden. In many cases, identifying the obstacles in as much detail as possible helps to suggest specific methods to remove those obstacles.

4. Identify the methods.

What are you going to do to reach a solution? What is your plan of attack? What steps will eliminate each obstacle?

5. Carry out the plan.

6. Check the results.

Have you solved the problem?

▨ ACTIVITY I. FOLLOWING THE PROBLEM-SOLVING SEQUENCE IN A POEM

The purpose of this activity is to identify the steps in the problem-solving sequence as one poet uses them.

1. Read Robert Frost's poem "A Minor Bird" (page 253).

2. State the problem faced by the speaker.

3. What are the **givens** in the speaker's situation?

4. What is the **obstacle**?

5. What is the speaker's **method**, or plan?

6. Does the speaker **carry out the plan**?

7. Check the results. Is the plan a success?

8. What further decision does the speaker make?

▨ ACTIVITY II. DEFINING A PROBLEM IN A POEM

The purpose of this activity is to apply the steps in the problem-solving sequence to any poem in this book.

1. Select and read a poem. Your **goal** is to gain an understanding of the poem.

2. State the **givens** of the situation. The poem itself is the basic given. However, do not forget to state any background knowledge you have of the poem's subject, as well as any personal experience you may have about the poem's subject.

3. State the **obstacles** to solving the problem. List everything you do not understand about the poem.

4. Describe the **methods**, or the plan, you will use to find the answers to your questions.

5. Carry out the plan by making an oral statement or writing out what you think the poem means.

6. Check the results by comparing your interpretation with interpretations by other people. Remember that there may be more than one satisfying answer. Do you find your interpretation satisfying? Have you solved the problem?

LESSON 3: Inductive Inquiry

■ DEFINITION

Inductive inquiry is a way to *discover* meaning by observation. In fact, it is sometimes called discovery learning. When you inquire inductively, you observe several examples of a thing and discover how they are alike. You discover what features they share—that is, what they have in common. You also discover how the examples differ from one another.

■ EXAMPLE

If you have read newspaper articles about news events, read someone's autobiography or biography, or seen a documentary movie, then you have experienced nonfiction. The Nonfiction unit in this book includes selections that are different from each other in a number of ways. However, they are all nonfiction. They deal with different topics and are written in different styles. What, then, makes them nonfiction?

■ EXPLANATION

In order to **inquire** into the special features of the idea of nonfiction, you first need to **find some examples** of nonfiction. You may, for example, choose three selections you have read from the unit called "Nonfiction" in this book.

Your next step is to **identify the general characteristics** of each of the nonfiction selections you have chosen. Then, after you have identified those characteristics, you **identify which characteristics are common** to all of the nonfiction selections.

Making a chart to **display** all of the characteristics is often very helpful. A chart that displays the general characteristics of nonfiction might look something like the chart at the top of the next column.

Characteristics	Work 1	Work 2	Work 3
Thesis statement	+	+	+
Realistic details	+	+	+
Verifiability	+	+	+
Narrative	+	–	–
Exposition	–	+	–
Persuasion	–	–	+

The plus and minus signs indicate whether or not a selection has (+) or does not have (–) that characteristic. Looking closely at the chart, you see that three characteristics—thesis statement, realistic details, and verifiability—are common to all the examples you examined. Once you have identified common characteristics, you can more accurately and easily recognize any new example of nonfiction.

It is also useful to **test your findings** against examples that are not likely to share the characteristics. In this case, it would be a good idea to test your findings about nonfiction against an example of fiction. Add one more column to your chart, a column for a fiction selection, a non-example.

Characteristics	Work 1	Work 2	Work 3	Non-example
Thesis statement	+	+	+	–
Realistic details	+	+	+	+
Verifiability	+	+	+	–
Narrative	+	–	–	+
Exposition	–	+	–	–
Persuasion	–	–	+	–

Looking closely at this chart, you see that the non-example does share two characteristics of nonfiction—realistic details and narrative. But the chart shows that those two characteristics are not enough to make a work of nonfiction. The non-example still does not share any of the other characteristics. Adding more examples and non-examples will give more support to your findings.

PROCEDURES

1. In order to inquire into a particular idea, first **examine familiar examples** of the idea.

2. **List all the general characteristics** you can think of that are true of each of the examples.

3. **Display the list** in a way that helps you see the pattern of common characteristics.

4. **Identify the pattern** of common characteristics.

5. **Test your findings** by comparing what you found to be true of the idea with the characteristics of a non-example. You will find some characteristics that are special to your idea and that do not occur in the non-example.

ACTIVITY I. INQUIRING INTO AN IDEA IN NONFICTION

The purpose of this activity is to apply the steps of inductive inquiry to discover the common characteristics of communities presented in nonfiction.

1. What does the word *community* mean to you? List the general characteristics of some familiar communities. Then **identify at least two examples** of communities described in nonfiction in this book.

2. Using the nonfiction selections chosen for step 1, **list all the general characteristics** that are true of each community. For example, does the group have a purpose? A leader? Where does the group live? What experiences are shared?

3. **Display the list** in a way that helps you see the pattern of common characteristics.

4. **Identify the pattern.**

5. **Test your findings** by comparing what you found to be true of the examples of community with the characteristics of a closely related non-example. (Consider other kinds of groups, such as a mob or a crowd.)

6. **Write a brief summary** of the characteristics of the idea of community as you found it shown in nonfiction. Support your findings with the specific examples you used.

ACTIVITY II. INQUIRING INTO THE IDEA OF HAPPINESS IN LITERATURE

1. Using any work of nonfiction, fiction, poetry, or drama that you have read, **identify five examples** of happiness.

2. **List all the general characteristics** you can think of that are true of each example. Did happiness come from achieving a goal, from winning something, from doing something, from not doing something? Did happiness last for a moment or for a long time?

3. **Display the list** in a way that helps you see the pattern of common characteristics.

4. **Identify the pattern.**

5. **Test your findings** by comparing what you found to be true of the examples with the characteristics of a closely related non-example, such as unhappiness.

6. **Write a brief summary** of the characteristics of the idea of happiness as you have found it shown in literature. Support your findings with the specific examples.

LESSON 4: *Logical Reasoning*

DEFINITION

Logical reasoning is a way of thinking. It is a way of putting together an explanation that can stand up to a challenge. When you reason logically, you state the *conditions that are necessary* for the explanation to hold. You then determine whether there is *sufficient evidence* to conclude that the conditions have actually been met.

In order for logical reasoning to be effective, you and your audience must share the same set of assumptions. **Assumptions** are the ideas you and your audience take for granted without needing any evidence or support. For example, if you were comparing the performance of two cars, you would assume that both cars were in working condition.

EXAMPLE

Some characters in stories, plays, and movies are called *heroes*. The conditions that are necessary for them to be called heroes are actions in a particular set of circumstances—that is, what they do in certain situations. The hero often faces a threatening situation, is forceful and decisive, solves a problem or removes a danger, and is self-sacrificing.

If you wanted to reason logically to convince someone that a character in a certain drama is a hero, you would begin by identifying the conditions which are necessary for a character to be considered heroic. (In this case, you would point to a threatening situation, forcefulness and decisiveness, problem solving, the removal of a danger, and self-sacrifice.) Then you would show that there is sufficient evidence (details in the drama) to meet these conditions. You would also expect that your audience shares your assumptions that this same set of conditions is required for a character to be considered a hero.

EXPLANATION

Both you and your audience assume that the conditions that are necessary for a character to be a hero are threatening circumstances, decisive action, and solving a problem or removing a danger. In addition, some heroes also sacrifice their lives. Is this last quality—sacrificing life—a necessary condition for heroism?

It will help you to make a chart to display the features of each example of a character you are trying to classify as a hero. On this chart you can examine the features of each character to see whether they match the necessary conditions. Such a chart might look like this:

Features	Example 1	Example 2	Example 3
Threatening situation	+	+	+
Decisive action	+	+	+
Removing danger	+	+	+
Loss of life	−	+	−

Example 2 has all the features of heroism that we have identified. But examples 1 and 3 do not share the feature of loss of life. These three examples show that it is not absolutely necessary for a character to sacrifice life in order to be a hero. On the other hand, the three examples are sufficient evidence to suggest that the other features are necessary conditions for heroism. When you demonstrate that any character meets the *necessary conditions* for heroism, you engage in *logical reasoning*.

PROCEDURES

1. **State what you believe** to be true.

2. **Identify all the conditions that are necessary** for the situation to be true.

3. Show how the necessary conditions have been met. **Give specific examples that constitute sufficient evidence** to support your position.

4. **Identify the important assumptions** you and your audience must share in order for your position to be convincing.

◼ ACTIVITY I. REASONING LOGICALLY ABOUT A WORK OF DRAMA

The plays in the Drama unit of this book (pages 349–437) describe many different kinds of love. The purpose of this activity is to determine whether a particular play provides sufficient evidence to reveal one kind of love to the audience.

1. **Choose an example** of one kind of love that is illustrated in a play you have read or seen. Consider romantic love, love of country, love for a parent, or love for a child.

2. **List the conditions that are necessary** for this type of love to be evident—that is, tell how the characters might be expected to act in order to demonstrate their feelings of love.

3. On a chart **identify specific examples** from the play—evidence—that would be sufficient to support your idea that this kind of love is presented in the play.

4. **Identify the assumptions** that you and your audience share about the kind of love being presented.

5. **Write a brief statement** in which you present your position and state logical reasons supporting your position—the necessary conditions and sufficient evidence.

◼ ACTIVITY II. REASONING LOGICALLY ABOUT A LITERARY CHARACTER

The purpose of this activity is to demonstrate logically that a literary character possesses a certain character trait, or quality.

1. **Choose any literary character** you like. Identify one outstanding character trait.

2. **Describe the conditions** under which this character would necessarily demonstrate this trait.

3. **Find examples** of this character's actions that constitute sufficient evidence to show that the character's behavior indeed demonstrates that trait.

4. **Describe what you assume to be true** of the character and why that trait would show up under certain conditions.

5. **Write a brief statement** describing your position and the logical reasons for it.

LESSON 5: *Evaluation*

■ DEFINITION

When you **evaluate** something, you make a judgment about it. Evaluation requires determining the value, beauty, effectiveness, truthfulness, or reliability of something. In order to evaluate properly, you need to apply an appropriate criterion. A **criterion** is a standard, rule, or test on which a judgment can be based.

■ EXAMPLE

In order to promote school spirit, the English teachers at a certain school are conducting an essay contest on the topic "Our School's Most Interesting Character." The contest rules are the following:

1. The subject may be anyone who attended the school for at least two years.

2. The essay must be 950 to 1,000 words in length.

3. There may be no false information, exaggeration, or ridicule in the essay.

4. The essay must be written on white lined paper in ink or typed.

5. Essays with more than three errors in spelling or grammar will be disqualified.

6. The winner's essay will be printed in the school paper, and the winner will be presented with twenty-five free movie passes.

■ EXPLANATION

The essays will be evaluated according to the contest rules. The rules are the criteria. Good evaluation requires appropriate and clear criteria. According to the rules for this contest, would an essay about a former principal of the school be accepted or rejected? Would an essay written on a word processor be accepted? Would an essay containing grammatically incorrect quotations be accepted? Answers to these questions suggest that criteria are not always as simple and clear as they appear to be. In doing evaluative thinking, it is always a good idea to think carefully first about the criteria to be used. Only after the criteria are clear and complete should we apply them and make the judgment.

■ PROCEDURES

1. **Start with a reason or purpose** for evaluation.

2. **Identify the criteria**—the rules, tests, or standards you will use to make a judgment.

3. **Apply the criteria**.

4. **Draw a conclusion**. Your conclusion will be your evaluation.

■ ACTIVITY I. DEVELOPING CRITERIA FOR EVALUATING MYTHS AND FOLK TALES

The purpose of this activity is to create a set of criteria.

1. Review the unit called "Greek Myths and American Folk Tales" (pages 439–499) to find characteristics typical of heroes. The word *hero* can refer to a person admired for courage, fortitude, prowess, nobility, and so on. It can also refer to the principal character in a play, story, or poem. Not all principal characters are to be admired, but sometimes they are heroes.

606   *Thinking Skills Handbook*

What you are to look for, however, are *characteristics* we admire, such as courage, power to endure pain or hardship, valor, or skill.

2. **Compile a list** of such characteristics for each hero you find.

3. When you have made a list for each hero, **compare the lists**.

4. **Select the most frequently occurring characteristics** from each list, and list them separately.

5. These frequently occurring characteristics of the heroes in this unit will be the criteria you can use for evaluating other heroes.

6. **Compare your criteria** with those of other students. Note the specific criteria that are like those of other students. Note the criteria you listed that are different. Be prepared to give reasons why you selected each criterion on your list. Be prepared to ask questions about any criterion with which you do not agree or that you do not understand.

ACTIVITY II. EVALUATING SUPERHEROES

1. **Select three of four superheroes** from television or the movies.

2. **Apply your criteria** for evaluating heroes to each of the superheroes on your list. You may want to make a chart to display the criteria you are applying to each hero.

3. **Evaluate today's superheroes**. Do today's superheroes have any of the same qualities as those found in Greek mythology and American folklore? What qualities are different? Do today's heroes have more of certain qualities? Do they have less of certain qualities? Are today's heroes more or less interesting than the heroes of the past?

4. Use the criteria to **evaluate some of the villains** in today's television shows or movies. What characteristics do the villains lack that the heroes have? In what ways are villains similar to heroes?

5. **Identify the main differences** between villains and heroes, based on your evaluation.

LESSON 6: *Synthesis*

DEFINITION

Synthesis involves combining elements from different sources into some kind of organized product. The product must be more than an essay discussing some element from two or more pieces of literature. In a synthesis there has to be some evidence of a pattern or structure that you are noticing—a pattern or structure that was not obvious before your thought about the individual pieces. Synthesis involves the creation of something new.

EXAMPLE

John is preparing a report on the recent award of a literary prize. He must consider both sides of a controversy: Two groups disagree about who should have been given the award. He must create a synthesis, a conclusion.

EXPLANATION

The key elements in John's report are the two different points of view, the supporting evidence for each point of view, and the conclusion he will construct. His conclusion should be a well-organized statement that did not exist before he constructed it.

John's **purpose** is clear—to examine the situation and clarify it for his audience, presenting a conclusion based on differing points. He **identifies the elements** he has to work with—the two points of view. He **states a relationship** between the elements—that they are opposed on the main issue but agree on many other points. He **constructs an original product**—a report that expresses the relationship between the two sides. His report is a synthesis, a combining of information into something new, something that did not exist before he made it.

PROCEDURES

1. **Identify the purpose** of the activity.

2. **Identify the elements** to be combined.

3. **State a relationship** among the elements, and represent the relationship in a graphic form if possible.

4. **Construct an original product** that expresses the relationship. The product may be a plan, a statement of the relationship, a written work, or the application of a particular point of view to something.

ACTIVITY I. PLANNING A LETTER ON AMERICA

The purpose of this activity is to develop a plan for writing a letter on America as it is described in literature. The letter is from your class to another group of students of the same age in another country.

1. **Brainstorm** to identify literary selections you have read that describe America in some way.

2. **Identify the concepts and facts** in each selection that tell you something important about living in America—both in the past and in the present. Make a list of concepts and facts for each selection.

3. **Group together the facts** that deal with similar topics, such as America's heroes, nature, history, art, and politics. Note: Some selections may relate to more than one topic; be sure to consider all selections on a given topic.

4. **Develop a plan** for the letter. **Discuss the topics** you want to develop. **Consider** the follow-

608   *Thinking Skills Handbook*

ing questions:

- How many topics will you write about?
- Which topics of all those listed will you include? Why?
- How will you organize the letter?
- What pictures, drawings, or photos will you include?

ACTIVITY II. EXAMINING DIFFERENT POINTS OF VIEW

The purpose of this activity is to examine different points of view regarding the causes of specific events.

1. Working in small groups, **select a work of literature** that focuses on a problem. (Each group should choose a different selection.)

2. **Identify a series of events or actions** within the selection. **Label them** in some way. (For example, "Mary wins prize" might be the label of one event in the short story "Mary" on page 103.) It is important to agree on the nature of the events and their labels before proceeding to the next step.

3. **Divide the small group** into two teams. Team A will **develop the argument** that the events occurred the way they did primarily because of specific decisions of the individuals involved. Team B will **develop the opposite point of view**—namely, that individuals are not really in control of the events because of forces beyond their control or because of luck.

   Note: Each team should outline its argument. You do not necessarily have to believe that your team's argument is really correct. That is, you may believe that the event was caused by individual decisions but be on the team that has to present the opposite point of view.

4. Each small group should **present the two opposing arguments** (one from team A and one from team B) to the rest of the class. Each presentation should be no longer than three to five minutes.

5. As a whole class consider whether there is some position in between those expressed by the A teams and the B teams.

ACTIVITY III. DEFINING HEROISM

The purpose of this analysis is to establish a definition of heroism that is realistic—an ideal for real people to achieve.

1. Each group should **select a genre** (short stories, nonfiction, drama, myths, or folk tales) that includes selections focusing on the theme of heroism.

2. **Identify selections** within the genre that relate to heroism. **Review the events and character traits** of the heroes or heroines in those selections.

3. Still working in small groups, **construct a definition** of heroism that fits the events and character traits within the chosen genre. Each group should include in its definition at least three examples of heroism from the selections.

4. **Share** the **definition** with the whole class.

5. As a class, **reflect on the different definitions** of heroism. For each definition, **decide** whether human beings could in fact ever achieve the various traits and behaviors included in that definition.

6. Still working as a whole class, **construct a definition** of heroism that humans could achieve.

Thinking Skills Handbook 609

READING AND STUDY SKILLS HANDBOOK

Each of the four lessons in this handbook provides students with a direct instructional model of a reading skill or a study skill important for the active reading and study of literature. Each lesson is literature-based and emphasizes the application of a particular skill so that the student may more fully understand the ideas of a literary selection.

Each lesson is structured in the following way:

- EXPLANATION AND EXAMPLES— A definition of the reading or study skill, with clear examples drawn from students' own experiences. Each example is explained as the student is walked through each step in the application of the skill.
- PRACTICE—Literature-based activities for using the reading or study skill and examining how it is used.
- FURTHER ASSIGNMENTS—All assignments are literature-based. Those assignments keyed to specific literary selections give the students the opportunity to apply the skill. Those assignments not keyed to specific literary selections provide the opportunity to transfer the reading or study skill to any literary situation.

The detailed lessons in this handbook are not the only application of reading and study skills in the *Scribner Literature Series*. Throughout each book students also practice and reinforce reading and study skills through the following features:

- Purpose-setting questions
- Study Questions divided into Recalling, Interpreting, and Extending categories
- Reading and Literary Focuses
- Models for Active Reading
- Active Reading end-of-unit pages

LESSON 1: *Finding the Main Idea of a Whole Selection*

■ EXPLANATION AND EXAMPLES

When it is necessary to read many pieces of literature, identifying the main idea of each selection will help you both to clarify your thoughts and to retain the information for future use. Identifying the main idea will come in useful with your school work now and later in life also.

Each *paragraph* that you read has a main idea—the most important point that the writer wants to make about the subject of the paragraph. Sometimes the writer states the main idea directly, but most of the time he or she does not. If the author does not state the main idea, you need to study the details in the paragraph, using them to figure out the main idea on your own.

Most of what we read is longer than one paragraph. Think about your most recent reading assignment in science. How long was it? Three paragraphs? Two pages? One chapter? What about your literature assignment? Aren't you usually told to read an *entire* story—not just one paragraph?

Rather than thinking of reading assignments as being three or more separate paragraphs that just *happen* to be grouped together, regard them instead as pieces of a whole . . . like parts of a bicycle. Taken individually, the parts might include two wheels, two pedals, handlebars, seat, chain, brakes, reflectors, etc. Only when they are put together do you have a bicycle. It is the same with reading selections that are longer than a paragraph: You must understand that the individual paragraphs—and individual main ideas—add up to something significant.

■ NOTING ORGANIZATION

It will probably help if you first decide how the material you are reading has been organized. Keep in mind the following types of text structures. (You might want to turn to the examples in this book and check them out yourself.)

Problem/Solution

Some selections deal with solving a problem. A detective story like the one about Sherlock Holmes (page 503) illustrates this type of selection. Obviously, the main idea of such a selection has to do with the problem and its solution.

Antecedent/Consequences

In this type of selection, one event or situation will bring about certain consequences, or results. You might want to call this the "if this, then" type of selection. The short passage "Adjusting Rate of Reading" (page 26) is this type of writing. It basically says, "*If* you are reading this type of material, *then* you will read faster, but *if* you are reading another type of material, *then* you will need to read slower."

Comparison/Contrast

This kind of selection either compares two items (tells how they are the same) or contrasts them (tells how they are different). The section entitled "Recognizing Differences and Similarities" (page 24) is a shining example of this type of writing. It talks about how several types of literature are different and how they are the same.

610   *Reading and Study Skills Handbook*

come based on these clues. As you continue reading, you gather more clues. These additional clues will lead you to one of the following conclusions about each of your predictions:

1. Keep it.
2. Discard it and make another prediction about the outcome.
3. Change the prediction slightly based on the new information.

PRACTICE

Read the following paragraph, and use the clues to predict what will happen next.

Joe was in his room practicing his violin. He practiced his violin every day after school for an hour. His parents said he had to finish his practicing before he could go out and play with his friends. He sure didn't want to be there that day. Looking out his window, he could see all his friends playing football in the empty lot next door. Suddenly his mother called upstairs, "Joe, I've got a meeting with a potential buyer for that house I'm trying to sell on the other side of town. I'm going to meet with them downtown at the office. I'll be home in a couple of hours. Tell your father when he gets home. He should be here in another hour." Joe continued practicing a little while longer. Then he looked outside. His mother's car was no longer in the driveway.

- What will Joe probably do?
- What clues help you make your prediction?

ASSIGNMENTS

1. Turn to page 64, and read the first paragraph of the story "Thank you, M'am" by Langston Hughes. Read only the first paragraph.

- Write your prediction of what will happen next.
- Write the clues in the paragraph that led you to this prediction.
- What knowledge from personal experience did you have that led you to this prediction?

2. In the story "Spring Victory" by Jesse Stuart, the father has been sick for a long time and the family is running out of food and money. Use the clues provided in the following short excerpt from that story to make your best prediction about what will eventually happen. In this excerpt the mother is talking to two of the children:

"Son, we are not whipped yet," Mom said to me. "Your Pa is asleep now. I'll tell you what we are going to do."

I walked over beside Mom's chair. Sophie stood beside her too.

"Sophie can do the cooking," Mom said. "Can't you bake bread and cook potatoes, Sophie?"

"Yes, Mom."

"And you can use an ax well for a boy ten years old," Mom said.

"It's easy for me to chop with my pole-ax."

"Then you take your ax and go to the hills," Mom said pointing from the front window to the steep snow-covered bluff east of our house. "You can find all kinds of tough-butted white oaks on the bluff over there. Cut them down, trim them and scoot them over the hill. We're going to make baskets out of them."

- What do you predict will happen next?
- What clues in the story led you to make this prediction?

LESSON 3:   *Studying for a Test*

■■■ EXPLANATION AND EXAMPLES

"Boy do I ever have to cram tonight. I've got a test tomorrow morning in lit class and I've still got five stories to read. With my luck the teacher will decide that these are the most important stories to test."

There's a better way to study for a test than cramming. This lesson will present some alternatives to cramming. As you read about them, think about how you can integrate them into your present study strategies.

In general, this better approach is *Don't CRAM; do PLAN.* Let's go through it step by step, first looking at what you should not do when you need to study for a test. (HINT FOR REMEMBERING: Look at the first letter of the first word following the four *Don'ts*. Notice how they spell *CRAM.*)

1. **DON'T cling to bad study habits**.
   Do you, for example, read your assignments without establishing a reason for reading? Do you stay up late every night even though you have to be at school at eight in the morning? Do you daydream in class instead of listening to points the teacher and classmates are making about the story? You must avoid these bad study habits. Don't cling to them. Throw them out!

   - Before you read anything, decide why you are reading. (It may be to solve a problem, for example.)
   - Get plenty of rest so you are alert in school.
   - Pay attention in class.

2. **DON'T read all the material for the very first time the night before your test**.
   Spread your reading out over a period. Read the material when it is assigned so you only have to *review* it the night before the test.

3. **DON'T allow other interests to take you away from your studying.**
   If you carefully plan your time, you can frequently attend to other interests also. Just do them *after* studying, not before.

4. **DON'T make excuses for not studying.**
   Some excuses can be quite creative: "Joe was holding my book while I tied my shoe, and I forgot to get it back from him." "I forgot the assignment." "The assignment isn't due until next week." The time wasted on making up creative excuses is just that—wasted.

   Now let's look at what you *should* do. Do plan. (HINT FOR REMEMBERING: The first letters of these *do* items spell *PLAN*.)

1. **DO participate in class**.
   The more you are actively involved, the better you will remember points that might appear later on a test. Participation means answering questions. It also means *asking* questions. If you do not understand something, ask for an explanation.

2. **DO listen carefully for hints from the teacher about what is important.**
   For example, your teacher might write several main points from the story on the board. Jot these down. Then again, your teacher might say, "This is a key point" or "This is vital information" or even "This would be a good test question." Clues like these should signal you to pay particular attention to these areas. Again, you might want to jot them down in your notebook.

614   *Reading and Study Skills Handbook*

3. **DO ask the teacher questions about the test**.

- What kinds of questions will there be? Essay? Short answer?
- Will you have to know the authors?
- Will you need to put story events in order?
- Will you need to identify characters by what they said?
- How many questions will there be on the test?
- Will there be questions about all of the stories?
- Will you need to explain what a novel (short story, poem, etc.) *is*?

No test should be a supreme surprise. The answers to your questions will help you choose what is and what is not important to review.

4. **DO notice "hints" of key points in your textbook**.

These will be pieces of information that you will want to study for the test. There are many such hints in your literature book. For example, before each selection there is a short paragraph about the author ending with questions about the selection. This question is a hint. (The question in the paragraph preceding Pearl S. Buck's story "Christmas Day in the Morning" is "What understanding does the man in the story reach by the story's end?") The questions at the end of the reading selection will also be good reviews. Also look for diagrams of concepts (like the one about plot on page 41) or bold print.

■ PRACTICE

Read the following examples of students' studying (or not studying). Identify which *Don't CRAM; do PLAN* point applies.

1. Joan is sitting in lit class. Her book is open to the story the class is talking about, but Joan is thinking about the new outfit she saw yesterday at the mall.

2. Jeff is trying to find out more about the test he's going to have next week: "Mr. Lesman, are we going to be tested on *all* of the stories? What will you ask about them?"

3. While listening to the class discuss the story "Charles" one day, Pamela hears Ms. Everett say, "The clues the author provides about Charles's identity are known as foreshadowing. This is an important technique for you to recognize and use." Pamela writes down the word *foreshadowing* in her notebook.

■ ASSIGNMENT

Think of the last time you studied for a test. Explain how your approach to studying used (or did *not* use) the *Don't CRAM; do PLAN* strategies. What (if anything) will you do differently when you study for the next test?

LESSON 4: Outlining Information

■■ EXPLANATION AND EXAMPLES

"What happened to my white socks? They're pink!"

"Oh, I threw all the clothes you had piled on the floor in the same load of wash. I didn't know your red socks would bleed all over the light stuff. Wait until you see your white shirt."

The preceding is an example of what happens when a simple project like the laundry is not organized properly. An important first step in washing clothes is to sort them by color, then by special treatment (such as gentle cycle with cold water). Red socks in the wrong load can be a disaster!

Similarly, when we read, we need to organize all the information we're processing. We need to sort—or classify—the details into their proper groups. This process will aid us in remembering the writers' important ideas and the points they want to make about the ideas.

Outlining a selection is one way to organize its information into a logical arrangement. Basically, when you outline, you are illustrating the underlying structure of a passage. You have probably seen a building under construction. The first thing the carpenters do is construct the frame. When you look at the frame, you can easily decide whether it will be a house or store. Although the skeleton is missing certain aspects—such as roofing, windows, doors, and siding—the basic structure is there.

The first step in outlining is to identify the author's structure. Look at the structure of this lesson. There are three main sections: Explanation, Practices, Assignments. Let's jot these points down in outline form with some supporting details.

Explanation: An explanation of outlining information is presented.

- The importance of organizing information is discussed.
- Organizing information helps us remember writers' ideas.
- Outlining organizes information by providing a skeleton of the passage.
- Indenting and numbering indicates the order of ideas.

Practice: Two activities to practice outlining are provided.

Assignments: Three independent assignments about outlining are given.

Notice how the supporting details for *Explanation* have been indented. If you want to add details about the details, you will indent again. Another way to indicate structure in an outline is to use a consistent system of lettering and numbering. The most common system is to use Roman numerals (I, II, III) for the major headings, capital letters (A, B, C) for the next level of details, and Arabic numerals (1, 2, 3) for the next level, as follows:

I. Explanation: An explanation of outlining information is presented.
   A. The importance of organizing information is discussed.
   B. Organizing information helps us remember writers' ideas.
   C. Outlining organizes information by providing a skeleton of the passage.
      1. It is similar to the frame of a building.
      2. You can guess what the building is by the frame.
   D. Indenting and numbering indicates the order of ideas.

II. Practice: Two activities to practice outlining are provided.

III. Assignments: Three independent assignments for outlining are given.

Outlining is a tool that lets you organize the information you read. The outlined information shows the relationships of the various ideas presented by the writer. Your outline will help you remember the important points and how they are interrelated.

■ PRACTICE

1. The short section on page 249 entitled "The Form of Poetry" is partially outlined below. Read page 249, and then complete the outline by copying it onto your paper and filling in the blanks.

    I. All poems have form—an overall structure and organization.
        ____. Form is created by patterns of sound, images, ideas, and words placed on the page.
        ____. Form is fundamental to experiencing the whole poem.
    _. Two forms of poems are open and closed.
        A. Closed _____
            1. Poets who write closed poems are like dancers who follow painted footprints on the floor.
            2. _____
        B. Open _____
            1. _____
            2. _____

2. Finish the outline in the next column by copying it over on a separate sheet of paper and filling in the blanks. This is an outline of *The Diary of Anne Frank* (page 366).

I. *The Diary of Anne Frank* is based on a real-life diary kept by a Jewish girl named Anne Frank living in the 1930s and 1940s.
    A. Hitler and the Nazi party come into power in Germany.
        1. Hitler blames the Jews for the country's economic problems.
        2. Anne's family moves to Holland.
    __. Anne receives the diary as a present for her birthday and writes what happens to the family in Holland.
        1. _____
        2. _____
        3. _____
        4. _____
    __. The Nazis find the Frank family and send them to concentration camps.
        _. Anne dies _____
        _. _____

II. (another idea whose weight is equal to that in I).

■ ASSIGNMENTS

1. Read the material on pages 4–5 entitled "The Short Story." Put its ideas into outline form. Remember, you are outlining so that *you* will recognize the main points and their relationships to each other.

2. Read the story by L. M. Montgomery beginning on page 131. Then outline the important ideas and events. Be sure to use a consistent system of numbering and lettering for the ideas.

3. Apply the principles of outlining to any other selection in this book.

The Writing About Literature Handbook guides students through the types of writing assignments that they are most likely to encounter in literature classes. Six lessons focus on analytical topics; four lessons, on creative or personal writing. The lessons can be taught in any order; they cover the genres of fiction, poetry, nonfiction, and drama.

The handbook follows a writing-process approach to the various assignments, beginning with prewriting and continuing through writing and revising. Clearly sequenced instructions with specific examples reinforce students' familiarity with the writing process.

ANSWERING AN ESSAY QUESTION

Focusing on the task of answering an essay question about a literary work, this first lesson introduces students to a writing-process approach to writing about literature. You may want to teach this lesson in conjunction with your first writing assignment on the material in the unit "Enjoying Literature." Since the lesson uses examples from the story "A Day's Wait," you may want to assign that story before you teach this lesson. Under "Assignments" on the following page, you will find cross-references to appropriate Composition assignments throughout this textbook.

In your *Teacher's Resource Book* you will find these related blackline masters: Chart for Answering an Essay Question; Checklist for Revising a Paper About a Literary Work.

WRITING ABOUT LITERATURE HANDBOOK

LESSON 1: *Answering an Essay Question*

This lesson will show that the actual writing is only one part of answering an essay question.

CONCEPTS TO REMEMBER

1. Your answer to an essay question may be only one paragraph long or may be several paragraphs long.
2. In an essay answer of several paragraphs, the introductory paragraph usually begins with a **thesis statement,** which states your central idea and makes clear the purpose your essay will serve. The middle paragraphs develop various aspects of the thesis statement. The concluding paragraph restates your central idea.
3. The details that you use in support of your idea may be facts or examples from the selection.

PREWRITING

1. Read the essay question, copying down important words that tell you what is expected.

Example of Essay Question

   Write a short essay in which you give your general opinion about a particular work of literature. Explain your response by answering the following questions: (a) Did the characters in the selection seem believable? (b) Were the time and place in which the selection occurred vividly described? (c) Did the action in the selection interest you? (d) Did you like the outcome of the selection?

2. Make a chart on which to jot down ideas in note form. The chart should have room for (a) the

SAMPLE CHART: ANSWERING AN ESSAY QUESTION			
SELECTION: "A Day's Wait"			
BELIEVABLE CHARACTERS?	**VIVID SETTING?**	**INTERESTING ACTION?**	**SATISFYING OUTCOME?**
the boy ill, pale, dark areas under eyes, shivering; stares blankly ahead; tries to protect others from his illness; faces "death" quietly but cries with relief *the parent* concerned for son, sits with him, reads to him; knows illness is not serious, leaves the boy for hunting; reassures boy about not dying	winter, bright, cold day, sleet, outdoors "varnished with ice," "glassy surface" of creek, covey of quail, overhanging brush; boy is cold, closes window, sits by fire	A simple error causes a boy to face his own "death." He does so bravely and protects others from his illness and his "death." The reader does not at first understand the boy's motivation; the reader feels suspense.	The boy's mistake is corrected. The truth explains his unusual behavior: staring blankly, sending others from the room. His crying shows his relief.
OVERALL REACTION TO THE SELECTION: ___X Favorable ___ Unfavorable			

618   *Writing About Literature Handbook*

general answer to the essay question and (b) each of the specific points that you must discuss in order to fulfill all the requirements of the essay question. The chart at the bottom of page 590 is based on "A Day's Wait."

WRITING PARAGRAPH BY PARAGRAPH

After you have put your thoughts down as notes on a chart, you may follow these steps to present them in carefully constructed paragraphs.

1. Restate the question as a statement. This sentence will be your thesis statement, a clear statement of your central idea. You may follow the thesis statement with one or more sentences telling how your answer will proceed.

Example of Introductory Paragraph and Thesis Statement

"A Day's Wait" by Ernest Hemingway is a touching story with believable characters, clear description of place, an element of suspense in the action, and a satisfying outcome. The following paragraphs will offer details in support of this general reaction and will discuss each element separately.

2. Begin each of the middle paragraphs of your answer with a **topic sentence,** which states the main idea, purpose, or plan for the paragraph. Each sentence that follows the topic sentence should support it.

Example of Topic Sentence and Supporting Detail for Second Paragraph

Both main characters in "A Day's Wait," the son and the father, seem very real. The boy is ill, pale, and shivering with dark areas under his eyes. He is having a common misunderstanding about his temperature. He faces his "death" bravely and protects others from his illness and dying. The father sits with the boy and reads to him. However, he is not aware of the boy's fears and leaves the boy alone in order to do some hunting.

3. Write a concluding paragraph. Begin it with the idea expressed in your thesis statement, but use different words. You may round out this paragraph by adding other thoughts about your reaction to the story.

WRITING A ONE-PARAGRAPH ANSWER

If your answer is limited to one paragraph, begin with a strong topic sentence that restates the question in the essay assignment. Each of your following sentences should develop one aspect of the topic sentence. You still must give evidence to support your topic sentence.

REVISING AND EDITING

Now that you have completed the first draft, it is important that you review your work. Use the following checklist to revise, edit, and proofread your written work. Prepare a final version.

  I. Content and Organization
    A. Have you turned the assignment question into a thesis statement?
    B. Does each following paragraph have a topic sentence and supporting details?
    C. Does the concluding paragraph restate the thesis statement and perhaps add further insights and comments?
 II. Grammar, Usage, Mechanics
    A. Have you used complete sentences?
    B. Have you used correct punctuation, capitalization, and spelling?
III. Word Choice, Style
    A. Have you used appropriate words?
    B. Have you avoided wordiness?
    C. Have you varied sentence length?

ASSIGNMENTS

1. Finish the answer to the question about "A Day's Wait" presented in this lesson. You may use the information on the chart.
2. Do an assignment called "Answering an Essay Question" (page 63 or 462).

Writing About Literature Handbook 619

LESSON 2: *Writing About Plot*

Writing about the **plot** (the sequence of events or actions in a selection) requires paying attention to all the ways in which a selection moves ahead—through actions and through dialogue.

TYPICAL ESSAY QUESTION

When you are asked to write about the plot of a story, you will often have to answer a question like the following one:

State whether the outcome of the plot follows logically from the events of the story. Give at least two reasons for your opinion of the outcome. Support each reason with examples.

PREWRITING

Break down the assignment into its various parts. Draw a chart with space in which to make notes about each part of the assignment. A sample chart appears at the top of the opposite page. Use the following guidelines and questions as aids to your thinking and note making.

1. Identify the outcome of the selection. In other words, how does the selection end?
2. List the main events of the selection in the order in which they occur.
3. Form your opinion about whether the outcome follows logically from the events of the story.
4. State at least two reasons for the opinion you formed in Prewriting 3.
5. List the examples you can use in support of your reasons.

WRITING PARAGRAPH BY PARAGRAPH

Convert your notes to sentences and paragraphs, following the steps listed here. (If your answer is just one paragraph long, think of these steps as applying to each sentence rather than to each paragraph.)

1. In your introductory paragraph write a thesis statement, putting the central idea of the essay question into your own words. You may follow the thesis statement with one or more sentences.

Example of Introductory Paragraph with Thesis Statement

The plot of "A Day's Wait" by Ernest Hemingway prepares us for an outcome in which the boy learns he is well and gains our sympathy. Throughout the story there are hints that the situation is not very grave and that the little boy is suffering much more than he has to.

2. In each of the middle paragraphs present a topic sentence that expands an aspect of your thesis statement. Give examples to show the truth of your topic sentence.

Example of a Middle Paragraph with Topic Sentence and Supporting Detail

If the situation had been grave, the father, who seems to be very caring, would have expressed more anxiety. He calls in a doctor and keeps track of the boy's temperature and medication schedule, but he does not panic or in any other way express concern that the boy's illness is serious. He reads to the boy, advises him to sleep, and then gives in to the boy's request to be left alone for a while. This is not the sort of father who would go off hunting if there were anything gravely wrong with his son.

3. In your concluding paragraph restate your thesis statement, using different words from those in your introductory paragraph. You may wish to add an additional comment or two about the story in general.

620 *Writing About Literature Handbook*

SAMPLE CHART: WRITING ABOUT PLOT
SELECTION: "A Day's Wait"

OUTCOME OF SELECTION:	The boy discovers that he is not deathly ill after all, and we feel sympathy for the way the boy suffered.
EVENTS IN SELECTION:	1. Father notices nine-year-old son is sick. 2. Son insists he is all right. 3. Doctor takes boy's temperature (102 degrees) and leaves medication for him. 4. Son appears very detached as father tries to make him feel better. 5. Son suggests father leave him alone. 6. Father returns, takes son's temperature, and realizes that the boy is very upset about something. 7. Son asks question, and father realizes the boy is afraid he is going to die. Then the father and son realize that the son has had the wrong idea about the meaning of his temperature. 8. The son relaxes and becomes a little boy again.
OPINION OF OUTCOME:	follows logically from the events of the story

REASONS	EXAMPLES
The story has prepared us for an ending in which the boy realizes he is not deathly ill. Throughout the story the father is calm about the boy's illness. If there had been anything to worry about, the father, who is very caring, would have acted differently.	*Examples of the father's caring behavior:* tells son to go to bed; calls the doctor; is a careful nurse, writing down the boy's temperature and medication schedule; reads to the boy; leaves to go hunting only when he knows the boy will be all right alone
The story has prepared us for an ending in which we feel sympathy for the little boy. When we learn that the boy feared he was dying, we understand why he acted as he did during the day.	*Examples of boy's behavior during the day:* won't allow himself to fall asleep; is worried that the situation—his "dying"—will bother his father; worries that others will catch what he has

▬▬ REVISING AND EDITING

See Lesson 1 for detailed reminders about improving your writing.

▬▬ ASSIGNMENTS

1. Use the chart given in this lesson and ideas of your own to write about the outcome of "A Day's Wait" (page 2). State whether the outcome of the plot follows logically from the events of the story. Give at least two reasons for your opinion of the outcome. Support each reason with examples from the story.

2. Complete an assignment called "Writing About Plot" (page 41, 243, or 273).

LESSON 3: *Writing About Character*

A **character** is an individual in a piece of literature. The main character is usually developed so completely that he or she seems like a real person whom you may meet and get to know. To judge whether a character seems real, you can ask yourself whether the character's key traits seem true to life, whether the character's motivations seem believable, and whether any changes in the character seem understandable.

CONCEPTS TO REMEMBER

1. A character in literature has key, or outstanding, traits. *Trait* is simply another word for "quality" or "characteristic." *Key* or *outstanding* in this usage means "most important." You can determine the character's key traits by studying the character's appearance, speech, thoughts, and feelings.
2. **Motivation** refers to the reasons that a character acts as he or she does.
3. Not all characters change, but you should always look to see if a character does change and, if so, how.

TYPICAL ESSAY QUESTION

When you are asked to write about character in a piece of literature, you will often be asked to do an assignment such as the following:

Select a character, and tell whether the character seems true to life.

PREWRITING

1. Select a character who interests you. When you have decided on a character, review the selection, asking yourself the following questions:

Key Traits
a. Does the character look like a true-to-life person?
b. Does the character talk like a real person?

c. Do the character's thoughts and feelings seem realistic?

Motivation
d. Does the character act in ways you think a real person would act?

Change
e. Does the character change in a way that seems realistic?

2. To help you organize your ideas about the character, record your thoughts about the character on a chart. The sample chart on the next page is based on "Charles."

WRITING PARAGRAPH BY PARAGRAPH

If your answer is just one paragraph long, think of the following steps as applying to each sentence rather than to each paragraph.

1. Begin your introductory paragraph with a thesis statement in which you identify the character, name the work in which the character appears, and give your overall opinion of whether or not the character seems true to life and why. In the rest of this paragraph, you can tell how your composition will proceed.

Example of Introductory Paragraph with Thesis Statement

In Shirley Jackson's "Charles" the character of Laurie is true to life. Laurie, who has just started to go to school, reveals traits that are typical for a child of his age. To illustrate this idea, the following paragraphs will offer details of Laurie's traits, his motivations, and the changes that he undergoes.

2. In each of your following paragraphs, take up one of the main points of your thesis statement—the character's key traits, the character's motivation, or the character's change. Use a

622   *Writing About Literature Handbook*

ANALYSIS OF CHARACTER SELECTION: "Charles" CHARACTER: Laurie			
QUESTION	**GENERAL ANSWER**	**EXAMPLES**	**TRUE TO LIFE?**
WHAT ARE THE CHARACTER'S KEY TRAITS, BASED ON APPEARANCE, SPEECH, ACTIONS, AND THOUGHTS AND FEELINGS?	*Appearance:* wants to be more adult	wears jeans with belt	YES
	Speech: enjoys school and talking with parents	tells parents a great deal about school	YES
	Actions: independent; wants attention	swaggers, does not wave good-by to mother; slams door and shouts	YES YES
WHAT IS THE CHARACTER'S MOTIVATION?	He enjoys attention and is trying to adjust to school.	He talks a great deal about school. The teacher says that adjusting takes time.	YES
HOW WOULD YOU DESCRIBE THE CHANGE, IF ANY, IN THE CHARACTER?	He is becoming better adjusted to school.	The teacher says he has become a "fine little helper."	YES
OVERALL IMPRESSION OF CHARACTER: **X** TRUE TO LIFE ___ **NOT TRUE TO LIFE**			

topic sentence, followed by details that support your topic sentence.

Example of Topic Sentence and Supporting Details

Laurie has at least four key traits, which are revealed through his appearance, his speech, and his actions. Because he is starting school, Laurie wants to be treated more like an adult—his first key trait. He refuses to wear overalls and wears jeans with a belt instead. Another key trait is his enjoyment of school. We know he enjoys it because he talks about it a great deal with his parents. A third key trait is Laurie's wish to be independent. One example of this trait is his failure to wave to his mother as he leaves for school. At the same time he seeks attention—his fourth key trait. He demonstrates this trait when he slams the door and shouts.

3. In your concluding paragraph restate the idea expressed in your thesis statement, and add other general ideas about the character.

■ ASSIGNMENTS

1. Use the chart in this lesson and ideas of your own to write about the character of Laurie in "Charles" (page 53). State whether the character is true to life.

2. Do an assignment called "Writing About Character" (page 77, 107, 139, or 270).

Writing About Literature Handbook   623

This lesson guides students through the process of writing an original short story. The lesson reinforces the textbook's teaching about short story elements such as character, plot, and setting; in addition, it gives students practice in writing dialogue. The lesson develops a specific story from general idea to outline form. Under "Assignments" on the final page of this lesson, you will find a cross-reference to a story-writing Composition assignment in this textbook.

In your *Teacher's Resource Book* you will find these related blackline masters: Charts for Writing a Story; Outline for a Story; Checklists for Revising Creative Writing.

LESSON 4: *Writing a Story*

Writing a story is a craft, or skill, that requires an understanding of the important elements and techniques of the short story. A vivid imagination may add sparkle to a good story, but anyone familiar with the basic tools of the short story writer can produce an effective story.

▬ CONCEPTS TO REMEMBER

1. **Plot** is the sequence of events, or what happens in a story. Each event causes or leads to the next. At the center of a plot is a problem, or conflict, that the main character faces. For example, this problem may be a difficult decision, a disagreement with another person, or a struggle against hardship. The story builds toward its point of highest interest, the climax. The character solves the problem and learns something about himself or herself.

2. A **character** is an individual in a story. Most stories have only a few major characters. They should have believable personality or character traits and clear motivations for their actions.

3. The **setting** is the time and place in which a story happens. It often provides a story with mood, or atmosphere.

▬ TYPICAL ASSIGNMENT

You may be given an assignment like this one:

Write a short story that has a logical sequence of events. Describe your characters and setting clearly.

▬ PREWRITING

1. To find an idea for your story, try to think of an interesting problem, an unusual person, or a colorful place. Most people write best when they write about things they know. Perhaps your hobbies and interests—for example, tennis or gardening—can inspire you. You may also want to page through a magazine or travel book. Some action, face, or location may give you an idea.

624 *Writing About Literature Handbook*

2. When you have chosen the plot and characters for your story, ask yourself the following questions.

   a. What problem, or conflict, does the main character face?
   b. What is the character's reaction?
   c. What obstacles prevent the character from solving the problem?
   d. In what way does the character finally solve the problem?
   e. What is the final outcome?

3. Try to imagine how your characters look, sound, and act. Then fill in a chart like the one on the next page called "Characters." You may not use all this information in the actual story, but the chart will help you to picture the characters. The sample chart contains information about characters that one writer has in mind for a story.

4. Picture your setting or settings. Then fill in a chart like the one on the next page called "Settings."

5. Write an outline to help organize your thoughts. In the outline that follows, the sections printed in bold type are the steps that every story outline should include. The sections in italics are examples from the two charts on the next page.

STORY OUTLINE

I. **Beginning**
   A. **Introduce the main character.** *Mark, fourteen years old, works on his family's farm.*
   B. **Describe the setting.** *The barn is musty and hot. It is cluttered with old machinery.*
   C. **Begin the plot.** *Mark is bored and tired of chores. He hears a strange noise. He follows the sound and finds a time machine.*

II. **Middle**
   A. **Introduce the character's problem.** *Mark wants adventure and a rest from chores. He asks the machine to take him to ancient Egypt.*

CHARACTERS

CHARACTER	PHYSICAL TRAITS					PERSONALITY OR CHARACTER TRAITS		
	AGE	SIZE	HAIR	DRESS	FEATURES	PERSONALITY	SPEECH	BEHAVIOR
Mark	14	tall, muscular	red	over-alls, work shoes	tanned, serious face	easily bored, impatient, eager for excitement, respectful	soft, slow	keeps to himself, hard working
Pharaoh	50s	tall, thin	black, long, under royal headdress	bright red royal robes	scornful smile	domineering, selfish, cruel	booming, clear	demands respect, bullies his subjects
Rokah, a boy of ancient Egypt	14	short, very thin	black, long	dirty, torn, brown robe	drawn, tired face, warm smile	friendly and enthusiastic in spite of a difficult life of hard work	high, fast, excited	always active, eager to help others

SETTINGS

SETTING	HISTORICAL PERIOD, SEASON, YEAR, TIME OF DAY	PLACE (CITY, COUNTRY, INDOORS, OUTDOORS)	WEATHER	OTHER DETAILS
midwestern farm	present day, late summer, noon	inside an old barn	very warm and bright	clutter of old machinery, sun streaming through holes in roof
building site	ancient Egypt, late summer, noon	outdoors in front of building under construction	very warm and bright	hundreds of workers and overseers, large blocks of stone, dust

B. **Describe a new setting, if necessary.** *Mark is suddenly in ancient Egypt at a construction site for a new temple.*

C. **Introduce minor characters.** *Mark meets Rokah, an Egyptian boy of fourteen. As the boys talk, the Pharaoh passes.*

D. **Build toward the point of highest interest, or climax.** *The Pharoah notices the time machine and orders his guards to keep watch over it. Mark realizes that he may not be able to get home. He is then forced to labor on the construction.*

III. **Ending**

A. **Reach the point of highest interest.** *After days of hard work, Mark faints in the strong sun. The Pharaoh sees and threatens to punish him. Mark tells him about the time machine. The Pharaoh demands a demonstration. Mark asks the machine to take him home.*

B. **Wind down the action.** *Mark arrives home.*

C. **Give the final outcome.** *Mark is pleased to do his own chores again.*

Writing About Literature Handbook 625

6. When you have completed your outline, recite your plot aloud. Be sure that your plot builds in interest to a climax and then tells how the problem was finally solved.

7. Plan to use dialogue, or conversation between characters. Dialogue makes your story more realistic and more exciting. Remember the following points when you write dialogue.

   a. All words spoken by characters must be surrounded by quotation marks. A direct quotation can come at the beginning or the end of a sentence.

   b. A direct quotation begins with a capital letter. If a quotation is interrupted, the second part begins with a small letter.

   c. A direct quotation is set off from the rest of a sentence by commas. If a direct quotation is interrupted, commas are placed before and after the interruption. The comma before a direct quotation falls outside the quotation marks. The comma—or any punctuation—after a direct quotation falls inside the quotation marks.

Examples
- He frowned and thought, "Lunch is over, and I have to get back to the fields."
- "A farm sounds like a wonderful place to live," reflected Rokah.
- "Guards," boomed the Pharaoh, "keep watch over this strange device. Let no one near its magic."

   d. Dialogue is less formal than other kinds of writing. To make your characters sound natural, you may use short sentences and contractions in dialogue.

   e. In a conversation between characters, start a new paragraph each time the speaker changes.

   f. Be careful not to use the word *said* too often. Use other, livelier verbs, such as *whispered, yelled, mumbled, crowed,* and *confessed*.

8. When you have completed your outline, choose a title for your story. The title may refer to an important event, object, character, setting, statement, or idea from your story.

WRITING PARAGRAPH BY PARAGRAPH

1. Following your outline, begin your first paragraph by describing your main character and your setting. The first paragraph should also introduce the plot with one important action. You may wish to use dialogue.

Example

   Mark, fourteen, brushed his red hair from his eyes and sighed deeply. He frowned and thought, "Lunch is over, and I have to get back to the fields." Bored with farm chores, he sat in the musty old barn and watched the sun stream through a hole in the roof. Suddenly he heard a sound like the whirring and beeping of a computer. It seemed to be coming from behind a rusty clutter of old machinery. When he explored, he found an old machine that he had never noticed before. Across its side in large, old-fashioned print, it said "Time Machine"!

2. In the next paragraph or paragraphs introduce the character's problem. Describe it in detail, and include the character's reaction. If your story includes a change of setting, describe the second setting and its effect on the main character. Describe minor characters who are involved in the problem.

3. In the paragraph or paragraphs that follow, build suspense as the story moves toward the point of highest interest, the climax, and the character tries to solve his or her problem. Be sure that the character behaves according to information in the chart.

4. In the final paragraph or two, present the climax. Be sure that the solution to the character's problem is believable. End by showing what the character learned from the problem.

626 *Writing About Literature Handbook*

■■■ REVISING AND EDITING

Read your story aloud, and use the following checklist to revise, edit, and proofread your first draft into a polished second draft.

I. Content
  A. Does your title point to something important in the story and grab the reader's interest?
  B. Have you included details that describe your characters and setting?
  C. Do you present the main character's problem clearly? Does each event of the plot grow logically from what happened before?
  D. Is your climax a clear solution to the problem? Does your plot end soon after the climax? Do you show the main character's reaction to the climax?
  E. Do you use dialogue to make the story more interesting and realistic?
II. Style
  A. Have you cut out unnecessary details?
  B. Have you used colorful adjectives and verbs wherever possible?
  C. Does your dialogue sound real?
  D. Do you use both long and short sentences for variety?
III. Grammar, Usage, Mechanics
  A. Is each sentence complete (no fragments, no run-ons)?
  B. Are all words spelled correctly? If you are not sure of the spelling of a word, have you consulted a dictionary?
  C. Have you punctuated and capitalized your sentences correctly? In dialogue have you used quotation marks and capital letters correctly?
  D. Do you begin a new paragraph whenever the subject, time, or place changes or whenever the speaker in a dialogue changes?

■■■ ASSIGNMENTS

1. Complete the story begun in this lesson by using the charts. You may follow the outline to the end of the story, or you may create your own ending if you wish. Give the story a title.
2. Do an assignment called "Writing a Story" (page 107 or 167).

Writing About Literature Handbook 627

This lesson guides students through the process of writing about a poem. The lesson reinforces the textbook's teaching about poetic elements such as sound devices, imagery, figurative language, and total effect. You may want to teach this lesson in conjunction with the final subunit in the Poetry unit in this textbook. Since the lesson uses examples from the poem "Willow and Ginkgo," you may want to assign that poem before you teach this lesson. Under "Assignments" on the following page, you will find cross-references to Composition assignments that focus on writing about poetry.

In your *Teacher's Resource Book* you will find these related blackline masters: Chart for Writing About Poetry; Checklist for Revising a Paper About a Literary Work.

LESSON 5: *Writing About Poetry*

A poem is like a magical machine. It has many separate parts that can be examined individually, but when they work together, they produce a magical, unpredictable effect.

▥ CONCEPTS TO REMEMBER

1. The **total effect** of a poem is the overall impact that it has on the reader or listener.
2. **Sound devices:** Many sound devices contribute to the poem's effect. These devices include

   alliteration: the repeating of consonant sounds, usually at the beginnings of words
   onomatopoeia: the use of a word or phrase whose sound imitates or suggests its meaning
   rhythm: the pattern created by arranging stressed and unstressed syllables
   rhyme: the repeating at regular intervals of similar or identical sounds

3. **Images:** The poet also relies on images, or mental pictures created with words, which appeal to one or more of the senses.
4. **Figurative language:** The poet uses language that stretches words beyond their usual meanings. Common figures of speech are

   simile: A simile is a stated comparison between two otherwise unlike things. The comparison uses the word *like* or *as*.
   metaphor: A metaphor is an implied comparison between two things. The comparison does not use the word *like* or *as*.
   personification: Personification is a figure of speech in which the poet gives human qualities to an animal, object, or idea.

▥ TYPICAL ESSAY QUESTION

When you are asked to write about poetry, you may find yourself answering an assignment such as the following:

Write about the total effect of a poem. First describe the poem's overall impact on you. Explain the poem's meaning. Then give examples of the sounds, imagery, and figurative language that help to create the poem's impact.

▥ PREWRITING

1. Read the poem out loud. Then reread it silently, thinking about its **meaning,** or the central idea or emotion behind the poem. If it will help you, paraphrase the poem, restating it in your own words. If you still have difficulty grasping the poem's meaning, ask yourself these questions:

   a. Does the poem spotlight a person, place, thing, idea, or feeling?
   b. What emotion do you feel when you read the poem?

2. Read the poem again, asking yourself the following questions about the techniques in the poem:

   a. **Sound:** What is the rhythm of the poem? Is it regular or irregular? Fast or slow? Gentle or driving? Does the poet use alliteration, onomatopoeia, or rhyme? How does each of these techniques add to the poem's meaning, emotion, and music?
   b. **Imagery:** What images does the poet use? Which seems most vivid? To which senses does each image appeal? What do these images add to the meaning and emotion of the poem?
   c. **Figurative language:** What examples of simile, metaphor, and personification can you find? What do these figures of speech contribute to the poem?

3. After you have thought about the meaning of the poem and have looked carefully at the techniques used in the poem, prepare a chart that will help you see how the techniques contribute

TOTAL EFFECT OF A POEM SELECTION: "Willow and Ginkgo"			
MEANING	**SOUND**	**IMAGERY**	**FIGURATIVE LANGUAGE**
Paraphrase: People appreciate delicate beauty—the willow—but they admire and sympathize with toughness and survival—the ginkgo. *Emotion:* love of beauty, pride in survival	*Rhythm:* regular with exceptions *Alliteration:* "*g*rows, there is *g*reen and *g*old"; "*w*illow dips to the *w*ater"; "*P*rotected and *p*recious" *Rhyme:* occasional end rhyme	*Images of sight:* "an etching / fine-lined against the sky"; "streaming hair"; "green and gold"; "gray concrete"; "metal sky" *Images of sound:* "like a soprano, / delicate and thin"; "like a chorus with everyone joining in" *Images of touch:* "sleek as a velvet-nosed calf"; "leathery as an old bull"; "silken thread"; "stubby rough wool"	*Simile:* "like an etching"; "like a crude sketch"; "like a soprano"; "like a chorus"; "sleek as a velvet-nosed calf"; "leathery as an old bull"; "like silken thread"; "like stubby rough wool"; "like a nymph"; "like the king's favorite daughter"; "Like a city child" *Metaphor:* "metal sky" *Personification:* "My eyes feast"

to the meaning and how the poem as a whole affects you. One reader of "Willow and Ginkgo" (page 244) prepared the sample chart in this lesson.

WRITING PARAGRAPH BY PARAGRAPH

If your answer is just one paragraph, think of the following steps as applying to each sentence rather than to each paragraph.

1. Begin your introductory paragraph with a thesis statement, which should restate the major points made in the assignment. In other words, the thesis statement should refer briefly to the poem's impact on you, its meaning, and those techniques that the poet uses to create the poem's impact. The introductory paragraph can also include other general thoughts about the poem before you go on to discuss the specifics.

Example of Thesis Statement

Eve Merriam's poem "Willow and Ginkgo" uses sense images, rhythm, rhyme, alliteration, and figurative language to compare delicate beauty with toughness. The result is a

touching poem that is full of a love of beauty and a pride in survival.

2. In each of the following paragraphs, focus on one technique. Supply examples of each.
3. In the concluding paragraph restate your thesis, using different words.

REVISING AND EDITING

For detailed reminders about how to improve your writing, see Lesson 1 in this Writing About Literature Handbook.

ASSIGNMENTS

1. Use the chart in this lesson and ideas of your own to finish writing about the total effect of "Willow and Ginkgo" (page 244).
2. Do an assignment called "Writing About Poetry" (page 284, or page 288), or choose another poem from this book and write about its total effect. First describe the poem's overall impact on you. Explain the poem's meaning. Then give examples of the sounds, imagery, and figurative language that help to create the poem's impact.

Writing About Literature Handbook 629

This lesson guides students through the process of writing an original poem. The lesson reinforces the textbook's teaching about concrete and figurative language, imagery, sound devices, and poetic form. A series of specific exercises (for example, using colorful details, writing metaphors) helps students generate material for original poems. Then the lesson guides students step by step through the process of writing a poem. Under "Assignments" on the final page of this lesson, you will find cross-references to Composition assignments on writing a poem, along with several additional ideas to stimulate students to write poems.

In your *Teacher's Resource Book* you will find these related blackline masters: Charts for Writing a Poem; Outline for Poetry Notes; Checklists for Revising Creative Writing.

LESSON 6: *Writing a Poem*

To write effective poetry, you should understand how images, ideas, and emotions work together.

CONCEPTS TO REMEMBER

1. Poetry contains colorful language. **Concrete language** is specific language that appeals to the senses. **Images** are pictures made with words. **Figurative language**—similes, metaphors, and personifications—makes unusual comparisons. A **simile** compares seemingly unlike things using a comparing word such as *like* or *as*. A **metaphor** compares seemingly unlike things without direct comparing words. **Personification** gives human characteristics to an object, animal, or idea.

2. Poetry uses several sound techniques. **Repetition** is the repeated use of sounds, words, phrases, or lines. **Alliteration** is the repetition of consonant sounds, often at the beginnings of words. **Rhythm** is the pattern of beats made by stressed and unstressed syllables. **Onomatopoeia** is the use of words whose sounds imitate or suggest their meanings.

3. Every poem has an overall pattern, or **form.** Some poems are broken up into groups of lines, or **stanzas.** Some have a set number of syllables in each line.

4. A poem can be about anything at all, but it should include the poet's attitude or feelings toward the subject.

TYPICAL ASSIGNMENT

You may be given an assignment like this one:

Write a poem on any subject. Use at least three of the following techniques: images, figurative language (simile, metaphor, and personification), repetition, alliteration, and onomatopoeia. Use concrete language that appeals to the senses. Choose the form of your poem; do not use rhyme.

630 *Writing About Literature Handbook*

PRACTICING POETIC TECHNIQUES

Practice poetic techniques to prepare yourself to write a poem and to help you find a subject.

1. **Colorful details:** Choose one of the following items, or name any item you wish: an onion, a tiger, lemonade, fog, celery, a banana. Then fill in a chart like the one that follows. On your chart write five sense descriptions of the item. Appeal to all five of the senses. After each description tell which sense is involved.

ITEM	SENSE DESCRIPTIONS	SENSE
onion	1. brown, papery skin 2. green-white rings 3. a sharp sting 4. bittersweet to taste 5. small globe with points	sight, touch sight taste, smell taste sight

2. **Similes:** Choose one of the following items, or name any item of your choice: a fire siren, a football field, the moon, winter, popcorn, a lawn, a saw, a light bulb, sadness, a new car, school. Write five similes that describe the same object. Use *like* in three of your similes; use *as* in two.

Examples
- The fire siren is like a screech owl's song.
- The fire siren is as shrill as the cry of a trapped cat.

3. **Metaphors:** Choose five items from one of the following categories: vegetables, colors, liquids, sports. Write a metaphor to describe each of your five items.

Examples
- A stalk of asparagus is a soldier in a helmet.
- A head of cabbage is a clump of laundry.
- A carrot is a sharpened crayon.

4. **Personification:** Choose four of the following items, or name any items of your choice: a grandfather clock, a hockey stick, the New Year, a sneaker, friendship, a pencil, a toothbrush, a mosquito, a dinosaur, winter. For each item write a sentence that personifies, or gives human qualities to, that item.

Example
Winter spread her linen tablecloth across my lawn.

5. **Vivid verbs:** Replace the italicized verbs in the following sentences with vivid verbs.

Example
- The plane *flew* through the sky.
  The plane sailed through the sky.

  a. The stars are *shining* in the sky.
  b. The silvery fish *swam* in the clear brook.
  c. The cowboy *walked* into the general store.
  d. The rain *wet* the ground.
  e. The audience *cheered* with excitement.

6. **Alliteration:** Write a three-line nonrhyming poem in which almost every word in a line begins with the same consonant sound. You may change the sound with each line. You may use one of the following subjects, or you may use a subject of your own: lordly lions, giggling gorillas, friendly flowers, bouncing basketballs, swirling snowflakes.

Example
*D*ogs *d*utifully *d*ig *d*uring the *d*aytime.

7. **Onomatopoeia:** Choose one of the following items, or name any item of your choice: an alarm clock, a computer, windshield wipers, rocket blastoff, a waterfall, a vacuum cleaner, the wind. Write a sentence with onomatopoeia about the item. To do this, use words that imitate the sound of your item.

Example
The kicking alarm clock clanged and howled.

8. **Repetition:** Write an eight-line nonrhyming poem that uses repetition. Begin the first line with the words "Freedom is _____." Complete the line with an imaginative statement. Begin the second line with the words "Freedom makes me _____," followed by another vivid statement. Repeat and alternate these beginnings through the entire poem.

Example
Freedom is a broad blue sky.
Freedom makes me soar.

9. **Rhythm and Rhyme:** Write a two-line poem with rhythm and rhyme. Begin by finding two words that rhyme. Make each the last word in a line. Then fill in the beginning of each line. Try to give each line the same number of stressed syllables.

Example
Whose woods these are I think I know.
His house is in the village though;
— "Stopping by the Woods on a Snowy Evening" by Robert Frost

10. **Form:** Write a poem that has two stanzas with four lines in each stanza. In the first stanza describe an item from column A. In the second stanza describe the matching item in column B.

COLUMN A	COLUMN B
an alarm clock	the dismissal bell
a beach in summer	a beach in winter
training for a game	the big game
snow	how snow makes you feel
a vegetable market	a salad
a parade	the spectators

PREWRITING

1. An idea for a poem can come to you in many ways. You may see a striking image in your mind. You may want to express a strong emo-

tion. You may hear a word and like its sound. You may begin a brief practice exercise (such as those above) and find yourself writing a whole poem. If you have difficulty finding a subject, the following list of general ideas may help.

a. a person (you, a stranger, a celebrity)
b. an animal (real or imaginary)
c. an object (natural or artificial)
d. a scene (real or imaginary)
e. an event (real or imaginary)
f. an emotion (something you feel or you would like to feel)

2. After you choose your subject, close your eyes, and try to picture it in detail. Ask yourself what you see, hear, taste, smell, and touch when you think of the subject. How does the subject make you feel?

3. To help you to explore your thoughts, prepare notes for your poem. In the following sample of notes, the sections printed in bold type are advice for every writer of a poem. The sections in italics are one writer's ideas for a poem.

POETRY NOTES

I. Content
  A. State the subject of your poem. *a city in the rain*
  B. Tell how the subject makes you feel. *delighted, excited*
II. Language
  A. Write specific images that apply to your subject and that appeal to the senses.
    1. Write an image of sight. *people rushing through revolving doors*
    2. Write an image of sound. *boots slopping through puddles*
    3. Write an image of taste. *the fresh rain*
    4. Write an image of smell. *fumes from slowing traffic*
    5. Write an image of touch. *the wind pulling an umbrella inside out*

  B. Write figurative language.
    1. Write at least one simile. *Shop awnings are like eyes blinking and crying.*
    2. Write at least one metaphor. *Umbrellas bloom everywhere.*
    3. Write at least one example of personification. *Cabs in yellow slickers push and shove.*
III. Sound
  Decide what sounds fit your subject and your images.
  A. Write at least one example of alliteration. *The wind whips up whirlpools of leaves and litter.*
  B. Write at least one example of onomatopoeia. *shoes slopping and splashing through puddles*
  C. Write at least one phrase or line that you will repeat in the poem. *red and yellow, blue and black umbrellas*
IV. Form
  Describe the form of your poem. *two stanzas of four lines each, no strict pattern of beats*

▮▮ WRITING LINE BY LINE

1. In your first line identify your subject. Use concrete language and sense details.

Example
A rush of rain. The city street turns slick.

2. In the lines that follow, use the ideas and words that occurred to you when you worked on your poetry notes. Use one of these details per line, or combine two on a single line. Add connecting words (*and, but, or, for, since, because*), colorful adjectives, and vivid verbs.

Example
Cold liquid leaks beneath my collar.
Shop awnings blink and cry like eyes,
And shoes slop and splash through puddles.

3. If you have chosen a specific form for your

632 *Writing About Literature Handbook*

poem, try to fit your ideas into this form. You may need to change the word order and to leave out some of your ideas. If you have not chosen a specific form, decide whether or not you will break your poem into stanzas.

4. The last line or lines of your poem should present a striking image. This image should sum up your feelings about the subject, or it should repeat an important phrase from the poem.

Examples
- I cannot wait for another rush of rain.
- Sunshine glistens on my umbrella garden.
- Umbrellas blooming everywhere.
- Red and yellow, blue and black umbrellas.

5. When you have finished the first draft of your poem, chose a title. It can be the subject, an important image, or a phrase from the poem.

▰▰▰ REVISING AND EDITING

Once you have finished the first draft, you must take time to polish it into an improved second draft.

1. Read your poem aloud.
2. Do you use striking images that appeal to several senses?
3. Do you use at least one simile, metaphor, and personification?
4. Do you use alliteration, onomatopoeia, and repetition?
5. Do you use colorful adjectives and vivid verbs?
6. Is your poem written in complete sentences and punctuated correctly? Does it flow naturally?
7. Is the form of your poem consistent throughout?

▰▰▰ ASSIGNMENTS

1. Complete the poem begun in the lesson. First look at the sample lines, and choose those you want to use. Then add connecting words. In addition, add one striking image, one simile, and one metaphor of your own. Give the poem a title.

2. Do an assignment on writing a poem (page 238, 247, 261, 275, or 279). Be sure to use at least three of the following techniques: images, figurative language (simile, metaphor, and personification), repetition, alliteration, and onomatopoeia. Use concrete language that appeals to the senses. You may choose the form of your poem, but do not use rhyme.

3. Choose a poem that you enjoyed from this book (pages 219–295). Write down the first and last words of each of that poem's lines. Then fill in the rest of each line with your own thoughts. Use vivid words and original images and figures of speech.

4. Write a tanka, a Japanese poetry form of five lines. The first and third lines should have five syllables each. The second, fourth, and fifth lines should have seven syllables each.

5. Look through a magazine, and find a picture that impresses you in some way. For example, it may move you with its beauty, or it may upset you or make you laugh. Write a nonrhyming poem of two stanzas about this picture. In the first stanza describe the picture. In the second stanza describe the effect that the picture had on you. Tape the picture to a piece of paper, and write the poem neatly below it.

This lesson guides students through the process of writing about a nonfiction work. The lesson reinforces the textbook's teaching about central idea and supporting information such as facts, examples, and details. You may want to teach this lesson in conjunction with the Nonfiction unit in this textbook. Since the lesson uses examples from *Growing Up,* you may want to assign that work before you teach this lesson. Under "Assignments" on the following page, you will find cross-references to Composition assignments that focus on writing about nonfiction.

In your *Teacher's Resource Book* you will find these related blackline masters: Chart for Writing About Nonfiction; Checklist for Revising a Paper About a Literary Work.

LESSON 7: *Writing About Nonfiction*

Nonfiction is factual prose writing. It provides true accounts of real people in real situations. Autobiographies, biographies, diaries, journals, essays, and magazine and newspaper articles are all examples of this kind of writing. Whether a piece of nonfiction is only a few paragraphs or as long as a book, you can analyze it using the same approach. First identify its central ideas, and then discuss the various techniques that the author uses to communicate that idea.

TYPICAL ESSAY QUESTION

When you are asked to write about a piece of nonfiction, you are often asked to do an assignment such as the following:

A piece of nonfiction always has a central idea. To convey the central idea the author may use various techniques. For example, the author may provide facts, describe details, and give examples. What is the central idea in this piece of nonfiction? Mention the general techniques that the author uses to convey this idea, and give specific instances of each technique.

PREWRITING

1. Think about the central idea of the selection. If you have difficulty determining what the central idea is, ask yourself questions such as the following:

   a. What, if anything, does the title suggest about the author's opinion of the subject discussed in the selection?

   b. What opinion about life is suggested by the experiences that the author relates?

   c. What opinion about people in general is suggested by the experiences that the author relates?

   d. What ideas about the world in general are suggested by the details of setting?

634   *Writing About Literature Handbook*

2. Once you have determined the central idea of the selection, prepare a chart on which to record specific instances of the techniques that the author uses to convey that idea. After reading the excerpt from *Growing Up* by Russell Baker (page 8), you might prepare the chart that appears in this lesson.

WRITING PARAGRAPH BY PARAGRAPH

If your answer is just one paragraph long, think of the following steps as applying to each sentence rather than to each paragraph.

1. Begin your introductory paragraph with a thesis statement that (a) states the central idea and (b) indicates in general terms which techniques the author uses to convey that central idea.

   Example of Thesis Statement
   In the excerpt from *Growing Up,* Russell Baker uses facts, descriptive details, and examples to show that when a young person is recognized for his talents he can gain confidence about his future.

   The rest of the introductory paragraph may say more about the central idea itself.

2. In each of the following paragraphs, show how the author uses one particular technique to communicate the selection's central idea. Following the topic sentence, give specific occurrences of that technique within the selection.

3. In the concluding paragraph restate your thesis statement from your introductory paragraph, using different words. This is also the place where you can tell whether you think the author supported the central idea as well as possible.

REVISING AND EDITING

For detailed reminders about how to improve your writing, see Lesson 1 in this Writing About Literature Handbook.

ANALYZING NONFICTION		
SELECTION: excerpt from *Growing Up*		
CENTRAL IDEA: Being recognized for your real talents when you are young can have a tremendous impact on your future plans.		
TECHNIQUES USED TO CONVEY CENTRAL IDEA		
FACTS	**DESCRIPTIVE DETAILS**	**EXAMPLES**
Baker had no plans for a career after high school. The only thing that interested him was writing, not a field at which he could earn a living. Baker chose as an essay topic ''The Art of Eating Spaghetti'' and wrote the essay to please himself. The entire class enjoys the humorous essay. Mr. Fleagle praises it. A writing career became a real possibility.	A large family laughingly argues the ''socially respectable method for moving spaghetti from plate to mouth.'' ''. . . the entire class was listening. Listening attentively. Then somebody laughed, then the entire class was laughing, and not in contempt and ridicule, but with openhearted enjoyment.''	*of boredom:* found grammar dull, wrote poor compositions, thought classics ''deadening'' *of pleasure in writing ''The Art of Eating Spaghetti'':* ''warmth and good feeling,'' writing for personal joy, reliving a happy time, not worrying about rules of composition *of attitudes about writing career:* writing done only by the rich, not real work, not possible to earn a living, only real skill he has, his words have power to make people laugh

ASSIGNMENTS

1. Using the chart provided in this lesson for the excerpt from *Growing Up,* discuss Baker's central idea, and explain how he conveys that idea.

2. Do the assignment called ''Writing About Autobiography'' (page 305), ''Writing About Description'' (page 323), or ''Writing About Exposition'' (page 328). Discuss the author's central idea and the techniques used to convey that idea. Give examples of each technique.

This lesson guides students through the process of writing an original nonfiction narrative about a personal experience. The lesson reinforces the textbook's teaching about nonfiction elements such as purpose, audience, and main idea, as well as techniques drawn from fiction—for example, plot, conflict, and dialogue. The lesson develops a specific narrative from general idea to outline form. Under "Assignments" on the final page of this lesson, you will find cross-references to Composition assignments on writing a nonfiction narrative, along with several ideas to stimulate personal narratives.

In your *Teacher's Resource Book* you will find these related blackline masters: Charts for Writing a Nonfiction Narrative; Outline for a Narrative; Checklists for Revising Creative Writing.

LESSON 8: *Writing a Nonfiction Narrative*

A **nonfiction narrative** is factual prose writing that tells a true story. When you read a news story, you are reading a nonfiction narrative. When you write about some event in your journal, you are writing a nonfiction narrative.

CONCEPTS TO REMEMBER

1. The **purpose** of a work of nonfiction is the author's reason for writing—to entertain, to inform, or to persuade. The **audience** is the type of reader for whom the work is intended. Every work contains a **central idea,** or general statement about life.

2. Effective nonfiction uses many techniques of fiction. **Plot** is the sequence of events, what happens in a narrative. At the center of a plot is a problem, or **conflict.** As a person in the narrative tries to solve his or her problem, the plot builds to the point of highest interest, or the **climax.** Nonfiction also uses **dialogue,** or conversation between individuals. In addition, descriptions of people and places help to make a narrative interesting and lifelike.

TYPICAL ASSIGNMENT

When asked to write a nonfiction narrative, you may be asked to do an assignment like this one:

Write a nonfiction narrative telling about a true experience in which you learned something about yourself or something about another person.

PREWRITING

1. To find a subject, think about the important people and events of your life. You may wish to look for an idea in your journal or in a family photo album or school publication. Choose one experience that caused you to learn something about yourself or another person. In choosing an event, consider your audience—for exam-

ple, your teacher and classmates. The experience you choose should be something that you wish to share with them. You may wish to choose a happy event. The following chart may help you to remember an appropriate experience.

POSSIBLE SUBJECTS	
first day of school	recital or play
birth of brother or sister	school event
being excluded from a group	moving
something lost or found	serious mistake
accident	school project
trying to improve grades	prize or trophy
learning a new skill	getting lost
helping a friend	helping at home
making a friend	having a job

2. In one or two sentences write the lesson that you learned from the experience. These sentences will state your central idea. The purpose of your narrative is to explain this lesson.

Examples

- I learned that being helpful is good but that I should not force my will on others.
- I learned that people with different personalities and different interests can still be friends.

3. Think about the sequence of events that made up your true experience. Then answer the following questions.

  a. In what way did your experience begin?
  b. What problem, or conflict, did you face?
  c. What was your reaction to the problem?
  d. What obstacles prevented you from solving the problem?
  e. In what way did you solve the problem?
  f. What was your reaction to the solution?
  g. What was the final outcome?

  List the events of your experience in chrono-

636   *Writing About Literature Handbook*

PEOPLE IN NONFICTION NARRATIVE

PERSON	PHYSICAL TRAITS	CHARACTER TRAITS	BEHAVIOR / REACTION	WHAT I LEARNED ABOUT MYSELF OR ANOTHER PERSON
ME	blond, wearing colorful pants and tops	friendly, enthusiastic, athletic, sometimes inconsiderate	funny, energetic, insistent, social	Being helpful is good, but I must not force my will on others.
CHERYL	small, dark, wearing skirts	sensitive about being nonathletic, honest	quiet, lonely, emotional	Cheryl's personality and her interests are different from mine, but the two of us can still be friends.

SETTING FOR NONFICTION NARRATIVE

PLACE	TIME OF DAY / YEAR	WEATHER	DETAILS OF SETTING
school cafeteria	lunchtime at school, fall	sunny and cool	large, brightly lit room with hundreds of students, a buzz of conversation, and the smells of different foods
school hockey field	fall, after school	cloudy and windy	closely mown field of grass with red goals, cheers from spectators

logical order. Be sure that each part of the experience leads clearly to the next.

4. Remember how you and the others in your narrative looked, dressed, sounded, and acted. Remember how you felt. Then fill in a chart like the one above. The sample chart contains information about one writer's plan for the people in a narrative.

5. Picture the setting, or the time and place, in which your true experience happened. Remember what you saw, heard, smelled, tasted, and touched in this setting. Then fill in a chart like the one above. The sample chart contains information about one writer's plan for the setting in a narrative.

6. Write an outline to help organize your thoughts. In the outline that follows, the sections printed in bold type are the steps that every narrative outline should include. The sections in italics are examples from the two charts on this page.

Continued on page 638

Writing About Literature Handbook   637

NARRATIVE OUTLINE

I. Beginning

  A. Describe the setting. *I was in the school cafeteria. It was fall, the first week of school in the seventh grade.*

  B. Give important background information including your age at the time. *I was talking and laughing with some friends about our field hockey club.*

  C. Begin to tell what happened. *I noticed a new girl, and I introduced myself to her.*

II. Middle

  A. Introduce and briefly describe the other people involved. *The new girl was Cheryl, who had just moved into town with her family.*

  B. Introduce a conflict, or problem. *I convinced Cheryl to join the hockey club in spite of her claim that she was not athletic. At practice she played poorly and was embarrassed. The other players blamed me for adding a weak player to the club.*

  C. Show your reaction to the conflict with a direct statement. *I felt responsible for making Cheryl and my teammates unhappy. I was unhappy whenever Cheryl made a mistake on the field.*

  D. Build toward a climax, the point of highest interest. *Near the end of an important game with a tied score, Cheryl shot for an unblocked goal and missed. She ran off the field.*

III. Ending

  A. Write a climax. *After the game I met Cheryl near the field. She said that she had never wanted to play hockey but that I forced her to play.*

  B. Give your reaction to the climax. *I apologized to Cheryl. I realized that she was not interested in sports but that we could still be friends. I also realized that I must not force my interests on others.*

638 *Writing About Literature Handbook*

7. Review the tips for writing dialogue, or conversation, in Lesson 4.

8. When you have completed your outline, choose a title for your narrative. The title may refer to what happens or to the lesson that you learned. It may also refer to a person, object, or setting.

▪ WRITING PARAGRAPH BY PARAGRAPH

1. Follow your outline. In the first paragraph tell where and when your true experience happens. Use sense details to describe the setting. Then give background information about yourself and the event, including your age at the time.

Example

    I met my friend Cheryl one year ago. I was twelve, and it was the first week of school in the seventh grade. I was in the school cafeteria with some of my friends from the field hockey club. We sat in the brightly lit room that smelled of hamburgers and tomato soup and told stories about the club. I noticed a new girl sitting by herself at the next table and went over to introduce myself.

2. In the second paragraph introduce the other people who are involved in the experience. Briefly describe them and your feelings toward them. If you wish, use dialogue.

Example

    Cheryl looked very small and was dressed in a skirt while almost everyone else wore jeans. She seemed eager to make friends and smiled broadly when I said hello. I liked her and knew that we would be friends.

    "You are new here," I said.

    "Yes, my family just moved into town. I just started in Mr. Benton's eighth-grade class."

3. In the third paragraph introduce your problem, or conflict, Be sure to include your feelings about the problem.

Example

I invited Cheryl to join me and my other friends. Because much of our conversation was about the hockey club, I urged Cheryl to join. When she said that she was not an athlete, I laughed. "Cheryl, we do not consider ourselves athletes. We enjoy the game, and it certainly is a great way to make friends." Cheryl joined the club later that week. From the beginning she played poorly. My other friends in the club blamed me for bringing in a weak player, and Cheryl seemed unhappy whenever we played. I began to feel responsible for everyone's unhappiness.

4. In the paragraph or paragraphs that follow, build suspense as the narrative moves toward a climax and you try to solve your problem. Continue to recount your actions and to reveal your feelings about what happens.
5. In the next-to-last paragraph present the point of highest interest, or climax. Give your reaction to what happens.
6. In the last paragraph wind down the action, and give the final outcome of the experience. Be sure to tell what you learned about yourself or another person.

▨ REVISING AND EDITING

Once you have finished the first draft, you must take time to polish it into an improved second draft. Read your narrative aloud, and use the following checklist to revise your writing.

I. Content
  A. Does your title point to something important and grab the reader's interest?
  B. Does your narrative reveal the kind of person you are? If your narrative concerns another person, do you reveal something about his or her personality?
  C. Do you present events in chronological order?
  D. Do you use sense details and dialogue to make the narrative more interesting and realistic?
  E. Do you use a first-person narrator, referring to yourself as "I"?
  F. Do you clearly tell what you learned about yourself or someone else from the experience in your narrative?
II. Style
  See Lesson 4 for detailed reminders about improving the style of your writing.
III. Grammar, Usage, Mechanics
  See Lesson 4 for detailed reminders about improving the grammar, usage, and mechanics of your writing.

▨ ASSIGNMENTS

1. Imagine that you are the young hockey player in the narrative outline in this lesson. Complete the narrative begun in this lesson by using the charts. You may follow the outline to the end of the narrative, or you may create your own ending if you wish. Give the narrative a title. Be sure to explain what the experience in the narrative taught you about yourself or another person.
2. Do an assignment called "Writing a Nonfiction Narrative" (page 102 or 305). Your narrative should tell about an interesting experience in which you learned something about yourself or something about another person.
3. Keep a journal that is a record of important experiences that happen to you. Describe each experience, and tell what your reaction to the experience was. Then tell what you learned about yourself or about another person from the experience. You may want to include photographs and drawings in your journal.

Writing About Literature Handbook 639

This lesson guides students through the process of writing a review of a book or play. The lesson reinforces the textbook's teaching about plot, character, and setting. You may want to teach this lesson in conjunction with the Short Story, Drama, or Novel units in this textbook. Since the lesson uses examples from the one-act play *The Romancers,* you may want to assign that work before you teach this lesson. Under "Assignments" on the following page, you will find cross-references to Composition assignments that focus on drama and book reviews.

In your *Teacher's Resource Book* you will find these related black-line masters: Outline for Writing a Book or Drama Review; Questions to Explore a Literary Work; Checklist for Revising a Paper About a Literary Work.

LESSON 9: *Writing a Book or Drama Review*

A book or drama review is one person's written opinion of a particular literary selection. When you are asked to write a review, you must read the selection carefully, weighing its strengths and weaknesses. You must then support your opinions with specific examples from the text. Include the title of the work, brief information about the work's contents, biographical facts about the author that directly relate to the work, and judgments about the content and literary elements in the work.

TYPICAL ESSAY QUESTION

When you are asked to write a book or drama review, you may be asked to do an assignment like the following one:

Write a book [or drama] review. Begin with facts about the book [or drama]—such as the work's title, critics' opinions of it, date of publication, and awards if any. Describe the setting of the story. Then go on to describe the main characters and to summarize the plot. Conclude by giving your opinion of the book [or drama] backed by supporting details from the work.

You may be asked to write a drama review based on the printed version only or on an actual performance.

PREWRITING

1. Collect as much of the following information about the work as possible:

   a. whether or not the work is well known
   b. if it is an early, later, typical, or unusual work by the author
   c. what the author's general reputation is
   d. when and where the author lived
   e. what awards the work has received

   This information often appears on the book jacket, in the program of a play, or in a reference book.

2. Ask yourself questions such as the following about each of the literary elements:

   a. **Setting:** Is the setting realistic or at least believable?
   b. **Characters:** Are they believable? Do you come to care about the characters?
   c. **Plot:** Does the plot grow logically out of the characters' actions, decisions, and personalities? Does suspense build to a climax? Is the conflict settled in a satisfying way?

3. Prepare an outline for your review. In the suggested outline that follows, the sections printed in bold type are useful for all reviews. The sections in italics are examples based on the script for *The Romancers* (page 351).

OUTLINE FOR REVIEW

I. **Introduction**
   General information about the work
   1. **Title:** *The Romancers*
   2. **Critics' opinion of the work:** *highly praised and adapted*
   3. **Date:** *1894*
   4. **Place in author's career:** *his first play*
   5. **Awards:** *author elected to the French Academy*

II. **Body of Review**
   A. **Setting**
      1. **Where and when:** *a garden divided by a high wall, anywhere, at any time*
      2. **Appropriateness of setting:** *The garden is appropriate to romance; the wall shows the division between families.*
   B. **Main characters**
      1. **Names and key descriptions:**
         Sylvette, a romantic young woman
         Percinet, a romantic young man
         Pasquinot, Sylvette's father
         Bergamin, Percinet's father
         Straforel, a swordsman

2. Believability of characters:

Sylvette and Percinet are consistent as a typical "starry-eyed" couple. The fathers are interesting because they pretend to be enemies when they are really friends.

C. Plot

1. Brief summary:
Sylvette and Percinet fall in love although they believe their fathers to be enemies. In fact, the fathers are old friends who wish their children to marry. They stage a kidnapping in which Percinet "saves" Sylvette. The fathers then give their blessings to the wedding.

2. Believability of plot:
The play is not true to life because people do not pretend to be enemies and stage kidnappings. The plot, however, is lively with a duel and a kidnapping. It has unexpected twists; for example, the two fathers are actually friends.

III. Conclusion

A. General opinion of the work:
an enjoyable, lively, and witty play that has an unrealistic plot but has consistent characters

B. Recommendations to others:
particularly to those who enjoy comedy or who have seen one of the other versions of the play

▬ WRITING PARAGRAPH BY PARAGRAPH

1. In your first paragraph begin with a thesis statement. Tell which elements you will review.

Example of Thesis Statement

   The Romancers by Edmond Rostand is an enjoyable short play that has survived so long because of its believable characters, twisting plot, and appropriate setting.

You can fill out the introductory paragraph with other facts about the work. (See, for example, I.A. on the outline.)

2. In each of the following paragraphs, discuss one literary element and its appropriateness. For each element, give a topic sentence and at least one example to support it. The following paragraph discusses setting. Other paragraphs could take up characters and plot.

Example of Topic Sentence and Detail

   Both the young people and the adults in *The Romancers* are appropriate characters to convey the lengths that people will go to for love. The fathers love their children so much that they pretend for many years to be enemies. They want their children to marry and hide their friendship so that the young people do not feel that their marriage was arranged. The young people will not allow their fathers' feud to come between them, and the young man is willing to risk his life to rescue his love.

3. In your concluding paragraph give your overall opinion of the work. Then tell who else would enjoy the work.

▬ REVISING AND EDITING

See Lesson 1 for detailed reminders about improving your writing.

▬ ASSIGNMENTS

1. Use the outline in this lesson for *The Romancers* to complete a review of the play.
2. Do one of the assignments called "Writing a Drama Review" (page 23 or 431) or the assignment called "Writing a Book Review" (page 582).

This lesson guides students
through the process of writing an
original dramatic scene. The lesson reinforces the textbook's
teaching about dramatic elements such as dialogue and
stage directions. It also reviews
elements of fiction such as plot
structure, conflict, character, and
setting. The lesson develops a
specific scene from general idea
to outline form. Under "Assignments" on the final page of this
lesson, you will find cross references to scene-writing Composition assignments in this textbook.

In your *Teacher's Resource Book*
you will find these related black-
line masters: Charts for Writing a
Dramatic Scene; Outline for a
Dramatic Scene; Checklists for
Revising Creative Writing.

LESSON 10: *Writing a Scene*

A play is a story that is meant to be acted out for
an audience. When you see a play, you actually
see the action, characters, and settings. When you
write a play, you should be able to picture your play
as it would appear on a stage.

CONCEPTS TO REMEMBER

1. A **scene** is a very short play or part of a play.
   A scene usually concerns a single event and
   happens in a single setting.
2. The script of a play contains (1) **dialogue,** or
   the conversation of the characters, and (2)
   stage directions, or descriptions of actions,
   characters, and settings.
3. Drama uses many of the same techniques as
   the short story. The plot of a play usually concerns a problem, or **conflict.** As the characters
   try to solve this problem, the play builds to its
   point of highest interest, or **climax.** The characters in a play should have believable personality traits and clear motivations for their actions. They reveal their personalities by their
   words and actions.

TYPICAL ASSIGNMENT

When asked to write a scene, you will often be
given an assignment like this one:

Write a dramatic scene with believable plot, characters, and setting.

PREWRITING

1. To find an idea for your dramatic scene, think
   first about characters. Because you will need at
   least two characters in order to have dialogue,
   try to think of interesting combinations of people. Then think of a problem, or conflict, that
   such people might share. List some different
   ideas on a chart like the one on the next page.
2. From your chart choose the characters and
   problem for your scene. Ask yourself the following questions: How will a problem occur between the two characters? In what ways will
   each character react to the problem? How will
   the problem be solved?
3. Try to imagine how your characters look, sound,
   and act. Then fill in a chart like the one called
   "Characters" on the next page. The sample
   contains information about characters that one
   writer has in mind for a scene.
4. Picture your setting. When and where does the
   action take place? What background scenery
   will your scene need? What furniture and objects, or props, are on the stage? Fill in a chart
   like the one called "Setting" on the next page.
5. To help you to organize your thoughts, prepare
   an outline for your scene. In the following sample outline, the sections printed in bold type are
   steps that every outline for a dramatic scene
   should include. The sections in italics are examples of one writer's ideas for a scene.

POSSIBLE IDEAS FOR A DRAMATIC SCENE

FIRST CHARACTER	SECOND CHARACTER	PROBLEM
airplane pilot	passenger	nervousness about flying
baseball player	baseball fan	an error during a big game
teen-ager	parent	desire for driving lessons
travel agent	customer	desire for the ideal vacation
submarine navigator	submarine commander	lost at sea
football coach	football player	being dropped from the team
robot	robot	what it is like to be human
American	foreign tourist	different cultures
customer	clerk at complaint desk	defective merchandise
student	wrestling coach	knee injury

CHARACTERS

CHARACTER	JOB	AGE	SIZE	FEATURES	GESTURES	DRESS	SPEECH	PERSONALITY
Max Meyeron	student	15	tall, muscular	short, dark hair, shy smile	looks down while speaking, crosses arms	school wrestling team uniform	slow, quiet, thoughtful	tough but shy, proud of skill at wrestling, considerate
Mr. Andrew Hamilton	junior high school wrestling coach	40s	tall, muscular	short blond hair and beard, a friendly smile	calm, uses hands for emphasis when speaking	blue slacks, white shirt, jacket, and cap	slow, loud, forceful	friendly, strong, enjoys working with student athletes

SETTING

HISTORICAL PERIOD, SEASON, TIME	PLACE	BACKGROUND	FURNITURE	LIGHT	PROPS
present day, winter, early evening	school gymnasium	tile walls, hardwood floors	bleachers ready for a match, wrestling mats	Windows are dark; room brightly lit.	wrestling helmets and knee pads

Writing About Literature Handbook 643

DRAMATIC SCENE OUTLINE

I. Cast of characters
List your characters in order of appearance with some identification for each. *Max Meyeron, 15, a junior-varsity wrestler Mr. Hamilton, the school wrestling coach Mrs. Meyeron, Max's mother Emily, 14, the girl whom Max likes*

II. Setting the stage
A. Describe the background scenery, furniture, and lighting. *The scene is a modern junior high school gymnasium just before a wrestling match. The tile walls and hardwood floors are covered with wrestling mats. Although it is cold and dark outside, the room is warm and brightly lit. Wrestling equipment litters the floor. A door on the right leads to the coach's office.*

B. Tell which characters are on stage and what they are doing as the scene begins. *Max, a tall, muscular wrestler, is pacing in front of the coach's office. The door opens, and Mr. Hamilton stands in the doorway. He is carrying a clipboard.*

III. Beginning
A. Make it clear who your characters are and how they are related. *Max and his coach exchange greetings.*

B. Give background information that is important to the plot. *Hamilton asks Max about his injured knee. Max says that his doctor has given permission for him to wrestle again.*

C. Introduce the problem, or conflict. *Hamilton says that Max should rest his knee longer.*

IV. Middle
A. Show the reactions of characters to the conflict. *Max insists that he can wrestle tonight. Emily, a girl he likes, has promised to watch the match tonight.*

B. Build toward the point of highest interest, or climax. *Hamilton learns that two of his best wrestlers are ill. He agrees to let Max wrestle. Max's match begins.*

C. Introduce minor characters, and show their relationship to others. *Emily enters and sits next to Max's mother. Mrs. Meyeron worries about Max's knee. Emily says that she likes Max because of his shyness and consideration.*

V. Ending
A. Reach the point of highest interest. *The match is very close. Suddenly Max is pinned down and cries out in pain. He is holding his knee and is unable to stand.*

B. Show the characters' reactions to the climax. *Mrs. Meyeron runs to a phone to call the doctor. Emily shyly approaches.*

C. Show the final outcome. *Max tells Emily that he may have to give up wrestling. Emily says that she is sure he will succeed at anything else he takes up instead.*

6. When your outline is complete, practice writing dialogue. Write at least one line for each character. You may want to ask friends for help in writing realistic dialogue. Assign the part of one character to each friend. Then have them improvise a short conversation as the characters.

7. Choose a title for your dramatic scene. The title may refer to an important event, object, character, setting, or statement in the scene.

▉ WRITING LINE BY LINE

1. Write your title. Beneath it write *Cast of Characters*. Under this heading list the characters in order of appearance. Identify each character briefly.

2. On a new line write the word *Scene*. Then state the time and place. Describe the scenery, furniture, and lighting. Tell which characters are on stage. Describe them briefly and tell what they are doing as the scene begins.

644   *Writing About Literature Handbook*

Example

Scene: The setting is the gymnasium of a junior high school just before an important junior varsity wrestling match. Although it is cold and dark outside, the room is warm and brightly lit. The tile walls and hardwood floor are covered with wrestling mats. Wrestling equipment is scattered about the floor. On the right is a door that leads to the coach's office. As the scene begins, MAX MEYERON, a fifteen-year-old member of the junior varsity wrestling team, is pacing before this door. He is wearing the red and blue wrestling uniform of the school. The door opens, and MR. HAMILTON stands in the doorway. He is tall and muscular with short blond hair and beard. He is dressed in blue slacks with a white shirt and jacket. He is carrying a clipboard.

3. Write the name of the first character to speak on the next line, followed by a colon. Then write what this character says. Place stage directions, descriptions of the character's movements and speech, inside brackets. Begin a new line each time a different character speaks.

Example

HAMILTON: [His voice is friendly.] Hello, Max. You are early tonight as usual.
MAX: [He makes a small waving greeting gesture.] This is a big match, Coach. I think we can qualify for the finals tonight. [He claps his hands with excitement.]

4. Following your outline, continue to use dialogue and stage directions to introduce the problem, or conflict. Develop the sequence of events.
5. In the dialogue that follows, build suspense as the scene moves toward the climax.
6. Use dialogue and stage directions to introduce any additional characters.
7. Present the climax. Be sure that the solution to the problem is believable. Show the characters'

reaction to the climax. Write final stage directions that tell what the characters are doing as the scene ends.

▬ REVISING AND EDITING

Use the following checklist to revise your writing.

I. Content
  A. Does your title point to something important and grab the audience's interest?
  B. Do you list and identify your characters?
  C. Have you described the scenery, lighting, and furniture? Do you tell what the characters are doing as the scene begins?
  D. Do your stage directions describe the speech and actions of characters? Do they include information about props?
  E. Does your dialogue provide necessary background information?
  F. Does your dialogue show the problem, its solution, and the characters' reactions?
II. Style
  A. Have you put colons after the characters' names before they speak? Have you enclosed stage directions in parentheses?
  B. See Lesson 4 for further reminders.
III. Grammar, Usage, Mechanics
  A. Is each sentence complete (no fragments, no run ons)?
  B. Are all words spelled correctly? If you are not sure of the spelling of a word, have you consulted a dictionary?
  C. Have you punctuated sentences correctly?

▬ ASSIGNMENTS

1. Complete the scene begun in this lesson by using the charts. You may follow the outline to the end of the scene, or you may create your own ending if you wish. Give the scene a title.
2. Do an assignment called "Writing a Scene" (page 23, 189, or 431).

In this Handbook you will find all of the reading and literary terms taught in *Introducing Literature*. Each entry defines a term and then briefly discusses it, elaborating with examples from the selections. Each entry ends with a cross-reference to the pages that teach the literary term and, in some cases, to related entries in this Handbook.

READING AND LITERARY TERMS HANDBOOK

ALLITERATION   *The repetition of consonant sounds, most often at the beginning of words.* For example, the *n* sound is repeated in part of a line from Poe's "Raven" (page 239):

> While I *n*odded, *n*early *n*apping

See page 224.

ALLUSION   *A reference in a work of literature to a person, place, or event from history, another work of literature, or a work of art.* In "Crime on Mars" by Arthur Clarke (page 87), the narrator makes an allusion when he says the robbery of the Siren Goddess would be like a theft of the *Mona Lisa,* an extremely valuable painting.

See page 453.

ANECDOTE   *A brief account of a true event, meant to add depth and color to writing.* Anecdotes are often used in nonfiction to help reveal personality. For example, the anecdote in Agnes De Mille's autobiography (page 298) demonstrates that Kosloff was generous.

See page 312.

ASSONANCE   *The repetition of similar vowel sounds.* For example, in line 8 of Keats's "On the Grasshopper and the Cricket" (page 228) the repetition of the *ē* sound suggests the coziness of the Grasshopper's retreat:

> He rests at *ea*se beneath some pleasant weed.

See page 227.
See also ALLITERATION.

ATMOSPHERE   *The mood, or feeling, that runs through a work of literature.* Atmosphere is created largely through an author's choice of details and language. The atmosphere of a work may be one of gloom, happiness, mystery, and so on.

For example, the dust, wind, and poverty of the prairie town in William Stafford's "Osage Orange Tree" (page 68) create an atmosphere of sadness.

See page 92.

AUDIENCE   *The type of reader for whom a literary work is intended.* For example, Edward Abbey's "Havasu" (page 313) was probably written in particular for readers who enjoy adventure and suspense.

See pages 297, 486.

AUTOBIOGRAPHY   *The story of a person's life written by that person.* Russell Baker's *Growing Up* (page 8) is an example of autobiography.

See pages 297, 304.
See also NONFICTION.

BIOGRAPHY   *The story of a person's life written by someone other than that person.* "Harriet Tubman: The Moses of Her People" (page 306) is an example of biography.

See pages 297, 312.
See also NONFICTION.

CAUSE AND EFFECT   *A relationship between events in which one event—the cause—makes another event—the effect—happen.* For example, in "A Game of Catch" (page 74) Scho's teasing causes Glennie and Monk to call off their game. This response, in turn, encourages Scho to continue annoying them.

See page 47, 318.
See also MOTIVATION.

CHARACTER   *A person in a story, novel, poem, or play.* Each character has certain qualities, or

646   *Reading and Literary Terms Handbook*

character traits, that the reader discovers as the work unfolds. **Major characters** are well-developed, often complex personalities. For example, in Katherine Mansfield's "Mary" (page 103) Kass first does something very generous for Mary but keeps it a secret. Later, Kass regrets her "sacrifice" so much that she almost reveals the secret in order to hurt her sister. **Minor characters,** like James Keller in *The Miracle Worker* (page 12) are less developed and less likely to change.

> See pages 67, 566.
> See also CHARACTERIZA-
> TION, MOTIVATION.

CHARACTERIZATION   *The personality of a character and the way in which an author reveals that personality.* An author may directly state opinions about a character. For instance, in "The Brother Who Failed" (page 131) the author explains that Robert Monroe had never thought himself a failure until he overheard Aunt Isabel call him one. An author may also reveal a character's personality indirectly through the character's words and actions. For example, in "The Six Rows of Pompons" (page 140) the uncle's defense of Tatsuo indirectly reveals that the uncle loves his nephew.

> See pages 85, 566.
> See also CHARACTER,
> MOTIVATION.

CHRONOLOGICAL ORDER   *The time order in which events naturally happen.* In a literary work that follows chronological order, the event that takes place first is described first, and so on. Most narrative works of literature, such as "Spring Victory" by Jesse Stuart (page 32), are told in chronological order.

> See pages 47, 318.
> See also FLASHBACK.

CLIMAX   *The point of the reader's highest interest and emotional involvement in a story, novel, or play.* For example, in *The Romancers* (page 351) the climax occurs when Percinet fights Straforel.

> See pages 41, 430.
> See also CONFLICT, PLOT,
> RESOLUTION.

COMEDY   *A play that treats human problems lightly. The Romancers* by Edmond Rostand (page 351) is a comedy.

> See pages 349, 350.
> See also DRAMA, TRAGEDY.

COMPARISON AND CONTRAST   *A similarity (comparison) or difference (contrast) drawn between two or more items.* For example, in "On Summer" (page 324) Lorraine Hansberry contrasts summer with the other seasons of the year.

> See page 211.

CONCRETE LANGUAGE   Specific words that appeal to the five senses and are used to create images. Concrete language is specific rather than abstract or general. For instance, in "Counting-Out Rhyme" (page 222) the phrases "Silver bark of beech" and "Stripe of green in moose wood maple" create sharp visual images.

> See page 238.
> See also FIGURATIVE
> LANGUAGE, IMAGE.

CONCRETE POEM   *A poem shaped to look like its subject.* The placement of letters, words, lines, and punctuation creates a striking visual effect. "Seal" (page 233) is a concrete poem.

CONFLICT   *In the plot of a story, novel, or play, a struggle between two or more opposing forces.* An **external conflict** is a character's struggle against an outside force, such as nature, fate, or another person. For instance, in Jessamyn West's "Then He Goes Free" (page 78) Edwin's parents and Cress's parents have an angry discussion about their children's behavior. An **internal conflict** is a struggle that takes place within a char-

Reading and Literary Terms Handbook   647

acter's mind. For example, in Langston Hughes's short story "Thank You M'am" (page 64) Roger must choose between his desire to escape from Mrs. Jones's house and his desire to win Mrs. Jones's trust.

> See page 52.
> See also CLIMAX, PLOT, RESOLUTION.

COUPLET *Two consecutive lines of poetry that rhyme.* The two lines in a couplet often have the same length and rhythm and express a single, complete idea. For example, the entire text of the poem "Night Thought of a Tortoise Suffering from Insomnia on a Lawn" (page 264) is a couplet:

> The world is very flat—
> There is no doubt of that.

> See page 253.
> See also STANZA.

DEDUCTIVE REASONING *Logical thinking that begins with a general rule or assumption and then uses evidence to reach a specific conclusion.*

> See page 583.

DESCRIPTION *The type of writing that creates a vivid, exact picture of a person, animal, object, place, or event.* Description is used in both fiction and nonfiction.

> See pages 297, 323.
> See also DETAILS, ESSAY, EXPOSITION, NARRATION, PERSUASION.

DETAILS *Particular features of an item, used to make descriptive writing more precise and life-like.* For example, in "On Summer" (page 324) Lorraine Hansberry helps the reader understand her childhood dislike of summer when she associates summer with the following details: "the too-grainy texture of sand; the too-cold coldness of the various waters we constantly try to escape into, and the icky-perspiry feeling of bathing caps."

> See pages 73, 96, 212, 290, 323.
> See also DESCRIPTION.

DIALECT *The special form of speech that belongs to a particular group or region.* For example, in *All Things Bright and Beautiful* (page 319) the farmer Robert Corner speaks in the dialect of the British region of Yorkshire.

> See page 102.

DIALOGUE *The conversation between characters in a literary work.* In drama dialogue is the most important method by which the author gives information about the characters.

> See pages 189, 349, 364.
> See also DRAMA.

DRAMA *A literary work meant to be performed for an audience.* The written script of a play contains **dialogue**—the conversation of the characters—and **stage directions**—the writer's descriptions of sets, characters, and actions. Some plays, like *The Romancers* by Edmond Rostand (page 351), are **one-act plays.** Others, like *The Diary of Anne Frank* (page 366), are **full-length plays** that contain two or more acts.

> See pages 22, 349, 364.
> See also COMEDY, TRAGEDY.

END–STOPPED LINE *In poetry a line in which a pause occurs naturally at the end of the line.* The pause may be created by a period or semicolon, for example. Line 4 of Robert Francis' "Preparation" (page 224) is an end-stopped line:

> All winter long the land lay fallow.

> See page 252.
> See also RUN-ON LINE.

ESSAY *A short piece of nonfiction writing on any subject.* An essay uses facts, examples, and

648 *Reading and Literary Terms Handbook*

reasons to express an idea or opinion. For example, in "On Summer" (page 324) Lorraine Hansberry relates examples and incidents from her own life to explain how her feelings about summer have changed over the years.

> See pages 11, 297.
> See also DESCRIPTION, EXPOSITION, NARRATION, NONFICTION, PERSUASION.

EXPOSITION *The type of writing that presents facts or explains ideas.* Lorraine Hansberry's "On Summer" (page 324) is an example of an expository essay.

> See pages 297, 327.
> See also DESCRIPTION, ESSAY, NARRATION, PERSUASION, THESIS STATEMENT.

FABLE *A brief folk tale told to teach a moral, or lesson.* Often, the characters in fables are animals.

> See page 139.
> See also FOLK TALE, MYTH.

FALLACY *A mistake in reasoning.* One type of fallacy is known as **traits in common.** This type of fallacy incorrectly assumes that two items with several traits in common are identical in every other way. Another type of fallacy is known as **mistaken reverse.** This type of fallacy incorrectly assumes that two things that are opposite in one respect are opposite in every other respect.

> See page 584.

FICTION *Prose narrative works of the imagination including novels and short stories.*

FIGURATIVE LANGUAGE *Imaginative language used for descriptive effect and not meant to be taken as the literal truth.* For example, "drives its dark arrows" in Robert Francis' poem "Preparation" (page 224) is figurative language that suggests the force with which the rain penetrates the earth. Instances of figurative language are called **figures of speech. Similes** and **metaphors** are common figures of speech.

> See pages 245, 247.
> See also METAPHOR, PERSONIFICATION, SIMILE.

FLASHBACK *In a narrative, a scene that breaks the normal time order of the plot to show an event that happened in the past.* For example, in *The Diary of Anne Frank* (page 368) the first scene takes place in 1945, and the next scene is a flashback to 1942.

> See pages 63, 430.
> See also CHRONOLOGICAL ORDER.

FOLK TALE *An anonymous story that was originally passed down orally, or by word of mouth.* Folk tales usually reflect the beliefs, goals, and customs of a people. Folk tales differ from myths in that folk tales do not generally involve gods and goddesses. "Strong Wind, the Invisible" (page 483) is a folk tale.

> See pages 469, 471.
> See also FABLE, MYTH, TALL TALE.

FORESHADOWING *The use of clues by an author to prepare the reader for future developments in a story, novel, or play.* For example, in *The Hound of the Baskervilles* (page 503) the physical description of Beryl Stapleton hints that she may not be Mr. Stapleton's sister.

> See pages 57, 130, 458, 566.

FREE VERSE *Poetry that has irregular rhythms and line lengths.* Free verse usually does not rhyme, and it reflects the rhythms of everyday speech. Alice Walker's "For My Sister Molly Who in the Fifties" (page 284) is an example of a free verse poem.

> See page 260.
> See also RHYTHM.

Reading and Literary Terms Handbook 649

HAIKU *A three-line poem, usually on the subject of nature, with five syllables each in the first and third lines and seven syllables in the second line.* The following poem by Bashō is an example:

Song of the cuckoo:
　in the grove of great bamboos,
　　moonlight seeping through.

HERO *The central character in a work of literature.* A hero may be either male or female. In myths and folk tales heroes often have superhuman abilities. In most modern works heroes are more like ordinary people. For instance, Laurie is the hero of Shirley Jackson's story "Charles" (page 53).

See page 449.

IMAGE *A picture, or likeness, that is created with words.* Images are most often visual, but they may appeal to any of the five senses (sight, sound, touch, taste, and smell). For example, lines 11–12 of Frost's "Stopping by Woods on a Snowy Evening" (page 230) appeal to the senses of hearing, sight, and touch:

The only other sound's the sweep
Of easy wind and downy flake.

See page 238.
See also CONCRETE
LANGUAGE, IMAGERY.

IMAGERY *Language that appeals to the senses.* Imagery is the combination or collection of images in a literary work.

See page 238.
See also CONCRETE
LANGUAGE, IMAGE.

INFERENCE *A conclusion that can be drawn from the available information.* In literary works details about appearance and behavior help reveal a character's personality. For example, in Jessamyn West's "Then He Goes Free" (page 78), when the schoolchildren tear their bouquets apart and the teacher makes Edwin clean up the mess, we can infer that his classmates and teacher are scornful of Edwin because he is different.

See pages 73, 96, 406.
See also CHARACTERIZA-
TION, MOTIVATION.

IRONY *A difference between the way things seem to be and the way they actually are.* For example, *The Romancers* (page 351) contains an instance of irony when it turns out that the fathers are not enemies after all but are actually good friends.

See page 189.

LYRIC POEM *A poem that expresses a personal thought or emotion.* Most lyric poems are short, musical, and full of vivid images. Edna St. Vincent Millay's "Counting-Out Rhyme" (page 222) is a lyric poem that expresses the poet's delight in the richness of both nature and language.

See page 275.
See also NARRATIVE POEM.

METAPHOR *A figure of speech that compares or equates two basically different things.* For example, in "Paul Revere's Ride" (page 266) Longfellow compares death and war in a metaphor when he calls the graveyard a "night encampment" (line 43).

See page 247.
See also SIMILE.

MOTIVATION *A feeling, idea, or goal that causes a character to act in a certain way.* For example, in Ursula K. Le Guin's "The Rule of Names" (page 121) Birt takes Palani away from the island because he fears that the dragon will attack her.

See pages 77, 462.
See also CHARACTER,
INFERENCE.

MYTH *An ancient anonymous story that conveys the beliefs and ideals of a culture and usu-*

650　*Reading and Literary Terms Handbook*

ally involves gods and goddesses. Myths often provide examples of the way humans should behave. For instance, the story of Phaethon (page 450) warns mortals against attempting to be as powerful as the gods. A **mythology** refers to the collection of myths of a particular people.

See page 440.
See also FOLK TALE.

NARRATION *The type of writing that tells a story.* A narrative work may be either fiction or nonfiction. Types of narrative writing include autobiographies, biographies, narrative essays, short stories, novels, and narrative poems.

See pages 297, 318.
See also DESCRIPTION, ESSAY, EXPOSITION, PERSUASION.

NARRATIVE POEM *A poem that tells a story.* Narrative poems usually include setting, characters, action, and conflict. Henry Wadsworth Longfellow's "Paul Revere's Ride" (page 266) is a narrative poem.

See page 273.
See also LYRIC POEM.

NARRATOR *In a short story or novel, the person who tells the story.* A **first-person narrator** is a character in the work who tells the story as he or she experiences it. For example, in "Christmas Day in the Morning" (page 59) the first-person narrator describes the Christmas morning he milked the cows by himself and then waited eagerly for his father to return from the barn. A **third-person narrator** is an outside observer—not a character in the story—who refers to the characters as "he" and "she." A third-person narrator can usually describe the thoughts of all the characters in the work. Isaac Bashevis Singer's "The Mixed-Up Feet and the Silly Bridegroom" (page 42) has a third-person narrator.

See pages 107, 120, 550.
See also POINT OF VIEW.

NONFICTION *Factual prose writing.* Nonfiction always tells about incidents that actually happened and people who actually lived. Nonfiction includes **autobiography, biography,** and **essay.**

See pages 10, 297.
See also AUTOBIOGRAPHY, BIOGRAPHY, ESSAY.

NOVEL *A long work of narrative fiction written in prose.* Conan Doyle's *The Hound of the Baskervilles* (page 503) is a novel.

See page 501.
See also SHORT STORY.

ONOMATOPOEIA *The use of a word or phrase that imitates or suggests the sound of what it describes.* For instance, in line 11 of Keats's "On the Grasshopper and the Cricket" (page 228) the word *shrills* helps the reader hear the cricket's song.

See page 234.

OPINION *A statement expressing an individual's personal belief.* An opinion is not a **fact,** which is a statement that can be proven true. For example, in "Harriet Tubman: The Moses of Her People" (page 306) Langston Hughes states a fact when he says that Harriet Tubman was one of eleven children. He expresses an opinion when he says that "there was no one with a greater capacity for leadership than she had."

See page 342.
See also PERSUASION.

PARAPHRASE *A restatement in the reader's own words of the content of a written work.* By paraphrasing a written work the reader gains a better understanding of the writer's meaning.

See pages 287, 330.

PERSONIFICATION *A figure of speech in which an animal, object, or idea is given the characteristics of a human being.* For example, in "Mushrooms" (page 226) the mushrooms take on hu-

Reading and Literary Terms Handbook 651

man qualities by speaking and referring to their "toes" and "noses."

See page 248.
See also FIGURATIVE LANGUAGE.

PERSUASION *The type of writing in which an author attempts to make the reader accept an opinion or take action of some kind.* The Gettysburg Address (page 329) is persuasive writing.

See pages 297, 330.
See also DESCRIPTION, ESSAY, EXPOSITION, NARRATION.

PLOT *The sequence of events in a story, novel, play, or narrative poem.* The events in the plot usually develop into one or more **conflicts,** or struggles between opposing forces. The **climax** is the point of the reader's highest interest in the plot. The **resolution** reveals the final outcome of the plot. Some longer works have one or more **subplots,** or secondary but related plots within the main plot. The story of Selden in *The Hound of the Baskervilles* (page 503) is a subplot.

See pages 41, 430, 501.
See also CLIMAX, CONFLICT, RESOLUTION.

POETRY *Imaginative writing in which language, images, sound, and rhythm combine to create a special emotional effect.* Poetry is usually arranged in lines. Many poems have a regular **rhythm,** or pattern of beats, and some have **rhyme.**

See pages 7, 219.
See also LYRIC POEM, NARRATIVE POEM.

POINT OF VIEW *The relationship of the narrator, or storyteller, to the story.*

See pages 107, 120, 550.
See also NARRATOR, SPEAKER.

652 *Reading and Literary Terms Handbook*

PROSE *The kind of writing that is used in short stories, novels, works of nonfiction, journalism, and so forth.* Prose is distinguished from poetry. Unlike poetry, prose is usually written in lines that run from margin to margin across a page. Prose is also divided into sentences and paragraphs, and it sounds more like everyday speech than poetry does.

See also POETRY.

PURPOSE *The author's intention or goal in writing a particular work.* A writer's purpose may be to inform, entertain, or persuade the reader, or to express an idea. For example, Abraham Lincoln's purpose in writing the Gettysburg Address (page 329) was to persuade his listeners that they must dedicate themselves to the preservation of the United States and its ideals of freedom and democracy.

See pages 297, 305.
See also AUDIENCE, NONFICTION.

QUATRAIN *A group of four consecutive lines of poetry that form a unit.* The lines may or may not have the same length and rhythm, but together they usually express a complete thought. For instance, Robert Frost's "Stopping by Woods on a Snowy Evening" (page 230) is made up of four quatrains.

See page 255.
See also STANZA.

REFRAIN *In some songs and poems a line or group of lines repeated at regular intervals.* For example, in "The Raven" (page 239) several stanzas end with the refrain "Quoth the Raven 'Nevermore.'"

See also REPETITION.

REPETITION *The repeated use of sounds, words, phrases, or lines.* Repetition stresses important items and helps unify the poem or other work of literature. For example, in "Ring Out,

Wild Bells'' (page 232) the phrases *ring out* and *ring in* are repeated several times.

See page 224.
See also ALLITERATION, ASSONANCE, REFRAIN, RHYME.

RESOLUTION   *In a story, novel, or play, the part of the plot that presents the final outcome.* The resolution in *The Diary of Anne Frank* (page 368) occurs when Mr. Frank reveals that everyone else who had lived in the attic has died.

See page 41.
See also CLIMAX, PLOT.

RHYME   *The repetition, in two or more words, of stressed vowel sounds and the consonants that come after them.* The most common type of rhymes are **end rhymes,** which occur at the ends of lines. **Near,** or **approximate, rhymes** are words that almost rhyme, like *note* and *pot*.

See page 228.
See also COUPLET, RHYME SCHEME

RHYME SCHEME   *The pattern made by the end rhymes in a poem.* The rhyme scheme of a poem is indicated by the assignment of a different alphabet letter to each new rhyme. For example, the rhyme scheme of the first stanza of "Ring Out, Wild Bells" (page 232) is *abba:*

Ring out, wild bells, to the wild sky,	*a*
The flying cloud, the frosty light;	*b*
The year is dying in the night;	*b*
Ring out, wild bells, and let him die.	*a*

See page 228.
See also RHYME.

RHYTHM   *The pattern of beats made by stressed and unstressed syllables in the lines of a poem.* A poem's rhythm usually reflects its meaning. For instance, a fast rhythm fits a poem of action, while a slower rhythm is appropriate in a poem that expresses a calm feeling. Rhythm may be regular and follow a repeated pattern, or it may be irregular. For example, Shakespeare's "When Icicles Hang by the Wall" (page 237) follows a regular pattern of alternating unstressed and stressed syllables:

When all aloud the wind doth blow,
And coughing drowns the parson's saw

See page 231.

RUN-ON LINE   *In poetry a line in which the meaning continues beyond the line.* The line does not end with a mark of punctuation or other break. For example, lines 1 and 2 of Francis' "Preparation" (page 224) are run-on lines:

Last fall I saw the farmer follow
The plow that dug the long dark furrow

See page 252.
See also END-STOPPED LINE.

SCANNING   *A method of reading in which the reader searches quickly through a work for a particular word, phrase, or piece of information.*

See page 27.
See also SKIMMING.

SETTING   *The time and place in which a work of literature happens.* For example, the setting of Stuart's "Spring Victory" (page 32) is a country farm during the bitterly cold, snow-filled winter.

See pages 92, 101, 581.
See also ATMOSPHERE.

SHORT STORY   *A brief account in prose of fictional events.* Most stories have one or more **characters** and occur in a particular time and place, or **setting.** The **plot** is the sequence of events that happen in the story. A story's **theme** is the main idea the writer is expressing.

See pages 4, 31.
See also CHARACTER, NARRATOR, PLOT, SETTING, THEME.

SIMILE *A figure of speech that uses* like *or* as *to directly compare two seemingly unlike things.* For example, in "Paul Revere's Ride" (page 266) the sound of the wind was "like a sentinel's tread" (line 45).

See page 245.
See also FIGURATIVE
LANGUAGE, METAPHOR.

SKIMMING *A method of reading in which the reader glances quickly through a written work in order to preview it.* The reader skims through a work by noting title, table of contents, headings, boldfaced or italicized terms, and illustrations.

See page 27.
See also SCANNING.

SPEAKER *In a poem the voice that utters the words of the poem.* The speaker may be the poet or may be a character that the poet has created. Some poets even use animals or inanimate objects as their speakers. For example, in "Mushrooms" (page 226) the speakers are mushrooms.

See page 279.

STAGE DIRECTIONS *In drama the writer's instructions for performing the work and descriptions of sets, characters, and actions.*

See pages 22, 349.
See also DRAMA.

STAGING *The acting, costumes, scenery, lighting, sound effects, and other special effects that bring a play to life.*

See pages 349, 365.
See also DRAMA.

STANZA *A group of lines forming a unit in a poem.* Stanzas, which are separated by a space, often represent units of meaning. For example, Poe's "Raven" (page 239) has six- line stanzas.

See pages 7, 258.
See also COUPLET,
QUATRAIN.

654 *Reading and Literary Terms Handbook*

SUSPENSE *The reader's growing interest in the outcome of a literary work.* Hemingway creates suspense in "A Day's Wait" (page 2) because the reader is eager to learn why Schatz is upset.

See page 57.

TALL TALE *A story of unbelievable events told with perfect seriousness.* "Paul Bunyan's Cornstalk" (page 472) is a tall tale.

See page 471.
See also FOLK TALE.

THEME *The main idea of a literary work, usually expressed as a generalization.* A **stated theme** is one that the author expresses directly in the work. For example, the first line of Keats's "On the Grasshopper and the Cricket" (page 228) states this poem's theme: "The poetry of earth is never dead." An **implied theme** is not stated directly in the work but is suggested by the work's other elements. For example, Helen's discovery of language in *The Miracle Worker* (page 12) suggests the work's theme: "Language is the vital link between human beings."

See pages 139, 145, 276, 277.

THESIS STATEMENT *A sentence or group of sentences expressing the author's central idea in a work of nonfiction.* For example, the thesis statement of "Harriet Tubman: The Moses of Her People" (page 306) is "Before the War, like Frederick Douglass, Harriet Tubman devoted her life to the cause of freedom, and after the War to the advancement of her people."

See page 327.
See also TOPIC SENTENCE.

TITLE *The name of a work of literature.* The title sometimes refers to an important character or event, sets the work's mood, or provides a clue to the work's main idea. For example, the title "Gentleman of Río en Medio" (page 93) suggests two things about Don Anselmo: that he is dignified and that he is gentle.

See pages 139, 265.

TOPIC SENTENCE *The sentence that expresses the main idea of a paragraph of nonfiction.* The topic sentence usually appears very early in the paragraph, and the rest of the paragraph develops the idea stated in that sentence. For example, in "Havasu" the sixth paragraph on page 314 begins with the following topic sentence: "After the first wave of utter panic had passed I began to try to think." The rest of the paragraph shows the line of thought that Abbey began to follow.

See page 305.
See also THESIS
STATEMENT.

TRAGEDY *A serious play that ends sadly.* The opposite of tragedy is **comedy.**

See page 350.
See also COMEDY, DRAMA.

WORD CHOICE *The selection of words in a literary work to convey meaning, suggest the author's attitude, and create images.* For example, in "Mushrooms" (page 226) words like *discreetly, acquire, voiceless,* and *nudgers* encourage the reader to view the mushrooms as sinister, almost human creatures.

See page 243.

WORDPLAY *The skillful manipulation of words, often for humorous effect.* A **pun**—a joke based on words that have the same sound but different spellings or meanings—is a type of wordplay. The mouse-father in Stafford's "Mouse Night: One of Our Games" (page 251) makes a pun when he says "we'll be brainwashed/for sure if head-sized chunks of water hit us."

See page 223.

GLOSSARY

GLOSSARY

In the Glossary you will find the more difficult words in the selections, along with pronunciations and definitions of the words as they are used in the selections. In addition, you will find the Glossary words for each selection listed in the teacher's materials for that selection in your *Teacher's Resource Book.*

The following Glossary lists words that are from the selections but may be unfamiliar to you. Many of the words have several different meanings. However, they are defined here only as they are used in the selections. Some words may be familiar to you in other contexts but may have unusual meanings in this text.

Each Glossary entry contains a pronunciation, a part of speech, and a definition. Some words are used in more than one way in the textbook and therefore have more than one definition. Occasionally a word has more than one part of speech. Related words are often combined in one entry: The main form (for example, the adjective *absurd*) is defined, and another form (for example, the noun *absurdity*) is listed after the main definition. Adverbs ending in *-ly* are usually listed after the definition of the adjective form.

Some unusual words or meanings of words are labeled ARCHAIC (old-fashioned). Other special usage labels include INFORMAL, CHIEFLY BRITISH, and so on.

The following abbreviations are used in this Glossary:

n.	noun	*adv.*	adverb
v.	verb	*conj.*	conjunction
adj.	adjective	*n. pl.*	plural noun

A key to pronunciations may be found in the lower right-hand corner of each right-hand page of the Glossary.

A

abduct [ab dukt'] *v.* to kidnap or carry off without legal right to do so. — **abduction,** *n.*

abhor [ab hôr'] *v.* to hate; look on with disgust and dislike.

ablaze [ə blāz'] *adj.* on fire; in flames.

abominable [ə bom'ə nə bəl] *adj.* very unpleasant.

abound [ə bound'] *v.* to have many of; be filled with.

abrupt [ə brupt'] *adj.* sudden; unexpected. — **abruptly,** *adv.*

abstract [ab strakt'] *v.* to remove; take away.

absurdity [ab sur'də tē, ab zur'də tē] *n.* the state of being ridiculous; foolishness.

accelerate [ak sel'ə rāt'] *v.* to speed up; hasten.

accentuate [ak sen'choo āt'] *v.* to emphasize; stress.

accordingly [ə kôr'ding lē] *adv.* therefore.

acquainted [ə kwān'tid] *adj.* known to each other, but not close friends.

acquiescent [ak'wē es'ənt] *adj.* agreeing; not resisting.

acquire [ə kwīr'] *v.* to gain possession of something.

acute [ə kūt'] *adj.* intense; strong; severe. — **acutely,** *adv.*

adjacent [ə jā'sənt] *adj.* lying next to or near; adjoining.

adjourn [ə jurn'] *v.* to postpone; put off to a later time.

admirable [ad'mər ə bəl] *adj.* worthwhile; important; highly regarded.

adversary [ad'vər ser'ē] *n.* an enemy; opponent.

advisable [əd vī'zə bəl] *adj.* sensible. — **advisability,** *n.*

aesthetic [es thet'ik] *adj.* of or relating to art or beauty. — **aesthetically,** *adv.*

afford [ə fôrd'] *v.* to give or provide.

aggravate [ag'rə vāt'] *v.* to annoy, irritate.

aghast [ə gast'] *adj.* horrified; amazed.

agonized [ag'ə nīz'] *v.* to feel great pain; suffer greatly.

allusion [ə loo'zhən] *n.* a reference made in passing.

alter [ôl'tər] *v.* to change; make different.

amble [am'bəl] *v.* to walk slowly in a relaxed way; stroll.

amiable [ā'mē ə bəl] *adj.* friendly; good-natured; pleasant. — **amiably,** *adv.*

amiss [ə mis'] *adj.* wrong.

amongst [ə mungst'] *prep.* among; in the company of.

amorous [am'ər us] *adj.* showing love.

analysis [ə nal'ə sis] *n.* a careful and detailed examination.

anguish [ang'gwish] *n.* great mental or physical pain; agony.

antagonist [an tag'ə nist] *n.* an opponent, often in battle.

anteroom [an'tē room'] *n.* a room outside a main room.

anticipate [an tis'ə pāt'] *v.* **1.** to know, understand, or react to something or someone in advance. **2.** to come before.

anxious [angk'shəs, ang'shəs] *adj.* uneasy; concerned. — **anxiously,** *adv.*

apex [ā'peks] *n.* highest, most important point.

appendix [ə pen'diks] *n.* a section of additional information, usually at the end of a written work.

applicable [ap'li kə bəl, ə plik'ə bəl] *v.* that can be applied; suitable. — **applicability,** *n.*

apprehension [ap'ri hen'shən] *n.* a fear of what may happen.

approbation [ap'rə bā'shən] *n.* praise; approval.

apt [apt] *adj.* suitable and to the point. — **aptly,** *adv.*

aptitude [ap'tə tood', ap'tə tūd'] *n.* a natural ability or talent.

arbitrary [är'bə trer'ē] *adj.* based on rules that are often unreasonable.

arrogance [ar'ə gəns] *n.* too much pride mixed with a lack of respect for other people.

articulate [är tik'yə lit] *adj.* able to speak.

artifact [är'tə fakt'] *n.* an object made by humans, often a weapon or tool used in ancient times.

ascertain [as'ər tān'] *v.* to find out with certainty; determine.

ascot [as'kət, as'kot] *n.* a scarf that is tied around the neck with one end placed over the other.

asperity [as per'ə tē, əs per'ə tē] *n.* a severe, bitter tone or manner.

assertion [ə sur'shən] *n.* a positive statement; declaration.

astraddle [ə strad'əl] *adv.* seated on an animal with a leg on either side of it.

astute [əs toot', əs tūt'] *adj.* wise; smart; having the ability to understand quickly. — **astutely,** *adv.*

atone [ə tōn'] *v.* to make up for wrongs done.

atrocious [ə trō'shəs] *adj.* extremely bad; dreadful.

attentive [ə ten'tiv] *adj.* with concentration and thoughtful consideration.

attire [ə tīr'] **1.** *v.* to dress. **2.** *n.* clothes.

audacious [ô dā'shəs] *adj.* bold; daring.

audible [ô'də bəl] *adj.* loud enough to be heard.

austere [ôs tēr'] adj. **1.** severe; not warm or kindly. **2.** serious and plain.

autocrat [ô'tə krat'] n. a person who takes, has, and keeps complete authority over others.

avail [ə vāl'] v. to be able to do something.

avenge [ə venj'] v. to injure and harm someone in return for an act done by that person; get revenge.

awe [ô] v. to fill with wonder and fear.

azure [azh'ər, ā'zhər] adj. clear blue color, like the sky.

B

bandanna [ban dan'ə] n. a cloth like a large handkerchief, often brightly colored, worn around the head or used for carrying things.

barometer [bə rom'ə tər] n. anything that indicates changes.

bask [bask] v. to take pleasure in; enjoy.

bazaar [bə zär'] n. a place where many different goods are sold.

bedim [bi dim'] v. to obscure; make dim.

beggarly [beg'ər lē] adj. poor; pitiful; slight.

beguile [bi gīl'] v. to amuse; charm.

beset [bi set'] v. to attack from all sides.

betray [bi trā'] v. to reveal or point out.

bewilder [bi wil'dər] v. to confuse or puzzle completely.

bias [bī'əs] **1.** n. a leaning too much toward one point of view. **2.** v. to influence someone's thinking or opinions.

blanch [blanch] v. to become white and pale.

bleak [blēk] adj. cold and dreary; without cheer.

bluff [bluf] n. a high cliff.

bog [bog, bôg] n. a wet, swampy area.

boisterous [bois'tər əs, bois'trəs] adj. noisy, often enthusiastic and without control.

botanical [bə tan'i kəl] adj. relating to plants.

bourgeois [boor zhwä', boor'zhwä] adj. of or relating to the middle class.

bravado [brə vä'dō] n. one who acts boldly and with daring to hide a true feeling of fear.

breach [brēch] n. a breaking of friendly relations; quarrel.

bridle [brīd'əl] v. to harness a horse.

bristle [bris'əl] n. short, stiff hairs, as in a toothbrush.

broach [brōch] v. to introduce or bring up a subject for the first time.

C

cajole [kə jōl'] v. to persuade; coax.

calamity [kə lam'ə tē] n. a dreadful happening; disaster.

candid [kan'did] adj. honest and fair; sincere.

capacity [kə pas'ə tē] n. ability; power to do something.

captivate [kap'tə vāt'] v. to enchant; fascinate; hold the attention.

cardiac [kär'dē ak'] adj. relating to the heart.

cascade [kas kād'] n. a waterfall.

catastrophe [kə tas'trə fē'] n. a great and sudden disaster.

charade [shə rād'] n. a false display for the purpose of deceiving.

chasm [kaz'əm] n. an enormous crack or opening in the earth's surface.

chivalry [shiv'əl rē] n. qualities of an ideal knight, such as generosity, honorable behavior, and courtesy.

choleric [kol'ər ik] adj. easily angered or irritated.

chortle [chôrt'əl] n. a chuckle or laugh.

circumstantial [sur'kəm stan'shəl] adj. relating to events, often events at the time of a crime.

claimant [klā'mənt] n. one who declares his or her right to a certain property.

cleave [klēv] v. to divide; split into parts.

coherent [kō hēr'ənt, kō her'ənt] adj. **1.** easily understood. **2.** connected in a reasonable way. – **coherently,** adv.

commence [kə mens'] v. to begin; start.

commit [kə mit'] v. to do or perform (something wrong).

commitment [kə mit'mənt] n. an obligation; pledge.

commonplace [kom'ən plās] adj. dull; ordinary; lacking interest.

commotion [kə mō'shən] n. noisy disturbance; excited behavior.

commutation [kom'yə tā'shən] n. a reduction or change in a prison sentence.

compensate [kom'pən sāt'] v. to make up for.

compensation [kom'pən sā'shən] n. a payment or reward for work or service.

complacent [kəm plā'sənt] adj. satisfied, especially with oneself.

comprehend [kom pri hend'] v. to understand fully and completely.

concave [kon kāv', kon'kav] adj. curving inward.

conceive [kən sēv'] v. to think of or imagine.

condemn [kən dem'] v. to sentence.

confide [kən fīd'] v. to tell very personal information, such as secrets.

conical [kon'i kəl] adj. shaped like a cone, as an ice-cream cone.

conjecture [kən jek'chər] n. a guess; opinion not based on facts.

connoisseur [kon'ə sur'] n. an expert who can make judgments on a particular subject.

conscientious [kon'shē en'shəs] adj. **1.** aware of right and wrong and in the habit of choosing to do the right thing. **2.** having thought and care. – **conscientiously,** adv.

conscious [kon'shəs] n. state of mental awareness.

consecrate [kon'sə krāt'] v. to set aside as sacred or holy.

consequent [kon'sə kwent', kon'sə kwənt] adj. following, coming after and as a result of. – **consequently,** adv.

conservatory [kən sur'və tôr'ē] n. a school where the fine arts and music are taught.

conspicuous [kən spik'ū əs] adj. easily seen; displayed in an important way.

contemplate [kon'tem plāt'] v. to consider; think about.

contempt [kən tempt'] n. scorn; a feeling that a person is worthless.

contort [kən tôrt'] v. to twist; bend out of normal shape.

contrivance [kən trī'vəns] n. a clever scheme or plan.

---

at; āpe; cär; end; mē; it; īce; hot; ōld; fôrk; wood; fool; oil; out; up; ūse; turn; ə in ago, taken, pencil, lemon, circus; bat; chin; dear; five; game; hit; hw in white; joke; kit; lid; man; not; singer; pail; ride; sat; shoe; tag; thin; this; very; wet; yes; zoo; zh in treasure; кн in loch, German ach; N in French bon; œ in French feu, German schön

---

Glossary 657

convalescence [kon′və les′əns] *n.* a period during which someone recovers health after an illness.

convex [kon veks′, kən veks′, kon′veks] *adj.* curved outward.

convulsive [kən vul′siv] *adj.* with violent shaking movements.

coordination [kō ôr′di nā′shən] *n.* control of body movements so that actions take place in order and harmony.

cordial [kor′jəl] *adj.* warm and friendly; welcoming.

corduroy [kor′də roi′, kor′də roi′] *n.* a soft cloth with uneven, ribbed surface, often used in clothing.

corrupt [kə rupt′] *v.* to make something evil or useless.

countenance [koun′tə nəns] *n.* the expression on the face.

counteract [koun′tər akt′] *v.* to act against the effect or force of.

cower [kou′ər] *v.* to crouch or huddle as if in fear.

crevice [krev′is] *n.* a narrow crack or opening.

croon [krōōn] *v.* to sing softly or hum.

curriculum [kə rik′yə ləm] *n.* all the classes of study in a school.

D

daub [dôb] *v.* to cover or smear with a soft substance.

daunt [dônt] *v.* to make fearful or timid.

decree [di krē′] *v.* to order; rule.

default [di fôlt′] *n.* the absence of something needed.

defy [di fī′] *v.* to resist boldly or openly. – **defiance**, *n.* – **defiant**, *adj.* – **defiantly**, *adv.*

dejection [di jek′shən] *n.* sadness; lowness of spirits.

deluge [del′ūj] *n.* a downpour; heavy rain.

denounce [di nouns′] *v.* to criticize severely; blame.

describe [di skrīb′] *v.* to draw or trace the outline of.

desolate [des′ə lit] *adj.* sad; miserable; lonely.

desperado [des′pə rä′dō, des′pə rä′dō] *n.* a reckless, violent, bold criminal.

desperation [des′pə rā′shən] *n.* recklessness that comes from lack of hope.

despondency [di spon′dən sē] *n.* a loss of heart or hope; sadness.

detached [di tacht′] *adj.* not connected; unattached.

devastate [dev′əs tāt′] *v.* to destroy.

dictate [dik′tāt] *n.* a rule or principle that must be obeyed.

dilapidated [di lap′ə dā′tid] *adj.* broken down; ruined.

dilate [dī lāt′] *v.* to make larger or wider.

dilemma [di lem′ə] *n.* a difficult problem.

diligent [dil′ə jənt] *adj.* careful; painstaking.

diminish [di min′ish] *v.* to grow smaller.

diploma [di plō′mə] *n.* certificate given to a student when he or she graduates from a school.

direful [dīr′fəl] *adj.* dreadful; terrible.

disapproval [dis′ə prōō′vəl] *n.* an unfavorable opinion or feeling; dislike.

disavow [dis′ə vou′] *v.* to refuse to recognize.

discern [di surn′, di zurn′] *v.* to see; recognize.

disciple [di sī′pəl] *n.* a follower of a particular teacher.

discreet [dis krēt′] *adj.* having good judgment in speech and action.

disdain [dis dān′] *n.* scorn; feeling that someone or something is not important or worthwhile.

disfigure [dis fig′yər] *v.* to spoil the appearance of.

disgruntle [dis grunt′əl] *v.* to make displeased or cross.

disheveled [di shev′əld] *adj.* rumpled; untidy.

dismal [diz′məl] *adj.* **1.** causing gloom or sadness. **2.** dreadful; terrible.

disown [dis ōn′] *v.* to reject; cut one's ties with.

dispatch [dis pach′] *v.* to get rid of something; send away.

dissuade [di swād′] *v.* to keep someone from doing something by advice or persuasion.

distinct [dis tingkt′] *adj.* clear. – **distinctly**, *adv.*

divine [di vīn′] *adj.* related to the gods.

domain [do mān′] *n.* the land owned by one person or family; estate.

douse [dous] *v.* to throw water over; drench.

droll [drōl] *adj.* odd and amusing.

duration [dōō rā′shən, dyoo rā′shən] *n.* the length of time something lasts.

dutiful [dōō′ti fəl, dū′ti fəl] *adj.* doing what one is obliged or required to do. – **dutifully**, *adv.*

dwell [dwel] *v.* to make one's home; reside.

dwelt [dwelt] a past tense of **dwell**.

dwindle [dwind′əl] *v.* to become smaller; shrink.

E

earnest [ur′nist] *adj.* serious or sincere in feeling. – **earnestly**, *adv.*

ecstasy [ek′stə sē] *n.* a feeling of complete joy; happiness; delight. – **ecstatic**, *adj.*

edible [ed′ə bəl] *adj.* something fit to be eaten.

efface [i fās′] *v.* to wipe away or erase.

effigy [ef′i jē] *n.* a doll-like form made to resemble a person or animal, often made of straw or cloth.

elaborate [i lab′ər it] *adj.* highly detailed; worked out with great care. – **elaborately**, *adv.*

elicit [i lis′it] *v.* to bring out or draw forth.

eloquence [el′ə kwəns] *n.* the quality of being expressive or effective. – **eloquent**, *adj.*

emigrate [em′ə grāt′] *v.* to move from one country in order to settle and live in another country.

encounter [en koun′tər] *v.* to meet or come upon unexpectedly.

endorse [en dôrs′] *v.* to write one's name; sign.

engulf [en gulf′] *v.* to crowd around; surround and overcome.

entail [en tāl′] *v.* to involve; cause; bring.

epidemic [ep′ə dem′ik] *n.* the sudden spread or appearance of a disease among many people at the same time.

equestrian [i kwes′trē ən] *adj.* relating to a person mounted on horseback.

erupt [i rupt′] *v.* to throw forth something suddenly and violently. – **eruption**, *n.*

esteem [es tēm′] *v.* to have a high opinion of someone or something.

etching [ech′ing] *n.* a picture made by metal pressing paper onto an inked metal plate into which a drawing has been scratched.

exalt [ig zôlt′] *v.* to praise; honor.

exasperate [ig zas′pə rāt′] *v.* to annoy greatly; make angry.

excavator [eks′kə vā′tər] *n.* a machine that digs up and clears away rubble and parts of fallen buildings.

exceedingly [ek sē′ding lē] *adv.* unusually; extremely.

exclamation [eks′klə mā′shən] *n.* word or words spoken or cried out suddenly.

execute [ek′sə kūt′] v. to produce, especially according to plan or design.

exhilarate [ig zil′ə rāt′] v. to excite; stimulate.

expanse [iks pans′] n. a large area.

expedient [iks pē′dē ənt] n. a means or way of accomplishing something.

exposure [iks pō′zhər] n. the act of being seen or looked at.

extract [iks trakt′] v. to pull or take out.

extricate [eks′trə kāt′] v. to pull free from a knot or tangle.

exuberant [ig zōō′bər ənt] adj. overflowing with high spirits.

exult [eg zult′] v. to rejoice greatly; be joyful. – **exultant**, adj. – **exultation**, n.

F

famine [fam′in] n. a widespread lack of food, resulting in extreme hunger and starvation.

fanatic [fə nat′ik] n. a person who is completely and unreasonably devoted to an idea. – **fanatical**, adj.

fantasist [fan′tə sist] n. one who believes in and invents make-believe ideas and stories.

farce [färs] n. a joke; mockery.

fatalist [fāt′əl ist] n. one who believes that events are decided by fate and that human action cannot change the outcome.

feud [fūd] n. a long-lasting hatred and struggle between groups.

fiend [fēnd] n. a devil; evil spirit.

finesse [fi nes′] n. skill; ability to handle difficult situations gracefully.

finicky [fin′i kē] adj. fussy.

flail [flāl] v. to wave or swing violently.

flaxen [flak′sən] adj. having a pale yellow color, like the color of straw.

fledgling [flej′ling] n. a very young bird.

flush [flush] v. **1.** to drive an animal or person out from cover or a hiding place. **2.** to glow with a reddish color.

foliage [fō′lē ij] n. the growth of leaves on a tree or other plant.

forbear [fôr bār′] v. to keep from doing something; hold back.

foreman [fôr′mən] n. a supervisor in charge of a group of workers.

formidable [fôr′mi də bəl] adj. **1.** causing fear or dread because of great strength or size. **2.** difficult to deal with.

fret [fret] v. to be upset, unhappy, or worried.

furtive [fur′tiv] adj. half-hidden; secret.

G

gallant [gal′ənt] adj. brave, noble, like a hero. – **gallantly**, adv. – **gallantry**, n.

gape [gāp] v. to open or be opened wide.

gaunt [gônt] adj. very thin and hollow-eyed.

gazelle [gə zel′] n. a small African or Asian antelope, having yellow-brown coat and large, shining eyes.

gesticulate [jes tik′yə lāt′] v. to move head and parts of the body to express thoughts or feelings.

gird [gurd] v. to put on and fasten.

gist [jist] n. a main idea.

gloat [glōt] v. to look upon something with satisfaction.

gnarled [närld] adj. rough, with many knoblike shapes on the surface.

gratify [grat′ə fī′] v. to please; give pleasure and satisfaction. – **gratification**, n.

grave [grāv] adj. serious. – **gravely**, adv.

grievance [grē′vəns] n. a wrong that causes anger or distress.

grotesque [grō tesk′] adj. ugly in shape or appearance.

gullet [gul′it] n. the throat.

H

habitation [hab′ə tā′shən] n. a place to live in.

haggard [hag′ərd] adj. looking tired and worn out.

hailstorm [hāl′stôrm] n. a storm during which bits of ice fall.

hark [härk] v. to go back, as to a previous time in one's memory.

harry [har′ē] v. to trouble; annoy.

haul [hôl] v. to pull; drag.

haunch [hônch] n. the leg and loin of an animal.

hazard [haz′ərd] n. a risk of danger or accident.

hearten [härt′ən] v. to encourage; cheer.

heft [heft] v. INFORMAL. to test the weight of something by lifting it.

hilt [hilt] n. the handle of a sword or dagger.

hinder [hin′dər] v. to make difficult or delay the progress of something.

hoist [hoist] v. to lift, pull up.

hollow [hol′ō] n. a valley.

hulk [hulk] n. a large mass, as the body of a ship.

humiliate [hū mil′ē āt′, ū mil′ē āt′] v. to embarrass; make ashamed.

hypothesis [hī poth′ə sis] n. a theory or explanation that is based on known facts but has not been proved.

I

illiteracy [i lit′ər ə sē] n. a lack of ability to read or write.

immobile [i mō′bil, i mō′bēl] adj. fixed in one place; still; not moving.

impair [im pār′] v. to weaken; damage.

impassive [im pas′iv] adj. having or showing no emotion; unmoved.

impending [im pend′ing] adj. about to happen; threatening.

impenetrable [im pen′ə trə bəl] adj. impossible to pass through.

imperious [im pēr′ē əs] adj. urgent. – **imperiously**, adv.

at; āpe; cär; end; mē; it; īce; hot; ōld; fôrk; wood; fōōl; oil; out; up; ūse; turn; ə in ago, taken, pencil, lemon, circus; bat; chin; dear; five; game; hit; hw in white; joke; kit; lid; man; not; singer; pail; ride; sat; shoe; tag; thin; this; very; wet; yes; zoo; zh in treasure; кн in loch, German ach; N in French bon; œ in French feu, German schön

implicate [im′plə kāt′] *v.* to show that someone or something is involved, usually in a crime.

implicit [im plis′it] *adj.* without question. – **implicitly**, *adv.*

implore [im plôr′] *v.* to plead with; ask earnestly.

imprudent [im prōōd′ənt] *adj.* unwise; rash.

inaccessible [in′ək ses′ə bəl] *adj.* impossible to reach or touch.

inadequacy [in ad′ə kwə sē] *n.* a failure to meet required or desired standard.

inadvertent [in′əd vurt′ənt] *adj.* accidental; not planned or intended. – **inadvertently**, *adv.*

inapplicable [in ap′li kə bəl, in ə plik′ə bəl] *adj.* not suited.

incessant [in ses′ənt] *adj.* never ending; continuous.

incisive [in sī′siv] *adj.* sharp; clear; to the point.

incompatible [in′kəm pat′ə bəl] *adj.* not able to exist in harmony or agreement.

inconspicuous [in′kən spik′ū əs] *adj.* likely to escape notice.

indicate [in′di kāt] *v.* to be a sign of; show. – **indication**, *n.*

indignation [in′dig nā′shən] *n.* anger aroused by something unfair.

indignity [in dig′nə tē] *n.* an act or remark that insults or injures.

indulgent [in dulj′ənt] *adj.* giving in to the wishes of others. – **indulgently**, *adv.*

ineffectual [in′i fek′chōō əl] *adj.* without results. – **ineffectually**, *adv.*

inert [i nurt′] *adj.* without power to move or act.

inevitable [i nev′ə tə bəl] *adj.* certain to happen, not possible to avoid. – **inevitably**, *adv.*

inexorable [i nek′sər ə bəl] *adj.* that does not change or stop, no matter what is said or done.

inexplicable [in′iks plik′ə bəl, in əks′pli kə bəl] that cannot be explained. – **inexplicability**, *n.*

infernal [in furn′əl] *adj.* terrible; hateful.

infest [in fest′] *v.* to overrun in large numbers so as to overcome and harm.

infirm [in furm′] *adj.* physically weak, as from old age.

infuriate [in fyoor′ē āt′] *v.* to make furious; enrage.

ingenious [in jēn′yəs] *adj.* clever; imaginative.

inherit [in her′it] *v.* to receive or come into possession of in any way.

injunction [in jungk′shən] *n.* order; command.

innumerable [i nōō′mər ə bəl, i nū′mər ə bəl] *adj.* too many to count.

inquest [in′kwest] *n.* an inquiry made by a jury to decide whether there has been a criminal act.

inquisitive [in kwiz′ə tiv] *adj.* eager for knowledge; curious.

insignia [in sig′nē ə] *n.* a mark or emblem.

insignificant [in′sig nif′ə kənt] *adj.* not important; having little meaning.

insolent [in′sə lənt] *adj.* rude or bold. – **insolently**, *adv.*

insomnia [in som′nē ə] *n.* the inability to sleep.

institution [in′sti tōō′shən, in′sti tū′shən] *n.* a person or practice that occupies a regular and important place.

intact [in takt′] *adj.* untouched or whole.

intent [in tent′] *adj.* firmly directed or fixed. – **intently**, *adv.*

intercourse [in′tər kôrs′] *n.* an exchange; relationship.

interrogate [in ter′ə gāt′] *v.* to examine; ask questions.

interval [in′tər vəl] *n.* a period of time.

intimate [in′tə mit] *adj.* closely related to, well acquainted. – **intimacy**, *n.*

intoxicate [in tok′sə kāt′] *v.* to excite greatly.

introspective [in′trə spek′tiv] *adj.* characterized by the examination of one's own thoughts and feelings.

intuition [in′tōō ish′ən, in′tū ish′ən] *n.* the ability to sense the truth without having been told.

invaluable [in val′ū ə bəl, in val′yə bəl] *adj.* priceless.

invariable [in vār′ē ə bəl] *adj.* not changing; always the same. – **invariably**, *adv.*

invoke [in vōk′] *v.* to call upon.

irresolute [i rez′ə lōōt′] *adj.* hesitating; uncertain. – **irresolution**, *n.*

irreverent [i rev′ər ənt] *adj.* lacking in respect.

itinerant [ī tin′ər ənt, i tin′ər ənt] *adj.* going from place to place.

J

jaunt [jônt, jänt] *n.* a short trip, usually for pleasure.

jostle [jos′əl] *v.* to push, bump, or shove.

jounce [jouns] *v.* to move up and down with rough, bouncing movements.

jubilation [jōō′bə lā′shən] *n.* a feeling of joy or triumph.

juncture [jungk′chər] *n.* a point in time.

K

knave [nāv] *n.* a person with no principles or moral standards.

L

labyrinth [lab′ə rinth′] *n.* a place with confusing, winding, and connecting passages in which it is easy to get lost.

lackluster [lak′lus′tər] *adj.* dull; of little or no interest.

lag [lag] *v.* to fall behind; decline.

languid [lang′gwid] *adj.* lacking interest and concern.

languish [lang′wish] *v.* to weaken.

lank [langk] *adj.* thin and tall.

lateral [lat′ər əl] *adj.* sideways; to one side.

laurel [lôr′əl, lor′əl] *n.* a medium-sized bush with shiny green leaves.

levity [lev′ə tē] *n.* light, carefree, happy behavior.

liable [lī′ə bəl] *adj.* INFORMAL. likely.

linger [ling′gər] *v.* to go at a slow pace.

literate [lit′ər it] *adj.* able to read and write.

litigation [lit′ə gā′shən] *n.* a legal action against another party, usually involving court action.

loiter [loi′tər] *v.* to move slowly or with frequent pauses. – **loiterer**, *n.*

lopsided [lop′sī′did] *adj.* not the same on both sides; leaning to one side.

lumberjack [lum′bər jak′] *n.* a person who cuts down trees and gets them ready to be shipped to a sawmill.

lurch [lurch] *v.* to roll or sway to one side.

luxury [luk′shər ē, lug′zhər ē] *n.* something that adds to a person's comfort and pleasure.

660 *Glossary*

maestro [mīs′trō] *n.* one who is an expert in a special field or area.

malformation [mal′fôr mā′shən] *n.* a misshaped part of the body.

malignant [mə lig′nənt] *adj.* evil; ready to do harm. — **malignantly,** *adv.*

maneuver [mə nōō′vər] *v.* to move skillfully and carefully.

manifest [man′ə fest′] *v.* show; make visible.

manipulate [mə nip′yə lāt′] *v.* to move or work, using the hands.

mariner [mar′ə nər] *n.* a sailor.

matronly [mā′trən lē] *adj.* like or belonging to a grown woman.

matted [mat′əd] *adj.* entangled or entwined in a thick mass.

maxim [mak′sim] *n.* a short statement expressing a general truth.

meager [mē′gər] *adj.* small; thin.

meditate [med′ə tāt′] *v.* to think seriously and carefully.

meek [mēk] *adj.* gentle; mild in manner.

melancholy [mel′ən kol′ē] *adj.* sad; low in spirits.

merchandise [mur′chən dīz′, mur′chən dīs′] *n.* goods that are for sale.

meticulous [mi tik′yə ləs] *adj.* very careful about details. — **meticulously,** *adv.*

mettlesome [met′əl səm] *adj.* having spirit and courage.

miasma [mī az′mə] *n.* a poisonous gas formerly believed to rise from the earth and pollute the air. — **miasmatic,** *adj.*

midway [mid′wā′] *adj.* in the middle of the way.

mire [mīr] *n.* an area of wet, muddy, soft ground.

morass [mə ras′] *n.* an area of wet ground; marsh; swamp.

morose [mə rōs′] *adj.* appearing to be gloomy or sullen.

mortification [môr′tə fi kā′shən] *n.* a feeling of deep embarrassment or shame.

mosaic [mō zā′ik] *n.* a picture or design made of small bits of colored stone or other hard material.

mottle [mot′əl] *v.* to mark or cover with spots or patches.

multitude [mul′tə tōōd′, mul′tə tūd′] *n.* a great number of people.

muzzle [muz′əl] *n.* the opening at the front end of a gun.

mysticism [mis′tə siz′əm] *n.* of or related to beliefs that have hidden or secret meanings.

naivete [nä ēv′tā′] *n.* the quality of being innocent or simple.

negligent [neg′li jənt] *adj.* careless; neglectful.

negotiate [ni gō′shē āt′] *v.* to manage; make something work.

negotiation [ni gō′shē ā′shən] *n.* a discussion in order to come to an agreement.

neutral [nōō′tral, nyōō′trəl] *adj.* not taking either side in an issue or conflict. — **neutrality,** *n.*

newfangled [nōō′fang′gəld, nū′fang′əld] *adj.* recently come into fashion; modern.

nocturnal [nok turn′əl] *adj.* happening at night.

nonchalance [non′shə läns′, non′chə läns′] *n.* a casual attitude of not caring.

notable [nō′tə bəl] *adj.* remarkable; worth noticing.

notorious [nō tôr′ē əs] *adj.* well-known, usually having a somewhat bad reputation.

obedience [ō bē′dē əns] *n.* the act of obeying or carrying out the orders and ideas of a person in authority.

obligation [ob′lə gā′shən] *n.* something by which one is bound, such as a promise or sense of duty.

obscure [əb skyoor′] **1.** *v.* to hide. **2.** *adj.* not easily seen.

onslaught [on′slôt′, on′slot] *n.* a destructive attack.

oppression [ə presh′ən] *n.* cruel and unfair control, usually by force.

orator [ôr′ə tər, or′ə tər] *n.* a skillful speech maker.

ordain [ôr dān′] *v.* to command by authority.

organic [ôr gan′ik] *adj.* of or relating to an organ of the body, such as the heart.

ostentatious [os′tən tā′shəs] *adj.* showy; in a way that attracts attention. — **ostentatiously,** *adv.*

outstrip [out′strip′] *v.* to race ahead of others.

overhaul [ō′vər hôl′] *v.* to catch up with and overtake.

pageantry [paj′ən trē] *n.* an elaborate spectacle or display.

palate [pal′it] *n.* the sense of taste.

pallid [pal′id] *adj.* pale; without color.

palpable [pal′pə bəl] *adj.* able to be observed by means of the senses; noticeable.

pandemonium [pan′də mō′nē əm] *n.* noisy disorder or uproar.

paroxysm [par′ək siz′əm] *n.* a sudden physical reaction.

parson [pär′sən] *n.* a church official, such as a minister.

particle [pär′ti kəl] *n.* a small piece of material.

passion [pash′ən] *n.* a fit or spell of emotion, such as love or anger. — **passionate,** *adj.* — **passionately,** *adv.*

paternal [pə turn′əl] *adj.* belonging or relating to a father.

peerless [pēr′lis] *adj.* without equal; matchless.

peevish [pē′vish] *adj.* irritable; cranky.

penetrate [pen′ə trāt′] *v.* to go through something.

pensive [pen′siv] *adj.* thoughtful.

perceive [pər sēv′] *v.* to become aware of. — **perception,** *n.*

perceptible [pər sep′tə bəl] *adj.* noticeable; easily seen. — **perceptibly,** *adv.*

peremptory [pə remp′tər ē] *adj.* determined; unconditional; final.

peril [per′əl] *n.* an extremely dangerous situation.

perpetual [pər pech′ōō əl] *adj.* lasting a very long time or forever.

---

at; āpe; cär; end; mē; it; īce; hot; ōld; fôrk; wood; fōōl; oil; out; up; ūse; turn; ə in ago, taken, pencil, lemon, circus; bat; chin; dear; five; game; hit; hw in white; joke; kit; lid; man; not; singer; pail; ride; sat; shoe; tag; thin; this; very; wet; yes; zoo; zh in treasure; ᴋʜ in loch, German ach; ɴ in French bon; œ in French feu, German schön

Glossary 661

persecution [pur′sə kū′shən] *n.* a continual, cruel treatment.

perseverance [pur′sə vēr′əns] *n.* an ability to continue a plan of action in spite of difficulties.

persistent [pər sist′ənt] *adj.* continuing firmly despite opposition.

perverse [pər vurs′] *adj.* unreasonable and unnecessary.

petition [pə tish′ən] *n.* a request for action.

petty [pet′ē] *adj.* of little importance or value.

phenomenal [fə nom′ən əl] *adj.* remarkable; extraordinary.

phosphorus [fos′fər əs, fos fôr′əs] *n.* an element that produces a glow that is visible in the dark.

pittance [pit′əns] *n.* a small allowance, usually of money.

placid [plas′id] *adj.* calm; peaceful.

poise [poiz] *n.* a state of balance.

pompous [pom′pəs] *adj.* full of ceremony.

ponder [pon′dər] *v.* to consider; think over in a careful way.

porous [pôr′əs] *adj.* having many small openings or pores through which air and liquids may pass.

portal [pôrt′əl] *n.* an entrance, often a gate or doorway.

post-mortem [pōst′môr′təm] *adj.* taking place after death.

posture [pos′chər] *n.* the way of holding or carrying the head and body.

preachment [prēch′mənt] *n.* a speech, especially a long speech.

precipice [pres′ə pis] *n.* a high, steep face of rock.

predict [pri dikt′] *v.* to announce or declare beforehand. — **predictable**, *adj.*

preliminary [pri lim′ə ner′ē] **1.** *n.* a word or action serving as an introduction to a main event. **2.** *adj.* coming before the main event.

premises [prem′is əz] *n. pl.* land and the buildings on it.

prescribe [pri skrīb′] *v.* to recommend or order, often by a doctor for a medicine.

pretext [prē′tekst′] *n.* a false reason or excuse given to hide a true reason.

prim [prim] *adj.* stiffly polite; formal. — **primly**, *adv.*

prodigious [prə dij′əs] *adj.* marvelous; amazing. — **prodigiously**, *adv.*

profanity [prō fan′ə tē, prə fan′ə tē] *n.* coarse speech.

promenade [prom′ə nād′, prom′ə näd′] *n.* a place or area for taking walks.

prominent [prom′ə nənt] *adj.* very noticeable.

prophet [prof′it] *n.* one who can tell what will happen in the future.

proposition [prop′ə zish′ən] *n.* a suggestion for a plan of action.

prosperous [pros′pər əs] *adj.* successful; wealthy; flourishing.

prostrate [pros′trāt] *adj.* lying on the ground.

protrude [prō trōōd′] *v.* to stick out; project.

prow [prou] *n.* the forward part of a boat or ship.

prune [prōōn] *v.* to cut off branches of trees, usually to improve their growth or appearance.

psychology [sī kol′ə jē] *n.* the study of the mind and mental processes.

pugnacious [pug nā′shəs] *adj.* ready and eager to fight.

punctual [pungk′chōō əl] *adj.* prompt; on time.

punctuate [pungk′chōō āt′] *v.* to interrupt from time to time.

purloin [pur loin′] *v.* to steal.

purposeful [pur′pəs fəl] *adj.* having direction and determination.

Q

quaint [kwānt] *adj.* charming in an old-fashioned way.

R

radiant [rā′dē ənt] *adj.* shining, glowing, often with happiness and joy. — **radiance**, *n.*

radical [rad′i kəl] *adj.* tending toward revolutionary change in society.

random [ran′dəm] *adj.* lacking in pattern or clear and definite purpose.

rash [rash] *adj.* inclined to act hastily and without thinking.

ravage [rav′ij] *n.* a destructive action resulting in harm and injury.

ravisher [rav′ish ər] *n.* one who kidnaps someone or something.

rawhide [rô′hīd′] *n.* animal skin or hide that has not been tanned.

reassure [rē′ə shoor′] *v.* to give confidence or support. — **reassuringly**, *adv.*

rebellious [ri bel′yəs] *adj.* resisting authority and control; inclined to disobey.

recline [ri klīn′] *v.* to lie back or down.

recollection [rek′ə lek′shən] *n.* something remembered.

reconcile [rek′ən sīl′] *v.* **1.** to restore a friendship after a quarrel. **2.** to make things or events fit together in meaning, as to put the events of a story in order.

reek [rēk] *v.* to give off a very strong odor or smell.

reformation [ref′ər mā′shən] *n.* a complete change, usually for the better.

refusal [ri fū′zəl] *n.* the act of rejecting a suggestion or proposed action.

relevant [rel′ə vənt] *adj.* having to do with the matter at hand. — **relevancy**, *n.*

relinquish [ri ling′kwish] *v.* to let go of something.

remedy [rem′ə dē] *n.* a treatment designed to cure a problem or illness.

reminiscence [rem′ə nis′əns] *n.* an account of something remembered.

rendezvous [rän′də vōō′, rän′dā vōō′] *n.* an agreed-upon meeting place.

renown [ri noun′] *n.* fame; widespread reputation.

repentant [ri pent′ənt] *adj.* feeling sorrow for something one has done.

replica [rep′li kə] *n.* a close copy, often smaller than the original.

repose [ri pōz′] *n.* rest; sleep.

repress [ri pres′] *v.* to check or hold back.

residue [rez′ə dōō′, res′ə dū′] *n.* the remaining part of something, after the main part has been given or taken away.

resignation [rez′ig nā′shən] *n.* an attitude of accepting and submitting to someone or something.

resolute [rez′ə lōōt′] *adj.* showing great determination.

resonant [rez′ə nənt] *adj.* having a full, rich sound.

restless [rest′lis] *adj.* changing position constantly; unable to stop moving. — **restlessly**, *adv.*

retain [ri tān′] *v.* to preserve.

retrospection [ret′rə spek′shən] *n.* a survey or review of past events.

revel [rev′əl] *n.* a noisy festivity or party.

reverence [rev′ər əns, rev′rəns] *n.* a feeling of deep respect. — **reverent,** *adj.*

reversion [ri vur′zhən, ri vur′shən] *n.* a return to an earlier condition.

roguery [rō′gər ē] *n.* dishonest behavior.

rotary [rō′tər ē] *adj.* having a part or parts that turn.

rudiments [rōō′də mənts] *n. pl.* beginnings or early stages of something.

ruse [rōōz] *n.* an action designed to trick, deceive, or mislead.

rustic [rus′tik] *adj.* plain; simple; relating to country life.

S

sable [sā′bəl] *adj.* the color black.

sap [sap] *v.* to weaken gradually.

sapling [sap′ling] *n.* a young tree.

saunter [sôn′tər, sän′tər] *v.* to walk in a relaxed way.

savory [sā′vər ē] *adj.* smelling and tasting good.

scan [skan] *v.* to look at closely and carefully.

score [skôr] *n.* a set or group of twenty.

scornful [skôrn′fəl] *adj.* showing a feeling of hatred or contempt.

scowl [skoul] *v.* to frown angrily.

scuttle [skut′əl] *v.* to move rapidly, usually with short, fast steps.

semantic [si man′tik] *adj.* having to do with the meanings of words.

senility [si nil′ə tē] *n.* a weakening of mental powers that may occur in old age.

sequence [sē′kwəns] *n.* an orderly series of connected things.

serene [sə rēn′] *adj.* calm; without worry.

sever [sev′ər] *v.* to separate by cutting.

sham [sham] *n.* something false; fraud.

sheer [shēr] *adj.* straight up and down.

sidle [sīd′əl] *v.* to move sideways.

significant [sig nif′i kənt] *adj.* important; of special value.

signify [sig′nə fī′] *v.* to represent; mean.

silo [sī′lō] *n.* a building in which food for animals, usually dried grass and cornstalks, is stored.

simultaneous [sī′məl tā′nē əs, sim′əl tā′nē əs] *adj.* happening at the same time. — **simultaneously,** *adv.*

singe [sinj] *v.* to burn lightly.

sinister [sin′is tər] *adj.* evil; dangerous.

skein [skān] *n.* a coil of yarn or thread.

skitter [skit′ər] *v.* to slip along a surface.

skulk [skulk] *v.* to move in a sneaking way.

slack [slak] *adj.* loose; not tight or firm.

slay [slā] *v.* to kill, with violence.

slew [slōō] the past tense of **slay.**

slither [slith′ər] *v.* to slide, as on a slippery surface.

slog [slog] *v.* to move with great effort; plod.

slovenly [sluv′ən lē] *adj.* untidy; careless.

smite [smīt] *v.* to affect strongly with powerful feeling.

smitten [smit′ən] a past tense of **smite.**

sober [sō′bər] *adj.* serious; grave. — **soberly,** *adv.*

sojourn [sō′jurn, sō jurn′] *v.* to live briefly in a place.

solitary [sol′ə ter′ē] *adj.* lonely.

sovereign [sov′rən, sov′ər ən] *n.* a ruler.

sparse [spärs] *adj.* thin and spare.

specialization [spesh′əl ī zā′shən] *n.* a concentration on a single area of learning.

species [spē′shēz] *n.* a kind or type.

specious [spē′shəs] *adj.* apparently true but actually false.

specter [spek′tər] *n.* something that threatens or causes fear.

spectral [spek′trəl] *adj.* ghostly.

spry [sprī] *adj.* lively and nimble.

stability [stə bil′ə tē] *n.* steadiness.

stagnant [stag′nənt] *adj.* still; not flowing.

stature [stach′ər] *n.* the relative place or rank of something.

stench [stench] *n.* a very unpleasant smell.

stimulus [stim′yə ləs] *n.* something that causes a reaction.

straddle [strad′əl] *v.* to sit with one leg on each side of something.

strident [strīd′ənt] *adj.* loud; harsh; shrill.

subconscious [sub kon′shəs] *n.* the part of the mind that holds memories that are below the surface of everyday thinking and that are hard to bring back to awareness.

submission [səb mish′ən] *n.* the act of giving in; accepting without resistance.

subtle [sut′əl] *adj.* sly; crafty. — **subtlety,** *n.*

suede [swād] *adj.* made of a soft leather with a velvety surface.

suffocate [suf′ə kāt] *v.* to interrupt the breathing of.

sullen [sul′ən] *adj.* dismal; gloomy.

supernatural [sōō′pər nach′ər əl] *adj.* beyond the natural world; relating to ghosts.

supple [sup′əl] *adj.* **1.** easily bent. **2.** moving or thinking rapidly.

supremacy [sə prem′ə sē, sōō prem′ə sē] *n.* the quality of being greatest in power and authority.

surge [surj] *v.* to rise suddenly.

surgery [sur′jər ē] *n.* the removal or repair of injured parts of the body. — **surgical,** *adj.*

surmise [sər mīz′, sur′mīz] *n.* a guess.

surpass [sər pas′] *v.* to go beyond; be better than.

surveillance [sər vā′ləns, sər vāl′yəns] *n.* a close watch over a person in order to obtain information.

surveyor [sər vā′ər] *n.* one who examines, measures, and reports on land for its owner.

sustenance [sus′tə nəns] *n.* something that supports life, usually food.

swathe [swāth] *v.* to bind or wrap.

sympathize [sim′pə thīz′] *v.* to understand and share the feelings of another.

---

at; āpe; cär; end; mē; it; īce; hot; ōld; fôrk; wood; fōōl; oil; out; up; ūse; turn; ə in ago, taken, pencil, lemon, circus; bat; chin; dear; five; game; hit; hw in white; joke; kit; lid; man; not; singer; pail; ride; sat; shoe; tag; thin; this; very; wet; yes; zoo; zh in treasure; кн in loch, German ach; ɴ in French bon; œ in French feu, German schön

Glossary 663

syndrome [sin′drōm′] *n.* a number of signs that indicate a particular disease.

T

tactful [takt′fəl] *adj.* sensitive to the feelings of others.
taint [tānt] *v.* to spoil or damage.
tangible [tan′jə bəl] *adj.* capable of being touched.
taunt [tônt, tänt] *v.* to tease or mock with insults.
technician [tek nish′ən] *n.* a trained, skillful worker in any field.
tenderhearted [ten′dər här′tid] *adj.* gentle; sympathetic.
throng [thrông, throng] *v.* to fill; crowd into.
tragic [traj′ik] *adj.* dealing with plots and events that end in sadness or disaster.
tranquil [trang′kwəl] *adj.* quiet; peaceful; having little or no movement.
transfusion [trans fū′zhən] *n.* the transfer of liquid, often blood, from a container or an individual into the body of another individual.
transmit [trans mit′, tranz mit′] *v.* to send out; communicate.
trappings [trap′ingz] *n. pl.* brightly colored and decorated cloth spread over horses.
tread [tred] *v.* to walk on or along.
trodden [trod′ən] a past tense of **tread.**

U

unaccountable [un′ə koun′tə bəl] *adj.* impossible to explain or give a reason for.
unbounding [un boun′ding] *adj.* without limits.
uncanny [un kan′ē] *adj.* strange; eerie; weird.
unendurable [un en door′ə bəl, un en dyoor′ə bəl] *adj.* very painful; impossible to bear.
unmitigated [un mit′ə gā tid] *adj.* complete; total.
unprovoked [un prə vōkt′] *adj.* without cause.
unresilient [un ri zil′yənt, un ri zil′ē ənt] *adj.* stiff; unable to spring back into earlier condition.
unrestrained [un ri strānd′] *adj.* free; without regulation.
unsettle [un set′əl] *v.* to confuse; upset.
unwonted [un wôn′tid, un wōn′tid] *adj.* unusual; not customary.

V

vacate [vā′kāt] *v.* to leave empty.
vacuous [vak′ū əs] *adj.* empty; lacking intelligence.
vale [vāl] *n.* a valley.
valiant [val′yənt] *adj.* brave; courageous.
vapor [vā′pər] *n.* a gas, like a cloud of steam.
varnish [vär′nish] *v.* to cover with a substance that produces a clear and shining surface.
vault [vôlt] *n.* a high arch. **– vaulty,** *adj.*
venerable [ven′ər ə bəl] *adj.* deserving respect because of age.
verge [vurj] CHIEFLY BRITISH *n.* the grassy border of a road.
verify [ver′ə fī] *v.* to make sure that something is true and accurate.
vexation [vek sā′shən] *n.* an annoyance; irritation.
vicinity [vi sin′ə tē] *n.* the area near a particular place.
vulnerable [vul′nər ə bəl] *adj.* able to be physically wounded or injured.

W

waft [waft, wôft] *v.* **1.** to float. **2.** to carry lightly through the air or over water.
wallow [wol′ō] *v.* to roll around or move about happily.
wary [wâr′ē] *adj.* watchful; cautious.
waver [wā′vər] *v.* to move from side to side or up and down; sway.
wayward [wā′wərd] *adj.* irregular. **– waywardness,** *n.*
wheel [hwēl] *v.* to turn; pivot.
whim [hwim, wim] *n.* an unexpected notion or idea.
whimsical [hwim′zi kəl, wim′zi kəl] *adj.* having odd notions or ideas.
willful [wil′fəl] *adj.* determined to do as one pleases; stubborn.
work [wurk] *v.* to act to accomplish a definite purpose, task, or goal.
wrath [rath] *n.* violent anger; rage.
wretched [rech′id] *adj.* very unhappy; poor; pitiful.
wrought [rôt] past tense of **work.**

Z

zeal [zēl] *n.* an enthusiastic effort and interest.

VOCABULARY REVIEW

In addition to the words listed in the Glossary and the words covered in the word study sections throughout this book, each of the following words is presented to help you prepare for standardized tests of verbal skills. The page numbers at the right tell where you can find these words treated in *Enjoying Literature*.

apex	328	epidemic	5	lingering	41
articulate	582	esteemed	582	loam	227
attired	312	exceedingly	47	meek	227
bluff	41	exclamation	11	merchandise	47
calamity	449	execute	458	morose	312
candid	130	feud	232	pallid	582
capacity	312	finesse	582	peril	449
commenced	5	fledgling	458	pondered	47
commitment	328	formidable	328	prescribed	5
commotion	47	foul	232	purposeful	328
countenance	312	gaping	130	reeked	130
cowered	130	gaunt	73	remedy	47
cranny	227	gist	86	sable	449
default	130	grief	232	sapling	41
dejection	156	hauled	41	saps	232
detached	156	herons	458	saunter	86
diminished	86	hoist	449	slack	5
diploma	73	impassive	156	slithered	5
discreetly	227	impulse	458	slovenly	582
dismal	156	invaluable	312	surging	11
doused	86	jaunt	86	tranquil	73
ecstasy	11	lackluster	11	wild	232
edible	227	liable	41		

Vocabulary Review   665

This index groups all of the selections according to the themes that they address. Every selection is listed at least once; many are listed more than once. You may want to use this index to help students examine the presentation of a particular theme in different selections.

INDEX OF TITLES BY THEMES

666　Index of Titles by Theme

This index lists the skills covered under the following heads in the postselection study aids: Reading and Literary Focus, Composition, Vocabulary. The index identifies the pages on which the skills are taught or reinforced. For example, every Composition assignment is listed in the Composition Skills section of this index. Page numbers in boldface indicate entries in the Writing About Literature Handbook. Page numbers in italics indicate entries in the Handbook of Reading and Literary Terms.

INDEX OF SKILLS

Page numbers in boldface italics indicate entries in the Writing About Literature Handbook.
Page numbers in italics indicate entries in the Handbook of Reading and Literary Terms.

READING AND LITERARY SKILLS

Act, 364
Alliteration, 224, 282, **600, 602,** *618*
Allusion, 453, *618*
Anecdote, 312, 331, 333, *618*
Assonance, *227, 618*
Atmosphere, 92, 165, *618*
Audience, 25, 297, 330, 486, *618*
Autobiography, 11, 297, 304, *618*

Biography, 11, 297, 312, *618*

Cause and effect, 47, 318, 341, 494, *618*
Characterization, 67, 85, 160, 406, 430, **594, 596,** *618, 619*
   character traits, 67, 160, 430, **594, 596,** *618*
   techniques of, 85, 406, **594, 596,** *619*
Characters, 67, 77, 430, 462, 468, 496, 566, **594, 596,** *618*
   change in, 468
   major and minor, 566
   motives of, 77, 462, 496
Chronological order, 47, 159, 318, 332, *619*
Climax, 41, 166, 430, *619*
Comedy, 349, 350, *619*
Comparison and contrast, 211, *619*
Concrete language, 238, *619*
Concrete poetry, 234, *619*
Conflict, 52, 165, 430, *619*
Couplet, 253, *620*

Deductive reasoning, 583, *620*
Description, 297, 323, 333, *620*
Details, 73, 96, 212, 290, 291, 292, 323, 432, **590,** *620*
Dialect, 102, *620*
Dialogue, 22, 189, 349, 364, **614,** *620*
Drama, 22, 349, 364, 430, 432, 433, **612, 614,** *620*

End-stopped line, 252, *620*
Essay, 11, 297, 318, 327, 331, *620*
Exaggeration, 475
Exposition, 297, 327, 340, *621*
Expository essay, 297, 327

Fable, 471, *621*
Fact, 342, 343
Fallacy, 584, *621*
Fantasy, 494
Fiction, *621*
Figurative language, 245, 247, 248, 282, **600, 602,** *621, 622, 623, 626*
   metaphor, 247, **600, 602,** *622*
   personification, 248, **600, 602,** *623*

simile, 245, **600, 602,** *626*
Flashback, 63, 430, *621*
Flexibility, 25, 26, 27
Folk tale and folk literature, 469, 471, 486, *621*
Foreshadowing, 57, 130, 160, 458, 566, *621*
Free verse, 260, *621*
Full-length play, 349, 364

Generalizations, 139

Hero, 449, *622*
Humor, 475

Imagery, 7, 238, 282, **600,** *622*
Inferring, 73, 96, 213, 292, 406, *622*
   about characters, 73, 406
   about setting, 96
Irony, 189, *622*

Lyric poetry, 275, *622*

Main idea, 327, 335, **606**
Metaphor, 247, **600, 602,** *622*
Mood, *92*
Motivation, 77, 462, 495, *622*
Mystery, 502
Myth, 439, 440, *622*

Narration, 297, 318, 332, *623*
Narrative poetry, 273, *623*
Narrator, 107, 120, 550, *623*
   first-person, 107, 550
   third-person, 120, 550
Nonfiction, 10, 297, 318, 323, 327, 330, **606, 608,** *623*
   descriptive, 323
   distinguished from fiction, 297, **606, 608**
   expository, 327
   narrative, 318
   persuasive, 330
Novel, 501, *623*

One-act play, 349, 364
Onomatopoeia, 234, **600, 602,** *623*
Opinion, 342, 343, *623*
Oral tradition, 349

Paraphrasing, 287, **590,** *623*
Personification, 248, **600, 602,** *623*
Persuasion, 297, 330, 344, *624*
Plot, 41, 47, 52, 57, 63, 157, 430, 458, 501, 566, 581, **592, 596,** *624*
   cause and effect, 47
   chronological order, 47
   climax and resolution, 41
   conflict, 52
   in drama, 430
   flashback, 63
   foreshadowing, 57, 458, 566

COMPOSITION SKILLS

Page numbers in boldface italics indicate entries in the Writing About Literature Handbook.

ANALYTICAL
Writing *about* the following:

Writing the following analytical essays:

CREATIVE
Writing the following:

Index of Skills   669

Newspaper story, 41
Nonfiction narrative, 305, **608**
Onomatopoeia, 234
Persuasion, 365
Poem, 229, 265, 275, 279, 285, **602**
Scene, 23, 189, 431, **614**
Speech, 330, 449
Story, 5, 107, 167, **596**
Title, 289
Wordplay, 223

VOCABULARY SKILLS

TEST-TAKING SKILLS

Analogies, 73, 328
Antonyms, 156, 232, 449
Sentence completions, 47, 227
Synonyms, 5, 41, 130, 312

WORD STUDY

Compound words, 493
Context clues, 11, 86, 365, 458, 581
Dialect, 102
Dictionary, 58, 482
Glossary, 96
Homonyms / homophones, 229
Jargon / technical words, 305

Prefixes, 270
Pronunciation key, 393
Roots, 258
Shades of meaning, 453
Suffixes, 245
Thesaurus, 179
Word origins, 260, 318
Words often confused, 225

CHALLENGES

Bibliography, 5
Children's book, 47
Collage, 92
Description, 229
Diorama, 243
Exhibit, 289
Further reading, 283, 312, 468, 493
Illustration, 255
Interview, 582
Literary criticism, 102, 179, 261, 406
Mapmaking, 225
Memorizing, 330
Outlining, 328
Recordings, 486
Research, 23, 67, 145, 227, 265, 458
Research and oral report, 52, 167, 231, 252
Songs, 482
Staging, 365
Tribute, 247

Continued from page v

Little, Brown and Company
EDITH HAMILTON: "Phaethon" from *Mythology.* Copyright 1942 by Edith Hamilton; Copyright © renewed 1969 by Dorian Fielding Reid and Doris Fielding Reid, Executrix of the will of Edith Hamilton. Reprinted by permission of Little, Brown and Company.

Macmillan Publishing Company
JAMES STEPHENS: "The Wind" from *Collected Poems.* Copyright 1915 by Macmillan Publishing Co., Inc., renewed 1943 by James Stephens. Reprinted by permission of Macmillan Publishing Company.

Harold Matson Company, Inc.
JAMES STREET: "Weep No More, My Lady." Copyright © 1941 by James Street, © renewed 1969 by Lucy Nash Street. Reprinted by permission of Harold Matson Company, Inc.

Scott Meredith Literary Agency, Inc.
ARTHUR C. CLARKE: "Crime on Mars." Reprinted by permission of the author and the author's agents, Scott Meredith Literary Agency, Inc., 845 Third Avenue, New York, New York 10022.

Robert Nemiroff
LORRAINE HANSBERRY: "On Summer." © 1960 by Robert Nemiroff. All rights reserved. Reprinted by permission of Robert Nemiroff.

The New Yorker Magazine, Inc.
RICHARD WILBUR: "A Game of Catch" from *The New Yorker,* July 15, 1953 issue. © 1953, 1981 The New Yorker Magazine, Inc. Reprinted by permission of The New Yorker.

Harold Ober Associates, Incorporated
PEARL S. BUCK: "Christmas Day in the Morning" from *Collier's,* December 23, 1955. Copyright © 1955 by Pearl S. Buck. Copyright renewed 1983.
AGNES DE MILLE: "The Kosloff School" from *Dance to the Piper.* Copyright 1951, 1952 by Agnes de Mille. Copyright renewed 1979, 1980 by Agnes de Mille.
JAMES HERRIOT. Excerpt from *All Things Bright and Beautiful.* Copyright © 1973, 1974 by James Herriot.
LANGSTON HUGHES. "Harriet Tubman" from *Famous American Negroes.* Copyright 1954 by Langston Hughes. Copyright renewed 1982 by George Houston Bass. "Thank You M'am" from *The Langston Hughes Reader* copyright 1958 by Langston Hughes.
The preceding selections were reprinted by permission of Harold Ober Associates Incorporated.

Rand McNally & Company
THOR HEYERDAHL: Excerpt from *Kon-Tiki.* © 1950 by Thor Heyerdahl. Copyright renewed 1978. Published in the U.S. by Rand McNally & Company. Reprinted by permission of Rand McNally & Company.

Random House, Inc./Alfred A. Knopf, Inc.
FRANCES GOODRICH AND ALBERT HACKETT: Excerpt from *The Diary of Anne Frank.* Copyright 1954, 1956 as an unpublished work. Copyright © 1956 by Albert Hackett, Frances Goodrich Hackett, and Otto Frank. Reprinted by permission of Random House, Inc.

LANGSTON HUGHES: "The Dream Keeper" from *The Dream Keeper and Other Poems.* Copyright 1932, and renewed 1960 by Langston Hughes. Reprinted by permission of Alfred A. Knopf, Inc.
SYLVIA PLATH: "Mushroom" from *The Colossus and Other Poems.* Copyright © 1960 by Sylvia Plath. Reprinted by permission of Alfred A. Knopf, Inc.

Read Magazine
EDWIN A. HOEY: "Foul Shot" from *Read Magazine,* 1962. Published by Xerox Education Publications. © 1962, Xerox Corp. Reprinted by permission of *Read Magazine.*

Flora Roberts, Inc.
WILLIAM GIBSON: Two scenes from *The Miracle Worker.* © 1956 by William Gibson.
FRANCES GOODRICH AND ALBERT HACKETT: *The Diary of Anne Frank.* Copyright 1954 by Albert Hackett, Frances Goodrich Hackett, and Otto Frank.
The preceding selections were reprinted by permission of Flora Roberts, Inc.

Russell & Volkening, Inc.
JESSAMYN WEST: "Then He Goes Free" from *Cress Delahanty.* Copyright 1948, 1954, renewed 1982 by Jessamyn West. Reprinted by permission of Russell & Volkening, Inc. as agents for the author.

St. Martin's Press, Inc.
RUSSELL BAKER: Excerpt from *Growing Up.* Copyright © 1982 by Russell Baker. Reprinted by permission of Congdon & Weed, Inc. and St. Martin's Press, Inc.
JAMES HERRIOT: Excerpt from *All Things Bright and Beautiful.* Copyright © 1973, 1974 by James Herriot. Reprinted by permission of St. Martin's Press, Inc.

Charles Scribner's Sons
ERNEST HEMINGWAY: "A Day's Wait" from *Winner Take Nothing.* Copyright 1933 Charles Scribner's Sons; copyright renewed 1961 Mary Hemingway. Reprinted by permission of Charles Scribner's Sons.

Argelia L. Sedillo
JUAN A. A. SEDILLO: "Gentleman of Río en Medio." Reprinted by permission of Argelia L. Sedillo.

Simon Schuster, Inc.
LOUIS UNTERMEYER. "The Dog of Pompeii" from *The Fireside Book of Dog Stories,* edited by Jack Goodman. Copyright © 1943 by Simon & Schuster, Inc., renewed © 1971 by Simon & Schuster, Inc. Reprinted by permission of Simon & Schuster, Inc.

William Jay Smith
WILLIAM JAY SMITH: "Seal" from *Laughing Time: Nonsense Poems.* Published by Delacorte Press, 1980. Copyright © 1955, 1957, 1980 by William Jay Smith. Reprinted by permission of William Jay Smith.

The Society of Authors
KATHERINE MANSFIELD: "Mary." Reprinted by permission of The Society of Authors as the literary representative of the Estate of Katherine Mansfield.
JAMES STEPHENS: "The Wind." Reprinted by permission of

671

The Society of Authors on behalf of the copyright owner, Mrs. Iris Wise.

William Stafford

WILLIAM STAFFORD: "The Osage Orange Tree." Reprinted by permission of William Stafford.

The Jesse Stuart Foundation

JESSE STUART: "Spring Victory" from *Tales from the Plum Grove Hills.* Reprinted by permission of the Jesse Stuart Foundation/Eastern Kentucky University/Richmond, Ky. 40475/J. C. Powell, Chairman.

University of Massachusetts Press

ROBERT FRANCIS: "Preparation" from *Robert Francis: Collected Poems, 1936–1976.* Copyright © 1944, 1972 by Robert Francis. Reprinted by permission of The University of Massachusetts Press.

Viking Penguin Inc.

ADRIEN STOUTENBURG: A slightly abridged version of "Hammerman" and "Pecos Bill, Coyote Cowboy" from *American Tall Tales.* Copyright © 1966 by Adrien Stoutenburg. Reprinted by permission of Viking Penguin Inc.

Western Publishing Company, Inc.

ANNE TERRY WHITE: "Daedalus" from *Golden Treasury of Myths and Legends.* © 1959 by Western Publishing Company, Inc. Reprinted by permission of Western Publishing Company, Inc.

Max Wilkinson

JOHN D. MACDONALD: "Fire!" Copyright © 1980 by John D. MacDonald Publishing, Inc. Reprinted by permission of Max Wilkinson as agent for John D. MacDonald.

CREDITS

Illustration Credits:

Cover: David Frampton

Jim Barkley, 49, 50–51; Debbi Chabrian, 70; William Cigliano, 34, 38; Bill Cleaver, 81, 83; Helen Cogencherry, 105; Len Ebert, 442, 447; Shelley Freshman, 466, 467; Don Gates, 3; Jim Hays, 500–501, 502, 503, 506, 509, 512, 516, 520–521, 525, 528–529, 532, 536, 540, 546, 551, 558, 560, 565, 567, 569, 574, 579; Marilyn Janovitz, 98–99, 226; Larry Johnson, 488, 491; Angie Kimball, 240, 241; Jacob Knight, 266, 268, 269; Ed Martinez, 184, 187; Bob Masheris, 110, 113, 116, 119; Michael McNelly, 212; Verlin Miller, 438–439, 473; Sal Murdocca, 30–31, 171, 176–177, 479; Beverly Pardee, 193, 197, 201, 204, 209; Rodney Pate, 61, 65; Jerry Pinkney, 94; Yuri Salzman, 43, 45; Karen Schwartz, 256–257; Joel Snyder, 484; Sandy Speidel, 133, 137; David Wenzel, 123, 125, 128; Chuck Wimmer, 90; Larry Winborg, 30–31, 148, 153; Fred Winkowski, 54, 55.

Photo Credits: © Clara Aich, 246. Animals Animals: © Willard Luce, 245. Peter Arnold, Inc.: © C. Allan Morgan, 334. Courtesy of Russell Baker, 9. Courtesy of Ballantine Books: Photograph by Charles Adams, 87. Courtesy of Bantam Books, Inc.: Photograph by Harry Snavely, 190. The Bettmann Archive, 168, 180, 221T, 250C, 262C, 263T, 324, 329. Black Star: © Mark Morrow, 32; © Werner Wolff, 53. © Derry Brabbs, 320, 321. Brown Brothers, 131, 158, 236B, 262B, 472. Courtesy of B. J. Chute, 146. The Cleveland Museum of Art, 143. Bruce Coleman, Inc.: © Carl Roessler, 336T; © Jane Shaw, 336C; © Norman O. Tomalin, 244R; © Bill Wood, 337BR. Colour Library International, 163L. Culver Pictures, Inc., xiv–1T, 6, 14, 18, 59, 97, 103, 220T, 221TC & BC, 235B, 249B, 280T, BC, & B, 350, 476, 502. Leo deWys, Inc.: © Steve Vidler, 325. DRK Photo: © S. J. Krasemann, 274. Courtesy of E. P. Dutton: Photograph by Renée Abbey, 313. Earth Scenes: © J. C. Stevenson, 316. Fantastics of University Theatre, University of Illinois, Urbana, 348–349, 351, 354, 360–361, 363. Photo Fred Fehl, 367, 368, 370, 377, 398, 411, 417, 425, 428. The Folger Shakespeare Library, Washington, D.C., 235T. Folio Inc.: © Robert Madden, 264. Courtesy of Harper & Row, 68, 249T. Courtesy of Thor Heyerdahl, 336B, 337T. Historical Picture Service, Chicago, 470. Courtesy of Edwin A. Hoey, 250B. Courtesy of Evelyn Tooley Hunt, 236C. The Image Bank: © Aram Gesar, 230; © D. William Hamilton, 286; © Richard Nowitz, 224; © Marc Solomon, 259; © F. Whitney, 218–219B, 244L. Courtesy of Michael Joseph, London, 319. The Library of Congress: Photograph by Lindsley, 309. Magnum Photos, Inc.: © Burt Glinn, 250T; © Erich Hartmann, 222; © McClullin, 296–297B, 321. © Steven Y. Mori, 140. National Museum, Naples, 450, 459. New York Public Library: Lincoln Center, Performing Arts Research Center, 302; Picture Collection, 220C. The New York Times: 8, 236T; © Jack Manning, 332. Penguin Books Ltd., London, 262T. Photo Researchers, Inc.: © John Bryson, 2. Phototeque: From the Collection of Carlos Clarens, 21. PhotoUnique: © John Barstow, 315. Picture Archive, 237. Rainbow: © Dan McCoy, 218–219T, 288. Courtesy of Flora Roberts, Inc., 12. © Editta Sherman, 108. Kunsthistorisches Museum, 461. Shostal Associates, © Eric G. Carle, 163R. Stock Boston: © J. Albertson, 251. © Time Inc.: Enrico Ferorelli/Life Magazine, 296–297, 325; Lisa Kroeber/Time Magazine, 121; Carl Mydams/Time Magazine, 48; Gordon Parks/Life Magazine, 381, 391, 396, 403, 419; Gordon Tinney/Life Magazine, 302. UPI/Bettmann Archive, 64, 263C & B. Vatican Museum, Rome, 450, 459. Wide World, 366, 367T. Woodfin Camp & Associates: © Julie Habel, xiv–1B, 6, 75, 237; © Stephanie Maze, 278.

672

INDEX OF AUTHORS AND TITLES

Index of Authors and Titles 673

INDEX OF AUTHORS AND TITLES

This index is an alphabetical listing of all the selections and authors included in this textbook. Page numbers in italics indicate biographical information.

TEACHER'S PERSONAL RECORD

Most Successful Assignments and Projects

Page   Notes

_____

_____

_____

_____

_____

_____

_____

_____

_____

_____

_____

_____

_____

_____

_____

_____

_____

_____

TEACHER'S PERSONAL RECORD

Most Successful Assignments and Projects

Page   Notes

_____

_____

_____

_____

_____

_____

_____

_____

_____

_____

_____

_____

_____

_____

_____

_____

_____

_____

_____

TEACHER'S PERSONAL RECORD

Most Successful Pairings or Groupings of Selections

_____

_____

_____

_____

_____

_____

_____

_____

_____

_____

_____

_____

_____

_____

_____

_____

_____

TEACHER'S PERSONAL RECORD

Most Successful Pairings or Groupings of Selections

_____

_____

_____

_____

_____

_____

_____

_____

_____

_____

_____

_____

_____

_____

_____

_____

TEACHER'S PERSONAL RECORD

Original Assignments and Projects

Literary work
being taught

My original
assignment or project

_____

_____

_____

_____

_____

_____

_____

_____

_____

_____

_____

_____

_____

_____

_____

_____

_____

_____

_____

TEACHER'S PERSONAL RECORD

Original Assignments and Projects

Literary work
being taught

My original
assignment or project

_____

_____

_____

_____

_____

_____

_____

_____

_____

_____

_____

_____

_____

_____

_____

_____

TEACHER'S PERSONAL RECORD

Additional Resources

Literary work
being taught

Title and location of article,
illustration, recording, film, etc.

_____

_____

_____

_____

_____

_____

_____

_____

_____

_____

_____

_____

_____

_____

_____

_____

TEACHER'S PERSONAL RECORD

Additional Resources

Literary work
being taught

Title and location of article,
illustration, recording, film, etc.

_____

_____

_____

_____

_____

_____

_____

_____

_____

_____

_____

_____

_____

_____

_____

_____

E. Dickinson   Wilbur Faulkner   Tom Wolfe

Gerard M. Hopkins S.J.   Mark Twain   Rudyard Kipling

Gwendolyn Brooks   Randall Jarrell   Joseph Conrad

Stephen Spender   R M Rilke   C Brontë   Virginia Woolf

John Keats   Arthur Conan Doyle   Sidney Lanier

[illegible]   Robert Burns   A Bradstreet   William Shakespeare

A Lincoln   Henry W. Longfellow   Marianne Moore

James Joyce   Fred'k Douglass   W Blake   J. Austen

Wallace Stevens   Robert Burns   Phillis Wheatley   [illegible]

C Brontë   James Thurber   F Scott Fitzgerald